High Lights in English Literature

In came Bob Cratchit with Tiny Tim on his shoulder.—CHRISTMAS CAROL.

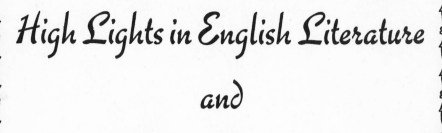

High Lights in English Literature

and

Other Selectons

By

OLA PAULINE SRYGLEY

And

OTSIE VERNONA BETTS

Granger Index Reprint Series

Originally published by
BANKS UPSHAW AND COMPANY
Dallas

BOOKS FOR LIBRARIES PRESS
FREEPORT, NEW YORK

Copyright 1940 by Banks Upshaw and Company

Reprinted 1971 by arrangement with
National Textbook Company

INTERNATIONAL STANDARD BOOK NUMBER:
0-8369-6289-3

LIBRARY OF CONGRESS CATALOG CARD NUMBER:
76-167484

PRINTED IN THE UNITED STATES OF AMERICA

PREFACE

Literature is recognized as an integral part of life, being at once its reflection and its interpretation. For this reason the selections in HIGH LIGHTS IN ENGLISH LITERATURE are grouped under themes bearing directly upon the lives of people, themes of enduring interest to them. Such an arrangement enables one to read with greater comprehension and to see literature and life in their proper relationship and enjoy both to a greater degree.

Themes chosen deal chiefly with the racial inheritance and the environment of the British in such a way as to reveal their traits, ideals, and achievements. The themes are, therefore, ones to which we, their American kinsmen, are responsive. The first unit is Humor in Literature. Others are Mainly About People, The Quest for Happiness, Standards and Ideals, Many Moods of Love, The Charm of the Unusual, Faith and Reverence, Love of Freedom, The Futility and Destruction of War, Good Will to Men, and Nature and Reflection.

The text includes numbers of new selections and many that are universally known. Such a story as "Beltarbet's Pride"—the account of a man's pride in his family, of his love for his horse, and of his love and loyalty to his servant—makes appeal to all readers, for all admire these loyalties. "The Magic Formula," another twentieth century selection, with its reminiscence of boyhood days, its discussion of attitudes toward life, its questions relative to the permanence of the civilization we are building, is pertinent and full of charm. A certain schoolboy's reaction to this essay was, "It is the best thing I have ever read."

The biographical sketches, in common with the selections, have personal appeal. They portray the authors not merely as meritorious writers but also as interesting persons. Literary selections, biographical sketches, introductory notes, and questions for thought and discussion were tested in schools of various types before being incorporated in the text.

Macbeth, because of its traditional and its present interest, is included. Such a character as Macbeth, a king magnificent in prowess and achievement, and yet a destructive criminal and colossal failure, captures and holds the attention of readers, even those of today, accustomed as they are to the spectacular and tragic careers of criminals of the twentieth century.

Literary works before the time of Shakespeare are omitted in order that emphasis may be placed on modern material. Readers desirous of making a study of early English literature may find elsewhere significant and entertaining writings of the Anglo-Saxon, the Anglo-Norman, and the Chaucerian periods. Chief among these selections are *Beowulf*, "The Seafarer," "The Pearl," "Piers Plowman," and Chaucer's *Canterbury Tales*.

Milton's pastorals, "L'Allegro" and "Il Penseroso," are placed with the nature poems among which are many of the selections of the Romantic Period. Poems by Tennyson and Browning, both versatile writers, are listed under several themes. "If," "The Ballad of East and West," "The Spires of Oxford," and "On the Road" are representative of twentieth century idealism and realism.

Emphasis is placed on prose. There is sufficient basic material for a short story course and an essay course, should pupils and teachers desire to make an intensive study of these types. Among the short stories included by other than English writers are "The Substitute," French; "The Bet," Russian; and "The Christmas Guest," Swedish. These have an emotional appeal and, at the same time, touch upon topics of civic and economic welfare.

Upon one theme, The Futility and Destruction of War, World War poets have voiced unmistakable convictions, which are given recognition in the text. Unfortunately, however, literary people have not yet caught the *Gleam* clearly enough to show that the way of peace lies through building up good will between individuals and between nations. National and international good will and the economic depression, too, with its terrible lesson on inadequate economic organization have yet to find, as they will find, an interpreter who will teach the world that the way to happiness lies through realizing the interdependence of individual and of general welfare.

In recognizing the social trends in literature, the primary aim of reading for pleasure has not been ignored. Many selections are included for their esthetic value alone, and much study and work, creative in approach and content, is suggested for the artistic minority capable of sharing experiences with others in such a way as to add to their enjoyment.

Because of recognized differences in reading ability even among pupils of secondary schools, material suitable for a wide range of developmental levels is provided. Not by accident does "Moti Guj" find a place beside *Macbeth* and as for "The Ancient Mariner," usually placed in the eighth or ninth grade, it is the conviction of the compilers of this text that a pupil must reach a certain maturity before he can have an appreciation for Coleridge's themes or for his figurative and highly descriptive language.

Whatever the preferred method of approach and instruction, HIGH LIGHTS IN ENGLISH LITERATURE AND OTHER SELECTIONS is designed to meet the desires and the needs of both pupils and teachers.

It has certain features which simplify the study of literature. In the first place the organization by themes offers a more natural approach by encouraging study along specific lines of interest. The plan offers a group of selections from which the pupil may make comparisons of points of view and of different treatment of the same topic. His mental horizon is broadened by class discussions from which he has an opportunity to gain a wealth of ideas.

The inclusion of both prose and poetry in every section simplifies and enriches the sections. The pupil who finds poetry difficult to understand will be assisted by this plan, and the pupil who has an aversion to poetry is more likely to become interested. He passes over form to a consideration of content. Passing from one type to another in the same section simplifies study, because the pupil's interest shifts from form to content.

The title page preceding each section attracts attention at the outset. Voluntarily the pupil scans this page for familiar names and titles. This arrangement by appealing to his visual memory enables him to learn titles and authors easily.

Illustrations which are appropriate arouse the interest of pupils who enjoy finding the passage which the artist used as a basis for her work. Youthful photographs of authors likewise are attractive to young people.

For those who prefer it a chronological index is provided. This and an adequate historical section offer admirable means of adaptation to the chronological method of instruction. Those following this latter plan will begin with a study of the historical section and will take up in order the works of the Elizabethan Age and of each succeeding period.

An index by types and a section entitled "Types of Literature" make provision for pupils and teachers who favor studying by types. Reading the simple and diverting short story is excellent for initiating the type study.

Regardless of approach, classes should read the twelfth section of the text and make constant reference to it. They should read also introductory notes and footnotes and follow instructions given for thought and discussion.

A study manual, *Each Day's Work,* has been prepared to be used in connection with the text. This solves for the pupil the difficult problem of finding a point of attack and opens to him new avenues of enjoyment through literature.

Attention is called to the exercise How to Use Your Book which acquaints a class with the organization of the text and enables pupils to study more systematically.

HIGH LIGHTS IN ENGLISH LITERATURE is designed for the last year of high school. The compilers feel that all those who complete their work in high school should have the opportunity to read the literature which is the heritage of English speaking people wherever they may be.

ACKNOWLEDGMENTS

For their assistance and helpful suggestions grateful acknowledgment is made to the following:

From Fort Worth, Texas, Mr. W. M. Green, Superintendent of the Public Schools; Mr. W. A. Meacham, Assistant Superintendent; Mrs. E. M. Myres, Head of the English Department, Arlington Heights High School; Miss Agnes Edens, Head of the English Department, Paschal High School; Mr. E. L. Callihan, Head of the Journalism Department, Arlington Heights High School, and the following teachers: Miss Lena Austin, Mrs. Bonnie Crone, Mr. Mayhew Mantor, Miss Clara Agnes Deen, Miss Louise Langley, and Miss Julia Monk.

Miss Mabel Major, Professor of English, Texas Christian University, Fort Worth; Mr. M. M. Hoover, Assistant to the Director, University Extension, Columbia University; Miss Mattie M. Allison, Teaching Supervisor of High School English, Southwest Texas State Teachers College and San Marcos Public Schools, San Marcos, Texas; Dr. B. F. Fronabarger, Head of the English Department, West Texas State Teachers College, Canyon, Texas; Mr. Merril Bishop, Director of the Curriculum of San Antonio Public Schools, San Antonio, Texas; Mrs. Bertie M. Mothershead, Librarian of Texas Christian University, Fort Worth.

For permission to use copyrighted selections grateful acknowledgment is made to the following:

Walter Baker Company for "What Men Live By" by Leo Tolstoy, adapted by Virginia Church.

The Clarendon Press, Oxford, for "Dear Lady, When Thou Frownest" and "To the United States of America," from *October and Other Poems*, by Robert Bridges.

Thomas Y. Crowell Company for "How Much Land Does a Man Require" by Leo Tolstoy.

Curtis Brown, Ltd., and the author for *The Boy Comes Home* by A. A. Milne and for "The Memory of a Midnight Express," from *Yet Again*, by Max Beerbohm.

Dodd, Mead and Company, Inc., for *Life of Johnson* by James Boswell; "The Soldier" and "The Dead," from *Collected Poems*, by Rupert Brooke, copyright 1915, used by permission of Dodd, Mead and Company, Inc.

Doubleday, Doran & Company, Inc., for "From One Generation to Another," from *The Matador of Five Towns and Other Stories*, copyright 1912, and "Controlling the Mind," from *How to Live on 24 Hours a Day*, by Arnold Bennett, copyright 1910, by Doubleday, Doran & Company, Inc.; "A Christmas Guest," from

Invisible Links, by Selma Lagerlöf, copyright 1899, 1927, by Doubleday, Doran & Company, Inc., reprinted by permission of Doubleday, Doran & Company, Inc.

E. P. Dutton & Company, Inc., for "The Spires of Oxford," taken from *The Spires of Oxford and Other Poems*, by Winifred M. Letts, published and copyrighted by E. P. Dutton & Company, Inc., New York.

E. P. Dutton & Company, Inc., taken from *The Roadmender*, by Michael Fairless, published by E. P. Dutton & Company, Inc., New York.

E. P. Dutton & Company, Inc., and the author for "Does It Matter?" by Siegfried Sassoon; for "Running Wolf," taken from *The Wolves of God*, by Algernon Blackwood, published and copyrighted by E. P. Dutton & Company, Inc., New York.

Harper & Brothers for "The Substitute," from *Ten Tales*, by François Coppée.

Houghton Mifflin Company for "Sing a Song of Sixpence," from *The Runagates Club*, by John Buchan, used by permission of, and by arrangement with, Houghton Mifflin Company.

Alfred A. Knopf, Inc., for *Green Mansions* by W. H. Hudson, and "Story of a Piebald Horse," reprinted from *Tales of the Pampas*, by W. H. Hudson, by permission of and special arrangement with Alfred A. Knopf, Inc., authorized publishers.

Little, Brown & Company for "The True History of the Hare and the Tortoise," from *Fifty-One Tales* by Lord Dunsany; "The Lighthouse Keeper of Aspinwall," by Henryk Sienkiewicz.

David Lloyd for "Leisure" and "The Rainbow" by William H. Davies, from the *Poems* of W. H. Davies (1934) by permission of Jonathan Cape, Ltd., copyright 1916 by William H. Davies.

Robert M. McBride & Co. and the author for "The Turkish Trench Dog," from *Poems*, by Geoffrey Dearmer.

Macmillan Company and the author for "An Old Woman of the Roads," from *Wild Earth*, by Padraic Colum; "Battle: Hit," "Between the Lines," "The Going," "On the Road," from *Collected Poems* by W. W. Gibson; "A Consecration," "Sea Fever," from *Collected Poems* by John Masefield; "The Lake Isle of Innisfree," from *Early Poems and Other Stories* by William Butler Yeats; *Lord Alfred Tennyson: A Memoir* by Hallam Tennyson.

Macmillan Company, London, for *Florence Nightingale* by Sir Edward Cook.

Modern Library for "The Bet" by Anton Chekhov.

Alida Monro for "Overheard on a Salt Marsh," from "Children of Love," 1915, reprinted in *Collected Poems* in 1934, by Harold Monro.

A. D. Peters for "On Dropping Anchor" by Hilaire Belloc.

Walter de la Mare, his publishers, and his representatives, Pinker & Morrison, Inc., for *Memoirs of a Midget* by Walter de la Mare.

George Runnell Preedy for "Beltarbet's Pride" by George Runnell Preedy.

Mary Leonard Pritchett and Adrienne Morrison for "Letter to a Young Man," from *Cry Havoc,* by Beverley Nichols.

Siegfried Sassoon for "Does It Matter?," "Counter-Attack," from *Counter-Attack,* "Aftermath," from *Picture-Show,* by Siegfried Sassoon.

Charles Scribner's Sons for selections by John Galsworthy: "American and Briton," from *Another Sheaf;* "Courage," from *Moods, Songs, and Doggerel; "Quality,"* from *The Inn of Tranquillity;* "A Sad Affair"; for "Invictus" and "A Late Lark Twitters," from *Poems,* by William Ernest Henley; for "Juggling Jerry," from *Poems,* by Charles Meredith; for selections by Robert Louis Stevenson: "The Hunter's Family," from *Silverado Squatters;* "Pan's Pipes," from *Virginibus Puerisque;* "Requiem," "The Vagabond," from *Complete Poems;* "The Sire de Malétroit's Door," from *New Arabian Nights;* and for "To a Snowflake" by Francis Thompson.

Sidgwick and Jackson, London, for "Ducks," from *Ducks & Other Verses,* by Frederick William Harvey.

Frederick A. Stokes Company for "The Highwayman," from *Collected Poems,* Vol. I, by Alfred Noyes.

The Viking Press, Inc., for "Futility" by Wilfred Owen.

Ann Watkins, Inc., for "Paternity" by Warwick Deeping.

A. P. Watt & Son, London, and Doubleday, Doran and Company, Inc., the American publishers, for "The Ballad of East and West," and "Gunga Din," from the *Barrack Room Ballads,* copyright 1892 and 1899 by Rudyard Kipling; "If," from *Rewards and Fairies,* copyright 1910, by Rudyard Kipling; "Moti Guj, Mutineer," from *Life's Handicap,* copyright 1891 and 1918 by Rudyard Kipling, and reprinted by permission of these firms and Mr. Kipling.

The Wilson Bulletin for permission to use references for "Periods and Types of Literature."

CONTENTS

SECTION THREE

THE QUEST FOR HAPPINESS

SECTION FOUR

STANDARDS AND IDEALS OF LIVING

SECTION FIVE

MANY MOODS OF LOVE

SECTION SIX

THE CHARM OF THE UNUSUAL

SECTION SEVEN

FAITH AND REVERENCE

SECTION TEN

GOOD WILL TO MEN

SECTION ELEVEN

NATURE AND REFLECTION

SECTION TWELVE

PERIODS AND TYPES OF LITERATURE

FOREWORD TO THE READER

No matter what kind of reading you enjoy, or whether you, as a rule, enjoy any kind of reading, we challenge you to browse through *High Lights in English Literature* without finding something which will catch and hold your attention.

One of the desirable features of the book is that it is so arranged that you can easily locate material upon a given theme, material that you will be responsive to in all your varying moods. The group arrangement of selections of similar theme, we believe, will enable you to derive more pleasure as well as more profit from your studies. The wide range of material in this text gives you the opportunity to choose the selections of the greatest interest to you. To see how different writers treat the same subjects provides interesting variations in your work.

If it is a little nonsense you desire, you have at hand, in the section, Humor, many selections over which you can smile and smile for quite some time and which you will probably read again and again.

If it is something out of the ordinary—adventure, mystery on land and sea, or a fairy story of the type that seems real—you will wish to turn to the section called Charm of the Unusual. Perhaps you will not like every selection, but we promise you that you will read with pleasure some one or more of them. The probability is that you will finish the whole section and then search through your library for the books and articles mentioned in the list of additional readings.

Perhaps you do not like love stories, but more than likely you do. If so, Many Moods of Love is the section after your own heart, for it contains love stories of all types—humorous, gay, whimsical, and grave and tender.

Your class, perhaps, will be asked to arrange a Christmas, Thanksgiving, Armistice, or Easter program for the school, or perhaps you will be asked to read over a radio program on some special occasion. If so, you will be likely to find the particular selection you are searching for in the section called Good Will to Men, or Love of Freedom, or Nature and Reflection.

You are constantly being asked to speak in a school club or in other organizations such as a church or a club. Why not, on such occasions, quote by way of inspiration or illustration from some of the poems or essays or stories in the two sections, Standards and Ideals and Faith and Reverence?

Silent reading is excellent personal pastime; reading aloud is a source of pastime for oneself and for others, and the person who knows literature and reads and quotes it effectively is in constant demand as a public speaker. The chances are that the popular congressman of your district spends much time in the study of literature, and you would show intelligence to follow his example, particularly if you wish to follow in his footsteps. In biblical phraseology an apt quotation is, to the public speaker, "like apples of gold in pictures of silver."

How shall you read? As your inclination or the necessity demands, read for sheer pleasure, read reflectively, read as many readers do in this period of unrest to gain a feeling of security, poise, and peace, and read, upon occasion, purposefully, with the idea of getting a better understanding of life and social and civic problems through the works of writers who have made a particular study of such problems.

Desirable Study Procedures for a Pupil

Read the general introduction to the section, the editorial opposite the title page.

Read the introductory notes before each selection.

Read the selection through for pleasure; refer to the footnotes as you read.

Follow the directions given in For Thought and Discussion.

Be sure you know the meaning and pronunciation of each word.

Discover the glow of satisfaction which comes from making a thorough study of a selection, and surprise yourself and your teacher by completing at least a part of the assignments suggested by the Plus Work, or better still, some creative work you initiate yourself.

Introduce yourself to new book friends by reading the lives of the authors. You will take delight in finding out what an author was like as a boy and what caused him to want to make the *literary wheels go round*. Becoming familiar with a writer's life will add to your enjoyment of his works.

We hope that an understanding of the selections in this book will make your life richer and give you some of the happiness which we have experienced in reading for *high lights*.

HOW TO USE YOUR BOOK

Before one can study, he must know how to use his book. The following exercise may be oral or written.

1. Study the table of contents on pages IX to XV inclusive. How many sections are in the book? Upon what subjects?

II. Find title pages of the sections entitled The Quest for Happiness, Nature and Reflection, The Charm of the Unusual, The Futility and Destruction of War. Find the introductions to the same sections.

III. What is included under the section entitled Periods and Types of Literature? Name the main historical and literary periods.

IV. Name the different types of literature. Turn to the Introduction to Types of Literature, page 841. Find the index to types. Look up one selection for each type.

V. Find the author's index on page 858. How many selections by Robert Browning are printed in this text? Is one of Galsworthy's stories included? On what page? Turn to that page.

VI. Find the pronouncing index. Look up the pronunciation of Galsworthy, Abou Ben Adhem, Baiae, Banquo, Caithness, Cawdor.

VII. Refer to the general index. Look up the Age of Elizabeth, the seventeenth century, free verse, narrative poetry, drama, the short story, ballad, dramatic monologue, the essay, the lyric. Look up "The Bet," "A Sad Affair," "The Christmas Guest," "The Boy Comes Home," "The Soldier," "On the Road."

VIII. Find the biographies of William Wordsworth, Sir Walter Scott, Robert Browning, and Robert Louis Stevenson.

IX. Look up the map of the British Isles. Locate Edinburgh, Ayr, English Lake District, Stratford-on-Avon, Oxford, London, Innisfree, Dublin.

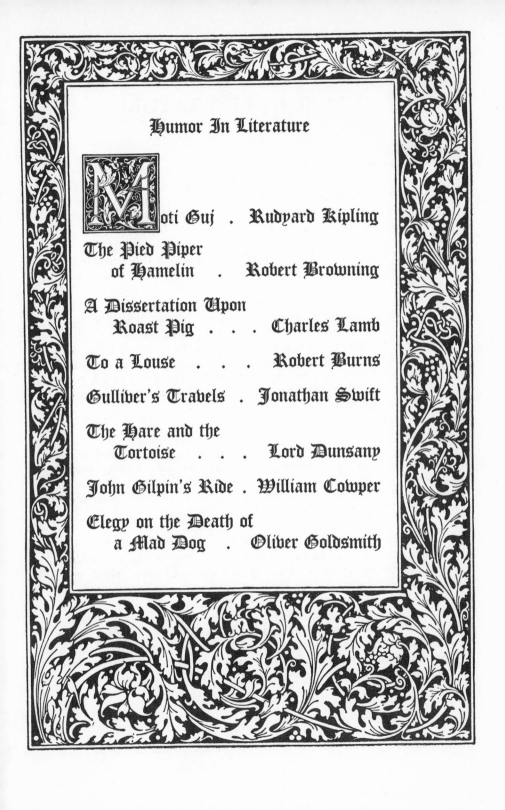

Humor In Literature

HUMOR IN LITERATURE

WHAT a prosaic world this would be if there were no non-sense—nothing but sobriety. It might be a very bad world, too, for nonsense is quite often inverted wisdom, and the humorist is one of the best possible ambassadors to pleasant relationships. Think, for instance, how by word of mouth and pen Will Rogers made the world a pleasanter place in which to live.

True humor is one of the kindest qualities in the universe and one of the most potent. It is a leaven compounded of love and wit which works good to all with which it comes in contact. The genuine humorist is a philosopher who accepts situations as they are and then laughs himself out of them; furthermore he has a measure of good-humored tolerance for the weakness of others. The true humorist is a big man—in spirit he is an optimist who wastes no time in pitying himself; and, when he speaks, or writes, he makes others forget to pity themselves. There is nothing petty or mean about him; he sees every angle of a situation; he is not swayed by anger or fear or jealousy.

Humor has such infinite variety that it never grows stale. Let these words suggest some of its many types—puckish, jovial, droll, whimsical, shrewd, hilarious, ludicrous, waggish, comic, subtle, ironical, inscrutable—all these with only a difference in proportion to distinguish the dry from the merry, the broad from the delicate, the nimble from the clumsy.

Common acceptation to the contrary, the English have a most delightful sense of humor; rarely boisterous or caustic, seldom obtrusive, theirs is, as a rule, a quiet bubbling humor which only occasionally bursts into merriment, and even less occasionally, as in the case of Swift, takes on the acid of satire. Some English humor is sheer nonsense; some is tonic and purposeful; some closely akin to pathos. Really England has as many types of humor as she has humorists; and Swift, Goldsmith, Burns, Lamb, and Kipling are but a few of the many English men of letters who have made delightful additions to the literature of humor.

"DEESA·WOULD·EMBRACE·HIS·TRUNK
AND · WEEP · AND · CALL · HIM · HIS
LOVE · AND · HIS · LIFE · AND · GIVE
HIM · SOME · LIQUOR."

MOTI GUJ—MUTINEER[1]

RUDYARD KIPLING

ONCE upon a time there was a coffee planter in India who wished to clear some forest land for coffee planting. When he had cut down all the trees and burned the underwood, the stumps still remained. Dynamite is expensive and slow fire slow. The happy medium for stump clearing is the lord of all beasts, who is the elephant. He will either push the stump out of the ground with his tusks, if he has any, or drag it out with ropes. The planter, therefore, hired elephants by ones and twos and threes, and fell to work. The very best of all the elephants belonged to the very worst of all the drivers or mahouts; and this superior beast's name was Moti Guj. He was the absolute property of his mahout, which

would never have been the case under native rule; for Moti Guj was a creature to be desired by kings, and his name, being translated, meant the Pearl Elephant. Because the British government was in the land, Deesa, the mahout, enjoyed his property undisturbed. He was dissipated. When he had made much money through the strength of his elephant, he would get extremely drunk and give Moti Guj a beating with a tent peg over the tender nails of the forefeet. Moti Guj never trampled the life out of Deesa on these occasions, for he knew that after the beating was over, Deesa would embrace his trunk and weep and call him his love and his life and the liver of his soul, and give him some liquor. Moti Guj was very fond of liquor—arrack for choice, though

[1] *Moti Guj* (mō′ tĭ gōōj).

- 3 -

he would drink palm-tree toddy if nothing better offered. Then Deesa would go to sleep between Moti Guj's forefeet, and as Deesa generally chose the middle of the public road, and as Moti Guj mounted guard over him, and would not permit horse, foot, or cart to pass by, traffic was congested till Deesa saw fit to wake up.

There was no sleeping in the daytime on the planter's clearing; the wages were too high to risk. Deesa sat on Moti Guj's neck and gave him orders, while Moti Guj rooted up the stumps—for he owned a magnificent pair of tusks; or pulled at the end of a rope—for he had a magnificent pair of shoulders—while Deesa kicked him behind the ears and said he was the king of elephants. At evening time Moti Guj would wash down his three hundred pounds' weight of green food with a quart of arrack, and Deesa would take a share, and sing songs between Moti Guj's legs till it was time to go to bed. Once a week Deesa led Moti Guj down to the river, and Moti Guj lay on his side luxuriously in the shallows, while Deesa went over him with a coir swab and a brick. Moti Guj never mistook the pounding blow of the latter for the smack of the former that warned him to get up and turn over on the other side. Then Deesa would look at his feet and examine his eyes, and turn up the fringes of his mighty ears in case of sores or budding ophthalmia. After inspection the two would "come up with a song from the sea," Moti Guj, all black and shining, waving a torn tree branch twelve feet long in his trunk, and Deesa knotting up his own long wet· hair.

It was a peaceful, well-paid life till Deesa felt the return of the desire to drink deep. He wished for an orgy. The little draughts that led nowhere were taking the manhood out of him.

He went to the planter, and "My mother's dead," said he, weeping.

"She died on the last plantation, two months ago, and she died once before that when you were working for me last year," said the planter, who knew something of the ways of nativedom.

"Then it's my aunt, and she was just the same as a mother to me," said Deesa, weeping more than ever. "She has left eighteen small children entirely without bread, and it is I who must fill their little stomachs," said Deesa, beating his head on the floor.

"Who brought you the news?" said the planter.

"The post," said Deesa.

"There hasn't been a post here for the past week. Get back to your lines!"

"A devastating sickness has fallen on my village, and all my wives are dying," yelled Deesa, really in tears this time.

"Call Chihun, who comes from Deesa's village," said the planter. "Chihun, has this man got a wife?"

"He?" said Chihun. "No. Not a woman of our village would look at him. They'd sooner marry the elephant."

Chihun snorted. Deesa wept and bellowed.

"You will get into a difficulty in a minute," said the planter. "Go back to your work!"

"Now I will speak Heaven's truth," gulped Deesa, with an inspiration. "I haven't been drunk for two months. I desire to depart in order to get properly drunk afar off and distant from this heavenly plantation. Thus I shall cause no trouble."

A flickering smile crossed the planter's face. "Deesa," said he, "you've spoken the truth, and I'd give you leave on the spot if anything could be done with Moti Guj while you're away. You know that he will only obey your orders."

"May the light of the heavens live forty thousand years. I shall be absent but ten little days. After that, upon my faith and honor and soul, I return. As to the inconsiderable interval, have I the gracious permission of the heaven-born to call up Moti Guj?"

Permission was granted, and in answer to Deesa's shrill yell, the mighty tusker swung out of the shade of a clump of trees where he had been squirting dust over himself till his master should return.

"Light of my heart, protector of the drunken, mountain of might, give ear!" said Deesa, standing in front of him.

Moti Guj gave ear, and saluted with his trunk. "I am going away," said Deesa.

Moti Guj's eyes twinkled. He liked jaunts as well as his master. One could snatch all manner of nice things from the roadside then.

"But you, you fussy old pig, must stay behind and work."

The twinkle died out as Moti Guj tried to look delighted. He hated stump-hauling on the plantation. It hurt his teeth.

"I shall be gone for ten days, oh, delectable one! Hold up your near forefoot and I'll impress the fact upon it, warty toad of a dried mud-puddle." Deesa took a tent peg and banged Moti Guj ten times on the nails. Moti Guj grunted and shuffled from foot to foot.

"Ten days," said Deesa, "you will work and haul and root the trees as Chihun here shall order you. Take up Chihun and set him on your neck!" Moti Guj curled the tip of his trunk, Chihun put his foot there and was swung on to the neck. Deesa handed Chihun the heavy *ankus*, the iron elephant goad.

Chihun thumped Moti Guj's bald head as a paver thumps a curbstone.

Moti Guj trumpeted.

"Be still, hog of the backwoods! Chihun's your mahout for ten days. And now bid me good-by, beast after mine own heart. Oh, my lord, my king! Jewel of all created elephants, lily of the herd, preserve your honored health; be virtuous. Adieu!"

Moti Guj lapped his trunk round Deesa and swung him into the air twice. That was his way of bidding him good-by.

"He'll work now," said Deesa to the planter. "Have I leave to go?"

The planter nodded, and Deesa dived into the woods. Moti Guj went back to haul stumps.

Chihun was very kind to him, but he felt unhappy and forlorn for all that. Chihun gave him a ball of spices, and tickled him under the chin, and Chihun's little baby cooed to him after work was over, and Chihun's wife called him a darling; but Moti Guj was a bachelor by instinct, as Deesa was. He did not understand the domestic emotions. He wanted the light of his universe back again — the drink and the drunken slumber, the savage beatings and the savage caresses.

None the less he worked well, and the planter wondered. Deesa had wandered along the roads till he met a marriage procession of his own caste, and, drinking, dancing, and tippling, had drifted with it past all knowledge of the lapse of time.

The morning of the eleventh day dawned, and there returned no Deesa. Moti Guj was loosed from his ropes for the daily stint. He swung clear, looked round, shrugged his shoulders, and began to walk away, as one having business elsewhere.

"Hi! ho! Come back you!" shouted Chihun. "Come back and put me on your neck, misborn mountain! Return, splendor of the hillsides! Adornment of all India, heave to, or I'll bang every toe off your fat forefoot!"

Moti Guj gurgled gently, but did not obey. Chihun ran after him with a rope and caught him up. Moti Guj put his ears forward, and Chihun knew what that meant, though he tried to carry it off with high words.

"None of your nonsense with me," said he. "To your pickets, devil-son!"

"Hrrump!" said Moti Guj, and that was all—that and the forebent ears.

Moti Guj put his hands in his pockets, chewed a branch for a toothpick, and strolled about the clearing, making fun of the other elephants who had just set to work.

Chihun reported the state of affairs to the planter, who came out with a dog-whip and cracked it furiously. Moti Guj paid the white man the compliment of charging him nearly a quarter of a mile across the clearing and "Hrrumphing" him into his veranda. Then he stood outside the house, chuckling to himself and shaking all over with the fun of it, as an elephant will.

"We'll thrash him," said the planter. "He shall have the finest thrashing ever elephant received. Give Kala Nag and Nazim twelve foot of chain apiece, and tell them to lay on twenty."

Kala Nag — which means Black Snake—and Nazim were two of the biggest elephants in the lines, and one of their duties was to administer the graver punishment, since no man can beat an elephant properly.

They took the whipping-chains and rattled them in their trunks as they sidled up to Moti Guj, meaning to hustle him between them. Moti Guj had never, in all his life of thirty-nine years, been whipped, and he did not intend to begin a new experience. So he waited, waving his head from right to left and measuring the precise spot in Kala Nag's fat side where a blunt tusk could sink deepest. Kala Nag had no tusks; the chain was the badge of his authority; but for all that, he swung wide of Moti Guj at the last minute, and tried to appear as if he had brought the chain out for amusement. Nazim turned round and went home early. He did not feel fighting fit that morning, and so Moti Guj was left standing alone with his ears cocked.

That decided the planter to argue no more, and Moti Guj rolled back to his amateur inspection of the clearing. An elephant who will not work and is not tied up is about as manageable as an eighty-one-ton gun loose in a heavy seaway. He slapped old friends on the back and asked them if the stumps were coming away easily; he talked nonsense concerning labor and the inalienable rights of elephants to a long "nooning"; and, wandering to and fro, he thoroughly demoralized the garden till sundown, when he returned to his picket for food.

"If you won't work you shan't eat," said Chihun, angrily. "You're a wild elephant, and no educated animal at all. Go back to your jungle."

Chihun's little brown baby was rolling on the floor of the hut, and stretching out its fat arms to the huge shadow in the doorway. Moti Guj knew well that it was the dearest thing on earth to Chihun. He swung out his trunk with a fascinating crook at the end, and the brown baby threw itself, shouting, upon it. Moti Guj made fast and pulled up till the brown baby was crowing in the air twelve feet above his father's head.

"Great Lord!" said Chihun. "Flour

cakes of the best, twelve in number, two feet across and soaked in rum, shall be yours on the instant, and two hundred pounds' weight of fresh-cut young sugar cane therewith. Deign only to put down safely that insignificant brat who is my heart and my life to me!"

Moti Guj tucked the brown baby comfortably between his forefeet, that could have knocked into toothpicks all Chihun's hut, and waited for his food. He ate it, and the brown baby crawled away. Moti Guj dozed and thought of Deesa. One of many mysteries connected with the elephant is that his huge body needs less sleep than anything else that lives. Four or five hours in the night suffice—two just before midnight, lying down on one side; two just after one o'clock, lying down on the other. The rest of the silent hours are filled with eating and fidgeting, and long grumbling soliloquies.

At midnight, therefore, Moti Guj strode out of his pickets, for a thought had come to him that Deesa might be lying drunk somewhere in the dark forest with none to look after him. So all that night he chased through the undergrowth, blowing and trumpeting and shaking his ears. He went down to the river and blared across the shallows where Deesa used to wash him, but there was no answer. He could not find Deesa, but he disturbed all the other elephants in the lines, and nearly frightened to death some gypsies in the woods.

At dawn Deesa returned to the plantation. He had been very drunk indeed, and he expected to get into trouble for outstaying his leave. He drew a long breath when he saw that the bungalow and the plantation were still uninjured, for he knew something of Moti Guj's temper, and reported himself with many lies and salaams. Moti Guj had gone to his pickets for breakfast. The night exercise had made him hungry.

"Call up your beast," said the planter; and Deesa shouted in the mysterious elephant language that some mahouts believe came from China at the birth of the world, when elephants and not men were masters. Moti Guj heard and came. Elephants do not gallop. They move from places at varying rates of speed. If an elephant wished to catch an express train he could not gallop, but he could catch the train. So Moti Guj was at the planter's door almost before Chihun noticed that he had left his pickets. He fell into Deesa's arms trumpeting with joy, and the man and beast wept and slobbered over each other, and handled each other from head to heel to see that no harm had befallen.

"Now we will get to work," said Deesa. "Lift me up, my son and my joy!"

Moti Guj swung him up, and the two went to the coffee clearing to look for difficult stumps.

The planter was too astonished to be very angry.

For Thought and Discussion

1. Why did the planter give Deesa permission to leave the plantation?
2. Give some of the titles of endearment Deesa bestowed upon Moti Guj.
3. What did Moti Guj do on the eleventh day?
4. How did Moti Guj force Chihun to feed him?

5. How long does an elephant sleep?
6. What human traits did Moti Guj have?
7. What purpose is served by the title of this story?
8. What features entitle this story to be termed humorous?
9. Aside from humor, what features add to the interest of the selection?
10. Indicate differences in the temperament of Eastern and Western peoples, particularly in regard to truth and humor and extravagance of language.
11. How do you think Kipling obtained material for this story?
12. Study the discussion of the short story in the section "A Brief Introduction to Types of Literature" found in the last section of the book.

RUDYARD KIPLING 1865-1936

Early Life. In Bombay, India, there was born an English boy who was destined to interpret to England her far-away colonial subjects in India, in Canada, in South Africa, and in Australia. Kipling's early life fitted him for this special work, for his first impressions were of the strange land of his birth with its two-fold association,—his British parents and the native household servants. In this congenial home the boy passed six happy years in an environment of affection and sympathetic understanding.

School Days. When the time came for an education to be taken seriously, Kipling and his little sister were placed in a boarding school in England. The story of this experience of a misunderstood child, as told in "Baa, Baa, Black Sheep," is one of the saddest stories in literature. It deserves a few readings in every lifetime. Because of its vivid portrayal of boys' interests, *Stalky and Company,* which gives a picture of his life in a second and a happier school setting, will probably one day be used by the moving pictures. In this second school were a large number of boys who had been born abroad, and as three-fourths of them were sons of army officers or of others in the service, naturally they talked about and looked forward to the time when they would be army men. It seems rather fitting, therefore, that one of them, Kipling, should eventually write songs of the soldiers. Through editing his school paper, Kipling received his first training in writing, and the fact that he chose newspaper work for his career is a sufficient indication that his early training was both pleasant and profitable.

Return to India. Whether directed by the spirit of adventure, by chance, or by good judgment, Kipling chose to return to India. Accordingly, the seventeen-year-old youth was soon at work on a small daily paper, learning his trade under the most strenuous conditions, habitually overworked because the staff, too small at best, was usually reduced further by the frequent attacks of tropical fever. As a special reporter Kipling visited out-of-the-way places and in addition to his regular work stored up material

RUDYARD KIPLING

---

which he was in time to write as songs of the joys and sorrows of
the British soldier. When they were printed, readers criticized
them vigorously for their rough expressions but read them avidly.
For seven years—until he was sure of himself in his chosen work—
India held Kipling.

Travels. His travels took him to many places—Italy, Australia,
New Zealand, Cape Town, the United States, and to London,

where he decided to remain. Within a year he was discovered and became at twenty-five the most popular English writer, and those stories which earlier had been refused were now eagerly sought by editors. In London he married an American wife and left for a trip around the world but turned back at Tokyo because of the failure of the bank there. The Kiplings spent their first winter in an isolated farm house in New England, where in a tiny study with snowdrifts up to the window sills, Kipling wrote stories. Later they built a home, "Naulahka," near Brattleboro, Vermont, and from this residence there came several stories with an American background, among them *Captains Courageous*. In a few years the Kiplings returned to England, where they made their home, leaving often, however, for trips to the far corners of the British Empire. For seven years the family, including the parents, children, governess, and servants, went to South Africa for a few months of the year. Kipling said that the children were so much at home on the steamer that they felt that they owned the Union Castle Steamship Line. In South Africa they were close neighbors of Cecil Rhodes, who lived on an interesting estate, which had as its chief attraction for the Kipling children a very wonderful zoo. This background of South Africa was used by Kipling for many stories.

His Popularity. Kipling wrote too many volumes for a full enumeration of titles; these include verse, short stories, and longer stories. One may say with assurance that he is one of the most interesting and widely read writers of all time. Something of the wide interest in his work was revealed upon the occasion of his illness in a New York hotel. So many inquiries were received that hourly bulletins from his physician were posted in the lobby; the numbers of people from all classes who came to read them were a sufficient indication of the extensive appeal of his writing. In 1907 world recognition was given to him by the award of the Nobel prize for idealism in literature.

Short Stories. For those who enjoy stories of the adventure type, Kipling's are of absorbing interest. He mastered the art of writing stories which captivate children, as is evidenced by the large numbers who have read *The Jungle Books*, *Puck of Pook's Hill*, and *Plain Tales from the Hills*; the last, as the title indicates, is of the hill people in India. One of the favorite Indian stories is "Wee Willie Winkie," which has for its hero the sturdy six-year-old "Winkie," whose high code of honor has endeared him to readers, both young and old.

Poetry. The soldier poems, *Departmental Ditties* and *Barrack Room Ballads*, which are usually written in the Cockney dialect of *Tommy*, have given many happy hours to those who enjoy vigorous verse. Among the single selections which are favorites are "If," "The Recessional," "Gunga Din," and "The Ballad of the East and West."

Last Years. Kipling's last years were passed in his home in England. He spent a great deal of time out of doors; roving the countryside in a Norfolk jacket and knickerbockers, he could easily have been taken for a Sussex farmer. After the death of his son in the World War, he had few associations with the outside world; his desire for seclusion was respected by the villagers, who were exceedingly vague about directions when tourists wished to see his home. An account of his life, *Something of Myself*, published after his death, is written with that same magic which was ever his when he had a story to tell.

THE PIED PIPER OF HAMELIN

ROBERT BROWNING

[The child for whom "The Pied Piper of Hamelin" was written was Willie Macready, the small son of Robert Macready, the actor, who produced Browning's drama "Strafford." The poem was written to amuse the little boy during an illness, and he spent hours of his convalescence in making original drawings to illustrate it. The selection was based on an old German legend.]

HAMELIN Town's in Brunswick,[1]
  By famous Hanover city;
The river Weser, deep and wide,
Washes its wall on the southern side;
A pleasanter spot you never spied;   5
  But when begins my ditty,
Almost five hundred years ago,
To see the townsfolk suffer so
  From vermin was a pity.

Rats!   10
They fought the dogs and killed the
    cats,
  And bit the babies in the cradles,
And ate the cheeses out of the vats,
  And licked the soup from the
    cooks' own ladles,
Split open the kegs of salted sprats,   15
Made nests inside men's Sunday hats,
And even spoiled the women's chats
  By drowning their speaking
  With shrieking and squeaking
In fifty different sharps and flats.   20

---

[1]*Brunswick*, a state in Germany.

At last the people in a body
  To the Town Hall came flocking.
"'Tis clear," cried they, "our Mayor's
  a noddy;
And as for our Corporation—shocking
To think we buy gowns lined with
  ermine   25
For dolts that can't or won't deter-
  mine
What's best to rid us of our vermin!
You hope, because you're old and
  obese,
To find in the furry civic robe ease?
Rouse up, sirs! Give your brains a
  racking   30
To find the remedy we're lacking,
Or, sure as fate, we'll send you pack-
  ing!"
At this the Mayor and Corporation
Quaked with a mighty consternation.

An hour they sat in council.   35
  At length the Mayor broke silence:
"For a guilder I'd my ermine gown
  sell;
  I wish I were a mile hence!
It's easy to bid one rack one's brain—
I'm sure my poor head aches again,   40
I've scratched it so, and all in vain.
Oh, for a trap, a trap, a trap!"
Just as he said this, what should hap
At the chamber door but a gentle
  tap?
"Bless us," cried the Mayor, "what's
  that?"   45

(With the Corporation as he sat,
Looking little though wondrous fat;
Nor brighter was his eye, nor moister
Than a too-long-opened oyster,
Save when at noon his paunch grew
  mutinous   50
For a plate of turtle, green and glu-
  tinous)
"Only a scraping of shoes on the mat?
Anything like the sound of a rat
Makes my heart go pit-a-pat!"

"Come in!"—the Mayor cried, look-
  ing bigger;   55
And in did come the strangest figure!
His queer long coat from heel to head
Was half of yellow and half of red,
And he himself was tall and thin,
With sharp blue eyes, each like a
  pin,   60
And light loose hair, yet swarthy skin,
No tuft on cheek nor beard on chin,
But lips where smiles went out and in;
There was no guessing his kith and
  kin;
And nobody could enough admire 65
The tall man and his quaint attire.
Quoth one: "It's as my great-grand-
  sire,
Starting up at the Trump of Doom's
  tone,
Had walked this way from his painted
  tombstone!"

He advanced to the council-table: 70
And, "Please your honors," said he,
  "I'm able,
By means of a secret charm, to draw
  All creatures living beneath the
  sun,
  That creep or swim or fly or run,
After me so as you never saw! 75
And I chiefly use my charm
On creatures that do people harm,
The mole and toad and newt and
  viper;
And people call me the Pied Piper."

(And here they noticed round his
  neck   80
A scarf of red and yellow stripe,
To match with his coat of the self-
  same check;
And at the scarf's end hung a pipe;
And his fingers, they noticed, were
  ever straying
As if impatient to be playing 85
Upon this pipe, as low it dangled
Over his vesture so old-fangled.)
"Yet," said he, "poor piper as I am,
In Tartary I freed the Cham,[3]
  Last June, from his huge swarms of
  gnats;   90
I eased in Asia the Nizam[4]
  Of a monstrous brood of vampire-
  bats;
And as for what your brain bewilders,
If I can rid your town of rats
Will you give me a thousand guild-
  ers?"[5]   95
"One? fifty thousand!"—was the ex-
  clamation
Of the astonished Mayor and Cor-
  poration.

Into the street the Piper stepped,
  Smiling first a little smile,
As if he knew what magic slept 100
  In his quiet pipe the while;
Then, like a musical adept,
To blow the pipe his lips he wrinkled,
And green and blue his sharp eyes
  twinkled,
Like a candle-flame where salt is
  sprinkled;   105
And ere three shrill notes the pipe
  uttered,
You heard as if an army muttered;
And the muttering grew to a grumb-
  ling;
And the grumbling grew to a mighty
  rumbling;

---

[3]*Cham,* Khan, ruler of the Tartar
Empire in Central Asia.
[4]*Nizam,* the ruler of Hyderabad in
India.
[5]*guilder,* an old coin worth about
forty cents.

And out of the houses the rats came
    tumbling.   110
Great rats, small rats, lean rats,
    brawny rats,
Brown rats, black rats, gray rats,
    tawny rats,
Grave old plodders, gay young frisk-
    ers,
    Fathers, mothers, uncles, cousins,
Cocking tails and pricking whiskers,
    Families by tens and dozens,   116
Brothers, sisters, husbands, wives—
Followed the Piper for their lives.
From street to street he piped advanc-
    ing,
And step for step they followed danc-
    ing,   120
Until they came to the river Weser,
    Wherein all plunged and perished!
—Save one who, stout as Julius
    Caesar,
Swam across and lived to carry
    (As he, the manuscript he cher-
    ished)   125
To Rat-land home his commentary;
Which was, "At the first shrill notes
    of the pipe,
I heard a sound as of scraping tripe,
And putting apples, wondrous ripe,
Into a cider-press's gripe;   130
And a moving away of pickle-tub-
    boards,
And a leaving ajar of conserve-cup-
    boards,
And a drawing the corks of train-oil-
    flasks,
And a breaking the hoops of butter-
    casks;
And it seemed as if a voice   135
    (Sweeter far than by harp or by
    psaltery
Is breathed) called out, 'O rats, re-
    joice!
    The world is grown to one vast
    dry-saltery!
So munch on, crunch on, take your
    nuncheon,   139
Breakfast, supper, dinner, luncheon!'
And just as a bulky sugar-puncheon,

All ready staved, like a great sun
    shone
Glorious scarce an inch before me,
Just as methought it said, 'Come, bore
    me!'   144
—I found the Weser rolling o'er me."

You should have heard the Hamelin
    people
Ringing the bells till they rocked the
    steeple.
"Go," cried the Mayor, "and get long
    poles,
Poke out the nests and block up the
    holes!
Consult with carpenters and builders,
And leave in our town not even a
    trace   151
Of the rats!"—when suddenly, up the
    face
Of the Piper perked in the market-
    place,
With a, "First, if you please, my
    thousand guilders!"

A thousand guilders! The Mayor
    looked blue;   155
So did the Corporation, too.
For council dinners made rare havoc
With Claret, Moselle, Vin-de-Grave,
    Hock;
And half the money would replenish
Their cellar's biggest butt with Rhen-
    ish.   160
To pay this sum to a wandering fel-
    low
With a gypsy coat of red and yellow!
"Beside," quoth the Mayor with
    knowing wink,
"Our business was done at the river's
    brink;
We saw with our eyes the vermin
    sink,   165
And what's dead can't come to life, I
    think.
So, friend, we're not the folks to
    shrink
From the duty of giving you some-
    thing for drink,

And a matter of money to put in your
    poke[6];
But as for the guilders, what we spoke
Of them, as you very well know, was
    in joke.   171
Beside, our losses have made us
    thrifty.
A thousand guilders!   Come, take
    fifty!"

The Piper's face fell, and he cried,
"No trifling! I can't wait, beside!   175
I've promised to visit by dinner time
Bagdat, and accept the prime
Of the head-cook's pottage, all he's
    rich in,
For having left, in the Caliph's kitch-
    en,
Of a nest of scorpions no survivor. 180
With him I proved no bargain-driver;
With you, don't think I'll bate a
    stiver[7]!
And folks who put me in a passion
May find me pipe after another fash-
    ion."

---

[6]poke, bag.
[7]stiver, a Dutch coin worth about
two cents.

"How?" cried the Mayor, "d'ye think
    I brook   185
Being worse treated than a cook?
Insulted by a lazy ribald
With idle pipe and vesture piebald?
You threaten us, fellow? Do your
    worst,   189
Blow your pipe there till you burst!"

Once more he stepped into the street
    And to his lips again
Laid his long pipe of smooth, straight
    cane;
    And ere he blew three notes (such
        sweet,
Soft notes as yet musician's cunning
    Never gave the enraptured air)   196
There was a rustling that seemed like
    a bustling
Of merry crowds justling at pitching
    and hustling;
Small feet were pattering, wooden
    shoes clattering,
Little hands clapping and little
    tongues chattering,   200
And, like fowls in a farm-yard when
    barley is scattering,
Out came the children running.

All the little boys and girls,
With rosy cheeks and flaxen curls,
And sparkling eyes and teeth like
    pearls, 205
Tripping and skipping, ran merrily
    after
The wonderful music with shouting
    and laughter.

The Mayor was dumb, and the Coun-
    cil stood
As if they were changed into blocks
    of wood,
Unable to move a step, or cry 210
To the children merrily skipping by,
—Could only follow with the eye
That joyous crowd at the Piper's
    back.
But how the Mayor was on the
    rack,[8]—
And the wretched Council's bosoms
    beat, 215
As the Piper turned from the High
    Street
To where the Weser rolled its waters
Right in the way of their sons and
    daughters!
However, he turned from south to
    west,
And to Koppelberg Hill his steps ad-
    dressed, 220
And after him the children pressed;
Great was the joy in every breast.
"He never can cross that mighty top!
He's forced to let the piping drop,
And we shall see our children stop!"
When, lo, as they reached the moun-
    tain-side, 226
A wondrous portal opened wide,
As if a cavern was suddenly hol-
    lowed;
And the Piper advanced and the chil-
    dren followed,
And when all were in to the very last,
The door in the mountain-side shut
    fast. 231
Did I say all? No! One was lame,

---

[8] *on the rack,* in torment.

And could not dance the whole of
    the way;
And in after years, if you would
    blame
His sadness, he was used to say—
"It's dull in our town since my play-
    mates left! 236
I can't forget that I'm bereft
Of all the pleasant sights they see,
Which the Piper also promised me.
For he led us, he said, to a joyous land,
Joining the town and just at hand,
Where waters gushed and fruit-trees
    grew, 242
And flowers put forth a fairer hue,
And everything was strange and new;
The sparrows were brighter than pea-
    cocks here, 245
And their dogs outran our fallow
    deer,
And honey-bees had lost their stings,
And horses were born with eagles'
    wings.
And just as I became assured
My lame foot would be speedily
    cured, 250
The music stopped and I stood still,
And found myself outside the hill,
Left alone against my will,
To go now limping as before,
And never hear of that country
    more!" 255

Alas, alas for Hamelin!
    There came into many a burgher's
      pate
    A text which says that heaven's
      gate
    Opes to the rich at as easy rate
As the needle's eye takes a camel in!
The Mayor sent east, west, north, and
    south, 261
To offer the Piper, by word of mouth,
    Wherever it was men's lot to find
      him,
Silver and gold to his heart's content,
If he'd only return the way he went,
    And bring the children behind
      him. 266

But when they saw 'twas a lost en-
    deavor,
And Piper and dancers were gone for-
    ever,
They made a decree that lawyers
    never
    Should think their records dated
        duly   270
If, after the day of the month and
    year,
These words did not as well appear,
"And so long after what happened
    here
    On the Twenty-second of July,
Thirteen hundred and seventy-six."
And the better in memory to fix   276
The place of the children's last re-
    treat,
They called it the Pied Piper's
    Street—
Where anyone playing on pipe or ta-
    bor
Was sure for the future to lose his
    labor.   280
Nor suffered they hostelry or tavern
    To shock with mirth a street so sol-
    emn;
But opposite the place of the cavern
    They wrote the story on a column,
And on the great church-window
    painted   285

The same, to make the world ac-
    quainted
How their children were stolen away,
And there it stands to this very day.
And I must not omit to say   289
That in Transylvania[9] there's a tribe
Of alien people who ascribe
The outlandish ways and dress
On which their neighbors lay such
    stress,
To their fathers and mothers having
    risen   294
Out of some subterraneous prison
Into which they were trepanned[10]
Long time ago in a mighty band
Out of Hamelin town in Brunswick
    land,
But how or why, they don't under-
    stand.

So, Willy, let me and you be wipers
Of scores out with all men—especial-
    ly pipers!   301
And, whether they pipe us free from
    rats or from mice,
If we've promised them aught, let us
    keep our promise!

_____

[9]*Transylvania,* in Hungary.
[10]*trepanned,* ensnared.

For Thought and Discussion

1. How is the interest of a child enlisted and held by this story?
2. Which of the terms, *ridiculous* or *comical,* do you think more applicable to the mayor? Which to the piper?
3. Which seems to you the more vivid, the rush of the rats or the rush of the children?
4. By the promise of what pleasures do you think present-day children might be attracted?
5. What is the moral of this poem? Do you think Browning violated good poetical form in appending a moral? Why so or why not?
6. Do you think Robert Browning's inconsistency in verse form in this poem is faulty? Why so or why not?
7. A study of narrative verse in "A Brief Introduction to Types of Literature" in the last section of the book will enable you to discuss this selection as a specific type of poetry.

A DISSERTATION UPON ROAST PIG
CHARLES LAMB

Jowes ratherish unwell
Ch⁵ Lamb

[Charles Lamb, 1775-1834, one of that famous trio of which Wordsworth and Coleridge were the other members, is well known for his humorous essays, *The Essays of Elia,* which reveal his gentle, whimsical nature. In Lamb's early manhood the great tragedy which was to color the life of this lovable, kindly character took place. His mother met a violent death at the hands of his sister, who was temporarily insane. During the rest of his life he lavished care and devotion upon his sister, who suffered from occasional attacks of insanity. The two collaborated on writing the volume, *Tales from Shakespeare,* Shakespeare's plays in narrative form.]

MANKIND, says a Chinese manuscript, which my friend M. was obliging enough to read and explain to me, for the first seventy thousand ages ate their meat raw, clawing or biting it from the living animal, just as they do in Abyssinia to this day. This period is not obscurely hinted at by their great Confucius in the second chapter of his *Mundane Mutations,* where he designates a kind of golden age by the term *Chofang,* literally the Cooks' Holiday. The manuscript goes on to say that the art of roasting, or rather broiling (which I take to be the elder brother), was accidentally discovered in the manner following. The swineherd, Ho-ti, having gone out into the woods one morning, as his manner was, to collect mast for his hogs, left his cottage in the care of his eldest son, Bo-bo, a great lubberly boy, who being fond of playing with fire, as younkers of his age commonly are, let some sparks escape into a bundle of straw, which kindling quickly, spread the conflagration over every part of their poor mansion, till it was reduced to ashes. Together with the cottage (a sorry antediluvian makeshift of a building, you may think it), what was of much more importance, a fine litter of new-farrowed pigs, no less than nine in number, perished. China pigs have been esteemed a luxury all over the East, from the remotest periods that we read of. Bo-bo was in the utmost consternation, as you may think, not so much for the sake of the tenement, which his father and he could easily build up again with a few dry branches, and the labor of an hour or two, at any time, as for the loss of the pigs. While he was thinking what he should say to his father, and wringing his hands over the smoking remnants of one of those untimely sufferers, an odor assailed his nostrils, unlike any scent which he had before experienced. What could it proceed from? —not from the burnt cottage—he had smelt that smell before—indeed, this was by no means the first accident of the kind which had occurred through the negligence of this unlucky young firebrand. Much less did it resemble that of any known herb, weed, or flower. A premonitory moistening at the same time overflowed his nether lip. He knew not what to think. He next stooped down to feel the pig, if there were any signs of life in it. He burnt his fingers, and to cool them he applied them in his booby fashion to his mouth. Some of the crumbs of the scorched skin had come away with his fingers, and for the first time in his life (in the world's life indeed, for before him no man had known it) he tasted—*crackling!* Again he felt and fumbled at the pig. It did not burn him so much now; still he licked his fingers from a sort of habit. The truth at length broke into his slow understanding, that it was the pig that smelt so, and the pig that tasted so delicious; and, surrendering himself up to the new-born pleasure, he fell to tearing up whole handfuls of the scorched skin with the flesh next it, and was cramming it down his throat in his beastly fashion when his sire entered amid the smoking rafters, armed with retributory cudgel, and finding how affairs stood, began to rain blows upon the young rogue's shoulders, as thick as hailstones, which Bo-bo heeded not any more than if they had been flies. The tickling pleasure, which he experienced in his lower regions, had rendered him quite callous to any inconveniences he might feel in those remote quarters. His father might lay on, but he could not beat him from his pig, till he had fairly made an end of it, when, becoming a little more sensible of his situation, something like the following dialogue ensued:

"You graceless whelp, what have you got there devouring? Is it not enough that you have burned me down three houses with your dog's tricks, and be hanged to you, but you must be eating fire, and I know not what—what have you got there, I say?"

"O father, the pig, the pig, do come and taste how nice the burnt pig eats."

The ears of Ho-ti tingled with horror. He cursed his son, and he cursed himself that ever he should beget a son that should eat burnt pig.

Bo-bo, whose scent was wonderfully sharpened since morning, soon raked out another pig, and fairly rending it asunder, thrust the lesser half by main force into the fists of Ho-ti, still shouting out, "Eat, eat, eat the burnt pig, father, only taste— O Lord"—with such-like barbarous ejaculations, cramming all the while as if he would choke.

Ho-ti trembled in every joint while he grasped the abominable thing, wavering whether he should not put his son to death for an unnatural young monster, when the crackling scorching his fingers, as it had done his son's, and applying the same remedy to them, he in his turn tasted some of its flavor, which, make what sour mouths he would for a pretense, proved not altogether displeasing to him. In conclusion (for the manuscript here is a little tedious) both father and son fairly sat down to the mess, and never left off till they had dispatched all that remained of the litter.

Bo-bo was strictly enjoined not to let the secret escape, for the neighbors would certainly have stoned them for a couple of abominable wretches, who could think of improving upon the

good meat which God had sent them. Nevertheless, strange stories got about. It was observed that Ho-ti's cottage was burned down now more frequently than ever. Nothing but fires from this time forward. Some would break out in broad day, others in the night-time. As often as the sow farrowed, so sure was the house of Ho-ti to be in a blaze; and Ho-ti himself, which was the more remarkable, instead of chastising his son, seemed to grow more indulgent to him than ever. At length they were watched, the terrible mystery discovered, and father and son summoned to take their trial at Pekin, then an inconsiderable assize town. Evidence was given, the obnoxious food itself produced in court, and verdict about to be pronounced, when the foreman of the jury begged that some of the burnt pig, of which the culprits stood accused, might be handed into the box. He handled it, and they all handled it, and burned their fingers, as Bo-bo and his father had done before them, and nature prompting to each of them the same remedy, against the face of all the facts, and the clearest charge which judge had ever given—to the surprise of the whole court, townfolk, strangers, reporters, and all present—without leaving the box, or any manner of consultation whatever, they brought in a simultaneous verdict of Not Guilty.

The judge, who was a shrewd fellow, winked at the manifest iniquity of the decision; and when the court was dismissed, went privily and bought up all the pigs that could be had for love or money. In a few days his lordship's town-house was observed to be on fire. The thing took wing, and now there was nothing to be seen but fires in every direction. Fuel and pigs grew enormously dear all over the district. The insurance offices, one and all, shut up shop. People built slighter and slighter every day, until it was feared that the very science of architecture would in no long time be lost to the world. Thus this custom of firing houses continued, till in process of time, says my manuscript, a sage arose, like our Locke, who made a discovery that the flesh of swine, or indeed of any other animal, might be cooked (*burnt,* as they called it) without the necessity of consuming a whole house to dress it. Then first began the rude form of a gridiron. Roasting by the string or spit came in a century or two later, I forget in whose dynasty. By such slow degrees, concludes the manuscript, do the most useful, and seemingly the most obvious arts, make their way among mankind.

Without placing too implicit faith in the account above given, it must be agreed that if a worthy pretext for so dangerous an experiment as setting houses on fire (especially in these days) could be assigned in favor of any culinary object, that pretext and excuse might be found in ROAST PIG.

Of all the delicacies in the whole *mundus edibilis,* I will maintain it to be the most delicate—*princeps obsoniorum.*

I speak not of your grown porkers —things between pig and pork— those hobbledehoys—but a young and tender suckling—under a moon old —guiltless as yet of the sty—with no original speck of the *amor immunditiae,* the hereditary failing of the first parent, yet manifest—his voice as yet not broken, but something between a childish treble and a grumble —the mild forerunner, or *praeludium,* of a grunt.

He must be roasted. I am not ignorant that our ancestors ate them seethed, or boiled—but what a sacrifice of the exterior tegument!

There is no flavor comparable, I will contend, to that of the crisp, tawny, well-watched, not over-roasted, *crackling,* as it is well called—the very teeth are invited to their share of the pleasure at this banquet in overcoming the coy, brittle resistance—

with the adhesive oleaginous—O call it not fat! but an indefinable sweetness growing up to it—the tender blossoming of fat—fat cropped in the bud—taken in the shoot—in the first innocence—the cream and quintessence of the child-pig's yet pure food —the lean, no lean, but a kind of animal manna—or, rather, fat and lean (if it must be so) so blended and running into each other, that both together make but one ambrosian result or common substance.

Behold him. while he is "doing"— it seemeth rather a refreshing warmth, than a scorching heat, that he is so passive to. How equably he twirleth round the string! Now he is just done. To see the extreme sensibility of that tender age! he hath wept out his pretty eyes — radiant jellies — shooting stars—

See him in the dish, his second cradle, how meek he lieth! Wouldst thou have had this innocent grow up to the grossness and indocility which too often accompany maturer swinehood? Ten to one he would have proved a glutton, a sloven, an obstinate, disagreeable animal—wallowing in all manner of filthy conversation— from these sins he is happily snatched away—

Ere sin could blight, or sorrow fade, Death came with timely care—

his memory is odoriferous—no clown curseth, while his stomach half rejecteth, the rank bacon—no coalheaver bolteth him in reeking sausages —he hath a fair sepulcher in the grateful stomach of the judicious epicure—and for such a tomb might be content to die.

He is the best of Sapors. Pineapple is great. She is indeed almost too transcendent—a delight, if not sinful, yet so like to sinning, that really a tender-conscienced person would do well to pause—too ravishing for mortal taste, she woundeth and excoriateth the lips that approach her —like lovers' kisses, she biteth—she is a pleasure bordering on pain from the fierceness and insanity of her relish—but she stoppeth at the palate —she meddleth not with the appetite —and the coarsest hunger might barter her consistently for a mutton chop.

Pig—let me speak his praise—is no less provocative of the appetite than he is satisfactory to the criticalness of the censorious palate. The strong man may batten on him, and the weakling refuseth not his mild juices.

Unlike to mankind's mixed characters, a bundle of virtues and vices, inexplicably intertwisted, and not to be unraveled without hazard, he is—good throughout. No part of him is better or worse than another. He helpeth, as far as his little means extend, all around. He is the least envious of banquets. He is all neighbors' fare.

I am one of those who freely and ungrudgingly impart a share of the good things of this life which fall to their lot (few as mine are in this kind) to a friend. I protest I take as great an interest in my friend's pleasures, his relishes, and proper satisfactions, as in mine own. "Presents," I often say, "endear Absents." Hares, pheasants, partridges, snipes, barn-door chickens (those "tame villatic fowl"), capons, plovers, brawn, barrels of oysters, I dispense as freely as I receive them. I love to taste them, as it were, upon the tongue of my friend. But a stop must be put somewhere. One would not, like Lear, "give everything." I make my stand upon pig. Methinks it is an ingratitude to the Giver of all good favors, to extradomiciliate, or send out of the

house, slightingly (under pretext of friendship, or I know not what), a blessing so particularly adapted, predestined, I may say, to my individual palate. It argues an insensibility.

I remember a touch of conscience in this kind at school. My good old aunt, who never parted from me at the end of a holiday without stuffing a sweetmeat, or some nice thing, into my pocket, had dismissed me one evening with a smoking plum-cake, fresh from the oven. In my way to school (it was over London Bridge) a grayheaded old beggar saluted me (I have no doubt at this time of day that he was a counterfeit). I had no pence to console him with, and in the vanity of self-denial, and the very coxcombry of charity, schoolboy-like, I made him a present of—the whole cake! I walked on a little, buoyed up, as one is on such occasions, with a sweet soothing of self-satisfaction; but before I had got to the end of the bridge, my better feelings returned, and I burst into tears, thinking how ungrateful I had been to my good aunt, to go and give her good gift away to a stranger, that I had never seen before, and who might be a bad man for aught I knew; and then I thought of the pleasure my aunt would be taking in thinking that I— I myself, and not another—would eat her nice cake—and what should I say to her the next time I saw her—how naughty I was to part with her pretty present—and the odor of that spicy cake came back upon my recollection, and the pleasure and the curiosity I had taken in seeing her make it, and her joy when she sent it to the oven, and how disappointed she would feel that I had never had a bit of it in my mouth at last—and I blamed my impertinent spirit of almsgiving, and out-of-place hypocrisy of goodness, and above all I wished never to see the face again of that insidious, good-for-nothing, old gray impostor.

Our ancestors were nice in their method of sacrificing these tender victims. We read of pigs whipped to death, with something of a shock, as we hear of any other obsolete custom. The age of discipline is gone by, or it would be curious to inquire (in a philosophical light merely) what effect this process might have toward intenerating and dulcifying a substance naturally so mild and dulcet as the flesh of young pigs. It looks like refining a violet. Yet we should be cautious, while we condemn the inhumanity, how we censure the wisdom of the practice. It might impart a gusto—

I remember an hypothesis, argued upon by the young students, when I was at St. Omer's, and maintained with much learning and pleasantry on both sides, "Whether, supposing that the flavor of a pig who obtained his death by whipping (*per flagellationem extremam*) superadded a pleasure upon the palate of a man more intense than any possible suffering we can conceive in the animal, is man justified in using that method of putting the animal to death?" I forget the decision.

His sauce should be considered. Decidedly, a few bread crumbs, done up with his liver and brains, and a dash of mild sage. But, banish, dear Mrs. Cook, I beseech you, the whole onion tribe. Barbecue your whole hogs to your palate, steep them in shalots, stuff them out with plantations of the rank and guilty garlic; you cannot poison them, or make them stronger than they are—but consider, he is a weakling—a flower.

For Thought and Discussion

1. How do the introductory sentences indicate that the subject of roast pig is to be treated in a pretentious and seemingly serious fashion?
2. What effect is produced by references to a Chinese manuscript, to the customs in Abyssinia, and to Confucius?
3. What is the effect of using the names *Ho-ti, Bo-bo,* and *swineherd?*
4. How did Bo-bo naturally and accidentally taste roast pig? How do the father's curses heighten the humorous effect?
5. Does bringing the court into the story seemingly add dignity? How does the trial become a farce? How is the judge and how are the people in turn ridiculed on the subject of learning how to cook meat?
6. What tribute does the author pay to roast pig? Is this a popular dish in England? How does his description of this appetizing delicacy appeal to the senses?
7. Why was pineapple a much greater delicacy in Lamb's day than it is in our day?
8. How does Lamb lead up to a climax?
9. What makes the incident on giving away the plum cake humorous? Is one who is inclined to be altruistic likely to be led at times by his emotion to grounds beyond himself?

10. How in the end does Lamb accentuate the delicate flavor of roast pig?
11. How often can you compare reactions of people in the essay to similar reactions of your own?
12. How does Lamb succeed in giving to this favored delicacy, roast pig, a humorous history?
13. Can you find examples of high-sounding and pretentious words? Compile a list of interesting words from this essay. Learn the definitions.

Plus Work

After the manner of Lamb write an essay of your own on the origin of some such dish as roast turkey or pumpkin pie. The story may have an Indian background.

TO A LOUSE

On seeing one on a lady's bonnet at church

ROBERT BURNS

HA! whare ye gaun,[1] ye crowlan ferlie[2]!
Your impudence protects you sairlie;[3]
I canna say but ye strunt rarely
    Owre[4] gawze and lace;
Though faith! I fear ye dine but sparely   5
    On sic[5] a place.

Ye ugly, creepan, blastet wonner,[6]
Detested, shunned by saunt an' sinner,
How daur[7] ye set your fit[8] upon her,
    Sae fine a lady?   10
Gae somewhere else and seek your dinner
    On some poor body.

Swith, in some beggar's hauffet[9] squattle;

There ye may creep, an' sprawl, an' sprattle,
Wi' ither kindred, jumping cattle,   15
    In shoals and nations;
Whare horn[10] or bane ne'er daur unsettle
    Your thick plantations.

Now haud you there, ye're out o' sight,
Below the fatt'rells,[11] snug an' tight;
Na, faith ye yet! ye'll no be right   21
    'Till ye've got on it—
The vera tapmost, towrin height
    O' Miss's bonnet.

My sooth! right bauld[12] ye set your nose out,   25
As plump an' gray as onie grozet;[13]
O for some rank, mercurial rozet,[14]
    Or fell, red smeddum,[14]
I'd gie ye sic a hearty dose o't,
    Wad dress your droddum!   30

---

[1]*gaun*, going.
[2]*ferlie*, wonder.
[3]*sairlie*, surely.
[4]*owre*, over.
[5]*sic*, such.
[6]*wonner*, wonder.
[7]*daur*, dare.
[8]*fit*, foot.
[9]*hauffet*, temples, hair at temples.

[10]*horn, bane*, horn or bone comb.
[11]*fatt'rells*, trimmings.
[12]*bauld*, bold.
[13]*grozet*, gooseberry.
[14]*rozet, smeddum*, fatal drugs.

I wad na been surprised to spy
You on an auld wife's flainen toy;
Or aiblins some bit duddie[15] boy,
　　On's wylecoat;
But Miss's fine Lunardi![16] fye!   35
　　How daur ye do't?

O Jenny, dinna toss your head,
An' set your beauties a' abroad!
Ye little ken[17] what cursèd speed

---

[15]*duddie*, ragged.
[16]*Lunardi*, balloon-shaped bonnet.
[17]*ken*, know.

The blastie's makin!   40
Thae winks an' finger-ends, I dread,
　　Are notice takin.

O wad some Power the giftie gie us
To see oursels as others see us!
It wad frae monie a blunder free us,
　　An' foolish notion;   46
What airs in dress an' gait wad lea'e
us,
　　And ev'n devotion!

For Thought and Discussion

1. Why has this poem been read widely?
2. Why did Burns refuse to leave "To a Louse" out of his collection, even though the publisher did not consider it refined?
3. Burns could find even in a small incident a universal truth, one touching the lives of people the world over. Compare the truth expressed in this poem with that expressed in his sympathetic poem, "To a Mouse."

ROBERT BURNS 1759-1796

Poverty in Early Life. The father of the poet, Robert Burns, was a tenant farmer oppressed by poverty, and consequently Robert learned to follow the plough at an early age, working long hours and having only a few weeks of school in the summer. In this life of want and hardship the bright spot was the home, in which tenderness, kindness, honesty, and good sense prevailed. The Scotch respect for education was responsible for the teaching which the children received from the father at the home fireside after the day's hard work was over.

After the father's death Burns and his brother Gilbert moved to another farm, on which they fared badly. It was at this time that the young ploughman began composing love songs, among which are "Jean," to Jean Armour, whom he afterwards married; and "Highland Mary" and "Sweet Afton," to Mary Campbell, whose death saddened his life.

Triumph in Edinburgh. Because of adversity and general unhappiness Burns decided to emigrate to Jamaica, and to pay his expenses he collected and published his poems. The recognition and appreciation which were immediately accorded his work changed his plans, and he moved to Edinburgh, where he was cordially received in fashionable circles and where he thoroughly enjoyed himself the first winter.

The Poet's Description of Himself. For a picture of this young genius one may turn to the poet himself: "A man who had

ROBERT BURNS

little art in making money, and still less in keeping it; but was, however, a man of some sense, a great deal of honesty, and unbounded good will to every creature, rational and irrational.

"As he was but little indebted to scholastic education, and bred at the plough-tail, his performances must be strongly tinctured with his unpolished, rustic way of life; but as I believe they are really his own, it may be some entertainment to a curious observer of human nature to see how a ploughman thinks and feels under pressure of love, ambition, anxiety, grief, and the like cares and passions, which, however diversified by the modes and manners of life, operate pretty much alike, I believe, on all the species." These simple heartfelt sentiments expressed in his poems have endeared them to readers.

Disappointments. The fortunes of Burns, which had risen like a skyrocket, descended almost as rapidly. He found life in Edinburgh disappointing; for various reasons he lost his friends and became melancholy. Leaving Edinburgh, he married Jean Armour and returned to farming, which, as usual with him, proved unprofitable. The necessity for earning a living caused him to accept a position as exciseman, but this divided purpose—for he knew that he was neglecting his one great gift, poetry—made life difficult and brought unhappiness. At Dumfries he spent his last tragic years, and there, although his health was undermined, he wrote some of his beautiful songs and his long humorous poem "Tam o' Shanter."

Early Death.   Broken in spirit and health and disappointed with life, he died at the age of thirty-seven years. The notice of his death aroused the public to the fact that Scotland had lost her great poet, and recognition and sympathy, so sadly lacking in the last years of his life, were given him when crowds of people came to his grave to pay tribute. A* very imposing monument was erected to his memory.

❧

GULLIVER'S TRAVELS

JONATHAN SWIFT

A VOYAGE TO LILLIPUT

From Part I

[*Gulliver's Travels,* a story which is read widely because it tells of Gulliver's amusing adventures among pygmies and giants, was really written as an ironical criticism of the times, the early part of the eighteenth century. Jonathan Swift uses a fantastic voyage for describing under disguise the life of the Western world. In the first voyage he reduces the proportions of life to pygmy size, and in the second voyage he enlarges the proportions of life to giant size. In both accounts he holds up to scorn the pettiness of human life. There are a few things which he does not ridicule, those aspects of life which he feels do not change when belittled, such as intelligence, courage, altruism, and devotion. He does not condemn religion, but he does condemn religious quarrels and corruption in the church. In this allegorical story of English court life, Lilliput is England; Flimnap, the prime minister Horace Walpole; a Nardac, a nobleman. The Big Endians and the Little Endians are different religious parties, and the wearers of low and high heels are High and Low Churchmen. Gulliver himself, in the first voyage, is a typical ordinary person.]

CHAPTER I

The author gives some account of himself and family, his first inducements to travel. He is shipwrecked, and swims for his life, gets safe on shore in the country of Lilliput, is made a prisoner, and carried up the country.

MY father had a small estate in Nottinghamshire; I was the third of five sons. He sent me to Emanuel College in Cambridge, at fourteen years old, where I resided three years, and applied myself close to my studies; but the charge of maintaining me (although I had a very scanty allowance) being too great for a narrow fortune, I was bound apprentice to Mr. James Bates, an eminent surgeon in London, with whom I continued four years; and my father now and then sending me small sums of money, I laid them out in learning navigation, and other parts of the mathematics, useful to those who intend to travel, as I always believed it would be some time or other my fortune to do. When I left Mr. Bates, I went down to my father; where by the assistance of him and my Uncle John, and some other relations, I got forty pounds, and a promise of thirty pounds a year to maintain me at Leyden: there I studied physic two years and seven months, knowing it would be useful in long voyages.

Soon after my return from Leyden, I was recommended by my good master Mr. Bates, to be surgeon to the *Swallow*, Captain Abraham Pannell, Commander; with whom I continued three years and a half, making a voyage or two into the Levant, and some other parts. When I came back, I resolved to settle in London, to which Mr. Bates, my master, encouraged me, and by him I was recommended to several patients. I took part of a small house in the Old Jewry; and being advised to alter my condition, I married Mistress Mary Burton, second daughter to Mr. Edmond Burton, hosier in Newgate Street, with whom I received four hundred pounds for a portion.

But, my good master Bates dying in two years after, and I having few friends, my business began to fail; for my conscience would not suffer me to imitate the bad practice of too many among my brethren. Having, therefore, consulted with my wife, and some of my acquaintance, I determined to go again to sea. I was surgeon successively in two ships, and made several voyages, for six years, to the East and West Indies, by which I got some addition to my fortune. My hours of leisure I spent in reading the best authors, ancient and modern, being always provided with a good number of books; and when I was ashore, in observing the manners and dispositions of the people, as well as learning their language, wherein I had a great facility by the strength of my memory.

The last of these voyages not proving very fortunate, I grew weary of the sea and intended to stay at home with my wife and family. I removed from the Old Jewry to Fetter Lane, and from thence to Wapping, hoping to get business among the sailors; but it would not turn to account. After three years' expectation that things would mend, I accepted an advantageous offer from Captain William Prichard, Master of the *Antelope*, who was making a voyage to the South Sea. We set sail from Bristol, May 4th, 1699, and our voyage at first was very prosperous.

It would not be proper, for some reasons, to trouble the reader with the particulars of our adventures in those seas: let it suffice to inform him, that in our passage from thence to the East Indies, we were driven by a violent storm to the northwest of Van Diemen's Land. By an observation, we found ourselves in the latitude of 30 degrees 2 minutes south. Twelve of our crew were dead by immoderate labour, and ill food; the rest were in a very weak condition. On the fifth of November, which was the beginning of summer in those parts, the weather being very hazy, the seamen spied a rock, within half a cable's length of the ship; but the wind was so strong that we were driven directly upon it, and immediately split. Six of the crew, of whom I was one, having let down the boat into the sea, made a shift to get clear of the ship, and the rock. We rowed by my computation about three leagues, till we were able to work no longer, being already spent with labour while we were in the ship. We therefore trusted ourselves to the mercy of the waves, and in about half an hour the boat was overset by a sudden flurry from the north. What became of my companions in the boat, as well as of those who escaped on the rock, or were left in the vessel, I cannot tell, but conclude they were all lost. For my own part, I swam as fortune directed me, and was pushed forward by wind and tide. I often let my legs drop, and could feel no bottom, but when I was almost gone, and able to struggle no longer, I found myself within my depth; and by this time the storm was much abated. The declivity was so small, that I walked near a mile before I got to the shore, which I conjectured was about eight o'clock in the evening. I then advanced forward near half a mile, but could not discover any sign of houses or inhabitants; at least I was in so weak a condition that I did not observe them. I was extremely tired, and with that, and the heat of the weather, and about half a pint of brandy that I drank as I left the ship, I found myself much inclined to sleep. I lay down on the grass, which was very short and soft, where I slept sounder than ever I remember to have done in my life, and as I reckoned, above nine hours; for when I awaked, it was just day-light. I attempted to rise, but was not able to stir: for as I happened to lie on my back, I found my arms and legs were strongly fastened on each side to the ground; and my hair, which was long and thick, tied down in the same manner. I likewise felt several slender ligatures across my body, from my armpits to my thighs. I could only look upwards, the sun began to grow hot, and the light offended mine eyes. I heard a confused noise about me, but in the posture I lay, could see nothing except the sky. In a little time I felt something alive moving on my left leg, which advancing gently forward over my breast, came almost up to my chin;

when bending mine eyes downwards as much as I could, I perceived it to be a human creature not six inches high, with a bow and arrow in his hands and a quiver at his back. In the meantime, I felt at least forty more of the same kind (as I conjectured) following the first. I was in the utmost astonishment, and roared so loud, that they all ran back in a fright, and some of them, as I was afterwards told, were hurt with the falls they got by leaping from my sides upon the ground. However, they soon returned, and one of them, who ventured so far as to get a full sight of my face, lifting up his hands and eyes by way of admiration, cried out in a shrill but distinct voice, *Hekinah degul.* The others repeated the same words several times, but I then knew not what they meant. I lay all this while, as the reader may believe, in great uneasiness; at length, struggling to get loose, I had the fortune to break the strings, and wrench out the pegs that fastened my left arm to the ground, for, by lifting it up to my face, I discovered the methods they had taken to bind me, and, at the same time, with a violent pull, which gave me excessive pain, I a little loosened the strings that tied down my hair on the left side, so that I was just able to turn my head about two inches. But the creatures ran off a second time, before I could seize them; whereupon there was a great shout in a very shrill accent, and after it had ceased, I heard one of them cry aloud, *Tolgo phonac;* when in an instant I felt above an hundred arrows discharged on my left hand, which pricked me like so many needles; and besides they shot another flight into the air, as we do bombs in Europe, whereof many, I suppose, fell on my body, (though I felt them not) and some on my face, which I immedi-

ately covered with my left hand. When this shower of arrows was over, I fell a groaning with grief and pain, and then striving again to get loose, they discharged another volley larger than the first, and some of them attempted with spears to stick me in the sides; but, by good luck, I had on me a buff jerkin, which they could not pierce. I thought it the most prudent method to lie still, and my design was to continue so till night, when my left hand being already loose, I could easily free myself: and as for the inhabitants, I had reason to believe I might be a match for the greatest armies they could bring against me, if they were all of the same size with him that I saw. But fortune disposed otherwise of me. When the people observed I was quiet, they discharged no more arrows: but by the noise I heard, I knew their numbers increased; and about four yards from me, over against my right ear, I heard a knocking for above an hour, like that of people at work; when turning my head that way, as well as the pegs and strings would

permit me, I saw a stage erected about a foot and a half from the ground, capable of holding four of the inhabitants, with two or three ladders to mount it, from whence one of them, who seemed to be a person of quality, made me a long speech, whereof I understood not one syllable. But I should have mentioned, that before the principal person began his oration, he cried out three times *Langro dehul san:* (these words and the former were afterwards repeated and explained to me). Whereupon, immediately about fifty of the inhabitants came and cut the strings that fastened the left side of my head, which gave me the liberty of turning it to the right, and of observing the person and gesture of him that was to speak. He appeared to be of a middle age, and taller than any of the other three who attended him, whereof one was a page that held up his train and seemed to be somewhat longer than my middle finger; the other two stood one on each side to support him. He acted every part of an orator, and I could observe many periods of threatening, and others of promises, pity and kindness. I answered in a few words, but in the most submissive manner, lifting up my left hand and both mine eyes to the sun, as calling him for a witness; and being almost famished with hunger, having not eaten a morsel for some hours before I left the ship, I found the demands of nature so strong upon me that I could not forbear showing my impatience (perhaps against the strict rules of decency) by putting my finger frequently on my mouth, to signify that I wanted food. The *hurgo* (for so they call a great lord, as I afterwards learnt) understood me very well. He descended from the stage and commanded that several ladders should be applied to my sides, on which above an hundred of the inhabitants mounted, and walked towards my mouth, laden with baskets full of meat, which had been provided and sent thither by the king's orders upon the first intelligence he received of me. I observed there was the flesh of several animals, but could not distinguish them by the taste. There were shoulders, legs and loins shaped like those of mutton, and very well dressed, but smaller than the wings of a lark. I ate them by two or three at a mouthful, and took three loaves at a time, about the bigness of musket bullets. They supplied me as they could, showing a thousand marks of wonder and astonishment at my bulk and appetite. I then made another sign that I wanted drink. They found by my eating that a small quantity would not suffice me, and being a most ingenious people, they slung up with great dexterity one of their largest hogsheads, then rolled it towards my hand, and beat out the top; I drank it off at a draught, which I might well do, for it did not hold half a pint, and tasted like a small wine of Burgundy, but much more delicious. They brought me a second hogshead, which I drank in the same manner, and made signs for more, but they had none to give me. When I had performed these wonders, they shouted for joy, and danced upon my breast, repeating several times as they did at first, *Hekinah degul.* They made me a sign that I should throw down the two hogsheads, but first warning the people below to stand out of the way, crying aloud, *Borach mivola,* and when they saw the vessels in the air, there was an universal shout of *Hekinah degul.* I confess I was often tempted, while they were passing backwards and forwards on my body, to seize forty or fifty of the first that came in my reach, and dash them against the ground. But the remembrance of what I had felt, which probably might not be the worst they could do, and the promise of honour I made them, for so I interpreted my submissive behaviour, soon drove out these imaginations. Besides, I now considered myself as bound by the laws of hospitality to a people who had treated me with so much expense and magnificence. However, in my thoughts I could not sufficiently wonder at the intrepidity of these diminutive mortals, who durst venture to mount and walk upon my body, while one of my hands was at liberty, without trembling at the very sight of so prodigious a creature as I must appear to them. After some time, when they observed that I made no more demands for meat, there appeared before me a person of high rank from his Imperial Majesty. His Excellency having mounted on the small of my right leg, advanced forwards up to my face, with about a dozen of his retinue. And producing his credentials under the signet royal, which he applied close to mine eyes, spoke about ten minutes, without any signs of anger, but with a kind of determinate resolution; often pointing forwards which as I afterwards found, was towards the capital city, about half a mile distant, whither it was agreed by his majesty in council that I must be conveyed. I answered in few words, but to no purpose, and made a sign with my hand that was loose, putting it to the other (but over his excellency's head, for fear of hurting him or his train) and then to my own head and body, to signify that I desired my liberty. It appeared that he understood me well enough, for he shook his head by way of disapprobation, and held his hand in a posture to show that I must be carried as a prisoner. However, he made other signs to let me understand that I should have meat and drink enough, and very good treatment. Whereupon I once more thought of attempting to break my bonds, but again, when I felt the smart of their arrows, upon my face and hands, which were all in blisters, and many of the darts still sticking in them, and observing likewise that the number of my enemies increased, I gave tokens to let them know that they might do with me what they pleased. Upon this the *hurgo* and his train withdrew with much civility and cheerful countenances. Soon after I heard a general shout, with frequent repetitions of the words, *Peplom selan*, and I felt great numbers of the people on my left side relaxing the cords to such a degree, that I was able to turn upon my right . . . . . But before this, they had daubed my face and both my hands with a sort of ointment very pleasant to the smell, which in a few minutes removed all the smart of their arrows. These circumstances added to the refreshment I had received by their victuals and drink, which were very nourishing, disposed me to sleep. I slept about eight hours, as I was afterwards assured; and it was no wonder, for the physicians, by the Emperor's order, had mingled a sleepy potion in the hogsheads of wine.

It seems that upon the first moment I was discovered sleeping on the ground after my landing, the Emperor had early notice of it by an express, and determined in council that I should be tied in the manner I have related (which was done in the night while I slept), that plenty of meat and drink should be sent to me, and a machine prepared to carry me to the capital city.

This resolution perhaps may appear very bold and dangerous, and I am confident would not be imitated by any prince in Europe on the like occasion; however, in my opinion it was extremely prudent as well as generous. For supposing these people had endeavored to kill me with their spears and arrows while I was asleep, I should certainly have waked with the first sense of smart, which might so far have roused my rage and strength, as to have enabled me to break the strings wherewith I was tied; after which, as they were not able to make resistance, so they could expect no mercy.

These people are most excellent mathematicians and arrived to a great perfection in mechanics by the countenance and encouragement of the emperor, who is a renowned patron of learning. This prince hath several machines fixed on wheels for the carriage of trees and other great weights. He often builds his largest men of war, whereof some are nine feet long, in the woods where the timber grows, and has them carried on these engines three or four hundred yards to the sea. Five hundred carpenters and engineers were immediately set at work to prepare the greatest engine they had. It was a frame of wood raised three inches from the ground, about seven feet long and four wide, moving upon twenty-two wheels. The shout I heard was upon the arrival of this engine, which it seems set out in four hours after my landing. It was brought parallel to me as I lay. But the principal difficulty was to raise and place me in this vehicle. Eighty poles, each of one foot high, were erected for this purpose, and very strong cords of the bigness of packthread were fastened by hooks to many bandages, which the workmen had girt round my neck, my hands, my body, and my legs. Nine hundred of the strongest men were employed to draw up these cords by many pulleys fastened on the poles, and thus in less than three hours, I was raised and slung into the engine, and there tied fast. All this I was told, for while the whole operation was performing, I lay in a profound sleep, by the force of that soporiferous medicine infused into my liquor. Fifteen hundred of the emperor's largest horses, each about four inches and an half high, were employed to draw me towards the metropolis, which, as I said, was half a mile distant.

About four hours after we began our journey, I awakened by a very ridiculous accident; for the carriage being stopped a while to adjust something that was out of order, two or three of the young natives had the curiosity to see how I looked when I was asleep; they climbed up into the engine, and advancing very softly to my face, one of them, an officer in the guards, put the sharp end of his half-pike a good way up into my left nostril, which tickled my nose like a straw, and made me sneeze violently; whereupon they stole off unperceived, and it was three weeks before I knew the cause of my awaking so suddenly. We made a long march the remaining part of that day, and rested at night with five hundred guards on each side of me, half with torches, and half with bows and arrows, ready to shoot me if I should offer to stir. The next morning at sunrise we continued our march, and arrived within two hundred yards of the city gates about noon. The emperor, and all his court, came out to meet us, but his great officers would by no means suffer his majesty to endanger his person by mounting on my body.

At the place where the carriage stopped, there stood an ancient temple, esteemed to be the largest in the whole kingdom, which having been polluted some years before by an unnatural murder, was, according to the zeal of those people, looked on as profane, and therefore had been applied to common use, and all the ornaments and furniture carried away. In this edifice it was determined I should lodge. The great gate fronting to the north, was about four feet high and almost two feet wide, through which I could easily creep. On each side of the gate was a small window not above six inches from the ground: into that on the left side, the king's smiths conveyed fourscore and eleven chains, like those that hang to a lady's watch in Europe, and almost as large, which were locked to my left leg with six and thirty padlocks. Over against this temple, on the other side of the great highway, at twenty feet distance, there was a turret at least five feet high. Here the emperor ascended with many principal lords of his court, to have an opportunity of viewing me, as I was told, for I could not see them. It was reckoned that above an hundred thousand inhabitants came out of the town upon the same errand; and in spite of my guards, I believe there could not be fewer than ten thousand, at several times, who mounted upon my body by the help of ladders. But a proclamation was soon issued to forbid it upon pain of death. When the workmen found it was impossible for me to break loose, they cut all the strings that bound me; whereupon I rose up with as melancholy a disposition as ever I had in my life. But the noise and astonishment of the people at seeing me rise and walk are not to be expressed. The chains that held my left leg were about two yards long, and gave me not only the liberty of walking backwards and forwards in a semicircle; but being fixed within four inches of the gate, allowed me to creep in, and lie at my full length in the temple.

CHAPTER IV

Milendo, the metropolis of Lilliput, described, together with the emperor's palace. A conversation between the author and a principal secretary, concerning the affairs of that empire: The Author's offers to serve the emperor in his wars.

The first request I made after I had obtained my liberty, was, that I might have license to see Milendo, the metropolis; which the emperor easily granted me, but with a special charge to do no hurt, either to the inhabitants, or their houses. The people had notice by proclamation of my design to visit the town. The wall which encompassed it is two feet and a half high, and at least eleven inches broad, so that a coach and horses may be driven very safely round it; and it is flanked with strong towers at ten feet distance. I stepped over the great

western gate, and passed very gently, and sideling through the two principal streets, only in my short waistcoat, for fear of damaging the roofs and eves of the houses with the skirts of my coat. I walked with the utmost circumspection, to avoid treading on any stragglers, that might remain in the streets, although the orders were very strict, that all people should keep in their houses, at their own peril. The garret windows and tops of houses were so crowded with spectators, that I thought in all my travels I had not seen a more populous place. The city is an exact square, each side of the wall being five hundred feet long. The two great streets, which run cross and divide it into four quarters, are five feet wide. The lanes and alleys, which I could not enter, but only viewed them as I passed, are from twelve to eighteen inches. The town is capable of holding five hundred thousand souls. The houses are from three to five stories. The shops and markets well provided.

The emperor's palace is in the center of the city, where the two great streets meet. It is inclosed by a wall of two feet high, and twenty feet distant from the buildings. I had his majesty's permission to step over this wall; and the space being so wide between that and the palace, I could easily view it on every side. The outward court is a square of forty feet, and includes two other courts: in the inmost are the royal apartments, which I was very desirous to see, but found it extremely difficult; for the great gates, from one square into another, were but eighteen inches high, and seven inches wide. Now the buildings of the outer court were at least five feet high, and it was impossible for me to stride over them, without infinite damage to the pile, though the walls were strongly built of hewn stone, and four inches thick. At the same time the emperor had a great desire that I should see the magnificence of his palace; but this I was not able to do till three days after, which I spent in cutting down with my knife some of the largest trees in the Royal Park, about an hundred yards distant from the city. Of these trees I made two stools, each about three feet high, and strong enough to bear my weight. The people having received notice a second time, I went again through the city to the palace, with my two stools in my hands. When I came to the side of the outer court, I stood upon one stool, and took the other in my hand: this I lifted over the roof, and gently set it down on the space between the first and second court, which was eight feet wide. I then stepped over the buildings very conveniently from one stool to the other, and drew up the first after me with a hooked stock. By this contrivance I got into the inmost court; and lying down upon my side, I applied my face to the windows of the middle stories which were left open on purpose, and discovered the most splendid apartments that can be imagined. There I saw the empress, and the young princes in their several lodgings, with their chief attendants about them. Her imperial majesty was pleased to smile very graciously upon me, and gave me out of the window her hand to kiss.

But I shall not anticipate the reader with farther descriptions of this kind, because I reserve them for a greater work, which is now almost ready for the press, containing a general description of this empire, from its first erection, through a long series of princes, with a particular account of their wars and politics, laws, learning, and religion: their plants and animals, their peculiar manners and customs, with other matters very curious and useful; my chief design at present being only to relate such events and transactions as happened to the public, or to myself, during a residence of about nine months in that empire.

One morning, about a fortnight after I had obtained my liberty, Reldresal, principal secretary (as they style him) of private affairs, came to my house, attended only by one servant. He ordered his coach to wait at a distance, and desired I would give him an hour's audience; which I readily consented to, on account of his quality and personal merits, as well as the many good offices he had done me during my solicitations at court. I offered to lie down, that he might the more conveniently reach my ear; but he chose rather to let me hold him in my hand during our conversation. He began with compliments on my liberty, said he might pretend to some merit in it: but, however, added, that if it had not been for the present situation of things at court, perhaps I might not have obtained it so soon. For said he, as flourishing a condition as we may appear to be in to foreigners, we labour under two mighty evils; a violent faction at home, and the danger of an invasion by a most potent enemy from abroad. As to the first, you are to understand, that for above seventy moons past, there have been two struggling parties in this empire, under the names of Tramecksan, and Slamecksan, from the high and low heels on their shoes, by which they distinguish themselves. It is alleged indeed that the high heels are most agreeable to our ancient constitution: but however this be, his majesty hath determined to make use of only low heels in the administration of the government, and all offices in the gift of the crown, as you cannot but observe; and particularly, that his majesty's imperial heels are lower at least by a drurr than any of his court (drurr is a measure about the fourteenth part of an inch). The animosities between these two parties run so high, that they will neither eat nor drink, nor talk with each other. We compute the Tramecksan, or high-heels, to exceed us in number; but the power is wholly on our side. We apprehend his imperial highness, the heir to the crown, to have some tendency towards the high-heels; at least, we can plainly discover one of his heels higher than the other, which gives him a hobble in his gait. Now, in the midst of these intestine disquiets, we are threatened with an invasion from the island of Blefuscu, which is the other great empire of the universe, almost as large and powerful as this of his majesty. For as to what we have heard you affirm, that there are other kingdoms and states in the world, inhabited by human creatures as large as yourself, our philosophers are in much doubt, and would rather conjecture that you dropped from the moon, or one of the stars; because it is certain, that an hundred mortals of your bulk would, in a short time, destroy all the fruits and cattle of his majesty's dominions. Besides, our histories of six thousand moons make no mention of any other regions, than the two great empires of Lilliput and Blefuscu, which two mighty powers have, as I was going to tell you, been engaged in a most obstinate war for six and thirty moons past. It began upon the following occasion. It is allowed on all hands, that the primitive way of breaking eggs before we eat them, was upon the larger end; but his present majesty's grandfather, while he was a boy, going to eat an egg, and breaking it according to the ancient practice, happened to cut one of his fingers. Whereupon the emperor, his father, published an edict, commanding all his subjects, upon great penalties to break the smaller end of their eggs. The people so highly resented this law, that our histories tell us there have been six rebellions raised on that account; wherein one emperor lost his life, and another his crown. These civil commotions were constantly fomented by the monarchs of Blefuscu and when they were quelled, the exiles always fled for refuge to that empire. It is computed, that eleven thousand persons have, at several times, suffered death, rather than submit to break their eggs at the smaller end. Many hundred large volumes have been published upon this controversy: but the books of the Big-Endians have been long forbidden, and the whole party rendered incapable by law of holding employments. During the course of these troubles, the emperors of Blefuscu did frequently expostulate by their ambassadors, accusing us of making a schism in religion, by offending against a fundamental doctrine of our great prophet Lustrog, in the fifty-fourth chapter of the Blundecral, (which is their Alcoran). This, however, is thought to be a mere strain upon the text: for the words are these: *That all true believers shall break their eggs at the convenient end:* and which is the convenient end, seems, in my humble opinion, to be left to every man's conscience, or at least in the power of the chief magistrate to determine. Now, the Big-Endian exiles have found so much credit in the emperor of Blefuscu's court, and so much private assistance and encouragement from their party here at home, that a bloody war hath been carried on between the two empires for six and thirty moons with various success;

during which time we have lost forty capital ships, and a much greater number of smaller vessels, together with thirty thousand of our best seamen and soldiers; and the damage received by the enemy is reckoned to be somewhat greater than ours. However, they have now equipped a numerous fleet, and are just preparing to make a descent upon us; and his imperial majesty placing great confidence in your valour and strength, hath commanded me to lay this account of his affairs before you.

I desired the secretary to present my humble duty to the emperor, and to let him know, that I thought it would not become me, who was a foreigner, to interfere with parties; but I was ready, with the hazard of my life, to defend his person and state against all invaders.

CHAPTER VI

Of the inhabitants of Lilliput; their learning, laws, and customs, the manner of educating their children. The author's way of living in that country. His vindication of a great lady.

Although I intend to leave the description of this empire to a particular treatise, yet in the mean time I am content to gratify the curious reader with some general ideas. As the common size of the natives is somewhat under six inches high, so there is an exact proportion in all other animals, as well as plants and trees: for instance the tallest horses and oxen are between four and five inches in height, the sheep an inch and a half, more or less; their geese about the bigness of a sparrow, and so the several gradations downwards, till you come to the smallest, which, to my sight, were almost invisible; but nature hath adapted the eyes of the Lilliputians to all objects proper for their view. They

see with great exactness, but at no great distance. And to show the sharpness of their sight, toward objects that are near, I have been much pleased observing a cook pulling a lark, which was not so large as a common fly; and a young girl threading an invisible needle with invisible silk. Their tallest trees are about seven feet high. I mean some of those in the great Royal Park, the tops whereof I could but just reach with my fist clenched. The other vegetables are in the same proportion; but this I leave to the reader's imagination.

I shall say but little at the present of their learning, which for many ages hath flourished in all its branches among them: but their manner of writing is very peculiar being neither from the left to the right, like the Europeans; nor from the right to the left, like the Arabians, nor from up to down, like the Chinese; nor from down to up, like the Cascagians; but aslant from one corner of the paper to the other, like ladies in England.

They bury their dead with their heads directly downwards, because they hold an opinion, that in eleven thousand moons they are all to rise again, in which period the earth (which they conceive to be flat) will turn upside down, and by this means they shall, at their resurrection, be found ready standing on their feet. The learned among them confess the absurdity of this doctrine, but the practice still continues, in compliance to the vulgar.

There are some laws and customs in this empire very peculiar; and if they were not so directly contrary to those of my own dear country, I should be tempted to say a little in their justification. It is only to be wished, that they were as well executed. The first I shall mention, relates to informers. All crimes against the state are punished here with the utmost severity; but if the person accused maketh his innocence plainly to appear upon his trial, the accuser is immediately put to an ignominious death; and out of his goods or lands, the innocent person is quadruply recompensed for the loss of his time, for the danger he underwent, for the hardship of his imprisonment, and for all the charges he hath been at in making his defence. Or, if that fund be deficient, it is largely supplied by the crown. The emperor does also confer on him some public mark of his favour, and proclamation is made of his innocence through the whole city.

They look upon fraud as a greater crime than theft, and therefore seldom fail to punish it with death; for they allege, that care and vigilance, with a very common understanding, may preserve a man's goods from thieves, but honesty has no fence against superior cunning: and since it is necessary that there should be a perpetual intercourse of buying and selling, and dealing upon credit, where fraud is permitted or connived at, or hath no law to punish it, the honest dealer is always undone, and the knave gets the advantage. I remember when I was once interceding with the king for a criminal who had wronged his master of a great sum of money, which he received by order, and ran away with; and happening to tell his majesty, by way of extenuation, that it was only a breach of trust; the emperor thought it monstrous in me to offer as a defence, the greatest aggravation of the crime: and truly I had little to say in return, farther than the common answer, that different nations had different customs; for, I confess, I was heartily ashamed.

Although we usually call reward and punishment the two hinges upon which all government turns, yet I could never observe this maxim to be put in practice by any nation except that of Lilliput. Whoever can there bring sufficient proof that he hath strictly observed the laws of his country for seventy-three moons, hath a claim to certain privileges, according to his quality and condition of life, with a proportionable sum of money out of a fund appropriated for that use: he likewise acquires the title of *Snilpall*, or *Legal*, which is added to his name, but does not descend to his posterity. And these people thought it a prodigious defect of policy among us, when I told them that our laws were enforced only by penalties without any mention of reward. It is upon this account that the image of justice, in their courts of judicature, is formed with six eyes, two before, as many behind, and on each side one, to signify circumspection; with a bag of gold open in her right hand, and a sword sheathed in her left, to show she is more disposed to reward than to punish.

In choosing persons for all employments, they have more regard to good morals than to great abilities; for, since government is necessary to mankind, they believe that the common size of human understandings is fitted to some station or other, and that providence never intended to make the management of public affairs a mystery, to be comprehended only by a few persons of sublime genius, of which there seldom are three born in an age: but they suppose truth, justice, temperance, and the like, to be in every man's power; the practice of which virtues, assisted by experience and a good intention, would qualify any man for the service of his country, except where a course of study is required. But they thought the want of moral virtues was so far from being supplied by superior endowments of the mind, that employments could never be put into such dangerous hands as those of persons so qualified; and at least, that the mistakes committed by ignorance in a virtuous disposition, would never be of such fatal consequence to the public weal, as the practices of a man whose inclinations led him to be corrupt, and had great abilities to manage and multiply, and defend his corruptions.

In like manner, the disbelief of a divine providence renders a man uncapable of holding any public station; for since kings avow themselves to be the deputies of providence, the Lilliputians think nothing can be more absurd than for a prince to employ such men as disown the authority under which he acts.

In relating these and the following laws, I would only be understood to mean the original institutions, and not the most scandalous corruptions into which these people are fallen by the degenerate nature of man. For as to that infamous practice of acquiring great employments by dancing on the ropes, or badges of favour and distinction by leaping over sticks, and creeping under them, the reader is to observe that they were first introduced by the grandfather of the emperor now reigning, and grew to the present height, by the gradual increase of party and faction.

Ingratitude is among them a capital crime, as we read it to have been in some other countries; for they reason thus, that whoever makes ill returns to his benefactor, must needs be a common enemy to the rest of mankind, from whom he hath received no obligation, and therefore such a man is not fit to live.

Their notions relating to the duties of parents and children differ extremely from ours. Their opinion is, that parents are the last of all others to be trusted with the education of their own children: and therefore they have in every town public nurseries, where all parents, except cottagers and labourers, are obliged to send their infants of both sexes to be reared and educated when they come to the age of twenty moons, at which time, they are supposed to have some rudiments of docility. These schools are of several kinds, suited to different qualities, and to both sexes. They have certain professors well skilled in preparing children for such a condition of life as befits the rank of their parents, and their own capacities as well as inclinations. I shall first say something of the male nurseries, and then of the female.

The nurseries for males of noble or eminent birth, are provided with grave and learned professors, and their several deputies. The clothes and food of the children are plain and simple. They are bred up in the principles of honour, justice, courage, modesty, clemency, religion, and love of their country; they are always employed in some business, except in the times of eating and sleeping, which are very short, and two hours for diversions, consisting of bodily exercises. They are dressed by men till four years of age, and then are obliged to dress themselves, although their quality be ever so great; and the women attendants, who are aged proportionably to ours at fifty, perform only the most menial offices. They are never suffered to converse with servants, but go together in small or greater numbers to take their diversions, and always in the presence of a professor, or one of his deputies; whereby they avoid those early bad impressions of folly and vice to which our children are subject. Their parents are suffered to see them only twice a year; the visit is to last but an hour. They are allowed to kiss the child at meeting and parting; but a professor, who always stands by on those occasions, will not suffer them to whisper, or use any fondling expressions, or bring any presents of toys, sweet-meats, and the like.

The pension from each family for the education and entertainment of a child, upon failure of due payment, is levied by the emperor's officers.

The nurseries for children of ordinary gentlemen, merchants, traders, and handicrafts, are managed proportionably after the same manner; only those designed for trades, are put out apprentices at eleven years old, whereas those of persons of quality continue in their nurseries till fifteen, which answers to one and twenty with us: but the confinement is gradually lessened for the last three years.

In the female nurseries, the young girls of quality are educated much like the males, only they are dressed by orderly servants of their own sex, but always in the presence of a professor or deputy, till they come to dress themselves, which is at five years old. And if it be found that these nurses ever presume to entertain the girls with frightful or foolish stories, or the common follies practised by chamber-maids among us, they are publicly whipped thrice about the city, imprisoned for a year, and banished for life to the most desolate part of the country. Thus the young ladies there are as much ashamed of being cowards and fools, as the men, and despise all personal ornaments beyond decency and cleanliness: neither did I perceive any difference in their education, made by their difference of sex, only that the exercises of the females were not altogether so robust; and that some rules were given them relating to domestic life,

and a smaller compass of learning was enjoined them: for the maxim is, that among people of quality, a wife should be always a reasonable and agreeable companion, because she cannot always be young. When the girls are twelve years old, which among them is the marriageable age, their parents or guardians take them home, with great expressions of gratitude to the professors, and seldom without tears of the young lady and her companions.

In the nurseries of females of the meaner sort, the children are instructed in all kinds of works proper for their sex, and their several degrees: those intended for apprentices, are dismissed at nine years old, the rest are kept to thirteen.

The meaner families, who have children at these nurseries, are obliged, besides their annual pension, which is as low as possible, to return to the steward of the nursery a small monthly share of their gettings, to be a portion for the child, and therefore all parents are limited in their expenses by the law. For the Lilliputians think nothing can be more unjust, than for people to bring children into the world, and leave the burden of supporting them on the public. As to persons of quality, they give security to appropriate a certain sum for each child, suitable to their condition; and these funds are always managed with good husbandry, and the most exact justice.

The cottagers and labourers keep their children at home, their business being only to till and cultivate the earth, and therefore their education is of little consequence to the public; but the old and diseased among them are supported by hospitals: for begging is a trade unknown in this kingdom.

And here it may perhaps divert the curious reader, to give some account of my domestic, and my manner of living in this country, during a residence of nine months and thirteen days. Having a head mechanically turned, and being likewise forced by necessity, I had made for myself a table and chair convenient enough, out of the largest trees in the royal park. Two hundred seamstresses were employed to make me ·shirts, and linen for my bed and table, all of the strongest and coarsest kind they could get; which, however, they were forced to quilt together in several folds, for the thickest was some degrees finer than lawn. Their linen is usually three inches wide, and three feet make a piece. The seamstresses took my measure as I lay on the ground, one standing at my neck, and another at my mid-leg, with a strong cord extended, that each held by the end, while the third measured the length of the cord with a rule of an inch long. Then they measured my right thumb, and desired no more; for by a mathematical computation, that twice round the thumb is once round the wrist, and so on to the neck and the waist, and by the help of my old shirt, which I displayed on the ground before them for a pattern, they fitted me exactly. Three hundred tailors were employed in the same manner to make me clothes; but they had another contrivance for taking my measure. I kneeled down, and they raised a ladder from the ground to my neck; upon this ladder one of them mounted, and let fall a plum-line from my collar to the floor, which just answered the length of my coat; but my waist and arms I measured myself. When my clothes were finished, which was done in my house, (for the largest of theirs would not be able to hold them) they looked like the patch-work made by the ladies in England, only that mine were all of a colour.

I had three hundred cooks to dress my victuals, in little convenient huts built about my house, where they and their families lived, and prepared me two dishes a-piece. I took up twenty waiters in my hand, and placed them on the table, an hundred more attended below on the ground, some with dishes of meat, and some with barrels of wine, and other liquors, slung on their shoulders; all which the waiters above drew up as I wanted, in a very ingenious manner, by certain cords, as we draw the bucket up a well in Europe. A dish of their meat was a good mouthful, and a barrel of their liquor a reasonable draught. Their mutton yields to ours, but their beef is excellent. I have had a sirloin so large, that I have been forced to make three bits of it; but this is rare. My servants were astonished to see me eat it bones and all, as in our country we do the leg of a lark. Their geese and turkeys I usually eat at a mouthful, and I must confess they far exceed ours. Of their smaller fowl I could take up twenty or thirty at the end of my knife.

One day his imperial majesty being informed of my way of living, desired that himself and his royal consort, with the young princes of the blood of both sexes, might have the happiness (as he was pleased to call it) of dining with me. They came accordingly, and I placed them upon chairs of state on my table, just over-against me, with their guards about them. Flimnap the lord high treasurer attended there likewise, with his white staff; and I observed he often looked on me with a sour countenance, which I would not seem to regard, but eat more than usual in honour to my dear country, as well as to fill the court with admiration. I have some private reasons to believe, that this visit from his majesty gave Flimnap an opportunity of doing me ill offices to his master. That minister had always been my secret enemy, though he outwardly caressed me more than was usual to the moroseness of his nature. He represented to the emperor the low condition of his treasury; that he was forced to take up money at great discount; that exchequer bills would not circulate under nine per cent. below par; that in short I had cost his majesty above a million and half of sprugs, (their greatest gold coin, about the bigness of a spangle); and upon the whole, that it would be advisable in the emperor to take the first fair occasion of dismissing me.

I am here obliged to vindicate the reputation of an excellent lady, who was an innocent sufferer upon my account. The treasurer took a fancy to be jealous of his wife, from the malice of some evil tongues, who informed him that her grace had taken a violent affection for my person, and the court scandal ran for some time, that she once came privately to my lodging. This I solemnly declare to be a most infamous falsehood, without any grounds, farther than that her grace was pleased to treat me with all innocent marks of freedom and friendship. I own she came often to my house, but always publicly, nor ever without three more in the coach, who were usually her sister and young daughter, and some particular acquaintance; but this was common to many other ladies of the court. And I still appeal to my servants round, whether they at any time saw a coach at my door without knowing what persons were in it. On those occasions, when a servant had given me notice,

my custom was to go immediately to the door: and, after paying my respects, to take up the coach and two horses very carefully in my hands, (for if there were six horses, the postillion always unharnessed four) and place them on a table, where I had fixed a movable rim quite round, of five inches high, to prevent accidents. And I have often had four coaches and horses at once on my table full of company, while I sat in my chair, leaning my face towards them; and when I was engaged with one set, the coachman would gently drive the others round my table. I have passed many an afternoon very agreeably in these conversations. But I defy the treasurer, or his two informers, (I will name them, and let 'em make their best of it) Clustril and Drunlo, to prove that any person ever came to me incognito, except the Secretary Reldresal, who was sent by express command of his imperial majesty, as I have before related. I should not have dwelt so long upon this particular, if it had not been a point wherein the reputation of a great lady is so nearly concerned, to say nothing of my own; though I had then the honour to be a Nardac, which the treasurer himself is not; for all the world knows he is only a Glumglum, a title inferior by one degree, as that of a marquis is to a duke in England, although I allow he preceded me in right of his post. These false informations, which I afterwards came to the knowledge of, by an accident not proper to mention, made Flimnap, the treasurer, show his lady for some time an ill countenance, and me a worse; and although he were at last undeceived and reconciled to her, yet I lost all credit with him, and found my interest decline very fast with the emperor himself, who was indeed too much governed by that favourite.

For Thought and Discussion

1. In Chapter IV what are some of the evils mentioned by Rel-dresal? What does Swift ridicule?
2. In Chapter VI what criticism is made of the prosecution of innocent people?
   Is that still a weak point in judicial systems?
   What does Swift say about crime and fraud?
   What does he say of the importance of morals and abilities for public officers? What do you consider the relative value of the two?
3. Swift believed that in the eighteenth century the parent often tyrannized over the child? How has the situation changed?

A VOYAGE TO BROBDINGNAG[1]

From Part II

[When Gulliver goes to the land of the giants, he is a Lilliputian and is very much like those people whom he ridiculed in the first voyage. The giants are an idealized race who have common sense and soundness of judgment, but they are ignorant and have few ideas. The enlargement of the scale of life, represented by the giants, rids the personality of some of its pride and folly, but it also strips human beings of their grace and charm.]

CHAPTER I

A great storm described, the long-boat sent to fetch water, the author goes with it to discover the country. He is left on shore, is seized by one of the natives, and carried to a farmer's house. His reception there, with several accidents that happened there. A description of the inhabitants.

Having been condemned by nature and fortune to an active and restless life, in ten months after my return, I again left my native country, and took shipping in the Downs on the 20th day of June 1702, in the *Adventure,* Captain John Nich-

[1]*Brobdingnag* (brŏb' dĭng năg).

olas, a Cornish man, commander, bound for Surat. We had a very prosperous gale till we arrived at the Cape of Good Hope, where we landed for fresh water, but discovering a leak we unshipped our goods, and wintered there; for the captain falling sick of an ague, we could not leave the Cape till the end of March. We then set sail, and had a good voyage till we passed the Straits of Madagascar; but having got northward of that island, and to about five degrees south latitude, the winds, which in those seas are observed to blow a constant equal gale between the north and west from the beginning of December to the beginning of May, on the 19th of April began to blow with much greater violence, and more westerly than usual, continuing so for twenty days together, during which time we were driven a little to the east of the Molucca Islands, and about three degrees northward of the line, as our captain found by an observation he took the 2nd of May, at which time the wind ceased, and it was a perfect calm, whereat I was not a little rejoiced. But he being a man well experienced in the navigation of those seas, bid us all prepare against a storm, which accordingly happened the day following: for a southern wind, called the southern monsoon, began to set in.

Finding it was like to overblow, we took in our spritsail, and stood by to hand the foresail; but making foul weather, we looked if the guns were all fast, and handed the mizzen. The ship lay very broad off, so we thought it better spooning before the sea, than trying or hulling. We reefed the foresail and set him, we hauled aft the foresheet; the helm was hard a-weather. The ship wore bravely. We belayed the fore-down-hall; but the sail was split, and we hauled down the yard, and got the sail into the ship, and unbound all the things clear of it. It was a very fierce storm; the sea broke strange and dangerous. We hauled off upon the lanyard of the whip-staff, and helped the man at helm. We would not get down our top-mast, but let all stand, because she scudded before the sea very well, and we knew that the top-mast being aloft, the ship was the wholesomer, and made better way through the sea, seeing we had sea-room. When the storm was over, we set foresail and mainsail, and brought the ship to. Then we set the missen, maintop-sail and the foretop-sail. Our course was east northeast, the wind was at southwest. We got the starboard tacks aboard, we cast off our weather-braces and lifts; we set in the lee-braces, and hauled forward by the weather-bowlings, and hauled them tight, and belayed them, and hauled over the missen tack to windward, and kept her full and by as near as she could lie.

During this storm, which was followed by a strong wind west southwest, we were carried, by my computation, about five hundred leagues to the east, so that the oldest sailor on board could not tell in what part of the world we were. Our provisions held out well, our ship was staunch, and our crew all in good health; but we lay in the utmost distress for water. We thought it best to hold on the same course, rather than turn more northerly, which might have brought us to the north-west parts of great Tartary, and into the frozen sea.

On the 16th day of June, 1703, a boy on the topmast discovered land. On the 17th we came in full view of a great island or continent (for we knew not whether) on the south-side whereof was a small neck of land jutting out into the sea, and a creek too shallow to hold a ship of above one hundred tons. We cast anchor within a league of this creek, and our captain sent a dozen of his men well armed in the long boat, with vessels for water, if any could be found. I desired his leave to go with them, that I might see the country, and make what discoveries I could. When we came to land we saw no river or spring, nor any sign of inhabitants. Our men therefore wandered on the shore to find out some fresh water near the sea, and I walked alone about a mile on the other side, where I observed the country all barren and rocky. I now began to be weary, and seeing nothing to entertain my curiosity, I returned gently down towards the creek; and the sea being full in my view, I saw our men already got into the boat, and rowing for life to the ship. I was going to holloa after them, although it had been to little purpose, when I observed a huge creature walking after them in the sea, as fast as he could. He waded not much deeper than his knees, and took prodigious strides, but our men had the start of him half a league, and the sea thereabouts being full of sharp-pointed rocks, the monster was not able to overtake the boat. This I was afterwards told, for I durst not stay to see the issue of that adventure; but ran as fast as I could the way I first went; and then climbed up a steep hill, which gave me some prospect of the country. I found it fully cultivated; but that which first surprised me was the length of the grass, which in those grounds that seemed to be kept for hay, was above twenty feet high.

I fell into a high road, for so I took it to be, though it served to the inhabitants only as a foot path through a field of barley. Here I walked on for some time, but could see little on either side, it being now near harvest, and the corn rising at least forty feet. I was an hour walking to the end of this field, which was fenced in with a hedge of at least one hundred and twenty feet high, and the trees so lofty that I could make no computation of their altitude. There was a stile to pass from this field into the next. It had four steps, and a stone to cross over when you came to the uppermost. It was impossible for me to climb this stile, because every step was six feet high, and the upper stone above twenty. I was endeavouring to find some gap in the hedge, when I discovered one of the inhabitants in the next field, advancing towards the stile, of the same size with him whom I saw in the sea, pursuing our boat. He appeared as tall as an ordinary spire-steeple, and took about ten yards at every stride, as near as I could guess. I was struck with the utmost fear and astonishment, and ran to hide myself in the corn, from whence I saw him at the top of the style, looking back into the next field on the right hand, and heard him call

in a voice many degrees louder than a speaking trumpet; but the noise was so high in the air, that at first I certainly thought it was thunder. Whereupon seven monsters like himself came towards him with reaping-hooks in their hands, each hook about the largeness of six scythes. These people were not so well clad as the first, whose servants or labourers they seemed to be, for upon some words he spoke, they went to reap the corn in the field where I lay. I kept from them at as great a distance as I could, but was forced to move with extreme difficulty, for the stalks of the corn were sometimes not above a foot distant, so that I could hardly squeeze my body betwixt them. I made a shift to go forward till I came to a part of the field where the corn had been laid by the rain and wind. Here it was impossible for me to advance a step; for the stalks were so interwoven that I could not creep through, and the beards of the fallen ears so strong and pointed that they pierced through my clothes into my flesh. At the same time I heard the reapers not above an hundred yards behind me. Being quite dispirited with toil, and wholly overcome by grief and despair, I lay down between two ridges, and heartily wished I might there end my days. I bemoaned my desolate widow, and fatherless children. I lamented my own folly and willfulness in attempting a second voyage against the advice of all my friends and relations. In this terrible agitation of mind I could not forbear thinking of Lilliput, whose inhabitants looked upon me as the greatest prodigy that ever appeared in the world: where I was able to draw an imperial fleet in my hand, and perform those other actions which will be recorded for ever in the chronicles of that empire, while posterity shall hardly believe them, although attested by millions. I reflected what a mortification it must prove to me to appear as inconsiderable in this nation as one single Lilliputian would be among us. But this I conceived was to be the least of my misfortunes: for, as human creatures are observed to be more savage and cruel in proportion to their bulk, what could I expect but to be a morsel in the mouth of the first among these enormous barbarians that should happen to seize me? Undoubtedly philosophers are in the right when they tell us that nothing is great or little otherwise than by comparison. It might have pleased fortune to let the Lilliputians find some nation, where the people were as diminutive with respect to them, as they were to me. And who knows but that even this prodigious race of mortals might be equally overmatched in some distant part of the world, whereof we have yet no discovery?

Scared and confounded as I was, I could not forbear going on with these reflections, when one of the reapers approached within ten yards of the ridge where I lay, made me apprehend that with the next step I should be squashed to death under his foot, or cut in two with his reaping-hook. And therefore when he was again about to move, I screamed as loud as fear could make me. Whereupon the huge creature trod short, and looking round about under him for some time, at last espied me as I lay on the ground. He considered a while with the caution of one who endeavours to lay hold on a small dangerous animal in such a manner that it may not be able either to scratch or to bite him, as I myself have sometimes done with a weasel in England. At length he ventured to take me up behind by the middle between his forefinger

and thumb, and brought me within three yards of his eyes, that he might behold my shape more perfectly. I guessed his meaning, and my good fortune gave me so much presence of mind, that I resolved not to struggle in the least as he held me in the air, about sixty feet from the ground, although he grievously pinched my sides, for fear I should slip through his fingers. All I ventured was to raise mine eyes towards the sun, and place my hands together in a supplicating posture, and to speak some words in an humble and melancholy tone, suitable to the condition I then was in. For I apprehended every moment that he would dash me against the ground, as we usually do any little hateful animal which we have a mind to destroy. But my good star would have it, that he appeared pleased with my voice and gestures, and began to look upon me as a curiosity, much wondering to hear me pronounce articulate words, although he could not understand them. In the meantime I was not able to forbear groaning and shedding tears, and turning my head towards my sides; letting him know, as well as I could, how cruelly I was hurt by the pressure of his thumb and finger. He seemed to apprehend my meaning; for, lifting up the lappet of his coat, he put me gently into it, and immediately ran along with me to his master, who was a substantial farmer, and the same person I had first seen in the field.

The farmer having (as I supposed by their talk) received such an account of me as his servant could give him, took a piece of a small straw, about the size of a walking staff, and therewith lifted up the lappets of my coat; which it seems he thought to be some kind of covering that nature had given me. He blew my hairs aside •to take a better view of my face. He called his hands about him, and asked them (as I afterwards learned) whether they had ever seen in the fields any little creature that resembled me? He then placed me softly on the ground upon all fours, but I got immediately up, and walked slowly backwards and forwards, to let those people see I had no intent to run away. They all sat down in a circle about me, the better to observe my motions. I pulled off my hat, and made a low bow towards the farmer. I fell on my knees, and lifted up my hands and eyes, and spoke several words as loud as I could: I took a purse of gold out of my pocket, and humbly presented it to him. He received it on the palm of his hand, then applied it close to his eye, to see what it was, and afterwards turned it several times with the point of a pin (which he took out of his sleeve), but could make nothing of it. Whereupon I made a sign that he should place his hand on the ground. I took the purse, and opening it, poured all the gold into his palm. There were six Spanish pieces of four pistoles each, besides twenty or thirty smaller coins. I saw him wet the tip of his little finger upon his tongue, and take up one of my largest pieces, and then another, but he seemed to be wholly ignorant what they were. He made me a sign to put them again into my purse, and the purse again into my pocket, which after offering to him several times, I thought it best to do.

The farmer by this time was convinced I must be a rational creature. He spoke often to me, but the sound of his voice pierced my ears like that of a water-mill, yet his words were articulate enough. I answered as loud as I could, in several languages, and he often laid his ear within two yards of me; but all in vain, for we were wholly unintelligible to each other. He then sent his servants to their work, and taking his handkerchief out of his pocket, he doubled and spread it on his left hand, which he placed flat on the ground, with the palm upwards, making me a sign to step into it, as I could easily do, for it was not above a foot in thickness. I thought it my part to obey, and for fear of falling, laid myself at length upon the handkerchief, with the remainder of which he lapped me up to the head for further security, and in this manner carried me home to his house. There he called his wife, and showed me to her; but she screamed and ran back, as women in England do at the sight of a toad or a spider. However, when she had a while seen my behaviour, and how well I observed the signs her husband made, she was soon reconciled, and by degrees grew extremely tender of me.

It was about twelve at noon, and a servant brought in dinner. It was only one substantial dish of meat (fit for the plain condition of an husbandman) in a dish of about four and twenty feet diameter. The company were the farmer and his wife, three children, and an old grandmother: when they were sat down, the farmer placed me at some distance from him on the table, which was thirty feet high from the floor. I was in a terrible fright, and kept as far as I could from the edge for fear of falling. The wife minced a bit of meat, then crumbled some bread on a trencher, and placed it before me. I made her a low bow, took out my knife and fork, and fell to eat, which gave them exceeding delight. The mistress sent her maid for a small dram-cup, which held about three gallons, and filled it with drink. I took up the vessel with much difficulty in both hands, and in a most respectful manner drank to her ladyship's health, expressing the words as loud as I could in English, which made the company laugh so heartily, that I was almost deafened with the noise. This liquor tasted like a small cider, and was not unpleasant. Then the master made me a sign to come to his trencher-side; but as I walked on the table, being in great surprize all the time, as the indulgent reader will easily conceive and excuse, I happened to stumble against a crust, and fell flat on my face, but received no hurt. I got up immediately, and observing the good people to be in much concern, I took my hat (which I held under my arm out of good manners) and waving it over my head, made three huzzas to show I had got no mischief by my fall. But advancing forwards toward my master (as I shall henceforth call him) his youngest son who sat next him, an arch boy of about ten years old, took me up by the legs, and held me so high in the air, that I trembled in every limb; but his father snatched me from him, and at the same time gave him such a box on the left ear, as would have felled an European troop of horse to the earth, ordering him to be taken from the table. But being afraid the boy might owe me a spite, and well remembering how mischievous all children among us naturally are to sparrows, rabbits, young kittens, and puppy dogs, I fell on my knees, and pointing to the boy, made my master to understand, as well as I could, that I desired his son might be pardoned. The father complied, and the lad took his seat again; whereupon I went to him and kissed his hand, which my master took, and made him stroke me gently with it.

In the midst of dinner, my mistress's favourite cat leaped into her lap. I heard a noise behind me like that of a dozen stocking-weavers at work; and turning my head I found it proceeded from the purring of this animal, who seemed to be three times larger than an ox, as I computed by the view of her head, and one of her paws, while her mistress was feeding and stroking her. The fierceness of this creature's countenance altogether discomposed me; though I stood at the further end of the table, above fifty feet off, and although my mistress held her fast for fear she might give a spring, and seize me in her talons. But it happened there was no danger; for the cat took not the least notice of me when my master placed me within three yards of her. And as I have been always told, and found true by experience in my travels, that flying, or discovering fear before a fierce animal, is a certain way to make it pursue or attack you, so I resolved in this dangerous juncture to show no manner of concern. I walked with intrepidity five or six times before the very head of the cat, and came within half a yard of her; whereupon she drew herself back, as if she were more afraid of me: I had less apprehension concerning the dogs, whereof three or four came into the room, as it is usual in farmers' houses; one of which was a mastiff, equal in bulk to four elephants, and a greyhound somewhat taller than the mastiff, but not so large.

I remember when I was at Lilliput, the complexions of those diminutive people appeared to me the fairest in the world, and talking upon this subject with a person of learning there, who was an intimate friend of mine, he said that my face appeared much fairer and smoother when he looked on me from the ground, than it did upon a nearer view when I took him up in my hand, and brought him close, which he confessed was at first a very shocking sight. He said he could discover great holes in my skin; that the stumps of my beard were ten times stronger than the bristles of a boar, and my complexion made up of several colours altogether disagreeable: although I must beg leave to say for myself, that I am as fair as most of my sex and country, and very little sun-burned by my travels. On the other side, discoursing of the ladies in that emperor's court, he used to tell me, one had freckles, another too wide a mouth, a third too large a nose, nothing of which I was able to distinguish. I confess this reflection was obvious enough; which however I could not forbear, lest the reader might think those vast creatures were actually deformed: for I must do them justice to say they are a comely race of people; and particularly the features of my master's countenance, although he were but a farmer, when I beheld him from the height of sixty feet, appeared very well proportioned.

When dinner was done, my master went out to his labourers, and as I could discover by his voice and gesture, gave his wife a strict charge to take care of me. I was very much tired and disposed to sleep, which my mistress perceiving, she put me on her own bed, and covered me with a clean white handkerchief, but larger and coarser than the main-sail of a man of war.

I slept about two hours, and dreamed I was at home with my wife and children, which aggravated my sorrows when I awaked and found myself alone in a vast room, between two and three hundred feet wide, and above two hundred high, lying in a bed twenty yards wide. My mistress was gone about her household affairs and had locked me in. The bed was eight yards from the floor. I durst not presume to call, and if I had, it would have been in vain, with such a voice as mine, at so great a distance as from the room where I lay to the kitchen where the family kept. While I was under these circumstances, two rats crept up the curtains, and ran smelling backwards and forwards on the bed. One of them came up almost to my face, whereupon I rose in a fright, and drew out my hanger to defend myself. These horrible animals had the boldness to attack me on both sides, and one of them held his fore-feet at my collar; but I had the good fortune to rip up his belly before he could do me any mischief. He fell down at my feet, and the other seeing the fate of his comrade, made his escape, but not without one good wound on the back, which I gave him as he fled, and made the blood run trickling from him. After this exploit, I walked gently to and fro on the bed, to recover my breath and loss of spirits. These creatures were of the size of a large mastiff, but infinitely more nimble and fierce, so that if I had taken off my belt before I went to sleep, I must have infallibly been torn to pieces and devoured. I measured the tail of the dead rat, and found it to be two yards long, wanting an inch; but it went against my stomach to drag the carcass off the bed, where it lay still bleeding; I observed it had yet some life, but with a strong slash across the neck I thoroughly dispatched it.

Soon after my mistress came into the room, who seeing me all bloody, ran and took me up in her hand. I pointed to the dead rat, smiling and making other signs to show I was not hurt, whereat she was extremely rejoiced, calling the maid to take up the dead rat with a pair of tongs, and throw it out of the window. Then she set me on a table, where I showed her my hanger all bloody, and wiping it on the lappet of my coat, returned it to the scabbard.

I hope the gentle reader will excuse me for dwelling on these and the like particulars, which however insignificant they may appear to groveling, vulgar minds, yet will certainly help a philosopher to enlarge his thoughts and imagination, and apply them to the benefit of public as well as private life, which was my sole design in presenting this and other accounts of my travels to the world; wherein I have been chiefly studious of truth, without affecting any ornaments of learning or of style. But the whole scene of this voyage made so strong an impression on my mind and is so deeply fixed in my memory, that in committing it to paper I did not omit one material circumstance: however, upon a strict review, I blotted out several passages of less moment which were in my first copy, for fear of being censured as tedious and trifling, whereof travellers are often, perhaps not without justice, accused.

CHAPTER II

A description of the farmer's daughter. The author carried to a market-town, and then to the metropolis. The particulars of his journey.

My mistress had a daughter of nine years old, a child of toward parts for her age, very dextrous at her needle, and skilful in dressing her baby. Her mother and she contrived to fit up the baby's cradle for me against night: the cradle was put into a small drawer of a cabinet, and the drawer placed upon a hanging-shelf, for fear of the rats. This was my bed all the time I stayed with those people, though made more convenient by degrees, as I began to learn their language, and make my wants known. This young girl was so handy, that after I once

or twice pulled off my clothes before her, she was able to dress and undress me, though I never gave her that trouble when she would let me do either myself. She made me seven shirts, and some other linen, of as fine cloth as could be got, which indeed was coarser than sackcloth; and these she constantly washed for me with her own hands. She was likewise my school-mistress to teach me the language: when I pointed to anything she told me the name of it in her own tongue, so that in a few days I was able to call for whatever I had a mind to. She was very good-natured, and not above forty feet high, being little for her age. She gave me the name of Grildrig, which the family took up, and afterwards the whole kingdom. The word imports what the Latins call *nanunculus*, the Italians *homunceletino*, and the English *mannikin*. To her I chiefly owe my preservation in that country: we never parted while I was there. I called her my *Glumdalclitch*, or little nurse: and I should be guilty of great ingratitude if I omitted this honourable mention of her care and affection towards me, which I heartily wish it lay in my power to requite as she deserves, instead of being the innocent but unhappy instrument of her disgrace, as I have too much reason to fear.

It now began to be known and talked of in the neighborhood, that my master had found a strange animal in the field about the bigness of a *splacnuck*, but exactly shaped in every part like a human creature; which it likewise imitated in all its actions; seemed to speak in a little language of its own, had already learned several words of theirs, went erect upon two legs, was tame and gentle, would come when it was called, do whatever it was bid, had the finest limbs in the world, and a complexion fairer than a nobleman's daughter of three years old. Another farmer who lived hard by, and was a particular friend of my master, came on a visit on purpose to inquire into the truth of this story. I was immediately produced, and placed upon a table, where I walked as I was commanded, drew my hanger, put it up again, made my reverence to my master's guest, asked him in his own language how he did, and told him he was welcome, just as my little nurse had instructed me. This man who was old and dim sighted, put on his spectacles to behold me better, at which I could not forbear laughing very heartily, for his eyes appeared like the full-moon shining into a chamber at two windows. Our people, who discovered the cause of my mirth, bore me company in laughing, at which the old fellow was fool enough to be angry and out of countenance. He had the character of a great miser, and to my misfortune he well deserved it by the cursed advice he gave my master to show me as a sight upon a market-day in the next town, which was half an hour's riding, about two and twenty miles from our house. I guessed there was some mischief contriving, when I observed my master and his friend whispering long together, sometimes pointing at me; and my fears made me fancy that I overheard and understood some of their words. But, the next morning Glumdalclitch my little nurse, told me the whole matter, which she had cunningly picked out from her mother. The poor girl laid me on her bosom, and fell a weeping with shame and grief. She apprehended some mischief would happen to me from rude vulgar folks, who might squeeze me to death or break one of my limbs by taking me in their hands. She had

also observed how modest I was in my nature, how nicely I regarded my honour, and what an indignity I should conceive it to be exposed for money as a public spectacle to the meanest of the people. She said, her papa and mamma had promised that Grildrig should be hers, but now she found they meant to serve her as they did last year, when they pretended to give her a lamb, and yet, as soon as it was fat, sold it to a butcher. For my own part, I may truly affirm that I was less concerned than my nurse. I had a strong hope which never left me, that I should one day recover my liberty; and as to the ignominy of being carried about for a monster, I considered myself to be a perfect stranger in the country, and that such a misfortune could never be charged upon me as a reproach if ever I should return to England; since the king of Great Britain himself, in my condition, must have undergone the same distress.

My master, pursuant to the advice of his friend, carried me in a box the next market day to the neighbouring town, and took along with him his little daughter, my nurse, upon a pillion behind him. The box was close on every side, with a little door for me to go in and out, and a few gimlet-holes to let in air. The girl had been so careful to put the quilt of her baby's bed into it, for me to lie down on. However, I was terribly shaken and discomposed in this journey, though it were but of half an hour; for the horse went about forty feet at every step, and trotted so high, that the agitation was equal to the rising and falling of a ship in a great storm, but much more frequent: our journey was somewhat further than from London to St. Alban's. My master alighted at an inn which he used to frequent; and after consulting a while with the inn-keeper, and making some necessary preparations, he hired the *grultrud,* or crier to give notice through the town of a strange creature to be seen at the sign of the Green Eagle not so big as a *splacnuck* (an animal in that country very finely shaped, about six feet long) and in every part of the body resembling an human creature, could speak several words, and perform an hundred diverting tricks.

I was placed upon a table in the largest room of the inn, which might be near three hundred feet square. My little nurse stood on a low stool close to the table, to take care of me, and direct what I should do. My master, to avoid a crowd, would suffer only thirty people at a time to see me. I walked about on the table as the girl commanded: she asked me questions as far as she knew my understanding of the language reached, and I answered them as loud as I could. I turned about several times to the company, paid my humble respects, said they were welcome, and used some other speeches I had been taught. I took up a thimble filled with liquor, which Glumdalclitch had given me for a cup, and drank their health. I drew out my hanger, and flourished with it after the manner of fencers in England. My nurse gave me part of a straw, which I exercised as a pike, having learned the art in my youth. I was that day shown to twelve sets of company, and as often forced to go over again with the same fopperies, till I was half dead with weariness and vexation. For, those who had seen me made such wonderful reports, that the people were ready to break down the doors to come in. My master for his own interest would not suffer any one to touch me except my nurse; and, to prevent danger, benches were set round the table at such a distance as put me out of everybody's reach. However, an unlucky school-boy aimed a hazel nut directly at my head, which very narrowly missed me; otherwise, it came with so much violence that it would have infallibly knocked out my brains, for it was almost as large as a small pumpkin, but I had the satisfaction to see the young rogue well beaten, and turned out of the room.

My master gave public notice, that he would show me again the next market-day, and in the meantime he prepared a more convenient vehicle for me which he had reason enough to do; for I was so tired with my first journey, and with entertaining company for eight hours together, that I could hardly stand upon my legs, or speak a word. It was at least three days before I recovered my strength; and that I might have no rest at home, all the neighbouring gentlemen from an hundred miles round, hearing of my fame, came to see me at my master's own house. There could not be fewer than thirty persons with their wives and children (for the country was very populous); and my master demanded the rate of a full room whenever he showed me at home, although it were only to a single family: so that for some time I had but little ease every day of the week (except Wednesday, which is their Sabbath) although I were not carried to the town.

My master finding how profitable I was like to be, resolved to carry me to the most considerable cities of the kingdom. Having therefore provided himself with all things necessary for a long journey, and settled his affairs at home, he took leave of his wife, and upon the 17th of August 1703, about two months after my arrival, we set out for the metropolis, situated near the middle of that empire, and about three thousand miles distance from our house. My master made his daughter, Glumdalclitch, ride behind him. She carried me on her lap in a box tied about her waist. The girl had lined it on all sides with the softest cloth she could get, well quilted underneath, furnished it with her baby's bed, provided me with linen and other necessaries, and made everything as convenient as she could. We had no other company but a boy of the house, who rode after us with the luggage.

My master's design was to show me in all the towns by the way, and to step out of the road for fifty or an hundred miles, to any village or person of quality's house where he might expect custom. We made easy journies of not above seven or eight-score miles a day. For Glumdalclitch, on purpose to spare me, complained she was tired with the trotting of the horse. She often took me out of my box at my own desire, to give me air, and show me the country, but always held me fast by a leading-string. We passed over five or six rivers many degrees broader and deeper than the Nile or the Ganges; and there was hardly a rivulet so small as the Thames at London-Bridge. We were ten weeks in our journey, and I was shown in eighteen large towns besides many villages and private families.

On the 26th day of October, we arrived at the metropolis, called in their language Lorbrulgrud, or Pride of the Universe. My master took a lodging in the principal street of the city, not far from the royal palace, and put out bills in the usual form, containing an exact description of my person and parts. He hired a large room between three and four hundred feet wide. He provided a table sixty feet in diameter, upon which I was to act my part, and palisadoed it round three feet from the edge, and as many high, to prevent my falling over. I was shown ten times a day to the wonder and satisfaction of all people. I could now speak the language tolerably well, and perfectly understood every word that was spoken to me. Besides, I had learned their alphabet, and could make a shift to explain a sentence here and there; for Glumdalclitch had been my instructor while we were at home, and at leisure hours during our journey. She carried a little book in her pocket, not much larger than a Sanson's Atlas; it was a common treatise for the use of young girls, giving a short account of their religion; out of this she taught me my letters, and interpreted the words.

CHAPTER VI

Several contrivances of the author to please the king and queen. He shows his skill in music. The king inquires into the state of Europe, which the author relates to him. The king's observations thereon.

I used to attend the king's levee once or twice a week, and had often seen him under the barber's hand, which indeed was at first very terrible to behold: for the razor was almost twice as long as an ordinary scythe. His majesty, according to the custom of the country, was only shaved twice a week. I once prevailed on the barber to give me some of the suds or lather, out of which I picked forty or fifty of the strongest stumps of hair. I then took a piece of fine wood, and cut it like the back of a comb, making several holes in it at equal distance with as small a needle as I could get from Glumdalclitch. I fixed in the stumps so artificially, scraping and sloping them with my knife towards the points, that I made a very tolerable comb; which was a seasonable supply, my own being so much broken in the teeth, that it was almost useless: neither did I know any artist in that country so nice and exact, as would undertake to make me another.

And this puts me in mind of an amusement wherein I spent many of my leisure hours. I desired the queen's woman to save for me the combings of her majesty's hair, whereof in time I got a good quantity, and consulting with my friend the cabinet-maker, who had received general orders to do little jobs for me, I directed him to make two chair-frames, no larger than those I had in my box, and then to bore little holes with a fine awl round those parts where I designed the backs and seats; through these holes I wove the strongest hairs I could pick out, just after the manner of cane-chairs in England. When they were finished, I made a present of them to her majesty, who kept them in her cabinet, and used to show them for curiosities, as indeed they were the wonder of everyone that beheld them. The queen would have had me sit upon one of these chairs, but I absolutely refused to obey her, protesting I would rather die a thousand deaths than place part of my body on those precious hairs that once adorned her majesty's head. Of these hairs (as I had always a mechanical genius) I likewise made a neat little purse about five feet long, with her majesty's name deciphered in gold letters, which I gave to Glumdalclitch, by the queen's consent. To say the truth, it was more for show than use, being not of strength to bear the weight of the larger coins, and therefore she kept nothing in it, but some little toys that girls are fond of.

The king, who delighted in music, had frequent consorts at court, to which I was sometimes carried, and set in my box on a table to hear them: but, the noise was so great, that I could hardly distinguish the tunes. I am confident that all the drums and trumpets of a royal army, beating and sounding together just at your ears, could not equal it. My practice was to have my box removed from the places where the performers sat, as far as I could, then to shut the doors and windows of it, and draw the window-curtains; after which I found their music not disagreeable.

I had learned in my youth to play a little upon the spinet. Glumdalclitch kept one in her chamber, and a master attended twice a week to teach her: I call it a spinet, because it somewhat resembled that instrument, and was played upon in the same manner. A fancy came into my head that I would entertain the king and queen with an English tune upon this instrument. But this appeared extremely difficult: for, the spinet was nearly sixty feet long, each key being almost a foot wide, so that, with my arms extended, I could not reach to above five keys, and to press them down required a good smart stroke with my fist, which would be too great a labour, and to no purpose. The method I contrived was this. I prepared two round sticks about the bigness of common cudgels; they were thicker at one end than the other, and I covered the thicker ends with a piece of a mouse's skin, that by rapping on them, I might neither damage the tops of the keys, nor interrupt the sound. Before the spinet a bench was placed about four feet below the keys, and I was put upon the bench.

I ran sideling upon it that way and this, as fast as I could, banging the proper keys with my two sticks, and made a shift to play a jigg, to the great satisfaction of both their majesties: but it was the most violent exercise I ever underwent, and yet I could not strike above sixteen keys, nor, consequently, play the bass and treble together, as other artists do; which was a great disadvantage to my performance.

The king, who, as I before observed, was a prince of excellent understanding, would frequently order that I should be brought in my box, and set upon the table in his closet: he would then command me to bring one of my chairs out of the box, and sit down within three yards distance upon the top of the cabinet, which brought me almost to a level with his face. In this manner I had several conversations with him. I one day took the freedom to tell his majesty, that the contempt he discovered towards Europe, and the rest of the world, did not seem answerable to those excellent qualities of the mind he was master of. That reason did not extend itself with the bulk of the body: on the contrary, we observed in our country, that the tallest persons were usually least provided with it; that among other animals, bees and ants had the reputation of more industry, art, and sagacity, than many of the larger kinds; and that, as inconsiderable as he took me to be, I hoped I might live to do his majesty some signal service. The king heard me with attention, and began to conceive a much better opinion of me than he had ever before. He desired I would give him as exact an account of the government of England, as I possibly could; because, as fond as princes commonly are of their own customs (for so he conjectured of other monarchs by my former discourses), he should be glad to hear of anything that might deserve imitation.

Imagine with thyself, courteous reader, how often I then wished for the tongue of Demosthenes or Cicero, that might have enabled me to celebrate the praise of my own dear native country in a style equal to its merits and felicity.

I began my discourse by informing his majesty that our dominions consisted of two islands, which composed three mighty kingdoms under one sovereign, besides our plantations in America. I dwelt long upon the fertility of our soil, and the temperature of our climate. I then spoke at large upon the constitution of an English parliament, partly made up of an illustrious body called the house of peers, persons of the noblest blood, and of the most ancient and ample patrimonies. I described that extraordinary care always taken of their education in arts and arms, to qualify them for being counsellors born to the king and kingdom; to have a share in the legislature; to be members of the highest court of judicature, from whence there could be no appeal; and to be champions always ready for the defence of their prince and country, by their valour, conduct and fidelity. That these were the ornament and bulwark of the kingdom, worthy followers of their most renowned ancestors, whose honour had been the reward of their virtue, from which their posterity were never once known to degenerate. To these were joined several holy persons, as part of that assembly, under the title of bishops, whose peculiar business it is to take care of religion, and of those who instruct the people therein. These were searched, and sought out, through the whole nation, by the prince and his wisest counsellors, among such of the priesthood as were most deservedly distinguished by the sanctity of their lives, and the depth of their erudition, who were indeed the spiritual fathers of the clergy and the people.

That, the other part of the parliament consisted of an assembly called the house of commons, who were all principal gentlemen, freely picked and culled out by the people themselves, for their great abilities and love of their country, to represent the wisdom of the whole nation. And these two bodies make up the most august assembly in Europe, to whom, in conjunction with the prince, the whole legislature is committed.

I then descended to the courts of justice, over which the judges, those venerable sages and interpreters of the law presided, for determining the disputed rights and properties of men, as well as for the punishment of vice, and protection of innocence. I mentioned the prudent management of our treasury, the valour and achievements of our forces by sea and land. I computed the number of our people, by reckoning how many millions there might be of each religious sect, or political party among us. I did not omit even our sports and pastimes, or any other particular which I thought might redound to the honour of my country. And I finished all with a brief historical account of affairs and events in England for about an hundred years past.

This conversation was not ended under five audiences, each of several hours, and the king heard the whole with great attention, frequently taking notes of what I spoke, as well as memorandums of all questions he intended to ask me.

When I had put an end to these long discourses, his majesty in a sixth audience consulting his notes, proposed many doubts, queries, and objections, upon every article. He asked what methods were used to cultivate the minds and bodies of our young nobility, and in what kind of business they commonly spent the first and teachable part of their lives. What course was taken to supply that assembly when any noble family became extinct. What qualifications were necessary in those who are to be created new lords: whether the humour of the prince, a sum of money to a court lady or a prime minister, or a design of strengthening a party opposite to the public interest, ever happened to be motives in those advancements. What share of knowledge these lords had in the laws of their country, and how they came by it, so as to enable them to decide the properties of their fellow-subjects in the last resort. Whether they were always so free from avarice, partialities, or want, that a bribe, or some other sinister view, could have no place among them. Whether those holy lords I spoke of were always promoted to that rank upon account of their knowledge in religious matters, and the sanctity of their lives, had never been compliers with the times while they were common priests, or slavish prostitute chaplains to some nobleman, whose opinions they continued servilely to follow after they were admitted into that assembly.

He then desired to know what arts were practised in electing those whom I called commoners: whether a stranger with a strong purse might not influence the vulgar voters to choose him before their own landlord, or the most considerable gentleman in the neighbourhood. How it came to pass, that people were so violently bent upon getting into this assembly, which I allowed to be a great trouble and expense, often to the ruin of their families, without any salary or pension: because this appeared such an exalted strain of virtue and public spirit, that his majesty seemed to doubt it might possibly not be always sincere: and he desired to know whether such zealous gentlemen could have any views of refunding themselves for the charges and trouble they were at, by sacrificing the public good to the designs of a weak and vicious prince in conjunction with a corrupted ministry. He multiplied his questions, and sifted me thoroughly upon every part of this head, proposing numberless inquiries and objections, which I think it not prudent or convenient to repeat.

Upon what I said in relation to our courts of justice, his majesty desired to be satisfied in several points: and this I was the better able to do, having been formerly almost ruined by a long suit in the chancery, which was decreed for me with costs. He asked what time was usually spent in determining between right and wrong, and what degree of expense. Whether advocates and orators had liberty to plead in causes manifestly known to be unjust, vexatious, or oppressive. Whether party in religion or politics were observed to be of any weight in the scale of justice. Whether those pleading orators were persons educated in the general knowledge of equity or only in provincial, national, and other local customs. Whether they or their judges had any part in penning those laws which they assumed the liberty of interpreting and glossing upon at their pleasure. Whether they had ever at different times pleaded for and against the same cause, and cited precedents to prove contrary opinions. Whether they were a rich or a poor corporation. Whether they received any pecuniary reward for pleading or delivering their opinions. And particularly, whether they were ever admitted as members in the lower senate.

He fell next upon the management of our treasury, and said, he thought my memory had failed me, because I computed our taxes at about five or six millions a year, and when I came to mention the issues, he found they sometimes amounted to more than double; for the notes he had taken were very particular in this point, because he hoped, as he told me, that the knowledge of our conduct might be useful to him, and he could not be deceived in his calculations. But, if what I told him were true, he was still at a loss how a kingdom could run out of its estate like a private person. He asked me, who were our creditors; and where we should find money to pay them. He wondered to hear me talk of such chargeable and extensive wars; that certainly we must be a quarrelsome people, or live among very bad neighbours, and that our generals must needs be richer than our kings. He asked what business we had out of our own islands, unless upon the score of trade or treaty, or to defend the coasts with our fleet. Above all, he was amazed to hear me talk of a mercenary standing army in the midst of peace, and among a free people. He said, if we were governed by our own consent in the persons of our representatives, he could not imagine of whom we were afraid, or against whom we were to fight, and would hear my opinion, whether a private man's house might not better be defended by himself, his children, and family, than by half a dozen rascals picked up at a venture in the streets, for small wages, who might get an hundred times more by cutting their throats.

He laughed at my odd kind of arithmetic (as he was pleased to call it) in reckoning the numbers of our people by a computation drawn from the several sects among us in religion and politics. He said, he knew no reason, why those who entertain opinions prejudicial to the public, should be obliged to change or should not be obliged to conceal them. And as it was tyranny in any government to require the first, so it was weakness not to enforce the second: for a man may be allowed to keep poisons in his closet, but not to vend them about for cordials.

He observed, that among the diversions of our nobility and gentry, I had mentioned gaming. He desired to know at what age this entertainment was usually taken up, and when it was laid down; how much of their time it employed; whether it ever went so high as to affect their fortunes: whether mean vicious people, by their dexterity in that art, might not arrive at great riches, and sometimes keep our very nobles in dependence, as well as habituate them to vile companions, wholly take them from the improvement of their minds, and force them, by the losses they have received, to learn and practise that infamous dexterity upon others.

He was perfectly astonished with the historical account I gave him of our affairs during the last century, protesting it was only an heap of conspiracies, rebellions, murders, massacres, revolutions, banishments, the very worst effects that avarice, faction, hypocrisy, perfidiousness, cruelty, rage, madness, hatred, envy, lust, malice, or ambition, could produce.

His majesty in another audience was at the pains to recapitulate the sum of all I had spoken, compared the questions he made with the answers I had given; then taking me into his hands, and stroking me gently, delivered himself in these words, which I shall never forget, nor the manner he spoke them in: my little friend Grildrig, you have made a most admirable panegyric upon your country: you have clearly proved that ignorance, idleness and vice may be sometimes the only ingredients for qualifying a legislator: that laws are best explained, interpreted, and applied by those whose interest and abilities lie in perverting, confounding, and eluding them. I observe among you some lines of an institution, which in its original might have been tolerable, but these half erased, and the rest wholly blurred and blotted by corruptions. It doth not appear from all you have said, how any one virtue is required towards the procurement of any one station among you, much less that men were ennobled on account of their virtue, that priests were advanced for their piety or learning, soldiers for their conduct or valour, judges for their integrity, senators for the love of their country, or counsellors for their wisdom. As for yourself (continued the king), who have spent the greatest part of your life in travelling, I am well disposed to hope you may hitherto have escaped many vices of your country. But by what I have gathered from your own relation, and the answers I have with much pain wringed and extorted from you, I cannot but conclude the bulk of your natives to be the most pernicious race of little odious vermin that nature ever suffered to crawl upon the surface of the earth.

For Thought and Discussion

1. In Chapter I what kind of people does Gulliver encounter?
2. In Chapter II is the affection and devotion of Glumdalclitch ever ridiculed? What is the writer's attitude toward tenderness and kindness?
3. In Chapter VI discuss the writer's attitude toward actual and ideal conditions on such questions as qualifications of members of Parliament, interpretation and enforcement of the law, honesty of judges, advancement of the clergy, religious quarrels, and efficient national government.
4. From his two voyages what were some of the lessons learned by Gulliver on honor, titles, official life, party strife, and religious quarrels?
5. In his humorous, ironical fashion Swift criticizes people, customs, and institutions in order to indicate which values remain unchanged, regardless of conditions. What qualities does he find worthy?

Plus Work

Read the volume *Gulliver's Travels.*

~❧

THE TRUE HISTORY OF THE HARE AND THE TORTOISE
LORD DUNSANY

[Lord Dunsany, 1878—, served with distinction in the Boer War and in the World War. He is more distinguished, however, as a writer of romantic, highly imaginative literature. His use of allegory and symbolism is one of the marked characteristics of his work.]

FOR a long time there was doubt with acrimony among the beasts as to whether the hare or the tortoise could run the swifter. Some said the hare was the swifter of the two because he had such long ears, and others said that the tortoise was the swifter because any one whose shell was so hard as that should be able to run hard too. And lo, the forces of estrangement and disorder perpetually postponed a decisive contest.

But when there was nearly war among the beasts, at last an arrangement was come to and it was decided that the hare and the tortoise should run a race of five hundred yards so that all should see who was right.

"Ridiculous nonsense!" said the hare, and it was all his backers could do to get him to run.

"The contest is most welcome to me," said the tortoise. "I shall not shirk it."

Oh, how his backers cheered.

Feeling ran high on the day of the race; the goose rushed at the fox and nearly pecked him. Both sides spoke loudly of the approaching victory up to the very moment of the race.

"I am absolutely confident of success," said the tortoise. But the hare said nothing; he looked bored and cross. Some of his supporters deserted him then and went to the other side, who were loudly cheering the tortoise's inspiriting words. But many remained with the hare. "We shall not be disappointed in him," they said. "A beast with such long ears is bound to win."

"Run hard," said the supporters of the tortoise.

And "run hard" became a kind of catch-phrase which everybody repeated to one another. "Hard shell and hard living. That's what the country wants. Run hard," they said. And these words were never uttered but multitudes cheered from their hearts.

Then they were off, and suddenly there was a hush.

The hare dashed off for about a hundred yards, then he looked round to see where his rival was.

"It is rather absurd," he said, "to race with a tortoise." And he sat down and scratched himself. "Run hard! Run hard!" shouted some. "Let him rest," shouted others. And "let him rest" became a catch-phrase too.

And after a while his rival drew near to him.

"There comes that tortoise," said the hare, and he got up and ran as hard as he could so that he should not let the tortoise beat him.

"Those ears will win," said his friends. "Those ears will win; and establish upon an incontestable footing the truth of what we have said." And some of them turned to the backers of the tortoise and said: "What about your beast now?"

"Run hard," they replied. "Run hard."

The hare ran on for nearly three hundred yards, nearly in fact as far as the winning-post, when it suddenly struck him what a fool he looked running races with a tortoise who was nowhere in sight, and he sat down again and scratched.

"Run hard. Run hard," said the crowd, and, "Let him rest."

"Whatever is the use of it?" said the hare, and this time he stopped for good. Some say he slept.

There was desperate excitement for an hour or two, and then the tortoise won.

"Run hard. Run hard," shouted his backers. "Hard shell and hard living; that's what has done it." And then they asked the tortoise what his achievement signified, and he went and asked the turtle. And the turtle said: "It is a glorious victory for the forces of swiftness." And then the tortoise repeated it to his friends. And all the beasts said nothing else for years. And even to this day "a glorious victory for the forces of swiftness" is a catch-phrase in the house of the snail.

And the reason that this version of the race is not widely known is that very few of those that witnessed it survived the great forest-fire that happened shortly after. It came up over the weald by night with a great wind. The hare and the tortoise and a very few of the beasts saw it far off from a high bare hill that was at the edge of the trees, and they hurriedly called a meeting to decide what messenger they should send to warn the beasts in the forest.

They sent the tortoise.

For Thought and Discussion

1. How does Dunsany make use of Aesop's fable in this story?
2. How does he remove this story from the realm of the animal world to that of people?
3. What two different types of people do the hare and the tortoise represent?

4. How does Dunsany satirize cant phrases? Name some of them.
5. People pick up and repeat catch-phrases to save themselves from thinking. Make a list of such phrases and examine them for sense and meaning.
6. Why does this story sound like a political campaign?
7. What does the author satirize?
8. Are speeches to the masses often stocked with catch-phrases, designed to appeal to the emotions and prejudices rather than to the reason?
9. How do political speakers depend upon mass psychology? Do political speakers depend upon easily aroused emotions to sway their audiences? Can the radio be utilized for swaying large audiences? Are political slogans catch-phrases? Give examples of them.

JOHN GILPIN'S RIDE
WILLIAM COWPER[1]

[William Cowper, 1731-1800, a shy and often melancholy man, lived a deeply religious life and wrote many famous church hymns, among them "Oh! for a Closer Walk with God." He also wrote didactic poems, but even the most serious-minded people sometime turn to nonsense as Cowper did in "John Gilpin" of whom he said, "I made him on purpose to laugh at, and he served his purpose well."]

JOHN GILPIN was a citizen
  Of credit and renown,
A trainband[2] captain eke was he
  Of famous London town.

John Gilpin's spouse said to her dear, 5
  "Though wedded we have been
These twice ten tedious years, yet we
  No holiday have seen.

"To-morrow is our wedding day,
  And we will then repair   10

Unto the Bell at Edmonton,[3]
  All in a chaise and pair.[4]

"My sister, and my sister's child,
  Myself, and children three,
Will fill the chaise; so you must ride
  On horseback after we."   16

He soon replied,—"I do admire
  Of womankind but one,
And you are she, my dearest dear,
  Therefore it shall be done.   20

"I am a linendraper bold,
  As all the world doth know,
And my good friend the calender[5]
  Will lend his horse to go."

Quoth Mistress Gilpin, "That's well said;   25
  And for that wine is dear,

---

[1]Cowper, (kōō pẽr).
[2]Trainband captain, leader of a company of trained citizen soldiers.

[3]Bell at Edmonton, an inn in Edmonton, near London.
[4]Chaise (shāz) and pair, a carriage usually drawn by one horse, but for this occasion drawn by a pair of horses.
[5]Calender, the operator of a calender machine which was used for pressing and finishing cloth.

We will be furnished with our own,
  Which is both bright and clear."

John Gilpin kissed his loving wife;
  O'erjoyed was he to find   30
That, though on pleasure she was
      bent,
  She had a frugal mind.

The morning came, the chaise was
      brought,
  But yet was not allowed
To drive up to the door, lest all   35
  Should say that she was proud.

So three doors off the chaise was
      stayed,
  Where they did all get in;
Six precious souls, and all agog
  To dash through thick and thin.   40

Smack went the whip, round went the
      wheels;
  Were never folks so glad;
The stones did rattle underneath,
  As if Cheapside were mad.

John Gilpin at his horse's side   45
  Seized fast the flowing mane;
And up he got, in haste to ride,
  But soon came down again;

For saddletree scarce reached had he,
  His journey to begin,   50
When, turning round his head, he saw
  Three customers come in.

So down he came; for loss of time,
  Although it grieved him sore,
Yet loss of pence, full well he knew, 55
  Would trouble him much more.

'Twas long before the customers
  Were suited to their mind,
When Betty screaming came down
      stairs,
  "The wine is left behind!"   60

"Good lack!" quoth he, "yet bring it
      me
  My leathern belt likewise,
In which I bear my trusty sword
  When I do exercise."

Now Mistress Gilpin (careful soul!) 65
  Had two stone bottles found,

To hold the liquor that she loved,
And keep it safe and sound.

Each bottle had a curling ear,
Through which the belt he drew, [70]
And hung a bottle on each side
To make his balance true.

Then over all, that he might be
Equipped from top to toe,
His long red cloak, well brushed and
neat, [75]
He manfully did throw.

Now see him mounted once again
Upon his nimble steed,
Full slowly pacing o'er the stones,
With caution and good heed. [80]

But finding soon a smoother road
Beneath his well-shod feet,
The snorting beast began to trot,
Which galled him in his seat.

So "Fair and softly," John he cried, [85]
But John he cried in vain;
That trot became a gallop soon,
In spite of curb and rein.

So stooping down, as needs he must
Who cannot sit upright, [90]
He grasped the mane with both his
hands,
And eke with all his might.

His horse, who never in that sort
Had handled been before,
What thing upon his back had got [95]
Did wonder more and more.

Away went Gilpin, neck or nought;
Away went hat and wig;
He little dreamt, when he set out,
Of running such a rig. [100]

The wind did blow, the cloak did fly,
Like streamer long and gay,
Till, loop and button failing both,
At last it flew away.

Then might all people well discern [105]
The bottles he had slung;
A bottle swinging at each side,
As hath been said or sung.

The dogs did bark, the children
screamed;
Up flew the windows all; [110]
And every soul cried out, "Well
done!"
As loud as he could bawl.

Away went Gilpin—who but he?
His fame soon spread around;
"He carries weight!" "He rides a
race!" [115]
"'Tis for a thousand pound!"

And still as fast as he drew near,
'Twas wonderful to view
How in a trice the turnpike men
Their gates wide open threw. [120]

And now, as he went bowing down,
His reeking head full low,
The bottles twain behind his back
Were shattered at a blow.

Down ran the wine into the road, [125]
Most piteous to be seen,
Which made his horse's flanks to
smoke
As they had basted been.

But still he seemed to carry weight,
With leathern girdle braced; [130]
For all might see the bottle necks
Still dangling at his waist.

Thus all through merry Islington,
These gambols he did play,
Until he came unto the Wash [135]
Of Edmonton so gay;

And there he threw the Wash about,
On both sides of the way,
Just like unto a trundling mop,
Or a wild goose at play. [140]

At Edmonton, his loving wife
From the balcony spied
Her tender husband, wondering much
To see how he did ride.

"Stop, stop, John Gilpin!—Here's the
house!" 145
They all at once did cry;
"The dinner waits, and we are
tired."—
Said Gilpin, "So am I!"

But yet his horse was not a whit
Inclined to tarry there; 150
For why?—his owner had a house
Full ten miles off, at Ware.

So like an arrow swift he flew,
Shot by an archer strong;
So did he fly—which brings me to 155
The middle of my song.

Away went Gilpin, out of breath,
And sore against his will,
Till, at his friend the calender's,
His horse at last stood still. 160

The calender, amazed to see
His neighbor in such trim,
Laid down his pipe, flew to the gate,
And thus accosted him:

"What news? what news? your tid-
ings tell; 165
Tell me you must and shall—
Say why bareheaded you are come,
Or why you come at all?"

Now Gilpin had a pleasant wit,
And loved a timely joke; 170
And thus unto the calender,
In merry guise, he spoke:

"I came because your horse would
come;
And, if I well forbode,
My hat and wig will soon be here—175
They are upon the road."

The calender, right glad to find
His friend in merry pin,[6]
Returned him not a single word,
But to the house went in; 180

When straight he came, with hat and
wig—
A wig that flowed behind,
A hat not much the worse for wear,
Each comely in its kind.

He held them up, and in his turn, 185
Thus showed his ready wit:
"My head is twice as big as yours,
They therefore needs must fit.

"But let me scrape the dirt away
That hangs upon your face; 190
And stop and eat, for well you may
Be in a hungry case."

Said John—"It is my wedding day,
And all the world would stare,
If wife should dine at Edmonton 195
And I should dine at Ware."

So turning to his horse, he said,
"I am in haste to dine;
'Twas for your pleasure you came
here—
You shall go back for mine." 200

Ah! luckless speech, and bootless
boast,
For which he paid full dear;
For while he spake, a braying ass
Did sing most loud and clear;

Whereat his horse did snort, as he 205
Had heard a lion roar,
And galloped off with all his might,
As he had done before.

Away went Gilpin, and away
Went Gilpin's hat and wig: 210
He lost them sooner than at first,
For why?—they were too big.

6*Pin*, mood.

Now Mistress Gilpin, when she saw
  Her husband posting down
Into the country far away,   215
  She pulled out half a crown;

And thus unto the youth she said,
  That drove them to the Bell,
"This shall be yours, when you bring
    back
  My husband safe and well."   220

The youth did ride, and soon did meet
  John coming back amain;
Whom in a trice he tried to stop
  By catching at his rein;

But not performing what he meant,
  And gladly would have done,   226
The frighted steed he frighted more
  And made him faster run.

Away went Gilpin, and away
  Went postboy at his heels;   230
The postboy's horse right glad to miss
  The lumbering of the wheels.

Six gentlemen upon the road,
  Thus seeing Gilpin fly,
With postboy scampering in the
    rear,   235
  They raised a hue and cry:

"Stop thief! stop thief!—a highway-
    man!"
  Not one of them was mute;
And all and each that passed that way
  Did join in the pursuit.   240

And now the turnpike-gates again
  Flew open in short space,
The toll-men thinking as before,
  That Gilpin rode a race.

And so he did, and won it too,   245
  For he got first to town,
Nor stopped till where he had got up
  He did again get down.

Now let us sing long live the King,
  And Gilpin, long live he;   250
And when he next doth ride abroad,
  May I be there to see!

For Thought and Discussion

1. Why did John Gilpin and his wife decide to have a holiday?
2. Where did they live and where did they decide to go?
3. Why did John ride a horse and why did he start later than the others?
4. What part of the lunch did Mrs. Gilpin forget?
5. When John raced through the town with the bottles on either side of his saddle, what did the people think about his ride?
6. How did losing his cloak, hat, and wig add to the humor?
7. Where did his horse take him before stopping?
8. Why did his horse's flanks smoke?
9. As he raced back, what did the people cry?
10. How does the author poke fun at the wrong impressions which people often get from outward appearances?

Plus Work

Can you write a humorous story or poem about a run-a-way automobile or plane?

ELEGY ON THE DEATH OF A MAD DOG

OLIVER GOLDSMITH

GOOD people all, of every sort,
  Give ear unto my song;
And if you find it wondrous short,
  It cannot hold you long.

In Islington there was a man   5
  Of whom the world might say
That still a godly race he ran,
  Whene'er he went to pray.

A kind and gentle heart he had,
  To comfort friends and foes;   10
The naked every day he clad,
  When he put on his clothes.

And in that town a dog was found,
  As many dogs there be,
Both mongrel, puppy, whelp, and
    hound,   15
  And curs of low degree.

This dog and man at first were
    friends;
  But when a pique began,

The dog, to gain his private ends,
  Went mad, and bit the man.   20

Around from all the neighboring
    streets
  The wondering neighbors ran,
And swore the dog had lost his wits,
  To bite so good a man.

The wound it seemed both sore and
    sad   25
  To every Christian eye;
And while they swore the dog was
    mad,
  They swore the man would die.

But soon a wonder came to light,
  That showed the rogues they lied;
The man recovered of the bite;   31
  The dog it was that died.

❧

Additional Readings

Bennett, Arnold: *Buried Alive*
Bunner, H. C.: *Short Sixes*
Carroll, Lewis: *Alice in Wonderland*
Dickens, Charles: *Dialogues*
  The Pickwick Papers
Douglas, James: *The Bunch Book*
Gilbert, Sir William Schwenk: *Bab Ballads*
Gregory, Lady: *Spreading the News*
Herbert, A. P.: *On Drawing*
Kipling, Rudyard: *Namgay Doola*

Lucas, E. V.: *If Dogs Could Write*
Madigan, Benjamin de Cassera: *When Huck Finn Went Highbrow*
O'Sullivan, Maurice: *Twenty Years A-Growing*
Swift, Jonathan: *Gulliver's Travels*
Thackeray, W. M.: *The Rose and the Ring*
Wodehouse, P. G.: *The Story of Webster*
  Dear Old Squiffy

Mainly About People

MAINLY ABOUT PEOPLE

*L*ITERATURE about people is indispensable and will continue to be so as long as the world is inhabited by human beings. Long before the platitudinous Pope affirmed that the proper study of mankind is man, readers delighted in viewing man in his seven stages from morning infancy to evening childhood.

There would be few books, and they would be in little demand, were no people mentioned in them. How could there be a book called *Alice in Wonderland* if there were no Alice? Who would care to read the account of a treasure island for which no people were searching? What interest would there be in a stormy main unpeopled by the colorful ghosts of departed buccaneers like Captain Kidd and gallant heroes like Sir Richard Grenville? How could there be today a dissertation upon roast pig had there been no little boy to touch burnt flesh and stick his fingers in his mouth to cool them? Would even a *crowlan ferlie* like Burns's louse have provoked a smile had there been no lady on whose bonnet he could have shown his plump and impudent nose?

All people are interesting. Even a village school-master, as presented by Goldsmith, becomes a personage; and Swift's pigmy from Lilliput vies in interest with his giant from Brobdingnag.

Try to feature a library bereft of diaries and biographies and autobiographies—a library without a Pepys or a Florence Nightingale or a Queen Victoria. Try to conceive of narrative poems and dramas and short stories and novels with no mention of such arresting and companionable and heroic characters as Ulysses, the Lady of the Lake, Macbeth, King Arthur and his Knights of the Round Table, Wee Willie Winkie, Silas Marner, and Sidney Carton. Try to imagine the literature of the nineteenth and twentieth centuries minus characters like those created by Kipling, Stevenson, Eliot, Galsworthy, Hardy, and Tolstoy. Such a literature would be but empty words lacking the breath of life.

"MY DAUGHTER DOES NOT SEE STRANGERS, SIR, WITHOUT MY KNOWLEDGE AND PERMISSION."

PATERNITY
WARWICK DEEPING

[Warwick Deeping, 1877—, had opportunity to observe human nature closely while he studied medicine in Middlesex Hospital, in London, and during his service as a physician in the Gallipoli Campaign and in France. Now that he has deserted the profession followed by his father and his grandfather, he spends his time in writing and in working in the open about his country home.]

HER father was a little snuffy man, who, after living for fifteen years as a widower in the white house at the end of Prospect Terrace, had developed mannerisms and personal peculiarities that were neither criticized nor questioned by his daughter.

"Mary, I'm waiting."

He called her peremptorily. At a quarter to eleven every Sunday morning he would stand on the dining-room hearthrug, holding his top hat and his cane and his gloves, waiting for his daughter to go to church. Always he said the same things, and said them at the same time in the same way.

He had a habit of sniffing; also, a long pinched nose with blue veins on it, a narrow forehead, a precise mouth. Every button of him was done up. When he walked up the aisle of the parish church, he carried his top hat in his right hand and just as high as his shoulder. He joined in all the responses. During the sermon he sat bolt upright and as stiff as a backboard, sniffing rhythmically, and on his face an expression of alert skepticism, as though he were waiting to catch the preacher tripping.

His hobby was catching people out. He was the sort of person who, when he read a novel, scattered question marks and scrawls in pencil here and there, and if he found a mistake in the grammar he wrote to the author about it. He addressed frequent letters to the *Times*. He was fond of sending anonymous postcards to prominent people with whose views he disagreed.

"Sir: I beg to suggest that your opinions are dangerous and fallacious. I beg to protest...."

He was always protesting in his fussy, futile way, blowing his long nose like a trumpet, and sniffing his way through life toward an evangelical Elysium.

Mary was lame.

But her lameness was less an affliction than was her father, Mr. Frederick Fishenden of 17, Prospect Terrace, Barham-on-Sea. Mr. Fishenden had been a civil servant, and had retired on a pension and five thousand pounds or so invested in trustee stocks....

Mary had an allowance of twenty pounds a year, out of which she had to pay for her postage and her traveling expenses, such as they were. She was plain—pleasantly plain—and romance in its conventional form had not entered her life. Her father, neither in his person nor in his opinions, encouraged romance. Any young man hesitating outside the green door of No. 17, Prospect Terrace, and meeting that little old cock-sparrow of a man, might well have turned tail and sought adventure elsewhere.

Mary was useful to her father. She ran the house and kept the books, and was expected to darn his socks, and every Saturday evening she had to produce her weekly accounts.

"The books, my dear."

His audit was a solemn business. He sat in a cane-backed chair, jigging a foot and sniffing, and checking each item.

"Four bloaters—on Tuesday. How's that?"

"Two in the kitchen, father."

Usually he queried the amount of milk consumed. He was very touchy upon the matter of milk. He would say that he was convinced that those two wenches below stairs washed their faces in it.

"I abhor waste, my dear."

And every week she had to convince him that the maids did not use milk for their ablutions.

He was not only a tiresome and pompous little person, he was also a most tempestuous tyrant. Mary was allowed a little room of her own on the first floor at the back of the house. It had a high window looking out upon a narrow garden shut in by brick walls. An old pear tree grew in the garden and in the spring it was a smother of white, and in the autumn a pillar of fire. Mary loved the pear tree. Her father was always threatening to have it cut down, not because it perpetrated any definite offense, but because he liked to interfere with things and to exercise his authority.

Mary's room was supposed to be a work room. It was. She dealt with the mending there. Also, she had an old, flat-topped desk by the window, and the desk had drawers, and one of the drawers could be locked. She kept the key of it in her pocket, for in those flouncy days women had pockets. The locked drawer was her one secret in that dull, Victorian little house.

Mary's secret was that she wrote. She had scribbled for years. As a child she had spun wonderful and impossible stories about princes and fairies and haunted castles; but now she did not write of impossible things. She had her moments of peace during the day when Mr. Fishenden was out of the house. He took a walk from eleven o'clock till a quarter to one, marching out in his top hat with a cane tucked under his arm; he pottered up and down the parade, and met other quidnuncs, and set the world right. From two o'clock to three he slept on the sofa in the dining room with a handkerchief over his face and his hands crossed upon his tight little tummy. In spring and summer and autumn he took another little walk after tea, and then turned into the local Liberal Club for half an hour. He did not smoke and he did not drink.

So Mary had her secret hours when she was supposed to be mending the house linen and meditating upon the complete rightness of her lot. She would wait for the closing of the green front door, and then get out her papers and set herself down at the desk and escape into that other world. It was a wonderful world quite beyond Mr. Frederick Fishenden's ken.

Mary was writing a novel. She had written other novels. She belonged to that unexpected world of the Brontës and the Eliots; ostensibly she knew nothing of life, and yet the Mary who wrote somehow knew everything. The world seemed to look in at her window. The pear tree was a tree of heaven.

But her father was as inquisitive as a meddlesome child. One evening when Mary had gone to a party at Dr. Hale's—a musical party so-called —Mr. Fishenden felt fussy. He went exploring. Once a week he visited the gas meter, and poked his long nose into the linen cupboard; and on this particular evening he went rummaging in his daughter's room. He discovered the locked drawer in the desk. It annoyed him. He considered that nothing in his house should be locked against him. He tried his own bunch of keys on the drawer, but none of the keys would fit.

When Mary returned, he was waiting for her. He had no qualms about asking the most impertinent questions.

He said, "I found a drawer locked in your desk. Why do you keep it locked? I expect to be told."

Mary was very patient with her father. She had to be patient.

"It is my private drawer, father."

"Private!"

His tone implied that his daughter need no privacies.

"I keep letters and photos and things there."

"Letters! What letters? You don't get any letters that are private."

He was so utterly outside her real world that sometimes she wondered at him, and was exasperated even while she wondered.

"All letters from friends are private."

"What friends?" he asked irritably.

"Some of the girls I knew at school."

"O, girls' letters."

He sniffed. Such stuff could be passed over. And he remembered the gas meter.

"We have used too much gas this week. I expect those wenches have been keeping the jets flaring downstairs. You had better go down and look sometimes. Surprise them."

She stood observing him, seeing him all round as she saw the characters in her novel. He expected her to be a sort of domestic sneak.

"The days are getting shorter. They have to use more gas."

He snapped at her.

"Don't argue, my dear; see to it."

But he had not discovered her novel. It was beyond the capacity of his little, narrow, flat-backed head to conceive the wildness of his daughter perpetrating a novel. On the whole, he did not approve of novels—anything after Scott and Dickens. George Eliot he considered a monstrosity; women shouldn't do such things. He had read Trollope. Stevenson was in the air; but Mr. Fishenden thought Stevenson thin, flimsy stuff. The fellow's style was histrionic. Scott and Dickens had produced novels; the moderns perpetrated fiction.

One day in the spring of the year when the pear tree was in blossom, Mary did up a very neat parcel. It was the manuscript of her novel *Martin Hume*, and the manuscript was as neat as the parcel, for Mary wrote a beautiful, flowing hand. She was tempting adventure. Other and earlier novels had been relegated to an old sugar box in the attic where they lay concealed under piles of *Sunday at Home* and missionary journals; but *Martin Hume* was different, a grown man created by a woman who had genius. The parcel was addressed to Messrs. Lovell & Burnside, publishers, of Covent Garden, London, and Mary had chosen a time when her father was out in order to slip out and launch her parcel.

But as luck would have it, she met her father at the corner of Prospect Terrace just by the white portico of the Royal Hotel, and he stopped and pointed with his stick.

"What's that—what's that?"

Her tolerant and wise gray eyes concealed amusement. She was feeling very much in blossom, like the pear tree.

"Patterns, father."

"Patterns! Patterns for what?"

"New curtains."

"Where? We don't want any new curtains."

"My bedroom. I thought of buying them myself."

"Nonsense. New curtains. The old ones are not worn out, are they?"

She smiled at him.

"Evolution is life. Everything should change once in five years, even curtains," and she walked on past him, leaving him with a puzzled and disapproving look on his face. Evolution! Abominable word, smelling of Huxley and Darwin. Mr. Fishenden was a Liberal, but his liberalism was progress according to Fishenden. What nonsense women talked! As if a man's opinions and his personality were like lace curtains to be taken down and washed, or changed according to the fashion.

Meanwhile, Mary limped up the High Street of Barham-on-Sea to the post office, which still persisted in living in a white, bow-fronted building which was altogether charming. It belonged to the Barham of Nelson and William IV, when gentlemen wore coats of blue and bottle-green, and used the English language vigorously, and had not become too sensitive about the benighted heathen and wenches who wore white stockings. Mary had her parcel registered. She came out with a slight flush upon her pleasant, plain, wise face. She went and sat on a seat near the flagstaff on the cliffs and watched the shipping and the clouds coming up over the sea.

Messrs. Lovell & Burnside were a firm with traditions and courtesy. They acknowledged the receipt of Mary's novel, but not on a postcard, so that Mr. Fishenden was none the wiser when he scrutinized the envelope. He had all the letters that came placed beside his plate on the breakfast table, and if there happened to be one for his daughter, he doled it out to her.

"Who's that from?"

"The pattern people, I think."

She had to wear such a mask while living with Mr. Fishenden that she was able to conceal her excitement. She carried the letter upstairs with her to her room, and opened and read it, but was ready to hide it away should the little god of No. 17 contemplate interference. The letter acknowledged the receipt of the manuscript of her novel, and informed her that the novel was in the hands of Messrs. Lovell & Burnside's reader.

Three weeks passed. The pear tree had dropped its blossoms and had put on a coat of shining green, and the vine on the stable was beginning to weave a pattern with gilded leaves. Every year Mary's father had the little front garden above the area decorously stuffed with red geraniums, lobelia, and white marguerites; and it so happened that this bedding scheme was in progress when a gentleman and a valise arrived in a cab at the Royal Hotel. The gentleman wore an eyeglass; he had a largeness and an air of importance, and a pair of observant and ironic blue eyes. The Royal Hotel received him debonairly, for obviously he was made to be received in such a way.

He questioned old Tom, the head waiter, who invariably had a serviette over his left arm. It was said that old Tom would appear in heaven carrying that serviette.

"Whereabouts is Prospect Terrace?"

"Just here, sir. Turn to the right when you get outside."

The gentleman had lunch, lit a cigar, and wandered out and about; he surveyed Prospect Terrace, and the green door and green balcony of No.

17. He was interested in No. 17, and in the whole atmosphere of Prospect Terrace. But he was in no hurry; he idled to the cliffs and sat down on a seat and finished his cigar, and realized Barham-on-Sea as being not all Prospect Terrace. It had the sea and the sky and the shipping, and a certain, quiet, catholic flavor. It had produced a famous sea-dog, and now it had produced something else.

It was about a quarter to three when the gentleman strolled back to Prospect Terrace. Mr. Fishenden had emerged somewhat prematurely from his white handkerchief and his slumber in order to stand on the doorstep and overlook the activities of the jobbing gardener who was filling the front garden with pelargoniums.

So the gentleman with the eyeglass met Mary's father on the doorstep of No. 17, Prospect Terrace, and they observed each other. Mr. Fishenden detested monocles; they produced in his Liberal opinion and prejudices the redness of an extreme radicalism.

The gentleman with the monocle raised his hat to Mr. Fishenden. It was a gesture.

"Excuse me, I believe Miss Fishenden lives here."

Paterfamilias stared. His little, waspish plume of sandy gray hair seemed to erect itself.

He said, "I am Mr. Fishenden."

Obviously he considered the announcement to be final and sufficient. And who was this fellow with the eyeglass and his air of self-assurance who was asking for Mary? Paterfamilias bristled.

Said the man with the monocle, "My name's Burnside. I have come down from town to see Miss Fishenden."

Possibly Mr. Burnside considered that the information would act as "open sesame," but he did not know

Mr. Fishenden or the amount that Mary's father did not know. Anyway this little cock-sparrow of a man remained on the doorstep, with his hands in the pockets of his tight trousers, and his Pickwickian tummy stuck out.

"My daughter's busy."

Mr. Burnside began to appreciate his curmudgeon.

"Is that so? When will she be at liberty to see me?"

"When I choose, I think, sir. What is your business?"

"My business is with your daughter, Mr. Fishenden."

Mr. Fishenden was nonplussed. Who the devil was this fellow, a flash-bagman, a super-tout? Or was it possible that the fellow was matrimonially inclined, and that Mary had been concealing some romance?

He said, "My daughter does not see strangers, sir, without my knowledge and permission."

Mr. Burnside began to smile.

"I think I told you that my name is Burnside."

"It might be Smith, sir, or Jones, or Robinson."

"It is neither Smith, nor Jones, nor Robinson. I belong to the firm of Lovell & Burnside."

Mr. Fishenden had a lapse. He remembered the hypothetical new curtains, and the parcel of patterns. But then—the eyeglass?

"Ah—you've come about the curtains?"

Mr. Burnside's monocle twinkled.

"Not exactly. We are a firm of publishers. Possibly you may have seen our name. It has been known for some seventy years."

Mr. Fishenden was both surprised and annoyed.

"Ha, of course! I do know the name. But I fail to see—what my daughter—. We get our books from the local library."

"I dare say you do, sir. But I have come down from town to see your daughter about a book."

"What book, sir?"

"Her book."

"My daughter's book? I fail to understand you, sir."

"The book, Mr. Fishenden, written by your daughter, and sent to us about a month ago."

For the moment Mr. Fishenden's prim little mouth hung open. He looked rather like a fish with sandy gray spines on its head.

"A book! My daughter—written a book! I have had nothing to do with it."

Said Mr. Burnside sardonically, "I don't suppose you have."

But, obviously, something had to be done about it; even Mr. Fishenden realized the inevitableness of the situation. Incensed and astonished he might be. His daughter and a book! Incredible! And she had said nothing about it; she had maintained a most undaughterly silence; she had not even availed herself of his acumen as a critic. Incredible! Most unwomanly! And the member of an eminent firm of publishers standing on the doorstep!

But the book! What sort of trash? A novel—of course.

He moistened his lips. He became aware of the jobbing gardener kneeling there doing nothing, listening with a trowel and flowerpot idle in his hands. Wasting Mr. Fishenden's time.

He said, "What is this book? A novel?"

"Yes, a novel, sir."

"Fiction. Of course. May I say, sir, that my daughter never asked my permission—?"

"Is that so, sir? You surprise me. Possibly you will be surprised, Mr. Fishenden."

"Probably not, sir. Sentimental trash, sir, probably, sir. How could my daughter—?"

"I admit—the miracle. No doubt —from your point of view—"

Mr. Fishenden's face seemed to narrow to an edge. Was this fellow being ironical? Was he poking fun at an ex-member of Her Majesty's Civil Service? Confound him.

He said, "You had better come in, sir. We will discuss the matter."

Mr. Burnside grew more bland in response to Mr. Fishenden's pomposity.

"Really, you must excuse me, but I have come to discuss the matter with your daughter. It is her book, Mr. Fishenden."

"Granted, sir. I have had nothing to do with it."

"Let me assure you that I do not hold you responsible. My opinion of the book is—that it is a piece of genius."

"Genius, sir?"

"Yes, genius. Believe me, I absolve you from all responsibility."

Mr. Fishenden began to feel quite sure that this publisher fellow was indulging in irony, and Mr. Fishenden did not approve of irony save when he used it himself, heavily and with emphasis.

He said, "You'd better come in," and he let Burnside into the hall, and going to the foot of the stairs, shouted peremptorily—"Mary, Mary, come downstairs at once!" She came. She was aware of a stranger standing in the hall who was gazing with an air of ironic joy at the back of her father's head. His monocled glance raised itself to her. He looked at her with curiosity, interest. He held his hat in his left hand.

"Miss Mary Fishenden, I presume?"

"Yes."

He held out a hand.

"My name is Burnside. I have come down to see you about *Martin Hume*. May I congratulate you on that book?"

She colored up, and her gray eyes looked coy.

"You are Mr. Burnside, the publisher?"

"I am."

"I'm very glad."

And then she became aware of her father posed in the dining room doorway rather like a dog who had sat up to beg and was not being noticed. He sniffed. She knew from his expression that he was about to exert authority.

"Mr. Burnside, am I to understand that you have come to interview my daughter on business?"

Burnside looked first at Mary, and then at her father.

"I may say—pleasure and business. We should like to publish Miss Fishenden's book."

Her father raised a hand as though he were signaling to traffic and ordering it to abate its pace or to stop.

"One moment, sir; I have not seen this book; I expect to read this book before I allow it to be published."

He tightened his tummy. He was the little, paternal censor guarding the morals and the autocracies of Prospect Terrace. And Mr. Burnside fixed him with his monocle and looked amused.

"Indeed! But surely, sir, you have read some of your daughter's work?"

"Never."

He turned an accusing glance upon his daughter.

"Scribbling in secret. Must be

ashamed of it. I won't allow my daughter to rush into print without my—approval."

"I can assure you, sir, there is no need for alarm. Besides, I think it is Miss Fishenden's authority that we need. If she says 'Publish,' we publish. It is a question of terms. I am here to discuss terms."

His ironic and friendly monocle glimmered at Mary.

"Do you say 'Publish,' Miss Fishenden, provided we agree—?"

She stood on the last step, and ignored her father.

"Of course, publish, Mr. Burnside. Would you care to come up to my study to discuss details?"

She turned and climbed the stairs, and Burnside followed her, carrying his hat with a certain jauntiness. He expected paterfamilias to protest, but he had a glimpse of Mr. Fishenden left on one leg, with his face screwed up, and most illiberally inarticulate.

Closing the door of Mary's study, he gave her a little bow and a quizzical look.

"Remarkable man your father, Miss Fishenden, nearly as remarkable as your book."

Messrs. Lovell & Burnside were men of business, but on this occasion Mary and her book appeared to appeal to other-worldliness. Mr. Burnside had come down to Barham-on-Sea with the idea of proposing to buy Mary's book outright, but instead of doing so he advised her to accept a royalty agreement. Mr. Fishenden had performed one service. He had made of Burnside a cavalier and a partisan, and had pushed authoress and publisher into a conspiracy of understanding.

"I suppose you are of legal age, Miss Fishenden?"

"Yes, I'm twenty-nine."

So Mr. Burnside departed, and Mary met her father at tea, and poured out his tea for him, and he was portentously solemn. He had received a shock; he did not like to confess it even to himself, but his daughter was different; it is possible that he was just a little shy and afraid of her. He asked her no questions about the book, or about Mr. Burnside, or the terms of publication. He cultivated an official and departmental silence. Actually this silence continued for three months.

A week before the publication of *Martin Hume*, Mary came down to tea and presented her father with a copy of the book.

"Perhaps you would like to read it."

Mr. Fishenden read *Martin Hume*. He sat up till eleven o'clock reading it. He was astonished, shocked, a little bewildered. He could not understand how a daughter of his could have written such a book. Things happened in it which were not supposed to happen in a respectable English household. And the language in places! And the hero was nothing less than an infidel! The little, authoritative soul of Mary's father gibbered and protested. And yet, in a sense, the book overwhelmed him; it was beyond and over and around him; it had the bewildering bigness of a strange city in which Mr. Fishenden's conventions and opinions were lost. He wanted to shout at the book, to write an official letter beginning with a peremptory and protesting "Sir."

At breakfast Mary found *Martin Hume* lying beside her plate. Her father's face wore the expression it assumed just before going to church.

She poured out his tea for him. There was silence. The presence of *Martin Hume* was ignored. She knew that her father did not approve. She did not expect him to approve.

And yet, three years later, when Mary had a little house of her own in town, and had visited America, and was very much a figure in the great world, Mr. Fishenden was walking up and down the parade of Barham-on-Sea with his top hat more at an angle, and looking more of a cock-sparrow than ever. He had assimi-lated and digested his daughter's fame. He had pinned it in his but-tonhole. He wore it, too, as he wore his trousers.

He had the air of assuming himself to be a celebrity.

"Yes. That's Frederick Fishenden —the father of Mary Fishenden. Very exceptional man, obviously, to have produced such a daughter."

Obviously.

For Thought and Discussion

1. Have you ever met a person who reminds you of Mr. Fishenden?
2. What harmony is there between Mr. Fishenden's appearance and his character?
3. What terms does the author use to describe Mary? Do you like her? Do you blame her for the bit of deceit about the patterns? In what respect is the term, *patterns,* true and appropriate? Recall Amy Lowell's use of the term *patterns* in her poem of that title.
4. What was Mary's method of escape from unpleasantness? Is your way as profitable as hers was?
5. Why did Mr. Burnside change his mind and offer Mary a royalty instead of buying the book from her outright?
6. Explain the two-fold shock Mr. Fishenden experienced in connection with his daughter's writing.
7. What descriptive terms applied to Mr. Fishenden do you consider most comic? Is there an element of pathos about him?
8. What changes, if any, does Mary's success bring to her and to her father?

STORY OF A PIEBALD HORSE
WILLIAM HENRY HUDSON

[W. H. Hudson, 1846-1922, born in Argentina of an English father and a New England mother, was a naturalist who not only catalogued his accurate scientific observations for the purpose of research but also used them to enhance the field of romantic fiction. Hudson knew human nature as he knew history, and his philoso-phical studies present charming and sympathetic views of both. As a naturalist, yet with a poet's imagina-tion, he wrote of birds and butter-flies and plants and animals; and, as a romanticist, he used his loved out-of-doors for the setting of his stories. His style is simple and marked by a sensitive and almost poetic beauty of sound and cadence. His stories are at the same time realistic enough and virile enough to appeal to lovers of adventure, as is attested by the fact that *Green Mansions* was a favorite among Admiral Byrd's men in Little America. *Green Mansions*, a novel; *Idle Days in Patagonia; Far Away and Long Ago*, his marvelous biography; *Afoot in England; The Book of the Naturalist; The Purple Land;* and *Tales of the Pampas*, in which appears "El Ombu," called by some the greatest short story in the English language, are among his contributions to scientific and literary studies.]

THIS is all about a piebald. People there are like birds that come down in flocks, hop about chattering, gobble up their seed, then fly away, forgetting what they have swallowed. I love not to scatter grain for such as these. With you, friend, it is different. Others may laugh if they like at the old man of many stories, who puts all things into his copper memory. I can laugh, too, knowing that all things are ordered by destiny; otherwise I might sit down and cry.

The things I have seen! There was the piebald that died long ago; I could take you to the very spot where his bones used to lie bleaching in the sun. There is a nettle growing on the spot. I saw it yesterday. What important things are these to remember and talk about! Bones of a dead horse and a nettle; a young bird that falls from its nest in the night and is found dead in the morning; puffballs blown about by the wind; a little lamb left behind by the flock bleating at night amongst the thorns and thistles, where only the fox or wild dog can hear it! Small matters are these, and our lives, what are they? And the people we have known, the men and women who have spoken to us and touched us with warm hands —the bright eyes and red lips! Can we cast these things like dead leaves on the fire? Can we lie down full of heaviness because of them, and sleep and rise in the morning without them? Ah, friend!

Let us to the story of the piebald. There was a cattle marking at neighbor Sotelo's *estancia*,[1] and out of a herd of three thousand head we had to part all the yearlings to be branded. After that, dinner and a dance. At sunrise we gathered, about thirty of us; all friends and neighbors, to do the work. Only with us came one person nobody knew. He joined us when we were on our way to the cattle; a young man, slender, well formed, of pleasing countenance and dressed as few could dress in those days. His horse also shone with silver trappings. And what an animal! Many horses have I seen in this life, but never one with such a presence as this young stranger's piebald.

Arrived at the herd, we began to separate the young animals, the men riding in couples through the cattle, so that each calf when singled out could be driven by two horsemen, one on each side, to prevent it from doubling back. I happened to be mounted on a demon with a fiery mouth—there was no making him work, so I had to leave the parters and stand with little to do, watching the yearlings already parted, to keep them from returning to the herd.

Presently neighbor Chapaco rode up to me. He was a good-hearted man, well spoken, half Indian and half Christian; but he also had another half, and that was devil.

"What! neighbor Lucero, are you riding on a donkey or a goat, that you remain here doing boy's work?"

---

[1] *estancia,* a Spanish-American term for a ranch.

I began telling him about my horse, but he did not listen; he was looking at the parters.

"Who is that young stranger?" he asked.

"I see him today," I replied, "and if I see him again tomorrow then I shall have seen him twice."

"And in what country of which I have never heard did he learn cattle-parting?" said he.

"He rides," I answered, "like one presuming on a good horse. But he is safe, his fellow-worker has all the danger."

"I believe you," said Chapaco. "He charges furiously and hurls the heifer before his comrade, who has all the work to keep it from doubling, and all the danger, for at any moment his horse may go over it and fall. This our young stranger does knowingly, thinking that no one here will resent it. No, Lucero, he is presuming more on his long knife than on his good horse."

Even while we spoke, the two we were watching rode up to us. Chapaco saluted the young man, taking off his hat, and said—"Will you take me for a partner, friend?"

"Yes; why not, friend?" returned the other; and together the two rode back to the herd.

Now I shall watch them, said I to myself, to see what this Indian devil intends doing. Soon they came out of the herd driving a very small animal. Then I knew what was coming. "May your guardian angel be with you to avert a calamity, young stranger!" I exclaimed. Whip and spur those two came towards me like men riding a race and not parting cattle. Chapaco kept close to the calf, so that he had the advantage, for his horse was well trained. At length he got a little ahead, then, quick as lightning, he forced the calf round square before the other. The piebald struck it full in the middle, and fell because it had to fall. But, Saints in Heaven! why did not the rider save himself? Those who were watching saw him throw up his feet to tread his horse's neck and leap away; nevertheless man, horse, and calf came down together. They plowed the ground for some distance, so great had been their speed, and the man was under. When we picked him up he was senseless, the blood flowing from his mouth. Next morning, when the sun rose and God's light fell on the earth, he expired.

Of course there was no dancing that night. Some of the people, after eating, went away; others remained sitting about all night, talking in low tones, waiting for the end. A few of us were at his bedside watching his white face and closed eyes. He breathed, and that was all. When the sunlight came over the world he opened his eyes, and Sotelo asked him how he did. He took no notice, but presently his lips began to move, though they seemed to utter no sound. Sotelo bent his ear down to listen. "Where does she live?" he asked. He could not answer—he was dead.

"He seemed to be saying many things," Sotelo told us, "but I understood only this—'Tell her to forgive me . . . I was wrong. She loved him from the first . . . I was jealous and hated him . . . Tell Elaria not to grieve —Anacleto will be good to her.' Alas! my friends, where shall I find his relations to deliver this dying message to them?"

The Alcalde[2] came that day and made a list of the dead man's possessions, and bade Sotelo take charge of them till the relations could be found. Then, calling all the people together, he bade each person cut on his whip-handle and on the sheath of his knife the mark branded on the flank of the piebald, which was in shape like a horseshoe with a cross

inside, so that it might be shown to all strangers, and made known through the country until the dead man's relations should hear of it.

When a year had gone by, the Alcalde told Sotelo that, all inquiries having failed, he could now take the piebald and the silver trappings for himself. Sotelo would not listen to this, for he was a devout man and coveted no person's property, dead or alive. The horse and things, however, still remained in his charge.

Three years later I was one afternoon sitting with Sotelo, taking maté,[3] when his herd of dun mares were driven up. They came galloping and neighing to the corral and ahead of them, looking like a wild horse, was the piebald, for no person ever mounted him.

"Never do I look on that horse," I remarked, "without remembering the fatal marking, when its master met his death."

"Now you speak of it," said he, "let me inform you that I am about to try a new plan. That noble piebald and all those silver trappings hanging in my room are always reproaching my conscience. Let us not forget the young stranger we put under ground. I have had many masses said for his soul's repose, but that does not quite satisfy me. Somewhere there is a place where he is not forgotten. Hands there are, perhaps, that gather wild flowers to place them with lighted candles before the image of the Blessed Virgin; eyes there are that weep and watch for his coming. You know how many travelers and cattle-drovers going to Buenos Aires from the south call for refreshment at the pulpería.[4] I in-

---

[2]the Alcalde, an officer equivalent to the mayor.

[3]maté, a drink made from the maté plant.

[4]pulpería, a Spanish term for tavern or saloon.

tend taking the piebald and tying him every day at the gate there. No person calling will fail to notice the horse, and some day perhaps some traveler will recognize the brand on its flank and will be able to tell us what department and what *estancia* it comes from."

I did not believe anything would result from this, but said nothing, not wishing to discourage him.

Next morning the piebald was tied up at the gate of the *pulpería*, at the roadside, only to be released again when night came, and this was repeated every day for a long time. So fine an animal did not fail to attract the attention of all strangers passing that way; still several weeks went by and nothing was discovered. At length, one evening, just when the sun was setting, there appeared a troop of cattle driven by eight men. It had come a great distance, for the troop was a large one—about nine hundred head—and they moved slowly, like cattle that had been many days on the road. Some of the men came in for refreshments; then the storekeeper noticed that one remained outside leaning on the gate.

"What is the *capatas*[5] doing that he remains outside?" said one of the men.

"Evidently he has fallen in love with that piebald," said another, "for he cannot take his eyes off it."

At length the *capatas*, a young man of good presence, came in and sat down on a bench. The others were talking and laughing about the strange things they had all been doing the day before; for they had been many days and nights on the road, only nodding a little in their saddles, and at length becoming de-

---

[5]*capatas*, foreman or manager of the ranch.

lirious from want of sleep, they had begun to act like men that are half-crazed.

"Enough of the delusions of yesterday," said the *capatas*, who had been silently listening to them, "but tell me, boys, am I in the same condition today?"

"Surely not!" they replied. "Thanks to those horned devils being so tired and footsore, we all had some sleep last night."

"Very well then," said he, "now you have finished eating and drinking, go back to the troop, but before you leave look well at that piebald tied at the gate. He that is not a cattle drover may ask, 'How can my eyes deceive me?' but I know that a crazy brain makes us see many strange things when the drowsy eyes can only be held open with the fingers."

The men did as they were told, and when they had looked well at the piebald, they all shouted out, "He has the brand of the *estancia de Silva* on his flank, and no counter-brand—claim the horse, *capatas*, for he is yours." And after that they rode away to the herd.

"My friend," said the *capatas* to the storekeeper, "will you explain how you came possessed of this piebald horse?"

Then the other told him everything, even the dying words of the young stranger, for he knew all.

The *capatas* bent down his head, and covering his face shed tears. Then he said, "And you died thus, Torcuato, amongst strangers! From my heart I have forgiven you the wrong you did me. Heaven rest your soul, Torcuato; I cannot forget that we were once brothers. I, friend, am that Anacleto of whom he spoke with his last breath."

Sotelo was then sent for, and when

he arrived and the *pulpería* was closed for the night, the *capatas* told his story, which I will give you in his own words, for I was also present to hear him. This is what he told us:

I was born on the southern frontier. My parents died when I was very small, but Heaven had compassion on me and raised up one to shelter me in my orphanhood. Don Loreto Silva took me to his *estancia* on the Sarandi, a stream half a day's journey from Tandil, towards the setting sun. He treated me like one of his own children, and I took the name of Silva. He had two other children, Torcuato, who was about the same age as myself, and his daughter, Elaria, who was younger. He was a widower when he took charge of me, and died when I was still a youth. After his death we moved to Tandil, where we had a house close to the little town; for we were all minors, and the property had been left to be equally divided between us when we should be of age. For four years we lived happily together; then when we were of age we preferred to keep the property undivided. I proposed that we should go and live on the *estancia*, but Torcuato would not consent, liking the place where we were living best. Finally, not being able to persuade him, I resolved to go and attend to the *estancia* myself. He said that I could please myself and that he should stay where he was with Elaria. It was only when I told Elaria of these things that I knew how much I loved her. She wept and implored me not to leave her.

"Why do you shed tears, Elaria?" I said; "is it because you love me? Know, then, that I also love you with all my heart, and if you will be mine,

nothing can ever make us unhappy. Do not think that my absence at the *estancia* will deprive me of this feeling which has ever been growing up in me."

"I do love you, Anacleto," she replied, "and I have also known of your love for a long time. But there is something in my heart which I cannot impart to you; only I ask you, for the love you bear me, do not leave me, and do not ask me why I say this to you."

After this appeal I could not leave her, nor did I ask her to tell me her secret. Torcuato and I were friendly, but not as we had been before this difference. I had no evil thoughts of him; I loved him and was with him continually; but from the moment I announced to him that I had changed my mind about going to the *estancia,* and was silent when he demanded the reason, there was a something in him which made it different between us. I could not open my heart to him about Elaria, and sometimes I thought that he also had a secret which he had no intention of sharing with me. This coldness did not, however, distress me very much, so great was the happiness I now experienced, knowing that I possessed Elaria's love. He was much away from the house, being fond of amusements, and he had also begun to gamble. About three months passed in this way, when one morning Torcuato, who was saddling his horse to go out, said, "Will you come with me today, Anacleto?"

"I do not care to go," I answered.

"Look, Anacleto," said he, "once you were always ready to accompany me to a race or dance or cattle-marking. Why have you ceased to care for these things? Are you growing devout before your time, or does my company no longer please you?"

"It is best to tell him everything and have done with secrets," said I to myself, and so replied—

"Since you ask me, Torcuato, I will answer you frankly. It is true that I now take less pleasure than formerly in these pastimes; but you have not guessed the reason rightly."

"What then is this reason of which you speak?"

"Since you cannot guess it," I replied, "know that it is love."

"Love for whom?" he asked quickly, and turning very pale.

"Do you need ask? Elaria," I replied.

I had scarcely uttered the name before he turned on me full of rage.

"Elaria!" he exclaimed. "Do you dare tell me of love for Elaria! But you are only a blind fool, and do not know that I am going to marry her myself."

"Are you mad, Torcuato, to talk of marrying your sister?"

"She is no more my sister than you are my brother," he returned. "I," he continued, striking his breast passionately, "am the only child of my father, Loreto Silva. Elaria, whose mother died in giving her birth, was adopted by my parents. And because she is going to be my wife, I am willing that she should have a share of the property; but you, a miserable foundling, why were you lifted up so high? Was it not enough that you were clothed and fed till you came to man's estate? Not a hand's-breadth of the *estancia* land should be yours by right, and now you presume to speak of love for Elaria."

My blood was on fire with so many insults, but I remembered all the benefits I had received from his father, and did not raise my hand against him. Without more words he left me. I then hastened to Elaria and told her what had passed.

"This," I said, "is the secret you would not impart to me. Why, when you knew these things, was I kept in ignorance?"

"Have pity on me, Anacleto," she replied, crying. "Did I not see that you two were no longer friends and brothers, and this without knowing of each other's love? I dared not open my lips to you or to him. It is always a woman's part to suffer in silence. God intended us to be poor, Anacleto, for we were both born of poor parents, and had this property never come to us, how happy we might have been!"

"Why do you say such things, Elaria? Since we love each other, we cannot be unhappy, rich or poor."

"Is it a little matter," she replied, "that Torcuato must be our bitter enemy? But you do not know everything. Before Torcuato's father died, he said he wished his son to marry me when we came of age. When he spoke about it we were sitting together by his bed."

"And what did you say, Elaria?" I asked, full of concern.

"Torcuato promised to marry me. I only covered my face, and was silent, for I loved you best even then, though I was almost a child, and my heart was filled with grief at his words. After we came here, Torcuato reminded me of his father's words. I answered that I did not wish to marry him, that he was only a brother to me. Then he said that we were young and he could wait until I was of another mind. This is all I have to say; but how shall we three live together any longer? I cannot bear to part from you, and every moment I tremble to think what may happen when you two are together."

"Fear nothing," I said. "Tomorrow morning you can go to spend a week at some friend's house in the town;

then I will speak to Torcuato, and tell him that since we cannot live in peace together we must separate. Even if he answers with insults I shall do nothing to grieve you, and if he refuses to listen to me, I shall send some person we both respect to arrange all things between us."

This satisfied her, but as evening approached she grew paler, and I knew she feared Torcuato's return. He did not, however, come back that night. Early next morning she was ready to leave. It was an easy walk to the town, but the dew was heavy on the grass, and I saddled a horse for her to ride. I had just lifted her to the saddle when Torcuato appeared. He came at great speed, and throwing himself off his horse, advanced to us. Elaria trembled and seemed ready to sink upon the earth to hide herself like a partridge that has seen the hawk. I prepared myself for insults and perhaps violence. He never looked at me; he only spoke to her.

"Elaria," he said, "something has happened—something that obliges me to leave this house and neighborhood at once. Remember when I am away that my father, who cherished you and enriched you with his bounty, and who also cherished and enriched this ingrate, spoke to us from his dying bed and made me promise to marry you. Think what his love was; do not forget that his last wish is sacred, and that Anacleto has acted a base, treacherous part in trying to steal you from me. He was lifted out of the mire to be my brother and equal in everything except this. He has got a third part of my inheritance —let that satisfy him; your own heart, Elaria, will tell you that a marriage with him would be a crime before God and man. Look not for my return tomorrow nor for many days.

But if you two begin to laugh at my father's dying wishes, look for me, for then I shall not delay to come back to you, Elaria, and to you, Anacleto. I have spoken."

He then mounted his horse and rode away. Very soon we learned the cause of his sudden departure. He had quarreled over his cards and in a struggle that followed had stabbed his adversary to the heart. He had fled to escape the penalty. We did not believe that he would remain long absent; for Torcuato was very young, well off, and much liked, and this was, moreover, his first offense against the law. But time went on and he did not return, nor did any message from him reach us, and we at last concluded that he had left the country. Only now after four years have I accidentally discovered his fate through seeing his piebald horse.

After he had been absent over a year, I asked Elaria to become my wife. "We cannot marry till Torcuato returns," she said. "For if we take the property that ought to have been all his, and at the same time disobey his father's dying wish, we shall be doing an evil thing. Let us take care of the property till he returns to receive it all back from us; then, Anacleto, we shall be free to marry."

I consented, for she was more to me than lands and cattle. I put the *estancia* in order and leaving a trustworthy person in charge of everything I invested my money in fat bullocks to resell in Buenos Aires, and in this business I have been employed ever since. From the *estancia* I have taken nothing, and now it must all come back to us—his inheritance and ours. This is a bitter thing and will give Elaria great grief.

Thus ended Anacleto's story, and when he had finished speaking and still seemed greatly troubled in his mind, Sotelo said to him, "Friend, let me advise you what to do. You will now shortly be married to the woman you love, and probably some day a son will be born to you. Let him be named Torcuato, and let Torcuato's inheritance be kept for him. And if God gives you no son, remember what was done for you and for the girl you are going to marry, when you were orphans and friendless, and look out for some unhappy child in the same condition, to protect and enrich him as you were enriched."

"You have spoken well," said Anacleto. "I will report your words to Elaria, and whatever she wishes done that will I do."

So ends my story, friend. The cattle-drover left us that night and we saw no more of him. Only before going he gave the piebald and the silver trappings to Sotelo. Six months after his visit, Sotelo also received a letter from him to say that his marriage with Elaria had taken place; and the letter was accompanied with a present of seven cream-colored horses with black manes and hoofs.

For Thought and Discussion

1. What kind of people does the author describe in the second sentence?
2. Who was Chapaco?
3. Who was Torcuato?
4. Was Torcuato's death entirely accidental?
5. Why did Torcuato make no effort to save himself?
6. What overwhelming circumstances in his life caused him to place a very slight value upon his own life?
7. Is his reaction true to life in many cases?
8. What part did jealousy play in the story?
9. Do you think Sotelo's main object in seeking to find the dead man's relatives was to return to them his possessions? Why?
10. What redeeming feature do you find in Torcuato?
11. How did Torcuato fail to meet the test that life chanced to make for him?
12. What advice was given to Anacleto by Sotelo? Was it practical or idealistic or both?
13. How is the love story made a part of the narrative?
14. What is the author's purpose in this story?
15. Will you read the discussion of the short story from the section "A Brief Introduction to Types of Literature"? With your knowledge of the main characteristics of the short story, re-read this story to determine how it exhibits these characteristics.

Plus Work

Far Away and Long Ago by Hudson is the story of his life in South America. After reading it you realize how completely he understood the world of nature.

THE THREE STRANGERS
THOMAS HARDY

AMONG the few features of agricultural England which retain an appearance but little modified by the lapse of centuries, may be reckoned the high grassy and furzy downs, coombs,[1] or ewe-leases, as they are indifferently called, that fill a large area of certain counties in the south and southwest. If any mark of human occupation is met with hereon, it usually takes the form of the solitary cottage of some shepherd.

Fifty years ago such a lonely cottage stood on such a down, and may possibly be standing there now. In spite of its loneliness, however, the spot, by actual measurement, was not more than five miles from a county town.....

Higher Crowstairs, as the house was called, stood quite detached and undefended. The only reason for its precise situation seemed to be the crossing of two footpaths at right angles hard by, which may have crossed there and thus for a good five hundred years. Hence the house was exposed to the elements on all sides .... When the shepherd and his family who tenanted the house were pitied for their sufferings from the exposure, they said that upon the whole they were less inconvenienced by "wuzzes and flames" (hoarses and phlegms) than when they had lived by the stream of a snug neighboring valley.

The night of March 28, 182-, was precisely one of the nights that were wont to call forth these expressions of commiseration. The level rainstorm smote walls, slopes, and hedges like the clothyard shafts of Senlac

and Crécy.[2] Such sheep and outdoor animals as had no shelter stood with their buttocks to the winds; while the tails of little birds trying to roost on some scraggy thorn were blown inside-out like umbrellas. The gable end of the cottage was stained with wet, and the eavesdroppings flapped against the wall. Yet never was commiseration for the shepherd more misplaced. For that cheerful rustic was entertaining a large party in glorification of the christening of his second girl.

The guests had arrived before the rain began to fall, and they were all now assembled in the chief or living room of the dwelling. A glance into the apartment at eight o'clock on this eventful evening would have resulted in the opinion that it was as cozy and comfortable a nook as could be wished for in boisterous weather. The calling of its inhabitant was proclaimed by a number of highly polished sheep-crooks without stems that were hung ornamentally over the fireplace, the curl of each shining crook varying from the antiquated type engraved in the patriarchal pictures of old family Bibles to the most approved fashion of the last local sheep-fair. The room was lighted by half a dozen candles, having wicks only a trifle smaller than the grease which enveloped them, in candlesticks that were never used but at high-days, holy-days, and family feasts. The lights were scattered about the room,

---

[1]*coombs,* circular valleys with narrow inlets.

[2]*Senlac and Crécy.* The battle of Senlac is better known as the battle of Hastings (1066) in which William the Conqueror defeated Harold, the last of the Saxon kings. At Crécy, Edward, the Black Prince, defeated the French king in 1346.

two of them standing on the chimney piece. This position of candles was in itself significant. Candles on the chimney piece always meant a party.

On the hearth, in front of a back-brand to give substance, blazed a fire of thorns, that crackled "like the laughter of the fool."

Nineteen persons were gathered here. Of these, five women, wearing gowns of various bright hues, sat in chairs along the wall; girls shy and not shy filled the window-bench; four men, including Charley Jake, the hedge carpenter, Elijah New, the parish clerk, and John Pitcher, a neighboring dairyman, the shepherd's father-in-law, lolled in the settle; a young man and maid, who were blushing over tentative *pourparlers* on a life-companionship, sat beneath the corner cupboard; and an elderly engaged man of fifty or upward moved restlessly about from spots where his betrothed was not to the spot where she was. Enjoyment was pretty general, and so much the more prevailed in being unhampered by conventional restrictions. Absolute confidence in one another's good opinion begat perfect ease, while the finishing stroke of manner, amounting to a truly princely serenity, was lent to the majority by the absence of any expression or trait denoting that they wished to get on in the world, enlarge their minds, or do any eclipsing thing whatever — which nowadays so generally nips the bloom and *bonhomie*[3] of all except the two extremes of the social scale.

Shepherd Fennel had married well, his wife being a dairyman's daughter from a vale at a distance who brought fifty guineas in her pocket—and kept them there, till they should be required for ministering to the needs of a coming family. This frugal woman had been somewhat exercised as to the character that should be given to the gathering. A sit-still party had its advantages; but an undisturbed position of ease in chairs and settles was apt to lead on the men to such an unconscionable deal of toping that they would sometimes fairly drink the house dry. A dancing party was the alternative; but this, while avoiding the foregoing objection on the score of good drink, had a counterbalancing disadvantage in the matter of good victuals, the ravenous appetites engendered by the exercise causing immense havoc in the buttery. Shepherdess Fennel fell back upon the intermediate plan of mingling short dances with short periods of talk and singing, so as to hinder any ungovernable rage in either. But this scheme was entirely confined to her own gentle mind; the shepherd himself was in the mood to exhibit the most reckless phases of hospitality.

The fiddler was a boy of those parts, about twelve years of age, who had a wonderful dexterity in jigs and reels, though his fingers were so small and short as to necessitate a constant shifting for the high notes, from which he scrambled back to the first position with sounds not of unmixed purity of tone. At seven the shrill tweedle-dee of this youngster had begun, accompanied by a booming ground-bass from Elijah New, the parish clerk, who had thoughtfully brought with him his favorite musical instrument, the serpent.[4] Dancing was instantaneous, Mrs. Fennel privately enjoining the players on no account to let the dance exceed the length of a quarter of an hour.

But Elijah and the boy, in the excitement of their position, quite

[3]*bonhomie,* good fellowship.

[4]*serpent,* a musical instrument twisting like a snake.

forgot the injunction. Moreover, Oliver Giles, a man of seventeen, one of the dancers, who was enamored of his partner, a fair girl of thirty-three rolling years, had recklessly handed a new crown-piece to the musicians, as a bribe to keep going as long as they had muscle and wind. Mrs. Fennel, seeing the steam begin to generate on the countenances of her guests, crossed over and touched the fiddler's elbow and put her hand on the serpent's mouth. But they took no notice, and fearing she might lose her character of genial hostess if she were to interfere too markedly, she retired and sat down helpless. And so the dance whizzed on with cumulative fury, the performers moving in their planet-like courses, direct and retrograde, from apogee to perigee, till the hand of the well-kicked clock at the bottom of the room had traveled over the circumference of an hour.

While these cheerful events were in course of enactment within Fennel's pastoral dwelling, an incident having considerable bearing on the party had occurred in the gloomy night without. Mrs. Fennel's concern about the growing fierceness of the dance corresponded in point of time with the ascent of a human figure to the solitary hill of Higher Crowstairs from the direction of the distant town. This personage strode on through the rain without a pause following the little-worn path which, further on in its course, skirted the shepherd's cottage.

It was nearly the time of the full moon, and on this account, though the sky was lined with a uniform sheet of dripping cloud, ordinary objects out of doors were readily visible. The sad wan light revealed the lonely pedestrian to be a man of supple frame; his gait suggested that he had somewhat passed the period of perfect and instinctive agility, though not so far as to be otherwise than rapid of motion when occasion required. In point of fact, he might have been about forty years of age. He appeared tall, but a recruiting sergeant, or other person accustomed to the judging of men's heights by the eye, would have discerned that this was chiefly owing to his gauntness, and that he was not more than five-feet-eight or nine.

Notwithstanding the regularity of his tread, there was caution in it, as in that of one who mentally feels his way; and despite the fact that it was not a black coat nor a dark garment of any sort that he wore, there was something about him which suggested that he naturally belonged to the black-coated tribes of men. His clothes were of fustian, and his boots hobnailed, yet in his progress he showed not the mud-accustomed bearing of hobnailed and fustianed peasantry.

By the time that he had arrived abreast of the shepherd's premises the rain came down, or rather came along, with yet more determined violence. The outskirts of the little settlement partially broke the force of wind and rain, and this induced him to stand still. The most salient of the shepherd's domestic erections was an empty sty at the forward corner of his hedgeless garden, for in these latitudes the principle of masking the homelier features of your establishment by a conventional frontage was unknown. The traveler's eye was attracted to this small building by the pallid shine of the wet slates that covered it. He turned aside, and, finding it empty, stood under the pent-roof for shelter.

While he stood, the boom of the serpent within the adjacent house, and the lesser strains of the fiddler, reached the spot as an accompaniment to the surging hiss of the flying rain on the sod, its louder beating on the cabbage leaves of the garden, on the eight or ten beehives just discernible by the path, and its dripping from the eaves into a row of buckets and pans that had been placed under the walls of the cottage. For at Higher Crowstairs, as at all such elevated domiciles, the grand difficulty of housekeeping was an insufficiency of water; and a casual rainfall was utilized by turning out, as catchers, every utensil that the house contained. Some queer stories might be told of the contrivances for economy in suds and dishwaters that are absolutely necessitated in upland habitations during the droughts of summer. But at this season there were no such exigencies; a mere acceptance of what the skies bestowed was sufficient for an abundant supply.

At last the notes of the serpent ceased and the house was silent. This cessation of activity aroused the solitary pedestrian from the reverie into which he had lapsed, and emerging from the shed, with an apparently new intention, he walked up the path to the house door. Arrived here, his first act was to kneel down on a large stone beside the row of vessels, and to drink a copious draft from one of them. Having quenched his thirst he rose and lifted his hand to knock, but paused with his eye upon the panel. Since the dark surface of the wood revealed absolutely nothing, it was evident that he must be mentally looking through the door, as if he wished to measure thereby all the possibilities that a house of this sort might include, and how they might bear upon the question of his entry.

In his indecision he turned and surveyed the scene around. Not a soul was anywhere visible. The garden path stretched downward from his feet, gleaming like the track of a snail; the roof of the little well (mostly dry), the well cover, the top rail of the garden gate, were varnished with the same dull liquid glaze; while, far away in the vale, a faint whiteness of more than usual extent showed that the rivers were high in the meads. Beyond all this winked a few bleared lamplights through the beating drops, —lights that denoted the situation of the county town from which he had appeared to come. The absence of all notes of life in that direction seemed to clinch his intentions, and he knocked at the door.

Within, a desultory chat had taken the place of movement and musical sound. The hedge carpenter was suggesting a song to the company, which nobody just then was inclined to undertake, so that the knock afforded a not unwelcome diversion.

"Walk in," said the shepherd promptly.

The latch clicked upward, and out of the night our pedestrian appeared upon the doormat. The shepherd arose, snuffed two of the nearest candles, and turned to look at him.

Their light disclosed that the stranger was dark in complexion and not unprepossessing as to feature. His hat, which for a moment he did not remove, hung low over his eyes, without concealing that they were large, open, and determined, moving with a flash rather than a glance round the room. He seemed pleased with the survey, and, baring his shaggy head, said, in a rich deep voice, "The rain is so heavy, friends, that I ask leave to come in and rest awhile."

"To be sure, stranger," said the shepherd. "And faith, you've been lucky in choosing your time, for we are having a bit of a fling for a glad cause . . . ."

"And what may be this glad cause?" asked the stranger.

"A birth and christening," said the shepherd.

The stranger hoped his host might not be made unhappy either by too many or too few of such episodes, and being invited by a gesture to a pull at the mug, he readily acquiesced. His manner, which, before entering, had been so dubious, was now altogether that of a careless and candid man.

"Late to be traipsing athwart this coomb—hey?" said the engaged man of fifty.

"Late it is, master, as you say. I'll take a seat in the chimney corner, if you have nothing to urge against it, ma'am; for I am a little moist on the side that was next the rain."

Mrs. Shepherd Fennel assented, and made room for the self-invited comer, who, having got completely inside the chimney corner, stretched out his legs and his arms with the expansiveness of a person quite at home.

"Yes, I am rather cracked in the vamp," he said freely, seeing that the eyes of the shepherd's wife fell upon his boots, "and I am not well fitted either. I have had some rough times lately, and have been forced to pick up what I can get in the way of wearing, but I must find a suit better fit for working-days when I reach home."

"One of hereabouts?" she inquired.

"Not quite that—farther up the country."

"I thought so. And so am I; and by your tongue you come from my neighborhood."

"But you would hardly have heard of me," he said, quickly. "My time would be long before yours, ma'am, you see,"

This testimony to the youthfulness of his hostess had the effect of stopping her cross-examination.

"There is only one thing more wanted to make me happy," continued the new-comer, "and that is a little baccy, which I am sorry to say I am out of."

"I'll fill your pipe," said the shepherd.

"I must ask you to lend me a pipe likewise."

"A smoker, and no pipe about 'ee?"

"I have dropped it somewhere on the road."

The shepherd filled and handed him a new clay pipe, saying, as he did so, "Hand me your baccy-box—I'll fill that too, now I am about it."

The man went through the movement of searching his pockets.

"Lost that too?" said his entertainer, with some surprise.

"I am afraid so," said the man, with some confusion. "Give it to me in a screw of paper." Lighting his pipe at the candle with a suction that drew the whole flame into the bowl, he resettled himself in the corner and bent his looks upon the faint steam from his damp legs, as if he wished to say no more.

Meanwhile the general body of guests had been taking little notice of this visitor by reason of an absorbing discussion in which they were engaged with the band about a tune for the next dance. The matter being settled, they were about to stand up when an interruption came in the shape of another knock at the door.

At sound of the same the man in the chimney corner took up the poker and began stirring the brands as if doing it thoroughly were the one aim of his existence; and a second time the shepherd said, "Walk in!" In a moment another man stood upon the straw-woven doormat. He too was a stranger.

This individual was one of a type radically different from the first. There was more of the commonplace in his manner, and a certain jovial cosmopolitanism sat upon his features. He was several years older than the first arrival, his hair being slightly frosted, his eyebrows bristly, and his whiskers cut back from his cheeks. His face was rather full and flabby, and yet it was not altogether a face without power. A few grog-blossoms marked the neighborhood of his nose. He flung back his long drab greatcoat, revealing that beneath it he wore a suit of cinder-gray shade throughout; large heavy seals of some metal or other that would take a polish, dangling from his fob as his only personal ornament. Shaking the water drops from his low-crowned glazed hat, he said, "I must ask for a few minutes' shelter, comrades, or I shall be wetted to my skin before I get to Casterbridge."[5]

"Make yourself at home, master," said the shepherd, perhaps a trifle less heartily than on the first occasion. Not that Fennel had the least tinge of niggardliness in his composition; but the room was far from large, spare chairs were not numerous, and damp companions were not altogether desirable at close quarters for the women and girls in their bright-colored gowns.

However, the second comer, after taking off his greatcoat, and hanging his hat on a nail in one of the ceiling beams as if he had been specially invited to put it there, advanced and sat down at the table. This had been pushed so closely into the chimney corner, to give all available room to the dancers, that its inner edge grazed

the elbow of the man who had ensconced himself by the fire; and thus the two strangers were brought into close companionship. They nodded to each other by way of breaking the ice of unacquaintance, and the first stranger handed his neighbor the family mug—a huge vessel of brown ware, having its upper edge worn away like a threshold by the rub of whole generations of thirsty lips that had gone the way of all flesh, and bearing the following inscription burned upon its rotund side in yellow letters:

THERE IS NO FUN
UNTILL I CUM

The other man, nothing loath, raised the mug to his lips, and drank on, and on, and on—till a curious blueness overspread the countenance of the shepherd's wife, who had regarded with no little surprise the first stranger's free offer to the second of what did not belong to him to dispense.

"I knew it!" said the toper to the shepherd with much satisfaction. "When I walked up your garden before coming in, and saw the hives all of a row, I said to myself, 'Where there's bees there's honey, and where there's honey there's mead.' But mead of such a truly comfortable sort as this I really didn't expect to meet in my older days." He took yet another pull at the mug, till it assumed an ominous elevation.

"Glad you enjoy it!" said the shepherd warmly.

"It is goodish mead," assented Mrs. Fennel, with an absence of enthusiasm which seemed to say that it was possible to buy praise for one's cellar at too heavy a price. "It is trouble enough to make—and really I hardly think we shall make any more. For

_____
[5]*Casterbridge,* a name Hardy uses for Dorchester.

honey sells well, and we ourselves can make shift with a drop o' small mead and metheglin for common use from the comb-washings."

"Oh, but you'll never have the heart!" reproachfully cried the stranger in cinder-gray, after taking up the mug a third time and setting it down empty. "I love mead when 'tis old like this, as I love to go to church o' Sundays, or to relieve the needy any day of the week."

"Ha, ha, ha!" said the man in the chimney corner, who, in spite of the taciturnity induced by the pipe of tobacco, could not or would not refrain from this slight testimony to his comrade's humor.

Now, the old mead of those days, brewed of the purest first-year or maiden honey, four pounds to the gallon—with its due complement of white of eggs, cinnamon, ginger, cloves, mace, rosemary, yeast, and processes of working, bottling, and cellaring—tasted remarkably strong; but it did not taste so strong as it actually was. Hence, presently the stranger in cinder-gray at the table, moved by its creeping influence, unbuttoned his waistcoat, threw himself back in his chair, spread his legs, and made his presence felt in various ways.

"Well, well, as I say," he resumed, "I am going to Casterbridge, and to Casterbridge I must go. I should have been almost there by this time; but the rain drove me into your dwelling, and I'm not sorry for it."

"You don't live in Casterbridge?" said the shepherd.

"Not as yet, though I shortly mean to move there."

"Going to set up in trade, perhaps?"

"No, no," said the shepherd's wife. "It is easy to see that the gentleman is rich, and don't want to work at anything."

The cinder-gray stranger paused, as if to consider whether he would accept that definition of himself. He presently rejected it by answering, "Rich is not quite the word for me, dame. I do work, and I must work. And even if I only get to Casterbridge by midnight I must begin work there at eight tomorrow morning. Yes, het or wet, blow or snow, famine or sword, my day's work tomorrow must be done."

"Poor man! Then, in spite o' seeming, you be worse off than we," replied the shepherd's wife.

" 'Tis the nature of my trade, men and maidens. 'Tis the nature of my trade more than my poverty . . . . But really and truly I must up and off, or I shan't get a lodging in the town." However, the speaker did not move, and directly added, "There's time for one more draft of friendship before I go; and I'd perform it at once if the mug were not dry."

"Here's a mug o' small," said Mrs. Fennel. "Small, we call it, though to be sure 'tis only the first wash o' the combs."

"No," said the stranger disdainfully. "I won't spoil your first kindness by partaking o' your second."

"Certainly not," broke in Fennel. "We don't increase and multiply every day, and I'll fill the mug again." He went away to the dark place under the stairs where the barrel stood. The shepherdess followed him.

"Why should you do this?" she said reproachfully, as soon as they were alone. "He's emptied it once, though it held enough for ten people; and now he's not contented wi' the small, but must needs call for more o' the strong! And a stranger unbeknown to any of us. For my part, I don't like the look o' the man at all."

"But he's in the house, my honey; and 'tis a wet night, and a christening. Daze it, what's a cup of mead more or less? There'll be plenty more next bee-burning."

"Very well—this time, then," she answered, looking wistfully at the barrel. "But what is the man's calling, and where is he one of, that he should come in and join us like this?"

"I don't know. I'll ask him again."

The catastrophe of having the mug drained dry at one pull by the stranger in cinder-gray was effectually guarded against this time by Mrs. Fennel. She poured out his allowance in a small cup, keeping the large one at a discreet distance from him. When he had tossed off his portion the shepherd renewed his inquiry about the stranger's occupation.

The latter did not immediately reply, and the man in the chimney corner, with sudden demonstrativeness, said, "Anybody may know my trade—I'm a wheelwright."

"A very good trade for these parts," said the shepherd.

"And anybody may know mine—if they've the sense to find it out," said the stranger in cinder-gray.

"You may generally tell what a man is by his claws," observed the hedge carpenter, looking at his own hands. "My fingers be as full of thorns as an old pincushion is of pins."

The hands of the man in the chimney corner instinctively sought the shade, and he gazed into the fire as he resumed his pipe. The man at the table took up the hedge carpenter's remark, and added smartly, "True; but the oddity of my trade is that, instead of setting a mark upon me, it sets a mark upon my customers."

No observation being offered by anybody in elucidation of this enigma, the shepherd's wife once more called for a song. The same obstacles presented themselves as at the former

time—one had no voice, another had forgotten the first verse. The stranger at the table, whose soul had now risen to a good working temperature, relieved the difficulty by exclaiming that, to start the company, he would sing himself. Thrusting one thumb into the armhole of his waistcoat, he waved the other hand in the air, and, with an extemporizing gaze at the shining sheepcrooks above the mantel piece began:

"O, my trade it is the rarest one,
    Simple shepherds all—
My trade is a sight to see;
For my customers I tie, and take them
        up on high,
And waft 'em to a far countree!"

The room was silent when he had finished the verse—with one exception, that of the man in the chimney corner, who, at the singer's word, "Chorus!" joined him in a deep bass voice of musical relish—

"And waft 'em to a far countree!"

Oliver Giles, John Pitcher the dairyman, the parish clerk, the engaged man of fifty, the row of young women against the wall, seemed lost in thought not of the gayest kind. The shepherd looked meditatively on the ground, the shepherdess gazed keenly at the singer, and with some suspicion; she was doubting whether this stranger were merely singing an old song from recollection, or was composing one there and then for the occasion. All were as perplexed at the obscure revelation as the guests at Belshazzar's Feast, except the man in the chimney corner, who quietly said, "Second verse, stranger," and smoked on.

The singer thoroughly moistened himself from his lips inward, and went on with the next stanza as requested:

"My tools are but common ones,
　Simple shepherds all—
My tools are no sight to see;
A little hempen string, and a post
　whereon to swing,
Are implements enough for me!"

Shepherd Fennel glanced round. There was no longer any doubt that the stranger was answering his question rhythmically. The guests one and all started back with suppressed exclamations. The young woman engaged to the man of fifty fainted halfway, and would have proceeded, but finding him wanting in alacrity for catching her she sat down trembling.

"O, he's the——!" whispered the people in the background, mentioning the name of an ominous public officer. "He's come to do it! 'Tis to be at Casterbridge jail tomorrow—the man for sheep stealing—the poor clockmaker we heard of, who used to live away at Shottsford and had no work to do — Timothy Summers, whose family were a-starving, and so he went out of Shottsford by the highroad, and took a sheep in open daylight, defying the farmer and the farmer's wife and the farmer's lad, and every man jack among 'em. He" (and they nodded toward the stranger of the deadly trade) "is come from up the country to do it because there's not enough to do in his own county town, and he's got the place here now our own county man's dead; he's going to live in the same cottage under the prison wall."

The stranger in cinder-gray took no notice of this whispered string of observations, but again wetted his lips. Seeing that his friend in the chimney corner was the only one who

reciprocated his joviality in any way, he held out his cup toward that appreciative comrade, who also held out his own. They clinked together, the eyes of the rest of the room hanging upon the singer's actions. He parted his lips for the third verse, but at that moment another knock was audible upon the door. This time the knock was faint and hesitating.

The company seemed scared; the shepherd looked with consternation towards the entrance, and it was with some effort that he resisted his alarmed wife's deprecatory glance, and uttered for the third time the welcoming words, "Walk in!"

The door was gently opened, and another man stood upon the mat. He, like those who had preceded him, was a stranger. This time it was a short, small personage, of fair complexion, and dressed in a decent suit of dark clothes.

"Can you tell me the way to ——?" he began; when, gazing round the room to observe the nature of the company amongst whom he had fallen, his eyes lighted on the stranger in cinder-gray. It was just at the instant when the latter, who had thrown his mind into his song with such a will that he scarcely heeded the interruption, silenced all whispers and inquiries by bursting into his third verse:

"Tomorrow is my working day,
　Simple shepherds all—
Tomorrow is a working day for me:
For the farmer's sheep is slain, and the
　lad who did it ta'en,
　And on his soul may God ha'
　merc-y!"

The stranger in the chimney corner, waving cups with the singer so heartily that his mead splashed over

the hearth, repeated in his bass voice as before:

"And on his soul may God ha' merc-y!"

All this time the third stranger had been standing in the doorway. Finding now that he did not come forward or go on speaking, the guests particularly regarded him. They noticed to their surprise that he stood before them the picture of abject terror—his knees trembling, his hand shaking so violently that the door latch by which he supported himself rattled audibly; his white lips were parted, and his eyes fixed on the merry officer of justice in the middle of the room. A moment more and he had turned, closed the door, and fled.

"What a man can it be?" said the shepherd.

The rest, between the awfulness of their late discovery and the odd conduct of this third visitor, looked as if they knew not what to think, and said nothing. Instinctively they withdrew further and further from the grim gentleman in their midst, whom some of them seemed to take for the Prince of Darkness himself, till they formed a remote circle, an empty space of floor being left between them and him—

". . . circulus, cujus centrum diabolus."[6]

The room was so silent—though there were more than twenty people in it—that nothing could be heard but the patter of the rain against the window shutters, accompanied by the occasional hiss of a stray drop that fell down the chimney into the fire, and the steady puffing of the man in the corner, who had now resumed his pipe of long clay.

The stillness was unexpectedly broken. The distant sound of a gun reverberated through the air—apparently from the direction of the county town.

[6]*circulus, cujus centrum diabolus,* Latin, a little circle the center of which is the devil.

"Be jiggered!" cried the stranger who had sung the song, jumping up.

"What does that mean?" asked several.

"A prisoner escaped from the jail—that's what it means."

All listened. The sound was repeated, and none of them spoke but the man in the chimney corner, who said quietly, "I've often been told that in this county they fire a gun at such times; but I never heard it till now."

"I wonder if it is *my* man?" murmured the personage in cinder-gray.

"Surely it is!" said the shepherd involuntarily. "And surely we've zeed him! That little man who looked in at the door by now, and quivered like a leaf when he zeed ye and heard your song!"

"His teeth chattered, and the breath went out of his body," said the dairyman.

"And his heart seemed to sink within him like a stone," said Oliver Giles.

"And he bolted as if he'd been shot at," said the hedge carpenter.

"True—his teeth chattered, and his heart seemed to sink; and he bolted as if he'd been shot at," slowly summed up the man in the chimney corner.

"I didn't notice it," remarked the hangman.

"We were all a-wondering what made him run off in such a fright," faltered one of the women against the wall, "and now 'tis explained."

The firing of the alarm gun went on at intervals, low and sullenly, and their suspicions became a certainty. The sinister gentleman in cinder-gray roused himself. "Is there a constable here?" he asked, in thick tones. "If so, let him step forward."

The engaged man of fifty stepped quavering out from the wall, his betrothed beginning to sob on the back of the chair.

"You are a sworn constable?"

"I be, sir."

"Then pursue the criminal at once, with assistance, and bring him back here. He can't have gone far."

"I will, sir, I will—when I've got my staff. I'll go home and get it, and come sharp here, and start in a body."

"Staff!—never mind your staff; the man'll be gone!"

"But I can't do nothing without my staff—can I, William, and John, and Charles Jake? No; for there's the King's royal crown a-painted on en in yaller and gold, and the lion and the unicorn, so as when I raise en up and hit my prisoner, 'tis made a lawful blow thereby. I wouldn't 'tempt to take up a man without my staff—no, not I. If I hadn't the law to gie me courage, why, instead o' my taking up him he might take up me!"

"Now, I'm a King's man myself, and can give you authority enough for this," said the formidable officer in gray. "Now then, all of ye, be ready. Have ye any lanterns?"

"Yes—have ye any lanterns?—I demand it!" said the constable.

"And the rest of you able-bodied—"

"Able-bodied men—yes—the rest of ye!" said the constable.

"Have you some good stout staves and pitchforks—"

"Staves and pitchforks—in the name o' the law! And take 'em in yer hands and go in quest, and do as we in authority tell ye!"

Thus aroused, the men prepared to give chase. The evidence was, indeed, though circumstantial, so convincing, that but little argument was needed to show the shepherd's guests that after what they had seen it would look very much like connivance if they did not instantly pursue the unhappy third stranger, who could not as yet have gone more than a few hundred yards over such uneven country.

A shepherd is always well provided with lanterns; and, lighting these hastily, and with hurdle staves in their hands, they poured out of the door, taking a direction along the crest of the hill, away from the town, the rain having fortunately a little abated.

Disturbed by the noise, or possibly by unpleasant dreams of her baptism, the child who had been christened began to cry heart-brokenly in the room overhead. These notes of grief came down through the chinks of the floor to the ears of the women below, who jumped up one by one, and seemed glad of the excuse to ascend and comfort the baby, for the incidents of the last half hour greatly oppressed them. Thus in the space of two or three minutes the room on the ground floor was deserted quite.

But it was not for long. Hardly had the sound of footsteps died away when a man returned round the corner of the house from the direction the pursuers had taken. Peeping in at the door, and seeing nobody there, he entered leisurely. It was the stranger of the chimney corner, who had gone out with the rest. The motive of his return was shown by his helping himself to a cut piece of skimmer-cake that lay on a ledge beside where he had sat, and which he had apparently forgotten to take with him. He also poured out half a cup more mead from the quantity that remained, ravenously eating and drinking these as he stood. He had not finished when another figure came in just as quietly —his friend in cinder-gray.

"O—you here?" said the latter, smiling. "I thought you had gone to help in the capture." And this speaker also revealed the object of his return by looking solicitously round for the fascinating mug of old mead.

"And I thought you had gone," said the other, continuing his skimmer-cake with some effort.

"Well, on second thoughts, I felt there were enough without me," said the first, confidentially, "and such a night as it is, too. Besides, 'tis the business o' the government to take care of its criminals—not mine."

"True; so it is. And I felt as you did, that there were enough without me."

"I don't want to break my limbs running over the humps and hollows of this wild country."

"Nor I neither, between you and me."

"These shepherd-people are used to it—simple-minded souls, you know, stirred up to anything in a moment. They'll have him ready for me before the morning, and no trouble to me at all."

"They'll have him, and we shall have saved ourselves all labor in the matter."

"True, true. Well, my way is to Casterbridge; and 'tis as much as my legs will do to take me that far. Going the same way?"

"No, I am sorry to say! I have to get home over there" (he nodded indefinitely to the right), "and I feel as you do, that it is quite enough for my legs to do before bedtime."

The other had by this time finished the mead in the mug, after which, shaking hands heartily at the door, and wishing each other well, they went their several ways.

In the meantime the company of pursuers had reached the end of the hog's-back elevation which dominated this part of the down. They had decided on no particular plan of action; and, finding that the man of the baleful trade was no longer in their company, they seemed quite unable to form any such plan now. They descended in all directions down the hill, and straightway several of the party fell into the snare set by Nature for all misguided midnight ramblers over this part of the cretaceous formation. The "lanchets," or flint slopes, which belted the escarpment at intervals of a dozen yards, took the less cautious ones unawares, and losing their footing on the rubbly steep they slid sharply downward, the lanterns rolling from their hands to the bottom, and there lying on their sides till the horn was scorched through.

When they had again gathered themselves together, the shepherd, as the man who knew the country best, took the lead, and guided them round these treacherous inclines. The lanterns, which seemed rather to dazzle their eyes and warn the fugitive than to assist them in the exploration, were extinguished, due silence was observed; and in this more rational order they plunged into the vale. It was a grassy, briery, moist defile, affording some shelter to any person who had sought it; but the party perambulated it in vain, and ascended on the other side. Here they wandered apart, and after an interval closed together again to report progress. At the second time of closing in they found themselves near a lonely ash, the single tree on this part of the coomb, probably sown there by a passing bird some fifty years before. And here, standing a little to one side of the trunk, as motionless as the trunk itself, appeared the man they were in quest of, his outline being well defined against the sky beyond. The band noiselessly drew up and faced him.

"Your money or your life!" said the constable sternly to the still figure.

"No, no," whispered John Pitcher. " 'Tisn't our side ought to say that. That's the doctrine of vagabonds like him, and we be on the side of the law."

"Well, well," replied the constable impatiently; "I must say something, mustn't I? and if you had all the weight o' this undertaking upon your mind, perhaps you'd say the wrong thing too!—Prisoner at the bar, surrender, in the name of the Father—the Crown, I mane!"

The man under the tree seemed now to notice them for the first time, and, giving them no opportunity whatever for exhibiting their courage, he strolled slowly toward them. He was, indeed, the little man, the third stranger; but his trepidation had in a great measure gone.

"Well, travelers," he said, "did I hear ye speak to me?"

"You did: you've got to come and be our prisoner at once!" said the constable. "We arrest 'ee on the charge of not biding in Casterbridge jail in a decent proper manner to be hung tomorrow morning. Neighbors, do your duty, and seize the culpet!"

On hearing the charge, the man seemed enlightened, and, saying not another word, resigned himself with preternatural civility to the search-party, who, with their staves in their hands, surrounded him on all sides, and marched him back toward the shepherd's cottage.

It was eleven o'clock by the time they arrived. The light shining from the open door, a sound of men's voices within, proclaimed to them as they approached the house that some new events had arisen in their absence.

On entering they discovered the shepherd's living room to be invaded by two officers from Casterbridge jail, and a well-known magistrate who lived at the nearest country seat, intelligence of the escape having become generally circulated.

"Gentlemen," said the constable, "I have brought back your man—not without risk and danger; but every one must do his duty! He is inside this circle of able-bodied persons, who have lent me useful aid, considering their ignorance of Crown work. Men, bring forward your prisoner!" And the third stranger was led to the light.

"Who is this?" said one of the officials.

"The man," said the constable.

"Certainly not," said the turnkey; and the first corroborated his statement.

"But how can it be otherwise?" asked the constable. "Or why was he so terrified at sight o' the singing instrument of the law who sat there?" Here he related the strange behavior of the third stranger on entering the house during the hangman's song.

"Can't understand it," said the officer coolly. "All I know is that it is not the condemned man. He's quite a different character from this one; a gauntish fellow, with dark hair and eyes, rather good-looking, and with a musical bass voice that if you heard it once you'd never mistake as long as you lived."

"Why, souls—'twas the man in the chimney corner!"

"Hey—what?" said the magistrate, coming forward after inquiring particulars from the shepherd in the background. "Haven't you got the man after all?"

"Well, sir," said the constable, "he's the man we were in search of, that's true; and yet he's not the man we were in search of. For the man we were in search of was not the man we wanted, sir, if you understand my everyday way; for 'twas the man in the chimney corner!"

"A pretty kettle of fish altogether!" said the magistrate. "You had better start for the other man at once."

The prisoner now spoke for the first time. The mention of the man in the chimney corner seemed to have moved him as nothing else could do. "Sir," he said, stepping forward to the magistrate, "take no more trouble about me. The time is come when I may as well speak. I have done nothing; my crime is that the condemned man is my brother. Early this afternoon I left home at Shottsford to tramp it all the way to Casterbridge jail to bid him farewell. I was benighted, and called here to rest and ask the way. When I opened the door I saw before me the very man, my brother, that I thought to see in the condemned cell at Casterbridge. He was in the chimney corner and jammed close to him, so that he could not have got out if he had tried, was the executioner who'd come to take his life, singing a song about it and not knowing that it was his victim who was close by, joining in to save appearances. My brother looked a glance of agony at me, and I knew he meant, 'Don't reveal what you see; my life depends on it.' I was so terror-struck that I could hardly stand, and, not knowing what I did, I turned and hurried away."

The narrator's manner and tone had the stamp of truth, and his story made a great impression on all around. "And do you know where your brother is at the present time?" asked the magistrate.

"I do not. I have never seen him since I closed this door."

"I can testify to that, for we've been between ye ever since," said the constable.

"Where does he think to fly to?— what is his occupation?"

"He's a watch- and clock-maker, sir."

" 'A said 'a was a wheelwright—a wicked rogue," said the constable.

"The wheels of clocks and watches he meant, no doubt," said Shepherd Fennel. "I thought his hands were palish for's trade."

"Well, it appears to me that nothing can be gained by retaining this poor man in custody," said the magistrate; "your business lies with the other, unquestionably."

And so the little man was released offhand; but he looked nothing the less sad on that account, it being beyond the power of magistrate or constable to raze out the written troubles in his brain, for they concerned another whom he regarded with more solicitude than himself. When this was done, and the man had gone his way, the night was found to be so far advanced that it was deemed useless to renew the search before the next morning.

Next day, accordingly, the quest for the clever sheep stealer became general and keen, to all appearance at least. But the intended punishment was cruelly disproportioned to the transgression, and the sympathy of a great many country-folk in that district was strongly on the side of the fugitive. Moreover, his marvelous coolness and daring in hob-and-nobbing with the hangman, under the unprecedented circumstances of the shepherd's party, won their admiration. So that it may be questioned if all those who ostensibly made themselves so busy in exploring woods and fields and lanes were quite so thorough when it came to the private examination of their own lofts and outhouses. Stories were afloat of a mysterious figure being occasionally seen in some old overgrown trackway or other, remote from turnpike roads; but when a search was instituted in any of these suspected quarters nobody was found. Thus the days and weeks passed without tidings.

In brief, the bass-voiced man of the chimney corner was never recaptured. Some said that he went across the sea, others that he did not, but buried himself in the depths of a populous city. At any rate, the gentleman in cinder-gray never did his morning's work at Casterbridge, nor met anywhere at all, for business purposes, the genial comrade with whom he had passed an hour of relaxation in the lonely house on the coomb.

The grass has long been green on the graves of Shepherd Fennel and his frugal wife; the guests who made up the christening party have mainly followed their entertainers to the tomb; the baby in whose honor they all had met is a matron in the sere and yellow leaf. But the arrival of the three strangers at the shepherd's that night, and the details connected therewith, is a story as well known as ever in the country about Higher Crowstairs.

For Thought and Discussion

1. How do you account for the fact that Higher Crowstairs was rather isolated, although near a town?
2. Who were the most interesting guests at the party?
3. What problem did Shepherd Fennel's wife have in planning the party?
4. How did the first stranger stop the cross-examination from Shepherd Fennel's wife?
5. Contrast the characters of Fennel and his wife.

6. How was the occupation of the second stranger made known? What effect did knowing his occupation have upon the party?
7. Why did Timothy Summers have the sympathy of the public? What admirable traits of character did he have?
8. Why are your sympathies with the guilty man?
9. Would you have, at least passively, aided in his final escape? Why?
10. What impression does Hardy give of the people in his description of their reluctant chase for the supposed criminal?
11. Do you think that theft under the conditions mentioned here deserves the death penalty?
12. What does such a severe penalty indicate concerning the English attitude toward property?
13. How is the conduct of the constable made humorous?
14. Are officers of the law responsible for its enforcement?
15. What effect does public opinion have upon law enforcement?
16. Should laws not supported by the public in general be repealed? Why?
17. Is strict enforcement of law necessary for the stability of society? Why?
18. What part does coincidence play in the plot of this story?

Plus Work

Topics for Report:
    Hardy's Use of Coincidence and Character Drawing
    Evidences of Hardy's Training as an Architect
    Read Galsworthy's *A Man of Property* and discuss the English attitude toward property. This may be read as one of your parallel readings.
    Using the heading "Am I My Brother's Keeper?" or some other appropriate title, write a paper or give an oral discussion of the last five of the questions under "For Thought and Discussion."

Thomas Hardy 1840-1928

Early Life. Thomas Hardy was born three miles from the village of Dorchester, which was to become well-known through his depiction of its people in relation to their environment. In this region he remained through his boyhood. He attended the village school and was taught at the same time by his mother. He spent his leisure hours out-of-doors, observing with a sensitive eye the aged oaks and beech-woods, the hills, the fields, and the people at work—all of which he eventually interpreted for the reading world in his Wessex novels. Wessex was unusually interesting on account of the survival there of folk plays and other old customs and celebrations and superstitions concerning Midsummer Eve, the time when maidens were supposed to meet their future husbands.

His Profession and His Recreational Activities.   Hardy's father was a master-builder or "contractor," and Hardy himself studied under a local architect, who sent him out to procure measurements and make drawings of old houses which were being restored. Through this work Hardy incidentally increased his knowledge of the Wessex country. When not engaged in his professional duties, he read classical and modern literature and the Bible. He liked poetry, preferring the works of Shelley, Wordsworth, and Tennyson.

In London.   Seeking greater opportunities, Hardy, at the age of twenty-one, went to London, where he continued his study of architecture, attended evening classes at King's College, and spent much time in the art galleries, familiarizing himself with the paintings exhibited. During these years he wrote some poetry and became so much interested in writing that when the time came for him to begin his career he questioned whether he should follow architecture. He did follow that profession, for a time, but he continued writing also.

Literary Work.   He wrote little but poetry for a number of years, but as the editors would not publish it, he turned to prose. When he was twenty-five years old, he had his first short story published. Two years later he wrote his first novel; it was rejected. Apparently undaunted, he began another which he published at his own expense. This book received some praise but attracted few readers. Not until he was thirty-four years old was a novel to appear with his own name on the title page. This one, *A Pair of Blue Eyes,* was published first as a serial, as were all of his later novels. Its popularity made it possible for him to give up architecture and devote himself entirely to writing. The year of its publication Hardy left Weymouth, where he had lived seven years, and returned to London. In 1885 he established a permanent home in Dorchestershire, but he continued to spend a few months in London each year. It seems fitting that the last years of his life were spent in the "hills of Wessex," which had been a rich storehouse of material for him. After his death in 1928 his heart was buried in the little grave-yard of Stinsford Church near Dorchester at the same time that his ashes were placed with impressive ceremonies in the Poets' Corner of Westminster Abbey.

A Realist and a Fatalist.   Hardy, a realist and a fatalist, held that fate in the form of natural environment and blind chance plays an inescapable part in man's destiny and used the silent somber forces of his own Wessex heaths and woodlands to vindicate his deeply sad and sometimes bitter philosophy. His characters are not weaklings; they are simple, primitive beings, strong, as a rule, but hopelessly involved in a valiant struggle against malign natural forces over which they have no influence and to which they must inevitably succumb. As in the case of homely, poised, resolute, but reticent Gabriel Oaks and handsome, impulsive, contradictory Bathsheba Everdene, characters are effectively used as foils for each other. His plots, like his characters, are strong; they are neither slight nor poorly constructed. Technically they are flawless examples of literary architecture.

A Master of the Novel and the Short Story. *Far from the Madding Crowd, The Return of the Native, The Mayor of Casterbridge,* and *Tess of the D'Urbervilles* rank as the greatest and most representative of Hardy's novels. His short stories, which have practically all the earmarks of his novels, like the novels, treat of the Wessex region and deal with people of the soil. Since Hardy was ambitious to become a great poet, he must have been pleased with the critic who affirmed that the poem "Dynasts" is by far his greatest work. Perhaps the critic is correct in his judgment; as yet, however, Hardy is far better known as one of the masters in English novel and short story writing.

❧

A MEMORY OF A MIDNIGHT EXPRESS
MAX BEERBOHM

[Max Beerbohm was born in London and received his education at Oxford. He is distinguished as a clever caricaturist and as a writer of sketches, essays, and stories. His interest is in the "play of ideas," and he consciously uses trifles rather than conventional impressions. His work appeals particularly to the sophisticated because of its amusing satire and to the "literati" because of its adroit expression. This sketch, "A Memory of a Midnight Express," arouses a responsive mood, since many people suffer from imaginary misfortunes.]

OFTEN I have presentiments of evil; but, never having had one of them fulfilled, I am beginning to ignore them. I find that I have always walked straight, serenely imprescient, into whatever trap Fate has laid for me. When I think of any horrible thing that has befallen me, the horror is intensified by recollection of its suddenness. 'But a moment before, I had been quite happy, quite secure. A moment later—' I shudder. Why be thus at Fate's mercy always, when with a little ordinary second sight. . . . Yet no! That is the worst of a presentiment: it never averts evil, it does but unnerve the victim. Best, after all, to have only false presentiments like mine. Bolts that cannot be dodged strike us kindliest from the blue.

And so let me be thankful that my sole emotion as I entered an empty compartment at Holyhead was that craving for sleep which, after midnight, overwhelms every traveller — especially the Saxon traveller from tumultuous and quick-witted little Dublin.[1] Mechanically, comfortably, as I sank into a corner, I rolled my rug round me, laid my feet against the opposite cushions, twitched up my coat collar above my ears, twitched down my cap over my eyes.

———
[1] *Dublin*, capital of Ireland.

It was not the jerk of the starting train that half awoke me, but the consciousness that someone had flung himself into the compartment when the train was already in motion. I saw a small man putting something in the rack — a large black hand-bag. Through the haze of my sleep I saw him, vaguely resented him. He had no business to have slammed the door like that, no business to have jumped into a moving train, no business to put that huge hand-bag into a rack which was 'for light baggage only,' and no business to be wearing, at this hour and in this place, a top hat. These four peevish objections floated sleepily together round my brain. It was not till the man turned round, and I met his eye, that I awoke fully—awoke to danger. I had never seen a murderer, but I knew that the man who was so steadfastly peering at me now . . . I shut my eyes. I tried to think. Could I be dreaming? In books I had read of people pinching themselves to see whether they were really awake. But in actual life there was never any doubt on that score. The great thing was that I should keep all my wits about me. Everything might depend on presence of mind. Perhaps this murderer was mad. If you fix a lunatic with your eye. . . .

Screwing up my courage, I fixed the man with my eye. I had never seen such a horrible little eye as his. It was a sane eye, too. It radiated a cold and ruthless sanity. It belonged not to a man who would kill you wantonly, but to one who would not scruple to kill you for a purpose, and would do the job quickly and neatly, and not be found out. Was he physically strong? Though he looked very wiry, he was little and narrow, like his eyes. He could not overpower me by force, I thought (and instinctively I squared my shoulders against the cushions, that he might realize the impossibility of overpowering me), but I felt he had enough 'science' to make me less than a match for him. I tried to look cunning and determined. I longed for a mustache like his, to hide my somewhat amiable mouth. I was thankful I could not see his mouth —could not know the worst of the face that was staring at me in the lamplight. And yet what could be worse than his eyes, gleaming from the deep shadow cast by the brim of his top-hat? What deadlier than that square jaw, with the bone so sharply delineated under the taut skin?

The train rushed on, noisily swaying through the silence of the night. I thought of the unseen series of placid landscapes that we were passing through, of the unconscious cottagers snoring there in their beds, of the safe people in the next compartment to mine—to his. Not moving a muscle, we sat there, we two, watching each other, like two hostile cats. Or rather, I thought, he watched me as a snake watches a rabbit, and I like a rabbit, could not look away. I seemed to hear my heart beating time to the train. Suddenly my heart was at a standstill, and the double beat of the train receded faintly. The man was pointing upward . . . I shook my head. He had asked me, in a low voice, whether he should pull the hood across the lamp.

He was standing now with his back turned towards me, pulling his hand-bag out of the rack. He had a furtive back—the back of a man who, in his time, had borne many an alias. To this day I am ashamed that I did not spring up and pinion him, there and then. Had I possessed one ounce of physical courage, I should have done so. A coward, I let slip the opportunity. I thought of the communication-cord; but how could I move to it? He would be too quick for me. He would be very angry with me. I would sit quite still and wait. Every moment was a long reprieve to me now. Something might intervene to save me. There might be a collision on the line. Perhaps he was a quite harmless man ... I caught his eye, and shuddered ....

His bag was open on his knees. His right hand was groping in it. (Thank heaven he had not pulled the hood over the lamp!) I saw him draw out something—a limp thing, made of black cloth, not unlike the thing that a dentist places over your mouth when laughing-gas is to be administered. 'Laughing-gas, no laughing matter'—the irrelevant and idiotic embryo of a pun dangled itself for an instant in my brain. What other horrible thing would come out of the bag? Perhaps some gleaming instrument? ... He closed the bag with a snap, laid it beside him. He took off his top-hat, laid that beside him. I was surprised (I know not why) to see that he was bald. There was a gleaming highlight on his bald, round head. The limp, black thing was a cap, which he slowly adjusted with both hands, drawing it down over the brow and behind the ears. It seemed to me as though he were, after all, hooding the lamp; in my feverish fancy the compartment grew darker when the orb of his head was hidden. The shadow of another simile for his action came surging up. ... He had put on the cap so gravely, so judicially. Yes, that was it: he had assumed the black cap, that decent symbol which indemnifies the taker of a life; and might the Lord have mercy on my soul... Already he was addressing me.

... What had he said? I asked him to repeat it. My voice sounded even further away than his. He repeated that he thought we had met before. I heard my voice saying politely, somewhere in the distance, that I thought not. He suggested that I had been staying at some hotel in Colchester six years ago. My voice, drawing a little nearer to me, explained that I had never been at Colchester. He begged my pardon and hoped no offence would be taken where none had been meant. My voice, coming right back into its own quarters, reassured him that of course I had taken no offence at all, adding that I myself very often mistook one face for another. He replied, rather inconsequently, that the world was a small place.

Evidently he must have prepared this remark to follow my expected admission that I *had* been at that hotel in Colchester six years ago, and have thought it too striking a remark to be thrown away. A guileless creature evidently, and not a criminal at all. Then I reflected that most of the successful criminals succeed rather through the incomparable guilelessness of the police than through any devilish cunning in themselves. Besides, this man looked the very incarnation of ruthless cunning. Surely, he must but have dissembled. My suspicions of him resurged. But, somehow, I was no longer afraid of him. Whatever crimes he might have been committing, and be going to commit, I felt that he meant no harm to me. After all, why should I have imagined myself to be in danger? Meanwhile, I would try to draw the man out, pitting my wits against his.

I proceeded to do so. He was very voluble, in a quiet way. Before long I was in possession of all the materials for an exhaustive biography of him. And the strange thing was that I could not, with the best will in the world, believe that he was lying to me. I had never heard a man telling so obviously the truth. And the truth about any one, however commonplace, must always be interesting. Indeed, it is the commonplace truth—the truth of the widest application—that is the most interesting of all truths.

I do not now remember many details of this man's story; I remember merely that he was 'travelling in lace,' that he had been born at Boulogne (this was the one strange feature of the narrative), that somebody had once left him £100 in a will, and that he had a little daughter who was 'as pretty as a pink.' But at the time I was enthralled. Besides, I liked the man immensely. He was a kind and simple soul, utterly belying his appearance. I wondered how I ever could have feared him and hated him. Doubtless, the reaction from my previous state intensified the kindliness of my feelings. Anyhow, my heart went out to him. I felt that we had known each other for many years. While he poured out his recollections I felt that he was an old crony, talking over old days which were mine as well as his. Little by little, however, the slumber which he had scared from me came hovering back. My eyelids drooped; my comments on his stories became few and muffled. 'There!' he said, 'you're sleepy. I ought to have thought of that!' I protested feebly. He insisted kindly. 'You go to sleep,' he said, rising and drawing the hood over the lamp.

It was dawn when I awoke. Some one in a top-hat was standing over me and saying: 'Euston.'—'Euston?' —'Yes, this is Euston. Good day to you.'—'Good day to you,' I repeated mechanically, in the grey dawn.

Not till I was driving through the cold empty streets did I remember the episode of the night, and who it was that had awakened me. I wished I could see my friend again. It was horrible to think that perhaps I should never see him again. I had liked him so much, and he had seemed to like me. I did not think he was a happy man. There was something melancholy about him. I hoped he would prosper. I had a foreboding that some great calamity was in store for him, and I wished I could avert it. I thought of his little daughter who was 'as pretty as a pink.' Perhaps Fate was going to strike him through her. Perhaps when he got home he would find that she was dead. There were tears in my eyes when I alighted on my doorstep.

Thus, within a little space of time, did I experience two deep emotions, for neither of which was there any real justification. I experienced terror, though there was nothing to be afraid of, and I experienced sorrow, though there was nothing at all to be sorry about. And both my terror and my sorrow were, at the time, overwhelming.

You have no patience with me? Examine yourselves. Examine one another. In everyone of us the deepest emotions are constantly caused by some absurdly trivial thing, or by nothing at all. Conversely, the great things in our lives—the true occasions for wrath, anguish, rapture, what not—very often leave us quite calm. We never can depend on any right adjustment of emotion to circumstance. That is one of many reasons which prevent the philosopher from taking himself and his fellow beings quite so seriously as he would wish.

For Thought and Discussion

1. Explain the meaning of "Bolts that cannot be dodged strike us kindliest from the blue." Do you agree with the statement?
2. Why did the writer lose his fear of his fellow traveler?
3. Are first impressions of people often misleading?
4. Upon what are first impressions based?
5. What two deep emotions did the writer experience because he allowed his imagination to run away with him?
6. Is every person likely to let his imagination run away with him at some time or other?
7. What is the meaning of this essay?
8. A study of the essay as defined in the section "A Brief Introduction to Types of Literature" will make this selection more interesting.

❦

THE HUNTER'S FAMILY
From *The Silverado Squatters*
ROBERT LOUIS STEVENSON

THERE is quite a large race or class of people in America, for whom we scarcely seem to have a parallel in England. Of pure white blood, they are unknown or unrecognizable in towns; inhabit the fringe of settlements and the deep, quiet places of the country; rebellious to all labor, and pettily thievish, like the English gypsies; rustically ignorant, but with a touch of wood lore and the dexterity of the savage. Whence they came is a moot point. At the time of the war,[1] they poured north in crowds to escape the conscription; lived during the summer on fruits, wild animals, and petty theft; and at the approach of winter, when these supplies failed, built great fires in the forest, and there died stoically by starvation. They are widely scattered, however, and easily recognized. Loutish, but not ill-looking, they will sit all day, swinging their legs on a field fence, the mind seemingly as devoid of all reflection as a Suffolk peasant's, careless of politics, for the most part incapable of reading, but with a rebellious vanity and a strong sense of independence. Hunting is their most congenial business, or if the occasion offers, a little amateur detection. In tracking a criminal, following a particular horse along a beaten highway, and drawing inductions from a hair or a footprint, one of those somnolent, grinning Hodges will suddenly display activity of body and finesse of mind. By their names ye may know them, the women figuring as Loveina, Larsenia, Serena, Leanna, Orreana; the men answering to Alvin, Alva, or Orion, pronounced Orrion, with the accent on the first. Whether they are indeed a race, or whether this is the form of degeneracy common to all backwoodsmen, they are at least known by a generic byword, as Poor Whites or Lowdowners.

I will not say that the Hanson family was Poor White, because the name savors of offense; but I may go

---

[1] *war*, the Civil War.

as far as this—they were, in many points, not unsimilar to the people usually so called. Rufe himself combined two of the qualifications, for he was both a hunter and an amateur detective. It was he who pursued Russel and Dollar, the robbers of the Lakeport stage, and captured them the very morning after the exploit, while they were still sleeping in a hayfield. Russel, a drunken Scotch carpenter, was even an acquaintance of his own, and he expressed much grave commiseration for his fate. In all that he said and did, Rufe was grave. I never saw him hurried. When he spoke, he took out his pipe with ceremonial deliberation, looked east and west, and then, in quiet tones and few words, stated his business or told his story. His gait was to match; it would never have surprised you if, at any step, he had turned round and walked away again, so warily and slowly, and with so much seeming hesitation did he go about. He lay long in bed in the mornings—rarely, indeed, rose before noon; he loved all games, from poker to clerical croquet, and in the Toll House croquet ground I have seen him toiling at the latter with the devotion of a curate. He took an interest in education, was an active member of the local school board, and when I was there, he had recently lost the schoolhouse key. His wagon was broken, but it never seemed to occur to him to mend it. Like all truly idle people, he had an artistic eye. He chose the print stuff for his wife's dresses, and counselled her in the making of a patchwork quilt, always, as she thought, wrongly, but to the more educated eye, always with bizarre and admirable taste—the taste of an Indian. With all this, he was a perfect, unoffending gentleman in word and act. Take his clay pipe from him, and he was fit for any society but that of fools. Quiet as he was, there burned a deep, permanent excitement in his dark blue eyes; and when this grave man smiled, it was like sunshine in a shady place.

Mrs. Hanson (née, if you please, Lovelands) was more commonplace than her lord. She was a comely woman, too, plump, fair-colored, with wonderful white teeth; and in her print dresses (chosen by Rufe) and with a large sunbonnet shading her valued complexion, made, I assure you, a very agreeable figure. But she was on the surface, what there was of her, outspoken and loudspoken. Her noisy laughter had none of the charm of one of Hanson's rare, slow-spreading smiles; there was no reticence, no mystery, no manner about the woman; she was a first-class dairymaid, but her husband was an unknown quantity between the savage and the nobleman. She was often in and out with us, merry, and healthy, and fair; he came far seldomer—only, indeed, when there was business, or now and again, to pay a visit of ceremony, brushed up for the occasion, with his wife on his arm, and a clean clay pipe in his teeth. These visits, in our forest state, had quite the air of an event, and turned our red canyon into a salon.

Such was the pair who ruled in the old Silverado Hotel, among the windy trees, on the mountain shoulder overlooking the whole length of Napa Valley, as the man aloft looks down on the ship's deck. There they kept house, with sundry horses and fowls, and a family of sons, Daniel Webster, and I think George Washington, among the number. Nor did they want visitors. An old gentleman, of singular stolidity, and called Breedlove—I think he had crossed the plains in the same caravan with Rufe—housed with them for a while during our stay; and they had besides a permanent lodger, in the form of Mrs. Hanson's brother, Irvine Lovelands. I spell Irvine by guess; for I could get no information on the subject, just as I could never find out, in spite of many inquiries, whether or not Rufe was a contraction for Rufus. They were all cheerfully at sea about their names in that generation. And this is surely the more notable where the names are all so strange, and even the family names appear to have been coined. At one time, at least, the ancestors of all these Alvins and Alvas, Loveinas, Lovelands, and Breedloves, must have taken serious counsel and found a certain poetry in these denominations; that must have been, then, their form of literature. But still times change; and their next descendants, the George Washingtons and Daniel Websters, will at least be clear upon the point. And anyway, and however his name should be spelled, this Irvine Lovelands was the most unmitigated Caliban I ever knew.

Our very first morning at Silverado, when we were full of business, patching up doors and windows, making beds and seats, and getting our rough lodging into shape, Irvine and his sister made their appearance together, she for neighborliness and general curiosity; he, because he was working for me, to my sorrow, cutting firewood at I forget how much a day. The way that he set about cutting wood was characteristic. We were at that moment patching up and unpacking in the kitchen. Down he sat on one side, and down sat his sister on the other. Both were chewing pine-tree gum, and he, to my annoyance, accompanied that simple pleasure with profuse expectoration. She rattled away, talking up hill and down dale, laughing, tossing her head,

showing her brilliant teeth. He looked on in silence, now spitting heavily on the floor, now putting his head back and uttering a loud, discordant, joyless laugh. He had a tangle of shock hair, the color of wool; his mouth was a grin; although as strong as a horse, he looked neither heavy nor yet adroit, only leggy, coltish, and in the road. But it was plain he was in high spirits, thoroughly enjoying his visit; and he laughed frankly whenever we failed to accomplish what we were about. This was scarcely helpful: it was even, to amateur carpenters, embarrassing; but it lasted until we knocked off work and began to get dinner. Then Mrs. Hanson remembered she should have been gone an hour ago; and the pair retired, and the lady's laughter died away among the nutmegs down the path. That was Irvine's first day's work in my employment—the devil take him!

The next morning he returned and, as he was this time alone, he bestowed his conversation upon us with great liberality. He prided himself on his intelligence; asked us if we knew the schoolma'am. *He* didn't think much of her anyway. He had tried her, he had. He had put a question to her. If a tree a hundred feet high were to fall a foot a day, how long would it take to fall right down? She had not been able to solve the problem. "She don't know nothing," he opined. He told us how a friend of his kept a school with a revolver, and chuckled mightily over that; his friend could teach school, he could. All the time he kept chewing gum and spitting. He would stand a while looking down; and then he would toss back his shock of hair, and laugh hoarsely, and spit, and bring forward a new subject. A man, he told us, who bore a grudge against him, had poisoned his dog. "That was a low thing for a man to do now, wasn't it? It wasn't like a man, that, nohow. But I got even with him: I pisoned *his* dog." His clumsy utterance, his rude embarrassed manner, set a fresh value on the stupidity of his remarks. I do not think I ever appreciated the meaning of two words until I knew Irvine—the verb, loaf, and the noun, oaf; between them, they complete his portrait. He could lounge, and wriggle, and rub himself against the wall, and grin, and be more in everybody's way than any other two people that I ever set my eyes on. Nothing that he did became him; and yet you were conscious that he was one of your own race, that his mind was cumbrously at work, revolving the problem of existence like the quid of gum, and in his own cloudy manner enjoying life, and passing judgment on his fellows. Above all things, he was delighted with himself. You would not have thought it, from his uneasy manners and troubled, struggling utterance; but he loved himself to the marrow, and was happy and proud like a peacock on a rail.

His self-esteem was, indeed, the one joint in his harness. He could be got to work, and even kept at work, by flattery. As long as my wife stood over him, crying out how strong he was, so long exactly he would stick to the matter in hand; and the moment she turned her back, or ceased to praise him, he would stop. His physical strength was wonderful; and to have a woman stand by and admire his achievements, warmed his heart like sunshine. Yet he was as cowardly as he was powerful, and felt no shame in owning to the weakness. Something was once wanted from the crazy platform over the shaft, and he at once refused to venture there— "did not like," as he said, "foolin' round them kind o' places," and let

my wife go instead of him, looking on with a grin. Vanity, where it rules, is usually more heroic: but Irvine steadily approved himself, and expected others to approve him; rather looked down upon my wife, and decidely expected her to look up to him, on the strength of his superior prudence.

Yet the strangest part of the whole matter was perhaps this, that Irvine was as beautiful as a statue. His features were, in themselves, perfect; it was only his cloudy, uncouth, and coarse expression that disfigured them. So much strength residing in so spare a frame was proof sufficient of the accuracy of his shape. He must have been built somewhat after the pattern of Jack Sheppard; but the famous housebreaker, we may be certain, was no lout. It was by the extraordinary powers of his mind no less than by the vigor of his body, that he broke his strong prison with such imperfect implements, turning the very obstacles to service. Irvine, in the same case, would have sat down and spat, and grumbled curses. He had the soul of a fat sheep, but, regarded as an artist's model, the exterior of a Greek god. It was a cruel thought to persons less favored in their birth, that this creature, endowed—to use the language of theatres—with extraordinary "means," should so manage to misemploy them that he looked ugly and almost deformed. It was only by an effort of abstraction, and after many days, that you discovered what he was.

By playing on the oaf's conceit, and standing closely over him, we got a path made round the corner of the dump to our door, so that we could come and go with decent ease; and he even enjoyed the work, for in that there were boulders to be plucked up bodily, bushes to be uprooted, and other occasions for athletic display: but cutting wood was a different matter. Anybody could cut wood; and besides, my wife was tired of supervising him, and had other things to attend to. And, in short, days went by, and Irvine came daily, and talked and lounged and spat; but the firewood remained intact as sleepers on the platform or growing trees upon the mountainside. Irvine as a woodcutter, we could tolerate; but Irvine as a friend of the family, at so much a day, was too bald an imposition, and at length, on the afternoon of the fourth or fifth day of our connection, I explained to him, as clearly as I could, the light in which I had grown to regard his presence. I pointed out to him that I could not continue to give him a salary for spitting on the floor; and this expression, which came after a good many others, at last penetrated his obdurate wits. He rose at once, and said if that was the way he was going to be spoke to, he reckoned he would quit. And, no one interposing, he departed.

So far, so good. But we had no firewood. The next afternoon, I strolled down to Rufe's and consulted him on the subject. It was a very droll interview, in the large, bare north room of the Silverado Hotel, Mrs. Hanson's patchwork on a frame, and Rufe, and his wife, and I, and the oaf himself, all more or less embarrassed. Rufe announced there was nobody in the neighborhood but Irvine who could do a day's work for anybody. Irvine, thereupon, refused to have any more to do with my service; he "wouldn't work no more for a man as had spoke to him 's I had done." I found myself on the point of the last humiliation—driven to beseech the creature whom I had just dismissed with insult: but I took the high hand in despair, said there

must be no talk of Irvine coming back unless matters were to be differently managed; that I would rather chop firewood for myself than be fooled; and, in short, the Hansons being eager for the lad's hire, I so imposed upon them with merely affected resolution, that they ended by begging me to re-employ him again on a solemn promise that he should be more industrious. The promise, I am bound to say, was kept. We soon had a fine pile of firewood at our door; and if Caliban gave me the cold shoulder and spared me his conversation, I thought none the worse of him for that, nor did I find my days much longer for the deprivation.

The leading spirit of the family was, I am inclined to fancy, Mrs. Hanson. Her social brilliancy somewhat dazzled the others, and she had more of the small change of sense. It was she who faced Kelmar, for instance; and perhaps, if she had been alone, Kelmar would have had no rule within her doors. Rufe, to be sure, had a fine, sober, open-air attitude of mind, seeing the world without exaggeration—perhaps, we may even say, without enough; for he lacked, along with the others, that commercial idealism which puts so high a value on time and money. Sanity itself is a kind of convention. Perhaps Rufe was wrong; but, looking on life plainly, he was unable to perceive that croquet or poker were in any way less important than, for instance, mending his wagon. Even his own profession, hunting, was dear to him mainly as a sort of play; even that he would have neglected, had it not appealed to his imagination. His hunting-suit, for instance, had cost I should be afraid to say how many bucks— the currency in which he paid his way: it was all befringed, after the Indian fashion, and it was dear to his heart. The pictorial side of his daily business was never forgotten. He was even anxious to stand for his picture in those buckskin hunting clothes; and I remember how he once warmed almost into enthusiasm, his dark blue eyes growing perceptibly larger, as he planned the composition in which he should appear, "with the horns of some real big bucks, and dogs, and a camp on a crick" (creek, stream).

There was no trace in Irvine of this woodland poetry. He did not care for hunting, nor yet for buckskin suits. He had never observed scenery. The world, as it appeared to him, was almost obliterated by his own great grinning figure in the foreground: Caliban Malvolio. And it seems to me as if, in the persons of these brothers-in-law, we had the two sides of rusticity fairly well represented: the hunter living really in nature; the clodhopper living merely out of society: the one bent up in every corporal agent to capacity in one pursuit, doing at least one thing keenly and thoughtfully, and thoroughly alive to all that touches it; the other in the inert and bestial state, walking in a faint dream, and taking so dim an impression of the myriad sides of life that he is truly conscious of nothing but himself. • It is only in the fastnesses of nature, forests, mountains, and the back of man's beyond, that a creature endowed with five senses can grow up into the perfection of this crass and earthy vanity. In towns or the busier country sides, he is roughly reminded of other men's existence; and if he learns no more, he learns at least to fear contempt. But Irvine had come scathless through life, conscious only of himself, of his great strength and intelligence; and in the silence of the universe, to which he did not listen, dwelling with delight on the sound of his own thoughts.

For Thought and Discussion

1. What are the general characteristics of the class of people described in the first paragraph?
2. Describe the characters, Mrs. Hanson, Rufe, and Irvine, bringing out contrasts in the latter two. What admirable traits do these three people lack?
3. How does Stevenson poke fun at himself in the incident about re-hiring Irvine?
4. What distinction is there between "mending the wagon" and playing "croquet or poker"?
5. What are the characteristics of Stevenson's style?
6. Compare this essay with the preceding, "A Memory of a Midnight Express."

ROBERT LOUIS STEVENSON 1850-1894

"From the sick child, now well and old,
   Take, nurse, the little book you hold."[1]

These lines, "To Alison Cunningham, From Her Boy," were written by Robert Louis Stevenson to "Cummie," the nurse who cared for him so tenderly and faithfully throughout his childhood.

---

[1]The dedication of Child's Garden of Verses.

The main facts of his early life, particularly the accounts of the long hours the child spent in bed amusing himself with imaginary stories, are usually as familiar as the favorite poems from *Child's Garden of Verses*—"Where Go the Boats?" "My Shadow," "The Friendly Cow All Red and White," "The Wind," "Birdie with a Yellow Bill," "Singing," and "Foreign Lands."

School. Notwithstanding the fact that Stevenson's early schooling was informal because of his ill health, he followed the family tradition by studying engineering at the University of Edinburgh, returning later to study law after he had found engineering too uninteresting for a life career. His father feared that starvation was in store for him, if he relied upon writing for a means of livelihood, but when both engineering and law had failed entirely to arouse his interest, he was free to turn to writing.

Travels and Marriage. The stories imagined by the child became realities when Stevenson grew older; throughout his life he spent much time in ships, searching for health and adventure, always finding the latter. Leaving the raw climate of Scotland for sunnier climes, in the company of his cousin, he set out in his boat to find charming out-of-the-way places tucked away from the rest of the world. On one of his return trips he stopped at an artists' colony near Paris. All were very much interested in this unusual person, wearing unconventional, colorful clothes, tense and eager, brimming with stories of amusing adventures. The first evening when the entire colony went to inspect the boat, there was an eight year old boy present, Lloyd Osbourne, who was highly entertained because Stevenson took the trouble to explain to him the workings of the sails and masts. Later the two became fast friends, and soon Stevenson was very much in love with Mrs. Osbourne, Lloyd's mother. The three spent many happy hours together, "Luly," as Lloyd called him, amusing the boy with jolly stories "out of his own head." The happy trio were separated for a short time; "Luly" was sadly missed when he went to England, and Mrs. Osbourne and Lloyd returned to America. Later Stevenson and Mrs. Osbourne were married in California and spent their honeymoon in an abandoned mining camp, the scene of "The Hunter's Family," which was written later in France.

Fame and Fortune. For a time Stevenson suffered from depression of spirits; illness and failure to secure recognition for his writings made a trying combination of unhappy circumstances. The Stevensons returned to England, later went to the Alps for the winters, and eventually established a home in France. Stevenson became so ill that another change in climate was necessary, and when the decision to return to New Mexico and Colorado was made, he was delighted with the idea. When they landed in New York, *Treasure Island*, *Dr. Jekyll and Mr. Hyde*, and *Kidnapped* had made him a celebrity. His boat was met by crowds of newspaper reporters and photographers. Later on, when he was ready to travel, the railroad company placed a private car at his disposal.

Along with fame had come fortune through a legacy from his father and satisfactory remuneration for his writing.

Samoan Home. In San Francisco the Stevensons chartered a boat. They cruised in the Pacific three years, stopping at different islands in search of an ideal climate for Stevenson, who was ill with tuberculosis. They settled on one of the Samoan islands, where they built a home, Vailima (Five Waters). Stevenson lived happily the last four years of his life, entertaining often—for he liked jolly parties—making friends with the natives, to whom he became a sort of chieftain who was consulted so frequently that some of the islanders were usually to be seen on the "Road of the Loving Heart," the name which they gave to the road built to his home by Mataafa chiefs in appreciation for his kindness during their imprisonment after a revolution. In these last years of his life, though often ill, Stevenson wrote constantly, frequently consulting his wife and Lloyd Osbourne, his step-son, with whom he did some collaborative work.

Death. Stevenson's last birthday, not long before his death, was celebrated with a jolly party, attended by more than a hundred guests. Stevenson, who enjoyed the gay nonsense of a happy child, introduced pantomimes which afforded much hilarity, and as usual he was the most vivacious of all the merrymakers. The gladness, which seemed to remain with him afterwards, was responsible for many plans for the future which were stopped short by death, which struck so suddenly that he died as he had always hoped he would, "with his boots on." When the news of his death spread, the natives crowded into his home to mourn for their dear friend, bringing the customary precious gifts. Large numbers of them volunteered to cut the road to the top of the mountain on which he wished to be buried. His tomb may be seen there engraved with his own inscription:

REQUIEM

Under the wide and starry sky
Dig the grave and let me lie.
Glad did I live and gladly die,
    And I laid me down with a will.

This be the verse you grave for me:
Here he lies where he longed to be;
Home is the sailor, home from the sea,
    And the hunter home from the hill.

Style. The advice usually given to young writers who would acquire an easy, graceful style is "Read Stevenson." His long sentences move along with the rhythm of a smooth flowing river. Such perfection as his is gained only through devotion to a task and the persistence which few have the patience to exercise. With this in mind, it is interesting to learn that Stevenson considered the real fun of writing to be in re-writing and revising, which is drudgery to the average person.

Philosophy of Life. Stevenson was a Victorian in his optimistic outlook on life. Misfortune never quelled his spirit for any appreciable length of time. That his high spirits always seem spontaneous makes his attitude more attractive. Perhaps life has no greater gift to offer a person than the capacity for resisting unhappiness and depression of spirits when fortune seemingly deserts one. On Stevenson that gift was bestowed in a full measure.

His Books. Stevenson's clear, joyous outlook on life is reflected in his writings. It is singular that he has written for all ages, beginning with verses for children and including adventure stories and essays for youthful and older readers. Among the well-known titles are: *Child's Garden of Verses, Treasure Island, Kidnapped, The Strange Case of Dr. Jekyll and Mr. Hyde, An Inland Voyage, Travels with a Donkey, Virginibus Puerisque, A Lodging for the Night, Memories and Portraits,* and *Studies of Men and Books.*

JUGGLING JERRY

GEORGE MEREDITH

[Victorian writers were notably long-lived, perhaps fortunately so, since many of them had to wait long years for recognition. Among this group is Meredith, 1828-1909, whose works in some respects resemble Browning's and in some respects resemble George Eliot's. Meredith's style corresponds to Browning's in its intellectual pithiness and brilliance and to Eliot's in minute character analysis. It must be remembered, however, that while Eliot deals with the individual, Meredith deals with type characters, whose failings, such as pride and sentimentalism, he attacks not as a moral teacher, but as a satirist, albeit a kindly one, whose mocking laughter is untinged with malice. Though Meredith is too much of a philosopher to be a popular favorite, there is a growing regard for his novels. His long poems, many of which express radical opinions on the emancipation of women, probably will never be widely read, but his shorter poems are received with appreciation.

The dramatic monologue, "Juggling Jerry," with its mingling of pathos and humor, describes the death of an old juggler. The scene is laid in the heath country of southern England; the language is colloquial; but the homely philosophy expressed touches a responsive chord in the heart of almost every reader.]

PITCH here the tent, while the old horse grazes;
    By the old hedge-side we'll halt a stage.
It's nigh my last above the daisies;
    My next leaf'll be man's blank page.

Yes, my old girl! and it's no use crying, [5]
    Juggler, constable, king, must bow.
One that outjuggles all's been spying
    Long to have me, and he has me now.

We've traveled times to this old common;
    Often we've hung our pots in the gorse. [10]
We've had a stirring life, old woman!
    You, and I, and the old gray horse.
Races, and fairs, and royal occasions,
    Found us coming to their call;
Now they'll miss us at our stations; [15]
    There's a Juggler outjuggles all!

Up goes the lark, as if all were jolly!
    Over the duck-pond the willow shakes.
Easy to think that grieving's folly,
    When the hand's firm as driven stakes! [20]
Ay, when we're strong, and braced, and manful,
    Life's a sweet fiddle; but we're a batch
Born to become the Great Juggler's han'ful;
    Balls he shies up, and is safe to catch.

Here's where the lads of the village cricket; [25]
    I was a lad not wide[1] from here;
Couldn't I whip off the bail[2] from the wicket?
    Like an old world those days appear!
Donkey, sheep, geese and thatched ale-house—I know them!

---

[1]*wide,* far.
[2]*bail,* a piece of wood which was to be knocked off a wicket in the game of cricket.

They are old friends of my halts, and seem,   30
Somehow, as if kind thanks I owe them;
  Juggling don't hinder the heart's esteem.

Juggling's no sin, for we must have victual;
  Nature allows us to bait for the fool.
Holding one's own makes us juggle no little;   35
  But, to increase it, hard juggling's the rule.
You that are sneering at my profession,
  Haven't you juggled a vast amount?
There's the prime minister, in one Session,
  Juggles more games than my sins 'll count.   40

I've murdered insects with mock thunder[3];

Conscience, for that, in men don't quail.
I've made bread from the bump of wonder;
  That's my business, and there's my tale.
Fashion and rank all praised the professor;   45
  Ay! and I've had my smile from the Queen;
Bravo, Jerry! she meant—God bless her!
  Ain't this a sermon on that scene?

I've studied men from my topsy-turvy
  Close, and, I reckon, rather true.   50
Some are fine fellows; some, right scurvy;
  Most, a dash between the two.
But it's a woman, old girl, that makes me
  Think more kindly of the race;
And it's a woman, old girl, that shakes me   55
  When the Great Juggler I must face.

[3]*mock thunder*, blank cartridges, which jugglers often use in performances of magic.

We two were married, due and legal;
  Honest we've lived since we've been
  one.
Lord! I could then jump like an eagle;
  You danced bright as a bit o' the
  sun.   60
Birds in a May-bush we were! right
  merry!
  All night we kissed, we juggled all
  day.
Joy was the heart of Juggling Jerry!
  Now from his old girl he's juggled
  away.

It's past parsons to console us;   65
  No, nor no doctor fetch for me;
I can die without my bolus[4];
  Two of a trade, lass, never agree!
Parson and doctor!—don't they love
  rarely
  . Fighting the devil in other men's
  fields!   70
Stand up yourself and match him
  fairly;
  Then see how the rascal yields!

I, lass, have lived no gypsy, flaunting
  Finery while his poor helpmate
  grubs;
Coin I've stored, and you won't be
  wanting;   75
  You shan't beg from the troughs
  and tubs.
Nobly you've stuck to me, though in
  his kitchen
  Many a Marquis would hail you
  Cook!
Palaces you could have ruled and
  grown rich in,
  But your old Jerry you never for-
  sook.   80

----

[4]*bolus*, doctor's pill of large size, colloquial for something hard to swallow.

Hand up the chirper[5]! ripe ale winks
  in it;
  Let's have comfort and be at peace.
Once a stout draught made me light
  as a linnet.
  Cheer up! the Lord must have his
  lease.
Maybe—for none see in that black
  hollow—   85
  It's just a place where we're held in
  pawn,
And, when the Great Juggler makes
  as to swallow.
  It's just the sword trick—I ain't
  quite gone!

Yonder came smells of the gorse, so
  nutty,
  Gold-like and warm; it's the prime
  of May.   90
Better than mortar, brick, and putty,
  Is God's house on a blowing day.
Lean me more up the mound; now I
  feel it—
  All the old heath-smells! Ain't it
  strange?
There's the world laughing, as if to
  conceal it,   95
  But He's by us, juggling the
  change.

I mind it well, by the seabeach lying,
  Once—it's long gone—when two
  gulls we beheld.
Which, as the moon got up, were
  flying
  Down a big wave that sparkled and
  swelled.   100
Crack, went a gun: one fell; the
  second
  Wheeled round him twice, and was
  off for new luck;
There in the dark her white wing
  beckoned—
  Drop me a kiss—I'm the bird dead-
  struck!

----

[5]*chirper,* a mug of ale.

For Thought and Discussion

1. What is the situation?
2. What incident recalled by Juggling Jerry indicates that he was indeed a skilful juggler?
3. Into what three classes does Jerry place the people one finds in the world?
4. Why does Jerry want to die in the open?
5. Where is pathos most evident in the poem?
6. Why is Jerry an admirable character?
7. What is the old man's philosophy or view of life?
8. How does dialect add to the interest of the poem?

✎

A NOW—OF A COLD DAY
London Journal, December 3, 1834

LEIGH HUNT

[If the name, Leigh Hunt, 1784-1859, were as well known as is the title of his familiar poem, "Abou Ben Adhem," it would be almost a household term. Hunt's delightful essay, though not so universally known as the selection mentioned above, entitles him to a place among his close literary friends, Lamb, Wordsworth, Coleridge, Keats, Shelley, Byron, Browning, Tennyson, and Carlyle.]

A friend tells us, that having written a 'Now,' descriptive of a hot day, we ought to write another, descriptive of a cold one; and accordingly we do so. It happens that we are, at this minute, in a state at once fit and unfit for the task, being in the condition of the little boy at school, who, when asked the Latin for 'cold,' said he had it 'at his fingers' ends'; but this helps us to set off with a right taste of our subject, and the fire, which is clicking in our ear, shall soon enable us to handle it comfortably in other respects.

Now, then, to commence.—But first, the reader who is good-natured enough to have a regard for these papers may choose to be told of the origin of the use of this word *Now*, in case he is not already acquainted with it. It was suggested to us by the striking convenience it affords to descriptive writers, such as Thomson and others, who are fond of beginning their paragraphs with it, thereby saving themselves a world of trouble in bringing about a nicer conjunction of the various parts of their subject.

Now when the first foul torrent of the brooks—

Now flaming up to heaven, the potent sun—

Now when the cheerless empire of the sky—

But now—

When now—

Where now—

For now—, &c.

We say nothing of similar words among other nations, or of a certain *But* of the Greeks, which was as useful to them on all occasions as the *And so* of the little children's stories. Our business is with our old indigenous friend. No other *Now* can be so present, so instantaneous, so extremely *Now* as our own Now. The

Now of the Latins,—*Nunc*, or *Jam*, as he sometimes calls himself,—is a fellow of past ages. He is no Now. And the *Nun* of the Greek is older. How can there be a *Now* which was *Then?* a '*Now-then*,' as we sometimes barbarously phrase it. 'Now *and* then' is intelligible; but 'Now-then' is an extravagance, fit only for the delicious moments of a gentleman about to crack his bottle, or to run away with a lady, or to open a dance, or to carve a turkey and chine, or to pelt snowballs, or to commit some other piece of ultra-vivacity, such as excuses a man from the nicer proprieties of language.

But to begin.

Now, the moment people wake in the morning, they perceive the coldness with their faces, though they are warm with their bodies, and exclaim, 'Here's a day,' and pity the poor little sweep, and the boy with the water-cresses. How anybody can go to a cold ditch, and gather water-cresses, seems marvellous. Perhaps we hear great lumps in the street of something falling; and, looking through the window, perceive the roofs of the neighbouring houses thick with snow. The breath is visible, issuing from the mouth as we lie. Now we hate getting up, and hate shaving, and hate the empty grate in one's bedroom, and water freezes in ewers, and you must set the towel upright on its own hardness, and the window-panes are frost-whitened, or it is foggy, and the sun sends a dull, brazen beam into one's room; or, if it is fine, the windows outside are stuck with icicles; or a detestable thaw has begun, and they drip; but, at all events, it is horribly cold, and delicate shavers fidget about their chambers, looking distressed, and cherish their hard-hearted enemy, the razor, in their bosoms, to warm him a little, and coax him into a consideration of their chins. Savage is a cut, and makes them think destiny really too hard.

Now breakfast is fine; and the fire seems to laugh at us as we enter the breakfast-room, and say, 'Ha! ha! here's a better room than the bed-chamber!' and we always poke it before we do anything else; and people grow selfish about seats near it; and little boys think their elders tyrannical for saying, 'Oh, *you* don't want the fire; your blood is young.' And truly that is not the way of stating the case, albeit young blood is warmer than old. Now the butter is too hard to spread; and the rolls and toast are at their maximum; and the former look glorious as they issue, smoking, out of the flannel in which they come from the baker's; and people who come with single knocks at the door are pitied; and the voices of boys are loud in the street, sliding, or throwing snowballs; and the dustman's bell sounds cold; and we wonder how anybody can go about selling fish, especially with that hoarse voice; and schoolboys hate their slates, and blow their fingers, and detest infinitely the no-fire at school; and the parish-beadle's nose is redder than ever.

Now sounds in general are dull, and smoke out of chimneys looks warm and rich, and birds are pitied, hopping about for crumbs, and the trees look wiry and cheerless, albeit they are still beautiful to imaginative eyes, especially the evergreens, and the birch with boughs like dishevelled hair. Now mud in roads is stiff, and the kennel ices over, and boys make illegal slides in the pathways, and ashes are strewed before doors; or you crunch the snow as you tread, or kick mud-flakes before you, or are horribly muddy in cities. But if it is a hard frost, all the world is buttoned up and great-coated, except ostentatious elderly gentlemen, and pretended beggars with naked feet; and the delicious sound of 'All hot' is heard from roasted apple and potato-stalls, the vendor himself being cold, in spite of his 'hot,' and stamping up and down to warm his feet; and the little boys are astonished to think how he can eat bread and cold meat for his dinner, instead of the smoking apples.

Now skaters are on the alert; the cutlers' shopwindows abound with their swift shoes; and as you approach the scene of action (pond or canal) you can hear the dull grinding noise of the skates to and fro, and see tumbles, and Banbury-cake men and blackguard boys playing 'hockey,' and ladies standing shivering on the banks, admiring anybody but their brother, especially the gentleman who is cutting figures of eight, who, for his part, is admiring his own figure. Beginners affect to laugh at their tumbles, but are terribly angry, and long to thump the bystanders. On thawing days, idlers persist to the last in skating or sliding amidst the slush and bending ice, making the Humane-Society man ferocious. He feels as if he could give them the deaths from which it is his business to save them. When you have done skating, you come away feeling at once warm and numb in the feet, from the tight effect of the skates; and you carry them with an ostentatious air of indifference, as if you had done wonders; whereas you have fairly had three slips, and can barely achieve the inside edge.

Now riders look sharp, and horses seem brittle in the legs, and old gentlemen feel so; and coachmen, cabmen, and others, stand swinging their arms across at their sides to warm themselves; and blacksmiths' shops look pleasant, and potato shops detestable; the fishmongers' still more so. We wonder how he can live in that plash of wet and cold fish, without even a window. Now clerks in offices envy the one next the fireplace; and men from behind counters hardly think themselves repaid by being called out to speak to a Countess in her chariot; and the wheezy and effeminate pastry-cook, hatless and aproned, and with his hands in his breeches-pockets (as the graphic Cruikshank noticeth in his almanac) stands outside his door, chilling his household warmth with attending to the ice which is brought him, and seeing it unloaded into his cellar like coals. Comfortable look the Miss Joneses, coming this way with their muffs and furs; and the baker pities the maid-servant cleaning the steps, who, for her part, says, she is not cold, which he finds it difficult to believe.

Now dinner rejoiceth the gatherers together, and cold meat is despised, and the gout defieth the morrow, thinking it but reasonable, on such a day, to inflame itself with 't'other bottle'; and the sofa is wheeled round to the fire after dinner, and people proceed to burn their legs in their boots, and little boys their faces; and young ladies are tormented between the cold and their complexions, and their fingers freeze at the pianoforte, but they must not say so, because it will vex their poor comfortable grand-aunt, who is sitting with her knees in the fire, and who is anxious that they should not be spoilt.

Now the muffin-bell soundeth sweetly in the streets, reminding us, not of the man, but his muffins, and of twilight, and evening, and curtains, and the fireside. Now playgoers get cold feet, and invalids stop up every crevice in their rooms, and make themselves worse; and the streets are comparatively silent; and the wind rises and falls in moanings; and fires burn blue and crackle; and an easy chair with your feet by it on a stool, the lamp or candles a little behind you, and an interesting book just opened where you left off, is a bit of heaven upon earth. People in cottages crowd close into the chimney, and tell stories of ghosts and murders, the blue flame affording something like evidence of the facts.

The owl, with all her feathers, is a-cold,[1]

or you think her so. The whole country feels like a petrifaction of slate

---

[1]Keats, in *The Eve of St. Agnes*. Mr. Keats gave us some touches in our account of the 'Hot Day' (first published in *The Indicator*) as we sat writing it in his company thirteen or fourteen years back. We have here made him contribute to our 'Cold Day.' Thus it is to have immortal friends, whose company never forsakes us.

and stillness, cut across by the wind; and nobody in the mail-coach is warm but the horses, who steam pitifully when they stop. The 'oldest man' makes a point of never having 'seen such weather.' People have a painful doubt whether they have any chins or not; ears ache with the wind; and the waggoner goes puckering up his teeth, and thinking the time will never arrive when he shall get to the Five Bells.

At night, people get sleepy with the fireside, and long to go to bed, yet fear it on account of the different temperature of the bedroom; which is furthermore apt to wake them up. Warming-pans and hot-water bottles are in request; and naughty boys eschew their night-shirts and go to bed in their socks.

'Yes,' quoth a little boy, to whom we read this passage, 'and make their younger brother go to bed first.'

For Thought and Discussion

1. What is the effect of the use of "now" in the beginning of this selection?
2. What are the signs of a cold day that you perceive indoors? outdoors? What signs does Hunt mention?
3. At school what are the signs of a cold day?
4. Contrast winter sports of Leigh Hunt's time and of today.
5. Contrast living conditions of the early nineteenth century with those of today.
6. Does Hunt appeal more often through imagination or through the senses of sight, taste, and hearing?
7. Contrast this essay with "A Memory of a Midnight Express."

❧

From HIS DIARY

SAMUEL PEPYS

[One of the most interesting characters of the Restoration was Samuel Pepys (peeps, peps), known through the most readable diary in English literature. His accounts of events during the years 1660-1669 include the Restoration of King Charles II, who even the loyal Pepys was forced to admit fell short of the mark; the London fire, which destroyed a large part of the city; the plague which took so many lives that blocks of shops were closed and grass grew in the streets. As Secretary of the Admiralty, Pepys held a position of trust and importance and performed his duties ably and conscientiously. He raised the standards of the navy but was unable to correct many abuses which he knew should be corrected.

The diary reveals the foibles and very human character of the author. We smile and sympathize with him over his fondness for good clothes. He says: "I have bought me a new suit which becomes me well; the Lord help me to pay for it." One feels a kinship with him when he tells of losing his temper over a trifle and kicking up a big fuss and of feeling ashamed of himself afterward. Naturally such a frank piece of work was not written for publication. When it was discovered after his death among his books left to Magdalen (môd′ lĭn) College, it was translated from the shorthand in which it was written and was published.]

NOVEMBER 4th (Lord's day), 1660. My wife seemed very pretty to-day, it being the first time I had given her leave to wear a black patch.[1]

22. Mr. Fox came in presently and did receive us with a great deal of respect; and then did take my wife and I to the Queen's presence-chamber, where he got my wife placed behind the Queen's chair, and I got into the crowd, and by and by the Queen and the two Princesses came to dinner. The Queen a very little plain old woman, and nothing more in her presence in any respect nor garb than an ordinary woman. The

Princess of Orange I had often seen before. The Princess Henrietta is very pretty, but much below my expectation; and her dressing of herself with her hair frized short up to her ears, did make her seem so much the less to me. But my wife standing near her with two or three black patches on, and well dressed, did seem to me much handsomer than she.

January 3d, 1661. To Will's, where Spicer and I eat our dinner of a roasted leg of pork which Will did give us, and after that to the Theatre, where was acted "Beggars' Bush," it being very well done; and here the first time that ever I saw woman come upon the stage.

26th. Within all the morning. About noon comes one that had formerly known me and I him, but I know not his name, to borrow £5 of me, but I had the wit to deny him.

April 24th, 1661. To the Opera, and there saw "Hamlet, Prince of Denmark," done with scenes very well, but above all, Betterton did the prince's part beyond imagination.

July 4th, 1662. By and by comes Mr. Cooper, mate of the Royall Charles, of whom I intend to learn mathematiques, and do begin with him to-day, he being a very able man, and no great matter, I suppose, will content him. After an hour's being with him at arithmetique (my first attempt being to learn the multiplicacion-table); then we parted till to-morrow.

9th. Up by four o'clock, and at my multiplicacion-table hard, which is all the trouble I meet withal in my arithmetique.

11th. Up by four o'clock, and hard at my multiplicacion-table, which I am now almost master of.

19th. In the afternoon I went upon the river to look after some tar I

---

[1] *black patch,* beauty patch.

am sending down and some coles, and so home again; it raining hard upon the water, I put ashore and sheltered myself, while the King came by in his barge, going down towards the Downs to meet the Queen: the Duke being gone yesterday. But methought it lessened my esteem of a king, that he should not be able to command the rain.

Oct. 19th, 1662. (Lord's day). Got me ready in the morning and put on my first new lace-band; and so neat it is, that I am resolved my great expense shall be lace-bands, and it will set off anything else the more.

November 27th, 1626. At my waking, I found the tops of the houses covered with snow, which is a rare sight, that I have not seen these three years. We all went to the next house upon Tower Hill, to see the coming by of the Russia Embassador; for whose reception all the City trained-bands do attend in the streets, and the King's life-guards, and most of the wealthy citizens in their black velvet coats, and gold chains. I could not see the Embassador in his coach; but his attendants in their habits and fur caps very handsome, comely men, and most of them with hawkes upon their fists to present to the King. But Lord! to see the absurd nature of Englishmen, that cannot forbear laughing and jeering at everything that looks strange.

April 19th (Easter day), 1663. Up and this day put on my close-kneed coloured suit, which, with new stockings of the colour, with belt, and new gilt-handled sword, is very handsome.

March 9th, 1656. This night my wife had a new suit of flowered ash-coloured silke, very noble.

13th. This day my wife begun to wear light-coloured locks, quite white almost, which, though it makes her look very pretty, yet not being na-tural, vexes me, that I will not have her wear them.

May 13th, 1665. So home and late at my office. But, Lord! to see how much of my old folly and childishnesse hangs upon me still that I cannot forbear carrying my watch in my hand in the coach all this afternoon, and seeing what o'clock it is one hundred times, and am apt to think with myself, how could I be so long without one; though I remember since, I had one, and found it a trouble, and resolved to carry one no more about me while I lived.

Sept. 3rd, 1666. (The London Fire). About four o'clock in the morning, my Lady Batten sent me a cart to carry away all my money, and plate, and best things to Sir W. Rider's at Bednall-greene. Which I did, riding myself in my night-gowne in the cart; and, Lord! to see how the streets and the highways are crowded with people running and riding, and getting of carts at any rate to fetch away things. The Duke of Yorke come this day by the office, and spoke to us, and did ride with his guard up and down the City to keep all quiet (he being now Generall, and having the care of all). At night lay down a little upon a quilt of W. Hewer's in the office, all my owne things being packed up or gone; and after me my poor wife did the like, we having fed upon the remains of yesterday's dinner, having no fire nor dishes, nor any opportunity of dressing any thing.

5th. About two in the morning my wife calls me up and tells me of new cryes of fire, it being come to Barking Church, which is the bottom of our lane. I up, and finding it so, resolved presently to take her away, and did, and took my gold, which was about £2,350, W. Hewer, and Jane, down by Proundy's boat to Woolwich; but, Lord! what a sad sight it was by moone-light to see the City almost on fire, that you might see it plain at Woolwich, as if you were by it. .... I up to Barkeing steeple, and there I saw the saddest sight of desolation that I ever saw, every where great fires, oyle-cellars, and brimstone, and other things burning. I became afeard to stay there long, ... and to Sir W. Pen's, and there eat a piece of cold n.eat, having eaten nothing since Sunday, but the remains of a Sunday dinner.

8th. I met with many people undone, and more that have extraordinary great losses. People speaking their thoughts variously about the be-ginning of the fire, and the rebuilding of the City. Then to Sir W. Batten's, and took my brother with me, and there dined with a great company of neighbours, and much good discourse; among others, of the low spirits of some rich men in the City, in sparing any encouragement to the poor people that wrought for the saving their houses.

December 27th. Up; and called up by the King's trumpets, which cost me 10s. So to the office, where we sat all the morning. From hence to the Duke's house, and there saw "Macbeth" most excellently acted, and a most excellent play for variety.

For Thought and Discussion

1. In the sixteenth century boys whose voices were high and light played the rôles of the women characters. What change does Pepys remark upon after the Restoration of Charles II in 1660?
2. How much time does Pepys seem to have required for learning the multiplication table?
3. What criticism of his countrymen does Pepys make upon the occasion of the parade in honor of the "Russian Embassador"? Is this kind of behavior typical today?
4. Why do you suppose that watches were a novelty in Pepys's day?
5. What great calamity does Pepys describe? Is such a disaster likely to occur now? Give reasons for your answer.
6. For a background of the seventeenth century you may read "The Age of Milton and the Restoration."

Plus Work

Read Pepys's *Diary* and make a class report on one of these subjects:

The Personality of Pepys
The Influence of the Diary of Samuel Pepys upon Present Day Journalism

Write a diary fashioned after the style of Pepys.

From LIFE OF JOHNSON

JAMES BOSWELL

[Samuel Johnson, 1709-1784, noted for his knowledge on many and various subjects, his interesting conversations, which resembled orations, his idiosyncrasies of character, his strange and unusual prejudices, his charity toward the unfortunate, and his edition of the English Dictionary, was for many years the literary dictator of London. In the Johnson Circle, which gathered around him and organized into a club, were such men as Sir Joshua Reynolds, the famous painter; Edmund Burke, known as an orator and a statesman; Gibbons, the historian; Garrick, the popular actor; Oliver Goldsmith; and James Boswell, the hero-worshiper in the group. Boswell became Johnson's close friend and took great delight in recording the sayings of the great man, both the trivial and the significant. The biography he wrote is one of the greatest in English literature.]

First Meeting of Boswell and Johnson

I WAS much agitated; and recollecting his prejudice against the Scotch, of which I had heard so much, I said to Davies, "Don't tell him where I come from."

"From Scotland," cried Davies, roguishly.

"Mr. Johnson," said I, "I do indeed come from Scotland, but I cannot help it."

I am willing to flatter myself that I mean this as light pleasantry to soothe and conciliate him, and not as an humiliating abasement at the expense of my country. But however that might be, this speech was somewhat unlucky; for with that quickness of wit for which he was so re-markable, he seized the expression "come from Scotland," which I used in the sense of being from that country; and, as if I had said that I had come away from it, or left it, retorted, "That, Sir, I find, is what a very great many of your countrymen cannot help."

Johnson's Remarks on Intellectual Superiority

"In barbarous society, superiority of parts is of real consequence. Great strength or great wisdom is of much value to an individual. But in more polished times there are people to do everything for money; and then there are a number of other superiorities, such as those of birth and fortune and rank, that dissipate men's attention, and leave no extraordinary share of respect for personal and intellectual superiority. This is wisely ordered by providence, to preserve some equality among mankind."

Johnson's Account of the Publication of *The Vicar of Wakefield*

"I received one morning a message from poor Goldsmith that he was in great distress, and as it was not in his power to come to me, begging that I would come as soon as possible. I sent him a guinea, and promised to come to him directly. I went accordingly as soon I was drest, and found that his landlady had arrested him for his rent, at which he was in a violent passion. I perceived that he had already changed my guinea, and had got a bottle of Madeira and a glass before him. I put the cork into the bottle, desired he would be calm, and began to talk to him of the means by which he might be extricated. He then told me that he had a novel ready for the press which he produced to me. I looked into it, and saw its merit; told the landlady I should return, and having gone to a bookseller, sold it for sixty pounds. I brought Goldsmith the money, and he discharged his rent, not without rating his landlady in a high tone for having used him so ill."

The English Dictionary

On Tuesday, August 2 (the day of my departure from London having been fixed for the 5th), Dr. Johnson did me the honour to pass a part of the morning with me at my chambers. He said "he always felt an inclination to do nothing." I observed that it was strange to think that the most indolent man in Britain had written the most laborious work, *The English Dictionary*.

London

Johnson was much attached to London: he observed that a man stored his mind better there than anywhere else, and that in remote situations a man's body might be feasted, but his mind starved, and his faculties apt to degenerate, from want of exercise and competition. No place, he said, cured a man's vanity or arrogance, so well as London; for as no man was either great or good 'per se,' but as compared with others not so good or great, he was sure to find in the metropolis many his equals, and some his superiors. He observed that a man in London was in less danger of falling in love indiscreetly than anywhere else; for there the difficulty of deciding between the conflicting pretensions of a vast variety of objects kept him safe.

Johnson's Account of the Death of Goldsmith

"Of poor dear Dr. Goldsmith there is little to be told, more than his papers have been made public. He died of a fever made, I am afraid, more violent by uneasiness of mind. His debts began to be heavy, and all resources were exhausted. Sir Joshua is of the opinion that he owed not less than two thousand pounds. Was ever a poet so trusted before?"

Liberty

Johnson. "He is young, my Lord: looking to his lordship with an arch smile, all boys love liberty, till experience convinces them they are not fit to govern themselves as they imagined. We are all agreed as to our own liberty; we would have as much of it as we can get; but we are not agreed as to the liberty of others: for in proportion as we take, others must lose. I believe we hardly wish that the mob should have liberty to govern us. When that was the case some time ago, no man was at liberty to have candles in his windows."

Ramsey. "The result is, that order cannot be had but by subordination."

Wealth

On the subject of the right employment of wealth, Johnson observed, "A man cannot make a bad use of his money, so far as regards Society if he does not hoard it; for if he either spends it or lends it out, Society has the benefit. It is in general better to spend money than to give it away; for industry is more promoted by spending money than by giving it away. A man who spends ten thousand a year will do more good than a man who spends two thousand and gives away eight."

His Cat, Hodge

Nor would it be just under this head, to omit the fondness which he showed for animals which he had taken under his protection. I never shall forget the indulgence with which he treated Hodge, his cat; for whom he himself used to go out and buy oysters, lest the servants having trouble, should take a dislike to the poor creature. I am, unluckily, one of those who have an antipathy to a cat, so that I am uneasy when in the room with one, and I own, I frequently suffered a good deal from the presence of this same Hodge. I recollect him one day scrambling up Dr. Johnson's breast, apparently with much satisfaction, while my friend smiling and half-whistling, rubbed down his back, and pulled him by the tail; and when I observed he was a fine cat, saying "Why, yes, Sir, but I have had cats whom I liked better than this"; and then as if perceiving Hodge to be out of countenance, adding, "but he is a very fine cat indeed."

Johnson's Distinction Between a Well-bred and Ill-bred Man

The difference, he observed, between a well-bred and an ill-bred man is this: "One immediately attracts your liking, the other your aversion. You love the one till you find reason to hate him: you hate the other till you find reason to love him."

Johnson's Advice

"Get as much force of mind as you can. Live within your income. Always have something saved at the end of the year. Let your imports be more than your exports, and you'll never go far wrong."

For Thought and Discussion

1. Name the members of the famous Johnson Circle. In what century did they live?
2. For what was Johnson famous?
3. Do you agree with Johnson's ideas on the distribution of money and talents and intellectual superiority?
4. Why did Johnson prefer to live in London?
5. Find in "The Age of Classicism," the brief treatment of the trends of the eighteenth century, the latter part of which has been called "The Age of Johnson."

Plus Work

Make class reports on the following topics:

The First English Dictionary
Are Dr. Johnson's Ideas about Wealth Economically Sound?
English Booksellers of Johnson's Time
Johnson's Letter to the Earl of Chesterfield (the Literary Declaration of Independence)
Dr. Johnson's Conviction on Liberty

From LIFE OF FLORENCE NIGHTINGALE
SIR EDWARD COOK[1]

[Florence Nightingale, 1820-1910, was one of those rare people who have the good fortune to find the work for which they are fitted. The happiness which came to her through doing her great work was a result of the unselfishness which led her to perform distinguished services for England and the rest of the world. She was the first to establish scientific care for wounded soldiers. Her manual on the administration of army hospitals is still in use.

Ruskin's quotation, "Let every dawn of morning be to you as the beginning of life, and every setting sun be to you as its close—then let every one of these short lives leave its sure record of some kindly thing done for others," was used by Miss Nightingale as her New Year's greeting in 1889. It is an epitome of her life and works.]

Appearance, Manner, and Interests in Later Years

OCCASIONALLY Miss Nightingale would be seen standing or moving about in her room; what was then remarked was the grace and dignity of her bearing, though the "willowy figure" which distinguished her in earlier years had now become large. More often she received her visitors in bed or on her couch. What they then observed was the head, the face, the hands. Her head, in girlhood and early womanhood, had been remarked as small. Possibly it had grown somewhat, and something must be put down to the increased size of the face as affecting the appearance; but at any rate her head in later years was certainly large. An Army Surgeon who visited Miss Nightingale frequently in the 'eighties and 'nineties tells me that he was always struck by the massiveness of the head, comparable, he thought, to Mr. Gladstone's. There was an unusually fine rounded form of the fore-part of the head just above where the hair begins. The eyes were not specially remarkable, though there was a suggestion of intellectual keenness in them. The nose was fine and rather prominent; the mouth, small and firm. The hands were small and refined. Every one who saw her felt that he was in the presence of a woman of personality —of marked character, energy, and capacity. As her visitor entered, Miss Nightingale would bend forward from her bed or couch with a smile of welcome; the visitor would be invited to an easy chair beside her, and talk would begin.

In her youth Miss Nightingale was a brilliant talker, as witnesses cited in an earlier chapter have told us. In later years, too, she had flashes of brilliance. Madame Mohl, whose standard was high, wrote to her husband from Lea Hurst in 1873: "Mr. Jowett spent three days here. He is a man of mind; I think he would suit you. He is very fond of flow, which also would suit you. She is here, and her conversation is most nourishing. I would give a great deal for you to be here to enjoy it. She is really eloquent. Yesterday she quite surprised me."[2] But for the most part Miss Nightingale's talk was rather earnest, inquiring, sometimes searching, than sparkling or eloquent. "She is worse than a Royal Commission to answer," said Colonel Yule; "and, in the most gracious,

---

[1]Cook: *Life of Florence Nightingale*, Vol. 2.

[2]*Julius and Mary Mohl*, p. 342.

FLORENCE NIGHTINGALE

charming manner possible, immediately finds out all I don't know."[3] Younger visitors sometimes felt in awe of her; she could flash out a searching question upon a rash generalization as formidably as Mr. Gladstone himself. She was interested in everything except what was trivial. Her intellectual vitality was remarkable; visitors who knew nothing of her special interests or pursuits were yet delighted by the stimulating freshness of her talk. She liked to keep herself *au courant* with all that was going on in the political and learned worlds. The letters to her from more than one Indian Viceroy show that the pleasant gossip

from the lobbies or the Universities, with which she relieved her discourses on drains, was keenly appreciated. If the visitor talked of matters which appealed to her, she was instantly curious of detail.....

Miss Nightingale, except in the few travel-years of her youth, had little enjoyment from nature in its grander or larger aspects, but she knew how to find pleasure in the commoner sights and sounds; in flowers and birds, and in London skies. There was a tree in the garden of Dorchester House where the birds used to gather, and from which they flew to be fed at Miss Nightingale's window. She had studied the dietary of birds as carefully as of hospital patients, and imparted the

[3]Memoirs of Colonel Sir Henry Yule, by his Daughter, prefixed to the 3rd ed. (1903) of his translation of *The Book of Ser Marco Polo*, p. 65.

rudiments of such lore to the "Dicky-Bird Society."[4] In the country she liked to have a view from her bedroom of trees and flowers, and often in the early morning watches she wrote down her observations. Her balcony at Lea Hurst gave her a great deal of pleasure. It is large, being the top of the drawing-room bow; you see a wide stretch of sky from it, and it commands the view described by Mrs. Gaskell.[5] At Claydon she had her pet birds and squirrels, and used to write about them to Sir Harry's grandchildren. She took a great interest in elementary education, and insisted almost as much upon the importance of simple nature studies as upon that of physical training. "On very fine noondays in London," she wrote (Dec. 1888), "when there is nearly as much light as there is in a country dusk, the storm-like effects of the sun peeping out are more like the light streaming from the Glory in Heaven of the old Italian Masters than anything I know. And I wonder whether the poor people see it. And in old days when I walked out of doors, the murky effect at the end of the perspective of a long dull street running E. and W. was a real peep into heaven. I should teach these things in Board Schools to children condemned to live their lives in the streets of London, as I would teach the botany of leaves and trees and flowers to country children." Cheap popular books were much wanted giving account of "the habits, structure, and characters (what they are about, not classification) of plants as living beings"; and of birds treated in like fashion, and not from the point of view of ornithological classification. "I had a lovely little popular

book with woodcuts, published in Calcutta," she wrote,[6] "on the plants of Bengal. The author, an Englishman, offered me to write one on English plants in the same fashion; but one of the most popular and enterprising of all our publishers refused on the ground that it would not tell in Board School examinations and therefore would not pay."

A New Year Letter from Benjamin Jowett to Miss Nightingale in 1879

I cannot let the new year begin without sending my best and kindest wishes for you and for your work: I can only desire that you should go on as you are doing, in your own way. Lessening human suffering and speaking for those who cannot make their voices heard, with less of suffering to yourself, if this, as I fear, be not a necessary condition of the life you have chosen. There was a great deal of romantic feeling about you 23 years ago when you came home from the Crimea (I really believe that you might have been a Duchess if you had played your cards better!). And now you work on in silence, and nobody knows how many lives are saved by your nurses in hospitals (you have introduced a new era in nursing); how many thousand soldiers who would have fallen victims to bad air, bad water, bad drainage and ventilation, are now alive owing to your forethought and diligence; how many natives of India (they might be counted probably by hundreds of thousands) in this generation and in generations to come have been preserved from famine and oppression and the load of debt by the energy of a sick lady who can scarcely rise from her bed. The

[4]Bibliography A, No. 136.
[5]See Vol. I, p. 8.

[6]Letter to the secretary of the Pure Literature Society, March 30, 1891.

world does not know all this or think about it. But I know it and often think about it, and I want you to, so that in the later years of your course you may see (with a side of sorrow) what a blessed life yours is and has been. Is there anything which you could do, or would wish to do, other than you are doing? though you are overtaxed and have a feeling of oppression at the load which rests upon you. I think that the romance, too, which is with the past, did a great deal of good. Like Dr. Pusey, you are a Myth in your own life-time. Do you know that there are thousands of girls about the age of 18 to 23 named after you? As you once said to me "the world has not been unkind." Everybody has heard of you and has a sweet association with your name. It is about 17 years since we first became friends. How can I thank you properly for all your kindness and sympathy—never failing—when you had so many other things to occupy your mind? I have not been able to do so much as you expected of me, and probably never shall be, though I do not give up ambition. But I have been too much distracted by many things; and not strong enough for the place. I shall go on as quietly and industriously as I can. If I ever do much more, it will be chiefly owing to you: your friendship has strengthened and helped me, and never been a source of the least pain or regret. Farewell. May the later years of your life be clearer and happier and more useful than the earlier! If you will believe it, this may be so.

Reminiscences of a Nurse Concerning Her Beloved Chief

I was then Sister of one of the surgical wards at King's College Hospital. It was on a Saturday in February,

about midday, just as I was due to attend the operation cases from my ward, that a one-armed commissionaire appeared at the ward door: "A note for Sister Philippa from Miss Nightingale," he said. The request it contained was characteristic of the writer—decisive, yet kindly. Would I leave in three days' time for service in the Soudan? if so, I must be at her house for instructions on Monday at 8:30 A. M., at Marlborough House to be interviewed by Queen Alexandra (then Princess of Wales) at 11 A. M.; and immediately afterwards at Messrs. Cappers, Gracechurch Street, to be fitted for my war uniform. Would I also breakfast with her on Wednesday, so that she "might check the fit of my uniform, and wish me Godspeed." Months afterwards, when the war was over, and we were quietly chatting over things at Claydon, how she enjoyed hearing the numerous trivial details of that three days' rush! Again and again she would refer to that afternoon when I had to stand by the patient's side in the operating theatre, mechanically waiting on the surgeons, outwardly placid, yet inwardly, as I told her, in a fever of excitement, not so much at the thought of going to the front, as at the fact that I had been chosen by her to follow in her footsteps.

On the Monday above referred to, punctually at half-past eight, I arrived at South Street, wondering what my reception would be, but before ten minutes had passed all wonder and speculation had given place to unbounded admiration and (even at that early acquaintanceship) affection for the warm-hearted old lady who counselled me as a nurse, mothered me as an out-put from her Home, and urged me to spare no point—myself specially—where the soldiers were concerned. "Remember," she said, "when you are far away up-country, possibly the only English woman there, that those men will note and remember your every action, not only as a nurse, but as a woman; your life to them will be as the rings a pebble makes when thrown into a pond—reaching far, reaching wide—each ripple gone beyond your grasp, yet remembered almost to exaggeration by those soldiers lying helpless in their sickness. See that your every word and act is worthy of your profession and your womanhood." Then she asked me to accept an India-rubber travelling bath as "her parting gift to a one-time probationer who had once reminded her that cleanliness was next to Godliness," and in spite of the merry twinkle in her eye as she said this, there were tears of anxious kindness as she added, "God guard you in His safe keeping and make you worthy of His trust—our soldiers."

I saw nothing more of her till Wednesday morning. The troopship in which we were to go out left Tilbury Docks at 11 o'clock, and I was to breakfast with Miss Nightingale at half-past seven. It was rather a rush to manage it, but it was well worth any amount of inconvenience to have that last hour with her, and it was a picture that will always remain above all others in my memory. Propped up in bed, the pillows framing her kindly face with its lace-covered silvery hair, and twinkling eyes. I often think her sense of humour must have been as strong a bond between her and the soldiers as her sympathy was. The coffee, toast, eggs, and honey, "a real English breakfast, dear child," she said, "and it is good to know you will have honestly earned the next one you eat in England." "And suppose I don't return to eat one at all?" I asked. "Well! you will

have earned that too, dear heart," she answered quietly. Who can be surprised that we worshipped our Chief? Other nurses were going out in the same ship as I, and when we entered our cabins we found a bouquet of flowers for each of us, attached to which was "Godspeed from Florence Nightingale."

Six months after, in the glare and heat of an August afternoon, when the Egyptian campaign was a thing of the past, a ship-load of sick and wounded soldiers glided slowly into the docks at Southampton. While I was helping to transfer some of the most serious cases to Netley, a telegram was handed to me. It was from Miss Nightingale: "Am staying at Claydon, cleaners and painters in possession of 10 South Street, but two rooms, Mrs. Neild (the Housekeeper), and a warm welcome are awaiting your arrival there. Use them as long as you wish." On arriving at South Street I found it all just as she had said, and by the first post next day came a letter from Claydon, such a home welcome! It was well worth all the heat and glare of a Soudan summer, all the absence of water, and presence of insects, and the hundred and one other uncomfortable things that flesh is heir to during similar circumstances, to get such a letter of welcome as that. It ended up with "make South Street your headquarters till your work is finished" (there was much detail to complete in connection with the National Aid Society before I could leave London), "and then come to me at Claydon." So after a couple of weeks' work in London, I went to Claydon, and there, during a month's rest in one of the most beautiful of England's country homes, I learned to know and understand Miss Nightingale, to realize what the friendship of a character like hers means. "The essence of Friendship," says Emerson, "is tenderness and trust." No words better describe our Chief than these. . . . .

The last chapter was largely concerned with Miss Nightingale's activity in public affairs and with acquaintanceships which she formed in connection with them. In such affairs she was forcible, clear-sighted, methodical. Sir Bartle Frere, on first making her acquaintance, had said to a friend that it was "a great pleasure to meet such a good man of business as Miss Nightingale." But she was many-sided, and even in her converse with men or women on public affairs she was generally something more than a good "man of business." Much of her influence was due to the fact that so many of those who first saw her as a matter of affairs became her friends, and that to the qualities of a good man of business she added those of a richly sympathetic nature.

This aspect of Miss Nightingale's life and character has already been illustrated sufficiently in the case of her relations with Matrons, Superintendents, and Nurses. It may be discerned clearly enough, too, in the account of her official work with Sidney Herbert and other of her earlier allies. But it was as marked in her later as in her earlier years, and in relation to the men as to the women with whom she was brought into touch. In reading her collection of letters from various doctors and officials of all sorts, I have been struck many times with a quick change of atmosphere. The correspondence begins on a formal note. Her correspondent will be "pleased to make the acquaintance of a lady so justly esteemed," etc., etc. The interview has taken place, or a few letters have passed, and then the note alters. Wives or sons or daughters have been

to see her, or kindly inquiries and messages have been sent, and the correspondence becomes as between old family friends. Young and old alike felt the sympathetic touch of Miss Nightingale's manner.

Relations with Her Family

The affectionate sympathy which Miss Nightingale gave to her friends was not lacking to her relations. In 1889 one of the dearest of them, her "Aunt Mai," had died at the age of 91. Her husband, the "Uncle Sam" of earlier chapters, had died eight years before; and the widow's bereavement seems to have done away with such estrangement as there had been between her and her niece. They resumed their former affectionate correspondence on religious matters, and Miss Nightingale was again the "loving Flo" of earlier years. "Dearest friend," she wrote on the card sent with flowers when her aunt died; "lovely, loving soul; humble mind of high and holy thought."

Miss Nightingale was not one of those persons who keep their tact and kindly consideration for the outside world and think indolent indifference or rough candour good enough for the family circle. I have been told a little anecdote which is instructive in this connection. Miss Irby came into the garden hall at Lea Hurst one day, fresh from an interview with Miss Nightingale. "I must tell you," she said, laughing, to one of Miss Nightingale's younger cousins, "what Florence has just said; it's so like her. She said to me, 'I wonder whether R. remembered to have that branch taken away that fell across the south drive.' I said, 'I will ask her.' 'Oh, no,' said Florence, 'don't ask her that. Ask her *whom* she asked to take the branch away.' " This is only a trifle; but the method of the thing was very characteristic. Miss Nightingale was a diplomatist in small affairs as in great. She was careful not to run a risk of making mischief through intermediaries. She took real trouble to that end, and never seemed to find anything in this sort too much to do. Her influence with every member of her family was used to make relations between them better and more affectionate. With many of the younger generation of her cousins and other kinsfolk she maintained affectionate relations. She regulated her hours very strictly, as we have heard, but she found time, especially in her later years, to see some of these young friends repeatedly. When she did not see them, she liked to be informed of their comings and goings, their doings and prospects, their marriages and belongings. She held in deep affection the memory of Arthur Hugh Clough, and she loved tenderly her cousin, Mr. Shore Smith. She entertained a generous solicitude for Mr. Clough's family; and the family of her cousin, Shore, were especially close to her. A little note to Mrs. Shore Smith—one of hundreds—illustrates incidentally Miss Nightingale's love of flowers and their insect friends:—

10 South Street, *April* 24, 1894. Dearest, I feel so anxious to know how you are. Thank you so much for your beautiful Azaleas which have come out splendidly, and the yellow tulips. The smell of the Azaleas reminds me so of Embley. On a tulip sat a poor little tiny, tiny, pretty little snail of a sort unknown to me. He said: "I was so happy in my garden on my tulip, and I was kidnapped into that horrid box. And whatever am I to do?" So we carried him out and carefully put him among the shrubs in the boxes on the leads (lilacs). But

my opinion is that he is very particular about his diet and that his opinion was that he could find nothing worthy of his acceptance there. He must either have been drowned in the water-spout, or dree'd the penalty of being particular.

The Lesson of Life. (To Norman Bonham Carter.) 10 South Street, August 2 [1895] . . . . .

You will see by the accounts of the General Election how the Conservatives have got in by an enormous majority, and the Liberals are discomfited. But I am an old fogey, and have been at this work for 40 years. And I have always found that the man who has the genius to know how to find details, and the still greater genius of knowing how to apply them will win, and party does not signify at all. My masters[7]—that is, Sir Robert Peel's school, never cared for place, but always worked for both sides alike. I learn the lesson of life from a little kitten of mine, one of two. The old cat comes in and says, very cross, "I didn't ask you in here, I like to have my Missis to myself!" And he runs at them. The bigger and handsomer kitten runs away, but the littler one *stands her ground*, and when the old enemy comes near enough kisses his nose, and makes the peace. That is the lesson of life, to kiss one's enemy's nose, always standing one's ground. I am rather sorry for Lord Salisbury. A majority is always in the wrong.

Attitude toward Law Breakers and Law Enforcers

She had a soft place in her heart even for criminals who despitefully

---

[7]She was writing, it will be observed, on the anniversary of Sidney Herbert's death.

used her. In July, 1892, burglary was committed in her house in South Street. It was in the early morning, and she espied the burglar resting for a moment with his spoils (some of her plate and her maid's money) in a hiding-place behind the house. If her maids or the police or both had been more alert, the malefactor would have been arrested. Her sense for efficiency was outraged, but she relented when the Inspector came to see her. "Perhaps it was just as well that you didn't catch the man," she said with a twinkle, "for I am afraid you don't do them much good when you lock them up." She was fond of the police, and during the Jubilee year admired from her window their handling of the crowds. She noted the long hours; made friends with the Inspector at Grosvenor Gate, and sent supplies of hot tea and cakes for his men.....

In the Army, too, Miss Nightingale continued to take a lively interest, and Sir Douglas Galton was still within—not always instant—call to give her information or advice:—

Miss Nightingale to Sir Douglas Galton, 10 South Street, Nov. 24 (1895).

Oh you Turk, oh you rascal, Sir Douglas, not to tell me that you were in London, not to reward me for my good resolution in not troubling you. I would have asked but few questions, but these called for haste. (i.) Most important: How the troops for Kumassi are to be supplied with water, day and night, fit to drink? Spirit ration only as medicine? Are they to have salt pork and beef? Then about their shoes, stockings, and boots? Are these things now recognized at Head Quarters? Probably I am disquieting myself in vain. Lord Lansdowne is so overwhelmed with amateur schemes

for W. O. reform—not that I am in that line of business now at all; but I do not like to write to him just now. (ii.) Barracks at Newcastle-on-Tyne, depot where 5th Fusiliers are quartered, said to be in an awful state of bad drainage: not denied, but remedy "would cost too much." I know nothing of it personally. "Ladies Sanitary Association" dying to interfere. Sir Thomas Crawford dead, or I should have asked *his* advice. (iii.) We have another Nurse (a Sister of St. Thomas's) going out to India to join the Army Nursing Staff. Three are going out in three ships—they don't know where—each goes alone. (The I. O. sends them out like the famous *pair* of Painted Marmots who came over in *three* ships, on the crust of a two penny loaf which served them for provisions during the voyage.) Mine asks me for an Army Medical Book. Don't misunderstand: the Nurses must not know anything about anything, to be looked well on by the Doctors, whose treatment is, I believe, what it was 40 years ago. But if there is a book which could put her up to things, not excepting the terrible increase of the vicious disease, do recommend it me if you can.

Types of Nurses—Angels and Others

She was deeply interested in a nurse who volunteered for plague-service in India: "The deepest, quietest, most striking person I have seen from our present staff, and so pretty. Not enthusiastic except in the good old original sense: God in us. She is firmly and cautiously determined to go to the Plague." After a series of interviews with nurses and letters from them (1898), Miss Nightingale noted some impressions of types. She valued efficiency, but she deplored a tendency

which she detected to substitute professionalism for heart. Who are the "ministering angels"? she asked. "The Angels are *not* they who go about scattering flowers: any naughty child would like to do that, even any rascal. The Angels are they who, like Nurse or Ward-maid or Scavenger, do disgusting work, removing injury to health or obstacles to recovery, emptying slops, washing patients, etc., for all of which they receive no thanks. These are the Angels.....

Florence Nightingale was by no means a Plaster Saint. She was a woman of strong passions—not overgiven to praise, not quick to forgive; somewhat prone to be censorious, not apt to forget. She was not only a gentle angel of compassion; she was more of a logician than a sentimentalist; she knew that to do good work requires a hard head as well as a soft heart. It was said by Miss Nightingale of a certain great lady that "with the utmost kindness and benevolent intentions she is in consequence of want of practical habits of business nothing but good and bustling, a time-waster and an impediment." Miss Nightingale knew hardly any fault which seemed worse to her in a man than to be unbusiness-like; in a woman, than to be "only enthusiastic." She found no use for "angels without hands." She was essentially a "man of facts" and a "man of action." She had an equal contempt for those who act without knowledge, and for those whose knowledge leads to no useful action. She was herself laborious of detail and scrupulously careful of her premises. "Though I write positively," she once said, "I do not think positively." She weighed every consideration; she sought much competent advice; but when once her decision was taken, she was resolute and masterful — not lightly

turned from her course, impatient of
delay, not very tolerant of opposition.

Something of this spirit appears in
her view of friendship and in the conduct of her affections. Men and
women are placed in the world in
order, she thought, to work for the
betterment of the human race, and
their work should be the supreme consideration. . . . .

It is Miss Nightingale herself who,
unconsciously, has said the last words
on her Life and Character. In prais-
ing one of her fellow-workers, and,
next, in giving counsel to some fel-
low-seekers after good, she used
phrases which may well be applied to
herself:—

"One whose life makes a great difference for all: *all* are better off than
if he had not lived; and this better-
ness is for always, it does not die with
him—that is the true estimate of a
great LIFE."

"Live your life while you have it.
Life is a splendid gift. There is nothing small in it. For the greatest
things grow by God's law out of the
smallest. But to live your life, you
must discipline it. You must not
fritter it away in 'fair purpose, erring
act, inconstant will'; but must make
your thought, your words, your acts
all work to the same end, and that end
not self but God. This is what we
call CHARACTER."

FLORENCE NIGHTINGALE'S CARRIAGE
AT THE SEAT OF WAR 1856

For Thought and Discussion

1. What was Florence Nightingale's New Year's greeting for the
   year 1889?
2. What did Florence Nightingale learn about birds?
3. What was her idea on the value of nature studies to children?
4. Give the quotation from Emerson which was used by a nurse
   to describe Miss Nightingale.
5. Relate the incident of clearing the drive which showed the tact
   Miss Nightingale had with those nearest her.

6. How did her influence affect the members of her family?
7. What did Miss Nightingale do for the snail?
8. What did Miss Nightingale think determined whether or not a man would be elected to office?
9. What was her attitude toward law breakers?
10. How did she describe "ministering angels"?
11. Justify applying the term *versatile* to Miss Nightingale.
12. Explain the term *au courant* as applied to her.
13. Name her dominant trait of character.
14. What remark did she make in regard to what she called "the lesson of life"?
15. How did her life coincide with her definition of a great life and character?
16. Compare the biography of Florence Nightingale with that of Samuel Johnson.

~~

LONDON IN 1685

From *History of England*

THOMAS BABINGTON MACAULAY

[Thomas Babington Macaulay, 1800-1859, was outstanding as a statesman and as a writer. His oratorical eloquence attracted throngs of people when it was known that he was to speak in Parliament. He was a formidable opponent in debate because of his astute reasoning and his prodigious memory, which enabled him to learn verbatim *Paradise Lost* and *Pilgrim's Progress*. To posterity, however, he has been famous as a writer of clear prose, which includes articles, essays, and history, the *History of England*, in five volumes, popular at the time of its publication and also in the present day.]

THE position of London, relatively to the other towns of the empire, was, in the time of Charles the Second, far higher than at present. For at present the population of London is little more than six times the population of Manchester or of Liverpool. In the days of Charles the Second the population of London was more than seventeen times the population of Bristol or of Norwich. It may be doubted whether any other instance can be mentioned of a great kingdom in which the first city was more than seventeen times as large as the second. There is reason to believe that, in 1685, London had been, during about half a century, the most populous capital in Europe. The inhabitants, who are now at least nineteen hundred thousand, were then probably a little more than half a million. London had in the world only one commercial rival, now long outstripped, the mighty and opulent Amsterdam. English writers boasted of the forest of masts and yard arms which covered the river from the bridge to the Tower, and of the incredible sums which were collected at the Custom-House in Thames Street. There is, indeed, no doubt that the trade of the metropolis then bore a far greater proportion than at present to the whole trade of the country; yet to our generation the honest vaunting of our ancestors must appear almost ludicrous. The shipping which they thought incredibly great appears not to have exceeded seventy thousand tons. This was, indeed, then more than a third of the whole tonnage of the kingdom, but is now less than a fourth of the tonnage of Newcastle, and is nearly equaled by the tonnage of the steam vessels of the Thames. The customs of London amounted, in 1685, to about three hundred and thirty thousand pounds a year. In our time the net duty paid annually, at the same place, exceeds ten millions.

Of the metropolis, the City, properly so called, was the most important division. At the time of the Restoration it had been built, for the most part, of wood and plaster; the few bricks that were used were ill baked; the booths where goods were exposed to sale projected far into the streets, and were overhung by the upper stories. A few specimens of this architecture may still be seen in those districts which were not reached by the great fire. That fire had, in a few days, covered a space of little less than a square mile with the ruins of eighty-nine churches and of thirteen thousand houses. But the city had risen again with a celerity which had excited the admiration of neighboring countries. Unfortunately, the old lines of the streets had been to a great extent preserved; and those lines, originally traced in an age when even princesses performed their journeys on horseback, were often too narrow to allow wheeled carriages to pass each other with ease, and were therefore ill adapted for the residence of wealthy persons in an age when a coach and six was a fashionable luxury. The style of building was, how-

ever, far superior to that of the city which had perished. The ordinary material was brick, of much better quality than had formerly been used. On the sites of the ancient parish churches had arisen a multitude of new domes, towers, and spires which bore the mark of the fertile genius of Wren. In every place save one the traces of the great devastation had been completely effaced. But the crowds of workmen, the scaffolds, and the masses of hewn stone were still to be seen where the noblest of Protestant temples was slowly rising on the ruins of the old cathedral of St. Paul.

The houses were not numbered. There would indeed have been little advantage in numbering them; for of the coachmen, chairmen, porters, and errand boys of London, a very small portion could read. It was necessary to use marks which the most ignorant could understand. The shops were therefore distinguished by painted signs, which gave a gay and grotesque aspect to the streets. The walk from Charing Cross to Whitechapel lay through an endless succession of Saracen's Heads, Royal Oaks, Blue Bears, and Golden Lambs, which disappeared when they were no longer required for the direction of the common people.

When the evening closed in, the difficulty and danger of walking about London became serious indeed. The garret windows were opened, and pails were emptied, with little regard to those who were passing below. Falls, bruises, and broken bones were of constant occurrence. For, till the last year of the reign of Charles the Second, most of the streets were left in profound darkness. Thieves and robbers plied their trade with impunity; yet they were hardly so terrible to peaceable citizens as another class of ruffians. It was a favorite amusement of dissolute young gentlemen to swagger by night about the town, breaking windows, upsetting sedans, beating quiet men, and offering rude caresses to pretty women. Several dynasties of these tyrants had, since the Restoration, domineered over the streets. The Muns and Tityre Tus had given place to the Hectors, and the Hectors had been recently succeeded by the Scourers. At a later period arose the Nicker, the Hawcubite, and the yet more dreaded name of Mohawk. The machinery for keeping the peace was utterly contemptible. There was an act of Common Council which provided that more than a thousand watchmen should be constantly on the alert in the city, from sunset to sunrise, and that every inhabitant should take his turn of duty. But the act was negligently executed. Few of those who were summoned left their homes; and those few generally found it more agreeable to tipple in ale-houses than to pace the streets.

It ought to be noticed that, in the last year of the reign of Charles the Second, began a great change in the police of London,—a change which has perhaps added as much to the happiness of the great body of the people as revolutions of much greater fame. An ingenious projector, named Edward Heming, obtained letters patent conveying to him, for a term of years, the exclusive right of lighting up London. He undertook, for a moderate consideration, to place a light before every tenth door, on moonless nights, from Michaelmas to Lady Day, and from six to twelve of the clock. Those who now see the capital all the year round, from dusk to dawn, blazing with a splendor compared with which the illuminations for La Hogue and Blenheim would have looked pale, may perhaps smile to think of Heming's lanterns, which glimmered feebly before one house in ten during a small part of one night in three. But such was not the feeling of his contemporaries. His scheme was enthusiastically applauded and furiously attacked. The friends of improvement extolled him as the greatest of all the benefactors of his city. What, they asked, were the boasted inventions of Archimedes when compared with the achievement of the man who had turned the nocturnal shades into noonday? In spite of these eloquent eulogies, the cause of darkness was not left undefended. There were fools in that age who opposed the introduction of what was called the new light as strenuously as fools in our age have opposed the introduction of vaccination and railroads, as strenuously as the fools of an age anterior to the dawn of history doubtless opposed the introduction of the plough and of alphabetical writing. Many years after the date of Heming's patent, there were extensive districts in which no lamp was seen.

For Thought and Discussion

1. Why were the houses in London not numbered?
2. Why was walking on the street after night unsafe?
3. When and how were the streets first lighted? Why did some people oppose lighting the streets?

THE COFFEE-HOUSES

From *History of England*

THOMAS BABINGTON MACAULAY

THE coffee-house must not be dismissed with a cursory mention. It might indeed, at that time, have been not improperly called a most important political institution. No parliament had sate for years. The municipal council of the city had ceased to speak the sense of the citizens. Public meetings, harangues, resolutions, and the rest of the modern machinery of agitation had not yet come into fashion. Nothing resembling the modern newspaper existed. In such circumstances, the coffee-houses were the chief organs through which the public opinion of the metropolis vented itself.

The first of these establishments had been set up, in the time of the Commonwealth, by a Turkey merchant, who had acquired among the Mahometans a taste for their favorite beverage. The convenience of being able to make appointments in any part of the town, and of being able to pass evenings socially at a very small charge, was so great that the fashion spread fast. Every man of the upper or middle class went daily to his coffee-house to learn the news and to discuss it. Every coffee-house had one or more orators to whose eloquence the crowd listened with admiration, and who soon became, what the journalists of our own time have been called, a fourth estate of the realm. The court had long seen with uneasiness the growth of this new power in the state. An attempt had been made, during Danby's administration, to close the coffee-houses. But men of all parties missed their usual places of resort so much that there was a universal outcry. The

government did not venture, in opposition to a feeling so strong and general, to enforce a regulation of which the legality might well be questioned. Since that time ten years had elapsed, and, during those years, the number and influence of the coffee-houses had been constantly increasing. Foreigners remarked that the coffee-house was that which especially distinguished London from all other cities; that the coffee-house was the Londoner's home, and that those who wished to find a gentleman commonly asked, not whether he lived in Fleet Street or Chancery Lane, but whether he frequented the Grecian or the Rainbow. Nobody was excluded from these places who laid down his penny at the bar. Yet every rank and profession and every shade of religious and political opinion had its own headquarters. There were houses near St. James's Park where fops congregated, their heads and shoulders covered with black or flaxen wigs, not less ample than those which are now worn by the chancellor and by the speaker of the House of Commons. The wig came from Paris, and so did the rest of the fine gentleman's ornaments, his embroidered coat, his fringed gloves, and the tassel which upheld his pantaloons. The conversation was in that dialect which, long after it had ceased to be spoken in fashionable circles, continued, in the mouth of Lord Foppington, to excite the mirth of theatres. The atmosphere was like that of a perfumer's shop. Tobacco in any other form than that of richly scented snuff was held in abomination. If any clown, ignorant of the usages of the house, called for

a pipe, the sneers of the whole assembly and the short answers of the waiters soon convinced him that he had better go somewhere else. Nor, indeed, would he have had far to go. For, in general, the coffee-rooms reeked with tobacco like a guard room; and strangers sometimes expressed their surprise that so many people should leave their own firesides to sit in the midst of eternal fog and stench. Nowhere was the smoking more constant than at Will's. That celebrated house, situated between Covent Garden and Bow Street, was sacred to polite letters. There the talk was about poetical justice and the unities of place and time. There was a faction for Perrault and the moderns, a faction for Boileau and the ancients. One group debated whether *Paradise Lost* ought not to have been in rhyme. To another an envious poetaster demonstrated that *Venice Preserved* ought to have been hooted from the stage. Under no roof was a greater variety of figures to be seen, —earls in stars and garters, clergymen

in cassocks and bands, pert templars, sheepish lads from the universities, translators and index-makers in ragged coats of frieze. The great press was to get near the chair where John Dryden sate. In winter, that chair was always in the warmest nook by the fire; in summer, it stood in the balcony. To bow to him, and to hear his opinion of Racine's last tragedy or of Bossu's treatise on epic poetry, was thought a privilege. A pinch from his snuff-box was an honor sufficient to turn the head of a young enthusiast. There were coffee-houses where the first medical men might be consulted. Doctor John Radcliffe, who, in the year 1685, rose to the largest practice in London, came daily, at the hour when the Exchange was full, from his house in Bow Street, then a fashionable part of the capital, to Garraway's, and was to be found surrounded by surgeons and apothecaries at a particular table. There were Puritan coffee-houses where no oath was heard, and where lank-haired men discussed election and reprobation through their noses; Jew coffee-houses where dark-eyed money-changers from Venice and Amsterdam greeted each other; and Popish coffee-houses where, as good Protestants believed, Jesuits planned, over their cups, another great fire, and cast silver bullets to shoot the king.

These gregarious habits had no small share in forming the character of the Londoner of that age. He was, indeed, a different being from the rustic Englishman. There was not then the intercourse which now exists between the two classes. Only very great men were in the habit of dividing the year between town and country. Few esquires came to the capital thrice in their lives. Nor was it yet the practice of all citizens in easy circumstances to breathe the fresh air of the fields and woods during some weeks of every summer. A cockney, in a rural village, was stared at as much as if he had intruded into a Kraal of Hottentots. On the other hand, when the lord of a Lincoln-shire or Shropshire manor appeared in Fleet Street, he was as easily distinguished from the resident population as a Turk or a Lascar. His dress, his gait, his accent, the manner in which he stared at the shops, stumbled into the gutters, ran against the porters, and stood under the waterspouts marked him out as an excellent subject for the operations of swindlers and banterers. Bullies jostled him into the kennel. Hackney coachmen splashed him from head to foot. Thieves explored with perfect security the huge pockets of his horseman's coat, while he stood entranced by the splendor of the Lord Mayor's show. Money-droppers, sore from the cart's tail, introduced themselves to him, and appeared to him the most honest, friendly gentlemen that he had ever seen. If he asked his way to St. James's, his informants sent him to Mile End. If he went into a shop, he was instantly discerned to be a fit purchaser of everything that nobody else would buy, of second-hand embroidery, copper rings, and watches that would not go. If he rambled into any fashionable coffee-house, he became a mark for the insolent derision of fops and the grave waggery of templars. Enraged and mortified, he soon returned to his mansion, and there, in the homage of his tenants and the conversation of his boon companions, found consolation for the vexations and humiliations which he had undergone. There he once more felt himself a great man; and he saw nothing above him except when at the assizes he took his seat on the bench near the judge or when at the muster of the militia he saluted the lord lieutenant.

For Thought and Discussion

1. Why could the coffee-houses have been called political institutions?
2. Why was Will's coffee-house famous? Who was John Dryden?
3. Could the coffee-house be termed the predecessor of the modern club? Why or why not?
4. What change has taken place in the attitude of the Londoner and the country squire toward each other?

SUNDAY WITH SIR ROGER

From *The Sir Roger De Coverley Papers*

JOSEPH ADDISON

I AM always very well pleased with a country Sunday, and think if keeping holy the seventh day were only a human institution, it would be the best method that could have been thought of for the polishing and civilizing of mankind. It is certain the country people would soon degenerate into a kind of savages and barbarians, were there not such frequent returns of a stated time in which the whole village meet together with their best faces and in their cleanliest habits to converse with one another upon indifferent subjects, hear their duties explained to them, and join together in adoration of the Supreme Being. Sunday clears away the rust of the whole week, not only as it refreshes in their minds the notions of religion, but as it puts both the sexes upon appearing in their most agreeable forms and exerting all such qualities as are apt to give them a figure in the eye of the village. A country fellow distinguishes himself as much in the churchyard as a citizen does upon the Change, the whole parish politics being generally discussed in that place either after sermon or before the bell rings.

My friend Sir Roger, being a good churchman, has beautified the inside of his church with several texts of his own choosing. He has likewise given a handsome pulpit cloth, and railed in the communion table at his own expense. He has often told me that at his coming to his estate he found his parishioners very irregular; and that in order to make them kneel and join in the responses, he gave every one of them a hassock and a Common Prayer Book, and at the same time employed an itinerant singing-master, who goes about the country for that purpose, to instruct them rightly in the tunes of the Psalms; upon which they now very much value themselves, and indeed outdo most of the country churches that I have ever heard.

As Sir Roger is landlord to the whole congregation, he keeps them in very good order and will suffer nobody to sleep in it besides himself; for if by chance he has been surprised into a short nap at sermon, upon recovering out of it he stands up and looks about him and, if he sees anybody else nodding, either wakes them himself or sends his servant to them. Several other of the old knight's particularities break out upon these occasions; sometimes he will be lengthening out a verse in the Singing Psalms half a minute after the rest of the congregation have done with it; sometimes when he is pleased with the matter of his devotion, he pronounces "Amen" three or four times to the same prayer; and sometimes stands up when everybody else is upon their knees to count the congregation or see if any of his tenants are missing.

I was yesterday very much surprised to hear my old friend in the midst of the service calling out to one John Matthews to mind what he was about and not disturb the congregation. This John Matthews, it seems, is remarkable for being an idle fellow, and at that time was kicking his heels for his diversion. This authority of the knight, though exerted in that odd manner which accompanies him in all circumstances of life, has a very good effect upon the parish, who are not polite enough to see anything ridiculous in his behavior; besides that, the general good sense and worthiness of his character make his friends observe these little singularities as foils that rather set off than blemish his good qualities.

As soon as the sermon is finished, nobody presumes to stir till Sir Roger is gone out of the church. The knight walks down from his seat in the chancel between a double row of his tenants, that stand bowing to him on each side, and every now and then inquires how such a one's wife, or mother, or son, or father do, whom he does not see at church—which is understood as a secret reprimand to the person that is absent. The chaplain has often told me that upon a catechising day, when Sir Roger had been pleased with a boy that answers well, he has ordered a Bible to be given him next day for his encouragement, and sometimes accompanies it with a flitch of bacon to his mother. Sir Roger has likewise added five pounds a year to the clerk's place, and that he may encourage the young fellows to make themselves perfect in the church service, has promised upon the death of the present incumbent, who is very old, to bestow it according to merit.

The fair understanding between Sir Roger and his chaplain and their mutual concurrence in doing good is the more remarkable because the very next village is famous for the differences and contentions that rise between the parson and the squire, who live in a perpetual state of war. The parson is always preaching at the squire; and the squire, to be revenged on the parson, never comes to church. The squire has made all his tenants atheists and tithe-stealers; while the parson instructs them every Sunday in the dignity of his order and insinuates to them in almost every sermon that he is a better man than his patron. In short, matters have come to such an extremity that the squire has not said his prayers either in public or private this half year; and that the parson threatens him, if he does not mend his manners, to pray for him in the face of the whole congregation.

Feuds of this nature, though too frequent in the country, are very fatal to the ordinary people; who are so used to be dazzled with riches that they pay as much deference to the understanding of a man of an estate as of a man of learning; and are very hardly brought to regard any truth, how important soever it may be, that is preached to them, when they know there are several men of five hundred a year who do not believe it.

L.

For Thought and Discussion

1. What reasons does Addison give for observing Sunday?
2. What did the country people discuss when they met at church?
3. How did Sir Roger encourage his parishioners to come to church?
4. What incidents illustrate the affection which the people had for Sir Roger?
5. Whose tenants were said to be tithe-stealers? In respect to tithes and atheism how do you account for the difference between these tenants and those of Sir Roger?
6. Contrast "A Sunday with Sir Roger" with "A Now—Of a Cold Day."

Plus Work

Write a letter in which you describe spending a Sunday with Sir Roger.

Joseph Addison 1672-1719

Addison's Pleasant Youth. Born in Wiltshire in 1672, the son of an English clergyman and author, Joseph Addison was reared in an atmosphere of culture and pleasantness. Like his brothers and sisters, he was a gifted child. He attended a number of schools in which he behaved after the manner of a typical, healthy, mischievous boy and at the same time made an enviable record, particularly in the classics. He became so proficient in the writing of Latin verse that he was said to excel all makers of Latin verse after the time of Virgil.

Distinguishing Traits. As a man, Addison was of such unimpeachable character, and so correct and gracious in his manner, and so fluent in diction that he was variously termed a parson in a tye-wig, the most elegant literary figure of his day, and the master of English style. In an age of bitter, cutting satire, he achieved a style noted for quiet humor and kindly ridicule, far more influential and lasting in effect than the brilliant, caustic irony of his contemporaries. By nature he was a close observer of life and an admirer of social virtues and graces. These attributes, together with certain qualities acquired from association with Dick Steele, the impulsive, warm-hearted, rollicking, somewhat weak and heedless but always high-minded Irishman who was his closest friend, made Addison the wisest and sunniest reformer of his time.

The Tattler and The Spectator Papers. Except for his association with Steele, it is doubtful that Addison would have become known as the genial Spectator of Coffee-House fame, the companion of gallant Will Honeycomb, amiable Sir Roger De Coverley, entertaining but idle Will Wimble, and others of those typical characters who make us see vividly the town life and country life described in *The Tatler* and in *The Spectator Papers*.

Poems and Essays. In his own day Addison was given higher acclaim as a poet than as an essayist. First, his poem to Dryden brought him favorable notice; then, the selection, "The Peace of Ryswick," attracted the notice of King William, and Addison was given a pension that enabled him to go abroad "to learn French and diplomacy"; finally, "The Campaign," a poem celebrating the winning of the battle of Blenheim, led to his appointment as Secretary of State, an office from which he retired because of his inability to make speeches.

Today Addison's poems, with the exception of his church hymns, are little known; but his essays with their literary flavor and their graceful, unhurried, conversational style are read with pleasure.

LUCY GRAY

WILLIAM WORDSWORTH

[This ballad-like poem was based
on an actual incident.]

OFT I had heard of Lucy Gray—
   And when I crossed the wild,
I chanced to see at break of day
The solitary child.

No mate, no comrade Lucy knew;   5
She dwelt on a wide moor,
The sweetest thing that ever grew
Beside a human door!

You yet may spy the fawn at play,
The hare upon the green;   10
But the sweet face of Lucy Gray
Will never more be seen.

"Tonight will be a stormy night—
You to the town must go;
And take a lantern, child, to light   15
Your mother through the snow."

"That, father! will I gladly do.
'Tis scarcely afternoon—
The minster-clock has just struck
   two,
And yonder is the moon!"   20

At this the father raised his hook,
And snapped a faggot-band;
He plied his work—and Lucy took
The lantern in her hand.

Not blither is the mountain roe;   25
With many a wanton stroke
Her feet disperse the powdery snow,
That rises up like smoke.

The storm came on before its time;
She wandered up and down;   30
And many a hill did Lucy climb,
But never reached the town.

The wretched parents all that night
Went shouting far and wide;
But there was neither sound nor sight
To serve them for a guide.   36

At daybreak on a hill they stood
That overlooked the moor;
And thence they saw the bridge of
   wood
A furlong from their door.   40

They wept—and, turning homeward,
   cried,
"In heaven we all shall meet!"
—When in the snow the mother spied
The print of Lucy's feet.

Then downward from the steep hill's
   edge   45
They tracked the footmarks small;
And through the broken hawthorn
   hedge
And by the long stone wall.

And then an open field they crossed;
The marks were still the same.   50
They tracked them on, nor ever lost,
And to the bridge they came.

They followed from the snowy bank
Those footmarks, one by one,
Into the middle of the plank;   55
And further there were none!

—Yet some maintain that to this day
She is a living child;
That you may see sweet Lucy Gray
Upon the lonesome wild.   60

O'er rough and smooth she trips
   along,
And never looks behind;
And sings a solitary song
That whistles in the wind.

For Thought and Discussion

1. What is a minster-clock?
2. For what were faggot bands used?
3. The setting for "Lucy Gray" is said to have been near where Wordsworth lived. What impression does the poem give you of the surrounding country?
4. Describe Lucy's disposition.
5. State what seemed to be the attitude of the parents and the poet toward little Lucy.
6. What suggestion is made in the last stanza?
7. What other poem in this section ends in a similar manner?
8. What effect is produced by the ending?

THE SOLITARY REAPER

WILLIAM WORDSWORTH

BEHOLD her, single in the field,
  Yon solitary highland lass!
Reaping and singing by herself;
Stop here, or gently pass!
Alone she cuts and binds the grain,
And sings a melancholy strain;   6
O listen! for the vale profound
Is overflowing with the sound.

No nightingale did ever chaunt
More welcome notes to weary bands
Of travelers in some shady haunt,
Among Arabian sands;   12
A voice so thrilling ne'er was heard
In springtime from the cuckoo-bird,
Breaking the silence of the seas   15
Among the farthest Hebrides.

Will no one tell me what she sings?
Perhaps the plaintive numbers flow
For old, unhappy, far-off things,
And battles long ago;   20
Or is it some more humble lay,
Familiar matter of today?
Some natural sorrow, loss, or pain,
That has been, and may be again!

Whate'er the theme, the maiden sang
As if her song could have no ending;
I saw her singing at her work,   27
And o'er the sickle bending—
I listened, motionless and still;
And, as I mounted up the hill,   30
The music in my heart I bore
Long after it was heard no more.

For Thought and Discussion

1. Why was Wordsworth so attracted by this girl that he wrote about her?
2. Recall a similar experience of your own which left with you long afterwards a vivid impression of a stranger.
3. You will more fully appreciate the literary significance of Wordsworth, the outstanding writer of the nineteenth century, after reading "The Age of Romanticism."

Plus Work

Read Dorothy Wordsworth's *Journal* and report upon her influence upon the poet.

WILLIAM WORDSWORTH

WILLIAM WORDSWORTH[1] 1770-1850

Wordsworth, the Boy. As a small boy Wordsworth was vigorous, violent-tempered, and somewhat moody—so much so, in fact, that his mother was greatly concerned about his future. She predicted for him a life out of the ordinary, one either very bad or very good. Mrs. Wordsworth died when William was but eight

---

[1]Wordsworth (Words' worth), words rhymes with birds.

years old, and his father lived only a few years longer. Both, however, were able to recognize signs of their son's genius, and the father encouraged William in his poetic tendencies by having him memorize long passages from the great English poets. Because of his parents' influence and that of his sister Dorothy, together with the wise training he received at Hawkshead, where he was sent to school after his mother's death, William soon outgrew much of his moodiness. He enjoyed the many sports at Hawkshead, but being of an unsocial disposition, he did not care particularly for his companions. DeQuincy says of him at a later period: "I do not conceive that Wordsworth could have been an amiable boy; he was austere and unsocial, I have reason to think, in his habits, not generous and not self-denying. I am pretty certain that no consideration would have induced Wordsworth to burden himself with a lady's parasol, reticule, or anything exacting trouble and attention. Mighty must be the danger which would induce him to lead her horse by the bridle. Nor would he, without some demur, stop to offer her his hand over a stile. Freedom—unlimited, careless, insolent freedom—unoccupied possession of his own arms—absolute control over his own legs and motions—these have always been so essential to his comfort that in any case where they were likely to become questionable, he would have declined to make one of the party." Another writer once affirmed that Wordsworth could well have dispensed with books, but that conclusion may be questioned. Wordsworth always enjoyed reading; sometimes he so lost himself in that pleasure that he forgot even the joy of fishing, a sport of which he was quite fond.

University Life and Travels. Wordsworth's uncles sent him to St. John's College at Cambridge, from which he was graduated in 1791 with no special distinction. Save for an interest in sports, his study during the years of his college life was centered on poetry and mathematics. While on a trip abroad he became intensely interested in the French Revolution and might have been guillotined along with the leaders of the Girondists, with whom he sympathized, had not his relatives cut off his zeal for the revolutionary cause by withholding his allowance, thus hastening his return to England.

His Family and His Friends. Many lines in the biographical poem, "The Prelude," indicate Wordsworth's love for his parents, and, though after the death of his father and his mother, the five children of the family were placed in different homes, they, too, were closely knit in their affections. All of them won some measure of success in their chosen fields. One brother was a solicitor, one a churchman, who came to be master of Trinity College, Cambridge, and one was in the service of the East India Company. So much did the poet love and respect the last-mentioned brother that in a poem, "The Happy Warrior," he gave to his hero characteristics which he attributed, and probably justly so, to this brother.

His uncles, especially during the days when William could not decide upon a vocation, were somewhat mistrustful of him—not so his sister Dorothy. Her name means *gift of God* and a veritable *gift of God* she was to the boy, to the man, and to the poet Wordsworth. This little bird-like, gypsy-skinned woman, whose eye caught every tone of color, whether soft or glowing, and whose ears were attuned to every murmur of stream and breeze, was, like nature itself, a source of constant inspiration to her brother. She had a remarkable intellect and was as keenly sensitive to humanity as she was responsive to nature. Not once, but often, "the long remembered beggar" was her guest.   She had such unbounded energy that she never seemed to tire of accompanying her brother on his endless walking journeys, and she made it a part of her joy to enter his notes and copy his poems for him.   Though not a good conversationalist, Dorothy, a close observer, was fluent in written speech; for this reason it was to her notes that her brother often betook himself when his own vivid memory needed refreshing.

Wordsworth had few close friends, but those few were of the truest fibre. They gave unto him without stint. A friend made possible for him his chosen work; a friend gave direction to his genius. The first friend was Rawley Calvert, whom the poet nursed through a fatal siege of consumption. Out of gratitude Calvert left Wordsworth a few hundred pounds with the request that he devote his life to poetry. The second friend, a close companion for many years, was Samuel Taylor Coleridge, with whom Wordsworth collaborated in writing *Lyrical Ballads*, a publication which established a new era in the development of poetry.

A Pen Picture of the Poet. The third friend, Thomas De-Quincy, who was an almost worshipful admirer of Wordsworth, in his delightful sketches of the Lake Poets expressed himself as being astonished to note in a portrait of Milton an amazing likeness to Wordsworth. He pointed out, too, the fact that Haydon in his masterpiece, "Christ's Entry into Jerusalem," introduces Wordsworth as one of the disciples, while he depicts Voltaire[1] as a sneering Jewish Elder. DeQuincy says, however, that on the whole Wordsworth was far from prepossessing in either features or form. According to him the massive pile of his friend's forehead was out of proportion to his chin, his chest was much too narrow for a walker, and a sculptor would have complained of the contour of his limbs.   In his opinion, Wordsworth's eyes, which radiated a spiritual "light such as never glowed on land or sea," were his best features.

Dove Cottage at Grasmere. In 1799 Wordsworth and Dorothy moved to Dove Cottage at Grasmere and for thirteen years made their home in the cottage destined to become the shrine of the Lake Region. It was here that the poet wrote his best poems. Many of these reflect the serene loveliness of the lakes and the rugged beauty of the hills surrounding the little grey stone cottage at Gras-

---

[1]Voltaire, a French philosopher and author.

mere. Truly, Wordsworth continually looked toward the hills from whence came his strength.

His Happy Marriage. In 1802 Wordsworth married his cousin and childhood playmate, Mary Hutchinson, and their marriage was ideally happy. The world marvels that one man should have been so blessed with the devotion of two women, a sister and a wife, both of whom made his happiness their one aim. Though Wordsworth was notably lacking the domestic graces of a husband and a father, his wife seemed unaware of his failing. Because of her own tranquil sweetness and sunny radiance of manner she richly deserved the tribute paid to her by Wordsworth in "She Was a Phantom of Delight."

His Belated Recognition. During his long lifetime of eighty years Wordsworth devoted himself almost exclusively to poetry, but not until the evening twilight of his life did he reap the reward of popular favor. In 1830 the foremost university of England acclaimed his the greatest name since Milton. In 1843, when the poet was seventy-three, the honor of the laureateship was conferred upon him.

His Resting Place in Death. Wordsworth's body, together with that of his wife, lies as he requested between the grave of his sister and that of his daughter Dora in the churchyard at Grasmere. There he lived and loved and sang; there he lies under the yew trees which he himself planted.

MY LAST DUCHESS

FERRARA

ROBERT BROWNING

[Not even the best movie-tones of the present day can delineate character better than does this fifty-six line portrait of the haughty Duke of Ferrara. In this dramatic monologue the lips, the suggested glances, and the gestures of the tyrant connoisseur speak forth his own cruel, cultivated, and egotistical nature. And what a foil his pride-locked hardness is for the sincerity, charm, and responsive kindness of his wife.

The Duchess and Frà Pandolf (frä pän' dolf), the portrait, the sculptor, and the bronze Neptune are creations of the poet. The Duke, too, is probably a creation of his imagination, but his character is typical of the men of the House of Este, who were among the worst and yet the most accomplished rulers of the Italian Renascence. Ferrara, the scene of the poem, is not far from Vènice.]

THAT'S my last Duchess painted
    on the wall,
Looking as if she were alive. I call
That piece a wonder, now. Frà Pandolf's hands
Worked busily a day, and there she stands.
Will't please you sit and look at her?
    I said   5

"Frà Pandolf" by design, for never read
Strangers like you that pictured countenance,
The depth and passion of its earnest glance,
But to myself they turned (since none puts by
The curtain I have drawn for you, but I)   10
And seemed as they would ask me, if they durst,
How such a glance came there; so, not the first
Are you to turn and ask thus. Sir, 'twas not
Her husband's presence only, called that spot
Of joy into the Duchess' cheek; perhaps   15
Frà Pandolf chanced to say, "Her mantle laps
Over my lady's wrist too much," or "Paint
Must never hope to reproduce the faint

Half-flush that dies along her throat." Such stuff
Was courtesy, she thought, and cause enough   20
For calling up that spot of joy. She had
A heart—how shall I say?—too soon made glad,
Too easily impressed; she liked what-e'er
She looked on, and her looks went everywhere.
Sir, 'twas all one! My favor at her breast,   25
The dropping of the daylight in the West,
The bough of cherries some officious fool
Broke in the orchard for her, the white mule
She rode with round the terrace—all and each
Would draw from her alike the approving speech,   30
Or blush, at least. She thanked men—good!—but thanked

Somehow—I know not how—as if she ranked
My gift of a nine-hundred-years-old name
With anybody's gift. Who'd stoop to blame
This sort of trifling? Even had you skill ³⁵
In speech—(which I have not)—to make your will
Quite clear to such an one, and say, "Just this
Or that in you disgusts me; here you miss,
Or there exceed the mark"—and if she let
Herself be lessoned so, nor plainly set
Her wits to yours, forsooth, and made excuse, ⁴¹
—E'en then would be some stooping; and I choose
Never to stoop. Oh, sir, she smiled, no doubt,
Whene'er I passed her; but who passed without
Much the same smile? This grew; I gave commands; ⁴⁵
Then all smiles stopped together. There she stands
As if alive. Will't please you rise? We'll meet
The company below, then. I repeat,
The Count your master's known munificence
Is ample warrant that no just pretense
Of mine for dowry will be disallowed; ⁵¹
Though his fair daughter's self, as I avowed
At starting, is my object. Nay, we'll go
Together down, sir. Notice Neptune, though,
Taming a sea-horse, thought a rarity,
Which Claus of Innsbruck cast in bronze for me!

For Thought and Discussion

1. What is happening at the beginning of the poem?
2. Who is the speaker and whom is he addressing?
3. *Frà* is the Latin contraction for *frater*, brother, used as a title of respect for monks, many of whom were artists. Why do you suppose the Duke chose a monk as the artist to paint his wife's picture?
4. What terms do you think you would have to use, were you describing a picture of the Duke rather than one of his wife?
5. Did the Duke have an artist's or a husband's appreciation for his wife's portrait? Justify your answer.
6. How do you think the Duke wanted his wife to regard him? Justify your answer.
7. According to his standards what adverse criticism did his wife deserve? Do you agree with him?
8. What do you surmise were the commands given about his wife?
9. What did the Duke avow as his reason for wishing to marry the count's daughter?
10. How do you suppose the envoy regarded the Duke?
11. What interests of the Duke are revealed in the poem?
12. Read the explanation of the dramatic monologue as given in the section "Types of Literature." Can you explain why this poem is termed a dramatic monologue?

ROBERT BROWNING

(From a painting by his son)

Robert Browning 1812-1899

Master Robert Browning. "Handsome, vigorous, fearless"— these are the adjectives which were applied to young Master Robert Browning, and the record further states that his mother could keep him quiet only by telling him stories. His constant activity often led him into mischief, always motivated and never malicious, but destructive nevertheless. When a very small lisper, he was found one day burning a handsome piece of lace, his reason being "a pretty baze (pretty blaze), Mama."

Education at Home and Abroad. Partly to help a gentlewoman in reduced circumstances and partly, no doubt, to give his family a rest, Robert was sent at a very young age to a day school, where it is said, he learned so rapidly that the fond parents of the less talented and less studious children became jealous of his progress, and he, to save the teacher embarrassment, was withdrawn from school. After that he was enrolled in the Misses Macready's school and still later in their brother's preparatory school, where he remained until he was fourteen. He went for a short time to London University and later traveled in Russia. He said that Italy was his real university. As a youth Browning was allowed to study what and how he pleased. Those who would use him as an example of the effectiveness of the elective system, however, should be reminded that Browning was fond of study and that from his own desire, or perhaps because of encouragement of which he was not conscious, he made a well-balanced choice of studies, including among other subjects, history, English, Latin, music, art, fencing, boxing, dancing, and riding. In preparation for his chosen profession of literature it is said that he read and "digested" the whole of Johnson's dictionary. Considering this study of the dictionary and the fact that his father, who was a fluent Latin scholar and also a master of verse forms, taught him from babyhood English words and Latin declensions by means of putting them into rhyme, it is no wonder that Browning had an extraordinary command both of words and of verse forms.

A Happy Family. Browning was born May 7, 1812, and one might whimsically affirm that all the good fairies were present at his christening and that naught but good fortune was bestowed upon him. A student of eugenics could truthfully assert that few children are blessed with a combination of heredity and environment so favorable as that with which he was blessed. His mother was a cultured scholar and gentlewoman, the daughter of a German merchant and shipowner who had settled in Scotland; his father, typically British, though with a Creole strain, was, as were his forbears, engaged in the banking business for a livelihood but in literary and artistic pursuits for pleasure.

The devotion which the Browning family had for one another was remarkable. Many delightful stories are told of Browning and of his sister and of their kindness to their many pets. Browning had a deep affection for his mother. According to biographers it was his habit as long as he remained under the parental roof to bid his mother goodnight even when it was late enough to admit himself with a latchkey. He did this not from a sense of compulsion or duty but because of his very close regard for her. His mother was a very devout woman, and her influence upon his spiritual development was great. As for the relationship between Browning and his father, few parents and sons have been bound together by closer bonds of affection. Very often during the poet's youth and even after his return from Italy, he consulted his father about various phases of his work, and never did the critical judgment of that cultured gentleman fail his son.

Browning's Romance. In 1846 Browning eloped with Elizabeth Barrett, a poet whose fame at that time was greater than his own. Without question their romance is one of the most ideal love stories of all time. One biographer spoke of it as having the wonder and beauty of a medieval romance. After their marriage they spent fifteen radiant years in Italy. The Browning home, first at Pisa and later at Florence, was a Mecca of delight for the literary people of the time, and many selections written by contemporary writers recount interesting events of those years.

After Mrs. Browning's death in 1861 Browning took his young son back to England and thereafter spent part of his time in his own land and part in his adopted land, Italy.

Browning's Forte and His Challenges. Browning's *The Ring and the Book* and his other long selections indicate clearly that his forte is the interpretation of the soul, but while the soul studies found in these longer poems will probably remain unexcelled, it is to his shorter dramatic monologues that Browning owes his enduring and increasing fame. His character analyses include men of all ages and all lands, all professions and all stages of life. None save Shakespeare approaches him in range of characterization.

The charge of obscurity is sometimes brought against Browning. Much of his so-called obscurity, however, is not obscurity at all. As Carlyle puts it, "It is not the dark place but the dim eye that hinders." No other writer so challenges his reader's utmost ability to think as does Browning. Both as a small boy and as a man he was intolerant of mental laziness. He said he never designedly tried to write to puzzle people, but that he did not offer his works as a substitute for such light entertainment as afternoon games or after-dinner cigars. Browning's works are a challenge to right thinking and to triumphant living.

Honored at Home and Abroad. England honors Browning as one of her greatest poets. His body lies in Westminster Abbey. Italy, too, honors her foster child. On the walls of the house in which he died there is a tablet bearing this two-line inscription from his poem, "De Gustibus":

"Open my heart and you will see
Graved inside of it, 'Italy.' "

Though in life Browning liked to join with mingling crowds of people, one somehow feels that had he been given his preference, he would have chosen for his final resting place not the great cathedral, where thronging thousands, some curious, some reverent, pass by his tomb daily, but a quiet spot beside the grave of his wife in the little cemetery at Florence.

THE DESERTED VILLAGE

OLIVER GOLDSMITH

SWEET Auburn! loveliest village
   of the plain,
Where health and plenty cheered the
   laboring swain[1];
Where smiling spring its earliest visit
   paid,
And parting summer's lingering
   blooms delayed;
Dear lovely bowers of innocence and
   ease,   5
Seats of my youth, when every sport
   could please,
How often have I loitered o'er thy
   green,
Where humble happiness endeared
   each scene;
How often have I paused on every
   charm,
The sheltered cot,[2] the cultivated
   farm,   10
The never-failing brook, the busy
   mill,
The decent church that topped the
   neighboring hill,
The hawthorn bush, with seats beneath the shade,
For talking age and whispering lovers
   made!
How often have I blessed the coming
   day,   15
When toil remitting lent its turn to
   play,

And all the village train, from labor
   free,
Led up their sports beneath the
   spreading tree;
While many a pastime circled in the
   shade,
The young contending as the old surveyed;   20
And many a gambol frolicked o'er the
   ground,
And sleights of art and feats of
   strength went round;
And still, as each repeated pleasure
   tired,
Succeeding sports the mirthful band
   inspired;
The dancing pair that simply sought
   renown   25
By holding out to tire each other
   down;
The swain mistrustless of his smutted
   face,
While secret laughter tittered round
   the place;
The bashful virgin's sidelong looks of
   love,
The matron's glance that would those
   looks reprove.   30
These were thy charms, sweet village!
   sports like these,
With sweet succession, taught e'en toil
   to please;
These round thy bowers their cheerful influence shed;

---

[1] swain, a country gallant.
[2] cot, a small cottage or hut.

These were thy charms—but all these charms are fled.

Sweet smiling village, loveliest of the lawn,   35
Thy sports are fled, and all thy charms withdrawn;
Amidst thy bowers the tyrant's hand is seen,
And desolation saddens all thy green;
One only master grasps the whole domain,
And half a tillage stints thy smiling plain.   40
No more thy glassy brook reflects the day,
But choked with sedges works its weedy way;
Along thy glades, a solitary guest,
The hollow-sounding bittern guards its nest;
Amidst thy desert walks the lapwing flies,   45
And tires their echoes with unvaried cries.
Sunk are thy bowers in shapeless ruin all,

And the long grass o'ertops the moldering wall;
And trembling, shrinking from the spoiler's hand,
Far, far away thy children leave the land.   50

Ill fares the land, to hastening ills a prey,
Where wealth accumulates, and men decay;
Princes and lords may flourish, or may fade;
A breath can make them, as a breath has made;
But a bold peasantry, their country's pride,   55
When once destroyed, can never be supplied.

A time there was, ere England's griefs began,
When every rood of ground maintained its man;
For him light labor spread her wholesome store,
Just gave what life required, but gave no more;   60

His best companions, innocence and
    health,
And his best riches, ignorance of
    wealth.

But times are altered; trade's un-
    feeling train
Usurp the land and dispossess the
    swain;
Along the lawn, where scattered ham-
    lets rose,   65
Unwieldy wealth and cumbrous pomp
    repose,
And every want to luxury allied,
And every pang that folly pays to
    pride.
Those gentle hours that plenty bade
    to bloom,
Those calm desires that asked but
    little room,   70
Those healthful sports that graced the
    peaceful scene,
Lived in each look and brightened all
    the green;
These, far departing, seek a kinder
    shore,
And rural mirth and manners are no
    more.

Sweet Auburn! parent of the bliss-
    ful hour,   75
Thy glades forlorn confess the ty-
    rant's power.
Here, as I take my solitary rounds
Amidst thy tangling walks and ruined
    grounds,
And, many a year elapsed, return to
    view
Where once the cottage stood, the
    hawthorn grew,   80
Remembrance wakes with all her
    busy train,
Swells at my breast, and turns the
    past to pain.

In all my wanderings round this
    world of care;
In all my griefs—and God has given
    my share—

I still had hopes, my latest hours to
    crown,   85
Amidst these humble bowers to lay
    me down;
To husband out life's taper at the
    close,
And keep the flame from wasting, by
    repose.
I still had hopes, for pride attends us
    still,
Amidst the swains to show my book-
    learned skill,   90
Around my fire an evening group to
    draw,
And tell of all I felt, and all I saw;
And as a hare whom hounds and
    horns pursue,
Pants to the place from whence at
    first she flew,
I still had hopes, my long vexations
    past,   95
Here to return—and die at home at
    last.

O blessed retirement, friend to
    life's decline,
Retreats from care, that never must
    be mine,
How happy he who crowns in shades
    like these
A youth of labor with an age of ease;
Who quits a world where strong
    temptations try,   101
And, since 'tis hard to combat, learns
    to fly!
For him no wretches, born to work
    and weep,
Explore the mine, or tempt the dan-
    gerous deep;
No surly porter stands, in guilty
    state,   105
To spurn imploring famine from the
    gate;
But on he moves to meet his latter
    end,
Angels around befriending virtue's
    friend;
Bends to the grave with unperceived
    decay,

While resignation gently slopes the
. way;   110
And, all his prospects brightening to
the last,
His heaven commences ere the world
be past.

Sweet was the sound, when oft at
evening's close,
Up yonder hill the village murmur
rose.
There, as I passed with careless steps
and slow,   115
The mingling notes came softened
from below;
The swain responsive as the milk-maid
sung,
The sober herd that lowed to meet
their young,
The noisy geese that gabbled o'er the
pool,
The playful children just let loose
from school,   120
The watchdog's voice that bayed the
whispering wind,
And the loud laugh that spoke the
vacant mind;
These all in sweet confusion sought
the shade,
And filled each pause the nightingale
had made.
But now the sounds of population
fail,   125
No cheerful murmurs fluctuate in the
gale,
No busy steps the grass-grown foot-
way tread,
But all the bloomy flush of life is
fled;
All but yon widowed, solitary thing,
That feebly bends beside the plashy
spring;.   130
She, wretched matron, forced in age,
for bread,
To strip the brook with mantling
cresses spread,
To pick her wintry fagot from the
thorn,

To seek her nightly shed, and weep
till morn—
She only left of all the harmless
train,   135
The sad historian of the pensive plain.

Near yonder copse, where once the
garden smiled,
And still where many a garden flower
grows wild;
There, where a few torn shrubs the
place disclose,
The village preacher's modest mansion
rose.   140
A man he was to all the country dear,
And passing rich with forty pounds a
year;
Remote from towns he ran his godly
race,
Nor e'er had changed, nor wished to
change, his place;
Unskillful he to fawn, or seek for
power,   145
By doctrines fashioned to the varying
hour;
Far other aims his heart had learned
to prize,
More bent to raise the wretched than
to rise.
His house was known to all the va-
grant train;
He chid their wanderings, but re-
lieved their pain;   150
The long-remembered beggar was his
guest,
Whose beard descending swept his
aged breast;
The ruined spendthrift, now no
longer proud,
Claimed kindred there, and had his
claims allowed;
The broken soldier kindly bade to
stay,   155
Sat by his fire, and talked the night
away,
Wept o'er his wounds, or, tales of
sorrow done,
Shouldered his crutch, and showed
how fields were won.

Pleased with his guests, the good man
    learned to glow,
And quite forgot their vices in their
    woe;   160
Careless their merits or their faults
    to scan,
His pity gave ere charity began.

    Thus to relieve the wretched was
    his pride,
And e'en his failings leaned to virtue's
    side;
But in his duty prompt at every
    call,   165
He watched and wept, he prayed and
    felt for all;
And, as a bird each fond endearment
    tries
To tempt its new-fledged offspring to
    the skies
He tried each art, reproved each dull
    delay,
Allured to brighter worlds, and led
    the way.   170

    Beside the bed where parting life
    was laid,
And sorrow, guilt, and pain by turns
    dismayed,
The reverend champion stood. At his
    control
Despair and anguish fled the strug-
    gling soul;
Comfort came down the trembling
    wretch to raise,   175
And his last faltering accents whis-
    pered praise.

    At church, with meek and un-
    affected grace,
His looks adorned the venerable place;
Truth from his lips prevailed with
    double sway,
And fools, who came to scoff, re-
    mained to pray.   180
The service past, around the pious
    man,
With steady zeal, each honest rustic
    ran;

Even children followed, with endear-
    ing wile,
And plucked his gown, to share the
    good man's smile.
His ready smile a parent's warmth
    expressed,   185
Their welfare pleased him, and their
    cares distressed;
To them his heart, his love, his griefs
    were given,
But all his serious thoughts had rest
    in heaven—
As some tall cliff that lifts its awful
    form,
Swells from the vale, and midway
    leaves the storm,   190
Though round its breast the rolling
    clouds are spread,
Eternal sunshine settles on its head.

    Beside yon straggling fence that
    skirts the way,
With blossomed furze³ unprofitably
    gay,
There, in his noisy mansion, skilled
    to rule,   195
The village master taught his little
    school.
A man severe he was, and stern to
    view;
I knew him well, and every truant
    knew;
Well had the boding tremblers learned
    to trace
The day's disasters in his morning
    face;   200
Full well they laughed with counter-
    feited glee
At all his jokes, for many a joke had
    he;
Full well the busy whisper, circling
    round,
Conveyed the dismal tidings when he
    frowned.
Yet he was kind, or if severe in
    aught,   205

---

³*furze*, an evergreen shrub often
used for fuel and fodder.

The love he bore to learning was in fault.
The village all declared how much he knew;
'Twas certain he could write and cipher too;
Lands he could measure, terms and tides presage,
And even the story ran that he could gauge. 210
In arguing, too, the parson owned his skill,
For, even though vanquished, he could argue still;
While words of learned length and thundering sound
Amazed the gazing rustics ranged around;
And still they gazed, and still the wonder grew, 215
That one small head should carry all he knew.

But past is all his fame. The very spot
Where many a time he triumphed, is forgot.
Near yonder thorn that lifts its head on high,
Where once the signpost caught the passing eye, 220
Low lies that house where nut-brown draughts inspired,
Where graybeard mirth and smiling toil retired,
Where village statesmen talked with looks profound,
And news much older than their ale went round.
Imagination fondly stoops to trace 225
The parlor splendors of that festive place;
The whitewashed wall, the nicely sanded floor,
The varnished clock that clicked behind the door;
The chest contrived a double debt to pay,

A bed by night, a chest of drawers by day, 230
The pictures placed for ornament and use,
The twelve good rules, the royal game of goose;
The hearth, except when winter chilled the day,
With aspen boughs, and flowers and fennel, gay;
While broken teacups, wisely kept for show, 235
Ranged o'er the chimney, glistened in a row.

Vain transitory splendors! Could not all
Reprieve the tottering mansion from its fall!
Obscure it sinks, nor shall it more impart
An hour's importance to the poor man's heart. 240
Thither no more the peasant shall repair
To sweet oblivion of his daily care;
No more the farmer's news, the barber's tale,
No more the woodman's ballad shall prevail;
No more the smith his dusky brow shall clear, 245
Relax his ponderous strength, and lean to hear;
The host himself no longer shall be found
Careful to see the mantling bliss go round;
Nor the coy maid, half willing to be pressed,
Shall kiss the cup to pass it to the rest. 250

Yes! let the rich deride, the proud disdain,
These simple blessings of the lowly train;
To me more dear, congenial to my heart,

One native charm, than all the gloss
of art:
Spontaneous joys, where nature has
its play,   255
The soul adopts, and owns their first-
born sway.
Lightly they frolic o'er the vacant
mind,
Unenvied, unmolested, unconfined.
But the long pomp, the midnight
masquerade,
With all the freaks of wanton wealth
arrayed,   260
In these, ere triflers half their wish
obtain,
The toiling pleasure sickens into pain;
And, even while fashion's brightest
arts decoy,
The heart distrusting asks if this be
joy.

Ye friends to truth, ye statesmen
who survey   265
The rich man's joys increase, the
poor's decay,
Tis yours to judge how wide the
limits stand
Between a splendid and a happy land.
Proud swells the tide with loads of
freighted ore,
And shouting Folly hails them from
her shore;   270
Hoards even beyond the miser's wish
abound,
And rich men flock from all the
world around.
Yet count our gains. This wealth is
but a name
That leaves our useful products still
the same.
Not so the loss. The man of wealth
and pride   275
Takes up a space that many poor supplied;
Space for his lake, his park's extended
bounds,
Space for his horses, equipage, and
hounds;

The robe that wraps his limbs in
silken sloth
Has robbed the neighboring fields of
half their growth;   280
His seat, where solitary sports are
seen,
Indignant spurns the cottage from
the green;
Around the world each needful product flies,
For all the luxuries the world supplies;
While thus the land adorned for
pleasure, all   285
In barren splendor feebly waits the
fall.

As some fair female, unadorned
and plain,
Secure to please while youth confirms
her reign,
Slights every borrowed charm that
dress supplies,
Nor shares with art the triumph of
her eyes;   290
But when those charms are past, for
charms are frail,
When time advances, and when lovers
fail,
She then shines forth, solicitous to
bless,
In all the glaring impotence of dress—
Thus fares the land by luxury be-
trayed,   295
In nature's simplest charms at first
arrayed,
But verging to decline, its splendors
rise,
Its vistas strike, its palaces surprise;
While, scourged by famine, from
the smiling land
The mournful peasant leads his
humble band;   300
And while he sinks, without one arm
to save,
The country blooms—a garden and
a grave!

Where then, ah! where shall poverty reside,
To escape the pressure of contiguous pride?
If to some common's fenceless limits strayed   305
He drives his flock to pick the scanty blade,
Those fenceless fields the sons of wealth divide,
And even the bare-worn common is denied.

If to the city sped—what waits him there?
To see profusion that he must not share;   310
To see ten thousand baneful arts combined
To pamper luxury, and thin mankind;
To see those joys the sons of pleasure know,
Extorted from his fellow-creature's woe.
Here while the courtier glitters in brocade,   315
There the pale artist plies the sickly trade;
Here while the proud their long-drawn pomps display,
There the black gibbet glooms beside the way.
The dome where pleasure holds her midnight reign,
Here, richly decked, admits the gorgeous train;   320
Tumultuous grandeur crowds the blazing square,
The rattling chariots clash, the torches glare.
Sure scenes like these no troubles e'er annoy!
Sure these denote one universal joy!
Are these thy serious thoughts?—Ah, turn thine eyes   325
Where the poor houseless shivering female lies.

She once, perhaps, in village plenty blessed,
Has wept at tales of innocence distressed;
Her modest looks the cottage might adorn,
Sweet as the primrose peeps beneath the thorn;   330
Now lost to all—her friends, her virtue, fled—
Near her betrayer's door she lays her head,
And, pinched with cold, and shrinking from the shower,
With heavy heart deplores that luckless hour,
When idly first, ambitious of the town,   335
She left her wheel, and robes of country brown.

Do thine, sweet Auburn, thine, the loveliest train,
Do thy fair tribes participate her pain?
Even now, perhaps, by cold and hunger led,
At proud men's doors they ask a little bread!   340

Ah, no! To distant climes,[4] a dreary scene,
Where half the convex world intrudes between,
Through torrid tracts with fainting steps they go,
Where wild Altama[5] murmurs to their woe.
Far different there from all that charmed before   345
The various terrors of that horrid shore;
Those blazing suns that dart a downward ray,
And fiercely shed intolerable day;

---

[4]*distant climes,* America probably.
[5]*Altama,* Altamaha, a river in Georgia.

Those matted woods where birds forget to sing;
But silent bats in drowsy clusters
 cling; 350
Those poisonous fields with rank
 luxuriance crowned,
Where the dark scorpion gathers
 death around;
Where at each step the stranger fears
 to wake
The rattling terrors of the vengeful
 snake;
Where crouching tigers wait their
 hapless prey, 355
And savage men more murderous still
 than they;
While oft in whirls the mad tornado
 flies,
Mingling the ravaged landscape with
 the skies.
Far different these from every former
 scene,
The cooling brook, the grassy-vested
 green, 360
The breezy covert of the warbling
 grove,
That only sheltered thefts of harmless love.

Good Heaven! what sorrows
 gloomed that parting day,
That called them from their native
 walks away;
When the poor exiles, every pleasure
 past, 365
Hung round the bowers, and fondly
 looked their last,
And took a long farewell, and wished
 in vain
For seats like these beyond the western main,
And shuddering still to face the distant deep,
Returned and wept, and still returned
 to weep. 370
The good old sire the first prepared
 to go
To new-found worlds, and wept for
 others' woe;

But for himself, in conscious virtue
 brave,
He only wished for worlds beyond
 the grave.
His lovely daughter, lovelier in her
 tears, 375
The fond companion of his helpless
 years,
Silent went next, neglectful of her
 charms,
And left a lover's for a father's arms.
With louder plaints the mother spoke
 her woes,
And blessed the cot where every pleas-
 ure rose, 380
And kissed her thoughtless babes with
 many a tear,
And clasped them close, in sorrow
 doubly dear,
Whilst her fond husband strove to
 lend relief
In all the silent manliness of grief.

O luxury! thou cursed by Heaven's
 decree, 385
How ill exchanged are things like
 these for thee!
How do thy potions, with insidious
 joy,
Diffuse their pleasure only to destroy!
Kingdoms, by thee to sickly greatness
 grown,
Boast of a florid vigor not their
 own. 390
At every draught more large and
 large they grow,
A bloated mass of rank unwieldy
 woe;
Till sapped their strength, and every
 part unsound,
Down, down they sink, and spread
 a ruin round.

Even now the devastation is begun, 395
And half the business of destruction
 done;
Even now, methinks, as pondering
 here I stand,
I see the rural Virtues leave the land.

Down where yon anchoring vessel spreads the sail
That idly waiting flaps with every gale, 400
Downward they move, a melancholy band,
Pass from the shore, and darken all the strand.
Contented Toil, and hospitable Care,
And kind connubial Tenderness, are there;
And Piety, with wishes placed above,
And steady Loyalty and faithful Love. 406
And thou, sweet Poetry, thou loveliest maid,
Still first to fly where sensual joys invade;
Unfit in these degenerate times of shame
To catch the heart, or strike for honest fame, 410
Dear charming nymph, neglected and decried,
My shame in crowds, my solitary pride;
Thou source of all my bliss, and all my woe,

That found'st me poor at first, and keep'st me so;
Thou guide by which the nobler arts excel, 415
Thou nurse of every virtue, fare thee well!
Farewell, and O! where'er thy voice be tried,
On Torno's cliffs[6] or Pambamarca's[7] side,
Whether where equinoctial fervors glow,
Or winter wraps the polar world in snow, 420
Still let thy voice, prevailing over time,
Redress the rigors of th' inclement clime;
Aid slighted truth with thy persuasive strain,
Teach erring man to spurn the rage of gain;
Teach him, that states of native strength possessed, 425

---

[6]*Torno's cliffs*, in Sweden.
[7]*Pambamarca*, a mountain near the equator.

Though very poor, may still be very blessed;
That trade's proud empire hastes to swift decay,
As ocean sweeps the labored mole away;
While self-dependent power can time defy,
As rocks resist the billows and the sky. 430

For Thought and Discussion

1. Have you ever seen a deserted village?
2. Is the picture of this village idealistic or realistic?
3. What causes villages or towns to be deserted?
4. What caused this village to be deserted?
5. According to the poet, upon what does the prosperity of a country depend?
6. Compare this writer's views upon trade with present day views.
7. What does Goldsmith condemn in this poem?
8. What does he think poetry should do, what mission perform?
9. What economic ills of the present day seem to forecast decay of social systems?
10. With what class of people does Goldsmith sympathize?
11. What new spirit is pervading life and literature and has become more or less dominant? Why?
12. What verse form does Goldsmith use?
13. How does his poem differ in content and spirit from the selections characteristic of such verse form?
14. After a study of "A Brief Introduction to Types of Literature," determine why this poem is termed didactic.

Plus Work

Compare Goldsmith's village preacher with Chaucer's poor parson in "The Prologue" to *Canterbury Tales*.

Make a study of the passages in *The Deserted Village* which describe the unhappy lot of the villagers who moved to the city. Explain to the class how these people were left without employment and why they were misfits in the city.

Compare this poem with one called "The Rising Village"[1] written by Oliver Goldsmith's nephew, a Canadian poet also named Oliver Goldsmith.

---

[1]From *A Book of Canadian Prose and Verse*.

COURTESY OF THE T. F. HEALY COLLECTION

OLIVER GOLDSMITH

Oliver Goldsmith 1728-1774

Early Life.   Two Irish villages, Pallas, Goldsmith's birthplace, and Lissoy, his childhood home, idealized in *The Deserted Village,* claim renown through his name.   In his early childhood he wrote verses so easily and spontaneously that his mother was convinced that he should receive a learned education, which did not begin auspiciously. From his schoolmaster, an old soldier, who often entertained his youthful scholars with tales of his travels in Queen Anne's Wars, Goldsmith seems to have gained only a reputation as a dunce and a laughing stock, and a propensity for wandering. Later under a sympathetic master, the lad was found to be quick and clever and progressed rapidly. When he went away to school, he committed one of those blunders which were characteristic of the boy, later of the man, who was often lost in his imagination and oblivious to his surroundings. Inquiring pompously for the best inn in town, he was directed by a wag to a private residence; there he ordered the household about sharply until he discovered his mistake and was overcome with embarrassment. This incident became the basis for that amusing comedy, *She Stoops to Conquer*. Possibly the vivid impression of this occasion caused him to say years afterward, "I brought nothing out of Ireland but a brogue and a blunder."

Trinity College. At the age of fifteen Goldsmith entered Trinity College, the University of Dublin. The circumstances of his college life conspired to make the experience unhappy in many respects. His father was the village preacher of *The Deserted Village*, "passing rich at forty pounds a year"; consequently it was necessary for Goldsmith to enter college as a Sizar, a student who paid his tuition by performing certain tasks considered menial in the eighteenth century for one of Goldsmith's station in life. For the sensitive high-spirited boy, the situation was galling, reflecting upon his happy disposition and causing him to become depressed, morose, and vindictive. Once in a fit of anger, he left school, determined to seek his fortune in foreign lands, but when he had time to take a calmer view of the question, he returned and remained until he took his degree.

During the years in Trinity he did not decide upon a career; he disappointed his family by failing to become a clergyman. He had received a prize for literary merit on his Christmas examinations, but he was not a serious student, and he left college, fitted for nothing in particular, excelling only as a pleasant companion.

Study of Medicine. With the first money earned after college he disappeared for a time on one of those wandering tours which held a great fascination for him. On his return he decided to begin earnest work. After considering law for a profession, he finally chose medicine and studied first in Edinburgh, later in Leyden. Again he set out to travel and drifted over Europe, playing his flute for food and lodging and faring very well until he came to Italy, where he received so little appreciation for his scant musical ability that he must have starved but for free lodging in the monasteries. The letters which he wrote describing people and places are very amusing, and the experiences of this trip made the background for one of his finest poems, *The Traveller*. At Padua he completed his studies which were too desultory to make a place for him in his profession.

Life in London.   In London he tried various occupations, failing everywhere.   Without money, friends, or influence he had great difficulty in establishing himself.   He tried to practice medicine, but his patients were so poor that he was forced to eke out a living by hack-writing.   He led a miserable life, living in the slums in a garret accessible by a steep stairway known as Breakneck Steps. Dr. Goldsmith spent his spare time writing, gradually becoming a master .of style, and at length he was completely absorbed in his literary work.   Recognition, though slow, came with the publication of *The Traveller*, for which he was well paid.

Goldsmith met Dr. Samuel Johnson, the foremost literary man in London, and became a member of the famous Johnson Club, which included the outstanding men of the day: Joshua Reynolds,[1] the painter; Edmund Burke,[2] the parliamentary orator; Garrick, the actor, and others.   By this time Goldsmith had a large income which should easily have exceeded his wants, but with his generosity to beggars, for whom he always emptied his pockets, his fondness for clothes and entertaining, and his propensity for gambling, at which he was invariably unlucky, the poet was usually in debt.

Works.   *The Traveller; The Vicar of Wakefield; She Stoops to Conquer*, popular in its day and always fresh upon revival; and *The Deserted Village*, whose charming and humorous descriptions have given it a permanent place in the hearts of readers, are the best known of Goldsmith's works.

In *The Traveller* he pictures his brother's home, which was pervaded by friendliness and kindness, traits characteristic of the poet himself.

> "Blest be that spot, where cheerful guests retire
> To pause from toil, and trim their evening fire;
> Blest that abode, where want and pain repair,
> And every stranger finds a ready chair;
> Blest be those guests with simple plenty crown'd,
> Where all the ruddy family around
> Laugh at the jests or pranks that never fail,
> Or sigh with pity at some mournful tale;
> Or press the bashful stranger to his food,
> And learn the luxury of doing good."

Death.   Goldsmith's fine generosity and his other lovable qualities of character endeared him to all who knew him, and his circle of friends was large.   The demands which came through his great generosity overtaxed his strength and income.   An illness which seemed slight developed rapidly to a dangerous stage, and he died very suddenly.   Many were saddened over his death, for truly few men ever had as many friends as had Oliver Goldsmith.

---

[1]*Reynolds* painted "The Age of Innocence" and "The Strawberry Girl."
[2]*Burke*, author of *Conciliation with America.*

AULD LANG SYNE[1]
ROBERT BURNS

[[1]*Auld Lang Syne*, long, long ago.
[2]*jo*, a friend. [3]*braes*, small hills.
[4]*pou'd*, pulled. [5]*gowans*, wild daisies.
[6]*mony*, many. [7]*fit*, foot. [8]*burn*,
brook. [9]*dine*, dinner time. [10]*braid*,
broad. [11]*fiere*, friend.]

SHOULD auld acquaintance be
  forgot,
  And never brought to mind?
Should auld acquaintance be forgot,
  And auld lang syne.

Chorus.—
For auld lang syne, my jo,[2]—   5
  For auld lang syne,
We'll tak a cup o' kindness yet,
  For auld lang syne.

And surely ye'll be your pint stowp
  And surely I'll be mine,   10

And we'll tak a cup o' kindness yet,
  For auld lang syne.
    For auld, etc.

We twa hae run about the braes,[3]
  And pou'd[4] the gowans[5] fine;   15
But we've wandered mony[6] a weary
    fit,[7]
  Sin' auld lang syne.
    For auld, etc.

We twa hae paidled i' the burn[8]
  Frae morning sun till dine[9];   20
But seas between us braid[10] hae roared
  Sin' auld lang syne.
    For auld, etc.

And there's a hand, my trusty fiere,[11]
  And gie's a hand o' thine,   25
And we'll tak a right gude-willie
    waught
  For auld lang syne.
    For auld, etc.

For Thought and Discussion

What sentiment is expressed in "Auld Lang Syne" that makes it
a popular song throughout the world?

Additional Readings

Allen, Frederick Lewis: *Only Yesterday*

Babel, Isaac: *Red Cavalry*

Bentley, Phyllis: *Inheritance*
A Modern Tragedy

Clark and Lieber: *Great Short Stories of the World*

Craik, Dinah Marie: *John Halifax, Gentleman*

Dimnet, Ernest: *Art of Thinking*

Fisher, Dorothy Canfield: *Why Stop Learning*

Galsworthy, John: *The Skin Game*

Gordon, Margery: *A Magic World*

Grahame, Kenneth: *The Golden Age*
Wind in the Willows

Hilton, James: *Good-bye, Mr. Chips!*

Ibsen, Henrik: *An Enemy of the People*

Knapp-Fisher, H. C.: *The Modern World: a Pageant of Today*

Sutton, Marvin: *The Children of Ruth*

Tennyson, Alfred: *Idylls of the King*

Thackeray, W. M.: *Henry Esmond*

Wells, H. G.: *The Shape of Things to Come*

The Quest For Happiness

THE QUEST FOR HAPPINESS

*W*HY are everybody's ideas of happiness different? How are those conceptions affected by age, by education, and by environment? A peculiar characteristic of the vague term *happiness* is that it often eludes those who seek it and comes to those who do not pursue it. It has been said that it comes from within one's own heart; it assuredly depends upon harmony of spirit. Possibly it more often falls to the lot of the unselfish, because they forget themselves in external interests.

Truly some of the difficulty of attaining happiness may be attributed to confusion of ideas, the inability to distinguish between immediate and ultimate worth, and the failure to realize that those things for which people care most are above price. It is particularly difficult to choose wisely in an age which offers very lovely material things to make life interesting and enjoyable.

The isolated lighthouse keeper who sees the importance of his work in the scheme of things finds peace and contentment, while the wealthy and influential man loses sight of human welfare and wonders why he has failed to realize harmony in his own life. One man loves wealth, another power, another mankind, and each is dominated by the influence of his interests. One finds pleasure in art, music, literature, sports, adventure, travel, and work. One idealizes the world; another criticizes and reforms it; and another enjoys it.

The complexity of modern life often destroys one's sense of harmony, and he longs to steal away to quiet, out-of-the-way places to escape the noise and discontent and to find calmness, poise, and peace. As symbols of peace and security create images of felicity, so do people cling to them. As varied and rich as life itself are the ways to happiness, which may be likened to skeins of brightly colored silks that float in the air, and fortunate are those upon whom they may fall.

"UNCLE DAN DROVE AWAY LIKE THE WIND, AND THE STABLE-BOY HAD ALL HE COULD DO TO CLAMBER UP BEHIND."

FROM ONE GENERATION TO ANOTHER
ARNOLD BENNETT

IT IS the greatest mistake in the world to imagine that, because the Five Towns is an industrial district, devoted to the manufacture of cups and saucers, marbles and doorknobs, therefore there is no luxury in it.

A writer, not yet deceased, who spent two nights there, and wrote four hundred pages about it, has committed himself to the assertion that there are no private carriages in its streets — only perambulators[1] and tramcars.[2] That writer's reputation is ruined in the Five Towns. For the Five Towns, although continually complaining of bad times, is immensely wealthy, as well as immensely poor —a country of contrasts, indeed— and private carriages, if they do not abound, exist at any rate in sufficient numbers.

Nay, more, automobiles of the most expensive French and English makes fly dashingly along its hilly roads and scatter in profusion the rich black mud thereof.

On a Saturday afternoon in last spring, such an automobile stood outside the garden entrance of Bleakridge House, just half-way between Hanbridge and Bursley. It belonged to young Harold Etches, of Etches, Limited, the great porcelain manufacturers.

It was a 20 h.p. Panhard, and was worth over a thousand pounds as it stood there, throbbing, and Harold was proud of it.

He was also proud of his young wife, Maud, who, clad in several hundred pounds' worth of furs, had taken her seat next to the steering-wheel,

[1]*perambulators,* baby carriages.
[2]*tramcars,* street cars, trolleys.

and was waiting for Harold to mount by her side. The united ages of this handsome and gay couple came to less than forty-five.

And they owned the motor-car, and Bleakridge House with its ten bedrooms, and another house at Llandudno, and a controlling interest in Etches, Limited, that brought them in seven or eight thousand a year. They were a pretty tidy example of what the Five Towns can do when it tries to be wealthy.

At this moment, when Harold was climbing into the car, a shabby old man who was walking down the road, followed by a boy carrying a carpet-bag, stopped suddenly and touched Harold on the shoulder.

"Bless us!" exclaimed the old man. And the boy and the carpet-bag halted behind him.

"What? Uncle Dan?" said Harold.

"Uncle Dan!" cried Maud, springing up with an enchanting smile. "Why, it's ages since——"

"And what d'ye reckon ye'n gotten here?" demanded the old man.

"It's my new car," Harold explained.

"And ca'st drive it, lad?" asked the old man.

"I should think I could!" said Harold confidently.

"H'm!" commented the old man, and then he shook hands, and thoroughly scrutinized Maud.

Now, this is the sort of thing that can only be seen and appreciated in a district like the Five Towns, where families spring into splendor out of nothing in the course of a couple of generations, and as often as not sink back again into nothing in the course of two generations more.

The Etches family is among the best known and the widest spread in the Five Towns. It originated in three brothers, of whom Daniel was

the youngest. Daniel never married; the other two did. Daniel was not very fond of money; the other two were, and they founded the glorious firm of Etches. Harold was the grandson of one brother, and Maud was the granddaughter of the other. Consequently, they both stood in the same relation to Dan, who was their great-uncle—addressed as uncle "for short."

There is a good deal of snobbery in the Five Towns, but it does not exist among relatives. The relatives in danger of suffering by it would never stand it. Besides, although Dan's income did not exceed two hundred a year, he was really richer than his grandnephew, since Dan lived on half his income, whereas Harold, aided by Maud, lived on all of his.

Consequently, despite the vast difference in their stations, clothes, and manners, Daniel and his young relatives met as equals. It would have been amusing to see anyone—even the Countess of Chell, who patronized the entire district—attempt to patronize Dan.

In his time he had been the greatest pigeon-fancier in the country.

"So you're paying a visit to Bursley, uncle?" said Maud.

"Ay!" Dan replied. "I'm back i' owd[3] Bosley. Sarah—my housekeeper, thou know'st——"

"Not dead?"

"No. Her inna' dead; but her sister's dead, and I've give her a week's play, and come away. Rat Edge'll see nowt o' me this side Easter."

Rat Edge was the name of the village, five miles off, which Dan had honored in his declining years.

"And what are you going to do now?" asked Harold.

"I'm going to owd Sam Shawn's

___
[3] owd, old.

by th' owd church, to beg a bed."

"But you'll stop with us, of course?" said Harold.

"Nay, lad," said Dan.

"Oh yes, uncle," Maud insisted.

"Nay, lass," said Dan.

"Indeed, you will, uncle!" said Maud positively. "If you don't, I'll never speak to you again."

She had a charming fire in her eyes, had Maud.

Daniel, the old bachelor, yielded at once, but in his own style.

"I'll try it for a night, lass," said he.

Thus it occurred that the carpet-bag was carried into Bleakridge House, and that after some delay Harold and Maud carried off Uncle Dan with them in the car. He sat in the luxurious tonneau behind, and Maud had quitted her husband in order to join him. Possibly she liked the humorous wrinkles round his gray eyes. Or it may have been the eyes themselves, and yet Dan was nearer seventy than sixty.

The car passed everything on the road; it seemed to be overtaking electric trams all the time.

"So ye'n been married a year?" said Uncle Dan, smiling at Maud.

"Oh yes; a year and three days. We're quite used to it."

"Us'n be in h—ll in a minute, wench!" exclaimed Dan, calmly changing the topic, as Harold swung the car within an inch of a brewer's dray, and skidded slightly in the process. No anti-skidding device would operate in that generous, oozy mud.

And, as a matter of fact, they were in Hanbridge the next minute—Hanbridge, the center of the religions, the pleasures, and the vices of the Five Towns.

"Bless us!" said the old man. "It's fifteen year and more since I were here."

"Harold," said Maud, "let's stop at the Piccadilly Café and have some tea."

"Café?" asked Dan. "What be that?"

"It's a kind of pub." Harold threw the explanation over his shoulder as he brought the car up with swift dexterity in front of the Misses Callear's newly-opened afternoon tea-rooms.

"Oh, well, if it's a pub,"[4] said Uncle Dan, "I dunna object."

He frankly admitted, on entering, that he had never seen a pub full of little tables and white cloths, and flowers, and young women, and silver teapots, and cake-stands. And though he *did* pour his tea into his saucer, he was sufficiently at home there to address the younger Miss Callear as "young woman," and to inform her that her beverage was lacking in Orange Pekoe. And the Misses Callear, who conferred a favor on their customers by serving them, didn't like it.

He became reminiscent.

"Ay!" he said, "when I left th' Five Towns fifty-two years sin' to go weaving i' Derbyshire wi' my mother's brother, tay[5] were ten shilling a pun'. Us had it when us were sick — which wasna' often. We worked too hard for be sick. Hafe past five i' th' morning till eight of a night, and then Saturday afternoon walk ten mile to Glossop with a week's work on ye' back, and home again wi' th' brass.

"They've lost th' habit of work nowadays, seemingly," he went on, as the car moved off once more, but slowly, because of the vast crowds emerging from the Knype football ground. "It's football, Saturday; bands of a Sunday; football, Monday;

---

[4]*pub*, public eating house.
[5]*tay*, tea.

ill i' bed and getting round, Tuesday; do a bit o' work Wednesday; football, Thursday; draw wages Friday night; and football, Saturday. And wages higher than ever. It's that as beats me—wages higher than ever—

"Ye canna' smoke with any comfort i' these cars," he added, when Harold had got clear of the crowds and was letting out. He regretfully put his pipe in his pocket.

Harold skirted the whole length of the Five Towns from south to north, at an average rate of perhaps thirty miles an hour; and quite soon the party found itself on the outer side of Turnhill, and descending the terrible Clough Bank, three miles long, and of a steepness resembling the steepness of the side of a house.

The car had warmed to its business, and Harold took them down that declivity in a manner which startled even Maud, who long ago had resigned herself to the fact that she was tied for life to a young man for whom the word "danger" had no meaning.

At the bottom they had a severe skid; but as there was plenty of room for eccentricities, nothing happened except that the car tried to climb the hill again.

"Well, if I'd known," observed Uncle Dan, "if I'd guessed as you were reservin' this treat for th' owd uncle, I'd ha' walked."

The Etches blood in him was pretty cool, but his nerve had had a shaking.

Then Harold could not restart the car. The engine had stopped of its own accord, and, though Harold lavished much physical force on the magic handle in front, nothing would budge. Maud and the old man both got down, the latter with relief.

"Stuck, eh?" said Dan. "No steam?"

"That's it!" Harold cried, slapping

his leg. "What an ass I am! She wants petrol,[6] that's all. Maud, pass a couple of cans. They're under the seat there, behind. No; on the left, child."

However, there was no petrol in the car.

"That's that cursed Durand" (Durand being the new chauffeur—French, to match the car). "I told him not to forget. Last thing I said to the fool! Maud, I shall chuck that chap!"

"Can't we do anything?" asked Maud stiffly, putting her lips together.

"We can walk back to Turnhill and buy some petrol, some of us!" snapped Harold. "That's what we can do!"

"Sithee," said Uncle Dan. "There's the Plume o' Feathers half-a-mile back. Th' landlord's a friend o' mine. I can borrow his mare and trap, and drive to Turnhill and fetch some o' thy petrol, as thou calls it."

"It's awfully good of you, uncle."

"Nay, lad, I'm doing it for please mysen. But Maud mun come wi' me. Give us th' money for th' petrol, as thou calls it."

"Then I must stay here alone?" Harold complained.

"Seemingly," the old man agreed.

After a few words on pigeons, and a glass of beer, Dan had no difficulty whatever in borrowing his friend's white mare and black trap. He himself helped in the harnessing. Just as he was driving triumphantly away, with that delicious vision Maud on his left hand and a stable-boy behind, he reined the mare in.

"Give us a couple o' penny smokes, matey," he said to the landlord, and lit one.

The mare could go, and Dan could make her go, and she did go. And

---

[6]*petrol,* gasoline.

then the whole turn-out looked extremely dashing when, ultimately, it dashed into the glare of the acetylene lamps which the deserted Harold had lighted on his car.

The red end of a penny smoke in the gloom of twilight looks exactly as well as the red end of an Havana. Moreover, the mare caracolled ornamentally in the rays of the acetylene, and the stable-boy had to skid down quick and hold her head.

"How much didst say this traction-engine had cost thee?" Dan asked, while Harold was pouring the indispensable fluid into the tank.

"Not far off twelve hundred," answered Harold lightly. "Keep that cigar away from here."

"Fifteen pun' 'ud buy this mare," Dan announced to the road.

"Now, all aboard!" Harold commanded at length. "How much shall I give to the boy for the horse and trap, uncle?"

"Nothing," said Dan. "I havena' finished wi' that mare yet. Didst think I was going to trust mysen i' that thing o' yours again? I'll meet thee at Bleakridge, lad."

"And I think I'll go with uncle, too, Harold," said Maud.

Whereupon they both got into the trap.

Harold stared at them astounded.

"But I say——" he protested, beginning to be angry.

Uncle Dan drove away like the wind, and the stable-boy had all he could do to clamber up behind.

Now, at dinner-time that night, in the dining-room of the commodious and well-appointed mansion of the youngest and richest of the Etches, Uncle Dan stood waiting and waiting for his host and hostess to appear. He was wearing a Turkish tasseled smoking-cap to cover his baldness, and he

had taken off his jacket and put on his light, loose overcoat instead of it, since that was a comfortable habit of his.

He sent one of the two parlormaids upstairs for his carpet slippers out of the carpet-bag, and he passed part of the time in changing his boots for his slippers in front of the fire. Then at length, just as a maid was staggering out under the load of those enormous boots, Harold appeared, very correct, but alone.

"Awfully sorry to keep you waiting, uncle," said Harold, "but Maud isn't well. She isn't coming down to-night."

"What's up wi' Maud?"

"Oh, goodness knows!" responded Harold gloomily. "She's not well—that's all."

"H'm!" said Dan. "Well, let's peck a bit."

So they sat down and began to peck a bit, aided by the two maids. Dan pecked with prodigious enthusiasm, but Harold was not in good pecking form. And as the dinner progressed, and Harold sent dish after dish up to his wife, and his wife returned dish after dish untouched, Harold's gloom communicated itself to the house in general.

One felt that if one had penetrated to the furthest corner of the furthest attic, a little parcel of spiritual gloom would have already arrived there. The sense of disaster was in the abode. The cook was prophesying like anything in the kitchen. Durand in the garage was meditating upon such of his master's pithy remarks as he had been able to understand.

When the dinner was over, and the coffee and liqueurs and cigars had been served, and the two maids had left the dining-room, Dan turned to his grandnephew and said—

"There's things as has changed since

my time, lad, but human nature inna'[7] one on 'em."

"What do you mean, uncle?" Harold asked awkwardly, self-consciously.

"I mean as thou'rt a dashed foo'!"

"Why?"

"But thou'lt get better o' that," said Dan.

Harold smiled sheepishly.

"I don't know what you're driving at, uncle," said he.

"Yes, thou dost, lad. Thou'st been and quarreled wi' Maud. And I say thou'rt a dashed foo'!"

"As a matter of fact——" Harold stammered.

"And ye've never quarreled afore. This is th' fust time. And so thou'st under the impression that th' world's come to an end. Well, th' fust quarrel were bound to come sooner or later."

"It isn't really a quarrel—it's about nothing——"

"I know—I know," Dan broke in. "They always are. As for it not being a quarrel, lad, call it a picnic if thou'st a mind. But her's sulking upstairs, and thou'rt sulking down here."

"She was cross about the petrol," said Harold, glad to relieve his mind. "I hadn't a notion she was cross till I went up into the bedroom. Not a notion! I explained to her it wasn't my fault. I argued it out with her very calmly. I did my best to reason with her——"

"Listen here, young 'un," Dan interrupted him. "How old art?"

"Twenty-three."

"Thou may'st live another fifty years. If thou'st a mind to spend 'em i' peace, thoud'st better give up reasoning wi' women. Give it up right now! It's worse nor drink, as a habit. Kiss 'em, cuddle 'em, beat 'em. But dunna' reason wi' 'em."

"What should you have done in my place?" Harold asked.

"I should ha' told Maud her was quite right."

"But she wasn't."

"Then I should ha' winked at mysen i' th' glass," continued Dan, "and kissed her."

"That's all very well——"

"Naturally," said Dan, "her wanted to show off that car i' front o' me. That was but natural. And her was vexed when it went wrong."

"But I told her—I explained to her."

"Her's a handsome little wench," Dan proceeded. "And a good heart. But thou'st got ten times her brains, lad, and thou ought'st to ha' given in."

"But I can't always be——"

"It's allus them as gives in as has their own way. I remember her grandfather—he was th' eldest o' us—he quarreled wi' his wife afore they'd been married a week, and she raced him all over th' town wi' a besom[8]——"

"With a besom, uncle?" exclaimed Harold, shocked at these family disclosures.

"Wi' a besom," said Dan. "That come o' reasoning wi' a woman. It taught him a lesson, I can tell thee. And afterwards he always said as nowt was worth a quarrel—nowt![9] And it isna'."

"I don't think Maud will race me all over the town with a besom," Harold remarked reflectively.

"There's worse things nor that," said Dan. "Look thee here, get out o' th' house for a' 'our. Go to th' Conservative Club, and then come back. Dost understand?"

"But what——"

"Hook it, lad!" said Dan curtly. And just as Harold was leaving the

---

[7] inna', is not.

[8] besom, a broom of twigs.
[9] nowt, nothing.

room, like a schoolboy, he called him in again.

"I havena' told thee, Harold, as I'm subject to attacks. I'm getting up in years. I go off like. It isna' fits; but I go off. And if it should happen while I'm here, dunna' be alarmed."

"What are we to do?"

"Do nothing. I come round in a minute or two. Whatever ye do, dunna' give me brandy. It might kill me—so th' doctor says. I'm only telling thee in case."

"Well, I hope you won't have an attack," said Harold.

"It's a hundred to one I dunna'," said Dan. And Harold departed.

Soon afterwards Uncle Dan wandered into a kitchen full of servants.

"Show me th' missis's bedroom, one on ye," he said to the crowd.

And presently he was knocking at Maud's door.

"Maudie!"

"Who is it?" came a voice.

"It's thy owd uncle. Can'st spare a minute?"

Maud appeared at the door, smiling and arrayed in a *peignoir*.

"*He's* gone out," said Dan, implying scorn of the person who had gone out. "Wilt come downstairs?"

"Where's he gone to?" Maud demanded.

She didn't even pretend she was ill.

"Th' Club," said Dan.

And in about a hundred seconds or so he had her in the drawing-room, and she was actually pouring out gin for him. She looked ravishing in that *peignoir*, especially as she was munching an apple, and balancing herself on the arm of a chair.

"So he's been quarreling with ye, Maud?" Dan began.

"No not quarreling, uncle."

"Well, call it what ye'n a mind," said Dan. "Call it a prayer-meeting.

I didn't notice as ye came down for supper—dinner, as ye call it."

"It was like this, uncle," she said. "Poor Harry was very angry with himself about that petrol. Of course, he wanted the car to go well while you were in it; and he came upstairs and grumbled at me for leaving him all alone and driving home with you."

"Oh, did he?" exclaimed Dan.

"Yes. I explained to him that of course I couldn't leave you all alone. Then he got hot. I kept quite calm. I reasoned it out with him as quietly as I could——"

"Maudie, Maudie," protested the old man, "thou'rt th' prettiest wench i' this town, though I *am* thy great-uncle, and thou'st got plenty o' brains—a sight more than that husband o' thine."

"Do you think so, uncle?"

"Ay, but thou hasna' made use o' 'em tonight. Thou'rt a foolish wench, wench. At thy time o' life, and after a year o' th' married state, thou ought'st to know better than reason wi' a man in a temper."

"But, really, uncle, it was so absurd of Harold, wasn't it?"

"Ay!" said Dan. "But why didst' na' give in and kiss him, and smack his face for him?"

"There was nothing to give in about, uncle."

"There never is," said Dan. "There never is. That's the point. Still, thou'rt nigh crying, wench."

"I'm not, uncle," she contradicted, the tears falling onto the apple.

"And Harold's using bad language all up Trafalgar Road, I lay," Dan added.

"It was all Harold's fault," said Maud.

"Why, in course it were Harold's fault. But nowt's worth a quarrel, my dear—*nowt*. I remember Harold's grandfeyther—he were th' second of us, your grandfeyther were the eldest, and I were the youngest—I remember Harold's grandfeyther chasing his wife all over th' town wi' a besom a week after they were married."

"With a besom!" murmured Maud, pained and forgetting to cry. "Harold's grandfather, not mine?"

"Wi' a besom," Dan repeated, nodding. "They never quarreled again—ne'er again. Th' old woman allus said after that as quarrels were for fools. And her was right."

"I don't see Harold chasing me across Bursley with a besom," said Maud primly. "But what you say is quite right, you dear old uncle. Men *are* queer—I mean husbands. You can't argue with them. You'd much better give in——"

"And have your own way after all."

"And perhaps Harold was——"

Harold's step could be heard in the hall.

"Oh, dear!" cried Maud. "What shall I do?"

"I'm not feeling very well," whispered Uncle Dan weakly. "I have these 'ere attacks sometimes. There's only one thing as'll do me any good—brandy."

And his head fell over one side of the chair, and he looked precisely like a corpse.

"Maud, what are you doing?"almost shouted Harold, when he came into the room.

She was putting a liqueur-glass to Uncle Dan's lips.

"Oh, Harold," she cried, "uncle's had an attack of some sort. I'm giving him some brandy."

"But you mustn't give him brandy," said Harold authoritatively to her.

"But I *must* give him brandy," said Maud. "He told me that brandy was the only thing to save him."

"Nonsense, child!" Harold persisted. "Uncle told *me* all about these attacks. They're perfectly harmless so long as he doesn't have brandy. The doctors have warned him that brandy will be fatal."

"Harold, you are absolutely mistaken. Don't you understand that uncle has only this minute told me that he *must* have brandy?"

And she again approached the glass to the pale lips of the old man. His tasseled Turkish smoking-cap had fallen to the floor, and the hemisphere of his bald head glittered under the gas.

"Maud, I forbid you!" And Harold put a hand on the glass. "It's a matter of life and death. You must have misunderstood uncle."

"It was you who misunderstood uncle," said Maud. "Of course, if you mean to prevent me by brute force——"

They both paused and glanced at Daniel, and then at each other.

"Perhaps you are right, dearest," said Harold, in a new tone.

"No, dearest," said Maud, also in the new tone. "I expect you are right. I must have misunderstood."

"No, no, Maud. Give him the brandy by all means. I've no doubt you're right."

"But if you think I'd better not give it him——"

"But I would prefer you to give it him, dearest. It isn't likely you would be mistaken in a thing like that."

"I would prefer to be guided by you, dearest," said Maud.

So they went on for several minutes, each giving way to the other in the most angelic manner.

"*And meantime I'm supposed to be dying, am I?*" roared Uncle Dan, suddenly sitting up. "You'd let th' old uncle peg out while you practice his precepts! A nice pair you make! I thought for see which on ye 'ud give way to the other, but I didn't anticipate as both on ye 'ud be ready to sacrifice my life for the sake of domestic peace."

"But, uncle," they both said later, amid the universal and yet rather shamefaced peace rejoicings, "you said *nothing* was worth a quarrel."

"And I said right," answered Uncle Dan; "I said right. Th' divorce court is full o' fools as have begun married life by trying to convince the other fool—instead o' humoring him—or *her*. Kiss us, Maud."

For Thought and Discussion

1. Where did this story take place?
2. What is the effect of the dialect used by Uncle Dan?
3. Why was there no snobbery among the relatives?
4. Why does the author say that Dan was richer than Harold? Do you agree with him?
5. What kind of character was Dan?
6. Why do old people usually talk about the changes in the times?
7. Why did Uncle Dan tell the story of the besom to Harold and Maud, each at a different time?
8. What contrasts in living conditions were there between the time of Dan's boyhood and the time of the story?
9. What is Uncle Dan's advice on how to get on peaceably? Is this advice practical?
10. Why would Harold and Maud continue to quarrel unless each adopted a different attitude?
11. What is Uncle Dan's philosophy of life?
12. Does the individualism of this age tend to produce happiness or unhappiness?
13. Why are happy homes essential to the stability of society?

Plus Work

Read *Clayhanger* by Arnold Bennett for another Five Towns story.

ARNOLD BENNETT 1867-1931

A Teller, Not a Reader of Tales. For Arnold Bennett, the writer who spent his life telling little tales, one visions a boyhood spent in reading, poring over fairy tales and legends of the past, and then amusing himself and others with stories of his own invention. Such was not true, however, in his case. He was authority for the statement that as a child he read very little; in his youth the books of Scott, Austen, Dickens, and others of the Victorians were almost unknown to him; *David Copperfield* he read for the first time at thirty.

His Decision to Write. Although he did a little newspaper work in his home town, in his early years he had no inspiration to write and no desire for literary fame. He began to write at night, it is said, to escape the boredom of his law office, in which he served as an expert compiler of bills and a "crack shorthand writer," and he decided upon a literary career because he saw in writing possibilities of making money. His first award, twenty-five guineas for a humorous condensation of a very poor novel, was small, but it became the nucleus of a considerable fortune. To what proportion it grew may be surmised when one knows that for years he wrote multiplied thousands of words daily.

His Method of Composition. Bennett's habit of composing was most unusual. Rain or shine, it was his custom to spend his forenoons walking, and as he walked, he composed. In the afternoons he put on paper in longhand his thoughts of the morning, and so perfect was his handwriting and so smooth and easy his composition that his manuscripts are specimens of beauty. He took pride in recounting that in writing *Old Wives' Tales*, possibly his most celebrated novel, he did not blot a single line. He composed mentally, never writing a line until everything was in order.

Sources of His Plots. The idea for *Old Wives' Tales* came to him five years before he wrote the book. One day while seated at a restaurant in Paris, he observed a fat old woman who was behaving in a very eccentric manner. He reflected, he said, that she had once been young and pretty; the story he wrote, however, was not about her but about two sisters, girls of Five Towns in the pottery district of Southern England, where he himself lived in his early life, and it recounted in detail the few eventful and the many uneventful happenings of their existence from childhood till death.

The brain beneath Bennett's shaggy mop of hair must have been literally stored with what to many would have been insignificant, prosaic commonplaces—all filed away in little orderly heaps ready to be transmuted into stories which people continue to read, probably because in so doing they are reminded of unforgettable incidents, bitter, sweet, or otherwise, in their own experiences.

A Portrayer of Life. Bennett excels in revealing lonely people shut up within themselves, circumscribed by the routine of home and of industrial life, hemmed in by the baffled desires of their own drab and colorless existence. Though his settings, as a rule, are laid in the pottery and smelting district of Five Towns, so far as his themes and his characters are concerned, he might as well have chosen the automobile district of Detroit or the stockyards and the packing house districts of Kansas City or Fort Worth, for what he is really portraying is the enigma of personal and industrial life the world over.

The Clayhanger Trilogy and "From One Generation to Another." Doubtless were Bennett alive today, he would make a trilogy of his play, *Milestones*, in which he would treat of this younger generation; but it is quite doubtful that he could again equal the Clayhanger trilogy, *Clayhanger, Hilda Lessways*, and *These Twain*. In one of the best of his short selections, "From One

Generation to Another," Bennett uses his characteristic setting of Five Towns and touches upon, though in a much lighter vein, a part of the theme he used in *Milestones*. Uncle Dan, the homely philosopher of "From One Generation to Another," understands human nature in general, and, likewise, the younger generation in particular, very well; hence, his humorous solution of the marital difficulties of his grandniece and his grandnephew sets his readers to chuckling in a fashion characteristic of Uncle Dan himself and quite convinces them, as it did the young people in question, that nothing is worth a quarrel.

◆

WHAT THE OLD MAN DOES IS ALWAYS RIGHT
HANS CHRISTIAN ANDERSEN

[Hans Christian Andersen, 1805-1875, is known to the world through his beautiful fairy stories, and his own homeland, Denmark, has honored him by erecting statues of his famous characters. The popularity of his fairy tales has so overshadowed his other work that the world has failed to give it the appreciation which it merits.]

I WILL tell you the story which was told to me when I was a little boy. Every time I thought of the story, it seemed to me to become more and more charming; for it is with stories as it is with many people—they become better as they grow older.

I take it for granted that you have been in the country, and seen a very old farmhouse with a thatched roof, and mosses and small plants growing wild upon the thatch. There is a stork's nest on the summit of the gable; for we can't do without the stork. The walls of the house are sloping, and the windows are low, and only one of the latter is made so that it will open. The baking-oven sticks out of the wall like a little fat body. The elder-tree hangs over the paling, and beneath its branches, at the foot of the paling, is a pool of water in which a few ducks are disporting themselves. There is a yard dog too, who barks at all comers.

Just such a farmhouse stood out in the country; and in this house dwelt an old couple—a peasant and his wife. Small as was their property, there was one article among it that they could do without—a horse, which made a living out of the grass it found by the side of the high-road. The old peasant rode into town on this horse; and often his neighbors borrowed it of him, and rendered the old couple some service in return for the loan of it. But they thought it would be best if they sold the horse, or exchanged it for something that might be more useful to them. But what might this something be?

"You'll know that best, old man," said the wife. "It is fair-day to-day, so ride into town, and get rid of the horse for money, or make a good exchange: whichever you do will be right for me. Ride off to the fair."

And she fastened his neckerchief for him, for she could do that better than he could; and she tied it in a double bow, for she could do that very prettily. Then she brushed his hat round and round with the palm of her hand, and gave him a kiss. So he rode away upon the horse that was to be sold or to be bartered for something else. Yes, the old man knew what he was about.

The sun shone hotly down, and not a cloud was to be seen in the sky. The road was very dusty, for many people who were all bound for the fair were driving, or riding, or walking upon it. There was no shelter anywhere from the sunbeams.

Among the rest, a man was trudging along, and driving a cow to the fair. The cow was as beautiful a creature as any cow can be.

"She gives good milk, I'm sure," said the peasant. "That would be a very good exchange—the cow for the horse."

"Hallo, you there with the cow!" he said; "I tell you what—I fancy a horse costs more than a cow, but I don't care for that; a cow would be more useful to me. If you like, we'll exchange."

"To be sure I will," said the man; and they exchanged accordingly.

So that was settled, and the peasant might have turned back, for he had done the business he came to do; but as he had once made up his mind to go to the fair, he determined to proceed, merely to have a look at it; and so he went on to the town with his cow.

Leading the animal, he strode sturdily on; and after a short time he overtook a man who was driving a sheep. It was a good fat sheep, with a fine fleece on its back.

"I should like to have that fellow," said our peasant to himself. "He would find plenty of grass by our palings, and in the winter we could keep him in the room with us. Perhaps it would be more practical to have a sheep instead of a cow. Shall we exchange?"

The man with the sheep was quite ready, and the bargain was struck. So our peasant went on in the high-road with his sheep.

Soon he overtook another man, who came into the road from a field, carrying a great goose under his arm.

"That's a heavy thing you have there. It has plenty of feathers and plenty of fat, and would look well tied to a string, and paddling in the water at our place. That would be something for my old woman; she could make all kinds of profit out of it. How often she has said, 'If we only had a goose!' Now, perhaps she can have one; and, if possible, it shall be hers. Shall we exchange? I'll give you my sheep for your goose, and thank you into the bargain."

The other man had not the least objection; and accordingly they exchanged, and our peasant became the proprietor of the goose.

By this time he was very near the town. The crowd on the high-road became greater and greater; there was quite a crush of men and cattle. They walked in the road, and close by the palings; and at the barrier they even walked into the toll-man's potato-field, where his own fowl was strutting about with a string to its leg, lest it should take fright at the crowd, and stray away, and so be lost. This fowl had short tail-feathers, and winked with both its eyes, and looked very cunning. "Cluck, cluck!" said the fowl. What it thought when it said this I cannot tell you; but directly our good man saw it, he thought, "That's the finest fowl I've ever seen in my life! Why, it's finer than our parson's brood hen. On my word, I should like to have that fowl. A fowl can always find a grain or two, and can almost keep itself. I think it would be a good exchange if I could get that for my goose.

"Shall we exchange?" he asked the toll-taker.

"Exchange!" repeated the man; "well, that would not be a bad thing."

And so they exchanged; the toll-taker at the barrier kept the goose, and the peasant carried away the fowl.

Now he had done a good deal of business on his way to the fair, and he was hot and tired. He wanted something to eat, and a glass of brandy to drink; and soon he was in front of the inn. He was just about to step in, when the ostler came out, so they met at the door. The ostler was carrying a sack.

"What have you in the sack?" asked the peasant.

"Rotten apples," answered the ostler; "a whole sackful of them— enough to feed the pigs with."

"Why, that's terrible waste! I should like to take them to my old woman at home. Last year the old tree by the turf-hole only bore a single apple, and we kept it in the cupboard till it was quite rotten and spoiled. 'It was always property,' my old woman said; but here she could see a quantity of property—a whole sackful. Yes, I shall be glad to show them to her."

"What will you give me for the sackful?" asked the ostler.

"What will I give? I will give my fowl in exchange."

And he gave the fowl accordingly, and received the apples, which he carried into the guest-room. He leaned the sack carefully by the stove, and then went to the table. But the stove was hot: he had not thought of that. Many guests were present— horse-dealers, ox-herds, and two Englishmen—and the two Englishmen were so rich that their pockets bulged out with gold coins, and almost burst; and they could bet too, as you shall hear.

Hiss-s-s! hiss-s-s! What was that by the stove? The apples were beginning to roast!

"What is that?"

"Why, do you know—" said our peasant.

And he told the whole story of the horse that he had changed for a cow, and all the rest of it, down to the apples.

"Well," said one of the two Englishmen. "There will be a disturbance."

"What?—give me what?" said the peasant. "She will kiss me, and say, 'What the old man does is always right.'"

"Shall we wager?" said the Englishman. "We'll wager coined gold by the ton—a hundred pounds to the hundred weight!"

"A bushel will be enough," replied the peasant. "I can only set the bushel of apples against it; and I'll throw myself and my old woman into the bargain—and I fancy that's piling up the measure."

"Done—taken!"

And the bet was made. The host's carriage came up, and the Englishmen got in, and the peasant got in; away they went, and soon they stopped before the peasant's farm.

"Good evening, old woman."

"Good evening, old man."

"I've made the exchange."

"Yes, you understand what you're about," said the woman.

And she embraced him, and paid no attention to the stranger guests, nor did she notice the sack.

"I got a cow in exchange for the horse," said he.

"Heaven be thanked!" said she. "What glorious milk we shall now have, and butter and cheese on the

table! That was a most capital exchange!"

"Yes, but I changed the cow for a sheep."

"Ah, that's better still!" cried the wife. "You always think of everything: we have just pasture enough for a sheep. Ewe's-milk and cheese, and woollen jackets and stockings! The cow cannot give those, and her hairs will only come off. How you think of everything!"

"But I changed away the sheep for a goose."

"Then this year we shall really have roast goose to eat, my dear old man. You are always thinking of something to give me pleasure. How charming that is! We can let the goose walk about with a string to her leg, and she'll grow fatter still before we roast her."

"But I gave away the goose for a fowl," said the man.

"A fowl? That *was* a good exchange!" replied the woman. "The fowl will lay eggs and hatch them, and we shall have chickens: we shall have a whole poultry-yard! Oh, that's just what I was wishing for."

"Yes, but I exchanged the fowl for a sack of shrivelled apples."

"What!—I must positively kiss you for that," exclaimed the wife. "My dear, good husband! Now I'll tell you something. Do you know you had hardly left me this morning before I began thinking how I could give you something very nice this evening. I thought it should be pancakes with savoury herbs. I had eggs, and bacon too; but I wanted herbs. I went over to the schoolmaster's—they have herbs there, I know—the schoolmistress is a mean woman, though she looks so sweet. I begged her to lend me a handful of herbs. 'Lend!' she answered me; 'nothing at all grows in our garden, not even a shrivelled apple. I could not even lend you a shrivelled apple, my dear woman.' But now I can lend *her*—ten, or a whole sackful. That I'm very glad of; that makes me laugh!" And with that she gave him a sounding kiss.

"I like that!" exclaimed both the

Englishmen together. "Always going downhill, and always merry; that's worth the money."

So they paid a hundred weight of gold to the peasant, who was not scolded, but kissed.

Yes, it always pays, when the wife sees and always asserts that her husband knows best, and that whatever he does is right.

You see, that is my story. I heard it when I was a child; and now you have heard it too, and know that "What the old man does is always right."

For Thought and Discussion

1. What truth about well-known stories is stated in the opening paragraph?
2. Why did the old couple decide to sell the horse?
3. Describe the exchanges made by the old man.
4. What did the Englishmen have to say about the old man's exchanges? What wager was made?
5. What did the wife say about the exchanges made by the old man?
6. What did the Englishmen say about losing the wager?
7. Explain how this story is an expression of the grace and delightful spirit of Hans Christian Andersen.
8. Compare the attitude of the old couple toward each other with that of Harold and Maud in "From One Generation to Another."

THE LIGHTHOUSE KEEPER OF ASPINWALL

HENRYK SIENKIEWICZ

[A foreign character in an American setting, heart hunger for the "old country" on the part of a wanderer, escape from the barren reality of a man's present into the soul-satisfying memory realm of his past—thus one may characterize this short story by the Polish novelist and short story writer, Henryk Sienkiewicz. Sienkiewicz was educated in his home land, Lithuania, but he did the greater part of his writing after he came to America. *Quo Vadis* is his best known novel; "The Lighthouse Keeper of Aspinwall" is his best short story.]

ON A time it happened that the lighthouse keeper in Aspinwall,[1] not far from Panama, disappeared without a trace. Since he disappeared during a storm, it was supposed that the ill-fated man went to the very edge of the small, rocky island on which the lighthouse stood, and was swept out by a wave. This supposition seemed the more likely, as his boat was not found next day in its rocky niche. The place of lighthouse keeper had become vacant. It was necessary to fill this place at the earliest moment

---

[1] *Aspinwall,* in Panama, now Colon.

possible, since the lighthouse had no small significance for the local movement as well as for vessels going from New York to Panama; Mosquito Bay[2] abounds in sandbars and banks. Among these, navigation, even in the daytime, is difficult; but at night, especially with the fogs which are so frequent on those waters warmed by the sun of the tropics, it is nearly impossible. The only guide at that time for the numerous vessels is the lighthouse.

The task of finding a new keeper fell to the United States consul living in Panama, and this task was no small one: first, because it was absolutely necessary to find a man within twelve hours; second, the man must be unusually conscientious—it was not possible, of course, to take the first comer at random; finally, there was an utter lack of candidates. Life on a tower is uncommonly difficult, and by no means enticing to people of the South, who love idleness and the freedom of vagrant life. That lighthouse keeper is almost a prisoner. He cannot leave his rocky island except on Sundays. A boat from Aspinwall brings him provisions and water once a day, and returns immediately; on the whole island, one acre in area, there is no inhabitant. The keeper lives in the lighthouse; he keeps it in order. During the day he gives signals by displaying flags of various colors to indicate changes of the barometer; in the evening he lights the lantern. This would be no great labor were it not that to reach the lantern at the summit of the tower he must pass over more than four hundred steep and very high steps; sometimes he must make this journey repeatedly during the day. In general, it is the life of a monk, and indeed more than that—

the life of a hermit. It was not wonderful, therefore, that Mr. Isaac Falconbridge was in no small anxiety as to where he should find a permanent successor to the recent keeper; and it is easy to understand his joy when a successor announced himself most unexpectedly on that very day. He was a man already old, seventy years or more, but fresh, erect, with the movements and bearing of a soldier. His hair was perfectly white, his face as dark as that of a Creole[3]; but, judging from his blue eyes, he did not belong to a people of the South. His face was somewhat downcast and sad, but honest. At the first glance he pleased Falconbridge. It remained only to examine him. Therefore the following conversation began:

"Where are you from?"

"I am a Pole."[4]

"Where have you worked up to this time?"

"In one place and another."

"A lighthouse keeper should like to stay in one place."

"I need rest."

"Have you served? Have you testimonials of honorable government service?"

The old man drew from his bosom a piece of faded silk, resembling a strip of an old flag, unwound it, and said:

"Here are the testimonials. I received this cross in 1830. This second one is Spanish from the Carlist War[5]; the third is the French legion; the fourth I received in Hungary. Afterward I fought in the States against the South; there they do not give crosses."

---

[2]*Mosquito Bay,* Central America on Caribbean Sea.

[3]*Creole,* of French or Spanish descent.

[4]*Pole,* a native of Poland.

[5]*Carlist War,* unsuccessful revolt to establish the claims of Carlos to Spanish throne.

Falconbridge took the paper and began to read.

"H'm! Skavinski? Is that your name? H'm! Two flags captured in a bayonet attack. You were a gallant soldier."

"I am able to be a conscientious lighthouse keeper."

"It is necessary to ascend the tower a number of times daily. Have you sound legs?"

"I crossed the plains on foot." (The immense steppes between the East and California are called "the plains.")

"Do you know sea service?"

"I served three years on a whaler."

"You have tried various occupations."

"The only one I have not known is quiet."

"Why is that?"

The old man shrugged his shoulders. "Such is my fate."

"Still you seem to me too old for a lighthouse keeper."

"Sir," exclaimed the candidate suddenly in a voice of emotion, "I am greatly wearied, knocked about. I have passed through much, as you see. This place is one of those which I have wished for most ardently. I am old, I need rest. I need to say to myself, 'Here you will remain; this is your port.' Ah, sir, this depends now on you alone. Another time perhaps such a place will not offer itself. What luck that I was in Panama! I entreat you—as God is dear to me, I am like a ship which if it misses the harbor will be lost. If you wish to make an old man happy—I swear to you that I am honest, but—I have enough of wandering."

The blue eyes of the old man expressed such earnest entreaty that Falconbridge, who had a good, simple heart, was touched.

"Well," said he, "I take you. You are lighthouse keeper."

The old man's face gleamed with inexpressible joy.

"I thank you."

"Can you go to the tower to-day?"

"I can."

"Then good-bye. Another word —for any failure in service you will be dismissed."

"All right."

That same evening, when the sun had descended on the other side of the isthmus, and a day of sunshine was followed by a night without twilight, the new keeper was in his place evidently, for the lighthouse was casting its bright rays on the water as usual. The night was perfectly calm, silent, genuinely tropical, filled with a transparent haze, forming around the moon a great colored rainbow with soft, unbroken edges; the sea was moving only because the tide raised it. Skavinski on the balcony seemed from below like a small black point. He tried to collect his thoughts and take in his new position; but his mind was too much under pressure to move with regularity. He felt somewhat as a hunted beast feels when at last it has found refuge from pursuit on some inaccessible rock or in a cave. There had come to him, finally, an hour of quiet; the feeling of safety filled his soul with a certain unspeakable bliss. Now on that rock he can simply laugh at his previous wanderings, his misfortunes and failures. He was in truth like a ship whose masts, ropes, and sails had been broken and rent by a tempest, and cast from the clouds to the bottom of the sea—a ship on which the tempest had hurled waves and spat foam, but which still wound its way to the harbor. The pictures of that storm passed quickly through his mind as he compared it with the calm future now beginning. A part of his wonderful adventures he had related to Falconbridge; he had not mentioned, however, thousands of other incidents. It had been his misfortune that as often as he pitched his tent and fixed his fireplace to settle down permanently, some wind tore out the stakes of his tent, whirled away the fire, and bore him on toward destruction. Looking now from the balcony of the tower at the illuminated waves, he remembered everything through which he had passed. He had campaigned in the four parts of the world, and in wandering had tried almost every occupation. Laborloving and honest, more than once had he earned money, and had always lost it in spite of every prevision and the utmost caution. He had been a gold-miner in Australia, a diamond-digger in Africa, a rifleman in public service in the East Indies. He established a ranch in California—the drought ruined him; he tried trading with wild tribes in the interior of Brazil—his raft was wrecked on the Amazon; he himself alone, weaponless, and nearly naked, wandered in the forest for many weeks living on wild fruits, exposed every moment to death from the jaws of wild beasts. He established a forge in Helena, Arkansas, and that was burned in a great fire which consumed the whole town. Next he fell into the hands of Indians in the Rocky Mountains, and only through a miracle was he saved by Canadian trappers. Then he served as a sailor on a vessel running between Bahia[6] and Bordeaux,[7] and as harpooner on a whaling-ship; both vessels were wrecked. He had a cigar factory in Havana, and was robbed by his partner while he himself was lying sick with the vomito.[8] At last he came to Aspinwall, and there was to be the end of his failures—for what

could reach him on that rocky island? Neither water nor fire nor men. But from men Skavinski had not suffered much; he had met good men oftener than bad ones.

But it seemed to him that all the four elements were persecuting him. Those who knew him said that he had no luck, and with that they explained everything. He himself became somewhat of a monomaniac. He believed that some mighty and vengeful hand was pursuing him everywhere, on all lands and waters. He did not like, however, to speak of this; only at times, when someone asked him whose hand that could be, he pointed mysteriously to the Polar Star, and said, "It comes from that place." In reality his failures were so continuous that they were wonderful, and might easily drive a nail into the head, especially of the man who had experienced them. But Skavinski had the patience of an Indian, and that great calm power of resistance which comes from truth of heart. In his time he had received in Hungary a number of bayonet-thrusts because he would not grasp at a stirrup which was shown as means of salvation to him, and cry for quarter. In like manner he did not bend to misfortune. He crept up against the mountain as industriously as an ant. Pushed down a hundred times, he began his journey calmly for the hundred and first time. He was in his way a most peculiar original. This old soldier, tempered, God knows in how many fires, hardened in suffering, hammered and forged, had the heart of a child. In the time of the epidemic in Cuba, the vomito attacked him because he had given to the sick all his quinine, of which he had a considerable supply, and left not a grain to himself.

There had been in him also this

---

[6]*Bahia* (bä ē′ ä), in Brazil.
[7]*Bordeaux* (bôr′ dō), in France.
[8]*vomito*, yellow fever.

wonderful quality — that after so many disappointments he was ever full of confidence, and did not lose hope that all would be well yet. In winter he grew lively, and predicted great events. He waited for these events with impatience, and lived with the thought of them whole summers. But the winters passed one after another, and Skavinski lived only to this—that they whitened his head. At last he grew old, began to lose energy; his endurance was becoming more and more like resignation, his former calmness was tending toward supersensitiveness, and that tempered soldier was degenerating into a man ready to shed tears for any cause. Besides this, from time to time he was weighed down by a terrible homesickness which was roused by any circumstance—the sight of swallows, gray birds like sparrows, snow on the mountains, or melancholy music like that heard on a time. Finally, there was one idea which mastered him—the idea of rest. It mastered the old man thoroughly, and swallowed all other desires and hopes. This ceaseless wanderer could not imagine anything more to be longed for, anything more precious, than a quiet corner in which to rest, and wait in silence for the end. Perhaps specially because some whim of fate had so hurried him over all seas and lands that he could hardly catch his breath, did he imagine that the highest human happiness was simply not to wander. It is true that such modest happiness was his due; but he was so accustomed to disappointments that he thought of rest as people in general think of something which is beyond reach. He did not dare to hope for it. Meanwhile, unexpectedly, in the course of twelve hours he had gained a position which was as if chosen for him out of all the world. We are not

to wonder, then, that when he lighted his lantern in the evening he became as it were dazed—that he asked himself if that was reality, and he did not dare to answer that it was. But at the same time reality convinced him with incontrovertible proofs; hence hours one after another passed while he was on the balcony. He gazed, and convinced himself. It might seem that he was looking at the sea for the first time in his life. The lens of the lantern cast into the darkness an enormous triangle of light, beyond which the eye of the old man was lost in the black distance completely, in the distance mysterious and awful. But that distance seemed to run toward the light. The long waves following one another rolled out from the darkness, and went bellowing toward the base of the island; and then their foaming backs were visible, shining rose-colored in the light of the lantern. The incoming tide swelled more and more, and covered the sandy bars. The mysterious speech of the ocean came with a fullness more powerful and louder, at one time like the thunder of cannon, at another like the roar of great forests, at another like the distant dull sound of the voices of people. At moments it was quiet; then to the ears of the old man came some great sigh, then a kind of sobbing, and again threatening outbursts. At last the wind bore away the haze, but brought black, broken clouds, which hid the moon. From the west it began to blow more and more; the waves sprang with rage against the rock of the lighthouse, licking with foam the foundation walls. In the distance a storm was beginning to bellow. On the dark, disturbed expanse certain green lanterns gleamed from the masts of ships. These green points rose high and then sank; now they swayed to the right, and now to the left. Skavinski descended to his room. The storm began to howl. Outside, people on those ships were struggling with night, with darkness, with waves; but inside the tower it was calm and still. Even the sounds of the storm hardly came through the thick walls, and only the measured tick-tack of the clock lulled the wearied old man to his slumber.

Hours, days, and weeks began to pass. Sailors assert that sometimes when the sea is greatly roused, something from out the midst of night and darkness calls them by name. If the infinity of the sea may call out thus, perhaps when a man is growing old, calls come to him, too, from another infinity still darker and more deeply mysterious; and the more he is wearied by life the dearer are those calls to him. But to hear them quiet is needed. Besides old age loves to put itself aside, as if with a foreboding of the grave. The lighthouse had become for Skavinski such a half grave. Nothing is more monotonous than life on a beacon-tower. If young people consent to take up this service they leave it after a time. Lighthouse keepers are generally men not young, gloomy, and confined to themselves. If by chance one of them leaves his lighthouse and goes among men, he walks in the midst of them like a person roused from deep slumber. On the tower there is a lack of minute impressions which in ordinary life teach men to adapt themselves to everything. All that a lighthouse keeper comes in contact with is gigantic and devoid of definitely outlined forms. The sky is one whole, the water another; and between those two infinities the soul of man is in loneliness. That is a life in which thought is continual meditation, and out of that meditation nothing rouses the keeper, not even his work. Day is like day as two beads in a rosary, unless changes of weather form the only variety. But Skavinski felt more happiness than ever in life before. He rose with the dawn, took his breakfast, polished the lens, and then sitting on the balcony gazed into the distance of the water; and his eyes were never sated with the pictures which he saw before him. On the enormous turquoise ground of the ocean were to be seen generally flocks of swollen sails gleaming in the rays of the sun so brightly that the eyes were blinking before the excess of light. Sometimes the ships, favored by the so-called trade winds, went in an extended line one after another, like a chain of sea-mews or albatrosses. The red casks indicating the channel swayed on the light wave with gentle movement. Among the sails appeared every afternoon gigantic grayish feather-like plumes of smoke. That was a steamer from New York which brought passengers and goods to Aspinwall, drawing behind it a frothy path of foam. On the other side of the balcony Skavinski saw, as if on his palm, Aspinwall and its busy harbor, and in it a forest of masts, boats, and craft; a little farther, white houses and the towers of the town. From the height of his tower the small houses were like the nests of sea-mews, the boats were like beetles, and the people moved around like small points on the white stone boulevard. From early morning a light eastern breeze brought a confused hum of human life, above which predominated the whistle of steamers. In the afternoon six o'clock came; the movements in the harbor began to cease; the mews hid themselves in the rents of the cliffs; the waves grew feeble and became in some sort lazy; and then on the land, on the sea, and on the tower came a time of stillness unbroken by anything.

The yellow sands from which the waves had fallen back glittered like golden stripes on the width of the waters; the body of the tower was outlined definitely in blue. Floods of sunbeams were poured from the sky on the water and the sands and the cliff. At that time a certain lassitude full of sweetness seized the old man. He felt that the rest which he was enjoying was excellent; and when he thought that it would be continuous nothing was lacking to him.

Skavinski was intoxicated with his own happiness; and since a man adapts himself easily to improved conditions, he gained faith and confidence by degrees; for he thought that if men built houses for invalids, why should not God gather up at last His own invalids? Time passed, and confirmed him in this conviction. The old man grew accustomed to his tower, to the lantern, to the rock, to the sand-bars, to solitude. He grew accustomed also to the sea-mews which hatched in the crevices of the rock, and in the evening held meetings on the roof of the lighthouse. Skavinski threw to them generally the remnants of his food; and soon they grew tame, and afterward, when he fed them, a real storm of white wings encircled him, and the old man went among the birds like a shepherd among sheep. When the tide ebbed he went to the low sandbanks, on which he collected savory periwinkles and beautiful pearl shells of the nautilus,[9] which receding waves had left on the sand. In the night by the moonlight and the tower he went to catch fish, which frequented the windings of the cliff in myriads. At last he was in love with his rocks and his treeless little island, grown over only with small thick plants exuding sticky resin. The distant views repaid him for the poverty of the island, however. During afternoon hours, when the air became very clear he could see the whole isthmus covered with the richest vegetation. It seemed to Skavinski at such times that he saw one gigantic garden—bunches of cocoa, and enormous musa, combined as it were in luxurious tufted bouquets, right there behind the houses of Aspinwall. Farther on, between Aspinwall and Panama, was a great forest over which every morning and evening hung a reddish haze of exhalations—a real tropical forest with its feet in stagnant water, interlaced with lianas and filled with the sound of one sea of gigantic orchids, palms, milk-trees, iron-trees, gum-trees.

Through his field-glass the old man could see not only trees and the broad leaves of bananas, but even legions of monkeys and great marabous[10] and flocks of parrots, rising at times like a rainbow cloud over the forest. Skavinski knew such forests well, for after being wrecked on the Amazon he had wandered whole weeks among similar arches and thickets. He had seen how many dangers and deaths lie concealed under those wonderful and smiling exteriors. During the nights which he had spent in them he heard close at hand the sepulchral voices of howling monkeys and the roaring of the jaguars; he saw gigantic serpents coiled like lianas on trees; he knew those slumbering forest lakes full of torpedo-fish and swarming with crocodiles; he knew under what a yoke man lives in those unexplored wildernesses in which are single leaves that exceed a man's size ten times—wildernesses swarming with blood-drinking mosquitoes, tree-leeches, and gigantic

9*nautilus,* a shell fish, having a spiral and chambered shell.

10*marabou,* a large stork.

poisonous spiders. He had experienced that forest life himself, had witnessed it, had passed through it; therefore it gave him the greater enjoyment to look from his height and gaze on those *matos,* admire their beauty, and be guarded from their treacherousness. His tower preserved him from every evil. He left it only for a few hours on Sunday. He put on then his blue keeper's coat with silver buttons, and hung his crosses on his breast. His milk-white head was raised with a certain pride when he heard at the door, while entering the church, the Creoles say among themselves, ''We have an honorable lighthouse keeper and not a heretic, though he is a Yankee.'' But he returned straightway after Mass to his island, and returned happy, for he had still no faith in the mainland. On Sunday also he read the Spanish newspaper which he bought in the town, or the *New York Herald,* which he borrowed from Falconbridge; and he sought in it European news eagerly. The poor old heart on that lighthouse tower, and in another hemisphere, was beating yet for its birthplace. At times too, when the boat brought his daily supplies and water to the island, he went down from the tower to talk with Johnson, the guard. But after a while he seemed to grow shy. He ceased to go to the town, to read the papers and to go down to talk politics with Johnson. Whole weeks passed in this way, so that no one saw him and he saw no one. The only signs that the old man was living were the disappearance of the provisions left on shore, and the light of the lantern kindled every evening with the same regularity with which the sun rose in the morning from the waters of those regions. Evidently, the old man had become indifferent to the world. Homesickness was not the cause, but

just this—that even homesickness had passed into resignation. The whole world began now and ended for Skavinski on his island. He had grown accustomed to the thought that he would not leave the tower till his death, and he simply forgot that there was anything else besides it. Moreover, he had become a mystic; his mild blue eyes began to stare like the eyes of a child, and were as if fixed on something at a distance. In presence of a surrounding uncommonly simple and great, the old man was losing the feeling of personality; he was ceasing to exist as an individual, was becoming merged more and more in that which inclosed him. He did not understand anything beyond his environment; he felt only unconsciously. At last it seems to him that the heavens, the water, his rock, the tower, the golden sand-banks, and the swollen sails, the sea-mews, the ebb and flow of the tide—all form a mighty unity, one enormous mysterious soul; that he is sinking in that mystery, and feels that soul which lives and lulls itself. He sinks and is rocked, forgets himself; and in that narrowing of his own individual existence, in that half-waking, half-sleeping, he has discovered a rest so great that it nearly resembles half-death.

But the awakening came.

On a certain day, when the boat brought water and a supply of provisions, Skavinski came down an hour later from the tower, and saw that besides the usual cargo there was an additional package. On the outside of this package were postage stamps of the United States, and the address: "Skavinski, Esq.," written on coarse canvas.

The old man, with aroused curiosity, cut the canvas, and saw books; he took one in his hand, looked at it, and

out it back; thereupon his hands began to tremble greatly. He covered his eyes as if he did not believe them; it seemed to him as if he were dreaming. The book was Polish— what did that mean? Who could have sent the book? Clearly, it did not occur to him at the first moment that in the beginning of his lighthouse career he had read in the *Herald,* borrowed from the consul, of the formation of a Polish society in New York, and had sent at once to that society half his month's salary, for which he had, moreover, no use on the tower. The society had sent him the books with thanks. The books came in the natural way; but at the first moment the old man could not seize those thoughts. Polish books in Aspinwall, on his tower, amid his solitude—that was for him something uncommon, a certain breath from past times, a kind of miracle. Now it seemed to him, as to those sailors in the night, that something was calling him by name with a voice greatly beloved and near-

ly forgotten. He sat for a while with closed eyes, and was almost certain that, when he opened them, the dream would be gone.

The package, cut open, lay before him, shown upon clearly by the afternoon sun, and on it was an open book. When the old man stretched his hand toward it again, he heard in the stillness the beating of his own heart. He looked; it was poetry. On the outside stood printed in great letters the title, underneath the name of the author. The name was not strange to Skavinski; he saw that it belonged to the great poet,[11] whose productions he had read in 1830 in Paris. Afterward, when campaigning in Algiers and Spain, he had heard from his countrymen of the growing fame of the great seer; but he was so accustomed to the musket at that time that he took no book in hand. In 1849 he went to America, and in

[11]*Mickiewicz* (mitskyevich), the greatest poet of Poland.

the adventurous life which he led he hardly ever met a Pole, and never a Polish book. With the greater eagerness, therefore, and with a livelier beating of the heart, did he turn to the title-page. It seemed to him then that on his lonely rock some solemnity is about to take place. Indeed it was a moment of great calm and silence. The clocks of Aspinwall were striking five in the afternoon. Not a cloud darkened the clear sky; only a few sea-mews were sailing through the air. The ocean was as if cradled to sleep. The waves on the shore stammered quietly, spreading softly on the sand. In the distance the white houses of Aspinwall, and the wonderful groups of palm, were smiling. In truth, there was something there solemn, calm, and full of dignity. Suddenly, in the midst of that calm of Nature, was heard the trembling voice of the old man, who read aloud as if to understand himself better:

"Thou art like health, O my birth-
    land Litva![12]
How much we should prize thee he
    only can know who has lost thee.
Thy beauty in perfect adornment
    this day
I see and describe, because I am yearn-
    ing for thee."

His voice failed Skavinski. The letters began to dance before his eyes; something broke in his breast, and went like a wave from his heart higher and higher, choking his voice and pressing his throat. A moment more he controlled himself, and read further:

"O Holy Lady, who guardest bright
    Chenstohova,
Who shinest in Ostrobrama and pre-
    servest

---

[12]*Litva*, Lithuania.

The castle town Novgrodek with its
    trusty people,
As Thou didst give me back to health
    in childhood,
When by my weeping mother placed
    beneath Thy care
I raised my lifeless eyelids upward,
And straightway walked unto Thy
    holy threshold,
To thank God for the life restored
    me,—
So by a wonder now restore us to the
    bosom of our birthplace."

The swollen wave broke through the restraint of his will. The old man sobbed, and threw himself on the ground; his milk-white hair was mingled with the sand of the sea. Forty years had passed since he had seen his country, and God knows how many since he heard his native speech; and now that speech had come to him itself—it had sailed to him over the ocean, and found him in solitude on another hemisphere—it so loved, so dear, so beautiful! In the sobbing which shook him there was no pain— only a suddenly aroused immense love, in the presence of which other things are as nothing. With that great weeping he had simply implored forgiveness of that beloved one, set aside because he had grown so old, had become so accustomed to his solitary rock, and had so forgotten it that in him even longing had begun to disappear. But now it returned as if by a miracle; therefore the heart leaped in him.

Moments vanished one after another; he lay there continually. The mews flew over the lighthouse, crying as if alarmed for their old friend. The hour in which he fed them with the remnants of his food had come; therefore, some of them flew down from the lighthouse to him; then more and more came, and began to pick and shake their wings over his head. The sound of the wings roused him. He had wept his fill, and had now a certain calm and brightness; but his eyes were as if inspired. He gave unwittingly all his provisions to the birds, which rushed at him with an uproar, and he himself took the book again. The sun had gone already behind the gardens and the forest of Panama, and was going slowly beyond the isthmus to the other ocean; but the Atlantic was full of light yet; in the open air there was still perfect vision; therefore, he read further:

"Now bear my longing soul to those
    forest slopes, to those green
    meadows."

At last the dusk obliterates the letters on the white paper—the dusk short as a twinkle. The old man rested his head on the rock, and closed his eyes. Then "She who defends bright Chenstohova" took his soul and transported it to "those fields colored by various grain." On the sky were burning yet those long stripes, red and golden, and on those brightnesses he was flying to beloved regions. The pine-woods were sounding in his ears; the streams of his native place were murmuring. He saw everything as it was; everything asked him, "Dost remember?" He remembers! he sees broad fields; between the fields, woods and villages. It is night now. At this hour his lantern usually illuminates the darkness of the sea; but now he is in his native village. His old head has dropped on his breast, and he is dreaming. Pictures are passing before his eyes quickly, and a little disorderly. He does not see the house in which he was born, for war had destroyed it; he does not see his father and mother, for they died when he was a child; but

still the village is as if he had left it yesterday—the line of cottages with lights in the windows, the mound, the mill, the two ponds opposite each other, and thundering all night with a chorus of frogs. Once he had been on guard in that village all night; now that past stood before him at once in a series of views. He is an Uhlan again, and he stands there on guard; at a distance is the public-house; he looks with swimming eyes. There is thundering and singing and shouting amid the silence of the night, with voices of fiddles and bass-viols "U-ha! U-ha!" Then the Uhlans[13] knock out fire with their horseshoes, and it is wearisome for him there on his horse. The hours drag on slowly; at last the lights are quenched; now as far as the eye reaches there is mist, and mist impenetrable; now the fog rises, evidently from the fields, and embraces the whole world with a whitish cloud. You would say, a complete ocean. But that is fields; soon the land-rail will be heard in the darkness, and the bitterns will call from the reeds. The night is calm and cool—in truth, a Polish night! In the distance the pine-wood is sounding without wind, like the roll of the sea. Soon dawn will whiten the east. In fact, the cocks are beginning to crow behind the hedges. One answers to another from cottage to cottage; the storks are screaming somewhere on high. The Uhlan feels well and bright. Someone had spoken of a battle to-morrow. Hei! that will go on, like all the others, with shouting, with fluttering of flaglets. The young blood is playing like a trumpet, though the night cools it. But it is dawning. Already night is growing pale; out of the shadows come forests, the thicket, a row

[13]*Uhlans*, members of heavy cavalry, especially in Prussia.

of cottages, the mill, the poplars. The well is squeaking like a metal banner on a tower. What a beloved land, beautiful in the rosy gleams of the morning! Oh, the one land, the one land!

Quiet! the watchful picket hears that someone is approaching. Of course, they are coming to relieve the guard.

Suddenly some voice is heard above Skavinski:

"Here, old man! Get up! What's the matter?"

The old man opens his eyes, and looks with wonder at the person standing before him. The remnants of the dream-visions struggle in his head with reality. At last the visions pale and vanish. Before him stands Johnson, the harbor guide.

"What's this?" asked Johnson; "are you sick?"

"No."

"You didn't light the lantern. You must leave your place. A vessel from St. Geromo was wrecked on the bar. It is lucky that no one was drowned, or you would go to trial. Get into the boat with me; you'll hear the rest at the Consulate."

The old man grew pale; in fact he had not lighted the lantern that night.

A few days later, Skavinski was seen on the deck of a steamer, which was going from Aspinwall to New York. The poor man had lost his place. There opened before him new roads of wandering; the wind had torn that leaf away again to whirl it over lands and seas, to sport with it till satisfied. The old man had failed greatly during those few days, and was bent over; only his eyes were gleaming. On his new road of life he held at his breast his book, which from time to time he pressed with his hand as if in fear that that too might go from him.

For Thought and Discussion

1. Why is the position of a lighthouse keeper a difficult one to fill?
2. How in his past life had Skavinski acquired characteristics desirable in a lighthouse keeper?
3. Why had he suffered so many misfortunes in his life?
4. Why had he not become embittered from his experiences?
5. Can you explain why the old man forgot to light his lantern?
6. At the close of the story, what had come into the old man's life to alleviate his loneliness?
7. What element of victory is there in his failure?
8. Explain why the old lighthouse keeper, feeling such a deep love for his native land, left home.
   Account for his taking service with various foreign armies.
9. Which pictures recalled to the old man his home land?
   What expressions had for him the sharpest patriotic appeal?
10. What poetic qualities are notable in this selection?

AN OLD WOMAN OF THE ROADS
PADRAIC COLUM

[Padraic Colum, an Irish poet, was born in Langford, Ireland. He has written fantasies, stories for children, and poetry about peasant life. Much of his work is rich in folk lore.]

O TO have a little house!
   To own the hearth and stool and all!
The heaped up sods upon the fire,
The pile of turf against the wall!

To have a clock with weights and chains   5
And pendulum swinging up and down!
A dresser filled with shining delph,
Speckled and white and blue and brown!

I could be busy all the day
Clearing and sweeping hearth and floor,   10
And fixing on their shelf again
My white and blue and speckled store!

I could be quiet there at night
Beside the fire and by myself,
Sure of a bed and loath to leave
The ticking clock and the shining delph!   16

Och! but I'm weary of mist and dark,
And roads where there's never a house nor bush,
And tired I am of bog and road,
And the crying wind and the lonesome hush!   20

And I am praying to God on high,
And I am praying Him night and day,
For a little house—a house of my own—
Out of the wind's and the rain's way.

For Thought and Discussion

1. Why do you think the setting of this poem is not in America?
2. What deep instincts does this poem express?
3. To what class does this old woman belong?
4. Find vivid descriptive phrases.
5. What do you think would constitute happiness for this old woman?
6. Is happiness of this type an individual or a social problem?
7. Why does this poem arouse your sympathy?
8. Can you recall seemingly trivial objects which you have longed for, not because of the intrinsic worth but because of what they typified to you?
9. You may be interested in studying the lyric form in "Types of Literature." What characteristics of the lyric can you find in "The Old Woman of the Roads"? Compare this poem with the three following, "The Lake Isle of Innisfree," "The Vagabond," and "Sea Fever."

THE LAKE ISLE OF INNISFREE
WILLIAM BUTLER YEATS

[William Butler Yeats was an Irish poet who wrote both poetry and prose, usually of peasant life or faerie lore. He was awarded the Nobel prize in 1923.]

I WILL arise and go now, and go to Innisfree,
And a small cabin build there, of clay and wattles made;
Nine bean rows will I have there, a hive for the honey bee,
And live alone in the bee-loud glade.

And I shall have some peace there, for peace comes dropping slow, ⁵
Dropping from the veils of the morning to where the cricket sings;
There midnight's all a-glimmer, and noon a purple glow,
And evening full of the linnet's wings.

I will arise and go now, for always night and day
I hear lake water lapping with low sounds by the shore; ¹⁰
While I stand on the roadway, or on the pavements gray,
I hear it in the deep heart's core.

For Thought and Discussion

1. What called Yeats to Innisfree?
2. List the details used in the description.
3. Why do the strenuous demands of modern life sometimes cause people to want a vacation in "Innisfree"?
4. In what respects is the poem similar to Wordsworth's "The Daffodils," to Colum's "An Old Woman of the Roads"?

THE VAGABOND
ROBERT LOUIS STEVENSON

GIVE to me the life I love,
  Let the lave go by me;
Give the jolly heaven above
  And the byway nigh me.
Bed in the bush with stars to see,   5
  Bread I dip in the river—
There's the life for a man like me,
  There's the life forever.

Let the blow fall soon or late,
  Let what will be o'er me;   10
Give the face of earth around
  And the road before me.
Wealth I seek not, hope, nor love,
  Nor a friend to know me;
All I seek, the heaven above   15
  And the road below me.

For Thought and Discussion

1. What phases of life appeal to the vagabond?
2. Could Stevenson speak from experience?
3. What does the writer place above everything else?
4. Is the poem romantic or realistic in mood?

SEA FEVER
JOHN MASEFIELD

I MUST go down to the seas again,
    to the lonely sea and the sky,
And all I ask is a tall ship and a star
    to steer her by,
And the wheel's kick and the wind's
    song and the white sail's shak-
    ing,
And a gray mist on the sea's face and
    a gray dawn breaking.

I must go down to the seas again, for
    the call of the running tide   5
Is a wild call and a clear call that may
    not be denied;

And all I ask is a windy day with
    the white clouds flying,
And the flung spray and the blown
    spume, and the sea gulls cry-
    ing.

I must go down to the seas again to
    the vagrant gypsy life,
To the gull's way and the whale's
    way where the wind's like a
    whetted knife;   10
And all I ask is a merry yarn from a
    laughing fellow rover,
And quiet sleep and a sweet dream
    when the long trick's over.

For Thought and Discussion

1. Name some of the things the writer longs for.
2. Why does Masefield write very convincingly of the sea?
3. Is this poem realistic or romantic?

Plus Work

Read "The Seafarer," an early English poem, and compare it with
"Sea Fever."

THE SELFISH GIANT

OSCAR WILDE

EVERY afternoon, as they were coming from school, the children used to go and play in the Giant's garden.

It was a large lovely garden, with soft green grass. Here and there over the grass stood beautiful flowers like stars, and there were twelve peach-trees that in the Spring-time broke out into delicate blossoms of pink and pearl, and in the autumn bore rich fruit. The birds sat on the trees and sang so sweetly that the children used to stop their games in order to listen to them. "How happy we are here!" they cried to each other.

One day the Giant came back. He had been to visit his friend the Cornish ogre, and had stayed with him for seven years. After the seven years were over he had said all that he had to say, for his conversation was limited, and he determined to return to his own castle. When he arrived he saw the children playing in the garden.

"What are you doing there?" he cried in a very gruff voice, and the children ran away.

"My own garden is my own garden," said the Giant; "anyone can understand that, and I will allow nobody to play in it but myself." So he built a high wall all round it, and put up a notice-board.

> TRESPASSERS
> WILL BE
> PROSECUTED

He was a very selfish Giant.

The poor children had now nowhere to play. They tried to play on the road, but the road was very dusty and full of hard stones, and they did not like it. They used to wander round the high wall when their lessons were over, and talk about the beautiful garden inside. "How happy we were there," they said to each other.

Then the Spring came, and all over the country there were little blossoms and little birds. Only in the garden of the Selfish Giant it was still winter. The birds did not care to sing in it, as there were no children, and the trees forgot to blossom. Once a beautiful flower put its head out from the grass, but when it saw the notice-board it was so sorry for the children that it slipped back into the ground again, and went off to sleep. The only people who were pleased were the Snow and the Frost. "Spring has forgotten this garden," they cried, "so we will live here all the year round." The Snow covered up the grass with her great white cloak, and the Frost painted all the trees silver. Then they invited the North Wind to stay with them, and he came. He was wrapped in furs, and he roared all day about the garden, and blew the chimney-pots down. "This is a delightful spot," he said; "we must ask the Hail on a visit." So the Hail came. Every day for three hours he rattled on the roof of the castle till he broke most of the slates, and then he ran round and round the garden as fast as he could go. He was dressed in gray, and his breath was like ice.

"I can not understand why the Spring is so late in coming," said the Selfish Giant, as he sat at the window and looked out at his cold white garden; "I hope there will be a change in the weather."

But the Spring never came, nor the Summer. The Autumn gave golden fruit to every garden, but to the Giant's garden she gave none. "He is too selfish," she said. So it was always Winter there, and the North Wind, and the Hail, and the Frost, and the Snow danced about through the trees.

One morning the Giant was lying awake in bed when he heard some lovely music. It sounded so sweet to his ears that he thought it must be the King's musicians passing by. It was really only a little linnet singing outside his window, but it was so long since he had heard a bird sing in his garden that it seemed to him to be the most beautiful music in the world. Then the Hail stopped dancing over his head, and the North Wind ceased roaring, and a delicious perfume came to him through the open casement. "I believe the Spring has come at last," said the Giant; and he jumped out of bed and looked out.

What did he see?

He saw a most wonderful sight. Through a little hole in the wall the children had crept in, and they were sitting in the branches of the trees. In every tree that he could see there was a little child. And the trees were so glad to have the children back again that they had covered themselves with blossoms, and were waving their arms gently above the children's heads. The birds were flying about and twittering with delight, and the flowers were looking up through the green grass and laughing. It was a lovely scene, only in one corner it was still winter. It was the farthest corner of the garden, and in it was standing a little boy. He was so small that he could not reach up to the branches of the tree, and he was wandering all round it, crying bitterly.

The poor tree was still quite covered with frost and snow, and the North Wind was blowing and roaring above it. "Climb up, little boy," said the Tree, and it bent its branches down as low as it could; but the boy was too tiny.

And the Giant's heart melted as he looked out. "How selfish I have been!" he said; "now I know why the Spring would not come here. I will put that poor little boy on the top of the tree, and then I will knock down the wall, and my garden shall be the children's playground for ever and ever." He was really very sorry for what he had done.

So he crept downstairs and opened the front door quite softly, and went out into the garden. But when the children saw him they were so frightened that they all ran away, and the garden became winter again. Only the little boy did not run, for his eyes were so full of tears that he did not see the Giant coming. And the Giant stole up behind him and took him gently in his hand, and put him up into the tree. And the tree broke at once into blossoms, and the birds came and sang on it, and the little boy stretched out his two arms and flung them round the Giant's neck and kissed him. And the other children, when they saw that the Giant was not wicked any longer, came running back, and with them came the Spring. "It is your garden now, little children," said the Giant, and he took a great axe and knocked down the wall. And when the people were going to market at twelve o'clock they found the Giant playing with the children in the most beautiful garden they had ever seen.

All day long they played, and in the evening they came to the Giant to bid him good-bye.

"But where is your little compan-

ion?" he said: "the boy I put into the tree." The Giant loved him the best because he had kissed him.

"We don't know," answered the children; "he has gone away."

"You must tell him to be sure and come here to-morrow," said the Giant. But the children said that they did not know where he lived, and had never seen him before; and the Giant felt very sad.

Every afternoon, when school was over, the children came and played with the Giant. But the little boy whom the Giant loved was never seen again. The Giant was very kind to all the children, yet he longed for his first little friend, and often spoke of him. "How I would like to see him!" he used to say.

Years went over, and the Giant grew very old and feeble. He could not play about any more, so he sat in a huge armchair, and watched the children at their games, and admired his garden. "I have many beautiful flowers," he said; "but the children are the most beautiful flowers of all."

One winter morning he looked out of his window as he was dressing. He did not hate the Winter now, for he knew that it was merely the Spring asleep, and that the flowers were resting.

Suddenly he rubbed his eyes in wonder, and looked and looked. It certainly was a marvelous sight. In the farthest corner of the garden was a tree quite covered with lovely white blossoms. Its branches were all golden, and silver fruit hung down from them, and underneath it stood the little boy he had loved.

Downstairs ran the Giant in great joy, and out into the garden. He hastened across the grass, and came near to the child. And when he came quite close his face grew red with anger, and he said, "Who hath dared to wound thee?" For on the palms of the child's hands were the prints of two nails, and the prints of two nails were on the little feet.

"Who hath dared to wound thee?"

cried the Giant; "tell me, that I may take my big sword and slay him."

"Nay!" answered the child; "but these are the wounds of Love."

"Who art thou?" said the Giant, and a strange awe fell on him, and he knelt before the little child.

And the child smiled on the Giant, and said to him, "You let me play once in your garden, to-day you shall come with me to my garden, which is Paradise."

And when the children ran in that afternoon, they found the Giant lying dead under the tree, all covered with white blossoms.

For Thought and Discussion

1. Describe the Giant's garden while he was away and after he came back. Why was it changed upon his return?
2. Who stayed in his garden after the note to trespassers was put up?
3. When did the garden change again?
4. Describe the tree under which stood the little boy loved by the Giant. Whom did the little boy represent?
5. Explain the meaning of the allegory.
6. Of what Biblical passages are you reminded?

~&

THE BET

ANTON CHEKHOV

[There is an authentic account of an American who, because of a bet with an English banker, served a voluntary imprisonment of ten years. Whether Chekhov, one of the greatest of Russia's short story writers, was familiar with the account and utilized it in "The Bet" or whether his seemingly limitless knowledge and understanding of human life enabled him to imagine such an amazing story is not easily determined. At any rate, his realistic, cynical, fatalistic version of "The Bet" shows with unforgetable clarity the tragic consequences which can result from a simple jest.]

IT WAS a dark autumn night. The old banker was pacing from corner to corner of his study, recalling to his mind the party he gave in the autumn fifteen years before. There were many clever people at the party and much interesting conversation. They talked among other things of capital punishment. The guests, among them not a few scholars and journalists, for the most part disapproved of capital punishment. They found it obsolete as a means of punishment, unfitted to a Christian State, and immoral. Some of them thought that capital punishment should be replaced universally by life-imprisonment.

"I don't agree with you," said the host. "I myself have experienced neither capital punishment nor life-imprisonment, but if one may judge a priori,[1] then in my opinion capital punishment is more moral and more humane than imprisonment. Execu-

---

[1] a priori, deduced from known causes, an assumption.

tion kills instantly, life-imprisonment kills by degrees. Who is the more humane executioner, one who kills you in a few seconds or one who draws the life out of you incessantly, for years?"

"They're both equally immoral," remarked one of the guests, "because their purpose is the same, to take away life. The State is not God. It has no right to take away that which it cannot give back, if it should so desire."

Among the company was a lawyer, a young man of about twenty-five. On being asked his opinion, he said:

"Capital punishment and life-imprisonment are equally immoral; but if I were offered the choice between them, I would certainly choose the second. It's better to live somehow than not to live at all."

There ensued a lively discussion. The banker who was then younger and more nervous suddenly lost his temper, banged his fist on the table, and turning to the young lawyer, cried out:

"It's a lie. I bet you two millions you wouldn't stick in a cell even for five years."

"If you mean it seriously," replied the lawyer, "then I bet I'll stay not five but fifteen."

"Fifteen! Done!" cried the banker. "Gentlemen, I stake two millions."

"Agreed. You stake two millions, I my freedom," said the lawyer.

So this wild, ridiculous bet came to pass. The banker, who at that time had too many millions to count, spoiled and capricious, was beside himself with rapture. During supper he said to the lawyer jokingly:

"Come to your senses, young man, before it's too late. Two millions are nothing to me, but you stand to lose three or four of the best years of your life. I say three or four, because you'll never stick it out any longer. Don't

forget either, you unhappy man, that voluntary is much heavier than enforced imprisonment. The idea that you have the right to free yourself at any moment will poison the whole of your life in the cell. I pity you."

And now the banker, pacing from corner to corner, recalled all this and asked himself:

"Why did I make this bet? What's the good? The lawyer loses fifteen years of his life and I throw away two millions. Will it convince people that capital punishment is worse or better than imprisonment for life? No, no! all stuff and rubbish. On my part, it was the caprice of a well-fed man; on the lawyer's, pure greed of gold."

He recollected further what happened after the evening party. It was decided that the lawyer must undergo his imprisonment under the strictest observation, in a garden wing of the banker's house. It was agreed that during the period he would be deprived of the right to cross the threshold, to see living people, to hear human voices, and to receive letters and newspapers. He was permitted to have a musical instrument, to read books, to write letters, to drink wine and smoke tobacco. By the agreement he could communicate, but only in silence, with the outside world through a little window specially constructed for this purpose. Everything necessary, books, music, wine, he could receive in any quantity by sending a note through the window. The agreement provided for all the minutest details, which made the confinement strictly solitary, and it obliged the lawyer to remain exactly fifteen years from twelve o'clock of November 14th, 1870, to twelve o'clock of November 14th, 1885. The least attempt on his part to violate the conditions, to escape if only for two minutes before the time, freed the banker from the obligation to pay him the two millions.

During the first year of imprisonment, the lawyer, as far as it was possible to judge from his short notes, suffered terribly from loneliness and boredom. From his wing day and night came the sound of the piano. He rejected wine and tobacco. "Wine," he wrote, "excites desires, and desires are the chief foes of a prisoner; besides, nothing is more boring than to drink good wine alone," and tobacco spoiled the air in his room. During the first year the lawyer was sent books of a light character; novels with a complicated love interest, stories of crime and fantasy, comedies, and so on.

In the second year the piano was heard no longer and the lawyer asked only for classics. In the fifth year, music was heard again, and the prisoner asked for wine. Those who watched him said that during the whole of that year he was only eating, drinking, and lying on his bed. He yawned often and talked angrily to himself. Books he did not read. Sometimes at night he would sit down to write. He would write for a long time and tear it all up in the morning. More than once he was heard to weep.

In the second half of the sixth year, the prisoner began zealously to study languages, philosophy, and history. He fell on these subjects so hungrily that the banker hardly had time to get books enough for him. In the space of four years about six hundred volumes were bought at his request. It was while that passion lasted that the banker received the following letter from the prisoner: "My dear jailer, I am writing these lines in six languages. Show them to experts. Let them read them. If they do not find one single mistake, I beg you to give orders to have a gun fired off in the garden. By the noise I shall know that my efforts have not been in vain. The geniuses of all ages and countries speak in different languages; but in them all burns the same flame. Oh, if you knew my heavenly happiness now that I can understand them!" The prisoner's desire was fulfilled. Two shots were fired in the garden by the banker's order.

Later on, after the tenth year, the lawyer sat immovable before his table and read only the New Testament. The banker found it strange that a man who in four years had mastered six hundred erudite volumes, should have spent nearly a year in reading one book, easy to understand and by no means thick. The New Testament was then replaced by the history of religions and theology.

During the last two years of his confinement the prisoner read an extraordinary amount, quite haphazard. Now he would apply himself to the natural sciences, then he would read Byron or Shakespeare. Notes used to come from him in which he asked to be sent at the same time a book on chemistry, a text-book of medicine, a novel, and some treatise on philosophy or theology. He read as though he were swimming in the sea among broken pieces of wreckage, and in his desire to save his life was eagerly grasping one piece after another.

The banker recalled all this, and thought:

"To-morrow at twelve o'clock he receives his freedom. Under the agreement, I shall have to pay him two millions. If I pay, it's all over with me. I am ruined forever . . ."

Fifteen years before he had too many millions to count, but now he was afraid to ask himself which he had more of, money or debts. Gambling

on the Stock-Exchange, risky speculation, and the recklessness of which he
could not rid himself even in old age,
had gradually brought his business to
decay; and the fearless, self-confident,
proud man of business had become an
ordinary banker, trembling at every
rise and fall in the market.

"That cursed bet," murmured the
old man clutching his head in despair
... "Why didn't the man die? He's
only forty years old. He will take
away my last farthing, marry, enjoy
life, gamble on the Exchange, and I
will look on like an envious beggar
and hear the same words from him
every day: 'I'm obliged to you for the
happiness of my life. Let me help
you.' No, it's too much! The only
escape from bankruptcy and disgrace
—is that the man should die."

The clock had just struck three.
The banker was listening. In the
house every one was asleep, and one
could hear only the frozen trees whining outside the windows. Trying to
make no sound, he took out of his
safe the key of the door which had
not been opened for fifteen years, put
on his overcoat, and went out of the
house. The garden was dark and cold.
It was raining. A damp, penetrating
wind howled in the garden and gave
the trees no rest. Though he strained
his eyes, the banker could see neither
the ground, nor the white statues, nor
the garden wing, nor the trees. Approaching the garden wing, he called
the watchman twice. There was no
answer. Evidently the watchman had
taken shelter from the bad weather
and was now asleep somewhere in the
kitchen or the greenhouse.

"If I have the courage to fulfil my
intention," thought the old man, "the
suspicion will fall on the watchman
first of all."

In the darkness he groped for the
steps and the door and entered the
hall of the garden wing, then poked
his way into a narrow passage and
struck a match. Not a soul was there.
Some one's bed, with no bedclothes
on it, stood there, and an iron stove
loomed dark in the corner. The seals
on the door that led into the prisoner's room were unbroken.

When the match went out, the old
man, trembling from agitation,
peeped into the little window.

In the prisoner's room a candle was
burning dimly. The prisoner himself
sat by the table. Only his back, the
hair on his head and his hands were
visible. Open books were strewn
about on the table, the two chairs, and
on the carpet near the table.

Five minutes passed and the prisoner never once stirred. Fifteen
years' confinement had taught him to
sit motionless. The banker tapped
on the window with his finger, but
the prisoner made no movement in
reply. Then the banker cautiously
tore the seals from the door and put
the key into the lock. The rusty lock
gave a hoarse groan and the door
creaked. The banker expected instantly to hear a cry of surprise and
the sound of steps. Three minutes
passed and it was as quiet inside as it
had been before. He made up his
mind to enter.

Before the table sat a man, unlike
an ordinary human being. It was a
skeleton, with tight-drawn skin, with
long curly hair like a woman's, and
a shaggy beard. The color of his face
was yellow, of an earthy shade; the
cheeks were sunken, the back long
and narrow, and the hand upon which
he leaned his hairy head was so lean
and skinny that it was painful to look
upon. His hair was already silvering
with gray, and no one who glanced
at the senile emaciation of the face
would have believed that he was only
forty years old. On the table, before

his bended head, lay a sheet of paper on which something was written in a tiny hand.

"Poor devil," thought the banker, "he's asleep and probably seeing millions in his dreams. I have only to take and throw this half-dead thing on the bed, smother him a moment with the pillow, and the most careful examination will find no trace of unnatural death. But, first, let us read what he has written here."

The banker took the sheet from the table and read:

"To-morrow at twelve o'clock midnight, I shall obtain my freedom and the right to mix with people. But before I leave this room and see the sun I think it necessary to say a few words to you. On my own clear conscience and before God who sees me I declare to you that I despise freedom, life, health, and all that your books call the blessings of the world.

"For fifteen years I have diligently studied earthly life. True, I saw neither the earth nor the people, but in your books I drank fragrant wine, sang songs, hunted deer and wild boar in the forests, loved women ... And beautiful women, like clouds ethereal, created by the magic of your poets' genius, visited me by night and whispered to me wonderful tales, which made my head drunken. In your books I climbed the summits of Elbruz[2] and Mont Blanc[3] and saw from there how the sun rose in the morning, and in the evening suffused the sky, the ocean and the mountain ridges with a purple gold. I saw from there how above me lightnings glimmered, cleaving the clouds; I saw green forests, fields, rivers, lakes, cities; I heard sirens singing, and the playing of the pipes of Pan; I touched the wings of beautiful devils who came flying to me to speak of God .... In your books I cast myself into bottomless abysses, worked miracles, burned cities to the ground, preached new religions. conquered whole countries ....

[2]*Elbruz*, in Europe, 18,526 feet.
[3]*Mont Blanc* (môn blän′), loftiest of Alps, 15,781 feet.

"Your books gave me wisdom. All that unwearying human thought created in the centuries is compressed to a little lump in my skull. I know that I am cleverer than you all.

"And I despise your books, despise all worldly blessings and wisdom. Everything is void, frail, visionary and delusive as a mirage. Though you be proud and wise and beautiful, yet will death wipe you from the face of the earth like the mice underground; and your posterity, your history, and the immortality of your men of genius will be as frozen slag, burnt down together with the terrestrial globe.

"You are mad, and gone the wrong way. You take falsehood for truth and ugliness for beauty. You would marvel if suddenly apple and orange trees should bear frogs and lizards instead of fruit, and if roses should begin to breathe the odor of a sweating horse. So do I marvel at you, who have bartered heaven for earth. I do not want to understand you.

"That I may show you in deed my contempt for that by which you live, I waive the two millions of which I once dreamed as of paradise; and which I now despise. That I may deprive myself of my right to them, I shall come out from here five minutes before the stipulated term, and thus shall violate the agreement."

When he had read, the banker put the sheet on the table, kissed the head of the strange man, and began to weep. He went out of the wing. Never at any other time, not even after his terrible losses on the Exchange, had he felt such contempt for himself as now. Coming home, he lay down on his bed, but agitation and tears kept him a long time from sleeping . . . .

The next morning the poor watchman came running to him and told him that they had seen the man who lived in the wing climb through the window into the garden. He had gone to the gate and disappeared. The banker instantly went with his servants to the wing and established the escape of his prisoner. To avoid unnecessary rumors he took the paper with the renunciation from the table and, on his return, locked it in his safe.

For Thought and Discussion

1. Of what was the banker thinking as the story opens?
2. Who had been his guests fifteen years previously?
3. Upon what subject had a division of opinion arisen at that time?
4. What was the banker's opinion upon the question?
5. What was the lawyer's opinion?
6. With which one do you agree?
7. What had resulted from their difference?
8. What decision did the banker come to as the time drew near for him to pay his bet? In effect, of what crime was he guilty?
9. Why didn't he carry out his intention?
10. What is the real meaning of this story?
11. What do you conclude from this story concerning the detrimental effects of imprisonment (long or short) upon the individual? upon society?
12. Are there means by which long terms of imprisonment could

be utilized somewhat to the advantage of both the individual and society?

13. What improvements can you suggest in regard to present day prison conditions?

14. Which to you is the more interesting study, the banker or the lawyer?

15. How does this story reflect upon the influence of books and their contribution to human happiness?

16. What elements of a good short story are noticeable in the selection?

17. In your interest in the story itself did you forget the purpose for which the bet was placed?

18. You may find a contrast between this French short story and the English ones in the text.

◆◇

From RABBI BEN EZRA

ROBERT BROWNING

[It would seem to be a strange God who would plan for the closing years of man's life to be less happy and worth while than the opening years—who would plan for the harvest of joy to be sadness. The beauty of the philosophy expounded in "Rabbi Ben Ezra" lies in its presentation of life as a joyful progression from youthful aspiration and ideals to a maturity of soul development worthy of youthful ambitions.

Rabbi Ben Ezra, the speaker in this dramatic monologue, was a Jewish scholar, poet, and physician, who lived in the eleventh century.]

I

GROW old along with me!
  The best is yet to be,
The last of life, for which the first
    was made;
  Our times are in His hand
  Who saith, "A whole I planned,   5
Youth shows but half; trust God; see
    all, nor be afraid!"

.   .   .   .

VI

Then, welcome each rebuff
That turns earth's smoothness
    rough,
Each sting that bids nor sit nor stand
    but go!
Be our joys three-parts pain!   10
Strive, and hold cheap the strain;
Learn, nor account the pang; dare,
    never grudge the throe!

VII

For thence—a paradox
Which comforts while it mocks—
Shall life succeed in that it seems to
    fail;   15
What I aspired to be,
And was not, comforts me;
A brute I might have been, but would
    not sink i' the scale.

.   .   .   .

X

Not once beat, "Praise be Thine!
I see the whole design,   20
I, who saw power, see now love per-
    fect too.

Perfect I call Thy plan;
Thanks that I was a man!
Maker, remake, complete — I trust
  what thou shalt do!"

.   .   .   .

XXVI

Ay, note that Potter's wheel,   25
That metaphor! and feel
Why time spins fast, why passive lies
  our clay—
Thou, to whom fools propound,
When the wine makes its round,
"Since life fleets, all is change; the
  past gone, seize today!"   30

XXVII

Fool! All that is, at all,
Lasts ever, past recall;
Earth changes, but thy soul and God
  stand sure:
What entered into thee,
That was, is, and shall be;   35

Time's wheel runs back or stops; Potter and clay endure.

.   .   .   .

XXXI

But I need, now as then,
  Thee, God, who moldest men;
And since, not even while the whirl
  was worst,
Did I—to the wheel of life,   40
  With shapes and colors rife,
Bound dizzily—mistake my end, to
  slake Thy thirst;

XXXII

So take and use Thy work;
  Amend what flaws may lurk,
What strain o' the stuff, what warp-
  ings past the aim!   45
My times be in Thy hand!
  Perfect the cup as planned!
Let age approve of youth, and death
  complete the same!

For Thought and Discussion

1. Often adults say to boys and girls, "These are the happiest days of your lives." Do you agree with them or with the first four lines of this poem?
2. Compare stanza XXVI with Isaiah 64:8 and Jeremiah 18:2-6. Who is the *Potter*? What is the *clay*? What is the *wheel*?
3. What sacred hymn is based upon this passage?
4. What does this poem reveal concerning Browning's attitude toward God? Quote in proof.
5. Do you agree with the philosophy incorporated in the various stanzas?
6. Why does Browning believe that one should be happier during the last part of life?
7. Point out figures of speech that add to the effectiveness of this poem.

Plus Work

Read the entire poem "Rabbi Ben Ezra." Comment on the philosophy of life expressed in the poem.

ON FIRST LOOKING INTO CHAPMAN'S HOMER

JOHN KEATS

[Keats had always wanted to read Homer's works but could not because they were written in Greek, which he never had an opportunity to study. When one of his friends brought him a copy of Chapman's translation, they sat up all night to read it. The next morning, Keats wrote this sonnet.

[1]*bards,* poets. [2]*in fealty,* loyalty. [3]*Apollo,* the sun god, also the god of music and poetry. [4]*Homer,* a famous Greek poet, author of the "Iliad" and "Odyssey." [5]*Córtez,* evidently a mistake, since Balboa was the discoverer. [6]*Darien,* on the Isthmus of Panama.]

MUCH have I traveled in the realms of gold
And many goodly states and kingdoms seen;
Round many western islands have I been

Which bards[1] in fealty[2] to Apollo[3] hold.
Oft of one wide expanse had I been told   5
That deep-browed Homer[4] ruled as his demesne;
Yet did I never breathe its pure serene
Till I heard Chapman speak out loud and bold.
Then felt I like some watcher of the skies
When a new planet swims into his ken;   10
Or like stout Córtez,[5] when with eagle eyes
He stared at the Pacific—and all his men
Looked at each other with a wild surmise—
Silent, upon a peak in Darien.[6]

For Thought and Discussion

1. What was the poet's reaction to reading Chapman's Homer?
2. Can you name a book from which you have derived as much pleasure as Keats did from reading Homer?

❧

ODE TO A NIGHTINGALE

JOHN KEATS

[Keats was in a melancholy mood on account of the death of his brother Tom. For a few hours he sat under a plum tree and listened to a nightingale's song. Afterwards he wrote this poem.

[1]*hemlock,* poison. [2]*Lethe,* a river in Hades signifying forgetfulness. [3]*dryad,* a tree nymph. [4]*Flora,* goddess of flowers. [5]*Provençal,* Provence, a section of southern France. [6]*Bacchus,* *and his pards,* god of wine in chariot drawn by leopards. [7]*fays,* fairies. [8]*requiem,* a song for the dead.]

MY heart aches, and a drowsy numbness pains
My sense, as though of hemlock[1] I had drunk,
Or emptied some dull opiate to the drains
One minute past, and Lethe-wards[2] had sunk;

'Tis not through envy of thy happy
  lot,   5
But being too happy in thine happiness—
    That thou, light-wingèd dryad[3]
    of the trees,
      In some melodious plot
Of beechen green, and shadows
  numberless,
    Singest of summer in full-
    throated ease.   10

O for a draught of vintage! that hath
  been
  Cooled a long age in the deep-
  delvèd earth,
Tasting of Flora[4] and the country
  green,
  Dance, and Provençal[5] song, and
  sunburnt mirth!
O for a beaker full of the warm
  South,   15
  Full of the true, the blushful Hip-
  pocrene,
    With beaded bubbles winking at
    the brim,
    And purple-stainèd mouth;
That I might drink, and leave the
  world unseen,
And with thee fade away into the
  forest dim—   20

Fade far away, dissolve, and quite forget
  What thou among the leaves hast
  never known,
The weariness, the fever, and the fret
Here, where men sit and hear each
  other groan;
Where palsy shakes a few, sad, last
  gray hairs,   25
  Where youth grows pale, and
  specter-thin, and dies;
    Where but to think is to be full
    of sorrow
    And leaden-eyed despairs;
Where beauty cannot keep her lustrous eyes,
  Or new love pine at them beyond
  tomorrow.   30

Away! away! for I will fly to thee,
  Not charioted by Bacchus and his
  pards,[6]
But on the viewless wings of Poesy,
  Though the dull brain perplexes
  and retards;
Already with thee! tender is the
  night,   35
  And haply the Queen-Moon is on
  her throne,
    Clustered around by all her
    starry fays[7];
    But here there is no light,
Save what from heaven is with the
  breezes blown
  Through verdurous glooms and
  winding mossy ways.   40

I cannot see what flowers are at my
  feet,
  Nor what soft incense hangs upon
  the boughs,
But, in embalmèd darkness, guess each
  sweet
  Wherewith the seasonable month
  endows
The grass, the thicket, and the fruit
  tree wild;   45
  White hawthorn, and the pastoral
  eglantine;
    Fast fading violets covered up in
    leaves;
    And mid-May's eldest child,
The coming musk-rose, full of dewy
  wine,
  The murmurous haunt of flies on
  summer eves.   50

Darkling I listen; and for many a
  time
  I have been half in love with ease-
  ful Death,
Called him soft names in many a
  musèd rime,
  To take into the air my quiet
  breath;
Now more than ever seems it rich to
  die,   55

To cease upon the midnight with
no pain,
While thou art pouring forth
thy soul abroad
In such an ecstasy!
Still wouldst thou sing, and I have
ears in vain—
To thy high requiem[8] become a
sod.   60

Thou wast not born for death, immortal bird!
No hungry generations tread thee
down;
The voice I hear this passing night was
heard
In ancient days by emperor and
clown;
Perhaps the selfsame song that found
a path   65
Through the sad heart of Ruth,
when, sick for home,
She stood in tears amid the alien
corn;

The same that ofttimes hath
Charmed magic casements, opening
on the foam
Of perilous seas, in faery lands forlorn.   70

Forlorn! the very word is like a bell
To toll me back from thee to my
sole self!
Adieu! The fancy cannot cheat so
well
As she is famed to do, deceiving elf.
Adieu! adieu! thy plaintive anthem
fades   75
Past the near meadows, over the
still stream,
Up the hillside; and now 'tis
buried deep
In the next valley-glades;
Was it a vision, or a waking dream?
Fled is that music.—Do I wake or
sleep?

For Thought and Discussion

1. What effect did the death of his brother have upon Keats?
2. What effect did the song of the nightingale have upon the poet?
3. How can the "viewless wings of Poesy" give the poet happiness and peace?
4. Why does he say that the bird is immortal?
5. What flowers would probably be named if this poem were by an American?
6. Why did the song of the nightingale attract Keats?
7. Forms of everlasting beauty attracted the poet. Why does the song of the nightingale represent this type of beauty?

Plus Work

After reading the Book of Ruth, from the Old Testament, tell the story and explain why the poet here refers to Ruth.

ODE ON A GRECIAN URN

JOHN KEATS

[Keats, always attracted by beauty, was impressed by a Grecian urn, which was probably in the British Museum. As he observed the various figures carved in the stone, he contrasted this loveliness, which had lasted through the ages, with earthly forms of beauty, which fade and perish.

[1]*Sylvan*, forest-like. [2]*deities*, gods. [3]*Tempe, Arcady*, beautiful sections of Greece. [4]*ecstasy*, overmastering joy or rapture. [5]*sensual*, earthly. [6]*cloyed*, surfeited, having too much. [7]*citadel*, fortress. [8]*Attic*, Grecian. [9]*brede*, braid, embroidery, hence ornamentation, the sculptured decorations on the urn. [10]*Pastoral*, rural.]

I

THOU still unravished bride of
    quietness,
  Thou foster-child of silence and
    slow time,
Sylvan[1] historian, who canst thus ex-
    press
A flowery tale more sweetly than
    our rime,
What leaf-fringed legend haunts
    about thy shape   5
  Of deities[2] or mortals, or of both,
    In Tempe[3] or the dales of Ar-
    cady?
What men or gods are these? What
    maidens loath?
    What mad pursuit? What struggle
    to escape?
    What pipes and timbrels? What
    wild ecstasy[4]?   10

II

Heard melodies are sweet, but those
    unheard

Are sweeter; therefore, ye soft
    pipes, play on;
Not to the sensual[5] ear, but, more en-
    deared,
Pipe to the spirit ditties of no tone.
Fair youth, beneath the trees, thou
    canst not leave   15
  Thy song, nor ever can those trees
    be bare;
    Bold lover, never, never canst
    thou kiss,
Though winning near the goal—yet,
    do not grieve;
  She cannot fade, though thou hast
    not thy bliss,
    Forever wilt thou love, and she
    be fair!   20

III

Ah, happy, happy boughs! that can-
    not shed
  Your leaves, nor ever bid the spring
    adieu;
And, happy melodist, unwearièd,
    Forever piping songs forever new;
More happy love! more happy, happy
    love!   25
    Forever warm and still to be en-
    joyed,
    Forever panting, and forever
    young;
All breathing human passion far
    above,
    That leaves a heart high-sorrowful
    and cloyed,[6]
    A burning forehead, and a
    parching tongue.   30

IV

Who are these coming to the sacrifice?
  To what green altar, O mysterious
    priest,
Lead'st thou that heifer lowing at the
    skies,

And all her silken flanks with garlands dressed?
What little town by river or sea-shore, [35]
Or mountain-built with peaceful citadel,[7]
Is emptied of this folk, this pious morn?
And, little town, thy streets for evermore
Will silent be; and not a soul to tell
Why thou art desolate, can e'er return. [40]

V

O Attic[8] shape! Fair attitude! with brede[9]
Of marble men and maidens over-wrought,
With forest branches and the trodden weed;
Thou, silent form, dost tease us out of thought
As doth eternity: Cold Pastoral![10] [45]
When old age shall this generation waste,
Thou shalt remain, in midst of other woe
Than ours, a friend to man, to whom thou say'st,
"Beauty is truth, truth beauty"—that is all
Ye know on earth, and all ye need to know.

For Thought and Discussion

1. Why did the marble urn attract the poet?
2. Why did these scenes on the vase represent to the poet a greater happiness than can be found in this world?
3. Why did Keats call the urn "Cold Pastoral"?
4. Why did he write about this urn? What ideas does he express?
5. Upon what subjects did Keats usually write?
6. Why may the poetry of Keats be termed romantic?
7. Compare and contrast the three poems by Keats. Read "Types of Literature" for a definition of the ode so that you may compare the odes of Keats with those of Shelley.

JOHN KEATS 1795-1821

Inborn Sense of Beauty.

A thing of beauty is a joy forever:
Its loveliness increases; it will never
Pass into nothingness; but still will keep
A bower of quiet for us, and a sleep
Full of sweet dreams, and health, and quiet breathing.
—"Endymion" (ĕn dĭm′ ĭ ŏn).

An intense appreciation of beauty is the dominant characteristic of the poetry of Keats. His sense of beauty was inborn; there was little in the earliest years of his life to foster it. His first home was in London over the Swan-and-Hoop livery stable, which his father kept. When the family prospered, they moved to a better neighborhood, as his parents, who seemed to have possessed many good

JOHN KEATS

qualities, were very anxious to give their children excellent educational opportunities. These early years were the only time that Keats was to have even a brief period of happiness.

Fondness for Reading. At Enfield School, although known to be quick to get into a fight, Keats was popular because of his fairness and high-mindedness. Here he became a close friend of Charles Cowden Clarke, the son of the headmaster. Clarke said later of him that he read widely and took off all the prizes in literature.

Apprenticeship to a Surgeon. Before Keats was ten, his father died, and six years later his mother. His guardian apprenticed him to a surgeon and apothecary so that he might fit himself for a life position. Although the study of medicine did not interest Keats, he applied himself to his task, passed his examination, and began work in a hospital.

Interest in Poetry. As the minds of other students have often been elsewhere rather than on the subject at hand, so did Keats's mind wander away from the lesson. He said to his friend Clarke, "The other day during the lecture, there came a sunbeam into the room, and with it a whole troop of creatures floating in the ray; and I was off with them to Oberon and fairy-land." He seems to have been so strongly attracted by poetry that it was impossible for him to direct his mind into other channels. In a letter to one of his friends he declared that he could not exist without poetry, that he must spend the entire day on it, and that he could not be happy unless he wrote verse. This intense interest in poetry was to absorb him completely during the remaining years of his brief life.

Keats was introduced to Leigh Hunt, in whose home he spent much time thereafter, listening to political harangues about liberty and revolution but enjoying the times the conversations veered to poetry, particularly to that of his favorites—Shakespeare, Milton, Spenser, and Chaucer. In the year 1816 he wrote "On First Looking into Chapman's Homer," and two years later "Endymion," a quotation of which is used at the beginning of this biography.

Unhappiness.   Life held many vicissitudes for John Keats. He missed his brother George, who left to make his home in America; later on his brother Tom, whom he had nursed for three months, died of tuberculosis. The poet's sadness was responsible for the melancholy tone of "Ode to a Nightingale," which was written after his brother's death. The reviewers had pounced upon "Endymion" so unmercifully that Byron wrote after Keats's death:

> " 'Who killed John Keats?'
> 'I,' says the Quarterly,
> So savage and Tartarly;
> ' 'Twas one of my feats.' "

This review, however, was not in any way responsible for Keats's death.

Another cause for his depressed spirits was his love affair with Fanny Brawne, who seemingly did not care for the poet as deeply as he for her.   Even though his health was already undermined and his finances were a source of worry, he continued his writing, and in the last few years of his life wrote "Hyperion," "The Eve of St. Agnes," "Ode on a Grecian Urn," "Ode to a Nightingale," and other poems.

Death of Poet.   He became so ill that it was necessary for him to go to a warmer climate for more sunshine, and in September of 1820 he sailed for Italy.   Shelley, who had met him and admired his work, extended him an invitation for a visit, which Keats was unable to accept.   Six months later he died of tuberculosis in Rome, on February 23, 1821.

Every year many travelers read on his tomb in the Protestant cemetery the unusual inscription, "Here Lies One Whose Name Was Writ in Water."   In spite of the despair expressed in the poet's epitaph and his protracted illness, he did gain, in his short life of twenty-six years, lasting fame.

Characteristics of His Poetry. An intense love of beauty is expressed in his poetry: "A thing of beauty is a joy forever." Music and art appealed to him as forms of everlasting beauty; the romance of medieval times which charmed him was in turn expressed in such poems as "La Belle Dame Sans Merci" and the "Eve of St. Agnes." These lines, the essence of music and romance, are from the "Eve of St. Agnes":

> "And they are gone: ay, ages long ago
> These lovers fled away into the storm."

The artistic standard which he consistently maintained and the unhappy circumstances under which he worked during the few years he wrote poetry are conclusive evidence of his genius. One feels that death did overtake him before he expressed all the beautiful fancies that filled his mind, that his short life was too brief for the full expression of all the beauty of which he was acutely sensitive.

TO A SKYLARK

PERCY BYSSHE SHELLEY

[This poem, according to Mrs. Shelley in the edition of her husband's poems published after his death, was written in 1820, while she and her husband were at Leghorn for a visit. It was, she said, inspired by the song of a skylark which they heard as they were wandering among lanes whose hedges were alight with fireflies. His method of describing the sweet singer is to give a series of lovely comparisons. It is interesting to note in stanza eight Shelley's theory concerning the mission of a poet.]

HAIL to thee, blithe spirit!
  Bird thou never wert,
That from heaven, or near it,
  Pourest thy full heart
In profuse strains of unpremeditated
    art.   5

Higher still and higher
  From the earth thou springest
Like a cloud of fire;

The blue deep thou wingest,
And singing still dost soar, and soar-
    ing ever singest.   10

In the golden lightning
  Of the sunken sun,
O'er which clouds are bright'ning,
  Thou dost float and run,
Like an unbodied joy whose race is
    just begun.   15

The pale purple even
  Melts around thy flight;
Like a star of heaven
  In the broad daylight
Thou art unseen, but yet I hear thy
    shrill delight,   20

Keen as are the arrows
  Of that silver sphere,
Whose intense lamp narrows
  In the white dawn clear,
Until we hardly see, we feel that it
    is there.   25

All the earth and air
  With thy voice is loud,
As, when night is bare,
  From one lonely cloud
The moon rains out her beams, and
  heaven is overflowed.   30

What thou art we know not;
  What is most like thee?
From rainbow clouds there flow not
  Drops so bright to see,
As from thy presence showers a rain
  of melody.   35

Like a poet hidden
  In the light of thought,
Singing hymns unbidden,
  Till the world is wrought
To sympathy with hopes and fears it
  heeded not;   40

Like a high-born maiden
  In a palace-tower,
Soothing her love-laden
  Soul in secret hour
With music sweet as love, which over-
  flows her bower;   45

Like a glowworm golden
  In a dell of dew,
Scattering unbeholden
  Its aërial hue
Among the flowers and grass, which
  screen it from the view;   50

Like a rose embowered
  In its own green leaves,
By warm winds deflowered,
  Till the scent it gives
Makes faint with too much sweet
  these heavy-wingèd thieves;   55

Sound of vernal showers
  On the twinkling grass,
Rain-awakened flowers,
  All that ever was
Joyous, and clear, and fresh, thy
  music doth surpass.   60

Teach us, sprite or bird,
  What sweet thoughts are thine.
I have never heard
  Praise of love or wine
That panted forth a flood of rapture
  so divine.   65

Chorus hymeneal,[1]
  Or triumphant chaunt,
Matched with thine would be all
  But an empty vaunt,
A thing wherein we feel there is
  some hidden want.   70

What objects are the fountains
  Of thy happy strain?
What fields, or waves, or moun-
  tains?
What shapes of sky or plain?
What love of thine own kind? What
  ignorance of pain?   75

With thy clear, keen joyance
  Languor cannot be;
Shadow of annoyance
  Never came near thee;
Thou lovest, but ne'er knew love's
  sad satiety.   80

Waking or asleep,
  Thou of death must deem
Things more true and deep
  Than we mortals dream,
Or how could thy notes flow in such
  a crystal stream?   85

We look before and after,
  And pine for what is not;
Our sincerest laughter
  With some pain is fraught;
Our sweetest songs are those that tell
  of saddest thought.   90

Yet if we could scorn
  Hate, and pride, and fear;
If we were things born
  Not to shed a tear,
I know not how thy joy we ever
  should come near.   95

_____

[1]*chorus hymeneal,* marriage chorus.

Better than all measures
Of delightful sound,
Better than all treasures
That in books are found,
Thy skill to poet were, thou scorner
of the ground!   100

Teach me half the gladness
That thy brain must know,
Such harmonious madness
From my lips would flow,
The world should listen then, as I
am listening now.

For Thought and Discussion

1. How does the English skylark differ from the American meadowlark?
2. Do the titles by which the skylark is addressed suggest earthly or ethereal qualities?
3. To what various objects is the bird compared?
4. Other things being equal, which artist or singer does the better work, the one who has known sorrow or the one who has not known sorrow?
5. When does the poet begin to think of himself?
6. For which of his qualities, one of which is much like that of the skylark, does the world remember Shelley today?
7. One critic indicates four divisions of this poem. Do you agree that there are four divisions, or do you see five or even six logical divisions? Summarize the divisions as you see them.

PERCY BYSSHE SHELLEY 1792-1822

The Wanderer and the Reformer. Wordsworth rebelled against the bondage of literary rule and established a new school of poetry. Shelley rebelled against society and, if he could have done so, would have established a new social order. While his sincerity is unquestioned, in some of his longer poems, notably "Prometheus Unbound," he is revealed as an unbalanced reformer. In others, such as "Alastor," he is revealed as a wandering dreamer, restless and hopeless, akin to nature in gentleness and, likewise, in wildness.

His Home. Shelley belonged to an old family, honored in both the literary and the political field. As a small child he lived in pleasant surroundings; he joined in the romping play with his brother and his four sisters; but he lived, too, in a dream world peopled with creations of his own imagination, which he sometimes tried to foist upon others through tricks of science and magic. He loved and was loved dearly by children, one of his early fancies being to adopt a child. In later life his affection for his own children was marked.

His School Life. The poet's first school teacher was a hard-hearted master whose school was in keeping with his own brutal

PERCY BYSSHE SHELLEY

nature. It seems a pity that Shelley, like Wordsworth, could not
have been under the care of an understanding teacher. Neither
this school with its flogging system nor Eton with its fagging
system was a place for a sensitive child like Shelley. The scholars
were cruel to him, and being of a high spirit, he retaliated in such
frenzy that he was called "Mad Shelley." It is no wonder that his
spirit so revolted that in all his later life he was in such a resentful
mood that he sought to break the very foundation of society.
Shelley was a good student, excellent in literature and in science.
With the proceeds of his first published story he gave a dinner to
some of his school friends and presented to them autographed books
as keepsakes. His life at Oxford gave promise of being pleasanter
for him, but after reading some of Homer's philosophy, he wrote a
tract on the necessity for atheism. Because of that article he was
expelled from school and was even denied the rights of his home.

His Chivalry. While he was living in London, Shelley met
Harriet Westbrook, and she fell deeply in love with him. Because

of his chivalry he felt that he must marry her, and he did so in 1811. He was but nineteen and she sixteen. The marriage was unhappy, and after her death in 1816 he married Mary Godwin, a very intellectual woman.

Refuge in Italy. There were some unpleasant incidents in connection with the marriage of Shelley and his second wife, and partly because of the constant censure which was theirs in England and partly because of Shelley's ill health, they went to Italy in 1818. They never returned to their native land. In 1822, at the age of thirty, Shelley was drowned off the coast of Italy. His body was cremated, and the ashes placed in the little Protestant cemetery in Rome, near the grave of his friend Keats, a copy of whose poems was in his pocket at the time he was drowned. The volume was placed upon his funeral pyre.

His Longer Selections. Because his characters are unreal, his plots improbable, and his solutions impractical, only genuine lovers of poetry who have an appreciation for exquisite spirit fancies and ethereal music will care for Shelley's dramas and his other long poems. "Alastor" is a series of fanciful pictures; the lyrical drama, "Prometheus Unbound," is likewise a dream, a dream of the golden age of justice and brotherhood; his revolutionary dramas, "Queen Mab," "The Witch of Atlas," and "The Revolt of Hellas" are dreams, too, wild, mad dreams, in which the existing forms of church, society, and state were to be overthrown; and even his lovely threnody, "Adonais," a tribute to his friend Keats, is very much more like a phantasy than a record of personal grief. Only one selection, "Cenci," has an air of reality, and no one but a lover of the morbid would care to read that record of guilt.

His Lyrics. Shelley's best lyrics, few in number, are even better than those of Wordsworth. They are the embodiment of delicacy and grace and imaginative fancy. In his exquisite lyrics his words poured forth like the melody of his own blithe bird, the skylark.

❧

Additional Readings

Binyon, Lawrence: *The Golden Treasury of Modern Lyrics*

Boileau, Ethel: *A Gay Family*

Bridges, Robert: *The Testament of Beauty*

Colum, Padraic: *The Big Tree of Bunlahy*

Forbes, Anita P.: *Modern Verse*

Ibsen, Henrik: *The Doll's House*

Kingsley, Charles: *Water Babies*

Lofting, Hugh: *The Story of Doctor Dolittle*

Lucas, E. V.: *Fireside and Sunshine*

Maeterlinck, Maurice: *The Blue Bird*

Malot, Hector: *The Adventures of Perrine*

Milne, A. A.: *Four Plays*

Negri, Ada: *Morning Star*

Tomlinson, H. M.: *The Snows of Helicon*

Untermeyer, Louis: *Modern British Poetry*

Standards and Ideals of Living

STANDARDS and IDEALS of LIVING

IF ONE tries to determine what standards and ideals have contributed to the advancement of humanity, he realizes that courage and honesty unquestionably deserve a high place. The courageous person makes life easier for himself and others, and the honest man has harmony of spirit and furnishes stability to the business world. Pope's well-known statement is that "An honest man's the noblest work of God," and one may continue by saying that an honest man values facts, and that in the present day one who does not have a reverential regard for facts has failed to understand the scientific spirit of his own times.

How does one acquire his standards and ideals? The answer is significant—from his environment; from his home, from his church, from his family, from his friends and associates, and from his reading. A change in environment may bring one in contact with different ideas, and by learning to make a distinction between prejudice and principle one acquires tolerance, kindness, and sympathy. Such an adjustment and enlargement of mind and spirit is an important phase of one's college education and of his training in the business world.

Whoever seeks a career in public life finds fundamental honesty and courage a protection and a defense, but he may well beware of ambition, essential and laudable in itself, unless he directs it properly. And whether one finds a career in business, in public life, or in a home, one's standards and ideals fix his place in the minds and hearts of his fellow associates and determine his character and reputation. One understands an individual by learning his ideals, and a nation by reading the literature in which its ideals are expressed.

In the twentieth century with its emphasis upon speed and quantity, the old shoemaker who valued fine workmanship failed to find the appreciation which was his due. Quality, which he prized, is one of those standards with which the world cannot well dispense.

"DOSE ARE NOD MY BOODS···
·····DOSE BIG VIRMS HAVE
NO SELF-RESPECT, DRASH!"

QUALITY
JOHN GALSWORTHY

I KNEW him from the days of my extreme youth, because he made my father's boots; inhabiting with his elder brother two little shops let into one, in a small by-street—now no more, but then most fashionably placed in the West End.

That tenement had a certain quiet distinction; there was no sign upon its face that he made for any of the Royal Family—merely his own German name of Gessler Brothers; and in the window a few pairs of boots. I remember that it always troubled me to account for those unvarying boots in the window, for he made only what was ordered, reaching nothing down, and it seemed so inconceivable that what he made could ever have failed to fit. Had he bought them to put there? That, too, seemed inconceivable. He would never have tolerated in his house leather on which he had not worked himself. Besides, they were too beautiful—the pair of pumps, so inexpressibly slim, the patent leathers with cloth tops, making water come into one's mouth, the tall brown riding boots with marvelous sooty glow, as if, though new, they had been worn a hundred years. Those pairs could only have been made by one who saw before him the Soul of Boot—so truly were they prototypes incarnating the very spirit of all footgear. These thoughts, of course, came to me later, though even when I was promoted to him, at the age of perhaps fourteen, some inkling haunted me of the dignity of himself and brother. For to make boots—such boots as he made—seemed to me then, and still seems to me, mysterious and wonderful.

I remember well my shy remark, one day, while stretching out to him my youthful foot:

- 231 -

"Isn't it awfully hard to do, Mr. Gessler?"

And his answer, given with a sudden smile from out of the sardonic redness of his beard: "Id is an Ardt!"

Himself, he was a little as if made from leather, with his yellow crinkly face, and crinkly reddish hair and beard, and neat folds slanting down his cheeks to the corners of his mouth, and his guttural and one-toned voice; for leather is a sardonic substance, and stiff and slow of purpose. And that was the character of his face, save that his eyes, which were gray-blue, had in them the simple gravity of one secretly possessed by the Ideal. His elder brother was so very like him—though watery, paler in every way, with a great industry—that sometimes in early days I was not quite sure of him until the interview was over. Then I knew that it was he, if the words, "I will ask my brudder," had not been spoken; and that, if they had, it was his elder brother.

When one grew old and wild and ran up bills, one somehow never ran them up with Gessler Brothers. It would not have seemed becoming to go in there and stretch out one's foot to that blue iron-spectacled glance, owing him for more than—say—two pairs, just the comfortable reassurance that one was still his client.

For it was not possible to go to him very often—his boots lasted terribly, having something beyond the temporary—some, as it were, essence of boot stitched into them.

One went in, not as into most shops, in the mood of, "Please serve me, and let me go!" but restfully, as one enters a church; and, sitting on the single wooden chair, waited—for there was never anybody there. Soon, over the top edge of that sort of well —rather dark, and smelling soothingly of leather—which formed the shop, there would be seen his face, or that of his elder brother, peering down. A guttural sound and the tip-tap of bast slippers beating the narrow wooden stairs, and he would stand before one without coat, a little bent, in leather apron, with sleeves turned back, blinking—as if awakened from some dream of boots, or like an owl surprised in daylight and annoyed at this interruption.

And I would say, "How do you do, Mr. Gessler? Could you make me a pair of Russia leather boots?"

Without a word he would leave me, retiring whence he came, or into the other portion of the shop, and I would continue to rest in the wooden chair, inhaling the incense of his trade. Soon he would come back, holding in his thin, veined hand a piece of gold-brown leather. With eyes fixed on it, he would remark, "What a beautiful biece!" When I, too, had admired it, he would speak again. "When do you wand dem?" And I would answer, "Oh! As soon as you conveniently can." And he would say, "Tomorrow fordnighd?" Or, if he were his elder brother, "I will ask my brudder!"

Then I would murmur, "Thank you! Good morning, Mr. Gessler." "Goot morning!" he would reply, still looking at the leather in his hand. And as I moved to the door, I would hear the tip-tap of his bast slippers restoring him, up the stairs, to his dream of boots. But if it were some new kind of footgear that he had not yet made me, then indeed he would observe ceremony—divesting me of my boot and holding it long in his hand, looking at it with eyes at once critical and loving, as if recalling the glow with which he had created it, and rebuking the way in which one had disorganized this masterpiece. Then, placing my foot on a piece of paper, he would two or three times tickle the outer edges with a pencil and pass his nervous fingers over my toes, feeling himself into the heart of my requirements.

I cannot forget that day on which I had occasion to say to him, "Mr. Gessler, that last pair of town walking boots creaked, you know."

He looked at me for a time without replying, as if expecting me to withdraw or qualify the statement, then said: "Id shouldn'd 'ave greaked."

"It did, I'm afraid."

"You goddem wed before dey found demselves?"

"I don't think so."

At that he lowered his eyes, as if hunting for memory of those boots, and I felt sorry I had mentioned this grave thing.

"Zend dem back!" he said. "I will look at dem."

A feeling of compassion for my creaking boots surged up in me, so well could I imagine the sorrowful long curiosity of regard which he would bend on them.

"Zome boods," he said slowly, "are bad from birdt. If I can do noding wid dem, I dake dem off your bill."

Once (once only) I went absent-mindedly into his shop in a pair of boots bought in an emergency at some large firm's. He took my order without showing me any leather, and I could feel his eyes penetrating the inferior integument of my foot. At last he said, "Dose are nod my boods."

The tone was not one of anger, nor of sorrow, not even of contempt, but there was in it something quiet that froze the blood. He put his hand down and pressed a finger on the place where the left boot, endeavoring to be fashionable, was not quite comfortable.

"Id 'urds you dere," he said. "Dose big virms 'ave no self-respect. Drash!" And then, as if something

had given way within him, he spoke long and bitterly. It was the only time I ever heard him discuss the conditions and hardships of his trade.

"Dey get id all," he said, "dey get id by adverdisement, not by work. Dey dake it away from us, who lofe our boods. Id gomes to dis—bresently I haf no work. Every year id gets less—you will see." And looking at his lined face I saw things I had never noticed before, bitter things and bitter struggle—and what a lot of gray hairs there seemed suddenly in his red beard!

As best I could, I explained the circumstances of the purchase of those ill-omened boots. But his face and voice made so deep an impression that during the next few minutes I ordered many pairs. Nemesis fell! They lasted more terribly than ever. And I was not able conscientiously to go to him for nearly two years.

When at last I went I was surprised to find that outside one of the two little windows of his shop another name was painted, also that of a boot-maker—making, of course, for the Royal Family. The old familiar boots, no longer in dignified isolation, were huddled in the single window. Inside, the now contracted well of the one little shop was more scented and darker than ever. And it was longer than usual, too, before a face peered down, and the tip-tap of the bast slippers began. At last he stood before me, and, gazing through those rusty iron spectacles, said, "Mr. ——, isn'd it?"

"Ah! Mr. Gessler," I stammered, "but your boots are really *too* good, you know! See, these are quite decent still!" And I stretched out to him my foot. He looked at it.

"Yes," he said, "beople do nod wand good boods, id seems."

To get away from his reproachful

eyes and voice I hastily remarked, "What have you done to your shop?"

He answered quietly, "Id was too exbensif. Do you wand some boods?"

I ordered three pairs, though I had only wanted two, and quickly left. I had I do not know quite what feeling of being part, in his mind, of a conspiracy against him; or not perhaps so much against him as against his idea of boot. One does not, I suppose, care to feel like that; for it was again many months before my next visit to his shop, paid, I remember, with the feeling, "Oh! well, I can't leave the old boy—so here goes! Perhaps it'll be his elder brother!"

For his elder brother, I knew, had not character enough to reproach me, even dumbly.

And, to my relief, in the shop there did appear to be his elder brother, handling a piece of leather.

"Well, Mr. Gessler," I said, "how are you?"

He came close, and peered at me. "I am breddy well," he said slowly, "but my elder brudder is dead."

And I saw that it was indeed himself—but how aged and wan! And never before had I heard him mention his brother. Much shocked, I murmured, "Oh! I am sorry!"

"Yes," he answered, "he was a good man, he made a good bood; but he is dead." And he touched the top of his head, where the hair had suddenly gone as thin as it had been on that of his poor brother, to indicate, I suppose, the cause of death. "He could nod ged over losing de oder shop. Do you wand any boods?" And he held up the leather in his hand; "Id's a beaudiful biece."

I ordered several pairs. It was very long before they came—but they were better than ever. One simply could not wear them out. And soon after that I went abroad.

It was over a year before I was again in London. And the first shop I went to was my old friend's. I had left a man of sixty, I came back to one of seventy-five, pinched and worn and tremulous, who genuinely, this time, did not at first know me.

"Oh! Mr. Gessler," I said, sick at heart; "how splendid your boots are! See, I've been wearing this pair nearly all the time I've been abroad; and they're not half worn out, are they?"

He looked long at my boots—a pair of Russia leather, and his face seemed to regain steadiness. Putting his hand on my instep, he said, "Do dey vid you here? I 'ad drouble wid dat bair, I remember."

I assured him that they had fitted beautifully.

"Do you wand any boods?" he said. "I can make dem quickly; id is a slack dime."

I answered, "Please, please! I want boots all round—every kind!"

"I will make a vresh model. Your food must be bigger." And with utter slowness, he traced round my foot, and felt my toes, only once looking up to say,

"Did I dell you my brudder was dead?"

To watch him was painful, so feeble had he grown; I was glad to get away.

I had given those boots up, when one evening they came. Opening the parcel, I set the four pairs out in a row. Then one by one I tried them on. There was no doubt about it. In shape and fit, in finish and quality of leather, they were the best he had ever made me. And in the mouth of one of the town walking boots I found his bill. The amount was the same as usual, but it gave me quite a shock. He had never before sent it in till quarter day. I flew downstairs, and wrote a check, and posted it at once with my own hand.

A week later, passing the little street, I thought I would go in and tell him how splendidly the new boots fitted. But when I came to where his shop had been, his name was gone. Still there, in the window, were the slim pumps, the patent leathers with cloth tops, the sooty riding boots.

I went in, very much disturbed. In the two little shops—again made into one—was a young man with an English face.

"Mr. Gessler in?" I said.

He gave me a strange, ingratiating look.

"No, sir," he said, "no. But we can attend to anything with pleasure. We've taken the shop over. You've seen our name, no doubt, next door. We make for some very good people."

"Yes, yes," I said; "but Mr. Gessler?"

"Oh!" he answered; "dead."

"Dead! But I only received these boots from him last Wednesday week."

"Ah!" he said; "a shockin' go. Poor old man starved 'imself."

"Good God!"

"Slow starvation, the doctor called it! You see he went to work in such a way! Would keep the shop on; wouldn't have a soul touch his boots except himself. When he got an order, it took him such a time. People won't wait. He lost everybody. And there he'd sit, goin' on and on—I will say that for him—not a man in London made a better boot! But look at the competition! He never advertised! Would 'ave the best leather, too, and do it all 'imself. Well, there it is. What could you expect with his ideas?"

"But starvation—!"

"That may be a bit flowery, as the sayin' is—but I know myself he was sittin' over his boots day and night, to the very last. You see I used to watch him. Never gave 'imself time to eat; never had a penny in the house. All went in rent and leather. How he lived so long I don't know. He regular let his fire go out. He was a character. But he made good boots."

"Yes," I said, "he made good boots."

And I turned and went out quickly, for I did not want that youth to know that I could hardly see.

For Thought and Discussion

1. How did the quiet air of distinction and the absence of advertising show the quality of the boots, called shoes by Americans?
2. How does the description of the boots in the window describe their maker?
3. Why did one never run up bills at Gessler Brothers?
4. What was Mr. Gessler's attitude toward his own imperfect workmanship, when told that a pair of boots had creaked?
5. How did he criticize the illy-made boot from another shop?
6. Why was it nearly two years before the customer returned for new shoes? Why did Mr. Gessler's customers require very few pairs of shoes?
7. Why did Mr. Gessler lose his trade? What were Mr. Gessler's standards and ideals?
8. How does the story get its name? Is the title well chosen?
9. What effect does the use of machines have upon the feeling of

the workman toward his goods? How is it possible for a workman to influence the quality of goods manufactured?

10. How is this story a criticism of modern manufacturing?
11. How is Galsworthy's style adapted to his subject?
12. Point out instances in which the author appeals to the senses of
touch and smell.

John Galsworthy 1867-1933

Glimpses of Home Life, College Days, and Travels. In his
fondness for horses and dogs, many of which he had on his estate
in the Kipling country of the Devonshire hills, Galsworthy reminds one of Scott. Like Scott, too, in his youth he was fond of
sports, being captain of the football squad in his undergraduate
days at Harrow. At Oxford he was graduated with honor and was
called to the bar in 1890. He did not like the practice of law,
however, and as he was a man of means, he left his practice and set
out to roam at will through Russia, Australia, New Zealand, the
Fiji Islands, British Columbia, and Canada. One pleasant event
of his travels was his meeting with Joseph Conrad, with whom he
formed a fast friendship.

Influence of His Wife on His Career. In early life Galsworthy
had no particular literary ambitions; moreover, men of his station
rarely took up literature as a profession; but the young woman
who was later to become his wife, recognizing his ability, insisted
that he turn to literature as a career, and he did so. Later, in ac-
counting for his action, he remarked that one might like to please
a person of whom one was fond.

Grace and Beauty of Style. Galsworthy composed seated in an
arm chair. He wrote rapidly in a bold hand; but his manuscripts, it
is said, were not very tidy, being full of erasures and corrections.
Of his first nine tales he affirmed that they had every fault. In
view of that remark, and considering that Galsworthy achieved a
style distinguished for correctness and beauty, would-be-writers
should find encouragement. They should remember, however,
that Galsworthy waited for inspiration; he did not, out of necessity
for monetary returns, have to force himself to write.

Those who knew the novelist personally speak of his dignity and
his reticence and then, at once, refer to the ease and graciousness of
his manner. His seemed to be the quiet distinction and charm of
the well-appointed drawing rooms and the flower-filled gardens described very beautifully in many of his books. One is not surprised
to learn of his love for art and music; the writer of poetic prose,
such as his, is always appreciative of color and design and sound.

Sense of Sympathy and Justice. Galsworthy is like Dickens
in his sympathy for the unfortunate. His play *Justice* so aroused
England that the whole prison system was reformed. Other evils
that he attacked were strife between labor and capital, unjust legis-

lation, the dole system, the caste system. In fact, his talent was arrayed against all forms of injustice, pretense, and incompetence in either the individual or the class. That he was truly sensitive to distress and suffering and sorrow may be sensed in the manner in which he depicts the loneliness of lost dogs, the loneliness of wistful children, and the more poignant loneliness and suffering of the bits of "flotsam and jetsam" which make up the "tatterdemalion" crowd—they whom the misfortunes of war and sin and disease have left a little touched or queer or weak or bad. With charity and with a delicate irony, never malicious, he pictures the virtues, the vices, the strength, and the weakness of his characters. He presents life as he saw it, and he saw some goodness, some beauty, some innate refinement in almost every character.

The Forsyte Saga and Other Selections. Well known among Galsworthy's works are his novels, *Jocelyn* and *The Forsyte Saga* series, following the fortunes of one family through three generations and occupying twenty-six years of the author's life; his plays—*The Silver Box, The Skin Game, The Family*, and *Loyalties;* his volumes of short stories and essays—*Caravan, Tatterdemalion*, and the later volume *Inn of Tranquillity*.

At least one of Galsworthy's books was written in the United States. In 1925 he lived in California and while there finished the novel, *Escape*. In 1930 he and his wife spent the winter in Arizona as near to the desert as they could go. Something of the quality of desert stillness and desert beauty with which he became familiar there is reflected in his later works.

∾

LABOR

From *Past and Present*

THOMAS CARLYLE

[One of the Victorians who believed in the dignity of labor was Thomas Carlyle, 1795-1881. Work was to him a religious rite, a source of happiness, a means by which man made his due contribution to the world and attained harmony with the universe. In this selection, typical of Carlyle's use of biblical reference and style, he pays tribute to Christopher Wren, builder of St. Paul's Cathedral, London, and to Christopher Columbus, whom he calls a soldier of the "World Marine-service" destined to discover new Americas.

Carlyle does not confine his remarks upon labor to generalizations; in *Captains of Industry* he denounces the industrial system of England and advocates protection of workmen. Note his peculiar manner of using capitals in ways in which they are not ordinarily used.]

FOR there is a perennial nobleness, and even sacredness, in Work. Were he never so benighted, forgetful of his high calling, there is always hope in a man that actually and earnestly works: in Idleness alone is there perpetual despair. Work, never so Mammonish, mean, *is* in communication with Nature; the real desire to get Work done will itself lead one more and more to truth, to Nature's appointments and regulations, which are truth.

The latest Gospel in this world is, Know thy work and do it. 'Know thyself': long enough has that poor 'self' of thine tormented thee; thou wilt never get to 'know' it, I believe! Think it not thy business, this of knowing thyself; thou art an unknowable individual: know what thou canst work at; and work at it, like a Hercules! That will be thy better plan.

It has been written, 'an endless significance lies in Work'; a man perfects himself by working. Foul jungles are cleared away, fair seed-fields rise instead, and stately cities; and withal the man himself first ceases to be a jungle and foul unwholesome desert thereby. Consider how, even in the meanest sorts of Labor, the whole soul of a man is composed into a kind of real harmony, the instant he sets himself to work! Doubt, Desire, Sorrow, Remorse, Indignation, Despair itself, all these like helldogs lie beleaguering the soul of the poor dayworker, as of every man; but he bends himself with free valor against his task, and all these are stilled, all these shrink murmuring far off into their caves. The man is now a man. The blessed glow of Labor in him, is it not as purifying fire, wherein all poison is burnt up, and of sour smoke itself there is made bright blessed flame!

Destiny, on the whole, has no other way of cultivating us. A formless Chaos, once set it *revolving,* grows round and ever rounder; ranges itself, by mere force of gravity, into strata, spherical courses; is no longer a Chaos, but a round compacted World. What would become of the Earth, did she cease to revolve? In the poor old Earth, so long as she revolves, all inequalities, irregularities disperse themselves; all irregularities are incessantly becoming regular. Hast thou looked on the Potter's wheel—one of the venerablest objects; old as the Prophet Ezechiel and far older? Rude lumps of clay, how they spin themselves up, by mere quick whirling, into beautiful circular dishes. And fancy the most assiduous Potter, but without his wheel; reduced to make dishes or rather amorphous botches, by mere kneading and baking! Even such a Potter were Destiny, with a human soul that would rest and lie at ease, that would not work and spin! Of an idle unrevolving man the kindest Destiny like the most assiduous Potter without wheel, can bake and knead nothing other than a botch; let her spend on him what expensive coloring, what gilding and enameling she will, he is but a botch. Not a dish; no, a bulging, kneaded, crooked, shambling, squint-cornered, amorphous botch,—a mere enameled vessel of dishonor! Let the idle think of this.

Blessed is he who has found his work; let him ask no other blessedness. He has a work, a life-purpose; he has found it, and will follow it! How, as a free-flowing channel, dug and torn by noble force through the sour mud-swamp of one's existence, like an ever-deepening river there, it runs and flows; — draining off the sour festering water, gradually from the root of the remotest grass-blade; making, instead of pestilential swamp, a green fruitful meadow with its clear-flowing stream. How blessed for the meadow itself, let the stream and *its* value be great or small! Labor is Life: from the inmost heart of the Worker rises his God-given Force, the sacred celestial Life-essence breathed into him by Almighty God; from his inmost heart awakens him to all nobleness,—to all knowledge, 'self-knowledge' and much else, so soon as Work fitly begins. Knowledge? The knowledge that will hold good in working, cleave thou to that; for Nature herself accredits that, says Yea to that. Properly thou hast no other knowledge but what thou hast got by working: the rest is yet all a hypothesis of knowledge; a thing to be argued of in schools, a thing floating in the clouds, in endless logic-vortices, till we try it and fix it. 'Doubt, of whatever kind, can be ended by Action alone.'

And again, hast thou valued Patience, Courage, Perseverance, Openness to light; readiness to own thyself mistaken, to do better next time? All these, all virtues, in wrestling with the dim brute Powers of Fact, in ordering of thy fellows in such wrestle, there and elsewhere not at all, thou wilt continually learn. Set down a brave Sir Christopher in the middle of black ruined Stone-heaps, of foolish unarchitectural Bishops, redtape Officials, idle Nell-Gwyn Defenders of the Faith; and see whether he will ever raise a Paul's Cathedral out of all that, yea or no! Rough, rude, contradictory are all things and persons, from the mutinous masons and Irish hodmen, up to the idle Nell-Gwyn Defenders, to blustering redtape Officials, foolish unarchitectural Bishops. All these things and persons are there not for Christopher's sake and his Cathedral's; they are there for their own sake mainly! Christopher will have to conquer and constrain all these,—if he be able. All these are against him. Equitable Nature herself, who carries her mathematics and architectonics not on the face of her,

but deep in the hidden heart of her,—Nature herself is but partially for him; will be wholly against him, if he constrain her not! His very money, where is it to come from? The pious munificence of England lies far-scattered, distant, unable to speak, and say, 'I am here';—must be spoken to before it can speak. Pious munificence, and all help, is so silent, invisible like the gods; impediment, contradictions manifold are so loud and near! O brave Sir Christopher, trust thou in those notwithstanding, and front all these; understand all these; by valiant patience, noble effort, insight, by man's-strength, vanquish and compel all these,—and, on the whole, strike down victoriously the last topstone of that Paul's Edifice; thy monument for certain centuries, the stamp 'Great Man' impressed very legibly on Portland-stone there!—

Yes, all manner of help, and pious response from Men or Nature, is always what we call silent; cannot speak or come to light, till it be seen, till it be spoken to. Every noble work is at first 'impossible.' In very truth, for every noble work the possibilities will lie diffused through Immensity; inarticulate, undiscoverable except to faith. Like Gideon thou shalt spread out thy fleece at the door of thy tent; see whether under the wide arch of Heaven there be any bounteous moisture, or none. Thy heart and life-purpose shall be as a miraculous Gideon's fleece, spread out in silent appeal to Heaven; and from the kind Immensities, what from the poor unkind Localities and town and country Parishes there never could, blessed dew-moisture to suffice thee shall have fallen!

Work is of a religious nature—work is of a *brave* nature; which it is the aim of all religion to be. All work of man is as the swimmer's; a waste ocean threatens to devour him; if he front it not bravely, it will keep its word. By incessant wise defiance of it, lusty rebuke and buffet of it, behold how it loyally supports him, bears him as its conqueror along. 'It is so,' says Goethe, 'with all things that man undertakes in this world.'

Brave Sea-captain, Norse Sea-king —Cólumbus, my hero, royalest Sea-king of all! it is no friendly environment this of thine, in the waste deep waters; around thee mutinous discouraged souls, behind thee disgrace and ruin, before thee the unpenetrated veil of Night. Brother, these wild water-mountains, bounding from their deep bases (ten miles deep, I am told), are not entirely there on thy behalf! Meseems *they* have other work than floating thee forward:— and the huge Winds, that sweep from Ursa Major to the Tropics and Equators, dancing their giant-waltz through the kingdoms of Chaos and Immensity, they care little about filling rightly or filling wrongly the small shoulder-of-mutton sails in this cockle-skiff of thine! Thou art not among articulate-speaking friends, my brother; thou art among immeasurable dumb monsters, tumbling, howling wide as the world here. Secret, far off, invisible to all hearts but thine, there lies a help in them: see how thou wilt get at that. Patiently thou wilt wait till the mad Southwester spend itself, saving thyself by dextrous science of defense, the while: valiantly, with swift decision, wilt thou strike in, when the favoring East, the Possible, springs up. Mutiny of men thou wilt sternly repress; weakness, despondency, thou wilt cheerily encourage: thou wilt swallow down complaint, unreason, weariness, weakness of others and thyself;—how much wilt thou swallow down! There shall be a depth of Silence in thee, deeper than this Sea, which is but ten miles deep: a Silence unsoundable; known to God only. Thou shalt be a Great Man. Yes, my World-Soldier, thou of the World Marine-service,— thou wilt have to be *greater* than this tumultuous unmeasured World here round thee is; thou, in thy strong soul, as with wrestler's arms, shalt embrace it, harness it down; and make it bear thee on,—to new Americas, or whither God wills!

For Thought and Discussion

1. Carlyle was noted for coining new words and forming unusual compounds. List expressions which illustrate this tendency.
2. Where is there a reference to the potter's wheel in the Bible? How do you account for Carlyle's reference to Ezechiel, usually spelled Ezekiel?
3. According to this essay, what are the virtues developed through work?
4. List literary allusions used by Carlyle.
5. Is Carlyle's style characterized by figures of speech?
6. The twentieth century has been called a materialistic age. In the style of Carlyle write a denunciation of our present materialistic tendency.
7. Is "Doubt can be ended by action alone" good psychology?
8. Who was Sir Christopher Wren and what did he accomplish?

A MAN'S A MAN FOR A' THAT

ROBERT BURNS

[¹*guinea*, a coin. ²*gowd*, gold.
³*a' that*, all that. ⁴*hamely fare*, homely food. ⁵*hoddin gray*, coarse, gray
woolen cloth. ⁶*birkie*, fellow. ⁷*guid*,
good. ⁸*mauna fa'*, cannot make. ⁹*bear
the gree*, win the prize. ¹⁰*warld*,
world.]

I

IS there, for honest poverty
  That hangs his head, an' a' that?
The coward-slave, we pass him by,
  We dare be poor for a' that!
For a' that, an' a' that,   5
  Our toils obscure, and a' that;
The rank is but the guinea's¹ stamp:
  The man's the gowd² for a' that.³

II

What though on hamely fare⁴ we
    dine,
  Wear hoddin gray,⁵ an' a' that? 10
Gi'e fools their silks, an' knaves their
    wine,
  A man's a man for a' that;
For a' that, an' a' that,
  Their tinsel show, and a' that—
The honest man, though e'er sae
    poor,   15
  Is king o' men for a' that.

III

Ye see yon birkie,⁶ ca'd a lord,
  What struts, an' stares, an' a' that;
Tho' hundreds worship at his word,
  He's but a coof for a' that;   20
For a' that, an' a' that,
  His riband, star, an' a' that—
The man o' independent mind,
  He looks an' laughs at a' that.

IV

A prince can make a belted knight, 25
  A marquis, duke, an' a' that,
But an honest man's aboon his
    might—
  Guid⁷ faith, he mauna fa'⁸ that!
For a' that, an' a' that,
  Their dignities, an' a' that,   30
The pith o' sense and pride o' worth
  Are higher ranks than a' that.

V

Then let us pray that come it may,
  —As come it will for a' that—
That sense and worth, o'er a' the
    earth,   35
  Shall bear the gree,⁹ an' a' that.
For a' that, an' a' that,
  It's comin' yet, for a' that—
That man to man, the warld¹⁰ o'er,
  Shall brothers be for a' that!   40

For Thought and Discussion

1. Why did Burns have much sympathy for the poor man?
2. What does the poet place above titles and rank?
3. Has the belief in the worth of the individual been generally accepted by the rest of the world? How has this belief affected governments?
4. Name different nations in the world which now have governments based upon democratic principles.
5. Is it correct to say that the theory of government in the United States rests upon the same belief in the worth of a common man that Burns expresses in this poem? Explain.

6. Does Burns place his faith in the masses or in the classes?
7. How has the progress in the New World justified the poet's views?
8. Why did Burns feel that the world is more likely to honor a man for his wealth and position than for his character? Do you think that this is true or just?

COURAGE

JOHN GALSWORTHY

COURAGE is but a word, and yet, of words,
The only sentinel of permanence,
The ruddy watch fire of cold winter days;
We steal its comfort, lift our weary swords,
And on. For faith—without it— has no sense;   5
And love to wind of doubt and tremor sways;
And life forever quaking marsh must tread.
Laws give it not, before it prayer will blush,
Hope has it not, nor pride of being true.
'Tis the mysterious soul which never yields,   10
But hales us on and on to breast the rush
Of all the fortunes we shall happen through.
And when Death calls across his shadowy fields—
Dying, it answers: "Here! I am not dead!"

For Thought and Discussion

1. How does courage strengthen faith and love?
2. Do you agree with Galsworthy that courage is the only symbol of permanence?
3. What answer does Courage make to Death?

INVICTUS[1]

WILLIAM ERNEST HENLEY

[William Ernest Henley had to wait a long time for recognition of his work; he knew what it meant to strive against the "bludgeonings of chance." Because of a tubercular infection of the bone, he was forced to have one foot amputated. Two years were spent in a hospital, yet his courage never flagged. This poem was written during that time.]

OUT of the night that covers me,
    Black as the Pit from pole to pole,
I thank whatever gods may be
    For my unconquerable soul.

---

[1] *invictus,* unconquered.

n the fell clutch of circumstance [5]
I have not winced nor cried aloud.
Under the bludgeonings of chance
My head is bloody, but unbowed.

Beyond this place of wrath and tears
Looms but the Horror of the shade, [10]

And yet the menace of the years
Finds, and shall find, me unafraid.

It matters not how strait the gate,
How charged with punishments the scroll,
I am the master of my fate; [15]
I am the captain of my soul.

For Thought and Discussion

1. What is the meaning of "night" in the first line?
2. What is the "fell clutch of circumstance" in the second stanza?
3. What is the author's attitude toward misfortune? What effect does such an attitude have upon an individual who is in trouble?

IF

RUDYARD KIPLING

IF YOU can keep your head when all about you
Are losing theirs and blaming it on you,
If you can trust yourself when all men doubt you,
But make allowance for their doubting too;
If you can wait and not be tired by waiting, [5]
Or being lied about, don't deal in lies,
Or being hated don't give way to hating,
And yet don't look too good, nor talk too wise;

If you can dream—and not make dreams your master;
If you can think—and not make thoughts your aim, [10]
If you can meet with Triumph and Disaster
And treat those two impostors just the same;

If you can bear to hear the truth you've spoken
Twisted by knaves to make a trap for fools,
Or watch the things you gave your life to, broken, [15]
And stoop and build them up with worn-out tools;

If you can make one heap of all your winnings
And risk it on one turn of pitch-and-toss,
And lose, and start again at your beginnings
And never breathe a word about your loss; [20]
If you can force your heart and nerve and sinew
To serve your turn long after they are gone,
And so hold on when there is nothing in you
Except the will which says to them: "Hold on!"

If you can talk with crowds and keep your virtue,   25
Or walk with kings—nor lose the common touch,
If neither foes nor loving friends can hurt you,
If all men count with you, but none too much;

If you can fill the unforgiving minute
With sixty seconds' worth of distance run,   30
Yours is the earth and everything that's in it,
And—which is more—you'll be a man, my son!

For Thought and Discussion

1. Express in your own words the meaning of this poem, stanza by stanza.
2. Read aloud the stanza which seems to you to be the most significant.
3. Would you include any traits that Kipling does not name?

Plus Work

Compare this poem with "Invictus," contrasting theme, point of view, mood, vocabulary, and striking lines. You may make your study more extensive by finding other poems on courage by different writers.

❧

GUNGA DIN

RUDYARD KIPLING

[¹*bhisti*, an Indian water-carrier.
²*Panee lao*, bring water quickly. ³*juldee*, speed. ⁴*mussick*, water bag.
⁵*Gunga Din*, gōōng gà dēn.]

YOU may talk o' gin and beer
  When you're quartered safe out 'ere,
An' you're sent to penny-fights an' Aldershot it;
But when it comes to slaughter
You will do your work on water, 5
An' you'll lick the bloomin' boots of 'im that's got it.
Now in Injia's sunny clime,
Where I used to spend my time
A-servin' of 'Er Majesty the Queen,
Of all them blackfaced crew 10
The finest man I knew

Was our regimental bhisti,¹ Gunga Din.
  He was "Din! Din! Din!
  "You limpin' lump o' brick-dust, Gunga Din!

"Hi! Slippy *hitherao!* 15
"Water, get it! *Panee lao*²
"You squidgy-nosed old idol, Gunga Din."

The uniform 'e wore
Was nothin' much before,
An' rather less than 'arf o' that be'ind, 20
For a piece o' twisty rag
An' a goatskin water-bag
Was all the field-equipment 'e could find.
When the sweatin' troop-train lay

In a sidin' through the day,   25
Where the 'eat would make your
    bloomin' eyebrows crawl,
We shouted "Harry By!"
Till our throats were bricky-dry,
Then we wopped 'im 'cause 'e
    couldn't serve us all.
        It was "Din! Din! Din!   30
    "You 'eathen, where the mischief
        'ave you been?
        "You put some *juldee*[3] in it
        "Or I'll *marrow* you this minute
        "If you don't fill up my helmet,
        Gunga Din!"

'E would dot an' carry one   35
Till the longest day was done;
An' 'e didn't seem to know the use o'
    fear.
If we charged or broke or cut,
You could bet your bloomin' nut,
'E'd be waitin' fifty paces right flank
    rear.   40
With 'is mussick[4] on 'is back,
'E would skip with our attack,
An' watch us till the bugles made
    "Retire."
An' for all 'is dirty 'ide
'E was white, clear white, inside   45

When 'e went to tend the wounded
    under fire!
    It was "Din! Din! Din!"
With the bullets kickin' dust-spots
    on the green;
    When the cartridges ran out,
    You could hear the front-ranks
        shout,   50
    "Hi! ammunition-mules an' Gunga
        Din!"[5]

I sha'n't forgit the night
When I dropped be'ind the fight
With a bullet where my belt-plate
    should 'a' been.
I was chokin' mad with thirst,   55
An' the man that spied me first
Was our good old grinnin', gruntin'
    Gunga Din.
'E lifted up my 'ead,
An' he plugged me where I bled,
An' 'e guv me 'arf-a-pint o' water
    green.   60
It was crawlin' and it stunk,
But of all the drinks I've drunk,
I'm gratefullest to one from Gunga
    Din.
        It was "Din! Din! Din!

" 'Ere's a beggar with a bullet
  through 'is spleen;   65
" 'E's chawin' up the ground,
"An' 'e's kickin' all around:
"For Gawd's sake git the water,
  Gunga Din!"

'E carried me away
To where a dooli lay,   70
An' a bullet come an' drilled the beg-
  gar clean.
'E put me safe inside,
An' just before 'e died,
"I 'ope you liked your drink," sez
  Gunga Din.
So I'll meet 'im later on   75

At the place where 'e is gone—
Where it's always double drill and no
  canteen.
'E'll be squattin' on the coals
Givin' drink to poor damned souls,
An' I'll get a swig in hell from Gunga
  Din!   80
  Yes, Din! Din! Din!
  You Lazarushian-leather Gunga
    Din!
    Though I've belted you and
      flayed you,
    By the livin' Gawd that made
      you,
    You're a better man than I am,
      Gunga Din!

For Thought and Discussion

1. What did the old veteran telling the story say that the soldier
   wanted most in war?
2. Why was Gunga Din's work difficult?
3. Why did the men belittle Gunga Din?
4. Why do you admire Gunga Din?
5. How does the use of dialect add to the interest of the poem?

Plus Work

Read *Barrack Room Ballads* and make a study of Kipling's poetry.
Read "Wee Willie Winkie" and make a class report on it.

~∾∾

THE SUBSTITUTE

FRANÇOIS COPPÉE

[The sacrificial theme of this story and the fact that Brander Matthews paid tribute to Coppée's poetic insight and to his sympathetic portrayal of character by ranking him as equal in suggestive picturing power with Maupassant and Daudet, other masters of the French short story, is sufficient reason for including "The Substitute" in an anthology of literature. Coppée lived from 1842 until 1908.]

HE WAS scarcely ten years old when he was first arrested as a vagabond.

He spoke thus to the judge:

"I am called Jean François Leturc, and for six months I was with the man who sings and plays upon a cord of catgut between the lanterns at the Place de la Bastille.[1] I sang the

[1] *Bastille* (bȧs tēl'), state prison of Paris, destroyed in 1789.

refrain with him, and after that I called, 'Here's all the new songs, ten centimes, two sous!' He was always drunk, and used to beat me. That is why the police picked me up the other night. Before that I was with the man who sells brushes. My mother was a laundress, her name was Adèle. At one time she lived with a man on the ground-floor at Montmartre.[2] She was a good work-woman and liked me. She made money because she had for customers waiters in the cafés, and they use a good deal of linen. On Sundays she used to put me to bed early so that she could go to the ball. On week-days she sent me to Les Frères, where I learned to read. Well, the sergent-de-ville whose beat was in our street used always to stop before our windows to talk with her—a good-looking chap, with a medal[3] from the Crimea. They were married, and after that everything went wrong. He didn't take to me, and turned mother against me. Every one had a blow for me, and so, to get out of the house, I spent whole days in the Place Clichy, where I knew the mountebanks. My father-in-law lost his place, and my mother her work. She used to go out washing to take care of him; this gave her a cough— the steam. . . She is dead at Lamboi-sière. She was a good woman. Since that I have lived with the seller of brushes and the catgut scraper.[4] Are you going to send me to prison?"

He said this openly, cynically, like a man. He was a little ragged street-arab, as tall as a boot, his forehead hidden under a queer mop of yellow hair.

---

[2]*Montmartre*, northern district of Paris, a former suburban village.
[3]*a medal from the Crimea*, a medal from the Crimean War.
[4]*catgut scraper*, fiddler, from catgut, a violin string.

Nobody claimed him, and they sent him to the Reform School.

Not very intelligent, idle, clumsy with his hands, the only trade he could learn there was not a good one —that of reseating straw chairs. However, he was obedient, naturally quiet and silent, and he did not seem to be profoundly corrupted by that school of vice. But when, in his seventeenth year, he was thrown out again on the streets of Paris, he un-happily found there his prison com-rades, all great scamps, exercising their dirty professions: teaching dogs to catch rats in the sewers, and black-ing shoes on ball nights in the passage of the Opera—amateur wrestlers, who permitted themselves to be thrown by the Hercules of the booths—or fishing at noontime from rafts; all of these occupations he followed to some ex-tent, and, some months after he came out of the house of correction, he was arrested again for a petty theft—a pair of old shoes prigged from a shop-window. Result: a year in the prison of Sainte Pélagie, where he served as valet to the political prisoners.

He lived in much surprise among this group of prisoners, all very young, negligent in dress, who talked in loud voices, and carried their heads in a very solemn fashion. They used to meet in the cell of one of the oldest of them, a fellow of some thirty years, already a long time in prison and quite a fixture at Sainte Pélagie— a large cell, the walls covered with colored caricatures, and from the win-dow of which one could see all Paris —its roofs, its spires, and its domes— and far away the distant line of hills, blue and indistinct upon the sky. There were upon the walls some shelves filled with volumes and all the old paraphernalia of a fencing-room: broken masks, rusty foils, breast-plates, and gloves that were losing their tow. It was there that the "politicians" used to dine together, adding to the everlasting "soup and beef," fruit, cheese, and pints of wine which Jean François went out and got by the can—a tumultuous repast interrupted by violent disputes, and where, during the dessert, the "Carmagnole"[5] and "Ça Ira" were sung in full chorus. They assumed, however, an air of great dignity on those days when a newcomer was brought in among them, at first entertaining him gravely as a citizen, but on the morrow using him with affectionate familiarity and calling him by his nickname. Great words were used there: Corporation, Responsibility, and phrases quite unintelligible to Jean François —such as this, for example, which he once heard imperiously put forth by a frightful little hunchback who blotted some writing-paper every night:

"It is done. This is the composition of the Cabinet: Raymond, the Bureau of Public Instruction; Martial, the Interior; and for Foreign Affairs, myself."

His time done, he wandered again around Paris, watched afar by the police, after the fashion of cockchafers,[6] made by cruel children to fly at the end of a string. He became one of those fugitive and timid beings whom the law, with a sort of coquetry, arrests and releases by turn— something like those platonic fishers who, in order that they may not exhaust their fish-pond, throw immediately back into the water the fish which has just come out of the net. Without a suspicion on his part that so much honor had been done to so

sorry a subject, he had a special bundle of memoranda in the mysterious portfolios of the Rue de Jérusalem.[7] His name was written in round hand on the gray paper of the cover, and the notes and reports, carefully classified, gave him his successive appellations: "Name, Leturc"; "the prisoner Leturc," and, at last, "the criminal Leturc."

He was two years out of prison, dining where he could, sleeping in night lodging-houses and sometimes in lime-kilns, and taking part with his fellows in interminable games of pitch-penny on the boulevards near the barriers. He wore a greasy cap on the back of his head, carpet slippers, and a short white blouse. When he had five sous he had his hair curled. He danced at Constant's at Montparnasse; bought for two sous to sell for four at the door of Bobino, the jack of hearts or the ace of clubs serving as a countermark; sometimes opened the door of a carriage; led horses to the horse-market. From the lottery of all sorts of miserable employments he drew a goodly number. Who can say if the atmosphere of honor which one breathes as a soldier, if military discipline might not have saved him? Taken, in a cast of the net, with some young loafers who robbed drunkards sleeping on the streets, he denied very earnestly having taken part in their expeditions. Perhaps he told the truth, but his antecedents were accepted in lieu of proof, and he was sent for three years to Poissy.[8] There he made coarse playthings for children, was tattooed on the chest, learned thieves' slang and the penal code. A new liberation, and a new plunge into the sink of Paris; but

---

[5]"Carmagnole" (kär' män' yōl'), this song and also "Ça Ira" were sung on occasions of revolt and discontent in the French republic.

[6]cockchafer (chäf' ĕr), a large European beetle destructive to vegetation.

[7]Rue de Jérusalem, street Jerusalem.

[8]Poissy (pwä sē), on the left bank of the Seine, eleven miles southwest of Versailles.

very short this time, for at the end of six months at the most he was again compromised in a night robbery, aggravated by climbing and breaking— a serious affair, in which he played an obscure rôle, half dupe and half fence. On the whole his complicity was evident, and he was sent for five years at hard labor. His grief in this adventure was above all in being separated from an old dog which he had found on a dungheap, and cured of the mange. The beast loved him.

Toulon,[9] the ball and chain, the work in the harbor, the blows from a stick, wooden shoes on bare feet, soup of black beans dating from Trafalgar, no tobacco money, and the terrible sleep in a camp swarming with convicts; that was what he experienced for five broiling summers and five winters raw with the Mediterranean wind. He came out from there stunned, was sent under surveillance to Vernon, where he worked some time on the river. Then, an incorrigible vagabond, he broke his exile and came again to Paris. He had his savings, fifty-six francs, that is to say, time enough for reflection. During his absence his former wretched companions had dispersed. He was well hidden, and slept in a loft at an old woman's to whom he represented himself as a sailor, tired of the sea, who had lost his papers in a recent shipwreck, and who wanted to try his hand at something else. His tanned face and his calloused hands, together with some sea phrases which he dropped from time to time, made his tale seem probable enough.

One day when he risked a saunter in the streets, and when chance had led him as far as Montmartre, where he was born, an unexpected memory stopped him before the door of Les

Frères, where he had learned to read. As it was very warm the door was open, and by a single glance the passing outcast was able to recognize the peaceable school-room. Nothing was changed: neither the bright light shining in at the great windows, nor the crucifix over the desk, nor the rows of benches with the tables furnished with inkstands and pencils, nor the table of weights and measures, nor the map where pins stuck in still indicated the operations of some ancient war. Heedlessly and without thinking, Jean François read on the blackboard the words of the Evangelist which had been set there as a copy: "Joy shall be in heaven over one sinner that repenteth, more than over ninety and nine just persons, which need no repentance."

It was undoubtedly the hour for recreation, for the Brother Professor had left his chair, and, sitting on the edge of a table, he was telling a story to the boys who surrounded him with eager and attentive eyes. What a bright and innocent face he had, that beardless young man, in his long black gown, and white necktie, and great ugly shoes, and his badly cut brown hair streaming out behind! All the simple figures of the children of the people who were watching him seemed scarcely less childlike than his; above all when, delighted with some of his own simple and priestly pleasantries, he broke out in an open and frank peal of laughter which showed his white and regular teeth, a peal so contagious that all the scholars laughed loudly in their turn. It was such a sweet, simple group in the bright sunlight, which lighted their dear eyes and their blond curls.

Jean François looked at them for some time in silence, and for the first time in that savage nature, all instinct and appetite, there awoke a mysteri-

---

[9] *Toulon* (tōō' lŏn), forty-two miles southeast of Marseilles.

ous, a tender emotion. His heart, that seared and hardened heart, unmoved when the convict's cudgel or the heavy whip of the watchman fell on his shoulders, beat oppressively. In that sight he saw again his infancy; and closing his eyes sadly, the prey to torturing regret, he walked quickly away.

Then the words written on the blackboard came back to his mind. "If it wasn't too late, after all!" he murmured; "if I could again, like others, eat honestly my brown bread, and sleep my fill without nightmare! The spy must be sharp who recognizes me. My beard, which I shaved off down there, has grown out thick and strong. One can burrow somewhere in the great ant-hill, and work can be found. Whoever is not worked to death in the hell of the galleys comes out agile and robust, and I learned there to climb ropes with loads upon my back. Building is going on everywhere here, and the masons need helpers. Three francs a day! I never earned so much. Let me be forgotten, and that is all I ask."

He followed his courageous resolution; he was faithful to it, and after three months he was another man. The master for whom he worked called him his best workman. After a long day upon the scaffolding, in the hot sun and the dust, constantly bending and raising his back to take the hod from the man at his feet and pass it to the man over his head, he went for his soup to the cook-shop, tired out, his legs aching, his hands burning, his eyelids struck with plaster, but content with himself, and carrying his well-earned money in a knot in his handkerchief. He went out now without fear, since he could not be recognized in his white mask, and since he had noticed that the suspicious glances of the policeman were seldom turned on the tired workman. He was quiet and sober. He slept the sound sleep of fatigue. He was free!

At last—oh, supreme recompense!
—he had a friend!

He was a fellow-workman like himself, named Savinien, a little peasant with red lips who had come to Paris with his stick over his shoulder and a bundle on the end of it, fleeing from the wine-shops and going to mass every Sunday. Jean François loved him for his piety, for his candor, for his honesty, for all that he himself had lost, and so long ago. It was a passion, profound and unrestrained, which transformed him by fatherly cares and attentions. Savinien, himself of a weak and egotistical nature, let things take their course, satisfied only in finding a companion who shared his horror of the wine-shop. The two friends lived together in a fairly comfortable lodging, but their resources were very limited. They were obliged to take into their room a third companion, an old Auvergnat, gloomy and rapacious, who found it possible out of his meager salary to save something with which to buy a place in his own country. Jean François and Savinien were always together. On holidays they together took long walks in the environs of Paris, and dined under an arbor in one of those small country inns where there are a great many mushrooms in the sauces and innocent rebuses on the napkins. There Jean François learned from his friend all that lore of which they who are born in the city are ignorant; learned the names of the trees, the flowers, and the plants; the various seasons for harvesting; he heard eagerly the thousand details of a laborious country life —the autumn sowing, the winter chores, the splendid celebrations of harvest and vintage days, the sound of the mills at the water-side, and the flails striking the ground, the tired horses led to water, and the hunting in the morning mist; and, above all, the long evenings around the fire of vine-shoots, that were shortened by some marvelous stories. He discovered in himself a source of imagination before unknown, and found a singular delight in the recital of events so placid, so calm, so monotonous.

One thing troubled him, however: it was the fear lest Savinien might learn something of his past. Sometimes there escaped from him some low word of thieves' slang, a vulgar gesture—vestiges of his former horrible existence—and he felt the pain one feels when old wounds reopen; the more because he fancied that he sometimes saw in Savinien the awakening of an unhealthy curiosity. When the young man, already tempted by the pleasures which Paris offers to the poorest, asked him about the mysteries of the great city, Jean François feigned ignorance and turned the subject; but he felt a vague inquietude for the future of his friend.

His uneasiness was not without foundation. Savinien could not long remain the simple rustic that he was on his arrival in Paris. If the gross and noisy pleasures of the wine-shop always repelled him, he was profoundly troubled by other temptations, full of danger for the inexperience of his twenty years. When spring came he began to go off alone, and at first he wandered about the brilliant entrance of some dancing-hall, watching the young girls who went in with their arms around each other's waists, talking in low tones. Then, one evening, when lilacs perfumed the air and the call to quadrilles was most captivating, he crossed the threshold, and from that time Jean François observed a change, little by little, in his manners and his visage. He became more frivolous, more extravagant. He often borrowed from his friend his scanty savings, and he forgot to repay. Jean François, feeling that he was abandoned, jealous and forgiving at the same time, suffered and was silent. He felt that he had no right to reproach him, but with the foresight of affection he indulged in cruel and inevitable presentiments.

One evening, as he was mounting the stairs to his room, absorbed in his thoughts, he heard, as he was about to enter, the sound of angry voices, and he recognized that of the old Auvergnat who lodged with Savinien and himself. An old habit of suspicion made him stop at the landing-place and listen to learn the cause of the trouble.

"Yes," said the Auvergnat, angrily, "I am sure that some one has opened my trunk and stolen from it the three louis that I had hidden in a little box; and he who has done this thing must be one of the two companions who sleep here, if it were not the servant Maria. It concerns you as much as it does me, since you are the master of the house, and I will drag you to the courts if you do not let me at once break open the valises of the two masons. My poor gold! It was here yesterday in its place, and I will tell you just what it was, so that if we find it again nobody can accuse me of having lied. Ah, I know them, my three beautiful gold-pieces, and I can see them as plainly as I see you! One piece was more worn than the others; it was of greenish gold, with a portrait of the great emperor. The other was a great old fellow with a queue and epaulettes,[10] and the third, which had on it a Philippe with whiskers, I had marked with my teeth. They don't trick me. Do you know that I only

[10]*epaulettes*, ornamental badge on the shoulder of a soldier's uniform.

wanted two more like that to pay for my vineyard? Come, search these fellows' things with me, or I will call the police! Hurry up!"

"All right," said the voice of the landlord, "we will go and search with Maria. So much the worse for you if we find nothing, and the masons get angry. You have forced me to it."

Jean François' soul was full of fright. He remembered the embarrassed circumstances and the small loans of Savinien and how sober he had seemed for some days. And yet he could not believe that he was a thief. He heard the Auvergnat panting in his eager search, and he pressed his closed fists against his breast as if to still the furious beating of his heart.

"Here they are!" suddenly shouted the victorious miser. "Here they are, my louis, my dear treasure; and in the Sunday vest of that little hypocrite of Limousin! Look, landlord, they are just as I told you. Here is the Napoleon, the man with a queue, and the Philippe that I have bitten. See the dents! Ah, the little beggar with the sanctified air. I should have much sooner suspected the other. Ah, the wretch! Well, he must go to the convict prison."

At this moment Jean François heard the well-known step of Savinien coming slowly up the stairs.

He is going to his destruction, thought he. Three stories. I have time!

And, pushing open the door, he entered the room, pale as death, where he saw the landlord and the servant stupefied in a corner, while the Auvergnat, on his knees, in the disordered heap of clothes, was kissing the pieces of gold.

"Enough of this," he said, in a thick voice; "I took the money, and put it in my comrade's trunk. But that is too bad. I am a thief, but not a Judas.[11] Call the police; I will not try to escape, only I must say a word to Savinien in private. Here he is."

In fact, the little Limousin had just arrived, and seeing his crime discovered, believing himself lost, he stood there, his eyes fixed, his arms hanging.

Jean François seized him forcibly by the neck, as if to embrace him; he put his mouth close to Savinien's ear, and said to him in a low, supplicating voice:

"Keep quiet."

Then turning towards the others: "Leave me alone with him. I tell you I won't go away. Lock us in if you wish, but leave us alone."

With a commanding gesture he showed them the door.

They went out.

Savinien, broken by grief, was sitting on the bed, and lowered his eyes without understanding anything.

"Listen," said Jean François, who came and took him by the hands. "I understand! You have stolen three gold-pieces to buy some trifle for a girl. That costs six months in prison. But one only comes out from there to go back again, and you will become a pillar of police courts and tribunals. I understand it. I have been seven years at the Reform School, a year at Sainte Pélagie, three years at Poissy, five years at Toulon. Now, don't be afraid. Everything is arranged. I have taken it on my shoulders."

"It is dreadful," said Savinien; but

hope was springing up again in his cowardly heart.

"When the elder brother is under the flag, the younger one does not go," replied Jean François. "I am your substitute, that's all. You care for me a little, do you not? I am paid. Don't be childish—don't refuse. They would have taken me again one of these days, for I am a runaway from exile. And then, do you see, that life will be less hard for me than for you. I know it all, and I shall not complain if I have not done you this service for nothing, and if you swear to me that you will never do it again. Savinien, I have loved you well, and your friendship has made me happy. It is through it that, since I have known you, I have been honest and pure, as I might always have been, perhaps, if I had, like you, a father to put a tool in my hands, a mother to teach me my prayers. It was my sole regret that I was useless to you, and that I deceived you concerning myself. To-day I have unmasked in saving you. It is all right. Do not cry, and embrace me, for already I hear heavy boots on the stairs. They are coming with the *posse*, and we must not seem to know each other so well before those chaps."

He pressed Savinien quickly to his breast, then pushed him from him, when the door was thrown wide open.

It was the landlord and the Auvergnat, who brought the police. Jean François sprang forward to the landing-place, held out his hands for the handcuffs, and said, laughing, "Forward, bad lot!"

To-day he is at Cayenne, condemned for life as an incorrigible.

[11]*Judas*, the disciple who betrayed Christ for thirty pieces of silver.

For Thought and Discussion

1. Where did this story take place?
2. Do you think that military discipline would have saved Leturc?

3. Why was Jean François Leturc sent to prison when arrested with some loafers?
4. What traits of character were revealed by his grief over losing his dog?
5. After his release from prison, what effect did seeing the bright happy school boys have upon Leturc?
6. Why did Leturc become devoted to Savinien?
7. Who was the stronger character, Leturc or Savinien?
8. Why did each become a thief?
9. Why did Leturc substitute for his friend?
10. Did the weakness of his friend, Savinien, in taking money dishonestly come to Jean as a complete surprise?
11. Which is the more conducive to tolerance and sympathy, happy or unhappy circumstances in one's own experience?

~❧

HOW MUCH LAND DOES A MAN REQUIRE?

LEO TOLSTOY

[A life as varied in experience as that of Count Leo Tolstoy, 1828-1910, forms a rich background for such powerful and moving works as those produced by this great Russian, who is ranked as one of the best of modern writers. He showed pronounced literary tastes at an early age, and, encouraged by his aunt, wrote, when he was a very young man, a novel which attracted considerable attention. He studied law and served in the army, becoming an officer in the Crimean War. Because of his extreme social and political views, he renounced his fortune and lived the life of a peasant in his latter years. He knew people of all classes from king to peasant, and from them he gained that knowledge of life and human nature which he put into his short stories and such longer works as *War and Peace* and *Anna Karenina*.]

I

AN elder sister came from the town to visit a younger one. The elder one was married to a tradesman, and the younger to a peasant.

As the two drank tea and talked, the elder sister began to boast and make much of her life in town—how she lived and went about in ease and comfort, dressed her children well, had nice things to eat and drink, and went skating, walking, and to the theater.

The younger sister was vexed at this, and retorted by running down the life of a tradesman's wife and exalting her own country one.

"For my part, I should not care to exchange my life for yours," she said. "I grant you ours is an uneventful existence and that we know no excitement; yet you, on the other hand, with all your fine living, must either do a very large trade indeed or be ruined. You know the proverb: 'Loss is Gain's elder brother.' Well, you may be rich today, but tomorrow you may find yourself in the street. We have a better way than that, here in the country. The peasant's stomach may be thin, but it is long. That is to say, he may never be rich, yet he will always have enough."

The elder sister took her up quickly.

" 'Enough' indeed?" she retorted. " 'Enough'—with nothing but your wretched pigs and calves? 'Enough' —with no fine dresses or company? Why, however hard your man may work, you have to live in mud, and will die there—yes, and your children after you."

"Oh, no," replied the younger. " 'Tis like this with us. Though we may live hardly, the land is at least our own, and we have no need to bow and scrape to anyone. But you in town—you live in an atmosphere of scandal. Today all may be well with you, but tomorrow the evil eye may look upon you, and your husband find himself tempted away by cards or wine or some light-of-love, and you and yours find yourselves ruined. Is it not so?"

Pakhom, the younger sister's husband, had been listening near the stove.

"That is true," he said. "I have been turning over our mother earth since my childhood, and so have had no time to get any foolishness into my head. Yet I have one grievance —too little land. Only give me land, and I fear no man—no, not even the devil himself."

The two women finished their tea, chattered a little longer about dress, washed up the crockery, and went to bed.

All this time the devil had been sitting behind the stove, and had heard everything. He was delighted when the peasant's wife led her husband on to brag—led him on to boast that, once given land, not even the devil himself should take it from him.

"Splendid!" thought the devil. "I will try a fall with you. I will give you much land—and then take it away again."

II

Near these peasants there lived a lady landowner, with a small property of 120 *dessiatins*.[1] Formerly she had got on well with the peasants and in no way abused her rights; but she now took as overseer a retired soldier, who began to persecute the peasants with fines. No matter how careful Pakhom might be, one of his horses would get into the lady's oats, or a cow stray into her garden, or the calves break into her meadows: and for all these things there would be fines levied.

Pakhom paid up, and then beat and abused his household. Much trouble did he get into with the overseer for the doings of the summer, so that he felt devoutly thankful to have got his cattle standing in the straw-yard again. He regretted the cost of their keep there, yet it cost him less anxiety in other ways.

That winter a rumour went abroad that the *Barina* was going to sell her land, and that the overseer was arranging to buy both it and the highway rights attached. This rumour reached the peasants, and they were dismayed.

"If," they thought, "the overseer gets the land he will worry us with fines even worse than he did under the *Barina*. We must get hold of the property somehow, as we all live round it in a circle."

So a deputation from the *Mir*[2] went to see the *Barina*, and besought her not to sell the land to the overseer, but to give them the refusal of it, and they would outbid their rival. To this the *Barina* agreed, and the peasants set about arranging for the *Mir* to purchase the whole of her estate. They held a meeting about it, and yet an-

---

[1] *a dessiatin*, 2.70 acres.
[2] *mir*, a Russian village.

other one, but the matter did not go through. The fact was that the Unclean One[3] always defeated their object by making them unable to agree. Then the peasants decided to try and buy the land in separate lots, each man as much as he could; and to this also the *Barina* said she was agreeable. Pakhom heard one day that a neighbour had bought twenty *dessiatins,* and that the *Barina* had agreed to let half the purchase money stand over for a year. Pakhom grew envious. "If," he thought, "the others buy up all the land, I shall feel left out in the cold." So he took counsel of his wife. "Everybody is buying some," he said, "so we too had better get hold of ten *dessiatins.* We can't make a living as things are now, for the overseer takes it all out of us in fines." So they took thought how to effect the purchase.

They had 100 roubles[4] laid by; so that by selling a foal[5] and half their bees, in addition to putting out their son to service, they managed to raise half the money.

Pakhom collected it all together, selected fifteen *dessiatins* and a small piece of timber land, and went to the *Barina* to arrange things. The bargain struck, they shook hands upon it, and Pakhom paid a deposit. Then he went to town, completed the conveyance[6] (half the purchase money to be paid now, and half within two years' time)—and lo! Pakhom was a landowner! He also borrowed a small sum of his brother-in-law, wherewith to purchase seed. This he duly sowed in his newly-acquired property, and a fine crop came up; so that within a

[3]*The Unclean One,* the devil.
[4]*rouble,* also ruble, silver coin, standard of money in Russia, worth about seventy-five cents in American money.
[5]*foal,* a colt.
[6]*conveyance,* an instrument in writing, as a deed, by which property is conveyed from one person to another.

year he had repaid both the *Barina* and his brother-in-law. He was now an absolute proprietor. It was his own land that he sowed, his own hay that he reaped, his own firewood that he cut, and his own cattle that he grazed. Whenever he rode out to his inalienable estate, either to plough or to inspect the crops and meadows, he felt overjoyed. The very grass seemed to him different to other grass, the flowers to bloom differently. Once, when he had ridden over his land, it was just—land; but now, although still land, it was land with a difference.

III

Thus did Pakhom live for a time, and was happy. Indeed, all would have been well if only the other peasants had left Pakhom's corn and pasture alone. In vain did he make repeated remonstrances. Shepherds would turn their flocks out into his meadows, and horses would somehow get into the corn at night. Again and again Pakhom drove them out and overlooked the matter, but at last he lost his temper and laid a complaint before the district court. He knew that the peasants only did it from lack of land, not maliciously; yet it could not be allowed, since they were eating the place up. He must teach them a lesson.

So he taught first one of them a lesson in court, and then another; had one fined, and then a second. This aroused feeling against him, and his neighbours now began, of set purpose, to steal his crops. One man got into the plantation at night and stripped the bark off no less than ten linden-trees. When Pakhom next rode that way and saw what had been done he turned pale. He drew nearer, and perceived that bark had been stripped off and thrown about, and trunks uprooted. One tree only had the miscreant left, after lopping all its branches, but the rest he had cleared entirely in his evil progress. Pakhom was furious. "Ah!" he thought, "if only I knew who had done this, I would soon get my own back on him!" He wondered and wondered who it could be. If anyone in particular, it must be Semka. So he went to see Semka, but got nothing out of him except bad language: yet he felt more certain than ever now that it *was* Semka who had done it. He laid a complaint against him, and they were both of them summoned to attend the court. The magistrates sat and sat, and then dismissed the case for want of evidence. This enraged Pakhom still more. He abused both the *Starshina* and the magistrates. "You magistrates," he said, "are in league with thieves. If you were honest men you would never have acquitted Semka." Yes, there was no doubt that Pakhom was ill pleased both with the magistrates and with his neighbours. He began to live more and more apart on his land, and to have less and less to do with the *Mir*.

At this time there arose a rumor that some of the peasantry thereabouts were thinking of emigrating. This made Pakhom think to himself: "But there is no reason why I should leave *my* land. If some of the others go, why, it will make all the more room for me. I can buy up their land, and so hedge myself in all round. I should live much more comfortably then. At present I am too cramped."

It happened soon afterwards that Pakhom was sitting at home one day when a traveling peasant dropped in. Pakhom gave him a night's lodging and a meal, and then questioned him, in the course of conversation, as to whence in the name of God he had come. To this the peasant replied that he had come from lower down

the river—from a spot beyond the Volga,[7] where he had been in service. Then he went on to relate how a settlement was being formed there, every settler being enrolled in the *Mir* and allotted ten *dessiatins* of land. It was *such* land, too, he said, and grew *such* rye! Why, the straw of the rye was tall enough to hide a horse, and thick enough together to make a sheaf per five handfuls! One peasant, he went on, who had arrived there a poor man and had had nothing but his two hands to work with, now grew his fifty *dessiatins* of wheat. Indeed, during the past year that man had made five thousand roubles by his wheat alone!

Pakhom's soul was fired by this, and he thought to himself: "Why should I stay here, poor and cramped up, when I might be making such a fine living as that? I will sell out here—both land and homestead—and go build myself a new house and farm there with the money. Here, in this cramped-up spot, life is one long worry. At any rate, I might take a trip there and make inquiries."

So when the summer came he got himself ready and set out. He took a steamer down the Volga to Samara, and thence tramped four hundred versts[8] till he came to the place. It was all as had been described. The peasants lived splendidly, with ten *dessiatins* of free land to each soul, and he was assured of a welcome by the *Mir*. Moreover, he was told that anyone who came there with money could buy additional land—as much as ever he wanted—right out and in perpetuity. For three roubles a *dessiatin* a man could have the very finest land possible, and to any extent.

---

[7] *Volga*, one of the principal rivers of Russia.
[8] *versts* (vurst) nearly two-thirds of a mile.

All this Pakhom learned, and then returned home in the autumn. He began straightway to sell out, and succeeded in disposing both of land, buildings, and stock at a profit. Then he took his name off the *Mir's* books, waited for the spring, and departed to the new place with his family.

IV

They duly arrived at their destination, and Pakhom was forthwith enrolled in the *Mir* of the great settlement (after moistening the elders' throats, of course, and executing the necessary documents). Then they took him and assigned him fifty *dessiatins* of land—ten for each soul of his family—in different parts of the estate, in addition to common pasturage. Pakhom built himself a homestead and stocked it, his allotted land alone being twice what he had formerly possessed in the old place. It was corn-bearing land, too. Altogether life was ten times better here than where he had come from, for he had at his disposal both arable and pasture land—sufficient of the latter always to keep as many cattle as he cared to have.

At first, while building and stocking, he thought everything splendid. Later, when he had settled down a bit, he began to feel cramped again. He wanted to grow white Turkish wheat as several others did, but there was hardly any wheat-bearing land among his five allotments. Wheat needed to be grown on grass, new, or fallow land,[9] and such land had to be sown one year and left fallow for two, in order that the grass might grow again. True, he had as much soft land as he wanted, but it would only bear rye. Wheat required hard land, and hard land found many ap-

plicants, and there was not enough for all. Moreover, such land gave rise to disputes. The richer peasants sowed their own, but the poorer had to mortgage theirs to merchants. The first year, Pakhom sowed his allotments with wheat, and got splendid crops. Then he wanted to sow them with wheat again, but they were not large enough to admit both of sowing new land and of leaving last year's land to lie fallow. He must get hold of some more. So he went to a merchant, and took a year's lease of some wheat land. He sowed as much of it as he could, and reaped a magnificent crop. Unfortunately, however, the land was a long way from the settlement—in fact, the crop had to be carted fifteen versts; so, as Pakhom had seen merchant farmers living in fine homesteads and growing rich in the district where the land lay, he thought to himself: "How would it be if I took a longer lease of it and built a homestead there the same as they have done? Then I should be right on the land." So he set about arranging to do so.

Thus did Pakhom live for five years, continually taking up land and sowing it with wheat. All the years were good ones, the wheat thrived, and the money came in. Yet just to live and live was rather tedious, and Pakhom began to tire of leasing land every year in a strange district and removing his stock there. Wherever there was a particularly good plot of land, there would be a rush made for it by the other peasants, and it would be divided up before he was ready to lease and sow it as a whole. Once he went shares with a merchant in leasing a plot of pasturage of some peasants, and plowed it up. Then the peasants lost it in a lawsuit, and his labor went for nothing. If only it had been his own land absolutely, he

---

[9] *fallow land,* untilled, unsowed land.

need have given in to no one and been put to no trouble.

So he began to cast about where he could buy an estate outright. In this endeavor he fell in with a certain peasant who had ruined himself and was ready to let him have his property of five hundred *dessiatins* cheap. Pakhom entered into negotiations with him, and, after much discussion, closed at a thousand roubles—half down, and half to stand over. One day after they had thus clinched the matter, a merchant drove up to Pakhom's homestead to bait his horses. They drank a teapot empty and talked. The merchant said he had come a long, long way—from the country of the Bashkirs,[10] in fact, where (so he said) he had just purchased five thousand *dessiatins* for only a thousand roubles! Pakhom went on to question him further, and the merchant to answer. "All I did," said the latter, "was to make the elders there a few presents (khilats, carpets, and a chest of tea), to distribute about a hundred roubles, and to stand vodka to anyone who felt inclined for it. In the result I got the land for twenty kopecks a *dessiatin*," and he showed Pakhom the deed. "The property," he concluded, "fronts upon a river, and is all of it open, grass, steppe land." Pakhom questioned him still further.

"You would not," went on the merchant, "find such land as that in a year. The same with all the Bashkir land. Moreover, the people there are simple as sheep. You can get things out of them absolutely for nothing."

"Well," thought Pakhom, "what is the good of my giving a thousand roubles for only five hundred *dessiatins*, and still leaving a debt round

my neck, when I might become a proprietor indeed for the same money?"

V

Pakhom inquired of the merchant as to how to reach the country of the Bashkirs, and as soon as his informant had departed he got ready for the journey. Leaving his wife at home, and taking with him only his workman, he set out first for the town, where he bought a chest of tea, *vodka*,[11] and other gifts, as the merchant had advised. Then the two drove on and on until they had covered 500 versts, and on the seventh day arrived at the camp of the Bashkirs. Everything turned out to be as the merchant had said. The people there lived in hide-tilted wagons, which were drawn up by the side of a river running through the open steppe. They neither ploughed the land nor ate corn, while over the steppe wandered droves of cattle and Cossack[12] horses, the foals being tied to the backs of the wagons and their dams driven up to them twice a day to give them milk. The chief sustenance of the people was mare's milk, which the women made into a drink called *kumiss*,[13] and then churned the *kumiss* into cheese. In fact, the only drink the Bashkirs knew was either *kumiss* or tea, their only solid food mutton, and their only amusement pipe-playing. Nevertheless they all of them looked sleek and cheerful, and kept holiday the whole year round. In education they were sadly deficient, and knew no Russian, but were kindly and attractive folk for all that.

As soon as they caught sight of

---

[10]*Bashkirs*, tribe of half-civilized subjects of Russia on the banks of the Ural and Volga rivers.

[11]*vodka*, a Russian alcoholic drink.
[12]*Cossack*, people living in the region north of the Black and Caspian seas.
[13]*kumiss*, a fermented drink.

Pakhom they came out of their wagons and surrounded the guest. An interpreter was found, and Pakhom told him that he had come to buy land. At once the people were delighted, and, embracing Pakhom fervently, escorted him to a well-appointed wagon, where they made him sit down on a pile of rugs topped with soft cushions, and set about getting some tea and *kumiss* ready. A sheep was killed, and a meal served of the mutton, after which Pakhom produced the gifts from his *tarantass*, distributed them round, and shared out also the tea. Then the Bashkirs fell to talking among themselves for a while, and finally bade the interpreter speak.

"I am to tell you," said the interpreter, "that they are greatly taken with you, and that it is our custom to meet the wishes of a guest in every possible way, in return for the presents given us. Since, therefore, you have given us presents, say now what there is of ours which you may desire, so that we may grant it you."

"What I particularly desire," replied Pakhom, "is some of your land. Where I come from," he continued, "there is not enough land, and what there is is ploughed out, whereas you have much land, and good land, such as I have never before beheld."

The interpreter translated, and the Bashkirs talked again among themselves. Although Pakhom could not understand what they were saying, he could see that they kept crying out something in merry tones and then bursting into laughter. At last they stopped and looked at Pakhom, while the interpreter spoke.

"I am to tell you," he said, "that in return for your kindness we are ready to sell you as much land as you may wish. Merely make a gesture with your hand to signify how much, and it shall be yours."

At this point, however, the people began to talk among themselves again, and to dispute about something. On Pakhom asking what it was, the interpreter told him: "Some of them say that the *Starshina* ought to be asked first about the land, and that nothing should be done without him, while others say that it is not necessary."

VI

Suddenly, while the Bashkirs were thus disputing, there entered the wagon a man in a foxskin cap, at whose entry everyone rose, while the interpreter said to Pakhom: "This is the *Starshina* himself." At once Pakhom caught up the best *Khalat* and offered it to the newcomer, as well as five pounds of tea. The *Starshina* duly accepted them, and then sat down in the place of honour, while the Bashkirs began to expound to him some matter or another. He listened and listened, then gave a smile, and spoke to Pakhom in Russian.

"Very well," he said, "pray choose your land wheresoever it pleases you. We have much land."

"So I am to take as much as I want!" thought Pakhom to himself. "Still, I must strengthen that bargain somehow. They might say, 'The land is yours,' and then take it away again."

"I thank you," he said aloud, "for your kind speech. As you say, you have much land, whereas I am in need of some. I only desire to know precisely which of it is to be mine; wherefore it might be well to measure it off by some method and duly convey it to me. God only is lord of life and death, and, although you are good people who now give it to me, it might befall that your children would take it away again."

The *Starshina* smiled.

"The conveyance," he said, "is already executed. This present meeting is our mode of confirming it—and it could not be a surer one."

"But," said Pakhom, "I have been told that a merchant visited you recently, and that you sold him land and gave him a proper deed of conveyance. Pray, therefore, do the same with me."

The *Starshina* understood now. "Very well," he replied. "We have a writer here, and will go to a town and procure the necessary seals."

"But what is your price for the land?" asked Pakhom.

"Our price," answered the *Starshina*, "is only 1000 roubles per day." Pakhom did not understand this day-rate at all.

"How many *dessiatins* would that include?" he inquired presently.

"We do not reckon in that way," said the *Starshina*. "We sell only by the day. That is to say, as much land as you can walk round in a day, that much land is yours. That is our measure, and the price is 1000 roubles."

Pakhom was astounded.

"Why, a man might walk round a great deal in a day," he said.

The *Starshina* smiled again.

"Well, at all events," he said, "it will be yours. *Only*, there is one condition—namely, that if on that same day you do not return to the spot whence you started, your money is forfeited."

"But how do you decide upon that spot?" asked Pakhom.

"We take our stand," replied the *Starshina*, "upon whatsoever spot you may select. I and my people remain there, while you start off and describe a circle. Behind you will ride some of our young men, to plant stakes wherever you may desire that to be

done. Thereafter, a plow will be driven round those stakes. Describe what circle you wish; only, by the time of the setting of the sun you must have returned to the place from which you started. As much land as you may circle, that much land will be yours."

So Pakhom accepted these terms, and it was agreed to make an early start on the morrow. Then the company talked again, drank more kumiss and ate more mutton, passing on thence to tea, and the ceremonies were prolonged until nightfall. At length Pakhom was led to a bed of down and the Bashkirs dispersed, after first promising to gather on the morrow beyond the river and ride out to the appointed spot before sunrise.

VII

Pakhom lay on his bed of down, but could not get a wink of sleep for thinking of the land which, as he said, "I am going to farm here."

"For I mean to mark out a very large 'Promised Land' tomorrow," he continued to himself. "I can cover at least fifty versts in the day, and fifty versts should inclose somewhere about ten thousand *dessiatins*. Then I shall be under nobody's thumb, and be able to afford a pair-ox plow and two labourers. I shall plow up the best land, and feed stock on the rest."

All that night Pakhom never closed his eyes, but dozed off for a short while just before dawn. The instant he did so he had a dream. He seemed to be lying in this identical wagon and listening to somebody laughing and talking outside. Wishing to see who it was that was laughing so much, he went outside, and saw the *Starshina* sitting on the ground and holding his sides as he rolled about in ecstasies of mirth. Then in his dream Pakhom walked up to him and asked him what the joke was—and immediately saw that it was not the *Starshina* at all, but the merchant who had so lately visited him about this land. Then again, he had scarcely so much as said to the merchant, "Did I not see you at my home a little while ago?" when the merchant suddenly changed into the peasant from away down the Volga who had called at his farm in the old country. Finally Pakhom perceived that this peasant was not a peasant at all, but the devil himself, with horns and hoofs, and that he was gazing fixedly at something as he sat there and laughed. Then Pakhom thought to himself: "What is he looking at, and why does he laugh so much?" And in his dream he stepped a little aside to look, and saw a man —barefooted, and clad only in a shirt and breeches—lying flat on his back, with his face as white as a sheet. And presently, looking yet more attentively at the man, Pakhom saw that the man was himself!

He gave a gasp and awoke—awoke feeling as if the dream were real. Then he looked to see if it were getting light yet, and saw that the dawn was near.

"It is time to start," he thought. "I must arouse these good people."

VIII

Pakhom arose, awakened his workman in the *tarantass,* and told him to put the horse in and go round to call the Bashkirs, since it was time to go out upon the steppe[14] and measure off the land. So the Bashkirs arose and got themselves ready, and the *Starshina* also arrived. They breakfasted off *kumiss,* and were for giving Pakhom some tea, but he could not wait. "If we are to go, let us go," he said.

---

[14]*steppe,* one of the vast tracts of land in southeastern Europe and Asia, level and without trees.

"It is fully time." So the Bashkirs harnessed up and set out, some on horseback, and some in carts, while Pakhom drove in his *tarantass* with his workman. They came out upon the steppe just as the dawn was breaking, and proceeded towards a little knoll—called in the Bashkir dialect a *shichan.* There the people in carts alighted, and everyone collected together. The *Starshina* approached Pakhom and pointed all round with his hand. "Whatsoever land you see from here," he said, "is ours. Choose whichsoever direction you like." Pakhom's eyes glowed, for all the land was grass, level as the palm of his hand, and black beneath the turf as a poppy-head. Only where there was a ravine was there a break in the grass —grass which was everywhere breast-high. The *Starshina* took off his fox-skin cap, and laid it in the exact centre of the knoll. "This," he said, "will be the mark. Lay you your money in it, and your servant shall remain beside it while you are gone. From this mark you will start, and to this mark you will return. As much land as you circle, all of it will be yours."

Pakhom took out his money, and laid it in the cap. Then he divested himself of his cloak, stripped himself to his waistcoat, tightened his belt round his stomach, thrust his wallet with some bread into his bosom, tied a flask of water to his shoulder-strap, pulled up his long boots and prepared to start. He kept debating within himself which direction it would be best to take, for the land was so good everywhere. "Oh, well, as it is all the same, I will walk towards the rising sun," he decided at length. So he turned his face that way, and kept trying his limbs while waiting for the sun to appear. "I must lose no time," he thought, "for I shall do my best walking while the air is yet cool."

Then the mounted Bashkirs also ascended the knoll, and stationed themselves behind Pakhom. No sooner had the sun shot his first rays above the horizon than Pakhom started forward and walked out into the steppe, the mounted men riding behind him.

He walked neither slowly nor hurriedly. After he had gone about a verst he stopped and had a stake put in. Then he went on again. He was losing his first stiffness and beginning to lengthen his stride. Presently he stopped again and had another stake put in. He looked up at the sun—which was now lighting the knoll clearly, with the people standing there —and calculated that he had now gone about five versts. He was beginning to grow warm now, so he took off his waistcoat, and then fastened up his belt again. Then he went on another five versts, and stopped. It was growing really hot now. He looked at the sun again, and saw that it was breakfast time. "One stage done!" he thought. "But there are four of them in the day, and it is early yet to change my direction. Nevertheless, I must take my boots off." So he sat down, took them off, and went on again. Walking was easier now. "As soon as I have covered another five versts," he reflected, "I will begin to bend round to the left. That spot was exceedingly well chosen. The farther I go, the better the land is." So he kept straight on, although, when he looked round, the knoll was almost out of sight, and the people on it looked like little black ants.

"Now," he said to himself at length, "I have made the circle large enough, and must bend round," He had sweated a good deal and was thirsty, so he raised the flask and took a drink. Then he had a stake put in that point, and bent round sharply to the left. On he went and on, through the high grass and the burning heat. He was beginning to tire now, and, glancing at the sun, saw that it was dinner time. "Now," he thought to himself, "I might venture to take a rest." So he stopped and ate some bread, though without sitting down, since he said to himself: "If I once sat down I should go on to lying down, and so end by going off to sleep." He waited a little, therefore, till he felt rested, and then went on again. At first he found walking easy, for the meal had revived his strength, but presently the sun seemed to grow all the hotter as it began to slant towards evening. Pakhom was nearly worn out now, yet he merely thought to himself: "An hour's pain may a century gain."

He had traversed about ten versts of this lap of the circle, and was about to bend inwards again to the left, when he caught sight of an excellent bit of land round a dry ravine. It would be a pity to leave that out. "Flax would grow so splendidly there!" he thought. So he kept straight on until he had taken in the ravine, and, having had a stake planted at the spot, again wheeled inwards. Looking toward the knoll, he could see that the people there were almost indistinguishable. They could not be less than fifteen versts away. "Well," he thought, "I have covered the two long laps of the circuit, and must take this last one by the shortest cut possible." So he started upon the last lap, and quickened his pace. Once again he looked at the sun. It was now drawing near to the time of the evening meal, and he had only covered two versts of the distance. The starting point was still thirteen versts away. ."I must hurry straight along now," he said to himself, "however rough the country be. I must not take in a single extra piece on the way. I have enclosed sufficient as it is." And Pakhom headed straight for the knoll.

IX

He pressed on straight in its direction, yet found walking very difficult now. His feet were aching badly, for he had chafed and bruised them, and they were beginning to totter under him. He would have given anything to have rested for a while, yet knew that he must not if he was ever to regain the knoll before sunset. The sun at least would not wait. Nay, it was like a driver ever lashing him on. From time to time he staggered. "Surely I have not miscalculated?" he thought to himself. "Surely I have not taken in too much land ever to get back, however much I hurry? There is such a long way to go yet, and I am dead beat. It cannot be that all my money and toil have gone in vain? Ah, well, I must do my best."

Pakhom pulled himself together, and broke into a run. He had torn his feet till they were bleeding, yet he still ran on, ran on, ran further and further. Waistcoat, boots, flask, cap —he flung them all away. "Ah!" was his thought, "I was too pleased with what I saw. Now everything is lost, and I shall never reach the mark before sunset." His fears served to render him only the more breathless, but he still ran on, his shirt and breeches clinging to his limbs with sweat, and his mouth parched. In his breast there were a pair of blacksmith's bellows working, and in his heart a steam hammer, while his legs seemed to be breaking under him and

to be no longer his own. He had lost all thought of the land now. All that he thought of was to avoid dying from exertion. Yet, although he was so afraid of dying, he could not stop. "To have gone so far," he thought, "and then to stop! Why, they would think me a fool!" By this time he could hear the Bashkirs cheering and shouting to him, and their cries stirred his heart with fresh spirit. On, on he ran with his last remaining strength, while the sun was just touching the horizon. Ah, but he was close to the spot now. He could see the people on the knoll waving their hands to him and urging him on. He could see the foxskin cap lying on the ground, the money in it, the *Starshina* sitting beside it with his hands pressed to his sides. Suddenly Pakhom remembered his dream. "Yet I have much land now," he thought, "if only God should bring me safe to live upon it. But my heart misgives me that I have killed myself." Still he ran on. For the last time he looked at the sun. Large and red, it had touched the earth, and was beginning to sink below the horizon. Pakhom reached the knoll just as it set. "Ah!" he cried in his despair, for he thought that everything was lost; suddenly, however, he remembered that he could not see from below so well as could the people on the knoll above him, and that to them the sun would still seem not to have set. He rushed at the slope, and could see as he scrambled up to it that the cap was still there. Then he stumbled and fell— yet in the very act of falling stretched out his hands toward the cap—and touched it!

"Ah, young man," cried the *Starshina*, "you have earned much land indeed!"

Pakhom's servant ran to his master and tried to raise him, but blood was running from his mouth. Pakhom lay there dead. The servant cried out in consternation, but the *Starshina* remained sitting on his haunches—laughing and holding his hands to his sides.

At length he got up, took a spade from the ground, and threw it to the servant.

"Bury him," was all he said.

The Bashkirs arose and departed. Only the servant remained. He dug a grave of the same length as Pakhom's form from head to heels—three Russian ells—and buried him.

For Thought and Discussion

1. What unhappy conditions caused Pakhom to become discontented the first time?
2. What effect did the depredations of the peasants have upon Pakhom's character?
3. After he moved to the new *Mir,* why did Pakhom begin to feel cramped?
4. Why were the Bashkirs a happy people?
5. What proposition did the *Starshina* make to Pakhom about the land?
6. Why did the devil laugh at Pakhom when he planned to walk around fifty versts of land?
7. Why did Pakhom fail to get his land?
8. How do people often lose life and happiness in pursuit of wealth?
9. How much money does a man need?
10. Is the good of society affected by the attitude each man has on question nine?

A SAD AFFAIR

A Forsyte Story

JOHN GALSWORTHY

IN 1866, at the age of nineteen, young Jolyon Forsyte left Eton[1] and went up to Cambridge, in the semi-whiskered condition of those days. An amiable youth of fair scholastic and athletic attainments, and more susceptible to emotions, aesthetic and otherwise, than most young barbarians, he went up a little intoxicated on the novels of Whyte-Melville. From continually reading about whis-

---

[1]*Eton, Harrow, Winchester,* famous English preparatory schools.

kered dandies, garbed to perfection and imperturbably stoical in the trying circumstances of debt and discomfiture, he had come to the conviction that to be whiskered and unmoved by Fortune was quite the ultimate hope of existence. There was something not altogether ignoble at the back of his creed. He passed imperceptibly into a fashionable set, and applied himself to the study of whist. All the heroes of Whyte-Melville played whist admirably; all rode horses to distraction. Young Jolyon joined the

Drag, and began to canter over to Newmarket, conveniently situated for Cambridge undergraduates. Like many youths before and after him, he had gone into residence with little or no idea of the value of money; and in the main this "sad affair" must be traced to the fact that while he had no idea of the value of money, and, in proportion to his standards, not much money, his sire, Old Jolyon, had much idea of the value of money, and still more money. The hundred pounds placed to his credit for his first term seemed to young Jolyon an important sum, and he had very soon none of it left. This surprised him, but was of no great significance, because all Whyte-Melville's dandies were in debt; indeed, half their merit consisted in an imperturbable indifference to mere financial liability. Young Jolyon proceeded, therefore, to get into debt. It was easy, and "the thing." At the end of his first term he had spent just double his allowance. He was not vicious nor particularly extravagant—but what, after all, was money? Besides to live on the edge of Fortune was the only way to show that one could rise above it. Not that he deliberately hired horses, bought clothes, boots, wine and tobacco, for that purpose; still, there was in a sense a principle involved. This is made plain, because it is exactly what was not plain to Old Jolyon later on. He, as a young man, with not half his son's allowance, had never been in debt, had paid his way, and made it. But then he had not had the advantages of Eton, Cambridge, and the novels of Whyte-Melville. He had simply gone into Tea.

Young Jolyon going up for his second term, with another hundred pounds from an unconscious sire, at once perceived that if he paid his debts, or an appreciable portion of them, he would have no money for the term's expenses. He therefore applied his means to the more immediate ends of existence—College fees, "wines," whist, riding, and so forth—and left his debts to grow.

At the end of his first year he was fully three hundred pounds to the bad, and beginning to be reflective. Unhappily, however, he went up for his second year with longer whiskers and a more perfect capacity for enjoyment than ever. He had the best fellows in the world for friends, life was sweet, Schools still far off. He was liked and he liked being liked. He had, in fact, a habit of existence eminently unsuited to the drawing-in of horns.

Now his set were very pleasant young men from Eton and Harrow and Winchester, some of whom had more worldly knowledge than young Jolyon, and some of whom had more money, but none of whom had more sense of responsibility. It was in the rooms of "Cuffs" Charwell (the name was pronounced Cherrell) who was taking Divinity Schools, and was afterwards the Bishop, that whist was first abandoned for baccarat, under the auspices of "Donny" Covercourt. That young scion of the Shropshire Covercourts had discovered this exhilarating pastime, indissolubly connected with the figure Nine, at a French watering-place during the Long Vacation, and when he returned to Cambridge was brimming over with it, in his admirably impassive manner. Now, young Jolyon was not by rights a gambler; that is to say, he was self-conscious about the thing, never properly carried away. Moreover, in spite of Whyte-Melville, he was by this time indubitably nervous about his monetary position—on all accounts, therefore, inclined to lose rather than to win. But when such cronies as "Cuffs" Charwell, "Feathers" Totteridge, Guy Winlow, and "Donny" himself—best fellows in the world—were bent on baccarat,[2] who could be a "worm" and wriggle away?

On the fourth evening his turn came to take the "bank." What with paying off his most pestiferous creditors and his College fees, so unfeelingly exacted in advance, he had just fifteen pounds left—the term being a fortnight spent. He was called on to take a "bank" of one hundred. With a sinking heart and a marbled countenance, therefore, he sat down at the head of the green board. This was his best chance, so far, of living up to his whiskers—come what would, he must not fail the shades of "Digby Grand," "Daisy Waters," and the "Honble. Crasher!"

He lost from the first moment; with one or two momentary flickers of fortune in his favor, his descent to Avernus was one of the steadiest ever made. He sat through it with his heart kept in by very straight lips. He rose languidly at the end of half an hour with the "bank" broken, and, wanly smiling, signed his I.O.U.'s, including one to "Donny" Covercourt for a cool eighty. Restoring himself with mulled claret, he resumed his seat at the board, but, for the rest of the evening, neither won nor lost. He went across the Quad to his own rooms with a queasy feeling—he was seeing his father's face. For this was his first unpayable debt of honour, so different from mere debts to tradesmen. And, sitting on his narrow bed in his six-foot by fifteen bedroom, he wrestled for the means of payment. Paid somehow it must be! Would his Bank let him

overdraw to the amount? He could see the stolid faces behind that confounded counter. Not they! And if they didn't! That brute Davids? Or—the Dad? Which was worse? Oh, the Dad was worse! For, suddenly, young Jolyon was perceiving that from the beginning he had lived up here a life that his father would not understand. With a sort of horror he visualized his effort to explain it to that high-domed forehead, and the straight glance that came from so deep behind. No! Davids was the ticket! After all, "Daisy Waters," "Digby Grand," the "Honble. Crasher," and the rest of the elect—had they jibbed at money-lenders? Not so! Did "Feathers," did "Donny"? What else were money-lenders for but lending money? Trying to cheer himself with that thought, he fell asleep from sheer unhappiness.

Next morning, at his Bank, very tight lips assured him that an overdraft without security was not in the day's work. Young Jolyon arched his eyebrows, ran fingers through a best whisker, drawled the words: "It's of no consequence!" and went away, stiffening his fallen crest. In front of him he saw again his father's face, and he couldn't stand it. He sought the rooms of "Feathers" Totteridge. The engaging youth had just had his "tosh" and was seated over devilled kidneys, in his dressing-gown.

Young Jolyon said:

"Feathers, old cock, give me a note to that brute Davids!"

Feathers stared. "What ho, friend!" he said, "Plucked? He'll skin you, Jo."

"Can't be helped," said young Jolyon, glumly.

He went away armed with the note, and in the afternoon sought the abode of Mr. Rufus Davids. The benefactor read the note, and bent on

---

[2]*baccarat,* a French card game.

young Jolyon the glance of criticism.

"How mutth do you want, Mithter Forthyte?" he said.

"One hundred and fifty."

"That will cotht you two hundred thicth month from now. I give good termth."

Good terms! Young Jolyon checked the opening of his lips. One didn't chaffer.

"I like to know my cuthtomerth, you know, Mithter Forthyte. To-morrow afternoon."

Young Jolyon nodded, and went out.

It hadn't been so bad, after all; and, cantering over to Newmarket, he almost forgot how *"Post equitem sedet atra cura."*[3]

In the afternoon of the following day he received one hundred and fifty pounds for his autograph, and seeking out "Donny" and the others who held his I.O.U.'s, discharged the lot. Not without a sense of virtue did he sit down to an evening collation in his rooms. He was eating cold wild duck, when his door was knocked on.

"Come in!" he shouted. And, there —in overcoat, top hat in hand—his father stood . . . .

Sitting in the City offices of those great tea-men, "Forsyte and Treffry," old Jolyon had been handed, with the country post, a communication marked: "Confidential!"

"Great Cury,
"Cambridge.
"Dear Sir—

"In accordance with your desire that we should advise you of anything unusual, expressed to us when you opened your son's account a year ago, we beg to notify you that Mr. Jolyon Forsyte, Junr., made application to us today for an overdraft of one hun-

dred pounds. We did not feel justified in granting this without your permission, but shall be happy to act in accordance with your decision in this matter.

"We are, dear Sir, with the compliments of the season,
"Your faithful servants,
"Brotherton and Darnett."

Old Jolyon had sat some time regarding this missive with grave and troubled eyes. He then placed it in the breast pocket of his frock coat, and taking out a little comb, had passed it through his grey Dundreary's and moustachios.

"I am going down to Cambridge, Timming. Get me a cab."

In the cab and in the train, and again in the cab from the station at Cambridge he had brooded, restless and unhappy. Why had the boy not come to *him?* What had he been doing to require an overdraft like that? He had a good allowance. He had never said anything about being pressed for money. This way and that way he turned it in his mind, and whichever way he turned it, the conclusion was that it showed weakness—weakness to want the money; above all, weakness not to have come to his father first. Of all things, Old Jolyon disliked weakness. And so there he stood, tall and grey-headed, in the doorway.

"I've come down, Jo. I've had a letter I don't like."

Through young Jolyon raced the thought: "Davids!" and his heart sank into his velvet slippers. He said, however, drawling:

"Charmed to see you, Sir. You haven't had dinner? Can you eat wild duck? This claret's pretty good."

Taking his father's hat and coat, he placed him with his back to the fire, plied the bellows, and bawled down

---

[3] *"Post equitem sedet atra cura,"* Heavy cares crouch behind the rider.

the stairway for forks and another wild duck. And while he bawled he felt as if he could be sick, for he had a great love for his father, and this was why he was afraid of him. And old Jolyon, who had a great love for his son, was not sorry to stand and warm his legs and wait.

They ate the wild duck, drank the claret, talking of the weather, and small matters. They finished, and young Jolyon said:

"Take that 'froust,' Dad"; and his heart tried to creep from him into the floor.

Old Jolyon clipped a cigar, handed another to his son, and sat down in the old leather chair on one side of the fire; young Jolyon sat in another old leather chair on the other side, and they smoked in silence, till old Jolyon took the letter from his pocket and handed it across.

"What's the meaning of it, Jo? Why didn't you come to me?"

Young Jolyon read the letter with feelings of relief, dismay, and anger with his Bank. Why on earth had they written? He felt his whiskers, and said:

"Oh! That!"

Old Jolyon sat looking at him with a sharp deep gravity.

"I suppose it means that you're in debt?" he said, at last.

Young Jolyon shrugged: "Oh! well, naturally. I mean, one must—"

"Must what?"

"Live like other fellows, Dad."

"Other fellows? Haven't you at least the average allowance?"

Young Jolyon had. "But that's just it," he said eagerly, "I'm not in an average set."

"Then why did you get into such a set, Jo?"

"I don't know, Sir. School and one thing and another. It's an awfully good set."

"H'm!" said old Jolyon, deeply. "Would this hundred pounds have cleared you?"

"Cleared me! Oh! well—yes, of what matters."

"What matters?" repeated old Jolyon. "Doesn't every debt matter?"

"Of course, Dad: but everybody up here owes money to tradesmen. I mean, they expect it."

Old Jolyon's eyes narrowed and sharpened.

"Tradesmen? What matters are not tradesmen? What then? A woman?" The word came out hushed and sharp.

Young Jolyon shook his head. "Oh! No."

Old Jolyon's attitude relaxed a little, as if with some intimate relief. He flipped the ash off his cigar.

"Have you been gambling, then, Jo?"

Struggling to keep his face calm and his eyes on his father's, young Jolyon answered:

"A little."

"Gambling!" Something of distress and consternation in the sound young Jolyon couldn't bear, and hastened on:

"Well, Dad, I don't mean to go on with it. But Newmarket, you know, and—and—one doesn't like to be a prig."

"Prig? For not gambling? I don't understand. A gambler!"

And, again, at that note in his voice, young Jolyon cried:

"I really don't care for it, Dad; I mean I'm just as happy without."

"Then why do you do it? It's weak. I don't like weakness, Jo."

Young Jolyon's face hardened. The Dad would never understand. To be a swell—superior to Fate! Hopeless to explain! He said lamely:

"All the best chaps—"

Old Jolyon averted his eyes. For

at least two minutes he sat staring at the fire.

"I've never gambled, or owed money," he said at last, with no pride in the tone of his voice, but with deep conviction. "I must know your position, Jo. What is it? Speak the truth. How much do you owe, and to whom?"

Young Jolyon had once been discovered cribbing. This was worse. It was as little possible as it had been then to explain that everybody did it. He said sullenly:

"I suppose—somewhere about three hundred, to tradesmen."

Old Jolyon's glance went through and through him.

"And that doesn't matter? What else?"

"I did owe about a hundred to fellows, but I've paid them."

"That's what you wanted the overdraft for, then?"

"Debts of honour—yes."

"Debts of honour," repeated old Jolyon. "And where did you get the hundred from?"

"I borrowed it."

"When?"

"Today."

"Who from?"

"A man called Davids."

"Money-lender?"

Young Jolyon bowed his head.

"And you preferred to go to a money-lender than to come to me?"

Young Jolyon's lips quivered; he pitched his cigar into the fire, not strong enough to bear it.

"I—I—knew you'd—you'd hate it so, Dad."

"I hate this more, Jo."

To both of them it seemed the worst moment they had ever been through, and it lasted a long time. Then old Jolyon said:

"What did you sign?"

"I borrowed a hundred and fifty, and promised to pay two hundred in six months."

"And how were you going to get that?"

"I don't know."

Old Jolyon, too, pitched his cigar into the fire, and passed his hand over his forehead.

Impulsively young Jolyon rose, and, oblivious of his whiskers, sat down on the arm of his father's chair, precisely as if he were not a swell. There were tears in his eyes.

"I'm truly sorry, Dad; only, you don't understand." Old Jolyon shook his head.

"No, I don't understand, Jo. That's the way to ruin."

"They were debts of honour, Dad."

"All debts are debts of honour. But that's not the point. It seems to me you can't face things. I know you're an affectionate chap, but that won't help you."

Young Jolyon got up.

"I _can_ face things," he said: "I—! Oh! You can't realize."

Scattering the logs with his slippered foot, he stared into the glow. His eyes felt burned, his inside all churned up; and while the "swell" within him drawled: "A fuss about money;" all his love for his father was raw and quivering. He heard old Jolyon say:

"I'll go now, Jo. Have a list of your debts for me tomorrow. I shall pay them myself. We'll go to that money-lender chap together."

Young Jolyon heard him getting up, heard him with his coat and hat, heard him open the door; and, twisting round, cried:

"Oh! Dad!"

"Good-night, Jo!" He was gone.

Young Jolyon stood a long time by the dying fire. His father did not, could not know what a fellow had to do, how behave—to be superior to fortune. He was old-fashioned! But, besides loving him, young Jolyon admired his father, admired him physically and mentally—as much—yes, more than the Honble. Crasher or Digby Grand. And he was miserable.

He sat up late, making a list of his debts as well as anyone could who had the habit of tearing up his bills. Repressed emotion tossed his slumbers, and when he woke the thought of the joint visit to Mr. Davids made him feel unwell.

Old Jolyon came at ten o'clock, looking almost haggard. He took the list from his son.

"Are these all, Jo?"

"As far as I can remember."

"Send any others in to me. Which of your friends are the gamblers?"

"You must excuse me, Dad."

Old Jolyon looked at him.

"Very well!" he said. "We'll go to this money-lender now."

They walked forth. By God's mercy no one had bounced in on his way to Newmarket. Young Jolyon caught sight of "Donny" Covercourt on the far side of the quadrangle and returned him no greeting. Quite silent, side by side, father and son passed out into the street. Except for old Jolyon's remark:

"There's no end to these Colleges, it seems," they did not speak until they reached the office of Mr. Davids, above a billiard room.

Old Jolyon ascended, stumping the stairs with his umbrella; young Jolyon followed with his head down. He was bitterly ashamed; it is probable that old Jolyon was even more so.

The money-lender was in his inner office, just visible through the half-open doorway. Old Jolyon pushed the door with his umbrella.

Mr. Davids rose, apparently surprised, and stood looking round his nose in an ingratiating manner.

"This is my father," said young Jolyon, gazing deeply at his boots.

"Mr. Davids, I think?" began old Jolyon.

"Yeth, Thir. What may I have the pleasure—"

"You were good enough yesterday to advance my son the sum of a hundred and fifty pounds, for which he signed a promissory note for an extortionate amount. Kindly give me that note, and take this cheque in satisfaction."

Mr. Davids washed his hands.

"For what amount ith your cheque, Thir?"

Old Jolyon took a cheque from his pocket and unfolded it.

"For your money, and one day's interest at ten per cent."

Mr. Davids threw up his well-washed hands.

"Oh! No, Mithter Forthyte; no! Thath not bithneth. Give me a cheque for the amount of the promithory note, and you can have it. I'm not ancthious to be paid—not at all."

Old Jolyon clapped his hat on his head.

"You will accept my cheque!" he said, and thrust it under the money-lender's eyes.

Mr. Davids examined it, and said:

"You take me for a fool, it theemth."

"I take you for a knave," said Old Jolyon. "Sixty-six per cent, forsooth!"

Mr. Davids recoiled in sheer surprise.

"I took great rithk to lend your thon that money."

"You took no risk whatever. One day's interest at ten per cent is ninepence three-farthings; I've made it tenpence. Be so good as to give me that note."

Mr. Davids shook his head.

"Very well," said old Jolyon. "I've made some inquiries about you. I go straight from here to the Vice-Chancellor."

Mr. Davids again began to wash his hands.

"And thuppothe," he said, "I go to your thon's College and tell them that I lend him thith money?"

"Do!" said old Jolyon; "do! Come Jo!" He turned and walked to the door, followed by his agonized but unmoved son.

"Thtop!" said Mr. Davids. "I don't want to make no trouble."

Old Jolyon's eyes twinkled under his drawn brows.

"Oh!" he said without turning, "you don't! Make haste, then. I give you two minutes," and he took out his watch.

Young Jolyon stood looking dazedly at the familiar golden object. Behind him he could hear Mr. Davids making haste.

"Here it ith, Mithter Forthyte, here it ith!"

Old Jolyon turned.

"Is that your signature, Jo?"

"Yes," said young Jolyon dully.

"Take it, then, and tear it up."

Young Jolyon took, and tore it savagely.

"Here's your cheque," said old Jolyon.

Mr. Davids grasped the cheque, changing his feet rapidly.

"Ith not bithneth, really ith not bithneth," he repeated.

"The deuce it isn't," said old Jolyon; "you may thank your stars I don't go to the Vice-Chancellor, into the bargain. Good-bye to you!" He stumped his umbrella and walked out. Young Jolyon followed, sheepishly.

"Where's the station, Jo?"

Young Jolyon led the way, and they walked on, more silent than ever.

At last old Jolyon said:

"This has been a sad affair. It's your not coming to me, Jo, that hurt."

Young Jolyon's answer was strangled in his throat.

"And don't gamble, my boy. It's weak-minded. Well, here we are!"

They turned into the station. Old Jolyon bought *The Times*. They stood together, silent on the platform, till the London train came in; then young Jolyon put his hand through his father's arm, and squeezed it. Old Jolyon nodded:

"I shan't allude to this again, Jo. But there's just one thing: If you must be a swell, remember that you're a gentleman too. Good-bye, my boy!" He laid his hand on his son's shoulder, turned quickly and got in.

Young Jolyon stood with bared head, watching the train go out. He then walked, as well as he knew how, back to College.

For Thought and Discussion

1. How did young Jolyon get his ideals, and what did he consider the most desirable type of life?
2. What is the "sad affair" referred to in the first paragraph?
3. Why did young Jolyon not write to his father for money rather than apply for an overdraft at the bank and later go to a money-lender?
4. Contrast young Jolyon's and his father's attitude toward debts to tradesmen? Is that difference of consequence for a stable business world?

5. Why did young Jolyon gamble? Why was it impossible for his father to understand his reasons?

6. How did old Jolyon deal with the money-lender and why was he able to settle the affair in this fashion?

7. What did old Jolyon mean by "If you must be a swell, remember that you are a gentleman, too"?

∾

THE DEFINITION OF A GENTLEMAN

From *The Idea of a University*

JOHN HENRY NEWMAN

[Cardinal Newman, 1801-1890, himself a genuine Christian gentleman, in his definition of the term *gentleman* stresses the virtues he considers desirable that a man possess. The accurate choice of words, the clear style, the tolerant tone, and the sweet spirit of this essay are characteristic of all Newman's writing.]

IT IS almost a definition of a gentleman to say he is one who never inflicts pain. This description is both refined and, as far as it goes, accurate. He is mainly occupied in removing the obstacles which hinder the free and unembarrassed action of those about him, and he concurs with their movements rather than takes the initiative himself. His benefits may be considered as parallel to what are called comforts or conveniences in arrangements of a personal nature; like an easy chair or a good fire, which do their part in dispelling cold and fatigue, though nature provides both means of rest and animal heat without them. The true gentleman in like manner carefully avoids whatever may cause a jar or a jolt in the minds of those with whom he is cast—all clashing of opinion, or collision of feeling, all restraint, or suspicion, or gloom, or resentment; his great concern being to make every one at their ease and at home. He has his eyes on all his company; he is tender towards the bashful, gentle towards the distant, and merciful towards the absurd; he can recollect to whom he is speaking; he guards against unreasonable allusions, or topics which may irritate; he is seldom prominent in conversation, and never wearisome. He makes light of favors while he does them, and seems to be receiving when he is conferring. He never speaks of himself except when compelled, never defends himself by a mere retort, he has no ears for slander or gossip, is scrupulous in imputing motives to those who interfere with him, and interprets everything for the best. He is never mean or little in his disputes, never takes unfair advantage, never mistakes personalities or sharp sayings for arguments, or insinuates evil which he dare not say out. From a long-sighted prudence, he observes the maxim of the ancient sage, that we should ever conduct ourselves towards our enemy as if he were one day to be our friend. He has too much good sense to be affronted at insults, he is too well employed to remember injuries, and too indolent to bear malice. He is patient, forbearing, and resigned, on philosophical principles; he submits to pain because it is inevitable, to bereavement because it is irreparable, and to death because it is his destiny. If he engages in controversy of any kind, his disciplined intellect preserves him from the blundering discourtesy of better, perhaps, but less educated minds, who, like blunt weapons, tear and hack, instead of cutting clean, who mistake the point in argument, waste their strength on trifles, misconceive their adversary, and leave the question more involved than they find it. He may be right or wrong in his opinion, but he is too clearheaded to be unjust; he is as simple as he is forcible, and as brief as he is decisive. Nowhere shall we find greater candor, consideration, indulgence; he throws himself into the minds of his opponents, he accounts for their mistakes. He knows the weakness of human reason as well as its strength, its province and its limits. If he be an unbeliever, he will be too profound and large-minded to ridicule religion or to act against it; he is too wise to be a dogmatist or fanatic in his infidelity. He respects piety and devotion; he even supports institutions as venerable, beautiful, or useful, to which he does not assent; he honors the ministers of religion, and it contents him to decline its mysteries without assailing or denouncing them. He is a friend of religious toleration, and that not only because his philosophy has taught him to look on all forms of faith with an impartial eye, but also from the gentleness and effeminacy of feeling which is the attendant on civilization.

For Thought and Discussion

1. What is the author's first qualification for a gentleman?
2. What is his attitude toward other people?
3. Why are "his benefits" compared to those of an "easy chair" or a "good fire"?
4. When there is a difference of opinion, what is the attitude of the gentleman?
5. How does the gentleman feel about favors which he may confer?
6. Why are insinuations one of the most evil forms of gossip?
7. What effect does tolerance have upon the individual? How does it affect general welfare?
8. Are the qualifications of a gentleman as given by Newman practical ideals?
9. What trait, if any, mentioned by Newman as desirable for a gentleman do you think non-essential or undesirable?
10. What trait, if any, not mentioned by Newman do you consider essential or desirable?
11. Compare the traits mentioned by Newman with those listed in Wordsworth's "Character of the Happy Warrior."

Plus Work

After the manner of Newman define the *all-round senior, the ideal chum, the true friend.*

Make a class report on Newman's ideas of education from *The Idea of a University.*

CHARACTER OF THE HAPPY WARRIOR

WILLIAM WORDSWORTH

[This poem, written as a tribute to Lord Nelson, is said to be descriptive of the character of Wordsworth's younger brother, a sea captain who was drowned in the same year that Nelson met his death at Trafalgar.]

WHO is the happy Warrior? Who is he
That every man in arms should wish to be?
—It is the generous spirit, who, when brought
Among the tasks of real life, hath wrought
Upon the plan that pleased his boyish thought;   5
Whose high endeavors are an inward light
That makes the path before him always bright;
Who, with a natural instinct to discern
What knowledge can perform, is diligent to learn;
Abides by this resolve, and stops not there,   10
But makes his moral being his prime care;
Who, doomed to go in company with pain
And fear and bloodshed, miserable train!
Turns his necessity to glorious gain;
In face of these doth exercise a power   15
Which is our human nature's highest dower;
Controls them and subdues, transmutes, bereaves
Of their bad influence, and their good receives;
By objects, which might force the soul to abate

Her feeling, rendered more compassionate;   20
Is placable—because occasions rise
So often that demand such sacrifice;
More skillful in self-knowledge, even more pure,
As tempted more; more able to endure,
As more exposed to suffering and distress;   25
Thence, also, more alive to tenderness.
—'Tis he whose law is reason; who depends
Upon that law as on the best of friends;
Whence, in a state where men are tempted still
To evil for a guard against worse ill,   30
And what in quality or act is best
Doth seldom on a right foundation rest,
He labors good on good to fix, and owes
To virtue every triumph that he knows;
—Who, if he rise to station of command,   35
Rises by open means; and there will stand
On honorable terms, or else retire,
And in himself possess his own desire;
Who comprehends his trust, and to the same
Keeps faithful with a singleness of aim;   40
And therefore does not stoop, nor lie in wait
For wealth or honors or for worldly state;
Whom they must follow; on whose head must fall,
Like showers of manna, if they come at all;

Whose powers shed round him in the common strife, 45
Or mild concerns of ordinary life,
A constant influence, a peculiar grace;
But who, if he be called upon to face
Some awful moment to which Heaven has joined
Great issues, good or bad for human kind, 50
Is happy as a lover; and attired
With sudden brightness, like a man inspired;
And, through the heat of conflict, keeps the law
In calmness made, and sees what he foresaw;
Or if an unexpected call succeed, 55
Come when it will, is equal to the need.
—He who, though thus endued as with a sense
And faculty for storm and turbulence,
Is yet a soul whose master-bias leans
To home-felt pleasures and to gentle scenes; 60
Sweet images! which, whereso'er he be,
Are at his heart; and such fidelity
It is his darling passion to approve;
More brave for this, that he hath much to love.
'Tis, finally, the man, who, lifted high, 65

Conspicuous object in a nation's eye,
Or left unthought-of in obscurity—
Who, with a toward or untoward lot,
Prosperous or adverse, to his wish or not—
Plays, in the many games of life, that one 70
Where what he most doth value must be won;
Whom neither shape of danger can dismay,
Nor thought of tender happiness betray;
Who, not content that former worth stand fast,
Looks forward, persevering to the last, 75
From well to better, daily self-surpassed;
Who, whether praise of him must walk the earth
Forever, and to noble deeds give birth,
Or he must fall to sleep without his fame,
And leave a dead, unprofitable name— 80
Finds comfort in himself and in his cause;
And, while the mortal mist is gathering, draws
His breath in confidence of Heaven's applause—
This is the happy Warrior; this is he
That every man in arms should wish to be.

For Thought and Discussion

1. What is the attitude of the happy Warrior toward himself? toward reason? toward a definite purpose in life? toward honor and praise here and in the hereafter?
2. Explain what the term "happy Warrior" means to you.
3. Did you ever hear of any one termed a "happy Warrior"? Who? Why?
4. Compare this poem with Kipling's "If."

THE EDUCATION OF A GENTLEWOMAN

From *Sesame and Lilies*

JOHN RUSKIN

[Ruskin, 1819-1900, a lover of nature, art, architecture, and humanity, and a student of industrialism and materialism, held educational and economic views which affected profoundly the thought of his time. He preached the gospel of love and joy and beauty, but he did not stop with lecturing on his views; he spent money (a not inconsiderable fortune) and time in seeing his theories placed in operation. As a lecturer he was in great demand. The address from which this excerpt is taken was delivered before a girls' school near Manchester.]

THE perfect loveliness of a woman's countenance can only consist in that majestic peace, which is founded in the memory of happy and useful years,—full of sweet records; and from the joining of this with that yet more majestic childishness, which is still full of change and promise; — opening always — modest at once, and bright, with hope of better things to be won, and to be bestowed. There is no old age where there is still that promise.

Thus, then, you have first to mold her physical frame, and then, as the strength she gains will permit you, to fill and temper her mind with all knowledge and thoughts which tend to confirm its natural instincts of justice, and refine its natural tact of love.

All such knowledge should be given her as may enable her to understand, and even to aid, the work of men: and yet it should be given, not as knowledge,—not as if it were, or could be, for her an object to know;

but only to feel, and to judge. It is of no moment, as a matter of pride or perfectness in herself, whether she knows many languages or one; but it is of the utmost, that she should be able to show kindness to a stranger, and to understand the sweetness of a stranger's tongue. It is of no moment to her own worth or dignity that she should be acquainted with this science or that; but it is of the highest that she should be trained in habits of accurate thought; that she should understand the meaning, the inevitableness, and the loveliness of natural laws; and follow at least some one path of scientific attainment, as far as to the threshold of that bitter Valley of Humiliation, into which only the wisest and bravest of men can descend, owning themselves forever children, gathering pebbles on a boundless shore. It is of little consequence how many positions of cities she knows, or how many dates of events, or how many names of celebrated persons—it is not the object of education to turn a woman into a dictionary; but it is deeply necessary that she should be taught to enter with her whole personality into the history she reads; to picture the passages of it vitally in her own bright imagination; to apprehend, with her fine instincts, the pathetic circumstances and dramatic relations, which the historian too often only eclipses by his reasoning, and disconnects by his arrangement: it is for her to trace the hidden equities of divine reward, and catch sight, through the darkness, of the fateful threads of woven fire that connect error with its retribution. But, chiefly of all, she is to be taught to extend the limits of her sympathy with respect to that history which is being forever determined as the moments pass in which she draws her peaceful breath; and to the contemporary calamity which, were it but rightly mourned by her, would recur no more hereafter. She is to exercise herself in imagining what would be the effects upon her mind and conduct, if she were daily brought into the presence of the suffering which is not the less real because shut from her sight. She is to be taught somewhat to understand the nothingness of the proportion which that little world in which she lives and loves, bears to the world in which God lives and loves;—and solemnly she is to be taught to strive that her thoughts of piety may not be feeble in proportion to the number they embrace, nor her prayer more languid than it is for the momentary relief from pain of her husband or her child, when it is uttered for the multitudes of those who have none to love them,—and is "for all who are desolate and oppressed."

. . . .

It is now long since the women of England arrogated, universally, a title which once belonged to nobility only; and, having once been in the habit of accepting the simple title of gentlewoman, as correspondent to that of gentleman, insisted on the privilege of assuming the title of "Lady," which properly corresponds only to the title of "Lord."

I do not blame them for this; but only for their narrow motive in this. I would have them desire and claim the title of Lady, provided they claim, not merely the title, but the office and duty signified by it. Lady means "bread-giver" or "loaf-giver," and Lord means "maintainer of laws," and both titles have reference, not to the law which is maintained in the house, nor to the bread which is given to the household; but to law maintained for the multitude, and to bread broken among the multitude. So that a Lord has legal claim only to his title in so far as he is the maintainer of the justice of the Lord of Lords; and a Lady has legal claim to her title, only so far as she communicates that help to the poor representatives of her Master, which women once, ministering to Him of their substance, were permitted to extend to that Master Himself; and when she is known, as He Himself once was, in breaking of bread.

For Thought and Discussion

1. What characteristics mentioned by Newman in his definition of a gentleman are also listed by Ruskin?
2. Have you noted faces which seemed to record undesirable traits and others which seemed to bear record of well-spent years?
3. Do you approve of the educational views Ruskin expressed?
4. Is he opposed to the study of foreign language, geography, history?
5. Mention specific means by which a girl may speak the language of kindness to which Ruskin refers.
6. What attitude does Ruskin hold toward God?
7. What scriptural text could Ruskin have used to refer to his gospel of ministering to the Master?

Plus Work

Read the other essays included in *Sesame and Lilies* and report on Ruskin's views on education for a boy; education for a girl; home; reading; work; war.

~❧

THE IDEAL WIFE
PROVERBS 31

WHO can find a virtuous woman? For her price is far above rubies. The heart of her husband doth safely trust in her, so that he shall have no need of spoil. She will do him good and not evil all the days of her life. She seeketh wool, and flax, and worketh willingly with her hands. She is like the merchants' ships; she bringeth her food from afar. She riseth also while it is yet night, and giveth meat to her household, and a portion to her maidens. She considereth a field, and buyeth it; with the fruit of her hands she planteth a vineyard. She girdeth her loins with strength, and strengtheneth her arms. She perceiveth that her merchandise is good; her candle goeth not out by night. She layeth her hands to the spindle, and her hands hold the distaff. She stretcheth out her hand to the poor; yea, she reacheth forth her hands to the needy. She is not afraid of the snow for her household, for all her household are clothed with scarlet. She maketh her coverings of tapestry; her clothing is silk and purple. Her husband is known in the gates, when he sitteth among the elders of the land. She maketh fine linen, and selleth it; and delivereth girdles unto the merchant. Strength and honor are her clothing, and she shall rejoice in time to come. She openeth her mouth with wisdom, and in her tongue is the law of kindness. She looketh well to the way of her household, and eateth not the bread of idleness. Her children arise up, and call her blessèd; her husband also, and he praiseth her. Many daughters have done virtuously, but thou excellest them all. Favor is deceitful, and beauty is vain, but a woman that feareth the Lord, she shall be praised. Give her of the fruit of her hands, and let her own works praise her in the gates.

~❧

ON DROPPING ANCHOR
HILAIRE BELLOC

[Hilaire Belloc, 1870—, is a Frenchman and an Englishman, his ancestry including French and English and Irish. At an early age he left his birthplace in France and went to England to live. He is an Oxford man and a naturalized Englishman. He has been named as "one of the three cleverest men in London"; the other two are Shaw and Chesterton. He is a poet, a novelist, and an essayist.]

THE best noise in all the world is the rattle of the anchor chain when one comes into harbor at last, and lets it go over the bows.

You may say that one does nothing of the sort, that one picks up moorings, and that letting go so heavy a thing as an anchor is no business for you and me. If you say that, you are wrong. Men go from inhabited place to inhabited place, and for pleasure from station to station, then pick up moorings as best they can, usually craning over the side and grabbing as they pass, and cursing the man astern for leaving such way on her and for passing so wide. Yes, I know that. You are not the only man who has picked up moorings. Not by many, many thousands. Many moorings have I picked up in many places, none without some sort of misfortune; therefore do I still prefer the rattle of the anchor chain.

Once — to be accurate, seventeen years ago — I had been out all night by myself in a boat called the *Silver Star*. She was a very small boat. She had only one sail; she was black inside and out, and I think about one hundred years old. I had hired her of a poor man, and she was his only possession.

It was a rough night in the late summer, when the rich are compelled in their detestable grind to go to the Solent. When I say it was night I mean it was the early morning, just late enough for the rich to be asleep aboard their boats; and the dawn was silent upon the sea. There was a strong tide running up the Medina. I was tired to death. I had passed the Royal Squadron grounds, and the first thing I saw was a very fine and noble buoy, new-painted, gay, lordly—moorings worthy of a man!

I let go the halyard very briskly, and I nipped forward and got my hand upon the great buoy — there was no hauling of it in-board; I took the little painter of my boat and made it fast to this noble buoy, and then

immediately I fell asleep. In this sleep of mine I heard, as in a pleasant dream, the exact motion of many oars rowed by strong men; and very soon afterwards I heard a voice with a Colonial accent swearing in an abominable manner; and I woke up and looked — and there was a man of prodigious wealth, all dressed in white, and with an extremely new cap on his head. His whiskers also were white and his face bright red, and he was in a great passion. He was evidently the owner or master of the buoy, and on either side of the fine boat in which he rowed were the rowers, his slaves. He could not conceive why I had tied the *Silver Star* to his magnificent great imperial moorings, to which he had decided to tie his own expensive ship, on which, no doubt, a dozen as rich as he were sailing the seas.

I told him that I was sorry I had picked up his moorings, but that, in this country, it was the common courtesy of the seas to pick up any spare moorings one could find. I also asked him the name of his expensive ship, but he only answered with curses. I told him the name of my ship was the *Silver Star*.

Then when I had cast off, I put out the sweeps and I rowed gently, for it was now slack water at the top of the tide, and I stood by while he tied his magnificent yacht to the moorings. When he had done that I rowed under the stern of that ship and read her name. But I will not print it here; only let me tell you it was the name of a ship belonging to a fabulously rich man. Riches, I thought then and I think still, corrupt the heart.

Under another occasion I came with one companion across the bar of Orford River, out of a very heavy wind outside and a very heavy sea.

I just touched as I crossed that bar, though I was on the top of the highest tide of the year, for it was just this time in September, the highest springs of the hunter's moon.

My companion and I sailed up·Orford River, and when we came to Orford Town we saw a buoy, and I said to my companion, "Let us pick up moorings."

Upon the bank of the river was a long line of men, all shouting and howling, and warning us not to touch that buoy. But we called out to them that we meant no harm. We only meant to pick up those moorings for a moment, so as to make everything snug on board, and that then we would take a line ashore and lie close to the wharf. Only the more did those numerous men (whom many others ran up to join as I called) forbid us with oaths to touch the buoy. Nevertheless, we picked up the little buoy, which was quite small and light, and we got it in-board, and held on, waiting for our boat to swing to it. But an astonishing thing happened! The boat paid not attention to the moorings, but went careering up-river, carrying the buoy with it, and apparently dragging the moorings along the bottom without the least difficulty. And this was no wonder, for we found out afterward that the little buoy had only been set there to mark a racing-point, and that the weights holding the line of it to the bottom were very light and few. So it was no wonder the men of Orford had been so angry. Soon it was dark, and we replaced the buoy stealthily, and when we came in to eat at the Inn we were not recognized.

It was on this occasion that was written the song: —

The men that lived in Orford stood
  Upon the shore to meet me;
Their faces were like carven wood,
  They did not wish to greet
    me. . . .

It has eighteen verses.

I say again, unless you have moorings of your own — an extravagant habit — picking up moorings is always a perilous and doubtful thing, fraught with accident and hatred and mischance. Give me the rattle of the anchor chain!

I love to consider a place I have never yet seen, but which I shall reach at last, full of repose, marking the end of those voyages, and security from the trouble of the sea.

This place will be a cove set round with high hills on which there shall be no house or sign of men, and it shall be enfolded by quite deserted land; but the westering sun will shine pleasantly upon it under a warm air. It will be a proper place for sleep.

The fairway into that haven shall lie behind a pleasant little beach of shingle, which shall run out aslant into the sea from the steep hillside, and shall be a breakwater made by God. The tide shall run up behind it smoothly, and in a silent way, filling the quiet hollow of the hills, brimming it all up like a cup — a cup of refreshment and of quiet, a cup of ending.

Then with what pleasure shall I put my small boat round, just round the point of that shingle beach, noting the shoal water by the eddies and the deeps by the blue color of them where the channel runs from the main into the fairway. Up that fairway shall I go, up into the cove, and the gates of it shall shut behind me, headland against headland, so that I shall not see the open sea any more, though I shall still hear its distant noise. But all around me, save for that distant echo of the surf from the high hills, will be silence; and the evening will be gathering already.

Under that falling light, all alone in such a place, I shall let go the anchor chain, and let it rattle for the last time. My anchor will go down into the clear salt water with a run, and when it touches I shall pay out four lengths or more so that she may swing easily and not drag, and then I shall tie up my canvas and fasten all for the night, and get me ready for sleep. And that will be the end of my sailing.

For Thought and Discussion

1. Why does the writer prefer anchor chains to moorings?
2. Describe the *Silver Star*.
3. Why is the wealthy man described in this selection unattractive?
4. Why is the second incident about moorings humorous?
5. Why do you think that the author is democratic?
6. How does the author pass from the subject of moorings to a deeper subject?
7. Explain the meaning of the essay.

RING OUT, WILD BELLS

From *In Memoriam*

ALFRED LORD TENNYSON

[*In Memoriam*, a collection of lyrics, was written in memory of Arthur Hallam, Tennyson's Cambridge schoolmate who died in Europe. The New Year's song marks the third New Year after Hallam's death.]

RING out, wild bells, to the wild
    sky,
  The flying cloud, the frosty light;
  The year is dying in the night;
Ring out, wild bells, and let him die.

Ring out the old, ring in the new,   5
  Ring, happy bells, across the
    snow;
  The year is going, let him go;
Ring out the false, ring in the true.

Ring out the grief that saps the mind,
  For those that here we see no
    more;   10
  Ring out the feud of rich and
    poor;
Ring in redress to all mankind.

Ring out a slowly dying cause,
  And ancient forms of party strife;

Ring in the nobler modes of life, 15
With sweeter manners, purer laws.

Ring out the want, the care, the sin,
  The faithless coldness of the times;
  Ring out, ring out my mournful
    rimes,
But ring the fuller minstrel in.   20

Ring out false pride in place and
    blood,
  The civic slander and the spite;
  Ring in the love of truth and
    right,
Ring in the common love of good.

Ring out old shapes of foul disease; 25
  Ring out the narrowing lust of
    gold;
  Ring out the thousand wars of
    old,
Ring in the thousand years of peace.

Ring in the valiant man and free,
  The larger heart, the kindlier
    hand;   30
  Ring out the darkness of the land,
Ring in the Christ that is to be.

For Thought and Discussion

1. How many of the problems named by Tennyson are important today?
2. Find the most musical lines.

❧

THE MAGIC FORMULA

LAWRENCE PEARSALL JACKS

[Lawrence Pearsall Jacks, born in Nottingham, England, attended London University and Harvard. Formerly an instructor in philosophy in one of the colleges of Oxford, he later became its principal. His essays and stories embody his philosophical ideas and offer a basis for a happier and more satisfactory social system. He makes a sharp distinction between

"Space Thinkers," who think only in terms of the present, and "Time Thinkers," who not only evaluate the past but also visualize the future —those see the whole of life through a long span of years—"time."

Appreciative audiences, who have sought him in times of stress and uncertainty, indicate that the world is interested in hearing his views about this society which we have built.]

I

MANY years ago I had a school-fellow and bosom friend whom I knew as Billy, but whose name as it stood in the Register was William Xavier Plosive. Where his family came from, or where they got their outlandish name, I know not. From its rarity I infer that the Plosive stock has not multiplied lavishly on the earth. No sooner, of course, was the name William X. Plosive seen on the outside of the poor boy's copy-books than a whisper passed through the whole school—"Billy Burst." And that name remained with him to the end. It was more appropriate than its bestowers knew.

"*When* did Billy burst?" "*Why* did Billy burst?" "Will Billy burst again?" and a hundred questions of the like order were asked all day long apropos of nothing. They were shouted in the playgrounds. They were whispered in the class. They broke the silence of the dormitory in the dead of night. One morning the Rev. Cyril Puttock, M. A., who "took" us in Divinity, saw written large on the blackboard in front of him these words: "What burst Billy?" I spent my next half-holiday in writing out the Beatitudes a hundred times.

Billy and I slept in the same dormitory and our beds were side by side. Both of us were bad sleepers, and

many a deep affinity did our souls discover in the silent watches of the night. This is the sort of thing that would go on:

"Billy, are you awake?"

"Yes; I knew *you* were."

"I say, we are going to have that beastly pudding for dinner to-morrow."

"That's just what I want to talk about."

"I've got an idea. Billy, I found out yesterday where they cook those puddings. They boil them in the copper of the out-house, and the cook leaves them there while she looks after the rest of the dinner."

"Ripping!" answered Billy. *"I'll* tell you what we'll do.—Hush! Is old Ginger awake? All right. Well, we'll sneak into the out-house to-morrow when the cook isn't looking, pinch the puddings out of the copper and chuck 'em in the pond."

"Why, Billy, that's just what I was going to say to you. But won't we scald ourselves?"

"I've thought of that. We'll get the garden fork and jab it into the puddings. They boil 'em in bags, you know."

Enterprises such as these, however, were episodic. The seat of our affinities lay deeper. Both Billy and I were persons with an "end" in life, and breathed in common the atmosphere of great designs. Few were the days of our companionship when we were not infatuated about something or other; and I sometimes doubt whether even yet I have outgrown the habit.

At the time this history begins the particular mania that afflicted me was the collecting of tramcar tickets. My friends used to save them for me; I begged them from passengers as they alighted from the cars; I picked them up in the street; and I had over seven thousand collected in a box. I thought that when the sum had risen to ten thousand the goal of my existence would be reached; and it may be said that I lived for little else.

Billy's mania was astronomy. He would spend the hours of his playtime lying on his stomach with a map of the stars spread out before him on the floor. Billy was a great astronomer —in secret. On the very day when he and I were being initiated into the mysteries of decimals, he whispered to me in class, "I say, I wonder how people found out the weight of the planets." Little did the master know what Billy was thinking of as he stared at the wall before him with his great, dreamy eyes—and not for ten thousand worlds would Billy have told him. He was thinking about the weight of the planets, and the problem lay heavy on his soul. At last he suddenly waked up and began to get top-marks not only in arithmetic but in every other subject as well. And later on, when we came to the quadratic equations and the higher geometry, the master was amazed to find that Billy required no teaching at all.

"What has happened to Billy?" asked somebody; and the answer came, "Why, of course, Billy has *burst*."

So he had. Billy had found out "how they weighed the planets," and the mass of darkness that oppressed him had been blown away in the explosion. About the same time I burst also. On counting up my tickets I found there were ten thousand of them.

Then came a pause, during which Billy and I wandered about in dry places seeking rest and finding none. We were both waiting for the new birth, or the new explosion, utterly unconscious of our condition. The usual exchange of measles and whoop-ing-cough had been going on in our school and Billy and I being convalescent from the latter complaint, were sent out one day to take an airing in the Park. On passing down a certain walk, shaded by planes, we noticed a very old gentleman seated in a bath-chair which had been wheeled under the shadow of one of the trees. He sat in the chair with his head bent forward on his chest, and his wasted hands were spread out on the cover. He seemed an image of decrepitude, a symbol of approaching death.

I think it was the immobility of the old man that first arrested our attention. The moment we saw him we stopped dead in our walk and stood, motionless as the figure before us, staring at what we saw.

Suddenly Billy Burst clutched my arm—he had a habit of doing that. "I say," he whispered, "let's go up to him and *ask him to tell us the time*."

We crept up to the bath-chair like two timid animals, literally sniffing the air as we went. The old man was still unaware of our presence.

"If you please," said Billy, "would you mind telling us the time?"

At the sound of Billy's voice the old man seemed to wake from his dream. He lifted his head and listened, as though he heard himself summoned from a far point in space; and his eyes wandered vaguely from side to side unable to focus the speaker. Then they fell to rest on Billy and his gaze was arrested. A look of indescribable pleasure overspread the withered face. It almost seemed as if, for a moment, youth returned to him, or as if a breath of spring had awakened in the midst of the winter's frost.

"The time, laddie?" said he. "Why, yes, of course I can give you the time; as much of it as you want. For, don't you see, I'm a very old fellow— ninety-one last birthday; which I should think is not more than eighty years older than you, my little man. So, I've plenty of time to spare. But don't take too much of it, my laddie. It's not good for little chaps like you. Now, how much of the time would you like?"

"The correct time, if you please, sir," said Billy, ignoring the quantitative form in which the question had been framed. So the old gentleman gave us the correct time.

"I'll tell you what," said Billy as soon as we were out of hearing. "I've found out something. It does old gentlemen good to ask them the time. Let's ask some more."

So for an hour or more we wandered about looking out for old gentlemen—"to do them good." Several whom we met were rejected by Billy on the ground that they were not old enough, and allowed to pass unquestioned. Some three or four came up to the standard and at each experiment we found that our magic formula worked with wonderful success. It provoked smiles and kind words; it pleased the old gentlemen; it did them good. Old hands were laid on young shoulders; old faces lit up; old watches were pulled out of old pockets. But, be it observed, Billy was the spokesman every time.

From that time onward, Billy and I were Masters in Magic, no less, infatuated with our calling and devoted to our formula. The star-books were bundled in Billy's play-box; and the ten thousand tramcar tickets were thrown into the fire. Never since the world began, thought we, had a more glorious game been invented. A world-wide mission to old gentlemen was ours. Who would have believed there were so many of them? They seemed to spring into existence, to gather themselves from the four quarters of the earth, in order that they might receive the healing touch of our formula. We met them in the street, in the Park, by the river, at the railway station, coming out of church—everywhere. And all were completely in our power. Oh, it was magnificent!

So it went on for three or four weeks. But a shock was in store for us. At first, as I have said, Billy was the spokesman. But there came a day when it seemed good that some independence of action should be introduced into the partnership. Billy went one way and I another.

Going on alone, I presently espied an old gentleman of promising antiquity, walking briskly down one of the gravel paths. He was intermittently reading a newspaper. Trotting up behind him, I observed that in the intervals of his reading he would be talking to himself. He would read for half a minute and then, whipping the newspaper behind his back, begin to declaim, as though he were making a speech, quickening his pace meanwhile, so that I was hard put to it to keep up with him. Indeed I had to run, and was out of breath when, coming up alongside, I popped out my question, "If you please, sir, what o'clock is it?"

"Go to the devil!" growled the old ruffian. And without pausing even to look at me he strode on, continuing his declamation. For the first time the formula had failed to work —had done the old gentleman no good. It cut me to the heart. I ran about in distress, seeking Billy, whom finding presently I informed in general terms of what had happened.

"What did you say to the old beast?" asked Billy.

"I said, 'If you please, sir, what o'clock is it?'"

"Oh, you ass!" cried Billy. "*Those are the wrong words*. If you'd said, 'Would you mind telling me the time?' he'd have gone down like a ninepin. Only cads say 'what o'clock.' He thought you were a cad! Oh, you idiot! Leave me to do it next time."

Thus it came to pass that the partnership was resumed on its old basis, with Billy as the predominant member and spokesman of the Firm.

And now we entered on what I still regard as an enterprise of pith and moment. We determined, after long colloquy in the bedroom to waylay this recalcitrant old gentleman once more, and repeat our question in its proper form, and with Billy as spokesman. For several days the declaiming gentleman, whom we now knew as "the old beast," and never called by any other name, failed to appear. But at last we caught sight of him, striding along and violently whipping his newspaper behind his back, just as before.

On the former occasion, when I was alone, I had operated from the rear, but with Billy in support, I proposed that we should attack from the front. So we threw ourselves in his path and marched steadily to meet him. On he came, and as he drew near, down went the newspaper, and, as though he were spitting poison, he hissed out from between his teeth a fearful sentence, of which the last words were: "the most iniquitous government that has ever betrayed and abused the confidence of a sovereign people"—staring meanwhile straight over our heads.

"If you please, sir," said Billy in his singing voice, "would you mind telling us the time?"

"Go to—" But at that moment the gentleman lowered his fierce old eyes and encountered the gaze of Billy, who was standing full in his path.

Have you ever seen a wild beast suddenly grow tame? I have not, but I saw something like it on the occasion of which I speak. Never did a swifter or more astonishing change pass over the countenance of any human being. I really think the old fellow suffered a physical shock, for he stepped back two paces and looked for a moment like one who has been seriously hurt. Then he recovered himself; lowered his spectacles to the tip of his nose; gazed over them at me for a moment, at Billy for a quarter of a minute, and finally broke out into a hearty laugh.

"Well," he exclaimed, in the merriest of voices, "you're a couple of young rascals. What are your names, and how old are you, and what school do you belong to, and who are your fathers?"

We answered his questions in a fairly business-like manner until we came to that about the fathers. Here there was an interlude. For Billy had to explain, in succession, that he had no father, and no mother, and no brothers, and no sisters—indeed, no relations at all that he knew of. And there was some emotion at this point.

"Bless my soul," said the old gentleman, "that's very sad—very sad indeed. But who pays for your schooling?"

"A friend of my mater's," said Billy. "He's very good to me and has me to his house for the holidays."

"And gives you plenty of pocketmoney?"

"Lots," answered Billy.

"Then you are not an unhappy boy?"

"Not a bit," answered Billy.

"Thank God for that! Thank God for that! I should be very sorry to learn you were unhappy. I hope you

never will be. You don't *look* unhappy."

All this time the old gentleman
seemed quite unconscious of my existence. But I was not hurt by that.
I was well used to being overlooked
when Billy was with me, and never
questioned for a moment the justice
of the arrangement. But now the old
gentleman seemed to recollect himself.

"What was it you asked me just
now?" said he.

"We asked if you would mind telling us the time."

"Ha, just so. Now are you quite
sure that what you asked for is what
you want? You said 'the time,' not
'time.' For you must know, my
dears, that there's a great difference
between 'time' and '*the* time.' "

Billy and I looked at each other,
perplexed and disgusted—perplexed
by the subtle distinction just drawn
by the old gentleman; disgusted at
being addressed as "my dears." ("He
might as well have given us a kiss
while he was about it," we thought.)

"We want *the* time, if you please,"
we said at length.

"What, the whole of it?" said the
old gentleman.

"No," answered Billy, "we only
want the bit of it that's going on
now."

"Which bit is that?" said our venerable friend.

"That's just what we want to
know," answered Billy.

This fairly floored the old gentleman. "You'll be a great Parliamentary
debater one day, my boy," he said,
"but the bit of time that's going on
now is not an easy thing to catch.
My watch can't catch it."

"Give us the best your watch can
do," answered Billy.

This made the old gentleman laugh
again. "Better and better," said he.

"Well, the best my watch can do is
a quarter past twelve. And that reminds me that you two young scamps
have made me late for an appointment. Now be good boys, both of
you; and don't forget to write to
your moth—to your friends. And
put that in your pockets." Whereupon he gave each of us half-a-
sovereign.

"It worked," said Billy at length.

"Rather!" I answered.

Presently we were greeted by the
Park-keeper, who was a friend of
ours.

"Well, young hopefuls," he said,
"and who have you been asking the
time of to-day?"

We pointed to the old gentleman
whose figure was still visible in the
distance.

"Him!" cried the Park-keeper.
"Well, bless your rascal impudence!
Do you know who *he* is?"

"No."

"Why, he's Lord——."

The name mentioned was that of a
distinguished member of the Cabinet
which had recently gone out of
office. Did we quail and cower at the
mention of that mighty name? Did
we cover ourselves with confusion?
Not we.

"What shall we do with those half-
sovereigns?" I asked.

"Keep them. Let's put a cross on
each of them at once."

So we took out the coins, and with
our pen-knives we scratched a cross
on the cheek of her gracious Majesty,
Queen Victoria. Both coins are now
in my possession. The cross on the
cheek of Queen Victoria has worked
wonders. It has brought me good
luck. In return I have hedged the
coins with safe-guards both moral and
material. When I am gone they will
be— But I am anticipating.

And now the fever was in full

possession of our souls. An ardent missionary fervour burned in our bones. As a preliminary step to the accomplishment of these great designs we resolved to ask ten thousand old gentlemen to tell us the time. Making a calculation, we reckoned that, at the normal rate of progress, nine years would be required to complete the task. In order to expedite matters, we resolved to include old ladies, and any young persons of either sex with grey hair, or who, in our opinion, showed other signs of prematurely growing old. This led on to further extensions. We agreed, first, that anyone who looked "miserable" should have the benefit of our formula; next, that all limitations whatsoever, save one, should be withdrawn, and the formula allowed a universal application. The outstanding limitation was that nobody should be asked the question until he had been previously viewed by Billy, who was a psychologist, and pronounced by him to be "the right sort."

As became a firm of businesslike magicians, Billy and I kept books, duly averaged and balanced, entering in them day by day the names of the persons to whom we had applied the formula. One of these books is before me now, and here are a few names, culled almost at random from its pages. It will be observed that in the last group our faculty of invention gave out and we were compelled to plagiarise:

Mr. Smoky, Mr. Shinytopper, Uncle Jellybones, Aunt Ginger, Lady Peppermint, Bishop Butter, Canon Sweaty, Dirty Boots, Holy Toad, Satan, Old Hurry, Old Bless-my-soul, Old Chronometer, Miss No-Watch, Dr. Beard, Lord Splutters, Aurora, Mrs. Proud, Polly Sniggers, Diamond Pin, Cigar, Cuttyperoozle, Jim, Alfred Dear! Mr. Just-engaged, Miss Ditto, Mr. Catch-his-train, Mr. Hot, The Reverend Hum, The Reverend Ha-Ha, So-there-you-be, Mrs. Robin, Mr. High-mind, Mr. Love-lust, Mr. Heady.

II

One night Billy and I were lying awake as usual, and the question "shall we talk?" had been asked and duly answered in the affirmative.

"Put your ear a little closer, Billy, and listen like mad. Suppose you were to meet a beautiful woman—what would you do?"

Quick as thought came the answer —"I should ask her to tell me the time."

Next day, the instant we were freed from school we bolted for the Park, exalted in spirit and full of resolution. A lovely Presence floated in the light above us and accompanied us as we ran. Arrived in the Park, we seemed to have reached the threshold of a new world. We stood on a peak in Darien[1]; and before us there shimmered an enchanted sea lit by the softest of lights and tinted with the fairest of colors. Forces as old as the earth and as young as the dawn were stirring within us; the breath of spring was in our souls, and a vision of living beauty, seen only in the faintest of glimpses, lured us on.

Think not that we lacked discrimination. "Let's wait, Billy," I said, as he made a dart forward at a girl in a white frock, "till we find one beautiful enough. That one won't do. Look at the size of her feet."

"We shall never find her here," said Billy. "Let's try the walk down by the river. They are better-looking down there, especially on Sunday

---

[1]*Darien,* isthmus of Panama. Balboa is supposed to have seen the Pacific Ocean first from here, and to have been overawed by the sight.

afternoon. And I'll bet you most of them have watches."

The very day on which Billy made this proposal another nasty thing happened to us. We were summoned into the Headmaster's study and informed that complaints had reached him concerning two boys who were in the habit of walking about in the Park and staring in the rudest manner at young ladies, and making audible remarks about their personal appearance. Were we the culprits? We confessed that we were. What did we mean by it? We were silent: not for a whole archipelago packed full of buried treasure would we have answered that question. The foolish man then gave himself away by telling us that whenever we met Miss Overbury's school on their daily promenade we were to walk on the other side of the road.

Necessity having thus combined with choice, the scene of our quest was now definitely shifted to the riverbank, where a broad winding path, with seats at intervals, ran under the willows. Here a new order of beauty seemed to present itself, and our hopes ran high. Several promising candidates presented themselves at once. One, I remember, wore a scarlet feather; another carried a gray muff. The scarlet feather was my fancy; the gray muff Billy's.

Billy went off to take a final look before deciding. In a minute he returned white as the table-cloth and trembling all over.

"Come on!" he gasped. "I've found the very one! Quick, quick, or she'll be gone!"

"What is she like, Billy?" I asked as we hurried away.

"She's—oh, *she's the exact image of my mater!*" he said.

Billy's mater had died about a year ago. At the age of twelve I had been deeply in love with her, and to this hour her image remains with me as the type of all that is most commendable in woman.

We turned the bend and came in sight of the seat where Billy had seen what he saw. The seat was empty. We looked round us: not a soul was in sight. Arrived at the seat, Billy felt it all over with his hands and finding nothing, flung himself face downwards on the turf and uttered the most lamentable cry I have ever heard.

"I knew she wouldn't wait," he moaned. "Oh, why weren't we quicker! Oh, why didn't I ask her the time the minute I saw her!"

As, shattered and silent, we crawled back to school, continually loitering to gaze at a world that was all hateful, I realized with a feeling of awe that I had discovered something deep in Billy's soul. And I inwardly resolved that, so far as I could, I would set the matter right, and put friendship on a footing of true equality, by telling Billy the deepest secret of *mine*.

The great adventure was over. It had ended in disaster and tears. Never again did Billy and I ask any human being the time.

III

In those days I was a great metaphysician. Unassisted by any philosopher, I had made a discovery in the metaphysical line. This discovery was *my* secret.

In the church-tower of the village where I was nurtured there was an ancient and curious clock, said to have been brought from Spain by a former owner of the parish. This clock was worked by an enormous pendulum which hung down, through a slit in the ceiling, into the body of the church, swinging to and fro at the west end of the nave. Its motion was even and beautiful; and the sight of it fascinated me continually through the hours of divine service. To those who were not attentive, the pendulum was inaudible; but if you listened you could detect a gentle tick, tock, between the pauses of the hymns or the parson's voice.

The question that haunted me was this: Did the pendulum *stop* on reaching the highest point of the ascending arc? Did it pause before beginning the descent? And if it stopped did *time* stop with it? I answered both questions in the affirmative. Well, then, what was a second? Did the stoppage at the end of the swing make the second, or was the second made by the swing, the movement between the two points of rest? I concluded that it was the stoppage. For, mark you, it takes a second for the pendulum to reach the stopping point on either side; therefore there can be no second till that point is reached; the second must *wait* for the stoppage to do the business. I saw no other way of getting any seconds. And if no seconds, no minutes; and if no minutes, no hours, no days, and therefore no time at all—which is absurd.

I found great peace in this conclusion; but none the less I continued to support it by collateral reasonings, and by observation. In particular I determined, for reasons of my own, to make a careful survey of the hands of the clock. With this object I borrowed my father's field-glass, and retiring to a convenient point of observation, focussed it on the clock-face. Instantly a startling phenomenon sprang into view. I saw that the big hand of the clock, instead of moving evenly as it seemed to do when viewed by the naked eye, was visibly jerking on its way, in time with the seconds that were being ticked off by the pendulum inside. By George, the hand was going jerk, jerk! The pendulum and the hand were moving together! Jerk went the hand: then a pause. What's happening now? thought I. Why the pendulum has just ticked and is going to tock. Tock it goes and—there you are! — jerk goes the hand again. "Why, of course," I said to myself, "that proves it. The hand *stops,* as well as the pendulum. The seconds *must* be the stoppages. There's nothing else for them to be."

Such was the secret which I resolved to impart to Billy in return for what he had disclosed to me. Some months after this amazing discovery Billy came down for the holidays. He arrived late in the afternoon, and I could hardly restrain my impatience while he was having his tea. Hardly had he swallowed the last mouthful when I had him by the jacket. "Come on, Billy," I cried. "I'm going to show you something"—and we ran together to the church. Arrived there, I placed him in front of the pendulum, which seemed to be swinging that afternoon with an even friendlier motion than usual.

"There!" I said, "look at him." Billy stood spell-bound.

"I say," he whispered, "*it knows us.* Here, old chap" (addressing the pendulum), "you know us, don't you? You're glad to see us, aren't you?"

"Tick, tock," said the pendulum.

"Can't he talk—just!" said Billy. "Look at his eye! He winked at me that time, I'll swear," and by the Powers, the very next time the pendulum reached the top of the arc I saw the crumpled metal in the middle of the disc double itself up and wink at *me* also, plain as plain.

"Billy," I said, "if we stare at him much longer we shall both go cracked.

Let's go into the churchyard. I've something else to show you."

There, among the mouldering tombstones, I expounded to Billy my new theory as to the nature of Time, reserving the crowning evidence until Billy had grasped the main principle.

"So you see," I concluded, "the seconds are the stoppages."

"There aren't any stoppages," said he. "Pendulums don't stop."

"Then where do the seconds come in?"

"They don't *come* in: they *are* in all along."

"Then," I said triumphantly, "look at that clock face. Can't you see how the big hand goes jerk, jerk?"

"Well, what of that?"

"What of that? Why, if the seconds aren't the stoppages, what becomes of time between the jerks?"

"Why," answered Billy, *"it's plugging ahead all the time."*

"All *what* time?" I countered, convinced now that I had him in a vicious circle.

"Blockhead!" cried Billy. "Don't you remember what that old Johnny told us in the Park? There's all the difference in the world between *the* time and *time*."

* * *

Ten years later when Billy, barely twenty-three, had half finished a book which would have made him famous, I handed him an essay by a distinguished philosopher, and requested him to read it. The title was "On Translating Time into Eternity." When Billy returned it, I asked him how he had fared. "Oh," he answered, "I translated time into eternity without much difficulty. *But it was plugging ahead all the time.*"

Shortly after that, Billy rejoined his mater—a victim to the same disease. Poor Billy! You brought luck to others; God knows you had little yourself. He died in a hospital, without kith or kin to close his eyes. The Sister who attended him brought me a small purse which she said Billy had very urgently requested her to give me. On opening the purse I found in it a gold coin, marked with a cross. The nurse also told me that an hour before he died Billy sat up suddenly in his bed and, opening his eyes very wide, said in a singing voice:

"If you please, Sir, would you mind telling me the time?"

For Thought and Discussion

1. Where did the writer and Billy know each other?
2. Why did they get so much pleasure from asking the time?
3. In what different hobbies did they indulge?
4. Why did Billy succeed in extracting an answer from the old gentleman after his friend had failed?
5. Whom did they finally include in their experiment?
6. Where is there pathos in the story?
7. In Section III what was the question about "time" that puzzled the narrator?
8. What distinction can you make between "time" and "the time"?
9. How will this distinction between "time" and "the time" affect your own career?

10. How does this distinction affect civilization?
11. Why is this distinction often not made in the United States?
12. Take account of the slender story thread and the ideas presented. What do you think is the author's purpose?

~~

OF STUDIES

FRANCIS BACON

[Francis (Lord) Bacon, 1561-1626, had an interesting career. As his father was Lord Keeper of the Great Seal under Queen Elizabeth, he had reason to look forward to a position of consequence at court, but his father's death left him adrift without the patronage necessary for preferment. Finally he gradually rose, holding one political office after another. It had long been customary for judges to receive gifts, but in Bacon's time public conscience was being aroused against the practice. On charge of bribery Bacon was tried and convicted, deprived of office, given a heavy fine, and excluded from public offices thereafter. As he had always been a student, he devoted himself entirely to his studies, continuing those investigations in science which made him the most famous scientist of his time. Also he wrote direct, compact, epigrammatic essays on various subjects.

[1]*Abeunt studia in mores*, studies influence manners or character.

[2]*cymini sectores*, cummin seed or hair splitters. The Schoolmen or scholars of the Middle Ages argued over fine points.]

STUDIES serve for delight, for ornament, and for ability. Their chief use for delight is in privateness and retiring; for ornament, is in discourse; and for ability, is in the judgment and disposition of business. For expert men can execute, and perhaps judge of particulars, one by one; but the general counsels, and the plots and marshaling of affairs, come best from those that are learned. To spend too much time in studies is sloth; to use them too much for ornament, is affectation; to make judgment wholly by their rules, is the humor of a scholar. They perfect nature, and are perfected by experience; for natural abilities are like natural plants, that need proyning by study; and studies themselves do give forth directions too much at large, except they be bounded in by experience. Crafty men contemn studies, simple men admire them, and wise men use them; for they teach not their own use; but that is a wisdom without them, and above them, won by observation. Read not to contradict and confute; nor to believe and take for granted; nor to find talk and discourse; but to weigh and consider. Some books are to be tasted, others to be swallowed, and some few to be chewed and digested; that is, some books are to be read only in parts; others to be read, but not curiously; and some few to be read wholly, and with diligence and attention. Some books also may be read by deputy, and extracts made of them by others; but that would be only in the less important arguments, and the meaner sort of books; else distilled books are like common distilled waters, flashy things. Reading maketh a full man; conference a ready man; and writing an exact man. And therefore, if a man write little, he had need have a great memory; if he confer little, he had need have a present wit; and if he read little, he had need have much cunning, to seem to know that he doth not. Histories make men wise; poets, witty; the mathematics, subtile; natural philosophy, deep; moral, grave; logic and rhetoric, able to contend. *Abeunt studia in mores.*[1] Nay, there is no stond or impediment in the wit but may be wrought out by fit studies; like as diseases of the body may have appropriate exercises. Bowling is good for the stone and reins; shooting for the lungs and breast; gentle walking for the stomach; riding for the head; and the like. So if a man's wit be wandering, let him study the mathematics; for in demonstrations, if his wit be called away never so little, he must begin again. If his wit be not apt to distinguish or find differences, let him study the Schoolmen; for they are *cymini sectores.*[2] If he be not apt to beat over matters, and to call up the thing to prove and illustrate another, let him study the lawyers' cases. So every defect of mind may have a special receipt.

For Thought and Discussion

1. According to Bacon why do people read?
2. Why do you read?
3. Should the purpose of the reader affect the type of reading he does?
4. What effect do reading, talking, and writing have upon one's ability?
5. How do Bacon's theories of different subjects, as history and mathematics, differ from present educational ideas?

❧

QUOTATIONS FROM POPE
ALEXANDER POPE

[Pope, 1688-1744, was the outstanding poet of the eighteenth century. His translation of Homer made him not only famous but also wealthy. He was able to make a comfortable living by his writing without the patronage of a lord—a fact remarkable in that he was the first to win that distinction. Ill all his life, Pope was not a very pleasant person nor a dependable friend, but constantly engaged in wrangles, lampooning his enemies unmercifully with his sharp pen. As he believed there was nothing new to be said, he emphasized correctness rather than originality. He wrote brilliant, epigrammatic, heroic couplets. On the Thames (tĕmz), near London, he built Twickenham, the home in which he entertained the witty and clever, both men and women, of his time. Among his well-known works are *Essay on Man, Essay on Criticism,* and *The Rape of the Lock.*]

From *Essay on Criticism*

'TIS with our judgments as our watches, none
Go just alike, yet each believes his own.

———

A little learning is a dangerous thing;
Drink deep, or taste not the Pierian
    spring:
There shallow drafts intoxicate the
    brain,
And drinking largely sobers us again.

Be not the first by whom the new is
    tried
Nor yet the last to lay the old aside.

Avoid extremes; and shun the fault
    of such
Who still are pleased too little or too
    much.

Some praise at morning what they
    blame at night;
But always think the last opinion
    right.

We think our fathers fools, so wise we
    grow;
Our wiser sons, no doubt, will think
    us so.

Be thou the first true merit to defend,
His praise is lost, who stays till all
    commend.

To err is human, to forgive, divine.

In all you speak, let truth and candor
    shine.

'Tis better sometimes your censure to
    restrain,
And charitable let the dull be vain.

Fools rush in where angels fear to
    tread.

Careless of censure nor too fond of
    fame;
Still pleased to praise, yet not afraid
    to blame,
Averse alike to flatter, or to offend;
Not free from faults nor yet too vain
    to mend.

From *Essay on Man*

Hope springs eternal in the human
    breast.

All nature is but Art, unknown to
    thee;
All Chance, Direction, which thou
    cans't not see;
All Discord, Harmony not under-
    stood;
All partial Evil, universal Good;
And, spite of Pride, in erring Reason's
    spite,
One Truth is clear, Whatever is, is
    right.

An honest man's the noblest work of
    God.

For Thought and Discussion

1. The lines from Pope are interesting if read aloud in class and discussed. How many of his opinions are true today and are profitable and practical ideals?
2. How many of these lines are an epigrammatic expression of what the world has long accepted as truth or fact?
3. To understand the writings of Alexander Pope and his place in his own time you should read "The Age of Classicism."

CONTROLLING THE MIND

From *How to Live on Twenty-Four Hours a Day*

ARNOLD BENNETT

PEOPLE say: "One can't help one's thoughts." But one can. The control of the thinking machine is perfectly possible. And since nothing whatever happens to us outside our own brain; since nothing hurts us or gives us pleasure except within the brain, the supreme importance of being able to control what goes on in that mysterious brain is patent. This idea is one of the oldest platitudes, but it is a platitude whose profound truth and urgency most people live and die without realizing. People complain of the lack of power to concentrate, not witting that they may acquire the power, if they choose.

And without the power to concentrate—that is to say, without the power to dictate to the brain its task and to ensure obedience—true life is impossible. Mind control is the first element of a full existence.

Hence, it seems to me, the first business of the day should be to put the mind through its paces. You look after your body, inside and out; you run grave danger in hacking hairs off your skin; you employ a whole army of individuals, from the milkman to the pig-killer, to enable you to bribe your stomach into decent behaviour. Why not devote a little attention to the far more delicate machinery of the mind, especially as you will require no extraneous aid? It is for this portion of the art and craft of living that I have reserved the time from the moment of quitting your door to the moment of arriving at your office.

"What? I am to cultivate my mind in the street, on the platform, in the train, and in the crowded street again?" Precisely. Nothing simpler! No tools required! Not even a book. Nevertheless, the affair is not easy.

When you leave your house, concentrate your mind on a subject (no matter what, to begin with). You will not have gone ten yards before your mind has skipped away under your very eyes and is larking round the corner with another subject.

Bring it back by the scruff of the neck. Ere you have reached the station you will have brought it back about forty times. Do not despair. Continue. Keep it up. You will succeed. You cannot by any chance fail if you persevere. It is idle to pretend that your mind is incapable of concentration. Do you not remember that morning when you received a disquieting letter which demanded a very carefully-worded answer? How you kept your mind steadily on the subject of the answer, without a second's intermission, until you reached your office; whereupon you instantly sat down and wrote the answer? That was a case in which *you* were roused by circumstances to such a degree of vitality that you were able to dominate your mind like a tyrant. You would have no trifling. You insisted that its work should be done, and its work was done.

By the regular practice of concentration (as to which there is no secret —save the secret of perseverance) you can tyrannise over your mind (which is not the highest part of *you*) every hour of the day, and in no matter what place. The exercise is a very convenient one. If you got into your morning train with a pair of dumb-bells for your muscles or an encyclopaedia in ten volumes for your learning, you would probably excite remark. But as you walk in the street, or sit in the corner of the compartment behind a pipe, or "straphang" on the Subterranean, who is to know that you are engaged in the most important of daily acts? What asinine boor can laugh at you?

I do not care what you concentrate on, so long as you concentrate. It is the mere disciplining of the thinking machine that counts. But still, you may as well kill two birds with one stone, and concentrate on something useful. I suggest—it is only a suggestion—a little chapter of Marcus Aurelius or Epictetus.

Do not, I beg, shy at their names. For myself, I know nothing more "actual," more bursting with plain common-sense, applicable to the daily life of plain persons like you and me (who hate airs, pose, and nonsense) than Marcus Aurelius or Epictetus. Read a chapter—and so short they are, the chapters!—in the evening and concentrate on it the next morning. You will see.

Yes, my friend, it is useless for you to try to disguise the fact. I can hear your brain like a telephone at my ear. You are saying to yourself: "This fellow was doing pretty well up to his seventh chapter. He had begun to interest me faintly. But what he says about thinking in trains, and concentration, and so on, is not for me. It may be well enough for some folks, but it isn't in my line."

It is for you, I passionately repeat; it is for you. Indeed, you are the very man I am aiming at.

Throw away the suggestion, and you throw away the most precious suggestion that was ever offered to you. It is not my suggestion. It is the suggestion of the most sensible, practical, hard-headed men that have walked the earth. I only give it you at second-hand. Try it. Get your mind in hand. And see how the process cures half the evils of life—especially worry, that miserable, avoidable, shameful disease—worry!

For Thought and Discussion

1. What does Bennett consider the first element of a full existence?
2. How can one learn to concentrate?
3. According to the author, what disease can be conquered by concentration?
4. If, as Bennett affirms, your mind "is not the highest part of *you*," what is higher?
5. Who were Marcus Aurelius and Epictetus? Did you have enough curiosity to read a chapter from either?
6. Can you recall an instance in which ability to concentrate was of distinct aid to you?
7. How do you spend your time on motor, train, and airplane trips over familiar territory? over unfamiliar territory?

BLESSED IS THE MAN

PSALM 1

BLESSED is the man that walketh not in the counsel of the ungodly,
Nor standeth in the way of sinners,
Nor sitteth in the seat of the scornful.
But his delight is in the law of the Lord;

And in his law doth he meditate day and night.
And he shall be like a tree planted by the rivers of water, that bringeth forth his fruit in his season;
His leaf also shall not wither;

And whatsoever he doeth shall prosper.
The ungodly are not so;
But are like the chaff which the wind driveth away.
Therefore the ungodly shall not stand in the judgment,

Nor sinners in the congregation of the righteous.
For the Lord knoweth the way of the righteous;
But the way of the ungodly shall perish.

❧

MACBETH

WILLIAM SHAKESPEARE

DRAMATIS PERSONAE

DUNCAN, King of Scotland.
MALCOLM ⎱ his sons.
DONALBAIN ⎰
MACBETH ⎱ generals of the king's
BANQUO ⎰ army.
MACDUFF
LENNOX
ROSS
MENTEITH ⎬ noblemen of Scotland.
ANGUS
CAITHNESS
FLEANCE, son to Banquo.
SIWARD, Earl of Northumberland, general of the English forces.
YOUNG SIWARD, his son.
SEYTON, an officer attending on Macbeth.

Boy, son to Macduff.
An English Doctor.
A Scotch Doctor.
A Soldier.
A Porter.
An Old Man.
LADY MACBETH.
LADY MACDUFF.
Gentlewoman attending on Lady Macbeth.
HECATE.
Three Witches.
Apparitions.
Lords, Gentlemen, Officers, Soldiers, Murderers, Attendants, and Messengers.

ACT I

SCENE: *Scotland; England.*

[Scotland has been attacked by Sweno, King of Norway, assisted by the Scotch traitor, the thane of Cawdor. The Norwegian forces are defeated by the brave generals, Macbeth and Banquo. On their way home, they are met by three witches who greet Macbeth as thane of Glamis, Cawdor, and king thereafter; Banquo they hail as father to a line of kings. King Duncan of Scotland appoints his eldest son, Malcolm, Prince of Cumberland, heir to the Scotch throne. Lady Macbeth, when informed by a letter from Macbeth of the witches' prophecies, determines to make Macbeth king. Together Macbeth and she plan to murder Duncan.]

SCENE I. *A desert place.*

Thunder and lightning. Enter three Witches.

FIRST WITCH. When shall we three meet again
In thunder, lightning, or in rain?
SECOND WITCH. When the hurly-burly's¹ done,
When the battle's lost and won.
THIRD WITCH. That will be ere the set of sun.   5
FIRST WITCH. Where the place?
SECOND WITCH. Upon the heath.²
THIRD WITCH. There to meet with Macbeth.
FIRST WITCH. I come, Graymalkin!
SECOND WITCH. Paddock³ calls.
THIRD WITCH. Anon!   10
ALL. Fair is foul, and foul is fair;
Hover through the fog and filthy air.⁴
                                    [*Exeunt.*]

---

¹*hurlyburly,* tumult.
²*heath,* a tract of waste land.
³*paddock,* toad. Cats and toads were supposed to consort with witches.
⁴*filthy air,* murky, dark, hazy air.

SCENE II. *A camp near Forres.*

Alarum within. Enter DUNCAN, MALCOLM, DONALBAIN, LENNOX, *with* Attendants, *meeting a bleeding* Sergeant.

DUNCAN. What bloody man is that? He can report,
As seemeth by his plight, of the revolt
The newest state.
MALCOLM. This is the sergeant
Who, like a good and hardy soldier, fought
'Gainst my captivity. Hail, brave friend!   5
Say to the king the knowledge of the broil
As thou didst leave it.
SERGEANT. Doubtful it stood;
As two spent swimmers, that do cling together
And choke their art. The merciless Macdonwald—
Worthy to be a rebel, for to that   10
The multiplying villainies of nature
Do swarm upon him—from the western isles⁵
Of kerns⁶ and gallowglasses⁷ is supplied;
And fortune, on his damnèd quarrel smiling,
Showed like a rebel's drab; but all's too weak;   15
For brave Macbeth—well he deserves that name—
Disdaining fortune, with his brandished steel,
Which smoked with bloody execution,
Like valor's minion carved out his passage
Till he faced the slave;   20

---

⁵*western isles,* Ireland.
⁶*kerns,* heavily armed soldiers.
⁷*gallowglasses,* light-armed soldiers, carrying javelins and daggers.

Which ne'er shook hands, nor bade
farewell to him,
Till he unseamed him from the nave
to the chaps,
And fixed his head upon our battle-
ments.
DUNCAN. O valiant cousin! worthy
gentleman!
SERGEANT. As whence the sun
'gins his reflection   25
Shipwrecking storms and direful
thunders break,
So from that spring whence comfort
seemed to come
Discomfort swells. Mark, king of
Scotland, mark.
No sooner justice had with valor
armed
Compelled these skipping kerns to
trust their heels,   30
But the Norweyan lord, surveying
vantage,
With furbished arms and new sup-
plies of men
Began a fresh assault.
DUNCAN.   Dismayed not this
Our captains, Macbeth and Banquo?
SERGEANT.   Yes,
As sparrows eagles, or the hare the
lion.   35
If I say sooth, I must report they were
As cannons overcharged with double
cracks, so they
Doubly redoubled strokes upon the
foe;
Except they meant to bathe in reek-
ing wounds,
Or memorize another Golgotha,[8]   40
I cannot tell.
But I am faint; my gashes cry for
help.
DUNCAN. So well thy words be-
come thee as thy wounds;
They smack of honor both. Go get
him surgeons.
[*Exit* Sergeant, *attended*.]

Who comes here?

Enter Ross.

MALCOLM. The worthy thane[9] of
Ross.   45
LENNOX. What a haste looks
through his eyes! So should he
look
That seems to speak things strange.
ROSS.   God save the king!
DUNCAN. Whence camest thou,
worthy thane?
ROSS.   From Fife, great king;
Where the Norweyan banners flout
the sky
And fan our people cold. Norway
himself,   50
With terrible numbers,
Assisted by that most disloyal traitor,
The thane of Cawdor,[10] began a dis-
mal conflict;
Till that Bellona's bridegroom,[11]
lapped in proof,
Confronted him with self-compari-
sons,   55
Point against point rebellious, arm
'gainst arm,
Curbing his lavish spirit; and, to con-
clude,
The victory fell on us.
DUNCAN.   Great happiness!
ROSS.   That now
Sweno, the Norways' king, craves
composition;
Nor would we deign him burial of his
men   60
Till he disbursèd at St. Colme's inch
Ten thousand dollars to our general
use.
DUNCAN. No more that thane of
Cawdor shall deceive
Our bosom interest. Go pronounce his
present death,
And with his former title greet Mac-
beth.   65

---

[8]*Golgotha* (gŏl' gŏthá), a reference
to the crucifixion of Christ at Calvary.

[9]*thane*, a Scotch noble.
[10]Cawdor, (kô' dŏr).
[11]*Bellona's bridegroom*, Bellona, Roman Goddess of war.

Ross.   I'll see it done.
Duncan. What he hath lost noble
Macbeth hath won.   [*Exeunt.*]

Scene III.   *A heath near Forres.*

Thunder.   Enter the three Witches.

First Witch. Where hast thou
been, sister?
Second Witch. Killing swine.
Third Witch. Sister, where thou?
First Witch. A sailor's wife had
chestnuts in her lap,
And munched, and munched, and
munched:—"Give me," quoth
I.   5
"Aroint thee, witch!" the rump-fed
ronyon cries.
Her husband's to Aleppo gone, master
o' the *Tiger.*[12]
But in a sieve I'll thither sail,
And, like a rat without a tail,[13]
I'll do, I'll do, and I'll do.   10
Second Witch. I'll give thee a
wind.
First Witch. Thou 'rt kind.
Third Witch. And I another.
First Witch. I myself have all the
other,
And the very ports they blow,   15
All the quarters that they know
I' the shipman's card.[14]
I will drain him dry as hay;
Sleep shall neither night nor day
Hang upon his pent-house lid;[15]   20
He shall live a man forbid;
Weary se'nnights nine times nine
Shall he dwindle, peak and pine;
Though his bark cannot be lost,
Yet it shall be tempest-tossed.   25
Look what I have.

____

[12]*Tiger,* common name for ship.
[13]*rat without a tail,* If a witch assumed the form of an animal, there
was always a defect or blemish to indicate the evil nature of the witch.
[14]*shipman's card,* a card on which
the points of the compass are indicated.
[15]*pent-house lid,* eyelid.

Second Witch. Show me, show
me.
First Witch. Here I have a pilot's
thumb,
Wrecked as homeward he did come.
[*Drum within.*]
Third Witch. A drum, a drum![30]
Macbeth doth come.
All. The weird sisters, hand in
hand,
Posters of the sea and land,
Thus do go about, about;
Thrice to thine and thrice to mine   35
And thrice again, to make up nine.
Peace! The charm's wound up.

Enter Macbeth *and* Banquo.

Macbeth. So foul and fair a day
I have not seen.
Banquo. How far is 't called to
Forres? What are these
So withered, and so wild in their
attire,   40
That look not like the inhabitants o'
the earth,
And yet are on 't? Live you? or are
you aught
That man may question? You seem
to understand me,
By each at once her choppy finger
laying
Upon her skinny lips. You should be
women,   45
And yet your beards forbid me to
interpret
That you are so.
Macbeth. Speak, if you can. What
are you?
First Witch. All hail, Macbeth!
Hail to thee, thane of Glamis!
Second Witch. All hail, Macbeth!
Hail to thee, thane of Cawdor!
Third Witch. All hail, Macbeth,
that shalt be king hereafter!   50
Banquo. Good sir, why do you
start; and seem to fear
Things that do sound so fair? I' the
name of truth,

"All hail, Macbeth! Hail to thee, thane of Glamis! All hail, Macbeth! Hail to thee, thane of Cawdor! All hail, Macbeth, that shall be king hereafter!"

Are ye fantastical,[16] or that indeed
Which outwardly ye show? My noble partner
You greet with present grace and great prediction   55
Of noble having and of royal hope,
That he seems rapt withal; to me you speak not.
If you can look into the seeds of time,
And say which grain will grow and which will not,
Speak then to me, who neither beg nor fear   60
Your favors nor your hate.

FIRST WITCH. Hail!

SECOND WITCH. Hail!

THIRD WITCH. Hail!

FIRST WITCH. Lesser than Macbeth and greater.   65

SECOND WITCH. Not so happy, yet much happier.

THIRD WITCH. Thou shalt get kings, though thou be none.

So all hail, Macbeth and Banquo!

FIRST WITCH. Banquo and Macbeth, all hail!

MACBETH. Stay, you imperfect speakers, tell me more;   70
By Sinel's death I know I am thane of Glamis;
But how of Cawdor? The thane of Cawdor lives,
A prosperous gentleman; and to be king
Stands not within the prospect of belief,
No more than to be Cawdor. Say from whence   75
You owe this strange intelligence, or why
Upon this blasted heath you stop our way
With such prophetic greeting? Speak, I charge you. [Witches *vanish*.]

BANQUO. The earth hath bubbles, as the water has,

---

[16]*fantastical*, imaginary.

And these are of them. Whither are
   they vanished?   80
MACBETH. Into the air; and what
   seemed corporal melted
As breath into the wind. Would
   they had stayed!
BANQUO. Were such things here as
   we do speak about?
Or have we eaten on the insane root[17]
That takes the reason prisoner?   85
MACBETH. Your children shall be
   kings.
BANQUO.   You shall be king.
MACBETH. And thane of Cawdor
   too. Went it not so?
BANQUO. To the selfsame tune and
   words. Who's here?

Enter ROSS *and* ANGUS.

ROSS. The king hath happily received, Macbeth,
The news of thy success; and when
   he reads   90
Thy personal venture in the rebels'
   fight,
His wonders and his praises do con-
   tend
Which should be thine or his; silenced
   with that,
In viewing o'er the rest o' the self-
   same day,
He finds thee in the stout Norweyan
   ranks,   95
Nothing afeard of what thyself didst
   make,
Strange images of death. As thick
   as hail
Came post with post; and every one
   did bear
Thy praises in his kingdom's great de-
   fence,
And poured them down before him.
ANGUS.   We are sent[100]
To give thee from our royal master
   thanks;
Only to herald thee into his sight,
Not pay thee.

ROSS. And, for an earnest of a
   greater honor,
He bade me, from him, call thee thane
   of Cawdor;   105
In which addition, hail, most worthy
   thane!
For it is thine.
BANQUO. What, can the devil
   speak true?
MACBETH. The thane of Cawdor
   lives. Why do you dress me
In borrowed robes?
ANGUS. Who was the thane lives
   yet;
But under heavy judgment bears that
   life   110
Which he deserves to lose. Whether
   he was combined
With those of Norway, or did line the
   rebel
With hidden help and vantage, or
   that with both
He labored in his country's wreck, I
   know not;
But treasons capital, confessed and
   proved,   115
Have overthrown him.
MACBETH. [*Aside*] Glamis, and
   thane of Cawdor!
The greatest is behind. [*To* ROSS *and*
   ANGUS] Thanks for your pains.
[*To* BANQUO] Do you not hope your
   children shall be kings,
When those that gave the thane of
   Cawdor to me
Promised no less to them?
BANQUO.   That trusted home[120]
Might yet enkindle you unto the
   crown,
Besides the thane of Cawdor. But 'tis
   strange.
And oftentimes, to win us to our
   harm,
The instruments of darkness[18] tell us
   truths,
Win us with honest[19] trifles, to be-
   tray's   125

---

[17]*insane root*, poison which destroys
reason, probably hemlock.

[18]*instruments of darkness*, evil forces.
[19]*honest*, truthful.

In deepest consequence.[20]
Cousins, a word, I pray you.

MACBETH. [*Aside*] Two truths are told,
As happy prologues to the swelling act
Of the imperial theme.—I thank you, gentlemen.
[*Aside*] This supernatural soliciting   130
Cannot be ill, cannot be good. If ill,
Why hath it given me earnest of success,
Commencing in a truth? I am thane of Cawdor.
If good, why do I yield to that suggestion
Whose horrid image doth unfix my hair   135
And make my seated heart knock at my ribs,
Against the use of nature? Present fears
Are less than horrible imaginings;
My thought, whose murder yet is but fantastical,
Shakes so my single state of man that function   140
Is smothered in surmise, and nothing is
But what is not.

BANQUO. Look, how our partner's rapt.

MACBETH. [*Aside*] If chance will have me king, why, chance may crown me,
Without my stir.

BANQUO. New honors come upon him,
Like our strange garments, cleave not to their mold   145
But with the aid of use.

MACBETH. [*Aside*] Come what come may,
Time and the hour runs through the roughest day.

---

[20]*deepest consequence*, evil.

BANQUO. Worthy Macbeth, we stay upon your leisure.

MACBETH. Give me your favor,
My dull brain was wrought
With things forgotten. Kind gentlemen, your pains   150
Are registered where every day I turn
The leaf to read them. Let us toward the king.
Think upon what hath chanced, and at more time,
The interim having weighed it, let us speak
Our free hearts each to other.

BANQUO.   Very gladly.[155]

MACBETH.   Till then, enough.
Come, friends.   [*Exeunt.*]

SCENE IV. *Forres. The palace.*

Flourish. Enter DUNCAN, MALCOLM,
DONALBAIN, LENNOX, *and*
Attendants.

DUNCAN. Is execution done on Cawdor? Are not those in commission yet returned?

MALCOLM.   My liege,
They are not yet come back. But I have spoke
With one that saw him die; who did report
That very frankly he confessed his treasons,   5
Implored your highness' pardon, and set forth
A deep repentance. Nothing in his life
Became him like the leaving it; he died
As one that had been studied in his death
To throw away the dearest thing he owed,[21]   10
As 'twere a careless trifle.

DUNCAN.   There's no art
To find the mind's construction in the face;
He was a gentleman on whom I built

---

[21]*owed*, owned.

An absolute trust.

Enter MACBETH, BANQUO, ROSS, *and*
ANGUS.

           O worthiest cousin!
The sin of my ingratitude even
   now   15
Was heavy on me; thou art so far before
That swiftest wing of recompense is
   slow
To overtake thee. Would thou hadst
   less deserved,
That the proportion both of thanks
   and payment
Might have been mine! Only I have
   left to say,   20
More is thy due than more than all
   can pay.
    MACBETH. The service and the loy-
   alty I owe,
In doing it, pays itself. Your highness'
   part
Is to receive our duties; and our duties
Are to your throne and state children
   and servants,   25
Which do but what they should, by
   doing every thing
Safe toward your love and honor.
    DUNCAN.   Welcome hither;
I have begun to plant thee, and will
   labor
To make thee full of growing. Noble
   Banquo,
That hast no less deserved, nor must
   be known   30
No less to have done so; let me infold
   thee
And hold thee to my heart.
    BANQUO.   There if I grow,
The harvest is your own.
    DUNCAN.   My plenteous joys,
Wanton in fulness, seek to hide them-
   selves
In drops of sorrow. Sons, kinsmen,
   thanes,   35
And you whose places are the nearest,
   know
We will establish our estate upon

Our eldest, Malcolm, whom we name
   hereafter
The Prince of Cumberland[22]; which
   honor must
Not unaccompanied invest him
   only,   40
But signs of nobleness, like stars, shall
   shine
On all deservers. From hence to
   Inverness,
And bind us further to you.
    MACBETH. The rest is labor, which
   is not used for you.
I'll be myself the harbinger[23] and
   make joyful   45
The hearing of my wife with your
   approach;
So humbly take my leave.
    DUNCAN.   My worthy Cawdor!
    MACBETH. [*Aside*] The Prince of
   Cumberland! That is a step
On which I must fall down, or else
   o'erleap,
For in my way it lies. Stars, hide
   your fires;   50
Let not light see my black and deep
   desires;
The eye wink at the hand; yet let
   that be,
Which the eye fears, when it is done,
   to see.
                     [*Exit.*]
    DUNCAN. True, worthy Banquo;
   he is full so valiant,
And in his commendations I am fed;[55]
It is a banquet to me. Let's after him,
Whose care is gone before to bid us
   welcome.
It is a peerless kinsman.
        [*Flourish. Exeunt.*]

SCENE V. *Inverness. Macbeth's
castle.*

Enter LADY MACBETH, *reading a
letter.*

---

[22]*The Prince of Cumberland* was the
successor to the throne.
[23]*harbinger,* one who rode ahead to
arrange for the King's lodging.

LADY MACBETH. "They met me in the day of success; and I have learned by the perfectest report, they have more in them than mortal knowledge. When I burned in desire to question them further, they made themselves air, into which they vanished. Whiles I stood rapt in the wonder of it, came missives from the king, who all-hailed me 'Thane of Cawdor,' by which title, before, these weird sisters saluted me, and referred me to the coming on of time, with 'Hail, king that shalt be!' This have I thought good to deliver thee, my dearest partner of greatness, that thou mightst not lose the dues of rejoicing, by being ignorant of what greatness is promised thee. Lay it to thy heart, and farewell."

Glamis thou art, and Cawdor; and shalt be
What thou art promised. Yet do I fear thy nature;
It is too full o' the milk of human kindness
To catch the nearest way. Thou wouldst be great;
Art not without ambition, but with-
out   20
The illness²⁴ should attend it. What thou wouldst highly,
That wouldst thou holily; wouldst not play false,
And yet wouldst wrongly win. Thou 'ldst have, great Glamis,
That which cries "Thus thou must do, if thou have it";
And that which rather thou dost fear to do   25
Than wishest should be undone. Hie thee hither,
That I may pour my spirits in thine ear;
And chastise with the valor of my tongue

_____
²⁴illness, evil nature.

All that impedes thee from the gold-
en round,
Which fate and metaphysical aid doth seem   30
To have thee crowned withal.

Enter a Messenger.

                    What is your tidings?
MESSENGER. The king comes here tonight.
LADY MACBETH. Thou'rt mad to say it.
Is not thy master with him? who, were 't so,
Would have informed for prepara-
tion.
MESSENGER. So please you, it is true; our thane is coming.   35
One of my fellows had the speed of him,
Who, almost dead for breath, had scarcely more
Than would make up his message.
LADY MACBETH. Give him tending;
He brings great news.
                    [*Exit* Messenger.]
            The raven himself is hoarse
That croaks the fatal entrance of Duncan   40
Under my battlements. Come, you spirits
That tend on mortal thoughts, unsex me here,
And fill me from the crown to the toe top-full
Of direst cruelty! make thick my blood;
Stop up the access and passage to remorse,   45
That no compunctious visitings of nature
Shake my fell purpose, nor keep peace between
The effect and it! Come to my wo-
man's breasts,
And take my milk for gall, you mur-
dering ministers,
Wherever in your sightless sub-
stances   50

You wait on nature's mischief! Come, thick night,
And pall thee in the dunnest smoke of hell,
That my keen knife see not the wound it makes,
Nor heaven peep through the blanket of the dark,
To cry "Hold, hold!"

Enter MACBETH.

Great Glamis! worthy Cawdor! 55
Greater than both, by the all-hail hereafter!
Thy letters have transported me beyond
This ignorant present, and I feel now
The future in the instant.
  MACBETH.   My dearest love,
Duncan comes here tonight.
  LADY MACBETH.   And when goes
    hence?   60
  MACBETH. Tomorrow, as he purposes.
  LADY MACBETH.   O, never
Shall sun that morrow see!
Your face, my thane, is as a book where men
May read strange matters. To beguile the time,
Look like the time; bear welcome in your eye,   65
Your hand, your tongue. Look like the innocent flower,
But be the serpent under 't. He that's coming
Must be provided for; and you shall put
This night's great business into my dispatch,
Which shall to all our nights and days to come   70
Give solely sovereign sway and masterdom.
  MACBETH. We will speak further.
  LADY MACBETH. Only look up clear;
To alter favor ever is to fear.
Leave all the rest to me.   [*Exeunt.*]

SCENE VI. *Before Macbeth's castle.*

Hautboys and torches. Enter DUNCAN, MALCOLM, DONALBAIN, BANQUO, LENNOX, MACDUFF, ROSS, ANGUS, *and* Attendants.

  DUNCAN. This castle hath a pleasant seat; the air
Nimbly and sweetly recommends itself
Unto our gentle senses.
  BANQUO.   This guest of summer,
The temple-haunting martlet,[25] does approve,
By his loved mansionry, that the heaven's breath   5
Smells wooingly here. No jutty, frieze,
Buttress, nor coign of vantage, but this bird
Hath made his pendent bed and procreant cradle.
Where they most breed and haunt, I have observed,
The air is delicate.

Enter LADY MACBETH.

  DUNCAN. See, see, our honored hostess!   10
The love that follows us sometime is our trouble,
Which still we thank as love. Herein I teach you
How you shall bid God 'ild us[26] for your pains,
And thank us for your trouble.
  LADY MACBETH.   All our service
In every point twice done and then done double   15
Were poor and single business to contend
Against those honors deep and broad wherewith
Your majesty loads our house; for those of old,
And the late dignities heaped up to them,

---

[25]*martlet,* martin, swallow, a bird that builds its nest in protected places.
[26]*God 'ild us,* God reward us.

We rest your hermits.[27]

DUNCAN. Where's the thane of
  Cawdor?   20
We coursed him at the heels, and had
  a purpose
To be his purveyor;[28] but he rides
  well,
And his great love, sharp as his spur,
  hath holp[29] him
To his home before us. Fair and
  noble hostess,
We are your guest tonight.

  LADY MACBETH. Your servants
    ever   25
Have theirs, themselves, and what is
  theirs, in compt,[30]
To make their audit at your highness'
  pleasure,
Still to return your own.

  DUNCAN. Give me your hand;
Conduct me to mine host. We love
  him highly,
And shall continue our graces to-
  wards him.   30
By your leave, hostess.

                    [*Exeunt.*]

SCENE VII. *Macbeth's castle.*

Hautboys and torches. Enter a Sewer,
and divers Servants *with dishes and
service, and pass over the stage.*

    Then enter MACBETH.

MACBETH. If it were done when
  'tis done, then 'twere well
It were done quickly. If the assassina-
  tion
Could trammel up the consequence,
  and catch
With his surcease[31] success; that but
  this blow
Might be the be-all and the end-all
  here,   5

But here, upon this bank and shoal
  of time,
We 'ld jump the life to come.[32] But
  in these cases
We still have judgment here; that
  we but teach
Bloody instructions, which being
  taught, return
To plague the inventor. This even-
  handed justice   10
Commends the ingredients of our
  poisoned chalice[33]
To our own lips. He's here in double
  trust:
First, as I am his kinsman and his
  subject,
Strong both against the deed; then,
  as his host,
Who should against his murderer shut
  the door,   15
Not bear the knife myself. Besides,
  this Duncan
Hath borne his faculties so meek,
  hath been
So clear in his great office, that his
  virtues
Will plead like angels, trumpet-
  tongued, against
The deep damnation of his taking-
  off;   20
And pity, like a naked new-born
  babe,
Striding the blast, or heaven's cher-
  ubin,[34] horsed
Upon the sightless couriers of the air,
Shall blow the horrid deed in every
  eye,
That tears shall drown the wind. I
  have no spur   25
To prick the sides of my intent, but
  only
Vaulting ambition, which o'erleaps
  itself
And falls on the other.

---

[27]*hermits,* beadsmen who pray for
a benefactor.
[28]*purveyor,* one who rides ahead to
arrange for supplies for the king.
[29]*holp,* helped.
[30]*compt,* in account.
[31]*surcease,* death.

[32]*life to come,* life after death—Macbeth would take a chance on punishment hereafter.
[33]*chalice,* cup.
[34]*cherubin,* child angels.

Enter LADY MACBETH.

How now! What news?

LADY MACBETH. He has almost
supped. Why have you left the
chamber?

MACBETH. Hath he asked for me?

LADY MACBETH. Know you not he
has?   30

MACBETH. We will proceed no further in this business;
He hath honored me of late, and I
have bought
Golden opinions from all sorts of
people,
Which would be worn now in their
newest gloss,
Not cast aside so soon.

LADY MACBETH. Was the hope
drunk   35
Wherein you dressed yourself? Hath
it slept since?
And wakes it now to look so green
and pale
At what it did so freely? From this
time
Such I account thy love. Art thou
afeard
To be the same in thine own act and
valor   40
As thou art in desire? Wouldst thou
have that
Which thou esteem'st the ornament of
life,
And live a coward in thine own esteem,
Letting "I dare not" wait upon "I
would,"
Like the poor cat i' the adage?³⁵

MACBETH.   Prithee, peace;   45
I dare do all that may become a man;
Who dares do more is none.

LADY MACBETH. What beast was't,
then,
That made you break this enterprise
to me?

---

³⁵*cat i' the adage,* "The cat would
eat fish and not wet her feet" is an
old proverb.

When you durst do it, then you were
a man;
And to be more than what you were,
you would   50
Be so much more the man. Nor
time nor place
Did then adhere, and yet you would
make both;
They have made themselves, and
that their fitness now
Does unmake you. I have given suck,
and know
How tender 'tis to love the babe that
milks me;   55
I would, while it was smiling in my
face,
Have plucked my nipple from his
boneless gums,
And dashed the brains out, had I so
sworn as you
Have done to this.

MACBETH.   If we should fail?

LADY MACBETH.   We fail.
But screw your courage to the stick-
ing-place,   60
And we'll not fail. When Duncan is
asleep—
Whereto the rather shall his day's
hard journey
Soundly invite him—his two cham-
berlains
Will I with wine and wassail so con-
vince
That memory, the warder of the
brain,   65
Shall be a fume, and the receipt of
reason
A limbeck only. When in swinish
sleep
Their drenchèd natures lie as in a
death,
What cannot you and I perform upon
The unguarded Duncan? what not
put upon   70
His spongy officers, who shall bear
the guilt
Of our great quell?³⁶

---

³⁶*Quell,* murder, slaughter.

MACBETH. Bring forth men-children only;
For thy undaunted mettle should compose
Nothing but males. Will it not be received,
When we have marked with blood those sleepy two   75
Of his own chamber and used their very daggers
That they have done 't?
    LADY MACBETH. Who dares receive it other,
As we shall make our griefs and clamor roar
Upon his death?
    MACBETH. I am settled, and bend up
Each corporal agent to this terrible feat.   80
Away, and mock the time with fairest show;
False face must hide what the false heart doth know.

                    [*Exeunt.*]

For Thought and Discussion

ACT I

SCENE 1.

1. Describe the stage setting of the opening scene.
2. What effect is created by thunder and lightning?
3. Describe the witches.
4. What is the effect of opening the play with the witches' scene?
5. In Shakespeare's day many people believed in witches. What line suggests the evil nature of the witches?

SCENE 2.

1. For what news is King Duncan anxiously waiting?
2. Does the fact that he is not with the army suggest that he is not a capable leader?
3. Who is Macbeth? What has he done to distinguish himself?
4. Who is the strongest and most outstanding figure in the play? Who has saved the country?
5. What other brave general has fought bravely in the battle?
6. Who is the traitor and what becomes of him?

SCENE 3.

1. What does this scene reveal about the character of the witches?
2. Explain the meaning of Macbeth's speech on "So fair and foul a day."
3. Why do the witches address Macbeth first rather than Banquo?
4. What prophecies do they make about him? How is he affected by these prophecies? Macbeth feels that he is entitled to the kingship by birth and by his outstanding bravery and leadership. Does the fact that Scotland suffered from both internal revolt and foreign invasion suggest that Duncan had been selected king over Macbeth by the nobles, because they could dominate Duncan?
5. What prophecies do the witches make about Banquo?

6. How do Macbeth and Banquo react to the news that Macbeth has been made thane of Cawdor?
7. What position does Macbeth now hope to obtain? Why does he think the prophecies cannot be good? cannot be evil?
8. Does Banquo feel that the prophecies are good or evil? Quote his speech.
9. Contrast the reaction of Macbeth and Banquo toward the witches' prophecies.

SCENE 4.

1. Why does Duncan praise Macbeth? What does he say about the thane of Cawdor?
2. How does he greet Macbeth and Banquo?
3. Why does Duncan decide to visit at Macbeth's castle?
4. What effect does the naming of Malcolm as Prince of Cumberland, heir to the throne, have upon Macbeth? Why does he feel that he has been treated unfairly?

SCENE 5.

1. What decision does Lady Macbeth make after she reads Macbeth's letter?
2. Does Lady Macbeth possess sufficient courage and will-power to commit the crime she plans?
3. Lady Macbeth was probably small and dainty. Does the fact that she calls upon evil spirits to assist her suggest that she is attempting a crime that will in the end, overtax her strength and conscience?
4. Why does she plan the crime? Answer carefully by reading lines from the text. Does she think of herself or of Macbeth? What is her most outstanding trait of character?
5. Why does she feel that Macbeth will not commit the deed without her assistance? Does she believe that he is too honest, too honorable, too kind, too weak in will-power?

SCENE 6.

1. What is the effect of the beautiful and peaceful scene at the beginning of this act? Why is the situation ironical?
2. How does Lady Macbeth's gracious reception of her guests add to the pleasant picture?
3. What impression of Duncan's character is gained from this scene?

SCENE 7.

1. Read aloud Macbeth's soliloquy. Why does he debate with himself over the murder? Does he fear his own conscience or discovery or punishment for the crime? What moral traits does he lack? What urges him on?
2. What reason does he give Lady Macbeth for changing his mind and refusing to proceed with the plans?
3. What two strong arguments does she use to goad him on to

commit the crime? How do her careful plans for escaping detection influence him?

4. What forces are combined to cause Macbeth to commit the murder?

5. What is the situation at the end of the first act?

A Study of Significant Passages

Select and read aloud the significant lines in this act. The following suggestions may assist in making the choice, as lines which show:

Indecision of character
Conflict between good and evil
Praise of a character
Dire forecasts of terrible events
Flattering speeches
Peaceful scenes
Forceful revelations of the thoughts of a character
Expression of universal truth
Poetic excellence in phrasing and expression of a sentiment

ACT II

[Macbeth murders Duncan but becomes terrified and brings the daggers away with him. Lady Macbeth takes them and smears the guards with blood to place the guilt upon them. Macduff finds the murdered king and spreads the alarm. Macbeth kills the guards who apparently had committed the crime. Fearing that their own lives are in danger, the king's two sons, Malcolm and Donalbain, flee to England and Ireland. People believe that they bribed the guards to murder their father. Macbeth is crowned king.]

SCENE I. *Court of Macbeth's castle.*

Enter BANQUO, *and* FLEANCE[37] *bearing a torch before him.*

BANQUO. How goes the night, boy?

FLEANCE. The moon is down; I have not heard the clock.

------

[37]*Fleance* (flē′ ans).

BANQUO. And she goes down at twelve.

FLEANCE. I take 't, 'tis later, sir.

BANQUO. Hold, take my sword. There's husbandry[38] in heaven; Their candles are all out. Take thee that too.   5

A heavy summons lies like lead upon me,

And yet I would not sleep. Merciful powers,

Restrain in me the cursèd thoughts that nature

Gives way to in repose!

Enter MACBETH, *and a* Servant *with a torch.*

                    Give me my sword.
Who's there?   10

MACBETH. A friend.

BANQUO. What, sir, not yet at rest? The king's a-bed;

------

[38]*husbandry,* economy, dark night without light from moon or stars.

He hath been in unusual pleasure, and
Sent forth great largess[39] to your of-
fices.
This diamond he greets your wife
withal,   15
By the name of most kind hostess;
and shut up
In measureless content.
   MACBETH.   Being unprepared,
Our will became the servant to de-
fect;
Which else should free have wrought.
   BANQUO.   All's well.
I dreamt last night of the three weird
sisters.   20
To you they have showed some truth.
   MACBETH.   I think not of them.
Yet, when we can entreat an hour to
serve,
We would spend it in some words
upon that business,
If you would grant the time.
   BANQUO. At your kind'st leisure.
   MACBETH. If you shall cleave to
my consent, when 'tis,   25
It shall make honor for you.
   BANQUO.   So I lose none
In seeking to augment it, but still
keep
My bosom franchised and allegiance
clear,
I shall be counseled.
   MACBETH. Good repose the while!
   BANQUO. Thanks, Sir; the like to
you!
[*Exeunt* BANQUO *and* FLEANCE.][30]
   MACBETH.   Go bid thy mistress,
when my drink is ready,
She strike upon the bell. Get thee
to bed.
             [*Exit* Servant.]
Is this a dagger which I see before me,
The handle toward my hand? Come,
let me clutch thee.
I have thee not, and yet I see thee
still.   35
Art thou not, fatal vision, sensible

"Is this a dagger which I see before me, the handle toward my hand? Come, let me clutch thee."

---

[39]*largess*, gifts of money.

To feeling as to sight? Or art thou but
A dagger of the mind, a false creation,
Proceeding from the heat-oppressèd brain?
I see thee yet, in form as palpable   40
As this which now I draw.
Thou marshal'st me the way that I was going;
And such an instrument I was to use.
Mine eyes are made the fools o' the other senses,
Or else worth all the rest; I see thee still,   45
And on thy blade and dudgeon[40] gouts[41] of blood,
Which was not so before. There's no such thing;
It is the bloody business which informs
Thus to mine eyes. Now o'er the one half-world
Nature seems dead, and wicked dreams abuse   50
The curtained sleep; witchcraft celebrates
Pale Hecate's[42] offerings, and withered murder,
Alarumed by his sentinel, the wolf,
Whose howl's his watch, thus with his stealthy pace,
With Tarquin's ravishing strides, towards his design   55
Moves like a ghost. Thou sure and firm-set earth,
Hear not my steps, which way they walk, for fear
Thy very stones prate of my whereabout,
And take the present horror from the time,
Which now suits with it. Whiles I threat, he lives;   60
Words to the heat of deeds too cold breath gives.   [A bell rings.]

---

[40]*dudgeon,* handle.
[41]*gouts,* drops of blood.
[42]*Hecate,* ruling spirit of witches.

I go, and it is done; the bell invites me.
Hear it not, Duncan; for it is a knell
That summons thee to heaven or to hell.   [*Exit.*]

SCENE II. *The same.*

Enter LADY MACBETH.

LADY MACBETH. That which hath made them drunk hath made me bold;
What hath quenched them hath given me fire. Hark! Peace!
It was the owl that shrieked, the fatal bellman,
Which gives the stern'st good-night. He is about it.
The doors are open; and the surfeited grooms   5
Do mock their charge with snores. I have drugged their possets,[43]
That death and nature do contend about them,
Whether they live or die.
MACBETH. [*Within*] Who's there? What, ho!
LADY MACBETH. Alack, I am afraid they have awaked,   10
And 'tis not done. The attempt and not the deed
Confounds us. Hark! I laid their daggers ready;
He could not miss 'em. Had he not resembled
My father as he slept, I had done 't.

Enter MACBETH.

                              My husband!
MACBETH. I have done the deed. Didst thou not hear a noise?   15
LADY MACBETH. I heard the owl scream and the crickets cry.
Did not you speak?
MACBETH. When?
LADY MACBETH. Now.
MACBETH.   As I descended?
LADY MACBETH. Ay.

---

[43]*possets,* drinks.

MACBETH. Hark!
Who lies i' the second chamber?
LADY MACBETH.   Donalbain. [20]
MACBETH. This is a sorry sight.
      [*Looking on his hands.*]
LADY   MACBETH.   A   foolish
   thought, to say a sorry sight.
MACBETH. There's one did laugh
   in 's sleep, and one cried "Mur-
   der!"
That they did wake each other. I
   stood and heard them;
But they did say their prayers, and
   addressed them   [25]
Again to sleep.
   LADY MACBETH.   There are two
      lodged together.
MACBETH. One cried "God bless
   us!" and "Amen!" the other,
As they had seen me with these hang-
   man's hands.
Listening their fear, I could not say
   "Amen!"
When they did say "God bless us!"
   LADY MACBETH. Consider it not
      so deeply.   [30]
MACBETH. But wherefore could not
   I pronounce "Amen"?
I had most need of blessing, and
   "Amen"
Stuck in my throat.
   LADY MACBETH. These deeds must
      not be thought
After these ways; so, it will make us
   mad.
MACBETH. Methought I heard a
   voice cry, "Sleep no more!   [35]
Macbeth doth murder sleep"—the in-
   nocent sleep,
Sleep that knits up the raveled sleave[44]
   of care,
The death of each day's life, sore
   labor's bath,
Balm of hurt minds, great nature's
   second course,[45]
Chief nourisher in life's feast—

LADY MACBETH.   What do you
   mean?   [40]
MACBETH. Still it cried, "Sleep no
   more!" to all the house;
"Glamis hath murdered sleep, and
   therefore Cawdor
Shall sleep no more; Macbeth shall
   sleep no more!"
   LADY MACBETH. Who was it that
      thus cried? Why, worthy thane,
You do unbend your noble strength,
   to think   [45]
So brainsickly of things. Go get some
   water,
And wash this filthy witness from
   your hand.
Why did you bring these daggers
   from the place?
They must lie there; go carry them;
   and smear
The sleepy grooms with blood.
   MACBETH.   I'll go no more. [50]
I am afraid to think what I have
   done;
Look on 't again I dare not.
   LADY MACBETH. Infirm of purpose!
Give me the daggers. The sleeping
   and the dead
Are but as pictures; 'tis the eye of
   childhood
That fears a painted devil. If he do
   bleed,   [55]
I'll gild the faces of the grooms
   withal;
For it must seem their guilt.
      [*Exit. Knocking within.*]
   MACBETH. Whence is that knock-
      ing?
How is 't with me, when every noise
   appals me?
What hands are here? Ha! they pluck
   out mine eyes.
Will all great Neptune's[46] ocean wash
   this blood   [60]
Clean from my hand? No, this my
   hand will rather
The multitudinous seas incarnadine,[47]

---

[44]*raveled sleave*, tangled threads.
[45]*second course*, main or meat course.

[46]*Neptune*, god of the sea.
[47]*incarnadine*, make red.

Making the green one red.

Re-enter LADY MACBETH.

LADY MACBETH. My hands are of your color; but I shame
To wear a heart so white. [*Knocking within.*] I hear a knocking [65]
At the south entry. Retire we to our chamber;
A little water clears us of this deed.
How easy is it, then! Your constancy
Hath left you unattended. [*Knocking within.*] Hark! More knocking.
Get on your nightgown, lest occasion call us [70]
And show us to be watchers. Be not lost
So poorly in your thoughts.

MACBETH. To know my deed, 't were best not know myself.
[*Knocking within.*]
Wake Duncan with thy knocking!
I would thou couldst! [*Exeunt.*]

SCENE III. *The same.*

Knocking within. Enter a Porter.

PORTER. Here's a knocking indeed! If a man were porter of hellgate, he should have old turning the key. [*Knocking within.*] Knock, knock, knock! Who's there, i' the name of Beelzebub?[48] Here's a farmer, that hanged himself on the expectation of plenty. Come in time; have napkins enow[49] about you; here you'll sweat for 't. [*Knocking within.*] Knock, knock! Who's there, in the other devil's name? Faith, here's an equivocator,[50] that could swear in both the scales against either scale; who committed treason enough for God's sake, yet could not equivocate to heaven: O, come in, equivocator. [*Knocking

within.] Knock, knock, knock! Who's there? Faith, here's an English tailor come hither, for stealing out of a French hose.[51] Come in, tailor; here you may roast your goose.[52] [*Knocking within.*] Knock, knock; never at quiet! What are you? But this place is too cold for hell. I'll devil-porter it no further; I had thought to have let in some of all professions that go the primrose way to the everlasting bonfire. [*Knocking within.*] Anon, anon! I pray you, remember the porter.   [*Opens the gate.*]

Enter MACDUFF *and* LENNOX.

MACDUFF. Was it so late, friend, ere you went to bed,
That you do lie so late?

PORTER. 'Faith, sir, we were carousing till the second cock.

MACDUFF. Is thy master stirring?

Enter MACBETH.

Our knocking has awaked him; here he comes.

LENNOX. Good morrow, noble sir.

MACBETH.   Good morrow, both.

MACDUFF. Is the king stirring, worthy thane?

MACBETH.   Not yet. [50]

MACDUFF. He did command me to call timely on him;
I have almost slipped the hour.

MACBETH.   I'll bring you to him.

MACDUFF. I know this is a joyful trouble to you;
But yet 'tis one.

MACBETH. The labor we delight in physics pain. [55]
This is the door.

MACDUFF. I'll make so bold to call,
For 't is my limited service. [*Exit.*]

LENNOX. Goes the king hence today?

---

[48]*Beelzebub* (bē el' zē bub), prince of demons.
[49]*napkins enow*, pocket handkerchiefs enough.
[50]*equivocator*, liar.

[51]*French hose*, tailors were accused of stealing out of material upon which they were working.
[52]*goose*, tailor's pressing iron.

MACBETH. He does; he did appoint so.

LENNOX. The night has been unruly. Where we lay,
Our chimneys were blown down; and, as they say, 60
Lamentings heard i' the air; strange screams of death,
And prophesying, with accents terrible,
Of dire combustion and confused events
New hatched to the woeful time; the obscure bird[53]
Clamored the livelong night; some say, the earth 65
Was feverous and did shake.

MACBETH. 'Twas a rough night.

LENNOX. My young remembrance cannot parallel
A fellow to it.

Re-enter MACDUFF.

MACDUFF. O horror, horror, horror! Tongue nor heart
Cannot conceive nor name thee!

MACBETH. ⎱ What's the matter? 70
LENNOX. ⎰

MACDUFF. Confusion[54] now hath made his masterpiece!
Most sacrilegious murder hath broke ope
The Lord's anointed temple, and stole thence
The life o' the building!

MACBETH. What is 't you say? the life?

LENNOX. Mean you his majesty?[75]

MACDUFF. Approach the chamber, and destroy your sight
With a new Gorgon.[55] Do not bid me speak;
See, and then speak yourselves.

----

[53]*obscure bird*, owl.
[54]*confusion*, murder, destruction.
[55]*Gorgon*, according to mythology the Gorgon sisters were evil monsters with snaky locks. One look at them would change a mortal to stone.

[*Exeunt* MACBETH *and* LENNOX.]
                          Awake, awake!
Ring the alarum-bell. Murder and treason!
Banquo and Donalbain! Malcolm! awake! 80
Shake off this downy sleep, death's counterfeit,
And look on death itself! Up, up, and see
The great doom's image! Malcolm! Banquo!
As from your graves rise up, and walk like sprites,
To countenance this horror! Ring the bell. [*Bell rings.*] 85

Enter LADY MACBETH.

LADY MACBETH. What's the business,
That such a hideous trumpet calls to parley
The sleepers of the house? Speak, speak!

MACDUFF. O gentle lady,
'Tis not for you to hear what I can speak;
The repetition, in a woman's ear, 90
Would murder as it fell.

Enter BANQUO.

                    O Banquo, Banquo,
Our royal master's murdered!

LADY MACBETH. Woe, alas!
What, in our house?

BANQUO. Too cruel anywhere.
Dear Duff, I prithee, contradict thyself,
And say it is not so. 95

Re-enter MACBETH *and* LENNOX,
with Ross.

MACBETH. Had I but died an hour before this chance,
I had lived a blessèd time; for, from this instant,
There's nothing serious in mortality[56];

----

[56]*mortality*, life.

All is but toys; renown and grace is
dead;
The wine of life is drawn, and the
mere lees[57]　　　　　　100
Is left this vault to brag of.

Enter MALCOLM *and* DONALBAIN.

DONALBAIN. What is amiss?
MACBETH. You are, and do not
know 't;
The spring, the head, the fountain of
your blood
Is stopped; the very source of it is
stopped.
MACDUFF. Your royal father's
murdered.
MALCOLM.　　　O, by whom? 105
LENNOX. Those of his chamber, as
it seemed, had done 't.
Their hands and faces were all badged
with blood;
So were their daggers, which unwiped
we found
Upon their pillows.
They stared, and were distracted; no
man's life　　　　　　110
Was to be trusted with them.
MACBETH. O, yet I do repent me
of my fury,
That I did kill them.
MACDUFF. Wherefore did you so?
MACBETH. Who can be wise,
amazed, temperate and furious,
Loyal and neutral, in a moment? No
man.　　　　　　115
The expedition[58] of my violent love
Outrun the pauser, reason. Here lay
Duncan.
His silver skin laced with his golden
blood,
And his gashed stabs looked like a
breach in nature
For ruin's wasteful entrance; there,
the murderers,　　　　　　120
Steeped in the colors of their trade,
their daggers

Unmannerly breeched with gore.[59]
Who could refrain,
That had a heart to love, and in that
heart
Courage to make 's love known?
LADY MACBETH. Help me hence,
ho!
MACDUFF. Look to the lady.
MALCOLM. [*Aside to* DONALBAIN]
Why do we hold our tongues, 125
That most may claim this argument
for ours?
DONALBAIN. [*Aside to* MALCOLM]
What should be spoken here,
where our fate,
Hid in an auger-hole, may rush, and
seize us?
Let's away;
Our tears are not yet brewed.
MALCOLM. [*Aside to* DONALBAIN]
Nor our strong sorrow　　　130
Upon the foot of motion.
BANQUO.　　　Look to the lady.

[LADY MACBETH *is carried out.*]

And when we have our naked frail-
ties[60] hid,
That suffer in exposure, let us meet,
And question this most bloody piece
of work,
To know it further. Fears and scru-
ples shake us;　　　　　　135
In the great hand of God I stand; and
thence
Against the undivulged pretence I
fight
Of treasonous malice.
MACDUFF.　　　And so do I.
ALL.　　　　　　So all.
MACBETH. Let's briefly put on
manly readiness,
And meet i' the hall together.
ALL.　　Well contented.　　140

[*Exeunt all but* MALCOLM *and*
DONALBAIN.]

---

[57]*lees*, dregs.
[58]*expedition*, haste.

[59]*gore*, blood.
[60]*frailties*, dressed ourselves; many
rushed out half-clothed to learn the
cause of the alarm.

MALCOLM. What will you do? Let's
not consort with them;
To show an unfelt sorrow is an office
Which the false man does easy. I'll to
England.
DONALBAIN. To Ireland, I; our
separated fortune
Shall keep us both the safer; where
we are,   145
There's daggers in men's smiles the
near in blood,
The nearer bloody.
MALCOLM. This murderous shaft
that's shot
Hath not yet lighted, and our safest
way
Is to avoid the aim. Therefore, to
horse;
And let us not be dainty of leave-
taking,   150
But shift away; there's warrant in
that theft
Which steals itself, when there's no
mercy left.   [*Exeunt.*]

SCENE IV. *Outside* MACBETH'S
castle.

Enter ROSS *and an* OLD MAN.

OLD MAN. Threescore and ten I
can remember well;
Within the volume of which time I
have seen
Hours dreadful and things strange;
but this sore night
Hath trifled former knowings.
ROSS.   Ah, good father,
Thou seest, the heavens, as troubled
with man's act,   5
Threaten his bloody stage; by the
clock, 'tis day,
And yet dark night strangles the
traveling lamp.[61]
Is 't night's predominance, or the
day's shame,
That darkness does the face of earth
entomb,

When living light should kiss it?
OLD MAN.   'Tis unnatural, [10]
Even like the deed that's done. On
Tuesday last,
A falcon, towering in her pride of
place,[62]
Was by a mousing owl hawked at and
killed.
ROSS. And Duncan's horses — a
thing most strange and certain—
Beauteous and swift, the minions of
their race,   [15]
Turned wild in nature, broke their
stalls, flung out,
Contending 'gainst obedience, as they
would make
War with mankind.
OLD MAN.   'Tis said they eat
each other.
ROSS. They did so, to the amaze-
ment of mine eyes
That looked upon 't. Here comes the
good Macduff.   [20]

Enter MACDUFF.

How goes the world, sir, now?
MACDUFF.   Why, see you not?
ROSS. Is 't known who did this
more than bloody deed?
MACDUFF. Those that Macbeth
hath slain.
ROSS.   Alas, the day!
What good could they pretend?
MACDUFF. They were suborned.[63]
Malcolm and Donalbain, the king's
two sons,   [25]
Are stolen away and fled; which puts
upon them
Suspicion of the deed.
ROSS.   'Gainst nature still!
Thriftless ambition, that wilt ravin
up[64]
Thine own life's means! Then 'tis
most like

---

[61]*lamp,* the sun.

[62]*falcon, towering in her pride of
place,* a pet hawk kept for sport, flying at her height.
[63]*suborned,* bribed.
[64]*ravin up,* destroy.

The sovereignty will fall upon Mac-
beth.   30
MACDUFF. He is already named,
and gone to Scone⁶⁵
To be invested.
Ross.   Where is Duncan's body?
MACDUFF. Carried to Colmekill,⁶⁶
The sacred storehouse of his prede-
cessors,
And guardian of their bones.

————————
⁶⁵*Scone*, an ancient Scotch city
which was the residence of kings.
⁶⁶*Colmekill* (kŏm' kĭl), one of the islands of the Hebrides (hĕb' rĭ dēz), at
one time very important.

Ross.   Will you to Scone?³⁵
MACDUFF. No, cousin, I'll to Fife.
Ross.   Well, I will thither.
MACDUFF. Well, may you see things
well done there. Adieu!
Lest our old robes sit easier than our
new!⁶⁷
Ross. Farewell, father.
OLD MAN. God's benison go with
you, and with those   40
That would make good of bad and
friends of foes!   [*Exeunt.*]

————————
⁶⁷*new*, distrust of the new king, Macbeth.

For Thought and Discussion
ACT II

SCENE 1.
1. Describe the stage setting.
2. Why is Banquo unable to sleep? What token of the King's gratitude to Lady Macbeth does Banquo give to Macbeth? What is the dramatic effect of Duncan's kindness?
3. Explain the meaning of Macbeth's speech to Banquo, "If you shall cleave to my consent." What differences in character are revealed in the men? Why is Banquo suspicious of Mac-beth?
4. While Macbeth waits for the signal for the murder, why does he see a dagger? How does it change while he looks at it? What side of Macbeth's nature is shown by this scene?

SCENE 2.
1. Of what is Lady Macbeth afraid while Macbeth is murdering Duncan? Why does she not commit the deed herself?
2. Contrast the reactions of Macbeth and Lady Macbeth to the murder. What do Macbeth's references to sleep suggest as to his peace of mind hereafter?
3. Why does Lady Macbeth return the daggers to the scene of the murder?
4. What is the dramatic effect of the knocking at the gate?

SCENE 3.
1. Why is the humorous scene of the drunken porter a relief? In what sense is the door to Macbeth's castle a "hell-gate"?
2. What is the dramatic effect of the storm on the night of the murder?
3. Who discovers the murder of Duncan?

4. What happens to the guards? Does Lady Macbeth really faint?
   Answer carefully.
5. How does Macbeth react to the discovery of the murder? What
   happens to the guards?
6. Why do Malcolm and Donalbain flee? Who is suspected of the
   crime?
7. What methods of crime detection unknown then are used
   now?

SCENE 4.

1. Who do the people believe bribed the guards to murder Duncan?
2. Who was crowned king and why?
3. What does Macduff think of Macbeth as king?
4. What is the situation at the end of the second act?

A Study of Significant Passages

Select and read aloud the significant lines in this act. The following suggestions may assist you in making your choice, as lines which show:

Macbeth's uncontrolled imagination
Lady Macbeth's affection for her father
Macbeth's sense of guilt
Lady Macbeth's determination
Foreshadowings of tragedy

———

ACT III

[Macbeth fears Banquo because the witches promised the throne to Banquo's posterity and because he has found Banquo incorruptible. He employs murderers to kill Banquo and his son Fleance. The plan is only a partial success, as Fleance escapes when his father is killed. At the banquet in the palace Banquo's ghost appears to Macbeth and terrorizes him so completely that Lady Macbeth is forced to ask the guests to leave. Lennox tells another lord that he suspects Macbeth of the murder of Duncan and Banquo, and he hopes that Macduff, who has fled to England, will return with an army to overthrow Macbeth.]

SCENE I. *Forres. The palace.*

Enter BANQUO.

BANQUO. Thou hast it now—king,
   Cawdor, Glamis, all,
As the weird women promised, and I
   fear,
Thou playedst most foully for 't; yet
   it was said
It should not stand in thy posterity,
But that myself should be the root
   and father   5
Of many kings. If there come truth
   from them—
As upon thee, Macbeth, their speeches
   shine—
Why, by the verities on thee made
   good,

May they not be my oracles as well,
And set me up in hope?   But hush!
No more.   10

Sennet sounded. Enter MACBETH, *as
king,* LADY MACBETH, *as queen,* LEN-
NOX, ROSS, Lords, Ladies,
and Attendants.

MACBETH. Here's our chief guest.
LADY MACBETH.   If he had been
forgotten,
It had been as a gap in our great feast,
And all-thing unbecoming.
MACBETH. Tonight we hold a sol-
emn supper, sir,
And I'll request your presence.
BANQUO.   Let your highness 15
Command upon me; to the which my
duties
Are with a most indissoluble tie
Forever knit.
MACBETH. Ride you this after-
noon?
BANQUO. Ay, my good lord.   20
MACBETH. We should have else de-
sired your good advice,
Which still[68] hath been both grave
and prosperous,
In this day's council; but we'll take
tomorrow.
Is 't far you ride?
BANQUO. As far, my lord, as will
fill up the time   25
'Twixt this and supper; go not my
horse the better,
I must become a borrower of the
night
For a dark hour or twain.
MACBETH.   Fail not our feast.
BANQUO. My lord, I will not.
MACBETH. We hear, our bloody
cousins[69] are bestowed   30
In England and in Ireland, not con-
fessing

Their cruel parricide,[70] filling their
hearers
With strange invention; but of that
tomorrow,
When therewithal we shall have cause
of state
Craving us jointly. Hie you to horse.
Adieu,   35
Till you return at night. Goes Fleance
with you?
BANQUO. Ay, my good lord; our
time does call upon 's.
MACBETH. I wish your horses swift
and sure of foot;
And so I do commend you to their
backs.
Farewell.   [*Exit* BANQUO.] 40
Let every man be master of his time
Till seven at night. To make society
The sweeter welcome, we will keep
ourself
Till supper-time alone. While then,[71]
God be with you!

[*Exeunt all but* MACBETH, *and an*
Attendant.]

Sirrah, a word with you.   Attend
those men   45
Our pleasure?
ATTENDANT. They are, my lord,
without the palace gate.
MACBETH. Bring them before us.
[*Exit* Attendant.]

To be thus is nothing;
But to be safely thus.—Our fears in
Banquo
Stick deep; and in his royalty of na-
ture   50
Reigns that which would be feared.
'Tis much he dares;
And, to that dauntless temper of his
mind,
He hath a wisdom that doth guide his
valor
To act in safety. There is none but
he

___

[68]*still,* always.
[69]*cousins,* Malcolm and Donalbain.

[70]*parricide,* murder of father.
[71]*while then,* until then.

Whose being I do fear; and under
  him,   55
My Genius is rebuked, as, it is said,
Mark Antony's was by Caesar.[72] He
  chid the sisters
When first they put the name of king
  upon me,
And bade them speak to him. Then
  prophet-like
They hailed him father to a line of
  kings;   60
Upon my head they placed a fruitless
  crown,
And put a barren scepter in my gripe,
Thence to be wrenched with an un-
  lineal hand,
No son of mine succeeding. If 't be
  so,
For Banquo's issue have I 'filed[73] my
  mind;   65
For them the gracious Duncan have I
  murdered;
Put rancors in the vessel of my peace
Only for them; and mine eternal
  jewel[74]
Given to the common enemy of man,
To make them kings, the seed of Ban-
  quo kings!   70
Rather than so, come fate into the list,
And champion me to the utterance![75]
Who's there?

  Re-enter Attendant, *with two*
        Murderers.

Now go to the door, and stay there
  till we call.   [*Exit* Attendant.]
Was it not yesterday we spoke to-
  gether?
  FIRST MURDERER. It was, so please
    your highness.
  MACBETH.   Well then, now   75
Have you considered of my speeches?
  Know

That it was he in the times past which
  held you
So under fortune, which you thought
  had been
Our innocent self; this I made good
  to you
In our last conference, passed in pro-
  bation[76] with you,   80
How you were borne in hand, how
  crossed, the instruments,
Who wrought with them, and all
  things else that might
To half a soul and to a notion crazed
Say "Thus did Banquo."
  FIRST MURDERER.   You made it
    known to us.
  MACBETH. I did so, and went fur-
    ther, which is now   85
Our point of second meeting.   Do
  you find
Your patience so predominant in your
  nature
That you can let this go?   Are you so
  gospeled
To pray for this good man and for
  his issue,
Whose heavy hand hath bowed you
  to the grave   90
And beggared yours forever?
  FIRST MURDERER.   We are men,
    my liege.
  MACBETH. Ay, in the catalogue ye
    go for men;
As hounds and greyhounds, mongrels,
  spaniels, curs,
Shoughs,[77]   water-rugs   and   demi-
  wolves, are clept[78]
All by the name of dogs; the valued
  file   95
Distinguishes the swift, the slow, the
  subtle,
The housekeeper, the hunter, every
  one
According to the gift which boun-
  teous nature

---

[72]*Caesar,* Caesar (Octavius) was Antony's superior.
  [73]*'filed,* defiled.
  [74]*eternal jewel,* soul.
  [75]*utterance,* last.

---

[76]*probation with you,* proved to you.
  [77]*shoughs,* (shocks), a dog with
coarse hair.
  [78]*clept,* called.

Hath in him closed; whereby he does receive
Particular addition, from the bill [100]
That writes them all alike; and so of men.
Now, if you have a station in the file,
Not i' the worst rank of manhood, say 't;
And I will put that business in your bosoms,
Whose execution takes your enemy off, [105]
Grapples you to the heart and love of us,
Who wear our health but sickly in his life,
Which in his death were perfect.
SECOND MURDERER. I am one, my liege,
Whom the vile blows and buffets of the world
Have so incensed that I am reckless what [110]
I do to spite the world.
FIRST MURDERER. And I another
So weary with disasters, tugged with fortune,
That I would set my life on any chance,
To mend it, or be rid on 't.
MACBETH. Both of you
Know Banquo was your enemy.
BOTH MURDERERS. True, my lord. [115]
MACBETH. So is he mine; and in such bloody distance,[79]
That every minute of his being thrusts
Against my near'st of life; and though I could
With barefaced power sweep him from my sight
And bid my will avouch it, yet I must not, [120]
For certain friends that are both his and mine,

Whose loves I may not drop, but wail his fall
Who I myself struck down; and thence it is,
That I to your assistance do make love,
Masking the business from the common eye [125]
For sundry weighty reasons.
SECOND MURDERER. We shall, my lord,
Perform what you command us.
FIRST MURDERER. Though our lives—
MACBETH. Your spirits shine through you. Within this hour at most
I will advise you where to plant yourselves;
Acquaint you with the perfect spy o' the time,[80] [130]
The moment on 't; for 't must be done tonight,
And something from the palace; always thought
That I require a clearness,[81] and with him—
To leave no rubs nor botches in the work—
Fleance his son, that keeps him company, [135]
Whose absence is no less material to me
Than is his father's, must embrace the fate
Of that dark hour. Resolve yourselves apart;
I'll come to you anon.
BOTH MURDERERS. We are resolved, my lord.
MACBETH. I'll call upon you straight; abide within.
[Exeunt Murderers.] [140]
It is concluded. Banquo, thy soul's flight,

---

[79]*bloody distance,* very near, as close as two combatants fighting for the death stroke.

[80]*spy o' the time,* know the time to catch him.
[81]*clearness,* that I seem clear of the deed, that I be uninvolved.

If it find heaven, must find it out tonight.   [*Exit.*]

SCENE II. *The palace.*

Enter LADY MACBETH *and a* Servant.

LADY MACBETH. Is Banquo gone from court?

SERVANT. Ay, madam, but returns again tonight.

LADY MACBETH. Say to the king, I would attend his leisure
For a few words.

SERVANT.   Madam, I will. [*Exit.*]

LADY MACBETH.   Naught 's had, all 's spent,
Where our desire is got without content;   5
'Tis safer to be that which we destroy
Than by destruction dwell in doubtful joy.

Enter MACBETH.

How now, my lord! why do you keep alone,
Of sorriest fancies your companions making,
Using those thoughts which should indeed have died   10
With them they think on? Things without all remedy
Should be without regard; what's done is done.

MACBETH. We have scotched[82] the snake, not killed it;
She'll close and be herself, whilst our poor malice[83]
Remains in danger of her former tooth.   15
But let the frame of things disjoint, both the worlds suffer,
Ere we will eat our meal in fear and sleep
In the affliction of these terrible dreams
That shake us nightly; better be with the dead,

Whom we, to gain our peace, have sent to peace,   20
Than on the torture of the mind to lie
In restless ecstasy.[84] Duncan is in his grave:
After life's fitful fever he sleeps well;
Treason has done his worst; nor steel, nor poison,
Malice domestic, foreign levy, nothing,   25
Can touch him further.

LADY MACBETH.   Come on;
Gentle my lord, sleek o'er your rugged looks;
Be bright and jovial among your guests tonight.

MACBETH. So shall I, love; and so, I pray, be you.
Let your remembrance apply to Banquo;   30
Present him eminence,[85] both with eye and tongue;
Unsafe the while, that we
Must lave our honors in these flattering streams,
And make our faces vizards[86] to our hearts,
Disguising what they are.

LADY MACBETH.   You must leave this.   35

MACBETH. O, full of scorpions is my mind, dear wife!
Thou know'st that Banquo, and his Fleance, lives.

LADY MACBETH. But in them nature's copy 's not eterne.[87]

MACBETH. There's comfort yet; they are assailable;
Then be thou jocund; ere the bat hath flown   40
His cloistered flight, ere to black Hecate's summons
The shard-borne beetle with his drowsy hums

---

[82]*scotched,* wounded.
[83]*malice,* endangered future.
[84]*ecstasy,* not joy but great grief.
[85]*eminence,* honor.
[86]*vizards,* masks, disguises.
[87]*eterne,* eternal, unassailable.

Hath rung night's yawning peal, there
  shall be done
A deed of dreadful note.
  LADY MACBETH. What's to be
    done?
  MACBETH. Be innocent of the
    knowledge, dearest chuck,   45
Till thou applaud the deed. Come,
  seeling night,
Scarf up the tender eye of pitiful day;
And with thy bloody and invisible
  hand
Cancel and tear to pieces that great
  bond[88]
Which keeps me pale! Light thickens,
  and the crow   50
Makes wing to the rooky wood;
Good things of day begin to droop
  and drowse;
Whiles night's black agents to their
  preys do rouse.
Thou marvel'st at my words; but hold
  thee still;
Things bad begun make strong them-
  selves by ill.   55
So, prithee, go with me.   [*Exeunt.*]

SCENE III. *A park near the palace.*

Enter three Murderers.

  FIRST MURDERER. But who did bid
    thee join with us?
  THIRD MURDERER.   Macbeth.
  SECOND MURDERER. He needs not
    our mistrust,[89] since he delivers
Our offices and what we have to do
To the direction just.
  FIRST MURDERER. Then stand with
    us.
The west yet glimmers with some
  streaks of day!   5
Now spurs the lated traveler apace
To gain the timely inn, and near ap-
  proaches
The subject of our watch.
  THIRD MURDERER. Hark! I hear
    horses.

---
[88]*bond,* Banquo's existence.
[89]*mistrust,* suspicion.

  BANQUO. [*Within*] Give us a light
    there, ho!
  SECOND MURDERER. Then 'tis he;
    the rest
That are within the note of expecta-
  tion[90]   10
Already are i' the court.
  FIRST MURDERER. His horses go
    about.
  THIRD MURDERER. Almost a mile;
    but he does usually,
So all men do, from hence to the
  palace gate
Make it their walk.
  SECOND MURDERER. A light, a
    light!

Enter BANQUO, *and* FLEANCE *with a*
torch.

  THIRD MURDERER.   'Tis he.
  FIRST MURDERER. Stand to 't.   15
  BANQUO. It will be rain tonight.
  FIRST MURDERER. Let it come
    down.
      [*They set upon* BANQUO.]
  BANQUO. O, treachery! Fly, good
    Fleance, fly, fly, fly!
Thou mayst revenge. O slave!
      [*Dies.* FLEANCE *escapes.*]
  THIRD MURDERER. Who did strike
    out the light?
  FIRST MURDERER. Was 't not the
    way?
  THIRD MURDERER. There's but one
    down; the son is fled.
  SECOND MURDERER. We have lost 20
Best half of our affair.
  FIRST MURDERER. Well, let's away,
    and say how much is done.
          [*Exeunt.*]

SCENE IV. *The same. Hall in the*
palace.

A banquet prepared. Enter MAC-
  BETH, LADY MACBETH, ROSS,
  LENNOX, *Lords, and* Attendants.

---
[90]*expectation,* all those expected at
court are there except Banquo, who is
late.

MACBETH. You know your own degrees; sit down; at first
And last the hearty welcome.
LORDS. Thanks to your majesty.
MACBETH.   Ourself will mingle with society.
And play the humble host.
Our hostess keeps her state,[91] but in best time   5
We will require her welcome.
LADY MACBETH. Pronounce it for me, sir, to all our friends;
For my heart speaks they are welcome.

First Murderer *appears at the door.*

MACBETH. See, they encounter thee with their hearts' thanks.
Both sides are even; here I'll sit i' the midst;   10
Be large in mirth, anon we'll drink a measure
The table round. [*Approaching the door.*] There's blood upon thy face.
MURDERER. 'Tis Banquo's then.
MACBETH. 'Tis better thee without than he within.
Is he dispatched?   15
MURDERER. My lord, his throat is cut; that I did for him.
MACBETH. Thou art the best o' the cut-throats; yet he's good
That did the like for Fleance; if thou didst it,
Thou art the nonpareil.[92]
MURDERER.   Most royal sir.
Fleance is 'scaped.   20
MACBETH. Then comes my fit again. I had else been perfect.
Whole as the marble, founded as the rock,
As broad and general as the casing[93] air;
But now I am cabined, cribbed, confined, bound in

To saucy doubts and fears. But Banquo's safe?   25
MURDERER. Ay, my good lord, safe in a ditch he bides,
With twenty trenchèd gashes on his head,
The least a death to nature.
MACBETH.   Thanks for that.
There the grown serpent lies; the worm that's fled
Hath nature that in time will venom breed;   30
No teeth for the present. Get thee gone. Tomorrow
We'll hear, ourselves again.
                    [*Exit* Murderer.]
LADY MACBETH.   My royal lord,
You do not give the cheer[94]; the feast is sold
That is not often vouched, while 'tis a-making,
'Tis given with welcome; to feed were best at home;   35
From thence the sauce to meat is ceremony;
Meeting were bare without it.
MACBETH.   Sweet remembrancer!
Now, good digestion wait on appetite,
And health on both!
LENNOX.   May 't please your highness sit.

[*The Ghost of* BANQUO *enters, and sits in* MACBETH's *place.*]

MACBETH. Here had we now our country's honor roofed,   40
Were the graced person of our Banquo present;
Who may I rather challenge for unkindness
Than pity for mischance!
ROSS.   His absence, sir,
Lays blame upon his promise. Please 't your highness
To grace us with your royal company.   45
MACBETH. The table's full.

---

[91]*keeps her state,* Lady Macbeth remains in her chair of state.
[92]*nonpareil,* unequalled.
[93]*casing,* encasing, surrounding.

[94]*cheer,* welcome.

LENNOX. Here is a place reserved, sir.

MACBETH. Where?

LENNOX. Here, my good lord. What is 't that moves your highness?

MACBETH. Which of you have done this?

LORDS.   What, my good lord?

MACBETH. Thou canst not say I did it; never shake   50
Thy gory locks at me.

ROSS. Gentlemen, rise; his highness is not well.

LADY MACBETH. Sit, worthy friends; my lord is often thus,
And hath been from his youth. Pray you, keep seat;
The fit is momentary; upon a thought   55
He will again be well; if much you note him,
You shall offend him and extend his passion.
Feed, and regard him not.—Are you a man?

MACBETH. Ay, and a bold one, that dare look on that
Which might appal the devil.

LADY MACBETH. O proper stuff!   60
This is the very painting of your fear;
This is the air-drawn dagger which, you said,
Led you to Duncan. O, these flaws and starts,
Impostors to true fear, would well become
A woman's story at a winter's fire,   65
Authorized by her grandam. Shame itself!
Why do you make such faces? When all 's done,
You look but on a stool.

MACBETH. Prithee, see there! Behold! Look! Lo! How say you?
Why, what care I? If thou canst nod, speak too.   70

If charnel-houses and our graves must send
Those that we bury back, our monuments
Shall be the maws[95] of kites.[96]
              [Ghost vanishes.]

LADY MACBETH. What, quite unmanned in folly?

MACBETH. If I stand here, I saw him.

LADY MACBETH. Fie, for shame!

MACBETH. Blood hath been shed ere now, i' the olden time,   75
Ere human statute purged the gentle weal;
Ay, and since too, murders have been performed
Too terrible for the ear. The time has been,
That, when the brains were out, the man would die,
And there an end; but now they rise again,   80
With twenty mortal murders on their crowns,
And push us from our stools. This is more strange
Than such a murder is.

LADY MACBETH. My worthy lord,
Your noble friends do lack you.

MACBETH.   I do forget.—
Do not muse at me, my most worthy friends;   85
I have a strange infirmity, which is nothing
To those that know me. Come, love and health to all;
Then I'll sit down. Give me some wine; fill full.
I drink to the general joy o' the whole table,
And to our dear friend Banquo, whom we miss;   90
Would he were here! to all, and him, We thirst,
And all to all.

LORDS. Our duties, and the pledge.

---

[95]*maws*, stomachs.
[96]*kites*, hawks.

Re-enter Ghost.

MACBETH. Avaunt! and quit my sight! Let the earth hide thee! Thy bones are marrowless, thy blood is cold;

Thou hast no speculation[97] in those eyes 95

Which thou dost glare with!

LADY MACBETH. Think of this, good peers,

But as a thing of custom; 'tis no other;

Only it spoils the pleasure of the time.

MACBETH. What man dare, I dare.

Approach thou like the rugged Russian bear, 100

The armed rhinoceros,[98] or the Hyrcan tiger[99]

Take any shape but that, and my firm nerves

Shall never tremble; or be alive again,

And dare me to the desert with thy sword:

If trembling I inhabit then, protest[100] me 105

The baby of a girl. Hence, horrible shadow!

Unreal mockery, hence!

[Ghost *vanishes*.]

Why, so; being gone,

I am a man again. Pray you, sit still.

LADY MACBETH. You have displaced the mirth, broke the good meeting,

With most admired disorder.

MACBETH. Can such things be, 110

And overcome us like a summer's cloud,

Without our special wonder? You make me strange

"Thy bones are marrowless, thy blood is cold; Thou hast no speculation in those eyes Which thou dost glare with!"

---

[97]*speculation,* reason.

[98]*armed rhinoceros,* well armed by his thick skin, which protects him.

[99]*Hyrcan* (hûr′ kăn) *tiger,* from Northern Asia.

[100]*protest,* proclaim.

Even to the disposition that I owe,
When now I think you can behold
  such sights,
And keep the natural ruby of your
  cheeks, ¹¹⁵
When mine is blanched with fear.
  Ross.   What sights,
  my lord?
  LADY MACBETH. I pray you, speak
  not; he grows worse and worse;
Question enrages him. At once, good
  night;
Stand not upon the order of your
  going,
But go at once.
  LENNOX.   Good night; and
  better health ¹²⁰
Attend his majesty!
  LADY MACBETH.   A kind good
  night to all!

[*Exeunt all but* MACBETH *and* LADY
            MACBETH.]

  MACBETH. It will have blood; they
  say, blood will have blood;
Stones have been known to move¹⁰¹
  and trees to speak;
Augurs¹⁰² and understood relations
  have
By magot-pies and choughs and
  rooks¹⁰³ brought forth   125
The secret'st man of blood. What
  is the night?
  LADY MACBETH. Almost at odds
  with morning, which is which.
  MACBETH. How say'st thou, that
  Macduff denies his person
At our great bidding?
  LADY MACBETH. Did you send to
  him, sir?
  MACBETH. I hear it by the way;
  but I will send;   130
There's not a one of them but in his
  house

---

¹⁰¹*move*, old belief that stones moved
at the touch of an innocent person.
¹⁰²*augurs*, wizards.
¹⁰³*rooks*, these birds would proclaim
the guilt of the murderer.

I keep a servant fee'd. I will tomor-
  row,
And betimes I will, to the weird sis-
  ters;
More shall they speak; for now I am
  bent to know,
By the worst means, the worst. For
  mine own good,   135
All causes shall give way. I am in
  blood
Stepped in so far that, should I wade
  no more,
Returning were as tedious as go o'er;
Strange things I have in head, that
  will to hand,
Which must be acted ere they may
  be scanned.   140
  LADY MACBETH. You lack the sea-
  son of all natures, sleep.
  MACBETH. Come we'll to sleep. My
  strange and self-abuse
Is the initiate fear that wants hard
  use;
We are yet but young in deed.
                    [*Exeunt.*]

SCENE V. *A heath.*

Thunder. Enter the three Witches,
meeting HECATE.

  FIRST WITCH. Why, how now, He-
  cate! you look angerly.
  HECATE. Have I not reason, bel-
  dams as you are,
Saucy and overbold? How did you
  dare
To trade and traffic with Macbeth
In riddles and affairs of death;   5
And I, the mistress of your charms,
The close contriver of all harms,
Was never called to bear my part,
Or show the glory of our art?
And, which is worse, all you have
  done   10
Hath been but for a wayward son,
Spiteful and wrathful, who, as others
  do,
Loves for his own ends, not for you.

But make amends now. Get you
gone,
And at the pit of Acheron[104]   15
Meet me i' the morning; thither he
Will come to know his destiny;
Your vessels and your spells provide,
Your charms and every thing beside.
I am for the air; this night I'll
spend   20
Unto a dismal and a fatal end;
Great business must be wrought ere
noon;
Upon the corner of the moon
There hangs a vaporous drop pro-
found;
I'll catch it ere it come to ground;   25
And that distilled by magic sleights[105]
Shall raise such artificial sprites[106]
As by the strength of their illusion
Shall draw him on to his confusion.
He shall spurn fate, scorn death, and
bear   30
His hopes 'bove wisdom, grace and
fear.
And you all know, security[107]
Is mortals' chiefest enemy.
[*Music and a song within*: "Come
away, come away," etc.]
Hark! I am called; my little spirit, see,
Sits in a foggy cloud, and stays for
me.   [*Exit.*]   35
FIRST WITCH. Come, let's make
haste; she'll soon be back again.
[*Exeunt.*]

SCENE VI. *Forres. The palace.*

Enter LENNOX *and another* Lord.

LENNOX. My former speeches have
but hit your thoughts,
Which can interpret further; only,
I say,
Things have been strangely borne.
The gracious Duncan

Was pitied of Macbeth; marry,[108] he
was dead.
And the right-valiant Banquo walked
too late;   5
Whom, you may say, if 't please you,
Fleance killed,
For Fleance fled; men must not walk
too late.
Who cannot want the thought how
monstrous
It was for Malcolm and for Donal-
bain
To kill their gracious father?   Damn-
èd fact!   10
How it did grieve Macbeth! Did he
not straight
In pious rage the two delinquents tear,
That were the slaves of drink and
thralls of sleep?
Was not that nobly done?   Ay, and
wisely too;
For 't would have angered any heart
alive   15
To hear the men deny 't. So that,
I say,
He has borne all things well; and I
do think
That had he Duncan's sons under his
key—
As, an 't please heaven, he shall not—
they should find
What 'twere to kill a father; so should
Fleance.   20
But, peace! For from broad words and
'cause he failed
His presence at the tyrant's feast, I
hear
Macduff lives in disgrace.   Sir, can
you tell
Where he bestows himself?
LORD.   The son of Duncan,
From whom this tyrant holds the due
of birth,   25
Lives in the English court, and is
received
Of the most pious Edward with such
grace

104*Acheron* (ăk' ēr ŏn), river in
Hades.
105*sleights*, tricks.
106*sprites*, spirits.
107*security*, a feeling of security
makes people careless.

108*marry*, an oath, originally, *Virgin
Mary.*

That the malevolence of fortune no-
thing
Takes from his high respect; thither
Macduff
Is gone to pray the holy king, upon
his aid   30
To wake Northumberland and war-
like Siward,
That, by the help of these—with Him
above
To ratify the work—we may again
Give to our tables meat, sleep to our
nights,
Free from our feasts and banquets
bloody knives,   35
Do faithful homage and receive free
honors,
All which we pine for now; and this
report
Hath so exasperate the king that he
Prepares for some attempt of war.
LENNOX.   Sent he to Macduff?

LORD. He did; and with an abso-
lute "Sir, not I,"   40
The cloudy messenger turns me his
back,
And hums, as who should say "You'll
rue the time
That clogs me with this answer."
LENNOX.   And that well might
Advise him to a caution, to hold what
distance
His wisdom can provide. Some holy
angel   45
Fly to the court of England and un-
fold
His message ere he come, that a swift
blessing
May soon return to this our suffering
country
Under a hand accursed!
LORD. I'll send my prayers with
him.
                                  [*Exeunt.*]

For Thought and Discussion

ACT III

SCENE 1.

1. What does Banquo's speech reveal about his suspicions of Macbeth? Why does he not accuse Macbeth of foul play?
2. What does Macbeth learn about Banquo's plans?
3. Why does he fear Banquo? What excuses does he find for
   murdering Banquo?
4. Why does he employ murderers rather than commit the crime
   himself? Is this a wise plan? These murderers are soldiers who
   think that they have not been treated fairly. How does Macbeth incense them against Banquo? Why is Fleance included
   in the plot?

SCENE 2.

1. Why is Lady Macbeth unhappy?
2. Why does Macbeth now spend much time alone? How does
   Lady Macbeth try to prevent him from brooding over the
   past? What does he say about Duncan?
3. Why does he not tell her about the plot against Banquo?
4. Contrast Macbeth's independence of Lady Macbeth in the murder of Banquo with his dependence upon her in the murder of
   Duncan. What effect does the murder of Duncan finally have
   upon Macbeth and Lady Macbeth's love for each other?

SCENE 3.
1. What happens in this scene?
2. Why is the escape of Fleance considered the turning point in the play?

SCENE 4.
1. Why is Macbeth desperate when he learns of Fleance's escape? How does Lady Macbeth try to break up his fit of musing and cause him to remember his guests?
2. Why does Macbeth see Banquo's ghost? How is he affected? Does anyone else see the ghost? Has Macbeth been subject to hallucinations before? When? Do you recall Banquo's promise to come to the feast?
3. How does Lady Macbeth explain Macbeth's strange conduct to the guests? How does she attempt to restore his poise? What complaints does Macbeth make? What does he say that he does not fear? Why does Lady Macbeth dismiss the guests?
4. Is Macbeth able to sleep now? When was his unrest mentioned first?
5. How has Macbeth's character changed since the beginning of the play?

SCENE 5.
1. Why is Hecate angry? What fate does she plan for Macbeth? What does she say is "mortal's chiefest enemy"?

SCENE 6.
1. Of what do Lennox and other lords now suspect Macbeth?
2. Is there a suggestion of an uprising against him?

A Study of Significant Passages

Select and read aloud the significant lines in this act. The following suggestions may assist you in making your choice, as lines which show:

Thoughts of an honest and fair mind
A dishonest person's fear and jealousy of an honest one
A climax of events
A mental retribution for evil acts

Read aloud other passages of your own choice and explain their meaning and significance.

ACT IV

[Macbeth again seeks the witches, who call apparitions to foretell his future. The first apparition, a helmeted head, really representing Macbeth, warns him to "Beware Macduff." The second, a bloody child, representing the infant Macduff, tells Macbeth that none of woman born shall harm Macbeth. The third, a crowned child with a tree in its hand, representing Malcolm, assures him that he shall be safe until Birnam forest shall move against Dunsinane, Macbeth's castle. A line of ghostly kings appears, followed by Banquo's ghost. Macbeth determines to kill all who oppose him. He has Lady Macduff and her children killed but misses Macduff, because he has gone to England to persuade Malcolm to lead a revolt against Macbeth. The news of the murder of his wife and children impels Macduff to seek immediate revenge upon Macbeth. Macduff, Malcolm, and the English general Siward with his soldiers march into Scotland and attack Macbeth.]

SCENE I. *A cavern. In the middle, a boiling cauldron.*

Thunder. Enter the three Witches.

FIRST WITCH. Thrice the brinded[109] cat hath mewed.

SECOND WITCH. Thrice and once the hedge-pig whined.

THIRD WITCH. Harpier[110] cries, " 'Tis time, 'tis time."

FIRST WITCH. Round about the cauldron go;

In the poisoned entrails throw.   5
Toad that under cold stone
Days and nights has thirty-one
Sweltered venom sleeping got,
Boil thou first i' the charmèd pot.

ALL. Double, double toil and trouble;   10
Fire burn and cauldron bubble.

SECOND WITCH. Fillet of a fenny snake,

In the cauldron boil and bake;
Eye of newt[111] and toe of frog,
Wool of bat and tongue of dog,[15]
Adders fork[112] and blind-worm's sting,

Lizard's leg and howlet's[113] wing,
For a charm of powerful trouble,
Like a hell-broth boil and bubble.

ALL. Double, double toil and trouble;   20
Fire burn and cauldron bubble.

THIRD WITCH. Scale of dragon, tooth of wolf,

Witches' mummy, maw and gulf[114]
Of the ravined salt-sea shark,
Root of hemlock digged i' the dark, 25
Liver of blaspheming Jew,
Gall of goat, and slips of yew
Slivered in the moon's eclipse,
Nose of Turk and Tartar's lips,
Finger of birth-strangled babe   30
Ditch-delivered by a drab,
Make the gruel thick and slab;
Add thereto a tiger's chaudron,[115]
For the ingredients of our cauldron.

ALL. Double, double toil and trouble;   35
Fire burn and cauldron bubble.

SECOND WITCH. Cool it with a baboon's blood,

Then the charm is firm and good.

Enter HECATE *to the other three* Witches.

HECATE. Oh, well done! I commend your pains;

And every one shall share i' the gains;   40
And now about the cauldron sing,
Live elves and fairies in a ring,
Enchanting all that you put in.

[*Music and a song:* "Black spirits," &c. HECATE *retires.*]

SECOND WITCH. By the pricking of my thumbs,

Something wicked this way comes. 45
Open, locks,
Whoever knocks!

---

[109]*brinded,* brindled.
[110]*Harpier,* harpy, evil monster.
[111]*newt,* lizard.
[112]*fork,* tongue of adder, which is forked.

[113]*howlet,* owl.
[114]*gulf,* gullet.
[115]*chaudron,* entrails.

Enter MACBETH.

MACBETH. How now, you secret,
    black, and midnight hags!
What is 't you do?
    ALL.   A deed without a name.
    MACBETH. I conjure you, by that
        which you profess,   50
Howe'er you come to know it, answer
        me—
Though you untie the winds and let
        them fight
Against the churches; though the
        yesty waves
Confound and swallow navigation
        up;
Though bladed corn be lodged and
        trees blown down;   55
Though castles topple on their war-
        ders' heads;
Though palaces and pyramids do
        slope
Their heads to their foundations;
        though the treasure
Of nature's germens[116] tumble all to-
        gether,
Even till destruction sicken; answer
        me   60
To what I ask you.
    FIRST WITCH.   Speak.
    SECOND WITCH.   Demand.
    THIRD WITCH.   We'll answer.
    FIRST WITCH. Say, if thou 'dst
        rather hear it from our mouths,
Or from our masters?
    MACBETH.   Call 'em; let me see
        'em.
    FIRST WITCH. Pour in sow's blood,
        that hath eaten
Her nine farrow,[117] grease that's
        sweaten   65
From the murderer's gibbet throw
Into the flame.
    ALL.   Come, high or low;
Thyself and office deftly show!

"How now, you se-
cret, black, and
midnight hags!
What is it you
do?

---

[116]*germens,* fruitful seeds.
[117]*farrow,* litter of pigs.

Thunder. First Apparition: *an armed Head.*

MACBETH. Tell me, thou unknown power—

FIRST WITCH.   He knows thy thought;

Hear his speech, but say thou naught.   70

FIRST APPARITION. Macbeth! Macbeth! Macbeth! Beware Macduff; Beware the thane of Fife. Dismiss me. Enough.

[*Descends.*]

MACBETH. Whate'er thou art, for thy good caution, thanks;

Thou hast harped my fear aright; but one word more—

FIRST WITCH. He will not be commanded; here's another,   75

More potent than the first.

Thunder. Second Apparition: *a bloody* Child.

SECOND APPARITION.   Macbeth! Macbeth! Macbeth!

MACBETH.   Had I three ears, I 'ld hear thee.

SECOND APPARITION. Be bloody, bold, and resolute; laugh to scorn

The power of man, for none of woman born   80

Shall harm Macbeth.

[*Descends.*]

MACBETH. Then live, Macduff. What need I fear of thee?

But yet I'll make assurance doubly sure,

And take a bond of fate; thou shalt not live,

That I may tell pale-hearted fear it lies,   85

And sleep in spite of thunder.

Thunder. Third Apparition: *a* Child *crowned, with a tree in his hand.*

What is this

That rises like the issue of a king,

And wears upon his baby-brow the round

And top of sovereignty?

ALL.   Listen, but speak not to 't.

THIRD APPARITION. Be lion-mettled, proud; and take no care   90

Who chafes, who frets, or where conspirers are;

Macbeth shall never vanquished be until

Great Birnam wood to high Dunsinane hill

Shall come against him. [*Descends.*]

MACBETH.   That will never be.

Who can impress the forest, bid the tree   95

Unfix his earth-bound root? Sweet bodements![118] Good!

Rebellion's head rise never till the wood

Of Birnam rise, and our high-placed Macbeth

Shall live the lease of nature, pay his breath

To time and mortal custom.   Yet my heart   100

Throbs to know one thing: tell me, if your art

Can tell so much, shall Banquo's issue ever

Reign in this kingdom?

ALL.   Seek to know no more.

MACBETH. I will be satisfied! Deny me this,

And an eternal curse fall on you! Let me know.   105

Why sinks that cauldron? And what noise is this?

[*Hautboys.*]

FIRST WITCH. Show!

SECOND WITCH. Show!

THIRD WITCH. Show!

ALL. Show his eyes, and grieve his heart;   110

Come like shadows, so depart!

---

[118]*bodements,* prophecies.

[*A show of* Eight Kings, *the last with a glass in his hand;* BANQUO's Ghost *following.*]

MACBETH. Thou art too like the spirit of Banquo; down!
Thy crown does sear mine eye-balls. And thy hair,
Thou other gold-bound brow, is like the first.
A third is like the former. Filthy hags!   115
Why do you show me this? A fourth? Start, eyes!
What, will the line stretch out to the crack of doom?
Another yet! A seventh! I'll see no more.
And yet the eighth appears, who bears a glass
Which shows me many more; and some I see   120
That two-fold balls[119] and treble scepters carry
Horrible sight! Now, I see, 'tis true;
For the blood-boltered[120] Banquo smiles upon me,
And points at them for his. [*Apparitions vanish.*] What, is this so?
FIRST WITCH. Ay, sir, all this is so. But why   125
Stands Macbeth thus amazedly?
Come, sisters, cheer we up his sprites,
And show the best of our delights;
I'll charm the air to give a sound,
While you perform your antic round,[121]   130
That this great king may kindly say
Our duties did his welcome pay.

[*Music. The* Witches *dance, and then vanish, with* HECATE.]

———
[119]*two-fold balls*, emblems of sovereignty, foretelling the double crowning of James I at Scone as king of Scotland and at Westminster Abbey as King of England.
[120]*blood-boltered*, blood clotted.
[121]*antic round*, quaint circle.

MACBETH. Where are they? Gone? Let this pernicious hour
Stand aye accursèd in the calendar!
Come in, without there!

[*Enter* LENNOX.]

LENNOX.   What's your grace's will?   135
MACBETH. Saw you the weird sisters?
LENNOX.   No, my lord.
MACBETH. Came they not by you?
LENNOX.   No, indeed, my lord.
MACBETH. Infected be the air whereon they ride;
And damned all those that trust them! I did hear
The galloping of horse; who was 't came by?   140
LENNOX. 'Tis two or three, my lord, that bring you word Macduff is fled to England.
MACBETH.   Fled to England!
LENNOX. Ay, my good lord.
MACBETH. Time, thou anticipatest[122] my dread exploits.
The flighty purpose never is o'ertook   145
Unless the deed go with it; from this moment
The very firstlings of my heart shall be
The firstlings of my hand. And even now,
To crown my thoughts with acts, be it thought and done.
The castle of Macduff I will surprise;   150
Seize upon Fife; give to the edge o' the sword
His wife, his babes, and all unfortunate souls
That trace him in his line. No boasting like a fool:
This deed I'll do before this purpose cool.
But no more sights!—Where are these gentlemen?   155

———
[122]*anticipatest*, foresees.

Come, bring me where they are.

[*Exeunt.*]

SCENE II. *Fife*. MACDUFF's *castle*.

Enter LADY MACDUFF, *her* Son, *and*
Ross.

LADY MACDUFF. What had he done
to make him fly the land?

Ross. You must have patience,
madam.

LADY MACDUFF.   He had none;
His flight was madness; when our
actions do not,
Our fears do make us traitors.

Ross.   You know not
Whether it was his wisdom or his
fear.   5

LADY MACDUFF. Wisdom! To leave
his wife, to leave his babes,
His mansion and his titles in a place
From whence himself does fly? He
loves us not;
He wants the natural touch[123]; for
the poor wren,
The most diminutive of birds, will
fight,   10
Her young ones in her nest, against
the owl.
All is the fear and nothing is the love;
As little is the wisdom, where the
flight
So runs against all reason.

Ross.   My dearest coz,
I pray you, school yourself; but for
your husband;   15
He is noble, wise, judicious, and best
knows
The fits o' the season.[124] I dare not
speak much further;
But cruel are the times, when we are
traitors
And do not know ourselves, when we
hold rumor
From what we fear, yet know not
what we fear,   20

But float upon a wild and violent sea
Each way and move. I take my leave
of you.
Shall not be long but I'll be here
again.
Things at the worst will cease, or else
climb upward
To what they were before. My pret-
ty cousin,   25
Blessing upon you!

LADY MACDUFF.   Fathered he is,
and yet he's fatherless.

Ross. I am so much a fool, should
I stay longer,
It would be my disgrace and your dis-
comfort;
I take my leave at once.   [*Exit.*]

LADY MACDUFF.   Sirrah, your
father's dead.   30
And what will you do now? How
will you live?

SON. As birds do, mother.

LADY MACDUFF.   What, with
worms and flies?

SON. With what I get, I mean;
and so do they.

LADY MACDUFF. Poor bird! thou
'ldst never fear the net nor
lime,[125]
The pitfall nor the gin.[126]   35

SON. Why should I, mother? Poor
birds they are not set for.
My father is not dead, for all your
saying.

LADY MACDUFF. Yes, he is dead.
How wilt thou do for a father?

SON. Nay, how will you do for a
husband?

LADY MACDUFF. Why, I can buy
me twenty at any market.   40

SON. Then you'll buy 'em to sell
again.

LADY MACDUFF. Thou speak'st
with all thy wit; and yet, i' faith,
With wit enough for thee.

---

[123]*natural touch*, affection.
[124]*fits o' the season*, the times or
what is best.

[125]*lime*, a substance used for ensnar-
ing birds.
[126]*gin*, trap.

SON. Was my father a traitor, mother?

LADY MACDUFF. Ay, that he was. [45]

SON. What is a traitor?

LADY MACDUFF. Why, one that swears and lies.

SON. And be all traitors that do so?

LADY MACDUFF. Every one that does so is a traitor, and must be hanged. [50]

SON. And must they all be hanged that swear and lie?

LADY MACDUFF. Every one.

SON. Who must hang them?

LADY MACDUFF. Why, the honest men. [54]

SON. Then the liars and swearers are fools, for there are liars and swearers enow to beat the honest men and hang up them.

LADY MACDUFF. Now, God help thee, poor monkey! But how wilt thou do for a father? [60]

SON. If he were dead, you'd weep for him; if you would not, it were a good sign that I should quickly have a new father.

LADY MACDUFF. Poor prattler, how thou talk'st!

Enter a Messenger.

MESSENGER. Bless you, fair dame! I am not to you known, [65] Though in your state of honor I am perfect.

I doubt some danger does approach you nearly.

If you will take a homely man's advice, Be not found here; hence, with your little ones.

To fright you thus, methinks, I am too savage; [70]

To do worse to you were fell cruelty, Which is too nigh your person. Heaven preserve you!

I dare abide no longer.

[*Exit.*]

LADY MACDUFF. Whither should I fly?

I have done no harm. But I remember now

I am in this earthly world, where to do harm [75]

Is often laudable, to do good sometime

Accounted dangerous folly. Why then, alas,

Do I put up that womanly defence, To say I have done no harm?

Enter Murderers.

What are these faces?

FIRST MURDERER. Where is your husband? [80]

LADY MACDUFF. I hope in no place so unsanctified

Where such as thou may'st find him.

FIRST MURDERER. He's a traitor.

SON. Thou liest, thou shag-haired[127] villain!

FIRST MURDERER. What, you egg!

[*Stabbing him.*]

Young fry of treachery!

SON. He has killed me, Mother!

Run away, I pray you! [85]

[*Dies.*]

[*Exit* LADY MACDUFF, *crying* "Murder!" *Exeunt* Murderers *following her.*]

SCENE III. *England. Before the king's palace.*

Enter MALCOLM *and* MACDUFF.

MALCOLM. Let us seek out some desolate shade, and there

Weep our sad bosoms empty.

MACDUFF.   Let us rather

Hold fast the mortal sword, and like good men

Bestride our down-fallen birthdom.[128]

Each new morn

New widows howl, new orphans cry, new sorrows [5]

---

[127]*shag-haired,* coarse haired.
[128]*down-fallen birthdom,* down-fallen country, Scotland.

Strike heaven on the face, that it re-
sounds
As if it felt with Scotland and yelled
out
Like syllable of dolor.
MALCOLM.   What I believe I'll
wail,
What know believe, and what I can
redress,
As I shall find the time to friend, I
will.   10
What you have spoke, it may be so
perchance.
This tyrant, whose sole name[129] blis-
ters our tongues,
Was once thought honest; you have
loved him well;
He hath not touched you yet. I am
young; but something
You may deserve of him through me,
and wisdom   15
To offer up a weak poor innocent
lamb
To appease an angry god.
MACDUFF. I am not treacherous.
MALCOLM.   But Macbeth is.
A good and virtuous nature may re-
coil
In an imperial charge. But I shall
crave your pardon;   20
That which you are my thoughts can-
not transpose.
Angels are bright still, though the
brightest fell.
Though all things foul would wear
the brows of grace,
Yet grace must still look so.
MACDUFF.   I have lost my hopes.
MALCOLM. Perchance even there
where I did find my doubts.   25
Why in that rawness[130] left you wife
and child,
Those precious motives, those strong
knots of love,
Without leave-taking? I pray you,

Let not my jealousies be your dis-
honors,
But mine own safeties. You may be
rightly just,   30
Whatever I shall think.
MACDUFF.   Bleed, bleed, poor
country!
Great tyranny, lay thou thy basis
sure,
For goodness dare not check thee!
Wear thou thy wrongs;
The title is affeered![131] Fare thee well,
lord.
I would not be the villain that thou
think'st   35
For the whole space that's in the ty-
rant's grasp,
And the rich East to boot.
MALCOLM.   Be not offended;
I speak not as in absolute fear of you.
I think our country sinks beneath
the yoke;
It weeps, it bleeds; and each new day
a gash   40
Is added to her wounds. I think
withal
There would be hands uplifted in my
right;
And here from gracious England
have I offer
Of goodly thousands; but, for all
this,
When I shall tread upon the tyrant's
head,   45
Or wear it on my sword, yet my poor
country
Shall have more vices than it had be-
fore,
More suffer and more sundry ways
than ever,
By him that shall succeed.
MACDUFF.   What should he be?
MALCOLM. It is myself I mean; in
whom I know   50
All the particulars of vice so grafted
That, when they shall be opened,
black Macbeth

---

[129]*sole name*, name alone.
[130]*rawness*, unprotected state.

[131]*affeered*, confirmed.

Will seem as pure as snow, and the
     poor state
Esteem him as a lamb, being compared
With my confineless harms.
     MACDUFF.   Not in the legions [55]
Of horrid hell can come a devil more
     damned
In evils to top Macbeth.
     MALCOLM.   I grant him bloody,
Luxurious, avaricious, false, deceit-
     ful,
Sudden, malicious, smacking of every
     sin
That has a name; but there's no bot-
     tom, none,   [60]
In my voluptuousness .... and my
     desire
All continent impediments would
     o'erbear
That did oppose my will. Better Mac-
     beth
Than such an one to reign.
     MACDUFF.   Boundless intem-
     perance
In nature is a tyranny; it hath been
The untimely emptying of the happy
     throne
And fall of many kings. But fear
     not yet
To take upon you what is yours; you [70]
     may
Convey your pleasures in a spacious
     plenty,
And yet seem cold, the time you may
     so hoodwink.
     MALCOLM.   With this there
     grows
In my most ill-composed affection
     such
A stanchless avarice that, were I king,
I should cut off the nobles for their
     lands,
Desire his jewels, and this other's
     house;   [80]
And my more-having would be as a
     sauce
To make me hunger more, that I
     should forge

Quarrels unjust against the good and
     loyal,
Destroying them for wealth.
     MACDUFF.   This avarice
Sticks deeper, grows with more perni-
     cious root   [85]
Than summer-seeming lust, and it
     hath been
The sword of our slain kings; yet do
     not fear;
Scotland hath foisons[132] to fill up your
     will,
Of your mere own; all these are por-
     table,[133]
With other graces weighed.   [90]
     MALCOLM. But I have none; the
     king-becoming graces,
As justice, verity, temperance, stable-
     ness,
Bounty, perseverance, mercy, lowli-
     ness,
Devotion, patience, courage, forti-
     tude,
I have no relish of them, but
     abound   [95]
In the division of each several crime.
Acting in many ways. Nay, had I
     power, I should
Pour the sweet milk of concord into
     hell,
Uproar[134] the universal peace, con-
     found
All unity of earth.
     MACDUFF.   O Scotland, Scot-
     land!   [100]
     MALCOLM. If such a one be fit to
     govern, speak;
I am as I have spoken.
     MACDUFF.   Fit to govern!
No, not to live. O nation miserable,
With an untitled tyrant bloody-scep-
     tered,
When shalt thou see thy wholesome
     days again,   [105]
Since that the truest issue of thy
     throne

132*foisons*, abundance, stores.
133*portable*, bearable.
134*uproar*, put in uproar.

By his own interdiction[135] stands accursed,

And does blaspheme his breed? Thy royal father

Was a most sainted king; the queen that bore thee,

Oftener upon her knees than on her feet,   110

Died every day she lived.[136] Fare thee well!

These evils thou repeat'st upon thyself

Have banished me from Scotland. O my breast,

Thy hope ends here!

MALCOLM.   Macduff, this noble passion,

Child of integrity, hath from my soul   115

Wiped the black scruples, reconciled my thoughts

To thy good truth and honor. Devilish Macbeth

By many of these trains[137] hath sought to win me

Into his power, and modest wisdom plucks me

From over-credulous haste; but God above   120

Deal between thee and me! For even now

I put myself to thy direction, and

Unspeak mine own detraction, here abjure

The taints and blames I laid upon myself,

For strangers to my nature. I am yet   125

Unknown to woman, never was forsworn,

Scarcely have coveted what was mine own,

At no time broke my faith, would not betray

The devil to his fellow and delight

No less in truth than life; my first false speaking   130

Was this upon myself. What I am truly,

Is thine and my poor country's to command;

Whither indeed, before thy hereapproach,

Old Siward, with ten thousand warlike men,

Already at a point,[138] was setting forth.   135

Now we'll together; and the chance of goodness

Be like our warranted quarrel! Why are you silent?

MACDUFF. Such welcome and unwelcome things at once

'Tis hard to reconcile.

Enter a Doctor.

MALCOLM. Well; more anon.— Comes the king forth, I pray you?   140

DOCTOR. Ay, sir; there are a crew of wretched souls

That stay his cure; their malady convinces

The great assay of art[139]; but at his touch[140]—

Such sanctity hath heaven given his hand—

They presently amend.

MALCOLM. I thank you, doctor.   145
[*Exit* Doctor.]

MACDUFF. What's the disease he means?

MALCOLM.   'Tis called the evil;

A most miraculous work in this good king;

---

[135]*interdiction,* confession, admission.

[136]*died every day she lived,* crucified her spirit in humility to God, was godly and devout.

[137]*trains,* tricks.

[138]*point,* gathered together.

[139]*assay of art,* defies skill of physicians.

[140]*touch,* the king was supposed to be able to cure scrofula with his royal touch.

Which often, since my here-remain
  in England,
I have seen him do. How he solicits
  heaven,
Himself best knows; but strangely-
  visited people,   150
All swoln and ulcerous, pitiful to the
  eye,
The mere despair of surgery, he cures,
Hanging a golden stamp about their
  necks,
Put on with holy prayers; and 'tis
  spoken,
To the succeeding royalty he leaves 155
The healing benediction. With this
  strange virtue,
He hath a heavenly gift of prophecy,
And sundry blessings hang about his
  throne,
That speak him full of grace.

Enter Ross.

MACDUFF.   See, who comes
  here?
MALCOLM. My countryman; but
  yet I know him not.   160
MACDUFF. My ever-gentle cousin,
  welcome hither.
MALCOLM. I know him now. Good
  God, betimes remove
The means that makes us strangers!
Ross.   Sir, amen.
MACDUFF. Stands Scotland where
  it did?
Ross.   Alas, poor country!
Almost afraid to know itself. It can-
  not   165
Be called our mother, but our grave;
  where nothing,
But who knows nothing, is once seen
  to smile;
Where sighs and groans and shrieks
  that rend the air
Are made, not marked; where vio-
  lent sorrow seems
A modern ecstasy. The dead man's
  knell   170
Is there scarce asked for who; and
  good men's lives

Expire before the flowers in their
  caps,
Dying or ere they sicken.
MACDUFF.   O, relation
Too nice, and yet too true!
MALCOLM.   What's the new-
  est grief?
Ross. That of an hour's age doth
  hiss the speaker;   175
Each minute teems[141] a new one.
MACDUFF.   How does my
  wife?
Ross. Why, well.
MACDUFF.   And all my chil-
  dren?
Ross.   Well too.
MACDUFF. The tyrant has not bat-
  tered at their peace?
Ross. No; they were well at peace
  when I did leave 'em.
MACDUFF. Be not a niggard of
  your speech. How goes 't?   180
Ross. When I came hither to
  transport the tidings,
Which I have heavily borne, there ran
  a rumor
Of many worthy fellows that were
  out;
Which was to my belief witnessed
  the rather,
For that I saw the tyrant's power
  a-foot.   185
Now is the time of help; your eye in
  Scotland
Would create soldiers, make our wo-
  men fight,
To doff[142] their dire distresses.
MALCOLM.   Be 't their com-
  fort.
We are coming thither. Gracious
  England hath
Lent us good Siward and ten thou-
  sand men;   190
An older and a better soldier none
That Christendom gives out.
Ross.   Would I could answer

---

[141]*teems*, starts.
[142]*doff*, free themselves.

This comfort with the like! But I
have words
That would be howled out in the
desert air,
Where hearing should not latch them.
MACDUFF.   What concern
they?   195
The general cause? or is it a fee-
grief[143]
Due to some single breast?
ROSS.   No mind that's honest
But in it shares some woe; though the
main part
Pertains to you alone.
MACDUFF.   If it be mine,
Keep it not from me, quickly let me
have it.   200
ROSS. Let not your ears despise my
tongue forever,
Which shall possess them with the
heaviest sound
That ever yet they heard.
MACDUFF.   Hum! I guess at it.
ROSS. Your castle is surprised;
your wife and babes
Savagely slaughtered; to relate the
manner,   205
Were, on the quarry of these mur-
dered deer,
To add the death of you.
MALCOLM.   Merciful heaven!
What, man! ne'er pull your hat upon
your brows;
Give sorrow words; the grief that
does not speak
Whispers the o'er-fraught heart and
bids it break.   210
MACDUFF. My children too?
ROSS.   Wife, children, serv-
ants, all
That could be found.
MACDUFF.   And I must be from
thence!
My wife killed too?
ROSS.   I have said.
MALCOLM.   Be comforted.

---

[143]*fee-grief*, personal.

Let's make us medicines of our great
revenge,
To cure this deadly grief.   215
MACDUFF. He has no children. All
my pretty ones?
Did you say all? O hell-kite! All?
What, all my pretty chickens and
their dam
At one fell swoop?
MALCOLM. Dispute it like a man.
MACDUFF.   I shall
do so: 220
But I must also feel it as a man.
I cannot but remember such things
were,
That were most precious to me. Did
heaven look on,
And would not take their part? Sin-
ful Macduff,
They were all struck for thee! Naught
that I am,   225
Not for their own demerits, but for
mine,
Fell slaughter on their souls. Heaven
rest them now!
MALCOLM. Be this the whetstone
of your sword; let grief
Convert to anger; blunt not the heart,
enrage it.
MACDUFF. O, I could play the
woman with mine eyes   230
And braggart with my tongue! But,
gentle heavens,
Cut short all intermission; front to
front
Bring thou this fiend of Scotland and
myself;
Within my sword's length set him;
if he 'scape,
Heaven forgive him too!
MALCOLM.   This tune goes
manly.   235
Come, go we to the king; our power
is ready;
Our lack is nothing but our leave.
Macbeth
Is ripe for shaking, and the powers
above

Put on their instruments.   Receive The night is long that never finds
    what cheer you may;   the day.   [*Exeunt.*] 240

For Thought and Discussion

ACT IV

SCENE 1.
1. Describe the stage setting.
2. Why are the ingredients of the witches' cauldron described?
3. Why does Macbeth consult the witches again?   Does he now consider them good or evil?   How does he greet them?
4. What is the first apparition summoned by the witches?   What does it represent?   What warning does it give Macbeth?
5. What is the second apparition?   What does it represent?   What advice and assurance does it give?
6. What is the third apparition?   What does it represent?   What promises of security does it give Macbeth?   Are the assurances made in good faith or merely to deceive him and lead him astray?
7. To what question does Macbeth demand an answer?   Why is Banquo's ghost shown?   What is Macbeth's attitude now toward all real or fancied opposition?   What change in his character is now evident?   Did he already have evil designs in his mind?   Whom does he plan to attack first?

SCENE 2.
1. What news is brought to Lady Macduff?
2. Notice the ironic humor in this scene.
   Compare the murder in this scene with the first one committed. How has Macbeth's character changed?

SCENE 3.
1. Why does Malcolm distrust Macduff?   Why does he describe himself as a demon?
2. When does Malcolm become convinced of Macduff's integrity and love for Scotland?
3. Can you find a reason for introducing the doctor in this scene?
4. What news does Ross bring to Macduff?   What is its effect upon Macduff?
5. What support from England does Malcolm have?   What do Malcolm and Macduff plan to do?

A Study of Significant Passages

Select and read aloud the significant lines in this act. The following suggestions may assist you in making your choice, as lines which show:

Evil nature of witches
Results of evil deeds

Read aloud other passages of your own choice and explain their meaning and significance.

ACT V

[Lady Macbeth walks in her sleep, talking disjointedly of the various crimes committed. As the English soldiers pass Birnam wood, they hew boughs from the trees and march on toward Dunsinane hill. The English soldiers are joined by many Scotch soldiers. The death of Lady Macbeth is announced, and Macbeth resolves to take part in the conflict. On the battlefield he meets and kills young Siward. Eventually he is slain by Macduff. Malcolm is declared king.]

SCENE I. *Dunsinane. Ante-room in the castle.*

Enter a Doctor of Physic *and a* Waiting-Gentlewoman.

DOCTOR. I have two nights watched with you, but can perceive no truth in your report. When was it she last walked?   4

GENTLEWOMAN. Since his majesty went into the field, I have seen her rise from her bed, throw her nightgown upon her, unlock her closet, take forth paper, fold it, write upon 't, read it, afterwards seal it, and again return to bed; yet all this while in a most fast sleep.   12

DOCTOR. A great perturbation in nature, to receive at once the benefit of sleep, and do the effects of watching! In this slumbery agitation, besides her walking and other actual performances, what, at any time, have you heard her say?   19

GENTLEWOMAN. That, sir, which I will not report after her.

DOCTOR. You may to me; and 'tis most meet you should.

GENTLEWOMAN. Neither to you nor any one, having no witness to confirm my speech.   26

Enter LADY MACBETH, *with a taper.*

Lo, you, here she comes! This is her very guise; and, upon my life, fast asleep. Observe her; stand close.

DOCTOR. How came she by that light?   31

GENTLEWOMAN. Why, it stood by her; she has light by her continually; 'tis her command.

DOCTOR. You see, her eyes are open.   36

GENTLEWOMAN. Ay, but their sense is shut.

DOCTOR. What is it she does now? Look, how she rubs her hands.   40

GENTLEWOMAN. It is an accustomed action with her, to seem thus washing her hands. I have known her continue in this a quarter of an hour.   45

LADY MACBETH. Yet here's a spot.

DOCTOR. Hark! she speaks. I will set down what comes from her, to satisfy my remembrance the more strongly.   50

LADY MACBETH. Out, damned spot! out, I say!—One; two; why, then, 'tis time to do 't.—Hell is murky!—Fie, my lord, fie! A soldier, and afeard? What need we fear who knows it, when none can call our power to account?—Yet who would have thought the old man to have had so much blood in him.   59

DOCTOR. Do you mark that?

LADY MACBETH. The thane of Fife had a wife. Where is she now?— What, will these hands ne'er be clean? —No more o' that, my lord, no more o' that; you mar all with this starting.   66

DOCTOR. Go to, go to; you have known what you should not.

GENTLEWOMAN. She has spoke what she should not, I am sure of that; heaven knows what she has known.

LADY MACBETH. Here's the smell of the blood still; all the perfumes of Arabia will not sweeten this little hand. Oh, oh, oh! [76]

DOCTOR. What a sigh is there! The heart is sorely charged.

GENTLEWOMAN. I would not have such a heart in my bosom for the dignity of the whole body. [81]

DOCTOR. Well, well, well—

GENTLEWOMAN. Pray God it be, sir.

DOCTOR. This disease is beyond my practice; yet I have known those which have walked in their sleep who have died holily in their beds. [88]

LADY MACBETH. Wash your hands, put on your nightgown; look not so pale.—I tell you yet again, Banquo's buried; he cannot come out on 's grave.

DOCTOR. Even so? [94]

LADY MACBETH. To bed, to bed! There's knocking at the gate; come, come, come, come, give me your hand. What's done cannot be undone.—To bed, to bed, to bed! [*Exit.*]

DOCTOR. Will she go now to bed?

GENTLEWOMAN. Directly. [101]

DOCTOR. Foul whisperings are
  abroad; unnatural deeds
Do breed unnatural troubles; infected
  minds [105]
To their deaf pillows will discharge
  their secrets;
More needs she the divine than the
  physician.
God, God forgive us all! Look after
  her; [111]
Remove from her the means of all annoyance,
And still keep eyes upon her. So,
  good night; [115]
My mind she has mated,[144] and
  amazed my sight.

"Here's the smell of
  blood still:
All the perfumes
of Arabia will not
sweeten this little
hand. Oh, oh, oh!"

---

[144]*mated*, amazed, confounded.

I think, but dare not speak.

GENTLEWOMAN.   Good night, good doctor.

[*Exeunt.*]

SCENE II.   *The Country near Dunsinane.*

Drum and colors. Enter MENTEITH, CAITHNESS, ANGUS, LENNOX, *and* Soldiers.

MENTEITH.   The English power is near, led on by Malcolm,
His uncle Siward and the good Macduff.
Revenges burn in them; for their dear causes
Would to the bleeding and the grim alarm
Excite the mortified man.
ANGUS.   Near Birnam wood ⁵
Shall we well meet them; that way are they coming.
CAITHNESS. Who knows if Donalbain be with his brother?
LENNOX.   For certain, sir, he is not; I have a file
Of all the gentry.   There is Siward's son,
And many unrough youths that even now ¹⁰
Protest their first of manhood.
MENTEITH.   What does the tyrant?
CAITHNESS.   Great Dunsinane he strongly fortifies.
Some say he's mad; others that lesser hate him
Do call it valiant fury; but, for certain,
He cannot buckle his distempered cause ¹⁵
Within the belt of rule.
ANGUS.   Now does he feel
His secret murders sticking on his hands;
Now minutely¹⁴⁵ revolts upbraid his faith-breach;

Those he commands move only in command,
Nothing in love; now does he feel his title ²⁰
Hang loose about him, like a giant's robe
Upon a dwarfish thief.
MENTEITH.   Who then shall blame
His pestered¹⁴⁶ senses to recoil and start,
When all that is within him does condemn
Itself for being there?
CAITHNESS.   Well, march we on, ²⁵
To give obedience where 'tis truly owed.
Meet we the medicine of the sickly weal,
And with him pour we in our country's purge
Each drop of us.
LENNOX.   Or so much as it needs,
To dew the sovereign flower and drown the weeds. ³⁰
Make we our march towards Birnam.
[*Exeunt, marching.*]

SCENE III.   *Dunsinane.   A room in the castle.*

Enter MACBETH, DOCTOR, *and* ATTENDANTS.

MACBETH.   Bring me no more reports; let them fly all.
Till Birnam wood remove to Dunsinane,
I cannot taint with fear.   What's the boy Malcolm?
Was he not born of woman?   The spirits that know
All mortal consequences have pronounced me thus: ⁵
"Fear not, Macbeth; no man that's born of woman

---

¹⁴⁵*minutely,* constantly.

¹⁴⁶*pestered,* disturbed, irritated.

Shall e'er have power upon thee."
Then fly, false thanes,
And mingle with the English epi-
cures;
The mind I sway by[147] and the heart
I bear
Shall never sag with doubt nor shake
with fear. 10

Enter a SERVANT.

The devil damn thee black, thou
cream-faced loon!
Where got'st thou that goose look?
SERVANT. There is ten thousand—
MACBETH. Geese, villain?
SERVANT. Soldiers, sir.
MACBETH. Go prick thy face, and
over-red thy fear,
Thou lily-livered[148] boy. What sol-
diers, patch?[149] 15
Death of thy soul! those linen cheeks
of thine
Are counselors to fear. What sol-
diers, whey-face?
SERVANT. The English force, so
please you.
MACBETH. Take thy face hence.
[*Exit* SERVANT.]
Seyton!—I am sick at
heart,
When I behold—Seyton, I say!—
This push[150] 20
Will cheer me ever, or disseat me now.
I have lived long enough; my way of
life
Is fallen into the sear, the yellow leaf;
And that which should accompany
old age,
As honor, love, obedience, troops of
friends, 25
I must not look to have; but, in their
stead,
Curses, not loud but deep, mouth-
honor, breath,
Which the poor heart would fain
deny, and dare not.
Seyton!

Enter SEYTON.

SEYTON. What is your gracious
pleasure?
MACBETH. What news
more? 30
SEYTON. All is confirmed, my
lord, which was reported.
MACBETH. I'll fight till from my
bones my flesh be hacked.
Give me my armor.
SEYTON. 'Tis not needed yet.
MACBETH. I'll put it on.
Send out moe horses; skirr[151] the
country round; 35
Hang those that talk of fear. Give
me mine armor.
How does your patient, doctor?
DOCTOR. Not so sick, my
lord,
As she is troubled with thick-coming
fancies,
That keep her from her rest.
MACBETH. Cure her of
that.
Canst thou not minister to a mind
diseased, 40
Pluck from the memory a rooted sor-
row,
Raze out the written troubles of the
brain,
And with some sweet oblivious anti-
dote
Cleanse the stuffed bosom of that
perilous stuff
Which weighs upon the heart?
DOCTOR. Therein the
patient 45
Must minister to himself.
MACBETH. Throw physic to the
dogs; I'll none of it.
Come, put mine armor on; give me
my staff.[152]

---

[147]*sway by,* am ruled by.
[148]*lily-livered,* cowardly.
[149]*patch,* fool.
[150]*push,* attack.

---

[151]*skirr,* scour.
[152]*staff,* lance.

Seyton, send out. Doctor, the thanes
fly from me.
Come, sir, dispatch.[153] If thou couldst,
doctor, cast   50
The water of my land, find her dis-
ease,
And purge it to a sound and pristine
health,
I would applaud thee to the very echo,
That should applaud again.—Pull 't
off, I say.—
What rhubarb, senna, or what purga-
tive drug,   55
Would scour these English hence?
Hear'st thou of them?
    DOCTOR. Ay, my good lord; your
    royal preparation
Makes us hear something.
    MACBETH.   Bring it after
    me.
I will not be afraid of death and
bane,
Till Birnam forest come to Duns-
inane.   60
    DOCTOR. [Aside] Were I from
    Dunsinane away and clear,
Profit again should hardly draw me
here.
                            [Exeunt.]

SCENE IV. Country near Birnam
wood.

Drum and colors. Enter MALCOLM,
old SIWARD and his SON, MACDUFF,
MENTEITH, CAITHNESS, ANGUS,
LENNOX, ROSS, and SOLDIERS, marching.

    MALCOLM. Cousins, I hope the
    days are near at hand
That chambers will be safe.
    MENTEITH.   We doubt it
    nothing.
    SIWARD. What wood is this before
    us?
    MENTEITH.   The wood of
    Birnam.

---

[153]dispatch, haste.

    MALCOLM. Let every soldier hew
    him down a bough
And bear 't before him; thereby shall
we shadow   5
The numbers of our host and make
discovery
Err in report of us.
    SOLDIERS.   It shall be done.
    SIWARD. We learn no other but
    the confident tyrant
Keeps still in Dunsinane, and will en-
dure
Our setting down before 't.
    MALCOLM.   'Tis his main
    hope;   10
For where there is advantage to be
given,
Both more and less have given him
the revolt,
And none serve with him but con-
strainèd things
Whose hearts are absent too.
    MACDUFF.   Let our just
    censures
Attend the true event, and put we
on   15
Industrious soldiership.
    SIWARD.   The time ap-
    proaches
That will with due decision make us
know
What we shall say we have and what
we owe.
Thoughts speculative their unsure
hopes relate,
But certain issue strokes must arbi-
trate,   20
Towards which advance the war.
                    [Exeunt, marching.]

SCENE V. Dunsinane. Within the
castle.

Enter MACBETH, SEYTON, and
SOLDIERS with drum and colors.

    MACBETH. Hang out our banners
    on the outward walls;
The cry is still "They come"; our
castle's strength

Will laugh a siege to scorn. Here
let them lie
Till famine and the ague eat them
up;
Were they not forced[154] with those
that should be ours,   5
We might have met them dareful,
beard to beard,
And beat them backward home.
      [*A cry of women within.*]
      What is that noise?
SEYTON.   It is the cry of women,
my good lord.
                        [*Exit.*]
MACBETH.   I have almost forgot
the taste of fears.
The time has been, my senses would
have cooled   10
To hear a night-shriek; and my fell
of hair
Would at a dismal treatise[155] rouse and
stir
As life were in 't; I have supped full
with horrors.
Direness, familiar to my slaughterous
thoughts,
Cannot once start me.

            Re-enter SEYTON.

      Wherefore was that cry?   15
SEYTON.   The queen, my lord, is
dead.
MACBETH.   She should have died
hereafter;
There would have been a time for
such a word.
Tomorrow, and tomorrow, and to-
morrow,
Creeps in this petty pace from day to
day   20
To the last syllable of recorded time,
And all our yesterdays have lighted
fools
The way to dusty death. Out, out,
brief candle!

Life's but a walking shadow, a poor
player
That struts and frets his hour upon
the stage   25
And then is heard no more; it is a
tale
Told by an idiot, full of sound and
fury,
Signifying nothing.

            Enter a MESSENGER.

Thou comest to use thy tongue; thy
story quickly.
MESSENGER.   Gracious my lord,   30
I should report that which I say I
saw,
But know not how to do it.
MACBETH.   Well, say, sir.
MESSENGER.   As I did stand my
watch upon the hill,
I looked toward Birnam, and anon,
methought,
The wood began to move.
MACBETH.   Liar and slave! 35
MESSENGER.   Let me endure your
wrath, if 't be not so;
Within this three mile you may see
it coming;
I say, a moving grove.
MACBETH.   If thou speak'st
false,
Upon the next tree shalt thou hang
alive,
Till famine cling[156] thee; if thy speech
be sooth,   40
I care not if thou dost for me as
much.
I pull[157] in resolution, and begin
To doubt the equivocation of the
fiend
That lies like truth: "Fear not, till
Birnam wood
Do come to Dunsinane"; and now a
wood   45
Comes toward Dunsinane.   Arm,
arm, and out!

154*forced,* reinforced with Macbeth's
soldiers who have turned against him.
155*treatise,* a story or tale.

156*famine cling,* starvation shrivel
you.
157*pull,* falter.

If this which he avouches does appear,
There is nor flying hence nor tarrying
    here.
I 'gin to be aweary of the sun,
And wish the estate o' the world were
    now undone.   50
Ring the alarum-bell! Blow, wind!
    Come, wrack![158]
At least we'll die with harness on
    our back.   [*Exeunt.*]

SCENE VI. *Dunsinane.   Before the
            castle.*

Drum and colors.   Enter MALCOLM,
old SIWARD, MACDUFF, *and their
    Army* with boughs.

MALCOLM.   Now near enough;
    your leafy screens throw down,
And show like those you are.   You,
    worthy uncle,
Shall, with my cousin, your right-
    noble son,
Lead our first battle[159]; worthy Mac-
    duff and we
Shall take upon 's what else remains to
    do,   5
According to our order.
    SIWARD.   Fare you well.
Do we but find the tyrant's power
    tonight,
Let us be beaten, if we cannot fight.
    MACDUFF.   Make all our trumpets
    speak; give them all breath,
Those clamorous harbingers[160] of
    blood and death.   10
                        [*Exeunt.*]

SCENE VII.   *Another part of the
                field.*

Alarums.   Enter MACBETH.

MACBETH.   They have tied me to a
    stake; I cannot fly,
But, bear-like, I must fight the course.
    What 's he

---

[158]*wrack*, ruin, misfortune.
[159]*battle*, division.
[160]*harbingers*, messengers.

That was not born of woman?   Such
    a one
Am I to fear, or none.

Enter young SIWARD.

YOUNG SIWARD.   What is thy
    name?
MACBETH.   Thou'lt be
    afraid to hear it.   5
YOUNG SIWARD.   No; though thou
    call'st thyself a hotter name
Than any is in hell.
    MACBETH.   My name's Mac-
    beth.
YOUNG SIWARD.   The devil himself
    could not pronounce a title
More hateful to mine ear.
    MACBETH.   No, nor more
    fearful.
YOUNG SIWARD.   Thou liest, ab-
    horrèd tyrant; with my sword   10
I'll prove the lie thou speakest.

[*They fight and young* SIWARD *is
                        slain.*]

MACBETH.   Thou wast
    born of woman.
But swords I smile at, weapons laugh
    to scorn,
Brandished by man that's of a woman
    born.
                        [*Exit.*]

Alarums.   Enter MACDUFF.

MACDUFF.   That way the noise is.
    Tyrant show thy face!
If thou be'st slain and with no stroke
    of mine,   15
My wife and children's ghosts will
    haunt me still.
I cannot strike at wretched kerns,[161]
    whose arms
Are hired to bear their staves,[162] either
    thou, Macbeth,
Or else my sword with an unbattered
    edge

---

[161]*kerns.* soldiers.
[162]*staves*, lances.

I sheathe again undeeded. There thou
   shouldst be;   20
By this great clatter, one of greatest
   note
Seems bruited.[163] Let me find him,
   fortune!
And more I beg not.
               [*Exit. Alarums.*]

Enter MALCOLM *and old* SIWARD.

SIWARD. This way, my lord; the
   castle's gently rendered;
The tyrant's people on both sides do
   fight;   25
The noble thanes do bravely in the
   war;
The day almost itself professes yours,
And little is to do.
   MALCOLM.   We have met with
   foes
That strike beside us.
   SIWARD.   Enter, sir, the
   castle.
           [*Exeunt. Alarums.*]

SCENE VIII. *Another part of the
   field.*

Enter MACBETH.

MACBETH. Why should I play the
   Roman fool,[164] and die
On mine own sword? Whiles I see
   lives, the gashes
Do better upon them.

Enter MACDUFF.

   MACDUFF.   Turn, hell-
   hound, turn!
MACBETH. Of all men else I have
   avoided thee;
But get thee back; my soul is too
   much charged   5
With blood of thine already.
   MACDUFF.   I have no words;
My voice is in my sword, thou blood-
   ier villain

---

[163]*bruited,* noised abroad.
[164]*Roman fool,* Marcus Brutus fell
upon his own sword rather than be
captured.

Than terms can give thee out!
               [*They fight.*]
   MACBETH.   Thou losest
   labor:
As easy mayst thou the intrenchant
   air
With thy keen sword impress as make
   me bleed;   10
Let fall thy blade on vulnerable
   crests;
I bear a charmèd life, which must not
   yield
To one of woman born.
   MACDUFF.   Despair thy
   charm;
And let the angel whom thou still
   hast served
Tell thee, Macduff was from his
   mother's womb   15
Untimely ripped.
   MACBETH. Accursed be that tongue
   that tells me so.
For it hath cowed my better part of
   man!
And be these juggling fiends no more
   believed,
That palter[165] with us in a double
   sense;   20
That keep the word of promise to our
   ear,
And break it to our hope. I'll not
   fight with thee.
   MACDUFF. Then yield thee, cow-
   ard,
And live to be the show and gaze o'
   the time;
We'll have thee, as our rarer monsters
   are,   25
Painted upon a pole, and underwrit,
"Here may you see the tyrant."
   MACBETH.   I will not
   yield,
To kiss the ground before young Mal-
   colm's feet,
And to be baited[166] with the rabble's
   curse.

---

[165]*palter,* play false, deceive us.
[166]*baited,* tormented, jeered, harassed.

Though Birnam wood be come to
Dunsinane,   30
And thou opposed, being of no wom-
an born,
Yet I will try the last.   Before my
body
I throw my warlike shield.   Lay on,
Macduff,
And damned be him that first cries,
"Hold, enough!"
        [*Exeunt, fighting. Alarums.*]

*Retreat.   Flourish.   Enter, with drum
and colors,* MALCOLM, *old* SIWARD,
ROSS, *the other* THANES, *and*
SOLDIERS.

MALCOLM.   I would the friends we
miss were safe arrived.   35
SIWARD.   Some must go off; and
yet, by these I see,
So great a day as this is cheaply
bought.
MALCOLM.   Macduff is missing, and
your noble son.
ROSS.   Your son, my lord, has paid
a soldier's debt.
He only lived but till he was a
man;   40
The which no sooner had his prowess
confirmed
In the unshrinking station where he
fought,
But like a man he died.
SIWARD.   Then he is dead?
ROSS.   Ay, and brought off the
field.   Your cause of sorrow
Must not be measured by his worth,
for then   45
It hath no end.
SIWARD.   Had he his hurts
before?
ROSS.   Ay, on the front.
SIWARD.   Why then, God's
soldier be he!
Had I as many sons as I have hairs,
I would not wish them to a fairer
death.
And so, his knell is knolled.

MALCOLM.   He's worth
more sorrow,   50
And that I'll spend for him.
SIWARD.   He's worth no
more.
They say he parted well, and paid his
score;
And so, God be with him!   Here
comes newer comfort.

Re-enter MACDUFF, *with* MACBETH'S
head.

MACDUFF.   Hail, king! for so thou,
art.   Behold, where stands
The usurper's cursèd head.   The time
is free.   55
I see thee compassed with thy kingdom's pearl,[167]
That speak my salutation in their
minds,
Whose voices I desire aloud with
mine.
Hail, King of Scotland!
ALL.   Hail, King of Scot-
land!
                   [*Flourish.*]
MALCOLM.   We shall not spend a
large expense of time   60
Before we reckon with your several
loves,
And make us even with you.   My
thanes and kinsmen,
Henceforth be earls, the first that
ever Scotland
In such an honor named.   What's
more to do,
Which would be planted newly with
the time,   65
As calling home our exiled friends
abroad
That fled the snares of watchful ty-
ranny;
Producing forth the cruel ministers
Of this dead butcher and his fiend-
like queen,
Who, as 'tis thought, by self and vio-
lent hands   70

_____

[167]*pearl*, nobility.

Took off her life,[168] this, and what needful else
That calls upon us, by the grace of Grace,

_____

[168]*took off her life,* committed suicide.

We will perform in measure, time and place.
So, thanks to all at once and to each one,
Whom we invite to see us crowned at Scone. [*Flourish. Exeunt.*] 75

For Thought and Discussion

ACT V

SCENE 1.

1. What does Lady Macbeth talk about in the sleep-walking scene? What different crimes do her disjointed speeches refer to? Why does she wash her hands? Was her courage when Duncan was murdered false or real?
2. Recall what Macbeth said in an early scene about the blood on his hands.

SCENE 2.

1. By this time what do many of Macbeth's subjects think about him?
2. What happens in this scene?

SCENE 3.

1. Why do Macbeth's forces desert him?
2. Upon what does he now place his hope of victory?
3. Read aloud Macbeth's famous soliloquy in which he reveals his bitterness and sense of failure. Why does he want to die?

SCENE 4.

1. What forces are now marching against Macbeth?
2. Which prophecy is fulfilled in this scene?

SCENE 5.

1. Why does he decide to fortify the castle? Is this a wise decision?
2. How does he receive the news of the Queen's death?
3. Why does he feel that life is not worth living? Read aloud the passage that reveals his feelings about the futility of life. What general conclusion can be made about crime?
4. Why does the report of the moving wood terrify Macbeth? What desperate measures does he now take? Is he still the valiant soldier?

SCENE 6.

1. What happens in this scene?

SCENE 7.

1. How does Macbeth exhibit bravery and courage?
2. How does Siward's death increase his hopes?

SCENE 8.

1. Why does he quail before Macduff?
2. How does Macbeth meet his death?
3. How has the audience been prepared for the news of the suicide of Lady Macbeth?
4. Who is now proclaimed king of Scotland?

A Study of Significant Passages

Select and read aloud the significant lines in this act. The following suggestions may assist you in making your choice, as lines which show:

> Retribution
> Moral cowardice
> Physical bravery
> Macbeth's own conviction that "crime does not pay"

Read aloud other passages of your own choice and explain their meaning and significance.

For Thought and Discussion of the Play as a Whole

1. Do you think the statement,
   > "Fair is foul, and foul is fair,"
   refers to the weather and the victory, to the evil nature of the witches, or to the good and evil in Macbeth's mind?
2. Why was Macbeth an admirable character at the beginning of the play?
3. What traits in Macbeth's character led him to murder Duncan?
4. How did the flight of the king's sons, Malcolm and Donalbain, assist Macbeth in escaping detection?
5. Why did Macbeth distrust Banquo?
6. What was the difference in character between Macbeth and Banquo?
7. Was Macbeth a good king? Give reasons for your answer.
8. Why did the witches wish to mislead Macbeth? How do evil forces usually mislead those who yield to their suggestion?
9. Which scenes in the play are the most dramatic?
10. By omitting the historical setting, would it be possible to use the plot for a modern play?
11. You will gain a more thorough understanding of the drama by reading "The Age of Elizabeth" in "Periods of Literature."

Plus Work

A cast from the class may present *Macbeth* as a radio play. One end of the room will be used as a studio. An announcer will introduce the players and give the setting of each act.

Members of the class may also dramatize scenes, such as the "dagger scene" or the "sleep-walking scene."

Give oral or written reports from *England of Song and Story* by
Mary I. Curtis:

> Attending an Elizabethan Play
> A Shakespearean Playhouse
> Styles of Dress in Elizabeth's Day
> Superstitions of the Elizabethan Age

Make a study of Elizabethan plays, masks, and pageants.
Make a study of the historical characters Macbeth and Duncan.
Make a scenario of *Macbeth*.

Conduct a mock trial in which Macbeth is tried for the death of
Duncan and the usurpation of his throne. This project has been
explained by James P. Morris, in the English Journal, January,
1934, under the title "Macbeth—Not Guilty."

Make an oral report on the source of *Macbeth*.

WILLIAM SHAKESPEARE 1564-1616

Early Life.   The known facts of the early life of Shakespeare
are meager; the year of his birth was 1564, the month April, but
the exact day is not known. The village in which he was born,
Stratford-on-Avon, has become famous as his birthplace. As
Shakespeare's father was a man of some importance in this village
during the poet's boyhood, William probably lived happily, attending grammar school and finding enjoyment in sports and out-door
life. Later on, his father lost his standing and property through
being a contentious man continually involved in law suits.

Youth.   If the current stories of Shakespeare's poaching deer
on Sir Thomas Lucy's game preserve, of his fleeing to London because of his escapade, of his earning a living there by holding horses
for the patrons of the theater are to be believed, literary historians
will never be able to point to young William Shakespeare as a model
youth—but how the writers of popular success-stories could make
capital of such episodes as these! No matter what the nature of his
first work was in London, certainly the habit acquired later of observing closely what theater-goers liked, his work in revising old
plays, and his training as a young actor in minor rôles proved valuable to him when he turned to writing as his chief interest and to
old manuscripts as the chief sources for his plots. This training together with his childhood interest in the characters of village life
with their virtues and vices, the fact that as a boy he kept his heart
and eyes open to the beauties of nature so generously displayed in
his native countryside, and, by no means least, his habitual persistence and his capacity for hard work—all contributed to the making
of a man known to us as the most powerful playwright of all time,
but known to his associates as the "gentle Shakespeare," a man of
unquestioned honesty and worth.

His Marriage.   Shakespeare at the age of seventeen, before his
reputed flight to London, had fallen in love with and married Anne

SHAKESPEARE COURTING ANNE HATHAWAY,
WHOM HE MARRIED

THE SECOND-BEST BED OF "ANNE HATH A WAY"

Hathaway. In view of the clause in his last will and testament giving to Anne the second-best bed one may wonder whether the couple was ideally happy, but the whole matter is merely one of conjecture. Moreover, who knows but that Anne, of whom it was said "Anne hath a way" may have preferred the second-best bed?

Early Success. It is interesting to note that Shakespeare, had he written no dramas, would yet have become famous because of his sonnets and his long poems. It is particularly interesting to discover that "Venus and Adonis" (à dŏ′ nĭs), one of the longer poems very popular in his own day, probably marked the beginning of his success. According to tradition the dedication of this poem to the Earl of Southampton brought to Shakespeare a gift of money which he invested wisely. Later he bought an interest in the Globe and the Blackfriars theaters. Both his literary and his financial success was amazing. Within ten years after his arrival in London he was accepted as one of the famous actors and literary men in England. So unaware was Shakespeare, however, of the great place later to be awarded his works that he made no attempt to preserve his plays. Chance, or some may prefer to say providence, alone was responsible for the preservation of the literary manuscripts almost universally ranked next in importance to the Bible.

Later Life. Famous as a playwright and a producer, his fortune made, Shakespeare returned to his native Stratford to spend the remainder of his life with his wife and daughters. He bought the old home, which had passed into other hands, remodeled and restored it, and prepared to pass his old age in honor, ease, and happiness.

Death. On April 16, 1616, the village of Stratford entertained Shakespeare's fellow playwright from London, Ben Jonson. Shakespeare was called upon to act as master of ceremonies, but as he was really so ill that he should not have left his room, he suffered a collapse immediately afterward and did not recover. He died April 23, probably the anniversary of his birth, and was buried in his native Stratford.

Works. Numerous classifications of Shakespeare's plays have been made, but, for the present purpose, three are given: comedy, tragedy, and the historical play. The best known comedies are *The Tempest, As You Like It, The Merchant of Venice;* tragedies, *Romeo and Juliet, Macbeth, Hamlet, Julius Caesar, King Lear, Othello;* the historical plays, which can also be included in the two preceding groups, are *Henry IV, Henry V, Richard II,* and *Richard III.*

His Art. Today, no less than in the lifetime of the great poet, when Shakespeare's dramas are presented by a company of notable actors, audiences are held spell-bound by the gaiety, the splendor, the love of life, the spirit of adventure, and the lofty idealism of the Elizabethan Age. Under the spell of this artist's imagination his many characters, the king, the courtier, the shepherd, the merchant, the doctor, and the good wife,—in fact, people of all professions of all the past ages, as they sweep before their enchanted auditors, become almost as real to them as their closest friends or their enemies. Nor is this most versatile of all English writers limited in his field to the vivid portrayal of human nature: when he tells of a shepherd's care for the sick sheep, we catch the odor of healing tar; when the country air delights him with its fragrance, to us, also, it "nimbly and sweetly recommends itself," and when the birds sing for him, they likewise charm us with their song. Just as few artists approach the bard of Avon (ā' vŏn) in his descriptive characterizations, so few excel him in naturalness and fidelity of setting. Views of the Forest of Arden, of old ruins, military camps and roads, and gray old castles—all spots familiar to his childhood— make a powerful appeal to lovers of picturesque beauty just as they made appeal to the vivid imagination of the boy who was later to charm his readers with their description. All in all, Shakespeare's strength and skill lie in his ability to create life-like characters, place them in realistic situations, and have them engage in conversations so natural and so revealing that they cease to be literary characters and become living beings.

Characters. What reader could ever forget the vivid personalities presented by Shakespeare? Daring, delightful Rosalind;

SHAKESPEARE'S BIRTHPLACE—STRATFORD-ON-AVON

Miranda, falling in love for the first time, almost as free from inhibitions as her modern sisters; Macbeth, passing majestically to his downfall, arousing pity when the realization of his crime comes upon him; Lady Macbeth, breaking under the strain; Hamlet, weighing life in the scales with death—these are among the great host of Shakespearean characters who, because of the universal truth they represent, belong to all time.

Additional Readings

Barrie, James: *What Every Woman Knows*
   A Kiss for Cinderella
Belloc, Hilaire: *Joan of Arc*
Bennett, Arnold: *Clayhanger*
Boswell, James: *Life of Johnson*
Deeping, Warwick: *Roper's Row*
Drinkwater, John: *Abraham Lincoln*
Eaton, Jeanette: *Marquis de Lafayette*
Ervine, St. John: *John Ferguson*
Galsworthy, John: *The Forsyte Saga*
Grand Duchess Marie: *Education of a Princess*
Hamsun, Knut: *August*
Hilton, James: *Good-bye, Mr. Chips!*

Kaphan, Mortimer: *Tell us a Dickens Story*
Maughham, Somerset: *Of Human Bondage*
McSpadden, J. W.: *Stories from Dickens*
Reid, Edith Gittings: *The Great Physician*
Robinson, Mabel L.: *Blue Ribbon Stories*
Scott, Sir Walter: *Kenilworth*
   The Talisman
Sweetser, Kate Dickinson: *Ten Boys from Dickens*
   Ten Girls from Dickens
Woolf, Virginia: *The Second Common Reader*

Many Moods of Love

MANY MOODS OF LOVE

"For thy sweet love rememb'red such wealth brings
That then I scorn to change my state with kings."

*A*LONG with the happiness of love come the crosses: differences in years and station, interference of friends and
family, and separation through war, illness, and death.   As today
youthful lovers complain over their sad lot, so did they in ages past.
Would two young people of this day say more or less on this subject than did Hermia and Lysander?[1]

LYSANDER.   The course of true love never did run smooth;
    But either it was different in blood,—
HERMIA.   O cross! too high to be enthralled to low.
LYSANDER.   Or else misgaffed in respect to years,—
HERMIA.   O spite! too old to be engag'd to young.
LYSANDER.   Or else it stood upon the choice of friends,—
HERMIA.   O hell! to choose love by another's eyes.
LYSANDER.   Or, if there were sympathy in choice.
    War, death, or sickness lay siege to it,
    Making it momentary as a sound,
    Swift as a shadow, short as any dream,
    Brief as the lightning in the collied night,
    That, in a spleen, unfolds both heaven and earth,
    And ere a man hath power to say 'Behold!'
    The jaws of darkness do devour it up;
    So bright things come to confusion.

The subject of love ever provokes interesting questions.   Does
one fall in love at first sight?   Does true love really endure forever?
From a great master[2] comes the answer:

"Who ever loved that loved not at first sight?"

· · · · · · · · · · · · · ·

".... Love is not love
Which alters when it alteration finds
Or bends with the remover to remove."

· · · · · · · · · · · · ·

"Love alters not with his brief hours and weeks
But bears it out even to the edge of doom.
If this be error, and upon me proved,
I never writ, nor no man ever loved."

[1]*Midsummer Night's Dream.*
[2]*Shakespeare.*

"THEN LOOK FOR ME BY MOONLIGHT
WATCH FOR ME BY MOONLIGHT
I'LL COME TO THEE BY MOONLIGHT
THOUGH HELL SHOULD BAR THE WAY."

THE HIGHWAYMAN[1]

ALFRED NOYES

[Alfred Noyes, 1880—, has the calm, level gaze of a modern business man, and perhaps he is a good business man even though a poet-professor. His general appearance denotes the close co-ordination of mind and muscle which belongs to an athlete of ability; hence one is not surprised to learn of his distinction as an Oxford oarsman and of his prowess as a swimmer. Noyes is well known to the American public, for since his marriage to an American girl, he has made a number of lecture tours in the United States and has served as visiting professor at Princeton.

In his writings Noyes shows great devotion to England, and numbers of his poems, particularly "Republic and Motherland," express an appreciation for the United States. Although unable, because of defective eyes, to enlist in the World War, he like Milton, served his country ably with his pen. His war poems are so grippingly realistic that they are being widely used as peace propaganda. *The Wine Press* is one of his best volumes of war verse. The poet's early poems, ballads of sea and land, such as, "The Forty Singing Seamen," "Robin Hood," and "Tales of the Mermaid Tavern," told with the swinging rhythm of a rolling boat or a galloping steed and alive with color and adventure, entitle him to high rank among the narrative poets of the present day. "The Highwayman," perhaps the favorite among his shorter selections, is a vividly

[1]Reprinted by permission from *Collected Poems*, Volume I, by Alfred Noyes. Copyright, 1906, by Frederick A. Stokes Company.

dramatic and tragic story, full of color, sound and emotion.]

PART ONE

I

THE wind was a torrent of darkness among the gusty trees,
The moon was a ghostly galleon tossed upon cloudy seas,
The road was a ribbon of moonlight over the purple moor,
And the highwayman came riding—
    Riding—riding— 5
The highwayman came riding, up to the old inn-door.

II

He'd a French cocked hat on his forehead, a bunch of lace at his chin,
A coat of the claret velvet, and breeches of brown doe-skin;
They fitted with never a wrinkle; his boots were up to the thigh!
And he rode with a jeweled twinkle, 10
    His pistol butts a-twinkle,
His rapier hilt a-twinkle, under the jeweled sky.

III

Over the cobbles he clattered and clashed in the dark inn-yard,
And he tapped with his whip on the shutters, but all was locked and barred;
He whistled a tune to the window, and who should be waiting there 15
But the landlord's black-eyed daughter,
    Bess, the landlord's daughter,
Plaiting a dark red love-knot into her long black hair.

IV

And dark in the dark old inn-yard a stable-wicket creaked
Where Tim the ostler listened; his face was white and peaked; 20
His eyes were hollows of madness, his hair like moldy hay,
But he loved the landlord's daughter,
    The landlord's red-lipped daughter,
Dumb as a dog he listened, and he heard the robber say—

V

"One kiss, my bonny sweetheart, I'm after a prize tonight, 25
But I shall be back with the yellow gold before the morning light;
Yet, if they press me sharply, and harry me through the day,
Then look for me by moonlight,
    Watch for me by moonlight,
I'll come to thee by moonlight, though hell should bar the way." 30

VI

He rose upright in the stirrups; he scarce could reach her hand,
But she loosened her hair i' the casement! His face burnt like a brand
As the black cascade of perfume came tumbling over his breast;
And he kissed its waves in the moonlight,
    (Oh, sweet black waves in the moonlight!) 35
Then he tugged at his rein in the moonlight, and galloped away to the West.

PART TWO

I

He did not come in the dawning; he did not come at noon;
And out o' the tawny sunset, before the rise o' the moon,
When the road was a gypsy's ribbon, looping the purple moor,

A redcoat troop came marching— 40
Marching—marching—
King George's men came marching,
up to the old inn-door.

II

They said no word to the landlord,
they drank his ale instead,
But they gagged his daughter and
bound her to the foot of her narrow bed;
Two of them knelt at her casement,
with muskets at their side! 45
There was death at every window;
And hell at one dark window;
For Bess could see, through her casement, the road that *he* would
ride.

III

They had tied her up to attention,
with many a sniggering jest;
They had bound a musket beside her,
with a barrel beneath her
breast! 50
"Now keep good watch!" and they
kissed her.
She heard the dead man say—
Look for me by moonlight;
Watch for me by moonlight;
I'll come to thee by moonlight,
though hell should bar the
way! 55

IV

She twisted her hands behind her;
but all the knots held good!
She writhed her hands till her fingers
were wet with sweat or blood!
They stretched and strained in the
darkness, and the hours crawled
by like years,
Till, now, on the stroke of midnight,
Cold, on the stroke of midnight, 60
The tip of one finger touched it! The
trigger at least was hers!

V

The tip of one finger touched it; she
strove no more for the rest!
Up, she stood up to attention, with
the barrel beneath her breast,
She would not risk their hearing, she
would not strive again;
For the road lay bare in the moonlight; 65
Blank and bare in the moonlight;
And the blood of her veins in the
moonlight throbbed to her love's
refrain.

VI

Tlot-tlot; tlot-tlot! Had they heard
it? The horse-hoofs ringing
clear;
Tlot-tlot, tlot-tlot, in the distance?
Were they deaf that they did not
hear?
Down the ribbon of moonlight, over
the brow of the hill, 70
The highwayman came riding—
Riding—riding!
The redcoats looked to their priming!
She stood up, straight and still!

VII

Tlot-tlot, in the frosty silence! *Tlot-*
tlot, in the echoing night!
Nearer he came and nearer! Her face
was like a light! 75
Her eyes grew wide for a moment;
she drew one last deep breath,
Then her finger moved in the moonlight,
Her musket shattered the
moonlight,
Shattered her breast in the moonlight
and warned him — with her
death.

VIII

He turned; he spurred to the West;
he did not know who stood 80

Bowed, with her head o'er the musket,
    drenched with her own red
    blood!
Not till the dawn he heard it; his face
    grew gray to hear
How Bess, the landlord's daughter,
    The landlord's black-eyed
    daughter,
Had watched for her love in the
    moonlight and died in the dark-
    ness there.   85

IX

Back, he spurred like a madman,
    shrieking a curse to the sky,
With the white road smoking behind
    him and his rapier brandished
    high!
Blood-red were his spurs i' the golden
    noon; wine-red was his velvet
    coat,
When they shot him down on the
    highway,
        Down like a dog on the high-
        way,   90
And he lay in his blood on the high-

way, with the bunch of lace at
    his throat.
.   .   .   .

X

And still of a winter's night, they say,
    when the wind is in the trees,
When the moon is a ghostly galleon
    tossed upon cloudy seas,
When the road is a ribbon of moon-
    light over the purple moor,
A highwayman comes riding—   95
        Riding—riding—
A highwayman comes riding, up to
    the old inn-door.

XI

Over the cobbles he clatters and
    clangs in the dark inn-yard;
He taps with his whip on the shut-
    ters, but all is locked and barred;
He whistles a tune to the window, and
    who should be waiting there   100
But the landlord's black-eyed daugh-
    ter,
        Bess, the landlord's daughter,
Plaiting a dark red love-knot into her
    long black hair.

For Thought and Discussion

1. What effect is produced by the description of the night?
2. What type of person do you imagine the highwayman to be?
3. Why does Tim report the highwayman?
4. Account for the use of italics in stanzas 10 and 11.
5. Why is the poem classified as a ballad?
6. Select and read aloud the most vivid passages.
7. What is the most dramatic episode in the poem?
8. Do you consider this poem romantic or realistic? Why?
9. Do you find yourself visualizing the sights and hearing the
   sounds described by the author? Which sights and sounds
   recur to you most vividly?
10. List the various tones, tints, or shades of red mentioned in the
    poem.
11. List the emotional reactions which heighten the effect of the
    story.
12. You will find the explanation of ballad form in the section
    "Introduction to Types of Literature."

DRINK TO ME ONLY WITH THINE EYES

BEN JONSON

DRINK to me only with thine
    eyes,
  And I will pledge with mine;
Or leave a kiss but in the cup
  And I'll not look for wine.
The thirst that from the soul doth
    rise   5
  Doth ask a drink divine;
But might I of Jove's nectar sup,
  I would not change for thine.

I sent thee late a rosy wreath,
  Not so much honoring thee   10
As giving it a hope that there
  It could not withered be;
But thou thereon didst only breathe
  And sent'st it back to me;
Since when it grows, and smells, I
    swear   15
  Not of itself, but thee!

For Thought and Discussion

1. Is the mood of this poem serious, tender, humorous?
2. Select a leader and sing the song in class.
3. Discover, if you can, to whom Jonson dedicated this poem.

A RED, RED ROSE

ROBERT BURNS

MY luve's like a red, red rose,
  That's newly sprung in June;
My luve's like the melodie,
  That's sweetly played in tune.

As fair art thou, my bonie lass,   5
  So deep in luve am I;
And I will luve thee still, my dear,
  'Till a' the seas gang dry.

'Till a' the seas gang dry, my dear,
  And the rocks melt wi' the sun;   10
And I will luve thee still, my dear,
  While the sands o' life shall run.

And fare thee well, my only luve!
  And fare thee well awhile!
And I will come again, my luve,   15
  Tho' it were ten thousand mile!

For Thought and Discussion

1. To what does Burns compare his love?
2. Read this poem aloud and observe how smoothly it flows along.
3. How does the clause of concession in line sixteen compare with
   the clause of concession in "The Highwayman"?

JEAN

ROBERT BURNS

[¹*airts*, directions. ²*blaw*, blow.
³*bonie*, pretty. ⁴*row*, roll. ⁵*monie*,
many. ⁶*shaw*, wood.]

O F a' the airts¹ the wind can blaw²
   I dearly like the west,
For there the bonie³ lassie lives,
   The lassie I lo'e best.
There wild woods grow, and rivers
   row,⁴   5
And monie⁵ a hill between;

But day and night my fancy's flight
   Is ever wi' my Jean.

I see her in the dewy flowers,
   I see her sweet and fair;   10
I hear her in the tunefu' birds,
   I hear her charm the air.
There's not a bonie flower that springs
   By fountain, shaw,⁶ or green,
There's not a bonie bird that sings   15
   But minds me o' my Jean.

For Thought and Discussion

1. What reminds the poet of Jean? Who is Jean?
2. What is the mood of this poem? Is the use of dialect effective?

BONIE DOON

ROBERT BURNS

[¹*braes*, banks, hillsides. ²*blume*,
bloom. ³*sae*, so. ⁴*fu'*, full. ⁵*fause*,
false. ⁶*wist na*, knew not. ⁷*aft hae*,
oft have. ⁸*ilka*, every. ⁹*pu'd*, pulled.
¹⁰*staw*, stole.]

Y E banks and braes¹ o' bonie Doon
   How can ye blume² sae fair!
How can ye chant, ye little birds,
And I sae³ fu'⁴ o' care!

Thou'll break my heart, thou bonie
   bird   5
   That sings upon the bough;
Thou minds me o' the happy days
   When my fause⁵ luve was true.

Thou'll break my heart, thou bonie
   bird   10
   That sings beside thy mate;
For sae I sat, and sae I sang,
   And wist na⁶ o' my fate.

Aft hae⁷ I roved by bonie Doon
   To see the woodbine twine,
And ilka⁸ bird sang o' its love;   15
   And sae did I o' mine.

Wi' lightsome heart I pu'd⁹ a rose
   Frae aff its thorny tree;
And my fause luver staw¹⁰ the rose
   But left the thorn wi' me.

For Thought and Discussion

1. Why does the bird's song make the poet unhappy?
2. Contrast the mood of this poem with that of the two preceding
   poems.

SCOTLAND—THE LAND OF BURNS

SWEET AFTON

ROBERT BURNS

FLOW gently, sweet Afton, among
   thy green braes,
Flow gently, I'll sing thee a song in
   thy praise;
My Mary's asleep by thy murmuring stream,
Flow gently, sweet Afton, disturb
   not her dream.

Thou stock-dove, whose echo re-
   sounds thro' the glen,   5
Ye wild whistling blackbirds in yon
   thorny den,
Thou green-crested lapwing, thy
   screaming forbear,
I charge you disturb not my slumbering fair.

How lofty, sweet Afton, thy neighboring hills,
Far marked with the courses of clear
   winding rills;   10

There daily I wander as noon rises
   high,
My flocks and my Mary's sweet cot
   in my eye.

How pleasant thy banks and green
   valleys below,
Where wild in the woodlands the
   primroses blow;
There oft, as mild Evening weeps
   over the lea,   15
The sweet-scented birk shades my
   Mary and me.

Thy crystal stream, Afton, how lovely it glides,
And winds by the cot where my Mary
   resides;
How wanton thy waters her snowy
   feet lave,
As gathering sweet flow'rets she stems
   thy clear wave.   20

Flow gently, sweet Afton, among thy
    green braes,
Flow gently, sweet river, the theme of
    my lays;

My Mary's asleep by thy murmuring
    stream,
Flow gently, sweet Afton, disturb
    not her dream.

For Thought and Discussion

1. Why does the poet write about the river Afton?
2. What effect do the long lines have?
3. Observe the tone of this poem.
4. Make a study of the love poems of Burns. This may be an
oral or written report.

❧

THE SIRE DE MALETROIT'S DOOR

ROBERT LOUIS STEVENSON

DENIS de Beaulieu[1] was not yet two-and-twenty, but he counted himself a grown man, and a very accomplished cavalier into the bargain. Lads were early formed in that rough, warfaring epoch; and when one has been in a pitched battle and a dozen raids, has killed one's man in an honorable fashion, and knows a thing or two of strategy and mankind, a certain swagger in the gait is surely to be pardoned. He had put up his horse with due care, and supped with due deliberation; and then, in a very agreeable frame of mind, went out to pay a visit in the gray of the evening. It was not a very wise proceeding on the young man's part. He would have done better to remain beside the fire or go decently to bed. For the town was full of the troops of Burgundy and England under a mixed command; and though Denis was there on safe-conduct, his safe-conduct was like to serve him little on a chance encounter.

It was September, 1429; the weather had fallen sharp; a flighty piping wind, laden with showers, beat about the township; and the dead leaves ran riot along the streets. Here and there a window was already lighted up; and the noise of men-at-arms making merry over supper within, came forth in fits and was swallowed up and carried away by the wind. The night fell swiftly; the flag of England, fluttering on the spire-top, grew ever fainter and fainter against the flying clouds—a black speck like a swallow in the tumultuous, leaden chaos of the sky. As the night fell the wind rose, and began to hoot under archways and roar amid the treetops in the valley below the town.

Denis de Beaulieu walked fast and was soon knocking at his friend's door; but though he promised himself to stay only a little while and make an early return, his welcome was so pleasant, and he found so much to delay him, that it was already long past midnight before he said good-by upon the threshold. The wind had fallen again in the meanwhile; the night was as black as the grave; not a star, nor a glimmer of moonshine, slipped through the canopy of cloud. Denis was

---

[1]*Denis de Beaulieu* (dē nē′ dē bō lē û′).

ill-acquainted with the intricate lanes of Chateau Landon; even by daylight he had found some trouble in picking his way; and in this absolute darkness he soon lost it altogether. He was certain of one thing only—to keep mounting the hill; for his friend's house lay at the lower end, or tail, of Chateau Landon, while the inn was up at the head, under the great church spire. With this clue to go upon, he stumbled and groped forward, now breathing more freely in open places where there was a good slice of sky overhead now feeling along the wall in stifling closes. It is an eerie and mysterious position to be thus submerged in opaque blackness in an almost unknown town. The silence is terrifying in its possibilities. The touch of cold window-bars to the exploring hand startles the man like the touch of a toad; the inequalities of the pavement shake his heart into his mouth; a piece of denser darkness threatens an ambuscade or a chasm in the pathway; and where the air is brighter, the houses put on strange and bewildering appearances, as if to lead him farther from his way. For Denis, who had to regain his inn without attracting notice, there was real danger as well as mere discomfort in the walk; and he went warily and boldly at once, and at every corner paused to make an observation.

He had been for some time threading a lane so narrow that he could touch a wall with either hand when it began to open out and go sharply downward. Plainly this lay no longer in the direction of his inn; but the hope of a little more light tempted him forward to reconnoiter. The lane ended in a terrace with a bartizan wall, which gave an outlook between high houses, as out of an embrasure, into the valley lying dark and form-less several hundred feet below. Denis looked down, and could discern a few treetops waving and a single speck of brightness where the river ran across a weir. The weather was clearing up, and the sky had lightened, so as to show the outline of the heavier clouds and the dark margin of the hills. By the uncertain glimmer, the house on his left hand should be a place of some pretensions; it was surmounted by several pinnacles and turret-tops; the round stern of a chapel, with a fringe of flying buttresses, projected boldly from the main block; and the door was sheltered under a deep porch carved with figures and overhung by two long gargoyles. The windows of the chapel gleamed through their intricate tracery with a light as of many tapers, and threw out the buttresses and the peaked roof in a more intense blackness against the sky. It was plainly the hotel of some great family of the neighborhood; and as it reminded Denis of a town house of his own at Bourges, he stood for some time gazing up at it and mentally gauging the skill of the architects and the consideration of the two families.

There seemed to be no issue to the terrace but the lane by which he had reached it; he could only retrace his steps, but he had gained some notion of his whereabouts, and hoped by this means to hit the main thoroughfare and speedily regain the inn. He was reckoning without that chapter of accidents which was to make this night memorable above all others in his career; for he had not gone back above a hundred yards before he saw a light coming to meet him, and heard loud voices speaking together in the echoing narrows of the lane. It was a party of men-at-arms going the night round with torches. Denis assured himself that they had all been making free with the wine-bowl, and were in no mood to be particular about safe-conducts or the niceties of chivalrous war. It was as like as not that they would kill him like a dog and leave him where he fell. The situation was inspiriting but nervous. Their own torches would conceal him from sight, he reflected; and he hoped that they would drown the noise of his footsteps with their own empty voices. If he were but fleet and silent, he might evade their notice altogether.

Unfortunately, as he turned to beat a retreat, his foot rolled upon a pebble; he fell against the wall with an ejaculation, and his sword rang loudly on the stones. Two or three voices demanded who went there—some in French, some in English; but Denis made no reply, and ran the faster down the lane. Once upon the terrace, he paused to look back. They still kept calling after him, and just then began to double the pace in pursuit, with a considerable clank of armor, and great tossing of the torchlight to and fro in the narrow jaws of the passage.

Denis cast a look around and darted into the porch. There he might escape observation, or—if that were too much to expect—was in a capital posture whether for parley or defense. So thinking, he drew his sword and tried to set his back against the door. To his surprise, it yielded behind his weight; and though he turned in a moment, continued to swing back on oiled and noiseless hinges, until it stood wide open on a black interior. When things fall out opportunely for the person concerned, he is not apt to be critical about the how or why, his own immediate personal convenience seeming a sufficient reason for the strangest oddities and revolutions in our sublunary things; and so Denis, without a moment's hesitation,

stepped within and partly closed the door behind him to conceal his place of refuge. Nothing was further from his thoughts than to close it altogether; but for some inexplicable reason—perhaps by a spring or a weight—the ponderous mass of oak whipped itself out of his fingers and clanked to, with a formidable rumble and a noise like the falling of an automatic bar.

The round, at that very moment, debouched upon the terrace and proceeded to summon him with shouts and curses. He heard them ferreting in the dark corners; the stock of a lance even rattled along the outer surface of the door behind which he stood; but these gentlemen were in too high a humor to be long delayed, and soon made off down a corkscrew pathway which had escaped Denis's observation, and passed out of sight and hearing along the battlements of the town.

Denis breathed again. He gave them a few minutes' grace for fear of accidents, and then groped about for some means of opening the door and slipping forth again. The inner surface was quite smooth, not a handle, not a molding, not a projection of any sort. He got his finger nails round the edges and pulled, but the mass was immovable. He shook it; it was as firm as a rock. Denis de Beaulieu frowned and gave vent to a little noiseless whistle. What ailed the door? he wondered. Why was it open? How came it to shut so easily and so effectually after him? There was something obscure and underhand about all this, that was little to the young man's fancy. It looked like a snare; and yet who could suppose a snare in such a quiet by-street and in a house of so prosperous and even noble an exterior? And yet—snare or no snare, intentionally or unintentionally—here he was, prettily trapped; and for the life of him he could see no way out of it again. The darkness began to weigh upon him. He gave ear; all was silent without, but within and close by he seemed to catch a faint sighing, a faint sobbing rustle, a little stealthy creak — as though many persons were at his side, holding themselves quite still, and governing even their respiration with the extreme of slyness. The idea went to his vitals with a shock, and he faced about suddenly as if to defend his life. Then, for the first time, he became aware of a light about the level of his eyes and at some distance in the interior of the house —a vertical thread of light, widening towards the bottom, such as might escape between two wings of arras over a doorway. To see anything was a relief to Denis; it was like a piece of solid ground to a man laboring in a morass; his mind seized upon it with avidity; and he stood staring at it and trying to piece together some logical conception of his surroundings. Plainly there was a flight of steps ascending from his own level to that of this illuminated doorway; and indeed he thought he could make out another thread of light, as fine as a needle and as faint as phosphorescence, which might very well be reflected along the polished wood of a handrail. Since he had begun to suspect that he was not alone, his heart had continued to beat with smothering violence, and an intolerable desire for action of any sort had possessed itself of his spirit. He was in deadly peril, he believed. What could be more natural than to mount the staircase, lift the curtain, and confront his difficulty at once? At least he would be dealing with something tangible; at least he would be no longer in the dark. He stepped

slowly forward with outstretched hands, until his foot struck the bottom step; then he rapidly scaled the stairs, stood for a moment to compose his expression, lifted the arras and went in.

He found himself in a large apartment of polished stone. There were three doors; one on each of three sides; all similarly curtained with tapestry. The fourth side was occupied by two large windows and a great stone chimney piece, carved with the arms of Malétroits. Denis recognized the bearings, and was gratified to find himself in such good hands. The room was strongly illuminated; but it contained little furniture except a heavy table and a chair or two, the hearth was innocent of fire, and the pavement was but sparsely strewn with rushes clearly many days old.

On a high chair beside the chimney, and directly facing Denis as he entered, sat a little old gentleman in a fur tippet. He sat with his legs crossed and his hands folded, and a cup of spiced wine stood by his elbow on a bracket on the wall. His countenance had a strongly masculine cast; not properly human, but such as we see in the bull, the goat, or the domestic boar; something equivocal and wheedling, something greedy, brutal, and dangerous. The upper lip was inordinately full, as though swollen by a blow or a toothache; and the smile, the peaked eyebrows, and the small, strong eyes were quaintly and almost comically evil in expression. Beautiful white hair hung straight all round his head, like a saint's, and fell in a single curl upon the tippet. His beard and mustache were the pink of venerable sweetness. Age, probably in consequence of inordinate precautions, had left no mark upon his hands; and the Malétroit hand was famous. It would be difficult to imagine anything at once so fleshy and so delicate in design; the taper, sensual fingers were like those of one of Leonardo's women; the fork of the thumb made a dimpled protuberance when closed; the nails were perfectly shaped, and of a dead, surprising whiteness. It rendered his aspect tenfold more redoubtable, that a man with hands like these should keep them devoutly folded like a virgin martyr—that a man with so intent and startling an expression of face should sit patiently on his seat and contemplate people with an unwinking stare, like a god, or a god's statue. His quiescence seemed ironical and treacherous, it fitted so poorly with his looks.

Such was Alain, Sire de Malétroit.[2] Denis and he looked silently at each other for a second or two.

"Pray step in," said the Sire de Malétroit. "I have been expecting you all the evening."

He had not risen, but he accompanied his words with a smile and a slight but courteous inclination of the head. Partly from the smile, partly from the strange musical murmur with which the Sire prefaced his observation, Denis felt a strong shudder of disgust go through his marrow. And what with disgust and honest confusion of mind, he could scarcely get words together in reply.

"I fear," he said; "that this is a double accident. I am not the person you suppose me. It seems you were looking for a visit; but for my part, nothing was further from my thoughts—nothing could be more contrary to my wishes—than this intrusion."

"Well, well," replied the old gentleman indulgently, "here you are, which is the main point. Seat your-

---

[2]*Malétroit* (mäl' ā trwä).

self, my friend, and put yourself entirely at your ease. We shall arrange our little affairs presently."

Denis perceived that the matter was still complicated with some misconception and he hastened to continue his explanations.

"Your door . . ." he began.

"About my door?" asked the other, raising his peaked eyebrows. "A little piece of ingenuity." And he shrugged his shoulders. "A hospitable fancy! By your own account, you were not desirous of making my acquaintance. We old people look for such reluctance now and then; when it touches our honor, we cast about until we find some way of overcoming it. You arrive uninvited, but believe me, very welcome."

"You persist in error, sir," said Denis. "There can be no question between you and me. I am a stranger in this countryside. My name is Denis, damoiseau de Beaulieu. If you see me in your house, it is only——"

"My young friend," interrupted the other, "you will permit me to have my own ideas on that subject. They probably differ from yours at the present moment," he added with a leer, "but time will show which of us is in the right."

Denis was convinced he had to do with a lunatic. He seated himself with a shrug, content to wait the upshot; and a pause ensued, during which he thought he could distinguish a hurried gabbling as of prayer from behind the arras immediately opposite him. Sometimes there seemed to be but one person engaged, sometimes two; and the vehemence of the voice, low as it was, seemed to indicate either great haste or an agony of spirit. It occurred to him that this piece of tapestry covered the entrance to the chapel he had noticed from without. The old gentleman meanwhile surveyed Denis from head to foot with a smile, and from time to time emitted little noises like a bird or a mouse, which seemed to indicate a high degree of satisfaction. This state of matters became rapidly insupportable; and Denis, to put an end to it, remarked politely that the wind had gone down.

The old gentleman fell into a fit of silent laughter, so prolonged and violent that he became quite red in the face. Denis got upon his feet at once, and put on his hat with a flourish.

"Sir," he said, "if you are in your wits, you have affronted me grossly. If you are out of them, I flatter myself I can find better employment for my brains than to talk with lunatics. My conscience is clear; you have made a fool of me from the first moment; you have refused to hear my explanations; and now there is no power under God will make me stay here any longer; and if I cannot make my way out in a more decent fashion, I will hack your door in pieces with my sword."

The Sire de Malétroit raised his right hand and wagged it at Denis with the fore and little fingers extended.

"My dear nephew," he said, "sit down."

"Nephew!" retorted Denis, "you lie in your throat"; and he snapped his fingers in his face.

"Sit down, you rogue!" cried the old gentleman, in a sudden, harsh voice, like the barking of a dog. "Do you fancy," he went on, "that when I had made my little contrivance for the door I had stopped short with that? If you prefer to be bound hand and foot till your bones ache, rise and try to go away. If you choose to remain a free young buck, agreeably conversing with an old gentleman—why, sit where you are in peace, and God be with you."

"Do you mean I am a prisoner?" demanded Denis.

"I state the facts," replied the other. "I would rather leave the conclusion to yourself."

Denis sat down again. Externally he managed to keep pretty calm, but within, he was now boiling with anger, now chilled with apprehension. He no longer felt convinced that he was dealing with a madman. And if the old gentleman was sane, what, in God's name, had he to look for? What absurd or tragical adventure had befallen him? What countenance was he to assume?

While he was thus unpleasantly reflecting, the arras that overhung the chapel door was raised, and a tall priest in his robes came forth and, giving a long, keen stare at Denis, said something in an undertone to Sire de Malétroit.

"She is in a better frame of spirit?" asked the latter.

"She is more resigned, messire," replied the priest.

"Now the Lord help her, she is hard to please!" sneered the old gentleman. "A likely stripling—not ill-born—and of her own choosing, too? Why, what more would the jade have?"

"The situation is not usual for a young damsel," said the other, "and somewhat trying to her blushes."

"She should have thought of that before she began the dance! It was none of my choosing, God knows that; but since she is in it, by Our Lady, she shall carry it to the end." And then addressing Denis, "Monsieur de Beaulieu," he asked, "may I present you to my niece? She has been waiting your arrival, I may say, with even greater impatience than myself."

Denis had resigned himself with a

good grace—all he desired was to know the worst of it as speedily as possible; so he rose at once, and bowed in acquiescence. The Sire de Malétroit followed his example and limped, with the assistance of the chaplain's arm, towards the chapel door. The priest pulled aside the arras, and all three entered. The building had considerable architectural pretensions. A light groining sprang from six stout columns, and hung down in two rich pendants from the center of the vault. The place terminated behind the altar in a round end, embossed and honeycombed with a superfluity of ornament in relief, and pierced by many little windows shaped like stars, trefoils, or wheels. These windows were imperfectly glazed, so that the night air circulated freely in the chapel. The tapers, of which there must have been half a hundred burning on the altar, were unmercifully blown about; and the light went through many different phases of brilliancy and semi-eclipse. On the steps in front of the altar knelt a young girl richly attired as a bride. A chill settled over Denis as he observed her costume; he fought with desperate energy against the conclusion that was being thrust upon his mind; it could not—it should not—be as he feared.

"Blanche," said the Sire, in his most flute-like tones, "I have brought a friend to see you, my little girl; turn round and give him your pretty hand. It is good to be devout; but it is necessary to be polite, my niece."

The girl rose to her feet and turned toward the newcomers. She moved all of a piece; and shame and exhaustion were expressed in every line of her fresh young body; and she held her head down and kept her eyes upon the pavement, as she came slowly forward. In the course of her advance, her eyes fell upon Denis de Beaulieu's feet—feet of which he was justly vain, be it remarked, and wore in the most elegant accouterment even while traveling. She paused—started, as if his yellow boots had conveyed some shocking meaning—and glanced suddenly up into the wearer's countenance. Their eyes met; shame gave place to horror and terror in her looks; the blood left her lips; with a piercing scream she covered her face with her hands and sank upon the chapel floor.

"That is not the man!" she cried. "My uncle, that is not the man!"

The Sire de Malétroit chirped agreeably. "Of course not," he said, "I expected as much. It was so unfortunate you could not remember his name."

"Indeed," she cried, "indeed, I have never seen this person till this moment—I have never so much as set eyes upon him—I never wish to see him again. Sir," she said, turning to Denis, "if you are a gentleman, you will bear me out. Have I ever seen you—have you ever seen me—before this accursed hour?"

"To speak for myself, I have never had that pleasure," answered the young man. "This is the first time, messire, that I have met with your engaging niece."

The old gentleman shrugged his shoulders.

"I am distressed to hear it," he said. "But it is never too late to begin. I had little more acquaintance with my own late lady ere I married her; which proves," he added, with a grimace, "that these impromptu marriages may often produce an excellent understanding in the long run. As the bridegroom is to have a voice in the matter, I will give him two hours to make up for lost time before we proceed with the ceremony." And he

turned toward the door, followed by the clergyman.

The girl was on her feet in a moment. "My uncle, you cannot be in earnest," she said. "I declare before God I will stab myself rather than be forced on that young man. The heart rises at it; God forbids such marriages; you dishonor your white hair. Oh, my uncle, pity me! There is not a woman in all the world but would prefer death to such a nuptial. Is it possible," she added, faltering—"is it possible that you do not believe me—that you still think this"—and she pointed at Denis with a tremor of anger and contempt—"that you still think *this* to be the man?"

"Frankly," said the old gentleman, pausing on the threshold, "I do. But let me explain to you once for all, Blanche de Malétroit, my way of thinking about this affair. When you took it into your head to dishonor my family and the name that I have borne, in peace and war, for more than threescore years, you forfeited

not only the right to question my designs, but that of looking me in the face. If your father had been alive, he would have spat on you and turned you out of doors. His was the hand of iron. You may bless your God you have only to deal with the hand of velvet, mademoiselle. It was my duty to get you married without delay. Out of pure good-will, I have tried to find your own gallant for you. And I believe I have succeeded. But before God and all the holy angels, Blanche de Malétroit, if I have not, I care not one jack-straw. So let me recommend you to be polite to our young friend; for upon my word, your next groom may be less appetizing."

And with that he went out, with the chaplain at his heels; and the arras fell behind the pair.

The girl turned upon Denis with flashing eyes.

"And what, sir," she demanded, "may be the meaning of all this?"

"God knows," returned Denis,

gloomily. "I am a prisoner in this house, which seems full of mad people. More I know not; and nothing do I understand."

"And pray how came you here?" she asked.

He told her as briefly as he could. "For the rest," he added, "perhaps you will follow my example, and tell me the answer to all these riddles, and what, in God's name, is like to be the end of it."

She stood silent for a little, and he could see her lips tremble and her tearless eyes burn with a feverish luster. Then she pressed her forehead in both hands.

"Alas, how my head aches!" she said wearily—"to say nothing of my poor heart! But it is due to you to know my story, unmaidenly as it must seem. I am called Blanche de Malétroit; I have been without father or mother for—oh! for as long as I can recollect, and indeed I have been most unhappy all my life. Three months ago a young captain began to stand near me every day in church. I could see that I pleased him; I am much to blame, but I was so glad that any one should love me; and when he passed me a letter, I took it home with me and read it with great pleasure. Since that time he has written many. He was so anxious to speak with me, poor fellow! and kept asking me to leave the door open some evening that we might have two words upon the stair. For he knew how much my uncle trusted me." She gave something like a sob at that, and it. was a moment before she could go on. "My uncle is a hard man, but he is very shrewd," she said at last. "He has performed many feats in war, and was a great person at court, and much trusted by Queen Isabeau in old days. How he came to suspect me I cannot tell;

but it is hard to keep anything from his knowledge; and this morning, as we came from mass, he took my hand into his, forced it open, and read my little billet, walking by my side all the while. When he finished, he gave it back to me with great politeness. It contained another request to have the door left open; and this has been the ruin of us all. My uncle kept me strictly in my room until evening, and then ordered me to dress myself as you see me—a hard mockery for a young girl, do you not think so? I suppose, when he could not prevail with me to tell him the young captain's name, he must have laid a trap for him, into which, alas! you have fallen in the anger of God. I looked for much confusion; for how could I tell whether he was willing to take me for his wife on these sharp terms? He might have been trifling with me from the first; or I might have made myself too cheap in his eyes. But truly I had not looked for such a shameful punishment as this! I could not think that God would let a girl be so disgraced before a young man. And now I tell you all; and I can scarcely hope that you will not despise me."

Denis made her a respectful inclination.

"Madam," he said, "you have honored me by your confidence. It remains for me to prove that I am not unworthy of the honor. Is Messire de Malétroit at hand?"

"I believe he is writing in the salle without," she answered.

"May I lead you thither, madam?" asked Denis, offering his hand with his most courtly bearing.

She accepted it; and the pair passed out of the chapel, Blanche in a very drooping and shamefast condition, but Denis strutting and ruffling in the consciousness of a mission, and the boyish certainty of accomplishing it with honor.

The Sire de Malétroit rose to meet them with an ironical obeisance.

"Sir," said Denis, with the grandest possible air, "I believe I am to have some say in the matter of this marriage; and let me tell you at once, I will be no party to forcing the inclination of this young lady. Had it been freely offered to me, I should have been proud to accept her hand, for I perceive she is as good as she is beautiful; but as things are, I have now the honor, messire, of refusing."

Blanche looked at him with gratitude in her eyes; but the old gentleman only smiled and smiled, until his smile grew positively sickening to Denis.

"I am afraid," he said, "Monsieur de Beaulieu, that you do not perfectly understand the choice I have offered you. Follow me, I beseech you, to this window." And he led the way to one of the large windows which stood open on the night. "You observe," he went on, "there is an iron ring in the upper masonry, and reeved through that, a very efficacious rope. Now, mark my words: if you should find your disinclination to my niece's person insurmountable, I shall have you hanged out of this window before sunrise. I shall only proceed to such an extremity with the greatest regret, you may believe me. For it is not at all your death that I desire, but my niece's establishment in life. At the same time, it must come to that if you prove obstinate. Your family, Monsieur de Beaulieu, is very well in its way; but if you sprang from Charlemagne, you should not refuse the hand of a Malétroit with impunity—not if she had been as common as the Paris road—not if she were as hideous as the gargoyle

over my door. Neither my niece nor you, nor my own private feelings, move me at all in this matter. The honor of my house has been compromised; I believe you to be the guilty person, at least you are now in the secret; and you can hardly wonder if I request you to wipe out the stain. If you will not, your blood be on your own head! It will be no great satisfaction to me to have your interesting relics kicking their heels in the breeze below my windows, but half a loaf is better than no bread, and if I cannot cure the dishonor, I shall at least stop the scandal."

There was a pause.

"I believe there are other ways of settling such imbroglios among gentlemen," said Denis. "You wear a sword, and I hear you have used it with distinction."

The Sire de Malétroit made a signal to the chaplain, who crossed the room with long silent strides and raised the arras over the third of the three doors. It was only a moment before he let it fall again; but Denis had time to see a dusky passage full of armed men.

"When I was a little younger, I should have been delighted to honor you, Monsieur de Beaulieu," said Sire Alain; "but I am now too old. Faithful retainers are the sinews of age, and I must employ the strength I have. This is one of the hardest things to swallow as a man grows up in years; but with a little patience, even this becomes habitual. You and the lady seem to prefer the salle for what remains of your two hours; and as I have no desire to cross your preference, I shall resign it to your use with all the pleasure in the world. No haste!" he added, holding up his hand, as he saw a dangerous look come into Denis de Beaulieu's face. "If your mind revolt against hanging, it will be time enough two hours hence to throw yourself out of the window or upon the pikes of my retainers. Two hours of life are always two hours. A great many things may turn up in even as little a while as that. And, besides, if I understand her appearance, my niece has something to say to you. You will not disfigure your last hours by a want of politeness to a lady?"

Denis looked at Blanche, and she made him an imploring gesture.

It is likely that the old gentleman was hugely pleased at this symptom of an understanding; for he smiled on both, and added sweetly: "If you will give me your word of honor, Monsieur de Beaulieu, to await my return at the end of the two hours before attempting anything desperate, I shall withdraw my retainers, and let you speak in greater privacy with mademoiselle."

Denis again glanced at the girl, who seemed to beseech him to agree.

"I give you my word of honor," he said.

Messire de Malétroit bowed, and proceeded to limp about the apartment, clearing his throat the while with that odd musical chirp which had already grown so irritating in the ears of Denis de Beaulieu. He first possessed himself of some papers which lay upon the table; then he went to the mouth of the passage and appeared to give an order to the men behind the arras; and lastly he hobbled out through the door by which Denis had come in, turning upon the threshold to address a last smiling bow to the young couple, and followed by the chaplain with a hand-lamp.

No sooner were they alone than Blanche advanced towards Denis with her hands extended. Her face was flushed and excited, and her eyes shone with tears.

"You shall not die!" she cried. "You shall marry me after all."

"You seem to think, madam," replied Denis, "that I stand much in fear of death."

"Oh, no, no," she said, "I see you are no poltroon. It is for my own sake—I could not bear to have you slain for such a scruple."

"I am afraid," returned Denis, "that you underrate the difficulty, madam. What you may be too generous to refuse, I may be too proud to accept. In a moment of noble feeling towards me, you forgot what you perhaps owe to others."

He had the decency to keep his eyes on the floor as he said this, and after he had finished, so as not to spy upon her confusion. She stood silent for a moment, then walked suddenly away, and falling on her uncle's chair, fairly burst out sobbing. Denis was in the acme of embarrassment. He looked round, as if to seek for inspiration, and seeing a stool, plumped down upon it for something to do. There he sat, playing with the guard of his rapier, and wishing himself dead a thousand times over, and buried in the nastiest kitchen-heap in France. His eyes wandered round the apartment, but found nothing to arrest them. There were such wide spaces between the furniture, the light fell so badly and cheerlessly over all, the dark outside air looked in so coldly through the windows that he thought he had never seen a church so vast, nor a tomb so melancholy. The regular sobs of Blanche de Malétroit measured out the time like the ticking of a clock. He read the device upon the shield over and over again, until his eyes became obscured; he stared into shadowy corners until he imagined they were swarming with horrible animals; and every now and again he awoke with a start, to remember that his last two hours were running, and death was on the march.

Oftener and oftener, as the time went on, did his glance settle on the girl herself. Her face was bowed forward and covered with her hands, and she was shaken at intervals by the convulsive hiccup of grief. Even thus she was not an unpleasant object to dwell upon, so plump and yet so fine, with a warm brown skin and the most beautiful hair, Denis thought, in the whole world of womankind. Her hands were like her uncle's; but they were more in place at the end of her young arms, and looked infinitely soft and caressing. He remembered how her blue eyes had shone upon him, full of anger, pity, and innocence. And the more he dwelt on her perfections, the uglier death looked, and the more deeply was he smitten with penitence at her continued tears. Now he felt that no man could have the courage to leave a world which contained so beautiful a creature; and now he would have given forty minutes of his last hour to have unsaid his cruel speech.

Suddenly a hoarse and ragged peal of cockcrow rose to their ears from the dark valley below the windows. And this shattering noise in the silence of all around was like a light in a dark place, and shook them both out of their reflections.

"Alas, can I do nothing to help you?" she said, looking up.

"Madam," replied Denis, with a fine irrelevancy, "if I have said anything to wound you, believe me, it was for your own sake and not for mine."

She thanked him with a tearful look.

"I feel your position cruelly," he went on. "The world has been bitter hard on you. Your uncle is a disgrace to mankind. Believe me, madam, there is no young gentleman in all France but would be glad of my opportunity, to die in doing you a momentary service."

"I know already that you can be very brave and generous," she answered. "What I *want* to know is whether I can serve you—now or afterwards," she added, with a quaver.

"Most certainly," he answered with a smile. "Let me sit beside you as if I were a friend, instead of a foolish intruder; try to forget how awkwardly we are placed to one another; make my last moments go pleasantly; and you will do me the chief service possible."

"You are very gallant," she added, with a yet deeper sadness . . ."very gallant . . . and it somehow pains me. But draw nearer, if you please; and if you find anything to say to me, you will at least make certain of a very friendly listener. Ah! Monsieur de Beaulieu," she broke forth—"ah! Monsieur de Beaulieu, how can I look you in the face?" And she fell to weeping again with a renewed effusion.

"Madam," said Denis, taking her hand in both of his, "reflect on the little time I have before me, and the great bitterness into which I am cast by the sight of your distress. Spare me, in my last moments, the spectacle of what I cannot cure even with the sacrifice of my life."

"I am very selfish," answered Blanche. "I will be braver, Monsieur de Beaulieu, for your sake. But think if I can do you no kindness in the future—if you have no friends to whom I could carry your adieus. Charge me as heavily as you can; every burthen will lighten, by so little, the invaluable gratitude I owe you. Put it in my power to do some-. thing more for you than weep."

"My mother is married again, and has a young family to care for. My brother Guichard will inherit my fiefs; and if I am not in error, that will content him amply for my death. Life is a little vapor that passeth away, as we are told by those in holy orders. When a man is in a fair way and sees all life open in front of him, he seems to himself to make a very important figure in the world. His horse whinnies to him; the trumpets blow and the girls look out of windows as he rides into town before his company; he receives many assurances of trust and regard—sometimes by express in a letter—sometimes face to face, with persons of great consequence falling on his neck. It is not wonderful if his head is turned for a time. But once he is dead, were he as brave as Hercules or as wise as Solomon, he is soon forgotten. It is not ten years since my father fell, with many other knights around him, in a very fierce encounter, and I do not think that any one of them, nor so much as the name of the fight, is now remembered. No, no, madam, the nearer you come to it, you see that death is a dark and dusty corner, where a man gets into his tomb and has the door shut after him till the judgment day. I have few friends just now, and once I am dead I shall have none."

"Ah, Monsieur de Beaulieu!" she exclaimed, "you forget Blanche de Malétroit."

"You have a sweet nature, madam, and you are pleased to estimate a little service far beyond its worth."

"It is not that," she answered. "You mistake me if you think I am easily touched by my own concerns. I say so, because you are the noblest man I have ever met; because I recognize in you a spirit that would have made even a common person famous in the land."

"And yet here I die in a mousetrap —with no more noise about it than my own squeaking," answered he.

A look of pain crossed her face and she was silent for a little while. Then a light came into her eyes, and with a smile she spoke again.

"I cannot have my champion think meanly of himself. Any one who gives his life for another will be met in Paradise by all the heralds and angels of the Lord God. And you have no such cause to hang your head. For . . . pray, do you think me beautiful?" she asked, with a deep flush.

"Indeed, madam, I do," he said.

"I am glad of that," she answered heartily. "Do you think there are many men in France who have been asked in marriage by a beautiful maiden—with her own lips—and who have refused her to her face? I know you men would half despise such a triumph; but believe me, we women know more of what is precious in love. There is nothing that should set a person higher in his own esteem; and we women would prize nothing more dearly."

"You are very good," he said; "but you cannot make me forget that I was asked in pity and not for love."

"I am not so sure of that," she replied, holding down her head. "Hear me to an end, Monsieur de Beaulieu. I know how you must despise me; I feel you are right to do so; I am too poor a creature to occupy one thought of your mind, although, alas! you must die for me this morning. But when I asked you to marry me, indeed, and indeed, it was because I respected and admired you, and loved you with my whole soul, from the very moment that you took my part against my uncle. If you had seen yourself, and now noble you looked, you would pity rather than despise me. And now," she went on, hurriedly checking him with her hand, "although I have laid aside all reserve and told you so much, remember that I know your sentiments towards me already. I would not, believe me, being nobly born, weary you with importunities into consent. I too have a pride of my own; and I declare before the holy mother of God, if you should now go back from your word already given, I would no more marry you than I would marry my uncle's groom."

Denis smiled a little bitterly.

"It is a small love," he said, "that shies at a little pride."

She made no answer, although she probably had her own thoughts.

"Come hither to the window," he said with a sigh. "Here is the dawn."

And indeed the dawn was already beginning. The hollow of the sky was full of essential daylight, colorless and clean; and the valley underneath was flooded with a gray reflection. A few thin vapors clung in the coves of the forest or lay along the winding course of the river. The scene disengaged a surprising effect of stillness, which was hardly interrupted when the cocks began once more to crow among the steadings. Perhaps the same fellow who had made so horrid a clangor in the darkness not half an hour before, now sent up the merriest cheer to greet the coming day. A little wind went bustling and eddying among the tree-tops underneath the windows. And still the daylight kept flooding insensibly out of the east, which was soon to grow incandescent and cast up that red-hot cannon-ball, the rising sun.

Denis looked out over all this with a bit of a shiver. He had taken her hand, and retained it in his almost unconsciously.

"Has the day begun already?" she said; and then illogically enough: "the night has been so long! Alas! what shall we say to my uncle when he returns?"

"What you will," said Denis, and he pressed her fingers in his.

She was silent.

"Blanche," he said, with a swift, uncertain, passionate utterance, "you have seen whether I fear death. You must know well enough that I would as gladly leap out of that window into the empty air as to lay a finger on you without your free and full consent. But if you care for me at all do not let me lose my life in a misapprehension; for I love you better than the whole world; and though I will die for you blithely, it would be like all the joys of Paradise to live on and spend my life in your service."

As he stopped speaking, a bell began to ring loudly in the interior of the house; and a clatter of armor in the corridor showed that the retainers were returning to their post, and the two hours were at an end.

"After all that you have heard?" she whispered, leaning toward him with her lips and eyes.

"I have heard nothing," he replied.

"The captain's name was Florimond de Champdivers," she said in his ear.

"I did not hear it," he answered, taking her supple body in his arms, and covering her wet face with kisses.

A melodious chirping was audible behind, followed by a beautiful chuckle, and the voice of Messire de Malétroit wished his new nephew a good morning.

For Thought and Discussion

1. Explain the international complications that made it wise for people to remain indoors after nightfall.
2. What reactions did Denis have to Sire de Malétroit's remarks and his unusual behavior? Do you share his feelings?
3. With what emotions did Blanche first view Denis? What meaning is conveyed by the italicised *this* in her question which concludes with the clause ". . . . . . that you think *this* to be the man?"
4. Does the way in which Denis first phrases his refusal to marry Blanche lower or raise him in your estimation?
5. By what gentlemanly procedure did he offer to settle the difficulty with Sire de Malétroit?
6. Do you think Blanche's proposal to Denis commendable or unladylike?
7. Why did Denis continue for some time to reject her proposal? In the end which do you think weighed more with Denis, fear of death or love for Blanche?
8. Do you think that Blanche's withdrawal of her consent to marry Denis by chance helped to change his feeling of pity for her to love?
9. What is the most effective means used by Stevenson to reveal the character of Sire de Malétroit?
10. Quote some philosophical comments made by Denis? Which of these are similar in tone to comments made by Macbeth? Why do they seem appropriate coming from Macbeth but surprising on the lips of Denis?
11. Do you find Denis attractive? Why?
12. Explain the passage "relics kicking their heels."
13. Quote passages that are apt in their portrayal of emotions—fear, anger, contempt, pity, respect, love.
14. What elements of story writing characteristic of Stevenson are noticeable in this selection?

꙳

LOCHINVAR

SIR WALTER SCOTT

OH, Young Lochinvar is come out
   of the west;
Through all the wide Border his steed
   was the best;
And save his good broadsword he
   weapons had none,
He rode all unarmed, and he rode all
   alone.

So faithful in love, and so dauntless
   in war,   5
There never was knight like the
   young Lochinvar!

He stayed not for brake, and he
   stopped not for stone;
He swam the Esk River where ford
   there was none;

But ere he alighted at Netherby gate
The bride had consented, the gallant
    came late;   10
For a laggard in love, and a dastard
    in war,
Was to wed the fair Ellen of brave
    Lochinvar.

So boldly he entered the Netherby
    Hall,
Among bride's-men, and kinsmen,
    and brothers, and all.
Then spoke the bride's father, his
    hand on his sword,   15
(For the poor craven bridegroom
    said never a word)
"O come ye in peace here, or come ye
    in war,
Or to dance at our bridal, young
    Lord Lochinvar?"—

"I long wooed your daughter, my suit
    you denied—
Love swells like the Solway, but ebbs
    like its tide—   20
And now am I come, with this lost
    love of mine,
To lead but one measure, drink one
    cup of wine;
There are maidens in Scotland more
    lovely by far,
That would gladly be bride to the
    young Lochinvar."

The bride kissed the goblet; the
    knight took it up,   25
He quaffed off the wine, and he threw
    down the cup.
She looked down to blush, and she
    looked up to sigh,
With a smile on her lips, and a tear
    in her eye.

He took her soft hand, ere her mother
    could bar—
"Now tread we a measure!" said
    young Lochinvar.   30

So stately his form, and so lovely
    her face,
That never a hall such a galliard did
    grace;
While her mother did fret, and her
    father did fume,
And the bridegroom stood dangling
    his bonnet and plume;
And the bride-maidens whispered,
    " 'Twere better by far   35
To have matched our fair cousin
    with young Lochinvar."

One touch to her hand and one word
    in her ear,
When they reached the hall door, and
    the charger stood near;
So light to the croupe the fair lady
    he swung,
So light to the saddle before her he
    sprung!   40
"She is won! we are gone, over bank,
    bush and scaur;
They'll have fleet steeds that follow,"
    quoth young Lochinvar.

There was mounting 'mong Graemes
    of the Netherby clan;
Forsters, Fenwicks, and Musgraves,
    they rode and they ran;
There was racing and chasing on
    Cannobie Lee,   45
But the lost bride of Netherby ne'er
    did they see.
So daring in love, and so dauntless
    in war,
Have ye e'er heard of gallant like
    young Lochinvar?

For Thought and Discussion

1. Why do you admire young Lochinvar?
2. Why do you dislike his rival?

3. When he asked to dance with fair Ellen, did you think that he intended to elope with her?
4. Why do you think that Ellen's parents wanted her to marry the other man?
5. Why is this poem a ballad?
6. Where did Scott get material for ballads?
7. An interesting study may be made by comparing the love lyrics of Burns with the love ballads of Scott. A contrast of these poems will reveal the essential differences between the lyric and the ballad. Refer to "Types of Literature."
8. Read the "Age of Romanticism" for a background of the early nineteenth century.

Plus Work

Stage this poem in pantomime with proper setting and costuming. As it is acted, ask a member of the class to read the poem.

Read the entire poem *Marmion* from which "Lochinvar" was taken.

JOCK OF HAZELDEAN
SIR WALTER SCOTT

[¹*sall*, shall. ²*sae*, so. ³*loot*, let. ⁴*fa'*, fall. ⁵*ha'*, hall. ⁶*kirk*, church.]

WHY weep ye by the tide, ladie?
  Why weep ye by the tide?
I'll wed ye to my youngest son,
  And ye sall[1] be his bride.
And ye sall be his bride, ladie,   5
  Sae[2] comely to be seen"—
But aye she loot[3] the tears down fa'[4]
  For Jock of Hazeldean.

"Now let this willfu' grief be done,
  And dry that cheek so pale;   10
Young Frank is chief of Errington
  And lord of Langley-dale;
His step is first in peaceful ha',[5]
  His sword in battle keen"—
But aye she loot the tears down fa'   15
  For Jock of Hazeldean.

"A chain of gold ye sall not lack,
  Nor braid to bind your hair;
Nor mettled hound, nor managed hawk,
  Nor palfrey fresh and fair;   20
And you, the foremost o' them a',
  Shall ride our forest queen"—
But aye she loot the tears down fa'
  For Jock of Hazeldean.

The kirk[6] was decked at morning-tide,   25
  The tapers glimmered fair;
The priest and bridegroom wait the bride,
  And dame and knight are there.
They sought her baith by bower and ha';
  The ladie was not seen!   30
She's o'er the Border, and awa'
  Wi' Jock of Hazeldean.

For Thought and Discussion

1. Who is the leading figure in this poem?
2. What reasons were given to persuade her to marry Frank of Errington?

3. Why did she dislike Frank of Errington?
4. Why did Scott use Scotch words in this ballad?
5. Compare this poem with "Lochinvar."

SIR WALTER SCOTT 1771-1832

Early Life. Five years before the American Revolution, Walter Scott was born in Edinburgh, Scotland. When he was very young, he had an attack of fever, which left him almost helpless. On the farm of his grandparents, to which he was sent for the benefit of the country air, he soon became the most important member of the household, receiving much attention from his grandparents and his Aunt Janet and the servants. His appreciation of vivid scenes in nature is revealed by an incident which occurred while he was on the farm. When a thunderstorm came up, he was missed from the household and was found alone on the knolls, where he had been left by an unreliable servant. Instead of being frightened by the storm, he was lying on his back, clapping his hands at every flash of lightning and shouting, "Bonny! Bonny!"

Interest in Border Tales. In the evenings Walter loved to sit before the great fireplace and listen to stories of the Scotch border. From his Aunt Janet he learned the tale of Hardy Knute, which he recited so continuously that the minister, Dr. Duncan, said, no doubt rather impatiently, "One might as well speak in a cannon's mouth as where that child is!"

When Scott was seven or eight years old, he was able to return to his home in Edinburgh in excellent health, a very sturdy boy, with the exception of a slight lameness.

His interest in the border, implanted by his Aunt Janet, colored his school life and eventually shaped his career. In grammar school he amused the boys at play-time with border tales, and in Edinburgh University, where he went to study law, he continued to read ballads and stories of the border. He spent his holidays walking through the country searching out old people who might add another story to his collection. When his work in the university was finished and he had entered his father's law firm, he continued his long tramps in the country, sometimes walking thirty miles a day in spite of his lameness, thus calling forth his father's remark that Walter seemed to be born to be a strolling peddler.

His Marriage. When Scott was barely out of college, there occurred in his life an episode of more than passing importance. One Sunday as he stood on the church porch for shelter from the rain, he caught sight of a very beautiful girl without an umbrella. He graciously and no doubt gratefully offered her his, and was allowed to accompany her home. It was a case of love at first sight, and had Scott's fortunes been equal to the young lady's, he would doubtless have asked for her hand in marriage at once. As it was,

ABBOTSFORD

when six years later he did propose, he learned of her engagement to another. Scott was deeply hurt. But some time afterward, when, as he said his "heart was handsomely pieced," he fell in love again, this time with a young lady whom he had seen out horseback riding. They were soon married, and lived happily throughout their lives.

Poems. Although Scott was successful and busy in his work in the law office, he found time to edit some old ballads. In 1805 he wrote *The Lay of the Last Minstrel*, which immediately became popular; in 1808 *Marmion*; and in 1810 *The Lady of the Lake*. Everybody from king to beggar read his books.

Historical Novels. A new writer, Lord Byron, began writing narrative poems which the public read so eagerly that Scott's work was overshadowed; Scott himself soon realized what had happened. Toward the end of his life when asked why he quit writing poetry, he answered, "Byron bet (beat) me at it." Because of Byron's success Scott turned to prose and eventually gave a permanent place in literature to the historical novel. In his stories knights held sway, and the romance of medieval times lived again. Among his well-known volumes are *The Talisman, Guy Mannering, Rob Roy, The Heart of Midlothian, The Bride of Lammermoor, Woodstock, Ivanhoe,* and *Kenilworth.*

Life at Abbotsford. Scott had long dreamed of building a feudal castle resembling those of the barons of old, and finally the

SIR WALTER SCOTT AND MEMBERS OF HIS FAMILY
IN SCOTTISH DRESS

dream was realized in the building of Abbotsford, which became his last home. He wrote an amusing description of his removal to this estate:

"The neighbors have been much delighted with the procession of my furniture, in which old swords, bows, targets, and lances made a very conspicuous show. A family of turkeys was accommodated within the helmet of some prominent chevalier of ancient border family; and the very cows, for aught I know, were bearing banners and muskets. I assure your ladyship that this caravan, attended by a dozen ragged, rosy peasant children carrying fishing rods and spears, and leading ponies, would, as it crossed the Tweed, have furnished no bad subject for the pencil, and really reminded me of one of the gypsy groups of Callot upon their march."[1]

In this new home, with a large number of retainers, the laird of Abbotsford lived happily and entertained his friends magnificently. A feudal estate is not complete without horses and dogs, and Scott's was not lacking in either. Captain, Lieutenant, and Brown Adam, his favorite horses, did not like to be fed by any hand except the master's. His dogs were Camp and Maida. Scott also had a pet hen and a pet pig that followed him around. To the great

[1]*Life of Scott*, Lockhart.

amusement of all except his embarrassed master, the pig once delayed a hunting party until a servant came to take it away.

Business Failure. Scott entered into a partnership with a printing and publishing company. Scott, who knew nothing of the business, trusted the management to other members of the firm. When they failed with heavy liabilities in 1826, that chivalrous sense of honor, which had always been his, asserted itself, and he refused to take advantage of the bankrupt law but insisted upon assuming responsibility for the entire debt, which he determined to clear by proceeds from his writing. He had two strokes of paralysis as a result of overwork, and when another soon followed, he was forced to take a rest. He consented at last to go to Italy. By this time appreciation of his work was so general that he had become a national figure. The government placed a ship at his disposal, and the voyage began, the course of the ship often being changed to include historic spots. On his return voyage he was too eager to write to realize that his health was completely broken. He died a few months after reaching Abbotsford. The debt which he had tried valiantly to pay was partially cleared by his insurance, and fifteen years later was canceled by the proceeds from sales of his books.

Literary Work. Scott lived sixty-one years, from 1771 to 1832. As a literary man, who established a reputation in two different fields, first as a writer of narrative poetry, second as a creator of the historical novel, Scott had an interesting career. As one who looked back to medieval times for color and interest and the ideals of chivalry, he holds our attention. Lines which apply to his life and character are:

"Sound, sound the clarion, fill the file!
　To all the sensual world proclaim,
One crowded hour of glorious life
　Is worth an age without a name."

∿

THE EVE OF ST. AGNES

JOHN KEATS

[In this series of lightly-strung-together pictures Keats creates an atmosphere, a mood, scarcely a plot, of beauty and romance. Religious rites and medieval superstitions are closely interwoven in his narrative. St. Agnes, a Roman maiden of the time of Diocletian, was supposed to have suffered martyrdom on January 21. Because of a vision which her parents were said to have had, the lamb became sacred to St. Agnes. In their vision they saw their daughter, accompanied by a lamb and surrounded by angels. For this reason, lambs were brought to the altar on the eve of St. Agnes, and afterward they were sheared and the wool was woven into priestly vestments by the nuns.

According to the superstition connected with St. Agnes' Eve, a maiden who performed certain ceremonies and went supperless to bed on that evening would have visions of her future husband. The sketchy plot of the poem tells of Madeline, a lovely medieval maiden, who, wishing to see a vision of the man she was to marry, followed scrupulously all the rites associated with St. Agnes' Eve. How the charm worked for her and her lover Porphyro (pôr′ fĭ rō) the poem tells.

For atmospheric effect Keats uses religious customs of the Roman Catholic church. The beadsman, a person who prayed for others, is represented as counting the beads of his rosary, prayer beads. According to legend the night of January 21 is the coldest of the year; hence the poet speaks of the beadsman's breath being visible as it passes the picture of the Virgin Mary.]

I

ST. Agnes' Eve—Ah, bitter chill was!
The owl, for all his feathers, was a-cold;
The hare limped trembling through the frozen grass,
And silent was the flock in woolly fold;
Numb were the Beadsman's fingers, while he told   5
His rosary, and while his frosted breath,
Like pious incense from a censer old,
Seemed taking flight for heaven, without a death,
Past the sweet Virgin's picture, while his prayer he saith.

II

His prayer he saith, this patient, holy man;   10

Then takes his lamp, and riseth from his knees,
And back returneth, meager, barefoot, wan,
Along the chapel aisle by slow degrees;
The sculptured dead, on each side, seem to freeze,
Emprisoned in black, purgatorial rails;[1]   15
Knights, ladies, praying in dumb orat'ries,[2]
He passeth by; and his weak spirit fails
To think how they may ache in icy hoods and mails.

III

Northward he turneth through a little door,
And scarce three steps, ere Music's golden tongue   20
Flattered to tears this agèd man and poor;
But no—already had his deathbell rung;
The joys of all his life were said and sung;
His was harsh penance[3] on St. Agnes' Eve;
Another way he went, and soon among   25
Rough ashes sat he for his soul's reprieve,
And all night kept awake, for sinners' sake to grieve.

IV

That ancient Beadsman heard the prelude soft;
And so it chanced, for many a door was wide,

---

[1]*purgatorial rails,* prayer rails in purgatory, where according to Catholic belief souls are purified before entering heaven.
[2]*orat'ries,* places for prayer.
[3]*penance,* suffering undergone to gain forgiveness of sin.

From hurry to and fro. Soon, up
    aloft,   30
The silver, snarling trumpets 'gan
    to chide;
The level chambers, ready with
    their pride,
Were glowing to receive a thousand
    guests;
The carvèd angels, ever eager-eyed,
Stared, where upon their heads the
    cornice rests,   35
With hair blown back, and wings put
    crosswise on their breasts.

V

At length burst in the argent rev-
    elry,
With plume, tiara, and all rich
    array,
Numerous as shadows, haunting
    faerily
The brain, new stuffed, in youth,
    with triumphs gay   40
Of old romance. These let us wish
    away,
And turn, sole-thoughted, to one
    lady there,
Whose heart had brooded, all that
    wintry day,
On love, and winged St. Agnes'
    saintly care,
As she had heard old dames full many
    times declare.   45

VI

They told her how, upon St. Agnes'
    Eve,
Young virgins might have visions
    of delight,
And soft adorings from their loves
    receive
Upon the honeyed middle of the
    night,
If ceremonies due they did
    aright;   50
As, supperless to bed they must re-
    tire,

And couch supine their beauties,
    lily white;
Nor look behind, nor sideways, but
    require
Of Heaven with upward eyes for all
    that they desire.

VII

Full of this whim was thoughtful
    Madeline: 55
The music, yearning like a god in
    pain,
She scarcely heard; her maiden eyes
    divine,
Fixed on the floor, saw many a
    sweeping train
Pass by—she heeded not at all; in
    vain
Came many a tiptoe, amorous cav-
    alier,   60
And back retired, not cooled by
    high disdain,
But she saw not—her heart was
    otherwhere:
She sighed for Agnes' dreams, the
    sweetest of the year.

VIII

She danced along with vague, re-
    gardless eyes,
Anxious her lips, her breathing
    quick and short: 65
The hallowed hour was near at
    hand; she sighs
Amid the timbrels, and the
    thronged resort
Of whisperers in anger or in sport;
'Mid looks of love, defiance, hate,
    and scorn,
Hoodwinked with faery fancy, all
    amort   70
Save to St. Agnes and her lambs
    unshorn,
And all the bliss to be before to-mor-
    row morn.

IX

So, purposing each moment to re-
    tire,
She lingered still. Meantime, across
    the moors,
Had come young Porphyro, with
    heart of fire   75
For Madeline. Beside the portal
    doors,
Buttressed from moonlight, stands
    he, and implores
All saints to give him sight of
    Madeline,
But for one moment in the tedious
    hours,
That he might gaze and worship all
    unseen;   80
Perchance speak, kneel, touch, kiss—
    in sooth such things have been.

X

He ventures in: let no buzzed
    whisper tell;
All eyes be muffled, or a hundred
    swords
Will storm his heart, Love's fev'r-
    ous citadel:
For him, those chambers held bar-
    barian hordes,   85
Hyena foemen, and hot-blooded
    lords,
Whose very dogs would execrations
    howl
Against his lineage; not one breast
    affords
Him any mercy, in that mansion
    foul,
Save one old beldame,[4] weak in body
    and in soul.   90

XI

Ah, happy chance! the aged crea-
    ture came,
Shuffling along with ivory-headed
    wand,

---

[4]*beldame,* old woman.

To where he stood, hid from the
    torch's flame,
Behind a broad hall-pillar, far be-
    yond
The sound of merriment and cho-
    rus bland: 95
He startled her; but soon she knew
    his face,
And grasped his fingers in her
    palsied hand,
Saying, "Mercy, Porphyro! hie thee
    from this place;
They are all here tonight, the whole
    bloodthirsty race!

XII

"Get hence! get hence! there's
    dwarfish Hildebrand;   100
He had a fever late, and in the fit
He cursèd thee and thine, both
    house and land;
Then there's that old Lord Maurice,
    not a whit
More tame for his gray hairs—Alas
    me! flit!
Flit like a ghost away."—"Ah,
    Gossip dear,   105
We're safe enough; here in this
    armchair sit,
And tell me how"—"Good Saints!
    not here, not here;
Follow me, child, or else these stones
    will be thy bier."

XIII

He followed through a lowly
    archèd way,
Brushing the cobwebs with his
    lofty plume;   110
And as she muttered "Well-a—
    well-a-day!"
He found him in a little moonlight
    room,
Pale, latticed, chill, and silent as a
    tomb.
"Now tell me where is Madeline,"
    said he,

"O tell me, Angela, by the holy
    loom   ¹¹⁵
Which none but secret sisterhood
    may see,
When they St. Agnes' wool are weav-
    ing piously."

XIV

"St. Agnes! Ah! it is St. Agnes'
    Eve—
Yet men will murder upon holy
    days;
Thou must hold water in a witch's
    sieve,   ¹²⁰
And be liege-lord of all the elves
    and fays,
To venture so; it fills me with
    amaze
To see thee, Porphyro!—St. Agnes'
    Eve!
God's help! my lady fair the con-
    jurer plays
This very night; good angels her
    deceive!   ¹²⁵
But let me laugh awhile, I've mickle
    time to grieve."

XV

Feebly she laugheth in the languid
    moon,
While Porphyro upon her face doth
    look,
Like puzzled urchin on an aged
    crone
Who keepeth closed a wonderous
    riddle-book,   ¹³⁰
As spectacled she sits in chimney
    nook.
But soon his eyes grew brilliant,
    when she told
His lady's purpose; and he scarce
    could brook
Tears, at the thought of those en-
    chantments cold,
And Madeline asleep in lap of legends
    old.   ¹³⁵

XVI

Sudden a thought came like a full-
    blown rose,
Flushing his brow, and in his painèd
    heart
Made purple riot; then doth he
    propose
A stratagem, that makes the bel-
    dame start:
"A cruel man and impious thou
    art!   ¹⁴⁰
Sweet lady, let her pray, and sleep,
    and dream
Alone with her good angels, far
    apart
From wicked men like thee. Go,
    go! I deem
Thou canst not surely be the same
    that thou didst seem."

XVII

"I will not harm her, by all saints
    I swear,"   ¹⁴⁵
Quoth Porphyro. "O may I ne'er
    find grace
When my weak voice shall whisper
    its last prayer,
If one of her soft ringlets I dis-
    place,
Or look with ruffian passion in her
    face!
Good Angela, believe me by these
    tears;   ¹⁵⁰
Or I will, even in a moment's space,
Awake, with horrid shout, my foe-
    men's ears,
And beard them, though they be more
    fanged than wolves and
    bears."

XVIII

"Ah, why wilt thou affright a
    feeble soul?
A poor, weak, palsy-stricken,
    churchyard thing,   ¹⁵⁵
Whose passing-bell may ere the
    midnight toll;

Whose prayers for thee, each morn
    and evening,
Were never missed." Thus plain-
    ing, doth she bring
A gentler speech from burning
    Porphyro;
So woeful, and of such deep sor-
    rowing,   160
That Angela gives promise she will
    do
Whatever he shall wish, betide her
    weal or woe.

XIX

Which was, to lead him, in close
    secrecy,
Even to Madeline's chamber, and
    there hide
Him in a closet, of such privacy   165
That he might see her beauty un-
    espied,
And win perhaps that night a peer-
    less bride,
While legioned faeries paced the
    coverlet,
And pale enchantment held her
    sleepy-eyed.
Never on such a night have lovers
    met,   170
Since Merlin[5] paid his demon all the
    monstrous debt.

XX

"It shall be as thou wishest," said
    the dame:
"All cates and dainties shall be
    storèd there
Quickly on this feast-night; by the
    tambour frame
Her own lute thou wilt see: no
    time to spare,   175
For I am slow and feeble, and
    scarce dare
On such a catering trust my dizzy
    head.

---

[5]*Merlin,* a wizard who became the
victim of his own magic.

Wait here, my child, with patience;
    kneel in prayer
The while. Ah, thou must needs
    the lady wed,
Or may I never leave my grave among
    the dead."   180

XXI

So saying, she hobbled off with
    busy fear.
The lover's endless minutes slowly
    passed.
The dame returned, and whispered
    in his ear
To follow her, with aged eyes
    aghast
From fright of dim espial. Safe at
    last,   185
Through many a dusky gallery,
    they gain
The maiden's chamber, silken,
    hushed, and chaste,
Where Porphyro took covert,
    pleased amain.
His poor guide hurried back, with
    agues in her brain.

XXII

Her faltering hand upon the balus-
    trade,   190
Old Angela was feeling for the
    stair,
When Madeline, St. Agnes'
    charmèd maid,
Rose, like a missioned spirit, un-
    aware.
With silver taper's light, and pious
    care,
She turned, and down the aged
    gossip led   195
To a safe level matting. Now pre-
    pare,
Young Porphyro, for gazing on
    that bed:
She comes, she comes again, like ring-
    dove frayed and fled.

XXIII

Out went the taper as he hurried
in;
Its little smoke, in pallid moonshine, died: 200
She closed the door, she panted, all
akin
To spirits of the air and visions
wide:
No uttered syllable, or woe betide!
But to her heart, her heart was voluble,
Paining with eloquence her balmy
side;   205
As though a tongueless nightingale
should swell
Her throat in vain, and die, heart-
stifled, in her dell.

XXIV

A casement high and triple-arched
there was,
All garlanded with carven imag'ries
Of fruits, and flowers, and bunches
of knot-grass,   210
And diamondèd with panes of
quaint device,
Innumerable of stains and splendid
dyes,
As are the tiger-moth's deep-dam-
asked wings;
And in the midst, 'mong thousand
heraldries,
And twilight saints, and dim em-
blazonings,   215
A shielded scutcheon blushed with
blood of queens and kings.

XXV

Full on this casement shone the
wintry moon,
And threw warm gules[6] on Madeline's fair breast,
As down she knelt for heaven's
grace and boon;
Rose-bloom fell on her hands, together pressed,   220

---

[6]*gules,* red color.

And on her silver cross soft ame-
thyst,
And on her hair a glory, like a
saint;
She seemed a splendid angel, newly
dressed,
Save wings, for heaven; Porphyro
grew faint;
She knelt, so pure a thing, so free
from mortal taint.   225

XXVI

Anon his heart revives; her vespers
done,
Of all its wreathèd pearls her hair
she frees;
Unclasps her warmèd jewels one by
one;
Loosens her fragrant bodice; by degrees
Her rich attire creeps rustling to
her knees;   230
Half-hidden, like a mermaid in seaweed,
Pensive awhile she dreams awake,
and sees,
In fancy, fair St. Agnes in her bed,
But dares not look behind, or all the
charm is fled.

XXVII

Soon, trembling in her soft and
chilly nest,   235
In sort of wakeful swoon, per-
plexed she lay,
Until the poppied warmth of sleep
oppressed
Her soothèd limbs, and soul fa-
tigued away;
Flown, like a thought, until the
morrow-day;
Blissfully havened both from joy
and pain;   240
Clasped like a missal[7] where swart
Paynims pray;
Blinded alike from sunshine and
from rain,
As though a rose should shut, and be
a bud again.

---

[7]*missal,* a prayer book.

XXVIII

Stol'n to this paradise, and so en-
    tranced,
Porphyro gazed upon her empty
    dress,   245
And listened to her breathing, if it
    chanced
To wake into a slumberous tender-
    ness;
Which when he heard, that minute
    did he bless,
And breathed himself; then from
    the closet crept,
Noiseless as fear in a wide wilder-
    ness,   250
And over the hushed carpet, silent,
    stepped,
And 'tween the curtains peeped,
    where, lo! how fast she slept.

XXIX

Then by the bedside, where the
    faded moon
Made a dim, silver twilight, soft he
    set
A table, and, half anguished, threw
    thereon   255
A cloth of woven crimson, gold,
    and jet—
O for some drowsy Morphean amu-
    let!
The boisterous, midnight, festive
    clarion,
The kettle-drum, and far-heard
    clarinet,
Affray his ears, though but in dy-
    ing tone—   260
The hall door shuts again, and all the
    noise is gone.

XXX

And still she slept an azure-lidded
    sleep,
In blanchèd linen, smooth, and
    lavendered,
While he from forth the closet
    brought a heap

Of candied apple, quince, and
    plum, and gourd;   265
With jellies soother than the creamy
    curd,
And lucent syrops, tinct with cin-
    namon;
Manna and dates, in argosy trans-
    ferred
From Fez; and spicèd dainties,
    every one,
From silken Samarcand to cedared
    Lebanon.   270

XXXI

These delicates he heaped with
    glowing hand
On golden dishes and in baskets
    bright
Of wreathèd silver: sumptuous
    they stand
In the retirèd quiet of the night,
Filling the chilly room with per-
    fume light.—   275
"And now, my love, my seraph
    fair, awake!
Thou art my heaven, and I thine
    eremite[8];
Open thine eyes, for meek St.
    Agnes' sake,
Or I shall drowse beside thee, so my
    soul doth ache."

XXXII

Thus whispering, his warm, un-
    nervèd arm   280
Sank in her pillow. Shaded was
    her dream
By the dusk curtains—'t was a mid-
    night charm
Impossible to melt as icèd stream;
The lustrous salvers in the moon-
    light gleam;
Broad golden fringe upon the car-
    pet lies.   285
It seemed he never, never could re-
    deem

---

[8]*eremite,* a hermit who prays to
heaven.

From such a stedfast spell his lady's
    eyes;
So mused awhile, entoiled in woofèd
    phantasies.

XXXIII

Awakening up, he took her hollow
    lute—
Tumultuous,—and in chords that
    tenderest be,   290
He played an ancient ditty, long
    since mute,
In Provence called "La belle dame
    sans mercy,"
Close to her ear touching the mel-
    ody;
Wherewith disturbed, she uttered a
    soft moan;
He ceased—she panted quick—and
    suddenly   295
Her blue affrayed eyes wide open
    shone;
Upon his knees he sank, pale as
    smooth-sculptured stone.

XXXIV

Her eyes were open, but she still
    beheld,
Now wide awake, the vision of her
    sleep:
There was a painful change that
    nigh expelled   300
The blisses of her dream so pure
    and deep;
At which fair Madeline began to
    weep,
And moan forth witless words with
    many a sigh,
While still her gaze on Porphyro
    would keep,
Who knelt, with joined hands and
    piteous eye,   305
Fearing to move or speak, she looked
    so dreamingly.

XXXV

"Ah, Porphyro!" said she, "but
    even now

Thy voice was at sweet tremble in
    mine ear,
Made tuneable with every sweetest
    vow;
And those sad eyes were spiritual
    and clear: 310
How changed thou art! how pallid,
    chill, and drear!
Give me that voice again, my Por-
    phyro,
Those looks immortal, those com-
    plainings dear!
Oh leave me not in this eternal woe,
For if thou diest, my love, I know not
    where to go."   315

XXXVI

Beyond a mortal man impassioned
    far
At these voluptuous accents, he
    arose,
Ethereal, flushed, and like a throb-
    bing star
Seen 'mid the sapphire heaven's
    deep repose;
Into her dream he melted, as the
    rose   320
Blendeth its odour with the vio-
    let—
Solution sweet: meantime the frost-
    wind blows
Like Love's alarum pattering the
    sharp sleet
Against the window-panes; St. Agnes'
    moon hath set.

XXXVII

'T is dark; quick pattereth the
    flaw-blown sleet.   325
"This is no dream, my bride, my
    Madeline!"
'T is dark; the icèd gusts still rave
    and beat.
"No dream, alas! alas! and woe is
    mine!
Porphyro will leave me here to fade
    and pine—

Cruel! what traitor could thee
    hither bring? 330
I curse not, for my heart is lost in
    thine,
Though thou forsakest a deceivèd
    thing,
A dove forlorn and lost, with sick un-
    prunèd wing."

XXXVIII

"My Madeline! sweet dreamer!
    lovely bride!
Say, may I be for aye thy vassal
    blest? 335
Thy beauty's shield, heart-shaped
    and vermeil dyed?
Ah, silver shrine, here will I take
    my rest
After so many hours of toil and
    quest,
A famished pilgrim—saved by mir-
    acle.
Though I have found, I will not
    rob thy nest 340
Saving of thy sweet self; if thou
    think'st well
To trust, fair Madeline, to no rude
    infidel.

XXXIX

"Hark! 'tis an elfin-storm from
    faery land,
Of haggard seeming, but a boon
    indeed;
Arise—arise! the morning is at
    hand— 345
The bloated wassailers will never
    heed—
Let us away, my love, with happy
    speed;
There are no ears to hear, or eyes to
    see—
Drowned all in Rhenish and the
    sleepy mead;
Awake! arise! my love, and fear-
    less be, 350
For o'er the southern moors I have a
    home for thee."

XL

She hurried at his words, beset with
    fears,
For there were sleeping dragons all
    around,
At glaring watch, perhaps, with
    ready spears—
Down the wide stairs a darkling
    way they found— 355
In all the house was heard no hu-
    man sound.
A chain-drooped lamp was flicker-
    ing by each door;
The arras, rich with horseman,
    hawk, and hound,
Fluttered in the besieging wind's
    uproar;
And the long carpets rose along the
    gusty floor. 360

XLI

They glide, like phantoms, into the
    wide hall;
Like phantoms, to the iron porch,
    they glide;
Where lay the porter, in uneasy
    sprawl,
With a huge empty flagon by his
    side;
The wakeful bloodhound rose, and
    shook his hide, 365
But his sagacious eye an inmate
    owns;
By one and one, the bolts full easy
    slide—
The chains lie silent on the foot-
    worn stones—
The key turns, and the door upon its
    hinges groans.

XLII

And they are gone; aye, ages long
    ago 370
These lovers fled away into the
    storm.
That night the Baron dreamt of
    many a woe;

And all his warrior-guests, with
    shade and form
Of witch, and demon, and large
    coffin-worm,
Were long be-nightmared. Angela
    the old   375
Died palsy-twitched, with meagre
    face deform.

The beadsman, after thousand aves[9]
    told,
For aye unsought-for slept among his
    ashes cold.

---

[9] *aves,* prayers, meaning "Hail," from
the Roman Catholic prayer Hail Mary
(Ave Maria).

For Thought and Discussion

1. Judging from this poem would you say that Keats has narrative or lyric power? Justify your answer.
2. Which makes the greatest appeal to you, the plot, the persons, or the pictures of this poem?
3. What day celebrated at the present time corresponds somewhat to St. Agnes' Eve?
4. If Scott had been telling this story, what difference would he have made in plot? Would his characters have been more or less real than those of Keats? Would there have been more or less action in the story?
5. Copy five figures of speech. To what sense, if any, does each make appeal?
6. What is the setting of the story?
7. How did Porphyro happen to conceive the plan for elopement with Madeline?
8. Is Keats's imagery effective or does he use too much or too little description?

9. Explain the suggestive quality in the expressions "hyena foe-
   man," "dim espial," "agues in her brain," "poppied warmth."
10. What became of the characters mentioned in the poem?

$\sim\!\!\sim$

THE SNOWSTORM
ALEXANDER PUSHKIN

[Alexander Pushkin, 1799-1837, belongs among the famous Russian writers. Usually his work is characterized by imagination and poetic insight.]

TOWARDS the end of the year 1811, a memorable period for us, the good Gavril Gavrilovitch R—— was living on his domain of Nenaradova. He was celebrated throughout the district for his hospitality and kind-heartedness. The neighbors were constantly visiting him: some to eat and drink; some to play at five kopek "Boston" with his wife, Praskovia Petrovna; and some to look at their daughter, Maria Gavrilovna, a pale, slender girl of seventeen. She was considered a wealthy match, and many desired her for themselves or for their sons.

Maria Gavrilovna had been brought up on French novels and consequently was in love. The object of her choice was a poor sub-lieutenant in the army, who was then on leave of absence in his village. It need scarcely be mentioned that the young man returned her passion with equal ardor, and that the parents of his beloved one, observing their mutual inclination, forbade their daughter to think of him, and received him worse than a discharged assessor.

Our lovers corresponded with one another and daily saw each other alone in the little pine wood or near the old chapel. There they exchanged vows of eternal love, lamented their cruel fate, and formed various plans. Corresponding and conversing in this way, they arrived quite naturally at the following conclusion:

If we cannot exist without each other, and the will of hard-hearted parents stands in the way of our happiness, why cannot we do without them?

Needless to mention that this happy idea originated in the mind of the young man, and that it was very congenial to the romantic imagination of Maria Gavrilovna.

The winter came and put a stop to their meetings, but their correspondence became all the more active. Vladimir Nikolaievitch in every letter implored her to give herself to him, to get married secretly, to hide for some time, and then to throw themselves at the feet of their parents, who would, without any doubt be touched at last by the heroic constancy and unhappiness of the lovers, and would infallibly say to them: "Children, come to our arms!"

Maria Gavrilovna hesitated for a long time, and several plans for a flight were rejected. At last she consented: on the appointed day she was not to take supper, but was to retire to her room under the pretext of a headache. Her maid was in the plot; they were both to go into the garden by the back stairs, and behind the garden they would find ready a sledge, into which they were to get, and then drive straight to the church of Jadrino, a village about five versts from Nenaradova, where Vladimir would be waiting for them.

On the eve of the decisive day, Maria Gavrilovna did not sleep the whole night; she packed and tied up her linen and other articles of apparel, wrote a long letter to a sentimental young lady, a friend of hers, and another to her parents. She took leave of them in the most touching terms, urged the invincible strength of passion as an excuse for the step she was taking, and wound up with the assurance that she should consider it the happiest moment of her life, when she should be allowed to throw herself at the feet of her dear parents.

After having sealed both letters with a Toula seal, upon which were engraved two flaming hearts with a suitable inscription, she threw herself upon her bed just before daybreak, and dozed off: but even then she was constantly being awakened by terrible dreams. First, it seemed to her that at the very moment when she seated herself in the sledge, in order to go and get married, her father stopped her, dragged her into a dark bottomless abyss, down which she fell headlong with an indescribable sinking of the heart. Then she saw Vladimir lying on the grass, pale and bloodstained. With his dying breath he implored her, in a piercing voice, to make haste and marry him . . . . Other fantastic and senseless visions floated before her, one after another. At last she arose, paler than usual, and with an unfeigned headache. Her father and mother observed her uneasiness; their tender solicitude and incessant inquiries: "What is the matter with you, Masha? Are you ill, Masha?" cut her to the heart. She tried to reassure them and to appear cheerful, but in vain.

The evening came. The thought that this was the last day she would pass in the bosom of her family weighed upon her heart. She was more dead than alive. In secret she took leave of everybody, of all the objects that surrounded her.

Supper was served; her heart began to beat violently. In a trembling voice she declared that she did not want any supper, and then took leave of her father and mother. They kissed her and blessed her as usual, and she could hardly restrain herself from weeping.

On reaching her own room, she threw herself into a chair and burst into tears. Her maid urged her to be calm and to take courage. Everything was ready. In half an hour Masha would leave forever her parents' house, her room, and her peaceful girlish life . . . .

Out in the courtyard the snow was falling heavily; the wind howled, the shutters shook and rattled, and everything seemed to her to portend misfortune.

Soon all was quiet in the house: everyone was asleep. Masha wrapped herself in a shawl, put on a warm cloak, took her small box in her hand, and went down the back staircase. Her maid followed her with two bundles. They descended into the garden. The snowstorm had not subsided; the wind blew in their faces as if trying to stop the young criminal. With difficulty they reached the end of the garden. In the road a sledge awaited them. The horses, half-frozen with the cold, would not keep still; Vladimir's coachman was walking up and down in front of them, trying to restrain their impatience. He helped the young lady and her maid into the sledge, placed the box and the bundles in the vehicle, seized the reins, and the horses dashed off.

Having intrusted the young lady to

the care of fate, and to the skill of Tereshka the coachman, we will return to our young lover.

Vladimir had spent the whole of the day in driving about. In the morning he paid a visit to the priest of Jadrino, and having come to an agreement with him after a great deal of difficulty, he then set out to seek for witnesses among the neighboring landowners. The first to whom he presented himself, a retired cornet of about forty years of age, and whose name was Dravin, consented with pleasure. The adventure, he declared, reminded him of his young days and his pranks in the Hussars. He persuaded Vladimir to stay to dinner with him, and assured him that he would have no difficulty in finding the other two witnesses. And indeed, immediately after dinner, appeared the surveyor Schmidt, with mustache and spurs, and the son of the captain of police, a lad of sixteen years of age, who had recently entered the Uhlans. They not only accepted Vladimir's proposal, but even vowed that they were ready to sacrifice their lives for him. Vladimir embraced them with rapture, and returned home to get everything ready.

It had been dark for some time. He dispatched his faithful Tereshka to Nenaradova with his sledge and with detailed instructions, and ordered for himself the small sledge with one horse, and set out alone, without any coachman, for Jadrino, where Maria Gavrilovna ought to arrive in about a couple of hours. He knew the road well, and the journey would only occupy about twenty minutes altogether.

But scarcely had Vladimir issued from the paddock into the open field, when the wind rose and such a snowstorm came on that he could see nothing. In one minute the road was completely hidden; all surrounding objects disappeared in a thick yellow fog, through which fell the white flakes of snow; earth and sky became confounded. Vladimir found himself in the middle of the field, and tried in vain to find the road again. His horse went on at random, and at every moment kept either stepping into a snowdrift or stumbling into a hole, so that the sledge was constantly being overturned. Vladimir endeavored not to lose the right direction. But it seemed to him that more than half an hour had already passed, and he had not yet reached the Jadrino wood. Another ten minutes elapsed—still no wood was to be seen. Vladimir drove across a field intersected by deep ditches. The snowstorm did not abate, the sky did not become any clearer. The horse began to grow tired, and the perspiration rolled from him in great drops, in spite of the fact that he was constantly being half buried in the snow.

At last Vladimir perceived that he was going in the wrong direction. He stopped, began to think, to recollect, and compare, and he felt convinced that he ought to have turned to the right. He turned to the right now. His horse could scarcely move forward. He had now been on the road for more than an hour. Jadrino could not be far off. But on and on he went, and still no end to the field —nothing but snowdrifts and ditches. The sledge was constantly being overturned, and as constantly being set right again. The time was passing; Vladimir began to grow seriously uneasy.

At last something dark appeared in the distance. Vladimir directed his course towards it. On drawing near, he perceived that it was a wood. "Thank Heaven," he thought, "I am not far off now." He drove

along by the edge of the wood, hoping by and by to fall upon the well-known road or to pass round the wood; Jadrino was situated just behind it. He soon found the road, and plunged into the darkness of the wood, now denuded of leaves by the winter. The wind could not rage here; the road was smooth, the horse recovered courage, and Vladimir felt reassured.

But he drove on and on, and Jadrino was not to be seen; there was no end to the wood. Vladimir discovered with horror that he had entered an unknown forest. Despair took possession of him. He whipped the horse; the poor animal broke into a trot, but it soon slackened its pace, and in about a quarter of an hour it was scarcely able to drag one leg after the other, in spite of all the exertions of the unfortunate Vladimir.

Gradually the trees began to get sparser, and Vladimir emerged from the forest; but Jadrino was not to be seen. It must now have been midnight. Tears gushed from his eyes; he drove on at random. Meanwhile the storm had subsided, the clouds dispersed, and before him lay a level plain covered with a white, undulating carpet. The night was tolerably clear. He saw, not far off, a little village, consisting of four or five houses. Vladimir drove towards it. At the first cottage he jumped out of the sledge, ran to the window and began to knock. After a few minutes the wooden shutter was raised, and an old man thrust out his gray beard.

"What do you want?"

"Is Jadrino far from here?"

"Is Jadrino far from here?"

"Yes, yes! Is it far?"

"Not far; about ten versts."

At this reply, Vladimir grasped his hair and stood motionless, like a man condemned to death.

"Where do you come from?" continued the old man.

Vladimir had not the courage to answer the question.

"Listen, old man," said he, "can you procure me horses to take me to Jadrino?"

"How should we have such things as horses?" replied the peasant.

"Can I obtain a guide? I will pay him whatever he asks."

"Wait," said the old man, closing the shutter. "I will send my son out to you; he will guide you."

Vladimir waited. But a minute had scarcely elapsed when he began knocking again. The shutter was raised, and the beard again reappeared.

"What do you want?"

"What about your son?"

"He'll be out presently; he is putting on his boots. Are you cold? Come in and warm yourself."

"Thank you; send your son out quickly."

The door creaked; a lad came out with a cudgel and went on in front, at one time pointing out the road, at another searching for it among the drifted snow.

"What is the time?" Vladimir asked him.

"It will soon be daylight," replied the young peasant. Vladimir spoke not another word.

The cocks were crowing, and it was already light when they reached Jadrino. The church was closed. Vladimir paid the guide and drove into the priest's courtyard. His sledge was not there. What news awaited him!....

But let us return to the worthy proprietors of Nenaradova, and see what is happening there.

Nothing.

The old people awoke and went into the parlor, Gavril Gavrilovitch in a night-cap, and flannel doublet, Praskovia Petrovna in a wadded dressing-gown. The tea-urn (samovar) was brought in, and Gavril Gavrilovitch sent a servant to ask Maria Gavrilovna how she was and how she had passed the night. The servant returned saying that the young lady had not slept very well, but that she felt better now, and that she would come down presently into the parlor. And indeed, the door opened and Maria Gavrilovna entered the room and wished her father and mother good morning.

"How is your head, Masha?" asked Gavril Gavrilovitch.

"Better, papa," replied Masha.

"Very likely you inhaled the fumes from the charcoal yesterday," said Praskovia Petrovna.

"Very likely, mamma," replied Masha.

The day passed happily enough, but in the night Masha was taken ill. A doctor was sent for from the town. He arrived in the evening and found the sick girl delirious. A violent fever ensued, and for two weeks the poor patient hovered on the brink of the grave.

Nobody in the house knew anything about her flight. The letters, written by her the evening before, had been burnt; and her maid, dreading the wrath of her master, had not whispered a word about it to anybody. The priest, the retired cornet, the mustached surveyor, and the little Uhlan were discreet, and not without reason. Tereshka, the coachman, never uttered one word too much about it, even when he was drunk. Thus the secret was kept by more than half a dozen conspirators.

But Maria Gavrilovna herself divulged her secret during her delirious ravings. But her words were so disconnected, that her mother, who never left her bedside, could only understand from them that her daughter was deeply in love with Vladimir Nikolaievitch, and that probably love was the cause of her illness. She consulted her husband and some of her neighbors, and at last it was unanimously decided that such was evidently Maria Gavrilovna's fate, that a woman cannot ride away from the man who is destined to be her husband, that poverty is not a crime, that one does not marry wealth, but a man, etc., etc. Moral proverbs are wonderfully useful in those cases where we can invent little in our own justification.

In the meantime the young lady began to recover. Vladimir had not been seen for a long time in the house of Gavril Gavrilovitch. He was afraid of the usual reception. It was resolved to send and announce to him an unexpected piece of good news: the consent of Maria's parents to his marriage with their daughter. But what was the astonishment of the proprietor of Nenaradova, when, in reply to their invitation, they received from him a half insane letter. He informed them that he would never set foot in their house again, and begged them to forget an unhappy creature whose only hope was death. A few days afterwards they heard that Vladimir had joined the army again. This was in the year 1812.

For a long time they did not dare to announce this to Masha, who was now convalescent. She never mentioned the name of Vladimir. Some months afterwards, finding his name in the list of those who had distinguished themselves and been severely wounded at Borodino, she fainted away, and it was feared that she would have another attack of fever. But, Heaven be thanked! the fainting fit had no serious consequences.

Another misfortune fell upon her: Gavril Gavrilovitch died, leaving her the heiress to all his property. But the inheritance did not console her; she shared sincerely the grief of poor Praskovia Petrovna, vowing that she would never leave her. They both quitted Nenaradova, the scene of so many sad recollections, and went to live on another estate.

Suitors crowded round the young and wealthy heiress, but she gave not the slightest hope to any of them. Her mother sometimes exhorted her to make a choice; but Maria Gavrilovna shook her head and became pensive. Vladimir no longer existed: he had died in Moscow on the eve of the entry of the French. His memory seemed to be held sacred by Masha; at least she treasured up everything that could remind her of him: books that he had once read, his drawings, his notes, and verses of poetry that he had copied out for her. The neighbors, hearing of all this, were astonished at her constancy, and awaited with curiosity the hero who should at last triumph over the melancholy fidelity of this virgin Artemisia.

Meanwhile the war had ended gloriously. Our regiments returned from abroad, and the people went out to meet them. The bands played the conquering songs: "Vive Henri-Quatre," Tyrolese waltzes and airs from "Joconde." Officers who had set out for the war almost mere lads returned grown men, with martial air, and their breasts decorated with crosses. The soldiers chatted gaily among themselves, constantly mingling French and German words in their speech. Time never to be forgotten! Time of glory and enthusiasm! How throbbed the Russian heart at the word "Fatherland!" How sweet were the tears of meeting! With what unanimity did we unite feelings of national pride with love for the Czar! And for him—what a moment!

The women, the Russian women, were then incomparable. Their enthusiasm was truly intoxicating, when, welcoming the conquerors, they cried "Hurrah!"

"And threw their caps high in the air!"

What officer of that time does not confess that to the Russian women he was indebted for his best and most precious reward?

At this brilliant period Maria Gavrilovna was living with her mother in the province of ———, and did not see how both capitals celebrated the return of the troops. But in the districts and villages the general enthusiasm was, if possible, even still greater. The appearance of an officer in those places was for him a veritable triumph, and the lover in a plain coat felt very ill at ease in his vicinity. We have already said that, in spite of her coldness, Maria Gavrilovna was, as before, surrounded by suitors. But all had to retire into the background when the wounded Colonel Bourmin of the Hussars, with the Order of St. George in his buttonhole and with an "interesting pallor," as the young ladies of the neighborhood observed, appeared at the castle. He was about twenty-six years of age. He had obtained leave of absence to visit his estate, which was contiguous to that of Maria Gavrilovna. Maria bestowed special attention upon him. In his presence her habitual pensiveness disappeared. It cannot be said that she coquetted with him, but a poet, observing her behavior, would have said:

"Se amor non e, che dunque?"[1]

Bourmin was indeed a very charming young man. He possessed that spirit which is eminently pleasing to women: a spirit of decorum and observation, without any pretensions, and yet not without a slight tendency towards careless satire. His behavior towards Maria Gavrilovna was simple and frank, but whatever she said or did, his soul and eyes followed her. He seemed to be of a quiet and modest disposition, though report said that he had once been a terrible rake; but this did not injure him in the opinion of Maria Gavrilovna, who — like all young ladies in general—excused with pleasure follies that gave indication of boldness and ardor of temperament.

But more than everything else—more than his tenderness, more than his agreeable conversation, more than his interesting pallor, more than his arm in a sling—the silence of the young Hussar excited her curiosity

---

[1] If it isn't love, what is it?

and imagination. She could not but confess that he pleased her very much. Probably he, too, with his perception and experience, had already observed that she made a distinction between him and the others. How was it then that she had not yet seen him at her feet or heard his declaration? What restrained him? Was it timidity, inseparable from true love, or pride or the coquetry of a crafty wooer? It was an enigma to her. After long reflection, she came to the conclusion that timidity alone was the cause of it, and she resolved to encourage him by greater attention and, if circumstances should render it necessary, even by an exhibition of tenderness. She prepared a most unexpected dénouement, and waited with impatience for the moment of the romantic explanation. A secret, of whatever nature it may be, always presses heavily upon the human heart. Her stratagem had the desired success; at least Bourmin fell into such a reverie, and his black eyes rested with such fire upon her, that the decisive moment seemed close at hand. The neighbors spoke about the marriage as if it were a matter already decided upon, and good Praskovia Petrovna rejoiced that her daughter had at last found a lover worthy of her.

On one occasion the old lady was sitting alone in the parlor, amusing herself with a pack of cards, when Bourmin entered the room and immediately inquired for Maria Gavrilovna.

"She is in the garden," replied the old lady; "go out to her, and I will wait here for you."

Bourmin went, and the old lady made the sign of the cross and thought: "Perhaps the business will be settled to-day!"

Bourmin found Maria Gavrilovna near the pond, under a willow-tree, with a book in her hands, and in a white dress: a veritable heroine of romance. After the first few questions and observations, Maria Gavrilovna purposely allowed the conversation to drop, thereby increasing their mutual embarrassment, from which there was no possible way of escape except only by a sudden and decisive declaration.

And this is what happened: Bourmin, feeling the difficulty of his position, declared that he had long sought for an opportunity to open his heart to her, and requested a moment's attention. Maria Gavrilovna closed her book and cast down her eyes, as a sign of compliance with his request.

"I love you," said Bourmin. "I love you passionately...."

Maria Gavrilovna blushed and lowered her head still more. "I have acted imprudently in accustoming myself to the sweet pleasure of seeing and hearing you daily...." (Maria Gavrilovna recalled to mind the first letter of St. Preux.) "But it is now too late to resist my fate; the remembrance of you, your dear incomparable image, will henceforth be the torment and the consolation of my life, but there still remains a grave duty for me to perform—to reveal to you a terrible secret which will place between us an insurmountable barrier."

"That barrier has always existed," interrupted Maria Gavrilovna hastily. "I could never be your wife."

"I know," replied he calmly. "I know that you once loved, but death and three years of mourning.... Dear, kind Maria Gavrilovna, do not try to deprive me of my last consolation: the thought that you would have consented to make me happy if..."

"Don't speak, for Heaven's sake, don't speak. You torture me."

"Yes, I know. I feel that you would have been mine, but I am the most miserable creature under the sun—I am already married!"

Maria Gavrilovna looked at him in astonishment.

"I am already married," continued Bourmin: "I have been married four years, and I do not know who is my wife, or where she is, or whether I shall ever see her again!"

"What do you say?" exclaimed Maria Gavrilovna. "How very strange! Continue: I will relate to you afterwards.... But continue, I beg of you."

"At the beginning of the year 1812," said Bourmin, "I was hastening to Vilna, where my regiment was stationed. Arriving late one evening at one of the post stations, I ordered the horses to be got ready as quickly as possible, when suddenly a terrible snowstorm came on, and the post master and drivers advised me to wait till it had passed over. I followed their advice, but an unaccountable uneasiness took possession of me: it seemed as if someone were pushing me forward. Meanwhile the snowstorm did not subside. I could endure it no longer, and again ordering out the horses, I started off in the midst of the storm. The driver conceived the idea of following the course of the river, which would shorten our journey by three versts. The banks were covered with snow; the driver drove past the place where we should have come out upon the road, and so we found ourselves in an unknown part of the country. The storm did not cease; I saw a light in the distance, and I ordered the driver to proceed towards it. We reached a village; in the wooden church there was a light. The church was open. Outside the railings stood several sledges, and people were passing in and out through the porch.

" 'This way! this way,' cried several voices.

"I ordered the driver to proceed.

" 'In the name of Heaven, where have you been loitering?' said somebody to me. 'The bride has fainted away; the priest does not know what to do, and we were just getting ready to go back. Get out as quickly as you can.'

"I got out of the sledge without saying a word and went into the church, which was feebly lit up by two or three tapers. A young girl was sitting on a bench in a dark corner of the church; another girl was rubbing her temples.

" 'Thank God!' said the latter. 'You have come at last. You have almost killed the young lady.'

"The old priest advanced towards me, and said:

" 'Do you wish me to begin?'

" 'Begin, begin, father,' replied I absently.

"The young girl was raised up. She seemed to me not at all bad looking . . . . Impelled by an incomprehensible, unpardonable levity, I placed myself by her side in front of the pulpit; the priest hurried on; three men and a chambermaid supported the bride and only occupied themselves with her. We were married.

" 'Kiss each other!' said the witnesses to us.

"My wife turned her pale face towards me. I was about to kiss her, when she exclaimed: 'Oh! it is not he! It is not he!' and fell senseless.

"The witnesses gazed at me in alarm. I turned round and left the church without the least hindrance, flung myself into the kibitka and cried: 'Drive off!' "

"My God!" exclaimed Maria Gavrilovna. "And you do not know what became of your poor wife?"

"I do not know," replied Bourmin; "neither do I know the name of the village where I was married nor the post station where I set out from. At that time I attached so little importance to the wicked prank, that on leaving the church I fell asleep, and did not awake till the next morning after reaching the third station. The servant, who was then with me, died during the campaign, so that I have no hope of ever discovering the woman upon whom I played such a cruel joke, and who is now so cruelly avenged."

"My God! my God!" cried Maria Gavrilovna, seizing him by the hand. "Then it was you! And you do not recognize me?"

Bourmin turned pale—and threw himself at her feet.

For Thought and Discussion

1. Describe Maria.
   How does Pushkin satirize French novels?
2. With whom did Maria fall in love?
3. How did the opposition of Maria's parents affect the young lovers? What conclusion did the young lovers make?
4. Why did Vladimir become lost on the road?
5. When did he arrive at the church at Jadrino?
6. Why did Maria's flight remain a secret?
7. When Maria became ill, what were some of the moral proverbs that were quoted?

Why does the author say that the people are prone to rely on proverbs at such a time?

8. Why did Vladimir no longer visit Gavril Gavrilovitch's home? Why did he not come when he was invited? Why did he join the army? What happened to him?

9. When the war was over, what treatment was accorded the returning soldiers?

10. Who was Colonel Bourmin of the Hussars? Why was he popular with the young ladies?

11. Why did Maria become interested in him?

12. Why is the ending of the story a surprise?

13. Why had Maria and Colonel Bourmin failed to recognize each other?

14. Where does the story take place? Why is the setting important? Can you devise a better title than "The Snowstorm"?

15. Does this story depend upon character portrayal or plot for its effectiveness?

16. Name the instances of coincidence upon which the story depends.

17. What omission in the first part of the story enabled the author to give a surprise ending to the narrative?

~~

SHE STOOPS TO CONQUER

OLIVER GOLDSMITH

DRAMATIS PERSONAE

MEN

Sir Charles Marlow _____
Young Marlow (his son) _____
Hardcastle _____
Hastings _____
Tony Lumpkin _____
Diggory _____

WOMEN

Mrs. Hardcastle _____
Miss Hardcastle _____
Miss Neville _____
Maid _____

Landlord, Servants, etc.

ACT I

SCENE I. *A chamber in an old-fashioned house.*

Enter MRS. HARDCASTLE *and* MR. HARDCASTLE.

MRS. HARDCASTLE. I vow, Mr. Hardcastle, you're very particular. Is there a creature in the whole country but ourselves that does not take a trip to town now and then, to rub off the rust a little? There's the two Miss Hoggs, and our neighbor, Mrs. Grigsby, go to take a month's polishing every winter.

HARDCASTLE. Aye, and bring back vanity and affectation to last them the whole year. I wonder why London cannot keep its own fools at home. In my time the follies of the town crept slowly among us, but now they travel faster than a stagecoach. Its fopperies come down not only as inside passengers, but in the very basket.

MRS. HARDCASTLE. Aye, your times were fine times indeed; you have been telling us of them for many a long year. Here we live in an old rumbling mansion, that looks for all the world like an inn, but that we never see company. Our best visitors are old Mrs. Oddfish, the curate's wife, and little Cripplegate, the lame dancing master; and all our entertainment your old stories of Prince Eugene and the Duke of Marlborough. I hate such old-fashioned trumpery.

HARDCASTLE. And I love it. I love everything that's old—old friends, old times, old manners, old books, old wine; and, I believe, Dorothy (*taking her hand*), you'll own I've been pretty fond of an old wife.

MRS. HARDCASTLE. Lord, Mr. Hardcastle, you're forever at your Dorothys, and your old wives. You may be a Darby, but I'll be no Joan, I promise you. I'm not so old as you'd make me, by more than one good year. Add twenty to twenty, and make money of that.

HARDCASTLE. Let me see; twenty added to twenty—makes just fifty and seven.

MRS. HARDCASTLE. It's false, Mr. Hardcastle; I was but twenty when Tony, son of Mr. Lumpkin, my first husband, was born; and he's not come to years of discretion yet.

HARDCASTLE. Nor ever will, I dare answer for him. Aye, you have taught him finely.

MRS. HARDCASTLE. No matter. Tony Lumpkin has a good fortune. My son is not to live by his learning. I don't think a boy wants much learning to spend fifteen hundred a year.

HARDCASTLE. Learning, quotha! a mere composition of tricks and mischief.

MRS. HARDCASTLE. Humor, my dear; nothing but humor. Come, Mr. Hardcastle, you must allow the boy a little humor.

HARDCASTLE. I'd sooner allow him a horsepond. If burning the footmen's shoes, frightening the maids, and worrying the kittens be humor, he has it. It was but yesterday he fastened my wig to the back of my chair, and when I went to make a bow, I popped my bald head in Mrs. Frizzle's face.

MRS. HARDCASTLE. And am I to blame? The poor boy was always too sickly to do any good. A school would be his death. When he comes to be a little stronger, who knows what a year or two's Latin may do for him?

HARDCASTLE. Latin for him! A cat and fiddle. No, no; the alehouse and the stable are the only schools he'll ever go to.

MRS. HARDCASTLE. Well, we must not snub the poor boy now, for I believe we shan't have him long among us. Anybody that looks in his face may see he's consumptive.

HARDCASTLE. Aye, if growing too fat be one of the symptoms.

MRS. HARDCASTLE. He coughs sometimes.

HARDCASTLE. Yes, when his liquor goes the wrong way.

MRS. HARDCASTLE. I'm actually afraid of his lungs.

HARDCASTLE. And truly, so am I; for he sometimes whoops like a speaking trumpet—(TONY *hallooing behind the scenes*)—Oh, there he goes —a very consumptive figure, truly!

Enter TONY, *crossing the stage.*

MRS. HARDCASTLE. Tony, where are you going, my charmer? Won't you give papa and I a little of your company, lovee?

TONY. I'm in haste, mother; I cannot stay.

MRS. HARDCASTLE. You shan't venture out this raw evening, my dear; you look most shockingly.

TONY. I can't stay, I tell you. The Three Pigeons expects me down every moment. There's some fun going forward.

HARDCASTLE. Aye; the alehouse, the old place; I thought so.

MRS. HARDCASTLE. A low, paltry set of fellows.

TONY. Not so low, neither. There's Dick Muggins, the exciseman; Jack Slang, the horse-doctor; little Aminadab, that grinds the music-box; and Tom Twist, that spins the pewter platter.

MRS. HARDCASTLE. Pray, my dear, disappoint them for one night, at least.

TONY. As for disappointing them, I should not so much mind; but I can't abide to disappoint myself.

MRS. HARDCASTLE. (*Detaining him.*) You shan't go.

TONY. I will, I tell you.

MRS. HARDCASTLE. I say you shan't.

TONY. We'll see which is strongest, you or I. [*Exit, hauling her out.*]

HARDCASTLE. (*Alone.*) Aye, there goes a pair that only spoil each other. But is not the whole age in a combination to drive sense and discretion out of doors? There's my pretty darling, Kate! the fashions of the times have almost infected her, too. By living a year or two in town, she is as fond of gauze and French frippery as the best of them.

Enter MISS HARDCASTLE.

HARDCASTLE. Blessing on my pretty innocence! Dressed out as usual, my Kate. Goodness! What a quantity of superfluous silk hast thou got about thee, girl! I could never teach the fools of this age that the indigent world could be clothed out of the trimmings of the vain.

MISS HARDCASTLE. You know our agreement, sir. You allow me the morning to receive and pay visits, and to dress in my own manner; and in the evening I put on my housewife's dress, to please you.

HARDCASTLE. Well, remember, I insist on the terms of our agreement; and, by the bye, I believe I shall have occasion to try your obedience this very evening.

MISS HARDCASTLE. I protest, sir, I don't comprehend your meaning.

HARDCASTLE. Then, to be plain with you, Kate, I expect the young gentleman I have chosen to be your husband, from town this very day. I have his father's letter, in which he informs me his son is set out, and that he intends to follow, himself, shortly after.

MISS HARDCASTLE. Indeed! I wish I had known something of this before. Bless me, how shall I behave? It's a thousand to one I shan't like him; our meeting will be so formal, and so like a thing of business, that I shall find no room for friendship or esteem.

HARDCASTLE. Depend upon it, child, I'll never control your choice; but Mr. Marlow, whom I have pitched upon, is the son of my old friend, Sir Charles Marlow, of whom you have heard me talk so often. The young gentleman has been bred a scholar, and is designed for an employment in the service of his country. I am told he's a man of an excellent understanding.

MISS HARDCASTLE. Is he?

HARDCASTLE. Very generous.

MISS HARDCASTLE. I believe I shall like him.

HARDCASTLE. Young and brave.

MISS HARDCASTLE. I'm sure I shall like him.

HARDCASTLE. And very handsome.

MISS HARDCASTLE. My dear papa, say no more (*kissing his hand*), he's mine—I'll have him.

HARDCASTLE. And, to crown all, Kate, he's one of the most bashful and reserved young fellows in all the world.

MISS HARDCASTLE. Eh! you have frozen me to death again. That word *reserved* has undone all the rest of his accomplishments. A reserved lover, it is said, always makes a suspicious husband.

HARDCASTLE. On the contrary, modesty seldom resides in a breast that is not enriched with nobler virtues. It was the very feature in his character that first struck me.

MISS HARDCASTLE. He must have more striking features to catch me, I promise you. However, if he be so young, so handsome, and so everything as you mention, I believe he'll do still. I think I'll have him.

HARDCASTLE. Aye, Kate, but there is still an obstacle. It's more than an even wager he may not have you.

MISS HARDCASTLE. My dear papa, why will you mortify one so?—Well, if he refuses, instead of breaking my heart at his indifference, I'll only break my glass for its flattery, set my cap to some newer fashion, and look out for some less difficult admirer.

HARDCASTLE. Bravely resolved! In the meantime, I'll go prepare the servants for his reception. As we seldom see company, they want as much training as a company of recruits the first day's muster. [*Exit.*]

MISS HARDCASTLE. (*Alone.*) Lud, this news of papa's puts me all in a flutter. Young, handsome—these he put last, but I put them foremost. Sensible, good-natured—I like all that. But then, reserved and sheepish—that's much against him. Yet, can't he be cured of his timidity by being taught to be proud of his wife?

Yes, and can't I—but I vow I'm disposing of the husband before I have secured the lover.

Enter MISS NEVILLE.

MISS HARDCASTLE. I'm so glad you're come, Neville, my dear. Tell me, Constance, how do I look this evening? Is there anything whimsical about me? Is it one of my well-looking days, child? Am I in face today?

MISS NEVILLE. Perfectly, my dear. Yet now I look again—bless me!—surely no accident has happened among the canary birds or the goldfishes? Has your brother or the cat been meddling? Or has the last novel been too moving?

MISS HARDCASTLE. No; nothing of all this. I have been threatened—I can scarce get it out—I have been threatened with a lover.

MISS NEVILLE. And his name—

MISS HARDCASTLE. Is Marlow.

MISS NEVILLE. Indeed!

MISS HARDCASTLE. The son of Sir Charles Marlow.

MISS NEVILLE. As I live, the most intimate friend of Mr. Hastings, my admirer. They are never asunder. I believe you must have seen him when we lived in town.

MISS HARDCASTLE. Never.

MISS NEVILLE. He's a very singular character, I assure you. Among women of reputation and virtue, he is the modestest man alive; but his acquaintance give him a very different character among creatures of another stamp; you understand me.

MISS HARDCASTLE. An odd character, indeed. I shall never be able to manage him. What shall I do? Pshaw, think no more of him, but trust to occurrences for success. But how goes on your own affair, my dear? Has my mother been courting you for my brother Tony, as usual?

MISS NEVILLE. I have just come

from one of our agreeable tête-à-têtes. She has been saying a hundred tender things, and setting off her pretty monster as the very pink of perfection.

MISS HARDCASTLE. And her partiality is such that she actually thinks him so. A fortune like yours is no small temptation. Besides, as she has the sole management of it, I'm not surprised to see her unwilling to let it go out of the family.

MISS NEVILLE. A fortune like mine, which chiefly consists in jewels, is no such mighty temptation. But, at any rate, if my dear Hastings be but constant, I make no doubt to be too hard for her at last. However, I let her suppose that I am in love with her son; and she never once dreams that my affections are fixed upon another.

MISS HARDCASTLE. My good brother holds out stoutly. I could almost love him for hating you so.

MISS NEVILLE. It is a good-natured creature at bottom, and I'm sure would wish to see me married to anybody but himself. But my aunt's bell rings for our afternoon's walk 'round the improvements. *Allons!* Courage is necessary, as our affairs are critical.

MISS HARDCASTLE. Would it were bedtime, and all were well. [*Exeunt.*]

SCENE II. *An alehouse room.*

Several shabby fellows with punch and tobacco. TONY *at the head of the table, a little higher than the rest, a mallet in his hand.*

OMNES. Hurrah! Hurrah! Hurrah! Bravo!

FIRST FELLOW. Now, gentlemen, silence for a song. The squire is going to knock himself down for a song!

OMNES. Aye, a song, a song!

TONY. Then I'll sing you, gentle-men, a song I made upon this alehouse, The Three Pigeons.

SONG

Let schoolmasters puzzle their brain
    With grammar, and nonsense, and learning;
Good liquor, I stoutly maintain,
    Gives *genus* a better discerning.
Let them brag of their heathenish gods,
    Their Lethes, their Styxes, and Stygians,
Their *quis,* and their *quæs,* and their *quods,*
    They're all but a parcel of Pigeons.
            Toroddle, toroddle, toroll.

. . . .

Then come, put the jorum about,
    And let us be merry and clever;
Our hearts and our liquors are stout,
    Here's the Three Jolly Pigeons forever.
Let some cry up woodcock or hare,
    Your bustards, your ducks, and your widgeons;
But of all the birds in the air,
    Here's a health to the Three Jolly Pigeons.
            Toroddle, toroddle, toroll.

OMNES. Bravo, bravo!

FIRST FELLOW. The squire has got some spunk in him.

SECOND FELLOW. I loves to hear him sing, bekeays he never gives us nothing that's low.

THIRD FELLOW. Oh, anything that's low; I cannot bear it.

FOURTH FELLOW. The genteel thing is the genteel thing any time; if so be that a gentleman bees in a concatenation accordingly.

THIRD FELLOW. I like the maxum of it, Master Muggins. What, though I am obligated to dance a bear, a man may be a gentleman for all that.

May this be my poison, if my bear ever dances but to the very genteelest of tunes—"Water Parted," or "The Minuet in Ariadne."

SECOND FELLOW. What a pity it is the squire is not come to his own. It would be well for all the publicans within ten miles round of him.

TONY. Ecod, and so it would, Master Slang. I'd then show what it was to keep choice of company.

SECOND FELLOW. Oh, he takes after his own father for that. To be sure, old Squire Lumpkin was the finest gentleman I ever set my eyes on. For winding the straight horn, or beating a thicket for a hare, he never had his fellow. It was a saying in the place that he kept the best horses and dogs in the whole county.

TONY. Ecod, and when I'm of age I'll be a true son, I promise you. I have been thinking of Bet Bouncer and the miller's gray mare to begin with. But come, my boys, drink about and be merry, for you pay no reckoning. Well, Stingo, what's the matter?

Enter LANDLORD.

LANDLORD. There be two gentlemen in a post-chaise at the door. They have lost their way upo' the forest; and they are talking something about Mr. Hardcastle.

TONY. As sure as can be, one of them must be the gentleman that's coming down to court my sister. Do they seem to be Londoners?

LANDLORD. I believe they may. They look woundily like Frenchmen.

TONY. Then desire them to step this way, and I'll set them right in a twinkling. (*Exit* LANDLORD.) Gentlemen, as they mayn't be good enough company for you, step down for a moment, and I'll be with you in the squeezing of a lemon.

[*Exeunt mob.*]

TONY. (*Alone.*) Father-in-law has been calling me whelp and hound this half year. Now, if I pleased, I could be so revenged upon the old grumbletonian. But then I'm afraid —afraid of what? I shall soon be worth fifteen hundred a year, and let him frighten me out of *that* if he can.

Enter LANDLORD, *conducting* MARLOW *and* HASTINGS.

MARLOW. What a tedious, uncomfortable day have we had of it! We were told it was but forty miles across the country, and we have come above threescore!

HASTINGS. And all, Marlow, from that unaccountable reserve of yours, that would not let us inquire more frequently on the way.

MARLOW. I own, Hastings, I am unwilling to lay myself under an obligation to everyone I meet; and often stand the chance of an unmannerly answer.

HASTINGS. At present, however, we are not likely to receive any answer.

TONY. No offense, gentlemen. But I'm told you have been inquiring for one Mr. Hardcastle, in these parts. Do you know what part of the country you are in?

HASTINGS. Not in the least, sir, but should thank you for information.

TONY. Nor the way you come?

HASTINGS. No, sir; but if you can inform us—

TONY. Why, gentlemen, if you know neither the road you are going, nor where you are, nor the road you came, the first thing I have to inform you is that—you have lost your way.

MARLOW. We wanted no ghost to tell us that.

TONY. Pray, gentlemen, may I be

so bold as to ask the place from whence you came?

MARLOW. That's not necessary to-ward directing us where we are to go.

TONY. No offense; but question for question is all fair, you know. Pray, gentlemen, is not this same Hardcastle a cross-grained, old-fashioned, whimsical fellow, with an ugly face, a daughter, and a pretty son?

HASTINGS. We have not seen the gentleman; but he has the family you mention.

TONY. The daughter, a tall, trapesing, trolloping, talkative maypole; the son, a pretty, well-bred, agreeable youth, that everybody is fond of!

MARLOW. Our information differs in this. The daughter is said to be well-bred and beautiful; the son, an awkward booby, reared up and spoiled at his mother's apron-string.

TONY. He-he-hem!—Then, gentlemen, all I have to tell you is, that you won't reach Mr. Hardcastle's house this night, I believe.

HASTINGS. Unfortunate!

TONY. It's a long, dark, boggy, dirty, dangerous way. Stingo, tell the gentlemen the way to Mr. Hardcastle's (*winking upon the* LANDLORD)—Mr. Hardcastle's of Quagmire Marsh, you understand me?

LANDLORD. Master Hardcastle's! Lack-a-daisy, my masters, you're come a deadly deal wrong. When you came to the bottom of the hill, you should have crossed down Squash Lane.

MARLOW. Cross down Squash Lane!

LANDLORD. Then you were to keep straight forward, till you came to four roads.

MARLOW. Come to where four roads meet?

TONY. Aye; but you must be sure to take only one of them.

MARLOW. Oh, sir, you're facetious.

TONY. Then, keeping to the right, you are to go sideways till you come upon Crack-skull Common; there you must look sharp for the track of the wheel, and go forward till you come to Farmer Murrain's barn. Coming to the farmer's barn, you are to turn to the right, and then to the left, and then to the right about again, till you find out the old mill—

MARLOW. Zounds, man! we could as soon find out the longitude.

HASTINGS. What's to be done, Marlow?

MARLOW. This house promises but a poor reception; though, perhaps, the landlord can accommodate us.

LANDLORD. Alack, master, we have but one spare bed in the whole house.

TONY. And to my knowledge, that's taken up by three lodgers already. (*After a pause in which the rest seem disconcerted.*) I have hit it. Don't you think, Stingo, our landlady could accommodate the gentlemen by the fireside, with—three chairs and a bolster?

HASTINGS. I hate sleeping by the fireside.

MARLOW. And I detest your three chairs and a bolster.

TONY. You do, do you?—then, let me see—what if you go on a mile farther, to the Buck's Head; the old Buck's Head on the hill, one of the best inns in the whole country?

HASTINGS. O ho! so we have escaped an adventure for this night, however.

LANDLORD. (*Apart to* TONY.) Sure, you ben't sending them to your father's as an inn, be you?

TONY. Mum, you fool, you. Let *them* find that out. (*To them.*) You have only to keep on straight forward, till you come to a large old house by the roadside. You'll see a pair of large horns over the door.

That's the sign. Drive up the yard, and call stoutly about you.

HASTINGS. Sir, we are obliged to you. The servants can't miss the way?

TONY. No, no; but I tell you, though, the landlord is rich, and going to leave off business; so he wants to be thought a gentleman, saving your presence, he! he! he! He'll be for giving you his company; and, ecod, if you mind him, he'll persuade you that his mother was an alderman, and his aunt a justice of peace.

LANDLORD. A troublesome old blade, to be sure; but a keeps as good wines and beds as any in the whole country.

MARLOW. Well, if he supplies us with these, we shall want no further connection. We are to turn to the right, did you say?

TONY. No, no, straight forward. I'll just step myself, and show you a piece of the way. (*To the* LANDLORD.) Mum!

LANDLORD. Ah, bless your heart, for a sweet, pleasant, mischievous son.

[*Exeunt.*]

ACT II

SCENE I. *An old-fashioned house.*

Enter HARDCASTLE, *followed by three or four awkward* SERVANTS.

HARDCASTLE. Well, I hope you are perfect in the table exercise I have been teaching you these three days. You all know your posts and your places, and can show that you have been used to good company, without ever stirring from home.

OMNES. Aye, aye.

HARDCASTLE. When company comes, you are not to pop out and stare, and then run in again, like frighted rabbits in a warren.

OMNES. No, no.

HARDCASTLE. You, Diggory, whom I have taken from the barn, are to make a show at the side table; and you, Roger, whom I have advanced from the plow, are to place yourself behind my chair. But you're not to stand so, with your hands in your pockets. Take your hands from your pockets, Roger; and from your head, you blockhead, you. See how Diggory carries his hands. They're a little too stiff, indeed, but that's no great matter.

DIGGORY. Aye, mind how I hold them. I learned to hold my hands this way when I was upon drill for the militia. And so being upon drill—

HARDCASTLE. You must not be so talkative, Diggory. You must be all attention to the guests. You must hear us talk, and not think of talking; you must see us drink, and not think of drinking; you must see us eat, and not think of eating.

DIGGORY. By the laws, your worship, that's parfectly unpossible. Whenever Diggory sees yeating going forward, ecod, he's always wishing for a mouthful himself.

HARDCASTLE. Blockhead! Is not a bellyful in the kitchen as good as a bellyful in the parlor? Stay your stomach with that reflection.

DIGGORY. Ecod, I thank your worship, I'll make a shift to stay my stomach with a slice of cold beef in the pantry.

HARDCASTLE. Diggory, you are too talkative. Then, if I happen to say a good thing, or tell a good story at table, you must not all burst out a-laughing, as if you made part of the company.

DIGGORY. Then, ecod, your worship must not tell the story of the Ould Grouse in the gun-room. I can't help laughing at that—he! he! he!—for the soul of me! We have laughed at that these twenty years— ha! ha! ha!

HARDCASTLE. Ha! ha! ha! The story is a good one. Well, honest Diggory, you may laugh at that—but still remember to be attentive. Suppose one of the company should call for a glass of wine, how will you behave? A glass of wine, sir, if you please (*to* DIGGORY)—Eh, why don't you move?

DIGGORY. Ecod, your worship, I never have courage till I see the eatables and drinkables brought upo' the table, and then I'm as bauld as a lion.

HARDCASTLE. What, will nobody move?

FIRST SERVANT. I'm not to leave this pleace.

SECOND SERVANT. I'm sure it's no pleace of mine.

THIRD SERVANT. Nor mine, for sartain.

DIGGORY. Wauns, and I'm sure it canna be mine.

HARDCASTLE. You numskulls! and so, while, like your betters, you are quarreling for places, the guests must be starved. O you dunces! I find I must begin all over again—But don't I hear a coach drive into the yard? To your posts, you blockheads! I'll go in the meantime and give my old friend's son a hearty reception at the gate.   [*Exit* HARDCASTLE.]

DIGGORY. By the elevens, my pleace is quite gone out of my head.

ROGER. I know that my pleace is to be everywhere.

FIRST SERVANT. Where the devil is mine?

SECOND SERVANT. My pleace is to be nowhere at all; and so Ize go about my business.

[*Exeunt* SERVANTS, *running about as if frightened, several ways.*]

Enter SERVANT, *with candles, showing in* MARLOW *and* HASTINGS.

SERVANT. Welcome, gentlemen, very welcome! This way.

HASTINGS. After the disappointments of the day, welcome once more, Charles, to the comforts of a clean room and a good fire. Upon my word, a very well-looking house; antique but creditable.

MARLOW. The usual fate of a large mansion. Having first ruined the master by good housekeeping, it at last comes to levy contributions as an inn.

HASTINGS. As you say, we passengers are to be taxed to pay all these fineries. I have often seen a good sideboard, or a marble chimney-piece, though not actually put in the bill, inflame a reckoning confoundedly.

MARLOW. Travelers, George, must pay in all places; the only difference is that in good inns you pay dearly for luxuries; in bad inns you are fleeced and starved.

HASTINGS. You have lived pretty much among them. In truth, I have been often surprised that you who have seen so much of the world, with your natural good sense, and your many opportunities, could never yet acquire a requisite share of assurance.

MARLOW. The Englishman's malady. But tell me, George, where could I have learned that assurance you talk of? My life has been chiefly spent in a college, or an inn, in seclusion from that lovely part of the creation that chiefly teach men confidence. I don't know that I was ever familiarly acquainted with a single modest woman—except my mother—but among females of another class, you know—

HASTINGS. Aye, among them you

are impudent enough, of all conscience!

MARLOW. They are of *us*, you know.

HASTINGS. But in the company of women of reputation I never saw such an idiot, such a trembler; you look for all the world as if you wanted an opportunity of stealing out of the room.

MARLOW. Why, man, that's because I do want to steal out of the room. Faith, I have often formed a resolution to break the ice, and rattle away at any rate. But I don't know how, a single glance from a pair of fine eyes has totally overset my resolution. An impudent fellow may counterfeit modesty, but I'll be hanged if a modest man can ever counterfeit impudence.

HASTINGS. If you could but say half the fine things to them that I have heard you lavish upon the barmaid of an inn, or even a college bedmaker—

MARLOW. Why, George, I can't say fine things to them; they freeze, they petrify me. They may talk of a comet, or a burning mountain, or some such bagatelle; but to me a modest woman, dressed out in all her finery, is the most tremendous object of the whole creation.

HASTINGS. Ha! ha! ha! At this rate, man, how can you ever expect to marry?

MARLOW. Never; unless, as among kings and princes, my bride were to be courted by proxy. If, indeed, like an Eastern bridegroom, one were to be introduced to a wife he never saw before, it might be endured. But to go through all the terrors of a formal courtship, together with the episode of aunts, grandmothers, and cousins, and at last to blurt out the broad staring question of, "Madam, will you marry me?" No, no, that's a strain much above me, I assure you.

HASTINGS. I pity you. But how do you intend behaving to the lady you are come down to visit at the request of your father?

MARLOW. As I behave to all other ladies. Bow very low, answer "Yes" or "No" to all her demands—but for the rest, I don't think I shall venture to look in her face till I see my father's again.

HASTINGS. I'm surprised that one who is so warm a friend can be so cool a lover.

MARLOW. To be explicit, my dear Hastings, my chief inducement down was to be instrumental in forwarding your happiness, not my own. Miss Neville loves you, the family don't know you; as my friend you are sure of a reception, and let honor do the rest.

HASTINGS. My dear Marlow! But I'll suppress the emotion. Were I a wretch, meanly seeking to carry off a fortune, you should be the last man in the world I would apply to for assistance. But Miss Neville's person is all I ask, and that is mine, both from her deceased father's consent, and her own inclination.

MARLOW. Happy man! You have talents and art to captivate any woman. I'm doomed to adore the sex, and yet to converse with the only part of it I despise. This stammer in my address, and this awkward, prepossessing visage of mine can never permit me to soar above the reach of a milliner's 'prentice, or one of the duchesses of Drury Lane. Pshaw! this fellow here to interrupt us.

Enter HARDCASTLE.

HARDCASTLE. Gentlemen, once more you are heartily welcome. Which is Mr. Marlow? Sir, you are heartily welcome. It's not my way, you see, to receive my friends with my back to the fire. I like to give them a hearty reception in the old style at my gate. I like to see their horses and trunks taken care of.

MARLOW. (*Aside.*) He has got our names from the servants already. (*To him.*) We approve your caution and hospitality, sir. (*To* HASTINGS.) I have been thinking, George, of changing our traveling dresses in the morning. I am grown confoundedly ashamed of mine.

HARDCASTLE. I beg, Mr. Marlow, you'll use no ceremony in this house.

HASTINGS. I fancy, George, you're right; the first blow is half the battle. I intend opening the campaign with the white and gold.

HARDCASTLE. Mr. Marlow — Mr. Hastings—gentlemen—pray be under no restraint in this house. This is Liberty Hall, gentlemen. You may do just as you please here.

MARLOW. Yet, George, if we open the campaign too fiercely at first, we may want ammunition before it is over. I think to reserve the embroidery to secure a retreat.

HARDCASTLE. Your talking of a retreat, Mr. Marlow, puts me in mind of the Duke of Marlborough, when we went to besiege Denain. He first summoned the garrison—

MARLOW. Don't you think the *ventre d'or* waistcoat will do with the plain brown?

HARDCASTLE. He first summoned the garrison, which might consist of about five thousand men—

HASTINGS. I think not; brown and yellow mix but very poorly.

HARDCASTLE. I say, gentlemen, as I was telling you, he summoned the garrison, which might consist of about five thousand men—

MARLOW. The girls like finery.

HARDCASTLE. Which might consist of about five thousand men, well appointed with stores, ammunition, and other implements of war. "Now," says the Duke of Marlborough to George Brooks, that stood next to him—you must have heard of George Brooks—"I'll pawn my dukedom," says he, "but I take that garrison without spilling a drop of blood." So—

MARLOW. What, my good friend, if you gave us a glass of punch in the meantime; it would help us to carry on the siege with vigor.

HARDCASTLE. Punch, sir! (*Aside.*) This is the most unaccountable kind of modesty I ever met with.

MARLOW. Yes, sir, punch! A glass of warm punch, after our journey, will be comfortable. This is Liberty Hall, you know.

HARDCASTLE. Here's a cup, sir.

MARLOW. (*Aside.*) So this fellow, in his Liberty Hall, will only let us have just what he pleases.

HARDCASTLE. (*Taking the cup.*) I hope you'll find it to your mind. I have prepared it with my own hands, and I believe you'll own the ingredients are tolerable. Will you be so good as to pledge me, sir? Here, Mr. Marlow, here is to our better acquaintance! [*Drinks.*]

MARLOW. (*Aside.*) A very impudent fellow this. But he's a character, and I'll humor him a little. Sir, my service to you. [*Drinks.*]

HASTINGS. (*Aside.*) I see this fellow wants to give us his company, and forgets that he's an innkeeper, before he has learned to be a gentleman.

MARLOW. From the excellence of your cup, my old friend, I suppose you have a good deal of business in this part of the country. Warm work, now and then, at elections, I suppose?

HARDCASTLE. No, sir, I have long given that work over. Since our betters have hit upon the expedient of electing each other, there is no business "for us that sell ale."

HASTINGS. So, then, you have no turn for politics, I find.

HARDCASTLE. Not in the least. There was a time, indeed, I fretted myself about the mistakes of government, like other people; but, finding myself every day grow more angry, and the government growing no better, I left it to mend itself. Since that, I no more trouble my head about Hyder Ally, or Ally Cawn, than about Ally Croaker. Sir, my service to you.

HASTINGS. So that, with eating above stairs, and drinking below, with receiving your friends within, and amusing them without, you lead a good, pleasant, bustling life of it.

HARDCASTLE. I do stir about a great deal, that's certain. Half the differences of the parish are adjusted in this very parlor.

MARLOW. (*After drinking.*) And you have an argument in your cup, old gentleman, better than any in Westminster Hall.

HARDCASTLE. Aye, young gentleman, that, and a little philosophy.

MARLOW. (*Aside.*) Well, this is the first time I ever heard of an innkeeper's philosophy.

HASTINGS. So then, like an experienced general, you attack them on every quarter. If you find their reason manageable, you attack it with your philosophy; if you find they have no reason, you attack them with this. Here's your health, my philosopher. [*Drinks.*]

HARDCASTLE. Good, very good, thank you; ha! ha! Your generalship puts me in mind of Prince Eugene, when he fought the Turks at the battle of Belgrade. You shall hear.

MARLOW. Instead of the battle of Belgrade, I believe it's almost time to talk about supper. What has your philosophy got in the house for supper?

HARDCASTLE. For supper, sir! — (*Aside.*) Was ever such a request to a man in his own house!

MARLOW. Yes, sir, supper, sir; I begin to feel an appetite. I shall make devilish work tonight in the larder, I promise you.

HARDCASTLE. (*Aside.*) Such a brazen dog, sure, never my eyes beheld. (*To him.*) Why, really, sir, as for supper I can't well tell. My Dorothy and the cook-maid settle these things between them. I leave these kind of things entirely to them.

MARLOW. You do, do you?

HARDCASTLE. Entirely. By the bye, I believe they are in actual consultation upon what's for supper this moment in the kitchen.

MARLOW. Then I beg they'll admit me as one of their privy-council. It's a way I have got. When I travel I always choose to regulate my own supper. Let the cook be called. No offense, I hope, sir.

HARDCASTLE. Oh, no, sir, none in the least; yet I don't know how; our Bridget, the cook-maid, is not very communicative upon these occasions. Should we send for her, she might scold us all out of the house.

HASTINGS. Let's see your list of the larder, then. I ask it as a favor. I always match my appetite to my bill of fare.

MARLOW. (*To* HARDCASTLE, *who looks at them with surprise.*) Sir, he's very right, and it's my way too.

HARDCASTLE. Sir, you have a right to command here. Here, Roger, bring us the bill of fare for tonight's supper; I believe it's drawn out. (*Exit* ROGER.) Your manner, Mr. Hastings, puts me in mind of my uncle, Colonel Wallop. It was a saying of his that no man was sure of his supper till he had eaten it.

HASTINGS. (*Aside.*) All upon the high ropes! His uncle a colonel! We shall soon hear of his mother being a justice of the peace. But let's hear the bill of fare.

MARLOW. (*Perusing.*) What's here? For the first course; for the second course; for the dessert. The devil, sir, do you think we have brought down the whole Joiners' Company, or the Corporation of Bedford, to eat up such a supper? Two or three little things, clean and comfortable, will do.

HASTINGS. But let's hear it.

MARLOW. (*Reading.*) For the first course, at the top, a pig, and prune sauce.

HASTINGS. Away with your pig, I say!

MARLOW. And away with your prune sauce, say I!

HARDCASTLE. And yet, gentlemen, to men that are hungry, pig with prune sauce is very good eating.

MARLOW. At the bottom, a calf's tongue and brains.

HASTINGS. Let your brains be knocked out, my good sir, I don't like them.

MARLOW. Or you may clap them on a plate by themselves. I do.

HARDCASTLE. (*Aside.*) Their impudence confounds me. (*To them.*) Gentlemen, you are my guests; make what alterations you please. Is there anything else you wish to retrench or alter, gentlemen?

MARLOW. Item: A pork pie, a boiled rabbit and sausages, a florentine, a shaking pudding, and a dish of tiff—taff—taffety cream!

HASTINGS. Confound your made dishes! I shall be as much at a loss in this house as at a green and yellow dinner at the French ambassador's table. I'm for plain eating.

HARDCASTLE. I'm sorry, gentlemen, that I have nothing you like, but if there be anything you have a particular fancy to—

MARLOW. Why, really, sir, your bill of fare is so exquisite that any one part of it is full as good as another. Send us what you please. So much for supper. And now to see that our beds are aired, and properly taken care of.

HARDCASTLE. I entreat you'll leave all that to me. You shall not stir a step.

MARLOW. Leave that to you! I protest, sir, you must excuse me, I always look to these things myself.

HARDCASTLE. I must insist, sir, you'll make yourself easy on that head.

MARLOW. You see I'm resolved on it.—(*Aside.*) A very troublesome fellow this, as ever I met with.

HARDCASTLE. Well, sir, I'm resolved at least to attend you. (*Aside.*) This may be modern modesty, but I never saw anything look so like oldfashioned impudence.

[*Exeunt* MARLOW *and* HARDCASTLE.]

HASTINGS. (*Alone.*) So I find this fellow's civilities begin to grow troublesome. But who can be angry at those assiduities which are meant to please him? Ha! what do I see? Miss Neville, by all that's happy!

Enter MISS NEVILLE.

MISS NEVILLE. My dear Hastings! To what unexpected good fortune, to what accident, am I to ascribe this happy meeting?

HASTINGS. Rather let me ask the same question, as I could never have hoped to meet my dearest Constance at an inn.

MISS NEVILLE. An inn! sure you mistake; my aunt, my guardian, lives here. What could induce you to think this house an inn?

HASTINGS. My friend, Mr. Marlow, with whom I came down, and I have been sent here as to an inn, I assure you. A young fellow, whom we accidentally met at a house hard by, directed us hither.

MISS NEVILLE. Certainly it must be one of my hopeful cousin's tricks, of whom you have heard me talk so often; ha! ha! ha!

HASTINGS. He whom your aunt intends for you? He of whom I have such just apprehensions?

MISS NEVILLE. You have nothing to fear from him, I assure you. You'd adore him if you knew how heartily he despises me. My aunt knows it, too, and has undertaken to court me for him, and actually begins to think she has made a conquest.

HASTINGS. Thou dear dissembler! You must know, my Constance, I have just seized this happy opportunity of my friend's visit here to get admittance into the family. The horses that carried us down are now fatigued with their journey, but they'll soon be refreshed; and, then, if my dearest girl will trust in her faithful Hastings, we shall soon be landed in France, where even among slaves the laws of marriage are respected.

MISS NEVILLE. I have often told you that though ready to obey you, I yet should leave my little fortune behind with reluctance. The greatest part of it was left me by my uncle, the India director, and chiefly consists in jewels. I have been for some time persuading my aunt to let me wear them. I fancy I'm very near succeeding. The instant they are put into my possession, you shall find me ready to make them and myself yours.

HASTINGS. Perish the baubles! Your person is all I desire. In the meantime, my friend Marlow must not be let into his mistake. I know the strange reserve of his temper is such that if abruptly informed of it, he would instantly quit the house before our plan was ripe for execution.

MISS NEVILLE. But how shall we keep him in the deception? Miss Hardcastle is just returned from walking; what if we still continue to deceive him?—This, this way—

[*They confer.*]

Enter MARLOW.

MARLOW. The assiduities of these good people tease me beyond bearing. My host seems to think it ill manners to leave me alone, and so he claps not only himself but his old-fashioned wife on my back. They talk of coming to sup with us, too; and then, I suppose, we are to run the gauntlet through all the rest of the family.—What have we got here?

HASTINGS. My dear Charles! Let me congratulate you!—The most fortunate accident!—Who do you think is just alighted?

MARLOW. Cannot guess.

HASTINGS. Our mistresses, boy, Miss Hardcastle and Miss Neville. Give me leave to introduce Miss Constance Neville to your acquaintance. Happening to dine in the neighborhood, they called on their return to take fresh horses here. Miss Hardcastle has just stepped into the next room, and will be back in an instant. Wasn't it lucky? Eh!

MARLOW. (*Aside.*) I have just been mortified enough of all conscience, and here comes something to complete my embarrassment.

HASTINGS. Well, but wasn't it the most fortunate thing in the world?

MARLOW. Oh, yes! Very fortunate—a most joyful encounter—But our dresses, George, you know, are in disorder—What if we should postpone the happiness till tomorrow?—

Tomorrow at her own house—It will be every bit as convenient—and rather more respectful—Tomorrow let it be. [*Offering to go.*]

MISS NEVILLE. By no means, sir. Your ceremony will displease her. The disorder of your dress will show the ardor of your impatience. Besides, she knows you are in the house, and will permit you to see her.

MARLOW. Oh, the devil! How shall I support it? Hem! Hem! Hastings, you must not go. You are to assist me, you know. I shall be confoundedly ridiculous. Yet, hang it! I'll take courage. Hem!

HASTINGS. Pshaw, man! it's but the first plunge, and all's over. She's but a woman, you know.

MARLOW. And, of all women, she that I dread most to encounter.

Enter MISS HARDCASTLE, *as returned from walking, a bonnet, etc.*

HASTINGS. (*Introducing them.*) Miss Hardcastle, Mr. Marlow; I'm proud of bringing two persons of such merit together, that only want to know, to esteem each other.

MISS HARDCASTLE. (*Aside.*) Now for meeting my modest gentleman with a demure face, and quite in his own manner. (*After a pause, in which he appears very uneasy and disconcerted.*) I'm glad of your safe arrival, sir—I'm told you had some accidents by the way.

MARLOW. Only a few, madam. Yes, we had some. Yes, madam, a good many accidents, but should be sorry—madam—or rather glad of any accidents—that are so agreeably concluded. Hem!

HASTINGS. (*To him.*) You never spoke better in your whole life. Keep it up, and I'll insure you the victory.

MISS HARDCASTLE. I'm afraid you flatter, sir. You that have seen so much of the finest company can find

little entertainment in an obscure corner of the country.

MARLOW. (*Gathering courage.*) I have lived, indeed, in the world, madam; but I have kept very little company. I have been but an observer upon life, madam, while others were enjoying it.

MISS NEVILLE. But that, I am told, is the way to enjoy it at last.

HASTINGS. (*To him.*) Cicero never spoke better. Once more, and you are confirmed in assurance forever.

MARLOW. (*To him.*) Hem! Stand by me then, and when I'm down, throw in a word or two to set me up again.

MISS HARDCASTLE. An observer, like you, upon life, were, I fear, disagreeably employed, since you must have had much more to censure than to approve.

MARLOW. Pardon me, madam. I was always willing to be amused. The folly of most people is rather an object of mirth than uneasiness.

HASTINGS. (*To him.*) Bravo, bravo. Never spoke so well in your whole life. Well, Miss Hardcastle, I see that you and Mr. Marlow are going to be very good company. I believe our being here will but embarrass the interview.

MARLOW. Not in the least, Mr. Hastings. We like your company of all things. (*To him.*) Zounds, George, sure you won't go? How can you leave us?

HASTINGS. Our presence will but spoil conversation, so we'll retire to the next room. (*To him.*) You don't consider, man, that we are to manage a little tête-à-tête of our own.

[*Exeunt.*]

MISS HARDCASTLE. (*After a pause.*) But you have not been wholly an observer, I presume, sir; the ladies, I should hope, have employed some part of your addresses.

MARLOW. (*Relapsing into timidity.*) Pardon me, madam, I—I—I—as yet have studied—only—to—deserve them.

MISS HARDCASTLE. And that, some say, is the very worst way to obtain them.

MARLOW. Perhaps so, madam. But I love to converse only with the more grave and sensible part of the sex.— But I'm afraid I grow tiresome.

MISS HARDCASTLE. Not at all, sir; there is nothing I like so much as grave conversation myself; I could hear it forever. Indeed, I have often been surprised how a man of sentiment could ever admire those light, airy pleasures, where nothing reaches the heart.

MARLOW. It's—a disease—of the mind, madam. In the variety of tastes there must be some who, wanting a relish—for—um—a—um—

MISS HARDCASTLE. I understand you, sir. There must be some, who, wanting a relish for refined pleasures, pretend to despise what they are incapable of tasting.

MARLOW. My meaning, madam, but infinitely better expressed. And I can't help observing—a—

MISS HARDCASTLE. (*Aside.*) Who could ever suppose this fellow impudent upon some occasions! (*To him.*) You were going to observe, sir—

MARLOW. I was observing, madam —I protest, madam, I forget what I was going to observe.

MISS HARDCASTLE. (*Aside.*) I vow and so do I. (*To him.*) You were observing, sir, that in this age of hypocrisy—something about hypocrisy, sir.

MARLOW. Yes, madam. In this age of hypocrisy there are few who upon strict inquiry do not—a—a—a—

MISS HARDCASTLE. I understand you perfectly, sir.

MARLOW. (*Aside.*) Egad! and that's more than I do myself.

MISS HARDCASTLE. You mean that in this hypocritical age there are a few who do not condemn in public what they practice in private, and think they pay every debt to virtue when they praise it.

MARLOW. True, madam; those who have most virtue in their mouths have least of it in their bosoms. But I'm sure I tire you, madam.

MISS HARDCASTLE. Not in the least, sir; there's something so agreeable and spirited in your manner, such life and force—pray, sir, go on.

MARLOW. Yes, madam, I was saying—that there are some occasions— when a total want of courage, madam, destroys all the—and puts us—upon —a—a—a—

MISS HARDCASTLE. I agree with you entirely; a want of courage upon some occasions assumes the appearance of ignorance, and betrays us when we most want to excel. I beg you'll proceed.

MARLOW. Yes, madam. Morally speaking, madam — but I see Miss Neville expecting us in the next room. I would not intrude for the world.

MISS HARDCASTLE. I protest, sir, I never was more agreeably entertained in all my life. Pray, go on.

MARLOW. Yes, madam, I was—but she beckons us to join her. Madam, shall I do myself the honor to attend you?

MISS HARDCASTLE. Well, then, I'll follow.

MARLOW. (*Aside.*) This pretty, smooth dialogue has done for me.
[*Exit.*]

MISS HARDCASTLE. (*Alone.*) Ha! ha! ha! Was there ever such a sober, sentimental interview? I'm certain he scarce looked in my face the whole time. Yet the fellow, but for his unaccountable bashfulness, is pretty

well, too. He has good sense, but
then so buried in his fears that it
fatigues one more than ignorance.
If I could teach him a little confidence, it would be doing somebody
that I know of a piece of service. But
who is that somebody?—That, faith,
is a question I can scarce answer.
                                                  [*Exit.*]

Enter TONY *and* MISS NEVILLE, *followed by* MRS. HARDCASTLE *and*
HASTINGS.

TONY. What do you follow me
for, cousin Con? I wonder you're
not ashamed to be so very engaging.
MISS NEVILLE. I hope, cousin, one
may speak to one's own relations and
not be to blame.
TONY. Aye, but I know what sort
of a relation you want to make me,
though; but it won't do. I tell you,
cousin Con, it won't do; so I beg
you'll keep your distance. I want
no nearer relationship.

[*She follows, coquetting him, to
the back scene.*]

MRS. HARDCASTLE. Well! I vow,
Mr. Hastings, you are very entertaining. There's nothing in the world
I love to talk of so much as London,
and the fashions, though I was never
there myself.
HASTINGS. Never there! You
amaze me! From your air and manner, I concluded you had been bred
all your life either at Ranelagh, St.
James's, or Tower Wharf.
MRS. HARDCASTLE. Oh, sir! you're
only pleased to say so. We country
persons can have no manner at all.
I'm in love with the town, and that
serves to raise me above some of our
neighboring rustics; but who can
have a manner, that has never seen
the Pantheon, the Grotto Gardens,
The Borough, and such places where
the nobility chiefly resort? All I
can do is to enjoy London at second-
hand. I take care to know every
tête-à-tête from the Scandalous Magazine, and have all the fashions, as
they come out, in a letter from the
two Miss Rickets of Crooked Lane.

Pray, how do you like this head, Mr. Hastings?

HASTINGS. Extremely elegant and *dégagée*, upon my word, madam. Your friseur is a Frenchman, I suppose?

MRS. HARDCASTLE. I protest, I dressed it myself from a print in the Ladies' Memorandum-book for the last year.

HASTINGS. Indeed! Such a head in a sidebox, at the playhouse, would draw as many gazers as my Lady Mayoress at a City Ball.

MRS. HARDCASTLE. I vow, since inoculation began, there is no such thing to be seen as a plain woman; so one must dress a little particular, or one may escape in the crowd.

HASTINGS. But that can never be your case, madam, in any dress. (*Bowing.*)

MRS. HARDCASTLE. Yet, what signifies my dressing, when I have such a piece of antiquity by my side as Mr. Hardcastle; all I can say will never argue down a single button from his clothes. I have often wanted him to throw off his great flaxen wig, and where he was bald, to plaster it over, like my Lord Pately, with powder.

HASTINGS. You are right, madam; for, as among the ladies there are none ugly, so among the men there are none old.

MRS. HARDCASTLE. But what do you think his answer was? Why, with his usual Gothic vivacity, he said I only wanted him to throw off his wig to convert it into a *tête* for my own wearing!

HASTINGS. Intolerable! At your age you may wear what you please, and it must become you.

MRS. HARDCASTLE. Pray, Mr. Hastings, what do you take to be the most fashionable age about town?

HASTINGS. Some time ago, forty was all the mode; but I'm told the ladies intend to bring up fifty for the ensuing winter.

MRS. HARDCASTLE. Seriously? Then I shall be too young for the fashion!

HASTINGS. No lady begins now to put on jewels till she's past forty. For instance, miss there, in a polite circle, would be considered as a child, a mere maker of samplers.

MRS. HARDCASTLE. And yet Mistress Niece thinks herself as much a woman, and is as fond of jewels, as the oldest of us all.

HASTINGS. Your niece, is she? And that young gentleman—a brother of yours, I should presume?

MRS. HARDCASTLE. My son, sir. They are contracted to each other. Observe their little sports. They fall in and out ten times a day, as if they were man and wife already. (*To them.*) Well, Tony, child, what soft things are you saying to your cousin Constance, this evening?

TONY. I have been saying no soft things; but that it's very hard to be followed about so. Ecod! I've not a place in the house now that's left to myself but the stable.

MRS. HARDCASTLE. Never mind him, Con, my dear. He's in another story behind your back.

MISS NEVILLE. There's something generous in my cousin's manner. He falls out before faces to be forgiven in private.

TONY. That's a confounded — crack.

MRS. HARDCASTLE. Ah! he's a sly one. Don't you think they're like each other about the mouth, Mr. Hastings? The Blenkinsop mouth to a T. They're of a size too. Back to back, my pretties, that Mr. Hastings may see you. Come, Tony.

TONY. You had as good not make me, I tell you. (*Measuring.*)

MISS NEVILLE. O lud! he has almost cracked my head.

MRS. HARDCASTLE. Oh, the monster! For shame, Tony. You a man, and behave so!

TONY. If I'm a man, let me have my fortin. Ecod! I'll not be made a fool of no longer.

MRS. HARDCASTLE. Is this, ungrateful boy, all that I'm to get for the pains I have taken in your education? I that have rocked you in your cradle, and fed that pretty mouth with a spoon! Did not I work that waistcoat to make you genteel? Did not I prescribe for you every day, and weep while the receipt was operating?

TONY. Ecod! you had reason to weep, for you have been dosing me ever since I was born. I have gone through every receipt in the Complete Huswife ten times over; and you have thoughts of coursing me through Quincy next spring. But, ecod! I tell you, I'll not be made a fool of no longer.

MRS. HARDCASTLE. Wasn't it all for your good, viper? Wasn't it all for your good?

TONY. I wish you'd let me and my good alone, then. Snubbing this way when I'm in spirits! If I'm to have any good, let it come of itself; not to keep dinging it, dinging it into one so.

MRS. HARDCASTLE. That's false; I never see you when you're in spirits. No, Tony, you then go to the alehouse or kennel. I'm never to be delighted with your agreeable wild notes, unfeeling monster!

TONY. Ecod! mamma, your own notes are the wildest of the two.

MRS. HARDCASTLE. Was ever the like? But I see he wants to break my heart, I see he does.

HASTINGS. Dear madam, permit me to lecture the young gentleman a little. I'm certain I can persuade him to his duty.

MRS. HARDCASTLE. Well! I must retire. Come, Constance, my love. You see, Mr. Hastings, the wretchedness of my situation. Was ever poor woman so plagued with a dear, sweet, pretty, provoking, undutiful boy?

[*Exeunt* MRS. HARDCASTLE *and* MISS NEVILLE.]

TONY. (*Singing.*) "There was a young man riding by, and fain would have his will. Rang do didlo dee." Don't mind her. Let her cry. It's the comfort of her heart. I have seen her and sister cry over a book for an hour together, and they said they liked the book better the more it made them cry.

HASTINGS. Then you're no friend to the ladies, I find, my pretty young gentleman?

TONY. That's as I find 'um.

HASTINGS. Not to her of your mother's choosing, I dare answer? And yet she appears to me a pretty, well-tempered girl.

TONY. That's because you don't know her as well as I. Ecod! I know every inch about her; and there's not a more bitter cantankerous toad in all Christendom!

HASTINGS. (*Aside.*) Pretty encouragement this for a lover!

TONY. I have seen her since the height of that. She has as many tricks as a hare in a thicket, or a colt the first day's breaking.

HASTINGS. To me she appears sensible and silent.

TONY. Aye, before company. But when she's with her playmates, she's as loud as a hog in a gate.

HASTINGS. But there is a meek modesty about her that charms me.

TONY. Yes, but curb her never so little, she kicks up, and you're flung in a ditch.

HASTINGS. Well, but you must allow her a little beauty.—Yes, you must allow her some beauty.

TONY. Bandbox! She's all a made-up thing, mun. Ah! could you but see Bet Bouncer of these parts, you might then talk of beauty. Ecod! she has two eyes as black as sloes, and cheeks as broad and red as a pulpit cushion. She'd make two of she.

HASTINGS. Well, what say you to a friend that would take this bitter bargain off your hands?

TONY. Anon!

HASTINGS. Would you thank him that would take Miss Neville, and leave you to happiness and your dear Betsy?

TONY. Aye; but where is there such a friend, for who would take her?

HASTINGS. I am he. If you but assist me, I'll engage to whip her off to France, and you shall never hear more of her.

TONY. Assist you! Ecod, I will, to the last drop of my blood. I'll clap a pair of horses to your chaise that shall trundle you off in a twinkling, and maybe get you a part of her fortin besides, in jewels, that you little dream of.

HASTINGS. My dear squire, this looks like a lad of spirit.

TONY. Come along, then, and you shall see more of my spirit before you have done with me. (*Singing.*)

We are the boys
That fear no noise,
Where the thundering cannons roar.

[*Exeunt.*]

ACT III

SCENE I. *The house.*

Enter HARDCASTLE, *alone.*

HARDCASTLE. What could my old friend Sir Charles mean by recommending his son as the modestest young man in town? To me he appears the most impudent piece of brass that ever spoke with a tongue. He has taken possession of the easy chair by the fireside already. He took his boots off in the parlor, and desired me to see them taken care of. I'm desirous to know how his impudence affects my daughter. She will certainly be shocked at it.

Enter MISS HARDCASTLE, *plainly dressed.*

HARDCASTLE. Well, my Kate, I see you have changed your dress, as I bade you; and yet, I believe, there was no great occasion.

MISS HARDCASTLE. I find such a pleasure, sir, in obeying your commands that I take care to observe them without ever debating their propriety.

HARDCASTLE. And yet, Kate, I sometimes give you some cause, particularly when I recommended my modest gentleman to you as a lover today.

MISS HARDCASTLE. You taught me to expect something extraordinary, and I find the original exceeds the description.

HARDCASTLE. I was never so surprised in my life! He has quite confounded all my faculties!

MISS HARDCASTLE. I never saw anything like it; and a man of the world, too!

HARDCASTLE. Aye, he learned it all abroad—what a fool was I, to think a young man could learn modesty by traveling. He might as soon learn wit at a masquerade.

MISS HARDCASTLE. It seems all natural to him.

HARDCASTLE. A good deal assisted by bad company and a French dancing-master.

MISS HARDCASTLE. Sure, you mistake, papa! A French dancing-master could never have taught him that timid look—that awkward address—that bashful manner—

HARDCASTLE. Whose look? Whose manner, child?

MISS HARDCASTLE. Mr. Marlow's; his *mauvaise honte,* his timidity, struck me at the first sight.

HARDCASTLE. Then your first sight deceived you; for I think him one of the most brazen first sights that ever astonished my senses.

MISS HARDCASTLE. Sure, sir, you rally! I never saw anyone so modest.

HARDCASTLE. And can you be serious! I never saw such a bouncing, swaggering puppy since I was born. Bully Dawson was but a fool to him.

MISS HARDCASTLE. Surprising! He met me with a respectful bow, a stammering voice, and a look fixed on the ground.

HARDCASTLE. He met me with a loud voice, a lordly air, and a familiarity that made my blood freeze again.

MISS HARDCASTLE. He treated me with diffidence and respect; censured the manners of the age; admired the prudence of girls that never laughed; tired me with apologies for being tiresome; then left the room with a bow, and "Madam, I would not for the world detain you."

HARDCASTLE. He spoke to me as if he knew me all his life before; asked twenty questions, and never waited for an answer; interrupted my best remarks with some silly pun; and when I was in my best story of the Duke of Marlborough and Prince Eugene, he asked if I had not a good hand at making punch. Yes, Kate, he asked your father if he was a maker of punch!

MISS HARDCASTLE. One of us must certainly be mistaken.

HARDCASTLE. If he be what he has shown himself, I'm determined he shall never have my consent.

MISS HARDCASTLE. And if he be the sullen thing I take him, he shall never have mine.

HARDCASTLE. In one thing, then, we are agreed—to reject him.

MISS HARDCASTLE. Yes—but upon conditions. For if you should find him less impudent, and I more presuming; if you find him more respectful, and I more importunate—I don't know—the fellow is well enough for a man—certainly we don't meet many such at a horse-race in the country.

HARDCASTLE. If we should find him so—but that's impossible. The first appearance has done my business. I'm seldom deceived in that.

MISS HARDCASTLE. And yet there may be many good qualities under that first appearance.

HARDCASTLE. Aye, when a girl finds a fellow's outside to her taste, she then sets about guessing the rest of his furniture. With her a smooth face stands for good sense, and a genteel figure for every virtue.

MISS HARDCASTLE. I hope, sir, a conversation begun with a compliment to my good sense won't end with a sneer at my understanding?

HARDCASTLE. Pardon me, Kate. But if young Mr. Brazen can find the art of reconciling contradictions, he may please us both, perhaps.

MISS HARDCASTLE. And as one of us must be mistaken, what if we go to make further discoveries?

HARDCASTLE. Agreed. But depend on't, I'm in the right.

MISS HARDCASTLE. And, depend on't, I'm not much in the wrong.

[*Exeunt.*]

Enter TONY, *running in with a casket.*

TONY. Ecod! I have got them. Here they are. My cousin Con's

necklaces, bobs and all. My mother shan't cheat the poor souls out of their fortin neither. Oh, my genus! Is that you?

Enter HASTINGS.

HASTINGS. My dear friend, how have you managed with your mother? I hope you have amused her with pretending love for your cousin, and that you are willing to be reconciled at last? Our horses will be refreshed in a short time, and we shall soon be ready to set off.

TONY. And here's something to bear your charges by the way, (*giving the casket*)—your sweetheart's jewels. Keep them; and hang those, I say, that would rob you of one of them!

HASTINGS. But how have you procured them from your mother?

TONY. Ask me no questions, and I'll tell you no fibs. I procured them by the rule of thumb. If I had not a key to every drawer in mother's bureau, how could I go to the alehouse so often as I do? An honest man may rob himself of his own at any time.

HASTINGS. Thousands do it every day. But to be plain with you: Miss Neville is endeavoring to procure them from her aunt this very instant. If she succeeds, it will be the most delicate way at least of obtaining them.

TONY. Well, keep them until you know how it will be. But I know how it will be well enough; she'd as soon part with the only sound tooth in her head.

HASTINGS. But I dread the effects of her resentment when she finds she has lost them.

TONY. Never you mind her resentment; leave *me* to manage that. I don't value her resentment the bounce of a cracker. Zounds! here they are! Morrice! Prance!

[*Exit* HASTINGS.]

Enter MRS. HARDCASTLE *and* MISS NEVILLE.

MRS. HARDCASTLE. Indeed, Constance, you amaze me. Such a girl as you want jewels? It will be time enough for jewels, my dear, twenty years hence, when your beauty begins to want repairs.

MISS NEVILLE. But what will repair beauty at forty will certainly improve it at twenty, madam.

MRS. HARDCASTLE. Yours, my dear, can admit of none. That natural blush is beyond a thousand ornaments. Besides, child, jewels are quite out at present. Don't you see half the ladies of our acquaintance, my Lady Kill-day-light, and Mrs. Crump, and the rest of them, carry their jewels to town, and bring nothing but paste and marcasites back?

MISS NEVILLE. But who knows, madam, but somebody that shall be nameless would like me best with all my little finery about me?

MRS. HARDCASTLE. Consult your glass, my dear, and then see if, with such a pair of eyes, you want any better sparklers. What do you think, Tony, my dear? Does your cousin Con want any jewels, in your eyes, to set off her beauty?

TONY. That's as thereafter may be.

MISS NEVILLE. My dear aunt, if you knew how it would oblige me.

MRS. HARDCASTLE. A parcel of old-fashioned rose and table-cut things. They would make you look like the court of King Solomon at a puppet-show. Besides, I believe I can't readily come at them. They may be missing, for aught I know to the contrary.

TONY. (*Apart to* MRS. HARD-CASTLE.) Then why don't you tell her so at once, as she's so longing for them? Tell her they're lost. It's the only way to quiet her. Say they're lost, and call me to bear witness.

MRS. HARDCASTLE. (*Apart to* TONY.) You know, my dear, I'm only keeping them for you. So if I say they're gone, you'll bear me witness, will you? He! he! he!

TONY. (*Apart to* MRS. HARD-CASTLE.) Never fear me. Ecod! I'll say I saw them taken out with my own eyes.

MISS NEVILLE. I desire them but for a day, madam. Just to be permitted to show them as relics, and then they may be locked up again.

MRS. HARDCASTLE. To be plain with you, my dear Constance, if I could find them, you should have them. They're missing, I assure you. Lost, for aught I know; but we must have patience wherever they are.

MISS NEVILLE. I'll not believe it; this is but a shallow pretense to deny me. I know they are too valuable to be so slightly kept, and as you are to answer for the loss—

MRS. HARDCASTLE. Don't be alarmed, Constance. If they be lost, I must restore an equivalent. But my son knows they are missing, and not to be found.

TONY. That I can bear witness to. They are missing, and not to be found; I'll take my oath on't.

MRS. HARDCASTLE. You must learn resignation, my dear; for though we lose our fortune, yet we should not lose our patience. See me, how calm I am.

MISS NEVILLE. Aye, people are generally calm at the misfortunes of others.

MRS. HARDCASTLE. Now, I wonder a girl of your good sense should waste a thought upon such trumpery. We shall soon find them; and, in the meantime, you shall make use of my garnets till your jewels be found.

MISS NEVILLE. I detest garnets!

MRS. HARDCASTLE. The most becoming things in the world to set off a clear complexion. You have often seen how well they look upon me. You *shall* have them.   [*Exit.*]

MISS NEVILLE. I dislike them of all things. You shan't stir. Was ever anything so provoking, to mislay my own jewels, and force me to wear her trumpery?

TONY. Don't be a fool. If she gives you the garnets, take what you can get. The jewels are your own already. I have stolen them out of her bureau, and she does not know it. Fly to your spark; he'll tell you more of the matter. Leave me to manage her.

MISS NEVILLE. My dear cousin!

TONY. Vanish. She's here, and has missed them already. [*Exit* MISS NEVILLE.] Zounds! how she fidgets and spits about like a Catherine wheel.

Enter MRS. HARDCASTLE.

MRS. HARDCASTLE. Confusion! Thieves! Robbers! We are cheated, plundered, broke open, undone.

TONY. What's the matter, what's the matter, mamma? I hope nothing has happened to any of the good family!

MRS. HARDCASTLE. We are robbed. My bureau has been broke open, the jewels taken out, and I'm undone.

TONY. Oh! is that all? Ha! ha! ha! By the laws I never saw it better acted in my life. Ecod, I thought you was ruined in earnest, ha! ha! ha!

MRS. HARDCASTLE. Why, boy, I *am* ruined in earnest. My bureau has been broke open and all taken away.

TONY. Stick to that; ha! ha! ha! stick to that. I'll bear witness, you know; call me to bear witness.

MRS. HARDCASTLE. I tell you,

Tony, by all that's precious, the jewels are gone, and I shall be ruined forever.

TONY. Sure, I know they're gone, and I am to say so.

MRS. HARDCASTLE. My dearest Tony, but hear me. They're gone, I say.

TONY. By the laws, mamma, you make me for to laugh, ha! ha! I know who took them well enough, ha! ha! ha!

MRS. HARDCASTLE. Was there ever such a blockhead, that can't tell the difference between jest and earnest! I can tell you I'm not in jest, booby!

TONY. That's right, that's right; you must be in a bitter passion, and then nobody will suspect either of us. I'll bear witness that they are gone.

MRS. HARDCASTLE. Was there ever such a cross-grained brute, that won't hear me! Can you bear witness that you're no better than a fool? Was ever poor woman so beset with fools on one hand, and thieves on the other!

TONY. I can bear witness to that.

MRS. HARDCASTLE. Bear witness again, you blockhead, you, and I'll turn you out of the room directly. My poor niece, what will become of her? Do you laugh, you unfeeling brute, as if you enjoyed my distress?

TONY. I can bear witness to that.

MRS. HARDCASTLE. Do you insult me, monster? I'll teach you to vex your mother, I will!

TONY. I can bear witness to that.

[*He runs off; she follows him.*]

Enter MISS HARDCASTLE *and* MAID.

MISS HARDCASTLE. What an unaccountable creature is that brother of mine, to send them to the house as an inn, ha! ha! I don't wonder at his impudence.

MAID. But what is more, madam, the young gentleman, as you passed by in your present dress, asked me if you were the barmaid. He mistook you for the barmaid, madam!

MISS HARDCASTLE. Did he? Then, as I live, I'm resolved to keep up the delusion. Tell me, Pimple, how do you like my present dress? Don't you think I look something like Cherry in *The Beaux' Stratagem?*

MAID. It's the dress, madam, that every lady wears in the country but when she visits or receives company.

MISS HARDCASTLE. And are you sure he does not remember my face or person?

MAID. Certain of it!

MISS HARDCASTLE. I vow I thought so; for though we spoke for some time together, yet his fears were such that he never once looked up during the interview. Indeed, if he had, my bonnet would have kept him from seeing me.

MAID. But what do you hope from keeping him in his mistake?

MISS HARDCASTLE. In the first place, I shall be seen, and that is no small advantage to a girl who brings her face to market. Then I shall perhaps make an acquaintance, and that's no small victory gained over one who never addresses any but the wildest of her sex. But my chief aim is to take my gentleman off his guard, and, like an invisible champion of romance, examine the giant's force before I offer to combat.

MAID. But are you sure you can act your part, and disguise your voice, so that he may mistake that, as he has already mistaken your person?

MISS HARDCASTLE. Never fear me. I think I have got the true bar cant. —Did your honor call?—Attend the lion there.—Pipes and tobacco for the angel.—The lamb has been outrageous this half hour.

MAID. It will do, madam. But he's here. [*Exit* MAID.]

Enter MARLOW.

MARLOW. What a bawling in every part of the house! I have scarce a moment's repose. If I go to the best room, there I find my host and his story; if I fly to the gallery, there we have my hostess with her curtsy down to the ground. I have at last got a moment to myself, and now for recollection. [*Walks and muses.*]

MISS HARDCASTLE. Did you call, sir? Did your honor call?

MARLOW. (*Musing.*) As for Miss Hardcastle, she's too grave and sentimental for me.

MISS HARDCASTLE. Did your honor call?

[*She still places herself before him, he turning away.*]

MARLOW. No, child! (*Musing.*) Besides, from the glimpse I had of her, I think she squints.

MISS HARDCASTLE. I'm sure, sir, I heard the bell ring.

MARLOW. No, no! (*Musing.*) I have pleased my father, however, by coming down, and I'll tomorrow please myself by returning.

[*Taking out his tablets and perusing.*]

MISS HARDCASTLE. Perhaps the other gentleman called, sir?

MARLOW. I tell you no.

MISS HARDCASTLE. I should be glad to know, sir. We have such a parcel of servants.

MARLOW. No, no, I tell you. (*Looks full in her face.*) Yes, child, I think I did call. I wanted—I wanted—I vow, child, you are vastly handsome!

MISS HARDCASTLE. O la, sir, you'll make one ashamed.

MARLOW. Never saw a more sprightly, malicious eye. Yes, yes, my dear, I did call. Have you got any of your—a—what d'ye call it, in the house?

MISS HARDCASTLE. No, sir, we have been out of that these ten days.

MARLOW. One may call in this house, I find, to very little purpose. Suppose I should call for a taste, just by way of trial, of the nectar of your lips; perhaps I might be disappointed in that, too?

MISS HARDCASTLE. Nectar? Nectar? That's a liquor there's no call for in these parts. French, I suppose. We keep no French wines here, sir.

MARLOW. Of true English growth, I assure you.

MISS HARDCASTLE. Then it's odd I should not know it. We brew all sorts of wines in this house, and I have lived here these eighteen years.

MARLOW. Eighteen years! Why, one would think, child, you kept the bar before you were born. How old are you?

MISS HARDCASTLE. Oh! sir, I must not tell my age. They say women and music should never be dated.

MARLOW. To guess at this distance, you can't be much above forty. (*Approaching.*) Yet nearer, I don't think so much. (*Approaching.*) By coming close to some women, they look younger still; but when we come very close indeed—

[*Attempting to kiss her.*]

MISS HARDCASTLE. Pray, sir, keep your distance. One would think you wanted to know one's age as they do horses, by mark of mouth.

MARLOW. I protest, child, you use me extremely ill. If you keep me at this distance, how is it possible you and I can be ever acquainted?

MISS HARDCASTLE. And who wants to be acquainted with you? I want no such acquaintance, not I. I'm sure you did not treat Miss Hardcastle, that was here a while ago, in this obstropalous manner. I'll warrant me, before her you looked dashed, and kept bowing to the ground, and talked, for all the world, as if you was before a justice of peace.

MARLOW. (*Aside.*) Egad, she has hit it, sure enough! (*To her.*) In awe of her, child? Ha! ha! ha! A mere awkward, squinting thing! No, no! I find you don't know me. I laughed and rallied her a little; but I was unwilling to be too severe. No, I could not be too severe, curse me!

MISS HARDCASTLE. Oh, then, sir, you are a favorite, I find, among the ladies?

MARLOW. Yes, my dear, a great favorite. And yet hang me, I don't see what they find in me to follow. At the Ladies' Club in town I'm called their agreeable Rattle. Rattle, child, is not my real name but one I'm known by. My name is Solomons; Mr. Solomons, my dear, at your service.

[*Offering to salute her.*]

MISS HARDCASTLE. Hold, sir; you are introducing me to your club, not to yourself. And you're so great a favorite there, you say?

MARLOW. Yes, my dear. There's Mrs. Mantrap, Lady Betty Blackleg, the Countess of Sligo, Mrs. Langhorns, old Miss Biddy Buckskin, and your humble servant, keep up the spirit of the place.

MISS HARDCASTLE. Then it's a very merry place, I suppose?

MARLOW. Yes, as merry as cards, suppers, wine, and old women can make us.

MISS HARDCASTLE. And their agreeable Rattle, ha! ha! ha!

MARLOW. (*Aside.*) Egad! I don't quite like this chit. She looks knowing, methinks. You laugh, child?

MISS HARDCASTLE. I can't but laugh to think what time they all have for minding their work or their family.

MARLOW. (*Aside.*) All's well; she don't laugh at me. (*To her.*) Do you ever work, child?

MISS HARDCASTLE. Aye, sure. There's not a screen or a quilt in the whole house but what can bear witness to that.

MARLOW. Odso! Then you must show me your embroidery. I embroider and draw patterns myself a little. If you want a judge of your work, you must apply to me.

[*Seizing her hand.*]

Enter HARDCASTLE, *who stands in surprise.*

MISS HARDCASTLE. Aye, but the colors don't look well by candlelight. You shall see all in the morning. [*Struggling.*]

MARLOW. And why not now, my angel? Such beauty fires beyond the power of resistance. —Pshaw! the father here! My old luck; I never nicked seven that I did not throw ambsace three times following.

[*Exit* MARLOW.]

HARDCASTLE. So, madam! So I find *this* is your *modest* lover. This is your humble admirer, that kept his eyes fixed on the ground, and only adored at humble distance. Kate, Kate, art thou not ashamed to deceive your father so?

MISS HARDCASTLE. Never trust me, dear papa, but he's still the modest man I first took him for; you'll be convinced of it as well as I.

HARDCASTLE. By the hand of my body, I believe his impudence is infectious! Didn't I see him seize your hand? Didn't I see him haul you about like a milkmaid? And now you talk of his respect and his modesty, forsooth!

MISS HARDCASTLE. But if I shortly convince you of his modesty, that he has only the faults that will pass off with time, and the virtues that will improve with age, I hope you'll forgive him.

HARDCASTLE. The girl would actually make one run mad! I tell you I'll not be convinced. I am convinced. He has scarcely been three hours in the house, and he has already encroached on all my prerogatives. You may like his impudence, and call it modesty; but my son-in-law, madam, must have very different qualifications.

MISS HARDCASTLE. Sir, I ask but this night to convince you.

HARDCASTLE. You shall not have half the time, for I have thoughts of turning him out this very hour.

MISS HARDCASTLE. Give me that hour, then, and I hope to satisfy you.

HARDCASTLE. Well, an hour let it be then. But I'll have no trifling with your father. All fair and open, do you mind me?

MISS HARDCASTLE. I hope, sir, you have ever found that I considered your commands as my pride; for your kindness is such that my duty as yet has been inclination. [*Exeunt.*]

ACT IV

SCENE I. *The house.*

Enter HASTINGS *and* MISS NEVILLE.

HASTINGS. You surprise me; Sir Charles Marlow expected here this night! Where have you had your information?

MISS NEVILLE. You may depend upon it. I just saw his letter to Mr. Hardcastle, in which he tells him he intends setting out a few hours after his son.

HASTINGS. Then, my Constance, all must be completed before he arrives. He knows me; and should he find me here, would discover my name, and perhaps, my designs, to the rest of the family.

MISS NEVILLE. The jewels, I hope, are safe?

HASTINGS. Yes, yes. I have sent them to Marlow, who keeps the keys of our baggage. In the meantime, I'll go to prepare matters for our elopement. I have had the squire's promise of a fresh pair of horses; and, if I should not see him again, will write him further directions. [*Exit.*]

MISS NEVILLE. Well, success attend you! In the meantime, I'll go amuse my aunt with the old pretense of a violent passion for my cousin. [*Exit.*]

Enter MARLOW, *followed by a* SERVANT.

MARLOW. I wonder what Hastings could mean by sending me so valuable a thing as a casket to keep for him, when he knows the only place I have is the seat of a post-coach at an inn-door. Have you deposited the casket with the landlady, as I ordered you? Have you put it into her own hands?

SERVANT. Yes, your honor.

MARLOW. She said she'd keep it safe, did she?

SERVANT. Yes; she said she'd keep it safe enough; she asked me how I came by it; and she said she had a great mind to make me give an account of myself. [*Exit* SERVANT.]

MARLOW. Ha! ha! ha! They're safe, however. What an unaccountable set of beings have we got amongst! This little barmaid, though, runs in my head most strangely, and drives out the absurdities of all the rest of the family. She's mine, she must be mine, or I'm greatly mistaken.

Enter HASTINGS.

HASTINGS. Bless me! I quite forgot to tell her that I intended to prepare at the bottom of the garden. Marlow here, and in spirits too!

MARLOW. Give me joy, George! Crown me, shadow me with laurels! Well, George, after all, we modest fellows don't want for success among the women.

HASTINGS. Some women, you mean. But what success has your honor's modesty been crowned with now, that it grows so insolent upon us?

MARLOW. Didn't you see the tempting, brisk, lovely little thing that runs about the house with a bunch of keys to its girdle?

HASTINGS. Well, and what then?

MARLOW. She's mine, you rogue, you. Such fire, such motion, such eyes, such lips—but, egad! she would not let me kiss them, though.

HASTINGS. But you are sure, so very sure of her?

MARLOW. Why, man, she talked of showing me her work above stairs, and I am to approve the pattern.

HASTINGS. But how can you, Charles, go about to rob a woman of her honor?

MARLOW. Pshaw! Pshaw! We all know the honor of the barmaid of an inn. I don't intend to rob her, take my word for it.

HASTINGS. I believe the girl has virtue.

MARLOW. And if she has, I should be the last man in the world that would attempt to corrupt it.

HASTINGS. You have taken care, I hope, of the casket I sent you to lock up? It's in safety?

MARLOW. Yes, yes. It's safe enough. I have taken care of it. But how could you think the seat of a post-coach at an inn-door a place of safety? Ah! numskull! I have taken better precautions for you than you did for yourself—I have—

HASTINGS. What?

MARLOW. I have sent it to the landlady to keep for you.

HASTINGS. To the landlady!

MARLOW. The landlady.

HASTINGS. You did!

MARLOW. I did. She's to be answerable for its forthcoming, you know.

HASTINGS. Yes, she'll bring it forth with a witness.

MARLOW. Wasn't I right? I believe you'll allow that I acted prudently upon this occasion.

HASTINGS. (*Aside.*) He must not see my uneasiness.

MARLOW. You seem a little disconcerted though, methinks. Sure, nothing has happened?

HASTINGS. No, nothing. Never was in better spirits in all my life. And so you left it with the landlady, who, no doubt, very readily undertook the charge?

MARLOW. Rather too readily. For she not only kept the casket, but, through her great precaution, was going to keep the messenger too. Ha! ha! ha!

HASTINGS. He! he! he! They're safe, however.

MARLOW. As a guinea in a miser's purse.

HASTINGS. (*Aside.*) So now all hopes of fortune are at an end, and we must set off without it. (*To him.*) Well, Charles, I'll leave you to your meditations on the pretty barmaid, and, he! he! he! may you be as successful for yourself as you have been for me! [*Exit.*]

MARLOW. Thank ye, George; I ask no more. Ha! ha! ha!

Enter HARDCASTLE.

HARDCASTLE. I no longer know my own house. It's turned all topsy-turvy. His servants have got drunk already. I'll bear it no longer; and yet, from my respect for his father,

I'll be calm. (*To him.*) Mr. Marlow, your servant. I'm your very humble servant. [*Bowing low.*]

MARLOW. Sir, your humble servant. (*Aside.*) What is to be the wonder now?

HARDCASTLE. I believe, sir, you must be sensible, sir, that no man alive ought to be more welcome than your father's son, sir. I hope you think so?

MARLOW. I do from my soul, sir. I don't want much entreaty. I generally make my father's son welcome wherever he goes.

HARDCASTLE. I believe you do, from my soul, sir. But though I say nothing to your own conduct, that of your servants is insufferable. Their manner of drinking is setting a very bad example in this house, I assure you.

MARLOW. I protest, my very good sir, that is no fault of mine. If they don't drink as they ought, they are to blame. I ordered them not to spare the cellar. I did, I assure you. (*To the side-scene.*) Here, let one of my servants come up. (*To him.*) My positive directions were that as I did not drink myself they should make up for my deficiencies below.

HARDCASTLE. Then they had your orders for what they do? I'm satisfied!

MARLOW. They had, I assure you. You shall hear it from one of themselves.

Enter SERVANT, *drunk.*

MARLOW. You, Jeremy! Come forward, sirrah! What were my orders? Were you not told to drink freely, and call for what you thought fit, for the good of the house?

HARDCASTLE. (*Aside.*) I begin to lose my patience.

JEREMY. Please your honor, liberty and Fleet Street forever! Though I'm but a servant, I'm as good as another man. I'll drink for no man before supper, sir! Good liquor will sit upon a good supper, but a good supper will not sit upon—hiccup—upon my conscience, sir. [*Exit.*]

MARLOW. You see, my old friend, the fellow is as drunk as he can possibly be. I don't know what you'd have more, unless you'd have the poor devil soused in a beer barrel.

HARDCASTLE. Zounds! he'll drive me distracted, if I contain myself any longer. Mr. Marlow: sir, I have submitted to your insolence for more than four hours, and I see no likelihood of its coming to an end. I'm now resolved to be master here, sir, and I desire that you and your drunken pack may leave my house directly.

MARLOW. Leave your house! — Sure, you jest, my good friend! What, when I am doing what I can to please you!

HARDCASTLE. I tell you, sir, you don't please me; so I desire you'll leave my house.

MARLOW. Sure, you cannot be serious? At this time of night, and such a night? You only mean to banter me.

HARDCASTLE. I tell you, sir, I'm serious! And, now that my passions are aroused, I say this house is mine, sir; this house is mine, and I command you to leave it directly.

MARLOW. Ha! ha! ha! A puddle in a storm. I shan't stir a step, I assure you. (*In a serious tone.*) This your house, fellow! It's my house. This is my house. Mine, while I choose to stay. What right have you to bid me leave this house, sir? I never met with such impudence, curse me; never in my whole life before.

HARDCASTLE. Nor I, confound me if ever I did! To come to my house, to call for what he likes, to turn me out of my own chair, to insult the family, to order his servants to get drunk, and then to tell me, "This house is mine, sir." By all that's impudent, it makes me laugh. Ha! ha! ha! Pray, sir (*bantering*), as you take the house, what think you of taking the rest of the furniture? There's a pair of silver candlesticks, and there's a firescreen, and here's a pair of brazen-nosed bellows; perhaps you may take a fancy to them?

MARLOW. Bring me your bill, sir; bring me your bill, and let's make no more words about it.

HARDCASTLE. There are a set of prints, too. What think you of the Rake's Progress for your own apartment?

MARLOW. Bring me your bill, I say; and I'll leave you and your infernal house directly.

HARDCASTLE. Then there's a mahogany table that you may see your face in.

MARLOW. My bill, I say.

HARDCASTLE. I had forgot the great chair for your own particular slumbers, after a hearty meal.

MARLOW. Zounds! bring me my bill, I say, and let's hear no more on't.

HARDCASTLE. Young man, young man, from your father's letter to me, I was taught to expect a well-bred, modest man as a visitor here, but now I find him no better than a coxcomb and a bully; but he will be down here presently, and shall hear more of it.   [*Exit.*]

MARLOW. How's this! Sure, I have not mistaken the house? Everything looks like an inn. The servants cry, "Coming." The attendance is awkward; the barmaid, too, to attend us. But she's here, and will further inform me. Whither so fast, child? A word with you.

Enter MISS HARDCASTLE.

MISS HARDCASTLE. Let it be short, then. I'm in a hurry. (*Aside.*) I believe he begins to find out his mistake. But it's too soon quite to undeceive him.

MARLOW. Pray, child, answer me one question. What are you, and what may your business in this house be?

MISS HARDCASTLE. A relation of the family, sir.

MARLOW. What, a poor relation?

MISS HARDCASTLE. Yes, sir. A poor relation, appointed to keep the keys, and to see that the guests want nothing in my power to give them.

MARLOW. That is, you act as the barmaid of this inn.

MISS HARDCASTLE. Inn! O law!— What brought that into your head? One of the best families in the county keep an inn!—Ha! ha! ha! old Mr. Hardcastle's house an inn!

MARLOW. Mr. Hardcastle's house! Is this Mr. Hardcastle's house, child?

MISS HARDCASTLE. Aye, sure. Whose else should it be?

MARLOW. So, then, all's out, and I have been infernally imposed on. Oh, confound my stupid head, I shall be laughed at over the whole town. I shall be stuck up in caricature in all the print-shops. The Dullissimo Macaroni. To mistake this house of all others for an inn, and my father's old friend for an innkeeper! What a swaggering puppy must he take me for! What a silly puppy do I find myself! There again, may I be hanged, my dear, but I mistook you for the barmaid.

MISS HARDCASTLE. Dear me! dear me! I'm sure there's nothing in my *behavior* to put me upon a level with one of that stamp.

MARLOW. Nothing, my dear, nothing. But I was in for a list of blunders, and could not help making you a subscriber. My stupidity saw everything the wrong way. I mistook your assiduity for assurance, and your simplicity for allurement. But it's over —this house I no more show *my* face in.

MISS HARDCASTLE. I hope, sir, I have done nothing to disoblige you. I'm sure I should be sorry to affront any gentleman who has been so polite, and said so many civil things to me. I'm sure I should be sorry (*pretending to cry*) if he left the family on my account. I'm sure I should be sorry people said anything amiss, since I have no fortune but my character.

MARLOW. (*Aside.*) By heaven! she weeps. This is the first mark of tenderness I ever had from a modest woman, and it touches me. (*To her.*) Excuse me, my lovely girl; you are the only part of the family I leave with reluctance. But to be plain with you, the difference of our birth, fortune, and education, makes an honorable connection impossible; and I can never harbor a thought of seducing simplicity that trusted in my honor, or bringing ruin upon one whose only fault was being too lovely.

MISS HARDCASTLE. (*Aside.*) Generous man! I now begin to admire him. (*To him.*) But I am sure my family is as good as Miss Hardcastle's; and though I'm poor, that's no great misfortune to a contented mind; and, until this moment, I never thought that it was bad to want fortune.

MARLOW. And why now, my pretty simplicity?

MISS HARDCASTLE. Because it puts me at a distance from one that if I had a thousand pounds I would give it all to.

MARLOW. (*Aside.*) This simplicity bewitches me so that if I stay I'm undone. I must make one bold effort, and leave her. (*To her.*) Your par-

tiality in my favor, my dear, touches me most sensibly, and were I to live for myself alone, I could easily fix my choice. But I owe too much to the opinion of the world, too much to the authority of a father; so that—I can scarcely speak it—it affects me. Farewell! [*Exit.*]

MISS HARDCASTLE. I never knew half his merit till now. He shall not go if I have power or art to detain him. I'll still preserve the character in which I *stooped to conquer,* but will undeceive my papa, who, perhaps, may laugh him out of his resolution. [*Exit.*]

Enter TONY *and* MISS NEVILLE.

TONY. Aye, you may steal for yourselves the next time. I have done my duty. She has got the jewels again, that's a sure thing; but she believes it was all a mistake of the servants.

MISS NEVILLE. But, my dear cousin, sure you won't forsake us in this distress? If she in the least suspects that I am going off, I shall certainly be locked up, or sent to my Aunt Pedigree's, which is ten times worse.

TONY. To be sure, aunts of all kinds are very bad things. But what can I do? I have got you a pair of horses that will fly like Whistlejacket; and I'm sure you can't say but I have courted you nicely before her face. Here she comes; we must court a bit or two more, for fear she should suspect us.

[*They retire and seem to fondle.*]

Enter MRS. HARDCASTLE.

MRS. HARDCASTLE. Well, I was greatly fluttered, to be sure. But my son tells me it was all a mistake of the servants. I shan't be easy, however, till they are fairly married, and then let her keep her own fortune. But what do I see? Fondling together, as I'm alive. I never saw

Tony so sprightly before. Ah! have I caught you, my pretty doves? What, billing, exchanging stolen glances, and broken murmurs? Ah!

TONY. As for murmurs, mother, we grumble a little now and then, to be sure. But there's no love lost between us.

MRS. HARDCASTLE. A mere sprinkling, Tony, upon the flame, only to make it burn brighter.

MISS NEVILLE. Cousin Tony promises to give us more of his company at home. Indeed, he shan't leave us any more. It won't leave us, cousin Tony, will it?

TONY. Oh, it's a pretty creature! No, I'd sooner leave my horse in a pound than leave you when you smile upon one so. Your laugh makes you so becoming.

MISS NEVILLE. Agreeable cousin! Who can help admiring that natural humor, that pleasant, broad, red, thoughtless (*patting his cheek*)—ah! it's a bold face!

MRS. HARDCASTLE. Pretty innocence!

TONY. I'm sure I always loved cousin Con's hazel eyes, and her pretty long fingers, that she twists this way and that over the haspicholls, like a parcel of bobbins.

MRS. HARDCASTLE. Ah! he would charm the bird from the tree. I was never so happy before. My boy takes after his father, poor Mr. Lumpkin, exactly. The jewels, my dear Con, shall be yours incontinently. You shall have them. Isn't he a sweet boy, my dear? You shall be married tomorrow, and we'll put off the rest of his education, like Dr. Drowsy's sermons, to a fitter opportunity.

Enter DIGGORY.

DIGGORY. Where's the squire? I have got a letter for your worship.

TONY. Give it to my mamma. She reads all my letters first.

DIGGORY. I had orders to deliver it into your own hands.

TONY. Who does it come from?

DIGGORY. Your worship mun ask that o' the letter itself. [*Exit* DIGGORY.]

TONY. I could wish to know, though. [*Turning the letter, and gazing on it.*]

MISS NEVILLE. (*Aside.*) Undone! undone! A letter to him from Hastings. I know the hand. If my aunt sees it, we are ruined forever. I'll keep her employed a little, if I can. (*To* MRS. HARDCASTLE.) But I have not told you, madam, of my cousin's smart answer just now to Mr. Marlow. We so laughed—you must know, madam.—This way a little, for he must not hear us. [*They confer.*]

TONY. (*Still gazing.*) A cramp piece of penmanship as ever I saw in my life. I can read your print-hand very well. But here there are such handles, and shanks, and dashes that one can scarce tell the head from the tail. "To Anthony Lumpkin, Esquire." It's very odd, I can read the outside of my letters, where my own name is, well enough. But when I come to open it, it's all—buzz. That's hard—very hard; for the inside of the letter is always the cream of the correspondence.

MRS. HARDCASTLE. Ha! ha! ha! Very well, very well. And so my son was too hard for the philosopher.

MISS NEVILLE. Yes, madam; but you must hear the rest, madam. A little more this way, or he may hear us. You'll hear how he puzzled him again.

MRS. HARDCASTLE. He seems strangely puzzled now himself, methinks.

TONY. (*Still gazing.*) An up and down hand, as if it was disguised in liquor. (*Reading*.) "Dear sir,"—aye, that's that. Then there's an M, and a T, and an S, but whether the next be an izzard or an R, confound me, I cannot tell!

MRS. HARDCASTLE. What's that, my dear? Can I give you any assistance?

MISS NEVILLE. Pray, aunt, let me read it. Nobody reads a cramp hand better than I. (*Twitching the letter from her.*) Do you know who it is from?

TONY. Can't tell, except from Dick Ginger, the feeder.

MISS NEVILLE. Aye, so it is. (*Pretending to read.*) Dear Squire, hoping that you're in health, as I am at this present. The gentlemen of the Shake-bag Club has cut the gentlemen of the Goose-green quite out of feather. The odds—um—odd battle—um—long fighting—um—here, here, it's all about cocks and fighting; it's of no consequence; here, put it up, put it up.

[*Thrusting the crumpled letter upon him.*]

TONY. But I tell you, miss, it's of all the consequence in the world! I would not lose the rest of it for a guinea! Here, mother, do you make it out. Of no consequence!

[*Giving* MRS. HARDCASTLE *the letter.*]

MRS. HARDCASTLE. How's this? (*Reads.*) "Dear Squire, I'm now waiting for Miss Neville, with a post-chaise and pair, at the bottom of the garden, but I find my horses yet unable to perform the journey. I expect you'll assist us with a pair of fresh horses, as you promised. Dispatch is necessary, as the *hag*—aye, the hag—your mother will otherwise suspect us. Yours, Hastings." Grant

me patience. I shall run distracted! My rage chokes me!

MISS NEVILLE. I hope, madam, you'll suspend your resentment for a few moments, and not impute to me any impertinence, or sinister design, that belongs to another.

MRS. HARDCASTLE. (*Curtsying very low.*) Fine spoken, madam; you are most miraculously polite and engaging, and quite the very pink of courtesy and circumspection, madam. (*Changing her tone.*) And you, you great ill-fashioned oaf, with scarce sense enough to keep your mouth shut; were you, too, joined against me? But I'll defeat all your plots in a moment. As for you, madam, since you have got a pair of fresh horses ready, it would be cruel to disappoint them. So, if you please, instead of running away with your spark, prepare this very moment to run off with *me*. Your old Aunt Pedigree will keep you secure, I'll warrant me. You too, sir, may mount your horse, and guard us upon the way. Here, Thomas, Roger, Diggory! I'll show you that I wish you better than you do yourselves.

[*Exit.*]

MISS NEVILLE. So, now I'm completely ruined.

TONY. Aye, that's a sure thing.

MISS NEVILLE. What better could be expected from being connected with such a stupid fool—and after all the nods and signs I made him!

TONY. By the laws, miss, it was your own cleverness, and not my stupidity, that did your business. You were so nice and so busy with your Shake-bags and Goose-greens that I thought you could never be making believe.

Enter HASTINGS.

HASTINGS. So, sir, I find by my servant that you have shown my letter, and betrayed us. Was this well done, young gentleman?

TONY. Here's another. Ask miss, there, who betrayed you. Ecod, it was her doing, not mine.

Enter MARLOW.

MARLOW. So I have been finely used here among you. Rendered contemptible, driven into ill-manners, despised, insulted, laughed at.

TONY. Here's another. We shall have old Bedlam broke loose presently.

MISS NEVILLE. And there, sir, is the gentleman to whom we all owe every obligation.

MARLOW. What can I say to him, a mere boy, an idiot, whose ignorance and age are a protection.

HASTINGS. A poor, contemptible booby that would but disgrace correction.

MISS NEVILLE. Yet with cunning and malice enough to make himself merry with all our embarrassments.

HASTINGS. An insensible cub.

MARLOW. Replete with tricks and mischief.

TONY. Baw! but I'll fight you both, one after the other—with baskets.

MARLOW. As for him, he's below resentment. But your conduct, Mr. Hastings, requires an explanation. You knew of my mistakes, yet would not undeceive me.

HASTINGS. Tortured as I am with my own disappointments, is this a time for explanations? It is not friendly, Mr. Marlow.

MARLOW. But, sir—

MISS NEVILLE. Mr. Marlow, we never kept on your mistake till it was too late to undeceive you. Be pacified.

Enter SERVANT.

SERVANT. My mistress desires you'll get ready immediately, madam. The horses are putting to. Your hat and things are in the next room. We are to go thirty miles before morning.

[*Exit* SERVANT.]

MISS NEVILLE. Well, well; I'll come presently.

MARLOW. (*To* HASTINGS.) Was it well done, sir, to assist in rendering me ridiculous? To hang me out for the scorn of all my acquaintance? Depend upon it, sir, I shall expect an explanation.

HASTINGS. Was it well done, sir, if you're upon that subject, to deliver what I entrusted to yourself, to the care of another, sir?

MISS NEVILLE. Mr. Hastings! Mr. Marlow! Why will you increase my distress by this groundless dispute? I implore, I entreat you—

Enter SERVANT.

SERVANT. Your cloak, madam. My mistress is impatient.

MISS NEVILLE. I come. (*Exit* SERVANT.) Pray, be pacified. If I leave you thus, I shall die with apprehension!

Enter SERVANT.

SERVANT. Your fan, muff, and gloves, madam. The horses are waiting.

MISS NEVILLE. Oh, Mr. Marlow! if you knew what a scene of constraint and ill-nature lies before me, I'm sure it would convert your resentment into pity.

MARLOW. I'm so distracted with a variety of passions that I don't know what I do. Forgive me, madam. George, forgive me. You know my hasty temper, and should not exasperate it.

HASTINGS. The torture of my situation is my only excuse.

MISS NEVILLE. Well, my dear Hastings, if you have that esteem for me that I think that I am sure you have, your constancy for three years will but increase the happiness of our future connection. If—

MRS. HARDCASTLE. (*Within.*) Miss Neville. Constance, why, Constance, I say.

MISS NEVILLE. I'm coming. Well, constancy, remember, constancy is the word.

[*Exit, followed by the* SERVANT.]

HASTINGS. My heart! how can I support this! To be so near happiness, and such happiness!

MARLOW. (*To* TONY.) You see now, young gentleman, the effects of your folly. What might be amusement to you is here disappointment, and even distress.

TONY. (*From a reverie.*) Ecod, I have hit it. It's here. Your hands. Yours, and yours, my poor Sulky. My boots there, ho!—Meet me two hours hence at the bottom of the garden; and if you don't find Tony Lumpkin a more good-natured fellow than you thought for, I'll give you leave to take my best horse, and Bet Bouncer into the bargain. Come along. My boots, ho!

[*Exeunt.*]

ACT V

SCENE I. *The house.*

Enter HASTINGS *and* SERVANT.

HASTINGS. You saw the old lady and Miss Neville drive off, you say?

SERVANT. Yes, your honor. They went off in a post-coach, and the young squire went on horseback. They're thirty miles off by this time.

HASTINGS. Then all my hopes are over.

SERVANT. Yes, sir. Old Sir Charles is arrived. He and the old gentleman of the house have been laughing at Mr. Marlow's mistake this half hour. They are coming this way.

HASTINGS. Then I must not be seen. So now to my fruitless appointment at the bottom of the garden. This is about the time. [*Exit.*]

Enter SIR CHARLES *and* HARDCASTLE.

HARDCASTLE. Ha! ha! ha! The peremptory tone in which he sent forth his sublime commands!

SIR CHARLES. And the reserve with which I suppose he treated all your advances.

HARDCASTLE. And yet he might have seen something in me above a common innkeeper, too.

SIR CHARLES. Yes, Dick, but he mistook you for an uncommon innkeeper; ha! ha! ha!

HARDCASTLE. Well, I'm in too good spirits to think of anything but joy. Yes, my dear friend, this union of our families will make our personal friendships hereditary; and though my daughter's fortune is but small—

SIR CHARLES. Why, Dick, will you talk of fortune to *me*? My son is possessed of more than a competence already, and can want nothing but a good and virtuous girl to share his happiness and increase it. If they like each other, as you say they do—

HARDCASTLE. *If,* man! I tell you they *do* like each other. My daughter as good as told me so.

SIR CHARLES. But girls are apt to flatter themselves, you know.

HARDCASTLE. I saw him grasp her hand in the warmest manner myself; and here he comes to put you out of your *ifs,* I warrant him.

Enter MARLOW.

MARLOW. I come, sir, once more, to ask pardon for my strange conduct. I can scarce reflect on my insolence without confusion.

HARDCASTLE. Tut, boy, a trifle. You take it too gravely. An hour or two's laughing with my daughter will set all to rights again. She'll never like you the worse for it.

MARLOW. Sir, I shall be always proud of her approbation.

HARDCASTLE. Approbation is but a cold word, Mr. Marlow; if I am not deceived, you have something more than approbation thereabouts. You take me?

MARLOW. Really, sir, I have not that happiness.

HARDCASTLE. Come, boy, I'm an old fellow, and know what's what as well as you that are younger. I know what has passed between you; but mum.

MARLOW. Sure, sir, nothing has passed between us but the most profound respect on my side, and the most distant reserve on hers. You don't think, sir, that my impudence has been passed upon all the rest of the family?

HARDCASTLE. Impudence; No, I don't say that—not quite impudence—though girls like to be played with, and rumpled a little, too, sometimes. But she has told no tales, I assure you.

MARLOW. I never gave her the slightest cause.

HARDCASTLE. Well, well, I like modesty in its place well enough. But this is over-acting, young gentleman. You *may* be open. Your father and I will like you the better for it.

MARLOW. May I die, sir, if I ever—

HARDCASTLE. I tell you she don't dislike you; and as I'm sure you like her—

MARLOW. Dear sir—I protest, sir—

HARDCASTLE. I see no reason why you should not be joined as fast as the parson can tie you.

MARLOW. But hear me, sir—

HARDCASTLE. Your father approves the match, I admire it; every moment's delay will be doing mischief, so—

MARLOW. But why won't you hear me? By all that's just and true, I never gave Miss Hardcastle the slightest mark of my attachment, or even the most distant hint to suspect me of affection. We had but one interview, and that was formal, modest, and uninteresting.

HARDCASTLE. (*Aside.*) This fellow's formal, modest impudence is beyond bearing.

SIR CHARLES. And you never grasped her hand, or made any protestations?

MARLOW. As heaven is my witness, I came down in obedience to your commands. I saw the lady without emotion, and parted without reluctance. I hope you'll exact no further proofs of my duty, nor prevent me from leaving a house in which I suffer so many mortifications. [*Exit.*]

SIR CHARLES. I'm astonished at the air of sincerity with which he parted.

HARDCASTLE. And I'm astonished at the deliberate intrepidity of his assurance.

SIR CHARLES. I dare pledge my life and honor upon his truth.

HARDCASTLE. Here comes my daughter, and I would stake my happiness upon her veracity.

Enter MISS HARDCASTLE.

HARDCASTLE. Kate, come hither, child. Answer us sincerely, and without reserve. Has Mr. Marlow made you any professions of love and affection?

MISS HARDCASTLE. The question is very abrupt, sir! But since you require unreserved sincerity, I think he has.

HARDCASTLE. (*To* SIR CHARLES.) You see.

SIR CHARLES. And pray, madam, have you and my son had more than one interview?

MISS HARDCASTLE. Yes, sir, several.

HARDCASTLE. (*To* SIR CHARLES.) You see.

SIR CHARLES. But did he profess any attachment?

MISS HARDCASTLE. A lasting one.

SIR CHARLES. Did he talk of love?

MISS HARDCASTLE. Much, sir.

SIR CHARLES. Amazing! And all this formally?

MISS HARDCASTLE. Formally.

HARDCASTLE. Now, my friend, I hope you are satisfied.

SIR CHARLES. And how did he behave, madam?

MISS HARDCASTLE. As most professed admirers do: said some civil things of my face, talked much of his want of merit, and the greatness of mine; mentioned his heart, gave a short, tragedy speech, and ended with pretended rapture.

SIR CHARLES. Now I'm perfectly convinced, indeed. I know his conversation among women to be modest and submissive. This forward, canting, ranting manner by no means describes him; and, I am confident, he never sat for the picture.

MISS HARDCASTLE. Then what, sir, if I should convince you to your face of my sincerity? If you and my papa, in about half an hour, will place yourselves behind that screen, you shall hear him declare his passion to me in person.

SIR CHARLES. Agreed. And if I find him what you describe, all my happiness in him must have an end. [*Exit.*]

MISS HARDCASTLE. And if you don't find him what I describe—I fear my happiness must never have a beginning.

[*Exeunt.*]

SCENE II. *The back of the garden.*

Enter HASTINGS.

HASTINGS. What an idiot am I, to wait here for a fellow who probably takes a delight in mortifying me. He never intended to be punctual, and I'll wait no longer. What do I see? It is he! And perhaps with news of my Constance.

Enter TONY, *booted and spattered.*

HASTINGS. My honest squire! I now find you a man of your word. This looks like friendship.

TONY. Aye, I'm your friend, and the best friend you have in the world, if you knew but all. This riding by night, by the bye, is cursedly tiresome. It has shook me worse than the basket of a stage-coach.

HASTINGS. But how? Where did you leave your fellow-travelers? Are they in safety? Are they housed?

TONY. Five-and-twenty miles in two hours and a half is no such bad driving. The poor beasts have smoked for it. Rabbit me, but I'd rather ride forty miles after a fox than ten with such varment.

HASTINGS. Well, but where have you left the ladies? I die with impatience.

TONY. Left them? Why, where should I leave them but where I found them?

HASTINGS. This is a riddle.

TONY. Riddle me this, then. What's that goes round the house, and round the house, and never touches the house?

HASTINGS. I'm still astray.

TONY. Why, that's it, mon. I have led them astray. By jingo, there's not a pond or a slough within five miles of the place but they can tell the taste of.

HASTINGS. Ha! ha! ha! I understand; you took them in a round while they supposed themselves going forward, and so you have at last brought them home again.

TONY. You shall hear. I first took them down Feather-bed Lane, where we stuck fast in the mud. I then rattled them crack over the stones of Up-and-down Hill. I then introduced them to the gibbet on Heavy-tree Heath; and from that, with a circumbendibus, I fairly lodged them in the horse-pond at the bottom of the garden.

HASTINGS. But no accident, I hope?

TONY. No, no. Only mother is confoundedly frightened. She thinks herself forty miles off. She's sick of the journey; and the cattle can scarce crawl. So, if your own horses be ready, you may whip off with cousin, and I'll be bound that no soul here can budge a foot to follow you.

HASTINGS. My dear friend, how can I be grateful?

TONY. Aye, now it's "dear friend," "noble squire." Just now, it was all "idiot," "cub." After we take a knock in this part of the country, we kiss and be friends. But if you had stabbed me, then I should be dead, and you might go kiss the hangman.

HASTINGS. The rebuke is just. But I must hasten to relieve Miss Neville; if you keep the old lady employed, I promise to take care of the young one.

TONY. Never fear me. Here she comes; vanish. (*Exit* HASTINGS.) She's got from the pond, and draggled up to the waist like a mermaid.

Enter MRS. HARDCASTLE.

MRS. HARDCASTLE. Oh, Tony, I'm killed. Shook! Battered to death! I shall never survive it. That last jolt, that laid us against the quickset-hedge, has done my business.

TONY. Alack, mamma, it was all your own fault. You would be for running away by night, without knowing one inch of the way.

MRS. HARDCASTLE. I wish we were at home again. I never met so many accidents in so short a journey. Drenched in the mud, overturned in a ditch, stuck fast in a slough, jolted to a jelly, and at last to lose our way! Whereabouts do you think we are, Tony?

TONY. By my guess we should be upon Crackskull Common, about forty miles from home.

MRS. HARDCASTLE. O lud! O lud! The most notorious spot in all the country. We only want a robbery to make a complete night on't.

TONY. Don't be afraid, mamma, don't be afraid. Two of the five that kept here are hanged, and the other three may not find us. Don't be afraid.—Is that a man that's galloping behind us? No; it's only a tree. —Don't be afraid.

MRS. HARDCASTLE. The fright will certainly kill me.

TONY. Do you see anything like a black hat moving behind the thicket?

MRS. HARDCASTLE. Oh, death!

TONY. No; it's only a cow. Don't be afraid, mamma, don't be afraid.

MRS. HARDCASTLE. As I'm alive, Tony, I see a man coming toward us. Ah! I am sure on't. If he perceives us, we are undone.

TONY. (*Aside.*) Father-in-law, by all that's unlucky, come to take one of his night walks. (*To her.*) Ah, it's a highwayman, with pistols as long as my arm. An ill-looking fellow!

MRS. HARDCASTLE. Good heaven defend us! He approaches.

TONY. Do you hide yourself in that thicket, and leave me to manage him. If there be any danger, I'll cough, and cry hem. When I cough, be sure to keep close. [MRS. HARD-CASTLE *hides behind a tree in the back scene.*]

Enter HARDCASTLE.

HARDCASTLE. I'm mistaken, or I heard voices of people in want of help. Oh, Tony, is that you? I did not expect you so soon back. Are your mother and her charge in safety?

TONY. Very safe, sir, at my Aunt Pedigree's. Hem.

MRS. HARDCASTLE. (*From behind.*) Ah, death! I find there's danger.

HARDCASTLE. Forty miles in three hours; sure that's too much, my youngster.

TONY. Stout horses and willing minds make short journeys, as they say. Hem.

MRS. HARDCASTLE. (*From behind.*) Sure, he'll do the dear boy no harm.

HARDCASTLE. But I heard a voice here; I should be glad to know from whence it came.

TONY. It was I, sir, talking to myself, sir. I was saying that forty miles in four hours was very good going. Hem. As to be sure it was. Hem. I have got a sort of cold by being out in the air. We'll go in, if you please. Hem.

HARDCASTLE. But if you talked to yourself, you did not answer yourself. I'm certain I heard two voices, and am resolved (*raising his voice*) to find the other out.

MRS. HARDCASTLE. (*From behind.*) Oh! he's coming to find me out. Oh!

TONY. What need you go, sir, if I tell you? Hem. I'll lay down my life for the truth—hem—I'll tell you all, sir.

[*Detaining him.*]

HARDCASTLE. I tell you I will not be detained. I insist on seeing. It's in vain to expect I'll believe you.

MRS. HARDCASTLE. (*Running forward from behind.*) O lud! he'll murder my poor boy, my darling! Here, good gentleman, whet your rage upon me. Take my money, my

life, but spare that young gentleman; spare my child, if you have any mercy.

HARDCASTLE. My wife, as I'm a Christian. From whence can she come? or what does she mean?

MRS. HARDCASTLE. (*Kneeling.*) Take compassion on us, good Mr. Highwayman. Take our money, our watches, all we have, but spare our lives. We will never bring you to justice; indeed we won't, good Mr. Highwayman.

HARDCASTLE. I believe the woman's out of her senses. What, Dorothy, don't you know *me*?

MRS. HARDCASTLE. Mr. Hardcastle, as I'm alive! My fears blinded me. But who, my dear, could have expected to meet you here, in this frightful place, so far from home? What has brought you to follow us?

HARDCASTLE. Sure, Dorothy, you have not lost your wits? So far from home, when you are within forty yards of your own door! (*To him.*) This is one of your old tricks, you graceless rogue, you. (*To her.*) Don't you know the gate and the mulberry tree; and don't you remember the horse-pond, my dear?

MRS. HARDCASTLE. Yes, I shall remember the horse-pond as long as I live; I have caught my death in it. (*To Tony.*) And is it to you, you graceless varlet, I owe all this? I'll teach you to abuse your mother, I will.

TONY. Ecod, mother, all the parish says you have spoiled me, and so you may take the fruits on't.

MRS. HARDCASTLE. I'll spoil you, I will.

[*Follows him off the stage.*]

HARDCASTLE. There's morality, however, in his reply.

[*Exit.*]

Enter HASTINGS *and* MISS NEVILLE.

HASTINGS. My dear Constance, why will you deliberate thus? If we delay a moment, all is lost forever. Pluck up a little resolution, and we shall soon be out of the reach of her malignity.

MISS NEVILLE. I find it impossible. My spirits are so sunk with the agitations I have suffered that I am unable to face any new danger. Two or three years' patience will at last crown us with happiness.

HASTINGS. Such a tedious delay is worse than inconstancy. Let us fly, my charmer. Let us date our happiness from this very moment. Perish fortune! Love and content will increase what we possess beyond a monarch's revenue. Let me prevail!

MISS NEVILLE. No, Mr. Hastings, no. Prudence once more comes to my relief, and I will obey its dictates. In the moment of passion fortune may be despised, but it ever produces a lasting repentance. I'm resolved to apply to Mr. Hardcastle's compassion and justice for redress.

HASTINGS. But though he had the will, he has not the power to relieve you.

MISS NEVILLE. But he has influence, and upon that I am resolved to rely.

HASTINGS. I have no hopes. But, since you persist, I must reluctantly obey you.

[*Exeunt.*]

SCENE III. *A room at* MR. HARD-CASTLE'S.

Enter SIR CHARLES MARLOW *and* MISS HARDCASTLE.

SIR CHARLES. What a situation am I in! If what you say appears, I shall then find a guilty son. If what he says be true, I shall then lose one that, of all others, I most wished for a daughter.

MISS HARDCASTLE. I am proud of your approbation; and to show I merit it, if you place yourselves as I directed, you shall hear his explicit declaration. But he comes.

SIR CHARLES. I'll to your father, and keep him to the appointment.

[*Exit* SIR CHARLES.]

Enter MARLOW.

MARLOW. Though prepared for setting out, I come once more to take leave; nor did I, till this moment, know the pain I feel in the separation.

MISS HARDCASTLE. (*In her own natural manner.*) I believe these sufferings cannot be very great, sir, which you can so easily remove. A day or two longer, perhaps, might lessen your uneasiness, by showing the little value of what you now think proper to regret.

MARLOW. (*Aside.*) This girl every moment improves upon me. (*To her.*) It must not be, madam; I have already trifled too long with my heart. My very pride begins to submit to my passion. The disparity of education and fortune, the anger of a parent, and the contempt of my equals begin to lose their weight; and nothing can restore me to myself but this painful effort of resolution.

MISS HARDCASTLE. Then go, sir; I'll urge nothing more to detain you. Though my family be as good as hers you came down to visit, and my education, I hope, not inferior, what are these advantages without equal affluence? I must remain contented with the slight approbation of imputed merit; I must have only the mockery of your addresses, while all your serious aims are fixed on fortune.

Enter HARDCASTLE *and* SIR CHARLES
MARLOW *from behind.*

SIR CHARLES. Here, behind this
screen.

HARDCASTLE. Aye, aye; make no
noise. I'll engage my Kate covers
him with confusion at last.

MARLOW. By heavens, madam,
fortune was ever my smallest consideration. Your beauty at first
caught my eye; for who could see
that without emotion? But every
moment that I converse with you
steals in some new grace, heightens
the picture, and gives it stronger expression. What at first seemed rustic
plainness, now appears refined simplicity. What seemed forward assurance, now strikes me as the result
of courageous innocence and conscious virtue.

SIR CHARLES. What can it mean?
He amazes me!

HARDCASTLE. I told you how it
would be. Hush!

MARLOW. I am now determined to
stay, madam, and I have too good an
opinion of my father's discernment,
when he sees you, to doubt his approbation.

MISS HARDCASTLE. No, Mr. Marlow, I will not, cannot detain you.
Do you think I could suffer a connection in which there is the smallest
room for repentance? Do you think I
would take the mean advantage of
a transient passion to load you with
confusion? Do you think I could
ever relish that happiness which was
acquired by lessening yours?

MARLOW. By all that's good, I can
have no happiness but what's in your
power to grant me! Nor shall I ever
feel repentance but in not having seen
your merits before. I will stay even
contrary to your wishes; and though
you should persist to shun me, I will

make my respectful assiduities atone
for the levity of my past conduct.

MISS HARDCASTLE. Sir, I must entreat you'll desist. As our acquaintance began, so let it end, in indifference. I might have given an hour or
two to levity; but seriously, Mr. Marlow, do you think I could ever submit to a connection where I must appear mercenary, and *you* imprudent?
Do you think I could ever catch at
the confident addresses of a secure admirer?

MARLOW. (*Kneeling.*) Does this
look like security? Does this look
like confidence? No, madam, every
moment that shows me your merit
only serves to increase my diffidence
and confusion. Here let me continue—

SIR CHARLES. I can hold it no
longer. Charles, Charles, how hast
thou deceived me! Is this your indifference, your uninteresting conversation?

HARDCASTLE. Your cold contempt;
your formal interview! What have
you to say now?

MARLOW. That I'm all amazement!
What can it mean?

HARDCASTLE. It means that you
can say and unsay things at pleasure;
that you can address a lady in private,
and deny it in public; that you have
one story for us, and another for my
daughter.

MARLOW. Daughter! — this lady
your daughter?

HARDCASTLE. Yes, sir, my only
daughter; my Kate; whose else should
she be?

MARLOW. Oh, the devil!

MISS HARDCASTLE. Yes, sir, that
very identical, tall, squinting lady you
were pleased to take me for (*curtsying*), she that you addressed as the
mild, modest, sentimental man of
gravity, and the bold, forward, agree-

able Rattle of the Ladies' Club. Ha! ha! ha!

MARLOW. Zounds! There's no bearing this; it's worse than death!

MISS HARDCASTLE. In which of your characters, sir, will you give us leave to address you? As the faltering gentleman, with looks on the ground, that speaks just to be heard, and hates hypocrisy; or the loud, confident creature, that keeps it up with Mrs. Mantrap, and old Miss Biddy Buckskin, till three in the morning? Ha! ha! ha!

MARLOW. Oh, curse on my noisy head. I never attempted to be impudent yet that I was not taken down. I must be gone.

HARDCASTLE. By the hand of my body, but you shall not. I see it was all a mistake, and I am rejoiced to find it. You shall not, sir, I tell you. I know she'll forgive you. Won't you forgive him, Kate? We'll all forgive you. Take courage, man.

[*They retire, she tormenting him, to the back scene.*]

Enter MRS. HARDCASTLE *and* TONY.

MRS. HARDCASTLE. So, so, they're gone off. Let them go, I care not.

HARDCASTLE. Who gone?

MRS. HARDCASTLE. My dutiful niece and her gentleman, Mr. Hastings, from town. He who came down with our modest visitor here.

SIR CHARLES. Who, my honest George Hastings? As worthy a fellow as lives, and the girl could not have made a more prudent choice.

HARDCASTLE. Then, by the hand of my body, I'm proud of the connection.

MRS. HARDCASTLE. Well, if he has taken away the lady, he has not taken her fortune; that remains in this family to console us for her loss.

HARDCASTLE. Sure, Dorothy, you would not be so mercenary?

MRS. HARDCASTLE. Aye, that's my affair, not yours.

HARDCASTLE. But, you know, if your son, when of age, refuses to marry his cousin, her whole fortune is then at her own disposal.

MRS. HARDCASTLE. Aye, but he's not of age, and she has not thought proper to wait for his refusal.

Enter HASTINGS *and* MISS NEVILLE.

MRS. HARDCASTLE. (*Aside.*) What, returned so soon! I begin not to like it.

HASTINGS. (*To* HARDCASTLE.) For my late attempt to fly off with your niece, let my present confusion be my punishment. We are now come back, to appeal from your justice to your humanity. By her father's consent, I first paid her my addresses, and our passions were first founded in duty.

MISS NEVILLE. Since his death, I have been obliged to stoop to dissimulation to avoid oppression. In an hour of levity, I was ready even to give up my fortune to secure my choice. But I am now recovered from the delusion, and hope from your tenderness what is denied me from a nearer connection.

MRS. HARDCASTLE. Pshaw! Pshaw! this is all but the whining end of a modern novel.

HARDCASTLE. Be it what it will, I'm glad they're come back to reclaim their due. Come hither, Tony, boy. Do you refuse this lady's hand whom I now offer you?

TONY. What signifies my refusing? You know I can't refuse her till I'm of age, father.

HARDCASTLE. While I thought concealing your age, boy, was likely to conduce to your improvement, I concurred with your mother's desire to keep it secret. But since I find she turns it to a wrong use, I must now declare you have been of age these three months.

TONY. Of age! Am I of age, father?

HARDCASTLE. Above three months.

TONY. Then you'll see the first use I'll make of my liberty. (*Taking* MISS NEVILLE's *hand.*) Witness all men, by these presents, that I, Anthony Lumpkin, Esquire, of BLANK place, refuse you, Constantia Neville, spinster, of no place at all, for my true and lawful wife. So Constance Neville may marry whom she pleases, and Tony Lumpkin is his own man again.

SIR CHARLES. O brave squire!

HASTINGS. My worthy friend!

MRS. HARDCASTLE. My undutiful offspring!

MARLOW. Joy, my dear George! I give you joy sincerely. And could I prevail upon my little tyrant here to be less arbitrary, I should be the happiest man alive, if you would return me the favor.

HASTINGS. (*To* MISS HARDCASTLE.) Come, madam, you are now driven to the very last scene of all your contrivances. I know you like him, I'm sure he loves you, and you must and shall have him.

HARDCASTLE. (*Joining their hands.*) And I say so too. And, Mr. Marlow, if she makes as good a wife as she has a daughter, I don't believe you'll ever repent your bargain. So now to supper. Tomorrow we shall gather all the poor of the parish about us, and the mistakes of the night shall be crowned with a merry morning. So, boy, take her; and as you have been mistaken in the mistress, my wish is, that you may never be mistaken in the wife.

[*Exeunt* OMNES.]

For Thought and Discussion

1. From the opening scene what does one learn about Mr. and Mrs. Hardcastle and Tony?
2. How does Tony assist in making the plot?
3. Why does Mr. Hardcastle attempt to train the servants in anticipation of Mr. Marlow's visit? How is this scene made humorous?
4. What trait of character possessed by young Marlow is used in developing the plot?
5. What part does Kate play in developing the plot?
6. What part do Miss Neville and Hastings take in the play?
7. Why is the discovery of the theft of the jewels humorous?
8. What are the most humorous sections of the play?
9. How does the play get its title?
10. Upon what actual incident did Goldsmith base this play?
11. Read the life of Oliver Goldsmith.

Class Production

Read the play until you can describe the following characters: Mr. Hardcastle, Mrs. Hardcastle, Kate Hardcastle, Tony, Miss Neville, young Marlow, Hastings.

Hand in a caste of the play from members of the class, including yourself for the part you want.

From these papers, the teacher or a committee will make a caste for class production.

Rehearsals, during the class period, in a vacant room will enable the players to catch the spirit of the play and improve the performance.

The front of the room will serve for a stage, and the members of the class and visitors will compose the audience.

The stage manager will set the stage. The actors will use their books but talk their lines to make the play dramatic and amusing.

∿

A BIRTHDAY

CHRISTINA ROSSETTI

[In theme and in treatment the poems of Christina Rossetti, 1830-1894, resemble greatly those of her artist brother, Dante Gabriel Rossetti. Like his, her works are artistically lovely and full of emotional quality; like his, her religious poems seem illumined with spiritual light. In the poem "A Birthday" she has embroidered joy and love into rich hangings of purple and gold and silver.]

MY heart is like a singing bird
    Whose nest is in a watered
        shoot;
My heart is like an apple tree

Whose boughs are bent with thick-
        set fruit;
My heart is like a rainbow shell   5
    That paddles in a halcyon sea;
My heart is gladder than all these
    Because my love is come to me.

Raise me a dais of silk and down;
    Hang it with vair and purple
        dyes;   10
Carve it in doves and pomegranates,
    And peacocks with a hundred eyes;
Work it in gold and silver grapes,
    In leaves and silver fleur-de-lis;
Because the birthday of my life   15
    Is come, my love is come to me.

For Thought and Discussion

1. Why are the similes used by Miss Rossetti particularly appropriate to her theme?
2. Define *halcyon, dais, vair.*
3. What word seems rather out of harmony with the grace and delicacy of the poet's expression?
4. Which do you find more pleasing, the outdoor setting of stanza one or the indoor setting of stanza two?

"DEAR LADY, WHEN THOU FROWNEST"
ROBERT BRIDGES

DEAR lady, when thou frownest,
  And my true love despisest,
And all thy vows disownest
  That sealed my venture wisest;
I think thy pride's displeasure   5
Neglects a matchless treasure
Exceeding price and measure.

But when again thou smilest,
  And love for love returnest,
And fear with joy beguilest,   10
  And takest truth in earnest;
Then, though I sheer adore thee,
The sum of my love for thee
Seems poor, scant, and unworthy.

For Thought and Discussion

1. What does he think when she frowns? When she smiles?
2. Why does this poem have the charm of old-fashioned love lyrics?

SHE WAS A PHANTOM OF DELIGHT
WILLIAM WORDSWORTH

[This poem addressed to the poet's wife was written in the third year of their marriage. Note the beauty and depth of feeling expressed in comparing his wife to objects lovely in the natural and in the spiritual world.]

SHE was a phantom of delight
  When first she gleamed upon my sight;
A lovely apparition, sent
To be a moment's ornament;
Her eyes as stars of twilight fair,   5
Like twilight's, too, her dusky hair;
But all things else about her drawn
From May-time and the cheerful dawn;
A dancing shape, an image gay,
To haunt, to startle, and waylay.   10

I saw her upon nearer view,
A spirit, yet a woman too!
Her household motions light and free.
And steps of virgin-liberty;
A countenance in which did meet   15
Sweet records, promises as sweet;
A creature not too bright or good
For human nature's daily food;
For transient sorrows, simple wiles,
Praise, blame, love, kisses, tears, and
    smiles.   20

And now I see with eye serene
The very pulse of the machine;
A being breathing thoughtful breath,
A traveler between life and death;
The reason firm, the temperate will,
Endurance, foresight, strength, and
    skill;   26
A perfect woman, nobly planned
To warn, to comfort, and command;
And yet a spirit still, and bright
With something of angelic light.   30

For Thought and Discussion

1. What features added to the charm of the woman's personal appearance?
2. What qualities of mind were in harmony with her personal appearance?

3. Does she seem to be an imaginary character or a real person?
4. Did Wordsworth believe that what a person thought and did was reflected in his face? Justify your answer.

Plus Work

Compare the character here described with the one in "Character of the Happy Warrior."

SONNET XXIX

WILLIAM SHAKESPEARE

WHEN in disgrace with fortune and men's eyes
I all alone beweep my outcast state,
And trouble deaf heaven with my bootless cries,
And look upon myself, and curse my fate,
Wishing me like to one more rich in hope, 5
Featured like him, like him with friends possessed,
Desiring this man's art, and that man's scope,
With what I most enjoy contented least;
Yet in these thoughts myself almost despising,
Haply I think on thee,—and then my state, 10
(Like to the lark at break of day arising
From sullen earth,) sings hymns at heaven's gate;
For thy sweet love remembered, such wealth brings
That then I scorn to change my state with kings.

For Thought and Discussion

1. Why is the poet unhappy? Of what does he envy his friends?
2. What makes him as happy as a lark?
3. Why does he forget his misfortunes and appreciate his lot in life?
4. Count the lines in this poem. Refer to the section "Periods and Types of Literature" to learn how to classify this lyric.

Plus Work

Make a study of Shakespeare's sonnets. Give an oral report on your work.

PROLOGUE TO "THE TWO POETS OF CROISIC"
ROBERT BROWNING

[These verses are the prologue to a long poem, "The Two Poets of Croisic." There is no record to indicate that the poem was a tribute to Browning's wife, but it is pleasing to think that "thy face" does refer to Mrs. Browning, for she was truly Browning's world and like a smile of God to him. Those who read the entire poem will find delightful Browning's version of the old Greek story which inspired the writing of the poem. The poet has a most charming conception of the dawn of beauty and love.]

SUCH a starved bank of moss
    Till, that May-morn,
Blue ran the flash across:
    Violets were born!

Sky—what a scowl of cloud   5
    Till, near and far,
Ray on ray split the shroud:
    Splendid, a star!

World—how it walled about
    Life with disgrace   10
Till God's own smile came out:
    That was thy face!

For Thought and Discussion

1. This poem is sometimes called "Apparitions." See the dictionary meaning of that term. Do you think it a fitting title for this poem? Why or why not?

2. What similarities do you find between these verses and Wordsworth's "Phantom of Delight"?

3. Memorize the verse containing the tribute to one who had helped Browning become a better poet.

SONNETS FROM THE PORTUGUESE
ELIZABETH BARRETT BROWNING

[¹*Theocritus*, a Greek bard of the third century, was the creator of the pastoral idyl.]

I

I THOUGHT once how Theocritus¹
    had sung
Of the sweet years, the dear and
    wished-for years,
Who each one in a gracious hand appears
To bear a gift for mortals, old or
    young;
And, as I mused it in his antique
    tongue,   5
I saw in gradual vision through my
    tears,
The sweet, sad years, the melancholy
    years,
Those of my own life, who by turns
    had flung
A shadow across me. Straightway I
    was 'ware,
So weeping, how a mystic Shape did
    move   10
Behind me, and drew me backward
    by the hair;
And a voice said in mastery while I
    strove,
"Guess now who holds thee?"—
    "Death," I said. But there,
The silver answer rang: "Not
    Death, but Love."

For Thought and Discussion

1. Sonnet I and Sonnet XLIII are from *Sonnets from the Portuguese*. To whom were these sonnets addressed?
2. What circumstances in Mrs. Browning's life probably occasioned the lines, "The sweet, sad years, the melancholy years," and what happy circumstances inspired the closing lines of the poem?
3. What game of childhood probably suggested the line "Guess now who holds thee"?
4. What or whose was the "voice of mastery"?

ROBERT BROWNING AND ELIZABETH BARRETT

XLIII

HOW do I love thee?   Let me count the ways.
I love thee to the depth and breadth and height
My soul can reach, when feeling out of sight
For the ends of being and ideal grace.
I love thee to the level of every day's ⁵
Most quiet need, by sun and candle-light.
I love thee freely, as men strive for right;
I love thee purely, as they turn from praise;
I love thee with the passion put to use
In my old griefs, and with my childhood's faith; ¹⁰
I love thee with a love I seemed to lose
With my lost saints.—I love thee with the breath,
Smiles, tears, of all my life!—and if God choose,
I shall but love thee better after death.

For Thought and Discussion

1. How many answers are made to the question in line one?
2. What are these answers?
3. Which answer seems to you to be most expressive of Mrs. Browning's devotion to her husband?
4. Does Mrs. Browning put self before God? Justify your answer.
5. How do these poems compare with many love songs of the present day? What differences and what likenesses do you find? Of the two types, which touches the deeper chords of feeling?

Plus Work

Read *Sonnets from the Portuguese.*

ELIZABETH BARRETT BROWNING 1806-1861

Two Interesting Children. While Master Robert Browning, the sturdy young poet living in the suburbs of London, was at the age of six writing verses in imitation of the poet Byron, a dreamy-eyed little girl in the woods of the Malvern Hills was likewise making verses and visioning herself as a velvet-clad poet-page to that same romantic Byron. Shortly afterward the boy Robert was organizing Homeric combats among his play fellows and teaching them to fight after the manner of the Greeks and the Trojans, and the girl, little eleven-year-old Elizabeth Barrett, was poring over her great epic "The Battle of the Marathon," fifty copies of which were published by her adoring father. These coincidences are not remarkable within themselves. Many children unknown to each other make verses and engage in similar games. What is remarkable is that coincidence continued to play an important part in the lives of these two particular children. As they grew older, each decided upon a literary career.

Happy Marriage. For a long time young Browning received little notice, but finally he gained some little recognition, and among the sincere admirers of his works was Elizabeth Barrett, already so famous as to be ranked with Tennyson and considered for the poet laureateship. In her poem, "Lady Geraldine's Courtship," she praised Browning. In appreciation, Browning, encouraged by Mr. Kenyon, Elizabeth Barrett's cousin and publisher, and later the greatest benefactor of the two poets, wrote requesting to be allowed to call. Love at first sight was the result. Soon literary England was amazed to learn that the virile and traveled Browning had eloped with the fragile invalid, Elizabeth Barrett, whose works were read everywhere, but who herself scarcely ever crossed her own threshold. It is singular (isn't it?) to speak of the elopement of two mature persons whose names are well known to

ELIZABETH BARRETT IN EARLY YOUTH

all England. The explanation lies in the unaccountable fact that Elizabeth's father, who was in many respects a most loving and indulgent one, had a tyrannical obsession that caused him to forbid any of his children to marry.

Never did marriage bring more ideal happiness than did the marriage of Robert Browning and Elizabeth Barrett. In sunny Italy the invalid began to regain her health, and both poets gave expression to their deep and abiding joy by writing better poetry than either had written before.

Recognition given Mrs. Browning has been overshadowed by that accorded her husband, even as she felt her happiness encompassed in his love. Sonnet VI from *Sonnets from the Portuguese* is expressive of the oneness of their lives.

> ". . . . . . yet I feel that I shall stand
> Henceforth in thy shadow. Nevermore
> Alone upon the threshold of my door
> Of individual life,. . . . ."

Sonnets from the Portuguese. The best-known of Mrs. Browning's works is her immortal *Sonnets from the Portuguese.* Of these sonnets, which were written to her husband alone, being an exquisite record of their ideal romance, Browning said: "I dared not reserve to myself the finest sonnets written in any language since Shakespeare."

Sonnet I and Sonnet XLIII are such favorites that they are included in almost every anthology of Victorian verse. Other of her well-known works are "Casa Guida's Window," a somewhat emotional political poem; the "Cry of the Children," a protest against child labor; "Aurora Leigh," a novel in verse similar in moral tone and social ideas to the works of Dickens and Eliot.

THE BLESSED DAMOZEL
DANTE GABRIEL ROSSETTI

[Dante Gabriel Rossetti, 1828-1882, belongs to the comparatively small group of youthful prodigies who continued to do meritorious work in mature life. Although he liked to think of himself as a painter rather than a poet, Rossetti began making verses very early in life and at nineteen wrote his best-known poem, "The Blessed Damozel." This appeared first in the journal of the Pre-Raphaelite Brotherhood, an organization of artists founded by Rossetti. When in 1862 the poet lost his wife, he had placed in her casket the manuscript of his famous love sonnets, but a number of years later, at the insistence of friends, the poems were taken from the casket and published. Because of their mystical quality Rossetti's poems are not easy to understand, but one does not read Rossetti for understanding but for delicate pictorial quality and beauty of cadence. One must observe closely in order to follow the recital of the *blessèd damozel,* who is represented as leaning on the rampart of a tower, and that of the man who had loved her before her death. The man's speeches are in parentheses.]

THE BLESSED damozel leaned out
  From the gold bar of Heaven,
Her eyes were deeper than the depth
  Of waters stilled at even;
She had three lilies in her hand,   5
  And the stars in her hair were seven.

Her robe, ungirt from clasp to hem,
  No wrought flowers did adorn,
But a white rose of Mary's gift,
  For service meetly worn;   10

Her hair that lay along her back
  Was yellow like ripe corn.

Herseemed she scarce had been a day
  One of God's choristers;
The wonder was not yet quite gone   15
  From that still look of hers;
Albeit, to them she left, her day
  Had counted as ten years.

(To one, it is ten years of years.
  . . . Yet now, and in this place,   20
Surely she leaned o'er me—her hair
  Fell all about my face. . . .
Nothing; the autumn fall of leaves.
  The whole year sets apace.)

It was the rampart of God's house   25
  That she was standing on;
By God built over the sheer depth
  The which is Space begun;
So high, that looking downward thence
  She scarce could see the sun.   30

She lies in Heaven, across the flood
  Of ether, as a bridge.
Beneath, the tides of day and night
  With flame and darkness ridge
The void, as low as where this earth [35]
  Spins like a fretful midge.

Around her, lovers, newly met
  'Mid deathless love's acclaims,
Spoke evermore among themselves
  Their heart-remembered names; [40]
And the souls mounting up to God
  Went by her like thin flames.

And still she bowed herself and
    stooped
  Out of the circling charm;
Until her bosom must have made [45]
  The bar she leaned on warm,
And the lilies lay as if asleep
  Along her bended arm.

From the fixed place of Heaven
    she saw
  Time like a pulse shake fierce [50]
Through all the worlds. Her gaze
    still strove
  Within the gulf to pierce
Its path; and now she spoke as when
  The stars sang in their spheres.

The sun was gone now; the curled
    moon [55]
  Was like a little feather
Fluttering far down the gulf; and
    now
  She spoke through the still
    weather.
Her voice was like the voice the stars
  Had when they sang together. [60]

(Ah sweet! Even now, in that bird's
    song,
  Strove not her accents there,

Fain to be hearkened? When those
    bells
  Possessed the midday air,
Strove not her steps to reach my [65]
    side
  Down all the echoing stair?)

"I wish that he were come to me,
  For he will come," she said.
"Have I not prayed in Heaven?—
    on earth,
  Lord, Lord, has he not prayed? [70]
Are not two prayers a perfect
    strength?
  And shall I feel afraid?

"When round his head the aureole
    clings,
  And he is clothed in white,
I'll take his hand and go with him [75]
  To the deep wells of light;
As unto a stream we will step down,
  And bathe there in God's sight.

"We two will stand beside that shrine,
  Occult, withheld, untrod, [80]
Whose lamps are stirred continually
  With prayer sent up to God;
And see our old prayers, granted,
    melt
  Each like a little cloud.

"We two will lie i' the shadow of [85]
  That living mystic tree
Within whose secret growth the Dove
  Is sometimes felt to be,
While every leaf that His plumes
    touch
  Saith His Name audibly. [90]

"And I myself will teach to him,
  I myself, lying so,
The songs I sing here; which his voice
  Shall pause in, hushed and slow,
And find some knowledge at each
    pause, [95]
  Or some new thing to know."

(Alas! We two, we two, thou say'st!
    Yea, one wast thou with me
That once of old. But shall God lift
    To endless unity   100
The soul whose likeness with thy soul
    Was but its love for thee?)

"We two," she said, "will seek the
        groves
    Where the lady Mary is,
With her five handmaidens, whose
        names   105
    Are five sweet symphonies—
Cecily, Gertrude, Magdalen,
    Margaret, and Rosalys.

"Circlewise sit they, with bound
        locks
    And foreheads garlanded;   110
Into the fine cloth white like flame
    Weaving the golden thread,
To fashion the birth-robes for them
    Who are just born, being dead.

"He shall fear, haply, and be
        dumb;   115
    Then will I lay my cheek
To his, and tell about our love,
    Not once abashed or weak;
And the dear Mother will approve
    My pride, and let me speak. 120

"Herself shall bring us, hand in hand,
    To Him round whom all souls
Kneel, the clear-ranged unnumbered
        heads
    Bowed with their aureoles;
And angels meeting us shall sing   125
    To their citherns and citoles.

"There will I ask of Christ the Lord
    Thus much for him and me:
Only to live as once on earth
    With Love—only to be,   130
As then awhile, forever now
    Together, I and he."

She gazed and listened and then said,
    Less sad of speech than mild—
"All this is when he comes." She
        ceased.   135
    The light thrilled towards her,
        filled
With angels in strong level flight.
    Her eyes prayed, and she smiled.

(I saw her smile.) But soon their
        path
    Was vague in distant spheres; 140
And then she cast her arms along
    The golden barriers,
And laid her face between her hands,
    And wept. (I heard her tears.)

For Thought and Discussion

1. Is there any significance in the numbers three and seven?
   Name other symbolical terms.
2. Quote lines revealing earthly beauty and others revealing heavenly beauty.
3. Quote lines that justify Rossetti's being called the painter's
   poet. Might he likewise be termed the musician's poet?
4. What emotions are revealed in the speeches of the two speakers?
   Describe each of them.
5. What request does the damsel affirm she will make?

Additional Readings

Alden, R. M.: *Poems of the English Race*

Austen, Jane: *Emma*

Pride and Prejudice

Barrie, James: *The Little Minister*

Beith, Janet: *No Second Spring*

Besier, Rudolf: *Barretts of Wimpole Street*

Blackmore, R. D.: *Lorna Doone*

Brontë, Charlotte: *Jane Eyre*

Eliot, George: *Mill on the Floss*

Galsworthy, John: *Maid in Waiting*

Flowering Wilderness

One More River

Heydrick, Benjamin A.: *Types of the Short Story*

Lang, Andrew: *The Blue Poetry Book*

Russell, Frances Theresa: *Two Poets, a Dog, and a Boy*

Storm, Theodore: *Immensée*

Undset, Sigrid: *Ida Elizabeth*

Woolf, Virginia: *Flush*

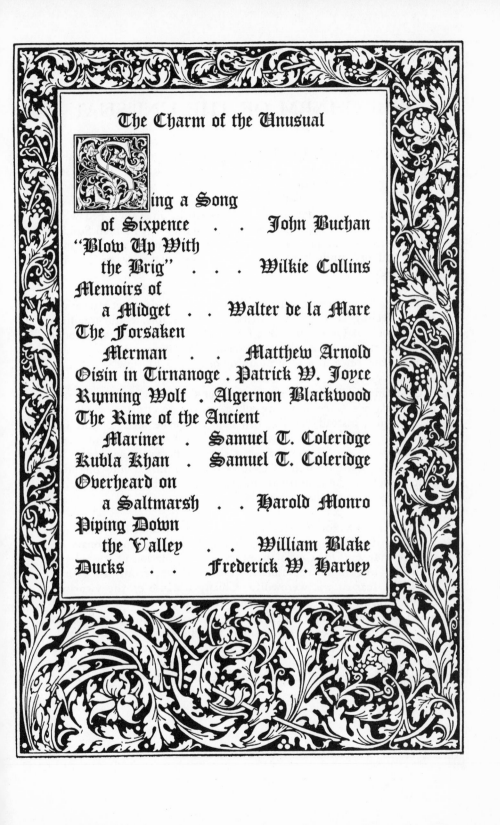

The Charm of the Unusual

THE CHARM OF THE UNUSUAL

GRANDMOTHER finds that wearing old shoes is comfortable. Father, despite the rush for the car or the subway, likes to seat himself in an accustomed place every day and read the morning paper on the way to the office. There is something satisfying about eating three meals a day and falling asleep in one's own bed when night comes. One likes the cheerful regularity with which Sunday is followed by Monday and Tuesday and so on until Sunday comes again and one finds himself seated in the usual pew singing the "Doxology."

There is assurance in realizing that the pyramids are centuries old and in feeling that certain institutions are stable, enduring, firm as the Rock of Gibraltar. But for all that, there is a charm about the rare, the unusual, the evanescent, the changing, that which happens but once in a blue moon or once in a lifetime.

Grandmother treasures a pair of silver slippers worn on a certain night. Father, once in a long while, makes no effort to catch the 8:20 train. Instead, he digs fish bait where he used to find fat, wriggly worms when he was a boy. Little brother likes mother's cookies every day of the year, but there's an extra twinkle in his eyes at the sight of lighted candles on a shining white birthday cake. Such a cake is unusual and, therefore, to be exulted over, as one exults over finding a four-leaf clover.

Our Anglo-Saxon forefathers loved their homes, but they also loved the thrill of adventure, the joy of landing their boats on strange shores. Our Celtic ancestors, in imagination at least, lived with the wee folks, the fairies. Our forbears from the North knew the fear of the werewolf. Chiefly because of the vicarious thrill of reading, all these, especially for the children of the mixed blood of America, have magic charm—the odor of brine, tall masts on a sailing ship, ice cliffs in a silent sea, the sound of church bells at evening time, and a mystery that has a clever solution or no solution at all. Selections by writers like Buchan, De La Mare, Blackwood, Coleridge, and Harvey are rich in romance and color and adventure.

"A ROTTEN NIGHT", I SAID. "IS SIXPENCE ANY GOOD TO YOU?"

SING A SONG OF SIXPENCE

JOHN BUCHAN

The effect of night, of any flowing water, of lighted cities, of the peep of day, of ships, of the open ocean, calls up in the mind an army of anonymous desires and pleasures. Something, we feel, should happen; we know not what, yet we proceed in quest of it.

R. L. Stevenson.

LEITHEN'S face had that sharp chiseling of the jaw and that compression of the lips which seem to follow upon high legal success. Also an overdose of German gas in '18 had given his skin an habitual pallor, so that he looked not unhealthy, but notably urban. As a matter of fact he was one of the hardest men I have ever known, but a chance observer might have guessed from his complexion that he rarely left the pavements.

Burminster, who had come back from a month in the grass countries with a face like a deep-sea mariner's, commented on this one evening.

"How do you manage always to look the complete Cit, Ned?" he asked. "You're as much a Londoner as a Parisian is a Parisian, if you know what I mean."

Leithen said that he was not ashamed of it, and he embarked on a eulogy of the metropolis. In London you met sooner or later everybody you had ever known; you could lay your hand on any knowledge you wanted; you could pull strings that controlled the innermost Sahara and the topmost Pamirs. Romance lay in wait for you at every street corner. It was the true City of the Caliphs.

"That is what they say," said Sandy Arbuthnot sadly, "but I never found it so. I yawn my head off in

- 469 -

London. Nothing amusing ever finds me out—I have to go and search for it, and it usually costs the deuce of a lot."

"I once stumbled upon a pretty generous allowance of romance," said Leithen, "and it cost me precisely sixpence."

Then he told us this story.

It happened a good many years ago, just when I was beginning to get on at the Bar. I spent busy days in court and chambers, but I was young and had a young man's appetite for society, so I used to dine out most nights and go to more balls than were good for me. It was pleasant after a heavy day to dive into a different kind of life. My rooms at the time were in Down Street, the same house as my present one, only two floors higher up.

On a certain night in February I was dining in Bryanston Square with the Nantleys. Mollie Nantley was an old friend, and used to fit me as an unattached bachelor into her big dinners. She was a young hostess and full of ambition, and one met an odd assortment of people at her house. Mostly political, of course, but a sprinkling of art and letters, and any visiting lion that happened to be passing through. Mollie was a very innocent lion hunter, but she had a partiality for the breed.

I don't remember much about the dinner, except that the principal guest had failed her. Mollie was loud in her lamentations. He was a South American president who had engineered a very pretty coup d'état the year before, and was now in England on some business concerning the finances of his state. You may remember his name—Ramon Pelem—he made rather a stir in the world for a year or two. I had read about him

in the papers, and had looked forward to meeting him, for he had won his way to power by extraordinary boldness and courage, and he was quite young. There was a story that he was partly English and that his grandfather's name had been Pelham. I don't know what truth there was in that, but he knew England well and Englishmen liked him.

Well, he had cried off on the telephone an hour before, and Mollie was grievously disappointed. Her other guests bore the loss with more fortitude, for I expect they thought he was a brand of cigar.

In those days dinners began earlier and dances later than they do today. I meant to leave soon, go back to my rooms and read briefs, and then look in at Lady Samplar's dance between eleven and twelve. So at nine-thirty I left.

Jervis, the old butler, who had been my ally from boyhood, was standing on the threshold, and in the square there was a considerable crowd, now thinning away. I asked what the trouble was.

"There's been an arrest, Mr. Edward," he said in an awestruck voice. "It 'appened when I was serving coffee in the dining room, but our Albert saw it all. Two foreigners, he said—proper rascals by their look—were took away by the police just outside this very door. The constables was very nippy and collared them before they could use their pistols—but they 'ad pistols on them and no mistake. Albert says he saw the weapons."

"Did they propose to burgle you?" I asked.

"I cannot say, Mr. Edward. But I shall give instruction for a very careful lockup tonight."

There were no cabs about, so I decided to walk on and pick one up. When I got into Great Cumberland

Place, it began to rain sharply, and I was just about to call a prowling hansom, when I put my hand into my pocket. I found that I had no more than one solitary sixpence.

I could, of course, have paid when I got to my flat. But as the rain seemed to be slacking off, I preferred to walk. Mollie's dining room had been stuffy, I had been in court all day, and I wanted some fresh air.

You know how in little things, when you have decided on a course, you are curiously reluctant to change it. Before I got to the Marble Arch, it had begun to pour in downright earnest. But I still stumped on. Only I entered the Park, for even in February there is a certain amount of cover from the trees.

I passed one or two hurried pedestrians, but the place was almost empty. The occasional lamps made only spots of light in a dripping darkness, and it struck me that this was a curious patch of gloom and loneliness to be so near to crowded streets, for with the rain had come a fine mist. I pitied the poor devils to whom it was the only home. There was one of them on a seat which I passed. The collar of his thin, shabby overcoat was turned up, and his shameful old felt hat was turned down, so that only a few square inches of pale face were visible. His toes stuck out of his boots, and he seemed sunk in a sodden misery.

I passed him and then turned back. Casual charity is an easy dope for the conscience, and I indulged in it too often. When I approached him he seemed to stiffen and his hands moved in his pockets.

"A rotten night," I said. "Is sixpence any good to you?" And I held out my solitary coin.

He lifted his face, and I started. For the eyes that looked at me were not those of a waster. They were bright, penetrating, authoritative—and they were young. I was conscious that they took in more of me than mine did of him.

"Thank you very much," he said, as he took the coin, and the voice was that of a cultivated man. "But I'm afraid I need rather more than sixpence."

"How much?" I asked. This was clearly an original.

"To be accurate, five million pounds."

He was certainly mad, but I was fascinated by this wisp of humanity. I wished that he would show more of his face.

"Till your ship comes home," I said, "you want a bed, and you'd be the better of a change. Sixpence is all I have on me. But if you come to my rooms, I'll give you the price of a night's lodging, and I think I might find you some old clothes."

"Where do you live?" he asked.

"Close by—in Down Street." I gave the number.

He seemed to reflect, and then he shot a glance on either side into the gloom behind the road. It may have been fancy, but I thought that I saw something stir in the darkness.

"What are you?" he asked.

I was getting abominably wet, and yet I submitted to be cross-examined by this waif.

"I am a lawyer," I said.

He looked at me again, very intently.

"Have you a telephone?" he asked.

I nodded.

"Right," he said. "You seem a good fellow and I'll take you at your word. I'll follow you .... Don't look back, please. It's important .... I'll be in Down Street as soon as you .... *Marchons.*"

It sounds preposterous, but I did

exactly as I was bid. I never looked back, but I kept my ears open for the sound of following footsteps. I thought I heard them, and then they seemed to die away. I turned out of the Park at Grosvenor Gate and went down Park Lane. When I reached the house which contained my flat, I looked up and down the street, but it was empty except for a waiting four-wheeler. But just as I turned in, I caught a glimpse of someone running at the Hertford Street end. The runner came to a sudden halt, and I saw that it was not the man I had left.

To my surprise I found the waif on the landing outside my flat. I was about to tell him to stop outside, but as soon as I unlocked the door he brushed past me and entered. My man, who did not sleep on the premises, had left the light burning in the little hall.

"Lock the door," he said in a tone of authority. "Forgive my taking charge, but I assure you it is important."

Then to my amazement he peeled off the sopping overcoat, and he kicked off his disreputable shoes. They were odd shoes, for what looked like his toes sticking out was really part of the makeup. He stood up before me in underclothes and socks, and I noticed that his underclothing seemed to be of the finest material.

"Now for your telephone," he said.

I was getting angry at these liberties.

"Who the devil are you?" I demanded.

"I am President Pelem," he said, with all the dignity in the world. "And you?"

"I?—oh, I am the German Emperor."

He laughed. "You know you invited me here," he said. "You've brought this on yourself." Then he stared at me. "Hullo, I've seen you before. You're Leithen. I saw you play at Lords'. I was twelfth man for Harrow that year.... Now for the telephone."

There was something about the fellow, something defiant and debonair and young, that stopped all further protest on my part. He might or might not be President Pelem, but he was certainly not a wastrel. Besides, he seemed curiously keyed up, as if the occasion were desperately important, and he infected me with the same feeling. I said no more, but led the way into my sitting room. He flung himself on the telephone, gave a number, was instantly connected, and began a conversation in monosyllables.

It was a queer jumble that I overheard. Bryanston Square was mentioned, and the Park, and the number of my house was given—to somebody. There was a string of foreign names —Pedro and Alejandro and Manuel and Alcaza—and short breathless inquiries. Then I heard—"a good fellow—looks as if he might be useful in a row," and I wondered if he was referring to me. Some rapid Spanish followed, and then, "Come round at once—they will be here before you. Have policemen below, but don't let them come up. We should be able to manage alone. Oh, and tell Burton to ring up here as soon as he has news." And he gave my telephone number.

I put some coals on the fire, changed into a tweed jacket, and lit a pipe. I fetched a dressing gown from my bedroom and flung it on the sofa. "You'd better put that on," I said when he had finished.

He shook his head.

"I would rather be unencumbered," he said. "But I should dearly love a cigarette.... and a liqueur brandy, if you have such a thing. That Park of yours is infernally chilly."

I supplied his needs, and he stretched himself in an armchair, with his stockinged feet to the fire.

"You have been very good-humoured, Leithen," he said. "Valdez—that's my aide-de-camp—will be here presently, and he will probably be preceded by other guests. But I think I have time for a short explanation which is your due. You believed what I told you?"

I nodded.

"Good. Well, I came to London three weeks ago to raise a loan. That was a matter of life or death for my big stupid country. I have succeeded. This afternoon the agreement was signed. I think I mentioned the amount to you—five million sterling."

He smiled happily and blew a smoke-ring into the air.

"I must tell you that I have enemies. Among my happy people there are many rascals, and I had to deal harshly with them. 'So foul a sky clears not without a storm'—that's Shakespeare, isn't it? I learned it at school. You see, I had Holy Church behind me, and therefore I had against me all the gentry who call themselves liberators. Red Masons, anarchists, communists, that sort of crew. A good many are now reposing beneath the sod, but some of the worst remain. In particular, six followed me to England with instructions that I must not return.

"I don't mind telling you, Leithen, that I have had a peculiarly rotten time the last three weeks. It was most important that nothing should happen to me till the loan was settled, so I had to lead the sheltered life. It went against the grain, I assure you,

for I prefer the offensive to the defensive. The English police were very amiable, and I never stirred without a cordon, your people and my own. The Six wanted to kill me, and as it is pretty easy to kill anybody if you don't mind being killed yourself, we had to take rather elaborate precautions. As it was, I was twice nearly done in. Once my carriage broke down mysteriously, and a crowd collected, and if I hadn't had the luck to board a passing cab, I should have had a knife in my ribs. The second was at a public dinner—something not quite right about the cayenne pepper served with the oysters. One of my staff is still seriously ill."

He stretched his arms.

"Well, that first stage is over. They can't wreck the loan, whatever happens to me. Now I am free to adopt different tactics and take the offensive. I have no fear of the Six in my own country. There I can take precautions, and they will find it difficult to cross the frontier or to live for six hours thereafter if they succeed. But here you are a free people, and protection is not so easy. I do not wish to leave England just yet—I have done my work and have earned a little respite. I know your land and love it, and look forward to seeing something of my friends. Also I want to attend the Grand National. Therefore, it is necessary that my enemies should be confined for a little, while I take my holiday. So for this evening I made a plan. I took the offensive. I deliberately put myself in their danger."

He turned his dancing eyes toward me, and I have rarely had such an impression of wild and mirthful audacity.

"We have an excellent intelligence system," he went on, "and the Six have been assiduously shadowed. But as I have told you, no precautions avail against the fanatic, and I do not wish to be killed on my little holiday. So I resolved to draw their fire —to expose myself as ground bait, so to speak, that I might have the chance of netting them. The Six usually hunt in couples, so it was necessary to have three separate acts in play, if all were to be gathered in. The first—"

"Was in Bryanston Square," I put in, "outside Lady Nantley's house?"

"True. How did you know?"

"I have just been dining there, and heard that you were expected. I saw the crowd in the square as I came away."

"It seems to have gone off quite nicely. We took pains to let it be known where I was dining. The Six, who mistrust me, delegated only two of their number for the job. They never put all their eggs in one basket. The two gentlemen were induced to make a scene, and since they proved to be heavily armed, were taken into custody and may get a six months' sentence. Very prettily managed, but unfortunately, it was the two that matter least—the ones we call Little Pedro and Alejandro the Scholar. Impatient, blundering children, both of them. That leaves four."

The telephone bell rang, and he made a long arm for the receiver. The news he got seemed to be good, for he turned a smiling face to me.

"I should have said two. My little enterprise in the Park has proved a brilliant success . . . . But I must explain. I was to be the bait for my enemies, so I showed myself to the remaining four. That was really rather a clever piece of business. They lost me at the Marble Arch and they did not recognize me as the scarecrow sitting on the seat in the rain. But they knew I had gone to earth there,

and they stuck to the scent like terriers. Presently they would have found me, and there would have been shooting. Some of my own people were in the shadow between the road and the railings."

"When I saw you, were your enemies near?" I asked.

"Two were on the opposite side of the road. One was standing under the lamp-post at the gate. I don't know where the fourth was at that moment. But all had passed me more than once . . . . By the way, you very nearly got yourself shot, you know. When you asked me if sixpence was any good to me . . . . That happens to be their password. I take great credit to myself for seeing instantly that you were harmless."

"Why did you leave the Park if you had your trap so well laid?" I asked.

"Because it meant dealing with all four together at once, and I do them the honor of being rather nervous about them. They are very quick with their guns. I wanted a chance to break up the covey, and your arrival gave it to me. When I went off, two followed, as I thought they would. My car was in Park Lane, and gave me a lift; and one of them saw me in it. I puzzled them a little, but by now they must be certain. You see, my car has been waiting for some minutes outside this house."

"What about the other two?" I asked.

"Burton has just telephoned that they have been gathered in. Quite an exciting little scrap. To your police it must have seemed a bad case of highway robbery—two ruffianly looking fellows hold up a peaceful elderly gentleman returning from dinner. The odds were not quite like that, but the men I had on the job are old soldiers of the Indian wars and can move softly . . . . I only wish I knew which two they have got. Burton was not sure. Alcaza is one, but I can't be certain about the other. I hope it is not the Irishman."

My bell rang very loud and steadily.

"In a few seconds I shall have solved that problem," he said gaily. "I am afraid I must trouble you to open the door, Leithen."

"Is it your aide-de-camp?"

"No. I instructed Valdez to knock. It is the residuum of the Six. Now, listen to me, my friend. These two, whoever they are, have come here to kill me, and I don't mean to be killed . . . . My first plan was to have Valdez here—and the others—so that my two enemies should walk into a trap. But I changed my mind before I telephoned. They are very clever men and by this time they will be very wary. So I have thought of something else."

The bell rang again and a third time insistently.

"Take these," and he held out a pair of cruel little bluish revolvers. "When you open the door, you will say that the President is at home and, in token of his confidence, offers them these. *'Une especes d'Irlandais, Messieurs. Vous commencez trop tard, et vous finissez trop tot.'* Then bring them here. Quick, now, I hope Corbally is one of them."

I did exactly as I was told. I cannot say that I had any liking for the task, but I was a good deal under the spell of that calm young man, and I was resigned to my flat being made a rendezvous for desperadoes. I had locked and chained and bolted the door, so it took me a few moments to open it.

I found myself looking at emptiness.

"Who is it?" I called. "Who rang?"

I was answered from behind me. It was the quickest thing I have ever seen, for they must have slipped through in the moment when my eyes were dazzled by the change from the dim light of the hall to the glare of the landing. That gave me some notion of the men we had to deal with.

"Here," said the voice. I turned and saw two men in waterproofs and felt hats, who kept their hands in their pockets and had a fraction of an eye on the two pistols I swung by the muzzles.

"M. le President will be glad to see you, gentlemen," I said. I held out the revolvers, which they seemed to grasp and flick into their pockets with a single movement. Then I repeated slowly the piece of rudeness in French.

One of the men laughed. "Ramon does not forget," he said. He was a young man with sandy hair and hot blue eyes and an odd break in his long drooping nose. The other was a wiry little fellow, with a grizzled beard and what looked like a stiff leg.

I had no guess at my friend's plan, and was concerned to do precisely as I was told. I opened the door of my sitting room, and noticed that the President was stretched on my sofa facing the door. He was smoking and was still in his underclothes. When the two men behind me saw that he was patently unarmed, they slipped into the room with a quick catlike movement and took their stand with their backs against the door.

"Hello, Corbally," said the President pleasantly. "And you, Manuel. You're looking younger than when I saw you last. Have a cigarette?" and he nodded toward my box on the table behind them. Both shook their heads.

"I'm glad you have come. You have probably seen the news of the loan in the evening papers. That should give you a holiday, as it gives me one. No further need for the hectic oversight of each other, which is so wearing and takes up so much time."

"No," said the man called Manuel, and there was something very grim about his quiet tones. "We shall take steps to prevent any need for that in the future."

"Tut, tut—that is your old self, Manuel. You are too fond of melodrama to be an artist. You are a priest at heart."

The man snarled. "There will be no priest at your deathbed." Then to his companion, "Let us get this farce over."

The President paid not the slightest attention, but looked steadily at the Irishman.

"You used to be a sportsman, Mike. Have you come to share Manuel's taste for potting the sitting rabbit?"

"We are not sportsmen; we are executioners of justice," said Manuel.

The President laughed merrily. "Superb! The best Roman manner." He still kept his eyes on Corbally.

"What's your game, Ramon?" the Irishman asked. His freckled face had become very red.

"Simply to propose a short armistice. I want a holiday. If you must know, I want to go to the Grand National."

"So do I."

"Well, let's call a truce. Say for two months or till I leave England, whichever period shall be the shorter. After that you can get busy again."

The one he had named Manuel broke into a spluttering torrent of Spanish, and for a little they all talked that language. It sounded like a commination service on the President, to which he good-humoredly replied. I had never seen this class of ruffian before, to whom murder was as simple as shooting a partridge, and I noted curiously the lean hands, the restless, wary eyes, and the ugly lips of the type. So far as I could make out, the President seemed to be getting on well with the Irishman, but to be having trouble with Manuel.

"Have you really and truly nothing on ye?" Corbally asked.

The President stretched his arms and revealed his slim figure in its close-fitting pants and vest.

"Nor him there?" and he nodded toward me.

"He is a lawyer; he doesn't use guns."

"Then I'm blamed if I touch ye. Two months it is. What's your fancy for Liverpool?"

This was too much for Manuel. I saw in what seemed to be one movement his hand slip from his pocket, Corbally's arm swing in a circle, and a plaster bust of Julius Caesar tumble off the top of my bookcase. Then I heard the report.

"Ye nasty little man," said Corbally as he pressed him to his bosom in a bear's hug.

"You are a traitor!" Manuel shouted. "How will we face the others? What will Alejandro say and Alcaza?"

"I think I can explain," said the President pleasantly. "They won't know for quite a time, and then only if you tell them. You two gentlemen are all that remain for the moment of your patriotic company. The other four have been victims of the English police—two in Bryanston Square, and two in the Park close to the Marble Arch."

"Ye don't say!" said Corbally, with

admiration in his voice. "Faith, that's smart work!"

"They, too, will have a holiday. A few months to meditate on politics, while you and I go to the Grand National."

Suddenly there was a sharp rat-tat at my door. It was like the knocking in Macbeth for dramatic effect. Corbally had one pistol at my ear in an instant, while a second covered the President.

"It's all right!" said the latter, never moving a muscle. "It's General Valdez, whom I think you know. That was another argument which I was coming to if I hadn't had the good fortune to appeal to Mr. Corbally's higher nature. I know you have sworn to kill me, but I take it that the killer wants to have a sporting chance of escape. Well, there wouldn't have been the faintest shadow of a chance here. Valdez is at the door, and the English police are below. You are brave men, I know, but even brave men dislike the cold gallows."

The knocker fell again. "Let him in, Leithen," I was told, "or he will be damaging your valuable door. He has not the Northern phlegm of you and me and Mr. Corbally."

A tall man in an ulster, which looked as if it covered a uniform, stood on the threshold. Someone had obscured the lights on the landing so that the staircase was dark, but I could see in the gloom other figures. "President Pelem," he began . . . .

"The President is here," I said. "Quite well and in great form. He is entertaining two other guests."

The General marched to my sitting room. I was behind him and did not see his face, but I can believe that it showed surprise when he recognized the guests. Manuel stood sulkily de-

fiant, his hands in his waterproof pockets, but Corbally's light eyes were laughing.

"I think you know each other," said the President graciously.

Valdez seemed to choke at the sight. "These swine! . . . . Excellency, I have—"

"You have nothing of the kind. These are friends of mine for the next two months, and Mr. Corbally and I are going to the Grand National together. Will you have the goodness to conduct them downstairs and explain to the inspector of police below that all has gone well and that I am perfectly satisfied, and that he will hear from me in the morning?"

I looked in at Lady Samplar's dance as I had meant to. Presently I saw a resplendent figure arrive—the President, with the ribbon of the Gold Star of Bolivar across his chest. He was no more the larky undergraduate, but the responsible statesman, the father of his country. There was a considerable crowd in his vicinity when I got near him and he was making his apologies to Mollie Nantley. She saw me and insisted on introducing me. "I so much wanted you two to meet. I had hoped it would be at my dinner—but anyhow I have managed it." I think she was a little surprised when the President took my hand in both of his. "I saw Mr. Leithen play at Lords' in '97," he said. "I was twelfth man for Harrow that year. It is delightful to make his acquaintance, I shall never forget this meeting."

"How English he is!" Mollie whispered to me as we made our way out of the crowd.

They got him next year. They were bound to, for in that kind of business you can have no real protection. But he managed to set his

country on its feet before he went
down ... No, it was neither Manuel
nor Corbally. I think it was Alejandro the Scholar.

For Thought and Discussion

1. Why did Leithen like London?
2. Why did he continue his walk from Mollie Nantley's house to his rooms in spite of the rain?
3. Why did he stop in the park to give money to the man on the bench?
4. Why did Leithen allow the stranger to go to his flat in Down Street?
5. When the stranger introduced himself as President Pelem, what was Leithen's reply?
6. Why did Leithen like Pelem?
7. On what two occasions had the Six attempted to assassinate President Pelem?
8. Why did Pelem desire to remain in England for a vacation? What does this decision reveal about his character?
9. What were the three separate acts in the play that Pelem planned? Where did the first take place? the second?
10. Why was Leithen's offer of a sixpence to the stranger dangerous?
11. Why did Pelem refuse to wear Leithen's dressing gown?
12. How did the two conspirators enter the hall when the door to the flat was opened to admit them?
13. Describe Manuel.
14. What type of character was Corbally?
15. Is the conclusion of this story logical? Why?
16. Why did Leithen have these adventures? Would Sandy Arbuthnot have had these adventures? Give reasons for your answer.
17. How does the introduction set the keynote for the entire story?
18. How does the story get its title?
19. Why have John Buchan's stories been compared to those of Robert Louis Stevenson?

❧

"BLOW UP WITH THE BRIG"

A Sailor's Story

WILKIE COLLINS[1]

I HAVE got an alarming confession to make. I am haunted by a Ghost. If you were to guess for a hundred years, you would never guess what

[1]Collins lived from 1824-1889.

my Ghost is. I shall make you laugh to begin with—and afterward I shall make your flesh creep. My Ghost is the ghost of a Bedroom Candlestick.

Yes, a bedroom candlestick and

candle, or a flat candlestick and candle—put it which way you like—that is what haunts me. I wish it was something pleasanter and more out of the common way; a beautiful lady, or a mine of gold and silver, or a cellar of wine and a coach and horses, and such like. But, being what it is, I must take it for what it is, and make the best of it; and I shall thank you kindly if you will help me out by doing the same.

I am not a scholar myself, but I make bold to believe that the haunting of any man with any thing under the sun begins with the frightening of him. At any rate, the haunting of me with a bedroom candlestick and candle began with the frightening of me with a bedroom candlestick and candle—the frightening of me half out of my life; and, for the time being, the frightening of me altogether out of my wits. That is not a very pleasant thing to confess before stating the particulars; but perhaps you will be the readier to believe that I am not a downright coward, because you find me bold enough to make a clean breast of it already, to my own great disadvantage so far.

Here are the particulars, as well as I can put them:

I was apprenticed to the sea when I was about as tall as my own walking-stick; and I made good enough use of my time to be fit for a mate's berth at the age of twenty-five years.

It was in the year eighteen hundred and eighteen, or nineteen, I am not quite certain which, that I reached the before-mentioned age of twenty-five. You will please to excuse my memory not being very good for dates, names, numbers, places, and such like. No fear, though, about the particulars I have undertaken to tell you of; I have got them all shipshape in my recollection; I can see

them, at this moment, as clear as noon-day in my own mind. But there is a mist over what went before, and, for the matter of that, a mist likewise over much that came after—and it's not very likely to lift at my time of life, is it?

Well, in eighteen hundred and eighteen, or nineteen, when there was peace in our part of the world—and not before it was wanted, you will say—there was fighting, of a certain scampering, scrambling kind, going on in that old battle-field which we sea-faring men know by the name of the Spanish Main.

The possessions that belonged to the Spaniards in South America had broken into open mutiny and declared for themselves years before. There was plenty of bloodshed between the new Government and the old; but the new had got the best of it, for the most part, under one General Bolivar—a famous man in his time, though he seems to have dropped out of people's memories now. Englishmen and Irishmen with a turn for fighting, and nothing particular to do at home, joined the general as volunteers; and some of our merchants here found it a good venture to send supplies across the ocean to the popular side. There was risk enough, of course, in doing this; but where one speculation of the kind succeeded, it made up for two, at the least, that failed. And that's the true principle of trade, wherever I have met with it, all the world over.

Among the Englishmen who were concerned in this Spanish-American business, I, your humble servant, happened, in a small way, to be one.

I was then mate of a brig belonging to a certain firm in the City, which drove a sort of general trade, mostly in queer out-of-the-way places, as far from home as possible;

and which freighted the brig, in the year I am speaking of, with a cargo of gunpowder for General Bolivar and his volunteers. Nobody knew anything about our instructions, when we sailed, except the captain; and he didn't half seem to like them. I can't rightly say how many barrels of powder we had on board, or how much each barrel held—I only know we had no other cargo. The name of the brig was the *Good Intent*—a queer name enough, you will tell me, for a vessel laden with gunpowder, and sent to help a revolution. And as far as this particular voyage was concerned, so it was. I mean that for a joke, and I hope you will encourage me by laughing at it.

The *Good Intent* was the craziest tub of a vessel I ever went to sea in, and the worst found in all respects. She was two hundred and thirty, or two hundred and eighty tons burden, I forget which; and she had a crew of eight, all told—nothing like as many as we ought by rights to have had to work the brig. However, we were well and honestly paid our wages; and we had to set that against the chance of foundering at sea, and, on this occasion, likewise the chance of being blown up into the bargain.

In consideration of the nature of our cargo, we were harassed with new regulations, which we didn't at all like, relative to smoking our pipes and lighting our lanterns; and, as usual in such cases, the captain, who made the regulations, preached what he didn't practice. Not a man of us was allowed to have a bit of lighted candle in his hand when he went below—except the skipper; and he used his light, when he turned in, or when he looked over his charts on the cabin table, just as usual.

This light was a common kitchen candle or "dip," and it stood in an old battered flat candlestick, with all the japan worn and melted off, and all the tin showing through. It would have been more seaman-like and suitable in every respect if he had had a lamp or a lantern; but he stuck to his old candlestick; and that same candlestick has ever afterward stuck to *me*. That's another joke, if you please, and a better one than the first, in my opinion.

Well (I said "well" before, but it's a word that helps a man on like), we sailed in the brig, and shaped our course, first, for the Virgin Islands, in the West Indies; and, after sighting them, we made for the Leeward Islands next, and then stood on due south, till the lookout at the masthead hailed the deck and said he saw land. That land was the coast of South America. We had had a wonderful voyage so far. We had lost none of our spars or sails, and not a man of us had been harassed to death at the pumps. It wasn't often the *Good Intent* made such a voyage as that, I can tell you.

I was sent aloft to make sure about the land, and I did make sure of it.

When I reported the same to the skipper, he went below, and had a look at his letter of instructions and the chart. When he came on deck again, he altered our course a trifle to the eastward—I forget the point on the compass, but that don't matter. What I do remember is, that it was dark before we closed in with the land. We kept the lead going, and hove the brig to in from four to five fathoms water, or it might be six— I can't say for certain. I kept a sharp eye to the drift of the vessel, none of us knowing how the currents ran on that coast. We all wondered why the skipper didn't anchor; but he said No, he must first show a light at the foretopmast-head, and wait for an answering light on shore. We did wait, and nothing of the sort appeared. It was starlight and calm. What little wind there was came in puffs off the land. I suppose we waited, drifting a little to the westward, as I made it out, best part of an hour before anything happened—and then, instead of seeing the light on shore, we saw a boat coming toward us, rowed by two men only.

We hailed them, and they answered "Friends!" and hailed us by our name. They came on board. One of them was an Irishman, and the other was a coffee-colored native pilot, who jabbered a little English.

The Irishman handed a note to our skipper, who showed it to me. It informed us that the part of the coast we were off was not oversafe for discharging our cargo, seeing that spies of the enemy (that is to say, of the old Government) had been taken and shot in the neighbourhood the day before. We might trust the brig to the native pilot; and he had his instructions to take us to another part of the coast. The note was signed by the proper parties; so we let the Irishman go back alone in the boat, and allowed the pilot to exercise his lawful authority over the brig. He kept us stretching off from the land' till noon the next day—his instructions, seemingly, ordering him to keep up well out of sight of the shore. We only altered our course in the afternoon, so as to close in with the land again a little before midnight.

This same pilot was about as ill-looking a vagabond as ever I saw; a skinny, cowardly, quarrelsome mongrel, who swore at the men in the vilest broken English, till they were every one of them ready to pitch him overboard. The skipper kept them quiet, and I kept them quiet; for the pilot being given us by our instructions, we were bound to make the best of him. Near nightfall, however, with the best will in the world to avoid it, I was unlucky enough to quarrel with him.

He wanted to go below with his pipe, and I stopped him, of course, because it was contrary to orders. Upon that he tried to hustle by me, and I put him away with my hand. I never meant to push him down; but somehow I did. He picked himself up as quick as lightning, and pulled out his knife. I snatched it out of his hand, slapped his murderous face for him, and threw his weapon overboard. He gave me one ugly look, and walked aft. I didn't think much of the look then, but I remembered it a little too well afterward.

We were close in with the land again, just as the wind failed us, between eleven and twelve that night, and dropped our anchor by the pilot's directions.

It was pitch-dark, and a dead, airless calm. The skipper was on deck, with two of our best men for watch. The rest were below, except the pilot, who coiled himself up, more like a snake than a man, on the forecastle. It was not my watch till four in the morning. But I didn't like the look of the night, or the pilot, or the state of things generally, and I shook myself down on deck to get my nap there, and be ready for anything at a moment's notice. The last I remember was the skipper whispering to me he didn't like the look of things either, and that he would go below and consult his instructions again. That is the last I remember, before the slow, heavy, regular roll of the old brig on the groundswell rocked me off to sleep.

I was awoke by a scuffle on the forecastle and a gag in my mouth.

There was a man on my breast and a man on my legs, and I was bound hand and foot in half a minute.

The brig was in the hands of the Spaniards. They were swarming all over her. I heard six heavy splashes in the water, one after another. I saw the captain stabbed to the heart as he came running up the companion, and I heard a seventh splash in the water. Except myself, every soul of us on board had been murdered and thrown into the sea. Why I was left, I couldn't think, till I saw the pilot stoop over me with a lantern and look, to make sure of who I was. There was a devilish grin on his face, and he nodded his head at me, as much as to say, *You* were the man who hustled me down and slapped my face, and I mean to play the game of cat and mouse with you in return for it!

I could neither move nor speak, but I could see the Spaniards take off the main hatch and rig the purchases for getting up the cargo. A quarter of an hour afterward I heard the sweeps of a schooner, or other small vessel, in the water. The strange craft was laid alongside of us, and the Spaniards set to work to discharge our cargo into her. They all worked hard except the pilot; and he came from time to time, with his lantern, to have another look at me, and to grin and nod always in the same devilish way. I am old enough now not to be ashamed of confessing the truth, and I don't mind acknowledging that the pilot frightened me.

The fright, and the bonds, and the gag, and the not being able to stir hand or foot, had pretty nigh worn me out by the time the Spaniards gave over work. This was just as the dawn broke. They had shifted a good part of our cargo on board their vessel, but nothing like all of it, and

they were sharp enough to be off with what they had got before daylight.

I need hardly say that I had made up my mind by this time to the worst I could think of. The pilot, it was clear enough, was one of the spies of the enemy, who had wormed himself into the confidence of our consignees without being suspected. He, or more likely his employers, had got knowledge enough of us to suspect what our cargo was; we had been anchored for the night in the safest berth for them to surprise us in; and we had paid the penalty of having a small crew, and consequently an insufficient watch. All this was clear enough—but what did the pilot mean to do with *me*?

On the word of a man, it makes my flesh creep now, only to tell you what he did with me.

After all the rest of them were out of the brig, except the pilot and two Spanish seamen, these last took me up, bound and gagged as I was, lowered me into the hold of the vessel, and laid me along on the floor, lashing me to it with ropes' ends, so that I could just turn from one side to the other, but could not roll myself fairly over, so as to change my place. They then left me. Both of them were the worse for liquor; but the devil of a pilot was sober—mind that!—as sober as I am at the present moment.

I lay in the dark for a little while, with my heart thumping as if it was going to jump out of me. I lay about five minutes or so when the pilot came down into the hold alone.

He had the captain's cursed flat candlestick and a carpenter's awl in one hand, and a long thin twist of cotton-yarn, well oiled, in the other. He put the candlestick, with a new "dip" candle lighted in it, down on the floor about two feet from my face, and close against the side of the vessel. The light was feeble enough; but it was sufficient to show a dozen barrels of gunpowder or more left all round me in the hold of the brig. I began to suspect what he was after the moment I noticed the barrels. The horrors laid hold of me from head to foot, and the sweat poured off my face like water.

I saw him go next to one of the barrels of powder standing against the side of the vessel in a line with the candle, and about three feet, or rather better, away from it. He bored a hole in the side of the barrel with his awl, and the horrid powder came trickling out, as black as hell, and dripped into the hollow of his hand, which he held to catch it. When he had got a good handful, he stopped up the hole by jamming one end of his oiled twist of cotton-yarn fast into it, and he then rubbed the powder into the whole length of the yarn till he had blackened every hair-breadth of it.

The next thing he did—as true as I sit here, as true as the heaven above us all—the next thing he did was to carry the free end of his long, lean, black, frightful slow-match to the lighted candle alongside my face. He tied it (the bloody-minded villain!) in several folds round the tallow dip, about a third of the distance down, measuring from the flame of the wick to the lip of the candlestick. He did that; he looked to see that my lashings were all safe; and then he put his face close to mine, and whispered in my ear, "Blow up with the brig!"

He was on deck again the moment after, and he and the two others shoved the hatch on over me. At the farthest end from where I lay they had not fitted it down quite true, and I saw a blink of daylight glimmering in when I looked in that direction. I heard the sweeps of the schooner fall into the water—splash! splash! fainter and fainter, as they swept the vessel out in the dead calm, to be ready for the wind in the offing. Fainter and fainter, splash, splash! for a quarter of an hour or more.

While those receding sounds were in my ears, my eyes were fixed on the candle.

It had been freshly lighted. If left to itself, it would burn for between six and seven hours. The slow-match was twisted round it about a third of the way down, and therefore the flame would be about two hours reaching it. There I lay, gagged, bound, lashed to the floor; seeing my own life burning down with the candle by my side—there I lay, alone on the sea, doomed to be blown to atoms, and to see that doom drawing on, nearer and nearer with every fresh second of time, through nigh on two hours to come; powerless to help myself, and speechless to call for help to others. The wonder to me is that I didn't cheat the flame, the slow-match, and the powder, and die of the horror of my situation before my first half-hour was out in the hold of the brig.

I can't exactly say how long I kept the command of my senses after I had ceased to hear the splash of the schooner's sweeps in the water. I can trace back everything I did and everything I thought, up to a certain point; but, once past that, I get all abroad, and lose myself in my memory now, much as I lost myself in my own feelings at the time.

The moment the hatch was covered over me, I began, as every other man would have begun in my place, with a frantic effort to free my hands. In the mad panic I was in, I cut my flesh with the lashings as if they had been knife-blades, but I never stirred them. There was less chance still of

freeing my legs, or of tearing myself from the fastenings that held me to the floor. I gave in when I was all but suffocated for want of breath. The gag, you will please to remember, was a terrible enemy to me; I could only breathe freely through my nose —and that is but a poor vent when a man is straining his strength as far as ever it will go.

- I gave in and lay quiet, and got my breath again, my eyes glaring and straining at the candle all the time. While I was staring at it, the notion struck me of trying to blow out the flame by pumping a long breath at it suddenly through my nostrils. It was too high above me, and too far away from me, to be reached in that fashion. I tried, and tried, and tried; and then I gave in again, and lay quiet again, always with my eyes glaring at the candle, and the candle glaring at *me*. The splash of the schooner's sweeps was very faint by this time. I could only just hear them in the morning stillness. Splash! splash!—fainter and fainter—splash! splash!

Without exactly feeling my mind going, I began to feel it getting queer as early as this. The snuff of the candle was growing taller and taller, and the length of the tallow between the flame and the slow-match, which was the length of my life, was getting shorter and shorter. I calculated that I had rather less than an hour and a half to live.

An hour and a half! Was there a chance in that time of a boat pulling off to the brig from shore? Whether the land near which the vessel was anchored was in possession of our side, or in possession of the enemy's side, I made out that they must, sooner or later, send to hail the brig merely because she was a stranger in those parts. The question for *me* was, how soon? The sun had not risen yet, as I could tell by looking through the chink in the hatch. There was no coast village near us, as we all knew, before the brig was seized, by seeing no lights on shore. There was no wind, as I could tell by listening, to bring any strange vessel near. If I had had six hours to live, there might have been a chance for me, reckoning from sunrise to noon. But with an hour and a half, which had dwindled to an hour and a quarter by this time—or, in other words, with the earliness of the morning, the uninhabited coast, and the dead calm all against me—there was not the ghost of a chance. As I felt that, I had another struggle—the last—with ny bonds, and only cut myself the deeper for my pains.

I gave in once more, and lay quiet, and listened for the splash of the sweeps.

Gone! Not a sound could I hear but the blowing of a fish now and then on the surface of the sea, and the creak of the brig's crazy old spars, as she rolled gently from side to side with the little swell there was on the quiet water.

An hour and a quarter. The wick grew terribly as the quarter slipped away, and the charred top of it began to thicken and spread out mushroom-shape. It would fall off soon. Would it fall off red-hot, and would the swing of the brig cant it over the side of the candle and let it down on the slow-match? If it would, I had about ten minutes to live instead of an hour.

This discovery set my mind for a minute on a new tack altogether. I began to ponder with myself what sort of a death blowing up might be. Painful! Well, it would be, surely, too sudden for that. Perhaps just one crash inside me, or outside me, or both; and nothing more! Perhaps not even a crash; that and death and the scattering of this living body of mine into millions of fiery sparks, might all happen in the same instant! I couldn't make it out; I couldn't settle how it would be. The minute of calmness in my mind left it before I had half done thinking; and I got all abroad again.

When I came back to my thoughts, or when they came back to me (I can't say which), the wick was awfully tall, the flame was burning with a smoke above it, the charred top was broad and red, and heavily spreading out to its fall.

My despair and horror at seeing it took me in a new way, which was good and right, at any rate, for my poor soul. I tried to pray—in my own heart, you will understand, for the gag put all lip-praying out of my power. I tried, but the candle seemed to burn it up in me. I struggled hard to force my eyes from the slow, murdering flame, and to look up through the chink in the hatch at the blessed daylight. I tried once, tried twice; and gave it up. I next tried only to shut my eyes, and keep them shut—once—twice—and the second time I did it. "God bless old mother, and sister Lizzie; God keep them both, and forgive *me*." That was all I had time to say, in my own heart, before my eyes opened again, in spite of me, and the flame of the candle flew into them, flew all over me, and burned up the rest of my thoughts in an instant.

I couldn't hear the fish blowing now; I couldn't hear the creak of the spars; I couldn't think; I couldn't feel the sweat of my own death agony on my face—I could only look at the heavy, charred top of the wick. It swelled, tottered, bent over to one side, dropped—red-hot at the moment of its fall—black and harmless, even before the swing of the brig had canted it over into the bottom of the candlestick.

I caught myself laughing.

Yes! laughing at the safe fall of the bit of wick. But for the gag, I should have screamed with laughing. As it was, I shook with it inside me—shook till the blood was in my head, and I was all but suffocated for want of breath. I had just sense enough left to feel that my own horrid laughter at that awful moment was a sign of my brain going at last. I had just sense enough left to make another struggle before my mind broke loose like a frightened horse, and ran away with me.

One comforting look at the blink of daylight through the hatch was what I tried for once more. The fight to force my eyes from the candle and to get that one look at the daylight was the hardest I had had yet; and I lost the fight. The flame had hold of my eyes as fast as the lashings had hold of my hands. I couldn't look away from it. I couldn't even shut my eyes, when I tried that next, for the second time. There was the wick growing tall once more. There was the space of unburned candle between the light and the slow-match shortened to an inch or less.

How much life did that inch leave me? Three-quarters of an hour? Half an hour? Fifty minutes? Twenty minutes? Steady! an inch of tallow-candle would burn longer than twenty minutes. An inch of tallow! the notion of a man's body and soul being kept together by an inch of tallow! Wonderful! Why, the greatest king that sits on a throne can't keep a man's body and soul together; and here's an inch of tallow that can do what the king can't! There's something to tell mother when I get home which will surprise her more than all the rest of my voyages put together. I laughed inwardly again at the thought of that, and shook and swelled and suffocated myself, till the light of the candle leaped in through my eyes, and licked up the laughter, and burned it out of me, and made me all empty and cold and quiet once more.

Mother and Lizzie. I don't know when they came back; but they did come back—not, as it seemed to me, into my mind this time, but right down bodily before me, in the hold of the brig.

Yes: sure enough, there was Lizzie, just as light-hearted as usual, laughing at me. Laughing? Well, why not? Who is to blame Lizzie for thinking I'm lying on my back, drunk in the cellar, with the beer-barrels all round me? Steady! She's crying now—spinning round and round in a fiery mist, wringing her hands, screeching out for help—fainter and fainter, like the splash of the schooner's sweeps. Gone—burned up in the fiery mist! Mist? fire? no; neither one nor the other. It's mother makes the light—mother knitting, with ten flaming points at the ends of her fingers and thumbs, and slow-matches hanging in bunches all round her face instead of her own grey hair. Mother in her old arm-chair, and the pilot's long skinny hands hanging over the back of the chair, dripping with gunpowder. No! no gunpowder, no chair, no mother—nothing but the pilot's face, shining red-hot, like a sun, in the fiery mist; turning upside down in the fiery mist; running backward and forward along the slow-match, in the fiery mist; spinning millions of miles in a minute, in the fiery mist—spinning itself smaller and smaller into one tiny point, and that point darting on a sudden straight into my head—and then, all fire and all mist—no hearing, no seeing, no thinking, no feeling—the brig, the sea, my own self, the whole world, all gone together!

After what I've just told you, I know nothing and remember nothing, till I woke up (as it seemed to me) in a comfortable bed, with two rough-and-ready men like myself sitting on each side of my pillow, and a gentleman standing watching me at the foot of the bed. It was about seven in the morning. My sleep (or what seemed like my sleep to me) had lasted better than eight months—I was among my own countrymen in the island of Trinidad—the men at each side of my pillow were my keepers, turn and turn about—and the gentleman standing at the foot of the bed was the doctor. What I said and did in those eight months, I never have known, and never shall. I woke out of it as if it had been one long sleep—that's all I know.

It was another two months or more before the doctor thought it safe to answer the questions I asked him.

The brig had been anchored, just as I had supposed, off a part of the coast which was lonely enough to make the Spaniards pretty sure of no interruption, so long as they managed their murderous work quietly under cover of night.

My life had not been saved from the shore, but from the sea. An American vessel, becalmed in the offing, had made out the brig as the sun rose; and the captain having his time on his hands in consequence of the calm, and seeing a vessel anchored where no vessel had any reason to be, had manned one of his boats and sent his mate with it, to look a little closer into the matter, and bring back a report of what he saw.

What he saw, when he and his men found the brig deserted and boarded her, was a gleam of candle-light through the chink in the hatchway. The flame was within about a thread's breadth of the slow-match when he lowered himself into the hold; and if he had not had the sense and coolness to cut the match in two with his knife before he touched the candle, he and his men might have been blown up along with the brig as well as me. The match caught and turned into sputtering red fire, in the very act of putting the candle out; and if the communication with the powder-barrel had not been cut off, the Lord only knows what might have happened.

What became of the Spanish schooner and the pilot, I have never heard from that day to this.

As for the brig, the Yankees took her, as they took me, to Trinidad, and claimed their salvage, and got it, I hope, for their own sakes. I was landed just in the same state as when they rescued me from the brig—that is to say, clean out of my senses. But please to remember, it was a long time ago; and, take my word for it, I was discharged cured, as I have told you. Bless your hearts, I'm all right now, as you may see. I'm a little shaken by telling the story, as is only natural—a little shaken, my good friends, that's all.

For Thought and Discussion

1. Who tells the story?
   What Ghost haunts the narrator?
   What does he say causes any man to be haunted by a ghost?
   Does his reasoning seem logical to you?
2. In what year did this story take place?
   What purpose is served by giving the date?
3. What famous general took part in the revolution?
4. Why did the merchants sell goods to the revolutionists?
5. What kind of cargo was on the ship?
   What was the name of the brig?
   Why was the name ironical?

6. What special regulations were passed on board the ship?
   How and why did the skipper fail to observe them?
7. Why do you distrust the pilot who took charge of the ship?
   Why did the mate and the pilot quarrel?
   Why did the pilot give the mate an "ugly look"?
8. What happened to the skipper and the rest of the crew?
9. Explain the pilot's plan for revenge.
10. What message did the pilot whisper in the mate's ear?
    How many hours of life did the mate believe were left to him
    after the pilot left the ship?
11. Why did the mate feel that he could scream with laughter?
    Why was he unable to look away from the candle?
    Who did he imagine was on the brig?
12. When the mate awoke, where was he?
    How was he rescued?
13. How does the story get its title?

From MEMOIRS OF A MIDGET

WALTER DE LA MARE

[Kinsman in spirit with Lewis Carrol and Robert Louis Stevenson, Walter de la Mare, 1873——, gained a secure place among writers of childlore. His poem, "Listeners," and the volume, *Memoirs of a Midget*, entitle him to an assured place in a broader field. The latter is, or so it seems, the life record of a creature so diminutive that in the author's words she belonged "among the smaller works of God" and yet so human that one sees her as a normal, intelligent person, adult in mind and spirit.]

CHAPTER ONE

SOME few years ago a brief account of me found its way into one or two country newspapers. I have been told, that it reappeared, later, in better proportion, in the Metropolitan Press! Fortunately, or unfortunately, very little of this account was true. It related, among other things, that I am accustomed to wear shoes with leaden soles to them to keep me from being blown away like thistledown in the wind, that as a child I had narrowly escaped being scalded to death in a soup tureen, that one of my ancestors came from Poland, that I am an expert painter of miniatures, that I am a changeling and can speak the fairy tongue. And so on and so forth.

I think I can guess where my ingenuous biographer borrowed these fables. He meant me no harm; he was earning his living; he made judicious use of his "no doubts" and "it may be supposed"; and I hope he amused his readers. But by far the greater part of his account was concerned with mere *physical* particulars. He had looked at me in fancy through spectacles which may or may not have been rosy, but which certainly minified. I do not deserve his inches and ounces, however flattering his intentions may have been. It is true that my body is among the smaller works of God. But I think he paid rather too much attention to this fact. He spared any reference not only to my soul (and I am not ungrateful for that), but also to my mind and heart. There may be too much of all three for some tastes in the following pages, and especially, perhaps, of the last. That cannot be helped. Finally, my anonymous journalist stated that I was born in Rutlandshire—because, I suppose, it is the smallest county in England.

That was truly unkind of him, for, as a matter of fact, and to begin at the (apparent) beginning, I was born in the village of Lyndsey in *Kent*—the prettiest country spot, as I believe, in all that county's million acres. So it remains to this day in spite of the fact that since my childhood its little church with its decaying stones and unfading twelfth—or is it thirteenth?—century glass has been "restored," and the lord of the manor has felled some of its finest trees, including a grove of sweet chestnuts on Bitchett Heath whose forefathers came over with the Romans. But he has not yet succeeded in levelling the barrow on Chizzel Hill. From my window I looked out (indeed, look out at this moment) to the wave-like crest of this beloved hill across a long straggling orchard, and pastures in the valley, where cattle grazed and sheep wandered, and unpolled willows stooped and silvered in the breeze. I never wearied of the hill, nor ever shall, and when, in my girlhood, my grandfather, aware of this idle, gazing habit of mine, sent me from Geneva a diminutive telescope, my day-dreams multiplied. His gift, as an old Kentish proverb goes, spread butter on bacon. With his spyglass to my eye I could bring a tapping green woodpecker as close as if it were actually laughing at me, and could all but snuff up the faint rich scent of the

cowslips—paggles, as we called them, in meadows a good mile away.

My father's house, Stonecote, has a rather ungainly appearance if viewed from across the valley. But it is roomy and open and fairly challenges the winds of the equinoxes. Its main windows are of shallow bow shape. One of them is among my first remembrances. I am seated in a bright tartan frock on a pomatum pot—a coloured picture of Mr. Shandy, as I remember, on its lid—and around me are the brushes, leather cases, knick-knacks, etc., of my father's dressing table. My father is shaving himself, his chin and cheeks puffed out with soapsuds. And now I look at him, and now at his reflection in the great looking-glass, and every time *that* happens he makes a pleasant grimace at me over his spectacles.

This particular moment of my childhood probably fixed itself on my mind because just as, with razor uplifted, he was about to attack his upper lip, a jackdaw, attracted maybe by my gay clothes, fluttered down on the sill outside, and fussing and scrabbling with wing and claw pecked hard with its beak against the glass. The sound and sight of this bird with its lively grey-blue eyes, so close and ardent, startled me. I leapt up, ran across the table, tripped over a hairbrush, and fell sprawling beside my father's watch. I hear its ticking, and also the little soothing whistle with which he was wont to comfort his daughter at any such mishap. Then perhaps I was five or six.

That is a genuine memory. But every family, I suppose, has its little pet traditions; and one of ours, relating to those early years, is connected with our kitchen cat, Miaou. She had come by a family of kittens, and I had crept, so it was said, into her shallow basket with them. Having, I suppose, been too frequently meddled with, this old mother cat lugged off her kittens one by one to a dark cupboard. The last one thus secured, she was discovered in rapt contemplation of myself, as if in debate whether or not it was her maternal duty to carry me off too. And there was I grinning up into her face. Such was our cook's—Mrs. Ballard's —story. What I actually remember is different. On the morning in question I was turning the corner of the brick-floored, dusky passage that led to the kitchen, when Miaou came trotting along out of it with her blind, blunt-headed bundle in her mouth. We were equally surprised at this encounter, and in brushing past she nearly knocked me over where I stood, casting me at the same moment the queerest animal look out of her eyes. So truth, in this case, was not so strange as Mrs. Ballard's fiction.

My father was then a rather corpulent man, with a high-coloured face, and he wore large spectacles. His time was his own, for we were comfortably off on an income derived from a half-share in the small fortune amassed by my grandfather and his partner in a paper mill. He might have been a more successful, though not perhaps a happier, man if he had done more work and planned to do less. But he only so far followed his hereditary occupation as to expend large quantities of its best "handmade" in the composition of a monograph; *The History of Paper Making*. This entailed a vast accumulation of books and much solitude. I fancy, too, he believed in the policy of sleeping on one's first thoughts.

Since he was engaged at the same time on similar compilations with the Hop and the Cherry for theme, he made indifferent progress in all three.

His papers, alas, were afterwards sold with his books, so I have no notion of what became of them or of their value. I can only hope that their purchaser has since won an easy distinction. These pursuits, if they achieved little else but the keeping of "the man of the house" quiet and contented, proved my father, at any rate, to be a loyal and enthusiastic Man of Kent; and I have seen to it that a fine Morello cherry-tree blossoms, fruits, and flourishes over his grave.

My father was something of a musician too, and could *pizzicato* so softly on his muted fiddle as not to jar even my too sensitive ear. He taught me to play chess on a little board with pygmy men, but he was apt to lose interest in the game when it went against him. Whereas it was then that our old friend, Dr. Grose, played his hardest. As my father's hands were rather clumsy in make, he took pains to be gentle and adroit with me. But even after shaving, his embrace was more of a discipline than a pleasure—a fact that may partly account for my own undemonstrativeness in this direction.

His voice, if anything, was small for his size, except when he discussed politics with Dr. Grose; religion or the bringing up of children with my godmother, Miss Fenne; or money matters with my mother. At such times, his noise—red face and gesticulations—affected one of his listeners, as eager as possible to pick up the crumbs, far more than ever thunder did, which is up in the clouds. My only other discomfort in his company was his habit of taking snuff. The stench of it almost suffocated me, and at tap of his finger-nail on the lid of his box, I would scamper off for shelter like a hare.

By birth he came of an old English

family, though no doubt with the usual admixtures. My mother's mother was French. She was a Daundelyon. The blood of that "sweet enemy" at times burned in her cheek like a flag; and my father needed his heaviest guns when the stormy winds did blow, and those colours were flying. At such moments I preferred to hear the engagement from a distance, not so much (again) because the mere discord grieved me, as to escape the din. But usually—and especially after such little displays—they were like two turtle-doves, and I did my small best to pipe a decoy.

My father had been a man past forty when he married my mother. She about fifteen years younger—a slim, nimble, and lovely being, who could slip round and encircle him in person or mind while he was pondering whether or not to say Bo to a goose. Seven years afterwards came I. Friends, as friends will, professed to see a likeness between us. And if my mother could have been dwindled down to be of my height and figure, perhaps they would have been justified.

But in hair and complexion, possibly in ways, too, I harked back to an aunt of hers, Kitilda, who had died of consumption in her early twenties. I loved to hear stories of my great-aunt Kitilda. She sang like a bird, twice ran away from her convent school, and was so fond of water that an old gentleman (a friend of Mr. Landor's, the poet) who fell in love with her, called her "the Naiad."

My mother, in her youth at Tunbridge Wells, had been considered "a beauty," and had had many admirers —at least so Mrs. Ballard, our cook, told Pollie: "Yes, and we know who might have turned out different if things hadn't been the same," was a cryptic remark she once made which

filled two "little pitchers" to overflowing. Among these admirers was a Mr. Wagginhorne who now lived at Maidstone. He had pocketed his passion but not his admiration; and being an artist in the same sense that my father was an author, he had painted my mother and me and a pot of azaleas in oils. How well I remember those interminable sittings, with the old gentleman daubing along, and cracking his beloved jokes and Kentish cobbs at one and the same time. Whenever he came to see us this portrait was taken out of a cupboard and hung up in substitution for another picture in the dining-room. What became of it when Mr. Wagginhorne died I could never discover. My mother would laugh when I inquired, and archly eye my father. It was clear, at any rate, that author was not jealous of artist!

My mother was gentle with me, and had need to be; and I was happier in her company than one might think possible in a world of such fleetingness. I would sit beside her workbox and she would softly talk to me, and teach me my lessons and small rhymes to say; while my own impulse and instinct taught me to sing and dance. What gay hours we shared. Sewing was at first difficult, for at that time no proportionate needles could be procured for me, and I hated to cobble up only coarse work. But she would give me little childish jobs to do, such as arranging her silks, or sorting her beads, and would rock me to sleep with her finger to a drone so gentle that it might have been a distant bee's.

Yet shadows there were, before the darkness came. Child that I was, I would watch gather over her face at times a kind of absentness, as if she were dreaming of something to which she could give no name, of some hope

or wish that was now never to be fulfilled. At this I would grow anxious
and silent, doubting, perhaps, that I
had displeased her; while, to judge
from her look, I might not have been
there at all.

Or again, a mischievousness and
mockery would steal into her mood.
Then she would treat me as a mere
trivial plaything, talking small things
to me, as if our alphabet consisted of
nothing but "little o"—a letter for
which I always felt a sort of pity; but
small affection. This habit saddened
my young days, and sometimes enraged me, more than I can say. I was
always of a serious cast of mind—
even a little priggish perhaps; and experience had already taught me that
I could share my mother's thoughts
and feelings more easily than she
could share mine.

CHAPTER TWO

When precisely I began to speculate
why I was despatched into this world
so minute and different I cannot say.
Pretty early, I fancy, though few opportunities for comparison were afforded me, and for some time I supposed that all young children were of
my stature. There was Adam Waggett, it is true, the bumpkin son of a
village friend of Mrs. Ballard's. But
he was some years older than I. He
would be invited to tea in the kitchen,
and was never at rest unless stuffing
himself out with bread-and-dripping
or dough-cake — victuals naturally
odious to me; or pestering me with his
coarse fooling and curiosity. He was
to prove useful in due season; but in
those days I had a distaste for him
almost as deep-rooted as that for
"Hoppy," the village idiot—though I
saw poor Hoppy only once.

Whatever the reason may be, except in extremely desperate moments,

I do not remember much regretting
that I was not of the common size.
Still, the realization was gradually
borne in on me that I was a disappointment and mischance to my parents. Yet I never dared to let fall a
question which was to be often in my
young thoughts: "Tell me, mamma,
are you *sorry* that your little daughter
is a Midget?" But then, does any one
ask questions like that until they cannot be answered?

Still, cross-examine her I did occasionally.

"Where did I come from, mamma?"

"Why, my dear, I am your
mother."

"Just," I replied, "like Pollie's
mother is *her* mother?"

She cast a glance at me from eyes
that appeared to be very small, unless
for that instant it was mine that I saw
reflected there.

"Yes, my dear," she replied at
length. "We come and we go." She
seemed tired with the heat of the day,
so I sat quietly, holding her finger,
until she was recovered.

Only, perhaps, on account of my
size was there any occasion for me to
be thoroughly ashamed of myself.
Otherwise I was, if anything, a rather
precocious child. I could walk a step
or two at eleven months, and began
to talk before the Christmas following the first anniversary of my birthday, August 30th. I learned my letters from the big black capitals in
the Book of Genesis; and to count and
cipher from a beautiful little Abacus
strung with beads of silver and garnets. The usual ailments came my
way, but were light come, light go.
I was remarkably sinewy and muscular, strong in the chest, and never
suffered from snuffling colds or from
chilblains, though shoes and gloves
have always been a difficulty.

I can perfectly recall my childish figure as I stood with endless satisfaction surveying my reflection in a looking-glass on the Christmas morning after my ninth birthday. My frock was of a fine puffed scarlet, my slippers loose at heel, to match. My hair, demurely parted in the middle, hung straight on my narrow shoulders (though I had already learned to plait it) and so framed my face; the eyebrows faintly arched (eyebrows darker and crookeder now); the nose in proportion; the lips rather narrow, and of a lively red.

My features wore a penetrating expression in that reflection because my keen look was searching them pretty close. But if it was a sharp look, it was not, I think, a bold or defiant; and then I smiled, as if to say, "So this is to be my companion, then?"

It was winter, and frost was on the window that day. I enjoyed the crisp air, for I was packed warm in lamb's-wool underneath. There I stood, my father's round red face beaming on one side of the table, my mother's smiling but enigmatic, scrutinizing my reflection on the other, and myself tippeting this way and that—a veritable miniature of Vanity.

Who should be ushered at this moment into the room, where we were so happy, but my godmother, Miss Fenne, come to bring my father and mother her Christmas greetings and me a little catechism sewn up in a pink silk cover. She was a bent-up old lady and a rapid talker, with a voice which, though small, jangled every nerve in my body, like a pencil on a slate. Being my godmother, she took great liberties in counselling my parents on the proper way of "managing" me. The only time, indeed, I ever heard my father utter an oath was when Miss Fenne was just beyond hearing. She peered across at me on this Christmas morning like a bird at a scorpion: "Caroline, Caroline," she cried, "for shame! The Shrimp! You will turn the child's head."

Shrimp! I had seen the loathsome, doubled-up creatures (in their boiled state) on a kitchen plate. My blood turned to vinegar; and in rage and shame I fell all of a heap on the table, hiding from her sight my face and my hands as best I could under my clothes, and wishing that I might vanish away from the world altogether.

My father's voice boomed out in protest; my mother took me into her arms to soothe and scold me; but long after the ruffled old lady had taken her departure I brooded on this affront. "Away, away!" a voice seemed to cry within; and I listened to it as if under a spell. All that day I nursed my wounded vanity, and the same evening, after candle light, I found myself for a moment alone in the kitchen. Pollie had gone to the wood-shed to fetch kindling, leaving the door into the garden ajar. The night air touched my cheek. Half beside myself with desire of I know not what, I sprang out from the doorstep into an inch or so of snow, and picking myself up, ran off into the darkness under the huge sky.

It was bitterly cold. Frost had crusted the virgin surface of the snow. My light footsteps can hardly have shattered its upper crystals. I ran on and on into the ghostly world, into this stiff, marvelous, gloating scene of frozen vegetation beneath that immense vacancy. A kind of stupor must have spread over my young mind. It seemed I was transported out of myself under the stars, in the mute presence of the Watchman of Heaven. I stood there lost in wonder in the grey, luminous gloom.

But my escapade was brief and humiliating. The shock of the cold, the excitement, quickly exhausted me. I threw myself down and covered my face with my hands, trying in vain to stifle my sobs. What was my longing? Where its satisfaction? Soft as wool a drowsiness stole over my senses that might swiftly have wafted me off on the last voyage of discovery. But I had been missed. A few minutes' search, and Pollie discovered me lying there by the frozen cabbage stalks. The woeful Maenad was carried back into the kitchen again—a hot bath, a hot posset, and a few anxious and thankful tears.

The wonder is, that, being an only child, and a sore problem when any question of discipline or punishment arose, I was not utterly spoiled. One person at least came very near to doing so, my grandfather, Monsieur Pierre de Ronville. To be exact, he was my step-grandfather, for my mother's charming mother, with her ringlets and crinoline, after my real grandfather's death, had married a second time. He crossed the English Channel to visit my parents when I was in my tenth year—a tall, stiff, jerky man, with a sallow face, speckled fur-like hair that stood in a little wall round his forehead, and the liveliest black eyes. His manners were a felicity to watch even at my age. You would have supposed he had come *courting* my mother; and he took a great fancy to me. He was extremely fond of salad, I remember; and I was proud of my mustard and cress—which I could gather for him myself with one of my own table-knives. So copiously he talked, with such a medley of joys and zests and surprises on his face, that I vowed soon to be mistress of my stepmother tongue. He could also conjure away reels and thimbles, even spoons and forks, with a skill that precluded my becoming a materialist for ever after. I *worshipped* my grandfather—and yet without a vestige of fear.

To him, indeed—though I think he was himself of a secular turn of mind—I owe the story of my birthday Saint, St. Rosa of Lima in Peru, the only saint, I believe, of the New World. With myself pinnacled on his angular knee, and devouring like a sweetmeat every broken English word as it slipped from his tongue, he told me how pious an infant my Saint had been; how, when her mother, to beautify her, had twined flowers in her hair, she had *pinned* them to her skull; how she had rubbed quicklime on her cheeks to disenchant her lovers (*"ses prétendants"*), and how it was only veritable showers of roses from heaven that had at last persuaded Pope Clement to make her a saint.

"Perhaps, *bon papa*," said I, "I shall dig and sow too when I am grown up, like St. Rosa, to support *my* mamma and papa when *they* are very old. Do you think I shall make enough money? Papa has a very good appetite?" He stared at me, as if in consternation.

"*Dieu vous en garde, ma p'tite*," he cried; and violently blew his nose.

So closely I took St. Rosa's story to heart that, one day, after bidding my beauty a wistful farewell in the glass, I rubbed my cheek too, but with the blue flowers of the—*brook*-lime. It stained them a little, but soon washed off. In my case a needless precaution; my *prétendants* have been few.

It was a mournful day when my grandfather returned to France, never to be seen by me again. Yet he was to remember me always; and at last when I myself had forgotten even my faith in his fidelity. Nearly all my personal furnishings and belongings were gifts of his from France, and many of them of his own making. There was my four-post bed, for instance; with a flowered silk canopy, a carved tester and half a dozen changes of linen and valance. There were chairs to match, a wardrobe, silk mats from Persia, a cheval glass, and clothes and finery in abundance, china and cutlery, top-boots and sabots. Even a silver-hooped bath-tub and a crystal toilet set, and scores of articles besides for use or ornament, which it would be tedious to mention. My grandfather had my measurements to a nicety, and as the years went by he sagaciously allowed for growth.

I learned to tell the time from an eight-day clock which played a sacred tune at matins and vespers; and later, he sent me a watch, the least bit too large for me to be quite comfortable, but an exquisite piece of workmanship. As my birthdays (and his) drew near, I could scarcely sleep for thinking what fresh entrancing novelty the festive morning would bring. The only one of his gifts—by no means the least ingenious — which never, after the first flush of excitement, gave me much pleasure, was a two-chambered thatched summer-house, set up on a pole, and reached by a wide, shallow ladder. The roof opened, so that on very hot days a block of ice could be laid within, the water from its slow melting running out by a gutter. But I loved sunshine. This was a plaything that ridiculously amused chance visitors; it attracted flies; I felt silly up in it: and gladly resigned it to the tits, starlings, and sparrows to quarrel over as they pleased.

My really useful furniture — of plain old Sheraton design—was set out in my bedroom. In one half of the room slept Pollie, a placid but, before her marriage, rather slow-witted creature about six years my senior. The other half was mine and had been made proportionate to my needs by a cabinet-maker from London. My father had had a low stone balcony built on beyond my window. This was fenced with fine trellis work to screen it from the colder winds. With its few extremely dwarf trees set along in green Nankin tubs, and the view it commanded, I could enjoy this eyrie for hours—never wearied of it in my youth, nor shall if I live to be a hundred.

I linger over these early recollections, simply because they are such very happy things to possess. And now for out-of-doors.

Either because my mother was shy of me, or because she thought vulgar attention would be bad for me, she seldom took me far abroad. Now and then Pollie carried me down to the village to tea with *her* mother, and once or twice I was taken to church. The last occasion, however, narrowly escaped being a catastrophe, and the experiment was not repeated. Instead, we usually held a short evening service, on Sundays, in the house, when my father read the lessons, "like a miner prophet," as I wrote and told Miss Fenne. He certainly dug away at the texts till the words glittered for me like lumps of coal. On weekdays more people were likely to be about, and in general I was secluded. A mistake, I think. But fortunately our high, plain house stood up in a delightful garden, sloping this way and that towards orchard and wood, with a fine-turfed lawn, few "cultivated" flowers, and ample drifts of shade. If Kent is the garden of England, then this was the garden of Kent.

I was forbidden to be alone in it. But Pollie would sometimes weary of her charge (in which I encouraged her) and when out of sight of the windows she would stray off to gossip with the gardener or with some friend from the village, leaving me to myself. To judge from the tales which I have read or have been told about

children, I must have been old for my age. But perhaps the workings of the mind and heart of a girl in her teens are not of general interest. Let me be brief. A stream of water ran on the southern side all the length of the garden, under a high rocky bank (its boundary) which was densely overhung with ash and willow, and hedges of brier and bramble looped with bindweed, goose-grass, and traveller's joy. On the nearer bank of this stream which had been left to its wild, I would sit among the mossy rocks and stones and search the green tops of my ambush as if in quest of Paradise.

When the sun's rays beat down too fiercely on my head I would make myself an umbrella of wild angelica or water parsnip.

Caring little for playthings, and having my smallest books with me chiefly for silent company, I would fall into a day-dream in a world that in my solitude became my own. In this fantastic and still world I forgot the misadventure of my birth, which had now really begun to burden me, forgot pride, vanity, and chagrin; and was at peace. There I had many proportionate friends, few enemies. An old carrion crow, that sulked out a black existence in this beauty, now and then alarmed me with his attentions; but he was easily scared off. The lesser and least of living things seemed to accept me as one of themselves. Nor (perhaps because I never killed them) had I any silly distaste for the caterpillars, centipedes, and satiny black slugs. Mistress Snail would stoop out at me like a foster-mother. Even the midges, which to his frenzy would swarm round my father's head like swifts round a steeple, left me entirely unmolested. Either I was too dry a prey, or they misliked the flavour of my blood.

My eyes dazzled in colours. The smallest of the marvels of flowers and flies and beetles and pebbles, and the radiance that washed over them, would fill me with a mute, pent-up rapture almost unendurable. Butterflies would settle quietly on the hot stones beside me as if to match their raiment against mine. If I proffered my hand, with quivering wings and horns they would uncoil their delicate tongues and quaff from it drops of dew or water. A solemn grasshopper would occasionally straddle across my palm, and with patience I made quite an old friend of a harvest mouse. They weigh only two to the half-penny. This sharp-nosed furry morsel would creep swiftly along to share my crumbs and snuggle itself to sleep in my lap. By-and-by, I suppose, it took to itself a wife; I saw it no more. Bees would rest there, the panniers of their thighs laden with pollen: and now and then a wasp, his jaws full of wood or meat. When sunbeetles or ants drew near, they would seem to pause at my whisper, as if hearkening. As if in their remote silence pondering and sharing the world with me. All childish fancy, no doubt; for I proved far less successful with the humans.

But how, it may be asked, seeing that there must have been a shrill piping of birds and brawling of water among the stones, how could Mademoiselle's delicate ear endure *that* racket? Perhaps it is because the birds being loose in the hollow of space, it carried away into its vacancy their cries. It is, too, the harsh, rather than the shrill, that frets me. As for the noise of the water, it was so full and limpid, yet made up of such infinitely entangled chimings and drummings, that it would lull me in-to a kind of trance, until to a strange eye I must have appeared like a lifeless waxen mammet on my stone.

What may wholly have been another childish fancy was that from the silvery darting flies and the rainbow-coloured motes in the sunbeams, fine and airy invisible shapes seemed to haunt and hover around me when all was still. Most of my fellow creatures to my young nose had an odour a good deal denser than the fainter scented flowers, and I can fancy such a fog, if intensified, would be distressing to beings so bodiless and rare. Whereas the air I disturbed and infected with my presence can have been but of shallow volume.

Fairies I never saw—I had a kind of fear and distaste for them even in books. Nor for that matter—perhaps because the stream here was too tumbling and opaque—a kingfisher. But whatever other company may have been mine, I had the clouds and the water and the insects and the stones—while pimpernel, mousetail, tormentil, the wild strawberry, the feathery grasses seemed to have been made expressly for my delight. Egocentric Midget that I was!

CHAPTER THREE

Not that in an existence so passive riddles never came my way. As one morning I brushed past a bush of lads' love (or maidens' ruin, as some call it), its fragrance sweeping me from top to toe, I stumbled on the carcass of a young mole. Curiosity vanquished the first gulp of horror. Holding my breath, with a stick I slowly edged it up in the dust and surveyed the white heaving nest of maggots in its belly with a peculiar and absorbed recognition. "Ah, ha!" a voice cried within me, "so this is what is in wait; this is how things are"; and I stooped with lips drawn back over my teeth to examine the stinking mystery more closely. That was a lesson I have never unlearned.

One of a rather different kind had another effect. I was sitting in the garden one day watching in the distance a jay huffling and sidling and preening its feathers on a bit of decrepit fencing. Suddenly there fell a sharp crack of sound. In a flash, with a derisive chattering, the jay was flown: and then I saw Adam Waggett, half doubled up, stealing along towards the place. I lay in wait for him. With catapult dangling in one hand, the other fist tight shut, he came along like a thief. And I cried hollowly out of my concealment, "Adam, what have you there?"

Such a picture of foolish shame I have never seen. He was compelled none the less to exhibit his spoil, an eye-shut, twinkle-tailed, needle-billed Jenny Wren crumpled up in his great, dirty paw. Fury burnt up in me like a fire. What I said to him I cannot remember, but it was nothing sweet; and it was a cowed Adam Waggett that loafed off as truculently as he could towards the house, his catapult and victim left behind him. But that was his lesson rather than mine, and one which *he* never forgot.

When in my serener moods Pollie's voice would be heard slyly hallooing for me, I would rouse up with a shock to realize again the little cell of my body into which I had been confined. Then she and I would eat our luncheon, a few snippets of biscuit, a cherry or two, or slice of apple for me, and for her a hunch of bread and bacon about half my size in length and thickness. I would turn my back on her, for I could not endure to see her gobble her meal, having an abhorrence of cooked flesh, and a dainty stomach. Still, like most children I

could be greedy, and curious of unfamiliar foods. To a few forbidden black currants which I reached up and plucked from their rank-smelling bush, and devoured, skin and all, I owe lesson Number 3. This one, however, had to be repeated.

Childhood quickly fleets away. Those happy, unhappy, far-away days seem like mere glimpses of a dragon-fly shimmering and darting over my garden stream, though at the actual time they more closely resembled, perhaps, a continuous dream broken into bits of vivid awakening.

As I grew older, my skirts grew longer, my desire for independence sharper, and my wits more inquiring. On my seventeenth birthday I put up my hair, and was confirmed by a bishop whom my godmother persuaded to officiate in the house. It was a solemn occasion; but my mother was a good deal concerned about the lunch, and I with the ballooning lawn sleeves and the two square episcopal finger-tips disposed upon my head. The experience cast a peaceful light into my mind and shook my heart, but it made me for a time a little self-concious of both my virtue and my sins. I began to brood not only on the deplorable state of my own soul, but also on Pollie's and Mrs. Ballard's, and became for a time a diminutive Miss Fenne. I suppose innocence is a precarious bliss. On the other hand, if one's mind is like a dead mole's belly, it is wise, I think, to examine it closely but not too often, and to repeat that confirmation for one's self every morning and evening.

As a young child I had been, of course, as naturally religious as a savage or an angel. But even then, I think, I never could quite believe that Paradise was a mere Fenne-land. Once I remember in the midst of my multiplication table I had broken out unannounced with, "Then God made the world, mamma?"

"Yes, my dear."

"And all things in the forests and the birds in the sky and—and moles, and this?" I held down my limp, coral-coloured arithmetic.

"Yes," said she.

I wondered a while, losing myself, as if in wanderings like Ariel's, between the clouds. "What, mamma, did He make them of?" my voice interrupted me.

"He made them," said my mother steadily, "of His Power and Love."

Rapidly I slid back into her company. "And can we, can I, make things of *my* power and love?"

"I suppose, my dear," replied my mother reflectively and perhaps thinking of my father in his study, over his Paper and Hops, "it is only *that* in life that is really worth doing."

"Then," I said sagely, "I *suspects* that's how Mullings does the garden, mamma."

Long before Miss Fenne's and the Bishop's visitation my mother had set about teaching me in earnest. A governess—a Miss Perry was our first experiment. Alas, apart from her tendency to quinsy, it was I who was found wanting. She complained of the strain on her nerves. My mother feared that quinsy was catching; and Miss Perry had no successor. Reading was always a difficulty. My father bought me as tiny old books as could be found, including a dwarf Bible, a midget Pickering, Shakespeare, and a grammar (with a menagerie for frontispiece) from which I learned that "irony is a figure which intends the reverse of what it speaks, and under the masque of praise, conceals the most biting satyr"; and the following stanza:—

Hail Energeia! hail my native tongue
Concisely full, and musically strong;
Thou with the pencil hold'st a glorious strife,
And paint'st the passions equal to the life.

My mother agreed that *strung* would be preferable to "*strong*," and explained that "the passions" did not signify merely ill-temper; while, if I pecked over-nicely at my food, my father would cry "Hail Energeia!" a challenge which rarely failed to persuade me to set to.

My grandfather sent me other pygmy books from Paris, including a minute masterpiece of calligraphy, *Une Anthologie de Chansons pour une Minuscule Aimante et Bienaimée par P. de R.* These I could easily carry about with me. I soon learned to accustom my arms and shoulders to bulkier and more cumbrous volumes. My usual method with a common-sized book was to prop it up towards the middle of the table and then to seat myself at the edge. The page finished, I would walk across and turn over a fresh leaf. Thus in my solitude I studied my lessons and read again and again my nursery favourites, some of them, I gather, now undeservedly out of fashion.

Perhaps even better than fiction or folk-tales, I liked books of knowledge.

There were two of these in particular, *The Observing Eye; or Lessons to Children on the Three Lowest Divisions of Animal Life—The Radiated, Articulated, and Molluscous*, and *The Childhood of the World*. Even at nine I remarked how nimbly the anonymous author of the former could skip from St Paul to the lobster; and I never wearied of brooding on Mr. Clodd's frontispiece. This depicts a large-headed and seemingly one-legged little girl in a flounced frock lying asleep under a wall on which ivy is sprawling. For pillow for herself and her staring doll there lies on the ground a full-sized human skull, and in the middle distance are seen the monoliths of Stonehenge. Beyond these gigantic stones, and behind the far mountains, rises with spiky rays an enormous Sun.

I was that child; and mine her sun that burned in heaven, and he a more obedient luminary than any lamp of man's. I would wonder what she would do when she awoke from sleep. The skull, in particular, both terrified and entranced me—the secret of all history seemed to lie hidden in the shadows beneath its dome. Indeed I needed no reminder from Mr. Clodd that "Children (and some grown-up people too) are apt to think that things are wonderful only when they are big, which is not true."

I knew already, out of nowhere, that "the bee's waxen cell is more curious than the chimpanzee's rough hut" (though I should have dearly liked to see the latter); and that "an ant is more wonderful than the huge and dull rhinoceros." Such is childishness, however: I pitied the poor rhinoceros his "dull." Over such small things as a nut, a shell, a drop of rainwater in a buttercup, a frond of frost (for there were cold winters at Lyndsey in those days), I would pore and pore, imbibing the lesson that the eye alone if used in patience will tell its owner far more about an object than it can merely see.

Among my few framed pictures I cannot resist mentioning one by a painter of the name of Bosch. Below the middle of it kneeled naked Adam and Eve with exquisite crimped hair on their shoulders; and between them stood God. All above and beneath them, roamed the animals, birds, insects, and infinitesimals of Eden, including a long-tailed monkey on an elephant, a jerboa, a dancing crocodile, and—who but our cat Miaou, carrying off a mouse! An astonishing, inexhaustible piece of thoughtfulness. I loved Mynheer Bosch.

Shameful dunce Miss M. may remain, but she did in her childhood supremely enjoy any simple book about the things of creation great or small. But I preferred my own notions of some of them. When my father of a dark, clear night would perch me up at a window to see the stars—Charles's Wain and the Chair; and told me that they were huge boiling suns, roaring their way through the vast pits of space, I would shake my head to myself, I was grateful for the science, but preferred to keep them just "stars." And though I loved to lave my hands in a trickle of light that had been numberless years on its journey to this earth, that of a candle also filled me with admiration, and I was unfeignedly grieved that the bleak moon was naught but a sheer hulk, *sans* even air or ice or rain or snow.

How much pleasanter it would be to think that her shine was the reflection of our cherry orchards, and that her shadows were just Kentish hay-ricks, barns, and oast-houses. It was, too, perhaps rather tactless of my father to beguile me with full-grown authors' accounts of the Lives of the Little. Accomplished writers they may be, but—well never mind. As for the Lives of the Great, I could easily adjust Monsieur Bon Papa's spyglass and reduce them to scale.

My father taught me also to swim in his round bath; and on a visit to Canterbury purchased for me the nimblest little dun Shetland pony, whom we called Mopsa. I learned to become a fearless rider. But hardy though her race may be, perhaps I was too light a burden to satisfy Mopsa's spirit. In a passing fit of temper she broke a leg. Though I had stopped my ears for an hour before the Vet came, I heard the shot.

My mother's lessons were never very burdensome. She taught me little, but she taught it well—even a morsel of Latin. I never wearied of the sweet oboe-like nasal sound of her French poems, and she instilled in me such a delight in words that to this day I firmly believe that things are at least twice the better and richer for being called by them. Apart from a kind of passionate impatience over what was alien to me—arithmetic, for instance, and "analysis"—and occasional fits of the sulks, which she allowed to deposit their own sediment at leisure, I was a willing, and, at times, even a greedy scholar. Apparently from infancy I was of a firm resolve to match my wits with those of the common-sized and to be "grown-up" some day.

So much for my education, a thing which it seems to me is likely to continue—and specially in respect of human nature—as long as I keep alive. With so little childish company, without rivalry, I was inclined to swell myself out with conceit and complacency. "It's easy holding down the latchet when nobody pulls the string." But whatever size we may be, in soul or body, I have found that the world wields a sharp pin, and is pitiless to bubbles.

Though inclined to be dreamy and idle when alone, I was, of course, my own teacher too. My senses were seven in number, however few my wits. In particular I loved to observe the clustering and gathering of plants, like families, each of a shape, size, and hue, each in their kind and season, though tall and lowly were intermingled. Now and then I would come on some small plant self-sown, shining and flourishing, free and clear, and even the lovelier for being alone in its kind amid its greater neighbours. I prized these discoveries, and if any one of them was dwarfed a little by its surroundings I would cosset it up and help it against them. How strange, thought I, if men so regarded each other's intelligence. If from pitying the dull-witted the sharp-witted slid to mere toleration, and from toleration to despising and loathing. What a contest would presently begin between the strong-bodied stupid and the feeble-bodied clever, and how soon there would be no strong-bodied stupid left in the world! They would dwindle away and disappear into Time like the mammoth and the woolly bear. And then I began to be sorry for the woolly bear and to wish I could go and have a look at him. Perhaps this is putting my old head on those young shoulders, but when I strive to re-enter the thoughts of those remote days, how like they seem to the noisy wasting stream beside which they flowed on, and of whose source and destination I was unaware.

All this egotism recalls a remark that Mrs. Ballard once made apropos of some little smart repartee from Miss M. as she sat beside her pasteboard and slapped away at a lump of dough, "Well I know a young lady who's been talking to the young man that rubbed his face with a brass candlestick."

For Thought and Discussion

1. By what means does the author, from the very beginning of the memoirs, get the reader to see the narrator of the memoirs as a normal person despite her diminutive size?
2. Is the reflection cast upon the Metropolitan press by the narrator true or false?
3. Where was the narrator born? What old Kentish proverb does she quote? Explain its meaning.
4. By what little device loved by small children did the father soothe the little girl when she was frightened?
5. Tell the cook's pet cat tradition.
6. Describe the midget's parents. How did they regard their little daughter?
7. What person or persons deserved the title "dreamer"?
8. Who in her family came nearest to spoiling the child?
9. Who was furthest from spoiling her and yet was harmful to her?
10. Which could enter more nearly into the feeling of the other, the mother or the daughter?
11. What kind of disposition did the midget have? Did she enjoy having people seem to be making an effort to speak on what they thought was her level?
12. Do children, as a rule, enjoy having people "talk down to them"?
13. In your opinion was it fortunate or unfortunate that the little girl had no brothers or sisters?
14. Do you think there is need of special training in courtesy toward people who differ in any way from the ordinary?
15. Was the midget precocious as a child? At what age do children usually begin to walk and to talk? At what age did she begin to talk and to walk?
16. From what did she learn her alphabet?
17. What books did she have? Which were her favorites?
18. Of what design was her furniture? Who made it? Name other gifts the donor gave her.
19. What characteristic quite common to children caused the midget to speak of herself as a "veritable miniature of Vanity"?
20. Tell the incident in connection with the name of the midget.
21. Where did the midget come nearest to finding peace and pleasure?
22. Quote references to indicate the author's interest in the various arts and in astronomy.
23. Describe the midget's education.
24. With what creature did the child make friends? How did she first come to think of death?
25. What incident indicates the midget's kindness and fearless bravery?

26. Is the question, "Then God made the world, Mamma?" a characteristic question of a child?
27. Quote figures of speech and proverbs and other epigrammatic remarks that indicate something of little Miss M.'s philosophy of life.
28. Define "paggles," "ego-centric," "pomatum," "pizziccato."

~∿~

THE FORSAKEN MERMAN
MATTHEW ARNOLD

[One reads "The Forsaken Merman" by Matthew Arnold, 1822-1888, as one reads poems by Rossetti —not in order to understand the poem but in order to feel an emotional response to the poet's recital. Here Arnold uses the familiar legend of a mortal lured to sea by a merman. In this instance, however, the merman has lost his mortal wife and is seeking her in the home of her childhood. The repetition of the first line of the poem adds to its pathos.]

COME, dear children, let us away;
  Down and away below!
Now my brothers call from the bay;
Now the great winds shorewards blow;
Now the salt tides seawards flow;
Now the wild white horses play,   6
Champ and chafe and toss in the spray.
  Children dear, let us away!
  This way, this way!

Call her once before you go—   10
  Call once yet!
In a voice that she will know:
  "Margaret! Margaret!"
Children's voices should be dear
(Call once more) to a mother's ear;   15
Children's voices, wild with pain—
Surely she will come again!

Call her once and come away;
This way, this way!

"Mother dear, we cannot stay!"   20
The wild white horses foam and fret.
Margaret! Margaret!

Come, dear children, come away
   down;
Call no more!
One last look at the white-walled
   town,   25
And the little gray church on the
   windy shore;
Then come down!
She will not come though you call
   all day—
Come away, come away!

Children dear, was it yesterday   30
We heard the sweet bells over the
   bay?
In the caverns where we lay,
Through the surf and through the
   swell,
The far-off sound of a silver bell?
Sand-strewn caverns, cool and deep, 35
Where the winds are all asleep;
Where the spent lights quiver and
   gleam;
Where the salt weed sways in the
   stream;
Where the sea-beasts, ranged all
   round,
Feed in the ooze of their pasture-
   ground;   40
Where the sea-snakes coil and twine,
Dry their mail and bask in the brine;
Where great whales come sailing by,
Sail and sail, with unshut eye,
Round the world forever and aye? 45
When did music come this way?
Children dear, was it yesterday?

Children dear, was it yesterday
(Call yet once) that she went away?
Once she sate with you and me,   50
On a red gold throne in the heart of
   the sea,
And the youngest sate on her knee.
She combed its bright hair, and she
   tended it well,
When down swung the sound of the
   far-off bell.
She sighed; she looked up through the
   clear, green sea;   55

She said: "I must go, for my kinsfolk pray
In the little gray church on the shore
   today.
'Twill be Easter-time in the world—
   ah, me!
And I lose my poor soul, merman,
   here with thee."
I said, "Go up, dear heart, through
   the waves;   60
Say thy prayer, and come back to the
   kind sea-caves."
She smiled; she went up through the
   surf in the bay.
   Children dear, was it yesterday?

Children dear, were we long alone?
"The sea grows stormy, the little ones
   moan.   65
Long prayers," I said, "in the world
   they say.
Come," I said, and we rose through
   the surf in the bay.
We went up the beach, by the sandy
   down
Where the sea-stocks bloom, to the
   white-walled town.
Through the narrow, paved streets,
   where all was still,   70
To the little gray church on the
   windy hill.
From the church came a murmur
   of folk at their prayers,
But we stood without in the cold,
   blowing airs.
We climbed on the graves, on the
   stones, worn with rains,
And we gazed up the aisle through
   the small, leaded panes   75
She sat by the pillar; we saw her clear:
"Margaret, hist! come quick, we are
   here!
Dear heart," I said, "we are long
   alone;
The sea grows stormy, the little ones
   moan."
But, ah, she gave me never a look, 80
For her eyes were sealed to the holy
   book.

Loud prays the priest; shut stands the
    door.
Come away, children, call no more!
Come away, come down, call no
    more!

Down, down, down!   85
Down to the depths of the sea!
She sits at her wheel in the humming
    town,
Singing most joyfully.
Hark, what she sings: "O joy, O joy,
For the humming street, and the
    child with its toy!   90
For the priest, and the bell, and the
    holy well;
For the wheel where I spun,
And the blessed light of the sun!"
And so she sings her fill,
Singing most joyfully,   95
Till the shuttle falls from her hand,
And the whizzing wheel stands still.
She steals to the window, and looks
    at the sand;
And over the sand at the sea;
And her eyes are set in a stare;   100
And anon there breaks a sigh,
And anon there drops a tear,
From a sorrow-clouded eye,
And a heart sorrow-laden,
A long, long sigh.   105
For the cold, strange eyes of a little
    mermaiden
And the gleam of her golden hair.

Come away, away, children!
Come, children, come down!

The salt tide rolls seaward.   110
Lights shine in the town;
She will start from her slumber
When gusts shake the door;
She will hear the winds howling,
Will hear the waves roar.   115
We shall see, while above us
The waves roar and whirl,
A ceiling of amber,
A pavement of pearl;
Singing, "Here came a mortal,   120
But faithless was she,
And alone dwell forever
The kings of the sea."

But, children, at midnight,
When soft the winds blow,   125
When clear falls the moonlight,
When springtides are low,
When sweet airs come seaward
From heaths starred with broom,
And high rocks throw mildly   130
On the blanched sands a gloom—
Up the still, glistening beaches,
Up the creeks we will hie;
Over banks of bright seaweed
The ebb-tide leaves dry.   135
We will gaze, from the sandhills,
At the white, sleeping town;
At the church on the hillside—
And then come back down,
Singing, "There dwells a loved one,140
But cruel is she;
She left lonely forever
The kings of the sea."

For Thought and Discussion

1. Since the poem is narrative as well as descriptive, it has a
   slight plot. Reveal the plot by following the actions of the
   merman.
2. Quote examples of various figures of speech.
3. What poetic devices seem to you most effective? Which are
   suggestive of Poe?
4. Contrast the appearance, action, and emotions of the woman as
   she sings and as she sighs.
5. Do you find yourself sympathizing more with the mortal wife
   or with the merman?

OISIN IN TIRNANOGE: OR, THE LAST OF THE FENA
PATRICK WESTON JOYCE

[Patrick Weston Joyce, the author of "Oisin in Tirnanoge," made extensive studies on many subjects, among them Irish music, education, history, superstitions, ancient stories, and legends.

The story of "Oisin in Tirnanoge," is of the hero-poet, who lived more than three hundred years, according to legend. He told St. Patrick •the story of his sojourn in the land of Tirnanoge (tir na nóg) the Land of Everlasting Youth. The inhabitants of this land were fairies, who lived in the green hills and were called Aes-shee, Dena-shee, *banshee*, or merely *shee*. In Irish literature there are many legendary stories of the *shee*, the woman of the fairy hills.]

According to an ancient legend, Finn's son Oisin, the hero-poet, survived to the time of St. Patrick, two hundred years (the legend makes it three hundred) after the other Fena. On a certain occasion, when the saint asked him how he had lived to such a great age, the old hero related the following story.

A SHORT time after the fatal battle of Gavra where so many of our heroes fell, we were hunting on a dewy morning near the brink of Lough Lein,[1] where the trees and hedges around us were all fragrant with blossoms, and the little birds sang melodious music on the branches. We soon roused the deer from the thickets, and as they bounded over the plain, our hounds followed after them in full cry.

We were not long so engaged, when we saw a rider coming swiftly towards us from the west; and we soon perceived that it was a maiden on a white steed. We all ceased from the chase on seeing the lady, who reined in as she approached. And Finn and the Fena were greatly surprised, for they had never before seen so lovely a maiden. A slender golden diadem encircled her head; and she wore a brown robe of silk, spangled with stars of red gold, which was fastened in front by a golden brooch, and fell from her shoulders till it swept the ground. Her yellow hair flowed far down over her robe in bright, golden ringlets. Her blue eyes were as clear as the drops of dew on the grass; and while her small, white hand held the bridle and curbed her steed with a golden bit, she sat more gracefully than the swan on Lough Lein. The white steed was covered with a smooth, flowing mantle. He was shod with four shoes of pure yellow gold, and in all Erin[2] a better or more beautiful steed could not be found.

As she came slowly to the presence of Finn, he addressed her courteously in these words—

"Who art thou, O lovely youthful princess? Tell us thy name and the name of thy country, and relate to us the cause of thy coming."

She answered in a sweet and gentle voice, "Noble king of the Fena, I have had a long journey this day, for my country lies far off in the Western Sea. I am the daughter of the king of Tirnanoge, and my name is Niam of the Golden Hair."

"And what is it that has caused thee to come so far across the sea? Has thy husband forsaken thee; or what other evil has befallen thee?"

"My husband has not forsaken me,

---

[1] *Lough Lein,* the Lakes of Killarney.

[2] *Erin,* Ireland.

for I have never been married or betrothed to any man. But I love
thy noble son, Oisin; and this is what
has brought me to Erin. It is not
without reason that I have given him
my love, and that I have undertaken
this long journey; for I have often
heard of his bravery, his gentleness,
and the nobleness of his person.
Many princes and high chiefs have
sought me in marriage; but I was
quite indifferent to all men, and never
consented to wed, till my heart was
moved with love for thy gentle son,
Oisin."

When I heard these words, and
when I looked on the lovely maiden
with her glossy, golden hair, I was
all over in love with her. I came
near, and taking her small hand in
mine, I told her she was a mild star
of brightness and beauty, and that I
preferred her to all the princesses in
the world for my wife.

"Then," said she, "I place you under gesa, which true heroes never
break through, to come with me on
my white steed to Tirnanoge, the
land of never-ending youth. It is
the most delightful and the most renowned country under the sun.
There is abundance of gold and silver and jewels, of honey and wine;
and the trees bear fruit and blossoms
and green leaves together all the year
round. You will get a hundred
swords and a hundred robes of silk
and satin, a hundred swift steeds,
and a hundred slender, keen-scented
hounds. You will get herds of cows
without number and flocks of sheep
with fleeces of gold; a coat of mail
that cannot be pierced, and a sword
that never missed a stroke and from
which no one ever escaped alive.
There are feasting and harmless pastimes each day. A hundred warriors
fully armed shall always await you at
call, and harpers shall delight you

with their sweet music. You will wear
the diadem of the king of Tirnanoge,
which he never yet gave to any one
under the sun, and which will guard
you day and night, in tumult and
battle and danger of every kind.
Lapse of time shall bring neither decay nor death, and you shall be forever young and gifted with unfading
beauty and strength. All these delights you shall enjoy, and many
others that I do not mention; and
I myself will be your wife if you
come with me to Tirnanoge."

I replied that she was my choice
above all the maidens in the world,
and that I would willingly go with
her to the Land of Youth.

When my father, Finn, and Fena
heard me say this, and knew that I
was going from them, they raised
three shouts of grief and lamentation.
And Finn came up to me and took my
hand in his, saying sadly—

"Woe is me, my son, that you are
going away from me, for I do not
expect that you will ever return to
me!"

The manly beauty of his countenance became quite dimmed with sorrow; and though I promised to return after a little time, and fully believed that I should see him again,
I could not check my tears, as I gently
kissed my father's cheek.

I then bade farewell to my dear
companions, and mounted the white
steed, while the lady kept her seat before me. She gave the signal, and the
steed galloped swiftly and smoothly
towards the west, till he reached the
strand; and when his gold-shod hoofs
touched the waves, he shook himself
and neighed three times. He made no
delay but plunged forward at once,
moving over the face of the sea with
the speed of a cloud-shadow on a
March day. The wind overtook the
waves and we overtook the wind, so

that we straightway lost sight of land; and we saw nothing but billows tumbling before us and billows tumbling behind us.

Other shores came into view, and we saw many wonderful things on our journey—islands and cities, lime-white mansions, bright greenans[3] and lofty palaces. A hornless fawn once crossed our course, bounding nimbly along from the crest of one wave to the crest of another; and close after, in full chase, a white hound with red ears. We saw also a lovely young maiden on a brown steed with a golden apple in her hand; and as she passed swiftly by a young warrior on a white steed plunged after her, wearing a long, flowing mantle of yellow silk, and holding a gold-hilted sword in his hand.

I knew naught of these things, and, marveling much, I asked the princess what they meant; but she answered—

"Heed not what you see here, Oisin; for all these wonders are as nothing compared with what you shall see in Tirnanoge."

At last we saw at a great distance, rising over the waves on the very verge of the sea, a palace more splendid than all the others; and, as we drew near, its front glittered like the morning sun. I asked the lady what royal house this was and who was the prince that ruled over it.

"This country is the Land of Virtues," she replied. "Its king is the giant, Fomor of the Blows, and its queen the daughter of the king of the Land of Life. The Fomor brought the lady away by force from her own country, and keeps her in his palace; but she has put him under gesa that he cannot break through, never to ask her to marry him till she can find a champion to fight him in single com-

[3]*greenans*, a summer house, one in a beautiful bright place.

bat. But she still remains in bondage; for no hero has yet come hither who has the courage to meet the giant."

"A blessing on you, golden-haired Niam," I replied; "I have never heard music sweeter than your voice; and although I feel pity for this princess, yet your story is pleasant to me to hear; for of a certainty I will go to the palace, and try whether I cannot kill this Fomor, and free the lady."

So we came to land; and as we drew nigh to the palace, the lovely young queen met us and bade us welcome. She led us in and placed us on chairs of gold; after which choice food was placed before us, and drinking-horns filled with mead, and golden goblets of sweet wine.

When we had eaten and drunk, the mild young princess told us her story, while tears streamed from her soft blue eyes; and she ended by saying—

"I shall never return to my own country and to my father's house, so long as this great cruel giant is alive!"

When I heard her sad words, and saw her tears falling, I was moved with pity, and telling her to cease from her grief, I gave her my hand as a pledge that I would meet the giant, and either slay him or fall myself in her defense.

While we were yet speaking, we saw the giant coming towards the palace, large of body, and ugly and hateful in appearance, carrying a load of deerskins on his back, and holding a great iron club in his hand. He threw down his load when he saw us, turned a surly look on the princess, and, without greeting us or showing the least mark of courtesy, he forthwith challenged me to battle in a loud, rough voice.

It was not my wont to be dismayed

by a call to battle, or to be terrified at the sight of an enemy; and I went forth at once without the least fear in my heart. But though I had fought many battles in Erin against wild boars and enchanters and foreign invaders, never before did I find it so hard to preserve my life. We fought for three days and three nights without food or drink or sleep; for the giant did not give me a moment for rest, and neither did I give him. At length, when I looked at the two princesses weeping in great fear, and when I called to mind my father's deeds in battle, the fury of my valor arose; and with a sudden onset I felled the giant to the earth; and instantly, before he could recover himself, I cut off his head.

When the maidens saw the monster lying on the ground dead, they uttered three cries of joy; and they came to me, and led me in the palace. For I was indeed bruised all over, and covered with gory wounds; and a sudden dizziness of brain and feebleness of body seized me. But the daughter of the king of the Land of Life applied precious balsam and healing herbs to my wounds; and in a short time I was healed, and my cheerfulness of mind returned.

Then I buried the giant in a deep and wide grave; and I raised a great carn over him, and placed on it a stone with his name graved in Ogam.

We rested that night, and at the dawn of the next morning Niam said to me that it was time for us to resume our journey to Tirnanoge. So we took leave of the daughter of the king of the Land of Life; and though her heart was joyful after her release, she wept at our departure, and we were not less sorry at parting from her. When we had mounted the white steed, he galloped towards the strand; and as soon as his hoofs touched the wave, he shook himself and neighed three times. We plunged forward over the clear, green sea, with the speed of a March wind on a hillside; and soon we saw nothing but billows tumbling before us and billows tumbling behind us. We saw again the fawn chased by the white hound with red ears; and the maiden with the golden apple passed swiftly by, followed by the young warrior in yellow silk on his white steed. And again we passed many strange islands and cities and white palaces.

The sky now darkened, so that the sun was hidden from our view. A storm arose, and the sea was lighted up with constant flashes. But though the wind blew from every point of the heavens, and the waves rose up and roared around us, the white steed kept his course straight on, moving as calmly and swiftly as before, through the foam and blinding spray, without being delayed or disturbed in the least, and without turning either to the right or to the left.

At length the storm abated, and after a time the sun again shone brightly; and when I looked up, I saw a country near at hand all green and full of flowers, with beautiful smooth plains, blue hills, and bright lakes and waterfalls. Not far from the shore stood a palace of surpassing beauty and splendor. It was covered all over with gold and with gems of every color—blue, green, crimson, and yellow; and on each side were greenans shining with precious stones, built by artists the most skilled that could be found. I asked Niam the name of that delightful country, and she replied—

"This is my native country, Tirnanoge; and there is nothing I have promised you that you will not find in it."

As soon as we reached the shore,

we dismounted; and now we saw advancing from the palace a troop of noble looking warriors, all clad in bright garments, who came forward to meet and welcome us. Following these we saw a stately glittering host, with the king at their head wearing a robe of bright yellow satin covered with gems, and a crown that sparkled with gold and diamonds. The queen came after, attended by a hundred lovely young maidens; and as they advanced towards us, it seemed to me that this king and queen exceeded all the kings and queens of the world in beauty and gracefulness and majesty.

After they had kissed their daughter, the king took my hand, and said aloud in the hearing of the host—

"This is Oisin, the son of Finn, for whom my daughter, Niam, traveled over the sea to Erin. This is Oisin, who is to be the husband of Niam of the Golden Hair. We give you a hundred thousand welcomes, brave Oisin. You will be forever young in this land. All kinds of delights and innocent pleasures are awaiting you, and my daughter, the gentle, golden-haired Niam, shall be your wife; for I am the king of Tirnanoge."

I gave thanks to the king, and I bowed low to the queen; after which we went into the palace, where we found a banquet prepared. The feasting and rejoicing lasted for ten days, and on the last day I was wedded to gentle Niam of the Golden Hair.

I lived in the Land of Youth more than three hundred years; but it appeared to me that only three years had passed since the day I parted from my friends. At the end of that time, I began to have a longing desire to see my father, Finn, and all my old companions, and I asked leave of Niam and of the king to visit Erin. The king gave permission, and Niam said—

"I will give consent, though I feel sorrow in my heart, for I fear much you will never return to me."

I replied that I would surely return, and that she need not feel any doubt or dread, for that the white steed knew the way, and would bring me back in safety. Then she addressed me in these words, which seemed very strange to me—

"I will not refuse this request, though your journey afflicts me with great grief and fear. Erin is not now as it was when you left it. The great king Finn and his Fena are all gone; and you will find instead of them, a holy father and hosts of priests and saints. Now, think well on what I say to you and keep my words in your mind. If once you alight from the white steed, you will never come back to me. Again I warn you, if you place your feet on the green sod in Erin, you will never return to this lovely land. A third time, O Oisin, my beloved husband, a third time I say to you, if you alight from the white steed, you will never see me again."

I promised that I would faithfully attend to her words, and that I would not alight from the white steed. Then, as I looked into her gentle face and marked her grief, my heart was weighed down with sadness, and my tears flowed plentifully; but even so, my mind was bent on coming back to Erin.

When I had mounted the white steed, he galloped straight towards the shore. We moved as swiftly as before over the clear sea. The wind overtook the waves and we overtook the wind, so that we straightway left the Land of Youth behind; and we passed by many islands and cities, till at length we landed on the green shores of Erin.

As I traveled on through the country, I looked closely around me; but I scarcely knew the old places, for everything seemed strangely altered. I saw no sign of Finn and his host, and I began to dread that Niam's saying was coming true. At length, I espied at a distance a company of little men and women, all mounted on horses as small as themselves; and when I came near, they greeted me kindly and courteously. They looked at me with wonder and curiosity, and they marveled much at my great size, and at the beauty and majesty of my person.

I asked them about Finn and the Fena; whether they were still living, or if any sudden disaster had swept them away. And one replied—

"We have heard of the hero Finn, who ruled the Fena of Erin in times of old, and who never had an equal for bravery and wisdom. The poets of the Gaels have written many books concerning his deeds and the deeds of the Fena, which we cannot now relate; but they are all gone long since, for they lived many ages ago. We have heard also, and we have seen it written in very old books, that Finn had a son named Oisin. Now this Oisin went with a young fairy maiden to Tirnanoge, and his father and his friends sorrowed greatly after him, and sought him long; but he was never seen again."

When I heard all this, I was filled with amazement, and my heart grew heavy with great sorrow. I silently turned my steed away from the wondering people, and set forward straightway for Allen of the mighty deeds, on the broad, green plains of Leinster. It was a miserable journey to me; and though my mind, being full of sadness at all I saw and heard, forecasted further sorrows, I was grieved more than ever when I reached Allen. For there, indeed, I found the hill deserted and lonely, and my father's palace all in ruins and overgrown with grass and weeds.

I turned slowly away, and afterwards fared through the land in every direction in search of my friends. But I met only crowds of little people, all strangers, who gazed on me with wonder; and none knew me. I visited every place throughout the country where I knew the Fena had lived; but I found their houses all like Allen, solitary and in ruins.

At length I came to Glenasmole, where many a time I had hunted in days of old with the Fena, and there I saw a crowd of people in the glen. As soon as they saw me, one of them came forward and said—

"Come to us, thou mighty hero, and help us out of our strait; for thou art a man of vast strength."

I went to them, and found a number of men trying in vain to raise a large, flat stone. It was half lifted from the ground; but those who were under it were not strong enough either to raise it further or to free themselves from its weight. And they were in great distress, and on the point of being crushed to death.

I thought it a shameful thing that so many men should be unable to lift this stone, which Oscar, if he were alive, would take in his right hand and fling over the heads of the feeble crowd. After I had looked a little while, I stooped forward and seized the flag with one hand; and, putting forth my strength, I flung it seven perches from its place, and relieved the little men. But with the great strain the golden saddle-girth broke, and, bounding forward to keep myself from falling, I suddenly came to the ground on my two feet.

The moment the white steed felt himself free, he shook himself and neighed. Then, starting off with the speed of a cloud-shadow on a March day, he left me standing helpless and sorrowful. Instantly a woeful change came over me: the sight of my eyes began to fade, the ruddy beauty of my face fled, I lost all my strength, and I fell to the earth, a poor, withered old man, blind and wrinkled and feeble.

The white steed was never seen again. I never recovered my sight, my youth, or my strength; and I have lived in this manner, sorrowing without ceasing for my gentle, golden-haired wife, Niam, and thinking ever of my father, Finn, and of the lost companions of my youth.

For Thought and Discussion

1. What is a legend?
   To whom did Oisin tell the story?
2. Give the descriptive details that make the account of the morning hunt very beautiful.
3. Describe the maiden who met the hunters.
   Describe the steed she rode.
4. Who was the maiden, and what was the purpose of her visit?
   Who was Oisin, and why is he famous?
   To what did Oisin compare the maiden after hearing her speak?
5. Where did Niam plan to take Oisin?
   How was Tirnanoge, the land of never-ending youth, described?
   Of what were the lovely things in that land symbolic?
6. Why did Finn grieve over his son's departure?
7. How did Niam and Oisin leave Ireland?
8. Name some of the wonders they saw on the sea.
9. What adventure did they encounter on the way to Tirnanoge?
   Whom did Oisin slay?
   How long did the fight last, and why was Oisin able to slay the giant?
   Of what is the giant's name suggestive?
10. How were Niam and Oisin received in Tirnanoge?
11. How long did Oisin remain in that land, and why did he wish to leave?
12. What warning did Niam give Oisin as he left?
13. When Oisin returned to Erin (Ireland), why was he disappointed?
    Why did he not return to Tirnanoge? Did you expect him to return? Why or why not?
14. Do the stories of the marriage of fairies and mortals usually have a happy ending?
15. Cite examples of the use of color, of extravagance, of unreality, and of symbolism.
16. Why is the setting of this story important?

Plus Work

Make a study of the fairy lore of Ireland. Give the class an oral report of your findings.

~❧~

RUNNING WOLF

ALGERNON BLACKWOOD

[Born in England, educated in Edinburgh University, Algernon Blackwood decided to try his fortune in Canada. He began with dairy farming but eventually drifted from one job to another in a desperate attempt to make a living. He has done almost every kind of work: he has posed for artists, given music lessons at twenty-five cents each, at different times taught shorthand and French and German, and acted as a secretary. By chance, upon the advice of a friend he sold some ghost stories. Then within three years he became a successful writer, and now he spends his time traveling and writing.]

LONELINESS in a backwoods camp brings charm, pleasure, and a happy sense of calm until, and unless, it comes too near. Once it has crept within short distance, however, it may easily cross the narrow line between comfort and discomfort."

The man who enjoys an adventure outside the general experience of the race, and imparts it to others, must not be surprised if he is taken for either a liar or a fool, as Malcolm Hyde, hotel clerk on a holiday, discovered in due course. Nor is "enjoy" the right word to use in describing his emotions; the word he chose was probably "survive."

When he first set eyes on Medicine Lake he was struck by its still, sparkling beauty, lying there in the vast Canadian backwoods; next, by its extreme loneliness; and, lastly—a good deal later, this—by its combination of beauty, loneliness, and singular atmosphere, due to the fact that it was the scene of his adventure.

"It's fairly stiff with big fish," said Morton of the Montreal Sporting Club. "Spend your holiday there— up Mattawa way, some fifteen miles west of Stony Creek. You'll have it all to yourself except for an old Indian who's got a shack there. Camp on the east side—if you'll take a tip from me." He then talked for half an hour about the wonderful sport; yet he was not otherwise very communicative, and did not suffer questions gladly, Hyde noticed. Nor had he stayed there very long himself. If it was such a paradise as Morton, its discoverer and the most experienced rod in the province, claimed, why had he himself spent only three days there?

"Ran short of grub," was the explanation offered; but to another friend he had mentioned briefly, "flies," and to a third, so Hyde learned later, he gave the excuse that his half-breed "took sick," necessitating a quick return to civilization.

Hyde, however, cared little for the explanations; his interest in these came later. "Stiff with fish" was the phrase he liked. He took the Canadian Pacific train to Mattawa, laid in his outfit at Stony Creek, and set off thence for the fifteen-mile canoe-trip without a care in the world.

Traveling light, the portages did not trouble him; the water was swift and easy, the rapids negotiable; everything came his way, as the saying is. Occasionally he saw big fish making for the deeper pools, and was sorely tempted to stop; but he resisted. He pushed on between the immense world of forests that stretched for hundreds of miles, known to deer, bear, moose, and wolf, but strange to any echo of human tread, a deserted and primeval wilderness. The autumn day was calm, the water sang and sparkled, the blue sky hung cloudless over all, ablaze with light. Toward evening he passed an old beaver-dam, rounded a little point, and had his first sight of Medicine Lake. He lifted his dripping paddle; the canoe shot with silent glide into calm water. He gave an exclamation of delight, for the loveliness caught his breath away.

Though primarily a sportsman, he was not insensible to beauty. The lake formed a crescent, perhaps four miles long, its width between a mile and half a mile. The slanting gold of sunset flooded it. No wind stirred its crystal surface. Here it had lain since the redskin's god first made it; here it would lie until he dried it up again. Towering spruce and hemlock trooped to its very edge, majestic cedars leaned down as if to drink, crimson sumachs shone in fiery patches, and maples gleamed orange and red beyond belief. The air was like wine, with the silence of a dream.

It was here the red men formerly "made medicine," with all the wild ritual and tribal ceremony of an ancient day. But it was of Morton, rather than of Indians, that Hyde thought. If this lonely, hidden para-dise was really stiff with big fish, he owed a lot to Morton for the information. Peace invaded him, but the excitement of the hunter lay below.

He looked about him with quick, practised eye for a camping-place before the sun sank below the forests and the half-lights came. The Indian's shack, lying in full sunshine on the eastern shore, he found at once; but the trees lay too thick about it for comfort, nor did he wish to be so close to its inhabitant. Upon the opposite side, however, an ideal clearing offered. This lay already in shadow, the huge forest darkening it toward evening; but the open space attracted. He paddled over quickly and examined it. The ground was hard and dry, he found, and a little brook ran tinkling down one side of it into the lake. This outfall, too, would be a good fishing spot. Also it was sheltered. A few low willows marked the mouth.

An experienced camper soon makes up his mind. It was a perfect site, and some charred logs, with traces of former fires, proved that he was not the first to think so. Hyde was delighted. Then, suddenly, disappointment came to tinge his pleasure. His kit was landed, and preparations for putting up the tent were begun, when he recalled a detail that excitement had so far kept in the background of his mind—Morton's advice. But not Morton's only, for the storekeeper at Stony Creek had reinforced it. The big fellow with straggling mustache and stooping shoulders, dressed in shirt and trousers, had handed him out a final sentence with the bacon, flour, condensed milk, and sugar. He had repeated Morton's half-forgotten words:

"Put yer tent on the east shore. I should," he said at parting.

He remembered Morton, too, apparently. "A shortish fellow, brown as an Indian and fairly smelling of the woods. Traveling with Jake, the half-breed." That assuredly was Morton. "Didn't stay long, now, did he?" he added in a reflective tone.

"Going Windy Lake way, are yer? Or Ten Mile Water, maybe?" he had first inquired of Hyde.

"Medicine Lake."

"Is that so?" the man said, as though he doubted it for some obscure reason. He pulled at his ragged mustache a moment. "Is that so, now?" he repeated. And the final words followed him downstream after a considerable pause—the advice about the best shore on which to put his tent.

All this now suddenly flashed back upon Hyde's mind with a tinge of disappointment and annoyance, for when two experienced men agreed, their opinion was not to be lightly disregarded. He wished he had asked the storekeeper for more details. He looked about him, he reflected, he hesitated. His ideal camping-ground lay certainly on the forbidden shore. What in the world, he wondered, could be the objection to it?

But the light was fading; he must decide quickly one way or the other. After staring at his unpacked dunnage and the tent, already half erected, he made up his mind with a muttered expression that consigned both Morton and the storekeeper to less pleasant places. "They must have some reason," he growled to himself; "fellows like that usually know what they're talking about. I guess I'd better shift over to the other side—for tonight, at any rate."

He glanced across the water before actually reloading. No smoke rose from the Indian's shack. He had seen no sign of a canoe. The man, he decided, was away. Reluctantly, then, he left the good camping-ground and paddled across the lake, and half an hour later his tent was up, firewood collected, and two small trout were already caught for supper. But the bigger fish, he knew, lay waiting for him on the other side by the little outfall, and he fell asleep at length on his bed of balsam boughs, annoyed and disappointed, yet wondering how a mere sentence could have persuaded him so easily against his own better judgment. He slept like the dead; the sun was well up before he stirred.

But his morning mood was a very different one. The brilliant light, the peace, the intoxicating air, all this was too exhilarating for the mind to harbor foolish fancies, and he marveled that he could have been so weak the night before. No hesitation lay in him anywhere. He struck camp immediately after breakfast, paddled back across the strip of shining water, and quickly settled in upon the forbidden shore, as he now called it, with a contemptuous grin. And the more he saw of the spot, the better he liked it. There was plenty of wood, running water to drink, an open space about the tent, and there were no flies. The fishing, moreover, was magnificent; Morton's description was fully justified, and "stiff with big fish" for once was not an exaggeration.

The useless hours of the early afternoon he passed dozing in the sun, or wandering through the underbrush beyond the camp. He found no sign of anything unusual. He bathed in a cool, deep pool; he reveled in the lonely little paradise. Lonely it certainly was, but the loneliness was part of its charm; the stillness, the peace, the isolation of this beautiful backwoods lake delighted him. The silence was divine. He was entirely satisfied.

After a brew of tea, he strolled toward evening along the shore, looking for the first sign of a rising fish. A faint ripple on the water, with the lengthening shadows, made good conditions. *Plop* followed *plop*, as the big fellows rose, snatched at their food, and vanished into the depths. He hurried back. Ten minutes later he had taken his rods and was gliding cautiously in the canoe through the quiet water.

So good was the sport, indeed, and so quickly did the big trout pile up in the bottom of the canoe that, despite the growing lateness, he found it hard to tear himself away. "One more," he said, "and then I really will go." He landed that "one more," and was in the act of taking it off the hook, when the deep silence of the evening was curiously disturbed. He became abruptly aware that some one watched him. A pair of eyes, it seemed, were fixed upon him from some point in the surrounding shadows.

Thus, at least, he interpreted the odd disturbance in his happy mood; for thus he felt it. The feeling stole over him without the slightest warning. He was not alone. The slippery big trout dripped from his fingers. He sat motionless, and stared about him.

Nothing stirred; the ripple on the lake had died away; there was no wind; the forest lay a single purple mass of shadow; the yellow sky, fast fading, threw reflections that troubled the eye and made distances uncertain. But there was no sound, no movement; he saw no figure anywhere. Yet he knew that some one watched him, and a wave of quite unreasoning terror gripped him. The nose of the canoe was against the bank. In a moment, and instinctively, he shoved it off and paddled into deeper water. The watcher, it came to him instinctively, was quite close to him upon

the bank. But where? And who? Was it the Indian?

Here, in deeper water, and some twenty yards from the shore, he paused and strained both sight and hearing to find some possible clue. He felt half ashamed, now that the first strange feeling passed a little. But the certainty remained. Absurd as it was, he felt positive that some one watched him with concentrated and intent regard. Every fiber in his being told him so; and though he could discover no figure, no new outline on the shore, he could even have sworn in which clump of willow bushes the hidden person crouched and stared. His attention seemed drawn to that particular clump.

The water dripped slowly from his paddle, now lying across the thwarts. There was no other sound. The canvas of his tent gleamed dimly. A star or two were out. He waited. Nothing happened.

Then, as suddenly as it had come, the feeling passed, and he knew that the person who had been watching him intently had gone. It was as if a current had been turned off; the normal world flowed back; the landscape emptied as if some one had left a room. The disagreeable feeling left him at the same time, so that he instantly turned the canoe in to the shore again, landed, and, paddle in hand, went over to examine the clump of willows he had singled out as the place of concealment. There was no one there, of course, or any trace of recent human occupancy. No leaves, no branches stirred, nor was a single twig displaced; his keen and practised sight detected no sign of tracks upon the ground. Yet, for all that, he felt positive that a little time ago some one had crouched among these very leaves and watched him. He remained absolutely convinced of it. The watcher, whether Indian, hunter, stray lumberman, or wandering half-breed, had now withdrawn, a search was useless, and dusk was falling. He returned to his little camp, more disturbed perhaps than he cared to acknowledge. He cooked his supper, hung up his catch on a string, so that no prowling animal could get at it during the night, and prepared to make himself comfortable until bed-time. Unconsciously, he built a bigger fire than usual, and found himself peering over his pipe into the deep shadows beyond the firelight, straining his ears to catch the slightest sound. He remained generally on the alert in a way that was new to him.

A man under such conditions and in such a place need not know discomfort until the sense of loneliness strikes him as too vivid a reality. Loneliness in a backwoods camp brings charm, pleasure, and a happy sense of calm until, and unless, it comes too near. It should remain an ingredient only among other conditions; it should not be directly, vividly noticed. Once it has crept within short range, however, it may easily cross the narrow line between comfort and discomfort, and darkness is an undesirable time for the transition. A curious dread may easily follow— the dread lest the loneliness suddenly be disturbed, and the solitary human feel himself open to attack.

For Hyde, now, this transition had been already accomplished; the too intimate sense of loneliness had shifted abruptly into the worse condition of no longer being quite alone. It was an awkward moment, and the hotel clerk realized his position exactly. He did not quite like it. He sat there, with his back to the blazing logs, a very visible object in the light, while all about him the darkness of the forest lay like an impenetrable wall. He could not see a foot beyond the small circle of his camp-fire; the silence about him was like the silence of the dead. No leaf rustled, no wave lapped; he himself sat motionless as a log.

Then again he became suddenly aware that the person who watched him had returned, and that same intent and concentrated gaze as before was fixed upon him where he lay. There was no warning; he heard no stealthy tread or snapping of dry twigs, yet the owner of those steady eyes was very close to him, probably not a dozen feet away. This sense of proximity was overwhelming.

It is unquestionable that a shiver ran down his spine. This time, moreover, he felt positive that the man crouched just beyond the firelight, the distance he himself could see being nicely calculated, and straight in front of him. For some minutes he sat without stirring a single muscle, yet with each muscle ready and alert, straining his eyes in vain to pierce the darkness, but only succeeding in dazzling his sight with the reflected light. Then, as he shifted his position slowly, cautiously, to obtain another angle of vision, his heart gave two big thumps against his ribs and the hair seemed to rise on his scalp with the sense of cold that shot horribly up his spine. In the darkness facing him he saw two small and greenish circles that were certainly a pair of eyes, yet not the eyes of Indian, hunter, or of any human being. It was a pair of animal eyes that stared so fixedly at him out of the night. And this certainty had an immediate and natural effect upon him.

For, at the menace of those eyes, the fears of millions of long dead hunters since the dawn of time woke in him. Hotel clerk though he was, heredity surged through him in an automatic wave of instinct. His hand groped for a weapon. His fingers fell on the iron head of his small camp ax, and at once he was himself again. Confidence returned; the vague, superstitious dread was gone. This was a bear or wolf that smelt his catch and came to steal it. With beings of that sort he knew instinctively how to deal, yet admitting, by this very instinct, that his original dread had been of quite another kind.

"I'll very quickly find out what it is," he exclaimed aloud, and snatching a burning brand from the fire, he hurled it with good aim straight at the eyes of the beast before him.

The bit of pitch-pine fell in a shower of sparks that lit the dry grass this side of the animal, flared up a moment, then died quickly down again. But in that instant of bright illumination he saw clearly what his unwelcome visitor was. A big timber wolf sat on its hind-quarters, staring steadily at him through the firelight. He saw its legs and shoulders, he saw its hair, he saw also the big hemlock trunks lit up behind it, and the willow scrub on each side. It formed a vivid, clear-cut picture shown in clear detail by the momentary blaze. To his amazement, however, the wolf did not turn and bolt away from the burning log, but withdrew a few yards only, and sat there again on its haunches, staring, staring as before. Heavens, how it stared! He "shoed" it, but without effect; it did not budge. He did not waste another good log on it, for his fear was dissipated now, and a timber wolf was a timber wolf, and it might sit there as long as it pleased, provided it did not try to steal his catch. No alarm was in him any more. He knew that wolves were harmless in the summer and autumn, and even when "packed"

in the winter, they would attack a man only when suffering desperate hunger. So he lay and watched the beast, threw bits of stick in its direction, even talked to it, wondering only that it never moved. "You can stay there forever, if you like," he remarked to it aloud, "for you cannot get at my fish, and the rest of the grub I shall take into the tent with me."

The creature blinked its bright green eyes, but made no move.

Why, then, if his fear was gone, did he think of certain things as he rolled himself in the Hudson Bay blankets before going to sleep? The immobility of the animal was strange, its refusal to turn and bolt was still stranger. Never before had he known a wild creature that was not afraid of fire. Why did it sit and watch him, as with purpose in its dreadf··l eyes? How had he felt its presence earlier and instantly? A timber wolf, especially a solitary timber wolf, was a timid thing, yet this one feared neither man nor fire. Now as he lay there wrapped in his blankets inside the cozy tent, it sat outside beneath the stars, beside the fading embers, the wind chilly in its fur, the ground cooling beneath its planted paws, watching him, steadily watching him, perhaps until the dawn.

It was unusual, it was strange. Having neither imagination nor tradition, he called upon no store of racial visions. Matter of fact, a hotel clerk on a fishing holiday, he lay there in his blankets, merely wondering and puzzled. A timber wolf was a timber wolf and nothing more. Yet this timber wolf—the idea haunted him—was different. In a word, the deeper part of his original uneasiness remained. He tossed about, he shivered sometimes in his broken sleep, he did not go out to see, but he woke early and unrefreshed.

Again, with the sunshine and the morning wind, however, the incident of the night before was forgotten, almost unreal. His hunting zeal was uppermost. The tea and fish were delicious, his pipe had never tasted so good, the glory of this lonely lake amid primeval forests went to his head a little; he was a hunter[1] before the Lord, and nothing else. He tried the edge of the lake, and in the excitement of playing a big fish, knew suddenly that *it*, the wolf, was there. He paused with the rod, exactly as if struck. He looked about him, he looked in a definite direction. The brilliant sunshine made every smallest detail clear and sharp—boulders of granite, burned stems, crimson sumach, pebbles along the shore in neat, separate detail—without revealing where the watcher hid. Then, his sight wandering farther inshore among the tangled undergrowth, he suddenly picked up the familiar, half-expected outline. The wolf was lying behind a granite boulder, so that only the head, the muzzle, and the eyes were visible. It merged in its background. Had he not known it was a wolf, he could never have separated it from the landscape. The eyes shone in the sunlight.

There it lay. He looked straight at it. Their eyes, in fact, actually met full and square. "Great Scot!" he exclaimed aloud, "why, it's like looking at a human being!" And from that moment, unwittingly, he established a singular personal relation with the beast. And what followed confirmed this undesirable impression, for the animal rose instantly and came down in leisurely fashion to the shore,

where it stood looking back at him. It stood and stared into his eyes like some great wild dog, so that he was aware of a new and almost incredible sensation—that it courted recognition.

"Well! well!" he exclaimed again, relieving his feelings by addressing it aloud, "if this doesn't beat everything I ever saw! What d' you want, anyway?"

He examined it now more carefully. He had never seen a wolf so big before; it was a tremendous beast, a nasty customer to tackle, he reflected, if it ever came to that. It stood there absolutely fearless and full of confidence. In the clear sunlight he took in every detail of it—a huge, shaggy, lean-flanked timber wolf, its wicked eyes staring straight into his own, almost with a kind of purpose in them. He saw its great jaws, its teeth, and its tongue, hung out, dropping saliva a little. And yet the idea of its savagery, its fierceness, was very little in him.

He was amazed and puzzled beyond belief. He wished the Indian would come back. He did not understand this strange behavior in an animal. Its eyes, the odd expression in them, gave him a queer, unusual, difficult feeling. Had his nerves gone wrong? He almost wondered.

The beast stood on the shore and looked at him. He wished for the first time that he had brought a rifle. With a resounding smack he brought his paddle down flat upon the water, using all his strength, till the echoes rang as from a pistol-shot that was audible from one end of the lake to the other. The wolf never stirred. He shouted, but the beast remained unmoved. He blinked his eyes, speaking as to a dog, a domestic animal, a creature accustomed to hu-

---

[1]*hunter*, a reference to Genesis 10:9, where Nimrod is called "A mighty hunter before the Lord."

man ways. It blinked its eyes in return.

At length, increasing his distance from the shore, he continued fishing, and the excitement of the marvelous sport held his attention—his surface attention, at any rate. At times he almost forgot the attendant beast; yet whenever he looked up, he saw it there. And worse; when he slowly paddled home again, he observed it trotting along the shore as though to keep him company. Crossing a little bay, he spurted, hoping to reach the other point before his undesired and undesirable attendant. Instantly the brute broke into that rapid, tireless lope that, except on ice, can run down anything on four legs in the woods. When he reached the distant point, the wolf was waiting for him. He raised his paddle from the water, pausing a moment for reflection; for this very close attention—there were dusk and night yet to come—he certainly did not relish. His camp was near; he had to land; he felt uncomfortable even in the sunshine of broad day, when, to his keen relief, about half a mile from the tent, he saw the creature suddenly stop and sit down in the open. He waited a moment, then paddled on. It did not follow. There was no attempt to move; it merely sat and watched him. After a few hundred yards, he looked back. It was still sitting where he left it. And the absurd, yet significant, feeling came to him that the beast divined his thought, his anxiety, his dread, and was now showing him, as well as it could, that it entertained no hostile feeling and did not meditate attack.

He turned the canoe toward the shore; he landed; he cooked his supper in the dusk; the animal made no sign. Not far away it certainly lay and watched, but it did not advance. And to Hyde, observant now in a new way, came one sharp, vivid reminder of the strange atmosphere into which his commonplace personality had strayed: he suddenly recalled that his relations with the beast, already established, had progressed distinctly a stage further. This startled him, yet without the accompanying alarm he must certainly have felt twenty-four hours before. He had an understanding with the wolf. He was aware of friendly thoughts toward it. He even went so far as to set out a few big fish on the spot where he had first seen it sitting the previous night. "If he comes," he thought, "he is welcome to them. I've got plenty, anyway." He thought of it now as "he."

Yet the wolf made no appearance until he was in the act of entering his tent a good deal later. It was close on ten o'clock, whereas nine was his hour, and late at that, for turning in. He had, therefore, unconsciously been waiting for him. Then, as he was closing the flap, he saw the eyes close to where he had placed the fish. He waited, hiding himself, and expecting to hear sounds of munching jaws; but all was silence. Only the eyes glowed steadily out of the background of pitch darkness. He closed the flap. He had no slightest fear. In ten minutes he was sound asleep.

He could not have slept very long, for when he woke up he could see the shine of a faint red light through the canvas, and the fire had not died down completely. He rose and cautiously peeped out. The air was very cold; he saw his breath. But he also saw the wolf, for it had come in, and was sitting by the dying embers, not two yards away from where he crouched behind the flap. And this time, at these very close quarters, there was something in the attitude of the big wild thing that caught his attention with a vivid thrill of startled surprise and a sudden shock of cold that held him spellbound. He stared, unable to believe his eyes; for the wolf's attitude conveyed to him something familiar that at first he was unable to explain. Its pose reached him in the terms of another thing with which he was entirely at home. What was it? Did his senses betray him? Was he still asleep and dreaming?

Then, suddenly, with a start of uncanny recognition, he knew. Its attitude was that of a dog. Having found the clue, his mind then made an awful leap. For it was, after all, no dog its appearance aped, but something nearer to himself, and more familiar still. Good heavens! It sat there with the pose, the attitude, the gesture in repose of something almost human. And then, with a second shock of biting wonder, it came to him like a revelation. The wolf sat beside that camp-fire as a man might sit.

Before he could weigh his extraordinary discovery, before he could examine it in detail or with care, the animal, sitting in this ghastly fashion, seemed to feel his eyes fixed on it. It slowly turned and looked him in the face, and for the first time Hyde felt a full-blooded, superstitious fear flood through his entire being. He seemed transfixed with that nameless terror that is said to attack human beings who suddenly face the dead, finding themselves bereft of speech and movement. This moment of paralysis certainly occurred. Its passing, however, was as singular as its advent. For almost at once he was aware of something beyond and above this mockery of human attitude and pose, something that ran along unaccustomed nerves and reached his feeling, even perhaps his heart. The revulsion was extraordinary, its result still more extraordinary and unexpected. Yet the fact remains. He was aware of another thing that had the effect of stilling his terror as soon as it was born. He was aware of appeal, silent, half-expressed, yet vastly pathetic. He saw in the savage eyes a beseeching, even a yearning, expression that changed his mood as by magic from dread to natural sympathy. The great gray brute, symbol of cruel ferocity, sat there beside his dying fire and appealed for help.

This gulf betwixt animal and human seemed in that instant bridged. It was, of course, incredible. Hyde, sleep still possibly clinging to his inner being with the shades and half-shapes of dreams yet about his soul, acknowledged, how he knew not, the amazing fact. He found himself nodding to the brute in half-consent, and instantly, without more ado, the lean gray shape rose like a wraith and trotted off swiftly, but with stealthy tread into the background of the night.

When Hyde woke in the morning his first impression was that he must have dreamed the entire incident. His practical nature asserted itself. There was a bite in the fresh autumn air; the bright sun allowed no half-lights anywhere; he felt brisk in mind and body. Reviewing what had happened, he came to the conclusion that it was utterly vain to speculate; no possible explanation of the animal's behavior occurred to him: he was dealing with something entirely outside his experience. His fear, however, had completely left him. The odd sense of friendliness remained. The beast had a definite purpose, and he himself was included in that purpose. His sympathy held good.

But with the sympathy there was also an intense curiosity. "If it shows itself again," he told himself, "I'll go up close and find out what it wants." The fish laid out the night before had not been touched.

It must have been a full hour after breakfast when he next saw the brute; it was standing on the edge of the clearing, looking at him in the way now become familiar. Hyde immediately picked up his ax and advanced toward it boldly, keeping his eyes fixed straight upon its own. There was nervousness in him, but kept well under; nothing betraying it; step by step he drew nearer until some ten yards separated them. The wolf had not stirred a muscle as yet. Its jaws hung open, its eyes observed him intently; it allowed him to approach without a sign of what its mood might be. Then, with these ten yards between them, it turned abruptly and moved slowly off, looking back first over one shoulder and then over the other, exactly as a dog might do, to see if he was following.

A singular journey it was they then made together, animal and man. The trees surrounded them at once, for they left the lake behind them, entering the tangled bush beyond. The beast, Hyde noticed, obviously picked the easiest track for him to follow; for obstacles that meant nothing to the four-legged expert, yet were difficult for a man, were carefully avoided with an almost uncanny skill, while yet the general direction was accurately kept. Occasionally there were windfalls to be surmounted; but though the wolf bounded over these with ease, it was always waiting for the man on the other side after he had laboriously climbed over. Deeper and deeper into the heart of the lonely forest they penetrated in this singular fashion, cutting across the arc of the lake's crescent, it seemed to Hyde; for after two miles or so, he recognized the big rocky bluff that overhung the water at its northern end. This outstanding bluff he had seen from his camp, one side of it falling sheer into the water; it was probably the spot, he imagined, where the Indians held their medicine-making ceremonies, for it stood out in isolated fashion, and its top formed a private plateau not easy of access. And it was here, close to a big spruce at the foot of the bluff upon the forest side, that the wolf stopped suddenly and for the first time since its appearance gave audible expression to its feelings. It sat down on its haunches, lifted its muzzle with open jaws, and gave vent to a subdued and long-drawn howl that was more like the wail of a dog than the fierce barking cry associated with a wolf.

By this time Hyde had lost not only fear, but caution, too; nor, oddly enough, did this warning howl revive a sign of unwelcome emotion in him. In that curious sound he detected the same message that the eyes conveyed—appeal for help. He paused, nevertheless, a little startled, and while the wolf sat waiting for him, he looked about him quickly. There was young timber here; it had once been a small clearing, evidently. Ax and fire had done their work, but there was evidence to an experienced eye that it was Indians and not white men who had once been busy here. Some part of the medicine ritual, doubtless, took place in the little clearing, thought the man, as he advanced again toward his patient leader. The end of their queer journey, he felt, was close at hand.

He had not taken two steps before the animal got up and moved very slowly in the direction of some low bushes that formed a clump just beyond. It entered these, first looking back to make sure that its companion watched. The bushes hid it; a moment later it emerged again. Twice it performed this pantomime, each time, as it reappeared, standing still and staring at the man with as distinct an expression of appeal in the eyes as an animal may compass, probably. Its excitement, meanwhile, certainly increased, and this excitement was, with equal certainty, communicated to the man. Hyde made up his mind quickly. Gripping his ax tightly, and ready to use it at the first hint of malice, he moved slowly nearer to the bushes, wondering with something of a tremor what would happen.

If he expected to be startled, his expectation was at once fulfilled; but it was the behavior of the beast that made him jump. It positively frisked about him like a happy dog. It frisked for joy. Its excitement was intense, yet from its open mouth no sound was audible. With a sudden leap, then, it bounded past him into the clump of bushes, against whose very edge he stood and began scraping vigorously at the ground. Hyde stood and stared, amazement and interest now banishing all his nervousness, even when the beast, in its violent scraping, actually touched his body with its own. He had, perhaps, the feeling that he was in a dream, one of those fantastic dreams in which things may happen without involving an adequate surprise; for otherwise the manner of scraping and scratching at the ground must have seemed an impossible phenomenon. No wolf, no dog certainly, used its paws in the way those paws were working. Hyde had the odd, distressing sensation that it was hands, not paws, he watched. And yet, somehow, the natural, adequate surprise he should have felt, was absent. The strange action seemed not entirely unnatural. In his heart some deep hidden spring of sympathy and pity stirred instead. He was aware of pathos.

The wolf stopped in its task and looked up into his face. Hyde acted without hesitation then. Afterward he was wholly at a loss to explain his own conduct. It seemed he knew what to do, divined what was asked, expected of him. Between his mind and the dumb desire yearning through the savage animal there was intelligent and intelligible communication. He cut a stake and sharpened it, for the stones would blunt his ax-edge. He entered the clump of bushes to complete the digging his four-legged companion had begun. And while he worked, though he did not forget the close proximity of the wolf, he paid no attention to it; often his back was turned as he stooped over the laborious clearing away of the hard earth; no uneasiness or sense of danger was in him any more. The wolf sat outside the clump and watched the operations. Its concentrated attention, its patience, its intense eagerness, the gentleness and docility of the gray, fierce, and probably hungry brute, its obvious pleasure and satisfaction, too, at having won the human to its mysterious purpose—these were colors in the strange picture that Hyde thought of later when dealing with the human herd in his hotel again. At the moment he was aware chiefly of pathos and affection. The whole business was, of course, not to be believed, but that discovery came later, too, when telling it to others.

The digging continued for fully half an hour before his labor was rewarded by the discovery of a small whitish object. He picked it up and examined it—the finger-bone of a man. Other discoveries then followed quickly and in quantity. The cache was laid bare. He collected nearly the complete skeleton. The skull, however, he found last, and might not have found at all but for the guidance of his strangely alert companion. It lay some few yards away from the central hole now dug, and the wolf stood nuzzling the ground with its nose before Hyde understood that he was meant to dig exactly in that spot for it. Between the beast's very paws his stake struck hard upon it. He scraped the earth from the bone and examined it carefully. It was perfect, save for the fact that some wild animal had gnawed it, the teethmarks being still plainly visible. Close beside it lay the rusty iron head of a tomahawk. This and the smallness of the bones confirmed him in his judgment that it was the skeleton not of a white man, but of an Indian.

During the excitement of the discovery of the bones one by one, and finally of the skull, but, more especially, during the period of intense interest while Hyde was examining them, he had paid little, if any, attention to the wolf. He was aware that it sat and watched him, never moving its keen eyes for a single moment from the actual operations, but of sign or movement it made none at all. He knew that it was pleased and satisfied; he knew also that he had now fulfilled its purpose in a great measure. The further intuition that now came to him, derived, he felt positive, from his companion's dumb desire, was perhaps the cream of the entire experience to him. Gathering the bones together in his coat, he carried them, together with the tomahawk, to the foot of the big spruce where the animal had first stopped. His leg actually touched the creature's muzzle as he passed. It turned its head to watch, but did not follow, nor did it move a muscle while he prepared the platform of boughs upon which he then laid the poor worn bones of an Indian who had been killed, doubtless, in a sudden attack of ambush, and to whose remains had been denied the last grace of proper burial. He wrapped the bones in bark; he laid the tomahawk beside the skull; he lit the circular fire round the pyre, and the blue smoke rose upward into the clear bright sunshine of the Canadian autumn morning till it was lost among the mighty trees far overhead.

In the moment before actually lighting the little fire he had turned to note what his companion did. It sat five yards away, he saw, gazing intently, and one of its front paws was raised a little from the ground. It made no sign of any kind. He finished the work, becoming so absorbed in it that he had eyes for nothing but the tending and guarding of his careful ceremonial fire. It was only when the platform of boughs collapsed, laying their charred burden gently on the fragrant earth among the soft wood ashes, that he turned again, as though to show the wolf what he had done, and seek, perhaps, some look of satisfaction in its curiously expressive eyes. But the place he searched was empty. The wolf had gone.

He did not see it again; it gave no sign of its presence anywhere; he was not watched. He fished as before, wandered through the bush about his camp, sat smoking round his fire after dark, and slept peacefully in his cozy little tent. He was not disturbed. No howl was ever audible in the distant forest, no twig snapped beneath a stealthy tread, he saw no eyes. The wolf that behaved like a man had gone forever.

It was the day before he left that Hyde, noticing smoke rising from the shack across the lake, paddled over to exchange a word or two with the Indian, who had evidently now returned. The redskin came down to meet him as he landed, but it was soon plain that he spoke very little English. He emitted the familiar grunts at first; then bit by bit Hyde stirred his limited vocabulary into action. The net result, however, was slight enough, though it was certainly direct:

"You camp there?" the man asked, pointing to the other side.

"Yes."

"Wolf come?"

"Yes."

"You see wolf?"

"Yes."

The Indian stared at him fixedly a moment, a keen, wondering look upon his coppery, creased face.

"You 'fraid wolf?" he asked after a moment's pause.

"No," replied Hyde, truthfully. He knew it was useless to ask questions of his own, though he was eager for information. The other would have told him nothing. It was sheer luck that the man had touched on the subject at all, and Hyde realized that his own best rôle was merely to answer, but to ask no questions. Then, suddenly, the Indian became comparatively voluble. There was awe in his voice and manner.

"Him no wolf. Him big medicine wolf. Him spirit wolf."

Whereupon he drank the tea the other had brewed for him, closed his lips tightly, and said no more. His outline was discernible on the shore, rigid and motionless, an hour later, when Hyde's canoe turned the corner of the lake three miles away, and landed to make the portages up the first rapid of his homeward stream.

It was Morton who, after some persuasion, supplied further details of what he called the legend. Some hundred years before, the tribe that lived in the territory beyond the lake began their annual medicine-making ceremonies on the big rocky bluff at the northern end; but no medicine could be made. The spirits, declared the chief medicine man, would not answer. They were offended. An investigation followed. It was discovered that a young brave had recently killed a wolf, a thing strictly forbidden, since the wolf was the totem animal of the tribe. To make matters worse, the name of the guilty man was Running Wolf. The offense being unpardonable, the man was cursed and driven from the tribe:

"Go out. Wander alone among the woods, and if we see you, we slay you. Your bones shall be scattered in the forest, and your spirit shall not enter the Happy Hunting Grounds till one of another race shall find and bury them."

"Which meant," explained Morton, laconically, his only comment on the story, "probably forever."

For Thought and Discussion

1. This legendary story is based upon stories told about a tragedy which took place in the Canadian woods.
2. Is a man who recounts an unusual experience often taken for a liar or a fool?
3. What place did Malcolm Hyde select for his unusual vacation?
4. Why was this place chosen?
5. What is the first suggestion of mystery?
6. Name the descriptive details that make Medicine Lake attractive.
7. How did this lake get its name?
8. Was it natural for Hyde to become uncomfortable when he felt someone watching him?
9. When does this writer say that loneliness becomes unpleasant?
10. Why did this timber wolf seem uncanny and unreal?
11. Can you point out stages of development in Hyde's relation with the wolf?
12. In the final analysis, with what two beings did Hyde compare the wolf?
13. How does the wolf's mysterious appeal for help connect the actual events of the fishing trip with the legendary story told by the Indians?
14. Why is the telling of the legendary story left until the end of the story?

ILLUSTRATION BY J. NOEL PATON

THE RIME OF THE ANCIENT MARINER
SAMUEL TAYLOR COLERIDGE

PART I

IT is an ancient mariner,[1]
And he stoppeth one of three.
"By thy long gray beard and glittering eye,
Now wherefore stopp'st thou me?

"The bridegroom's doors are opened wide,   5
And I am next of kin;
The guests are met, the feast is set—
May'st hear the merry din."

He holds him with his skinny hand,
"There was a ship," quoth he.   10
"Hold off! unhand me, graybeard loon!"
Eftsoons[2] his hand dropt he.

An ancient mariner meeteth three gallants bidden to a wedding feast, and detaineth one.

---

[1]*mariner*, a seaman or sailor.
[2]*eftsoons*, immediately.

The wedding guest is spell-bound by the eye of the old seafaring man, and constrained to hear his tale.	He holds him with his glittering eye— The wedding guest stood still, And listens like a three-years' child; 15 The mariner hath his will.

The wedding guest sat on a stone;
He cannot choose but hear;
And thus spake on that ancient man,
The bright-eyed mariner—   20

"The ship was cheered, the harbor cleared,
Merrily did we drop
Below the kirk, below the hill,
Below the lighthouse top.

The mariner tells how the ship sailed southward with a good wind and fair weather, till it reached the line.

"The sun came up upon the left,   25
Out of the sea came he!
And he shone bright, and on the right
Went down into the sea.

"Higher and higher every day,
Till over the mast at noon"—   30
The wedding guest here beat his breast,
For he heard the loud bassoon.[3]

The wedding guest heareth the bridal music, but the mariner continueth his tale.

The bride hath paced into the hall,
Red as a rose is she;
Nodding their heads before her goes   35
The merry minstrelsy.

The wedding guest he beat his breast,
Yet he cannot choose but hear;
And thus spake on that ancient man,
The bright-eyed mariner—   40

The ship driven by a storm towards the south pole.

"And now the storm blast came, and he
Was tyrannous and strong;
He struck with his o'ertaking wings,
And chased us south along.

"With sloping masts and dipping prow,   45
As who pursued with yell and blow
Still treads the shadow of his foe,
And forward bends his head,
The ship drove fast, loud roared the blast,
And southward aye we fled.   50

---

[3]*bassoon,* a deep-toned orchestral instrument.

ILLUSTRATION BY J. NOEL PATON

"And now there came both mist and snow,
And it grew wondrous cold;
And ice, mast-high, came floating by,
As green as emerald,

"And through the drifts the snowy clifts   55
Did send a dismal sheen;
Nor shapes of men nor beasts we ken—
The ice was all between.

The land of ice,
and of fearful
sounds, where no
living thing was
to be seen.

"The ice was here, the ice was there,
The ice was all around;   60
It cracked and growled, and roared and howled,
Like noises in a swound![4]

"At length did cross an albatross[5];
Thorough the fog it came;
As if it had been a Christian soul,   65
We hailed it in God's name.

Till a great sea-
bird, called the
albatross, came
through the
snow-fog, and
was received with
great joy and
hospitality.

[4]*swound,* a swoon, a faint.
[5]*albatross,* a sea bird.

"It ate the food it ne'er had eat,
And round and round it flew.
The ice did split with a thunder fit;
The helmsman steered us through!   70

And lo! the alba-
tross proveth a bird
of good omen, and
followeth the ship
as it returned
northward through
fog and floating
ice.

"And a good south wind sprung up behind;
The albatross did follow,
And every day, for food or play,
Came to the mariners' hollo!

"In mist or cloud, on mast or shroud,   75
It perched for vespers nine;
Whiles all the night, through fog-smoke white,
Glimmered the white moonshine."

The ancient
mariner inhospi-
tably killeth the
pious bird of
good omen.

"God save thee, ancient mariner,
From the fiends that plague thee thus!   80
Why look'st thou so?"—'With my crossbow
I shot the albatross!

PART II

"The sun now rose upon the right;
Out of the sea came he,
Still hid in mist, and on the left   85
Went down into the sea.

"And the good south wind still blew behind,
But no sweet bird did follow,
Nor any day for food or play,
Came to the mariners' hollo!   90

His shipmates cry
out against the
ancient mariner
for killing the bird
of good luck.

But when the fog
cleared off, they
justify the same,
and thus make
themselves
accomplices in
the crime.

The fair breeze
continues; the
ship enters the
Pacific Ocean,
and sails north-
.ward, even till it
reaches the Line.

"And I had done a hellish thing,
And it would work 'em woe;
For all averred, I had killed the bird
That made the breeze to blow.
'Ah wretch!' said they, 'the bird to slay,   95
That made the breeze to blow!'

"Nor dim nor red, like God's own head,
The glorious sun uprist;
Then all averred, I had killed the bird
That brought the fog and mist.   100
' 'Twas right,' said they, 'such birds to slay,
That bring the fog and mist.'

"The fair breeze blew, the white foam flew,
The furrow followed free;
We were the first that ever burst   105
Into that silent sea.

"Down dropt the breeze, the sails dropt down,
'Twas sad as sad could be;
And we did speak only to break
The silence of the sea!   110

The ship hath
been suddenly
becalmed.

"All in a hot and copper sky,
The bloody sun, at noon,
Right up above the mast did stand,
No bigger than the moon.

"Day after day, day after day,   115
We struck, nor breath nor motion;
As idle as a painted ship
Upon a painted ocean.

"Water, water, everywhere,   120
And all the boards did shrink;
Water, water, everywhere,
Nor any drop to drink.

And the alba-
tross begins to
be avenged.

"The very deep did rot.   O Christ!
That ever this should be!
Yea, slimy things did crawl with legs   125
Upon the slimy sea.

"About, about, in reel and rout,
The death-fires danced at night;
The water, like a witch's oils,
Burnt green and blue and white.   130

"And some in dreams assurèd were
Of the spirit that plagued us so;
Nine fathom deep he had followed us
From the land of mist and snow,

A spirit had fol-
lowed them; one
of the invisible
inhabitants of
this planet,
neither departed
souls nor angels.

"And every tongue, through utter drought,[6]   135
Was withered at the root;
We could not speak, no more than if
We had been choked with soot.

"Ah, well-a-day! what evil looks
Had I from old and young!   140
Instead of the cross, the albatross
About my neck was hung.

The shipmates,
in their sore dis-
tress, would fain
throw the whole
guilt on the
ancient mariner;
in sign whereof
they hang the
dead sea-bird
round his neck.

---

[6]*drought*, thirst.

ILLUSTRATION BY J. NOEL PATON

Part III

The ancient
mariner beholdeth
a sign in the ele-
ment afar off.

"There passed a weary time. Each throat
Was parched, and glazed each eye.
A weary time! a weary time!   145
How glazed each weary eye!
When, looking westward, I beheld
A something in the sky.

"At first it seemed a little speck,
And then it seemed a mist;   150
It moved and moved, and took at last
A certain shape, I wist.

"A speck, a mist, a shape, I wist!
And still it neared and neared;
As if it dodged a water-sprite,   155
It plunged and tacked and veered.

At its nearer
approach, it
seemeth him to
be a ship; and at
a dear ransom he
freeth his speech
from the bonds
of thirst.

"With throats unslaked, with black lips baked
We could nor laugh nor wail;
Through utter drought all dumb we stood!
I bit my arm, I sucked the blood,   160
And cried, 'A sail! a sail!'

"With throats unslaked, with black lips baked,
Agape they heard me call.
Gramercy! they for joy did grin,   A flash of joy;
And all at once their breath drew in,   165
As they were drinking all.

"'See! see!' I cried, 'she tacks no more
Hither, to work us weal—
Without a breeze, without a tide,
She steadies with upright keel!'   170

And horror fol-
lows. For can it
be a *ship* that
comes onward
without wind
or tide?

"The western wave was all aflame;
The day was well-nigh done;
Almost upon the western wave
Rested the broad bright sun;
When that strange shape drove suddenly   175
Betwixt us and the sun.

"And straight the sun was flecked with bars,   It seemeth him
(Heaven's Mother send us grace!)   but the skeleton
As if through a dungeon grate he peered   of a ship.
With broad and burning face.   180

"'Alas!' thought I, and my heart beat loud,
'How fast she nears and nears!
Are those her sails that glance in the sun,
Like restless gossameres?

"'Are those her ribs through which the sun   185
Did peer, as through a grate?
And is that woman all her crew?
Is that a Death? and are there two?
Is Death that woman's mate?'

And its ribs are
seen as bars on
the face of the
setting sun.
    The specter-
woman and her
Death-mate, and
no other on board
the skeleton ship.

"Her lips were red, her looks were free,   190
Her locks were yellow as gold;
Her skin was as white as leprosy,
The nightmare, Life-in-Death, was she,
Who thicks man's blood with cold.

Like vessel,
like crew!

"The naked hulk alongside came,   195
And the twain were casting dice;
'The game is done! I've won! I've won!'
Quoth she, and whistles thrice.

Death and Life-
in-Death have
diced for the
ship's crew, and
she (the latter)
winneth the
ancient mariner.

"The sun's rim dips; the stars rush out;
At one stride comes the dark;   200
With far-heard whisper, o'er the sea,
Off shot the specter bark.

No twilight within
the courts of the
sun.

At the rising of
the moon,

"We listened and looked sideways up!
Fear at my heart, as at a cup,
My lifeblood seemed to sip!   205
The stars were dim, and thick the night,
The steersman's face by his lamp gleamed white;
From the sails the dew did drip—
Till clomb above the eastern bar
The hornèd moon, with one bright star   210
Within the nether tip.

One after another,

"One after one, by the star-dogged moon,
Too quick for groan or sigh,
Each turned his face with a ghastly pang,
And cursed me with his eye.   215

His shipmates
drop down dead.

"Four times fifty living men
(And I heard nor sigh nor groan),
With heavy thump, a lifeless lump,
They dropped down one by one.

But Life-in-Death
begins her work on
the ancient
mariner.

"The souls did from their bodies fly—   220
They fled to bliss or woe!
And every soul, it passed me by,
Like the whizz of my crossbow!"

PART IV

The wedding guest
feareth that a spirit
is talking to him;

"I fear thee, ancient mariner!
I fear thy skinny hand!   225
And thou art long, and lank, and brown,
As is the ribbed sea sand.

"I fear thee and thy glittering eye,
And thy skinny hand, so brown!"—
"Fear not, fear not, thou wedding guest!   230
This body dropped not down.

But the ancient
mariner assureth
him of his bodily
life, and pro-
ceedeth to relate
his horrible
penance.

"Alone, alone, all, all alone,
Alone on a wide wide sea!
And never a saint took pity on
My soul in agony.   235

He despiseth the
creatures of the
calm,

"The many men, so beautiful!
And they all dead did lie;
And a thousand thousand slimy things
Lived on; and so did I.

And envieth that
they should live,
and so many lie
dead.

"I looked upon the rotting sea,   240
And drew my eyes away;
I looked upon the rotting deck,
And there the dead men lay.

"I looked to heaven, and tried to pray;
But or ever a prayer had gusht,   245
A wicked whisper came, and made
My heart as dry as dust.

"I closed my lids, and kept them close,
And the balls like pulses beat;
For the sky and the sea, and the sea and the sky,   250
Lay like a load on my weary eye,
And the dead were at my feet.

"The cold sweat melted from their limbs,
Nor rot nor reek did they;
The look with which they looked on me   255
Had never passed away.

But the curse liveth for him in the eye of the dead men.

"An orphan's curse would drag to hell
A spirit from on high;
But oh! more horrible than that
Is the curse in a dead man's eye!   260
Seven days, seven nights, I saw that curse,
And yet I could not die.

"The moving moon went up the sky,
And nowhere did abide;
Softly she was going up,   265
And a star or two beside.

In his loneliness and fixedness he yearneth towards the journeying moon, and the stars that still sojourn, yet still move onward; and everywhere the blue sky belongs to them, and is their appointed rest, and their native country, and their own natural homes, which they enter unannounced, as lords that are certainly expected, and yet there is a silent joy at their arrival.

"Her beams bemocked the sultry main,
Like April hoarfrost spread;
But where the ship's huge shadow lay,
The charmèd water burnt alway   270
A still and awful red.

"Beyond the shadow of the ship
I watched the water snakes;
They moved in tracks of shining white,
And when they reared, the elfish light   275
Fell off in hoary flakes.

By the light of the moon he beholdeth God's creatures of the great calm.

"Within the shadow of the ship
I watched their rich attire;
Blue, glossy green, and velvet black,
They coiled and swam; and every track   280
Was a flash of golden fire.

"O happy living things! no tongue
Their beauty might declare.
A spring of love gushed from my heart,

Their beauty and their happiness.

<table>
<tr><td>He blesseth them
in his heart.</td><td>And I blessed them unaware!
Sure my kind saint took pity on me,
And I blessed them unaware.</td><td>285</td></tr>
</table>

He blesseth them
in his heart.

And I blessed them unaware!
Sure my kind saint took pity on me,
And I blessed them unaware.

285

The spell begins
to break.

"The selfsame moment I could pray;
And from my neck so free
The albatross fell off, and sank
Like lead into the sea.

290

Part V

"O sleep! it is a gentle thing,
Beloved from pole to pole!
To Mary Queen the praise be given!
She sent the gentle sleep from heaven,
That slid into my soul.

295

By grace of the
holy Mother, the
ancient mariner
is refreshed with
rain.

"The silly buckets on the deck,
That had so long remained,
I dreamt that they were filled with dew;
And when I awoke, it rained.

300

"My lips were wet, my throat was cold,
My garments all were dank;
Sure I had drunken in my dreams,
And still my body drank.

"I moved, and could not feel my limbs;
I was so light—almost
I thought that I had died in sleep,
And was a blessèd ghost.

305

He heareth sounds
and seeth strange
sights and com-
motions in the sky
and the element.

"And soon I heard a roaring wind;
It did not come anear;
But with its sound it shook the sails.
That were so thin and sere.

310

"The upper air burst into life!
And a hundred fire flags sheen,
To and fro they were hurried about;
And to and fro, and in and out,
The wan stars danced between.

315

"And the coming wind did roar more loud,
And the sails did sigh like sedge;
And the rain poured down from one black
    cloud;
The moon was at its edge.

320

"The thick black cloud was cleft, and still
The moon was at its side.
Like waters shot from some high crag,
The lightning fell with never a jag,   325
A river steep and wide.

"The loud wind never reached the ship,
Yet now the ship moved on!
Beneath the lightning and the moon
The dead men gave a groan.   330

"They groaned, they stirred, they all uprose,
Nor spake, nor moved their eyes;
It had been strange, even in a dream,
To have seen those dead men rise.

"The helmsman steered, the ship moved on;   335
Yet never a breeze upblew;
The mariners all 'gan work the ropes,
Where they were wont to do;
They raised their limbs like lifeless tools—
We were a ghastly crew.   340

"The body of my brother's son
Stood by me, knee to knee;
The body and I pulled at one rope,
But he said naught to me."

"I fear thee, ancient mariner!"—   345
"Be calm, thou wedding guest!
'Twas not those souls that fled in pain,
Which to their corses⁷ came again,
But a troop of spirits blest;

"For when it dawned—they dropped their
        arms,   350
And clustered round the mast;
Sweet sounds rose slowly through their mouths,
And from their bodies passed.

"Around, around, flew each sweet sound,
Then darted to the sun;   365
Slowly the sounds came back again,
Now mixed, now one by one.

"Sometimes a-dropping from the sky
I heard the skylark sing;
Sometimes all little birds that are,   360

⁷*corses*, dead bodies.

The bodies of the
ship's crew are
inspired, and
the ship moves
on;

But not by the
souls of the men,
nor by demons of
earth or middle
air, but by a
blessèd troop of
angelic spirits,
sent down by the
invocation of the
guardian saint.

How they seemed to fill the sea and air
With their sweet jargoning!

"And now 'twas like all instruments,
Now like a lonely flute;
And now it is an angel's song,   365
That makes the heavens be mute.

"It ceased; yet still the sails made on
A pleasant noise till noon,
A noise like of a hidden brook
In the leafy month of June,   370
That to the sleeping woods all night
Singeth a quiet tune.

"Till noon we quietly sailed on,
Yet never a breeze did breathe;
Slowly and smoothly went the ship,   375
Moved onward from beneath.

The lonesome   "Under the keel nine fathom deep,
spirit from the   From the land of mist and snow,
south pole carries   The spirit slid; and it was he
on the ship as far   That made the ship to go.   380
as the Line, in   The sails at noon left off their tune,
obedience to the   And the ship stood still also.
angelic troop,
but still requireth   "The sun, right up above the mast,
vengeance.   Had fixed her to the ocean;
                      But in a minute she 'gan stir   385
                      With a short uneasy motion—
                      Backwards and forwards half her length,
                      With a short uneasy motion.

                      "Then, like a pawing horse let go,
The Polar Spirit's   She made a sudden bound;   390
fellow-demons, the   It flung the blood into my head,
invisible inhabit-   And I fell down in a swound.
ants of the element,
take part in his   "How long in that same fit I lay,
wrong; and two of   I have not to declare;
them relate, one to   But ere my living life returned,   395
the other, that   I heard, and in my soul discerned,
penance long and   Two voices in the air.
heavy for the
ancient mariner   " 'Is it he?' quoth one, 'is this the man?
hath been accorded   By Him who died on cross,
to the Polar   With his cruel bow he laid full low   400
Spirit, who return-   The harmless albatross.
eth southward.

" 'The spirit who bideth by himself
In the land of mist and snow,
He loved the bird that loved the man
Who shot him with his bow.'   405

"The other was a softer voice,
As soft as honeydew.
Quoth he, 'The man hath penance[8] done,
And penance more will do.'

Part VI

First Voice

" 'But tell me, tell me! speak again,   410
Thy soft response renewing—
What makes that ship drive on so fast?
What is the ocean doing?'

Second Voice

" 'Still as a slave before his lord,
The ocean hath no blast;   415
His great bright eye most silently
Up to the moon is cast—

" 'If he may know which way to go;
For she guides him, smooth or grim.
See, brother, see! how graciously   420
She looketh down on him.'

First Voice

" 'But why drives on that ship so fast,
Without or wave or wind?'

Second Voice

" 'The air is cut away before,   425
And closes from behind.

The mariner hath been cast into a trance; for the angelic power causeth the vessel to drive northward faster than human life could endure.

" 'Fly, brother, fly! more high, more high!
Or we shall be belated;
For slow and slow that ship will go,
When the mariner's trance is abated.'

"I woke, and we were sailing on   430
As in a gentle weather;
'Twas night, calm night, the moon was high;
The dead men stood together.

The supernatural motion is retarded; the mariner awakes, and his penance begins anew.

---

[8]*penance,* self-imposed suffering.

"All stood together on the deck
For a charnel dungeon fitter;   435
All fixed on me their stony eyes,
That in the moon did glitter.

"The pang, the curse, with which they died
Had never passed away;
I could not draw my eyes from theirs,   440
Nor turn them up to pray.

The curse is   "And now this spell was snapped; once more
finally expiated. I viewed the ocean green,
And looked far forth, yet little saw
Of what had else been seen—   445

"Like one that on a lonesome road
Doth walk in fear and dread,
And having once turned round walks on,
And turns no more his head,
Because he knows a frightful fiend   450
Doth close behind him tread.

"But soon there breathed a wind on me,
Nor sound nor motion made;
Its path was not upon the sea,
In ripple or in shade.   455

"It raised my hair, it fanned my cheek
Like a meadow gale of spring—
It mingled strangely with my fears,
Yet it felt like a welcoming.

"Swiftly, swiftly, flew the ship,   460
Yet she sailed softly too;
Sweetly, sweetly, blew the breeze—
On me alone it blew.

And the ancient   "Oh! dream of joy! is this indeed
mariner beholdeth   The lighthouse top I see?   465
his native country. Is this the hill?   Is this the kirk?
Is this mine own countree?

"We drifted o'er the harbor bar,
And I with sobs did pray—
'O let me be awake, my God!   470
Or let me sleep alway.'

"The harbor bay was clear as glass,
So smoothly it was strewn;
And on the bay the moonlight lay,   **475**
And the shadow of the moon.

"The rock shone bright, the kirk no less,
That stands above the rock;
The moonlight steeped in silentness
The steady weathercock.

"And the bay was white with silent light,   **480**   The angelic spirits
Till, rising from the same,   leave the dead
Full many shapes, that shadows were,   bodies,
In crimson colors came.

"A little distance from the prow   And appear in
Those crimson shadows were;   **485**   their own forms
I turned my eyes upon the deck—   of light.
O, Christ! what saw I there!

"Each corse lay flat, lifeless and flat,
And, by the holy rood!
A man all light, a seraph[9] man,   **490**
On every corse there stood.

"This seraph band, each waved his hand;
It was a heavenly sight!
They stood as signals to the land,
Each one a lovely light;   **495**

"This seraph band, each waved his hand,
No voice did they impart—
No voice; but oh! the silence sank
Like music on my heart.

                                                               500
"But soon I heard the dash of oars,
I heard the pilot's cheer;
My head was turned perforce away,
And I saw a boat appear.

"The pilot and the pilot's boy,   **505**
I heard them coming fast;
Dear Lord in heaven! it was a joy
The dead men could not blast.

"I saw a third—I heard his voice—
It is the hermit good!
He singeth loud his godly hymns   **510**

---
[9]*seraph,* an angel.

ILLUSTRATION BY J. NOEL PATON

That he makes in the wood.
He'll shrieve[10] my soul, he'll wash away
The albatross's blood.

PART VII

The hermit of the wood

"This hermit good lives in that wood
Which slopes down to the sea.   515
How loudly his sweet voice he rears!
He loves to talk with marineres
That come from a far countree.

"He kneels at morn and noon and eve;
He hath a cushion plump;   520
It is the moss that wholly hides
The rotted old oak stump.

"The skiff boat neared; I heard them talk,
'Why, this is strange, I trow!
Where are those lights so many and fair,   525
That signal made but now?'

---

[10]*shrieve*, hear confession and grant forgiveness.

" 'Strange, by my faith!' the hermit said—
'And they answered not our cheer!
The planks look warped! and see those sails,
How thin they are and sere!   630
I never saw aught like to them,
Unless perchance it were

" 'Brown skeletons of leaves that lag
My forest brook along,
When the ivy tod is heavy with snow,   535
And the owlet whoops to the wolf below,
That eats the she-wolf's young.'

" 'Dear Lord! it hath a fiendish look,'
The pilot made reply;
'I am afeared.'—'Push on, push on!'   540
Said the hermit cheerily.

"The boat came closer to the ship,
But I nor spake nor stirred;
The boat came close beneath the ship,
And straight a sound was heard.   545

"Under the water it rumbled on,
Still louder and more dread;
It reached the ship, it split the bay;
The ship went down like lead.

"Stunned by that loud and dreadful sound,   550
Which sky and ocean smote,
Like one that hath been seven days drowned,
My body lay afloat;
But swift as dreams, myself I found   555
Within the pilot's boat.

"Upon the whirl, where sank the ship,
The boat spun round and round;
And all was still, save that the hill
Was telling of the sound.

"I moved my lips—the pilot shrieked   560
And fell down in a fit;
The holy hermit raised his eyes,
And prayed where he did sit.

"I took the oars; the pilot's boy,   565
Who now doth crazy go,
Laughed loud and long, and all the while

Approacheth the ship with wonder.

The ship suddenly sinketh.

The ancient mariner is saved in the pilot's boat.

ILLUSTRATION BY J. NOEL PATON

His eyes went to and fro.
'Ha, ha!' quoth he, 'full plain I see,
The Devil knows how to row.'

"And now, all in my own countree,   570
I stood on the firm land!
The hermit stepped forth from the boat,
And scarcely he could stand.

The ancient
mariner earnestly
entreateth the
hermit to shrieve
him; and the
penance of life
falls on him.

" 'O shrieve me, shrieve me, holy man!'
The hermit crossed his brow.   575
'Say quick,' quoth he, 'I bid thee say—
What manner of man art thou?'

"Forthwith this frame of mine was wrenched
With a woeful agony,
Which forced me to begin my tale;   580
And then it left me free.

And ever and
anon throughout
his future life an
agony constraineth
him to travel from
land to land;

"Since then, at an uncertain hour,
That agony returns;
And till my ghastly tale is told,
This heart within me burns.   585

"I pass, like night, from land to land;
I have strange power of speech;
That moment that his face I see,
I know the man that must hear me;   590
To him my tale I teach.

"What loud uproar bursts from that door!
The wedding guests are there;
But in the garden bower the bride
And bridemaids singing are;   595
And hark the little vesper bell,
Which biddeth me to prayer!

"O wedding guest! this soul hath been
Alone on a wide wide sea:
So lonely 'twas, that God himself   600
Scarce seemèd there to be.

"O, sweeter than the marriage feast,
'Tis sweeter far to me,
To walk together to the kirk
With a goodly company—

                                                605

"To walk together to the kirk,
And all together pray,
While each to his great Father bends—
Old men, and babes, and loving friends,
And youths and maidens gay!

"Farewell, farewell! but this I tell   610
To thee, thou wedding guest!
He prayeth well who loveth well
Both man and bird and beast.

And to teach, by
his own example,
love and rever-
ence to all things
that God made
and loveth.

"He prayeth best who loveth best
All things both great and small;   615
For the dear God who loveth us,
He made and loveth all."

The mariner, whose eye is bright,
Whose beard with age is hoar,
Is gone; and now the wedding guest   620
Turned from the bridegroom's door.

He went like one that hath been stunned,
And is of sense forlorn;
A sadder and a wiser man
He rose the morrow morn.   625

For Thought and Discussion

1. Is the method of character portrayal used in "The Ancient Mariner" direct or indirect? Explain. Do you consider the method used more effective than the opposite method would have been? Why?

2. How does the nature of the crime committed by the mariner add to the effectiveness of such a story? Are his punishment and his absolution in keeping with the nature of the crime?

3. What phase of the ordeal undergone by the mariner do you consider most wracking?

4. How is the passage of time indicated in the poem itself?

5. Of what value, if any, did you find the marginal glosses of this selection?

6. The old English ballads upon which this selection was modeled were marked by lack of descriptive passages and by lack of expression concerning inner or personal feelings. Does it differ from the model in the first, in the last, or in both respects?

7. Which of the following features lend themselves best to a screen version of the story—the appearance of the real characters, the descriptive sea and sky pictures, the plot, the supernatural elements?

8. What do you think of the relative value of sights and sounds as utilized in the poem to create an air of beauty and mystery and charm? Quote passages that give beautiful pictorial effects.

9. If this had not been an assigned selection, would you have finished reading it? Do you think you would have continued reading it for the thread of the plot or for the beauty of the descriptive passages or for some other reason?

10. Would you have included lines 610-617? If not, why not? In making your answer, consider whether a tale of fantasy logically lends itself to ethical teachings.

11. How does this poem compare with certain prose mystery stories you have read? Wherein does it differ from them?

12. Compare the references to sleep in lines 292-296 with the passage in *Macbeth*, Act II, Scene II.

13. "The Ancient Mariner" resulted from a plan made by Coleridge and by Wordsworth to help them defray expenses while they, together with Dorothy Wordsworth, were on a walking tour. Articles written under such circumstances today would probably be termed "pot-boilers." Do you think the term applicable to this poem? Justify your answer.

KUBLA KHAN
SAMUEL TAYLOR COLERIDGE

["Kubla Khan"[1] was composed in a dream. Upon awakening Coleridge began to write it down just as he had dreamed it, but he was interrupted by a visitor. After the visitor left, Coleridge was unable to recall the remainder of the poem.]

IN Xanadu[2] did Kubla Khan
A stately pleasure-dome decree;
Where Alph, the sacred river, ran
Through caverns measureless to man
    Down to a sunless sea.   5

So twice five miles of fertile ground
With walls and towers were girdled round;
And here were gardens bright with sinuous rills,
Where blossomed many an incense-bearing tree;
And here were forests ancient as the hills, 10
Enfolding sunny spots of greenery.

But, oh! that deep romantic chasm which slanted
Down the green hill athwart a cedarn cover!
A savage place! as holy and enchanted
As e'er beneath a waning moon was haunted 15
By woman wailing for her demon-lover!
And from this chasm, with ceaseless turmoil seething,
As if this earth in fast, thick pants were breathing,
A mighty fountain momently was forced;
Amid whose swift, half-intermitted burst 20
Huge fragments vaulted like rebounding hail,

Or chaffy grain beneath the thresher's flail.
And 'mid these dancing rocks at once and ever
It flung up momently the sacred river.
Five miles meandering with a mazy motion 25
Through wood and dale the sacred river ran,
Then reached the caverns measureless to man,
And sank in tumult to a lifeless ocean.
And 'mid this tumult Kubla heard from far
Ancestral voices prophesying war! 30

The shadow of the dome of pleasure
Floated midway on the waves;
Where was heard the mingled measure
From the fountain and the caves.
It was a miracle of rare device, 35
A sunny pleasure-dome with caves of ice!

A damsel with a dulcimer
In a vision once I saw;
It was an Abyssinian maid,
And on her dulcimer she played, 40
Singing of Mount Abora.
Could I revive within me
Her symphony and song,
To such a deep delight 'twould win me,
That with music loud and long, 45
I would build that dome in air,
That sunny dome! those caves of ice!
And all who heard should see them there—
And all should cry, "Beware! Beware!—
His flashing eyes, his floating hair! 50
Weave a circle round him thrice,
And close your eyes with holy dread,
For he on honey-dew hath fed,
And drunk the milk of Paradise."

[1]*Kubla Khan*, Kubla the Khan, or Emperor.
[2]*Xanadu*, a region in Tartary.

For Thought and Discussion

1. Explain why "Kubla Khan" is considered by many the most perfect romantic poem in the English language.
2. What do you see and how do you feel as you read the poem aloud? Do you like the fantastic imagery and the sound?

SAMUEL TAYLOR COLERIDGE 1772-1834

Coleridge, the Precocious Child. That Coleridge[1] was precocious and that he was also unhappy as a child was due largely to his parents. His father, a gentle, kindly scholar, the pastor of a country church, and the teacher of a country school, contributed much to the genius of his son. Doubtless it was because of his teaching that the small boy, at the age of five, had read and could remember much from both the Bible and *The Arabian Nights*. His mother contributed to his unhappiness. For some reason she did not love her son.

Coleridge in a Charity School. In the charity school, Christ's Hospital, Coleridge, like his friend, Charles Lamb, who was there at the same time, was desperately unhappy. The following anecdote recounts one of the few pleasant incidents of that period of his life.

Coleridge, while walking along the street one day dreaming as usual over some medieval story, accidentally touched the pocket of an old gentleman who was passing. The man took him to be a pick-pocket and started to hand him over to the police. "I am not a pick-pocket, Sir," protested the boy; "I only thought I was Leander swimming the Hellespont!"

The story concludes with the statement that the man was so greatly pleased that he immediately took steps to see that the boy who so loved reading that he lost himself in it was supplied with books.

Coleridge at Cambridge. Although he stayed in college three years, Coleridge left there without having gained a degree. To him his college associations perhaps meant more than text-books, for it was at Cambridge that he met Southey, another ardent young revolutionary spirit with whom he later planned a Utopian pantisocracy, which if it had been successful, would have anticipated the Brook Farm experiment in America. It is interesting to note that his friend Southey, though not a poet of the first order, later had the poet-laureateship conferred upon him.

The Poet's Unhappy Marriage. It seemed fated that Coleridge, if he had a home, must have an unhappy one. He and Southey married sisters, but Coleridge was neither provident nor pleasant to live with, and soon the task of caring for both families

---

[1] *Coleridge*, long ō as in "coal."

SAMUEL TAYLOR COLERIDGE

fell to the lot of the less talented but more amiable and thrifty Southey.

A Slave to the Poppy Plant. It seems almost ironical that the nature-loving poet, Coleridge, should have brought down calumny upon himself because of the misuse of a flower. Some excuse his weakness in taking opium on the score of ill-health; others think he knowingly sought "the dream path of the poppy." However that may be, this weakness brought still more sorrow and misery into an already tragic life.

His Magic Wand. As a conversationalist, a minister, and a lecturer (although he could never be depended upon to fulfill lecture engagements), Coleridge was pre-eminent. Wordsworth says of him: "Throughout a long-drawn summer day would this man

talk to you in low, equable, but clear and musical tones concerning
things human and divine; marshalling all history, harmonizing all
experiments, probing the depth of your consciousness and revealing visions of glory and error to the imagination." Wordsworth,
a profound admirer of Coleridge, might be thought partisan in his
comment, but all Coleridge's friends and critics agree in this estimate. Hazlitt after listening to Coleridge on one occasion said, "As
he (Coleridge) gave out his text, his voice rose like a stream of
distilled perfumes . . . . it seemed to me as if the sound might
have floated in solemn silence through the universe" . . . . and
again he said: "His genius had angelic wings, and fed on manna.
He talked on forever. His thoughts did not seem to come with
labor and effort, but as if the wings of imagination lifted him off
his feet. His voice rolled on the ear like a pealing organ and its
sound alone was the music of thought." Thus did the man of grief
through the magic of his tongue bring to the world gladness.

Coleridge, the Scholar, Translator, and Critic. Coleridge was
a dreamer, but he was more; he was a profound scholar. He was
almost a life-long student of metaphysics, and because of his trip
to Germany with the poet Wordsworth, decided to translate into
English the teachings of the German philosopher Kant. Coleridge
is to be praised also for bringing to the field of criticism something
of the new romantic feeling, for criticism needed greatly to be
freed from the cold formalism of the eighteenth century.

Coleridge's Masterpieces. With what is known as the medieval aspect of the romantic movement in literature Coleridge is
inseparably connected, and he is also inseparably connected with
the movement emphasizing the beauty of the commonplace in nature and in humanity. He has, however, a quality which is peculiarly his own, one which stamps him as one of the first and most
interesting of the poets to use mystery and horror themes. His
characters suffer not physical but spiritual terror and are redeemed
by the power of love. Rich poetic diction and the charm of haunting and mysterious beauty characterize Coleridge's three great
imaginative poems, "Kubla Khan" (kōō′ blä khän), "Christabel,"
and "The Rime of the Ancient Mariner."

Coleridge's Death. The poet, whose sad and tragic life was
in marked contrast with the tranquil existence of his friend
Wordsworth, died in 1834 and was buried in High Gate. Some
critic has voiced the opinion that this stanza from "Remorse" is
a fitting epitaph for him:

"Hark, the cadence dies away on the quiet moonlit sea;
   The boatmen rest their oars and say 'Miserere Domini.' "
(Have pity, O, Lord.)

OVERHEARD ON A SALTMARSH
HAROLD MONRO

[So whimsical and colorful is this burst of imaginative fancy, characteristic of Harold Monro, that one has but to read the lines to see the nymph and the elf and hear the "No!" of the former in answer to the "Give them me" of the latter.]

NYMPH, nymph, what are your beads?
Green glass, goblin. Why do you stare at them?
Give them me.

    No.

Give them me. Give them me.

    No.

Then I will howl all night in the reeds,

Lie in the mud and howl for them.

Goblin, why do you love them so?

They are better than stars or water,
Better than voices of winds that sing,
Better than any man's fair daughter,
Your green glass beads on a silver ring.

Hush, I stole them out of the moon.

Give me your beads. I desire them.

    No.

I will howl in a deep lagoon
For your green glass beads, I love them so.
Give them me. Give them.

    No.

For Thought and Discussion

1. Is the love of fairy lore restricted to childhood or do you, on occasion, feel responsive to a touch of whimsy?
2. List poetic elements notable in the poem.

❧

PIPING DOWN THE VALLEYS WILD
WILLIAM BLAKE

[Critics ask, "Was the writer of songs like 'The Tiger' and 'Piping Down the Valleys Wild' mad or inspired?" Perhaps both. At any rate Blake, 1755-1827, lived a rather long life and was artist enough to illustrate the works of the best writers of his time and to engrave his own poems upon plates of original, beautiful, but startling design.]

PIPING down the valleys wild,
    Piping songs of pleasant glee,
On a cloud I saw a child,
    And he laughing said to me:

"Pipe a song about a lamb!"   5
    So I piped with merry cheer.
"Piper, pipe that song again."
    So I piped; he wept to hear.

"Drop thy pipe, thy happy pipe;
    Sing thy songs of happy cheer!" 10
So I sung the same again,
    While he wept with joy to hear.

"Piper, sit thee down and write
  In a book, that all may read."
So he vanished from my sight;   15
  And I plucked a hollow reed,

And I made a rural pen,
  And I stained the water clear,
And I wrote my happy songs
  Every child may joy to hear.

For Thought and Discussion

    1. Why did the child weep when he heard the piper?   Does happiness often have this effect on people?
    2. Why did the poet write his "happy songs"?

DUCKS

FREDERICK WILLIAM HARVEY

[Frederick William Harvey was in
the English army during the World
War. "The Bugler" is the most famous of his war poems. "Ducks" is
interesting for its humor and originality.]

I

FROM troubles of the world
    I turn to ducks,
Beautiful comical things
Sleeping or curled
Their heads beneath white wings   5
By water cool,
Or finding curious things
To eat in various mucks
Beneath the pool
Tails uppermost, or waddling   10
Sailor-like on the shores
Of ponds, or paddling
—Left! right!—with fanlike feet
Which are for steady oars
When they (white galleys) float   15
Each bird a boat
Rippling at will the sweet
Wide waterway. . . . .
When night is fallen *you* creep
Upstairs, but drakes and dillies   20
Nest with pale water stars,
Moonbeams and shadow bars,
And water lilies;
Fearful too much to sleep

Since they've no locks   25
To click against the teeth
Of weasel and fox.
And warm beneath
Are eggs of cloudy green
Whence hungry rats and lean   30
Would stealthily suck
New life, but for the mien,
The bold ferocious mien
Of the mother duck.

II

Yes, ducks are valiant things   35
On nests of twigs and straws,
And ducks are soothy things
And lovely on the lake
When the sunlight draws
Thereon their pictures dim   40
In colors cool.
And when beneath the pool
They dabble, and when they swim
And make their rippling rings,
Oh, ducks are beautiful things!   45

But ducks are comical things—
As comical as you.
Quack!
They waddle round, they do.
They eat all sorts of things,   50
And then they quack.
By barn and stable and stack
They wander at their will,

But if you go too near
They look at you through black ⁵⁵
Small topaz-tinted eyes
And wish you ill.
Triangular and clear
They leave their curious track
In mud at the water's edge, ⁶⁰
And there amid the sedge
And slime they gobble and peer
Saying, "Quack! quack!"

III

When God had finished the stars and
whirl of colored suns
He turned His mind from big things
to fashion little ones, ⁶⁵
Beautiful tiny things (like daisies)
He made, and then

He made the comical ones in case the
minds of men
Should stiffen and become
Dull, humorless and glum;
And so forgetful of their Maker be ⁷⁰
As to take even themselves—*quite
seriously.*
Caterpillars and cats are lively and
excellent puns;
All God's jokes are good—even the
practical ones!
And as for the duck, I think God
must have smiled a bit
Seeing those bright eyes blink on the
day He fashioned it. ⁷⁵
And He's probably laughing still at
the sound that came out of its
bill!

For Thought and Discussion

1. Why does the author write about ducks?
2. Is his description of them realistic?
3. Notice the verse form. Is it suited to the subject treated?
4. According to the poet why did God create comical things like ducks? Note the twofold purpose.
5. What do the above purposes suggest as to the conception the author holds of the Creator and His relation to men? Is this conception conventional?

Additional Readings

Barrie, James: *Farewell to Miss Julie Logan*

Buchan, John: *Huntingtower*
A Prince of Captivity
The Magic Walking-Stick

Colum, Padraic: *Poems*

De La Mare, Walter: *Peacock Pie*

Dunsany, Lord: *Tales of Wonder*
Plays of Gods and Men

Ervine, St. John: *Mary, Mary, Quite Contrary*

French, J. L.: *Great Sea Stories*

Hedin, Sven: *Across the Gobi Desert*

Masefield, John: *The Bird of Dawning*
A Tale of Troy
Mitchell, Captain Pryce: *Deep Water*
Morton, H. V.: *Land of Heather*
Reade, Charles: *The Cloister and the Hearth*
Sabatini, Rafael: *Scaramouche*
Captain Blood
Walpole, Hugh: *Harmer John*
Wetjen, Albert Richard: *Captains All*
Way for a Sailor!
Youth Walks on the Highway
Yeats, William Butler: *The Land of Heart's Desire*

Faith and Reverence

FAITH AND REVERENCE

"God's in His heaven—
All's right with the world!"

SO SANG the sunny-hearted little girl whom Browning described in "Pippa Passes," a little girl who, because her heart was singing with faith, helped to make happier the affairs of all who on a certain holiday overheard her song. Thus literature identifies the quality that makes right relationships between man and man and between man and God. Such literature is beautiful and inspiring. It pictures strong characters who exhibit staunch belief in themselves, in their fellowmen, and in God; characters who, though self-confident, are neither self-centered nor self-righteous but, instead, are men of reverent mien who believe in themselves because they are a part of the Infinite.

In a very practical sense faith is spoken of as what a man lives by. Upon faith he establishes his home and all the other institutions necessary to his life as an individual and as a member of society. In a spiritual sense, too, literature attributes man's achievements to faith. Faith is a source of inspiration to man. It is by faith that he sees and follows what Tennyson calls *The Gleam*. It is through faith that he has courage to go forward in the face of difficulties and disasters, confident in the belief that, though fear and doubt and grief may come and wrong apparently prevail for a time, these will never triumph, since, as Browning further affirms in "Asolando," men

".... fall to rise, are baffled to fight better,
Sleep to wake".... and
"Greet the unseen with a cheer."

Faith, reverence, immortality—writers of literature, sacred and profane, have dwelt upon these themes. Many have pictured faith as a guide, a shield, a protector. To many a person, faith is, as it was to Newman, a "pillar of cloud by day" and a "pillar of fire by night,"[1] leading him back toward the shores of eternity from whence he came, there to meet his "Pilot face to face"[2] and be reunited with those whom he "has loved long since and lost awhile."

---

[1]Nehemiah 9:19. See Newman's title for the song generally known as "Lead, Kindly Light" from which "has loved long since and lost awhile" is quoted.
[2]From Tennyson's "Crossing the Bar."

"THE YEAR'S AT THE SPRING,
THE DAY'S AT THE MORN;
MORNING'S AT SEVEN;
THE HILLSIDE'S DEW-PEARLED"

SONGS FROM "PIPPA PASSES"
ROBERT BROWNING

[Through her gift of happy song a little silk weaver, Pippa, transforms and inspires to higher conceptions of living the people who hear her as she passes along the streets of Asolo, a little mountain side town of North Italy. Such is the theme of the story —"Pippa Passes"—which Browning conceived one day as he walked along through the wood near London. He later developed the idea into a dramatic selection of four acts at the beginning of each of which he placed a lyric. The loveliest of these lyrics are "New Year's Hymn" and "The Year's at the Spring."]

NEW YEAR'S HYMN

ALL service ranks the same with God:
If now, as formerly he trod
Paradise, his presence fills
Our earth, each only as God wills
Can work—God's puppets, best and worst,   5
Are we; there is no last nor first.

THE YEAR'S AT THE SPRING

The year's at the spring
And day's at the morn;
Morning's at seven;
The hill-side's dew-pearled;   10
The lark's on the wing;
The snail's on the thorn:
God's in his heaven—
All's right with the world!

For Thought and Discussion

1. What is the central theme of the "New Year's Hymn," of "The Year's at the Spring"?

2. The rhyme scheme of the second poem is perhaps different from that of any other poem you have read. Indicate the scheme by letters.

Plus Work

From a study of Browning's poems indicate your opinion of his favorite themes, style of writing, and philosophy of life.

✦

TO A SNOWFLAKE

FRANCIS THOMPSON

[Francis Thompson was for a long time unsuccessful at everything he undertook. Finally he was discovered by an editor, and the publication of his poetry brought fame to him. "The Hound of Heaven" is his most famous poem.]

WHAT heart would have thought you?—
Past our devisal
(O filigree petal!)
Fashioned so purely,
Fragilely, surely,   5
From what Paradisal
Imagineless metal

Too costly for cost?
Who hammered you, wrought you,
From argentine vapor?—   10
"God was my shaper
Passing surmisal,
He hammered, He wrought me,
From curled silver vapor,
To lust of His mind—   15
Thou couldst not have thought me!
So purely, so palely,
Tinily, surely,
Mightily, frailly,
Insculped and embossed,   20
With His hammer of wind,
And His graver of frost."

For Thought and Discussion

1. How does Thompson describe the snowflake?
2. What question does he ask?
3. What does the answer tell you about the author?
4. Why does he call the snowflake a "filigree petal?"

Plus Work

Find a picture of a snowflake to bring to class. Look at a snowflake under the microscope and describe it to the class.

WHAT MEN LIVE BY
LEO TOLSTOY
An adaptation by VIRGINIA CHURCH

CHARACTERS

SIMON, *the cobbler*
MATRENA, *his wife*
MICHAEL, *his apprentice*
BARON AVEDEITCH, *a wealthy land-owner*
THEDKA, *his footman*
SONIA IVANICH, *a lady of means*
BRENIE ⎱ *her two adopted children,*
NIKITA ⎰ *little girls of about six years*
ANNA MALOSKA, *a widow, friend of MATRENA*
TROFINOFF, *debtor*
THE GUARDIAN ANGEL
A LITTLE DEVIL

(*About four feet below the level of the street, which is reached by a few stairs at the back leading to an outer door, is the basement occupied by SIMON. At the right of the door, on a line with the pavement, is a long narrow window through which one may see the feet of the passers-by.*

SIMON, who does most of the cobbling for the village, knows the way-farers by the boots which he has re-paired. Under the window, placed so as to catch the meagre light, is a cobbler's bench with tools on either side. At the left of the stairs are long gray curtains forming a kind of closet in which outer wraps are hung. In the corner is a small china-closet. In the left wall is a hearth; here, over the fire, the wife cooks the meals. Two old chairs huddle near the fire as if for warmth. A table, half concealed by a worn cloth, stands near the fire-place. Opposite the fireplace is a door leading into the inner room.)

SCENE I

[SIMON, *old, slow in movement, kindly of feature, is seated at his bench, mending a pair of rough hide shoes. His wife,* MATRENA, *as brown and dry as a chip, is on a stool by the fire, mending a tattered old sheepskin outer coat. Occasionally one sees the feet of pedestrians pass by the little window.* SIMON *glances up as they throw a shadow on his table.*]

MATRENA. And who was that went by, Simon?

SIMON. It was Thedka, my dear Matrena. Thedka, the footman of the Barina. The side-patch on his boot has lasted well.

MATRENA. Yes, you make them last for so long that they do not need to come to you and so you have little trade.

SIMON. But, Matrena, I could not put on patches that would not last; then I should have no trade at all. I must do my best. That is the kind of man I am.

MATRENA. Yes, yes, Simon, that is the kind of man you are and so this is the kind of home we have, with hardly enough flour in the bin for one baking.

SIMON. Don't fret, Matrena. We shall not starve. God is good.

MATRENA. Aye, God is good, but his handmen are far from the likeness in which He cast them. (*A girl trips by.*) Was that Rozinka went by?

SIMON. No, Rozinka has not such high heels. It was Ulka, the Barina's maid.

MATRENA. I might have guessed it, after Thedka had passed. The minx is as hard on his footsteps as a man's shadow on a sunny day. It's a pity, since you shoe all the servants in the Baron's household, that the master would not let you make boots for him.

SIMON. The boots of the nobilities are brought from Paris, and are cut from northern leather. Trofinoff told me he brought five pair from the station on his last trip.

MATRENA. Trofinoff, hm! Did you not tell me Trofinoff promised to come this afternoon to pay the eight roubles he has owed you three years coming Michaelmas?

SIMON. Aye, so he said.

MATRENA. So he said, but I'll warrant we never see a hair of his beard till he's come barefoot again. Now (*holding up the sheepskin*), I've done all I can to your sheepskin. It's so thin the cold doesn't have to seek the holes to creep in: it walks through. It's thankful I'll be when we can buy another skin so that I can get out of the house the same time you go.

SIMON. We'll buy a skin this very afternoon, my dear. When Trofinoff brings me the eight roubles, we shall add it to the three you have saved, and that ought to buy a good skin— if not a tanned one, at all events, a good rough one.

MATRENA. *If* Trofinoff brings the money.

SIMON. He'll bring it, or, by heaven, I'll have the cap off his head, so I will. That is the kind of man I am.

MATRENA. If he were to come in and tell you he is hard up, you would tell him not to worry his head about the roubles, that God is good.

SIMON. No, I shall say, "Am I not hard up as well?"

MATRENA. Very well, if he comes we shall see what kind of man **you** are. Who was that?

SIMON. It was your friend, Anna Maloska, who wears too small shoes for her.

MATRENA. She wore large shoes after she caught her husband; but now he is dead, she wears small shoes again to catch another.

SIMON. I wonder that she did not stop.

MATRENA. She will stop on her way back from market, for there will be more news.

SIMON (*looking out the window and rising happily*). But see here, Matrena, you wronged the good Trofinoff. He has come to pay the eight roubles, as he promised. (*There is a halting knock at the door.*) Coming! Coming! (*He limps slightly as he hastens up the steps.*)

MATRENA (*as she crosses to go into the room at the right*). Well, Simon, I shall be the last to be sorry if your faith has been rewarded. (*She goes out as SIMON opens the door to the street. He comes down with TROFINOFF, a middle-aged, sharp-faced little man with gray beard and keen, roving eyes. He carries a bundle wrapped in brown cloth.*)

SIMON. Welcome, Trofinoff. I salute you.

TROFINOFF. Welcome, fellow brother. I wish you everything that is good.

SIMON. I thank you, brother. Is all well at home?

TROFINOFF. Not as well as might be, alas! Fuel takes much money these days. I have a flat purse.

SIMON. Then it was doubly good of you, friend Trofinoff, to come to settle our account. My good wife has not a kaftan or a sheepskin to wear when it snows.

TROFINOFF. I regret, Simon, I was unable to bring you the roubles I owe you. I am so hard pressed.

SIMON (*with forced sternness*). Am I not hard up as well?

TROFINOFF. Aye, but you have not so many mouths to fill, nor cattle to feed, nor grain to dispose of with little profit.

SIMON. Friend Trofinoff, you have a hut and cattle, while I have all on my back. You grow your own bread; I have to buy mine. If you do not pay me, I shall not have money for bread.

TROFINOFF. You are not so grieved as I, brother; and had it been any one but you I should not have dared face him, but I knew the kind of man you are. I have heard you say, "Let us love one another."

SIMON. That is so, for love is of God.

TROFINOFF. So I said to my wife: "Anya, if it were anyone but Simon, the good Simon, I would not dare take him our little one's shoes, but I know what kind of man he is: he loves the children and would not that the least of these should suffer and he could help it."

(*He unwraps a tattered pair of shoes, belonging to a child.*)

SIMON. Aye, the little Sarah's shoes. They need soles badly, and a toe-cap.

TROFINOFF. You will repair them for her, Simon?

SIMON. Of course, brother, I— (*He looks nervously toward the door to the inner room.*) Could you not pay me something, Trofinoff?

TROFINOFF. Here are two co-pecks. They will buy a half loaf for the wife, Simon. (*He goes to the door.*)

SIMON. Thank you.

TROFINOFF. And you shall have your roubles in a day or so—as soon as my grain is paid for.

SIMON. I can get along very comfortably. While one of us has a warm coat, why should we fret? I can stay in by the fire. Only, of course, there's my wife. She keeps worrying about it.

TROFINOFF. Your wife has no cause to be anxious while she has such a kind husband, Simon. I will send for the boots shortly. Good day.

SIMON. Good day. God be with you, brother!

(TROFINOFF *goes out.* SIMON *lays the copecks on the bench, and is examining the small shoes when* MATRENA *enters. He puts them behind his back guiltily.*)

MATRENA. Well, what are you hiding there? Did he bring you a gift with your money?

SIMON (*sadly*). No, he—he assured me, he was quite destitute.

MATRENA (*enraged*). Do you mean he brought you not even your eight roubles? (SIMON *shakes his head.*) What did I tell you, eh?

SIMON. But he says he will bring them soon—when his money comes in. I railed at him, Matrena. I scored him roundly for not paying his just dues.

MATRENA. And what have you there? (SIMON *produces the shoes and* MATRENA *is further enraged.*) I thought as much. You've taken more work for the cheater. You let him hoodwink you out of your senses while your old wife may go hungry and cold? What's this?

SIMON. He gave me two copecks for bread.

(MATRENA *hurls them angrily on the floor at* SIMON'S *feet. The old man patiently picks them up.*)

MATRENA. Bread, bah! It would not buy half a loaf. The thief! It is a shame, a shame! (*She rocks herself, crying, then falls into a chair by the fire, her apron thrown over her head, and gives way to grief.*)

SIMON (*distressed*). Come now, Matrena, why will you wag your tongue so foolishly? If we have bread for the day, the morrow will provide for itself. As for the coat, I shall go to Vanya, the vender of skins, and get one on credit.

(*The* LITTLE DEVIL *peers in at the window, then disappears.*)

MATRENA. And who would give the likes of us credit with not a dessiatine of land to our share?

SIMON (*putting the shoes on the bench and preparing for outdoors*). Vanya will. I have bought many skins from him for my shoes. I have favored him in his turn.

MATRENA. Men forget past favors in the face of present desires. But if you are going out, you had better put my woollen jacket under your kaftan. The wind is bitter cold to-day.

(*She goes to the curtains to the left of the stairs and takes down a close-fitting woollen sack. From a shelf of the cupboard she lifts a jar and shakes into her hand some money.* SIMON *is drawing on woollen slippers over his shoes. He puts on* MATRENA'S *jacket, a woollen kaftan or smock over it, and throws the sheepskin about his shoulders. On his bald head he draws down a fur cap.*)

SIMON (*submitting to* MATRENA'S *ministrations*). Thank you, Matrena, I shall feel quite warm in this old sheepskin. I sha'n't want a new one in a lifetime.

(*He goes up the steps.*)

MATRENA. You won't get one, the way you conduct your business. Now, Simon, here are our three roubles; give these to Vanya on account and he should then let you have the skin.

SIMON. He will, wife, he will.

MATRENA. Now go, and mind you do not stop for vodka on the way— your tongue is loose enough as it is. And do not talk aloud to yourself, as is your custom, for if a thief learn you have the roubles, he will not be above killing you for them.

SIMON. God is my protection. May his good angel guard our house in my absence! Good day, Matrena!

MATRENA. Good day, Simon!

(*He goes out, closing the door. She looks after him affectionately, then goes to the closet and taking an iron pot from the shelf, hangs it before the fire. Seeing that all is well, she crosses and goes into the inner room. The basement is but dimly lighted. The* LITTLE DEVIL, *after peering through the window to see that the coast is clear, comes in from the street, closing the door after him. He moves quickly and is merry, as if about to reap some reward for his efforts. From out the curtains, by the stairs, steps the figure of the* GUARDIAN ANGEL *in long, flowing garments. The* ANGEL *remains in the shadows and is never clearly visible.*)

ANGEL. Why are you here?

(*The* DEVIL *goes to the hearth and sits in front of the fire. He shows no surprise at being spoken to by the* ANGEL, *and does not look in his direction.*)

DEVIL. To try my luck to see if I can win old Simon with my dice. He has begun to ask credit, and if he stop for vodka, as I shall see that he does, that will be one step in my direction.

ANGEL. His faith is strong.

DEVIL. So are my dice, ha! ha! (*He throws them.*) Three, six, nine! Good! The three means that he will have a little luck; it will make him drink vodka and forget his wife. Six, he will prosper, and when a man prospers in *this* world he forgets the next. Nine, nine, that is not so well. Nine means that I shall get him—if —yet "ifs" are so little in my way. So I shall get him, unless—

ANGEL. Unless?

DEVIL (*rising*). Unless a greater than thou come into his home to protect him.

ANGEL. I am his Guardian Angel.

DEVIL (*on the stairs*). I will make the roubles jingle in his pockets so that he shall not hear the voice of the Guardian Angel. If nine had been twelve—but we shall see. I am off now to the home of the Baron, who long ago drowned the voice of his angel in vodka. I mixed his first glass. There was fox's blood to make him grow cunning, wolf's blood to make him grow cruel, and swine's blood to turn him into a pig. On my way, I shall mix a glass for Simon, to bring up in him all the beast-blood there is.

ANGEL. His faith is great.

(*The* DEVIL *laughs derisively as he goes out and slams the door, and the* ANGEL *disappears again in the shadows. Feet go by the window and voices are heard. Then, just as* MATRENA *comes in and goes to the fire, there is a knock.*)

MATRENA. Come in.

(*A comely woman of middle age enters. She is rather overdressed in poor clothes that strive to imitate the rich. It is* ANNA MALOSKA.)

MATRENA. Ah, Anna, is it you? I thought I smelled smoke and came to tend our fire. Come in.

ANNA (*sniffing*). It smells like sulphur. That's bad luck. Who was it went out?

MATRENA. No one. Sit down. Simon has gone to buy a sheepskin. Is it cold out?

ANNA (*sitting and throwing back her wraps*). Bitter cold. It was on just such a day my poor husband caught pneumonia.

MATRENA (*sitting on the other side of the fire and tending the porridge*). I do hope Simon won't catch cold and I do hope the sheepskin-seller won't cheat him. That man of mine is a regular simpleton.

ANNA (*patting her hair*). They all are, poor dears!

MATRENA. Simon never cheats a soul himself, yet a little child can lead him by the nose. It's time he was back; he had only a short way to go.

ANNA. If it were poor dear Ivan, I should know he had stopped for a glass of vodka.

MATRENA (*walking to the window and looking out*). I hope he hasn't gone making merry, that rascal of mine.

ANNA. Ah, Matrena, they are all rascals. Ivan drank himself into a drunken stupor every evening; then he would come home and beat me, and beat little Fifi, my dog; but I have to remember that he was a man and men are like that. I shall never be happy again, now that he is in his grave.

(*She weeps.*)

MATRENA (*patting her shoulder*). There, there, poor Anna!

ANNA (*brightening*). Do you like my hat?

MATRENA. Aye, aye, it is very tasty; though, if I might say, a trifle youthful.

ANNA. Why shouldn't a woman cheat Father Time if she can? He's the only man she can get even with. He liked my hat.

MATRENA. Ivan?

ANNA. Oh, no, the poor dear died without seeing it. I mean Martin Pakhom. I just met him at the door and he said, "Good day, Anna, what a beautiful hat that is you're wearing!"

MATRENA. They say Martin drinks like a trout.

ANNA. Ah, they all do, poor dears (*gathering up her basket*). I must go on. Fifi will be wanting his supper, though neither of us has eaten anything since poor Ivan died. Fifi is so affectionate. We both cry an hour every morning. Sonka times us.

MATRENA. Poor Anna!

ANNA. Won't you walk a way with me?

MATRENA. Simon went out with all our clothes upon him and left me nothing to wear. Besides, I must have his supper ready, and clean out my sleeping-room.

ANNA (*at the stairs*). I wish *I* had someone to get supper for. (*She goes up to the door.*) Matrena, Martin said something rather pointed just now.

MATRENA. What did he say, Anna?

ANNA. He said, "Marriage is a lottery!"

MATRENA. Aye, aye, so it is.

ANNA. I was just wondering—

MATRENA. Yes?

ANNA. I was wondering if Martin were thinking of taking a chance. Good-bye, Matrena.

MATRENA. Good-bye, Anna.

(ANNA *goes out. MATRENA, stirring her porridge, sits near the fire. The feet of two men pass the window. They belong to* SIMON *and a stranger. The men enter. The stranger is a young man, tall and slender, with fine clear-cut features and a mild, gentle expression. He is without stockings, being clad in* SIMON'S *woollen slippers and kaftan. He stands hesitating at the foot of the steps.* MATRENA *has risen and regards the two men angrily. "What tramp is this now,* SIMON *has brought home?" she is wondering.*)

SIMON. Well, Matrena, here we are home again. (*The old man approaches his wife fearfully.* MATRENA, *after a scathing glance, turns her back on him, and tends her fire.*) We have brought our appetites with us. Get us some supper, will you? (*He takes off his sheepskin and cap,*

but still MATRENA *does not respond. He motions the stranger to a chair at the right.*) Sit you down, brother, and we will have some supper. Have you anything cooked that you could give us?

MATRENA (*facing him in a rage*). Yes, I have something cooked, but not for you. I can see you have drunk your senses away. (*He starts to protest.*) Do you think I cannot smell your breath? Where is our sheepskin? Did you drink up all the three roubles?

(SIMON *goes to the stranger and reaching in the pocket of the kaftan, takes out the roubles.*)

SIMON. No, Matrena, I did not get the sheepskin, because the vender would not let me have one unless I brought all the money. "Bring all the cash," he said, "and then you can pick what skin you like. We all of us know how difficult it is to get quit of a debt." But here are your roubles; I spent only two copecks for the merest drop to send the blood bubbling finely in my veins.

MATRENA (*eyeing the man*). I have no supper for a pair of drunkards like you. One cannot feed every drunkard that comes along when one has not enough in the pot for two.

SIMON. Hold your tongue, Matrena. Give me time to explain.

MATRENA. How much sense am I likely to hear from a drunken fool, indeed! My mother gave me some linen—and you drank it away! You go out to buy a sheepskin and drink that away, too.

SIMON. But I did not—

MATRENA (*beside herself with rage*). Give me my jacket! It's the only one I have, yet you sneak it off while I stay home for lack of clothes. (*As she snatches off the jacket and starts to the other room, her anger is burning off.*) You—you haven't told me who this fellow is.

SIMON. If you will give me a chance for a word, I will. I saw this man lying by the chapel yonder, half naked and frozen. It is not summer time, you must remember. God led me to him, else he must have perished. The Baron Avedeitch drove up and I thought he would stop, but he did not. I started on, saying to myself the man could be up to no good there and if I went back I might be robbed and murdered. Then I said, "Fie, Simon, for shame! Would you let a man die at your very door for want of clothing and food?" What could I do? I shared with him my covering and brought him here. Calm your temper, Matrena, for to give way to it is sinful. Remember we would all die, were it not for God.

(MATRENA *turns back from the door, sets a teapot on the table and pours some kvass, laying knives and forks by the plates and serving the porridge.*)

MATRENA. Here is kvass and porridge. There is no bread. (*They eat humbly.* MATRENA *stops before the stranger.*) What is your name?

MICHAEL (*lifting his serious eyes to her face*). Michael.

MATRENA. Where do you come from?

MICHAEL. From another part than this.

MATRENA. How did you come to the chapel?

MICHAEL. I cannot say.

MATRENA. Someone must have assaulted you, then?

MICHAEL. No, no one assaulted me. God was punishing me.

SIMON. Of course, all things come from God. Yet where were you bound for?

MICHAEL. For nowhere in particular.

SIMON. Do you know any trade?

MICHAEL. No, none.

MATRENA (*her heart warming within her*). You could learn. I know, Simon, he could learn, if you would teach him. He might stay with us. There is enough straw for another bed in the hallway.

MICHAEL. The Lord be good to you! I was lying frozen and unclothed, when Simon saw and took compassion on me. He shared with me his clothing and brought me hither. You have given me food and drink and shown me great kindness.

MATRENA. No, I was not kind. I am ashamed of myself. (*She goes to the cupboard and brings out the one bit of bread.*) And I lied. I said there was no bread. There is one crust and you shall have half.

MICHAEL. But you?

MATRENA (*gently*). Eat, we shall have enough. You are welcome to stay with us as long as you wish. (MICHAEL *turns and smiles radiantly on her.*) Let us eat.

MICHAEL. God's blessing on this house!

SCENE II

[*There is an air of greater prosperity than before. The cobbler's bench is new. There are flowers in the window-box and on the mantel. It is spring outside. The sound of hammering is heard within. The outer door opens and* MATRENA *enters with* ANNA MALOSKA. *The women have been to market.* MATRENA *is well, though quietly, dressed;* ANNA, *in bright colors.*]

MATRENA. Come in, Anna.

ANNA. The men are not here. I wish to ask Simon about my shoes.

MATRENA. They are inside, building another room. We have needed it since Michael came. Michael made the new bench.

ANNA. Michael seems to do everything well. Just like poor Ivan.

MATRENA (*enthusiastically*). Ah, he is wonderful! Everything that Simon teaches him he learns readily. The first day he learned to twine and twist the thread,—no easy task for the apprentice. The third day he was able to work as if he had been a cobbler all his life. He never makes mistakes, and he eats no more than a sparrow.

(*They sit down at the table.*)

ANNA. He is woefully solemn.

MATRENA. Aye, he works all day, only resting for a moment to look upward. He never wishes to go out of doors; never jests, nor laughs. He has smiled only once: it was the night he came.

ANNA. Has he any family—a wife?

MATRENA. He never speaks of his own affairs.

ANNA. I should manage to worm it out of him, trust me. Martin shall have no secrets that I don't know.

MATRENA. When are you to marry, Anna?

ANNA. Next month. It will be such a relief to let down. I shan't wear these tight stays any longer, nor such close boots. I can go to breakfast in my old wrapper and curl-papers. Now Martin has a way of dropping in to breakfast and I have to keep on my sleekest dress.

MATRENA. Martin was in for shoes last week.

ANNA. Yes, he says no one sews so strongly and so neatly as Michael.

MATRENA. People come to Simon from all the country around. Since Michael came his business has increased tenfold.

ANNA. Aye, Martin says the fame of Simon's apprentice has crept a-broad. (*Regarding her own shoes.*) Martin has small feet. He told me last night he wore a number seven. But I must go.

MATRENA. Here comes Simon now.

(SIMON *and* MICHAEL *enter from the right. The latter is in simple workman's clothes. He bows gravely without speaking and going to the bench bends over his work.* SIMON *approaches the women, who have risen.*)

SIMON. Ah, Anna Maloska, how fares the bride to-day?

ANNA. Well, thank you, Simon. I came to order some new shoes.

SIMON. Good, Anna. Shall we make them on the same last as before? Sixes, I believe?

ANNA. No, Simon, I wish sevens this time. Good-bye, Matrena. Good-bye, Simon.

SIMON and MATRENA. Farewell, Anna.

MATRENA. Come in again, Anna.

ANNA (*at the door*). Simon, are Martin's shoes finished?

SIMON. No, Anna, but don't worry; they will be. I had to send for more leather. He wears large boots, you know.

ANNA (*turning on the steps*). Large? Sevens?

SIMON. Elevens, Anna.

ANNA. Elevens—why—after all, Simon, I believe you may make my shoes nines. (*She opens the door.*)

SIMON. Very well, Anna.

ANNA (*looking out, becomes excited*). Oh, Matrena, a fine gentleman in a greatcoat is getting out here. He has two coachmen and a footman. I think it is the Baron. I must run out of his way. (*She disappears.* SIMON *and* MATRENA *together look out of the window.*)

MATRENA. It is the Baron Avedeitch, isn't it, Simon?

SIMON. There is no mistaking the

Baron, and he is coming here. (*The door has been left open and is presently filled by a huge form that has to bow his great head to enter the low portal. The* BARON *has a ruddy, bibulous countenance, a neck like a bull's, and a figure of cast iron. He straightens up just inside the door.*)

BARON (*in a loud, pompous tone*). Which of you is the master bootmaker?

SIMON (*stepping aside*). I am, your honor.

BARON (*calling out the door*). Hi, Thedka! Bring me the stuff here. (*He comes down into the room, followed by* THEDKA, *who places the bundle on the table.*) Untie it. (*The footman does so, disclosing two sheets of leather. He then withdraws.* MATRENA *curtsies every time anyone looks in her direction though no one heeds her.*) Look here, bootmaker. Do you see this?

SIMON. Yes, your nobility.

BARON. Do you know what it is?

SIMON. It is good leather.

BARON (*thundering for emphasis*). Good leather, indeed! You blockhead, you have never seen such leather in your life before. It is of northern make and cost twenty roubles. Could you make me a pair of boots out of it?

SIMON. Possibly so, your honor.

BARON. "Possibly so!" Well, first, listen. I want a pair of boots that shall last a year, will never tread over, and never split at the seams. If you can make such boots, then set to work and cut out at once; but if you cannot, do neither of these things. I tell you beforehand that if the new pair should split or tread over before the year is out, I will clap you in prison.

MATRENA. Oh, your honor!

BARON (*ignoring her*). But, if they should not do so, then I will pay you ten roubles for your work.

SIMON (*turning to* MICHAEL). What do you think about it, brother?

MICHAEL. Take the work, Simon.

SIMON. Very well, sir.

BARON (*he sits and extends his foot*). Hi—Thedka. (THEDKA *advances and draws off the boot. The* BARON *then motions to* SIMON. MICHAEL *has advanced.*)

BARON. Take my measure. (MICHAEL *kneels and takes the measure of the sole and of the instep. He has to fasten on an extra piece of paper to measure the calf, as the muscles of the* BARON's *leg are as thick as a beam.*) Take care you don't make them too tight in the leg. (*As* MICHAEL *draws back,* THEDKA *replaces the boot on his master's foot, then withdraws again to the door.*)

BARON (*indicating* MICHAEL). Who is this you have with you?

SIMON. That is my skilled workman who will sew your boots.

BARON (*standing and stamping into his boot*). Look you sharp, then, and remember this—that you are to sew them so that they will last a year. (MICHAEL *does not respond but stands gazing past the* BARON *as though he saw someone back of him. His face suddenly breaks into a smile and he brightens all over. The* BARON, *irritated, glances back of him, then scowls at* MICHAEL.) What are you grinning at, you fool? I see no one back of me to grin at. You had better see that the boots are ready when I want them. (*He stalks up the steps.*)

MICHAEL. They will be ready when you need them.

(*The* BARON *goes out.* THEDKA *follows, closing the door.*)

MATRENA. What a man!

SIMON. He is as hard as a flint stone.

MATRENA. Why wouldn't he get hardened with the life he leads? Even death itself would not take such an iron rivet of a man.

SIMON (*taking the leather to* MICHAEL *at the bench*). Well, Michael, we have undertaken the work and we must not go amiss over it. This leather is valuable stuff.

MATRENA. And the gentleman is short-tempered.

SIMON. Aye, there must be no mistakes. You have the sharper eyes, as well as the greater skill in your fingers, so take these measures and cut out the stuff, while I finish sewing those toe-caps.

MICHAEL. I will make them according to your needs.

(*The men sit working while* MATRENA *busies herself with the housework.*)

MATRENA. Oh, Simon, I forgot to tell you, Sonia Ivanich is coming by to get shoes for her two little girls. The little Nikita is hard to fit, but Madame has heard that Michael can fit even a lame foot.

(MICHAEL *drops his work and leans forward.*)

MICHAEL. A lame child?

MATRENA. Yes, poor little thing— but hush, I hear the clamp, clamp of a wooden foot. Come, Simon, and greet her. Madame has money; you are getting all the best trade now.

(SIMON *puts down his work and comes forward.* MATRENA *hastens up to the door and holds it open. A gentle, good-looking lady enters with* NIKITA *and* BRENIE, *two pretty little girls. They have round wide eyes, rosy cheeks, and wear smart little shawls and dresses.*)

SONIA. Good day to you, mistress.

MATRENA. The same to you, madame, and the young misses. Won't you sit down?

(SONIA *sits by the table, the two little girls burying their faces in her skirt from timidity. She pats them tolerantly.* MICHAEL *keeps regarding them, though he works.*)

SONIA. Thank you. Is this Master Simon?

SIMON. It is, mistress. What can we do for you?

SONIA. I wish a pair of boots made for each of these little girls to wear for the spring.

SIMON. Very well, madame. Will you have them leather throughout or lined with linen?

SONIA. I believe linen will be softer. (*Lame* NIKITA *has slipped over to* MICHAEL *and he takes her on his knee.*) Well, will you see Nikita? I have never known her to take to a stranger so.

MATRENA. All the children love Michael. He is Simon's skilled workman. He will take the measures. (MICHAEL *measures the little feet.* NIKITA *pats his head.*)

NIKITA. I love you. Have you a little girl?

MICHAEL (*gently*). No, I have no little girl.

SONIA. Take both sets of measures from this little girl and make one *baskmak* for the crooked foot and three ordinary ones. The children take the same size: they are twins.

MATRENA. How came she to be lame? Such a pretty little lady.

SONIA. Her mother, when dying, fell over her.

MATRENA (*surprised*). Then you are not their mother.

SONIA. No, I adopted them. But I love them as much as though they were my own, and they are as happy as the day is long; they know no difference.

SIMON. Whose children were they?

SONIA. The children of peasants. The father died on a Tuesday from the felling of a tree. The mother died that Friday. She was all alone, and in her death agony she threw herself across the baby and crushed its foot. When we found her, she was stiff in death, but the children were alive.

MATRENA. Poor little mother!

SONIA. I was the only one in the village with a young child, so they were given to me to nurse. God took my own little one unto Himself, but I have come to love these like my own flesh. I could not live without them. They are to me as wax is to the candle.

SIMON. It is a true saying which reads, "Without father and mother we may live, but without God— never."

(*All are drawn to look at* MICHAEL *who, sitting with his hands folded on his knees, is gazing upward and smiling as though at someone unseen by the others.*)

SONIA (*rising*). Good day, master! Come, Nikita, we shall stop in again to try the boots.

SIMON. In seven days, mistress. We thank you.

NIKITA. Good-bye, man!

MICHAEL. Good-bye, little one!

SONIA. Well, I never! The little dear!

(*She goes out with the children.*)

SIMON. Michael, if you will bring me the awl from the other room, I, too, will work.

(*He approaches the bench as* MICHAEL *goes into the other room for the awl. He suddenly cries aloud in dismay.*) What has he done? What can ail the fellow?

MATRENA. What is it? (*She hastens to his side.*)

SIMON (*groaning*). Oh! How is it that Michael, who has lived with me for a whole year without making a single mistake, should now make such a blunder as this? The Baron ordered high boots and Michael has gone

and sewn a pair of soleless slippers and spoiled the leather.

MATRENA (*aghast*). Michael has done this!

SIMON. Alas! yes, and you heard what the gentleman said. I could replace an ordinary skin, but one does not see leather like this every day. (MICHAEL *returns with the awl.*) My good fellow, what have you done? You have simply ruined me! The gentleman ordered high boots, but what have you gone and made instead?

(*Before* MICHAEL *has a chance to respond, there is a loud knock at the door.*)

SIMON. Come in!

(*The door is opened and* THEDKA, *the footman of the* BARON, *enters.* SIMON *pushes the slipper behind him.*)

THEDKA. Good day to you!

SIMON (*uneasily*). Good day! What can we do for you?

THEDKA. My mistress sent me about the boots.

SIMON. Yes? What about them?

(MICHAEL, *unseen by the others, goes into the other room.*)

THEDKA. My master will not want them now. He is dead.

MATRENA. What are you saying?

THEDKA. He died on the way home. When we went to help him alight, he lay limp as a meal-sack on the floor of the carriage.

MATRENA. God help us!

THEDKA. My mistress sent me to tell the bootmaker to use the leather for a pair of slippers for the corpse and to make them as quickly as he can.

(MATRENA *and* SIMON *look at each other with wonderment in their eyes. They turn to where* MICHAEL *stood by the inner door, but he has disappeared.*)

SIMON. You shall have them in an hour.

THEDKA. I shall return. Good day, my master, and good luck to you!

SIMON. And to you!

(THEDKA *goes out, leaving* SIMON *and* MATRENA *gazing at each other in awe.*)

MATRENA. Michael is no ordinary being. We might have guessed before this.

SIMON. You remember how he smiled?

MATRENA. He has smiled three times.

SIMON. Let us see what he is doing.

MATRENA. You do not suppose he would go from us without a word, do you?

(*They go into the other room. Immediately the* LITTLE DEVIL *appears in the doorway at the back and* THE GUARDIAN ANGEL *is seen in the shadow of the curtains at the left.*)

ANGEL. You have lost!

DEVIL (*with a stamp of his foot*). I have lost Simon's soul, but I have the Baron. He shall be my torch this night in hell.

ANGEL. The faith of Simon was great.

DEVIL. *Thou* didst not save him!

ANGEL. One greater than I saved Simon. It was God!

(*At the word, the* DEVIL *stamps his foot again, slams the door, and goes. The* ANGEL *disappears. From the other room come* MATRENA *and* SIMON, *crossing to the hearth.*)

SIMON. He was in prayer.

MATRENA. His face was illumined, and such a light shone from him that at first I thought it was a fire. Oh, Simon, who is this that has dwelt with us?

(MICHAEL *comes in from the other room; goes to the steps, where he turns and faces them.*)

MICHAEL. God has pardoned me, good master and mistress. Do you also pardon me?

SIMON. Tell us, Michael, who you are and why God punished you.

MICHAEL. I was an angel in Heaven and God punished me because I disobeyed Him. He sent me to earth to bear away a woman's soul. But the woman, who had given birth to twin babies, cried to me, "Angel of God, I cannot leave them! They will die. I have no kin to care for them. Do not take away my soul. Children cannot live without mother or father!" So I hearkened to the mother and flew back to God, saying, "Little children cannot live without mother or father, so I did not take away the mother's soul." Then God said to me, "Go thou and fetch away the soul of the childing woman, and before thou return to Heaven thou shalt learn three words. Thou shalt learn both what that is which dwelleth in men, and what that is which is not given men to know, and what that is whereby men live. When thou hast learned these words thou mayst return to Heaven."

MATRENA. Tell us what you did, Michael.

MICHAEL. I went to earth and took the soul of the childing woman, then I rose above the village and tried to bear the soul to God, but a wind caught me, so that my wings hung down and were blown from me. The soul returned alone to God, while I fell to earth along the roadside.

(SIMON *and* MATRENA *marvel;* SIMON *speaks.*)

SIMON. Tell me, Michael, why you smiled three times, and what were the three words of God.

MICHAEL. When you, Simon, took me to your home and Matrena's heart prompted her to share her last crust, I smiled because I knew the first word of God. "Thou shalt learn what that is which dwelleth in men," and I knew by your goodness that what dwelleth in men is love. I felt glad that God had seen fit to reveal this to me, and I smiled.

MATRENA. What was it you saw over the shoulder of the Baron that made you smile?

MICHAEL. I saw the Angel of Death. No one else saw him, and I thought: here is this man planning for boots that shall last a year, when he is to die before the nightfall. Then I smiled when I remembered that God had said, "Thou shalt learn what it is not given to men to know."

SIMON. What was it made you smile at the story of the good Sonia Ivanich?

MICHAEL. I recognized in the children the twins that I had thought would die. Yet this woman had fed them and loved them. In her I beheld love and pity of the living God, and I understood what that is whereby men live. And I smiled. This much do I tell you to repay your kindness: that men only appear to live by taking thought of themselves; in reality, they live by Love alone. He that dwelleth in Love dwelleth in God and God in him; for God is Love.

(*The room is suddenly black with night. Then a hymn bursts forth as though from a great choir of voices, and in the doorway* MICHAEL, *bathed in light, stands looking upward. Before him, at the foot of the stairs, kneel the two peasants.*)

(CURTAIN)

For Thought and Discussion

1. How does Simon recognize passers on the street?
2. What trait of character does the cobbler display in his opening speeches in Scene I?
3. Is this a marked characteristic of the modern workman?
4. What weakness in her husband's manner of dealing with customers does Matrena deplore?
5. What three things did God tell Michael he must learn?
6. Explain how he learns these three truths.

I WILL LIFT UP MINE EYES

PSALM 121

I WILL lift up mine eyes unto the hills,
From whence cometh my help.
My help cometh from the Lord,
Which made heaven and earth.
He will not suffer thy foot to be moved;
He that keepeth thee will not slumber.
Behold, he that keepeth Israel
Shall neither slumber nor sleep.
The Lord is thy keeper;

The Lord is thy shade upon thy right hand.
The sun shall not smite thee by day,
Nor the moon by night.
The Lord shall preserve thee from all evil;
He shall preserve thy soul.
The Lord shall preserve thy going out and thy coming in
From this time forth, and even for evermore.

From THE PILGRIM'S PROGRESS

JOHN BUNYAN

[Bunyan's *Pilgrim's Progress*, a book written by an unlearned man who had been cast into prison because of fidelity to his religious belief, became one of the world's best sellers.

In several respects John Bunyan, 1628-1688, was peculiarly fitted to write a great Puritan allegory. By nature he had common sense, affection for his family, tolerance for all people, and, what is more vital to the writing of an allegory, an excessively vivid imagination. In addition to this, he knew the Bible. While in prison he spent some time in making shoe laces to support his family, but he had leisure for meditation and reading. The hours he pored over his two books, the *King James Version of the Bible* and Foxe's *Book of Martyrs*, led to the writing of *Pilgrim's Progress*. The allegory is told in dialogue form, some of the speakers being like the wicked worldly companions of Bunyan's youth, others being devout as he was in later years, and others being good but weak and timorous, tossed about in belief as he was before his reformation. Bunyan's characters are not dreamlike and visionary as characters often are in allegories; instead they are exceedingly life-like and real. In terse, conversational prose, often voiced in the form of parables, they relate the temptations and difficulties of Christian's pilgrimage from the City of Destruction to the Celestial City of Mount Zion.

Many biblical passages are quoted verbatim in *Pilgrim's Progress*. In the original, references for these were listed in the text proper directly after the quotation. This book, following the plan adopted by recent editors, gives the references in footnotes.]

EVANGELIST. What doest thou here, Christian? said he: at which words Christian knew not what to answer; wherefore at present he stood speechless before him. Then said Evangelist further, Art not thou the man that I found crying without the walls of the city of Destruction?

JOHN BUNYAN

CHRISTIAN. Yes, dear sir, I am the man.

EVANGELIST. Did not I direct thee the way to the little wicket-gate?

CHRISTIAN. Yes, dear sir, said Christian.

EVANGELIST. How is it, then, thou art so quickly turned aside? For thou art now out of thy way.

CHRISTIAN. I met with a gentle-man so soon as I had got over the Slough of Despond, who persuaded me that I might, in the village before me, find a man that could take off my burden.

EVANGELIST. What was he?

CHRISTIAN. He looked like a gen-tleman, and talked much to me, and got me at last to yield: so I came hither: but when I beheld this hill, and how it hangs over the way, I suddenly made a stand, lest it should fall on my head.

EVANGELIST. What said that gentleman to you?

CHRISTIAN. Why, he asked me whither I was going; and I told him.

EVANGELIST. And what said he then?

CHRISTIAN. He asked me if I had a family; and I told him. But, said I, I am so laden with the burden that is on my back, that I cannot take pleasure in them as formerly.

EVANGELIST. And what said he then?

CHRISTIAN. He bid me with speed get rid of my burden; and I told him it was ease that I sought. And, said I, I am therefore going to yonder gate, to receive further direction how I may get to the place of deliverance. So he said that he would show me a better way, and short, not so attended with difficulties as the way, sir, that you set me in; which way, said he, will direct you to a gentleman's house that hath skill to take off these burdens; so I believed him, and turned out of that way into this, if haply I might be soon eased of my burden. But when I came to this place, and beheld things as they are, I stopped, for fear (as I said) of danger: but I now know not what to do.

EVANGELIST. Then said Evangelist, Stand still a little, that I show thee the words of God. So he stood trembling. Then said Evangelist, "See that ye refuse not Him that speaketh; for if they escaped not who refused him that spake on earth, much more shall not we escape, if we turn away from Him that speaketh from heaven."[1] He said, moreover, "Now the just shall live by faith; but if any man draw back, my soul shall have no pleasure

in him."[2] He also did thus apply them: Thou art the man that art running into this misery: thou hast begun to reject the counsel of the Most High, and to draw back thy foot from the way of peace, even almost to the hazarding of thy perdition.

Then Christian fell down at his feet as dead, crying, Woe is me, for I am undone! At the sight of which Evangelist caught him by the right hand, saying, "All manner of sin and blasphemies shall be forgiven unto men."[3] "Be not faithless, but believing."[4] Then did Christian again a little revive, and stood up trembling, as at first, before Evangelist.

Then Evangelist proceeded, saying, Give more earnest heed to the things that I shall tell thee of. I will now show thee who it was that deluded thee, and who it was also to whom he sent thee. That man that met thee is one Worldly Wiseman; and rightly is he so called; partly because he savoreth only of the doctrine of this world[5]: (therefore he always goes to the town of Morality to church) and partly because he loveth that doctrine best, for it saveth him from the cross,[6] and because he is of this carnal temper, therefore he seeketh to pervert my ways, though right. Now there are three things in this man's counsel that thou must utterly abhor.

1. His turning thee out of the way.

2. His laboring to render the cross odious to thee.

3. And his setting thy feet in that way that leadeth unto the administration of death.

First, Thou must abhor his turning thee out of the way; yea, and thine own consenting thereto because this is to reject the counsel of God

---

[1] Heb. 12:25.

[2] Heb. 10:38.   [3] Matt. 12:31.
[4] John 20:27.   [5] 1 John 4:5.   [6] Gal. 6:12.

for the sake of the counsel of a Worldly Wiseman. The Lord says, "Strive to enter in at the strait gate,"[7] the gate to which I send thee; "for strait is the gate that leadeth unto life, and few there be that find it."[8] From this little wicket-gate, and from the way thereto, hath this wicked man turned thee, to the bringing of thee almost to destruction; hate, therefore, his turning thee out of the way, and abhor thyself for hearkening to him.

Secondly, Thou must abhor his laboring to render the cross odious unto thee; for thou art to prefer it before the treasures of Egypt.[9] Besides, the King of glory hath told thee, that he that will save his life shall lose it. And he that comes after him, and hates not his father, and mother, and wife, and children, and brethren, and sisters, yea, and his own life also, he can not be his disciple.[10] I say, therefore, for man to labor to persuade thee that that shall be thy death, without which, the truth hath said, thou canst not have eternal life, this doctrine thou must abhor.

Thirdly, Thou must hate his setting of thy feet in the way that leadeth to the ministration of death. And for this thou must consider to whom he sent thee, and also how unable that person was to deliver thee from thy burden.

He to whom thou wast sent for ease, being by name Legality, is the son of the bondwoman which now is, and is in bondage with her children,[11] and is, in a mystery, this Mount Sinai, which thou hast feared will fall on thy head. Now if she with her children are in bondage, how canst thou expect by them to be made free? This Legality, therefore, is not able to set thee free from thy burden. No man was as yet ever rid of his burden by him; no, nor ever is like to be: ye can not be justified by the works of the law; for by the deeds of the law no man living can be rid of his burden. Therefore Mr. Worldly Wiseman is an alien, and Mr. Legality is a cheat; and for his son Civility, notwithstanding his simpering looks, he is but a hypocrite, and can not help thee. Believe me, there is nothing in all this noise that thou hast heard of these sottish men, but a design to beguile thee of thy salvation, by turning thee from the way in which I set thee. After this, Evangelist called aloud to the heavens for confirmation of what he had said; and with that there came words and fire out of the mountain under which poor Christian stood, which made the hair of his flesh stand up. The words were thus pronounced, "As many as are of the works of the law are under the curse; for it is written, Cursed is every one that continueth not in all things which are written in the book of the law to do them."[12]

Now Christian looked for nothing but death, and began to cry out lamentably; even cursing the time in which he met with Mr. Worldly Wiseman; still calling himself a thousand fools for hearkening to his counsel. He also was greatly ashamed to think that this gentleman's arguments, flowing only from the flesh, should have the prevalency with him so far as to cause him to forsake the right way. This done, he applied himself again to Evangelist in words and sense as follows.

CHRISTIAN. Sir, what think you? Is there any hope? May I now go back, and go up to the wicket-gate?

---

[7]Luke 13:24. [8]Matt. 12:13, 14.
[9]Heb. 11:25, 26. [10]Mark 8:38; John 12:25; Matt. 10:39; Luke 14:26.
[11]Gal. 4:21-27.

---

[12]Gal. 3:10.

Shall I not be abandoned for this, and sent back from thence ashamed? I am sorry I have hearkened to this man's counsel; but may my sin be forgiven?

Then said Evangelist to him, Thy sin is very great, for by it thou hast committed two evils; thou hast forsaken the way that is good, to tread in forbidden paths. Yet will the man at the gate receive thee, for he has good will for men; only, said he, take heed that thou turn not aside again, lest thou "perish from the way, when his wrath is kindled but a little."[13]

Then did Christian address himself to go back; and Evangelist, after he had kissed him, gave him one smile, and bid him God speed; so he went on with haste, neither spake he to any man by the way; nor if any man asked him, would he vouchsafe them an answer. He went like one that was all the while treading on forbidden ground, and could by no means think himself safe, till again he was got into the way which he had left to follow Mr. Worldly Wiseman's counsel. So, in process of time, Christian got up to the gate. Now, over the gate there was written, "Knock, and it shall be opened unto you."[14]

He knocked, therefore, more than once or twice, saying,

"May I now enter here? Will he within
Open to sorry me, though I have been
An undeserving rebel? Then shall I
Not fail to sing his lasting praise on high."

At last there came a grave person to the gate, named Goodwill, who asked who was there, and whence he came, and what he would have.

CHRISTIAN. Here is a poor burdened sinner. I come from the city of Destruction, but am going to Mount Zion, that I may be delivered from the wrath to come. I would therefore, sir, since I am informed that by this gate is the way thither, know if you are willing to let me in.

GOODWILL. I am willing with all my heart, said he; and with that he opened the gate.

So when Christian was stepping in, the other gave him a pull. Then said Christian, What means that? The other told him, A little distance from this gate there is erected a strong castle, of which Beelzebub is the captain; from thence both he and they that are with him shoot arrows at those that come up to this gate, if haply they may die before they can enter in. Then said Christian, I rejoice and tremble. So when he was got in, the man of the gate asked him who directed him thither.

CHRISTIAN. Evangelist bid me come hither and knock, as I did: and he said, that you, sir, would tell me what I must do.

GOODWILL. An open door is set before thee, and no man can shut it.

CHRISTIAN. Now I begin to reap the benefit of my hazards.

GOODWILL. But how is it that you came alone?

CHRISTIAN. Because none of my neighbors saw their dangers as I saw mine.

GOODWILL. Did any of them know of your coming?

CHRISTIAN. Yes, my wife and children saw me at the first and called after me to turn again: also, some of my neighbors stood crying and calling after me to return; but I put my fingers in my ears, and so came on my way.

GOODWILL. But did none of them follow you, to persuade you to go back?

---

[13]Ps. 2:12.   [14]Matt. 7:7.

CHRISTIAN. Yes, both Obstinate and Pliable: but when they saw that they could not prevail, Obstinate went railing back, but Pliable came with me a little way.

GOODWILL. But why did he not come through?

CHRISTIAN. We indeed came both together until we came to the Slough of Despond into the which we also suddenly fell. And then was my neighbor Pliable discouraged and would not venture farther. Wherefore, getting out again on the side next to his own house, he told me I should possess the brave country alone for him; so he went his way, and I came mine; he after Obstinate, and I to this gate.

GOODWILL. Then said Goodwill, Alas, poor man; is the celestial glory of so little esteem with him, that he counteth it not worth running the hazard of a few difficulties to obtain it?

CHRISTIAN. Truly, said Christian, I have said the truth of Pliable; and if I should also say all the truth of myself, it will appear there is no betterment betwixt him and myself. It is true, he went back to his own house, but I also turned aside to go into the way of death, being persuaded thereto by the carnal argument of one Mr. Worldly Wiseman.

GOODWILL. Oh, did he light upon you? What, he would have had you seek for ease at the hands of Mr. Legality. They are both of them a very cheat. But did you take his counsel?

CHRISTIAN. Yes, as far as I durst. I went to find out Mr. Legality, until I thought that the mountain that stands by his house would have fallen upon my head; wherefore there was I forced to stop.

GOODWILL. That mountain has been the death of many, and will be the death of many more: it is well you escaped being by it dashed in pieces.

CHRISTIAN. Why truly I do not know what had become of me there, had not Evangelist happily met me again as I was musing in the midst of my dumps; but it was God's mercy that he came to me again, for else I had never come hither. But now I am come, such a one as I am, more fit indeed for death by that mountain, than thus to stand talking with my Lord. But oh, what a favor is this to me, that yet I am admitted entrance here!

GOODWILL. We make no objections against any, notwithstanding all that they have done before they come hither: they in no wise are cast out.[15] And therefore, good Christian, come a little way with me, and I will teach thee about the way thou must go. Look before thee; dost thou see this narrow way? That is the way thou must go. It was cast up by the patriarchs, prophets, Christ and his apostles, and it is as straight as a rule can make it; this is the way thou must go.

CHRISTIAN. But, said Christian, are there no turnings nor windings, by which a stranger may lose his way?

GOODWILL. Yes, there are many ways abut down upon this; and they are crooked and wide: but thus thou mayst distinguish the right from the wrong, the right only being straight and narrow.[16]

Then I saw in my dream, that Christian asked him further, if he could not help him off with his burden that was upon his back. For as yet he had not got rid thereof, nor could he by any means get it off without help.

He told him, "As to thy burden, be content to bear it until thou comest to the place of deliverance;

---

[15]John 6:37. [16]Matt. 7:14.

for there it will fall from thy back of itself."

Then Christian began to gird up his loins, and to address himself to his journey. So the other told him, that by that he was gone some distance from the gate, he would come to the house of the Interpreter, at whose door he should knock, and he would show him excellent things. Then Christian took his leave of his friend, and he again bid him God-speed.

Then he went on till he came to the house of the Interpreter, where he knocked over and over. At last one came to the door, and asked who was there.

CHRISTIAN. Sir, here is a traveller, who was bid by an acquaintance of the good man of this house to call here for my profit; I would therefore speak with the master of the house.

So he called for the master of the house, who, after a little time, came to Christian, and asked him what he would have.

CHRISTIAN. Sir, said Christian, I am a man that am come from the city of Destruction, and am going to the Mount Zion; and I was told by the man that stands at the gate at the head of this way, that if I called here you would show me excellent things, such as would be helpful to me on my journey.

INTERPRETER. Then said Interpreter, Come in; I will show thee that which will be profitable to thee.[17] So he commanded his man to light the candle, and bid Christian follow him. So he had him into a private room, and bid his man open a door; the which when he had done, Christian saw the picture of a very grave person hang up against the wall; and

this was the fashion of it; it had eyes lifted up to heaven, the best of books in its hand, the law of truth was written upon its lips, the world was behind its back; it stood as if it pleaded with men, and a crown of gold did hang over its head.

CHRISTIAN. Then said Christian, What means this?

INTERPRETER. The man whose picture this is, is one of a thousand: And whereas thou seest him with his eyes lift up to heaven, the best of books in his hand, and the law of truth writ on his lips: it is to show thee, that his work is to know, and unfold dark things to sinners; even as also thou seest him stand as if he pleaded with men. And whereas thou seest the world as cast behind him, and that a crown hangs over his head; that is to show thee, that slighting and despising the things that are present, for the love that he hath to his Master's service, he is sure in the world that comes next to have glory for his reward. Now, said the Interpreter, I have showed thee this picture first, because the man whose picture this is, is the only man whom the Lord of the place whither thou art going hath authorized to be thy guide in all difficult places thou mayst meet with in the way: wherefore take good heed to what I have showed thee, and bear well in thy mind what thou hast seen, lest in thy journey thou meet with some that pretend to lead thee right, but their way goes down to death.

Then he took him by the hand, and led him into a very large parlor that was full of dust because never swept; the which after he reviewed it a little while, the Interpreter called for a man to sweep. Now, when he began to sweep, the dust began so abundantly to fly about, that Christian had almost therewith been choked. Then said the Interpreter to a damsel that stood

---

[17]Following the example of biblical writers, Bunyan here presents picture parables and gives an explanation of each.

by, "Bring hither water, and sprinkle the room"; the which when she had done, it was swept and cleansed with pleasure.

Then said Christian, What means this?

The Interpreter answered, This parlor is the heart of a man that was never sanctified by the sweet grace of the gospel. The dust is his original sin, and inward corruptions, that have defiled the whole man. He that began to sweep at first, is the law; but she that brought water, and did sprinkle it, is the gospel. Now whereas thou sawest, that as soon as the first began to sweep, the dust did so fly about, that the room could not by him be cleansed, but that thou was almost choked therewith; this is to show thee, that the law, instead of cleansing the heart (by its working) from sin, doth revive,[18] put strength into,[19] and increase it in the soul,[20] even as it doth discover and forbid it; for it doth not give power to subdue. Again, as thou sawest the damsel sprinkle the room with water, upon which it was cleansed with pleasure, this is to show thee, that when the Gospel comes in the sweet and precious influences thereof to the heart, then, I say, even as thou sawest the damsel lay the dust by sprinkling the floor with water, so is sin vanquished and subdued, and the soul made clean through the faith of it, and consequently fit for the King of glory to inhabit.[21]

I saw moreover in my dream, that the Interpreter took him by the hand, and led him into a little room, where sat two little children, each one in his chair. The name of the eldest was Passion, and the name of the other Patience. Passion seemed to be much discontented, but Patience was very quiet. Then Christian asked, "What is the reason of the discontent of Passion?" The Interpreter answered, "The governor of them would have him stay for his best things till the beginning of the next year, but he will have all now; but Patience is willing to wait."

Then I saw that one came to Passion, and brought him a bag of treasure, and poured it down at his feet; the which he took up, and rejoiced therein, and withal laughed Patience to scorn. But I beheld but a while, and he had lavished all away, and had nothing left him but rags.

CHRISTIAN. Then said Christian to the Interpreter, Expound this matter more fully to me.

INTERPRETER. So he said, These two lads are figures: Passion of the men of this world, and Patience of the men of that which is to come; for, as here thou seest, Passion will have all now, this year, that is to say, in this world; so are the men of this world; they must have all their good things now; they cannot stay till the next year, that is, until the next world, for their portion of good. That proverb, "A bird in the hand is worth two in the bush," is of more authority with them than are all the divine testimonies of the good of the world to come. But as thou sawest that he had quickly lavished all away, and had presently left him nothing but rags, so will it be with all such men at the end of this world.

CHRISTIAN. Then said Christian, Now I see that Patience has the best wisdom, and that upon many accounts. 1. Because he stays for the best things. 2. And also because he will have the glory of his, when the other has nothing but rags.

INTERPRETER. Nay, you may add another, to-wit, the glory of the next

18Rom. 7:9. 191 Cor. 15:56. 20Rom. 5:20. 21John 15:3; Eph. 5: 26; Acts 15:9, Rom. 16:25, 26.

world will never wear out; but these are suddenly gone. Therefore Passion had not so much reason to laugh at Patience because he had his good things first as Patience will have to laugh at Passion, because he had his best things last; for first must give place to last, because last must have his time to come; but last gives place to nothing; for there is not another to succeed; he therefore that hath his portion first, must needs have a time to spend it; but he that hath his portion last, must have it lastingly: therefore it is said of Dives, "In thy lifetime thou receivedst thy good things, and likewise Lazarus evil things: but now he is comforted, and thou art tormented."[22]

CHRISTIAN. Then I perceive it is not best to covet things that are now, but to wait for things to come.

INTERPRETER. You say truth: for the things that are seen are temporal, but the things that are not seen are eternal.[23] But though this be so, yet since things present, and our fleshly appetite, are such near neighbors one to another; and again, because things to come and carnal sense are such strangers one to another; therefore it is, that the first of these so suddenly fall into amity, and that distance is so continued between the second.[24]

Then I saw in my dream, that the Interpreter took Christian by the hand, and led him into a place where was a fire burning against a wall, and one standing by it, always casting much water upon it, to quench it; yet did the fire burn higher and hotter.

Then said Christian, What means this?

The Interpreter answered, This fire is the work of grace that is wrought in the heart; he that casts water upon it to extinguish and put it out, is the devil: but in that thou seest the fire, notwithstanding, burn higher and hotter, thou shalt also see the reason of that. So he had him about to the back side of the wall, where he saw a man with a vessel of oil in his hand, of the which he did also continually cast (but secretly) into the fire.

Then said Christian, What means this?

The Interpreter answered, This is Christ, who continually, with the oil of his grace, maintains the work already begun in the heart; by the means of which, notwithstanding what the devil can do, the souls of his people prove gracious still.[25] And in that thou sawest that the man stood behind the wall to maintain the fire; this is to teach thee, that it is hard for the tempted to see how this work of grace is maintained in the soul.

I saw also, that the Interpreter took him again by the hand, and led him into a pleasant place, where was built a stately palace, beautiful to behold; at the sight of which Christian was greatly delighted. He saw also upon the top thereof certain persons walking, who were clothed all in gold.

Then said Christian may we go in thither?

Then the Interpreter took him, and led him up towards the door of the palace; and behold, at the door stood a great company of men, as desirous to go in, but durst not. There also sat a man at a little distance from the door, at the table-side, with a book and his inkhorn before him, to take the names of them that should enter therein; he saw also that in the doorway stood many men in armor to keep it, being resolved to do to the men that would enter what hurt and

[22]Luke 16:25. [23]2 Cor. 4:18. [24]Rom. 7:15-25. [25]2 Cor. 12:9.

mischief they could. Now was Christian somewhat in amaze. At last, when every man started back for fear of the armed men, Christian saw a man of a very stout countenance come up to the man that sat there to write, saying, "Set down my name sir"; the which when he had done, he saw the man draw his sword, and put a helmet upon his head, and rush toward the door upon the armed men, who laid upon him with deadly force; but the man, not at all discouraged, fell to cutting and hacking most fiercely. So after he had received and given many wounds to those that attempted to keep him out[26]; he cut his way through them all and pressed forward into the palace, at which there was a pleasant voice heard from those that were within, even of those that walked upon the top of the palace saying,

Come in, come in,
Eternal glory shalt thou win.

So he went in, and was clothed with such garments as they. Then Christian smiled, and said, I think verily I know the meaning of this.

Now, said Christian, Let me go hence. Nay, stay, said the Interpreter, until I have showed thee a little more, and after that thou shalt go thy way. So he took him by the hand again, and led him into a very dark room, where there sat a man in an iron cage.

Now the man, to look on, seemed very sad; he sat with his eyes looking down to the ground, his hands folded together, and he sighed as if he would break his heart. Then said Christian, What means this? At which the Interpreter bid him talk with the man.

Then said Christian to the man, What art thou? The man answered, I am what I was not once.

CHRISTIAN. What wast thou once?

MAN. The man said, I was once a fair and flourishing professor,[27] both in mine own eyes, and also in the eyes of others: I once was, as I thought, fair for the celestial city, and had then even joy at the thoughts that I should get thither.

CHRISTIAN. Well, but what art thou now?

MAN. I am now a man of despair, and am shut up in it, as in this iron cage. I cannot get out; oh, now I cannot!

CHRISTIAN. But how camest thou into this condition?

MAN. I left off to watch and be sober: I laid the reins upon the neck of my lusts; I sinned against the light of the world, and the goodness of God; I have grieved the Spirit, and he is gone; I tempted the devil, and he is come to me; I have provoked God to anger, and he has left me: I have so hardened my heart, that I cannot repent.

Then said Christian to the Interpreter, But is there no hope for such a man as this? Ask him, said the Interpreter.

CHRISTIAN. Then said Christian, Is there no hope, but you must be kept in the iron cage of despair?

MAN. No, none at all.

CHRISTIAN. Why, the Son of the Blessed is very pitiful.

MAN. I have crucified him to myself afresh.[28] I have despised his person.[29] I have despised his righteousness; I have counted his blood an unholy thing; I have done despite to the Spirit of grace[30]; therefore I shut myself out of all the promises, and there now remains to me nothing but threatenings, dreadful threatenings, fearful threatenings of certain judg-

---

[26]Matt. 1:12; Acts 14:22.

[27]Luke 8:13. [28]Heb. 6:6.
[29]Luke 19:14. [30]Heb. 10:28,29.

ment and fiery indignation, which shall devour me as an adversary.

CHRISTIAN. For what did you bring yourself into this condition?

MAN. For the lusts, pleasures, and profits of this world; in the enjoyment of which I did then promise myself much delight; but now every one of those things also bite me, and gnaw me, like a burning worm.

CHRISTIAN. But canst thou not now repent and turn?

MAN. God hath denied me repentance. His word gives me no encouragement to believe; yea, himself hath shut me up in this iron cage: nor can all the men in the world let me out. Oh eternity! eternity! how shall I grapple with the misery that I must meet with in eternity.

Then said the Interpreter to Christian, Let this man's misery be remembered by thee, and be an everlasting caution to thee.

Well, said Christian, this is fearful! God help me to watch and to be sober, and to pray that I may shun the cause of this man's misery. Sir, is it not time for me to go on my way now?

INTERPRETER. Tarry till I shall show thee one thing more, and then thou shalt go on thy way.

So he took Christian by the hand again, and led him into a chamber where there was one rising out of bed; and as he put on his raiment, he shook and trembled. Then said Christian, Why doth this man thus tremble? The Interpreter then bid him tell to Christian the reason of his so doing.

So he began, and said, "This night, as I was in my sleep, I dreamed, and behold the heavens grew exceeding black; also it thundered and lightened in most fearful wise, that it put me into an agony. So I looked up in my dream, and saw the clouds rack at an unusual rate; upon which I heard a great sound of a trumpet, and saw also a man sitting upon a cloud, attended with the thousands of heaven: they were all in flaming fire; also the heavens were in a burning flame. I heard then a voice, saying, 'Arise, ye dead, and come to judgment.' And with that the rocks rent, the graves opened, and the dead that were therein came forth; some of them were exceeding glad, and looked upward; and some sought to hide themselves under the mountains. Then I saw the man that sat upon the cloud open the book, and bid the world draw near. Yet there was, by reason of a fierce flame that issued out and came from before him, a convenient distance between him and them, as between the judge and the prisoners at the bar.[31] I heard it also proclaimed to them that attended on the man that sat on the cloud, 'Gather together the tares, the chaff, and stubble, and cast them into the burning lake.'[32] And with that the bottomless pit opened, just whereabout I stood; out of the mouth of which there came, in an abundant manner, smoke, and coals of fire, with hideous noises. It was also said to the same persons, 'Gather my wheat into the garner.'[33] And with that I saw many catched up and carried away into the clouds, but I was left behind.[34] I also sought to hide myself, but I could not; for the man that sat upon the cloud still kept his eye upon me: my sins also came into my mind, and my conscience did accuse me on every side.[35] Upon this I awakened from my sleep.

CHRISTIAN. But what was it that made you so afraid of this sight?

[31] 1 Cor. 15; 1 Thess. 4:16; Jude 15; John 5:28, 29; 2 Thess. 1:8-10; Rev. 20: 11-14; Isa. 26:21; Micah 7:16, 17; Psa. 5:4; 50:1-3; Mal. 3:2, 3; Dan. 7:9, 10. [32] Matt. 3:12; 18:30; 24:30; Mal. 4:1. [33] Luke 3:17. [34] 1 Thess. 4:16, 17. [35] Rom. 2:14, 15.

By Dalziel after Watson

CHRISTIAN AT THE END OF HIS JOURNEY

MAN. Why I thought that the day of judgment was come, and that I was not ready for it: but this affrighted me most, that the angels gathered up several, and left me behind: also the pit of hell opened her mouth just where I stood. My conscience too afflicted me; and, as I thought, the Judge had always his eye upon me, showing indignation in his countenance.

Then said the Interpreter to Christian, Hast thou considered all these things?

CHRISTIAN. Yes, and they put me in hope and fear.

INTERPRETER. Well, keep all things so in thy mind, that they may be as a goad in thy sides, to prick thee, forward in the way thou must go. Then Christian began to gird up his loins, and to address himself to his journey. Then said the Interpreter, "The Comforter be always with thee, good Christian, to guide thee in the way that leads to the city." So Christian went on his way, saying,—

Here have I seen things rare and profitable,
Things pleasant, dreadful, things to make me stable
In what I have begun to take in hand:
Then let me think on them, and understand
Wherefore they showed me were, and let me be
Thankful, O good Interpreter, to thee.

Now I saw in my dream, that the highway up which Christian was to go, was fenced on either side with a wall, and that wall was called Salvation.[36] Up this way, therefore, did burdened Christian run, but not without great difficulty, because of the load on his back.

He ran thus till he came at a place somewhat ascending; and upon that place stood a cross, and a little below, in the bottom, a sepulchre. So I saw in my dream, that just as Christian came up with the cross, his burden loosed from off his shoulders, and fell from off his back, and began to tumble, and so continued to do till it came to the mouth of the sepulchre, where it fell in, and I saw it no more.

Then was Christian glad and lightsome, and said with a merry heart, "He hath given me rest by his sorrow, and life by his death." Then he stood still a while, to look and wonder; for it was very surprising to him that the sight of the cross should thus ease him of his burden. He looked, therefore, and looked again, even till the springs that were in his head sent the waters down his cheeks.[37] Now as he stood looking and weeping, behold, three Shining Ones came to him, and saluted him with, "Peace be to thee." So the first said to him, "Thy sins be forgiven thee"[38]; the second stripped him of his rags, and clothed him with change of raiment[39]; the third also set a mark on his forehead,[40] and gave him a roll with a seal upon it, which he bid him look on as he ran, and that he should give it in at the celestial gate; so they went their way.

---

[36]Isaiah 26:1.

[37]Zech. 12:10.   [38]Mark 2:5.
[39]Zech. 3:4.   [40]Eph. 1:13.

For Thought and Discussion

1. Where had Evangelist first found Christian?
2. With what was Christian burdened on his journey?
3. Into what trouble did Worldly Wiseman lure Christian?
4. What three counsels of Worldly Wiseman did Evangelist bid Christian beware?
5. With what other vice does Bunyan link cheating and hypocrisy?
6. Why was it necessary for Christian to pass through the wicket-gate?
7. Who opened the gate for Christian?
8. What danger beset the way of all who tried to enter the wicket-gate?
9. Who is Beelzebub?
10. Account for the names borne by the companions who started on the journey with Christian.

11. What is the meaning of each of the parables?
12. What proverb is suggestive of Benjamin Franklin?   Is the proverb from the Bible?
13. Why was it fitting that in his dream Christian was supplied with clean and shining raiment?
14. What type of literature is *Pilgrim's Progress*?

WE ARE SEVEN

WILLIAM WORDSWORTH

[As his contribution to the *Lyrical Ballads* Wordsworth set out to write about aspects of nature and simple, commonplace objects.

In "We Are Seven" his purpose is accomplished, and something of his mystic quality is revealed, a quality which seems a heritage more common to children and youth than to maturity.]

—A simple child.
That lightly draws its breath,
And feels its life in every limb,
What should it know of death?

I met a little cottage girl;   5
She was eight years old, she said;
Her hair was thick with many a curl
That clustered round her head.

She had a rustic, woodland air,
And she was wildly clad;   10
Her eyes were fair, and very fair;
—Her beauty made me glad.

"Sisters and brothers, little maid,
How many may you be?"
"How many? Seven in all," she said, 15
And wondering looked at me.

"And where are they? I pray you tell."
She answered, "Seven are we;
And two of us at Conway dwell,
And two are gone to sea.   20

"Two of us in the churchyard lie,
My sister and my brother;
And, in the churchyard cottage, I
Dwell near them with my mother."

"You say that two at Conway dwell,
And two are gone to sea,   26
Yet ye are seven! I pray you tell,
Sweet maid, how this may be."

Then did the little maid reply,
"Seven boys and girls are we;   30
Two of us in the churchyard lie;
Beneath the churchyard tree."

"You run about, my little maid,
Your limbs, they are alive;
If two are in the churchyard laid, 35
Then ye are only five."

"Their graves are green; they may be seen,"
The little maid replied,
"Twelve steps or more from my mother's door,
And they are side by side.   40

"My stockings there I often knit,
My kerchief there I hem;
And there upon the ground I sit,
And sing a song to them.

"And often after sunset, sir,   45
When it is light and fair,
I take my little porringer,
And eat my supper there.

"The first that died was sister Jane;
In bed she moaning lay,   50
Till God released her of her pain;
And then she went away.

"So in the churchyard she was laid;
And, when the grass was dry,
Together round her grave we
        played,   55
My brother John and I.

"And when the ground was white
        with snow,
And I could run and slide,

My brother John was forced to go,
And he lies by her side."   60

"How many are you, then," said I,
"If they two are in heaven?"
Quick was the little maid's reply,
"O master! we are seven."

"But they are dead; those two are
        dead!   65
Their spirits are in heaven!"
'Twas throwing words away; for still
The little maid would have her will,
And said, "Nay, we are seven!"

For Thought and Discussion

1. What is the girl's attitude toward her family? toward death?
2. What experiences of Wordsworth's own life are possibly reflected in this poem?
3. Does using the exact language of the speaker add to or detract from the interest of the story? What type of poetry often makes use of this device?
4. How does this poem contribute to the plan Coleridge and Wordsworth made for their lyrical ballads?

A LATE LARK TWITTERS

WILLIAM ERNEST HENLEY

A LATE lark twitters from the
        quiet skies;
And from the west,
Where the sun, his day's work ended,
Lingers as in content,
There falls on the old, gray city   5
An influence luminous and serene,
A shining peace.

The smoke ascends
In a rosy-and-golden haze. The spires
Shine, and are changed. In the val-
        ley   10
Shadows rise. The lark sings on. The
        sun,

Closing his benediction,
Sinks, and the darkening air
Thrills with a sense of the triumphing
        night—
Night with her train of stars   15
And her great gift of sleep.

So be my passing!
My task accomplished and the long
        day done,
My wages taken, and in my heart
Some late lark singing,   20
Let me be gathered to the quiet west,
The sundown splendid and serene,
Death.

For Thought and Discussion

1. What does the poet mention in the first stanza that suggests the close of day?
2. To what does he compare the close of day?

∽∾

PROSPICE

ROBERT BROWNING

[*Prospice* (pros′ pĭ kĕ or prŏs′ pĭ sē) means "Look Forward." Browning's poem of this name expresses the author's attitude toward death and his assurance of a reunion with his wife, who died a few months before the poem was written.

[1]*The Arch Fear*, death. [2]*guerdon*, reward. [3]*arrears*, the debt of gratitude for what life has given him.]

FEAR death?—to feel the fog in
  my throat,
The mist in my face,
When the snows begin, and the blasts
  denote
I am nearing the place,
The power of the night, the press of
  the storm,   5
The post of the foe;
Where he stands, the Arch Fear[1] in a
  visible form,
Yet the strong man must go;
For the journey is done and the sum-
  mit attained,
And the barriers fall,   10

Though a battle's to fight ere the
  guerdon[2] be gained,
The reward of it all.
I was ever a fighter, so—one fight
  more,
The best and the last!
I would hate that death bandaged my
  eyes, and forbore,   15
And bade me creep past.
No! let me taste the whole of it, fare
  like my peers,
The heroes of old,
Bear the brunt, in a minute pay glad
  life's arrears[3]
Of pain, darkness, and cold.   20
For sudden the worst turns the best
  to the brave,
The black minute's at end,
And the elements' rage, the fiend-
  voices that rave,
Shall dwindle, shall blend,
Shall change, shall become first a
  peace out of pain,   25
Then a light, then thy breast,
O thou soul of my soul! I shall clasp
  thee again,
And with God be the rest!

For Thought and Discussion

1. Who is the *Arch Fear,* and what is the last fight referred to in this poem?
2. Explain the meaning of the expression "I would hate that death bandaged my eyes."
3. Bring out clearly the mood expressed in each of the two divisions of the poem.
4. Whom does the poet address in the closing lines?
5. What is the poet's attitude toward God?

EPILOGUE TO ASOLANDO

ROBERT BROWNING

[This selection, Browning's last words to the world, came from the press on the day of his death, December 12, 1889. It is a triumphant expression of a person who faced life and death not only unafraid but with challenging and conquering faith.]

A T the midnight in the silence of
   the sleep-time,
When you set your fancies free,
Will they pass to where—by death,
   fools think, imprisoned—
Low he lies who once so loved you,
   whom you loved so
     —Pity me?   5

Oh to love so, be so loved, yet so mistaken!
What had I on earth to do
With the slothful, with the mawkish,
   the unmanly?

Like the aimless, helpless, hopeless, did
   I drivel
     —Being—who?   10

One who never turned his back but
   marched breast forward,
   Never doubted clouds would break,
Never dreamed, though right were
   worsted, wrong would triumph,
Held we fall to rise, are baffled to
   fight better,
     Sleep to wake.   15

No at noonday in the bustle of man's
   work-time
   Greet the unseen with a cheer!
Bid him forward, breast and back as
   either should be,
"Strive and thrive!" cry, "Speed,—
   fight on, fare ever
     There as here!"

For Thought and Discussion

1. For what type of person would one need to feel pity in death?
2. What question does Browning ask about himself?
3. How does the poet bid one greet eternity?
4. Why does a brave attitude toward life and death strengthen one?

From IN MEMORIAM

ALFRED LORD TENNYSON

CXXX

T HY voice is on the rolling air;
   I hear thee where the waters run;
Thou standest in the rising sun,
And in the setting thou art fair.

What art thou then? I cannot guess. 5
   But tho' I seem in star and flower
   To feel thee some diffusive power,
I do not therefore love thee less:

My love involves the love before;
   My love is vaster passion now; 10
Tho' mix'd with God and Nature thou,
I seem to love thee more and more.

Far off thou art, but ever nigh;
   I have thee still, and I rejoice;
   I prosper, circled with thy voice; 15
I shall not lose thee tho' I die.

For Thought and Discussion

1. What is Tennyson's final conclusion about life after death, or immortality?
2. Compare this poem with "Crossing the Bar."

∽✑

CROSSING THE BAR
ALFRED LORD TENNYSON

[Tennyson requested his son, Hallam Tennyson, to have this poem placed last in all the editions of his works.]

Sunset and evening star,
  And one clear call for me!
And may there be no moaning of the
    bar,
  When I put out to sea,

But such a tide as moving seems
    asleep,   5
  Too full for sound and foam,

When that which drew from out the
    boundless deep
  Turns again home.

Twilight and evening bell,
  And after that the dark!   10
And may there be no sadness of fare-
    well,
  When I embark;

For though from out our bourne of
    Time and Place
  The flood may bear me far,
I hope to see my Pilot face to face   15
  When I have crossed the bar.

For Thought and Discussion

1. What kind of death does Tennyson describe in "Crossing the Bar"?
2. Who is the Pilot?
3. Why does Tennyson often refer to the sea in his poems?
4. Since Tennyson was pre-eminently a Victorian, he is an outstanding representative of his own time. Re-read "The Victorian Age" in "Periods of Literature."
5. Compare this poem in mood, theme, and attitude toward death with "A Late Lark Twitters."

———

ALFRED LORD TENNYSON 1809-1892

Early Life. Alfred Tennyson was the fourth in a family of twelve children of eight boys and four girls. In this group of imaginative children there was no lack of entertainment; the deeds of knights, champions, and warriors, enacted again and again, never grew old. In the evenings as they sat around the fire, Alfred often cheered the circle with endless stories continued from day to day.

At first Alfred attended a grammar school which he detested; later he studied under his father, rector of Somersby, known as the "stern doctor." As Tennyson lived in the country, he spent much

ALFRED LORD TENNYSON

time walking, enjoying particularly the dreary scenes of the marshy sections, often drawn to the seashore by that deep attraction which the sea always had for him.

At Cambridge.   At nineteen when he entered Cambridge along with his brother Charles, he found his studies uninteresting and matter-of-fact but liked the congenial friends whom he met, especially those in a club known as *The Apostles*. One of the members, Henry Arthur Hallam, became Tennyson's closest friend.

Alfred did not do brilliant work in college but did receive the prize medal for poetry on his poem "Timbuctoo" on June 6, 1829. The next year *Poems by Two Brothers*, a joint edition by Alfred and Charles, appeared without attracting an unusual amount of attention.

A Romantic Meeting.   On one of Hallam's frequent visits to Somersby, walking with Emily Sellwood in Fairy Wood, he came upon Tennyson who, charmed with the attractive simplicity of the girl's costume, wondered if she were a "Dryad or an Oread." Later when his brother Charles married Louise Sellwood, Emily, the bridesmaid, was taken into the church by Alfred. Alfred saw Emily frequently after this, and there was a long engagement which was ended by Mr. Sellwood, who thought that a "poor" young poet could never make a comfortable living.

After College.   Alfred left college on account of the ill health of his father, who died soon afterward. In the next few years the most significant event for Tennyson was the death of his friend, Arthur Hallam, who died suddenly from fever while in Europe. For both Tennyson and his sister Emily, Hallam's fiancée, the shock was very great, one from which the poet never recovered completely. In memory of this friend Tennyson began the series of lyrics which was finally to be published in 1850 as *In Memoriam*, his most famous work. Having adopted poetry for his life work, Tennyson spent long hours writing, revising, polishing, and for a long time tossed practically everything aside as unworthy. The perfection of style which finally resulted from this strenuous study is no doubt responsible in part for the popularity of his poetry, which is unusually clear and musical.

Friends in London.   After the marriage of Charles, Mrs. Tennyson and her daughters moved near London, and Alfred spent much time in the city, becoming a member of the Sterling Club, among whose members were Carlyle, Dickens, Thackeray, Leigh Hunt, Landor, as well as some of his old friends, *The Apostles*, from Cambridge. Carlyle, whom he knew very well, wrote an excellent description of him:

"I think he must be under forty, not much under it. One of the finest looking men in the world. A great shock of rough, dusky dark hair; bright, laughing hazel eyes, massive aquiline face, most massive yet most delicate; of sallow brown complexion, almost Indian looking, clothes cynically loose, free-and-easy, smokes infinite tobacco. His voice is musical, metallic, fit for loud laughter and piercing wail, and for all that may lie between; speech and speculation free and plenteous; I do not meet in these late decades such company over a pipe. We shall see what he shall grow to."[1]

Mrs. Carlyle said of him: Read "Ulysses," and "Dora," and the "Vision of Sin," and you will find that we do not over-rate him. Besides he is a very handsome man, and a noble-hearted one, with something of the gypsy in his appearance, which for me is perfectly charming."[2]

Poems. "Locksley Hall" with its well-known quotation,

"In the spring a young man's fancy lightly turns
to thoughts of love,"

"Ulysses," and "Morte d'Arthur" (mŏrt där' thĕr) were published in 1842 and *The Princess* in 1844. Although well received, these poems did not furnish means for a sufficient income, but through the kind intervention of Carlyle, Tennyson became the recipient of a pension, which proved a welcome addition to his finances.

1850. The year 1850 was significant for Tennyson. *In Memoriam*, written in memory of his friend, Arthur Hallam, was published, eagerly read, and pronounced outstanding. In this year he was married to Emily Sellwood with whom he had been in love

---

[1]*"Alfred, Lord Tennyson, a Memoir,"* Hallam Tennyson.
[2]*Ibid.*

TENNYSON'S FARRINGFORD PORCH

fourteen years. Shortly after his marriage he was appointed poet laureate to succeed Wordsworth, whose death had occurred a few months previously.

Life at Farringford. A few years after his marriage Tennyson bought Farringford on the Isle of Wight, a quiet retreat from the world, a haven for work. Especially did he like the location near the sea. From this time on, many poems were published, "The Charge of the Light Brigade," *Maud, Idylls of the King,* and *Enoch Arden,* which had a sale of sixty thousand copies.

Aldworth. Tennyson was a sufferer from hay fever. For this reason he bought Aldworth in Sussex and spent many months of each year there. He probably was not very fond of this new home, since here he had to climb to a high point to get a glimpse of the sea. On account of the popularity of his work, so many visitors came to see him that he found difficulty in finding the leisure and quiet necessary for work. The Brownings, Charles Kingsley, John Ruskin, the Carlyles were among the literary people with whom he corresponded. Among his American admirers were Emerson, Hawthorne, Margaret Fuller, Edgar Allan Poe, Dr. Oliver Wendell Holmes, Walt Whitman, and Henry Wadsworth Longfellow, who sent him an Indian stone pipe, since Tennyson was known to be quite fond of pipes. His definition of a perfect dinner was "a beefsteak, a potato, a cut of cheese, a pint of port, and afterward a pipe (never a cigar)."[3]

[3]*Alfred, Lord Tennyson, a Memoir,* Hallam Tennyson.

TENNYSON IN HIS LIBRARY

Last Days. When Tennyson grew old, he continued to write, even though his health was affected. He no longer had that robust strength which had enabled him in his youth to pick up a pet pony and walk off with it. By this time recognition of his poetry had given him a place of honor and security. At last he had taken the title which he had at first refused; he had now become Alfred Lord Tennyson, accepting this new honor for the sake of literature and to accede to the wishes of Queen Victoria and her famous minister, Gladstone.

"Crossing the Bar," one of his clearest and most musical lyrics, which was written a year before his death, seemed a fitting close for a great literary career.

His devotion to literature, which was lifelong, is exemplified in his death. One evening he died peacefully, clasping the volume of Shakespeare for which he had asked shortly before. He was buried in Westminster Abbey next to Robert Browning and in front of the Chaucer monument. These lines on the passing of King Arthur belong to him:

> ". . . . . . 'The King is gone.'
> And therewithal came on him the weird rhyme,
> 'From the great deep to the great deep he goes.' "

"LEAD, KINDLY LIGHT"

At Sea, June 16, 1833

JOHN HENRY NEWMAN

LEAD, kindly Light, amid the encircling gloom,
　　Lead thou me on!
The night is dark, and I am far from home—
　　Lead thou me on!
Keep thou my feet; I do not ask to see　　　　5
The distant scene—one step enough for me.

I was not ever thus, nor prayed that thou
　　Shouldst lead me on.
I loved to choose and see my path; but now
　　Lead thou me on!　　10
I loved the garish day, and, spite of fears,
Pride ruled my will; remember not past years.

So long thy power hath blest me, sure it still
　　Will lead me on,
O'er moor and fen, o'er crag and torrent, till　　15
　　The night is gone;
And with the morn those angel faces smile
Which I have loved long since, and lost awhile.

REMEMBER NOW THY CREATOR

ECCLESIASTES 12

REMEMBER now thy Creator in the days of thy Youth,
While the evil days come not, nor the years draw nigh,
When thou shalt say, "I have no pleasure in them";

While the sun, or the light, or the moon,
Or the stars, be not darkened,　　5
Nor the clouds return after the rain;

In the days when the keepers of the house shall tremble,
And the strong men shall bow themselves . . .
And those that look out of the windows be darkened,

And the doors shall be shut in the streets, . . .　　10
And he shall rise up at the voice of the bird,
And all the daughters of music shall be brought low;

Also when they shall be afraid of that which is high,
And fears shall be in the way, and the almond tree shall flourish,
And the grasshopper shall be a burden,　　15

And desire shall fail;
Because man goeth to his long home,
And the mourners go about the streets.

Or ever the silver cord be loosed,
Or the golden bowl be broken,   20
Or the pitcher be broken at the foun-
    tain,
Or the wheel broken at the cistern,

Then shall the dust return to the
    earth as it was;
And the spirit shall return unto God
    who gave it.

ODE

ON INTIMATIONS OF IMMORTALITY
FROM RECOLLECTIONS OF EARLY CHILDHOOD
WILLIAM WORDSWORTH

[Reflected in this poem is Wordsworth's philosophy — that common
life is a fitting theme for poetry, that
God is reflected in nature, that the
child is akin to nature and to God,
and that the simple, natural pleasures
of childhood are the true criteria of
happiness, and, yet, that the passing
of the years brings to the mature man
a philosophic strength and faith and
joy which more than compensate for
the lost radiance of his youth.]

THERE was a time when meadow,
    grove, and stream,
The earth, and every common sight
    To me did seem
    Appareled in celestial light,
The glory and the freshness of a
    dream.   5
It is not now as it hath been of yore—
    Turn wheresoe'er I may,
        By night or day,
The things which I have seen I now
    can see no more.

    The rainbow comes and goes,   10
    And lovely is the rose;
    The moon doth with delight
Look round her when the heavens
    are bare;
    Waters on a starry night
    Are beautiful and fair;   15
    The sunshine is a glorious birth;
    But yet I know, where'er I go,
That there hath passed away a glory
    from the earth.

Now, while the birds thus sing a joy-
    ous song,
    And while the young lambs
    bound   20
        As to the tabor's sound,
To me alone there came a thought of
    grief;
A timely utterance gave that thought
    relief,
    And I again am strong.
The cataracts blow their trumpets
    from the steep;   25

No more shall grief of mine the sea-
    son wrong;
I hear the echoes through the moun-
    tains throng;
The winds come to me from the fields
    of sleep,[1]
    And all the earth is gay;
        Land and sea   30
    Give themselves up to jollity,
    And with the heart of May
    Doth every beast keep holiday.
        Thou child of joy,
Shout round me, let me hear thy
    shouts, thou happy shepherd-
    boy!   35
Ye blessèd creatures, I have heard the
    call
    Ye to each other make; I see
The heavens laugh with you in your
    jubilee;

---

[1]*fields of sleep*, distant places of
quiet and repose.

My heart is at your festival,
    My head hath its coronal,   40
The fullness of your bliss, I feel—I
    feel it all.
    O evil day! if I were sullen
    While earth herself is adorning
        This sweet May-morning,
    And the children are culling   45
        On every side,
    In a thousand valleys far and
        wide,
Fresh flowers; while the sun shines
    warm,
And the babe leaps up on his mother's
    arm—
    I hear, I hear, with joy I hear!   50
    —But there's a tree, of many,
        one,
A single field which I have looked
    upon;
Both of them speak of something that
    is gone.
        The pansy at my feet
        Doth the same tale repeat;   55
Whither is fled the visionary gleam?
Where is it now, the glory and the
    dream?

Our birth is but a sleep and a forget-
    ting;
The soul that rises with us, our life's
    star,
    Hath had elsewhere its setting   60
        And cometh from afar;
    Not in entire forgetfulness,
    And not in utter nakedness,
But trailing clouds of glory we do
    come
        From God, who is our
        home.   65
Heaven lies about us in our infancy!
Shades of the prison-house begin to
    close
        Upon the growing boy,
But he beholds the light, and whence
    it flows,
        He sees it in his joy;   70
The youth, who daily farther from
    the east

Must travel, still is nature's priest,
    And by the vision splendid
    Is on his way attended;
At length the man perceives it die
    away,   75
And fade into the light of common
    day.

Earth fills her lap with pleasures of
    her own;
Yearnings she hath in her own natu-
    ral kind,
And, even with something of a
    mother's mind
        And no unworthy aim,   80
    The homely nurse doth all she
    can
To make her foster-child, her inmate
    man,
        Forget the glories he hath
        known,
And that imperial palace whence he
    came.
Behold the child among his new-born
    blisses,   85
A six years' darling of a pigmy size!
See, where 'mid work of his own
    hand he lies,
Fretted by sallies of his mother's
    kisses,
With light upon him from his father's
    eyes!
See, at his feet, some little plan or
    chart,   90
Some fragment from his dream of
    human life,
Shaped by himself with newly-
    learnèd art;
        A wedding or a festival,
        A mourning or a funeral;
        And this hath now his
        heart,   95
    And unto this he frames his song.
        Then will he fit his tongue
To dialogues of business, love, or
    strife;
    But it will not be long
    Ere this be thrown aside,   100
    And with new joy and pride

The little actor cons another part;
Filling from time to time his "humor-
    ous stage"[2]
With all the persons, down to palsied
    age,
That life brings with her in her equip-
    age[3];   105
        As if his whole vocation
        Were endless imitation.

Thou, whose exterior semblance doth
    belie
        Thy soul's immensity;
Thou best philosopher, who yet dost
    keep   110
Thy heritage, thou eye among the
    blind,
That, deaf and silent, read'st the
    eternal deep,[4]
Haunted forever by the eternal
    mind—
        Mighty prophet! seer blest!
        On whom those truths do
        rest   115
Which we are toiling all our lives to
    find,
In darkness lost, the darkness of the
    grave;
Thou, over whom thy immortality[5]
Broods like the day, a master o'er a
    slave,
A presence which is not to be put
    by;   120
Thou little child, yet glorious in the
    might
Of heaven-born freedom on thy be-
    ing's height,
Why with such earnest pains dost
    thou provoke

The years to bring the inevitable
    yoke,
Thus blindly with thy blessedness at
    strife?   125
Full soon thy soul shall have her
    earthly freight,
And custom lie upon thee with a
    weight
Heavy as frost, and deep almost as
    life!
        O joy! that in our embers
        Is something that doth
        live,   130
        That nature yet remembers
        What was so fugitive!
The thought of our past years in me
    doth breed
Perpetual benediction; not indeed
For that which is most worthy to be
    blest,   135
Delight and liberty, the simple
    creed
Of childhood, whether busy or at
    rest,
With new-fledged hope still flutter-
    ing in his breast—
        Not for these I raise
        The song of thanks and
        praise;   140
But for those obstinate question-
    ings[6]
Of sense and outward things,
Fallings from us, vanishings;
Blank misgivings of a creature
Moving about in worlds not real-
    ized,   145
High instincts, before which our mor-
    tal nature
Did tremble like a guilty thing sur-
    prised.
        But for those first affec-
        tions,
        Those shadowy recollec-
        tions,
        Which, be they what they
        may,   150

---

[2]*humorous*, whimsical, fanciful, i. e.,
the stage in which the child in various
whims and moods acts out the parts of
the various characters whom he ima-
gines himself to be.

[3]*equipage*, retinue.

[4]*eternal deep*, mysteries of life.

[5]*thy immortality*, not a reference to
dying but a suggestion that he has a
light or understanding of the world
from which he has so recently come.

---

[6]*obstinate questionings*, doubts of
the existence of things in the physical
world.

Are yet the fountain-light of all our
    day,
Are yet a master-light of all our
    seeing;
    Uphold us, cherish, and have power
      to make
Our noisy years seem moments in
    the being
Of the eternal silence: truths that
    wake,   155
        To perish never;
Which neither listlessness, nor mad
    endeavor,
        Nor man nor boy,
Nor all that is at enmity with joy,
Can utterly abolish or destroy!   160
    Hence, in a season of calm weather
      Though inland far we be,
Our souls have sight of that immor-
    tal sea
        Which brought us hither;
        Can in a moment travel thith-
      er,   165
And see the children sport upon the
    shore,
And hear the mighty waters rolling
    evermore.

Then sing, ye birds, sing, sing a joy-
    ous song!
    And let the young lambs bound
    As to the tabor's sound!   170
    We, in thought, will join your
      throng,
        Ye that pipe and ye that play,
        Ye that through your hearts to-
        day
    Feel the gladness of the May!
What though the radiance which was
    once so bright   175
Be now forever taken from my sight,
    Though nothing can bring back
    the hour
Of splendor in the grass, of glory
    in the flower;

We will grieve not, rather find
Strength in what remains be-
    hind;   18
In the primal sympathy
Which having been must ever
    be;
In the soothing thoughts that
    spring
Out of human suffering;
In the faith that looks through
    death,   18
In years that bring the philosophic
    mind.

And O ye fountains, meadows, hills
    and groves,
Forbode not any severing of our
    loves!
Yet in my heart of hearts I feel your
    might;
I only have relinquished one delight 190
To live beneath your more habitual
    sway.
I love the brooks which down their
    channels fret
Even more than when I tripped light-
    ly as they;
The innocent brightness of a new-
    born day
        Is lovely yet;   19
The clouds that gather round the
    setting sun
Do take a sober coloring from an eye
That hath kept watch o'er man's
    mortality;
Another race hath been, and other
    palms are won.
Thanks to the human heart by which
    we live,   200
Thanks to the tenderness, its joys, and
    fears,
To me the meanest flower that blows
    can give
Thoughts that do often lie too deep
    for tears.

For Thought and Discussion

1. Considering the meaning of the chief words of the title and the contents of the poem, suggest other titles suitable for the selection.
2. Mention several lines in the poem that remind you of your own childhood experiences.
3. In what respects are the introduction and the conclusion of this poem somewhat parallel?
4. In what does Wordsworth's joy in nature consist?
5. What question rather expressive of a certain discontent is asked in stanza four? How do later stanzas answer the question?
6. What beautiful assertion concerning birth is made in stanza five?
7. Why, according to lines 42-57, does a child begin to forget the glories mentioned above? How do lines 123-128 add to this conception? Explain the term "eye among the blind."
8. What value does the poet place upon recollections?
9. Would the poet, if he could do so, shield people from doubt and fears and sorrows? Justify your answer.
10. Judging from the last stanza of the poem, does Wordsworth seem to think an adult's pleasure in nature is less, more, or merely different from that of a child?

Plus Work

Compare lines 85-105 with the "Seven Ages of Man" in *As You Like It*, Act II, Scene 7.

TRUST

CHRISTINA ROSSETTI

[This sonnet is, in spirit of self-effacement, love for another, and trust in God, akin to *Sonnets from the Portuguese*.]

If I could trust mine own self with
    your fate,
Shall I not rather trust it in God's
    hand?
Without whose will one lily doth not
    stand,
Nor sparrow fall at his appointed
    date;
Who numbereth the innumerable
    sand,   5
Who weighs the wind and water with
    a weight,
To whom the world is neither small
    nor great,
Whose knowledge foreknew every
    plan we planned.
Searching my heart for all that
    touches you,
I find there only love and love's good-
    will   10
Helpless to help and impotent to do,
Of understanding dull, of sight most
    dim;
And therefore I commend you back
    to him
Whose love your love's capacity can
    fill.

For Thought and Discussion

1. List the biblical passages referred to by the poet.
2. Quote lines indicative of human frailty and weakness and others indicative of God's limitless power and love.

THE LORD IS MY SHEPHERD

PSALM 23

[In this lyric David, the sweet singer of Israel, voices his confidence in Jehovah's protecting care. He couches his trust in figurative language drawn from his experience as a shepherd boy. For beauty of setting, suggestiveness of language, and depth of faith the poem is unexcelled.]

THE LORD *is* my shepherd; I shall not want.

He maketh me to lie down in green pastures:

He leadeth me beside the still waters.

He restoreth my soul:

He leadeth me in the paths of righteousness for his name's sake.

Yea, though I walk through the valley of the shadow of death,

I will fear no evil: for thou *art* with me;

Thy rod and thy staff they comfort me.

Thou preparest a table before me in the presence of mine enemies:

Thou anointest my head with oil;

My cup runneth over.

Surely goodness and mercy shall follow me all the days of my life:

And I will dwell in the house of the Lord forever.

For Thought and Discussion

1. For what temporal wants does David declare the Lord will provide?
2. For what spiritual needs is His grace sufficient?
3. Which of his experiences as a shepherd boy do you think suggested to David the various lines of this Psalm?
4. What New Testament scripture carries out this figure of Christ as a Good Shepherd?
5. Why does David speak of "still waters"?
6. What tendency of the sheep called forth the statement "He restoreth my soul"?

Plus Work

Arrange for a group of your classmates to give this Psalm and Psalm 24 as a choral reading.

Read aloud to the class *The Song of our Syrian Guest* by William Allen Knight.

❧

Additional Readings

Brierley, J.: *Ourselves and the Universe*

Dickens, Charles: *Life of Our Lord*

Kingsley, Charles: *Hypatia*

Mikels and Shoup: *Poetry of Today*

Powys, Llewelyn: *The Cradle of God A Pagan's Pilgrimage*

Rittenhouse, Jessie B.: *The Little Book of Modern Verse*

Russell, George W.: *Collected Poems*

Tagore, Rabindranath: *The Religion of Man*

Tennyson, Alfred Lord: *In Memoriam*

Thompson, Francis: *The Hound of Heaven*

Unamuno, Miguel de: *The Agony of Christianity*

Yogananda, Swami: *Whispers from Eternity*

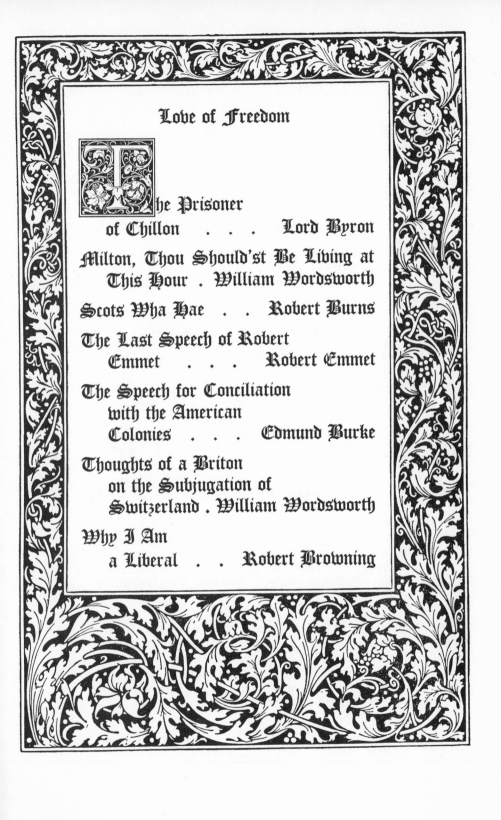

Love of Freedom

LOVE OF FREEDOM

THE freedom of birds in flight has ever been an inspiration to man, drawing him into the realm of fancy and reflection and giving zest to his spirit. An untrammeled spirit expands and leads, tempting the mind to greater achievement. Did man's desire to fly the heavens with the birds lead to the invention of the aeroplane? As freedom of the air is becoming a realization, freedom on the earth remains an unrealized ideal.

The countless numbers of men who have died for the cause of freedom indicate how precious the ideal is to humanity. In the twentieth century this love of freedom has expanded to include all classes in a measure never dreamed of in past ages. The same ideal was voiced by Voltaire when he said, "I disapprove of what you say, but I will defend to the death your right to say it." As long as the right to free speech is maintained, people will remain free, but when that right is lost, freedom is in the dust.

The free man initiates and builds. He is an asset because of his independence; the slave has lost the desire and capacity for progress and has become a liability, because his sense of responsibility has been destroyed. He cannot think for himself and can be dominated so that even his vote becomes a menace to society.

How is freedom lost? How can justice which insures freedom be made secure? Ideals and standards of fairness foster freedom. The man with authority and power, in any measure whatsoever, be it large or small, holds a potential influence for either freedom or servitude. If he respects human rights and feelings, he will make the world happier; if he crushes them, he leaves sadness and desolation in his wake. The right to authority and power should rest upon respect for human rights if man is to press forward to a fuller and better life.

Political freedom, racial freedom, religious freedom, and economic freedom are enjoyed in different degrees in different parts of the world. Crippled by prejudice but fostered by tolerance, freedom is crushed but rises again in turn. Depending upon its friends, courage and honesty, it marches on toward a goal which represents the inalienable rights of mankind.

"THEY CHAINED US EACH TO A
COLUMN STONE
AND WE WERE THERE YET
EACH ALONE"

THE PRISONER OF CHILLON

LORD BYRON

[Tourists still visit the castle of Chillon on Lake Geneva in Switzerland. Bonnivard was a political prisoner who was held for six years. Bonnivard's name and the fact that he had been imprisoned in Chillon fired Byron's imagination, and he wrote *The Prisoner of Chillon*.]

SONNET ON CHILLON

ETERNAL spirit of the chainless
mind!
Brightest in dungeons, Liberty, thou
art,
For there thy habitation is the heart—
The heart which love of thee alone
can bind;
And when thy sons to fetters are consigned—   5
To fetters, and the damp vault's day-
less gloom,

Their country conquers with their
martyrdom,
And Freedom's fame finds wings on
every wind.
Chillon! thy prison is a holy place,
And thy sad floor an altar—for 'twas
trod,   10
Until his very steps have left a trace
Worn, as if thy cold pavement were
a sod,
By Bonnivard!   May none those
marks efface!
For they appeal from tyranny to God.

THE PRISONER OF CHILLON

I

My hair is gray, but not with years,
Nor grew it white
In a single night,
As men's have grown from sudden
fears;

My limbs are bowed, though not with
   toil,   5
  But rusted with a vile repose,
For they have been a dungeon's spoil,
   And mine has been the fate of
    those
To whom the goodly earth and air
Are banned, and barred—forbidden
   fare;   10
But this was for my father's faith
I suffered chains and courted death;
That father perished at the stake
For tenets he would not forsake;
And for the same his lineal race   15
In darkness found a dwelling place;
We were seven—who now are one,
  Six in youth, and one in age,
Finished as they had begun,
   Proud of Persecution's rage;   20
One in fire, and two in field
Their belief with blood have sealed,
Dying as their father died,
For the God their foes denied;
Three were in a dungeon cast,   25
Of whom this wreck is left the last.

II

There are seven pillars of Gothic
   mold,
In Chillon's dungeons deep and old,
There are seven columns, massy and
   gray,
Dim with a dull imprisoned ray,   30
A sunbeam which hath lost its way
And through the crevice and the
   cleft
Of the thick wall is fallen and left;
Creeping o'er the floor so damp,
Like a marsh's meteor lamp.   35
And in each pillar there is a ring,
  And in each ring there is a chain;
That iron is a cankering thing,
   For in these limbs its teeth remain,
With marks that will not wear
   away,   40
Till I have done with this new day,
Which now is painful to these eyes,
Which have not seen the sun to rise

For years —I cannot count them o'er,
I lost their long and heavy score   45
When my last brother drooped and
   died,
And I lay living by his side.

III

They chained us each to a column
   stone,
And we were three—yet, each alone;
We could not move a single pace,   50
We could not see each other's face,
But with that pale and livid light
That made us strangers in our sight.
And thus together—yet apart,
Fettered in hand, but joined in
   heart,   55
'Twas still some solace, in the dearth
Of the pure elements of earth,
To hearken to each other's speech,
And each turn comforter to each
With some new hope, or legend
   old,   60
Or song heroically bold;
But even these at length grew cold.
Our voices took a dreary tone,
An echo of the dungeon stone,
  A grating sound, not full and
   free,   65
  As they of yore were wont to be;
  It might be fancy, but to me
They never sounded like our own.

IV

I was the eldest of the three,
  And to uphold and cheer the rest[70]
I ought to do—and did my best—
And each did well in his degree.
  The youngest, whom my father
   loved,
Because our mother's brow was given
To him, with eyes as blue as heav-
   en—   75
  For him my soul was sorely moved;
And truly might it be distressed
To see such bird in such a nest;
For he was beautiful as day—
  When day was beautiful to me   80

Castle of Chillon

As to young eagles, being free—
A polar day, which will not see
A sunset till its summer's gone,
  Its sleepless summer of long light,
The snow-clad offspring of the sun;[85]
  And thus he was as pure and
    bright,
And in his natural spirit gay,
With tears for naught but others'
    ills,
And then they flowed like mountain
    rills,
Unless he could assuage the woe   90
Which he abhorred to view below.

V

The other was as pure of mind,
But formed to combat with his kind;
Strong in his frame, and of a mood
Which 'gainst the world in war had
    stood   95
And perished in the foremost rank
  With joy—but not in chains to
    pine;
His spirit withered with their clank,
  I saw it silently decline—
    And so perchance in sooth did
      mine;   100

But yet I forced it on to cheer
Those relics of a home so dear.
He was a hunter of the hills,
  Had followed there the deer and
    wolf;
  To him this dungeon was a gulf,[105]
And fettered feet the worst of ills.

VI

  Lake Leman lies by Chillon's walls;
A thousand feet in depth below
Its massy waters meet and flow;
Thus much the fathom-line was
    sent   110
From Chillon's snow-white battle-
    ment,
  Which round about the wave en-
    thralls;
A double dungeon wall and wave
Have made—and like a living grave,
Below the surface of the lake   115
The dark vault lies wherein we lay;
We heard it ripple night and day;
  Sounding o'er our heads it knocked;
And I have felt the winter's spray
Wash through the bars when winds
    were high   120
And wanton in the happy sky;

And then the very rock hath rocked,
And I have felt it shake, un-
shocked,
Because I could have smiled to see
The death that would have set me
free.   125

VII

I said my nearer brother pined,
I said his mighty heart declined,
He loathed and put away his food;
It was not that 'twas coarse and rude,
For we were used to hunter's fare,   130
And for the like had little care.
The milk drawn from the mountain
goat
Was changed for water from the
moat;
Our bread was such as captives' tears
Have moistened many a thousand
years,   135
Since man first pent his fellow men
Like brutes within an iron den;
But what were these to us or him?
These wasted not his heart or limb;
My brother's soul was of that mold 140
Which in a palace had grown cold,
Had his free breathing been denied
The range of the steep mountain's
side;
But why delay the truth?—he died.
I saw, and could not hold his head, 145
Nor reach his dying hand—nor
dead—
Though hard I strove, but strove in
vain
To rend and gnash my bonds in
twain.
He died, and they unlocked his chain,
And scooped for him a shallow
grave   150
Even from the cold earth of our cave.
I begged them as a boon to lay
His corse in dust whereon the day
Might shine—it was a foolish thought,
But then within my brain it
wrought,   155

That even in death his free-born
breast
In such a dungeon could not rest.
I might have spared my idle prayer—
They coldly laughed, and laid him
there,
The flat and turfless earth above   160
The being we so much did love;
His empty chain above it leant,
Such murder's fitting monument!

VIII

But he, the favorite and the flower,
Most cherished since his natal hour, 165
His mother's image in fair face,
The infant love of all his race,
His martyred father's dearest thought,
My latest care, for whom I sought
To hoard my life, that his might be 170
Less wretched now, and one day free;
He, too, who yet had held untired
A spirit natural or inspired—
He, too, was struck, and day by day
Was withered on the stalk away.   175
Oh, God! it is a fearful thing
To see the human soul take wing
In any shape, in any mood;
I've seen it rushing forth in blood;
I've seen it on the breaking ocean 180
Strive with a swol'n convulsive mo-
tion,
I've seen the sick and ghastly bed
Of sin, delirious with its dread;
But these were horrors—this was woe
Unmixed with such—but sure and
slow.   185
He faded, and so calm and meek,
So softly worn, so sweetly weak,
So tearless, yet so tender—kind
And grieved for those he left behind;
With all the while a cheek whose
bloom   190
Was as a mockery of the tomb,
Whose tints as gently sunk away
As a departing rainbow's ray;
An eye of most transparent light,
That almost made the dungeon
bright;   195

And not a word of murmur, not
A groan o'er his untimely lot—
A little talk of better days,
A little hope my own to raise,
For I was sunk in silence—lost   200
In this last loss, of all the most;
And then the sighs he would suppress
Of fainting nature's feebleness,
More slowly drawn, grew less and
    less;
I listened, but I could not hear;   205
I called, for I was wild with fear;
I knew 'twas hopeless, but my dread
Would not be thus admonishèd;
I called, and thought I heard a
    sound—
I burst my chain with one strong
    bound,   210
And rushed to him—I found him not,
I only stirred in this black spot,
I only lived, I only drew
The accursèd breath of dungeon-dew;
The last, the sole, the dearest link   215
Between me and the eternal brink,
Which bound me to my failing race,
Was broken in this fatal place.
One on the earth, and one beneath—
My brothers—both had ceased to
    breathe.   220
I took that hand which lay so still,
Alas! my own was full as chill;
I had not strength to stir, or strive,
But felt that I was still alive—
A frantic feeling, when we know   225
That what we love shall ne'er be so.
    I know not why
    I could not die,
I had no earthly hope—but faith,
And that forbade a selfish death.   230

IX

What next befell me then and there
    I know not well—I never knew—
First came the loss of light, and air,
    And then of darkness too.
I had no thought, no feeling—
    none—   235
Among the stones I stood a stone,

And was scarce conscious what I wist,
As shrubless crags within the mist;
For all was blank, and bleak, and
    gray;
It was not night, it was not day;   240
It was not even the dungeon-light,
So hateful to my heavy sight,
But vacancy absorbing space,
And fixedness without a place;
There were no stars, no earth, no
    time,   245
No check, no change, no good, no
    crime,
But silence, and a stirless breath
Which neither was of life nor death;
A sea of stagnant idleness,
Blind, boundless, mute, and motion-
    less!   250

X

A light broke in upon my brain—
    It was the carol of a bird;
It ceased, and then it came again,
    The sweetest song ear ever heard,
And mine was thankful till my
    eyes   255
Ran over with the glad surprise,
And they that moment could not see
I was the mate of misery;
But then by dull degrees came back
My senses to their wonted track;   260
I saw the dungeon walls and floor
Close slowly round me as before,
I saw the glimmer of the sun
Creeping as it before had done,
But through the crevice where it
    came   265
That bird was perched, as fond and
    tame,
    And tamer than upon the tree;
A lovely bird, with azure wings,
And song that said a thousand things,
    And seemed to say them all for
        me!   270
I never saw its like before,
I ne'er shall see its likeness more;
It seemed like me to want a mate,
But was not half so desolate,

And it was come to love me when [275]
None lived to love me so again,
And cheering from my dungeon's
    brink,
Had brought me back to feel and
    think.
I know not if it late were free,
    Or broke its cage to perch on
        mine,   [280]
But knowing well captivity,
    Sweet bird! I could not wish for
        thine!
Or if it were, in wingèd guise,
A visitant from Paradise;
For—Heaven forgive that thought!
    the while   [285]
Which made me both to weep and
    smile—
I sometimes deemed that it might be
My brother's soul come down to me;
But then at last away it flew,
And then 'twas mortal well I
    knew,   [290]
For he would never thus have flown,
And left me twice so doubly lone,
Lone as the corse within its shroud,
Lone as a solitary cloud—
    A single cloud on a sunny day,   [295]
While all the rest of heaven is clear,
A frown upon the atmosphere,
That hath no business to appear
    When skies are blue, and earth is
        gay.

XI

A kind of change came in my fate; [300]
My keepers grew compassionate;
I know not what had made them so,
They were inured to sights of woe,
But so it was—my broken chain
With links unfastened did remain,   [305]
And it was liberty to stride
Along my cell from side to side,
And up and down, and then athwart,
And tread it over every part;
And round the pillars one by one,   [310]
Returning where my walk begun,
Avoiding only, as I trod,

My brothers' graves without a sod;
For if I thought with heedless tread
My step profaned their lowly bed,   [315]
My breath came gaspingly and thick,
And my crushed heart fell blind and
    sick.

XII

I made a footing in the wall,
    It was not therefrom to escape,
For I had buried one and all   [320]
    Who loved me in a human shape;
And the whole earth would hence-
    forth be
A wider prison unto me.
No child, no sire, no kin had I,
No partner in my misery;   [325]
I thought of this, and I was glad,
For thought of them had made me
    mad;
But I was curious to ascend
To my barred windows, and to bend
Once more, upon the mountains
    high,   [330]
The quiet of a loving eye.

XIII

I saw them, and they were the same,
They were not changed like me in
    frame;
I saw their thousand years of snow
On high—their wide long lake be-
    low,   [335]
And the blue Rhone in fullest flow;
I heard the torrents leap and gush
O'er channeled rock and broken
    bush;
I saw the white-walled distant town,
And whiter sails go skimming
    down;   [340]
And then there was a little isle,
Which in my very face did smile,
    The only one in view;
A small green isle; it seemed no more,
Scarce broader than my dungeon
    floor,   [345]
But in it there were three tall trees,
And o'er it blew the mountain breeze,

And by it there were waters flowing,
And on it there were young flowers
    growing,
  Of gentle breath and hue.   350
The fish swam by the castle wall,
And they seemed joyous each and all;
The eagle rode the rising blast,
Methought he never flew so fast
As then to me he seemed to fly;   355
And then new tears came in my eye,
And I felt troubled—and would fain
I had not left my recent chain;
And when I did descend again,
The darkness of my dim abode   360
Fell on me as a heavy load;
It was as is a new-dug grave,
Closing o'er one we sought to save—
And yet my glance, too much op-
    pressed
Had almost need of such a rest.   365

XIV

It might be months, or years, or days;
  I kept no count, I took no note,
I had no hope my eyes to raise,
  And clear them of their dreary
    mote;

At last men came to set me free;   370
  I asked not why, and recked not
    where;
It was at length the same to me,
Fettered or fetterless to be,
  I learned to love despair.
And thus when they appeared at   375
    last,
And all my bonds aside were cast,
These heavy walls to me had grown
A hermitage—and all my own!
And half I felt as they were come
To tear me from a second home;   380
With spiders I had friendship made,
And watched them in their sullen
    trade,
Had seen the mice by moonlight play,
And why should I feel less than they?
We were all inmates of one place, 385
And I, the monarch of each race,
Had power to kill—yet, strange to
    tell!
In quiet we had learned to dwell.
My very chains and I grew friends,
So much a long communion tends   390
To make us what we are—even I
Regained my freedom with a sigh.

For Thought and Discussion

1. Why does Byron say that liberty is brightest in dungeons?
2. Who was Bonnivard?
3. Why did Byron admire him?
4. Why does the poet place the sonnet before the poem proper?
5. Upon what general theme are the first eight lines of the sonnet? How do the last six lines relate to that theme?
6. Why were the three brothers imprisoned?
7. How had the different members of this family met their deaths?
8. Why do you sympathize with the youngest brother?
9. What was the ultimate fate of each brother?
10. What effect did imprisonment have upon the eldest brother?
11. Would a man be imprisoned now for his religious faith?
12. Explain the author's purpose in this poem.

Plus Work

The prison described here dates back to the sixteenth century. How far have we come toward the betterment of prison conditions and the solution of criminal problems?   In view of the difficulty of detecting crime and convicting criminals, what psychological and scientific methods would you offer as substitutes for inadequate and objectionable practices?

LORD BYRON

GEORGE NOEL GORDON, LORD BYRON 1788-1824

Early Life.   Dashing and extravagant Captain Byron of the army, the poet's father, died when George was very young. Mrs. Byron, who was Scotch, left London with her young son and went to Aberdeen, Scotland, to live on the small bit of property left from her fortune.   Sent to school before his fifth birthday, Byron exhibited a quick mind and learned easily.   Later on, in Aberdeen grammar school, he showed a fondness for all games and sports from which his lameness did not debar him, and enjoyed his reputation as a skillful marble player.   Even at this early period of life Byron was not happy, often moody; the inherent traits of his character—pride, restlessness, quick impatience, and resentment against restraint—were destined to shape his life. His mother, with many of the same traits, was incapable of teaching him that self-control which was essential to his happiness, and by her alternate abuse and grief over his lameness, she aroused his resentment so deeply that they were never able to live together peaceably for any length of time.

When Byron was ten years old, an uncle died and left him a title and Newstead Abbey, an estate which was more or less in ruins without an income sufficient for its maintenance. The proud, sensitive little boy was thrilled as well as slightly disappointed when, from his place in the carriage, he viewed for the first time beautiful Newstead Abbey, so sadly in need of repairs. Newstead Abbey was leased, and the family took lodgings. Byron first attended a small private school; later he enrolled in Harrow to prepare for Cambridge. He was usually lazy about his lessons but sometimes did brilliant work. At first he got on badly with the boys, fighting back resentfully at them, and they in turn retaliated by taunting him about his lameness, but his courage finally won their approval, and his relations with them became happy. At this time he read widely and excelled in athletics.

At Cambridge—Spirit of Revolt.   From 1805 to 1808 Byron was in Cambridge, interested in reading, in athletics, and in leading a fashionable life, with emphasis upon the latter. His now handsome income permitted his indulgence in the extravagant and unusual: he liked to ride and bought a horse which he named Oat-eater; in his rooms he had a tame bear, a wolf-hound, and a polished skull which was used as a wine cup. He liked to dream and write verses; he published his first poem, "Hours of Idleness," the title indicating that writing was a leisurely pastime. Eagerly waiting for its reception by the public, since he had already decided that he was to be a poet, he was deeply resentful of the severe criticism of the *Edinburgh Review.* The next year in retaliation he held up to ridicule many writers of the day, among them Scott, Coleridge, and Wordsworth, in "English Bards and Scotch Reviewers." Later on in life this youthful outburst of temper, as he termed it, was a source of humiliation, as his apologies on different occasions indicate.

At Newstead Abbey.   After leaving Cambridge, Byron lived at Newstead, giving weird parties which brought criticism upon him. The skull drinking cup, the tame bear, and the wolf-hound played a part in giving an uncanny atmosphere to the place, all of which no doubt delighted the young poet, who was always rather theatrical.

Travels Abroad.   Prompted by the spirit of adventure and restlessness, Byron and one of his friends from Cambridge left England to travel through Spain, Greece, and Turkey. On this trip swimming the Hellespont was one of the feats of interest to Byron, who derived genuine pleasure from visiting historic shrines. In 1812 Byron returned to London. While he attended to business affairs there in connection with the publication of his next poem, his mother, who had lived at Newstead during his absence, became ill and died very suddenly. Although they had never been congenial, Byron felt her death deeply. After her death he returned to London to wait impatiently for the publication of *Childe Harold*, the account of his travels. His dramatic account of the appearance of his poem was "I awoke one morning and found myself famous." The statement was true; in four weeks there were seven editions of his poem. Byron was instantly identified as the hero Childe Harold, and was lionized by London society. His popularity was no doubt increased by his personal beauty; he had wavy auburn hair, large expressive eyes, and a broad forehead. His melancholy mien, the slight lameness, and an extravagant wardrobe assisted in making him, in the eyes of the world, a very romantic person. Three years later, in 1815, he married Miss Millbanke, an heiress. His fortunes were soon completely changed, for when his wife left him, society criticized him so severely for the separation that he left London never to return. There seems to be no reason for doubting that his conduct was outrageous, nor is there any reason for not believing that the punishment which society inflicted upon him increased his bitter attitude toward life.

Last Years of Life. After leaving England, Byron visited Belgium, the Rhine, and Switzerland. He wrote Canto III of *Childe Harold* and "The Prisoner of Chillon" (shǐ lŏn'; Fr. shē yôn'). He went on into Italy, living in various cities for the next few years. He published many poems, among which were *Childe Harold*, Canto IV, *Manfred, Cain, The Vision of Judgment*, and *Don Juan* (dŏn jū' ăn; Sp. dōn whän), his most famous satire.

Interest in the Cause of Freedom. Tired of life, which brought neither content nor happiness, Byron was aroused through his love of freedom and spirit of revolt to join the Greeks in their fight for independence. He threw himself into their cause, using his income to equip a regiment to fight against the Turks. While assisting in the organization of forces at Mussolonghi, he contracted a fever and died on March 19, 1824, at the age of thirty-six.

Characteristics of Byron's Poetry. The proud sensitive hero who usually dominates Byron's works is the poet himself. The spirit of revolt, a distaste for sham and hypocrisy, and love of freedom characterize his poems. His strong narratives, particularly *Childe Harold*, captivated the reading public; his eloquent descriptions of the magnificent and powerful scenes of nature had a wide appeal. His keen and effective satire was a protest against the existing social organization.

Appreciation of his work was dimmed for a time by public disapproval of his revolutionary spirit, which passed into lawlessness not to be condoned by Englishmen; however, when time gave perspective to his life, his poetry was appreciated for its true worth, and Byron's permanent place among the poets was conceded.

∾

MILTON, THOU SHOULD'ST BE LIVING AT THIS HOUR

WILLIAM WORDSWORTH

[¹*hall and bower.* The hall was a Teutonic chieftain's public dwelling, while the bower was his private dwelling.]

MILTON! thou should'st be living at this hour;
England hath need of thee; she is a fen
Of stagnant waters; altar, sword, and pen,
Fireside, the heroic wealth of hall and bower,¹
Have forfeited their ancient English dower   5
Of inward happiness. We are selfish men;
Oh! raise us up, return to us again;
And give us manners, virtue, freedom, power.
Thy soul was like a star, and dwelt apart;
Thou hadst a voice whose sound was like the sea;   10
Pure as the naked heavens, majestic, free,
So didst thou travel on life's common way,
In cheerful godliness; and yet thy heart
The lowliest duties on herself did lay.

For Thought and Discussion

1. Do you think that the conditions described in this sonnet are applicable to America today?
2. Why was Milton a great leader?

∾

SCOTS WHA HAE

ROBERT BURNS

[In "Scots Wha Hae," written almost four centuries after the battle of Bannockburn, Burns voiced what he imagined was the speech by which Robert Bruce inspired his 30,000 Scots before they faced and defeated 100,000 Englishmen led by Edward II. In spirit the last fourteen lines of this poem are comparable to Patrick Henry's famous American "Give me liberty or give me death" oration.]

SCOTS, wha hae wi' Wallace bled,
Scots, wham Bruce has aften led;
Welcome to your gory bed,
  Or to victory!
Now's the day, and now's the hour;   5
See the front o' battle lour;
See approach proud Edward's power—
  Chains and slavery!

Wha will be a traitor knave?
Wha can fill a coward's grave?   10

Wha sae base as be a slave?
  Let him turn and flee!
Wha for Scotland's king and law
Freedom's sword will strongly draw,
Freeman stand, or Freeman fa',   15
  Let him follow me!

By oppression's woes and pains

By your sons in servile chains!
We will drain our dearest veins,
  But they shall be free!   20
Lay the proud usurpers low!
Tyrants fall in every foe!
Liberty's in every blow!—
  Let us do or die!

For Thought and Discussion

1. Aside from Bruce, what other Scotch patriot is mentioned in this poem?   How is this same leader referred to by Burns in his *Cotter's Saturday Night?*
2. By what means does Bruce appeal to his followers?
3. Of what other battle leader do the lines "Let him follow me," remind you?

THE LAST SPEECH OF ROBERT EMMET
ROBERT EMMET

[Robert Emmet, 1778-1803, an Irish patriot, was hanged for treason after an unsuccessful uprising against England.   At first he escaped; later he was captured when he returned to bid farewell to his fiancée.   The story is that his fiancée died of a broken heart two years later.   This address, delivered just before the sad close of his life, reveals his devotion to his native country and to the cause of liberty.]

MY LORDS:—What have I to say why sentence of death should not be pronounced on me according to law?   I have nothing to say that can alter your predetermination, nor that it will become me to say with any view to the mitigation of that sentence which you are here to pronounce, and I must abide by. But I have that to say which interests me more than life, and which you have labored (as was necessarily your office in the present circumstances of this oppressed country) to destroy.   I

have much to say why my reputation should be rescued from the load of false accusation and calumny which has been heaped upon it.   I do not imagine that, seated where you are, your minds can be so free from impurity as to receive the least impression from what I am going to utter. I have no hopes that I can anchor my character in the breast of a court constituted and trammeled as this is— I only wish, and it is the utmost I expect, that your lordships may suffer it to float down your memories untainted by the foul breath of prejudice, until it finds some more hospitable harbor to shelter it from the storm by which it is at present buffeted.

Was I only to suffer death after being adjudged guilty by *your* tribunal, I should bow in silence, and meet the fate that awaits me without a murmur; but the sentence of law which delivers my body to the executioner, will, through the ministry of that law, labor in its own vindication to consign my character to obloquy—for there must be guilt somewhere: whether in the sentence of the court or in the catastrophe, posterity must determine. A man in my situation, my lords, has not only to encounter the difficulties of fortune, and the force of power over minds which it has corrupted or subjugated, but the difficulties of established prejudice: the man dies, but his memory lives. That mine may not perish, that it may live in the respect of my countrymen, I seize upon this opportunity to vindicate myself from some of the charges alleged against me. When my spirit shall be wafted to a more friendly port; when my shade shall have joined the bands of those martyred heroes who have shed their blood on the scaffold and in the field, in defense of their country and of virtue, this is my hope: I wish that my memory and name may animate those who survive me, while I look down with complacency on the destruction of that perfidious government which upholds its domination by blasphemy of the Most High—which displays its power over man as over the beasts of the forest—which sets man upon his brother, and lifts his hand in the name of God against the throat of his fellow who believes or doubts a little more or a little less than the government standard—a government which is steeled to barbarity by the cries of the orphans and the tears of the widows which it has made.[1]

I appeal to the immaculate God—I swear by the throne of Heaven, before which I must shortly appear—by the blood of the murdered patriots who have gone before me—that my conduct has been through all this peril and all my purposes, governed only by the convictions which I have uttered, and by no other view, than that of their cure, and the emancipation of my country from the superinhuman oppression under which she has so long and too patiently travailed; and that I confidently and assuredly hope that, wild and chimerical as it may appear, there is still union and strength in Ireland to accomplish this noble enterprise. Of this I speak with the confidence of intimate knowledge, and with the consolation that appertains to that confidence. Think not, my lords, I say this for the petty gratification of giving you a transitory uneasiness; a man who never yet raised his voice to assert a lie, will not hazard his character with posterity by asserting a falsehood on a subject so important to his country, and on an occasion like this. Yes, my lords, a man who does not wish to have his epitaph written until his country is liberated, will not leave a weapon in the power of envy; nor a pretense to impeach the probity which he means to preserve even in the grave to which tyranny consigns him.[2]

Again I say, that what I have spoken was not intended for your lordship, whose situation I commiserate rather than envy—my expressions were for my countrymen; if there is a true Irishman present, let my last words cheer him in the hour of his affliction.[3]

---

[1]Lord Norbury here, as he did at several other times during the address, interrupted Emmet, censuring him for being one of what he termed an unwise and wicked group of enthusiasts who would never accomplish their purpose. From Emmet's remarks in reply as well as from his manner of addressing his lordship the points of interruption are easily determined.

[2]Lord Norbury interrupted a second time.
[3]A third time, Lord Norbury interrupted declaring he did not sit to hear treason.

I have always understood it to be the duty of a judge when a prisoner has been convicted, to pronounce the sentence of the law; I have also understood that judges sometimes think it their duty to hear with patience, and to speak with humanity; to exhort the victim of the laws, and to offer with tender benignity his opinions of the motives by which he was actuated in the crime, of which he had been adjudged guilty: that a judge has thought it his duty so to have done, I have no doubt—but where is the boasted freedom of your institutions, where is the vaunted impartiality, clemency, and mildness of your courts of justice, if an unfortunate prisoner, whom your policy, and not pure justice, is about to deliver into the hands of the executioner, is not suffered to explain his motives sincerely and truly, and to vindicate the principles by which he was actuated?

My lords, it may be a part of the system of angry justice, to bow a man's mind by humiliation to the purposed ignominy of the scaffold; but worse to me than the purposed shame, or the scaffold's terrors, would be the shame of such unfounded imputations as have been laid against me in this court: you, my lord (Lord Norbury), are a judge, I am the supposed culprit; I am a man, you are a man also; by a revolution of power, we might change places, tho we never could change characters; if I stand at the bar of this court, and dare not vindicate my character, what a farce is your justice? If I stand at this bar and dare not vindicate my character, how dare you calumniate it? Does the sentence of death which your unhallowed policy inflicts on my body, also condemn my tongue to silence and my reputation to reproach? Your executioner may abridge the period of my existence, but while I exist I shall not forbear to vindicate my character and motives from your aspersions; and as a man to whom fame is dearer than life, I will make the last use of that life in doing justice to that reputation which is to live after me, and which is the only legacy I can leave to those I honor and love, and for whom I am proud to perish. As men, my lord, we must appear at the great day at one common tribunal, and it will then remain for the searcher of all hearts to show a collective universe who was engaged in the most virtuous actions, or actuated by the purest motives—my country's oppressors or———[4]

My lord, will a dying man be denied the legal privilege of exculpating himself, in the eyes of the community, of an undeserved reproach thrown upon him during his trial, by charging him with ambition, and attempting to cast away, for a paltry consideration, the liberties of his country? Why did your lordship insult me? or rather why insult justice, in demanding of me why sentence of death should not be pronounced? I know, my lord, that form prescribes that you should ask the question; the form also presumes a right of answering. This no doubt may be dispensed with—and so might the whole ceremony of trial, since sentence was already pronounced at the castle, before your jury was impaneled; your lordships are but the priests of the oracle, and I submit; but I insist on the whole of the forms.

I am charged with being an emissary of France! An emissary of France! And for what end? It is alleged that I wished to sell the independence of my country! And for what end? Was this the object of

---

[4] Emmet was here adjured to listen to the sentence of the law.

my ambition? And is this the mode by which a tribunal of justice reconciles contradictions? No, I am no emissary; and my ambition was to hold a place among the deliverers of my country—not in power, nor in profit, but in the glory of the achievement! Sell my country's independence to France! And for what? Was it for a change of masters? No! But for ambition! O my country, was it personal ambition that could influence me? Had it been the soul of my actions, could I not by my education and fortune, by the rank and consideration of my family, have placed myself among the proudest of my oppressors? My country was my idol; to it I sacrificed every selfish, every endearing sentiment; and for it, I now offer up my life. O God! No, my lord; I acted as an Irishman, determined on delivering my country from the yoke of a foreign and unrelenting tyranny, and from the more galling yoke of a domestic faction, which is its joint partner and perpetrator in the parricide, for the ignominy of existing with an exterior of splendor and of conscious depravity. It was the wish of my heart to extricate my country from this doubly riveted despotism.

I wished to place her independence beyond the reach of any power on earth; I wished to exalt you to that proud station in the world.

Connection with France was indeed intended, but only as far as mutual interest would sanction or require. Were they to assume any authority inconsistent with the purest independence, it would be the signal for their destruction; we sought aid, and we sought it, as we had assurances we should obtain it—as auxiliaries in war and allies in peace.

Were the French to come as invaders or enemies, uninvited by the wishes of the people, I should oppose them to the utmost of my strength. Yes, my countrymen, I should advise you to meet them on the beach, with a sword in one hand, and a torch in the other; I would meet them with all the destructive fury of war; and I would animate my countrymen to immolate them in their boats, before they had contaminated the soil of my country. If they succeeded in landing, and if forced to retire before superior discipline, I would dispute every inch of ground, burn every blade of grass, and the last intrenchment of liberty should be my grave. What I could not do myself, if I should fall, I should leave as a last charge to my countrymen to accomplish; because I should feel conscious that life, any more than death, is unprofitable when a foreign nation holds my country in subjection.

But it was not as an enemy that the succors of France were to land. I looked indeed for the assistance of France; but I wished to prove to France and to the world that Irishmen deserved to be assisted!—that they were indignant at slavery, and ready to assert the independence and liberty of their country.

I wished to procure for my country the guarantee which Washington procured for America. To procure an aid, which, by its example, would be as important as its valor, disciplined, gallant, pregnant with science and experience; which would perceive the good, and polish the rough points of our character. They would come to us as strangers, and leave us as friends, after sharing in our perils and elevating our destiny. These were my objects—not to receive new taskmasters, but to expel old tyrants; these were my views, and these only became Irishmen. It was for these ends I sought aid from France; because France, even as an enemy, could not be more implacable than the enemy already in the bosom of my country.[5]

I have been charged with that importance in the efforts to emancipate my country, as to be considered the *keystone* of the combination of Irishmen; or, as your lordship expressed it, "the life and blood of conspiracy." You do me honor overmuch. You have given to the subaltern all the credit of a superior. There are men engaged in this *conspiracy*, who are not only superior to me, but even to your own conceptions of yourself, my lord; men, before the splendor of whose genius and virtues, I should bow with respectful deference, and who would think themselves dishonored to be called your friend—who would not disgrace themselves by shaking your bloodstained hand——[6]

What, my lord, shall you tell me, on the passage to that scaffold, which that tyranny, of which you are only the intermediary executioner, has erected for my murder, that I am accountable for all the blood that has and will be shed in this struggle of the oppressed against the oppressor? —shall you tell me this—and must I be so very a slave as not to repel it?

I do not fear to approach the omnipotent Judge, to answer for the conduct of my whole life; and am I to be appalled and falsified by a mere remnant of mortality here? By you, too, who, if it were possible to collect all the innocent blood that you have shed in your unhallowed ministry, in one great reservoir, your lordship might swim in it.[7]

Let no man dare, when I am dead,

to charge me with dishonor; let no man attaint my memory by believing that I could have engaged in any cause but that of my country's liberty and independence; or that I could have become the pliant minion of power in the oppression or the miseries of my countrymen. The proclamation of the provisional government speaks for our views; no inference can be tortured from it to countenance barbarity or debasement at home, or subjection, humiliation, or treachery from abroad; I would not have submitted to a foreign oppressor for the same reason that I would resist the foreign and domestic oppressor; in the dignity of freedom I would have fought upon the threshold of my country, and its enemy should enter only by passing over my lifeless corpse. Am I, who lived but for my country, and who have subjected myself to the dangers of the jealous and watchful oppressor, and the bondage of the grave, only to give my countrymen their rights, and my country her independence, and am I to be loaded with calumny, and not suffered to resent or repel it—no, God forbid!

If the spirits of the illustrious dead participate in the concerns and cares of those who are dear to them in this transitory life—oh, ever dear and venerated shade of my departed father, look down with scrutiny upon the conduct of your suffering son; and see if I have even for a moment deviated from those principles of morality and patriotism which it was your care to instil into my youthful mind, and for which I am now to offer up my life!

My lords, you are impatient for the sacrifice—the blood which you seek is not congealed by the artificial terrors which surround your victim; it circulates warmly and unruffled,

---

[5]Emmet was again interrupted.

[6]The dash marks a speech broken off by another interruption of the court.

[7]One senses here interference on the part of the judge.

through the channels which God created for noble purposes, but which you are bent to destroy, for purposes so grievous, that they cry to heaven. Be yet patient! I have but a few words more to say. I am going to my cold and silent grave: my lamp of life is nearly extinguished: my race is run: the grave opens to receive me, and I sink into its bosom! I have but one request to ask at my departure from this world—it is the charity of its silence! Let no man write my epitaph: for as no man who knows my motives dare now vindicate them, let not prejudice or ignorance asperse them. Let them and me repose in obscurity and peace, and my tomb remain uninscribed, until other times, and other men, can do justice to my character; when my country takes her place among the nations of the earth, then, and not till then, let my epitaph be written. I have done.

For Thought and Discussion

1. What motives actuated Robert Emmet?
2. Toward what goal were all his efforts directed?
3. When Emmet claimed the right to vindicate his character, why was the privilege granted to him?
4. Why had he been an emissary to France?
   What kind of connection with France did he hope to make?
   Was his motive worthy?
5. What did he say about Washington and America?
6. How did he desire to be regarded by posterity?
7. Notice the moving eloquence of this appeal.
8. How has American immigration been affected by England's unsuccessful attempts to deal with the Irish question?

From THE SPEECH FOR CONCILIATION WITH THE AMERICAN COLONIES
EDMUND BURKE

[Great Britain lost her most promising colonial possession, and America became a nation because Parliament, dominated by a king of German blood, refused to follow the policies advocated by Edmund Burke, 1729-1797, in his address, *The Speech for Conciliation with the American Colonies*. That Burke's policies were sound, time has proved; that Americans should be grateful that his just pleas in their behalf were not granted, no one who reads his speech will question. Everyone who would understand the issues that led to the American Revolution and everyone who appreciates a clear-cut argument should read Burke's *Speech on American Taxation*, *Speech for Conciliation with America*, and *Letter to the Sheriff of Bristol*. Although Burke received but little honor in his lifetime, year by year respect for his political philosophy and his literary ability grows. John Morley's prophecy is that in centuries to come Burke's name will be linked with the names of Shakespeare, Milton, and Bacon.]

EDMUND BURKE

THESE, sir, are my reasons for not entertaining that high opinion of untried force, by which many gentlemen, for whose sentiments in other particulars I have great respect, seem to be so greatly captivated. But there is still behind a third consideration concerning this object, which serves to determine my opinion on the sort of policy which ought to be pursued in the management of America, even more than its population and its commerce. I mean its *temper and character*.

In this character of the Americans, a love of freedom is the predominating feature which marks and distinguishes the whole; and as an ardent is always a jealous affection, your colonies become suspicious, restive, and untractable, whenever they see the least attempt to wrest from them by force, or shuffle from them by chicane, what they think the only advantage worth living for. This fierce spirit of liberty is stronger in the English colonies, probably, than in any other people of the earth; and this from a great variety of powerful causes, which, to understand the true temper of their minds, and the direction which this spirit takes, it will not be amiss to lay open somewhat more largely.

First, the people of the colonies are descendants of Englishmen. England, sir, is a nation which still, I hope, respects, and formerly adored, her freedom. The colonists emigrated from you when this part of your character was most predominant; and they took this bias and direction the moment they parted from your hands. They are therefore not only devoted to liberty, but to liberty according to English ideas, and on English principles. Abstract liberty, like other mere abstractions, is not to be found. Liberty inheres in some sensible object; and every nation has formed to itself some favorite point which, by way of eminence, becomes the criterion of their happiness. It happened, you know, sir, that the great contests for freedom in this country were from the earliest times chiefly upon the question of taxing. Most of the contests in the ancient commonwealths turned primarily on the right of election of magistrates, or on the balance among the several orders of the state. The question of money was not with them so immediate. But in England it was otherwise. On this point of taxes the ablest pens and most eloquent tongues have been exercised, the greatest spirits have acted and suffered. In order to give the fullest satisfaction concerning the importance of this point, it was not only necessary for those, who in argument defended the excellence of the English constitution, to insist on this privilege of granting money as a dry point of fact, and to prove that the right had been acknowledged in an-

cient parchments and blind usages to reside in a certain body called a House of Commons. They went much farther; they attempted to prove, and they succeeded, that in theory it ought to be so, from the particular nature of a House of Commons as an immediate representative of the people, whether the old records had delivered this oracle or not. They took infinite pains to inculcate, as a fundamental principle, that in all monarchies the people must in effect themselves, mediately or immediately, possess the power of granting their own money, or no shadow of liberty could subsist. The colonies draw from you, as with their lifeblood, these ideas and principles—their love of liberty, as with you, fixed and attached on this specific point of taxing. Liberty might be safe, or might be endangered, in twenty other particulars, without their being much pleased or alarmed. Here they felt its pulse; and as they found that beat, they thought themselves sick or sound. I do not say whether they were right or wrong in applying your general arguments to their own case. It is not easy, indeed, to make a monopoly of theorems and corollaries. The fact is that they did thus apply those general arguments; and your mode of governing them, whether through lenity or indolence, through wisdom or mistake, confirmed them in the imagination, that they, as well as you, had an interest in these common principles.

They were further confirmed in this pleasing error by the form of their provincial legislative assemblies. The governments are popular in a high degree; some are merely popular; in all, the popular representative is the most weighty; and this share of the people in their ordinary government never fails to inspire them with lofty sentiments, and with a strong aversion from whatever tends to deprive them of their chief importance.

If anything were wanting to this necessary operation of the form of government, religion would have given it a complete effect. Religion, always a principle of energy, in this new people is no way worn out or impaired; and their mode of professing it is also one main cause of this free spirit. The people are Protestants; and of that kind which is the most adverse to all implicit submission of mind and opinion. This is a persuasion not only favorable to liberty, but built upon it. I do not think, sir, that the reason of this averseness in the dissenting churches, from all that looks like absolute government, is so much to·be sought in their religious tenets as in their history. Every one knows that the Roman Catholic religion is at least coeval with most of the governments where it prevails; that it has generally gone hand in hand with them, and received great favor and every kind of support from authority. The Church of England too was formed from her cradle under the nursing care of regular government. But the dissenting interests have sprung up in direct opposition to all the ordinary powers of the world; and could justify that opposition only on a strong claim to natural liberty. Their very existence depended on the powerful and unremitted assertion of that claim. All Protestantism, even the most cold and passive, is a sort of dissent. But the religion most prevalent in our northern colonies is a refinement on the principle of resistance; it is the dissidence of dissent, and the Protestantism of the Protestant religion. This religion, under a variety of denominations agreeing in nothing but in the communion of the spirit of liberty, is predominant in most of the northern provinces, where the Church of England, notwithstanding its legal rights, is in reality no more than a sort of private sect, not composing most probably the tenth of the people. The colonists left England when this spirit was high, and in the emigrants was the highest of all, and even that stream of foreigners, which has been constantly flowing into these colonies, has, for the greatest part, been composed of dissenters from the establishments of their several countries, and have brought with them a temper and character far from alien to that of the people with whom they mixed.

Sir, I can perceive by their manner, that some gentlemen object to the latitude of this description, because in the southern colonies the Church of England forms a large body, and has a regular establishment. It is certainly true. There is, however, a circumstance attending these colonies, which, in my opinion, fully counterbalances this difference, and makes the spirit of liberty still more high and haughty than in those to the northward. It is, that in Virginia and the Carolinas they have a vast multitude of slaves. Where this is the case in any part of the world, those who are free are by far the most proud and jealous of their freedom. Freedom is to them not only an enjoyment, but a kind of rank and privilege. Not seeing there, that freedom, as in countries where it is a common blessing, and as broad and general as the air, may be united with much abject toil, with great misery, with all the exterior of servitude, liberty looks, amongst them, like something that is more noble and liberal. I do not mean, sir, to commend the superior morality of this sentiment, which has at least as much pride as virtue in it: but I cannot alter the nature of man. The fact is so; and these people of the southern colonies are much more strongly, and with a higher and more stubborn spirit, attached to liberty, than those to the northward. Such were all the ancient commonwealths; such were our Gothic ancestors; such in our days were the Poles; and such will be all masters of slaves who are not slaves themselves. In such a people, the haughtiness of domination combines with the spirit of freedom, fortifies it, and renders it invincible.

Permit me, sir, to add another circumstance in our colonies, which contributes no mean part towards the growth and effect of this untractable spirit. I mean their education. In no country perhaps in the world is the law so general a study. The profession itself is numerous and powerful; and in most provinces it takes the lead. The greater number of the deputies sent to the Congress were lawyers. But all who read (and most do read), endeavor to obtain some smattering in that science. I have been told by an eminent bookseller, that in no branch of his business, after tracts of popular devotion, were so many books as those on the law exported to the plantations. The colonists have now fallen into the way of printing them for their own use. I hear that they have sold nearly as many of Blackstone's Commentaries in America as in England. General Gage marks out this disposition very particularly in a letter on your table. He states that all the people in his government are lawyers, or smatterers in law; and that in Boston they have been enabled, by successful chicane, wholly to evade many parts of one of your capital penal constitutions. The smartness of debate will say that this knowledge ought to teach them more clearly the rights of legislature, their obligations to obedience, and the penalties of rebellion. All this is mighty well. But my honorable and learned friend on the floor, who condescends to mark what I say for animadversion, will disdain that ground. He has heard, as well as I, that when great honors and great emoluments do not win over this knowledge to the service of the state, it is a formidable adversary to government. If the spirit be not tamed and broken by these happy methods, it is stubborn and litigious. *Abeunt studia in mores* [studies develop into habits]. This study renders men acute, inquisitive, dexterous, prompt in attack, ready in defence, full of resources. In other countries, the people, more simple, and of a less mercurial cast, judge of an ill principle in government only by an actual grievance; here they anticipate the evil, and judge of the pressure of the grievance by the badness of the principle. They augur misgovernment at a distance, and snuff the approach of tyranny in every tainted breeze.

The last cause of this disobedient spirit in the colonies is hardly less powerful than the rest, as it is not merely moral, but laid deep in the natural constitution of things. Three thousand miles of ocean lie between you and them. No contrivance can prevent the effect of this distance in weakening government. Seas roll, and months pass, between the order and the execution; and the want of a speedy explanation of a single point is enough to defeat a whole system. You have, indeed, winged ministers of vengeance, who carry your bolts in their pounces to the remotest verge of the sea. But there a power steps in that limits the arrogance of raging passions and furious elements, and says, *So far shalt thou go, and no farther.* Who are you, that you should fret and rage, and bite the chains of nature? Nothing worse happens to you than does to all nations who have extensive empire; and it happens in all the forms into which empire can be thrown. In large bodies the circulation of power must be less vigorous at the extremities. Nature has said it. The Turk cannot govern Egypt and Arabia and Kurdistan as he governs Thrace; nor has he the same dominion in Crimea and Algiers which he has at Brusa and Smyrna. Despotism itself is obliged to truck and huckster. The Sultan gets such obedience as he can. He governs with a loose rein, that he may govern at all; and the whole of the force and vigor of his authority in his centre is derived from a prudent relaxation in all his borders. Spain, in her provinces, is, perhaps, not so well obeyed as you are in yours. She complies, too; she submits; she watches times. This is the immutable condition, the eternal law of extensive and detached empire.

Then, sir, from these six capital sources,—of descent, of form of government, of religion in the northern provinces, of manners in the southern, of education, of the remoteness of situation from the first mover of government,—from all these causes a fierce spirit of liberty has grown up. It has grown with the growth of the people in your colonies, and increased with the increase of their wealth; a spirit that, unhappily meeting with an exercise of power in England, which, however lawful, is not reconcilable to any ideas of liberty, much less with theirs, has kindled this flame that is ready to consume us.

I do not mean to commend either the spirit in this excess, or the moral causes which produce it. Perhaps a more smooth and accommodating spirit of freedom in them would be more acceptable to us. Perhaps ideas of liberty might be desired, more reconcilable with an arbitrary and boundless authority. Perhaps we might wish the colonists to be persuaded, that their liberty is more secure when held in trust for them by us (as their guardians during a perpetual minority), than with any part of it in their own hands. The question is, not whether their spirit deserves praise or blame, but—what, in the name of God, shall we do with it? You have before you the object, such as it is, with all its glories, with all its imperfections on its head. You see the magnitude; the importance; the temper; the habits; the disorders. By all these considerations we are strongly urged to determine something concerning it. We are called upon to fix some rule and line for our future conduct, which may give a little stability to our politics, and prevent the return of such unhappy deliberations as the present. Every such return will bring the matter before us in a still more untractable form. For what astonishing and incredible things have we not seen already! What monsters have not been generated from this unnatural contention! Whilst every principle of authority and resistance has been pushed, upon both sides, as far as it would go, there is nothing so solid and certain, either in reasoning or in practice, that has not been shaken.

Until very lately, all authority in America seemed to be nothing but an emanation from yours. Even the popular part of the colony constitution derived all its activity, and its first vital movement, from the pleasure of the crown. We thought, sir, that the utmost which the discontented colonists could do was to disturb authority; we never dreamt they could of themselves supply it; knowing in general what an operose business it is to establish a government absolutely new. But having, for our purposes in this contention, resolved that none but an obedient assembly should sit; the humors of the people there finding all passage through the legal channel stopped, with great violence broke out another way. Some provinces have tried their experiment, as we have tried ours; and theirs has succeeded. They have formed a government sufficient for its purposes, without the bustle of a revolution, or the troublesome formality of an election. Evident necessity and tacit consent have done the business in an instant. So well they have done it, that Lord Dunmore—the account is among the fragments on your table—tells you that the new institution is infinitely better obeyed than the ancient government ever was in its most fortunate periods. Obedience is what makes government, and not the names by which it is called; not the name of Governor, as formerly, or Committee, as at present. This new government has originated directly from the people; and was not transmitted through any of the ordinary artificial media of a positive constitution. It was not a manufacture ready formed, and transmitted to them in that condition from England. The evil arising from hence is this, that the colonists having once found the possibility of enjoying the advantages of order in the midst of a struggle for liberty, such struggles will not henceforward seem so terrible to the settled and sober part of mankind as they had appeared before the trial.

Pursuing the same plan of punishing by the denial of the exercise of government to still greater lengths, we wholly abrogated the ancient government of Massachusetts. We were confident that the first feeling, if not the very prospect of anarchy, would instantly enforce a complete submission. The experiment was tried. A new, strange, unexpected phase of things appeared. Anarchy is found tolerable. A vast province has now subsisted, and subsisted in a considerable degree of health and vigor, for near a twelvemonth, without Governor, without public council, without judges, without executive magistrates. How long it will continue in this state, or what may rise out of this unheard-of situation, how can the wisest of us conjecture? Our late experience has taught us that many of those fundamental principles formerly believed infallible, are either not of the importance they were imagined to be; or that we have not at all adverted to some other far more important and far more powerful principles, which entirely overrule those we had considered as omnipotent. I am much against any further experiments, which tend to put to the proof any more of these allowed opinions, which contribute too much to the public tranquillity. In effect, we suffer as much at home by this loosening of all ties, and this concussion of all established opinions, as we do abroad. For, in order to prove that the Americans have no right to their liberties, we are every day endeavoring to subvert the maxims which preserve the whole spirit of our own. To prove that the Americans ought not to be free, we are obliged to depreciate the value of freedom itself; and we never seem to gain a paltry advantage over them in debate, without attacking some of those principles, or deriding some of those feelings, for which our ancestors have shed their blood.

But, sir, in wishing to put an end to pernicious experiments, I do not mean to preclude the fullest inquiry. Far from it. Far from deciding on a sudden or partial view, I would patiently go round and round the subject, and survey it minutely in every possible aspect. Sir, if I were capable of engaging you to an equal attention, I would state that, as far as I am capable of discerning, there are but three ways of proceeding relative to this stubborn spirit, which prevails in your colonies, and disturbs your government. These are: to change that spirit, as inconvenient, by removing the causes; to prosecute it as criminal; or, to comply with it as necessary. I would not be guilty of an imperfect enumeration; I can think of but these three. Another has indeed been started, that of giving up the colonies; but it met so slight a reception that I do not think myself obliged to dwell a great while upon it. It is nothing but a little sally of anger, like the frowardness of peevish children, who, when they cannot get all they would have, are resolved to take nothing.

The first of these plans,—to change the spirit as inconvenient by removing the causes,—I think, is the most like a systematic proceeding. It is radical in its principle; but it is attended with great difficulties, some of them little short, as I conceive, of impossibilities. This will appear by examining into the plans which have been proposed.

As the growing population in the colonies is evidently one cause of their resistance, it was, last session, mentioned in both Houses, by men of weight, and received not without applause, that in order to check this evil it would be proper for the Crown to make no further grants of land. But to this scheme there are two objections. The first, that there is already so much unsettled land in private hands as to afford room for an immense future population, although the Crown not only withheld its grants but annihilated its soil. If this be the case, then the only effect of this avarice of desolation, this hoarding of a royal wilderness, would be to raise the value of the possessions in the hands of the great private monopolists, without any adequate check to the growing and alarming mischief of population.

But if you stopped your grants, what would be the consequence? The people would occupy without grants. They have already so occupied in many places. You cannot station garrisons in every part of these deserts. If you drive the people from one place, they will carry on their annual tillage, and remove with their flocks and herds to another. Many of the people in the back settlements are already little attached to particular situations. Already they have topped the Appalachian mountains. From thence they behold before them an immense plain, one vast, rich, level meadow; a square of five hundred miles. Over this they would wander without a possibility of restraint; they would change their manners with the habits of their life; would soon forget a government by which they were disowned; would become hordes of English Tartars; and, pouring down upon your unfortified frontiers a fierce and irresistible cavalry, become masters of your governors and your counsellors, your collectors and comptrollers, and of all the slaves that adhered to them. Such would, and in no long time must be, the effect of attempting to forbid as a crime and to suppress as an evil, the command and blessing of providence, *Increase and multiply*. Such would be the happy result of the endeavor to keep as a lair of wild beasts that earth which God, by an express charter, has given to the children of men. Far different, and surely much wiser, has been our policy hitherto. Hitherto we have invited our people, by every kind of bounty, to fixed establish-ments. We have invited the husband-man to look to authority for his title. We have taught him piously to be-lieve in the mysterious virtue of wax and parchment. We have thrown each tract of land, as it was peopled, into districts, that the ruling power should never be wholly out of sight. We have settled all we could; and we have carefully attended every settle-ment with government.

Adhering, sir, as I do, to this pol-icy, as well as for the reasons I have just given, I think this new project of hedging-in population to be neither prudent nor practicable.

To impoverish the colonies in gen-eral, and in particular to arrest the noble course of their marine enter-prises, would be a more easy task. I freely confess it. We have shown a disposition to a system of this kind, a disposition even to continue the re-straint after the offence, looking on ourselves as rivals to our colonies, and persuaded that of course we must gain all that they shall lose. Much mis-chief we may certainly do. The power inadequate to all other things is often more than sufficient for this. I do not look on the direct and immediate power of the colonies to resist our violence as very formidable. In this, however, I may be mistaken. But when I consider that we have colonies for no purpose but to be serviceable to us, it seems to my poor understanding a little preposterous to make them un-serviceable in order to keep them obedient. It is, in truth, nothing more than the old and, as I thought, ex-ploded problem of tyranny, which proposes to beggar its subjects into submission. But remember, when you have completed your system of im-poverishment, that Nature still pro-ceeds in her ordinary course; that dis-content will increase with misery; and that there are critical moments in the fortune of all states, when they who are too weak to contribute to your prosperity may be strong enough to complete your ruin. *Spoliatis arma supersunt* [Arms remain to the de-spoiled].

The temper and character which prevail in our colonies, are, I am afraid, unalterable by any human art. We cannot, I fear, falsify the pedigree of this fierce people, and persuade them that they are not sprung from a nation in whose veins the blood of freedom circulates. The language in which they would hear you tell them this tale would detect the imposition: your speech would betray you. An Englishman is the unfittest person on earth to argue another Englishman into slavery.

I think it is nearly as little in our power to change their republican re-ligion as their free descent; or to sub-stitute the Roman Catholic, as a pen-alty; or the Church of England, as an improvement. The mode of inquisi-tion and dragooning is going out of fashion in the Old World, and I should not confide much to their ef-ficacy in the New. The education of the Americans is also on the same un-alterable bottom with their religion. You cannot persuade them to burn their books of curious science; to ban-ish their lawyers from their courts of laws; or to quench the lights of their assemblies, by refusing to choose those persons who are best read in their privileges. It would be no less im-practicable to think of wholly anni-hilating the popular assemblies, in which these lawyers sit. The army, by which we must govern in their place, would be far more chargeable to us; not quite so effectual; and perhaps, in the end, full as difficult to be kept in obedience.

With regard to the high aristocratic spirit of Virginia and the southern colonies, it has been proposed, I know, to reduce it, by declaring a general enfranchisement of their slaves. This project has had its advocates and panegyrists; yet I never could argue myself into any opinion of it. Slaves are often much attached to their masters. A general wild offer of liberty would not always be accepted. History furnishes few instances of it. It is sometimes as hard to persuade slaves to be free, as it is to compel freemen to be slaves; and in this auspicious scheme we should have both these pleasing tasks on our hands at once. But when we talk of enfranchisement, do we not perceive that the American master may enfranchise too, and arm servile hands in defence of freedom? A measure to which other people have had recourse more than once, and not without success, in a desperate situation of their affairs.

Slaves as these unfortunate black people are, and dull as all men are from slavery, must they not a little suspect the offer of freedom from that very nation which has sold them to their present masters? from that nation, one of whose causes of quarrel with those masters is their refusal to deal any more in that inhuman traffic? An offer of freedom from England would come rather oddly, shipped to them in an African vessel, which is refused an entry into the ports of Virginia or Carolina, with a cargo of three hundred Angola negroes. It would be curious to see the Guinea captain attempting at the same instant to publish his proclamation of liberty, and to advertise his sale of slaves.

But let us suppose all these moral difficulties got over. The ocean re-mains. You cannot pump this dry; and as long as it continues in its present bed, so long all the causes which weaken authority by distance will continue. 'Ye gods, annihilate but space and time, and make two lovers happy!' was a pious and passionate prayer; but just as reasonable as many of the serious wishes of very grave and solemn politicians.

If then, sir, it seems almost desperate to think of any alternative course for changing the moral causes, and not quite easy to remove the natural, which produce prejudices irreconcilable to the late exercise of our authority, but that the spirit infallibly will continue, and, continuing, will produce such effects as now embarrass us; the second mode under consideration is to prosecute that spirit in its overt acts as criminal.

At this proposition I must pause a moment. The thing seems a great deal too big for my ideas of jurisprudence. It should seem to my way of conceiving such matters, that there is a very wide difference in reason and policy between the mode of proceeding on the irregular conduct of scattered individuals, or even of bands of men, who disturb order within the state, and the civil dissensions which may from time to time, on great questions, agitate the several communities which compose a great empire. It looks to me to be narrow and pedantic to apply the ordinary ideas of criminal justice to this great public contest. I do not know the method of drawing up an indictment against a whole people. I cannot insult and ridicule the feelings of millions of my fellow creatures as Sir Edward Coke insulted one excellent individual (Sir Walter Raleigh) at the bar. I hope I am not ripe to pass sentence on the gravest public bodies, intrusted with magistracies of great authority and dignity, and charged with the safety of their fellow citizens upon the very same title that I am. I really think that for wise men this is not judicious; for sober men, not decent; for minds tinctured with humanity, not mild and merciful.

Perhaps, sir, I am mistaken in my idea of an empire, as distinguished from a single state or kingdom. But my idea of it is this: that an empire is the aggregate of many states under one common head, whether this head be a monarch or a presiding republic. It does, in such constitutions, frequently happen (and nothing but the dismal, cold, dead uniformity of servitude can prevent its happening) that the subordinate parts have many local privileges and immunities. Between these privileges and the supreme common authority the line may be extremely nice. Of course disputes—often, too, very bitter disputes—and much ill blood will arise. But though every privilege is an exemption (in the case) from the ordinary exercise of the supreme authority, it is no denial of it. The claim of a privilege seems rather, *ex vi termini*, to imply a superior power. For to talk of the privileges of a state, or of a person, who has no superior, is hardly any better than speaking nonsense. Now, in such unfortunate quarrels among the component parts of a great political union of communities, I can scarcely conceive anything more completely imprudent than for the head of the empire to insist that, if any privilege is pleaded against his will or his acts, his whole authority is denied; instantly to proclaim rebellion, to beat to arms, and to put the offending provinces under the ban. Will not this, sir, very soon teach the provinces to make no distinctions on their part? Will it not teach them that the government, against which a claim of liberty is tantamount to high treason, is a government to which submission is equivalent to slavery? It may not always be quite convenient to impress dependent communities with such an idea.

We are, indeed, in all disputes with the colonies, by the necessity of things, the judge. It is true, sir. But I confess that the character of judge in my own cause is a thing that frightens me. Instead of filling me with pride, I am exceedingly humbled by it. I cannot proceed with a stern, assured, judicial confidence, until I find myself in something more like a judicial character. I must have these hesitations as long as I am compelled to recollect that, in my little reading upon such contests as these, the sense of mankind has, at least, as often decided against the superior as the subordinate power. Sir, let me add, too, that the opinion of my having some abstract right in my favor would not put me much at my ease in passing sentence, unless I could be sure that there were no rights which, in their exercise under certain circumstances, were not the most odious of all wrongs, and the most vexatious of all injustice. Sir, these considerations have great weight with me, when I find things so circumstanced that I see the same party, at once a civil litigant against me in point of right, and a culprit before me; while I sit as a criminal judge on acts of his, whose moral quality is to be decided upon the merits of that very litigation. Men are every now and then put, by the complexity of human affairs, into strange situations; but justice is the same, let the judge be in what situation he will.

There is, sir, also a circumstance which convinces me that this mode of criminal proceeding is not (at least in the present stage of our contest) altogether expedient; which is nothing less than the conduct of those very persons who have seemed to adopt that mode by lately declaring a rebellion in Massachusetts Bay, as they had formerly addressed to have traitors brought hither, under an Act of Henry the Eighth, for trial. For though rebellion is declared, it is not proceeded against as such, nor have any steps been taken towards the apprehension or conviction of any individual offender, either on our late or our former Address; but modes of public coercion have been adopted, and such as have much more resemblance to a sort of qualified hostility towards an independent power than the punishment of rebellious subjects. All this seems rather inconsistent; but it shows how difficult it is to apply these juridical ideas to our present case.

In this situation, let us seriously and coolly ponder. What is it we have got by all our menaces, which have been many and ferocious? What advantage have we derived from the penal laws we have passed, and which, for the time, have been severe and numerous? What advances have we made towards our object by the sending of a force which, by land and sea, is no contemptible strength? Has the disorder abated? Nothing less. When I see things in this situation after such confident hopes, bold promises, and active exertions, I cannot, for my life, avoid a suspicion that the plan itself is not correctly right.

If, then, the removal of the causes of this spirit of American liberty be for the greater part, or rather entirely, impracticable; if the ideas of criminal process be inapplicable—or, if applicable, are in the highest degree inexpedient—what way yet remains? No way is open but the third and last—to comply with the American spirit as necessary; or, if you please, to submit to it as a necessary evil.

If we adopt this mode,—if we mean to conciliate and concede—let us see of what nature the concession ought to be. To ascertain the nature of our concession, we must look at their complaint. The colonies complain that they have not the characteristic mark and seal of British freedom. They complain that they are taxed in a Parliament in which they are not represented. If you mean to satisfy them at all, you must satisfy them with regard to this complaint. If you mean to please any people, you must give them the boon which they ask; not what you may think better for them, but of a kind totally different. Such an act may be a wise regulation, but it is no concession; whereas our present theme is the mode of giving satisfaction.

Sir, I think you must perceive that I am resolved this day to have nothing at all to do with the question of the right of taxation. Some gentlemen startle—but it is true; I put it totally out of the question. It is less than nothing in my consideration. I do not indeed wonder, nor will you, sir, that gentlemen of profound learning are fond of displaying it on this profound subject. But my consideration is narrow, confined, and wholly limited to the policy of the question. I do not examine whether the giving away a man's money be a power excepted and reserved out of the general trust of government; and how far all mankind, in all forms of polity, are entitled to an exercise of that right by the charter of nature. Or whether, on the contrary, a right of taxation is necessarily involved in the general principle of legislation, and inseparable from the ordinary supreme power. These are deep questions, where great names militate against each other, where reason is perplexed, and an appeal to authorities only thickens the confusion. For high and reverend authorities lift up their heads on both sides, and there is no sure footing in the middle. This point is the great

Serbonian bog,
'Twixt Damiata and Mount Cassius old,
Where armies whole have sunk.

I do not intend to be overwhelmed in that bog, though in such respectable company.

The question with me is, not whether you have a right to render your people miserable, but whether it is not your interest to make them happy. It is not what a lawyer tells me I may do, but what humanity, reason, and justice tell me I ought to do. Is a politic act the worse for being a generous one? Is no concession proper, but that which is made from your want of right to keep what you grant? Or does it lessen the grace or dignity of relaxing in the exercise of an odious claim, because you have your evidence-room full of titles, and your magazines stuffed with arms to enforce them? What signify all those titles and all those arms? Of what avail are they, when the reason of the thing tells me that the assertion of my title is the loss of my suit; and that I could do nothing but wound myself by the use of my own weapons?

Such is steadfastly my opinion of the absolute necessity of keeping up the concord of this empire by a unity of spirit, though in a diversity of operations, that, if I were sure the colonists had, at their leaving this

country, sealed a regular compact of servitude; that they had solemnly abjured all the rights of citizens; that they had made a vow to renounce all ideas of liberty for them and their posterity to all generations; yet I should hold myself obliged to conform to the temper I found universally prevalent in my own day, and to govern two million of men, impatient of servitude, on the principles of freedom. I am not determining a point of law; I am restoring tranquillity; and the general character and situation of a people must determine what sort of government is fitted for them. That point nothing else can or ought to determine.

My idea, therefore, without considering whether we yield as matter of right, or grant as matter of favor, is to *admit the people of our colonies into an interest in the Constitution*; and, by recording that admission in the journals of Parliament, to give them as strong an assurance as the nature of the thing will admit, that we mean for ever to adhere to that solemn declaration of systematic indulgence.

Some years ago, the repeal of a Revenue Act, upon its understood principle, might have served to show that we intended an unconditional abatement of the exercise of a taxing power. Such a measure was then sufficient to remove all suspicion, and to give perfect content. But unfortunate events, since that time, may make something further necessary; and not more necessary for the satisfaction of the colonies, than for the dignity and consistency of our own future proceedings.

.   .   .   .

For Thought and Discussion

1. What did Burke declare were the outstanding characteristics not only of Americans but in all people of English descent?
2. Was Burke's plea for abstract liberty? If not, for what specific right did he plead?
3. Why was the question of religion brought into discussion?
4. What relationship did Burke profess to see between negro slavery in Virginia and the Carolinas and the stubborn spirit of liberty in those states?
5. What tribute was paid to early American legislators? Would such a tribute be deserved today? What is your impression of the fitness of men who hold political offices today?
6. What bearing did the distance between England and America have on the issues between the two?
7. State definitely six sources from which the spirit of American freedom springs.
8. List from the oration ten words for the meaning of which you had to consult the dictionary.
9. Did Burke believe in granting concessions the justice and wisdom of which had not been investigated?
10. What arguments did Burke use in trying to persuade England to grant privileges desired by America?
11. Which paragraph and which sentence of Burke's speech does it seem to you ought to have had most weight with his listeners?
12. Advance·Burke's argument against slavery.
13. What specific right did Burke advocate that Great Britain grant America?

Plus Work

In a paper of some length trace the probable course of history had Burke's pleas for America been granted.

❧

THOUGHTS OF A BRITON ON THE SUBJUGATION OF SWITZERLAND

WILLIAM WORDSWORTH

[Up until the time France annexed three cantons of Switzerland in 1798, Wordsworth's sympathy had been with Napoleon and the cause of the French. After that he joined in the antagonism Englishmen felt for Napoleon, who by 1803 had succeeded in becoming master of continental Europe and was threatening to overthrow England. Evidently the *two* *voices* to which Wordsworth refers are the voice of Switzerland and the voice of England.]

TWO voices are there. One is of the sea,
One of the mountains; each a mighty voice.
In both from age to age thou didst rejoice;

They were thy chosen music, Liberty!
There came a tyrant, and with holy
　　glee   5
Thou fought'st against him—but hast
　　vainly striven.
Thou from thy Alpine holds at length
　　art driven,
Where not a torrent murmurs heard
　　by thee.
—Of one deep bliss thine ear hath
　　been bereft;

Then cleave, O cleave to that which
　　still is left—   10
For, high-souled Maid, what sorrow
　　would it be
That mountain floods should thunder
　　as before,
And ocean bellow from his rocky
　　shore,
And neither awful voice be heard by
　　thee!

For Thought and Discussion

1. What is the present status of Switzerland?
2. What would your attitude be were an individual or a nation
   to threaten the liberty of Switzerland at this time?
3. Who is the tyrant referred to by Wordsworth?
4. Of what earlier British poet are you reminded by the personi-
   fied terms "Liberty" and "high-souled Maid"?
5. Do you think that figurative language is more effective in the
   poem than a literal expression of Wordsworth's feelings would
   have been? Why?
6. Why is it appropriate to speak of the ocean as the voice of
   England?

❧

WHY I AM A LIBERAL
ROBERT BROWNING

[Browning in this sonnet recognizes that narrowness, prejudice, and
convention are barriers to freedom
and achievement, and he affirms that
he is a liberal because he wishes for
others the same power to achieve
which he covets for himself.]

W**HY?"** Because all I haply can
　　and do,
All that I am now, all I hope to be—
Whence comes it save from fortune
　　setting free
Body and soul the purpose to pursue,
God traced for both? If fetters not
　　a few,   5

Of prejudice, convention, fall from
　　me,
These shall I bid men—each in his de-
　　gree
Also God-guided—bear, and gayly,
　　too?

But little do or can the best of us.
That little is achieved through Lib-
　　erty.   10
Who, then, dares hold, emancipated
　　thus,
His fellow shall continue bound? Not
　　I,
Who live, love, labor freely, nor dis-
　　cuss
A brother's right to freedom. That
　　is "Why."

For Thought and Discussion

1. Of what lines in Wordsworth's *Ode on Intimations of Immortality* does this poem remind you?
2. How can prejudice and convention be barriers to success?
3. Is it your observation that people of liberal tendencies are tolerant of the views of others?
4. Argue either for or against Browning's premise that whatever people accomplish is achieved through freedom.
5. Explain fortune can "set free body and soul."
6. Is convention sometimes a blessing instead of a barrier? Justify your opinion on this point.

~⌒~

Additional Readings

Auslander, Joseph and Hill, Frank Ernest: *The Winged Horse Anthology*

Browning, Robert: *Hervé Riel*

Collins, William: *How Sleep the Brave*

Gibson, Wilfrid Wilson: *Daily Bread*

Macaulay, Thomas Babington: *Lays of Ancient Rome*

Porter, Jane: *Thaddeus of Warsaw*

Sanders, Gerald De Witt and Nelson, John Herbert: *Chief Modern Poets of England and America*

Schiller, Johann: *William Tell*

Shelley, Percy Bysshe: *Prometheus Unbound*

Thomson, James: *Rule Brittania*

The Futility and Destruction of War

THE FUTILITY AND DESTRUCTION
OF WAR

FROM the dawn of history the glamour and glory of war have been extolled in literature. Once war was a phase of life, a national business which might offer to a young man an opportunity for a brilliant career. That it was inevitable and necessary may not have been a debatable question even as late as the nineteenth century, but with the turn of the century there came a new spirit which was to have a profound effect upon the lives of men thereafter.

Scientific investigation put the factual test upon the value of war as upon other existing customs and institutions. Does war have anything to offer the twentieth century which cannot better be accomplished by peaceful means? Before that question can be answered, it is necessary to make an analysis of causes and of gains and losses. War is recognized as an idealistic adventure which has failed to attain definite and worthy results; a tool for unprincipled leaders who have no respect for human life and happiness; a way for ruthless nations to advance themselves at the expense of helpless ones; an effective smoke-screen which conceals internal dissatisfaction and corrupt government; a defense against unprovoked attack.

In this modern age a moral distinction has been made between aggressive and defensive warfare. With the sympathies of enlightened nations enlisted upon the side of the nation under attack, the aggressor's loss of good will is a more serious matter than in times past.

Warfare in the twentieth century has certain terrible, distinguishing features. Deadly weapons annihilate on a vast scale and are directed not only against armies but also against the civilian population, including men, women, and children. Furthermore, it is a recognized fact that the threat of destruction and annihilation hangs over all the nations involved.

There is pathos in a situation which forces nations to spend overwhelming sums for necessary armament and which compels great leaders to devote their time and thought to questions of warfare rather than to programs of advancement. As large masses of people become aware of the futility of war, there is hope that because of the moral and economic value, they will choose peace.

"I saw the spires of Oxford
As I was passing by
My heart was with the Oxford men
Who went abroad to die"

THE SPIRES OF OXFORD

WINIFRED M. LETTS

[Winifred M. Letts was born in Ireland. Her literary work includes novels and stories for children as well as poems.]

I SAW the spires of Oxford
  As I was passing by,
The gray spires of Oxford
  Against a pearl-gray sky.
My heart was with the Oxford men 5
  Who went abroad to die.

The years go fast in Oxford,
  The golden years and gay;
The hoary colleges look down
  On careless boys at play. 10

But when the bugles sounded—War!
  They put their games away.

They left the peaceful river,
  The cricket field, the quad,
The shaven lawns of Oxford, 15
  To seek a bloody sod.
They gave their merry youth away
  For country and for God.

God rest you, happy gentlemen,
  Who laid your good lives down, 20
Who took the khaki and the gun
  Instead of cap and gown.
God bring you to a fairer place
  Than even Oxford town.

For Thought and Discussion

1. Why are the young men in college the first to go to war?
2. Can a country afford to lose this class?
3. How does this poem get its title?
4. What is the mood of this poem?

5. Suppose it were the custom to have the mature men called out first, what possible effect might this have on the readiness of a nation to declare war and what probable effect would the enlistment of these older men have upon the economic welfare of the country?

FUTILITY

WILFRED OWEN

[Wilfred Owen, 1893-1918, was honored for bravery under fire in the World War. His sympathy for his comrades took him back to the battle lines after he had earned the right to remain in England, and he was killed one week before the Armistice was signed. [1]*snow*, death. [2]*clay*, the soldier.]

M OVE him into the sun—
  Gently its touch awoke him once,

At home, whispering of fields unsown.
Always it woke him, even in France,
Until this morning and this snow.[1]
If anything might rouse him now 6
The kind old sun will know.

Think how it wakes the seeds,—
Woke, once, the clays of a cold star.
Are limbs, so dear-achieved, are sides,
Full-nerved—still warm—too hard to stir? 11
Was it for this the clay[2] grew tall?
—O what made fatuous sunbeams toil
To break earth's sleep at all?

For Thought and Discussion

1. Notice the tenderness and sympathy for the dead soldier. How does the poet describe the death of the young soldier?
2. When was the young soldier killed?
3. To what does the poet compare death?
4. Why does the poet say that war is symbolic of futility?

THE DESTRUCTION OF SENNACHERIB

LORD BYRON

[Sennacherib was king of Assyria for twenty-four years, 705-681 B. C. After he had gained many terrible victories over the Hebrews, he made an attack on Jerusalem, but the city was saved by a plague which fell upon his army, diminishing its numbers until Sennacherib was forced to retreat. [1]*The Assyrian*, Sennacherib. [2]*co-* horts, company. [3]*Galilee*, the sea of Galilee in Palestine. [4]*widows of Ashur*, widows of Assyria. [5]*Baal*, one of the Assyrian gods. [6]*Gentile*, Sennacherib.]

T HE Assyrian[1] came down like the wolf on the fold,
And his cohorts[2] were gleaming in purple and gold;

And the sheen of their spears was like
    stars on the sea,
When the blue wave rolls nightly on
    deep Galilee.[3]

Like the leaves of the forest when
    summer is green,   5
That host with their banners at sunset
    were seen;
Like the leaves of the forest when
    autumn hath blown,
That host on the morrow lay withered
    and strown.

For the Angel of Death spread his
    wings on the blast,
And breathed in the face of the foe
    as he passed;   10
And the eyes of the sleepers waxed
    deadly and chill,
And their hearts but once heaved, and
    forever grew still!

And there lay the steed with his nos-
    tril all wide,

But through it there rolled not the
    breath of his pride;
And the foam of his gasping lay white
    on the turf,   15
And cold as the spray of the rock-
    beating surf.

And there lay the rider distorted and
    pale,
With the dew on his brow and the
    rust on his mail;
And the tents were all silent, the ban-
    ners alone,
The lances unlifted, the trumpet un-
    blown.   20

And the widows of Ashur[4] are loud
    in their wail,
And the idols are broke in the temple
    of Baal[5];
And the might of the Gentile,[6] un-
    smote by the sword,
Hath melted like snow in the glance
    of the Lord!

For Thought and Discussion

1. Tell the story of the poem.
2. To what does the poet compare the plague?
3. Which lines of the poem rhyme?
4. Read the poem aloud to catch the martial rhythm.

THE BATTLE OF WATERLOO

From *Childe Harold*

Canto III

LORD BYRON

[Seized by the spirit of adventure, Lord Byron, accompanied by his friend, Hobhouse, traveled in Spain and in Greece. When he returned, he had written Cantos I and II of *Childe Harold's Pilgrimage*. Later on he visited Belgium, the Rhine, and Switzerland, and finally lived in Italy. At various times he wrote the other two cantos of *Childe Harold*. The hero, Childe Harold, is a traveler who recalls the past as he views historic places. In the selections given he describes the gay party at the home of the Duchess of Richmond, the evening before the Battle of Waterloo.]

THERE was a sound of revelry by
      night,
And Belgium's capital had gathered
      then
Her Beauty and her Chivalry, and
      bright
The lamps shone o'er fair women
      and brave men;
A thousand hearts beat happily;
      and when   5
Music arose with its voluptuous
      swell,
Soft eyes looked love to eyes which
      spake again,
And all went merry as a marriage
      bell;
But hush! hark! a deep sound strikes
      like a rising knell!

Did ye not hear it?—No; 'twas but
      the wind,   10
Or the car rattling o'er the stony
      street;
On with the dance! let joy be un-
      confined;
No sleep till morn, when Youth
      and Pleasure meet
To chase the glowing Hours with
      flying feet.—

But hark! that heavy sound breaks
      in once more,   15
As if the clouds its echo would re-
      peat;
And nearer, clearer, deadlier than
      before!
Arm! arm! it is!—it is—the cannon's
      opening roar!

.   .   .   .

Ah! then and there was hurrying
      to and fro,
And gathering tears, and trembl-
      ings of distress,   20
And cheeks all pale, which but an
      hour ago
Blushed at the praise of their own
      loveliness;
And there were sudden partings,
      such as press
The life from out young hearts,
      and choking sighs
Which ne'er might be repeated:
      who could guess   25
If ever more should meet those
      mutual eyes,
Since upon night so sweet such awful
      morn could rise!

For Thought and Discussion

1. What is the mood of and the impression given by the first eight lines?
2. What effect is produced by the ninth line?
3. In the third stanza what phases of war are made vivid?
4. How does Byron use contrast effectively in this poem?
5. Do we still seem to be hearing the echoes of Waterloo?

Plus Work

Make reports dealing with:
      The Battle of Waterloo
      Why Byron Has Been Called the Poet of Rebellion and
            Revolution
      Byron's Treatment of Nature

THE CHARGE OF THE LIGHT BRIGADE
ALFRED LORD TENNYSON

["The Charge of the Light Brigade" was written to celebrate the bravery of six hundred and seventy British soldiers who charged the Russian Army, through an order which their commander misinterpreted. They were not supported, and most of them were lost. Only one hundred and ninety-eight men survived. The attack took place during the Crimean War in 1854, when the English, French, and Turks fought against Russia.]

I

HALF a league, half a league,
Half a league onward,
All in the valley of death
  Rode the six hundred.
"Forward, the Light Brigade!   5
Charge for the guns!" he said;
Into the valley of death
  Rode the six hundred.

II

"Forward, the Light Brigade!"
Was there a man dismayed?   10
Not though the soldier knew
  Some one had blundered;
Theirs not to make reply,
Theirs not to reason why,
Theirs but to do and die;   15
Into the valley of death
  Rode the six hundred.

III

Cannon to right of them,
Cannon to left of them,
Cannon in front of them   20
  Volleyed and thundered;

Stormed at with shot and shell,
Boldly they rode and well,
Into the jaws of death
Into the mouth of Hell   25
  Rode the six hundred.

IV

Flashed all their sabers bare,
Flashed as they turned in air,
Sab'ring the gunners there,
Charging an army, while   30
  All the world wondered;
Plunged in the battery-smoke
Right through the line they broke;
Cossack and Russian
Reeled from the saber-stroke   35
  Shattered and sundered.
Then they rode back, but not—
  Not the six hundred.

V

Cannon to right of them,
Cannon to left of them,   40
Cannon behind them
  Volleyed and thundered;
Stormed at with shot and shell,
While horse and hero fell,
They that had fought so well   45
Came through the jaws of death,
Back from the mouth of Hell,
All that was left of them,
  Left of six hundred.

VI

When can their glory fade?   50
Oh, the wild charge they made!
  All the world wondered.
Honor the charge they made!
Honor the Light Brigade,
  Noble six hundred!   55

For Thought and Discussion

1. In the practical and scientific age in which we live, we question any system that sacrifices lives. Are there occupations and

professions that demand as much courage and bravery as war but which bring happiness to the world?

2. Was the Victorian poet's attitude toward war realistic or romantic?

3. Is the attitude of your age realistic or romantic? Why?

Plus Work

Compare "The Charge of the Light Brigade" with one of Siegfried Sassoon's poems on the World War. From this comparison bring out the difference between idealism and realism.

☙

THE REVENGE

A Ballad of the Fleet

ALFRED LORD TENNYSON

[Sir Richard Grenville, the English commander, with one ship fought the Spanish fleet of fifty-three ships for fifteen hours.]

I

AT Flores[1] in the Azores[2] Sir Richard Grenville lay,
And a pinnace,[3] like a fluttered bird, came flying from far away:
"Spanish ships of war at sea! we have sighted fifty-three!"
Then sware Lord Thomas Howard: " 'Fore God, I am no coward;
But I cannot meet them here, for my ships are out of gear,   5
And the half my men are sick. I must fly, but follow quick.
We are six ships of the line; can we fight with fifty-three?"

II

Then spake Sir Richard Grenville: "I know you are no coward;
You fly them for a moment to fight with them again.

But I've ninety men and more that are lying sick ashore.   10
I should count myself the coward if I left them, my Lord Howard,
To these Inquisition dogs and the devildoms of Spain."

III

So Lord Howard passed away with five ships of war that day,
Till he melted like a cloud in the silent summer heaven;
But Sir Richard bore in hand all his sick men from the land   15
Very carefully and slow,
Men of Bideford in Devon,
And we laid them on the ballast[4] down below:
For we brought them all aboard,
And they blessed him in their pain, that they were not left to Spain,   20
To the thumb-screw and the stake, for the glory of the Lord.

IV

He had only a hundred seamen to work the ship and to fight,

---

[1]*Flores*, one of the islands.
[2]*Azores*, a group of islands in the Atlantic.
[3]*pinnace*, flag or pennant.

[4]*ballast*, a heavy substance in the hold of the ship to give balance, hence a place of safety in the ship.

And he sailed away from Flores till
  the Spaniard came in sight,
With his huge sea-castles heaving up-
  on the weather bow.
"Shall we fight or shall we fly?   25
Good Sir Richard, tell us now,
For to fight is but to die!
There'll be little of us left by the time
  this sun be set."
And Sir Richard said again: "We be
  all good English men.
Let us bang these dogs of Seville, the
  children of the devil,   30
For I never turned my back upon
  Don or devil yet."

V

Sir Richard spoke and he laughed,
  and we roared a hurrah, and so
The little *Revenge* ran on sheer into
  the heart of the foe,
With her hundred fighters on deck,
  and her ninety sick below;
For half of their fleet to the right
  and half to the left were seen,   35
And the little *Revenge* ran on
  through the long sea-lane between.

VI

Thousands of their soldiers looked
  down from their decks and
  laughed,
Thousands of their seamen made
  mock at the mad little craft
Running on and on, till delayed
By their mountain-like *San Philip*
  that, of fifteen hundred tons,   40
And up-shadowing high above us
  with her yawning tiers of guns,
Took the breath from our sails, and
  we stayed.

VII

And while now the great *San Philip*
  hung above us like a cloud
Whence the thunderbolt will fall
Long and loud,   45

Four galleons[5] drew away
From the Spanish fleet that day,
And two upon the larboard[6] and two
  upon the starboard lay,
And the battle-thunder broke from
  them all.

VIII

But anon the great *San Philip,* she
  bethought herself and went,   50
Having that within her womb that
  had left her ill content;
And the rest they came aboard us, and
  they fought us hand to hand,
For a dozen times they came with
  their pikes and musqueteers,
And a dozen times we shook 'em off as
  a dog that shakes his ears
When he leaps from the water to
  the land.   55

IX

And the sun went down, and the stars
  came out far over the summer sea,
But never a moment ceased the fight
  of the one and the fifty-three.
Ship after ship, the whole night long,
  their high-built galleons came,
Ship after ship, the whole night long,
  with her battle-thunder and flame:
Ship after ship, the whole night long,
  drew back with her dead and her
  shame.   60
For some were sunk and many were
  shattered, and so could fight no
  more—
God of battles, was ever a battle like
  this in the world before?

X

For he said, "Fight on! fight on!"
Though his vessel was all but a wreck;
And it chanced that, when half of the
  short summer night was gone,   65

---

[5]*galleons,* three-deck ships, especially Spanish ships.
[6]*larboard,* landward or side toward
the land.

With a grisly wound to be dressed he
had left the deck,
But a bullet struck him that was
dressing it suddenly dead,
And himself he was wounded again
in the side and the head,
And he said, "Fight on! fight on!"

XI

And the night went down, and the
sun smiled out far over the summer
sea,   70
And the Spanish fleet with broken
sides lay round us all in a ring;
But they dared not touch us again,
for they feared that we still could
sting,
So they watched what the end would
be.
And we had not fought them in vain,
But in perilous plight were we,   75
Seeing forty of our poor hundred
were slain,
And half of the rest of us maimed for
life
In the crash of the cannonades and
the desperate strife:
And the sick men down in the hold
were most of them stark and cold,
And the pikes. were all broken or
bent, and the powder was all of it
spent;   80
And the masts and the rigging were
lying over the side;
But Sir Richard cried in his English
pride:
"We have fought such a fight for a
day and a night
As may never be fought again!
We have won great glory, my men! 85
And a day less or more
At sea or ashore,
We die—does it matter when?
Sink me the ship, Master Gunner—
sink her, split her in twain!
Fall into the hands of God, not into
the hands of Spain!"   90

XII

And the gunner said, "Ay, ay," but
the seamen made reply:
"We have children, we have wives,
And the Lord hath spared our lives.
We will make the Spaniard promise,
if we yield, to let us go;
We shall live to fight again and to
strike another blow."   95
And the lion there lay dying, and
they yielded to the foe.

XIII

And the stately Spanish men to their
flagship bore him then,
Where they laid him by the mast, old
Sir Richard caught at last,
And they praised him to his face with
their courtly foreign grace;
But he rose upon their decks, and he
cried: 100
"I have fought for Queen and Faith
like a valiant man and true;
I have only done my duty as a man is
bound to do.
With a joyful spirit I Sir Richard
Grenville die!"
And he fell upon their decks, and he
died.

XIV

And they stared at the dead that had
been so valiant and true,   105
And had holden the power and glory
of Spain so cheap
That he dared her with one little ship
and his English few;
Was he devil or man? He was devil
for aught they knew,
But they sank his body with honor
down into the deep,
And they manned the *Revenge* with
a swarthier alien crew,   110
And away she sailed with her loss and
longed for her own;
When a wind from the lands they had
ruined awoke from sleep,

And the water began to heave and the
    weather to moan,
And or ever that evening ended a
    great gale blew,
And a wave like the wave that is
    raised by an earthquake grew, 115
Till it smote on their hulls and their
sails and their masts and their flags,
And the whole sea plunged and fell
    on the shot-shattered navy of
    Spain,
And the little *Revenge* herself went
    down by the island crags
To be lost evermore in the main.

For Thought and Discussion

1. Make a report on the Spanish Armada.
2. Why did Lord Howard flee?
3. Why did Sir Richard stay to fight?
4. How long did the fight last?
5. Why did the seamen not wish to sink the ship?
6. Why did Sir Richard's death seem fitting?
7. Why were the Spaniards very gracious to Sir Richard after the surrender?
8. What outstanding traits of character did Sir Richard have?

Plus Work

The same kind of courage and bravery possessed by Sir Richard has been inherited by one of his family living in the twentieth century. Read and report on *Adrift on an Ice Pan* and *A Labrador Doctor* by Sir Wilfred Grenfell.

❦

INCIDENT OF THE FRENCH CAMP
ROBERT BROWNING

[Napoleon stormed Ratisbon in 1809. The incident described in this poem really occurred, except that the hero was a man instead of a boy.

[1]*Lannes*, Jean Lannes was one of Napoleon's field marshals. [2]*vans*, wing from the Latin term *vannue*, a fan.]

YOU know, we French stormed
    Ratisbon;
    A mile or so away,
On a little mound, Napoleon
    Stood on our storming-day,
With neck out-thrust, you fancy
    how,   5
    Legs wide, arms locked behind,
As if to balance the prone brow
    Oppressive with its mind.

Just as perhaps he mused, "My plans
    That soar, to earth may fall,   10
Let once my army-leader Lannes[1]
    Waver at yonder wall"—
Out 'twixt the battery-smokes there
    flew
A rider, bound on bound
Full-galloping; nor bridle drew   15
    Until he reached the mound.

Then off there flung in smiling joy,
    And held himself erect
By just his horse's mane, a boy;
    You hardly could suspect—   20
(So tight he kept his lips compressed,
    Scarce any blood came through)
You looked twice ere you saw his
    breast
    Was all but shot in two.

"Well," cried he, "Emperor, by God's grace   ²⁵
We've got you Ratisbon!
The Marshal's in the market-place,
And you'll be there anon
To see your flag-bird flap his vans[2]
Where I, to heart's desire,   ³⁰
Perched him!" The chief's eye flashed; his plans
Soared up again like fire.

The chief's eye flashed; but presently
Softened itself, as sheathes
A film the mother-eagle's eye   ³⁵
When her bruised eaglet breathes;
"You're wounded!" "Nay," the soldier's pride
Touched to the quick, he said;
"I'm killed, Sire!" And his chief beside
Smiling the boy fell dead.   ⁴⁰

For Thought and Discussion

1. What is the situation at the beginning of the poem?
2. According to the poet what was Napoleon's attitude toward the young soldier? What was the latter's attitude toward Napoleon? What other traits of character are here attributed to Napoleon?
3. Name the events of the poem in the order in which they happen.
4. If this were a twentieth century poem, do you think the poet would have been likely to use the last four lines of both the third and the last stanzas for the theme of his poem?

Plus Work

Make a study of the contrast in attitude toward war in nineteenth and twentieth century literature.

THE BOY COMES HOME
ALAN ALEXANDER MILNE

[During the World War, in which he served, Milne, while resting after an illness, dictated plays to his wife, one of which was *The Boy Comes Home*. In addition to plays he has written many children's books, *Christopher Robin*, *Story Book Reader*, and *Winnie-the-Pooh*.]

SCENE.—*A room in* UNCLE JAMES'S *house in the Cromwell Road.*

TIME.—*The day after the War.*

Any room in UNCLE JAMES'S *house is furnished in heavy mid-Victorian style; this particular morning-room is perhaps solider and more respectable even than the others, from the heavy table in the middle of it to the heavy engravings on the walls. There are two doors to it. The one at the back opens into the hall, the one at the side into the dining-room.*

PHILIP *comes in from the hall and goes into the dining-room. Apparently he finds nothing there, for he returns to the morning-room, looks about him for a moment and then rings the bell. It is ten o'-clock, and he wants his breakfast. He picks up the paper, and sits in a heavy arm-chair in front of the fire—a pleasant-looking well-built person of twenty-three, with an air of decisiveness about him.* MARY, *the parlour-maid, comes in.*

MARY. Did you ring, Master Philip?

PHILIP (*absently*). Yes; I want some breakfast, please, Mary.

MARY (*coldly*). Breakfast has been cleared away an hour ago.

PHILIP. Exactly. That's why I rang. You can boil me a couple of eggs or something. And coffee, not tea.

MARY. I'm sure I don't know what Mrs. Higgins will say?

PHILIP (*getting up*). Who is Mrs. Higgins?

MARY. The cook. And she's not used to being put about like this.

PHILIP. Do you think she'll say something?

MARY. I don't know *what* she'll say.

PHILIP. You needn't tell me, you know, if you don't want to. Anyway, I don't suppose it will shock me. One gets used to it in the Army. (*He smiles pleasantly at her.*)

MARY. Well, I'll do what I can, sir. But breakfast at eight sharp is the master's rule, just as it used to be before you went away to war.

PHILIP. Before I went away to the war I did a lot of silly things. Don't drag them up now. (*More curtly.*) Two eggs, and if there's a ham bring that along too. (*He turns away.*)

MARY (*doubtfully, as she prepares to go*). Well, I'm sure I don't know what Mrs. Higgins will say.

(*Exit* MARY.)

(*As she goes out she makes way for* AUNT EMILY *to come in, a kind-hearted mid-Victorian lady who has never had any desire for the vote.*)

EMILY. *There* you are, Philip! Good morning, dear. Did you sleep well?

PHILIP. Rather; splendidly, thanks, Aunt Emily. How are you? (*He kisses her.*)

EMILY. And did you have a good

breakfast? Naughty boy to be late for it. I always thought they had to get up so early in the Army.

PHILIP. They do. That's why. they're so late when they get out of the Army.

EMILY. Dear me! I should have thought a habit of four years would have stayed with you.

PHILIP. Every morning for four years, as I've shot out of bed, I've said to myself, "Wait! A time will come." (*Smiling.*) That doesn't really give a habit a chance.

EMILY. Well, I dare say you wanted your sleep out. I was so afraid that a really cosy bed would keep you awake after all those years in the trenches.

PHILIP. Well, one isn't in the trenches all the time. And one gets leave—if one's an officer.

EMILY (*reproachfully*). You didn't spend much of it with *us*, Philip.

PHILIP (*taking her hands*). I know; but you did understand, didn't you, dear?

EMILY. We're not very gay, and I know you must have wanted gaiety for the little time you had. But I think your Uncle James felt it. After all, dear, you've lived with us for some years, and he *is* your guardian.

PHILIP. I know. *You've* been a darling to me always, Aunt Emily. But (*awkwardly*) Uncle James and I——

EMILY. Of course, he is a *little* difficult to get on with. I'm more used to him. But I'm sure he really is very fond of you, Philip.

PHILIP. H'm! I always used to be frightened of him .... I suppose he's just the same. He seemed just the same last night—and he still has breakfast at eight o'clock. Been making pots of money, I suppose?

EMILY. He never tells me exactly, but he did speak once about the absurdity of the excess-profits tax.

You see, jam is a thing the Army wants.

PHILIP. It certainly gets it.

EMILY. It was so nice for him, because it made him feel he was doing his bit, helping the poor men in the trenches.

(*Enter* MARY.)

MARY. Mrs. Higgins wishes to speak to you, ma'am. (*She looks at* PHILIP *as much as to say, "There you are!"*)

EMILY (*getting up*). Yes, I'll come. (*To* PHILIP.) I think I'd better just see what she wants, Philip.

PHILIP (*firmly to* MARY). Tell Mrs. Higgins to come here. (MARY *hesitates and looks at her mistress.*) At once, please.

(*Exit* MARY.)

EMILY (*upset*). Philip, dear, I don't know what Mrs. Higgins will say——

PHILIP. No; nobody seems to. I thought we might really find out for once.

EMILY (*going towards the door*). Perhaps I'd better go——

PHILIP (*putting his arm round her waist*). Oh no, you mustn't. You see, she really wants to see *me*.

EMILY. *You?*

PHILIP. Yes; I ordered breakfast five minutes ago.

EMILY. Philip! My poor boy! Why didn't you tell me? and I dare say I could have got it for you. Though I don't know what Mrs. Higgins——

(*An extremely angry voice is heard outside, and* MRS. HIGGINS, *stout and aggressive, comes in.*)

MRS. HIGGINS (*truculently*). You sent for me, ma'am?

EMILY (*nervously*). Yes—er—I think if you—perhaps——

PHILIP (*calmly*). I sent for you, Mrs. Higgins. I want some breakfast. Didn't Mary tell you?

MRS. HIGGINS. Breakfast is at eight o'clock. It always has been as long as I've been in this house, and always will be until I get further orders.

PHILIP. Well, you've just got further orders. Two eggs, and if there's a ham——

MRS. HIGGINS. Orders. We're talking about orders. From whom in this house do I take orders, may I ask?

PHILIP. In this case from me.

MRS. HIGGINS (*playing her trump-card*). In that case, ma'am, I wish to give a month's notice from to-day. *Inclusive.*

PHILIP (*quickly, before his aunt can say anything*). Certainly. In fact, you'd probably prefer it if my aunt gave *you* notice, and then you could go at once. We can easily arrange that. (*To* AUNT EMILY, *as he takes out a fountain-pen and cheque-book.*) What do you pay her?

EMILY (*faintly*). Forty-five pounds.

PHILIP (*writing on his knee*). Twelves into forty-five . . . (*Pleasantly to* MRS. HIGGINS, *but without looking up.*) I hope you don't mind a Cox's cheque. Some people do; but this is quite a good one. (*Tearing it out.*) Here you are.

MRS. HIGGINS (*taken aback*). What's this?

PHILIP. Your wages instead of notice. Now you can go at once.

MRS. HIGGINS. Who said anything about going?

PHILIP (*surprised*). I'm sorry; I thought *you* did.

MRS. HIGGINS. If it's only a bit of breakfast, I don't say but what I mightn't get it, if I'm asked decent.

PHILIP (*putting back the cheque*). Then let me say again, "Two eggs, ham and coffee." And Mary can bring the ham up at once, and I'll get going on that. (*Turning away.*) Thanks very much.

MRS. HIGGINS. Well, I — well — well! (*Exit speechless.*)

PHILIP (*surprised*). Is that all she ever says? It isn't much to worry about.

EMILY. Philip, how could you! I should have been terrified.

PHILIP. Well, you see, I've done your job for two years out there.

EMILY. What job?

PHILIP. Mess President . . . I think I'll go and see about that ham.

(*He smiles at her and goes out into the dining-room.* AUNT EMILY *wanders round the room, putting a few things tidy as is her habit, when she is interrupted by the entrance of* UNCLE JAMES. JAMES *is not a big man, nor an impressive one in his black morning-coat; and his thin straggly beard, now going grey, does not hide a chin of any great power; but he has a severity which passes for strength with the weak.*)

JAMES. Philip down yet?

EMILY. He's just having his breakfast.

JAMES (*looking at his watch*). Ten o'clock. (*Snapping it shut and putting it back.*) Ten o'clock. I say ten o'clock, Emily.

EMILY. Yes, dear, I heard you.

JAMES. You don't say anything?

EMILY (*vaguely*). I expect he's tired after that long war.

JAMES. That's no excuse for not being punctual. I suppose he learnt punctuality in the Army?

EMILY. I expect he learnt it, James, but I understood him to say that he'd forgotten it.

JAMES. Then the sooner he learns it again the better. I particularly stayed away from the office to-day in order to talk things over with him, and (*looking at his watch*) here's ten o'clock—past ten—and no sign of him. I'm practically throwing away a day.

EMILY. What are you going to talk to him about?

JAMES. His future, naturally. I have decided that the best thing he can do is to come into the business at once.

EMILY. Are you really going to talk it over with him, James, or are you just going to tell him that he *must* come?

JAMES (*surprised*). What do you mean? What's the difference? Naturally we shall talk it over first, and —er—naturally he'll fall in with my wishes.

EMILY. I suppose he can hardly help himself, poor boy.

JAMES. Not until he's twenty-five, anyhow. When he's twenty-five he can have his own money and do what he likes with it.

EMILY (*timidly*). But I think you ought to consult him a little, dear. After all, he *has* been fighting for us.

JAMES (*with his back to the fire*). Now that's the sort of silly sentiment that there's been much too much of. I object to it strongly. I don't want to boast, but I think I may claim to have done my share. I gave up my nephew to my country, and I—er—suffered from the shortage of potatoes to an extent that you probably didn't realize. Indeed, if it hadn't been for your fortunate discovery about that time that you didn't really like potatoes, I don't know how we should have carried on. And, as I think I've told you before, the excess-profits tax seemed to me a singularly stupid piece of legislation—but I paid it. And I don't go boasting about how much I paid.

EMILY (*unconvinced*). Well, I think that Philip's four years out there have made him more of a man; he doesn't seem somehow like a boy who can be told what to do. I'm sure they've taught him something.

JAMES. I've no doubt that they've taught him something about—er—bombs and—er—which end a revolver goes off, and how to form fours. But I don't see that that sort of thing helps him to decide upon the most suitable career for a young man in after-war conditions.

EMILY. Well, I can only say you'll find him different.

JAMES. I didn't notice any particular difference last night.

EMILY. I think you'll find him rather more—I can't quite think of the word, but Mrs. Higgins could tell you what I mean.

JAMES. Of course, if he likes to earn his living any other way, he may; but I don't see how he proposes to do it so long as I hold the purse-strings. (*Looking at his watch.*) Perhaps you'd better tell him that I cannot wait any longer.

(EMILY *opens the door leading into the dining-room and talks through it to* PHILIP.)

EMILY. Philip, your uncle is waiting to see you before he goes to the office. Will you be long, dear?

PHILIP (*from the dining-room*). Is he in a hurry?

JAMES (*shortly*). Yes.

EMILY. He says he *is* rather, dear.

PHILIP. Couldn't he come and talk in here? It wouldn't interfere with my breakfast.

JAMES. No.

EMILY. He says he'd rather you came to *him*, darling.

PHILIP (*resigned*). Oh, well.

EMILY (*to James*). He'll be here directly, dear. Just sit down in front of the fire and make yourself comfortable with the paper. He won't keep you long. (*She arranges him.*)

JAMES (*taking the paper*). The

morning is not the time to make one-self comfortable. It's a most danger-ous habit. I nearly found myself dropping off in front of the fire just now. I don't like this hanging about, wasting the day. (*He opens the paper.*)

EMILY. You should have had a nice sleep, dear, while you could. We were up so late last night listening to Philip's stories.

JAMES. Yes, yes. (*He begins a yawn and stifles it hurriedly.*) You mustn't neglect your duties, Emily. I've no doubt you have plenty to do.

EMILY. All right, James, then I'll leave you. But don't be hard on the boy.

JAMES (*sleepily*). I shall be just, Emily; you can rely upon that.

EMILY (*going to the door*). I don't think that's quite what I meant. (*She goes out.*)

(JAMES, *who is now quite comfort-able, begins to nod. He wakes up with a start, turns over the paper, and nods again. Soon he is breath-ing deeply with closed eyes.*)

. . . .

PHILIP (*coming in*). Sorry to have kept you waiting, but I was a bit late for breakfast. (*He takes out his pipe.*) Are we going to talk business, or what?

JAMES (*taking out his watch*). A *bit* late! I make it just two hours.

PHILIP (*pleasantly*). All right, Uncle James. Call it two hours late. Or twenty-two hours early for to-morrow's breakfast, if you like. (*He sits down in a chair on the opposite side of the table from his uncle, and lights his pipe.*)

JAMES. You smoke now?

PHILIP (*staggered*). I what?

JAMES (*nodding at his pipe*). You smoke?

PHILIP. Good heavens! what do you think we *did* in France?

JAMES. Before you start smoking all over the house, I should have thought you would have asked your aunt's permission.

(PHILIP *looks at him in amazement, and then goes to the door.*)

PHILIP (*calling*). Aunt Emily! . . . Aunt Emily! . . . Do you mind my smoking in here?

AUNT EMILY (*from upstairs*). Of course not, darling.

PHILIP (*to* JAMES, *as he returns to his chair*). Of course not, darling. (*He puts back his pipe in his mouth.*)

JAMES. Now, understand once and for all, Philip, while you remain in my house I expect not only punctu-ality, but also civility and respect. I will *not* have impertinence.

PHILIP (*unimpressed*). Well, that's what I want to talk to you about, Uncle James. About staying in your house, I mean.

JAMES. I don't know what you do mean.

PHILIP. Well, we don't get on too well together, and I thought perhaps I'd better take rooms somewhere. You could give me an allowance until I came into my money. Or I suppose you could give me the money now if you really liked. I don't quite know how father left it to me.

JAMES (*coldly*). You come into your money when you are twenty-five. Your father very wisely felt that to trust a large sum to a mere boy of twenty-one was simply put-ting temptation in his way. Whether I have the power or not to alter his dispositions, I certainly don't propose to do so.

PHILIP. If it comes to that, I *am* twenty-five.

JAMES. Indeed? I had an impres-sion that that event took place in about two years' time. When did you become twenty-five, may I ask?

PHILIP (*quietly*). It was on the Somme. We were attacking the next day and my company was in support. We were in a so-called trench on the edge of a wood—a rotten place to be. The company commander sent back to ask if we could move. The C. O. said, "Certainly not; hang on." We hung on; doing nothing, you know—just hanging on and waiting for the next day. Of course, the Boche knew all about that. He had it on us nicely .... (*Sadly.*) Poor old Billy! he was one of the best—our company commander, you know. They got him, poor devil! That left *me* in command of the company. I sent a runner back to ask if I could move. Well, I'd had a bit of a scout on my own and found a sort of trench five hundred yards to the right. Not what *you'd* call a trench, of course, but compared to that wood—well, it was absolutely Hyde Park. I described the position and asked if I could go there. My man never came back. I waited an hour and sent another man. He went west too. Well, I wasn't going to send a third. It was murder. So I had to decide. We'd lost about half the company by this time, you see. Well, there were three things I could do—hang on, move to this other trench, against orders, or go back myself and explain the situation .... I moved.... And then I went back to the C. O. and told him I'd moved.... And then I went back to the company again.... (*Quietly.*) That was when I became twenty-five ... or thirty-five ... or forty-five.

JAMES (*recovering himself with an effort*). Ah, yes, yes. (*He coughs awkwardly.*) No doubt points like that frequently crop up in the trenches. I am glad that you did well out there, and I'm sure your Colonel would speak kindly of you; but when it comes to choosing a career for you now that you have left the Army, my advice is not altogether to be despised. Your father evidently thought so, or he would not have entrusted you to my care.

PHILIP. My father didn't foresee this war.

JAMES. Yes, yes, but you make too much of this war. All you young boys seem to think you've come back from France to teach us our business. You'll find that it is you who'll have to learn, not we.

PHILIP. I'm quite prepared to learn; in fact, I want to.

JAMES. Excellent. Then we can consider that settled.

PHILIP. Well, we haven't settled yet what business I'm going to learn.

JAMES. I don't think that's very difficult. I propose to take you into my business. You'll start at the bottom, of course, but it will be a splendid opening for you.

PHILIP (*thoughtfully*). I see. So you've decided it for me? The jam business.

JAMES (*sharply*). Is there anything to be ashamed of in that?

PHILIP. Oh no, nothing at all. Only it doesn't happen to appeal to me.

JAMES. If you knew which side your bread was buttered, it would appeal to you very considerably.

PHILIP. I'm afraid I can't see the butter for the jam.

JAMES. I don't want any silly jokes of that sort. You were glad enough to get it out there, I've no doubt.

PHILIP. Oh yes. Perhaps that's why I'm so sick of it now.... No, it's no good, Uncle James; you must think of something else.

JAMES (*with a sneer*). Perhaps *you've* thought of something else?

PHILIP. Well, I had some idea of being an architect——

JAMES. You propose to start learning to be an architect at twenty-three?

PHILIP (*smiling*). Well, I couldn't start before, could I?

JAMES. Exactly. And now you'll find it's too late.

PHILIP. Is it? Aren't there going to be any more architects, or doctors, or solicitors, or barristers? Because we've all lost four years of our lives, are all the professions going to die out?

JAMES. And how old do you suppose you'll be before you're earning money as an architect?

PHILIP. The usual time, whatever that may be. If I'm four years behind, so is everybody else.

JAMES. Well, I think it's high time you began to earn a living at once.

PHILIP. Look here, Uncle James, do you really think that you can treat me like a boy who's just left school? Do you think four years at the front have made no difference at all?

JAMES. If there had been any difference, I should have expected it to take the form of an increased readiness to obey orders and recognize authority.

PHILIP (*regretfully*). You are evidently determined to have a row. Perhaps I had better tell you once and for all that I refuse to go into the turnip and vegetable marrow business.

JAMES (*thumping the table angrily*). And perhaps I'd better tell *you*, sir, once and for all, that I don't propose to allow rudeness from an impertinent young puppy.

PHILIP (*reminiscently*). I remember annoying our Brigadier once. He was covered with red, had a very red face, about twenty medals, and a cold blue eye. He told me how angry he was for about five minutes while I stood to attention. I'm afraid you aren't nearly so impressive, Uncle James.

JAMES (*rather upset*). Oh! (*Recovering himself.*) Fortunately I have other means of impressing you. The power of the purse goes a long way in this world. I propose to use it.

PHILIP. I see. . . . Yes. . . that's rather awkward, isn't it?

JAMES (*pleasantly*). I think you'll find it very awkward.

PHILIP (*thoughtfully*). Yes.

(*With an amused laugh* JAMES *settles down to his paper as if the interview were over.*)

(*To himself.*) I suppose I shall have to think of another argument. (*He takes out a revolver from his pocket and fondles it affectionately.*)

JAMES (*looking up suddenly as he is doing this—amazed*). What on earth are you doing?

PHILIP. Souvenir from France. Do you know, Uncle James, that this revolver has killed about twenty Germans?

JAMES (*shortly*). Oh! Well, don't go playing about with it here, or you'll be killing Englishmen before you know where you are.

PHILIP. Well, you never know. (*He raises it leisurely and points it at his uncle.*) It's a nice little weapon.

JAMES (*angrily*). Put it down, sir. You ought to have grown out of monkey tricks like that in the Army. You ought to know better than to point an unloaded revolver at anybody. That's the way accidents always happen.

PHILIP. Not when you've been on a revolver course and know all about it. Besides, it *is* loaded.

JAMES (*very angry because he is*

frightened suddenly). Put it down at once, sir. (PHILIP *turns it away from him and examines it carelessly*.) What's the matter with you? Have you gone mad suddenly?

PHILIP (*mildly*). I thought you'd be interested in it. It's shot such a lot of Germans.

JAMES. Well, it won't want to shoot any more, and the sooner you get rid of it the better.

PHILIP. I wonder. Does it ever occur to you, Uncle James, that there are about a hundred thousand people in England who own revolvers, who are quite accustomed to them and—who have nobody to practice on now?

JAMES. No, sir, it certainly doesn't.

PHILIP (*thoughtfully*). I wonder if it will make any difference. You know, one gets so used to potting at people. It's rather difficult to realize suddenly that one oughtn't to.

JAMES (*getting up*). I don't know what the object of all this tom-foolery is, if it has one. But you understand that I expect you to come to the office with me to-morrow at nine

o'clock. Kindly see that you're punctual. (*He turns to go away*.)

PHILIP (*softly*). Uncle James.

JAMES (*over his shoulder*). I have no more——

PHILIP (*in his parade voice*). Stand to attention when you talk to an officer! (JAMES *instinctively turns round and stiffens himself*.) That's better; you can sit down if you like. (*He motions* JAMES *to his chair with the revolver*.)

JAMES (*going nervously to his chair*). What does this bluff mean?

PHILIP. It isn't bluff, it's quite serious. (*Pointing the revolver at his uncle*.) Do sit down.

JAMES (*sitting down*). Threats, eh?

PHILIP. Persuasion.

JAMES. At the point of the revolver? You settle your arguments by force? Good heavens, sir! this is just the very thing that we were fighting to put down.

PHILIP. *We* were fighting! *We! We!* Uncle, you're a humorist.

JAMES. Well, "you," if you prefer

it. Although those of us who stayed at home——

PHILIP. Yes, never mind about the excess profits now. I can tell you quite well what we fought for. We used force to put down force. That's what I'm doing now. You were going to use force—the force of money —to make me do what you wanted. Now I'm using force to stop it. (*He levels the revolver again.*)

JAMES. You're—you're going to shoot your old uncle?

PHILIP. Why not? I've shot lots of old uncles—Landsturmers.

JAMES. But those were Germans! It's different shooting Germans. You are in England now. You couldn't have a crime on your conscience like that.

PHILIP. Ah, but you mustn't think that after four years of war one has quite the same ideas about the sanctity of human life. How could one?

JAMES. You'll find that juries have kept pretty much the same ideas, I fancy.

PHILIP. Yes, but revolvers often go off accidentally. You said so yourself. This is going to be the purest accident. Can't you see it in the papers? "The deceased's nephew, who was obviously upset——"

JAMES. I suppose you think it's brave to come back from the front and threaten a defenceless man with a revolver? Is that the sort of fair play they teach you in the Army?

PHILIP. Good heavens! of course it is. You don't think that you wait until the other side has got just as many guns as you before you attack? You're really rather lucky. Strictly speaking, I ought to have thrown a half dozen bombs at you first. (*Taking one out of his pocket.*) As it happens, I've only got one.

JAMES (*thoroughly alarmed*). Put that back at once.

PHILIP (*putting down the revolver and taking it in his hands*). You hold it in the right hand—so—taking care to keep the lever down. Then you take the pin in the finger—so, and—but perhaps this doesn't interest you?

JAMES (*edging his chair away*). Put it down at once, sir. Good heavens! anything might happen.

PHILIP (*putting it down and taking up the revolver again*). Does it ever occur to you, Uncle James, that there are about three million people in England, who know all about bombs, and how to throw them, and——

JAMES. It certainly does not occur to me. I should never dream of letting these things occur to me.

PHILIP (*looking at the bomb regretfully*). It's rather against my principles as a soldier, but just to make things a bit more fair—(*generously*) you shall have it. (*He holds it out to him suddenly.*)

JAMES (*shrinking back again*). Certainly not, sir. It might go off at any moment.

PHILIP (*putting it back in his pocket*). Oh no; it's quite useless; there's no detonator . . . . (*Sternly.*) Now, then, let's talk business.

JAMES. What do you want me to do?

PHILIP. Strictly speaking, you should be holding your hands over your head and saying "Kamerad!"[1] However, I'll let you off that. All I ask from you is that you should be reasonable.

JAMES. And if I refuse, you'll shoot me?

PHILIP. Well, I don't quite know, Uncle James. I expect we should go through this little scene again to-mor-

---

[1]*Kamerad,* German for comrade.

row. You haven't enjoyed it, have you? Well, there's lots more of it to come. We'll rehearse it every day. One day, if you go on being unreasonable, the thing will go off. Of course, you think that I shouldn't have the pluck to fire. But you can't be quite certain. It's a hundred to one that I shan't—only I might. Fear— it's a horrible thing. Elderly men die of it sometimes.

JAMES. Pooh! I'm not to be bluffed like that.

PHILIP (*suddenly*). You're quite right; you're not that sort. I made a mistake. (*Aiming carefully.*) I shall have to do it straight off, after all. One—two——

JAMES (*on his knees, with uplifted hands, in an agony of terror*). Philip! Mercy! What are your terms?

PHILIP (*picking him up by the scruff, and helping him into the chair*). Good man, that's the way to talk. I'll get them for you. Make yourself comfortable in front of the fire till I come back. Here's the paper. (*He gives his uncle the paper, and goes out into the hall.*)

. . . .

(JAMES *opens his eyes with a start and looks round him in a bewildered way. He rubs his head, takes out his watch and looks at it, and then stares round the room again. The door from the dining-room opens, and* PHILIP *comes in with a piece of toast in his hand.*)

PHILIP (*his mouth full*). You wanted to see me, Uncle James?

JAMES (*still bewildered*). That's all right, my boy, that's all right. What have you been doing?

PHILIP (*surprised*). Breakfast. (*Putting the last piece in his mouth.*) Rather late, I'm afraid.

JAMES. That's all right. (*He laughs awkwardly.*)

PHILIP. Anything the matter? You don't look your usual bright self.

JAMES. I — er — seem to have dropped asleep in front of the fire. Most unusual thing for me to have done. Most unusual.

PHILIP. Let that be a lesson to you not to get up so early. Of course, if you're in the Army you can't help yourself. Thank heaven I'm out of it, and my own master again.

JAMES. Ah, that's what I wanted to talk to you about. Sit down, Philip. (*He indicates the chair by the fire.*)

PHILIP (*taking a chair by the table*). You have that, uncle; I shall be all right here.

JAMES (*hastily*). No, no; you come here. (*He gives* PHILIP *the armchair and sits by the table himself.*) I should be dropping off again. (*He laughs awkwardly.*)

PHILIP. Right-o. (*He puts his hand to his pocket.* UNCLE JAMES *shivers and looks at him in horror.* PHILIP *brings out his pipe, and a sickly grin of relief comes into* JAMES's *face.*)

JAMES. I suppose you smoked a lot in France?

PHILIP. Rather! Nothing else to do. It's allowed in here?

JAMES (*hastily*). Yes, yes, of course. (PHILIP *lights his pipe.*) Well now, Philip, what are you going to do, now you've left the Army?

PHILIP (*promptly*). Burn my uniform and sell my revolver.

JAMES (*starting at the word "revolver"*). Sell your revolver, eh?

PHILIP (*surprised*). Well, I don't want it now, do I?

JAMES. No .... Oh no .... Oh, most certainly not, I should say. Oh, I can't see why you should want it at all. (*With an uneasy laugh.*) You're in England now. No need for revolvers here—eh?

PHILIP (*staring at him*). Well, no, I hope not.

JAMES (*hastily*). Quite so. Well now, Philip, what next? We must find a profession for you.

PHILIP (*yawning*). I suppose so. I haven't really thought about it much.

JAMES. You never wanted to be an architect?

PHILIP (*surprised*). Architect?

(JAMES *rubs his head and wonders what made him think of architect.*)

JAMES. Or anything like that.

PHILIP. It's a bit late, isn't it?

JAMES. Well, if you're four years behind, so is everybody else. (*He feels vaguely that he has heard this argument before.*)

PHILIP (*smiling*). To tell the truth, I don't feel I mind much anyway. Anything you like—except a commissionaire. I absolutely refuse to wear a uniform again.

JAMES. How would you like to come into the business?

PHILIP. The jam business? Well, I don't know. You wouldn't want me to salute you in the morning?

JAMES. My dear boy, no!

PHILIP. All right, I'll try it if you like. I don't know if I shall be any good—what do you do?

JAMES. It's your experience in managing and—er—handling men which I hope will be of value.

PHILIP. Oh, I can do that all right. (*Stretching himself luxuriously.*) Uncle James, do you realize that I'm never going to salute again, or wear a uniform, or get wet —really wet, I mean—or examine men's feet, or stand to attention when I'm spoken to, or—oh, lots more

things? And best of all, I'm never going to be frightened again. Have you ever known what it is to be afraid—really afraid?

JAMES (*embarrassed*). I—er— well——— (*He coughs.*)

PHILIP. No, you couldn't—not really afraid of death, I mean. Well, that's over now. I could spend the rest of my life in the British Museum and be happy. . . .

JAMES (*getting up*). All right, we'll try you in the office. I expect you want a holiday first, though.

PHILIP (*getting up*). My dear uncle, this is holiday. Being in London is holiday. Buying an evening paper—wearing a waistcoat again— running after a bus—anything—it's all holiday.

JAMES. All right, then, come along with me now, and I'll introduce you to Mr. Bamford.

PHILIP. Right. Who's he?

JAMES. Our manager. A little stiff, but a very good fellow. He'll be delighted to hear that you are coming into the firm.

PHILIP (*smiling*). Perhaps I'd better bring my revolver, in case he isn't.

JAMES (*laughing with forced heartiness as they go together to the door*). Ha, ha! A good joke that! Ha, ha, ha! A good joke—but only a joke, of course. Ha, ha! He, he, he!

(PHILIP *goes out.* JAMES, *following him, turns at the door, and looks round the room in a bewildered way. Was it a dream, or wasn't it? He will never be quite certain.*)

[CURTAIN.]

For Thought and Discussion

1. Was Emily a realist or an idealist? Explain your answer.
2. Why was Philip able to get along with Mrs. Higgins?

3. What inconveniences did James suffer on account of the war?
4. Why did James and Philip fail to get on amicably?
5. What caused James to have his dream?
6. Why is the play true to life?
7. What is Philip's attitude toward war?
8. Why was the war profitable to James?
9. How does Milne suggest that the younger generation deals with facts in a straightforward way?
10. What effect does war usually have upon choice of careers?

Plus Work

Select a stage director to read the play with a committee and cast the characters for presenting the play as a radio skit. Use one end of the room as a studio. Select an announcer to present the program. The players should read the lines slowly and with dramatic expression.

✧

LETTER TO A YOUNG MAN
BEVERLEY NICHOLS

DEAR JOHN:
You have written to me telling me that your father is returning home next week, after a year in the Colonies, and that he is "utterly furious" with you because he has heard that at Oxford you voted for the famous Union resolution .... "That this house will in no circumstances fight for King and Country."

You quote him as saying, "If that is the sort of thing they teach you at Oxford, you had better leave, cut your schools, and go straight out to British East Africa, to get some sense knocked into your head." You are naturally worried by this ultimatum.[1] You are very fond of your father. At the same time, you were really serious when you recorded that vote. It was not merely a frivolous gesture. "I feel this whole thing too deeply to be stampeded into denying it," you write to me.

How would I have voted on this pacifist motion? I don't know. I have at last come to the conclusion that in certain circumstances I would fight in an international army, in an international cause, under some commander appointed by the League of Nations. This sounds extremely funny, and if your friends in the Tory[2] Club get to hear of it, they will be able to write delicious parodies about it. Lovely squibs and verses about me, forming fours in Geneva, and being told to "dress by the left," in bad French. Oh, yes. . . . I am handing them a rich gift of satire.

However, we are not worrying any longer about my case, but yours. You want to be able to defend that vote when your father returns. And you should have the courage to tell him, that though the motion was offensive to public taste, the meaning behind it was desperately sincere. For the

---

[1] ultimatum, final demand, last offer of conditions.

[2] Tory, a conservative, opposed to change.

young men know, only too well, how that phrase "King and Country" is abused by the politicians. Your "King and Country" may be in danger, certainly, but they may be in danger simply because of the folly of your country's ministers, or the aggressiveness of your country's policy. If you are going to abrogate your right to criticize those ministers and that policy, and also to deny the right of other nations to criticize it, you land yourself in the lunatic and criminal position of the man who says "my country, right or wrong." Which is as though a man were to say, "my sister, mad or sane, my brother, murderer or innocent." Just because a girl is your sister you do not claim the right to allow her to walk the streets as a homicidal lunatic. Just because a man is your brother you do not claim the right to assault those policemen who arrest him for murder. You do not do these things because you realize you are a social being, subject to certain laws which men have made for their own protection. You do not do these things because you believe in law as opposed to anarchy.

However, I realize only too well that when your father comes home, when his trunks have been carried upstairs, and the souvenirs produced, when you are eventually summoned to his study for this dreadful cross-examination, he will be little inclined to reason. He will drag out all the old questions, and you must be prepared to answer them. And I will wager ten to one that almost the first question he asks you will be:

"What would you do if you found a great hulking German attacking your sister? Wouldn't you fight then?"

This is the militarist's standard question. Having asked it, your father will lean back in his chair and survey you almost amiably, because, you see, he thinks there is no answer to the question. He thinks he's got you now, poor misguided lad that you are! And it would be ungentlemanly of him to exult too obviously in his intellectual triumph.

He is pitifully wrong, of course. There is not only an answer to this question . . . there are a great many answers, and you can vary them according to the temperament of the questioner. The quickest and most effective reply is, "I should behave exactly in the same way as if I found a great hulking Britisher attacking my sister—*i.e.*, I should give him a sock in the jaw."

As soon as you introduce this parallel, your father's argument becomes ridiculous. By giving the imaginary assailant of your sister a sock in the jaw you are merely temporarily taking the part of the police. . . .

However, the true argument, of course, goes deeper than that. It goes as deep as Christianity itself. The true argument is that if you wish to avoid the possibility of large numbers of women, of every nationality, being outraged, you must avoid war, at almost any cost. You will not drive out passion by passion. Soldiers are much alike, whatever uniform they may wear. But when they are in enemy territory, when they are doped with lies which make them believe that every German is a devil and that every German nurse tortures the wounded (or *vice versa*,[3] because the German stories about English nurses were exactly the same as ours), then you induce a state of mind which makes these soldiers feel that no treatment to which they could submit such she-devils could be too vile.

---

[3]*vice versa,* conversely, interchangeably.

You might also tell your father that this question about your sister is not only unintelligent, but cowardly. It is hitting below the belt. It is trying to trap you on a false analogy. It is confusing a vitally personal issue, which offers only one judgment and one method of treatment, with an entirely impersonal issue, which is open to many judgments and many methods of treatment. For what conceivable connection can be drawn between the blow which you deliver, in hot blood, against a man who is doing your family a great wrong, and the shot you fire, in cold blood, into the dark, in the hope that it may split the skull of some man you have never seen, some puzzled chap who, if the diplomatic wheel had spun another turn, might be your friend?

As the argument with your father quickens, he will probably ask you— "But don't you think that any cause can be just? Is there nothing you would fight for?"

Listen. You will begin, of course, by pointing out to your father that the "justice" or "injustice" of the cause has nothing whatever to do with the case. War does not settle who was right or wrong. It settles who was strongest. This is so childishly evident that I apologize for suggesting that your father needs to be told it.

What I am getting at is this. Sooner or later, in your argument, your father is bound to pin you down to the policy you tell me most of you really voted for, in that Oxford resolution, the policy of passive resistance. You are one of a large number of intelligent and representative young Englishmen who have deliberately chosen this as their programme in the event of war. Mind you, I don't go with you all the way—I don't believe the theory is workable. You do. And since you do, I implore you to

make the best of your case. Most of you seem to do your utmost to make the worst of it. You are flummoxed by your cross-examiners, who draw pictures of a nation in chains, a countryside laid waste, etc., etc. You know, as well as I do, that these pictures are silly little bogy pictures, which are not worthy of the serious consideration of an intelligent scullery-maid, but you do not seem able to convince your persecutors of this fact.

Your case for passive resistance can be proved in one way and one only, by imagining it put into practice in some specific instance, and by pinning your opponent down to the definite losses and injuries which, in his opinion, we should suffer, and by making him prove that these losses and injuries are likely to be greater than the losses and injuries we suffered in the last war. He must therefore prove that passive resistance would cost this country more than £9,590,000,000 and nearly 700,000 men killed, and more, morally, than is witnessed by the sense of utter futility and rottenness which broods over all our younger generation. These are the things that he must prove. And in order to prove them he must stick to facts. Here are the facts:

In the old days a conquered nation paid for its helplessness by four forms of tribute—by money, by services, by land, and by the surrender of various forms of booty which are best described as miscellaneous.

Let us see if and how these forms of tribute could be enacted from England, on the assumption that England was completely non-resistant . . . that we simply throw up our hands and say, "All right, come on, take what you want."

Firstly, *money*. We are constantly

being assured by all the big capitalists, especially the press lords, that the British people have reached the limit of taxation, and that further imposts will bring the whole of our financial edifice tumbling to the ground. We are also assured that the foundation of that edifice is the subtle cement called credit, which is more important in determining the value of the pound sterling than all the gold in the Bank of England. The pound sterling, too, as we are so often reminded, is an international currency. One-third of the world is on sterling. So that any severe shock to sterling reacts to the detriment of the whole economic structure of the world.

In the light of these facts, you might therefore ask your father what, exactly, a conquering nation will do, in this question of taking our money. Seize the gold in the Bank, for example? There is no statesman in the silliest part of the silliest country in Europe who would any longer advocate such a folly after the experience of the last few years. Nations now know, only too well, that a surplus of gold is only an encumbrance. We have just seen the ludicrous paradox whereby the richest citizen in the richest country in the world was unable to draw a single cent from his bank, gorged as it was with gold. (I refer, of course to the banking crisis which broke on the day of President Roosevelt's inauguration.) So we are not likely to see any nation taking away our gold, even if we open the vaults for them.

How else, then, are they to take our money? In stocks and shares? But these are only of value as long as our credit is good. Take away our credit and they are so much paper.

By doubling our taxes, then? But the economists and the press lords tell us that we can't be taxed any more.

It would send sterling down to zero. The international reactions would be appalling. Every country's currency would stagger. Who is going to risk that? The sturdy Germans? the canny French? The disciplined Italians? The hard-hit Americans? The ultra-Tory Japanese? The tortured Central Europeans? Well? Who wants sterling to go down?

Now we come to the second form of tribute—*services*. "We should be turned into a nation of slaves," we are informed. Very well. How? Where? When? In what way are we going to set to work for our conquerors? Remember, they have millions of unemployed of their own. It is hardly likely that out of mere spite they will employ Britons to engage in vast industrial or agricultural schemes when their own countrymen are chafing at their own idleness.

We therefore come to the third form of tribute which might be exacted—*land*. You must obviously face the problem of the annexation of the colonies. You must be prepared to say "All right—let 'em take the colonies." And having said that, I expect your father will lose his patience, and show you the door.

However, if, in the process of saying good-bye, you have an opportunity of asking him a few further questions, you might require him to be a little more particular as to who is to take what. It might be rather a large problem, for example, to "take" Canada. The only nation who would be wishful to take it would be America and one may reasonably ask what advantages America would gain thereby which she does not enjoy already. America and Canada form a geographical and economic unit. Along the vast frontier no single fort has been built, no single gun ever fires.

Lastly. *booty*. We are back again

in our frivolous mood, and the nature of this section is not going to help us escape it. For if your father draws for you a lurid picture of a band of alien savages marching into the National Gallery, all you have to do is to ask him when he last went to the National Gallery. Quite a long time ago, wasn't it? And what did he see there? Which masterpiece most impressed him? Oh, yes—you know all about Sargent's picture of Lord Ribblesdale, but that was in all the illustrated annuals last Christmas. Apart from Sargent's picture of Lord Ribblesdale, what is the name of the masterpiece that he, personally, would most miss?

And now, I'm almost through and the little jokes with which I have tried to enliven this utterly bitter subject no longer come to my pen. Because I am thinking of your brother, and how he was killed in that filthy way, on his first day, only 48 hours before the Armistice. Your father will be thinking of him too, during all this long and agonizing conversation—and so will you, I expect, though you were only a kid when he died. And your father may be comparing you two, in his mind, wondering how one son could be so fine and the other so contemptible. Yes—you might as well realize that's what he'll be thinking.

What must you do? You must walk up to him, and you must speak very quietly and calmly. You must say to him:

"Ted died for me. You told him,

and everybody else told him, that he was fighting in a war to end war. To end war. That was really what he died for. He didn't die for the mess we're in now. He didn't die in order that we should all be at each others' throats again, before the willow tree you planted on his grave had time to grow tall enough to throw its shadow.

"Please, father, don't hate me for reminding you of that. Ted wouldn't have hated me for it. Ted wasn't the hating sort. He just did what he thought was his duty. I believe I'm doing mine now, in the same way. It isn't as hard for me as it was for him, God knows. But it isn't easy, either. I do beg of you to believe me when I say that.

"Ted would have believed me. He might even have agreed with me. For do you think that he could rest happily if he were able to see me putting on the same old uniform, listening to the same old lies, marching to the same old tunes . . . to remind him that he died in vain? For if I have to go through it all again, did he not die in vain? Please, father, you must answer that. And if you answer it wrongly, I'm done. Just done."

And now my friend, I am done too. I don't know if this letter has been any help to you. I only know that the writing of it has been a help to me, in making me realize my deathless kinship with my brother man, and my love for him, beside which no hate can flourish.

BEVERLEY NICHOLS.

For Thought and Discussion

1. What is the traditional attitude toward war held by the father of the boy?
2. What are the arguments for war advanced by the father?
3. What false analogy does he use?

4. How does the writer point out the ineffectuality of war in solving problems?

5. Why are misrepresentations made about the enemy?

6. After balances are made between losses and gains in war, what is the final result?

7. How does the mere mention of the cause for which Ted died prove false those assumptions commonly regarded as legitimate causes for wars?

8. In the last sentence of this letter what does the writer name as the great principles which should govern men and nations? Why are these principles inimical to war?

9. The young men of the country go to war to protect the future of their country. If the young men are destroyed or maimed, why can it be said that both the present and the future of the country have been destroyed?

10. Does the fact that the United States and Canada have never built forts on their boundary seem to indicate that peace between two countries is a practical ideal?

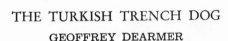

THE TURKISH TRENCH DOG

GEOFFREY DEARMER

[Geoffrey Dearmer now lives in London. *The Day's Delight* is the title of a charming volume of his poems.]

NIGHT held me as I crawled and scrambled near
The Turkish lines. Above, the mocking stars
Silvered the curving parapet, and clear
Cloud-latticed beams o'erflecked the land with bars;
I, crouching, lay between   5
Tense-listening armies peering through the night,
Twin giants bound by tentacles unseen.
Here in dim-shadowed light
I saw him, as a sudden movement turned
His eyes towards me, glowing eyes that burned   10
A moment ere his snuffling muzzle found
My trail; and then as serpents mesmerize
He chained me with those unrelenting eyes,
That muscle-sliding rhythm, knit and bound
In spare-limbed symmetry, those perfect jaws   15
And soft-approaching · pitter-patter paws.
Nearer and nearer like a wolf he crept—
That moment had my swift revolver leapt—
But terror seized me, terror born of shame
Brought flooding revelation. For he came   20
As one who offers comradeship deserved,
An open ally of the human race,
And sniffing at my prostrate form unnerved
He licked my face!

For Thought and Discussion

1. Where was the soldier? Why did he fear the dog?
2. Explain the meaning of this poem.

A plaque of Rupert Brooke

THE SOLDIER

RUPERT BROOKE

[Rupert Brooke, 1887-1915, was educated in England and won honors as a verse writer at both Rugby and Cambridge. He traveled and wrote vivid prose impressions of his travels. During the World War he was sent on the Dardanelles Expedition. He died of blood-poisoning on a French hospital ship off the coast of the Island of Skyros near Greece and was buried there. Knowing that he disliked the thought of growing old, possibly his friends should rejoice in the assurance that the world, in thinking of the spot where Brooke lies buried as "forever England," thinks also of the gallant soldier-poet as forever young.

Brooke, like Byron, was brilliant, handsome, exuberant, and defiantly adventurous; like Shelley he had a clear ethereal vision. In his youth, fearful of being termed the beautiful poet of beautiful themes, he evinced a rather coarse, hard realism, but with advancing · years the beauty of his lines grew deeper and more mellow; there was a transition from his humorous and somewhat cynical wit to a Wordsworthian tranquillity of recollected emotions. The beauty of his landscape scenes, particularly in *Grantchester,* and the deep patriotism expressed in his war poems remind one of Milton's pastorals and sonnets.]

IF I should die, think only this of me,
That there's some corner of a foreign field
That is forever England. There shall be

In that rich earth a richer dust concealed;
A dust whom England bore, shaped, made aware, 5
Gave, once, her flowers to love, her ways to roam,
A body of England's, breathing English air,
Washed by the rivers, blest by suns of home.
And think, this heart, all evil shed away,
A pulse in the eternal mind, no less 10
Gives somewhere back the thoughts by England given;
Her sights and sounds; dreams happy as her day;
And laughter, learnt of friends; and gentleness,
In hearts at peace, under an English heaven.

For Thought and Discussion

1. How does the soldier express his love for England?
2. What is the mood of this poem?

❧

THE DEAD

RUPERT BROOKE

[The closing lines might well be the author's epitaph.]

THESE hearts were woven of human joys and cares,
Washed marvelously with sorrow, swift to mirth;
The years had given them kindness. Dawn was theirs,
And sunset, and the colors of the earth.
These had seen movement, and heard music; known 5
Slumber and waking; loved; gone proudly friended;
Felt the quick stir of wonder; sat alone;

Touched flowers and furs and cheeks.
All this is ended.

There are waters blown by changing winds to laughter
And lit by the rich skies, all day. And after, 10
Frost, with a gesture, stays the waves that dance,
And wandering loveliness. He leaves a white
Unbroken glory, a gathered radiance,
A width, a shining peace, under the night.

For Thought and Discussion

1. How does the writer arouse your sympathy for the dead?
2. Read aloud the lines descriptive of death.

✌

THE GOING
To the Memory of Rupert Brooke
WILFRID WILSON GIBSON

[Present day critics accord to Wilfrid Wilson Gibson, the poet of the tenement and of the trench, a place of growing importance because of the value of his poetry as a social study. *Daily Bread*, published in 1912, reveals with power, fidelity, beauty, and pathos, the home life and labors of working people—miners, fisher folk, factory workers, housewives, and street waifs. Gibson's war poems are so lacking in patriotic patter and martial thrills and are so full of grim humor and sardonic horror that they have a tonic effect.]

HE'S gone.
   I do not understand.
I only know
That as he turned to go
And waved his hand   5
In his young eyes a sudden glory shone;
And I was dazzled by a sunset glow,
And he was gone.
        23d April, 1915

For Thought and Discussion

1. From this poem what type of character do you think Rupert Brooke was?
2. Of what lines in "The Dead" are you reminded?

✌

BATTLE: HIT
WILFRID WILSON GIBSON

OUT of the sparkling sea
   I drew my tingling body clear, and lay
On a low ledge the livelong summer day,
Basking, and watching lazily
White sails in Falmouth Bay.   5

My body seemed to burn
Salt in the sun that drenched it through and through,
Till every particle glowed clean and new
And slowly seemed to turn
To lucent amber in a world of blue   10

. . . .

I felt a sudden wrench—
A trickle of warm blood—
And found that I was sprawling in the mud
Among the dead men in the trench.

For Thought and Discussion

1. How does the writer express the soldier's enjoyment of life?
2. What happens?

BETWEEN THE LINES
WILFRID WILSON GIBSON

WHEN consciousness came back,
    he found he lay
Between the opposing fires, but could
    not tell
On which hand were his friends; and
    either way
For him to turn was chancy—bullet
    and shell
Whistling and shrieking over him, as
    the glare   5
Of searchlights scoured the darkness
    to blind day.
He scrambled to his hands and knees
    ascare,
Dragging his wounded foot through
    puddled clay,
And tumbled in a hole a shell had
    scooped
At random in a turnip-field be-
    tween   10
The unseen trenches where the foes
    lay cooped
Through that unending battle of un-
    seen,
Dead-locked, league-stretching ar-
    mies; and quite spent
He rolled upon his back within the
    pit,
And lay secure, thinking of all it
    meant—   15
His lying in that little hole, sore hit,
But living, while across the starry sky
Shrapnel and shell went screeching
    overhead—
Of all it meant that he, Tom Dodd,
    should lie
Among the Belgian turnips, while his
    bed . . .   20
If it were he, indeed, who'd climbed
    each night,
Fagged with the day's work, up the
    narrow stair,
And slipt his clothes off in the candle-
    light,

Too tired to fold them neatly on a
    chair
The way his mother'd taught him—
    too dog-tired   25
After the long day's serving in the
    shop,
Inquiring what each customer re-
    quired,
Politely talking weather, fit to
    drop . . .

And now for fourteen days and
    nights, at least,
He had n't had his clothes off, and
    had lain   30
In muddy trenches, napping like a
    beast
With one eye open, under sun and
    rain
And that unceasing hell-fire . . .
               It was strange
How things turned out—the chances!
    You'd just got   35
To take your luck in life, you
    couldn't change
Your luck.
        And so here he was lying shot
Who just six months ago had thought
    to spend
His days behind a counter. Still, per-
    haps . . .
And now, God only knew how he
    would end!

He'd like to know how many of the
    chaps   40
Had won back to the trench alive,
    when he
Had fallen wounded and been left for
    dead,
If any! . . .
        This was different, certainly,
From selling knots of tape and reels
    of thread
And knots of tape and reels of thread
    and knots   45

Of tape and reels of thread and knots
    of tape,
Day in, day out, and answering
    "Have you got" 's,
And "Do you keep" 's, till there
    seemed no escape
From everlasting serving in a shop,
Inquiring what each customer re-
    quired,   50
Politely talking weather, fit to drop,
With swollen ankles, tired . . .
                        But he was tired
Now.   Every bone was aching, and
    had ached
For fourteen days and nights in that
    wet trench—
Just duller when he slept than when
    he waked—   55
Crouching for shelter from the steady
    drench
Of shell and shrapnel . . .
                That old trench, it seemed
Almost like home to him.   He'd slept
    and fed
And sung and smoked in it, while
    shrapnel screamed
And shells went whining harmless
    overhead—   60
Harmless, at least, as far as he . . .
                        But Dick—
Dick had n't found them harmless
    yesterday,
At breakfast, when he'd said he
    could n't stick
Eating dry bread, and crawled out the
    back way,
And brought them butter in a lordly
    dish—   65
Butter enough for all, and held it
    high,
Yellow and fresh and clean as you
    could wish—
When plump upon the plate from out
    the sky
A shell fell bursting . . . Where the
    butter went,
God only knew! . . .
                And Dick . . .
                He dared not think   70

Of what had come to Dick . . . or
    what it meant—
The shrieking and the whistling and
    the stink
He'd lived in fourteen days and
    nights.   'T was luck
That he still lived . . . And queer how
    little then
He seemed to care that Dick . . . Per-
    haps 't was pluck   75
That hardened him—a man among
    the men—
Perhaps . . . Yet, only think things
    out a bit,
And he was rabbit-livered, blue with
    funk!
And he'd liked Dick . . . and yet when
    Dick was hit,
He had n't turned a hair. The meanest
    skunk   80
He should have thought would feel it
    when his mate
Was blown to smithereens—Dick,
    proud as punch,
Grinning like sin, and holding up the
    plate —
But he had gone on munching his dry
    hunch,
Unwinking, till he swallowed the last
    crumb.   85
Perhaps 'twas just because he dared
    not let
His mind run upon Dick, who'd been
    his chum.
He dared not now, though he could
    not forget.

Dick took his luck.   And, life or
    death, 't was luck
From first to last; and you'd just got
    to trust   90
Your luck and grin.   It was n't so
    much pluck
As knowing that you'd got to, when
    needs must,
And better to die grinning . . .
                        Quiet now
Had fallen on the night.   On either
    hand

The guns were quiet. Cool upon his brow 95
The quiet darkness brooded, as he scanned
The starry sky. He'd never seen before
So many stars. Although, of course, he'd known
That there were stars, somehow before the war
He'd never realised them—so thick-sown, 100
Millions and millions. Serving in the shop,
Stars did n't count for much; and then at nights
Strolling the pavements, dull and fit to drop,
You did n't see much but the city lights.
He'd never in his life seen so much sky 105
As he'd seen this last fortnight. It was queer
The things war taught you. He'd a mind to try
To count the stars—they shone so bright and clear.

One, two, three, four... Ah, God, but he was tired . . .
Five, six, seven, eight...
    Yes, it was number eight.
And what was the next thing that she required? 111
(Too bad of customers to come so late,
At closing time!) Again within the shop
He handled knots of tape and reels of thread,
Politely talking weather, fit to drop... 115
Whence once again the whole sky overhead
Flared blind with searchlights, and the shriek of shell
And scream of shrapnel roused him. Drowsily

He stared about him wondering. Then he fell
Into deep dreamless slumber. 120

. . . .

    He could see
Two dark eyes peeping at him, ere he knew
He was awake, and it again was day—
An August morning, burning to clear blue.
The frightened rabbit scuttled...
    Far away,
A sound of firing... Up there, in the sky 125
Big dragon-flies hung hovering... Snowballs burst
About them . . . Flies and snowballs! With a cry
He crouched to watch the airmen pass —the first
That he'd seen under fire. Lord, that was pluck—
Shells bursting all about them—and what nerve! 130
They took their chance, and trusted to their luck.
At such a dizzy height to dip and swerve,
Dodging the shell-fire...
    Hell! but one was hit,
And tumbling like a pigeon, plump...
    Thank Heaven,
It righted, and then turned; and after it 135
The whole flock followed safe—four, five, six, seven,
Yes, they were all there safe. He hoped they'd win
Back to their lines in safety. They deserved,
Even if they were Germans...'Twas no sin
To wish them luck. Think how that beggar swerved 140
Just in the nick of time!
    He, too, must try
To win back to the lines, though, likely as not,

He'd take the wrong turn: but he
couldn't lie
Forever in that hungry hole and rot,
He'd got to take his luck, to take his
chance   145
Of being sniped by foes or friends.
With any luck in Germany or France
He'd be

Or Kingdom-come, next morning . . .
                                          Drearily
The blazing day burnt over him. Shot
and shell
Whistling and whining ceaselessly.
But light   150
Faded at last, and as the darkness fell
He rose, and crawled away into the
night.

For Thought and Discussion

1. Of what did the wounded soldier think as he lay in a shell hole between the lines?
2. Do you think this incident described might have happened scores of times during the war?
3. Why did Dick crawl out the back way after butter?
4. Why did the soldier hope that the airmen would escape even though they were enemies? Were they enemies?
5. Why did the soldier never think of why he was fighting?
6. To what things did he seem to attach most value?
7. How does the poet make the incident real?
8. What do you think is the purpose of this selection?
9. Contrast the value of taking men out of their positions and putting them into the trenches to fight with that of using unemployed men to construct safer highways for travel, drain swamps and destroy breeding places for mosquitoes, construct protections against overflow waters and other such projects.

Plus Work

Ruskin's essays, *Sesame and Lilies*, *Unto This Last*, *The Crown of Wild Olives*, "Work," "Traffic," and "War" contain some challenging ideas on war, on industrialism, and on civic improvements. Note that though Ruskin's language is often as beautifully descriptive and rhythmical as poetry, his attitude toward the above problems is realistic rather than romantic.

❧

DOES IT MATTER?

SIEGFRIED SASSOON

[Siegfried Sassoon's experiences on the front were so vivid and so terrible that he became the outstanding poet depicting the suffering and anguish of war. Long before the armistice was signed, feeling the necessity for stopping the destruction of men, he spoke and wrote such bitter invectives against war that he was saved from imprisonment only by a brilliant war record. He had written several volumes of verse before he became embittered and convinced that the world must be made to realize the brutality of war. Before the World War he was graduated from Cambridge. In his university days he devoted himself largely to poetry, not, however, to the exclusion of outdoor sports. He continues to write and has received two prizes for excellent literary work. *Memoirs of a Fox-Hunting Man* and *Memoirs of an Infantry Officer* are his prose works.]

DOES it matter? — losing your leg?...
For people will always be kind,
And you must not show that you mind
When the others come in after hunting
To gobble their muffins and eggs.   5

Does it matter?—losing your sight?...
There's such splendid work for the blind;
And people will always be kind,
As you sit on the terrace remembering
And turning your face to the light. 10

Do they matter?—those dreams from the pit?...
You can drink and forget and be glad,
And people won't say that you're mad;
For they'll know that you fought for your country,
And no one will worry a bit.

For Thought and Discussion

1. Sassoon served in the English army in the World War. How does he make the lot of the disabled soldier vivid?
2. Would a brilliant war record repay the soldier who lost a leg, his eyesight, or all of his chance for the career he desired?

~&~

COUNTER-ATTACK

SIEGFRIED SASSOON

WE'D gained our first objective hours before
While dawn broke like a face with blinking eyes,
Pallid, unshaved and thirsty, blind with smoke.
Things seemed all right at first. We held their line,
With bombers posted, Lewis guns well placed,   5
And clink of shovels deepening the shallow trench.
The place was rotten with dead; green clumsy legs
High-booted, sprawled and grovelled along the saps;
And trunks, face downwards, in the sucking mud,

Wallowed like trodden sand-bags loosely filled;   10
And naked sodden buttocks, mats of hair,
Bulged, clotted heads slept in the plastering slime.

And then the rain began,—the jolly old rain!
A yawning soldier knelt against the bank,
Staring across the morning blear with fog;   15
He wondered when the Allemands would get busy;
And then, of course, they started with five-nines

Traversing, sure as fate, and never a
    dud.
Mute in the clamour of shells he
    watched them burst,
Spouting dark earth and wire with
    gusts from hell,   20
While posturing giants dissolved in
    drifts of smoke.
He crouched and flinched, dizzy with
    a galloping fear,
Sick for escape,—loathing the stran-
    gled horror
And butchered, frantic gestures of
    the dead.

An officer came blundering down the
    trench: 25
"Stand-to and man the fire-step!"
    On he went....
Gasping and bawling, "Fire-step ....
    Counter-attack!"
Then the haze lifted. Bombing on the
    right

Down the old sap; machine-guns on
    the left;
And stumbling figures looking out in
    front.   30
"O Christ, they're coming at us!"
    Bullets spat,
And he remembered his rifle ... rapid
    fire....
And started blazing wildly.... Then
    a bang
Crumpled and spun him sideways,
    knocked him out
To grunt and wriggle: none heeded
    him; he choked   35
And fought the flapping veils of
    smothering gloom,
Lost in a blurred confusion of yells
    and groans....
Down, and down, and down, he sank
    and drowned,
Bleeding to death. The counter-at-
    tack had failed.

For Thought and Discussion

1. After the war what impressions were most vivid in the mind
   of Sassoon?
2. Why is his poetry harsh and bitter?
3. In an age in which much scientific research is being made on
   learning to control and counteract disease, why is it rather
   paradoxical to countenance war, which places no value on human life?

❦

AFTERMATH

SIEGFRIED SASSOON

Have you forgotten yet? ...
For the world's events have rumbled
    on since those gagged days,
Like traffic checked awhile at the
    crossing of city ways:
And the haunted gap in your mind
    has filled with thoughts that flow
Like clouds in the lit heavens of life;
    and you're a man reprieved to
    go,   5

Taking your peaceful share of Time,
    with joy to spare.
*But the past is just the same—and
    War's a bloody game....*
Have you forgotten yet?...
*Look down, and swear by the slain of
    the War that you'll never forget.*

Do you remember the dark months
    you held the sector at Ma-
    metz—   10

The nights you watched and wired
and dug and piled sandbags on
parapets?

Do you remember the rats; and the
stench

Of corpses rotting in front of the
front-line trench—

And dawn coming, dirty-white, and
chill with a hopeless rain?

Do you ever stop and ask, "Is it all
going to happen again?"

For Thought and Discussion

1. How does the first line of the poem prepare the reader for the
last line? What is the poet's purpose?

VALLEY OF THE SHADOW

JOHN GALSWORTHY

GOD, I am traveling out to death's
sea,
I, who exulted in sunshine and
laughter,
Thought not of dying—death is such
a waste of me!
Grant me one prayer: Doom not
the hereafter

Of mankind to war, as though I had
died not—   5
I, who in battle, my comrade's arm
linking,

Shouted and sang—life in my pulses
hot,
Throbbing and dancing! Let not
my sinking

In dark be for naught, my death a
vain thing!
God, let me know it the end of
man's fever!   10
Make my last breath a bugle call,
carrying
Peace o'er the valleys and cold hills
forever!

For Thought and Discussion

1. What was the dying soldier's message to the world? Memorize the last two lines.

~~

Additional Readings

Aldington, Richard: *Roads to Glory*

Allen, Hervey: *Toward the Flame*

Brittain, Vera: *Testament of Youth*

Cunliffe, J. W.: *Poems of the Great War*

Dickens, Charles: *A Tale of Two Cities*

Gibbs, A. Hamilton: *Soundings*

Gibbs, Sir Philip: *The Cross of Peace Now It Can Be Told*

Gibson, Wilfrid Wilson: *Battle*

Morgan, Charles: *The Fountain*

Nichols, Beverley: *Cry Havoc*

Remarque, Erich Maria: *All Quiet on the Western Front*

Sassoon, Siegfried: *Collected War Poems*

Shaw, G. B.: *Arms and The Man*

Zweig, Arnold: *The Case of Sergeant Grischa*

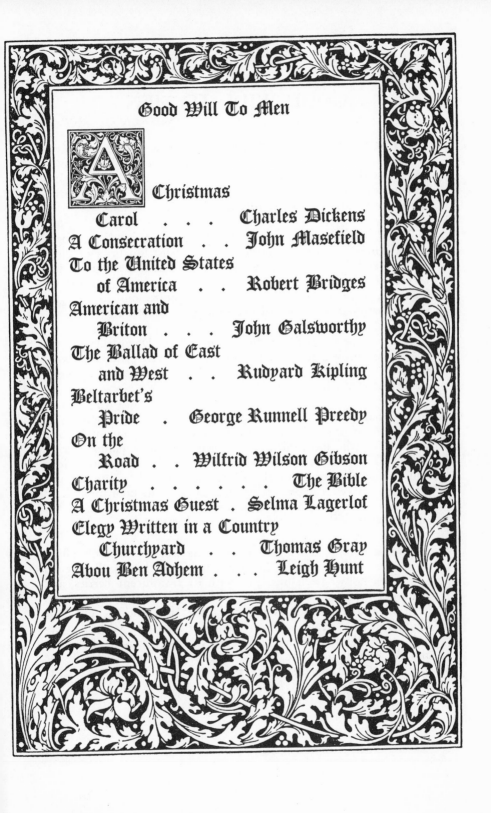

Good Will To Men

GOOD WILL TO MEN

*P*EACE on earth! Good will to men" was the message given to mankind long ago. It came from a heart filled to overflowing with kindness and sympathy for all the unfortunate. It is an expression of compassion for the man with "too weary a load," wherever he may be. It transcends classes and nations.

Prejudice and intolerance shrivel the heart, and generosity and kindness expand and enrich it. Unselfish qualities of character extend their influence beyond the threshold of the individual to include the underprivileged of all the world. Homes for the homeless, hospitals for the sick, and organizations to care for the unfortunate are material expressions of good will.

Good will is the cornerstone of democracy. Down through the ages it has proved its worth to mankind. Even primitive people possessed it and prospered because of it. It cherishes and preserves the fruits of civilization.

National good will is inclusive and extensive. It recognizes the obligation of the state to provide education, opportunity, and security for the individual. In an economic or a political crisis, good will among citizens preserves and stabilizes the state. Good will is necessary for national welfare and essential to international stability. It relies upon intelligence rather than upon prejudiced emotions, it employs co-operation rather than opposition, and it substitutes world peace for international wars.

Once a year good will reigns over the world. Happy, smiling people are on the streets, in the shops, and in the homes. Bright red and green holly, green mistletoe with its translucent berries, and pealing Christmas bells are symbolic of jollity and good cheer. Feasting and mirth hold sway, and "the larger heart" and "the kindlier hand" spread gladness throughout the land. Cheery greetings renew old friendships, gifts express the generosity of donors, and the beauty and good will of the season are symbolized in the glittering Christmas tree. The world echoes with "Merry Christmas to All," "A Happy New Year to All the World," and Tiny Tim's "God Bless Us, Every One."

"I AM THE GHOST OF CHRISTMAS PRESENT," SAID THE SPIRIT. "LOOK UPON ME!"

A CHRISTMAS CAROL

CHARLES DICKENS

STAVE ONE

MARLEY'S GHOST

MARLEY was dead: to begin with. There is no doubt whatever about that. The register of his burial was signed by the clergyman, the clerk, the undertaker, and the chief mourner. Scrooge signed it: and Scrooge's name was good upon 'Change, for anything he chose to put his hand to. Old Marley was as dead as a door-nail.

Mind! I don't mean to say that I know, of my own knowledge, what there is particularly dead about a door-nail. I might have been inclined, myself, to regard a coffin-nail as the deadest piece of ironmongery in the trade. But the wisdom of our ancestors is in the simile; and my unhal-lowed hands shall not disturb it, or the Country's done for. You will therefore permit me to repeat, emphatically, that Marley was as dead as a door-nail.

Scrooge knew he was dead? Of course he did. How could it be otherwise? Scrooge and he were partners for I don't know how many years. Scrooge was his sole executor, his sole administrator, his sole assign, his sole residuary legatee, his sole friend and sole mourner. And even Scrooge was not so dreadfully cut up by the sad event, but that he was an excellent man of business on the very day of the funeral, and solemnised it with an undoubted bargain.

The mention of Marley's funeral brings me back to the point I started from. There is no doubt that Marley was dead. This must be distinctly understood, or nothing wonderful can come of the story I am going to relate. If we were not perfectly convinced that Hamlet's Father died before the play began, there would be nothing more remarkable in his taking a stroll at night, in an easterly wind, upon his own ramparts, than there would be in any other middle-aged gentleman rashly turning out after dark in a breezy spot—say Saint Paul's Churchyard for instance —literally to astonish his son's weak mind.

Scrooge never painted out Old Marley's name. There it stood, years afterwards, above the warehouse door: Scrooge and Marley. The firm was known as Scrooge and Marley. Sometimes people new to the business called Scrooge Scrooge, and sometimes Marley, but he answered to both names: it was all the same to him.

Oh! But he was a tight-fisted hand at the grindstone, Scrooge! a squeezing, wrenching, grasping, scraping, clutching, covetous, old sinner! Hard and sharp as flint, from which no steel had ever struck out generous fire; secret, and self-contained, and solitary as an oyster. The cold within him froze his old features, nipped his pointed nose, shrivelled his cheek, stiffened his gait; made his eyes red, his thin lips blue; and spoke out shrewdly in his grating voice. A frosty rime was on his head, and on his eyebrows, and his wiry chin. He carried his own low temperature always about with him; he iced his office in the dog-days; and didn't thaw it one degree at Christmas.

External heat and cold had little influence on Scrooge. No warmth could warm, nor wintry weather chill him. No wind that blew was bitterer than he, no falling snow was more intent upon its purpose, no pelting rain less open to entreaty. Foul weather didn't know where to have him. The heaviest rain and snow, and hail, and sleet, could boast of the advantage over him in only one respect. They often "came down" handsomely, and Scrooge never did.

Nobody ever stopped him in the street to say, with gladsome looks, "My dear Scrooge, how are you? When will you come to see me?" No beggars implored him to bestow a trifle, no children asked him what it was o'clock, no man or woman ever once in all his life inquired the way to such and such a place, of Scrooge. Even the blind men's dogs appeared to know him; and when they saw him coming on, would tug their owners into doorways and up courts; and then would wag their tails as though they said, "No eye at all is better than an evil eye, dark master!"

But what did Scrooge care? It was the very thing he liked. To edge his way along the crowded paths of life, warning all human sympathy to keep its distance, was what the knowing ones call "nuts" to Scrooge.

Once upon a time—of all the good days in the year, on Christmas Eve— old Scrooge sat busy in his counting-house. It was cold, bleak, biting weather: foggy withal: and he could hear the people in the court outside go wheezing up and down, beating their hands upon their breasts, and stamping their feet upon the pavement-stones to warm them. The City clocks had only just gone three, but it was quite dark already: it had not been light all day: and candles were flaring in the windows of the neighbouring offices, like ruddy smears upon the palpable brown air. The fog came pouring in at every chink and keyhole, and was so dense without, that although the court was of the narrowest, the houses opposite were mere phantoms. To see the dingy cloud come drooping down, obscuring everything, one might have thought that Nature lived hard by, and was brewing on a large scale.

The door of Scrooge's countinghouse was open that he might keep his eye upon his clerk, who in a dismal little cell beyond, a sort of tank, was copying letters. Scrooge had a very small fire, but the clerk's fire was so very much smaller that it looked like one coal. But he couldn't replenish it, for Scrooge kept the coalbox in his own room; and so surely as the clerk came in with the shovel, the master predicted that it would be necessary for them to part. Wherefore the clerk put on his white comforter, and tried to warm himself at the candle; in which effort, not being a man of a strong imagination, he failed.

"A Merry Christmas, uncle! God save you!" cried a cheerful voice. It was the voice of Scrooge's nephew, who came upon him so quickly that this was the first intimation he had of his approach.

"Bah!" said Scrooge, "Humbug!"

He had so heated himself with rapid walking in the fog and frost, this nephew of Scrooge's, that he was all in a glow; his face was ruddy and handsome; his eyes sparkled, and his breath smoked again.

"Christmas a humbug, uncle!" said Scrooge's nephew. "You don't mean that, I am sure."

"I do," said Scrooge. "Merry Christmas! What right have you to be merry? What reason have you to be merry? You're poor enough."

"Come, then," returned the nephew, gayly. "What right have you to be dismal? What reason have you to be morose? You're rich enough."

Scrooge having no better answer ready on the spur of the moment, said, "Bah!" again; and followed it up with "Humbug."

"Don't be cross, uncle," said the nephew.

"What else can I be," returned the uncle, "when I live in such a world of fools as this? Merry Christmas! Out upon merry Christmas! What's Christmas time to you but a time for paying bills without money; a time for finding yourself a year older, but not an hour richer; a time for balancing your books and having every item in 'em through a round dozen of months presented dead against you? If I could work my will," said Scrooge, indignantly, "every idiot who goes about with 'Merry Christmas,' on his lips, should be boiled with his own pudding, and buried with a stake of holly through his heart. He should!"

"Uncle!" pleaded the nephew.

"Nephew!" returned the uncle, sternly, "keep Christmas in your own way, and let me keep it in mine."

"Keep it!" repeated Scrooge's nephew. "But you don't keep it."

"Let me leave it alone, then," said Scrooge. "Much good may it do you! Much good it has ever done you!"

"There are many things from which I might have derived good, by which I have not profited, I dare say," returned the nephew: "Christmas among the rest. But I am sure I have always thought of Christmas time, when it has come round—apart from the veneration due to its sacred name and origin, if anything belonging to it can be apart from that—as a good time: a kind, forgiving, charitable, pleasant time: the only time I know of, in the long calendar of the year, when men and women seem by one consent to open their shut-up hearts freely, and to think of people below them as if they really were fellow-passengers to the grave, and not another race of creatures bound on other journeys. And therefore, uncle, though it has never put a scrap of gold or silver in my pocket, I believe that it *has* done me good, and *will* do me good; and I say, God bless it!"

The clerk in the Tank involuntarily applauded: becoming immediately sensible of the impropriety, he poked the fire, and extinguished the last frail spark forever.

"Let me hear another sound from *you*," said Scrooge, "and you'll keep your Christmas by losing your situation." "You're quite a powerful speaker, Sir," he added, turning to his nephew. "I wonder you don't go into Parliament."

"Don't be angry, uncle. Come! Dine with us to-morrow."

Scrooge said that he would see him ——yes, indeed he did. He went the whole length of the expression, and said that he would see him in that extremity first.

"But why?" cried Scrooge's nephew. "Why?"

"Why did you get married?" said Scrooge.

"Because I fell in love."

"Because you fell in love!" growled Scrooge, as if that were the only one thing in the world more ridiculous than a merry Christmas. "Good afternoon!"

"Nay, uncle, but you never came to see me before that happened. Why give it as a reason for not coming now?"

"Good afternoon," said Scrooge.

"I want nothing from you; I ask nothing of you; why cannot we be friends?"

"Good afternoon," said Scrooge.

"I am sorry, with all my heart, to find you so resolute. We have never had any quarrel to which I have been

a party. But I have made the trial in homage to Christmas, and I'll keep my Christmas humour to the last. So A Merry Christmas, uncle!"

"Good afternoon!" said Scrooge.

"And A Happy New Year!"

"Good afternoon!" said Scrooge.

His nephew left the room without an angry word, notwithstanding. He stopped at the outer door to bestow the greetings of the season on the clerk, who, cold as he was, was warmer than Scrooge; for he returned them cordially.

"There's another fellow," muttered Scrooge; who overheard him: "my clerk, with fifteen shillings a-week, and a wife and family, talking about a merry Christmas. I'll retire to Bedlam."[1]

This lunatic, in letting Scrooge's nephew out, had let two other people in. They were portly gentlemen, pleasant to behold, and now stood, with their hats off, in Scrooge's office. They had books and papers in their hands, and bowed to him.

"Scrooge and Marley's, I believe," said one of the gentlemen, referring to his list. "Have I the pleasure of addressing Mr. Scrooge, or Mr. Marley?"

"Mr. Marley has been dead these seven years," Scrooge replied. "He died seven years ago, this very night."

"We have no doubt his liberality is well represented by his surviving partner," said the gentleman, presenting his credentials.

It certainly was; for they had been two kindred spirits. At the ominous word "liberality," Scrooge frowned, and shook his head, and handed the credentials back.

"At this festive season of the year, Mr. Scrooge," said the gentleman,

[1]*Bedlam,* meaning madhouse, from Bethlem or Bethlehem, an insane asylum in London.

taking up a pen, "it is more than usually desirable that we should make some slight provision for the poor and destitute, who suffer greatly at the present time. Many thousands are in want of common necessaries; hundreds of thousands are in want of common comforts, Sir."

"Are there no prisons?" asked Scrooge.

"Plenty of prisons," said the gentleman, laying down the pen again.

"And the Union workhouses[2]?" demanded Scrooge. "Are they still in operation?"

"They are. Still," returned the gentleman, "I wish I could say they were not."

"The Treadmill[3] and the Poor Law[4] are in full vigour, then?" said Scrooge.

"Both very busy, Sir."

"Oh! I was afraid, from what you said at first, that something had occurred to stop them in their useful course," said Scrooge. "I'm very glad to hear it."

"Under the impression that they scarcely furnish Christian cheer of mind or body to the multitude," returned the gentleman, "a few of us are endeavouring to raise a fund to buy the Poor some meat and drink, and means of warmth. We choose this time, because it is a time, of all others, when Want is keenly felt, and Abundance rejoices. What shall I put you down for?"

"Nothing!" Scrooge replied.

"You wish to be anonymous?"

"I wish to be left alone," said Scrooge. "Since you ask me what I wish, gentlemen, that is my answer.

I don't make merry myself at Christmas, and I can't afford to make idle people merry. I help to support the establishments I have mentioned: they cost enough: and those who are badly off must go there."

"Many can't go there; and many would rather die."

"If they would rather die," said Scrooge, "they had better do it, and decrease the surplus population. Besides—excuse me — I don't know that."

"But you might know it," observed the gentleman.

"It's not my business," Scrooge returned. "It's enough for a man to understand his own business, and not to interfere with other people's. Mine occupies me constantly. Good afternoon, gentlemen!"

Seeing clearly that it would be useless to pursue their point, the gentlemen withdrew. Scrooge resumed his labours with an improved opinion of himself, and in a more facetious temper than was usual with him.

Meanwhile the fog and darkness thickened so, that people ran about with flaring links,[5] proffering their services to go before horses in carriages, and conduct them on their way. The ancient tower of a church, whose gruff old bell was always peeping slyly down at Scrooge out of a gothic window in the wall, became invisible, and struck the hours and quarters in the clouds, with tremulous vibrations afterwards as if its teeth were chattering in its frozen head up there. The cold became intense. In the main street at the corner of the court, some labourers were repairing the gas-pipes, and had lighted a great fire in a brazier, round which a party of ragged men and boys were gath-

[2]*Union workhouses,* poor houses supported by the union of two or more parishes.

[3]*Treadmill,* used in prisons for punishment.

[4]*Poor Law,* law providing relief for the poor.

[5]*links,* torches carried by link-boys to light the way.

ered: warming their hands and winking their eyes before the blaze in rapture. The water-plug being left in solitude, its overflowings sullenly congealed, and turned to misanthropic ice. The brightness of the shops where holly sprigs and berries crackled in the lamp heat of the windows, made pale faces ruddy as they passed. Poulterers' and grocers' trades became a splendid joke: a glorious pageant, with which it was next to impossible to believe that such dull principles as bargain and sale had anything to do. The Lord Mayor, in the stronghold of the mighty Mansion House, gave orders to his fifty cooks and butlers to keep Christmas as a Lord Mayor's household should; and even the little tailor, whom he had fined five shillings on the previous Monday for being drunk and bloodthirsty in the streets, stirred up to-morrow's pudding in his garret, while his lean wife and the baby sallied out to buy the beef.

Foggier yet, and colder! Piercing, searching, biting cold. If the good Saint Dunstan[6] had but nipped the Evil Spirit's nose with a touch of such weather as that, instead of using his familiar weapons, then indeed he would have roared to lusty purpose. The owner of one scant young nose, gnawed and mumbled by the hungry cold as bones are gnawed by dogs, stooped down at Scrooge's keyhole to regale him with a Christmas carol: but at the first sound of

"God bless you, merry gentleman!
May nothing you dismay!"

Scrooge seized the ruler with such energy of action, that the singer fled in terror, leaving the keyhole to

---

[6]*Saint Dunstan,* when tempted by an Evil Spirit seized the spirit by the nose with red-hot tongs.

the fog and even more congenial frost.

At length the hour of shutting up the counting-house arrived. With an ill-will Scrooge dismounted from his stool, and tacitly admitted the fact to the expectant clerk in the Tank, who instantly snuffed his candle out, and put on his hat.

"You'll want all day to-morrow, I suppose?" said Scrooge.

"If quite convenient, Sir."

"It's not convenient," said Scrooge, "and it's not fair. If I was to stop half-a-crown for it, you'd think yourself ill-used, I'll be bound?"

The clerk smiled faintly.

"And yet," said Scrooge, "you don't think *me* ill-used, when I pay a day's wages for no work."

The clerk observed that it was only once a year.

"A poor excuse for picking a man's pocket every twenty-fifth of December!" said Scrooge, buttoning his great-coat to the chin. "But I suppose you must have the whole day. Be here all the earlier next morning!"

The clerk promised that he would; and Scrooge walked out with a growl. The office was closed in a twinkling, and the clerk, with the long ends of his white comforter dangling below his waist (for he boasted no great-coat), went down a slide on Cornhill, at the end of a lane of boys, twenty times, in honour of its being Christmas Eve, and then ran home to Camden Town as hard as he could pelt, to play at blindman's buff.

Scrooge took his melancholy dinner in his usual melancholy tavern; and having read all the newspapers, and beguiled the rest of the evening with his banker's-book, went home to bed. He lived in chambers which had once belonged to his deceased partner. They were a gloomy suite of rooms, in a lowering pile of building up a yard, where it had so little business to be, that one could scarcely help fancying it must have run there when it was a young house, playing at hide-and-seek with other houses, and have forgotten the way out again. It was old enough now, and dreary enough, for nobody lived in it but Scrooge, the other rooms being all let out as offices. The yard was so dark that even Scrooge, who knew its every stone, was fain to grope with his hands. The fog and frost so hung about the black old gateway of the house, that it seemed as if the Genius of the Weather sat in mournful meditation on the threshold.

Now, it is a fact, that there was nothing at all particular about the knocker on the door, except that it was very large. It is also a fact, that Scrooge had seen it, night and morning, during his whole residence in that place; also that Scrooge had as little of what is called fancy about him as any man in the City of London, even including—which is a bold word—the corporation, aldermen, and livery. Let it also be borne in mind that Scrooge had not bestowed one thought on Marley, since his last mention of his seven-years' dead partner that afternoon. And then let any man explain to me, if he can, how it happened that Scrooge, having his key in the lock of the door, saw in the knocker, without its undergoing any intermediate process of change: not a knocker, but Marley's face.

Marley's face. It was not in impenetrable shadow as the other objects in the yard were, but had a dismal light about it, like a bad lobster in a dark cellar. It was not angry or ferocious, but looked at Scrooge as Marley used to look: with ghostly spectacles turned up on its ghostly forehead. The hair was curiously stirred, as if by breath or hot air; and, though the eyes were wide open, they were perfectly motionless. That, and its livid colour, made it horrible; but its horror seemed to be in spite of the face and beyond its control, rather than a part of its own expression.

As Scrooge looked fixedly at this phenomenon, it was a knocker again.

To say that he was not startled, or that his blood was not conscious of a terrible sensation to which it had been a stranger from infancy, would be untrue. But he put his hand upon the key he had relinquished, turned it sturdily, walked in, and lighted his candle.

He *did* pause, with a moment's irresolution, before he shut the door; and he *did* look cautiously behind it first, as if he half-expected to be terrified with the sight of Marley's pigtail sticking out into the hall. But there was nothing on the back of the door, except the screws and nuts that held the knocker on; so he said "Pooh, pooh!" and closed it with a bang.

The sound resounded through the house like thunder. Every room above, and every cask in the wine-merchant's cellars below, appeared to have a separate peal of echoes of its own. Scrooge was not a man to be frightened by echoes. He fastened the door, and walked across the hall, and up the stairs: slowly too: trimming his candle as he went.

You may talk vaguely about driving a coach-and-six up a good old flight of stairs, or through a bad young Act of Parliament; but I mean to say you might have got a hearse up that staircase, and taken it broad-wise, with the splinter-bar towards the wall, and the door towards the balustrades: and done it easy. There was plenty of width for that, and room to spare; which is perhaps the reason why Scrooge thought he saw a locomotive hearse going on before him in the gloom. Half-a-dozen gas-lamps out of the street wouldn't have lighted the entry too well, so you may suppose that it was pretty dark with Scrooge's dip.

Up Scrooge went, not caring a button for that: darkness is cheap, and Scrooge liked it. But before he shut his heavy door, he walked through his rooms to see that all was right. He had just enough recollection of the face to desire to do that. Sitting-room, bedroom, lumber-room. All as they should be. Nobody under the table, nobody under the sofa; a small fire in the grate; spoon and basin ready; and the little saucepan of gruel (Scrooge had a cold in his head) upon the hob. Nobody under the bed; nobody in the closet; nobody in his dressing-gown, which was hanging up in a suspicious attitude against the wall. Lumber-room as usual. Old fire-guard, old shoes, two fish-baskets, washing-stand on three legs, and a poker.

Quite satisfied, he closed his door, and locked himself in; double-locked himself in, which was not his custom. Thus secured against surprise, he took off his cravat; put on his dressing-gown and slippers, and his nightcap; and sat down before the fire to take his gruel.

It was a very low fire indeed; nothing on such a bitter night. He was obliged to sit close to it, and brood over it, before he could extract the least sensation of warmth from such a handful of fuel. The fireplace was an old one, built by some Dutch merchant long ago, and paved all round with quaint Dutch tiles, designed to illustrate the Scriptures. There were Cains and Abels, Pharaoh's daughters, Queens of Sheba, Angelic messengers descending through the air on

clouds like feather-beds, Abrahams, Belshazzars, Apostles putting off to sea in butterboats, hundreds of figures, to attract his thoughts; and yet that face of Marley, seven years dead, came like the ancient Prophet's rod, and swallowed up the whole. If each smooth tile had been a blank at first, with power to shape some picture on its surface from the disjointed fragments of his thoughts, there would have been a copy of old Marley's head on every one.

"Humbug!" said Scrooge; and walked across the room.

After several turns, he sat down again. As he threw his head back in the chair, his glance happened to rest upon a bell, a disused bell, that hung in the room, and communicated for some purpose now forgotten with a chamber in the highest story of the building. It was with great astonishment, and with a strange, inexplicable dread, that as he looked, he saw this bell begin to swing. It swung so softly in the outset that it scarcely made a sound; but soon it rang out loudly, and so did every bell in the house.

This might have lasted half a minute, or a minute, but it seemed an hour. The bells ceased as they had begun, together. They were succeeded by a clanking noise, deep down below; as if some person were dragging a heavy chain over the casks in the wine-merchant's cellar. Scrooge then remembered to have heard that ghosts in haunted houses were described as dragging chains.

The cellar-door flew open with a booming sound, and then he heard the noise much louder, on the floors below; then coming up the stairs; then coming straight towards his door.

"It's humbug still!" said Scrooge. "I won't believe it."

His colour changed though, when,

without a pause, it came on through the heavy door, and passed into the room before his eyes. Upon its coming in, the dying flame leaped up, as though it cried "I know him! Marley's Ghost!" and fell again.

The same face: the very same. Marley in his pigtail, usual waistcoat, tights and boots; the tassels on the latter bristling, like his pigtail, and his coat-skirts, and the hair upon his head. The chain he drew was clasped about his middle. It was long, and wound about him like a tail; and it was made (for Scrooge observed it closely) of cash-boxes, keys, padlocks, ledgers, deeds, and heavy purses wrought in steel. His body was transparent; so that Scrooge, observing him, and looking through his waistcoat, could see the two buttons on his coat behind.

Scrooge had often heard it said that Marley had no bowels, but he had never believed it until now.

No, nor did he believe it even now. Though he looked the phantom through and through, and saw it standing before him; though he felt the chilling influence of its death-cold eyes; and marked the very texture of the folded kerchief bound about its head and chin, which wrapper he had not observed before: he was still incredulous, and fought against his senses.

"How now!" said Scrooge, caustic and cold as ever. "What do you want with me?"

"Much!" — Marley's voice, no doubt about it.

"Who are you?"

"Ask me who I *was*."

"Who *were* you then?" said Scrooge, raising his voice. "You're particular—for a shade." He was going to say "*to* a shade," but substituted this, as more appropriate.

"In life I was your partner, Jacob Marley."

"Can you—can you sit down?" asked Scrooge, looking doubtfully at him.

"I can."

"Do it then."

Scrooge asked the question, because he didn't know whether a ghost so transparent might find himself in a condition to take a chair; and felt that in the event of its being impossible, it might involve the necessity of an embarrassing explanation. But the Ghost sat down on the opposite side of the fireplace, as if he were quite used to it.

"You don't believe in me," observed the Ghost.

"I don't," said Scrooge.

"What evidence would you have of my reality beyond that of your senses?"

"I don't know," said Scrooge.

"Why do you doubt your senses?"

"Because," said Scrooge, "a little thing affects them. A slight disorder of the stomach makes them cheats. You may be an undigested bit of beef, a blot of mustard, a crumb of cheese, a fragment of an underdone potato. There's more of gravy than of grave about you, whatever you are!"

Scrooge was not much in the habit of cracking jokes, nor did he feel, in his heart, by any means waggish then. The truth is, that he tried to be smart, as a means of distracting his own attention, and keeping down his terror; for the spectre's voice disturbed the very marrow in his bones.

To sit, staring at those fixed, glazed eyes, in silence for a moment, would play, Scrooge felt, the very deuce with him. There was something very awful, too, in the spectre's being provided with an infernal atmosphere of its own. Scrooge could not feel it himself, but this was clearly the case;

for though the Ghost sat perfectly motionless, its hair, and skirts, and tassels, were still agitated as by the hot vapour from an oven.

"You see this toothpick?" said Scrooge, returning quickly to the charge, for the reason just assigned; and wishing, though it were only for a second, to divert the vision's stony gaze from himself.

"I do," replied the Ghost.

"You are not looking at it," said Scrooge.

"But I see it," said the Ghost, "notwithstanding."

"Well!" returned Scrooge. "I have but to swallow this, and be for the rest of my days persecuted by a legion of goblins, all of my own creation. Humbug, I tell you—humbug!"

At this the spirit raised a frightful cry, and shook its chain with such a dismal and appalling noise, that Scrooge held on tight to his chair, to save himself from falling in a swoon. But how much greater was his horror, when the phantom taking off the bandage round its head, as if it were too warm to wear indoors, its lower jaw dropped down upon its breast!

Scrooge fell upon his knees, and clasped his hands before his face.

"Mercy!" he said. "Dreadful apparition, why do you trouble me?"

"Man of the worldly mind!" replied the Ghost, "do you believe in me or not?"

"I do," said Scrooge. "I must. But why do spirits walk the earth, and why do they come to me?"

"It is required of every man," the Ghost returned, "that the spirit within him should walk abroad among his fellow-men, and travel far and wide; and if that spirit goes not forth in life, it is condemned to do so after death. It is doomed to wander through the world—oh, woe is me!—and witness what it cannot share, but

might have shared on earth, and turned to happiness!"

Again the spectre raised a cry, and shook its chain, and wrung its shadowy hands.

"You are fettered," said Scrooge, trembling. "Tell me why?"

"I wear the chain I forged in life," replied the Ghost. "I made it link by link, and yard by yard; I girded it on of my own free will, and of my own free will I wore it. Is its pattern strange to *you?*"

Scrooge trembled more and more.

"Or would you know," pursued the Ghost, "the weight and length of the strong coil you bear yourself? It was full as heavy and as long as this, seven Christmas Eves ago. You have laboured on it, since. It is a ponderous chain!"

Scrooge glanced about him on the floor, in the expectation of finding himself surrounded by some fifty or sixty fathoms of iron cable: but he could see nothing.

"Jacob," he said imploringly. "Old Jacob Marley, tell me more. Speak comfort to me, Jacob."

"I have none to give," the Ghost replied. "It comes from other regions, Ebenezer Scrooge, and is conveyed by other ministers, to other kinds of men. Nor can I tell you what I would. A very little more, is all permitted to me. I cannot rest, I cannot stay, I cannot linger anywhere. My spirit never walked beyond our counting-house—mark me!—in life my spirit never roved beyond the narrow limits of our money-changing hole; and weary journeys lie before me!"

It was a habit with Scrooge, whenever he became thoughtful, to put his hands in his breeches pockets. Pondering on what the Ghost had said, he did so now, but without lifting up his eyes, or getting off his knees.

"You must have been very slow about it, Jacob," Scrooge observed, in a business-like manner, though with humility and deference.

"Slow!" the Ghost repeated.

"Seven years dead," mused Scrooge. "And travelling all the time!"

"The whole time," said the Ghost. "No rest, no peace. Incessant torture of remorse."

"You travel fast?" said Scrooge.

"On the wings of the wind," replied the Ghost.

"You might have got over a great quantity of ground in seven years," said Scrooge.

The Ghost, on hearing this, set up another cry, and clanked its chain so hideously in the dead silence of the night, that the Ward would have been justified in indicting it for a nuisance.

"Oh! captive, bound, and double-ironed," cried the phantom, "not to know, that ages of incessant labour, by immortal creatures, for this earth must pass into eternity before the good of which it is susceptible is all developed. Not to know that any Christian spirit working kindly in its little sphere, whatever it may be, will find its mortal life too short for its vast means of usefulness. Not to know that no space of regret can make amends for one life's opportunity misused! Yet such was I! Oh! such was I!"

"But you were always a good man of business, Jacob," faltered Scrooge, who now began to apply this to himself.

"Business!" cried the Ghost, wringing its hands again. "Mankind was my business. The common welfare was my business; charity, mercy, forbearance, and benevolence, were, all, my business. The dealings of my trade were but a drop of water in the comprehensive ocean of my business!"

It held up its chain at arm's length, as if that were the cause of all its unavailing grief, and flung it heavily upon the ground again.

"At this time of the rolling year," the spectre said, "I suffer most. Why did I walk through crowds of fellow-beings with my eyes turned down, and never raise them to that blessed Star which led the Wise Men[7] to a poor abode! Were there no poor homes to which its light would have conducted *me!*"

Scrooge was very much dismayed to hear the spectre going on at this rate, and began to quake exceedingly.

"Hear me!" cried the Ghost. "My time is nearly gone."

"I will," said Scrooge. "But don't be hard upon me! Don't be flowery, Jacob! Pray!"

"How it is that I appear before you in a shape that you can see, I may not tell. I have sat invisible beside you many and many a day."

It was not an agreeable idea. Scrooge shivered, and wiped the perspiration from his brow.

"That is no light part of my penance," pursued the Ghost. "I am here to-night to warn you, that you have yet a chance and hope of escaping my fate. A chance and hope of my procuring, Ebenezer."

"You were always a good friend to me," said Scrooge. "Thank'ee!"

"You will be haunted," resumed the Ghost, "by Three Spirits."

Scrooge's countenance fell almost as low as the Ghost's had done.

"Is that the chance and hope you mentioned, Jacob?" he demanded, in a faltering voice.

"It is."

"I—I think I'd rather not," said Scrooge.

"Without their visits," said the

---

[7] *Wise Men,* led by a star to the manger of the infant Saviour, where they worshipped and offered gifts.

Ghost, "you cannot hope to shun the path I tread. Expect the first tomorrow, when the bell tolls one."

"Couldn't I take 'em all at once, and have it over, Jacob?" hinted Scrooge.

"Expect the second on the next night at the same hour. The third upon the next night when the last stroke of twelve has ceased to vibrate. Look to see me no more; and look that, for your own sake, you remember what has passed between us!"

When it had said these words, the spectre took its wrapper from the table, and bound it round its head, as before. Scrooge knew this, by the smart sound its teeth made, when the jaws were brought together by the bandage. He ventured to raise his eyes again, and found his supernatural visitor confronting him in an erect attitude, with its chain wound over and about its arm.

The apparition walked backward from him; and at every step it took, the window raised itself a little, so that when the spectre reached it, it was wide open. It beckoned Scrooge to approach, which he did. When they were within two paces of each other, Marley's Ghost held up its hand, warning him to come no nearer. Scrooge stopped.

Not so much in obedience, as in surprise and fear: for on the raising of the hand, he became sensible of confused noises in the air; incoherent sounds of lamentation and regret; wailings inexpressibly sorrowful and self-accusatory. The spectre, after listening for a moment, joined in the mournful dirge; and floated out upon the bleak, dark night.

Scrooge followed to the window: desperate in his curiosity. He looked out.

The air was filled with phantoms, wandering hither and thither in restless haste, and moaning as they went. Every one of them wore chains like Marley's Ghost; some few (they might be guilty governments) were linked together; none were free. Many had been personally known to Scrooge in their lives. He had been quite familiar with one old ghost, in a white waistcoat, with a monstrous iron safe attached to its ankle, who cried piteously at being unable to assist a wretched woman with an infant, whom it saw below, upon a door-step. The misery with them all was, clearly, that they sought to interfere, for good, in human matters, and had lost the power forever.

Whether these creatures faded into mist, or mist enshrouded them, he could not tell. But they and their spirit voices faded together; and the night became as it had been when he walked home.

Scrooge closed the window, and examined the door by which the Ghost had entered. It was doublelocked, as he had locked it with his own hands, and the bolts were undisturbed. He tried to say "Humbug!" but stopped at the first syllable. And being, from the emotion he had undergone, or the fatigues of the day, or his glimpse of the Invisible World, or the dull conversation of the Ghost, or the lateness of the hour, much in need of repose, went straight to bed, without undressing, and fell asleep upon the instant.

STAVE TWO

THE FIRST OF THE THREE SPIRITS

WHEN Scrooge awoke, it was so dark, that looking out of bed, he could scarcely distinguish the transparent window from the opaque walls of his chamber. He was endeavouring to pierce the darkness with his ferret eyes, when the chimes of a neighbouring church struck the four quarters. So he listened for the hour.

To his great astonishment the heavy bell went on from six to seven, and from seven to eight, and regularly up to twelve; then stopped. Twelve! It was past two when he went to bed. The clock was wrong. An icicle must have got into the works. Twelve!

He touched the spring of his repeater, to correct this most preposterous clock. Its rapid little pulse beat twelve; and stopped.

"Why, it isn't possible," said Scrooge, "that I can have slept through a whole day and far into another night. It isn't possible that anything has happened to the sun, and this is twelve at noon!"

The idea being an alarming one, he scrambled out of bed, and groped his way to the window. He was obliged to rub the frost off with the sleeve of his dressing-gown before he could see anything; and could see very little then. All he could make out was, that it was still very foggy and extremely cold, and that there was no noise of people running to and fro, and making a great stir, as there unquestionably would have been if night had beaten off bright day, and taken possession of the world. This was a great relief, because "three days after sight of this First of Exchange pay to Mr. Ebenezer Scrooge or his order," and so forth, would have become a mere United States' security if there were no days to count by.

Scrooge went to bed again, and thought, and thought, and thought it over and over and over, and could make nothing of it. The more he thought, the more perplexed he was; and the more he endeavoured not to think, the more he thought. Marley's Ghost bothered him exceedingly. Every time he resolved within himself, after mature inquiry, that it was all a dream, his mind flew back again, like a strong spring released, to its first position, and presented the same problem to be worked all through, "Was it a dream or not?"

Scrooge lay in this state until the chimes had gone three quarters more, when he remembered, on a sudden, that the Ghost had warned him of a visitation when the bell tolled one. He resolved to lie awake until the hour was passed; and, considering that he could no more go to sleep than go to Heaven, this was perhaps the wisest resolution in his power.

The quarter was so long, that he was more than once convinced he must have sunk into a doze unconsciously, and missed the clock. At length it broke upon his listening ear.

"Ding, dong!"

"A quarter past," said Scrooge, counting.

"Ding, dong!"

"Half-past!" said Scrooge.

"Ding, dong!"

"A quarter to it," said Scrooge.

"Ding, dong!"

"The hour itself," said Scrooge, triumphantly, "and nothing else!"

He spoke before the hour bell sounded, which it now did with a deep, dull, hollow, melancholy ONE. Light flashed up in the room upon the instant, and the curtains of his bed were drawn.

The curtains of his bed were drawn aside, I tell you, by a hand. Not the curtains at his feet, nor the curtains at his back, but those to which his face was addressed. The curtains of his bed were drawn aside; and Scrooge, starting up into a half-recumbent attitude, found himself face to face with the unearthly visitor who drew them: as close to it as I am now to you, and I am standing in the spirit at your elbow.

It was a strange figure—like a child: yet not so like a child as like an old man, viewed through some supernatural medium, which gave him the appearance of having receded from the view, and being diminished to a child's proportions. Its hair, which hung about its neck and down its back, was white as if with age; and yet the face had not a wrinkle in it, and the tenderest bloom was on the skin. The arms were very long and muscular; the hands the same, as if its hold were of uncommon strength. Its legs and feet, most delicately formed, were, like those upper members, bare. It wore a tunic of the purest white; and round its waist was bound a lustrous belt, the sheen of which was beautiful. It held a branch of fresh green holly in its hand; and, in singular contradiction of that wintry emblem, had its dress trimmed with summer flowers. But the strangest thing about it was, that from the crown of its head there sprang a bright clear jet of light, by which all this was visible; and which was doubtless the occasion of its using, in its duller moments, a great extinguisher for a cap, which it now held under its arm.

Even this, though, when Scrooge looked at it with increasing steadiness, was *not* its strangest quality. For as its belt sparkled and glittered now in one part and now in another, and what was light one instant, at another time was dark, so the figure itself fluctuated in its distinctness: being now a thing with one arm, now with one leg, now with twenty legs, now a pair of legs without a head, now a head without a body: of which dissolving parts, no outline would be visible in the dense gloom wherein they melted away. And in the very

wonder of this, it would be itself again; distinct and clear as ever.

"Are you the Spirit, Sir, whose coming was foretold to me?" asked Scrooge.

"I am!"

The voice was soft and gentle. Singularly low, as if instead of being so close beside him, it were at a distance.

"Who, and what are you?" Scrooge demanded.

"I am the Ghost of Christmas Past."

"Long past?" inquired Scrooge: observant of its dwarfish stature.

"No. Your past."

Perhaps, Scrooge could not have told anybody why, if anybody could have asked him; but he had a special desire to see the Spirit in his cap; and begged him to be covered.

"What!" exclaimed the Ghost, "would you so soon put out, with worldly hands, the light I give? Is it not enough that you are one of those whose passions made this cap, and force me through whole trains of years to wear it low upon my brow!"

Scrooge reverently disclaimed all intention to offend, or any knowledge of having wilfully "bonneted" the Spirit at any period of his life. He then made bold to inquire what business brought him there.

"Your welfare!" said the Ghost.

Scrooge expressed himself much obliged, but could not help thinking that a night of unbroken rest would have been more conducive to that end. The Spirit must have heard him thinking, for it said immediately:—

"Your reclamation, then. Take heed!"

It put out its strong hand as it spoke, and clasped him gently by the arm.

"Rise! and walk with me!"

It would have been in vain for Scrooge to plead that the weather and the hour were not adapted to pedestrian purposes; that bed was warm, and the thermometer a long way below freezing; that he was clad but lightly in his slippers, dressing-gown, and nightcap; and that he had a cold upon him at that time. The grasp, though gentle as a woman's hand, was not to be resisted. He rose: but finding that the Spirit made towards the window, clasped its robe in supplication.

"I am a mortal," Scrooge remonstrated, "and liable to fall."

"Bear but a touch of my hand *there*," said the Spirit, laying it upon his heart, "and you shall be upheld in more than this!"

As the words were spoken, they passed through the wall, and stood upon an open country road, with fields on either hand. The city had entirely vanished. Not a vestige of it was to be seen. The darkness and the mist had vanished with it, for it was a clear, cold, winter day, with snow upon the ground.

"Good Heaven!" said Scrooge, clasping his hands together, as he looked about him. "I was bred in this place. I was a boy here!"

The Spirit gazed upon him mildly. Its gentle touch, though it had been light and instantaneous, appeared still present to the old man's sense of feeling. He was conscious of a thousand odours floating in the air, each one connected with a thousand thoughts, and hopes, and joys, and cares long, long forgotten!

"Your lip is trembling," said the Ghost. "And what is that upon your cheek?"

Scrooge muttered, with an unusual catching in his voice, that it was a pimple; and begged the Ghost to lead him where he would.

"You recollect the way?" inquired the Spirit.

"Remember it!" cried Scrooge with fervour—"I could walk it blindfold."

"Strange to have forgotten it for so many years!" observed the Ghost. "Let us go on."

They walked along the road; Scrooge recognizing every gate, and post, and tree; until a little market-town appeared in the distance, with its bridge, its church, and winding river. Some shaggy ponies now were seen trotting towards them with boys upon their backs, who called to other boys in country gigs and carts, driven by farmers. All these boys were in great spirits, and shouted to each other, until the broad fields were so full of merry music, that the crisp air laughed to hear it.

"These are but shadows of the things that have been," said the Ghost. "They have no consciousness of us."

The jocund travellers came on; and as they came, Scrooge knew and named them every one. Why was he rejoiced beyond all bounds to see them! Why did his cold eye glisten, and his heart leap up as they went past! Why was he filled with gladness when he heard them give each other Merry Christmas, as they parted at cross-roads and by-ways, for their several homes! What was merry Christmas to Scrooge? Out upon merry Christmas! What good had it ever done to him?

"The school is not quite deserted," said the Ghost. "A solitary child, neglected by his friends, is left there still."

Scrooge said he knew it. And he sobbed.

They left the high-road, by a well-remembered lane, and soon approached a mansion of dull red brick, with a little weather-cock-surmounted cupola, on the roof, and a bell hanging in it. It was a large house, but one of broken fortunes; for the spacious offices were little used, their walls were damp and mossy, their windows broken, and their gates decayed. Fowls clucked and strutted in the stables; and the coach-houses and sheds were overrun with grass. Nor was it more retentive of its ancient state, within; for entering the dreary hall, and glancing through the open doors of many rooms, they found them poorly furnished, cold, and vast. There was an earthy savour in the air, a chilly bareness in the place, which associated itself somehow with too much getting up by candle-light, and not too much to eat.

They went, the Ghost and Scrooge, across the hall, to a door at the back of the house. It opened before them, and disclosed a long, bare, melancholy room, made barer still by lines of plain deal forms and desks. At one of these a lonely boy was reading near a feeble fire; and Scrooge sat down upon a form, and wept to see his poor forgotten self as he had used to be.

Not a latent echo in the house, not a squeak and scuffle from the mice behind the panelling, not a drip from the half-thawed water-spout in the dull yard behind, not a sigh among the leafless boughs of one despondent poplar, not the idle swinging of an empty store-house door, no, not a clicking in the fire, but fell upon the heart of Scrooge with softening influence, and gave a freer passage to his tears.

The Spirit touched him on the arm, and pointed to his younger self, intent upon his reading. Suddenly a man, in foreign garments: wonderfully real and distinct to look at: stood outside the window, with an axe stuck in his belt, and leading an ass laden with wood by the bridle.

"Why, it's Ali Baba!" Scrooge exclaimed in ecstasy. "It's dear old honest Ali Baba! Yes, yes, I know! One Christmas time, when yonder solitary child was left here all alone, he *did* come, for the first time, just like that. Poor boy! And Valentine," said Scrooge, "and his wild brother, Orson; there they go! And what's his name, who was put down in his drawers, asleep, at the Gate of Damascus; don't you see him! And the Sultan's Groom turned upside down by the Genii; there he is upon his head! Serve him right. I'm glad of it. What business had *he* to be married to the Princess!"

To hear Scrooge expending all the earnestness of his nature on such subjects, in a most extraordinary voice between laughing and crying; and to see his heightened and excited face; would have been a surprise to his business friends in the City, indeed.

"There's the Parrot!" cried Scrooge. "Green body and yellow tail, with a thing like a lettuce growing out of the top of his head; there he is! Poor Robin Crusoe, he called him, when he came home again after sailing round the island. 'Poor Robin Crusoe, where have you been, Robin Crusoe?' The man thought he was dreaming, but he wasn't. It was the parrot, you know. There goes Friday, running for his life to the little creek! Halloa! Hoop! Halloo!"

Then, with a rapidity of transition very foreign to his usual character, he said, in pity for his former self, "Poor boy!" and cried again.

"I wish," Scrooge muttered, putting his hand in his pocket, and looking about him, after drying his eyes with his cuff: "but it's too late now."

"What is the matter?" asked the Spirit.

"Nothing," said Scrooge. "Nothing. There was a boy singing a Christmas Carol at my door last night. I should like to have given him something: that's all."

The Ghost smiled thoughtfully, and waved its hand: saying as it did so, "Let us see another Christmas!"

Scrooge's former self grew larger at the words, and the room became a little darker and more dirty. The panels shrank, the windows cracked; fragments of plaster fell out of the ceiling, and the naked laths were shown instead; but how all this was brought about, Scrooge knew no more than you do. He only knew that it was quite correct; that everything had happened so; that there he was, alone again, when all the other boys had gone home for the jolly holidays.

He was not reading now, but walking up and down despairingly. Scrooge looked at the Ghost, and with a mournful shaking of his head, glanced anxiously towards the door.

It opened; and a little girl, much younger than the boy, came darting in, and putting her arms about his neck, and often kissing him, addressed him as her "Dear, dear brother."

"I have come to bring you home, dear brother!" said the child, clapping her tiny hands, and bending down to laugh. "To bring you home, home, home!"

"Home, little Fan?" returned the boy.

"Yes!" said the child, brimful of glee. "Home, for good and all. Home, for ever and ever. Father is so much kinder than he used to be, that home's like Heaven! He spoke so gently to me one dear night when I was going to bed, that I was not afraid to ask him once more if you might come home; and he said Yes, you should; and sent me in a coach to bring you. And you're to be a man!" said the child, opening her eyes, "and are never to come back here; but first, we're to be together all the Christmas long, and have the merriest time in all the world."

"You are quite a woman, little Fan!" exclaimed the boy.

She clapped her hands and laughed, and tried to touch his head; but being too little, laughed again, and stood on tiptoe to embrace him. Then she began to drag him, in her childish eagerness, towards the door; and he, nothing loath to go, accompanied her.

A terrible voice in the hall cried, "Bring down Master Scrooge's box, there!" and in the hall appeared the schoolmaster himself, who glared on Master Scrooge with a ferocious condescension, and threw him into a dreadful state of mind by shaking hands with him. He then conveyed him and his sister into the veriest old well of a shivering best-parlour that ever was seen, where the maps upon the wall, and the celestial and terrestrial globes in the windows, were waxy with cold. Here he produced a decanter of curiously light wine, and a block of curiously heavy cake, and administered instalments of those dainties to the young people: at the same time, sending out a meagre servant to offer a glass of "something" to the postboy, who answered that he thanked the gentleman, but if it was the same tap as he had tasted before, he had rather not. Master Scrooge's trunk being by this time tied on to the top of the chaise, the children bade the schoolmaster good-by right willingly; and getting into it, drove gayly down the garden-sweep: the quick wheels dashing the hoar-frost and snow from off the dark leaves of the evergreens like spray.

"Always a delicate creature, whom

a breath might have withered," said the Ghost. "But she had a large heart!"

"So she had," cried Scrooge. "You're right. I'll not gainsay it, Spirit. God forbid!"

"She died a woman," said the Ghost, "and had, as I think, children."

"One child," Scrooge returned.

"True," said the Ghost. "Your nephew!"

Scrooge seemed uneasy in his mind; and answered briefly, "Yes."

Although they had but that moment left the school behind them, they were now in the busy thoroughfares of a city, where shadowy passengers passed and repassed; where shadowy carts and coaches battled for the way, and all the strife and tumult of a real city were. It was made plain enough, by the dressing of the shops, that here too it was Christmas time again; but it was evening, and the streets were lighted up.

The Ghost stopped at a certain warehouse door, and asked Scrooge if he knew it.

"Know it!" said Scrooge. "Was I apprenticed here?"

They went in. At sight of an old gentleman in a Welsh wig, sitting behind such a high desk, that if he had been two inches taller he must have knocked his head against the ceiling, Scrooge cried in great excitement:—

"Why, it's old Fezziwig! Bless his heart; it's Fezziwig alive again!"

Old Fezziwig laid down his pen, and looked up at the clock, which pointed to the hour of seven. He rubbed his hands; adjusted his capacious waistcoat; laughed all over himself, from his shoes to his organ of benevolence; and called out in a comfortable, oily, rich, fat, jovial voice:—

"Yo ho, there! Ebenezer! Dick!"

Scrooge's former self, now grown a young man, came briskly in, accompanied by his fellow-'prentice.

"Dick Wilkins, to be sure!" said Scrooge to the Ghost. "Bless me, yes. There he is. He was very much attached to me, was Dick. Poor Dick! Dear, dear!"

"Yo ho, my boys!" said Fezziwig, "No more work to-night. Christmas Eve, Dick. Christmas, Ebenezer! Let's have the shutters up," cried old Fezziwig, with a sharp clap of his hands, "before a man can say Jack Robinson!"

You wouldn't believe how those two fellows went at it! They charged into the street with the shutters—one, two, three—had 'em up in their places—four, five, six—barred 'em and pinned 'em—seven, eight, nine—and came back before you could have got to twelve, panting like race-horses.

"Hilli-ho!" cried old Fezziwig, skipping down from the high desk, with wonderful agility. "Clear away, my lads, and let's have lots of room here! Hilli-ho, Dick! Chirrup, Ebenezer!"

Clear away! There was nothing they wouldn't have cleared away, or couldn't have cleared away, with old Fezziwig looking on. It was done in a minute. Every movable was packed off, as if it were dismissed from public life for evermore; the floor was swept and watered, the lamps were trimmed, fuel was heaped upon the fire; and the warehouse was as snug, and warm, and dry, and bright a ballroom, as you would desire to see upon a winter's night.

In came a fiddler with a music-book, and went up to the lofty desk, and made an orchestra of it, and tuned like fifty stomach-aches. In came Mrs. Fezziwig, one vast substantial smile. In came the three Miss Fezziwigs, beaming and lovable.

In came the six young followers whose hearts they broke. In came all the young men and women employed in the business. In came the housemaid, with her cousin, the baker. In came the cook, with her brother's particular friend, the milkman. In came the boy from over the way, who was suspected of not having board enough from his master; trying to hide himself behind the girl from next door but one, who was proved to have had her ears pulled by her mistress. In they all came, one after another; some shyly, some boldly, some gracefully, some awkwardly, some pushing, some pulling; in they all came, anyhow and everyhow. Away they all went, twenty couple at once, hands half round and back again the other way; down the middle and up again; round and round in various stages of affectionate grouping; old top couple always turning up in the wrong place; new top couple starting off again, as soon as they got there; all top couples at last, and not a bottom one to help them. When this result was brought about, old Fezziwig, clapping his hands to stop the dance, cried out, "Well done!" and the fiddler plunged his hot face into a pot of porter, especially provided for that purpose. But scorning rest upon his reappearance, he instantly began again, though there were no dancers yet, as if the other fiddler had been carried home, exhausted, on a shutter; and he were a bran-new man resolved to beat him out of sight, or perish.

There were more dances, and there were forfeits, and more dances, and there was cake, and there was negus, and there was a great piece of Cold Roast, and there was a great piece of Cold Boiled, and there were mince-pies, and plenty of beer. But the great effect of the evening came after

the Roast and Boiled, when the fiddler (an artful dog, mind! The sort of man who knew his business better than you or I could have told it him!) struck up "Sir Roger de Coverley."[8] Then old Fezziwig stood out to dance with Mrs. Fezziwig. Top couple, too; with a good stiff piece of work cut out for them; three or four and twenty pair of partners; people who were not to be trifled with; people who *would* dance, and had no notion of walking.

But if they had been twice as many: ah, four times: old Fezziwig would have been a match for them, and so would Mrs. Fezziwig. As to *her*, she was worthy to be his partner in every sense of the term. If that's not high praise, tell me higher, and I'll use it. A positive light appeared to issue from Fezziwig's calves. They shone in every part of the dance like moons. You couldn't have predicted, at any given time, what would become of 'em next. And when old Fezziwig and Mrs. Fezziwig had gone all through the dance; advance and retire, hold hands with your partner;

[8] *"Sir Roger de Coverley,"* an English country dance named for Sir Roger de Coverley.

bow and courtesy; corkscrew; thread-
the-needle, and back again to your
place; Fezziwig "cut"—cut so deftly,
that he appeared to wink with his
legs, and came upon his feet again
without a stagger.

When the clock struck eleven, this
domestic ball broke up. Mr. and Mrs.
Fezziwig took their stations, one on
either side the door, and shaking
hands with every person individually
as he or she went out, wished him or
her a Merry Christmas. When everybody had retired but the two 'pren-
tices, they did the same to them; and
thus the cheerful voices died away,
and the lads were left to their beds;
which were under a counter in the
back-shop.

During the whole of this time,
Scrooge had acted like a man out of
his wits. His heart and soul were in
the scene, and with his former self.
He corroborated everything, remembered everything, enjoyed everything,
and underwent the strangest agitation. It was not until now, when the
bright faces of his former self . and
Dick were turned from them, that he
remembered the Ghost, and became
conscious that it was looking full upon him, while the light upon its head
burnt very clear.

"A small matter," said the Ghost,
"to make these silly folks so full of
gratitude."

"Small!" echoed Scrooge.

The Spirit signed to him to listen
to the two apprentices, who were
pouring out their hearts in praise of
Fezziwig: and when he had done so,
said,

"Why! Is it not? He has spent but
a few pounds of your mortal money:
three or four, perhaps. Is that so
much that he deserves this praise?"

"It isn't that," said Scrooge, heated
by the remark, and speaking unconsciously like his former, not his latter,
self. "It isn't that, Spirit. He has
the power to render us happy or unhappy; to make our service light or
burdensome; a pleasure or a toil. Say
that his power lies in words and looks;
in things so slight and insignificant
that it is impossible to add and count
'em up: what then? The happiness he
gives, is quite as great as if it cost a
fortune."

He felt the Spirit's glance, and
stopped.

"What is the matter?" asked the
Ghost.

"Nothing particular," said Scrooge.

"Something, I think?" the Ghost
insisted.

"No," said Scrooge, "no. I should
like to be able to say a word or two
to my clerk just now! That's all."

His former self turned down the
lamps as he gave utterance to the
wish; and Scrooge and the Ghost
again stood side by side in the open
air.

"My time grows short," observed
the Spirit. "Quick!"

This was not addressed to Scrooge,
or to any one whom he could see, but
it produced an immediate effect. For
again Scrooge saw himself. He was
older now; a man in the prime of
life. His face had not the harsh and
rigid lines of later years; but it had
begun to wear the signs of care and
avarice. There was an eager, greedy,
restless motion in the eye, which
showed the passion that had taken
root, and where the shadow of the
growing tree would fall.

He was not alone, but sat by the
side of a fair young girl in a mourn-
ing-dress: in whose eyes there were
tears, which sparkled in the light that
shone out of the Ghost of Christmas
Past.

"It matters little," she said, softly.
"To you, very little. Another idol
has displaced me; and if it can cheer

and comfort you in time to come, as I would have tried to do, I have no just cause to grieve."

"What idol has displaced you?" he rejoined.

"A golden one."

"This is the even-handed dealing of the world!" he said. "There is nothing on which it is so hard as poverty; and there is nothing it professes to condemn with such severity as the pursuit of wealth!"

"You fear the world too much," she answered, gently. "All your other hopes have merged into the hope of being beyond the chance of its sordid reproach. I have seen your nobler aspirations fall off one by one, until the master-passion, Gain, engrosses you. Have I not?"

"What then?" he retorted. "Even if I have grown so much wiser, what then? I am not changed towards you."

She shook her head.

"Am I?"

"Our contract is an old one. It was made when we were both poor and content to be so, until, in good season, we could improve our worldly fortune by our patient industry. You *are* changed. When it was made, you were another man."

"I was a boy," he said impatiently.

"Your own feeling tells you that you were not what you are," she returned. "I am. That which promised happiness when we were one in heart, is fraught with misery now that we are two. How often and how keenly I have thought of this, I will not say. It is enough that I *have* thought of it and can release you."

"Have I ever sought release?"

"In words? No. Never."

"In what, then?"

"In a changed nature; in an altered spirit; in another atmosphere of life; another Hope as its great end. In everything that made my love of any worth or value in your sight. If this had never been between us," said the girl, looking mildly, but with steadiness, upon him; "tell me, would you seek me out and try to win me now? Ah, no!"

He seemed to yield to the justice of this supposition, in spite of himself. But he said with a struggle, "You think not."

"I would gladly think otherwise if I could," she answered, "Heaven knows! When *I* have learned a Truth like this, I know how strong and irresistible it must be. But if you were free to-day, to-morrow, yesterday, can even I believe that you would choose a dowerless girl—you who, in your very confidence with her, weigh everything by Gain: or, choosing her, if for a moment you were false enough to your one guiding principle to do so, do I not know that your repentance and regret would surely follow? I do; and I release you. With a full heart, for the love of him you once were."

He was about to speak; but with her head turned from him, she resumed.

"You may—the memory of what is past half makes me hope you will—have pain in this. A very, very brief time, and you will dismiss the recollection of it, gladly, as an unprofitable dream, from which it happened well that you awoke. May you be happy in the life you have chosen!"

She left him, and they parted.

"Spirit!" said Scrooge, "show me no more! Conduct me home. Why do you delight to torture me?"

"One shadow more!" exclaimed the Ghost.

"No more!" cried Scrooge. "No more. I don't wish to see it. Show me no more!"

But the relentless Ghost pinioned

him in both his arms, and forced him to observe what happened next.

They were in another scene and place; a room, not very large or handsome, but full of comfort. Near to the winter fire sat a beautiful young girl, so like the last that Scrooge believed it was the same, until he saw *her*, now a comely matron, sitting opposite her daughter. The noise in this room was perfectly tumultuous, for there were more children there, than Scrooge in his agitated state of mind could count; and, unlike the celebrated herd in the poem, they were not forty children conducting themselves like one, but every child was conducting itself like forty. The consequences were uproarious beyond belief; but no one seemed to care; on the contrary, the mother and daughter laughed heartily, and enjoyed it very much; and the latter, soon beginning to mingle in the sports, got pillaged by the young brigands most ruthlessly. What would I not have given to be one of them! Though I never could have been so rude, no, no! I wouldn't for the wealth of all the world have crushed that braided hair, and torn it down; and for the precious little shoe, I wouldn't have plucked it off, God bless my soul! to save my life. As to measuring her waist in sport, as they did, bold young brood, I couldn't have done it; I should have expected my arm to have grown around it for a punishment, and never come straight again. And yet I should have dearly liked, I own, to have touched her lips; to have questioned her, that she might have opened them; to have looked upon the lashes of her downcast eyes, and never raised a blush; to have let loose waves of hair, an inch of which would be a keepsake beyond price: in short, I should have liked, I do confess, to have had the lightest license

of a child, and yet been man enough to know its value.

But now a knocking at the door was heard, and such a rush immediately ensued that she with laughing face and plundered dress was borne towards it the centre of a flushed and boisterous group, just in time to greet the father, who came home attended by a man laden with Christmas toys and presents. Then the shouting and the struggling, and the onslaught that was made on the defenceless porter! The scaling him with chairs for ladders to dive into his pockets, despoil him of brown-paper parcels, hold on tight by his cravat, hug him round the neck, pommel his back, and kick his legs in irrepressible affection! The shouts of wonder and delight with which the development of every package was received! The terrible announcement that the baby had been taken in the act of putting a doll's frying-pan into his mouth, and was more than suspected of having swallowed a fictitious turkey, glued on a wooden platter! The immense relief of finding this a false alarm! The joy, and gratitude, and ecstacy! They are all indescribable alike. It is enough that by degrees the children and their emotions got out of the parlour and by one stair at a time, up to the top of the house; where they went to bed, and so subsided.

And now Scrooge looked on more attentively than ever, when the master of the house, having his daughter leaning fondly on him, sat down with her and her mother at his own fireside; and when he thought that such another creature, quite as graceful and as full of promise, might have called him father, and been a springtime in the haggard winter of his life, his sight grew very dim indeed.

"Belle," said the husband, turning to his wife with a smile, "I saw an old friend of yours this afternoon."

"Who was it?"

"Guess!"

"How can I? Tut, don't I know?" she added in the same breath, laughing as he laughed. "Mr. Scrooge."

"Mr. Scrooge it was. I passed his office window; and as it was not shut up, and he had a candle inside, I could scarcely help seeing him. His partner lies upon the point of death, I hear; and there he sat alone. Quite alone in the world, I do believe."

"Spirit!" said Scrooge in a broken voice, "remove me from this place."

"I told you these were shadows of the things that have been," said the Ghost. "That they are what they are, do not blame me!"

"Remove me!" Scrooge exclaimed, "I cannot bear it!"

He turned upon the Ghost, and seeing that it looked upon him with a face, in which in some strange way there were fragments of all the faces it had shown him, wrestled with it.

"Leave me! Take me back. Haunt me no longer!"

In the struggle, if that can be called a struggle in which the Ghost with no visible resistance on its own part was undisturbed by any effort of its adversary, Scrooge observed that its light was burning high and bright; and dimly connecting that with its influence over him, he seized the extinguisher-cap, and by a sudden action pressed it down upon his head.

The Spirit dropped beneath it, so that the extinguisher covered its whole form; but though Scrooge pressed it down with all his force, he could not hide the light, which streamed from under it, in an unbroken flood upon the ground.

He was conscious of being exhausted, and overcome by an irresistible drowsiness; and, further, of being in his own bedroom. He gave the cap a parting squeeze, in which his hand relaxed; and had barely time to reel to bed, before he sank into a heavy slumber.

STAVE THREE

THE SECOND OF THE THREE SPIRITS

AWAKING in the middle of a prodigiously tough snore, and sitting up in bed to get his thoughts together, Scrooge had no occasion to be told that the bell was again upon the stroke of One. He felt that he was restored to consciousness in the right nick of time, for the especial purpose of holding a conference with the second messenger despatched to him through Jacob Marley's intervention. But, finding that he turned uncomfortably cold when he began to wonder which of his curtains this new spectre would draw back, he put them every one aside with his own hands, and lying down again, established a sharp lookout all round the bed. For he wished to challenge the Spirit on the moment of its appearance, and did not wish to be taken by surprise and made nervous.

Gentlemen of the free-and-easy sort, who plume themselves on being acquainted with a move or two, and being usually equal to the time-of-day, express the wide range of their capacity for adventure by observing that they are good for anything from pitch-and-toss to manslaughter; between which opposite extremes, no doubt, there lies a tolerably wide and comprehensive range of subjects. Without venturing for Scrooge quite as hardily as this, I don't mind calling on you to believe that he was ready for a good broad field of strange appearances, and that nothing between a baby and rhinoceros would have astonished him very much.

Now, being prepared for almost anything, he was not by any means prepared for nothing; and, consequently, when the Bell struck One, and no shape appeared, he was taken with a violent fit of trembling. Five minutes, ten minutes, a quarter of an hour went by, yet nothing came. All this time, he lay upon his bed, the very core and centre of a blaze of ruddy light, which streamed upon it when the clock proclaimed the hour; and which, being only light, was more alarming than a dozen ghosts, as he was powerless to make out what it meant, or would be at; and was sometimes apprehensive that he might be at that very moment an interesting case of spontaneous combustion, without having the consolation of knowing it. At last, however, he began to think—as you or I would have thought at first; for it is always the person not in the predicament who knows what ought to have been done in it, and would unquestionably have done it too—at last, I say, he began to think that the source and secret of this ghostly light might be in the adjoining room, from whence, on further tracing it, it seemed to shine. This idea taking full possession of his mind, he got up softly and shuffled in his slippers to the door.

The moment Scrooge's hand was on the lock, a strange voice called him by his name, and bade him enter. He obeyed.

It was his own room. There was no doubt about that. But it had undergone a surprising transformation. The walls and ceiling were so hung with living green, that it looked a perfect grove, from every part of which, bright gleaming berries glistened. The crisp leaves of holly, mistletoe, and ivy reflected back the light as if so many little mirrors had been scattered there; and such a mighty blaze went roaring up the chimney, as that dull petrifaction of a hearth had never known in Scrooge's time, or Marley's, or for many and many a winter season gone. Heaped up on the floor, to form a kind of throne, were turkeys, geese, game, poultry, brawn, great joints of meat, sucking-pigs, long wreaths of sausages, mince-pies, plum-puddings, barrels of oysters, red-hot chestnuts, cherry-cheeked apples, juicy oranges, luscious pears, immense twelfth-cakes,[9] and seething bowls of punch, that made the chamber dim with their delicious steam. In easy state upon this couch, there sat a jolly Giant[10] glorious to see; who bore a glowing torch, in shape not unlike Plenty's horn, and held it up, high up, to shed its light on Scrooge, as he came peeping round the door.

"Come in!" exclaimed the Ghost. "Come in! and know me better, man!"

Scrooge entered timidly, and hung his head before this Spirit. He was not the dogged Scrooge he had been; and though the Spirit's eyes were clear and kind, he did not like to meet them.

"I am the Ghost of Christmas Present," said the Spirit. "Look upon me!"

Scrooge reverently did so. It was clothed in one simple deep green robe, or mantle, bordered with white fur. This garment hung so loosely on the figure, that its capacious breast was bare, as if disdaining to be warded or

---

[9]*twelfth-cakes*, eaten in honor of the Wise Men on Twelfth day, or the Epiphany, January 6, twelve days after Christmas. In the Twelfth Night festivities the person receiving the cake with a bean in it was master of ceremonies.

[10]*Giant*, Santa Claus.

concealed by any artifice. Its feet, observable beneath the ample folds of the garment, were also bare; and on its head it wore no other covering than a holly wreath set here and there with shining icicles. Its dark brown curls were long and free; free as its genial face, its sparkling eye, its open hand, its cheery voice, its unconstrained demeanour, and its joyful air. Girded round its middle was an antique scabbard; but no sword was in it, and the ancient sheath was eaten up with rust.

"You have never seen the like of me before!" exclaimed the Spirit.

"Never," Scrooge made answer to it.

"Have never walked forth with the younger members of my family; meaning (for I am very young) my elder brothers born in these later years?" pursued the Phantom.

"I don't think I have," said Scrooge. "I am afraid I have not. Have you had many brothers, Spirit?"

"More than eighteen hundred," said the Ghost.

"A tremendous family to provide for!" muttered Scrooge.

The Ghost of Christmas Present rose.

"Spirit," said Scrooge, submissively, "conduct me where you will. I went forth last night on compulsion, and I learnt a lesson which is working now. To-night, if you have aught to teach me, let me profit by it."

"Touch my robe!"

Scrooge did as he was told, and held it fast.

Holly, mistletoe, red berries, ivy, turkeys, geese, game, poultry, brawn, meat, pigs, sausages, oysters, pies, puddings, fruit, and punch, all vanished instantly. So did the room, the fire, the ruddy glow, the hour of night, and they stood in the city streets on Christmas morning, where (for the weather was severe) the people made a rough, but brisk and not unpleasant kind of music, in scraping the snow from the pavement in front of their dwellings, and from the tops of their houses: whence it was mad delight to the boys to see it come plumping down into the road below, and splitting into artificial little snow-storms.

The house fronts looked black enough, and the windows blacker, contrasting with the smooth white sheet of snow upon the roofs, and with the dirtier snow upon the ground; which last deposit had been ploughed up in deep furrows by the heavy wheels of carts and wagons; furrows that crossed and recrossed each other hundreds of times where the great streets branched off, and made intricate channels, hard to trace, in the thick yellow mud and icy water. The sky was gloomy, and the shortest streets were choked up with a dingy mist, half thawed, half frozen, whose heavier particles descended in a shower of sooty atoms, as if all the chimneys in Great Britain had, by one consent, caught fire, and were blazing away to their dear hearts' content. There was nothing very cheerful in the climate or the town, and yet was there an air of cheerfulness abroad that the clearest summer air and brightest summer sun might have endeavoured to diffuse in vain.

For, the people who were shovelling away on the house-tops were jovial and full of glee; calling out to one another from the parapets, and now and then exchanging a facetious snow-ball—better-natured missile far than many a wordy jest—laughing heartily if it went right and not less heartily if it went wrong. The poulterers' shops were still half open, and the fruiterers' were radiant in their glory. There were great, round, potbellied baskets of chestnuts, shaped like the waistcoats of jolly old gentlemen, lolling at the doors, and tumbling out into the street in their apoplectic opulence. There were ruddy, brown-faced, broad-girthed Spanish Onions, shining in the fatness of their growth like Spanish Friars; and winking from their shelves in wanton slyness at the girls as they went by, and glanced demurely at the hung-up mistletoe. There were pears and apples, clustered high in blooming pyramids; there were bunches of grapes, made, in the shopkeepers' benevolence, to dangle from conspicuous hooks, that people's mouths might water gratis as they passed; there were piles of filberts, mossy and brown, recalling, in their fragrance, ancient walks among the woods, and pleasant shufflings ankle deep through withered leaves; there were Norfolk Biffins,[11] squab, and swarthy, setting off the yellow of the oranges and lemons, and, in the great compactness of their juicy persons, urgently entreating and beseeching to be carried home in paper bags and eaten after dinner. The very gold and silver fish, set forth among these choice fruits in a bowl, though members of a dull and stagnant-blooded race, appeared to know that there was something going on; and, to a fish, went gasping round and round their little world in slow and passionless excitement.

The Grocers'! oh the Grocers'! nearly closed, with perhaps two shutters down, or one; but through those gaps such glimpses! It was not alone that the scales descending on the counter made a merry sound, or that the twine and roller parted company so briskly, or that the canisters were rattled up and down like juggling

―――――――
[11]*Norfolk Biffins,* fine red cooking apples.

tricks, or even that the blended scents of tea and coffee were so grateful to the nose, or even that the raisins were so plentiful and rare, the almonds so extremely white, the sticks of cinnamon so long and straight, the other spices so delicious, the candied fruits so caked and spotted with molten sugar as to make the coldest lookers-on feel faint and subsequently bilious. Nor was it that the figs were moist and pulpy, or that the French plums blushed in modest tartness from their highly-decorated boxes, or that everything was good to eat and in its Christmas dress: but the customers were all so hurried and so eager in the hopeful promise of the day, that they tumbled up against each other at the door, clashing their wicker baskets wildly, and left their purchases upon the counter, and came running back to fetch them, and committed hundreds of the like mistakes in the best humour possible; while the Grocer and his people were so frank and fresh that the polished hearts with which they fastened their aprons behind might have been their own, worn outside for general inspection, and for Christmas daws to peck at if they chose.

But soon the steeples called good people all, to church and chapel, and away they came, flocking through the streets in their best clothes, and with their gayest faces. And at the same time there emerged from scores of by-streets, lanes, and nameless turnings, innumerable people, carrying their dinners to the bakers' shops. The sight of these poor revellers appeared to interest the Spirit very much, for he stood with Scrooge beside him in a baker's doorway, and taking off the covers as their bearers passed sprinkled incense on their dinners from his torch. And it was a very uncommon kind of torch, for once or twice when there were angry words between some dinner-carriers who had jostled with each other, he shed a few drops of water on them from it, and their good humour was restored directly. For they said, it was a shame to quarrel upon Christmas Day. And so it was! God love it, so it was!

In time the bells ceased, and the bakers were shut up; and yet there was a genial shadowing forth of all these dinners and the progress of their cooking, in the thawed blotch of wet above each baker's oven; where the pavement smoked as if its stones were cooking too.

"Is there a peculiar flavour in what you sprinkle from your torch?" asked Scrooge.

"There is. My own."

"Would it apply to any kind of dinner on this day?" asked Scrooge.

"To any kindly given. To a poor one most."

"Why to a poor one most?" asked Scrooge.

"Because it needs it most."

"Spirit," said Scrooge, after a moment's thought, "I wonder you, of all the beings in the many worlds about us, should desire to cramp these people's opportunities of innocent enjoyment."

"I!" cried the Spirit.

"You would deprive them of their means of dining every seventh day, often the only day on which they can be said to dine at all," said Scrooge. "Wouldn't you?"

"I!" cried the Spirit.

"You seek to close these places on the Seventh Day?" said Scrooge. "And it comes to the same thing."

"I seek!" exclaimed the Spirit.

"Forgive me if I am wrong. It has been done in your name, or at least in that of your family," said Scrooge.

"There are some upon this earth of yours," returned the Spirit, "who lay claim to know us, and who do their deeds of passion, pride, ill-will, hatred, envy, bigotry, and selfishness in our name, who are as strange to us and all our kith and kin, as if they had never lived. Remember that, and charge their doings on themselves, not us."

Scrooge promised that he would; and they went on, invisible as they had been before, into the suburbs of the town. It was a remarkable quality of the Ghost (which Scrooge had observed at the baker's), that notwithstanding his gigantic size, he could accommodate himself to any place with ease; and that he stood beneath a low roof quite as gracefully and like a supernatural creature, as it was possible he could have done in any lofty hall.

And perhaps it was the pleasure the good Spirit had in showing off this power of his, or else it was his own kind, generous, hearty nature, and his sympathy with all poor men, that led him straight to Scrooge's clerk's; for there he went, and took Scrooge with him, holding to his robe; and on the threshold of the door the Spirit smiled, and stopped to bless Bob Cratchit's dwelling with the sprinklings of his torch. Think of that! Bob had but fifteen "Bob"[12] a-week himself; he pocketed on Saturdays but fifteen copies of his Christian name; and yet the Ghost of Christmas Present blessed his four-roomed house!

Then up rose Mrs. Cratchit, Cratchit's wife, dressed out but poorly in a twice-turned gown, but brave in ribbons, which are cheap and make a goodly show for sixpence; and she laid the cloth, assisted by Belinda Cratchit, second of her daughters, also brave in ribbons; while Master Peter

_____

12"*Bob,*" a shilling, worth about 24 cents.

Cratchit plunged a fork into the saucepan of potatoes, and getting the corners of his monstrous shirt collar (Bob's private property, conferred upon his son and heir in honour of the day) into his mouth, rejoiced to find himself so gallantly attired, and yearned to show his linen in the fashionable Parks. And now two smaller Cratchits, boy and girl, came tearing in, screaming that outside the baker's they had smelt the goose, and known it for their own; and basking in luxurious thoughts of sage-and-onion, these young Cratchits danced about the table, and exalted Master Peter Cratchit to the skies, while he (not proud, although his collars nearly choked him) blew the fire, until the slow potatoes bubbling up, knocked loudly at the saucepan-lid to be let out and peeled.

"What has ever got your precious father then?" said Mrs. Cratchit. "And your brother, Tiny Tim! And Martha warn't as late last Christmas Day by half-an-hour!"

"Here's Martha, mother!" said a girl, appearing as she spoke.

"Here's Martha, mother!" cried the two young Cratchits. "Hurrah! There's *such* a goose, Martha!"

"Why, bless your heart alive, my dear, how late you are!" said Mrs. Cratchit, kissing her a dozen times, and taking off her shawl and bonnet for her with officious zeal.

"We'd a deal of work to finish up last night," replied the girl, "and had to clear away this morning, mother!"

"Well! Never mind so long as you are come," said Mrs. Cratchit. "Sit ye down before the fire, my dear, and have a warm, Lord bless ye!"

"No, no! There's father coming," cried the two young Cratchits, who were everywhere at once. "Hide, Martha, hide!"

So Martha hid herself, and in came little Bob, the father, with at least three feet of comforter exclusive of the fringe, hanging down before him; and his threadbare clothes darned up and brushed, to look seasonable; and Tiny Tim upon his shoulder. Alas for Tiny Tim, he bore a little crutch and had his limbs supported by an iron frame!

"Why, where's our Martha?" cried Bob Cratchit, looking round.

"Not coming," said Mrs. Cratchit.

"Not coming!" said Bob, with a sudden declension in his high spirits; for he had been Tim's blood horse all the way from church, and had come home rampant. "Not coming upon Christmas Day!"

Martha didn't like to see him disappointed, if it were only in joke; so she came out prematurely from behind the closet door, and ran into his arms, while the two young Cratchits hustled Tiny Tim, and bore him off into the wash-house, that he might hear the pudding singing in the copper.

"And how did little Tim behave?" asked Mrs. Cratchit, when she had rallied Bob on his credulity, and Bob had hugged his daughter to his heart's content.

"As good as gold," said Bob, "and better. Somehow he gets thoughtful, sitting by himself so much, and thinks the strangest things you ever heard. He told me, coming home, that he hoped the people saw him in the church, because he was a cripple, and it might be pleasant to them to remember upon Christmas Day, who made lame beggars walk and blind men see."

Bob's voice was tremulous when he told them this, and trembled more when he said that Tiny Tim was growing strong and hearty.

His active little crutch was heard upon the floor, and back came Tiny

Tim before another word was spoken, escorted by his brother and sister to his stool before the fire; and while Bob, turning up his cuffs—as if, poor fellow, they were capable of being made more shabby — compounded some hot mixture in a jug with gin and lemons, and stirred it round and round and put it on the hob to simmer; Master Peter, and the two ubiquitous young Cratchits went to fetch the goose, with which they soon returned in high procession.

Such a bustle ensued that you might have thought a goose the rarest of all birds; a feathered phenomenon, to which a black swan was a matter of course—and in truth it was something very like it in that house. Mrs. Cratchit made the gravy (ready beforehand in a little saucepan) hissing hot; Master Peter mashed the potatoes with incredible vigour; Miss Belinda sweetened up the apple-sauce; Martha dusted the hot plates; Bob took Tiny Tim beside him in a tiny corner at the table; the two young Cratchits set chairs for everybody, not forgetting themselves, and mounting guard upon their posts, crammed spoons into their mouths, lest they should shriek for goose before their turn came to be helped. At last the dishes were set on, and grace was said. It was succeeded by a breathless pause, as Mrs. Cratchit, looking slowly all along the carving-knife, prepared to plunge it in the breast; but when she did, and when the long expected gush of stuffing issued forth, one murmur of delight arose all around the board, and even Tiny Tim, excited by the two young Cratchits, beat on the table with the handle of his knife, and feebly cried Hurrah!

There never was such a goose. Bob said he didn't believe there ever was such a goose cooked. Its tenderness and flavour, size and cheapness, were the themes of universal admiration. Eked out by the apple-sauce and mashed potatoes, it was a sufficient dinner for the whole family; indeed, as Mrs. Cratchit said with great delight (surveying one small atom of a bone upon the dish), they hadn't ate it all at last! Yet every one had had enough, and the youngest Cratchits in particular, were steeped in sage and onion to the eyebrows! But now, the plates being changed by Miss Belinda, Mrs. Cratchit left the room alone— too nervous to bear witness—to take the pudding up and bring it in.

Suppose it should not be done enough! Suppose it should break in turning out! Suppose somebody should have got over the wall of the back-yard, and stolen it, while they were merry with the goose—a supposition at which the two young Cratchits became livid! All sorts of horrors were supposed.

Hallo! A great deal of steam! The pudding was out of the copper. A smell like a washing-day! That was the cloth. A smell like an eating-house and a pastrycook's next door to each other, with a laundress's next door to that! That was the pudding! In half a minute Mrs. Cratchit entered—flushed, but smiling proudly —with the pudding, like a speckled cannon ball, so hard and firm, blazing in half of half-a-quartern of ignited brandy, and bedight with Christmas holly stuck into the top.

Oh, a wonderful pudding! Bob Cratchit said, and calmly too, that he regarded it as the greatest success achieved by Mrs. Cratchit since their marriage. Mrs. Cratchit said that now the weight was off her mind, she would confess she had had her doubts about the quantity of flour. Everybody had something to say about it, but nobody said or thought it was at all a small pudding for a large family. It would have been flat heresy to do so. Any Cratchit would have blushed to hint at such a thing.

At last the dinner was all done, the cloth was cleared, the hearth swept, and the fire made up. The compound in the jug being tasted, and considered perfect, apples and oranges were put upon the table, and a shovel-full of chestnuts on the fire. Then all the Cratchit family drew around the hearth, in what Bob Cratchit called a circle, meaning half a one; and at Bob Cratchit's elbow stood the family display of glass. Two tumblers, and a custard-cup without a handle.

These held the hot stuff from the jug, however, as well as golden goblets would have done; and Bob served it out with beaming looks, while the chestnuts on the fire sputtered and cracked noisily. Then Bob proposed:—

"A Merry Christmas to us all, my dears. God bless us!"

Which all the family re-echoed.

"God bless us every one!" said Tiny Tim, the last of all.

He sat very close to his father's side upon his little stool. Bob held his withered little hand in his, as if he loved the child, and wished to keep him by his side, and dreaded that he might be taken from him.

"Spirit," said Scrooge, with an interest he had never felt before, "tell me if Tiny Tim will live."

"I see a vacant seat," replied the Ghost, "in the poor chimney-corner, and a crutch without an owner, carefully preserved. If these shadows remain unaltered by the Future, the child will die."

"No, no," said Scrooge. "Oh, no, kind Spirit! say he will be spared."

"If these shadows remain unaltered by the Future, none other of my race," returned the Ghost, "will find him here. What then? If he be like to die, he had better do it, and decrease the surplus population."

Scrooge hung his head to hear his own words quoted by the Spirit, and was overcome with penitence and grief.

"Man," said the Ghost, "if man you be in heart, not adamant, forbear that wicked cant until you have discovered What the surplus is, and Where it is. Will you decide what men shall live, what men shall die? It may be, that in the sight of Heaven, you are more worthless and less fit to live than millions like this poor man's child. Oh God! to hear the Insect on the leaf pronouncing on the too much life among his hungry brothers in the dust!"

Scrooge bent before the Ghost's rebuke, and trembling cast his eyes upon the ground. But he raised them speedily, on hearing his own name.

"Mr. Scrooge!" said Bob; "I'll give you Mr. Scrooge, the Founder of the Feast!"

"The Founder of the Feast indeed!" cried Mrs. Cratchit, reddening. "I wish I had him here. I'd give him a piece of my mind to feast upon, and I hope he'd have a good appetite for it."

"My dear," said Bob, "the children! Christmas Day."

"It should be Christmas Day, I am sure," said she, "on which one drinks the health of such an odious, stingy, hard, unfeeling man as Mr. Scrooge. You know he is, Robert! Nobody knows it better than you do, poor fellow!"

"My dear," was Bob's mild answer, "Christmas Day."

"I'll drink his health for your sake and the Day's," said Mrs. Cratchit, "not for his. Long life to him! A Merry Christmas and a Happy

New Year! He'll be very merry and happy, I have no doubt!"

The children drank the toast after her. It was the first of their proceedings which had no heartiness in it. Tiny Tim drank it last of all, but he didn't care twopence for it. Scrooge was the Ogre of the family. The mention of his name cast a dark shadow on the party, which was not dispelled for full five minutes.

After it had passed away, they were ten times merrier than before, from the mere relief of Scrooge the Baleful being done with. Bob Cratchit told them how he had a situation in his eye for Master Peter, which would bring in, if obtained, full five and sixpence weekly. The two young Cratchits laughed tremendously at the idea of Peter's being a man of business; and Peter himself looked thoughtfully at the fire from between his collars, as if he were deliberating what particular investments he should favour when he came into the receipt of that bewildering income. Martha, who was a poor apprentice at a milliner's, then told them what kind of work she had to do, and how many hours she worked at a stretch, and how she meant to lie abed to-morrow morning for a good long rest; to-morrow being a holiday she passed at home. Also how she had seen a countess and a lord some days before, and how the lord "was much about as tall as Peter;" at which Peter pulled up his collars so high that you couldn't have seen his head if you had been there. All this time the chestnuts and the jug went round and round; and by-and-by they had a song, about a lost child travelling in the snow, from Tiny Tim, who had a plaintive little voice, and sang it very well indeed.

There was nothing of high mark in this. They were not a handsome family; they were not well dressed; their shoes were far from being water-proof; their clothes were scanty; and Peter might have known, and very likely did, the inside of a pawnbroker's. But, they were happy, grateful, pleased with one another, and contented with the time; and when they faded, and looked happier yet in the bright sprinklings of the Spirit's torch at parting, Scrooge had his eye upon them, and especially on Tiny Tim, until the last.

By this time it was getting dark, and snowing pretty heavily; and as Scrooge and the Spirit went along the streets, the brightness of the roaring fires in kitchens, parlours, and all sorts of rooms, was wonderful. Here, the flickering of the blaze showed preparations for a cosy dinner, with hot plates baking through and through before the fire, and deep red curtains, ready to be drawn to shut out cold and darkness. There, all the children of the house were running out into the snow to meet their married sisters, brothers, cousins, uncles, aunts, and be the first to greet them. Here, again, were shadows on the window-blind of guests assembling; and there a group of handsome girls, all hooded and fur-booted, and all chattering at once, tripped lightly off to some near neighbour's house; where, woe upon the single man who saw them enter—artful witches! well they knew it—in a glow!

But if you had judged from the numbers of people on their way to friendly gatherings, you might have thought that no one was at home to give them welcome when they got there, instead of every house expecting company, and piling up its fires half-chimney high. Blessings on it, how the Ghost exulted! How it bared its breadth of breast, and opened its capacious palm, and floated on, out-pouring, with a generous hand, its bright and harmless mirth on every-thing within its reach! The very lamplighter, who ran on before dot-ting the dusky street with specks of light, and who was dressed to spend the evening somewhere, laughed out loudly as the Spirit passed: though little kenned the lamplighter that he had any company but Christmas!

And now, without a word of warning from the Ghost, they stood upon a bleak and desert moor, where monstrous masses of rude stone were cast about, as though it were the burial-place of giants; and water spread itself wheresoever it listed, or would have done so, but for the frost that held it prisoner; and nothing grew but moss and furze, and coarse, rank grass. Down in the west the setting sun had left a streak of fiery red, which glared upon the desolation for an instant, like a sullen eye, and frowning lower, lower, lower yet, was lost in the thick gloom of darkest night.

"What place is this?" asked Scrooge.

"A place where Miners live, who labour in the bowels of the earth," returned the Spirit. "But they know me. See!"

A light shone from the window of a hut, and swiftly they advanced towards it. Passing through the wall of mud and stone, they found a cheerful company assembled round a glowing fire. An old, old man and woman, with their children and their children's children, and another gen-eration beyond that, all decked out gayly in their holiday attire. The old man, in a voice that seldom rose above the howling of the wind upon the barren waste, was singing them a Christmas song; it had been a very old song when he was a boy; and from time to time they all joined in.

the chorus. So surely as they raised their voices, the old man got quite blithe and loud; and so surely as they stopped, his vigour sank again.

The Spirit did not tarry here, but bade Scrooge hold his robe, and pass-ing on above the moor, sped whither? Not to sea? To sea. To Scrooge's horror, looking back, he saw the last of the land, a frightful range of rocks, behind them; and his ears were deafened by the thundering of water, as it rolled and roared, and raged among the dreadful caverns it had worn, and fiercely tried to under-mine the earth.

Built upon a dismal reef of sunken rocks, some league or so from shore, on which the waters chafed and dashed, the wild year through, there stood a solitary lighthouse. Great heaps of seaweed clung to its base, and storm-birds—born of the wind one might suppose, as seaweed of the water—rose and fell about it, like the waves they skimmed.

But even here, two men who watched the light had made a fire, that through the loophole in the thick stone wall shed out a ray of brightness on the awful sea. Join-ing their horny hands over the rough table at which they sat, they wished each other Merry Christmas in their can of grog; and one of them: the elder, too, with his face all damaged and scarred with hard weather, as the figure head of an old ship might be: struck up a sturdy song that was like a Gale in itself.

Again the Ghost sped on, above the black and heaving sea—on, on—until, being far away, as he told Scrooge, from any shore, they lighted on a ship. They stood beside the helmsman at the wheel, the look-out in the bow, the officers who had the watch; dark, ghostly figures in their several stations; but every man among them hummed a Christmas tune, or had a Christmas thought, or spoke below his breath to his companion of some by-gone Christmas Day, with homeward hopes belonging to it. And every man on board, waking or sleeping, good or bad, had had a kinder word for another on that day than on any day in the year; and had shared to some extent in its festivities; and had remembered those he cared for at a distance, and had known that they delighted to remember him.

It was a great surprise to Scrooge, while listening to the moaning of the wind, and thinking what a solemn thing it was to move on through the lonely darkness over an unknown abyss, whose depths were secrets as profound as Death: it was a great surprise to Scrooge, while thus engaged, to hear a hearty laugh. It was a much greater surprise to Scrooge to recognize it as his own nephew's and to find himself in a bright, dry, gleaming room, with the Spirit standing smiling by his side, and looking at that same nephew with approving affability.

"Ha, ha!" laughed Scrooge's nephew. "Ha, ha, ha!"

If you should happen, by any unlikely chance, to know a man more blest in a laugh than Scrooge's nephew, all I can say is, I should like to know him too. Introduce him to me, and I'll cultivate his acquaintance.

It is a fair, even-handed, noble adjustment of things, that while there is infection in disease and sorrow, there is nothing in the world so irresistibly contagious as laughter and good-humour. When Scrooge's nephew laughed in this way: holding his sides, rolling his head, and twisting his face into the most extravagant contortions: Scrooge's niece, by mar-riage, laughed as heartily as he. And their assembled friends being not a bit behindhand, roared out, lustily.

"Ha, ha! Ha, ha, ha, ha!"

"He said that Christmas was a humbug, as I live!" cried Scrooge's nephew. "He believed it too!"

"More shame for him, Fred!" said Scrooge's niece, indignantly. Bless those women; they never do anything by halves. They are always in earnest.

She was very pretty: exceedingly pretty. With a dimpled, surprised-looking, capital face; a ripe little mouth, that seemed made to be kissed —as no doubt it was; all kinds of good little dots about her chin, that melted into one another when she laughed; and the sunniest pair of eyes you ever saw in any little creature's head. Altogether she was what you would have called provoking, you know; but satisfactory, too. Oh, perfectly satisfactory!

"He's a comical old fellow," said Scrooge's nephew, "that's the truth; and not so pleasant as he might be. However, his offences carry their own punishment, and I have nothing to say against him."

"I'm sure he is very rich, Fred," hinted Scrooge's niece. "At least you always tell me so."

"What of that, my dear!" said Scrooge's nephew. "His wealth is of no use to him. He don't do any good with it. He don't make himself comfortable with it. He hasn't the satisfaction of thinking—ha, ha, ha! —that he is ever going to benefit Us with it."

"I have no patience with him," observed Scrooge's niece. Scrooge's niece's sisters, and all the other ladies, expressed the same opinion.

"Oh, I have!" said Scrooge's nephew. "I am sorry for him; I couldn't be angry with him if I tried. Who suffers by his ill whims? Himself, always. Here, he takes it into his head to dislike us, and he won't come and dine with us. What's the consequence? He don't lose much of a dinner."

"Indeed, I think he loses a very good dinner," interrupted Scrooge's niece. Everybody else said the same, and they must be allowed to have been competent judges, because they had just had dinner; and, with the dessert upon the table, were clustered around the fire, by lamplight.

"Well! I'm very glad to hear it," said Scrooge's nephew, "because I haven't any great faith in these young housekeepers. What do *you* say, Topper?"

Topper had clearly got his eye upon one of Scrooge's niece's sisters, for he answered that a bachelor was a wretched outcast, who had no right to express an opinion on the subject. Whereat Scrooge's niece's sister—the plump one with the lace tucker: not the one with the roses—blushed.

"Do go on, Fred," said Scrooge's niece, clapping her hands. "He never finishes what he begins to say! He is such a ridiculous fellow!"

Scrooge's nephew revelled in another laugh, and as it was impossible to keep the infection off; though the plump sister tried hard to do it with aromatic vinegar: his example was unanimously followed.

"I was only going to say," said Scrooge's nephew, "that the consequence of his taking a dislike to us, and not making merry with us, is, as I think, that he loses some pleasant moments, which could do him no harm. I am sure he loses pleasanter companions than he can find in his own thoughts, either in his mouldy old office, or his dusty chambers. I mean to give him the same chance every year, whether he likes it or not, for I pity him. He may rail at Christmas till he dies, but he can't help thinking better of it—I defy him—if he finds me going there, in good temper, year after year, and saying 'Uncle Scrooge, how are you?' If it only puts him in the vein to leave his poor clerk fifty pounds, *that's* something; and I think I shook him yesterday."

It was their turn to laugh now at the notion of his shaking Scrooge. But being thoroughly good-natured, and not much caring what they laughed at, so that they laughed at any rate, he encouraged them in their merriment, and passed the bottle joyously.

After tea, they had some music. For they were a musical family, and knew what they were about, when they sang a Glee or Catch, I can assure you: especially Topper, who could growl away in the bass like a good one, and never swell the large veins in his forehead, or get red in the face over it. Scrooge's niece played well upon the harp; and played among other tunes a simple little air (a mere nothing: you might learn to whistle it in two minutes), which had been familiar to the child who fetched Scrooge from the boarding-school, as he had been reminded by the Ghost of Christmas Past. When this strain of music sounded, all the things that Ghost had shown him, came upon his mind; he softened more and more; and thought that if he could have listened to it often, years ago, he might have cultivated the kindnesses of life for his own happiness with his own hands, without resorting to the sexton's spade that buried Jacob Marley.

But they didn't devote the whole evening to music. After a while they played at forfeits; for it is good to be children sometimes, and never better than at Christmas, when its mighty Founder was a child himself. Stop! There was first a game at blindman's buff. Of course there was. And I no more believe Topper was really blind than I believe he had eyes in his boots. My opinion is, that it was a done thing between him and Scrooge's nephew: and that the Ghost of Christmas Present knew it. The way he went after that plump sister in the lace tucker, was an outrage on the credulity of human nature. Knocking down the fire-irons, tumbling over the chairs, bumping up against the piano, smothering himself among the curtains, wherever she went, there went he. He always knew where the plump sister was. He wouldn't catch anybody else. If you had fallen up against him, as some of them did, and stood there; he would have made a feint of endeavouring to seize you, which would have been an affront to your understanding; and would instantly have sidled off in the direction of the plump sister. She often cried out that it wasn't fair; and it really was not. But when at last, he caught her; when, in spite of all her silken rustlings, and her rapid flutterings past him, he got her into a corner whence there was no escape; then his conduct was the most execrable. For his pretending not to know her; his pretending that it was necessary to touch her head-dress, and further to assure himself of her identity by pressing a certain ring upon her finger, and a certain chain about her neck; was vile, monstrous! No doubt she told him her opinion of it, when, another blindman being in office, they were so confidential together, behind the curtains.

Scrooge's niece was not one of the blindman's buff party, but was made comfortable with a large chair and a footstool, in a snug corner, where the Ghost and Scrooge were close behind her. But she joined in the forfeits, and loved her love to admiration with all the letters of the alphabet. Likewise at the game of How, When, and Where, she was very great, and to the secret joy of Scrooge's nephew, beat her sisters hollow; though they were sharp girls too, as Topper could have told you. There might have been twenty people there, young and old, but they all played, and so did Scrooge; for, wholly forgetting in the interest he had in what was going on, that his voice made no sound in their ears, he sometimes came out with his guess quite loud, and very often guessed quite right, too; for the sharpest needle, best Whitechapel, warranted not to cut in the eye, was not sharper than Scrooge: blunt as he took it in his head to be.

The Ghost was greatly pleased to find him in this mood, and looked upon him with such favour, that he begged like a boy to be allowed to stay until the guests departed. But this the Spirit said could not be done.

"Here is a new game," said Scrooge. "One half-hour, Spirit, only one!"

It is a Game called Yes and No, where Scrooge's nephew had to think of something, and the rest must find out what; he only answering to their questions yes or no, as the case was. The brisk fire of questioning to which he was exposed, elicited from him that he was thinking of an animal, a live animal, rather a disagreeable animal, a savage animal, an animal that growled and grunted sometimes, and talked sometimes, and lived in London, and walked about the streets, and wasn't made a show of, and wasn't led by anybody, and didn't live in a menagerie, and was never killed in a market, and was not a horse, or an ass, or a cow, or a bull, or a tiger, or a dog, or a pig, or a cat, or a bear. At every fresh question that was put to him, this nephew burst into a fresh roar of laughter; and was so inexpressibly tickled, that he was obliged to get up off the sofa and stamp. At last the plump sister, falling into a similar state, cried out:—

"I have found it out! I know what it is, Fred! I know what it is!"

"What is it?" cried Fred.

"It's your Uncle Scro-o-o-o-oge!"

Which it certainly was. Admiration was the universal sentiment, though some objected that the reply to "Is it a bear?" ought to have been "Yes;" inasmuch as an answer in the negative was sufficient to have diverted their thoughts from Mr. Scrooge, supposing they had ever had any tendency that way.

"He has given us plenty of merriment, I am sure," said Fred, "and it would be ungrateful not to drink his health. Here is a glass of mulled wine ready to our hand at the moment; and I say, 'Uncle Scrooge!'"

"Well! Uncle Scrooge!" they cried.

"A Merry Christmas and a Happy New Year to the old man, whatever he is!" said Scrooge's nephew. "He wouldn't take it from me, but may he have it, nevertheless. Uncle Scrooge!"

Uncle Scrooge had imperceptibly become so gay and light of heart, that he would have pledged the unconscious company in return, and thanked them in an inaudible speech, if the Ghost had given him time. But the whole scene passed off in the breath of the last word spoken by his nephew; and he and the Spirit were again upon their travels.

Much they saw, and far they went, and many homes they visited, but always with a happy end. The Spirit stood beside sick beds, and they were cheerful; on foreign lands, and they

were close at home; by struggling men, and they were patient in their greater hope; by poverty, and it was rich. In almshouse, hospital, and jail, in misery's every refuge, where vain man in his little brief authority had not made fast the door, and barred the Spirit out, he left his blessing, and taught Scrooge his precepts.

It was a long night, if it were only a night; but Scrooge had his doubts of this, because the Christmas Holidays appeared to be condensed into the space of time they passed together. It was strange, too, that while Scrooge remained unaltered in his outward form, the Ghost grew older, clearly older. Scrooge had observed this change, but never spoke of it, until they left a children's Twelfth Night party, when, looking at the Spirit as they stood together in an open place, he noticed that its hair was gray.

"Are spirits' lives so short?" asked Scrooge.

"My life upon this globe, is very brief," replied the Ghost. "It ends to-night."

"To-night!" cried Scrooge.

"To-night at midnight. Hark! The time is drawing near."

The chimes were ringing the three quarters past eleven at that moment.

"Forgive me if I am not justified in what I ask," said Scrooge, looking intently at the Spirit's robe, "but I see something strange, and not belonging to yourself, protruding from your skirts. Is it a foot or a claw?"

"It might be a claw, for the flesh there is upon it," was the Spirit's sorrowful reply. "Look here."

From the foldings of its robe, it brought two children; wretched, abject, frightful, hideous, miserable. They knelt down at its feet, and clung upon the outside of its garment.

"Oh, Man! look here. Look, look,

down here!" exclaimed the Ghost.

They were a boy and girl. Yellow, meagre, ragged, scowling, wolfish; but prostrate, too, in their humility. Where graceful youth should have filled their features out, and touched them with its freshest tints, a stale and shrivelled hand, like that of age, had pinched, and twisted them, and pulled them into shreds. Where angels might have sat enthroned, devils lurked, and glared out menacing. No change, no degradation, no perversion of humanity, in any grade, through all the mysteries of wonderful creation, has monsters half so horrible and dread.

Scrooge started back, appalled. Having them shown to him in this way, he tried to say they were fine children, but the words choked themselves, rather than be parties to a lie of such enormous magnitude.

"Spirit! are they yours?" Scrooge could say no more.

"They are Man's," said the Spirit, looking down upon them. "And they cling to me, appealing from their fathers. This boy is Ignorance. This girl is Want. Beware them both, and all of their degree, but most of all beware this boy, for on his brow I see that written which is Doom, unless the writing be erased. Deny it!" cried the Spirit, stretching out its hand toward the city. "Slander those who tell it ye! Admit it for your factious purposes, and make it worse! And bide the end!"

"Have they no refuge or resource?" cried Scrooge.

"Are there no prisons?" said the Spirit, turning on him for the last time with his own words. "Are there no workhouses?"

The bell struck twelve.

Scrooge looked about him for the Ghost, and saw it not. As the last stroke ceased to vibrate, he remem-bered the prediction of old Jacob Marley, and lifting up his eyes, beheld a solemn Phantom, draped and hooded, coming, like a mist along the ground, towards him.

STAVE FOUR

THE LAST OF THE SPIRITS

THE Phantom slowly, gravely, silently approached. When it came near him, Scrooge bent down upon his knee; for in the very air through which this Spirit moved it seemed to scatter gloom and mystery.

It was shrouded in a deep black garment, which concealed its head, its face, its form, and left nothing of it visible save one outstretched hand. But for this it would have been difficult to detach its figure from the night, and separate it from the darkness by which it was surrounded.

He felt that it was tall and stately when it came beside him, and that its mysterious presence filled him with a solemn dread. He knew no more, for the Spirit neither spoke nor moved.

"I am in the presence of the Ghost of Christmas Yet To Come?" said Scrooge.

The Spirit answered not, but pointed downward with its hand.

"You are about to show me shadows of the things that have not happened, but will happen in the time before us," Scrooge pursued. "Is that so, Spirit?"

The upper portion of the garment was contracted for an instant in its folds, as if the Spirit had inclined its head. That was the only answer he received.

Although well used to ghostly company by this time, Scrooge feared the silent shape so much that his legs trembled beneath him, and he found that he could hardly stand when he prepared to follow it. The Spirit paused a moment, as observing his condition, and giving him time to recover.

But Scrooge was all the worse for this. It thrilled him with a vague uncertain horror, to know that behind the dusky shroud there were ghostly eyes intently fixed upon him, while he, though he stretched his own to the utmost, could see nothing but a spectral hand and one great heap of black.

"Ghost of the Future!" he exclaimed, "I fear you more than any Spectre I have seen. But, as I know your purpose is to do me good, and as I hope to live to be another man from what I was, I am prepared to bear you company, and do it with a thankful heart. Will you not speak to me?"

It gave him no reply. The hand was pointed straight before them.

"Lead on!" said Scrooge. "Lead on! The night is waning fast, and it is precious time to me, I know. Lead on, Spirit!"

The Phantom moved away as it had come towards him. Scrooge followed in the shadow of its dress, which bore him up, he thought, and carried him along.

They scarcely seemed to enter the city; for the city rather seemed to spring up about them, and encompass them of its own act. But there they were, in the heart of it; on 'Change, amongst the merchants; who hurried up and down, and chinked the money in their pockets, and conversed in groups, and looked at their watches, and trifled thoughtfully with their great gold seals; and so forth, as Scrooge had seen them often.

The Spirit stopped beside one little knot of business men. Observing that the hand was pointed to them, Scrooge advanced to listen to their talk.

"No," said a great fat man with a monstrous chin, "I don't know much about it, either way. I only know he's dead."

"When did he die?" inquired another.

"Last night, I believe."

"Why, what was the matter with him?" asked a third, taking a vast quantity of snuff out of a very large snuff-box. "I thought he'd never die."

"God knows," said the first, with a yawn.

"What has he done with his money?" asked a red-faced gentleman with a pendulous excrescence on the end of his nose, that shook like the gills of a turkey-cock.

"I haven't heard," said the man with the large chin, yawning again. "Left it to his Company, perhaps. He hasn't left it to *me*. That's all I know."

This pleasantry was received with a general laugh.

"It's likely to be a very cheap funeral," said the same speaker; "for upon my life I don't know of anybody to go to it. Suppose we make up a party and volunteer?"

"I don't mind going if a lunch is provided," observed the gentleman with the excrescence on his nose. "But I must be fed, if I make one."

Another laugh.

"Well, I am the most disinterested among you, after all," said the first speaker, "for I never wear black gloves, and I never eat lunch. But I'll offer to go, if anybody else will. When I come to think of it, I'm not at all sure that I wasn't his most particular friend; for we used to stop and speak whenever we met. Bye, bye!"

Speakers and listeners strolled away, and mixed with other groups.

Scrooge knew the men, and looked towards the Spirit for an explanation.

The Phantom glided on into a street. Its finger pointed to two persons meeting. Scrooge listened again, thinking that the explanation might lie here.

He knew these men, also, perfectly. They were men of business: very wealthy, and of great importance. He had made a point always of standing well in their esteem: in a business point of view, that is; strictly in a business point of view.

"How are you?" said one.

"How are you?" returned the other.

"Well!" said the first. "Old Scratch has got his own at last, hey?"

"So I am told," returned the second. "Cold, isn't it?"

"Seasonable for Christmas time. You're not a skater, I suppose?"

"No. No. Something else to think of. Good morning!"

Not another word. That was their meeting, their conversation, and their parting.

Scrooge was at first inclined to be surprised that the Spirit should attach importance to conversations apparently so trivial; but feeling assured that they must have some hidden purpose, he set himself to consider what it was likely to be. They could scarcely be supposed to have any bearing on the death of Jacob, his old partner, for that was Past, and this Ghost's province was the Future. Nor could he think of any one immediately connected with himself, to whom he could apply them. But nothing doubting that to whomsoever they applied they had some latent moral for his own improvement, he resolved to treasure up every word he heard, and everything he saw; and especially to observe the shadow of himself when it appeared.

For he had an expectation that the conduct of his future self would give him the clew he missed, and would render the solution of these riddles easy.

He looked about in that very place for his own image; but another man stood in his accustomed corner, and though the clock pointed to his usual time of day for being there, he saw no likeness of himself among the multitudes that poured in through the Porch. It gave him little surprise, however; for he had been revolving in his mind a change of life, and thought and hoped he saw his new-born resolutions carried out in this.

Quiet and dark, beside him stood the Phantom, with its outstretched hand. When he roused himself from his thoughtful quest, he fancied from the turn of the hand, and its situation in reference to himself, that the Unseen Eyes were looking at him keenly. It made him shudder, and feel very cold.

They left the busy scene, and went into an obscure part of the town, where Scrooge had never penetrated before, although he recognized its situation, and its bad repute. The ways were foul and narrow; the shops and houses wretched; the people half-naked, drunken, slipshod, ugly. Alleys and archways, like so many cesspools, disgorged their offences of smell, and dirt, and life, upon the straggling streets; and the whole quarter reeked with crime, with filth, and misery.

Far in this den of infamous resort, there was a low-browed, beetling shop, below a pent-house roof, where iron, old rags, bottles, bones, and greasy offal, were bought. Upon the floor within, were piled up heaps of rusty keys, nails, chains, hinges, files, scales, weights, and refuse iron of all kinds. Secrets that few would like to scrutinize were bred and hidden in mountains of unseemly rags, masses of corrupt fat, and sepulchres of bones. Sitting in among the wares he dealt in, by a charcoal-stove, made of old bricks, was a gray-haired rascal, nearly seventy years of age; who had screened himself from the cold air without, by a frowzy curtaining of miscellaneous tatters, hung upon a line; and smoked his pipe in all the luxury of calm retirement.

Scrooge and the Phantom came into the presence of this man, just as a woman with a heavy bundle slunk into the shop. But she had scarcely entered, when another woman, similarly laden, came in too; and she was closely followed by a man in faded black, who was no less startled by the sight of them, than they had been upon the recognition of each other. After a short period of blank astonishment, in which the old man with the pipe had joined them, they all three burst into a laugh.

"Let the charwoman alone to be the first!" cried she who had entered first. "Let the laundress alone to be the second and let the undertaker's man alone to be the third. Look here, old Joe, here's a chance! If we haven't all three met here without meaning it!"

"You couldn't have met in a better place," said old Joe, removing his pipe from his mouth. "Come into the parlour. You were made free of it long ago, you know; and the other two an't strangers. Stop till I shut the door of the shop. Ah! How it skreeks! There an't such a rusty bit of metal in the place as its own hinges, I believe; and I'm sure there's no such old bones here, as mine. Ha, ha! We're all suitable to our calling, we're well matched. Come into the parlour. Come into the parlour."

The parlour was the space behind the screen of rags. The old man raked the fire together with an old stair-rod, and having trimmed his smoky lamp (for it was night) with the stem of his pipe, put it in his mouth again.

While he did this, the woman who had already spoken threw her bundle on the floor, and sat down in a flaunting manner on a stool; crossing her elbows on her knees, and looking with a bold defiance at the other two.

"What odds then! What odds, Mrs. Dilber?" said the woman. "Every person has a right to take care of themselves. *He* always did!"

"That's true, indeed!" said the laundress. "No man more so."

"Why, then, don't stand staring as if you was afraid, woman: who's the wiser? We're not going to pick holes in each other's coats, I suppose?"

"No, indeed!" said Mrs. Dilber and the man together. "We should hope not."

"Very well, then!" cried the woman. "That's enough. Who's the worse for the loss of a few things like these? Not a dead man, I suppose."

"No, indeed," said Mrs. Dilber, laughing.

"If he wanted to keep 'em after he was dead, a wicked old screw," pursued the woman, "why wasn't he natural in his lifetime? If he had been, he'd have had somebody to look after him when he was struck with Death, instead of lying gasping out his last there, alone by himself."

"It's the truest word that ever was spoke," said Mrs. Dilber. "It's a judgment on him."

"I wish it was a little heavier one," replied the woman; "and it should have been, you may depend upon it, if I could have laid my hands on anything else. Open that bundle, old Joe, and let me know the value of it. Speak out plain. I'm not afraid to be the first, nor afraid for them to see it. We knew pretty well that we were helping ourselves, before we met here, I believe. It's no sin. Open the bundle, Joe."

But the gallantry of her friends would not allow of this; and the man in faded black, mounting the breach first, produced *his* plunder. It was not extensive. A seal or two, a pencil-case, a pair of sleeve-buttons, and a brooch of no great value, were all. They were severally examined and appraised by old Joe, who chalked the sums he was disposed to give for each, upon the wall, and added them up into a total when he found there was nothing more to come.

"That's your account," said Joe, "and I wouldn't give another six-pence, if I was to be boiled for not doing it. Who's next?"

Mrs. Dilber was next. Sheets and towels, a little wearing apparel, two old-fashioned silver teaspoons, a pair of sugar-tongs, and a few boots. Her account was stated on the wall in the same manner.

"I always give too much to ladies. It's a weakness of mine, and that's the way I ruin myself," said old Joe. "That's your account. If you asked me for another penny, and made it an open question, I'd repent of being so liberal and knock off half-a-crown."

"And now undo *my* bundle, Joe," said the first woman.

Joe went down on his knees for the greater convenience of opening it, and having unfastened a great many knots, dragged out a large and heavy roll of some dark stuff.

"What do you call this?" said Joe. "Bed-curtains!"

"Ah!" returned the woman, laughing and leaning forward on her crossed arms. "Bed-curtains!"

"You don't mean to say you took

'em down, rings and all, with him lying there?" said Joe.

"Yes I do," replied the woman. "Why not?"

"You were born to make your fortune," said Joe, "and you'll certainly do it."

"I certainly shan't hold my hand, when I can get anything in it by reaching it out, for the sake of such a man as He was, I promise you, Joe," returned the woman, coolly. "Don't drop that oil upon the blankets, now."

"His blankets?" asked Joe.

"Whose else's do you think?" replied the woman. "He isn't likely to take cold without 'em, I dare say."

"I hope he didn't die of anything catching? Eh?" said old Joe, stopping in his work, and looking up.

"Don't you be afraid of that," returned the woman. "I ain't so fond of his company that I'd loiter about him for such things, if he did. Ah! you may look through that shirt till your eyes ache; but you won't find a hole in it, nor a threadbare place. It's the best he had, and a fine one too. They'd have wasted it, if it hadn't been for me."

"What do you call wasting of it?" asked old Joe.

"Putting it on him to be buried in, to be sure," replied the woman with a laugh. "Somebody was fool enough to do it, but I took it off again. If calico ain't good enough for such a purpose, it isn't good enough for anything. It's quite as becoming to the body. He can't look uglier than he did in that one."

Scrooge listened to this dialogue in horror. As they sat grouped about their spoil, in the scanty light afforded by the old man's lamp, he viewed them with a detestation and disgust, which could hardly have been greater, though they had been obscene demons, marketing the corpse itself.

"Ha, ha!" laughed the same woman, when old Joe, producing a flannel bag with money in it, told out their several gains upon the ground. "This is the end of it, you see! He frightened every one away from him when he was alive, to profit us when he was dead! Ha, ha, ha!"

"Spirit!" said Scrooge, shuddering from head to foot. "I see, I see. The case of this unhappy man might be my own. My life tends that way, now. Merciful Heaven, what is this!"

He recoiled in terror, for the scene had changed, and now he almost touched a bed: a bare, uncurtained bed: on which, beneath a ragged sheet, there lay a something covered up, which, though it was dumb, announced itself in awful language.

The room was very dark, too dark to be observed with any accuracy, though Scrooge glanced round it in obedience to a secret impulse, anxious to know what kind of room it was. A pale light, rising in the outer air, fell straight upon the bed; and on it, plundered and bereft, unwatched, unwept, uncared for, was the body of this man.

Scrooge glanced towards the Phantom. Its steady hand was pointed to the head. The cover was so carelessly adjusted that the slightest raising of it, the motion of a finger upon Scrooge's part, would have disclosed the face. He thought of it, felt how easy it would be to do, and longed to do it; but had no more power to withdraw the veil than to dismiss the spectre at his side.

Oh cold, cold, rigid, dreadful Death, set up thine altar here, and dress it with such terrors as thou hast at thy command: for this is thy dominion! But of the loved, revered, and honoured head, thou canst not turn one hair to thy dread purposes, or make one feature odious. It is not that the hand is heavy and will fall down when released; it is not that the heart and pulse are still; but that the hand WAS open, generous, and true; the heart brave, warm, and tender; and the pulse a man's. Strike, Shadow, strike! And see his good deeds springing from the wound, to sow the world with life immortal!

No voice pronounced these words in Scrooge's ears, and yet he heard them when he looked upon the bed. He thought, if this man could be raised up now, what would be his foremost thoughts? Avarice, hard dealing, griping cares? They have brought him to a rich end, truly!

He lay, in the dark empty house, with not a man, a woman, or a child, to say that he was kind to me in this or that, and for the memory of one kind word I will be kind to him. A cat was tearing at the door, and there was a sound of gnawing rats beneath the hearth-stone. What *they* wanted in the room of death, and why they were so restless and disturbed, Scrooge did not dare to think.

"Spirit!" he said, "this is a fearful place. In leaving it, I shall not leave its lesson, trust me. Let us go!"

Still the Ghost pointed with an unmoved finger to the head.

"I understand you," Scrooge returned, "and I would do it, if I could. But I have not the power, Spirit. I have not the power."

Again it seemed to look upon him.

"If there is any person in the town, who feels emotion caused by this man's death," said Scrooge quite agonized, "show that person to me, Spirit, I beseech you!"

The Phantom spread its dark robe before him for a moment, like a wing; and withdrawing it, revealed a room by daylight, where a mother and her children were.

She was expecting some one, and

with anxious eagerness; for she walked up and down the room; started at every sound; looked out from the window; glanced at the clock; tried, but in vain, to work with her needle; and could hardly bear the voices of the children in their play.

At length the long-expected knock was heard. She hurried to the door, and met her husband; a man whose face was careworn and depressed, though he was young. There was a remarkable expression in it now; a kind of serious delight of which he felt ashamed, and which he struggled to repress.

He sat down to the dinner that had been hoarding for him by the fire; and when she asked him faintly what news (which was not until after a long silence), he appeared embarrassed how to answer.

"Is it good," she said, "or bad?"—to help him.

"Bad," he answered.

"We are quite ruined?"

"No. There is hope yet, Caroline."

"If *he* relents," she said, amazed, "there is! Nothing is past hope, if such a miracle has happened."

"He is past relenting," said her husband. "He is dead."

She was a mild and patient creature if her face spoke truth; but she was thankful in her soul to hear it, and she said so, with clasped hands. She prayed forgiveness the next moment, and was sorry; but the first was the emotion of the heart.

"What the half-drunken woman whom I told you of last night, said to me, when I tried to see him and obtain a week's delay; and what I thought was a mere excuse to avoid me; turns out to have been quite true. He was not only very ill, but dying, then."

"To whom will our debt be transferred?"

"I don't know. But before that time we shall be ready with the money; and even though we were not, it would be bad fortune indeed to find so merciless a creditor in his successor. We may sleep to-night with light hearts, Caroline!"

Yes. Soften it as they would, their hearts were lighter. The children's faces, hushed, and clustered round to hear what they so little understood, were brighter; and it was a happier house for this man's death! The only emotion that the Ghost could show him, caused by the event, was one of pleasure.

"Let me see some tenderness connected with a death," said Scrooge; "or that dark chamber, Spirit, which we left just now, will be forever present to me."

The Ghost conducted him through several streets familiar to his feet; and as they went along, Scrooge looked here and there to find himself, but nowhere was he to be seen. They entered poor Bob Cratchit's house; the dwelling he had visited before; and found the mother and the children seated round the fire.

Quiet. Very quiet. The noisy little Cratchits were as still as statues in one corner, and sat looking up at Peter, who had a book before him. The mother and her daughters were engaged in sewing. But surely they were very quiet!

" 'And he took a child, and set him in the midst of them.' "

Where had Scrooge heard those words? He had not dreamed them. The boy must have read them out, as he and the Spirit crossed the threshold. Why did he not go on?

The mother laid her work upon the table, and put her hand up to her face.

"The colour hurts my eyes," she said.

The colour? Ah, poor Tiny Tim!

"They're better now again," said Cratchit's wife. "It makes them weak by candlelight; and I wouldn't show weak eyes to your father when he comes home, for the world. It must be near his time."

"Past it rather," Peter answered, shutting up his book. "But I think he's walked a little slower than he used, these few last evenings, mother."

They were very quiet again. At last she said, and in a steady cheerful voice, that only faltered once:—

"I have known him walk with—I have known him walk with Tiny Tim upon his shoulder, very fast indeed."

"And so have I," cried Peter. "Often."

"And so have I," exclaimed another. So had all.

"But he was very light to carry," she resumed, intent upon her work, "and his father loved him so, that it was no trouble—no trouble. And there is your father at the door!"

She hurried out to meet him; and little Bob in his comforter—he had need of it, poor fellow—came in. His tea was ready for him on the hob, and they all tried who should help him to it most. Then the two young Cratchits got upon his knees and laid, each child a little cheek, against his face, as if they said, "Don't mind it, father. Don't be grieved!"

Bob was very cheerful with them, and spoke pleasantly to all the family. He looked at the work upon the table, and praised the industry and speed of Mrs. Cratchit and the girls. They would be done long before Sunday he said.

"Sunday! You went to-day, then, Robert?" said his wife.

"Yes, my dear," returned Bob. "I wish you could have gone. It would have done you good to see how green a place it is. But you'll see it often. I promised him that I would walk there on a Sunday. My little, little child!" cried Bob. "My little child!"

He broke down all at once. He couldn't help it. If he could have helped it, he and his child would have been farther apart perhaps than they were.

He left the room, and went upstairs into the room above, which was lighted cheerfully, and hung with Christmas. There was a chair set close beside the child, and there were signs of some one having been there, lately. Poor Bob sat down in it, and when he had thought a little and composed himself, he kissed the little face. He was reconciled to what had happened, and went down again quite happy.

They drew about the fire, and talked; the girls and mother working still. Bob told them of the extraordinary kindness of Mr. Scrooge's nephew, whom he had scarcely seen but once, and who, meeting him in the street that day, and seeing that he looked a little—"just a little down you know," said Bob, inquired what had happened to distress him. "On which," said Bob, "for he is the pleasantest-spoken gentleman you ever heard, I told him. 'I am heartily sorry for it, Mr. Cratchit,' he said, 'and heartily sorry for your good wife.' By the bye, how he ever knew *that*, I don't know."

"Knew what, my dear?"

"Why, that you were a good wife," replied Bob.

"Everybody knows that!" said Peter.

"Very well observed, my boy!" cried Bob. "I hope they do. 'Heartily sorry,' he said, 'for your good wife. If I can be of service to you in any way,' he said, giving me his card, 'that's where I live. Pray come to me.' Now, it wasn't," cried Bob, "for the sake of anything he might be able to do for us, so much as for his kind way, that this was quite delightful. It really seemed as if he had known our Tiny Tim, and felt with us."

"I'm sure he's a good soul!" said Mrs. Cratchit.

"You would be surer of it, my dear," returned Bob, "if you saw and spoke to him. I shouldn't be at all surprised, mark what I say, if he got Peter a better situation."

"Only hear that, Peter," said Mrs. Cratchit.

"And then," cried one of the girls, "Peter will be keeping company with some one, and setting up for himself."

"Get along with you!" retorted Peter, grinning.

"It's just as likely as not," said Bob, "one of these days; though there's plenty of time for that, my dear. But however and whenever we part from one another, I am sure we shall none of us forget poor Tiny Tim—shall we—or this first parting that there was among us?"

"Never, father!" cried they all.

"And I know," said Bob, "I know, my dears, that when we recollect how patient and how mild he was; although he was a little, little child; we shall not quarrel easily among ourselves, and forget poor Tiny Tim in doing it."

"No, never, father!" they all cried again.

"I am very happy," said little Bob, "I am very happy!"

Mrs. Cratchit kissed him, his daughters kissed him, the two young Cratchits kissed him, and Peter and himself shook hands. Spirit of Tiny Tim, thy childish essence was from God!

"Spectre," said Scrooge, "something informs me that our parting moment is at hand. I know it, but I know not how. Tell me what man that was whom we saw lying dead?"

The Ghost of Christmas Yet To Come conveyed him, as before—though at a different time, he thought: indeed, there seemed no order in these latter visions, save that they were in the Future—into the resorts of business men, but showed him not himself. Indeed, the Spirit did not stay for anything, but went straight on, as to the end just now desired, until besought by Scrooge to tarry for a moment.

"This court," said Scrooge, "through which we hurry now, is where my place of occupation is, and has been for a length of time. I see the house. Let me behold what I shall be, in days to come!"

The Spirit stopped; the hand was pointed elsewhere.

"The house is yonder," Scrooge exclaimed. "Why do you point away?"

The inexorable finger underwent no change.

Scrooge hastened to the window of his office, and looked in. It was an office still, but not his. The furniture was not the same, and the figure in the chair was not himself. The Phantom pointed as before.

He joined it once again, and wondering why and whither he had gone, accompanied it until they reached an iron gate. He paused to look round before entering.

A churchyard. Here, then, the wretched man whose name he had now to learn, lay underneath the ground. It was a worthy place. Walled in by houses; overrun by grass and weeds, the growth of vegetation's death, not life; choked up with too much burying; fat with repleted appetite. A worthy place!

The Spirit stood among the graves, and pointed down to One. He advanced towards it trembling. The Phantom was exactly as it had been, but he dreaded that he saw new meaning in its solemn shape.

"Before I draw nearer to that stone to which you point," said Scrooge, "answer me one question. Are these the shadows of the things that Will be, or are they shadows of things that May be, only?"

Still the Ghost pointed downward to the grave by which it stood.

"Men's courses will foreshadow certain ends, to which, if persevered in, they must lead," said Scrooge. "But if the courses be departed from, the ends will change. Say it is thus with what you show me!"

The Spirit was immovable as ever.

Scrooge crept towards it, trembling as he went; and following the finger, read upon the stone of the neglected grave his own name, EBENEZER SCROOGE.

"Am *I* that man who lay upon the bed?" he cried, upon his knees.

The finger pointed from the grave to him, and back again.

"No, Spirit! Oh no, no!"

The finger still was there.

"Spirit!" he cried, tight clutching at its robe, "hear me! I am not the man I was. I will not be the man I must have been but for this intercourse. Why show me this, if I am past all hope!"

For the first time the hand appeared to shake.

"Good Spirit," he pursued, as down upon the ground he fell before it: "Your nature intercedes for me, and pities me. Assure me that I yet may change these shadows you have shown me, by an altered life!"

The kind hand trembled.

"I will honour Christmas in my heart, and try to keep it all the year.

I will live in the Past, the Present, and the Future. The Spirits of all Three shall strive within me. I will not shut out the lessons that they teach. Oh, tell me I may sponge away the writing on this stone!"

In his agony, he caught the spectral hand. It sought to free itself, but he was strong in his entreaty, and detained it. The Spirit, stronger yet, repulsed him.

Holding up his hands in one last prayer to have his fate reversed, he saw an alteration in the Phantom's hood and dress. It shrank, collapsed, and dwindled down into a bedpost.

STAVE FIVE

THE END OF IT

YES! and the bedpost was his own. The bed was his own, the room was his own. Best and happiest of all, the Time before him was his own, to make amends in!

"I will live in the Past, the Present, and the Future!" Scrooge repeated, as he scrambled out of bed. "The Spirits of all Three shall strive within me. Oh Jacob Marley! Heaven, and the Christmas Time be praised for this! I say it on my knees, old Jacob, on my knees!"

He was so fluttered and so glowing with his good intentions, that his broken voice would scarcely answer to his call. He had been sobbing violently in his conflict with the Spirit, and his face was wet with tears.

"They are not torn down," cried Scrooge, folding one of his bed-curtains in his arms, " they are not torn down, rings and all. They are here: I am here: the shadows of the things that would have been, may be dispelled. They will be. I know they will!"

His hands were busy with his garments all this time: turning them inside out, putting them on upside down, tearing them, mislaying them, making them parties to every kind of extravagance.

"I don't know what to do!" cried Scrooge, laughing and crying in the same breath; and making a perfect Laocoön of himself with his stockings. "I am as light as a feather, I am as happy as an angel, I am as merry as a schoolboy. I am as giddy as a drunken man. A Merry Christmas to everybody! A Happy New Year to all the world. Hallo here! Whoop! Hallo!"

He had frisked into the sitting-room, and was now standing there: perfectly winded.

"There's the saucepan that the gruel was in!" cried Scrooge, starting off again, and frisking round the fireplace. "There's the door, by which the Ghost of Jacob Marley entered! There's the corner where the Ghost of Christmas Present sat! There's the window where I saw the wandering Spirits! It's all right, it's all true, it all happened. Ha, ha, ha!"

Really, for a man who had been out of practice for so many years, it was a splendid laugh, a most illustrious laugh. The father of a long, long line of brilliant laughs!

"I don't know what day of the month it is!" said Scrooge. "I don't know how long I've been among the Spirits. I don't know anything. I'm quite a baby. Never mind. I don't care. I'd rather be a baby. Hallo! Whoop! Hallo here!"

He was checked in his transports by the churches ringing out the lustiest peals he had ever heard. Clash, clang, hammer, ding, dong, bell. Bell, dong, ding, hammer, clang, clash! Oh, glorious, glorious!

Running to the window, he opened it, and put out his head. No fog, no mist; clear, bright, jovial, stirring, cold; cold, piping for the blood to dance to; golden sunlight; heavenly sky; sweet fresh air; merry bells. Oh, glorious. Glorious!

"What's to-day?" cried Scrooge, calling downward to a boy in Sunday clothes, who perhaps had loitered in to look about him.

"Eh?" returned the boy, with all his might of wonder.

"What's to-day, my fine fellow?" said Scrooge.

"To-day!" replied the boy. "Why, CHRISTMAS DAY."

"It's Christmas Day!" said Scrooge to himself. "I haven't missed it. The Spirits have done it all in one night. They can do anything they like. Of course they can. Of course they can. Hallo, my fine fellow?"

"Hallo!" returned the boy.

"Do you know the Poulterer's, in the next street but one, at the corner?" Scrooge inquired.

"I should hope I did," replied the lad.

"An intelligent boy!" said Scrooge. "A remarkable boy! Do you know whether they've sold the prize Turkey that was hanging up there? Not the little prize Turkey: the big one?"

"What, the one as big as me?" returned the boy.

"What a delightful boy!" said Scrooge. "It's a pleasure to talk to him. Yes, my buck!"

"It's hanging there now," replied the boy.

"Is it?" said Scrooge. "Go and buy it."

"Walk-ER!"[13] exclaimed the boy.

"No, no," said Scrooge, "I am in earnest. Go and buy it, and tell 'em to bring it here, that I may give

---

[13]"*Walk-er!*" a slang term of surprise.

them the direction where to take it. Come back with the man, and I'll give you a shilling. Come back with him in less than five minutes, and I'll give you half a-crown!"

The boy was off like a shot. He must have had a steady hand at a trigger who could have got a shot off half so fast.

"I'll send it to Bob Cratchit's!" whispered Scrooge, rubbing his hands, and splitting with a laugh. "He shan't know who sends it. It's twice the size of Tiny Tim. Joe Miller[14] never made such a joke as sending it to Bob's will be!"

The hand in which he wrote the address was not a steady one, but write it he did, somehow, and went down stairs to open the street door, ready for the coming of the poulterer's man. As he stood there, waiting his arrival, the knocker caught his eye.

"I shall love it, as long as I live!" cried Scrooge, patting it with his hand. "I scarcely ever looked at it before. What an honest expression it has in its face! It's a wonderful knocker!—Here's the Turkey. Hallo! Whoop! How are you! Merry Christmas!"

It *was* a Turkey! He could never have stood upon his legs, that bird. He would have snapped 'em short off in a minute, like sticks of sealingwax.

"Why, it's impossible to carry that to Camden Town," said Scrooge. "You must have a cab."

The chuckle with which he said this, and the chuckle with which he paid for the turkey, and the chuckle with which he paid for the cab, and the chuckle with which he recompensed the boy, were only to be ex-

ceeded by the chuckle with which he sat down breathless in his chair again, and chuckled till he cried.

Shaving was not an easy task, for his hand continued to shake very much; and shaving requires attention, even when you don't dance while you are at it. But if he had cut the end of his nose off, he would have put a piece of sticking-plaster over it, and been quite satisfied.

He dressed himself "all in his best," and at last got out into the streets. The people were by this time pouring forth, as he had seen them with the Ghost of Christmas Present; and walking with his hands behind him, Scrooge regarded every one with a delighted smile. He looked so irresistibly pleasant, in a word, that three or four good-humoured fellows said, "Good morning, Sir! A Merry Christmas to you!" And Scrooge said often afterwards, that of all the blithe sounds he had ever heard, those were the blithest in his ears.

He had not gone far, when coming on towards him he beheld the portly gentleman, who had walked into his counting-house the day before and said, "Scrooge and Marley's, I believe?" It sent a pang across his heart to think how this old gentleman would look upon him when they met; but he knew what path lay straight before him, and he took it.

"My dear Sir," said Scrooge, quickening his pace, and taking the old gentleman by both his hands. "How do you do? I hope you succeeded yesterday. It was very kind of you. A Merry Christmas to you, Sir!"

"Mr. Scrooge?"

"Yes," said Scrooge. "That is my name, and I fear it may not be pleasant to you. Allow me to ask your pardon. And will you have the

---

[14]*Joe Miller,* a comic actor noted for his jokes.

goodness"—here Scrooge whispered in his ear.

"Lord bless me!" cried the gentleman, as if his breath were gone. "My dear Mr. Scrooge, are you serious?"

"If you please," said Scrooge. "Not a farthing less. A great many back-payments are included in it, I assure you. Will you do me that favour?"

"My dear Sir," said the other, shaking hands with him. "I don't know what to say to such munifi——"

"Don't say anything, please," retorted Scrooge. "Come and see me. Will you come and see me?"

"I will!" cried the old gentleman. And it was clear he meant to do it.

"Thank'ee," said Scrooge. "I am much obliged to you. I thank you fifty times. Bless you!"

He went to church, and walked about the streets, and watched the people hurrying to and fro, and patted children on the head, and questioned beggars, and looked down into the kitchens of houses, and up to the windows; and found that everything could yield him pleasure. He had never dreamed that any walk—that anything—could give him so much happiness. In the afternoon, he turned his steps towards his nephew's house.

He passed the door a dozen times, before he had the courage to go up and knock. But he made a dash, and did it:—

"Is your master at home, my dear?" said Scrooge to the girl. Nice girl! Very.

"Yes, Sir."

"Where is he, my love?" said Scrooge.

"He's in the dining-room, Sir, along with mistress. I'll show you upstairs, if you please."

"Thank'ee. He knows me," said Scrooge, with his hand already on the dining-room lock. "I'll go in here, my dear."

He turned it gently, and sidled his face in, round the door. They were looking at the table (which was spread out in great array); for these young housekeepers are always nervous on such points, and like to see that everything is right.

"Fred!" said Scrooge.

Dear heart alive, how his niece by marriage started! Scrooge had forgotten, for the moment, about her sitting in the corner with the foot-stool, or he wouldn't have done it, on any account.

"Why, bless my soul!" cried Fred, "who's that?"

"It's I. Your Uncle Scrooge. I have come to dinner. Will you let me in, Fred?"

Let him in! It is a mercy he didn't shake his arm off. He was at home in five minutes. Nothing could be heartier. His niece looked just the same. So did Topper when *he* came. So did the plump sister, when *she* came. So did everyone when *they* came. Wonderful party, wonderful games, wonderful unanimity, wonder-ful happiness!

But he was early at the office next morning. Oh, he was early there. If he could only be there first, and catch Bob Cratchit coming late! That was the thing he had set his heart upon.

And he did it; yes he did! The clock struck nine. No Bob. A quarter past. No Bob. He was full eighteen minutes and a half behind his time. Scrooge sat with his door wide open, that he might see him come into the Tank.

His hat was off, before he opened the door; his comforter too. He was on his stool in a jiffy; driving away with his pen, as if he were trying to overtake nine o'clock.

"Hallo!" growled Scrooge, in his accustomed voice as near as he could feign it. "What do you mean by coming here at this time of day?"

"I am very sorry, Sir," said Bob. "I *am* behind my time."

"You are?" repeated Scrooge. "Yes. I think you are. Step this way, Sir, if you please."

"It's only once a year, Sir," pleaded Bob, appearing from the Tank. "It shall not be repeated. I was making rather merry yesterday, Sir."

"Now, I'll tell you what, my friend," said Scrooge, "I am not going to stand this sort of thing any longer. And therefore," he continued, leaping from his stool, and giving Bob such a dig in the waistcoat that he staggered back into the Tank again: "and therefore I am about to raise your salary!"

Bob trembled, and got a little nearer to the ruler. He had a momentary idea of knocking Scrooge down with it; holding him; and calling to the people in the court for help and a strait waistcoat.

"A Merry Christmas, Bob!" said Scrooge, with an earnestness that could not be mistaken, as he clapped him on the back. "A merrier Christmas, Bob, my good fellow, than I have given you for many a year! I'll raise your salary, and endeavour to assist your struggling family, and we will discuss your affairs this very afternoon, over a Christmas bowl of smoking bishop, Bob! Make up the fires, and buy another coal-scuttle before you dot another i, Bob Cratchit!"

Scrooge was better than his word. He did it all, and infinitely more; and to Tiny Tim, who did NOT die, he was a second father. He became as good a friend, as good a master, and as good a man, as the good old city knew, or any other good old city, town, or borough, in the good old world. Some people laughed to see the alteration in him, but he let them laugh, and little heeded them; for he was wise enough to know that nothing ever happened on this globe, for good, at which some people did not have their fill of laughter in the outset; and knowing that such as these would be blind anyway, he thought it quite as well that they should wrinkle up their eyes in grins, as have the malady in less attractive forms. His own heart laughed: and that was quite enough for him.

He had no further intercourse with Spirits, but lived upon the Total Abstinence Principle, ever afterwards; and it was always said of him, that he knew how to keep Christmas well, if any man alive possessed the knowledge. May that be truly said of us, and all of us! And so, as Tiny Tim observed, God Bless Us, Every One!

For Thought and Discussion
STAVE ONE

1. Who was Marley? Describe Scrooge. Describe the weather on this particular Christmas Eve.
2. What kind of person was Scrooge's nephew? What was Scrooge's reply to the gentlemen who asked for contributions for the poor? What did Scrooge do when the carol singer came to his door? Was Scrooge willing to give his clerk a holiday on Christmas?
3. Describe Scrooge's lodgings. Why was Scrooge startled at the

appearance of the knocker? Why did Scrooge like the darkness on the stairway?

4. What strange apparition appeared in his room? What reason did it give for its appearance? Of what did it warn Scrooge?

STAVE TWO

1. Describe the first Spirit. What did it represent? What did it show Scrooge? Who was the lonely boy in the schoolroom, and why do you feel sorry for him? Why did Scrooge remember the carol singer? Who was little Fan, and why did Scrooge feel bad after seeing her?
2. Who was old Fezziwig? Why was Scrooge glad to see him?
3. Who was the fair young girl, and what idol took her place in Scrooge's heart? What became of the girl?

STAVE THREE

1. How had Scrooge's room been transformed? What Spirit presided over the room? How was it dressed?
2. What signs of Christmas did Scrooge see as he moved with the Spirit above the earth?
3. Why did the Spirit spill the sprinklings of his torch at Bob Cratchit's door? Why were the Cratchits happy? Why do you admire Tiny Tim and sympathize with him? What shadows threatened his life? How were the spirits of the family affected by the mention of Scrooge's name?
4. How was Christmas kept at the miner's home? at the lighthouse? on the ship at sea?
5. How was Scrooge affected by hearing himself discussed at the table of his nephew?

STAVE FOUR

1. What was the third Spirit, and what did it propose to show Scrooge?
2. When the Spirit stopped beside a group of business men, what were they discussing?
3. What did Scrooge learn about himself from his visit to the slums?

STAVE FIVE

1. When Scrooge waked from his dream, how did he determine to keep Christmas? How did he celebrate Christmas?

CHARLES DICKENS

—————

CHARLES DICKENS 1812-1870

Christmas Carol. Tiny Tim's shouts of joy at Christmas, "God Bless Us All! Every One of Us!" seem to belong to all Christmas celebrations. Surely at least once a year, particularly during the holiday season, there should be an hour for reading Dickens's *Christmas Carol.* Old Scrooge, selfish, lonely, and parsimonious, railing against those who are happy, whose heart is changed by the visions of his childhood, is as real as Tiny Tim, the merry little lame boy. Of all writers Dickens has given the largest troupe of interesting characters: David Copperfield and his Aunt Betsy Trotwood, eccentric, fearless, and outspoken—how satisfying it is to have Aunt Betsy Trotwood come into the story and put everybody in his place without any foolishness—Peggoty, David's faithful nurse; Barkis of the unique proposal "Barkis is willin'," which won for him Peggoty of the solid virtues; Mr. Micawber, the ne'er-do-well, never discouraged over the overwhelming misfortunes which he succeeded in bringing down upon himself and family, always believing that there would be a gold mine over the next hill.

Early Life. Many of the facts of the novel, *David Copperfield,* are autobiographical. Dickens's father was Mr. Micawber in the flesh, and probably his mother was strangely like Mrs. Micawber.

The Dickens family seemed to have enjoyed a comfortable living in the early years of Charles's life. Later when they moved from Portsmouth to London, the father was imprisoned for debt, and Charles became a wage earner for a few years until a legacy from his mother's relatives restored the elder Dickens to his family. For a few years Charles was in school, such a school as is described in *Nicholas Nickleby*. Later on he studied law and became a newspaper reporter. His work led him to many strange nooks in London and gave him that first-hand knowledge of the underworld which enabled him to portray so vividly and realistically such characters as Fagan in *Oliver Twist*.

Literary Work. Dickens wrote a series of articles called *Sketches by Boz*, which attracted the attention of the reading public. Then when his *Pickwick Papers* appeared some time later, presenting the humorous characters, Mr. Pickwick and his stupid servant, Sam Weller, blundering into all sorts of ridiculous situations, his position in the literary world became assured.

The works of Dickens are characterized by an understanding of human nature, a sense of the ridiculous, and pathos, particularly in connection with children who are the victims of misfortune with which they are unable to cope, as was Little Nell in *Old Curiosity Shop*, Little Dorrit in the novel of that name, Little Dombey in *Dombey and Son*, and little Oliver of *Oliver Twist*.

The large number of figurines of Dickens's characters to be found in shops is an indication of their popular appeal. America has long had an appreciation for his works. In the nineties *Harper's Magazine* bought the American rights to his novel *Great Expectations*, for the sum of 6000 dollars. In 1934 when the manuscript of *The Life of Christ*, which was written by Dickens for his children, was offered to the public, the American publishing rights were bought by the United Features Syndicate for 200,000 dollars, fifteen dollars a word.

Lectures and Theatricals. From his earliest years Dickens was an actor, frequently mimicking those around him for the amusement of his friends. Later in life he often took part in private theatricals, particularly toward the end of his life when he had leisure and financial security.

After his literary fame was established, Dickens was called upon for lectures, and probably undermined his health by this work. At the age of fifty-eight years, he died at his home in Gadshill, a very beautiful place which he purchased in later life, located on the Canterbury Road twenty miles out from London.

A CONSECRATION
JOHN MASEFIELD

NOT of the princes and prelates with periwigged charioteers
Riding triumphantly laureled to lap the fat of the years—
Rather the scorned—the rejected— the men hemmed in with the spears;

The men of the tattered battalion which fights till it dies,
Dazed with the dust of the battle, the din and the cries,   5
The men with the broken heads and the blood running into their eyes.

Not the be-medaled Commander, be- loved of the throne,
Riding cock-horse to parade when the bugles are blown,
But the lads who carried the koppie and cannot be known.

Not the ruler for me, but the ranker, the tramp of the road,   10
The slave with the sack on his shoul- ders pricked on with the goad,
The man with too weighty a burden, too weary a load.

The sailor, the stoker of steamers, the man with the clout,
The chantyman bent at the halliards putting a tune to the shout,
The drowsy man at the wheel and the tired look-out.   15

Others may sing of the wine and the wealth and the mirth,
The portly presence of potentates goodly in girth—
Mine be the dirt and the dross, the dust and scum of the earth!

Theirs be the music, the color, the glory, the gold;
Mine be a handful of ashes, a mouth- ful of mold.   20
Of the maimed, of the halt and the blind in the rain and the cold—
Of these shall my songs be fashioned, my tales be told. *Amen.*

For Thought and Discussion

1. Upon whom does the chance of victory in war largely depend?
2. How does Masefield arouse your sympathy for the worker? Why is he able to do this?
3. How does hard work often make better circumstances in life impossible for the worker?
4. The economic conditions from 1928 to 1934 showed beyond a doubt that the general welfare of society depends upon individual welfare, or employment for all. How will sympathy for the overworked man create a different and better world?
5. Read the section of the text called "The Twentieth Century" for an understanding of new themes in literature.

Plus Work

In Mrs. Browning's "Cry of the Children" there is a sympathetic though somewhat sentimental picture of child labor conditions, and there is also a sympathetic treatment in *Oliver Twist* by Charles Dickens. In Carlyle's essay, *Past and Present,* and in Ruskin's essays, *Unto This Last, The Crown of Wild Olives,* and "Work," the evils of the English economic system are attacked from a very practical standpoint. Galsworthy's plays, *Strife* and *The Pigeon,* deal realistically with the conflict between capital and labor and with organized charity. Make a report on one or more of these.

JOHN MASEFIELD 1874—

Democratic Sympathies. In his poem "A Consecration" John Masefield proclaims his democracy and expresses his sympathy for the lowly and his faith in their worth. These sentiments were probably deciding factors in his appointment to the office of poet laureate after the death of Robert Bridges in 1930.

Early Life. John Masefield, who has become famous in the past few years, was born in Herefordshire, Ledbury, in 1874. Both his father and his mother died when he was quite young, leaving his rearing to an aunt.

As he was restless and fond of adventure, he went to sea when he was fourteen years old and remained on board a merchant ship for three years. He later decided to live ashore awhile and landed in New York with five dollars and some clothes. He says that he was glad to get work of any kind at that time. At any rate he tried various ways of making a living. At first he worked in a livery stable, later was an assistant to the bar-tender in a saloon, and afterwards became a foreman in a carpet factory. During that time he became aware of his penchant for poetry and spent much time in the public library perusing his favorite authors. He read Milton's *Paradise Lost* and memorized long passages. By reading

Chaucer he was inspired to choose writing for his life work.

Literary Career. In 1897 he returned to England to begin his literary career. He reviewed books and did other journalistic work to make a living; he wrote poems to satisfy his own heart and mind. Gradually and quietly his poetry gained for him recognition in the literary world.

Works. Five years after his return to England he published *Salt Water Ballads,* his first volume of verse, which was enthusiastically received by the reading public. In this volume Masefield shows that his life on the sea had been a rich experience. Lines from different poems describe the various phases of that life; as, the harshness and hard work of a seaman's life in "Fever and Chills"; the lure in the voice of the "old Atlantic" in "A Wanderer's Song"; the beauty and the color of the waves and the sky in "Roadways" and in *Dauber.*

Dauber, which is one of his longer poems, is a vivid description of the colorful life on a ship, a powerful portraiture of its harshness and of its contempt for weakness and cowardice. Above all there is the never-to-be-forgotten weakling aboard, the "dauber," yearning to paint the sea, and lacking the strong qualities of manhood demanded by seamen, yet arousing the sympathy of the reader. Another of Masefield's long poems, *The Widow in Bye Street,* gripping in its pathos, is the old tragic story of a son who through an infatuation with an unworthy woman loses his own sense of right and wrong, deserts his mother, and brings ruin on himself. Such poems as *Dauber* and *The Widow in Bye Street* are vivid and lasting and implant a broad, sympathetic understanding of life.

Present Interests. Among his present interests along with his writing, mention must be made of Masefield's fondness for the theater, which finds expression in his interest in amateur plays. At his home at Boar's Hill he has a stage and properties. Sometimes he takes a part, but he really prefers directing the plays in which local people appear. The costumes are made under the direction of his wife and daughter. His interest in plays is second only to his pleasure in writing poems, which continue to receive critical as well as popular acclaim.

~✒~

TO THE UNITED STATES OF AMERICA

ROBERT BRIDGES

[Robert Bridges was a London physician who practiced his profession in the early part of his life. He was poet laureate from 1913 until his death in 1931.]

BROTHERS in blood! They who this wrong began
To wreck our commonwealth, will rue the day
When first they challenged freemen to the fray,

And with the Briton dared the American.

Now are we pledged to win the rights of man; 5

Labor and justice now shall have their way,

And in a League of Peace—God grant we may—

Transform the earth, not patch up the old plan.

Sure is our hope since he who led your nation

Spake for mankind; and ye arose in awe 10

Of that high call to work the world's salvation;

Clearing your minds of all estranging blindness

In the vision of beauty and the spirit's law,

Freedom and honor and sweet loving-kindness.

For Thought and Discussion

1. Why does the poet say "Brothers in blood"?
2. For what does he hope?
3. In the last line, what does he say the world needs?
4. How would these characteristics free the world of some of its ills?
5. If loving-kindness, good will between all nations, should exist, what would be the attitude of nations toward war?

~~

AMERICAN AND BRITON
JOHN GALSWORTHY

[There are Americans and Britons and people of many other nationalities. For what we think of them, for what they think of us, and for the probable effect of that mutual opinion upon civilization, read this thoughtful essay by a man whose chief study was private family life and national family life in Great Britain.]

ON the mutual understanding of each other by Britons and Americans the future happiness of nations depends more than on any other world cause.

I have never held a whole-hearted brief for the British character. There is a lot of good in it, but much which is repellent. It has a kind of deliberate unattractiveness, setting out on its journey with the words: "Take me or leave me." One may respect a person of this sort, but it is difficult either to know or to like him. I am told that an American officer said recently to a British staff officer in a friendly voice: "So we're going to clean up Brother Boche together!" and the British staff officer replied "Really!" No wonder Americans sometimes say: "I've got no use for those fellows."

The world is consecrate to strangeness and discovery, and the attitude of mind concreted in that "Really!" seems unforgivable, till one remembers that it is manner rather than matter which divides the hearts of American and Briton.

In a huge, still half-developed country, where every kind of national type and habit comes to run a new thread into the rich tapestry of American life and thought, people must find it almost impossible to conceive the life of a little old island where traditions persist generation after generation without anything to break them up; where blood remains undoctored by new strains; demeanor becomes crystallized for lack of contrasts and manner gets set like a plaster mask. The English manner of today, of what are called the classes, is the growth of only a century or so. There was probably nothing at all like it in the days of Elizabeth or even of Charles II. The English manner was still racy when the inhabitants of Virginia, as we are told, sent over to ask that there might be dispatched to them some hierarchical assistance for the good of their souls, and were answered: "D——n your souls, grow tobacco!" The English manner of today could not even have come into its own when that epitaph of a lady, quoted somewhere by Gilbert Murray, was written: "Bland, passionate, and deeply religious, she was second cousin to the Earl of Leitrim; of such are the Kingdom of Heaven." About that gravestone motto was a certain lack of the self-consciousness which is now the foremost characteristic of the English manner.

But this British self-consciousness is no mere fluffy *gaucherie* (gaw-shair-ié); it is our special form of what Germans would call "Kultur." Behind every manifestation of thought or emotion the Briton retains control of self, and is thinking: "That's all I'll let them see"; even "That's all I'll let myself feel." This stoicism is good in its refusal to be foundered; bad in that it fosters a narrow outlook; starves emotion, spontaneity, and· frank sympathy; destroys grace and what one may describe roughly as the lovable side of personality. The English hardly ever say just what comes into their heads. What we call "good form," the unwritten law which governs certain classes of the Briton, savors of the dull and glacial; but there lurks within it a core of virtue. It has grown up like callous shell round two fine ideals—suppression of the ego lest it trample on the corns of other people, and exaltation of the maxim: "Deeds before words." Good form, like any other religion, starts well with some ethical truth, but soon gets commonized and petrified till we can hardly trace its origin, and watch with surprise its denial and contradiction of the root idea.

Without doubt good form had become a kind of disease in England. A French friend told me how he witnessed in a Swiss hotel the meeting between an Englishwoman and her son, whom she had not seen for two years; she was greatly affected— by the fact that he had not brought a dinner jacket. The best manners are no "manners," or at all events no mannerisms; but many Britons who have even attained to this perfect purity are yet not free from the paralytic effects of "good form"; are still self-conscious in the depths of their souls, and never do or say a thing without trying not to show what they are feeling. All this guarantees a certain decency in life; but in intimate intercourse with people of other nations who have not this particular cult of suppression, we English disappoint, and jar, and often irritate. Nations have their differing forms of snobbery. At one time the English all wanted to be second cousins to the Earl of Leitrim, like that lady bland and passionate. Nowadays it is not so simple. The Earl of Leitrim has become etherealized. We no longer care how a fellow is born so long as he behaves as the Earl of Leitrim would have, never makes himself conspicuous or ridiculous, never shows too much what he's really feeling, never talks of what he's going to do, and always "plays the game." The cult is centered in our public schools and universities.

At a very typical and honored old public school the writer of this essay passed on the whole a happy time; but what a curious life, educationally speaking! We lived rather like young Spartans; and were not encouraged to think, imagine, or see anything that we learned in relation to life at large. It's very difficult to teach boys, because their chief object in life is not to be taught anything, but I should say we were crammed, not taught at all. Living as we did the herd-life of boys with little or no intrusion from our elders, and they men who had been brought up in the same way as ourselves, we were debarred from any real interest in philosophy, history, art, literature and music, or any advancing notions in social life or politics. I speak of the generality, not of the few black swans among us. We were reactionaries almost to a boy. I remember one summer term Gladstone came down to speak to us, and we repaired to the Speech Room with white collars and dark hearts, muttering what we would do to that Grand Old Man if we could have our way. But he contrived to charm us, after all, till we cheered him vociferously. In that queer life we had all sorts of unwritten rules of suppression. You must turn up your trousers; must not go out with your umbrella rolled. Your hat must be worn tilted forward; you must not walk more than two abreast till you reached a certain form, nor

be enthusiastic about anything, except such a supreme matter as a drive over the pavilion at cricket, or a run the whole length of the ground at football. You must not talk about yourself or your home people, and for any punishment you must assume complete indifference.

I dwell on these trivialities because every year thousands of British boys enter these mills which grind exceeding small, and because these boys constitute in after life the great majority of the official, military, academic, professional, and a considerable proportion of the business classes of Great Britain. They become the Englishmen who say: "Really!" and they are for the most part the Englishmen who travel and reach America. The great defense I have always heard put up for our public schools is that they form character. As oatmeal is supposed to form bone in the bodies of Scotsmen, so our public schools are supposed to form good, sound moral fiber in British boys. And there is much in this plea. The life does make boys enduring, self-reliant, good-tempered and honorable, but it most carefully endeavors to destroy all original sin of individuality, spontaneity, and engaging freakishness. It implants, moreover, in the great majority of those who have lived it the mental attitude of that swell, who when asked where he went for his hats, replied: "Blank's, of course. Is there another fellow's?"

To know all is to excuse all—to know all about the bringing up of English public school boys makes one excuse much. The atmosphere and tradition of those places is extraordinarily strong, and persists through all modern changes. Thirty-seven years have gone since I was a new boy, but cross-examining a young nephew who left not long ago, I found almost precisely the same features and conditions. The war, which has changed so much of our social life, will have some, but no very great, effect on this particular institution. The boys still go there from the same kind of homes and preparatory schools and come under the same kind of masters. And the traditional unemotionalism, the cult of a dry and narrow stoicism, is rather fortified than diminished by the time we live in. . . .

We are, deep down, under all our lazy mentality, the most combative and competitive race in the world, with the exception, perhaps, of the American. This is at once a spiritual link between the two peoples. We are not sure whether we are better men than Americans. Whether we are really better than French, Germans, Russians, Italians, Chinese, or any other race is, of course, more than a question; but those peoples are all so different from us that we are bound, I suppose, secretly to consider ourselves superior. But between Americans and ourselves, under all differences, there is some mysterious deep kinship which causes us to doubt and makes us irritable, as if we were continually being tickled by that question: Now am I really a better man than he? Exactly what proportion of American blood at this time of day is British, I know not; but enough to make us definitely cousins—always an awkward relationship. We see in Americans a sort of image of ourselves; feel near enough, yet far enough, to criticise and carp at the points of difference. It is as though a man went out and encountered, in the street, what he thought for the moment was himself, and, wounded in his *amour propre,* instantly began to disparage the appearance of that fellow. Probably community of language rather than of blood accounts for our sense of kinship, for a common means of expression cannot but mold thought and feeling into some kind of unity. One can hardly overrate the intimacy which a common literature brings. The lives of great Americans, Washington and Franklin, Lincoln and Lee and Grant, are unsealed for us, just as to Americans are the lives of Marlborough and Nelson, Pitt and Gladstone and Gordon. Longfellow and Whittier and Whitman can be read by the British child as simply as Burns and Shelley and Keats. Emerson and William James are no more difficult to us than Darwin and Spencer to Americans. Without an effort we rejoice in Hawthorne and Mark Twain, Henry James and Howells, as Americans can in Dickens and Thackeray, Meredith and Thomas Hardy. And, more than all, Americans own with ourselves all literature in the English tongue before the Mayflower sailed; Chaucer and Spenser and Shakespeare, Raleigh, Ben Jonson, and the authors of the English Bible Version are their spiritual ancestors as much as ever they are ours. The tie of language is all-powerful—for language is the food formative of minds. A volume could be written on the formation of character by literary humor alone. The American and Briton, especially the British townsman, have a kind of bone-deep defiance of Fate, a readiness for anything which may turn up, a dry, wry smile under the blackest sky, and an individual way of looking at things which nothing can shake. Americans and Britons both, we must and will think for ourselves, and know why we do a thing before we do it. We have that ingrained respect for the individual conscience which is at the bottom of all free institutions. Some years before the war an intelligent and cultivated

Austrian, who had lived long in England, was asked for his opinion of the British. "In many ways," he said, "I think you are inferior to us; but one great thing I have noticed about you which we have not. You think and act and speak for yourselves." If he had passed those years in America instead of in England he must needs have pronounced the same judgment of Americans. Free speech, of course, like every form of freedom, goes in danger of its life in wartime. The other day, in Russia, an Englishman came on a street meeting shortly after the first revolution had begun. An extremist was addressing the gathering and telling them that they were fools to go on fighting, that they ought to refuse and go home, and so forth. The crowd grew angry, and some soldiers were for making a rush at him; but the chairman, a big burly peasant, stopped them with these words: "Brothers, you know that our country is now a country of free speech. We must listen to this man, we must let him say anything he will. But, brothers, when he's finished, we'll bash his head in!"

I cannot assert that either Britons or Americans are incapable in times like these of a similar interpretation of "free speech." Things have been done in our country, and will be done in America, which should make us blush. But so strong is the free instinct in both countries that some vestiges of it will survive even this war,[1] for democracy is a sham unless it means the preservation and development of this instinct of thinking for oneself throughout a people. "Government of the people, by the people, for the people" means nothing unless individuals keep their consciences un-

fettered and think freely. Accustom people to be nose-led and spoon-fed, and democracy is a mere pretense. The measure of democracy is the measure of the freedom and sense of individual responsibility in its humblest citizens. And democracy—I say with solemnity—has yet to prove itself. . . .

Ever since the substantial introduction of democracy nearly a century and a half ago with the American War of Independence, Western civilization has been living on two planes or levels—the autocratic plane, with which is bound up the idea of nationalism, and the democratic, to which has become conjoined the idea of internationalism. Not only little wars, but great wars such as this, come because of inequality in growth, dissimilarity of political institutions between states; because this state or that is basing its life on different principles from its neighbors. The decentralization, delays, critical temper, and the importance of home affairs prevalent in democratic countries make them at once slower, weaker, less apt to strike, and less prepared to strike than countries where bureaucratic brains subject to no real popular check devise world policies which can be thrust, prepared to the last button, on the world at a moment's notice. The free and critical spirit in America, France, and Britain has kept our democracies comparatively unprepared for anything save their own affairs.

We fall into glib usage of words like democracy and make fetiches of them without due understanding. Democracy is inferior to autocracy from the aggressively national point of view; it is not necessarily superior to autocracy as a guarantee of general well-being; it may even turn out to be inferior unless we can improve

---

[1] *war*, the World War, 1914-1918.

it. But democracy is the rising tide; it may be dammed or delayed, but cannot be stopped. It seems to be a law in human nature that where, in any corporate society, the idea of self-government sets foot it refuses to take that foot up again. State after state, copying the American example, has adopted the democratic principle; the world's face is that way set. And civilization is now so of a pattern that the Western world may be looked on as one state and the process of change therein from autocracy to democracy regarded as though it were taking place in a single old-time country such as Greece or Rome. If throughout Western civilization we can secure the single democratic principle of government, its single level of state morality in thought and action, we shall be well on our way to unanimity throughout the world; for even in China and Japan the democratic virus is at work. It is my belief that only in a world thus uniform, and freed from the danger of pounce by autocracies, have states any chance to develop the individual conscience to a point which shall make democracy proof against anarchy and themselves proof against dissolution; and only in such a world can a League of Nations to enforce peace succeed.

But even if we do secure a single plane for Western civilization and ultimately for the world, there will be but slow and difficult progress in the lot of mankind. And unless we secure it, there will be only a march backward.

For this advance to a uniform civilization the solidarity of the English-speaking races is vital. Without that there will be no bottom on which to build.

The ancestors of the American people sought a new country because they had in them a reverence for the individual conscience; they came from Britain, the first large state in the Christian era to build up the idea of political freedom. The instincts and ideals of our two races have ever been the same. That great and lovable people, the French, with their clear thought and expression, and their quick blood, have expressed those ideals more vividly than either of us. But the phlegmatic and the dry tenacity of our English and American temperaments has ever made our countries the most settled and safe homes of the individual conscience, and of its children—Democracy, Freedom, and Internationalism. Whatever their faults—and their offenses cry aloud to such poor heaven as remains of chivalry and mercy— the Germans are in many ways a great race, but they possess two qualities dangerous to the individual conscience—unquestioning obedience and exaltation. When they embrace the democratic idea they may surpass us all in its logical development, but the individual conscience will still not be at ease with them. We must look to our two countries to guarantee its strength and activity, and if we English-speaking races quarrel and become disunited, civilization will split up again and go its way to ruin. We are the ballast of the new order.

I do not believe in formal alliances or in grouping nations to exclude and keep down other nations. Friendships between countries should have the only true reality of common sentiment, *and be animated by desire for the general welfare of mankind.* We need no formal bonds, but we have a sacred charge in common, to let no petty matters, differences of manner, or divergences of material interest, destroy our spiritual agreement. Our pasts, our geographical positions, our temperaments make us, beyond all other races, the hope and trustees of mankind's advance along the only lines now open—democratic internationalism. It is childish to claim for Americans or Britons virtues beyond those of other nations, or to believe in the superiority of one national culture to another; they are in this position of guardianship to the main line of human development; no need to pat ourselves on the back about it. But we are at a great and critical moment in the world's history—how critical none of us alive will ever realize. The civilization slowly built since the fall of Rome has either to break up and dissolve into jagged and isolated fragments through a century of war; or, unified and reanimated by a single idea, to move forward on one plane and attain greater height and breadth.

Under the pressure of this war there is, beneath the lip-service we pay to democracy, a disposition to lose faith in it because of its undoubted weakness and inconvenience in a struggle with states autocratically governed; there is even a sort of secret reaction to autocracy. On those lines there is no way out of a future of bitter rivalries, chicanery and wars, and the probable total failure of our civilization. The only cure which I can see lies in democratizing the whole world and removing the present weaknesses and shams of democracy by education of the individual conscience in every country. Goodby to that chance if Americans and Britons fall foul of each other, refuse to pool their thoughts and hopes, and to keep the general welfare of mankind in view. They have got to stand together, not in aggressive and jealous policies, but in defense and championship of the self-helpful, self-governing, "live and let live" philosophy of life.

The house of the future is always dark. There are few cornerstones to be discerned in the temple of our fate. But of these few one is the brotherhood and bond of the English-speaking races, not for narrow purposes, but that mankind may yet see faith and good-will enshrined, yet breathe a sweeter air, and know a life where Beauty passes, with the sun on her wings.

We want in the lives of men a "Song of Honor," as in Ralph Hodgson's poem:

The song of men all sorts and kinds,
As many tempers, moods and minds
    As leaves are on a tree,
As many faiths and castes and creeds,
As many human bloods and breeds,
    As in the world may be.

In the making of that song the English-speaking races will assuredly unite. What made this world we know not; the principle of life is inscrutable and will forever be; but we know that Earth is yet on the upgrade of existence, the mountain top of man's life not reached, that many centuries of growth are yet in front of us before Nature begins to chill this planet till it swims, at last, another moon, in space. In the climb to that mountain top of a happy life for mankind our two great nations are as guides who go before, roped together in perilous ascent. On their nerve, loyalty, and wisdom the adventure now hangs. What American or British knife will sever the rope?

He who ever gives a thought to the life of man at large, to his miseries and disappointments, to the waste and cruelty of existence, will remember that if American or Briton fail himself, or fail the other, there can but be for us both, and for all other peoples, a hideous slip, a swift and fearful fall into an abyss, whence all shall be to begin over again.

We shall not fail—neither ourselves, nor each other. Our comradeship will endure.

For Thought and Discussion

1. What are the ties between the people of America and the people of Great Britain? What are the notable differences between them?
2. What does Galsworthy consider the foundation of all free institutions?
3. What does the author affirm is the only certain basis of good will between nations?
4. What are the disadvantages and the advantages of conforming strictly to conventions?
5. Does the term *democracy* have great significance today? Or is it, as Galsworthy declares, too often but a fetich? Justify your answer.
6. Quote lines which are suggestive of poetry. Do you think these lines add to the effectiveness of Galsworthy's prose style?
7. Memorize a passage notable for strength and beauty.

≈≈

THE BALLAD OF EAST AND WEST
RUDYARD KIPLING

*Oh, East is East, and West is West,
   and never the twain shall meet,
Till Earth and Sky stand presently at
   God's great Judgment Seat;
But there is neither East nor West,
   Border, nor Breed, nor Birth,
When two strong men stand face to
   face, though they come from the
   ends of the earth.*

Kamal is out with twenty men to
   raise the Border side,   5
And he has lifted the Colonel's mare
   that is the Colonel's pride.
He has lifted her out of the stable-
   door between the dawn and the
   day,
And turned the calkins upon her
   feet, and ridden her far away.

Then up and spoke the Colonel's son
   that led a troop of the Guides:
"Is there never a man of all my men
   can say where Kamal hides?"   10
Then up and spoke Mohammed Khan,
   the son of the Ressaldar:
"If ye know the track of the morning mist, ye know where his pickets are.
At dusk he harries the Abazai—at dawn he is into Bonair,
But he must go by Fort Bukloh to his own place to fare.
So if ye gallop to Fort Bukloh as fast as a bird can fly,   15
By the favor of God ye may cut him off ere he win to the Tongue of Jagai.

But if he be past the Tongue of Jagai,
  right swiftly turn ye then,
For the length and the breadth of
  that grisly plain is sown with
  Kamal's men.
There is rock to the left, and rock to
  the right, and low lean thorn between,
And ye may hear a breech-bolt snick
  where never a man is seen."   20
The Colonel's son has taken a horse,
  and a raw rough dun was he,
With the mouth of a bell and the
  heart of Hell and the head of a
  gallows-tree.
The Colonel's son to the Fort has won,
  they bid him stay to eat—
Who rides at the tail of a Border
  thief, he sits not long at his meat.
He's up and away from Fort Bukloh
  as fast as he can fly,   25
Till he was aware of his father's mare
  in the gut of the Tongue of
  Jagai,
Till he was aware of his father's mare
  with Kamal upon her back,
And when he could spy the white of
  her eye, he made the pistol crack.
He has fired once, he has fired twice,
  but the whistling ball went wide.
"Ye shoot like a soldier," Kamal said.
  "Show now if ye can ride!"   30
It's up and over the Tongue of Jagai,
  as blown dust-devils go,
The dun he fled like a stag of ten, but
  the mare like a barren doe.
The dun he leaned against the bit and
  slugged his head above,
But the red mare played with the
  snaffle-bars, as a maiden plays
  with a glove.
There was rock to the left and rock
  to the right, and low lean thorn
  between,   35
And thrice he heard a breech-bolt
  snick tho' never a man was seen.
They have ridden the low moon out
  of the sky, their hoofs drum up
  the dawn,

The dun he went like a wounded bull,
  but the mare like a new-roused
  fawn.
The dun he fell at a water-course—
  in a woeful heap fell he,
And Kamal has turned the red mare
  back, and pulled the rider free. 40
He has knocked the pistol out of his
  hand—small room was there to
  strive,
" 'Twas only by favor of mine";
  quoth he, "ye rode so long alive;
There was not a rock for twenty mile,
  there was not a clump of tree,
But covered a man of my own men
  with his rifle cocked on his knee.
If I had raised my bridle-hand, as I
  have held it low,   45
The little jackals that flee so fast were
  feasting all in a row.
If I had bowed my head on my
  breast, as I have held it high,
The kite that whistles above us now
  were gorged till she could not
  fly."
Lightly answered the Colonel's son:
  "Do good to bird and beast,
But count who come for the broken
  meats before thou makest a
  feast.   50
If there should follow a thousand
  swords to carry my bones away,
Belike the price of a jackal's meal were
  more than a thief could pay.
They will feed their horse on the
  standing crop, their men on the
  garnered grain,
The thatch of the byres will serve
  their fires when all the cattle are
  slain.
But if thou thinkest the price be fair
  —thy brethren wait to sup,   55
The hound is kin to the jackal-spawn
  —howl, dog, and call them up!
And if thou thinkest the price be
  high, in steer and gear and stack,
Give me my father's mare again, and
  I'll fight my own way back!"

Kamal has gripped him by the hand
 and set him upon his feet.
"No talk shall be of dogs," said he,
 "when wolf and gray wolf
 meet.   60
May I eat dirt if thou hast hurt of
 me in deed or breath;
What dam of lances brought thee
 forth to jest at the dawn with
 Death?"
Lightly answered the Colonel's son:
 "I hold by the blood of my clan;
Take up the mare for my father's
 gift—by God, she has carried a
 man!"
The red mare ran to the Colonel's son,
 and nuzzled against his breast; 65
"We be two strong men," said Kamal then, "but she loveth the
 younger best.
So she shall go with a lifter's dower,
 my turquoise-studded rein,
My 'broidered saddle and saddle-
 cloth, and silver stirrups twain."
The Colonel's son a pistol drew, and
 held it muzzle end,
"Ye have taken the one from a foe,"

said he; "will ye take the mate
 from a friend?"   70
"A gift for a gift," said Kamal
 straight; "a limb for the risk of
 a limb.
Thy father has sent his son to me, I'll
 send my son to him!"
With that he whistled his only son,
 that dropped from a mountain
 crest—
He trod the ling like a buck in spring,
 and he looked like a lance in
 rest.
"Now here is thy master," Kamal
 said, "who leads a troop of the
 Guides,   75
And thou must ride at his left side
 as shield on shoulder rides.
Till Death or I cut loose the tie, at
 camp and board and bed,
Thy life is his—thy fate it is to guard
 him with thy head.
So, thou must eat the White Queen's
 meat, and all her foes are thine,
And thou must harry thy father's
 hold for the peace of the Bor-
 der-line.   80

And thou must make a trooper tough
  and hack thy way to power—
Belike they will raise thee to Ressaldar
  when I am hanged in Peshawur."

They have looked each other between
  the eyes, and there have found
  no fault,
They have taken the oath of the Bro-
  ther-in-Blood on leavened bread
  and salt;
They have taken the oath of Brother-
  in-Blood on fire and fresh-cut
  sod,   85
On the hilt and the haft of the
  Khyber knife, and the Wondrous
  Names of God.
The Colonel's son he rides the mare
  and the Kamal's boy the dun,
And two have come back to Fort
  Bukloh where there went forth
  but one.

And when they drew to the Quarter-
  Guard, full twenty swords flew
  clear—
There was not a man but carried his
  feud with the blood of the
  mountaineer.   90
"Ha' done! ha' done!" said the Colonel's son. "Put up the steel at
  your sides!
Last night ye had struck at a Border
  thief—tonight 'tis a man of the
  Guides!"

Oh, East is East, and West is West,
  and never the twain shall meet,
Till Earth and Sky stand presently at
  God's great Judgment Seat;
But there is neither East nor West,
  Border, nor Breed, nor Birth,   95
When two strong men stand face to
  face, though they come from the
  ends of the earth!

For Thought and Discussion

1. What is the purpose of the first stanza?
2. What country did the Colonel represent?
3. Who was Kamal?
4. Why was the Colonel's son allowed to ride unharmed by Kamal's men?
5. Why did Kamal refuse to take the mare?
6. What gifts did Kamal give the Colonel's son?
7. Who was the "White Queen"?
8. Why did Kamal want his son to be with the Colonel's son?
9. Is this the natural way for a parent to act, to want his son to have a better chance in life than he has had?
10. Why is this ballad popular?
11. What is the purpose of the author?
12. In what way are the Olympic Games expressive of the racial attitude portrayed in this poem?

Plus Work

Find and report on other poems by Kipling that show his respect for courage and faithfulness irrespective of color and race.

BELTARBET'S PRIDE
GEORGE RUNNELL PREEDY

[George Runnell Preedy has been interested since childhood in history. In school he studied architecture and drawing, but he adopted writing for his profession. He travels much and is especially fond of long walking tours. He is fond of animals, as this story shows.]

THERE'S Lord Maskell's steward been this hour in the parlor; shall I send him on his road again?"

"And what will Lord Maskell's steward be doing here?" was the impatient answer.

"Nothing that's good, my lord. Shall I put him on his road again?"

The young man to whom this eager question was addressed dismounted from his beautiful horse, hesitated, then said: "No, I'll see him."

The servant, now holding the dark horse's head, protested with a stern anxiety:

"You'll see him? And it's the steward — the gentleman not coming himself?"

Lord Beltarbet paused on the steps of his decayed mansion. The wind was blowing about his hair, the autumn leaves scurried round his feet; it was the earliest hour of a lovely, soft twilight.

"Maybe there's trouble," mused he, smiling wistfully at the servant. "I've heard there'll be more risings in County Clare — maybe in County Wicklow."

"That, my lord," replied the stately servant, with a hard, grim look, "will be no affair of Lord Maskell or his steward."

"They're English," said Beltarbet, with cold bitterness, and he entered his ancient, ill-kept house. He flung off his hat in the shabby hall and, still holding his riding whip behind him, entered the parlor where the Englishman waited.

The Englishman introduced himself—Mr. Simon Ware, Lord Maskell's agent; though his manner was respectful, the little neat man conveyed perfectly well that he knew he was one of the conquerors speaking to one of the conquered; his very civility had an air of pity.

To him the dark young man in the worn riding suit was merely a member of a despised and defeated race, the descendant of generations of rebels whose estates and titles were confiscated, and who was only suffered to retain such property and barren honors as he possessed through the charity of the British Government.

Lord Beltarbet had naturally another estimation of himself, and it was one that was shared by thousands of his countrymen. Beltarbet should have been one of the least of his titles and Fournaughts one of the least of his demesnes[1]; he was by right Clare and Thomond, this Murrough O'Brien, one of the most famous names in Ireland.

The O'Briens had been princes in Clare before the Romans entered Britain, and generations of them had fallen on foreign battlefields rather than submit to the English; but Beltarbet's father had come home to die, and through the intercession of kindly folk at St. James' this little parcel of land in Wicklow and this small title of honor had been allowed to the last of the Princes of Clare.

Lord Maskell, whose steward stood near him now, had been granted most of the Clare estate and it was rumored that the young Englishman, who had rendered brilliant service in the field, was soon to be rewarded with a revival in his favor of the ancient titles of Clare and Thomond. Lord Beltar-

[1]*demesne,* domain, land reserved for the lord of the manor.

bet, who had grown up with pride and poverty, bitter, reckless, thriftless, trained in nothing but loneliness, hated all the English, and hated more than any other man Lord Maskell, who ruled in Clare and who was on the Lord Lieutenant's staff—definitely one of the conquerors.

The agent was not discomposed by the young man's stormy glance, but came concisely and with no show of hesitation to the heart of his errand.

"Lord Maskell charged me to ask, sir, if you would reconsider your refusal in the matter of Diarmuid, the horse?"

"You've wasted your errand," returned Beltarbet, dryly; "six months ago I told your master that the horse was not for sale."

"Lord Maskell thought," said the Englishman, smoothly, "that possibly you had reconsidered. He is prepared to give even a higher price— he recognizes he is a very beautiful animal."

"There's no finer horse in Ireland," cried Beltarbet, with a flash.

"There'll be no finer price ever paid for a horse, if you take what Lord Maskell offers. It's fifteen thousand pounds, and that"—with a sly glance round the staring poverty of the room—"is a large sum, Lord Beltarbet."

"I'll not sell the horse—the money is nothing to me."

"You said as much before, Lord Beltarbet," the Englishman reminded him, slyly, "in the matter of Earl Sigurd's bowl."

My lord turned his back upon the speaker and struggled for control by tapping the handle of his riding-whip on the worn window-frame; in all his short, unhappy life he had never done anything that he reviewed with such remorse and regret as the selling of Earl Sigurd's bowl, the last treasure of his family, which, according to a lovingly credited tradition, had been taken from the defeated invader by an O'Brien on the fierce and bloody field of Clontarf.

"I sold the bowl to keep the horse," he muttered, "and that's enough."

"Fifteen thousand pounds?" queried Mr. Ware, distantly, casually.

Beltarbet faced him:

"You know my poverty; you do not know, it seems, some other things of me. The horse is not for sale."

"A pity!" The steward seemed to regret the sumptuous foolishness of this young man as well as the disappointment to his master. "Lord Maskell meant to enter him for the races. The Lord Lieutenant is entering Comet, the English horse—"

"And I am entering mine—Diarmuid," said Beltarbet, sternly.

Mr. Simon Ware was definitely surprised. His pursed lips and his raised eyebrows showed that he considered it an ostentatious and ridiculous gesture of defiance for a penniless young Irishman to dare to compete in races which were the diversion of the English gentlemen in Dublin.

"There'll be a good many guineas on him—all that I and my friends can scrape up," said Beltarbet, frowning him down.

"You'd be safer, sir, to take the money that's offered; it is a reckless risk to put all on the hazard of the winning of a race."

"My family," smiled Beltarbet, bitterly, "are used to living at a hazard, sir."

The Englishman rose, took his hat and cane, and smiled agreeably.

"Just one word of warning, sir," he said, with a dry compassion for the dark young man. "It is well for you to have some friend at the viceregal court.[2] . . . The times are difficult for one in your position. . . . Lord Maskell might be able, some day, to do you a service."

"The day when I shall ask Lord Maskell, or any other Englishman, to do me a service will never dawn," replied Beltarbet, quietly. "You may tell your master as much. He has got my estates and will have, I hear, my titles. He has Earl Sigurd's bowl, which was my last treasure. He shall not have the horse. I have no more to say, sir, nor any hospitality to offer you."

The Englishman bowed, by no means discomposed. "There are rumors of trouble," he said, flicking his gloves on his hat. "I live in Dublin. I hear a good deal that, perhaps, does not come to your Lordship's ears in Fournaughts. A Roman Catholic gentleman with Irish sympathies would do well to be very careful during the next few weeks."

"Careful!" cried Beltarbet. "And why should I be careful? I've neither wife nor child; I'm the last of my house; I have nothing to lose. Tell your master that, if he sent this warning."

"And you'll not sell the horse offered for in a fair and friendly fashion?"

"Good-day to you, Mr. Ware!"

Lord Maskell's steward drove away in his neat carriage from the demesne of Fournaughts. Beltarbet came out on to the sunken threshold step and into the sweet windy evening. Luke Tandy, the servant, was waiting there like a sentinel.

"He came to buy the horse," said

---

[2]*viceregal court,* court of the provincial viceroy, ruling with the authority of a king.

Beltarbet. "That was his errand, Luke."

"You've sent him away?" asked Tandy, eagerly.

"I've sent him away," smiled Beltarbet. "I'm putting Diarmuid into the October races and I'll ride the horse, though all the English in Ireland be there to laugh at me."

"Did he say anything of the troubles?" asked Luke Tandy, keenly scanning his master's face.

"He gave me some manner of warning," replied Beltarbet; "maybe from his master. But what's the matter for that to me. I've nothing in the world to lose—except the horse and you, Luke Tandy."

He smiled into the elder man's eyes.

They stood shoulder to shoulder, the same height, something of the same build; but forty years, and all the difference between royal and peasant blood, between them. They loved each other.

Luke Tandy had twice saved the life of Beltarbet's father in foreign battles; Luke Tandy had brought Beltarbet himself, as a small child, home to the miserable demesne that was all that was left to the heir of Clare. Luke Tandy had taught him all he knew of arms and horsemanship, and brought him up in love and lore of Ireland, the legends and history of it, the tales of the Shee[3] and other unseen folk that haunt the oppressed and desolate land. Luke Tandy had served him, without wage or thought of a wage, for a poor bare living; he had been his close companion, his loving teacher in wood and field, walking by the banks of the Liffey, strolling in the shaded valley of Clara, riding through the haunted hollows of Boyne fields, be-

[3] *Shee,* one of the Irish fairies living in the fairy hills.

neath the tombs of Irish kings, or climbing the noble sides of Slieve Donard, blue in the blue. To Luke Tandy, Beltarbet was a prince of ancient and pure race, and a boy dearer to him than his own two sons whom he had lost in the dreary hardships of long exile.

Beltarbet gazed earnestly at the face of his one friend, companion and servant.

"I had no right to refuse to sell the horse," he said. "There were pride and temper in that, although the animal is my own darling. I should have taken the money, and, maybe, built up the house again, and helped the creatures who starve to pay my rent, and see that you had more comfort and less work, Luke Tandy."

"There is no money could pay for the horse, my lord; haven't you bred him and broken him yourself, with perhaps some help from me? Isn't he famous not only in Ireland, but in England? Isn't he like a glory to the house, and an honor and a credit and a pride to you? We have so little —God help us!—for which to take honor and glory and credit."

Beltarbet knew that. The horse stood for beauty and nobility in his life, which was otherwise so thriftless and barren. The animal had always seemed to him of more than mortal grace and power, as if he came from the Shee, or was a descendant of the immortal steeds of fire and wings who had borne the Princes of Clare into a hundred battles.

But Beltarbet shook his head sadly and mocked at himself.

"I paid more than I could afford for the horse. I sold Earl Sigurd's bowl to keep him, and I had no right to refuse the price for him, Luke Tandy. This poverty is breaking the heart in me and I need the money, if it's only to pay for my journey away, so that the English shall not see how I die."

"You'll win the race and make a fortune," consoled the old servant, peering at his master lovingly and wistfully through the increasing azure twilight, so soft, so pure.

"I'll win the race," said Beltarbet, "but who'll put money on an Irish horse whose owner cannot afford to give him a rider but must ride him himself? The Catholic gentlemen have no money, Luke Tandy, and the English will bet on their own animals. But I'll do it, just to beat Maskell's horse—just for once in my life, Luke Tandy, to get the better of Lord Maskell. He's had everything—all of mine and, maybe, God'll not grudge me just the one moment when I ride Diarmuid to the winning-post."

Luke Tandy knew that there was more behind those words than the words themselves. The Englishman had indeed had everything—not only the estates, but the titles, the money, and the honors that should, in happier times for Ireland, have gone to the heir of Clare and Thomond; also the graces and favors of a lovely woman, fit bride for an O'Brien.

In Dublin last winter Beltarbet had allowed his heart to mislead him; proud, somber, galled and outfaced by the English and the Protestant Irish gentry, he had made but a short appearance at the stately court of the amiable Lord Lieutenant. Yet it had been long enough for him to meet, in the painted ballroom of Dublin Castle, a lady who had caused some dreams to stir in his desolate heart—dreams which might never come again; and he had been blinded enough to believe that she had favored him; but she was English and Protestant, and surrounded by

an ambitious family, and, before Beltarbet had left Dublin for the only retreat that his pride and poverty could tolerate, he had learned that the gay and splendid Kitty Archer was betrothed to Lord Maskell.

The only person in the world who knew of this secret and exquisite wound was Luke Tandy, who had stood by for many a steady month and watched the recklessness of grief, humbled pride and thwarted aspirations of the lonely young man; and comforted, strengthened and supported him as best he could—not by words, but by companionship and service, by being there in the midst of his desolation and humiliation—always Luke Tandy, a friend, a servant, a subject of the Princes of Clare.

Something of the poetry and romance of that brief, inarticulate and thwarted passion for the woman had passed into Beltarbet's feelings for the horse, this creature that seemed to have the wonder of all the four elements — the swiftness of the wind, the ardor of fire, the flowing grace of water, and the beauty of glittering earth.

With an instinct to escape from his present distresses, he went through the soft, gentle azure twilight down to the stables where Luke Tandy kept Diarmuid with a passion of tender care. Beltarbet leaned in the doorway and looked at the noble creature; he thought that the line and luster of him, the glow and color of him, were like an uprising poem or a swell of music.

The young man caressed the loving creature, who understood both his affection and his pain, and pressed his face against the smooth, warm, roan coat, and knew in his heart that he ought to have taken the English gold; that winter he and Luke Tandy and the few poor creatures who looked to him might be brought very low.

Beltarbet left the stables. He took a way that he could have found in the moonless dark, through a somber tangle of ashwood, to a little chapel. Here had stayed a great treasure, as safe in the lonely woods as if it had been in a safe in a London bank, for it was the last heirloom of the O'Briens and sacred to all the Irish —Earl Sigurd's bowl of silver gilt, with squares of flashing, angry-seeming, red and orange stone round it and strange lettering that no one had been skillful enough to decipher. Last year Beltarbet had sold this bowl to Lord Maskell in order to make some show in Dublin, without parting with his costly horse.

Beltarbet entered the chapel. A little old man greeted him. He sat down in the dim light, and opened his soul, not for the first time, to the sad, thoughtful priest; told him how Lord Maskell's agent had tempted him to sell Diarmuid, and of the arrest of men in Rathdrum, and soldiers in the Vale of Clara, of the peasantry gathering in Ballinalea, and how ill it went with him—a young man and strong, with a great name—to be there corrupting in idleness, and how he would rather die than live as he was living now, which was worse than a captive or an exile, outcast from all, denied everything . . . with ruin about him, and despair and idleness . . . .

Father Moran listened with loving patience. When Beltarbet had exhausted himself in overflowing speech, the priest spoke, and his kind voice was like a shadow and a chill over the bold despairing energy of the other. "Ireland cannot rise! How can a man who is shackled to the ground struggle to his feet? This will mean but more widows and orphans, more houses like your house, Lord Beltarbet, and churches like mine."

Luke Tandy had said the same; Beltarbet knew these two men, so different in their several ways, had spoken the dreadful truth. No revolt in Ireland could be anything but a desperate convulsion of extreme despair and would be most horribly punished.

"You have a responsibility," urged the priest, gently; "you must lead the people toward peace and submission, not toward a useless and costly striving which can have but one end. When the foot is on the neck and the yoke is on the shoulder, when the chain hangs heavy and the prison walls close round, there's nothing left but resignation."

Beltarbet received Father Moran's blessing; then turned and went back through the dark wood to his dark mansion.

The young man picked up the horn lantern in the hall and, holding it above his head, went from room to room, calling for Luke Tandy, to whom he wished to impart his resolution. . . . But a little waiting, and the race, and perhaps a few guineas from it, and then away! and escape from the humiliation of inaction . . . . "Eh, Luke! Luke Tandy!"

No answer though he searched from desolate chamber to chamber, went to the stables where his darling was safe, then round the whispering wood; he could not find his servant.

He was peering through the bushes with an increasing impatience and a growing dismay when a small, crying, ragged boy ran out from the dark and told him that when he had gone to see the priest the redcoats had ridden up to the house in haste and power, had arrested Luke Tandy and carried him off along the Dublin road....

Beltarbet mounted Diarmuid and pursued the soldiers through the mild, warm night. He came up with them when they were halfway to their destination; but little was the satisfaction Beltarbet got from the meeting. The prisoner was a known rebel who had been going about the country and stirring up the people against the government. He would be lodged that night in Dublin Castle.

Lord Beltarbet argued passionately with the British officer that it was a mistake; he could swear to it; his man would have done nothing without his knowledge.... Neither he nor Luke Tandy knew anything of the risings. He demanded deliverance of the pinioned prisoner. When he could not get a hearing, and the officer impatiently ignored him, he rode behind the cavalcade to Dublin, and his heart was like to fly out of his bosom with shame and grief.

That night Luke Tandy was flung into one of the evil cells in Dublin Castle, whose high-barred windows looked on to the courtyard called the Devil's Acre, from being the scene of floggings, executions and torments. Beltarbet and Diarmuid passed the night in a poor inn which was yet better than he could afford, and where he was treated with princely courtesy because his name was Murrough O'Brien.

The following morning, by use of grim patience and black determination, Beltarbet forced himself into the presence of the governor of the castle prison.

The interview with Luke Tandy he begged was denied him, but he got this news for his consolation:

Tomorrow the old man would be flogged in the Devil's Acre; he had refused any manner of confession; if he *did* confess and give the names of his accomplices he would be hanged; if he refused to confess he would be flogged again and, maybe, put to other tortures.

The English governor, a not unkindly man, was something confounded by the sight of Beltarbet's distress, but it was not in his power to grant him the interview, or, indeed, any privilege to any of his prisoners.

"Have you no friend at the court among the English?" he asked, curious, interested, a little sorry.

"A friend—I—an O'Brien?"

"I saw you with Lord Maskell last year; he has some influence, and the lady he is to marry is the commander-in-chief's daughter and high in the friendship of the Lord Lieutenant's wife — you might do something there."

"You send me to the man who has got my estates, will have my titles?" asked Beltarbet, thinking this an insult to his misery.

But the governor had not so intended his advice: "Lord Maskell might consider that an obligation; he is easy and generous—you should try him if you can think of no one else."

Easy and generous! The words beat bitterly in Beltarbet's distracted mind. Since he had come to Dublin he had heard the talk, which had now come to the coffee houses, that Lord Maskell and Brocas would be gazetted Earl of Clare and Thomond that winter....

That night he called at Lord Maskell's fine mansion in Kildare Street and waited, in vain, for a bitter hour. The Englishman was abroad—he had been occupied with the troubles, with his military duties. His distress, sharply increased by the delay, sent Beltarbet to a club in Merrion Square where my lord might be, and there, by chance, he found him with a number of his companions — English noblemen and officers, gay and splendid, animated by the successful crushing of the rebellion, the prospect of a struggle with the French.

Beltarbet sent in his name, and my lord left his gaming and came out to him.

The two men met in the high, elegant chamber, with its painted ceiling and the Italian marble chimney piece. Beltarbet was in his suit of an outdated fashion, shabby and worn, but brushed and mended by the landlord's daughter; the Englishman was in full regimentals, fair, handsome, confident.

"I have come about my horse, Diarmuid," Beltarbet said, sternly.

"You'll sell him?" asked Lord Maskell, agreeably.

"No, I'll not sell him, but I've come to bargain about him. And that's difficult, sir, for I cannot remember ever in my life having bargained before."

"Nor I," smiled the English officer, haughtily. "What, sir, can we have to bargain about?"

"Very little, as you may suppose," smiled Beltarbet, also grimly. "You have the titles and the estates which should go with the name I hold—it's a queer thing for a Murrough O'-Brien to come to an Englishman and talk of bargaining, is it not? There's little indeed I have left to trade with, Lord Maskell—only the horse, and it's desperate the plight I must be in before I talk of parting from him, for in all County Wicklow he's called 'Beltarbet's Pride.' "

"It's a beautiful horse," remarked the Englishman, smoothly; "I have always admired him, and I have offered you what I believe, Lord Beltarbet, is a fair and even a generous price."

"It's not the price I want," replied Murrough O'Brien, desperately. "There's a man of mine—a servant, a friend—in Dublin Castle, under suspicion of being implicated in these risings, and I can do nothing; I am a penniless, landless man with no influence, Lord Maskell; and there's none that'll be listening to me. But, if you lend me your influence for the sake of Luke Tandy, I'll give you the horse."

"A bribe!" murmured Lord Maskell, softly, with his hand on his hip, where his scarlet sash was knotted over his sword hilt.

"It will be in time for the races," added the Irishman. "He's not entered yet, and he'll win you the prize, for you'll have many friends that will put the golden guineas on him. I am offering you a large fortune, Lord Maskell—not that you need it, but money seldom comes amiss to any man."

"And what," asked the English officer, dryly, "precisely do you wish of me?"

Beltarbet told him, standing there in his worn, old-fashioned attire before the marble chimney piece, his youth and beauty haggard and wasted from days of anxiety and nights of despair.

"Luke Tandy is to be flogged tomorrow in what we call the Devil's Acre; it may be after that he'll be hanged, and maybe he'll be flogged again, and maybe he'll be put to some other torture; and that he's innocent I might take upon my honor; but, innocent or guilty, I'd have you use your influence to get him off, sir."

"I doubt I've influence enough to get a rebel pardoned," remarked Lord Maskell, slowly.

"There's your lady that's to be," suggested Beltarbet, quietly; "she's the daughter of the commander-in-chief—it may be she would say a word. Miss Kitty Archer was ever gentle and kind."

The two men glanced at each other and then away again; a little silence followed the mention of the lady's name.

Then Maskell asked:

"Who is this Luke Tandy?"

"He's the one friend I've left— the one servant and follower; he thinks of me still as if I were a Prince in Clare; he saved my father's life twice abroad and brought me home. He taught me all I know of action, as the priests have taught me all I know of thought. A brave and loyal man, Lord Maskell, he would do nothing to bring trouble on my house or me, knowing I'm deep enough in that already."

"I doubt if I can do anything," said the Englishman.

"You can stop the flogging."

Maskell was silent; his fair composed face was expressionless.

"And if you couldn't stop it," added the Irishman, with a heaving breast and a note of desperate earnestness in his soft voice, "maybe you could do this, Lord Maskell—allow me to stand beside him in the Devil's Acre while he takes his torment."

The Englishman glanced up with narrowed eyes.

"Perhaps I could do that," he conceded.

"And you'd give me your horse, for which I have offered fifteen thousand pounds, for so slight a favor?"

"No slight favor to me, Lord Maskell; the O'Briens have always stood by their friends and servants. I've no right to ask anything from you—we're not friends or equals," he added with a flash in eyes and voice, "and there's that between us should make us enemies. It has not been the easiest thing in the world for me to come to you, Lord Maskell; I'll call it a bargain—not the begging of favor."

"And I am to enter your horse," smiled the Englishman, "and win the race with him, and a power of guineas besides, eh? And who's to mount him? I hear you intended to ride him yourself."

"He would give his best with me. With others he's a fine horse, the most splendid animal in Ireland, but with me he's like a thing from the Shee— all wind and flame!" The Irishman lifted his head and his gray eyes gleamed. "I'll tell you this, Lord Maskell, if you'll do what you can for Luke Tandy, I'll ride the horse for you at the races."

"And yet you can have no cause to wish to serve me, Beltarbet."

"I've none! I've the wrongs of a hundred years and more between us. You, and the like of you, Lord Maskell, have made my own country so hateful to me that, until this came upon me, I was going abroad again and taking with me the horse and Luke Tandy and, maybe, the old priest—all of us becoming like the leaves on the road again in a foreign land where my forefathers died."

"And join our enemies?" suggested the Englishman, quietly.

"It may be," said Beltarbet. "What have we ever been but enemies—Irish and English—since the days when Strongbow landed?"

"If you would give up your property and serve the King," remarked Lord Maskell, "you might yet find life desirable. Such an existence as you lead, Beltarbet—idle, lonely—is damning to a man."

"I'll neither leave my faith nor serve the foreigner," replied Murrough O'Brien. "It wasn't to discuss this that I came here—but to

ask you to do what you can for
Luke Tandy. I have offered you the
horse and to ride him for you and
win the race—on my honor."

"You have no other friend—no
other hope?" Lord Maskell asked.

"None," replied the Irishman,
simply, "or I should never have come
to you."

"You hate me, I suppose," mused
the Englishman, "because my grandfather had your estates?"

"Hate? I don't know. They say
you'll be Clare and Thomond . . .
those are queer titles for a man
whose name is Henry Tresham. I'm
Murrough O'Brien and that's all the
difference there is between us. Now,
will you take my bargain or not?"

"What would you do if I refused?"
asked the Englishman, curiously.

"I could stand at the door of your
gaol tomorrow," flashed Murrough
O'Brien, "and hope that Luke Tandy
would know I was there. . . ."

"I'll see what I can do," said Maskell, negligently. "Will you stay and
entertain yourself with me and my
friends, Beltarbet?"

"Such is not my humor," replied
the Irishman, sternly. He gave the
address of the miserable hostelry on
the Howth Road where he was to be
found. "I'll be waiting there all night
for your news, Lord Maskell."

He left the warmly lit, aristocratic
mansion, with its company of gay,
laughing officers, gambling, drinking,
confident, walked to the poor inn
on the flats of the estuary, fetched
out Diarmuid, and rode for hours.

"Ah, my darling," he whispered to
the horse, "and if Luke Tandy can
be saved, I must ride the race with
you for another man, and then may
never mount you again. If Luke
Tandy is not to be saved, if the Englishman will do nothing, then you

and I must die, Diarmuid; some way,
not daring to live when we were useless at a push like this. We'll gallop into the sea, Diarmuid, my darling, where the Danish ravens went
down, and as the surf goes over us,
maybe Firvanna himself will catch
your bridle and lead us to the company of the Shee. Maybe we'll then
possess the land, my darling, and
ride over it day and night with the
English never seeing us."

In the blue dawn he led the beautiful horse to the dingy stable and
himself saw to his comfort, then
caressed him, and lingered long beside him, for he must hope that he
would not soon have to part with
him.

In the murky light, for it was not
yet full day, he saw Luke Tandy
standing eagerly waiting by the rough
table in the poor parlor.

"I'm free!" cried Luke Tandy,
hoarsely.

Not till after a full five minutes of
warm delight and gratitude did Beltarbet consider Diarmuid must go.

"And I'll be the Englishman's
jockey in the race!" And he wondered how he should give this news
to Luke Tandy, who would not consider himself worth such a price.

The servant caressed his master's
hand and talked to him wistfully,
eagerly, of their dear project of leaving Ireland and trying some fortune
abroad.

"And you've a friend, my lord,
who gave me this."

He put a letter into Beltarbet's
hand.

The Irishman opened it. It was
addressed to "The Earl of Clare and
Thomond."

"Why, who calls me this, Luke?—
the name that was lost a hundred
years ago, and never heard since save
in the mouths of foreigners."

He carried the letter to the mean window and in the pale light that entered read the large resolute hand:

My Lord:

Keep your titles, your servant, your horse. Indeed, no man can deprive you of them. I send you with this, passports which will see you all safely beyond the seas; for your affairs in Ireland I will be steward. Perhaps we shall meet on the battlefield. I recommend to you, my lord, a life of action. The titles which I now give you shall never be my signature; but I shall always remain

Your obedient servant, sir,

MASKELL AND BROCAS.

The bitterness of a hundred years lifted from the soul of Beltarbet—he had his horse, his servant, an open port, a generous enemy; as for his purse, the October races would line that very comfortably; for, unless God interfered, Diarmuid could not lose. And after that—a stern but noble fate would beckon him from his present ruin; cause and country were lost, but nothing would make his faith less than inviolate, and in the tumult of a world in arms one more Irishman might find an honorable foreign grave—nay, not so foreign, for it is difficult to discover a spot the blood of the exiles had not hallowed.

The sunshine was very fair and pleasant—the pale tender sunshine of Ireland shining through the pure azure veils on the Wicklow hills melting round Slieve Donard, on the gray-blue waters of Dublin Bay, and penetrating the mean court of a poor inn where two men and a horse set out on a long journey—"With, maybe, the unseen people to guide us," mused Beltarbet, "for I believe Firvanna walks at Diarmuid's head and tells him the Shee goes with us."

For Thought and Discussion

1. Where did this story take place?
2. How does the author arouse your interest and sympathy for Lord Beltarbet?
3. Why do you dislike Mr. Simon Ware, Lord Maskell's agent?
4. How much did Mr. Ware offer Beltarbet for the horse?
5. Why did Beltarbet refuse to sell the horse?
6. What advice did the priest give Beltarbet?
7. Why did Beltarbet offer the horse to Lord Maskell?
8. How did this offer change Maskell's attitude toward Beltarbet?
9. Why did Lord Maskell decide to use his influence to protect Luke Tandy?
10. Why was Beltarbet an admirable character?
11. How did Beltarbet meet and overcome a test of character?
12. Why was Lord Maskell an admirable character?
13. How did Lord Maskell meet and overcome a test of character?
14. Why is the story called "Beltarbet's Pride"?
15. What is the purpose of the story?
16. How was Beltarbet influenced by past events?
17. Why was it possible for these two men of different races to be generous enemies? Could they have become friends? Under what circumstances?

ON THE ROAD

WILFRID WILSON GIBSON

PERSONS

REUBEN APPLEBY.
JESSIE APPLEBY, *his wife.*
PETER NIXON, *a stonebreaker.*

REUBEN APPLEBY *and his wife sit under a hedge by the highway.*
REUBEN *is eating bread and cheese, while* JESSIE *is feeding her baby with milk out of a bottle.*

REUBEN. "Married!" he says,
And looks at me quite sharply—
"A boy like you!"
And civilly I answered:
"Not such a boy, sir;
I am nineteen, past."
"Nineteen!" says he, and laughs;
"And you a husband, with a wife to keep—
A wife and family, I suppose."
"We have a baby, sir."
"A baby! and you're just a child yourself!
What right have you to marry,
And bring into the world
A tribe of helpless children
To starve, and beg, and steal?"
With that he took his children by the hand,
And walked away.
I could have flung his money after him,
But I had labored for it
And was hungry,
And knew that you were famished;
And the boy must have his milk.
What right!—
I could have flung. . .
    JESSIE. Then, you had flung away
Your baby's life!
    REUBEN. Ay, lass, that stopt me,
And the thought of you;
And so, I took the sixpence,
And bought the bread and cheese and milk.
    JESSIE. You brought it just in time.
He'd cried himself to sleep;
But in my arms he lay so still and white,
That I was frightened.
    REUBEN. You were famished, lass.
    JESSIE. Yes; I was done.
I scarce could hold him,
Though he's light—
So thin and light.
But, when I laid him down, he cried so,
I could not bear. . .
    REUBEN. Well, he looks happy now.
He's drinking like a fish.
The milk will make him fat again.
But you eat nothing, Jessie.
    JESSIE. I cannot eat.
    REUBEN. You cannot?
    JESSIE. Not just now.
    REUBEN. Jessie, you must;
You'll die of hunger.
    JESSIE. I'm not hungry now;
But only weary.
After, perhaps. . .
    REUBEN. What right had I to marry!
What right had he—
He, with his wife and children,
To speak to me like that?
I could have flung. . .
    JESSIE. Nay, lad; don't vex yourself
With thought of such as he.
How can it matter what he said to you,
Now that it's over,
And the boy is fed?
    REUBEN. His money bought the milk—
Ay, and the bread and cheese.
    JESSIE. And do they not taste sweet?
You seem to relish them.

REUBEN. They're well enough.
But, would not any food taste sweet,
After starvation?
And I'd worked for it.
JESSIE. How could it be his money,
If you'd earned it?
REUBEN. True, lass.
Still, you eat nothing.
JESSIE. I cannot eat.
REUBEN. It's ill work tramping
    all the livelong day,
With naught but hunger in the belly,
As we did yesterday;
And then, at night,
To shelter 'neath a stack;
And lie, and think—
Too cold and tired to sleep—
To lie and think,
And wonder if to-morrow
Would bring us bite and sup;
Envying the very beast that they
    could feed
Upon the hay that bedded us.
And still, 'twas good to rest
From tramping the hard road.
But, you were plucky, lass;
And trudged so bravely.
JESSIE. Yet I could have dropped,
Had I not hoped to get him milk ere
    night.
REUBEN. Poor babe!
He cried all day.
My sleeve was wet with tears.
JESSIE. 'Twas a hard road, and
    long.
REUBEN. The road is hard and
    long the poor must travel.
JESSIE. Ay, and the end?
REUBEN. The end?
Where the end lies, who knows?
                    (A pause.)
Wife, he spake truly;
I'd no right to marry—
No right to wed, and bring into the
    world. . .
JESSIE. What's that you say?
You're wearied of me, husband?
REUBEN. Nay, wife, you know . . .
Still, he spake truly.

I never thought of it like this before;
I never should have thought of it at
    all,
Had he not spoken;
I'd not wits enough.
But now, I see;
I had no right to marry,
And bring into the world
A baby. . .
JESSIE. Don't you love your son?
REUBEN. Love him!
I wouldn't see him starve.
I had no right. . .
Yet, when we married,
Things looked so different, Jessie.
I earned my weekly wage,
Enough to live on,
And to keep a wife on;
And we were happy in our home,
Together, weren't we, wife?
JESSIE. Ay, we were happy, Reu-
    ben.
REUBEN. And then, the baby
    came,
And we were happier still;
For, how could we foresee
Bad times would follow,
And work be slack;
And all the mills be stopt;
And we be bundled out of house and
    home,
With naught to do
But take the road,
And look for work elsewhere?
It's a long looking. . .
Nay, but he spake truly. . .
I had no right. . .
JESSIE. Nay, Reuben, you talk
    foolishness;
Your head is light with fasting.
An empty belly makes an empty
    head.
Leave idle talking to the rich;
A poor man can't afford it.
And I've no patience with such folly.
REUBEN. Nay, it's not folly, lass,
But truth, the bitter truth.
Is it not true, we're on the road,
I, and my starving wife and babe?

JESSIE. Nay, husband; see!
He's drunk the milk;
And sleeps so sweetly.
　　REUBEN. But you're ill.
　　JESSIE. Ill?
Nay, I'm well enough.
　　REUBEN. Yet you're too ill to eat.
　　JESSIE. Nay, I was only tired.
But I'll eat now, lad,
If you've left me aught!
See how it goes!
　　REUBEN. I had no right. . .
　　JESSIE. Not if you did not love
me!
　　REUBEN. You know. . .
　　JESSIE. How can I tell?
You talk so strangely;
And say that you'd no right to wed
me. . .
Why did you wed me, then?
　　REUBEN. Because I couldn't
help. . .
I could not do without you.
I did not think. . .
How could I think, when I was mad
for you?
　　JESSIE. And yet you had no right?
　　REUBEN. Right! What thought I
of right?
I only thought of you, lass.
Nay, but I did not think. . .
I only felt,
And knew I needs must have you.
　　JESSIE. You loved me. . .
Then, was love not right enough?
Why talk of right?
Or, have you wearied of us—
Your wife and son?
Poor babe!
He doesn't love us any longer.
　　REUBEN. Nay, wife, you know. . .

(PETER NIXON, *an elderly man,*
gaunt and bent with labor, comes
slowly down the road, with his stone-
breaker's hammer on his shoulder.
He glances at REUBEN *and* JESSIE,
in passing; hesitates, then turns, and
comes towards them.)

　　PETER. Fine morning, mate and
mistress!
Might you be looking for a job, my
lad?
Well. . .there's a heap of stones to
break, down yonder.
I was just on my way. . .
But I am old:
And, maybe, a bit idle;
And you look young,
And not afraid of work,
Or I'm an ill judge of a workman's
hands.
And when the job's done, lad,
There'll be a shilling.
And there's worse work than break-
ing stones for bread.
And I'll just have a nap,
While you are busy,
And, maybe, sleep away the after-
noon,
Like the old, idle rascal that I am.
Nay, but there's naught to thank me
for.
I'm old;
And I've no wife and children,
And so, don't need the shilling.
But you are young;
And you must work for it,
While I sit by and watch you
And keep you at it.
I like to watch folk working
For I am old and idle.
Perhaps I'll sleep a bit, with one eye
open;
And when you think I'm nodding,
I'll come down on you like a load of
metal.
Don't fear!
I'll make you earn it;
You'll have to sweat,
Before that shilling's yours;
Unless you're proud—
Too proud to work. . .
Nay?
Well, the heap's down yonder—
There, at the turning
Ah, the bonnie babe!
We had no children, mistress.

And what can any old man do with shillings,
With no one but himself to spend them on—

An idle, good-for-nothing, lone old man?
(*He leads them to the turning of the road.*)

For Thought and Discussion

1. What harsh criticism of Reuben did his employer make?
2. Why was Reuben bitter?
3. What had happened to him?
4. Why did Peter offer him a job?
5. Contrast the first employer with Peter.
6. Why do you sympathize with Reuben, with Jessie, with the child, with Peter?
7. What is the author's purpose?
8. Why may this poem be said to be an answer to "Am I my brother's keeper"?
9. Is the suffering of the poor their own concern, or is it society's?
10. This poem represents actual conditions, the lot of thousands. The poet tells the story. There is much work that should be done; there are many who want to work; what is wrong?

BUT THE GREATEST OF THESE IS CHARITY
I CORINTHIANS 13

THOUGH I speak with the tongues of men and of angels and have not charity,[1] I am become as sounding brass or a tinkling cymbal. And though I have the gift of prophecy, and understand all mysteries, and all knowledge; and though I have all faith, so that I could remove mountains, and have not charity, I am nothing. And though I bestow all my goods to feed the poor, and though I give my body to be burned, and have not charity, it profiteth me nothing.

Charity suffereth long and is kind; charity envieth not; charity vaunteth not itself, is not puffed up; doth not behave itself unseemly, seeketh not her own, is not easily provoked, thinketh no evil; rejoiceth not in iniquity, but rejoiceth in the truth; beareth all things, believeth all things, hopeth all things, endureth all things. Charity never faileth; but whether there be prophecies, they shall fail; whether there be tongues, they shall cease; whether there be knowledge, it shall vanish away. For we know in part, and we prophesy in part.

But when that which is perfect is come, then that which is in part shall be done away. When I was a child, I spake as a child, I understood as a child, I thought as a child; but when I became a man I put away childish things. For now we see through a glass darkly, but then face to face; now I know in part, but then shall I know even as also I am known.

And now abideth faith, hope, charity, these three; but the greatest of these is charity.

[1]The revised versions usually substitute the word *love* as that term more nearly preserves the meaning of the original.

A CHRISTMAS GUEST

SELMA LAGERLÖF

[Those readers who are familiar with *The Wonderful Adventures of Nils* already have a delightful acquaintance with the author, Selma Lagerlöf. An early interest in Scandinavian legends led her further and further into that field so that it is not surprising that in time she should turn to writing.

Her first literary recognition came when she won a thirteen-hundred-dollar prize for a novel, which was a section of a longer work upon which she had been writing for years. The novel submitted for the prize was rewritten in eight days and finished on the last day of the contest, a significant fact in that it reveals the genius of the author. As Selma Lagerlöf continued to receive recognition for her stories, she gave up her work of teaching and turned entirely to writing. The award to her of the Nobel prize in 1909 was an international recognition of her literary achievement. The highest compliment that can be paid to any writer's work may be given hers: her stories are more charming each time they are read.]

O NE of those who had lived the life of a pensioner at Ekeby was little Ruster, who could transpose music and play the flute. He was of low origin and poor, without home and without relations. Hard times came to him when the company of pensioners were dispersed.

He then had no horse nor carriole, no fur coat nor red-painted luncheon-basket. He had to go on foot from house to house and carry his belongings tied in a blue striped cotton handkerchief. He buttoned his coat all the way up to his chin, so that no one should need to know in what condition his shirt and waistcoat were, and in its deep pockets he kept his most precious possessions: his flute taken to pieces, his flat brandy bottle, and his music-pen.

His profession was to copy music, and if it had been as in the old days, there would have been no lack of work for him. But with every passing year music was less practiced in Värm-land. The guitar, with its mouldy, silken ribbon and its worn screws, and the dented horn, with faded tassels and cord, were put away in the lumber-room in the attic, and the dust settled inches deep on the long, iron-bound violin boxes. Yet the less little Ruster had to do with flute and music-pen, so much the more must he turn to the brandy flask, and at last he became quite a drunkard. It was a great pity.

He was still received at the manor houses as an old friend, but there were complaints when he came and joy when he went. There was an odor of dirt and brandy about him, and if he had only a couple of glasses of wine or one toddy, he grew confused and told unpleasant stories. He was the torment of the hospitable houses.

One Christmas he came to Löfdala, where Liljekrona, the great violinist, had his home. Liljekrona had also been one of the pensioners of Ekeby, but after the death of the major's wife, he returned to his quiet farm and remained there. Ruster came to him a few days before Christmas, in the midst of all the preparations, and asked for work. Liljekrona gave him a little copying to keep him busy.

"You ought to have let him go immediately," said his wife: "now he

will certainly take so long with that
that we will be obliged to keep him
over Christmas."

"He must be somewhere," answered
Liljekrona.

And he offered Ruster toddy and
brandy, sat with him, and lived over
again with him the whole Ekeby
time. But he was out of spirits and
disgusted by him, like everyone else,
although he would not let it be seen,
for old friendship and hospitality
were sacred to him.

In Liljekrona's house for three
weeks now they had been preparing
to receive Christmas. They had been
living in discomfort and bustle, had
sat up with dip-lights[1] and torches
till their eyes grew red, had been
frozen in the outhouse with the salt-
ing of meat and in the brewhouse
with the brewing of beer. But both
the mistress and the servants gave
themselves up to it all without grumbling.

When all the preparations were
done and the holy evening come, a
sweet enchantment would sink down
over them. Christmas would loosen
all tongues, so that jokes and jests,
rhymes and merriment would flow of
themselves without effort. Everyone's feet would wish to twirl in the
dance, and from memory's dark corners words and melodies would rise,
although no one could believe that
they were there. And then everyone
was so good, so good!

Now when Ruster came, the whole
household at Löfdala thought that
Christmas was spoiled. The mistress
and the older children and the old
servants were all of the same opinion.
Ruster caused them a suffocating disgust. They were moreover afraid that
when he and Liljekrona began to rake
up the old memories, the artist's blood

---

[1] *dip-light,* a light made by floating
a wick in melted fat.

would flame up in the great violinist
and his home would lose him. Formerly he had not been able to remain
long at home.

No one can describe how they loved
their master on the farm, since they
had had him with them a couple of
years. And what he had to give!
How much he had to give! How
much he was to his home, especially at
Christmas! He did not take his place
on any sofa or rocking-stool, but on
a high, narrow wooden bench in the
corner of the fire-place. When he
was settled there he started off on adventures. He traveled about the
earth, climbed up to the stars, and
even higher. He played and talked
by turns, and the whole household
gathered about him and listened. Life
grew proud and beautiful when the
richness of that one soul shone on it.

Therefore they loved him as they
loved Christmas time, pleasure, the
spring sun. And when little Ruster
came, their Christmas peace was destroyed. They had worked in vain if
he was coming to tempt away their
master. It was unjust that the drunkard should sit at the Christmas table
in a happy house and spoil the Christmas pleasure.

On the forenoon of Christmas Eve
little Ruster had his music written
out, and he said something about going, although of course he meant to
stay.

Liljekrona had been influenced by
the general feeling and therefore said
quite lukewarmly and indifferently
that Ruster had better stay where he
was over Christmas.

Little Ruster was inflammable and
proud. He twirled his mustache and
shook back the black artist's hair that
stood like a dark cloud over his head.
What did Liljekrona mean? Should
he stay because he had nowhere else
to go? Oh, only think how they

stood and waited for him in the big iron works in the parish of Bro! The guest-room was in order, the glass of welcome filled. He was in great haste. He only did not know to which he ought to go first.

"Very well," answered Liljekrona, "you may go if you will."

After dinner little Ruster borrowed horse and sleigh, coat and furs. The stable boy from Löfdala was to take him to some place in Bro and drive quickly back, for it threatened snow.

No one believed that he was expected, or that there was a single place in the neighborhood where he was welcome. But they were so anxious to be rid of him that they put the thought aside and let him depart. "He wished it himself," they said; and then they thought that now they would be glad.

But when they gathered in the dining-room at five o'clock to drink tea and to dance round the Christmas tree, Liljekrona was silent and out of spirits. He did not seat himself on the bench; he touched neither tea nor punch; he could not remember any polka; the violin was out of order. Those who could play and dance had to do it without him.

Then his wife grew uneasy; the children were discontented, everything in the house went wrong. It was the most lamentable Christmas Eve.

The porridge turned sour; the candles sputtered; the wood smoked; the wind stirred up the snow and blew bitter cold into the rooms. The stable boy who had driven Ruster did not come home. The cook wept; the maids scolded.

Finally Liljekrona remembered that no sheaves had been put out for the sparrows, and he complained aloud of all the women about him who abandoned old custom and were newfangled and heartless. They understood well enough that what tormented him was remorse that he had let little Ruster go away from his home on Christmas Eve.

After a while he went to his room, shut the door, and began to play as he had not played since he had ceased roaming. It was full of hate and scorn, full of longing and revolt. You thought to bind me, but you must forge new fetters. You thought to make me as small-minded as yourselves, but I turn to larger things, to the open. Commonplace people, slaves of the home, hold me prisoner if it is in your power!

When his wife heard the music, she said: "Tomorrow he is gone, if God does not work a miracle in the night. Our inhospitableness has brought on just what we thought we could avoid."

In the meantime little Ruster drove about in the snowstorm. He went from one house to the other and asked if there was any work for him to do, but he was not received anywhere. They did not even ask him to get out of the sledge. Some had their houses full of guests, others were going away on Christmas Day. "Drive to the next neighbor," they all said.

He could come and spoil the pleasure of an ordinary day, but not of Christmas Eve. Christmas Eve came but once a year, and the children had been rejoicing in the thought of it all the autumn. They could not put that man at a table where there were children. Formerly they had been glad to see him, but not since he had become a drunkard. Where should they put the fellow, moreover? The servants' room was too plain and the guest room too fine.

So little Ruster had to drive from house to house in the blinding snow. His wet mustache hung limply down over his mouth; his eyes were blood-shot and blurred, but the brandy was blown out of his brain. He began to wonder and to be amazed. Was it possible, was it possible that no one wished to receive him?

Then all at once he saw himself. He saw how miserable and degraded he was, and he understood that he was odious to people. "It is the end of me," he thought. "No more copy-ing music, no more flute-playing. No one on earth needs me; no one has compassion on me."

The storm whirled and played, tore apart the drifts and piled them up again, took a pillar of snow in its arms and danced out into the plain, lifted one flake up to the clouds and chased another down into a ditch. "It is so, it is so," said little Ruster; "while one dances and whirls it is play, but when one must be buried in the drift and forgotten, it is sorrow and grief." But down they all have to go, and now it was his turn. To think that he had now come to the end!

He no longer asked where the man was driving him; he thought that he was driving in the land of death.

Little Ruster made no offerings to the gods that night. He did not curse flute-playing or the life of a pen-sioner; he did not think that it had been better for him if he had plowed the earth or sewn shoes. But he mourned that he was now a worn-out instrument, which pleasure could no longer use. He complained of no one, for he knew that when the horn is cracked and the guitar will not stay in tune, they must go. He became all at once a very humble man. He understood that it was the end of him, on this Christmas Eve. Hunger and cold would destroy him, for he understood nothing, was good for nothing, and had no friends.

The sledge stops, and suddenly it is light about him, and he hears friendly voices, and there is some one who is helping him into a warm room, and some one who is pouring warm tea into him. His coat is pulled off him, and several people cry that he is welcome, and warm hands rub life into his benumbed fingers.

He was so confused by it all that he did not come to his senses for nearly a quarter of an hour. He could not possibly comprehend that he had come back to Löfdala. He had not been at all conscious that the stable boy had grown tired of driving about in the storm and had turned home.

Nor did he understand why he was now so well received in Lil-jekrona's house. He could not know that Liljekrona's wife understood what a weary journey he had made that Christmas Eve, when he had been turned away from every door where he had knocked. She felt such compassion on him that she for-got her own troubles.

Liljekrona went on with the wild playing up in his room; he did not know that Ruster had come. The lat-ter sat meanwhile in the dining-room with the wife and the children. The servants who used also to be there on Christmas Eve, moved out into the kitchen away from their mis-tress's trouble.

The mistress of the house lost no time in setting Ruster to work. "You hear, I suppose," she said, "that Lil-jekrona does nothing but play all the evening, and I must attend to setting the table and the food. The children are quite forsaken. You must look after the two smallest."

Children were the kind of people with whom little Ruster had had least intercourse. He had met them neither in the bachelor's wing nor in the campaign tent, neither in wayside

inns nor in the highways. He was almost shy of them, and did not know what he ought to say that was fine enough for them.

He took out his flute and taught them how to finger the stops and holes. There was one of four years and one of six. They had a lesson on the flute and were deeply interested in it. "This is A," he said, "and this is C," and then he blew the notes. Then the young people wished to know what kind of an A and C it was that was to be played.

Ruster took out his score and made a few notes.

"No," they said, "that is not right." And they ran away for an A B C book.

Little Ruster began to hear their alphabet. They knew it and they did not know it. What they knew was not very much. Ruster grew eager; he lifted the little boys up, each on one of his knees, and began to teach them. Liljekrona's wife went out and in and listened quite in amazement. It sounded like a

game, and the children were laughing the whole time, but they learned.

Ruster kept on for awhile, but he was absent from what he was doing. He was turning over the old thoughts from out in the storm. It was good and pleasant, but nevertheless it was the end of him. He was worn out. He ought to be thrown away. And all of a sudden he put his hands before his face and began to weep.

Liljekrona's wife came quickly up to him.

"Ruster," she said, "I can understand that you think that all is over for you. You cannot make a living with your music, and you are destroying yourself with brandy. But it is not the end, Ruster."

"Yes," sobbed the little flute-player.

"Do you see that to sit as to-night with the children, that would be something for you? If you would teach the children to read and write, you would be welcomed everywhere. That is no less important an instrument on which to play, Ruster, than flute and violin. Look at them, Ruster!"

She placed the two children in front of him, and he looked up, blinking as if he had looked at the sun. It seemed as if his little, blurred eyes could not meet those of the children, which were big, clear, and innocent.

"Look at them, Ruster!" repeated Liljekrona's wife.

"I dare not," said Ruster, for it was like a purgatory to look through the beautiful child eyes to the unspotted beauty of their souls.

Liljekrona's wife laughed loud and joyously. "Then you must accustom yourself to them, Ruster. You can stay in my house as schoolmaster this year."

Liljekrona heard his wife laugh and came out of his room.

"What is it?" he asked. "What is it?"

"Nothing," she answered, "but that Ruster has come again, and that I have engaged him as schoolmaster for our little boys."

Liljekrona was quite amazed. "Do you dare?" he said, "do you dare? Has he promised to give up—"

"No," said the wife; "Ruster has promised nothing. But there is much about which he must be careful when he has to look little children in the eyes every day. If it had not been Christmas, perhaps I would not have ventured; but when our Lord dared to place a little child who was His own son among us sinners, so can I also dare to let my little children try to save a human soul."

Liljekrona could not speak, but every feature and wrinkle in his face twitched and twisted as always when he heard anything noble.

Then he kissed his wife's hand as gently as a child who asks for forgiveness and cried aloud: "All the children must come and kiss their mother's hand."

They did so, and then they had a happy Christmas in Liljekrona's house.

For Thought and Discussion

1. In what country did this story take place?
2. What was the nature of little Ruster's work?
3. How did the lack of money and position and his own weaknesses affect Ruster's welcome in the homes of his more fortunate friends?
4. Who was Liljekrona, and why was he especially loved by his household?
5. Why was Liljekrona out of spirits on Christmas Eve?
6. How did his spirit of unhappiness affect the household?
7. How did the family fear the Christmas celebration was to be spoiled?
8. What really threatened the Christmas spirit?
9. What finally caused little Ruster to understand why he no longer received a welcome at the homes of his friends?
10. Why on his return was he so well received at Liljekrona's house? In what did little Ruster's hope of reformation lie?
11. What effect did Liljekrona's wife hope the children would have upon Ruster?
12. Of what Bible text is this selection suggestive?

ELEGY WRITTEN IN A COUNTRY CHURCHYARD

THOMAS GRAY

THE curfew tolls the knell of
    parting day,
The lowing herd wind slowly o'er
    the lea,
The plowman homeward plods his
    weary way,
    And leaves the world to darkness
    and to me.

Now fades the glimmering landscape
    on the sight,   5
    And all the air a solemn stillness
    holds,
Save where the beetle wheels his dron-
    ing flight,
    And drowsy tinklings lull the dis-
    tant folds;

Save that from yonder ivy-mantled
    tower
    The moping owl does to the moon
    complain   10
Of such as wandering near her secret
    bower
    Molest her ancient solitary reign.

Beneath those rugged elms, that yew-
    tree's shade,
    Where heaves the turf in many a
    moldering heap,
Each in his narrow cell forever laid, 15
    The rude forefathers of the hamlet
    sleep.

The breezy call of incense-breathing
    morn,
    The swallow twittering from the
    straw-built shed,
The cock's shrill clarion, and the
    echoing horn,
    No more shall rouse them from
    their lowly bed.   20

For them no more the blazing hearth
    shall burn,

Or busy housewife ply her evening
    care;
No children run to lisp their sire's re-
    turn,
    Or climb his knees the envied kiss
    to share.

Oft did the harvest to their sickle
    yield,   25
    Their furrow oft the stubborn
    glebe has broke;
How jocund did they drive their
    team afield!
    How bowed the woods beneath
    their sturdy stroke!

Let not ambition mock their useful
    toil,
    Their homely joys, and destiny ob-
    scure;   30
Nor grandeur hear, with a disdainful
    smile,
    The short and simple annals of the
    poor.

The boast of heraldry, the pomp of
    power,
    And all that beauty, all that wealth
    e'er gave,
Awaits alike th' inevitable hour.   35
    The paths of glory lead but to the
    grave.

Nor you, ye proud, impute to these
    the fault,
    If memory o'er their tomb no tro-
    phies raise,
Where through the long-drawn aisle
    and fretted vault
    The pealing anthem swells the note
    of praise.   40

Can storied urn or animated bust
    Back to its mansion call the fleeting
    breath?

Can honor's voice provoke the silent dust,
　Or flatt'ry soothe the dull cold ear of death?

Perhaps in this neglected spot is laid [45]
　Some heart once pregnant with celestial fire;
Hands that the rod of empire might have swayed,
　Or waked to ecstasy the living lyre.

But knowledge to their eyes her ample page
　Rich with the spoils of time did ne'er unroll; [50]
Chill Penury repressed their noble rage,
　And froze the genial current of the soul.

Full many a gem of purest ray serene,
　The dark unfathomed caves of ocean bear;
Full many a flower is born to blush unseen, [55]
　And waste its sweetness on the desert air.

Some village Hampden,[1] that with dauntless breast
　The little tyrant of his fields withstood,
Some mute, inglorious Milton here may rest,
　Some Cromwell,[2] guiltless of his country's blood. [60]

Th' applause of listening senates to command,
　The threats of pain and ruin to despise,
To scatter plenty o'er a smiling land
　And read their history in a nation's eyes,

---

[1]*Hampden*, English statesman.
[2]*Cromwell*, the great Puritan general and statesman.

Their lot forbade; nor circumscribed alone [65]
　Their growing virtues, but their crimes confined;
Forbade to wade through slaughter to a throne,
　And shut the gates of mercy on mankind,

The struggling pangs of conscious truth to hide,
　To quench the blushes of ingenuous shame, [70]
Or heap the shrine of luxury and pride
　With incense kindled at the muse's flame.

Far from the madding crowd's ignoble strife,
　Their sober wishes never learned to stray;
Along the cool, sequestered vale of life [75]
　They kept the noiseless tenor of their way.

Yet ev'n these bones from insult to protect
　Some frail memorial still erected nigh,
With uncouth rimes and shapeless sculpture decked,
　Implores the passing tribute of a sigh. [80]

Their name, their years, spelled by th' unlettered muse,
　The place of fame and elegy supply;
And many a holy text around she strews,
　That teach the rustic moralist to die.

For who, to dumb forgetfulness a prey, [85]
　This pleasing anxious being e'er resigned,

Elegy written in a Country Church Yard 1750

Perhaps in this neglected Spot is laid
Some Heart once pregnant with celestial Fire
Hands that the Reins of Empire might have sway'd   Rod
Or waked to Ecstacy the living Lyre,

But Knowledge to their Eyes her ample Page
Rich with the Spoils of Time did n'ier unroll
Chill Penury repress'd their noble Rage,
And froze the genial Current of the Soul

Full many a Gem of purest Ray serene
The dark unfathom'd Caves of Ocean bear
Full many a Flower is born to blush unseen
And waste its Sweetness on the desert Air

Some Village Hambden that with dauntless Breast
The little Tyrant of his fields withstood,
Some mute inglorious Milton here may rest
Some Cromwell guiltless of his Country's Blood

Th' Applause of list'ning Senates to command
The Threats of Pain & Ruin to despise,
To scatter Plenty o'er a smiling Land,
And read their Hist'ry in a Nation's Eyes

Their Lot forbad nor circumscribed alone
Their growing Virtues, but their Crimes confined,
Forbad to wade thro' Slaughter to a Throne
Or shut the Gates of Mercy on Mankind,

The struggling Pangs of conscious Truth to hide.
To quench the Blushes of ingenuous Shame.
Or heap the Shrine of Luxury & Pride
With Incense kindled at the Muses Flame

Far from the madding Crowd's ignoble Strife,
Their sober Wishes never learn'd to stray.
Along the cool sequester'd Vale of Life
They kept the noiseless Tenour of their Way

publish'd in
Feb: y 1751
by Dodsley & four
went thro' about
Editions; in two
months, & a fifth
afterwards a fifth
6th, 7th & 8th; 9 & 10
& printed also in 1753
with Mr Bentley's
Designs; of which
there is a 2d Edition
& again by Dodsley
in his Miscellany
Vol: 4th & in a
Scotch Collection
call'd the Union
translated into
Latin by Chr: Anstey
Esq & the Revd Mr
Roberts, & publisht
in 1762; & again
in the same year
by Rob: Lloyd M: A.

Left the warm precincts of the cheerful day,
   Nor cast one longing lingering look
   behind?

On some fond breast the parting soul
   relies,
   Some pious drops the closing eye
   requires;   90
Even from the tomb the voice of na-
   ture cries,
   Even in our ashes live their wonted
   fires.

For thee, who mindful of th' unhon-
   ored dead
   Dost in these lines their artless tale
   relate;
If chance, by lonely contemplation
   led,   95
   Some kindred spirit shall inquire
   thy fate,

Haply some hoary-headed swain may
   say,
   "Oft have we seen him at the deep
   of dawn
Brushing with hasty steps the dews
   away
   To meet the sun upon the upland
   lawn.   100

"There at the foot of yonder nodding
   beech,
   That wreathes its old fantastic roots
   so high,
His listless length at noontide would
   he stretch,
   And pore upon the brook that bab-
   bles by.

"Hard by yon wood, now smiling as
   in scorn,   105
   Muttering his wayward fancies he
   would rove,
Now drooping, woeful-wan, like one
   forlorn,

Or crazed with care, or crossed in
   hopeless love.

"One morn I missed him on the cus-
   tomed hill,
   Along the heath and near his favorite tree;   110
Another came; nor yet beside the rill,
   Nor up the lawn, nor at the wood
   was he;

"The next with dirges due in sad array
   Slow through the church-way path
   we saw him borne.—
Approach and read (for thou canst
   read) the lay   115
   Graved on the stone beneath yon
   agèd thorn."

THE EPITAPH

*Here rests his head upon the lap of
   earth,
   A youth to fortune and to fame
   unknown.
Fair science frowned not on his humble birth,
   And melancholy marked him for
   her own.*   120

*Large was his bounty, and his soul
   sincere,
   Heaven did a recompense as largely
   send;
He gave to mis'ry all he had, a tear,
   He gained from heaven ('twas all
   he wished) a friend.*

*No farther seek his merits to dis-
   close,*   125
   *Or draw his frailties from their
   dread abode,*
*(There they alike in trembling hope
   repose)*
   *The bosom of his Father and his
   God.*

For Thought and Discussion

1. What details of description in the first four stanzas assist in creating a quiet twilight setting?
2. How does the poet describe the lives of those who are now buried in the churchyard?
3. What does the poet say about glory?
4. What handicap does he think may have prevented some of these men from becoming famous?
5. Of what class of people is this poem an appreciation?
6. What gift does the poet say heaven bestowed upon him?
7. In what way did Gray's "Elegy" point forward to a new era?
8. Was sympathy for the uneducated as general in the eighteenth century as it is in the twentieth century? Explain your answer.

THOMAS GRAY 1716-1771

The Quiet Years of Gray's College Life. Though Thomas Gray's father came by inheritance into a small fortune, he was so selfish and heartless that the fortune was of little benefit to his wife and to Thomas, the only surviving child of their large family. Fortunately Gray's mother was loving, resourceful, and ambitious for her son. With her own earnings she paid his way through Eton and Cambridge.

Because of his modest means Gray lived very frugally at college. While there he made no particular effort to become either popular or distinguished for scholarship; nevertheless in his own quiet way he made friends and was recognized as a student of merit. Horace Walpole, the son of the Prime Minister, was one of his college friends. Gray's first published poem was an elegy written in honor of another one of his college friends, Richard West. It is characteristic of Gray that he spent much time in writing and revising this poem which was not published until a number of years after it was begun.

His Clear Simple Style. Clearness, simplicity, and correctness of form are marks of his style. Indeed, Gray has been called the most scholarly and well-balanced of the early Romantic poets. Even Johnson, always grudging in his praise, voiced that opinion of him. His reputation was such that he was offered the poet laureateship, an honor which he refused with the statement that he did not care to be rat-catcher to His Majesty.

Pleasures During His Latter Years. During the latter years of his life Gray was made Professor of Modern History and Languages at Cambridge, a position of honor and of but little toil. The income and the leisure afforded him by his professorship enabled the shy, retiring poet to spend his days as he wished to spend them, in adding to his large collection of natural history specimen (collecting insects was his particular hobby), in travel through England and Scotland, and in literary and other cultural pursuits which gave him pleasure. His life, though quiet, was not idle; his chosen motto was ". . . . to be employed is to be happy." Gray was buried beside his mother in the little churchyard at Stoke Poges (stōk pŏgz; pōg' ĭs), a fitting resting place for one whose verse has immortalized "The short and simple annals of the poor," the poor who lie buried with him in that spot.

ABOU BEN ADHEM
LEIGH HUNT

[Leigh Hunt, 1784-1859, wrote some very good essays and a few poems. "Abou Ben Adhem" is his best work. He knew many literary men of his time, among whom were Byron, Shelley, and Keats. [1]*Abou Ben Adhem* (ä boo' běn äd' hěm). [2]*"Write . . . . fellow-men."* This line is on Hunt's tombstone.]

ABOU BEN ADHEM[1] (may his tribe increase!)
Awoke one night from a deep dream of peace,
And saw, within the moonlight in his room,
Making it rich, and like a lily in bloom,
An angel writing in a book of gold: 5
Exceeding peace had made Ben Adhem bold,
And to the presence in the room he said,

"What writest thou?"—The vision raised its head,
And, with a look made of all sweet accord,
Answered, "The names of those who love the Lord." 10
"And is mine one?" said Abou. "Nay, not so,"
Replied the angel. Abou spoke more low,
But cheery still; and said, "I pray thee, then,
Write me as one that loves his fellow-men."[2]

The angel wrote, and vanished. The next night 15
It came again, with a great wakening light,
And showed the names whom love of God had blessed,—
And lo! Ben Adhem's name led all the rest.

For Thought and Discussion

1. What was the angel writing in the book of gold?
2. Quote the line which Abou Ben Adhem asked the angel to write.

Additional Readings

Bond, F. Fraser: *The Woolly Lamb of God*

Buck, Pearl S.: *The Good Earth*
Sons

Deeping, Warwick: *Two Black Sheep*

Gibson, Wilfrid Wilson: *Daily Bread*
Livelihood
Neighbors

Hobart, Alice Tisdale: *Oil for the Lamps of China*

Hood, Thomas: *The Song of the Shirt*

Jerome, Jerome K.: *Passing of the Third Floor Back*

Lewis, Elizabeth Foreman: *Young Fu of the Upper Yangtze*

Sanders, Gerald De Witt and Nelson, John Herbert: *Chief Modern Poets of England and America*

Tolstoy, Leo: *What To Do Then*
War and Peace

Nature and Reflection

NATURE AND REFLECTION

NATURE is the wisest of philosophers. She speaks a universal language; there is no ear unto which her speech is not intelligible. "Day unto day uttereth speech," said the Hebrew poet, "and night unto night showeth knowledge."[1] Nature is all things to all men in all their varied moods; but it is when a man is in a reflective mood that he listens most closely to her wisdom. Then she is the source of his meditations; her symbols become the medium by which he gives expression to reflections on other phases of life. For every abstract idea like love, peace, happiness, anger, grief, fear, and futility, nature has supplied man with a symbol. The rock is a symbol of refuge; the hill, a symbol of strength and courage. The willow is a sign of mourning; the dove, a token of gentleness and peace. The eagle connotes vigor and daring; the wind, restlessness and longing. Musing on the shortness of life, the Psalmist-philosopher compared man to grass which today is and tomorrow is not,[2] and reflecting on the fruitfulness of a righteous life, he likened a good man to a tree planted by rivers of water.[3] Wordsworth, lamenting the corrupt condition of his times, called England a "fen of stagnant waters."[4]

Often a man's reveries are associated with the past. Because of the scent of a certain flower, the sight of a familiar landscape, the sound of a familiar strain of music, his memories are invoked and he is led to muse upon events of earlier years. When the wind whistles through the trees, it brings back to him the dreams of his youth; when the moonlight glimmers on the water, he finds himself re-living the past.

In the lyric, the nature essay, and in selections of the semi-essay short story type, nature and meditation find fullest expression and interpretation. For Conrad and Masefield, whose works reflect life on the sea, for Hudson, whose works reflect life on the land, nature and reflection were the alchemists who transmuted the base metal of ordinary experience into the romance of pure gold. For Michael Fairless, author of *The Roadmender*, nature and mediation opened doors to life temporal and eternal. For all who learn to interpret and to speak the language of nature, life has a fuller meaning.

---

[1]Psalms 19:2. [2]Psalms 103:15. [3]Psalms 1:3. [4]London, 1802.

"A HOST OF GOLDEN DAFFODILS
BESIDE THE LAKE, BENEATH THE TREES
FLUTTERING AND DANCING IN THE
BREEZE."

THE DAFFODILS

WILLIAM WORDSWORTH

[Many of Wordsworth's lines are illustrative of his theory that poetry is the product of "emotion recollected in tranquillity." Nowhere is the idea more clearly or beautifully expressed than in the closing stanza of "The Daffodils," the last four lines of which were written by the poet's wife. The poem is descriptive of a landscape scene viewed by Wordsworth and his sister Dorothy, who recorded the incident in her journal April 15, 1802.]

I WANDERED lonely as a cloud
  That floats on high o'er vales and
    hills,
When all at once I saw a crowd,
A host of golden daffodils,
Beside the lake, beneath the trees,   5
Fluttering and dancing in the breeze.

Continuous as the stars that shine
And twinkle on the milky way,
They stretched in never-ending line
Along the margin of a bay;   10
Ten thousand saw I at a glance
Tossing their heads in sprightly
    dance.

The waves beside them danced, but
    they
Outdid the sparkling waves in glee—
A poet could not but be gay   15
In such a jocund company!
I gazed—and gazed—but little
    thought
What wealth the show to me had
    brought;

For oft, when on my couch I lie
In vacant or in pensive mood,   20
They flash upon that inward eye
Which is the bliss of solitude;
And then my heart with pleasure fills,
And dances with the daffodils.

For Thought and Discussion

1. To what kind of wealth does the poet refer in stanza three?
2. Would you judge from this poem that the companionship of people was essential to Wordsworth's happiness?
3. What do you think of the tonic effect of nature upon people? How much park space should a city have? Is the effect of environment upon people sufficient to justify the expenditure of immense sums upon the improvement of public grounds: for example, school grounds, federal grounds, penitentiaries, and highways?

FLOWER IN THE CRANNIED WALL
ALFRED LORD TENNYSON

FLOWER in the cranied wall,
   I pluck you out of the crannies,
I hold you here, root and all, in my hand,
Little flower—but if I could understand
What you are, root and all, and all in all,   5
I should know what God and man is.

For Thought and Discussion

1. Do you think it likely that the "Thoughts that do often lie too deep for tears" referred to by Wordsworth in the closing lines of "Ode on Intimations of Immortality" are similar to the thoughts expressed in the closing lines of this poem?
2. Do you agree with Tennyson's assertion that if one could understand all about a flower, he would understand "what God and man is"?

THE EAGLE
Fragment
ALFRED LORD TENNYSON

HE clasps the crag with crooked hands;
Close to the sun in lonely lands,
Ring'd with the azure world, he stands.
The wrinkled sea beneath him crawls;
He watches from his mountain walls,   5
And like a thunderbolt he falls.

For Thought and Discussion

1. What are the details which make this picture realistic?
2. Why do you suppose Tennyson spoke of the eagle as having hands instead of talons or claws?
3. To what does the poet compare the flight of the eagle? Is the comparison fitting? Why or why not?

ON THE GRASSHOPPER AND THE CRICKET

JOHN KEATS

THE poetry of earth is never
  dead:
When all the birds are faint with the
  hot sun,
And hide in cooling trees, a voice
  will run
From hedge to hedge about the new-
  mown mead;
That is the grasshopper's—he takes
  the lead   5
In summer luxury,—he has never
  done
With his delights; for when tired out
  with fun

He rests at ease beneath some pleasant weed.
The poetry of earth is ceasing never;
On a lone winter evening, when the
  frost   10
Has wrought a silence, from the stove
  there shrills
The cricket's song, in warmth increasing ever,
And seems to one in drowsiness half
  lost,
The grasshopper's among some grassy
  hills.

For Thought and Discussion

1. At what time of the year does the grasshopper sing?
2. Why may the song of the cricket be called an echo?
3. Why does the poet say, "The poetry of earth is ceasing never"?
4. What does he mean by *poetry*?

THE BROOK

ALFRED LORD TENNYSON

I COME from haunts of coot and
  hern,
  I make a sudden sally,
And sparkle out among the fern,
  To bicker down a valley.

By thirty hills I hurry down,   5
  Or slip between the ridges,
By twenty thorps, a little town,
  And half a hundred bridges.

Till last by Philip's farm I flow
  To join the brimming river,   10
For men may come and men may go,
  But I go on forever.

I chatter over stony ways,
  In little sharps and trebles,

I bubble into eddying bays,   15
  I babble on the pebbles.

With many a curve my banks I fret
  By many a field and fallow,
And many a fairy foreland set
  With willow-reed and mallow.   20

I chatter, chatter, as I flow
  To join the brimming river,
For men may come and men may go,
  But I go on forever.

I wind about, and in and out,   25
  With here a blossom sailing,
And here and there a lusty trout,
  And here and there a grayling,

And here and there a foamy flake
  Upon me, as I travel   30
With many a silvery waterbreak
  Above the golden gravel,

And draw them all along, and flow
  To join the brimming river,
For men may come and men may go,[35]
  But I go on forever.

I steal by lawns and grassy plots,
  I slide by hazel covers;
I move the sweet forget-me-nots
  That grow for happy lovers.   40

I slip, I slide, I gloom, I glance,
  Among my skimming swallows;
I make the netted sunbeams dance
  Against my sandy shallows.

I murmur under moon and stars   45
  In brambly wildernesses;
I linger by my shingly bars;
  I loiter round my cresses;.

And out again I curve and flow
  To join the brimming river,   50
For men may come and men may go,
  But I go on forever.

For Thought and Discussion

1. Read "The Brook" aloud.
   Notice the measure in which this poem is written.
   Why does the poet use this particular measure?
2. What qualities of the brook does he wish to emphasize?
3. Why does he repeat the lines,

   "For men may come and men may go,
   But I go on forever"?

Plus Work

In your opinion is this poem more effective with the stanzas written consecutively as they are here or interspersed as they are in the complete poem by the love story of Katie and James Willows and by what seem to be personal reminiscences of the poet?

Make a study of Tennyson's nature poems. Compare them with modern nature lyrics.

THE CATARACT OF LODORE
ROBERT SOUTHEY

[Robert Southey, 1774-1843, Coleridge, and Wordsworth were known as the Lake Poets, because they lived for some time in the Lake District in northern England. In his own day Southey was rather famous. He was poet laureate from 1813 until his death in 1843.]

HOW does the water
  Come down at Lodore?"[1]
My little boy asked me
  Thus once on a time;
And moreover he tasked me   5
  To tell him in rhyme.

—————
[1]*Lodore*, a waterfall near which Southey lived.

Anon at the word
There first came one daughter
And then came another
    To second and third   10
The request of their brother
And to hear how the water
    Comes down at Lodore
    With its rush and its roar,
      As many a time   15
    They had seen it before.
    I told them in rhyme,
For of rhymes I had store:
    And 'twas in my vocation
      For their recreation   20
      That so I should sing;
    Because I was Laureate
    To them and the King.

From its sources which well[2]
    In the tarn[3] on the fell[4];   25
    From its fountains
    In the mountains,
    Its rills and its gills;
Through moss and through
    brake,[5]
    It runs and it creeps   30
    For awhile, till it sleeps
    In its own little lake.
And thence at departing,
Awakening and starting,
    It runs through the reeds   35
    And away it proceeds,
Through meadow and glade,
    In sun and in shade,
And through the wood-shelter,
    Among crags in its flurry,   40
    Helter-skelter,
    Hurry-scurry.
Here it comes sparkling,
And there it lies darkling;
Now smoking and frothing[45]
    Its tumult and wrath in,
    Till in this rapid race
      On which it is bent,
      It reaches the place
      Of its steep descent.   50

[2]*well,* begin.
[3]*tarn,* lake.
[4]*fell,* a moor, treeless upland.
[5]*brake,* fern.

The cataract strong
Then plunges along,
    Striking and raging
    As if a war waging
Its caverns and rocks among: 55
    Rising and leaping,
    Sinking and creeping,
    Swelling and sweeping,
Showering and springing,
    Flying and flinging,   60
    Writhing and ringing,
    Eddying and whisking,
    Spouting and frisking,
    Turning and twisting,
    Around and around   65
    With endless rebound!
    Smiting and fighting,
    A sight to delight in;
Confounding, astounding,
Dizzying and deafening the ear
    with its sound.   70

Collecting, projecting,
Receding and speeding,
And shocking and rocking,
And darting and parting,
And threading and spreading,
And whizzing and hissing,   76
And dripping and skipping,
And hitting and splitting,
And shining and twining,
And rattling and battling,   80
And shaking and quaking,
And pouring and roaring,
And waving and raving,
And tossing and crossing,
And flowing and going,   85
And running and stunning,
And foaming and roaming,
And dinning and spinning,
And dropping and hopping,
And working and jerking,   90
And guggling and struggling,
And heaving and cleaving,
And moaning and groaning;
And glittering and frittering,
And gathering and feather-   95
    ing,

And whitening and brighten-
ing,
And quivering and shivering,
And hurrying and skurrying,
And thundering and flounder-
ing;

Dividing and gliding and sliding,   100
And falling and brawling and
sprawling,
And driving and riving and
striving,
And sprinkling and twinkling
and wrinkling,
And sounding and bounding and
rounding,
And bubbling and troubling and
doubling,   105
And grumbling and rumbling
and tumbling,
And clattering and battering and
shattering;

Retreating and beating and
meeting and sheeting,

Delaying and straying and playing and spraying,
Advancing and prancing and
glancing and dancing,   110
Recoiling, turmoiling and toiling and boiling,
And gleaming and streaming and
steaming and beaming,
And rushing and flushing and
brushing and gushing,
And flapping and rapping and
clapping and slapping,
And curling and whirling and
purling and twirling,   115
And thumping and plumping
and bumping and jumping,
And dashing and flashing and
splashing and clashing;
And so never ending, but always
descending,
Sounds and motions for ever and
ever are blending,
All at once and all o'er, with a
mighty uproar;   120
And this way the water comes
down at Lodore.

For Thought and Discussion

1. How many of the poet's children gathered around him to
   hear how the water came down at Lodore?
2. The poet makes use of onomatopoeia, the use of words to imitate the sound of the thing described. Can you give other
   poems which also imitate sounds?
3. Compare this poem with "The Brook," by Tennyson. Read
   "The Cataract of Lodore" aloud to get the sound effects.

❧

FROM GREEN MANSIONS
WILLIAM HENRY HUDSON

[Only a naturalist with the imagination of a poet and a romancer could
have conceived the method used by
Hudson to create and interpret a
character at once so simple, so human,
so ethereal, so akin to the spirit of the
forest folk and the forces of nature
as was the bird-woman, the heroine

of *Green Mansions*, from which the
following sketches are taken.]

IN the midst of this leafy labyrinth
I sat down on a projecting root
to cool my blood before attempting
to make my way back to my former
position. After that tempest of mo-

tion and confused noises the silence of the forest seemed very profound; but before I had been resting many moments it was broken by a low strain of exquisite bird-melody, wonderfully pure and expressive, unlike any musical sound I had ever heard before. It seemed to issue from a thick cluster of broad leaves of a creeper only a few yards from where I sat. With my eyes fixed on this green hiding-place I waited with suspended breath for its repetition, wondering whether any civilised being had ever listened to such a strain before. Surely not, I thought, else the fame of so divine a melody would long ago have been noised abroad. I thought of the rialejo, the celebrated organ-bird or flute-bird, and of the various ways in which hearers are affected by it. To some its warbling is like the sound of a beautiful mysterious instrument, while to others it seems like the singing of a blithe-hearted child with a highly melodious voice. I had often heard and listened with delight to the singing of the rialejo in the Guayana forests, but this song, or musical phrase, was utterly unlike it in character. It was pure, more expressive, softer— so low that at a distance of forty yards I could hardly have heard it. But its greatest charm was its resemblance to the human voice — a voice purified and brightened to something almost angelic. Imagine, then, my impatience as I sat there straining my sense, my deep disappointment when it was not repeated! I rose at length very reluctantly and slowly began making my way back; but when I had progressed about thirty yards, again the sweet voice sounded just behind me, and turning quickly I stood still and waited. The same voice, but not the same song— not the same phrase; the notes were

different, more varied and rapidly enunciated, as if the singer had been more excited. The blood rushed to my heart as I listened; my nerves tingled with a strange new delight, the rapture produced by such music heightened by a sense of mystery. Before many moments I heard it again, not rapid now, but a soft warbling, lower than at first, infinitely sweet and tender, sinking to lisping sounds that soon ceased to be audible; the whole having lasted as long as it would take me to repeat a sentence of a dozen words. This seemed the singer's farewell to me, for I waited and listened in vain to hear it repeated; and after getting back to the starting-point I sat for upwards of an hour, still hoping to hear it once more!

. . . .

Have you ever observed a humming-bird moving about in an aërial dance among the flowers—a living prismatic gem that changes its colour with every change of position— how in turning it catches the sunshine on its burnished neck and gorget plumes—green and gold and flame-coloured, the beams changing to visible flakes as they fall, dissolving into nothing, to be succeeded by others and yet others? In its exquisite form, its changeful splendour, its swift motions and intervals of aërial suspension, it is a creature of such fairy-like loveliness as to mock all description. And have you seen this same fairy-like creature suddenly perch itself on a twig, in the shade, its misty wings and fanlike tail folded, the iridescent glory vanished, looking like some common dull-plumaged little bird sitting listless in a cage? Just so great was the difference in the girl, as I had seen her in the forest and as she now appeared under the smoky roof in the firelight. . . . .

For some moments I stood still on the ridge, struck by the somewhat weird aspect of the shadowed scene before me—the long strip of dull uniform green, with here and there a slender palm lifting its feathery crown above the other trees, standing motionless, in strange relief against the advancing blackness. Then I set out once more at a run, taking advantage of the downward slope to get well on my way before the tempest should burst. As I approached the wood there came a flash of lightning, pale, but covering the whole visible sky, followed after a long interval by a distant roll of thunder, which lasted several seconds, and ended with a succession of deep throbs. It was as if Nature herself, in supreme anguish and abandonment, had cast herself prone on the earth, and her great heart had throbbed audibly, shaking the world with its beats. No more thunder followed, but the rain was coming down heavily now in huge drops that fell straight through the gloomy, windless air. In half a minute I was drenched to the skin; but for a short time the rain seemed an advantage, as the brightness of the falling water lessened the gloom, turning the air from dark to lighter grey. This subdued rain-light did not last long: I had not been twenty minutes in the wood before a second and greater darkness fell on the earth, accompanied by an even more copious downpour of water. The sun had evidently gone down, and the whole sky was now covered with one thick cloud.

.   .   .   .

As I kept to the more open part of the wood, on its southernmost border, the red flame of the sinking sun was seen at intervals through the deep humid green of the higher foliage.

How every object it touched took from it a new wonderful glory! At one spot, high up where the foliage was scanty, and slender bush ropes and moss depended like broken cordage from a dead limb — just there, bathing itself in that glory-giving light, I noticed a fluttering bird, and stood still to watch its antics. Now it would cling, head downwards, to the slender twigs, wings and tail open; then, righting itself, it would flit from waving line to line, dropping lower and lower; and anon soar upwards a distance of twenty feet and alight to recommence the flitting and swaying and dropping towards the earth. It was one of those birds that have a polished plumage, and as it moved this way and that, flirting its feathers, they caught the beams and shone at moments like glass or burnished metal. Suddenly another bird of the same kind dropped down to it as if from the sky, straight and swift as a falling stone; and the first bird sprang up to meet the comer, and after rapidly wheeling round each other for a moment they fled away in company, screaming shrilly through the wood, and were instantly lost to sight, while their jubilant cries came back fainter and fainter at each repetition.

I envied them not their wings: at that moment earth did not seem fixed and solid beneath me, nor I bound by gravity to it. The faint, floating clouds, the blue infinite heaven itself, seemed not more ethereal and free than I, or the ground I walked on. The low, stony hills on my right hand, of which I caught occasional glimpses through the trees, looking now blue and delicate in the level rays, were no more than the billowy projections on the moving cloud of earth: the trees of unnumbered kinds —great mora, cecropia, and greenheart, bush and fern and suspended lianas, and tall palms balancing their feathery foliage on slender stems— all was but a fantastic mist embroidery covering the surface of that floating cloud on which my feet were set, and which floated with me near the sun.

. . . .

One night a moth fluttered in and alighted on my hand as I sat by the fire, causing me to hold my breath as I gazed on it. Its fore wings were pale grey, with shadings dark and light written all over in finest characters with some twilight mystery or legend; but the round underwings were clear amber-yellow, veined like a leaf with red and purple veins; a thing of such exquisite chaste beauty that the sight of it gave me a sudden shock of pleasure. Very soon it flew up circling about, and finally lighted on the palm-leaf thatch directly over the fire. The heat, I thought, would soon drive it from the spot; and, rising, I opened the door, so that it might find its way out again into its own cool, dark, flowery world. And standing by the open door I turned and addressed it: "O night-wanderer of the pale, beautiful wings, go forth, and should you by chance meet her somewhere in the shadowy depths, revisiting her old haunts, be my messenger——" Thus much had I spoken when the frail thing loosened its hold to fall without a flutter, straight and swift, into the white blaze beneath.

For Thought and Discussion

1. Are these sketches written in the language of a poet or of a naturalist? Give proof by quotations.
2. What hints do you find that the nature descriptions are given with the ulterior motive of interpreting character rather than for beauty of sight or sound?
3. How does this selection differ from "The Piebald Horse" in content, in treatment, and in tone?
4. Which of the two selections do you like the better? Why?
5. Does the hint of mystery, as a rule, add to the delight of an experience?
6. Quote examples of poetic diction.
7. Note the effective use of contrast in scene and in mood.

&

HOME THOUGHTS FROM ABROAD
ROBERT BROWNING

[Browning is not primarily a landscape artist, yet often his verses present glimpses of pastoral loveliness such as are found in this lyric of springtime. The poem offers evidence of his minute observation of and love for nature.]

OH, to be in England
Now that April's there,
And whoever wakes in England
Sees, some morning, unaware,
That the lowest boughs and the
    brushwood sheaf   5

Round the elm-tree bole are in tiny
    leaf,
While the chaffinch sings on the or-
    chard bough
In England—now!

And after April, when May follows,
And the whitethroat builds, and all
    the swallows!   10
Hark, where my blossomed pear-tree
    in the hedge
Leans to the field and scatters on the
    clover
Blossoms and dewdrops—at the bent
    spray's edge—

That's the wise thrush; he sings each
    song twice over,
Lest you should think he never could
    recapture   15
The first fine careless rapture!
And though the fields look rough
    with hoary dew,
All will be gay when noontide wakes
    anew
The buttercups, the little children's
    dower—
Far brighter than this gaudy melon-
    flower!

For Thought and Discussion

1. Judging from the selections in this book and from other poems by him which you have read, and from what you have read concerning his works, do you consider this poem typical of Browning? Why or why not?
2. Of what other poet's works does the poem remind you?
3. Does this selection seem more or less spontaneous than other poems by Browning with which you are familiar? Can you account for this?
4. For what purpose does Browning primarily make use of nature in his poetry?

From THE ROADMENDER
MICHAEL FAIRLESS

[Margaret Fairless Barber (Michael Fairless) lies "under the firs in the quiet churchyard" at Ashhurst, Sussex, England, a few miles from the farm house where she wrote *The Roadmender,* the group of simple and lovely prose lyrics from which this sketch is taken.]

THE coppice at our back is full of birds, for it is far from the road and they nest there undisturbed year after year. Through the still night I heard the nightingales calling, calling, until I could bear it no longer and went softly out into the luminous dark.

The little wood was manifold with sound, I heard my little brothers who move by night rustling in grass and tree. A hedgehog crossed my path with a dull squeak, the bats shrilled high to the stars, a white owl swept past me crying his hunting note, a beetle boomed suddenly in my face; and above and through it all the nightingales sang—and sang!

The night wind bent the listening trees, and the stars yearned earthward to hear the song of deathless love. Louder and louder the wonderful notes rose and fell in a passion of melody; and then sank to rest on that low thrilling call which it is said Death once heard, and stayed his hand.

They will scarcely sing again this year, these nightingales, for they are late on the wing as it is. It seems as if on such nights they sang as the swan sings, knowing it to be the last time—with the lavish note of one who bids an eternal farewell.

At last there was silence. Sitting under the big beech tree, the giant of the coppice, I rested my tired self in the lap of mother earth, breathed of her breath and listened to her voice in the quickening silence until my flesh came again as the flesh of a little child, for it is true recreation to sit at the foot-stool of God wrapped in a fold of His living robe, the while night soothes our tired face with her healing hands.

The grey dawn awoke and stole with trailing robes across earth's floor. At her footsteps the birds roused from sleep and cried a greeting; the sky flushed and paled conscious of coming splendour; and overhead a file of swans passed with broad strong flight to the reeded waters of the sequestered pool.

Another hour of silence while the light throbbed and flamed in the east; then the larks rose harmonious from a neighbouring field, the rabbits scurried with ears alert to their morning meal, the day had begun.

I passed through the coppice and out into the fields beyond. The dew lay heavy on leaf and blade and gossamer, a cool fresh wind swept clear over dale and down from the sea, and the clover field rippled like a silvery lake in the breeze.

There is something inexpressibly beautiful in the unused day, something beautiful in the fact that it is still untouched, unsoiled; and town and country share alike in this loveliness. At half-past three on a June morning even London has not assumed her responsibilities, but smiles and glows lighthearted and smokeless under the caresses of the morning sun.

Five o'clock. The bell rings out crisp and clear from the monastery where the Bedesmen of St. Hugh watch and pray for the souls on this labouring forgetful earth. Every hour the note of comfort and warning cries across the land, tells the Sanctus, the Angelus, and the Hours of the Passion, and calls to remembrance and prayer.

When the wind is north, the sound carries as far as my road, and companies me through the day; and if to His dumb children God in His mercy reckons work as prayer, most certainly those who have forged through the ages an unbroken chain of supplication and thanksgiving will be counted among the stalwart labourers of the house of the Lord.

Sun and bell together are my only clock: it is time for my water drawing; and gathering a pile of mushrooms, children of the night, I hasten home.

The cottage is dear to me in its quaint untidiness and want of rectitude, dear because we are to be its last denizens, last of the long line of toilers who have sweated and sown that others might reap, and have passed away leaving no trace.

I once saw a tall cross in a seaboard churchyard, inscribed, "To the memory of the unknown dead who have perished in these waters." There might be one in every village sleeping-place to the unhonoured many who made fruitful the land with sweat and tears. It is a consolation to think that when we look back on this stretch of life's road from beyond the first milestone, which, it is instructive to remember, is always a grave, we may hope to see the work of this world with open eyes, and to judge of it with a due sense of proportion.

A bee with laden honey - bag hummed and buzzed in the hedge as I got ready for work, importuning the flowers for that which he could not carry, and finally giving up the attempt in despair fell asleep on a buttercup, the best place for his weary little velvet body. In five minutes—they may have been five hours to him—he awoke a new bee, sensible and clear-sighted, and flew blithely away to the hive with his sufficiency—an example this weary world would be wise to follow.

My road has been lonely to-day. A parson came by in the afternoon, a stranger in the neighbourhood, for he asked his way. He talked awhile, and with kindly rebuke said it was sad to see a man of my education brought so low, which shows how the outside appearance may mislead the prejudiced observer. "Was it misfortune?" "Nay, the best of good luck," I answered, gaily.

The good man with beautiful readiness sat down on a heap of stones and bade me say on. "Read me a sermon in stone," he said, simply; and I stayed my hand to read.

He listened with courteous intelligence.

"You hold a roadmender has a vocation?" he asked.

"As the monk or the artist, for, like both, he is universal. The world is his home; he serves all men alike, ay, and for him the beasts have equal honour with the men. His soul is 'bound up in the bundle of life' with all other souls, he sees his father, his mother, his brethren in the children of the road. For him there is nothing unclean, nothing common; the very stones cry out that they serve."

Parson nodded his head.

"It is all true," he said; "beautifully true. But need such a view of life necessitate the work of roadmending? Surely all men should be roadmenders."

O wise parson, so to read the lesson of the road!

"It is true," I answered; "but some of us find our salvation in the actual work, and earn our bread better in this than in any other way. No man is dependent on our earning, all men on our work. We are 'rich beyond the dreams of avarice' because we have all that we need, and yet we taste the life and poverty of the very poor. We are, if you will, uncloistered monks, preaching friars who speak not with the tongue, disciples who hear the wise words of a silent master."

"Robert Louis Stevenson was a roadmender," said the wise parson.

"Ay, and with more than his pen," I answered. "I wonder was he ever so truly great, so entirely the man we know and love, as when he inspired the chiefs to make a highway in the wilderness. Surely no more fitting monument could exist to his memory than the Road of Gratitude, cut, laid, and kept by the pure-blooded tribe kings of Samoa."

Parson nodded.

He knew that the people who make no roads are ruled out from intelligent participation in the world's brotherhood. He filled his pipe, thinking the while, then he held out his pouch to me.

"Try some of this baccy," he said; "Sherwood of Magdalen sent it me from some outlandish place."

I accepted gratefully. It was such tobacco as falls to the lot of few roadmenders.

He rose to go.

"I wish I could come and break stones," he said, a little wistfully.

"Nay," said I, "few men have such weary roadmending as yours, and perhaps you need my road less than most men, and less than most parsons."

We shook hands, and he went down the road and out of my life.

He little guessed that I knew Sherwood, ay, and knew him too, for had not Sherwood told me of the man he delighted to honour.

Ah, well! I am no Browning Junior, and Sherwood's name is not Sherwood.

For Thought and Discussion

1. What is the setting for this selection?
2. What joy did the writer derive from the setting?
3. Enumerate qualities which entitle this selection to be called lyric prose.
4. How does the roadmender regard his work?
5. What symbolical significance does the parson give to roadmending?
6. In what two senses was Stevenson regarded as a roadmender?
7. In what sense was the parson regarded as a roadmender?
8. Was Michael Fairless responsive to beauty of a city scene as well as to that of a country scene?
9. Which would you say the author worshiped, beauty and nature or the Creator of these things?
10. Which do you enjoy more in the story, the description of nature or the allegorical teaching?
11. What suggests that Michael Fairless agrees with Browning's statement "All service ranks the same with God"?
12. In what senses does a country have to be a road-builder in order to participate in world affairs?

WRITTEN IN MARCH
WILLIAM WORDSWORTH

[This refreshing springtime poem is one of the best illustrations possible of Wordsworth's plan of presenting the bird, the stream, the fields, the clouds, and other phases of nature just as they are and letting them speak their own message. Burns, like Gray, often registered his own emotions in a poem. Wordsworth rarely ever did so.]

THE cock is crowing,
The stream is flowing,
The small birds twitter,
The lake doth glitter,

The green field sleeps in the sun;   5
The oldest and youngest
Are at work with the strongest;
The cattle are grazing,
Their heads never raising;
There are forty feeding like one!   10

Like an army defeated
The snow hath retreated,
And now doth fare ill
On the top of the bare hill;
The plowboy is whooping—anon-   15
anon:
There's joy in the mountains;

There's life in the fountains;
Small clouds are sailing,
Blue sky prevailing;
The rain is over and gone.

For Thought and Discussion

1. What is the emotion which every one except a hopeless grouch would feel while reading this lyric? What is responsible for the emotion?
2. With the passing of the era of "great open spaces" is there a likelihood of the passing of a certain joy from the earth?
3. Is providing joy for a people within the realm of governmental obligations? Are joyous people usually law-abiding?
4. Using the term in its literal sense, what provisions can municipal, state, and federal bodies make to insure for urban and suburban dwellers the sights and, therefore, the memories of "blue sky prevailing"?
5. Using the term in a figurative sense, name certain provisions made by the government to insure *blue skies* for hundreds of thousands of American citizens.

COMPOSED UPON WESTMINSTER BRIDGE
WILLIAM WORDSWORTH

[This poem was composed while the poet was riding on the top of a London coach on the way to France, while the companion poem, "It Is a Beauteous Evening," was written soon after the poet's arrival at Calais.]

EARTH has not anything to show more fair;
Dull would he be of soul who could pass by
A sight so touching in its majesty.
This city now doth, like a garment, wear
The beauty of the morning; silent, bare,   5
Ships, towers, domes, theaters, and temples lie
Open unto the fields, and to the sky—
All bright and glittering in the smokeless air.
Never did sun more beautifully steep
In his first splendor, valley, rock, or hill;   10
Ne'er saw I, never felt, a calm so deep!
The river glideth at his own sweet will.
Dear God! the very houses seem asleep;
And all that mighty heart is lying still!

IT IS A BEAUTEOUS EVENING
WILLIAM WORDSWORTH

[¹*Dear child! dear girl!* refers to a little girl who was walking with Wordsworth along the seashore.

²*Abraham's bosom* means in the presence of God. See Luke 16:22.]

I T IS a beauteous evening, calm and
 free;
The holy time is quiet as a nun
Breathless with adoration; the broad
 sun
Is sinking down in its tranquillity;
The gentleness of heaven broods o'er
 the sea.   5
Listen! the mighty being is awake,
And doth with his eternal motion
 make
A sound like thunder—everlastingly.
Dear child! dear girl!¹ that walkest
 with me here,
If thou appear untouched by solemn
 thought,   10
Thy nature is not therefore less di-
 vine—
Thou liest in Abraham's bosom² all
 the year,
And worship'st at the temple's inner
 shrine,
God being with thee when we know
 it not.

THE WORLD IS TOO MUCH WITH US
WILLIAM WORDSWORTH

[*Proteus* and *Triton* were sea gods, the first being the shepherd of Neptune's sheep; the latter, Neptune's son who had power to govern the winds by blowing upon his seashell. Wordsworth here expresses the idea that he would rather be a pagan with some sense of the Divinity in nature than to be a professed Christian, who because of his love and pursuit of power and wealth, is indifferent to that Divinity.]

T HE world is too much with us;
 late and soon,
Getting and spending, we lay waste
 our powers;
Little we see in Nature that is ours;
We have given our hearts away, a
 sordid boon!
The sea that bares her bosom to the
 moon;   5
The winds that will be howling at all
 hours,
And are upgathered now like sleep-
 ing flowers;
For this, for everything, we are out of
 tune;
It moves us not.—Great God! I'd
 rather be
A pagan suckled in a creed outworn;¹⁰
So might I, standing on this pleasant
 lea,
Have glimpses that would make me
 less forlorn;
Have sight of Proteus rising from the
 sea;
Or hear old Triton blow his wreathèd
 horn.

For Thought and Discussion

 1. What is the general theme of each of these sonnets—"Composed Upon Westminster Bridge," "It Is a Beauteous Evening," "The World Is Too Much With Us"?

2. What similarities do you note in the first two sonnets?
3. How do the poems vary in subject matter and in sentiment?
4. What attribute described in these poems do you think Words-worth admired most?
5. Do you think the conditions described in the third sonnet are applicable to America today?
6. Which of the figures of speech used do you think is most effective?
7. Indicate evidences of mysticism in these and in other of Wordsworth's poems.

~~

PAN'S PIPES
ROBERT LOUIS STEVENSON

[Only a chosen few of the people of the world catch the varied notes of terror and charm in the pipes of the great god Pan[1] as he pipes by the reeds in the river—only a few, like Stevenson and Mrs. Browning, see both the filth and the lilies in the reeds by the river—only a few recognize the relationship existing between the piper's notes of ugliness and cruelty and death, and his notes of beauty and joy and life.]

THE world in which we live has been variously said and sung by the most ingenious poets and philosophers: these reducing it to formulae and chemical ingredients, those striking the lyre in high-sounding measures for the handiwork of God. What experience supplies is of a mingled tissue, and the choosing mind has much to reject before it can get together the materials of a theory. Dew and thunder, destroying Attila and the Spring lambkins, belong to an order of contrasts which no repetition

---

[1]*Pan*, in Greek mythology, the chief god of pastures, forests, and flocks, a lover of music and dancing, credited with the invention of musical instruments. He was represented with the head of a man and with lower limbs like the hindquarters of a goat.

can assimilate. There is an uncouth, outlandish strain throughout the web of the world, as from a vexatious planet in the house of life. Things are not congruous and wear strange disguises: the consummate flower is fostered out of dung, and after nourishing itself awhile with heaven's delicate distillations, decays again into indistinguishable soil; and with Caesar's ashes, Hamlet tells us, the urchins make dirt pies and filthily besmear their countenance. Nay, the kindly shine of summer, when tracked home with the scientific spy-glass, is found to issue from the most portentous nightmare of the universe—the great, conflagrant sun: a world of hell's squibs, tumultuary, roaring aloud, inimical to life. The sun itself is enough to disgust a human being of the scene which he inhabits; and you would not fancy there was a green or habitable spot in the universe thus awfully lighted up. And yet it is by the blaze of such a conflagration, to which the fire of Rome was but a spark, that we do all our fiddling, and hold domestic tea-parties at the arbour door.

The Greeks figured Pan, the god of Nature, now terribly stamping his foot, so that armies were dispersed;

now by the woodside on a summer noon trolling on his pipe until he charmed the hearts of upland ploughmen. And the Greeks, in so figuring, uttered the last word of human experience. To certain smoke-dried spirits matter and motion and elastic ethers, and the hypothesis of this or that other spectacled professor, tell a speaking story; but for youth and all ductile and congenial minds, Pan is not dead, but of all the classic hierarchy alone survives in triumph; goat-footed, with a gleeful and an angry look, the type of the shaggy world: and in every wood, if you go with a spirit properly prepared, you shall hear the note of his pipe.

For it is a shaggy world, and yet studded with gardens; where the salt and tumbling sea receives clear rivers running from among reeds and lilies; fruitful and austere; a rustic world; sunshiny, lewd, and cruel. What is it the birds sing among the trees in pairing-time? What means the sound of the rain falling far and wide upon the leafy forest? To what tune does the fisherman whistle, as he hauls in his net at morning, and the bright fish are heaped inside the boat? These are all airs upon Pan's pipe; he it was who gave them breath in the exultation of his heart, and gleefully modulated their outflow with his lips and fingers. The coarse mirth of herdsmen, shaking the dells with laughter and striking out high echoes from the rock; the tune of moving feet in the lamp-lit city, or on the smooth ball-room floor; the hooves of many horses, beating the wide pastures in alarm; the song of hurrying rivers; the colour of clear skies; and smiles and the live touch of hands; and the voice of things, and their significant look, and the renovating influence they breathe forth—these are his joyful measures, to which the whole earth treads in choral harmony. To this music the young lambs bound as to a tabor, and the London shop-girl skips rudely in the dance. For it puts a spirit of gladness in all hearts; and to look on the happy side of nature is common, in their hours, to all created things. Some are vocal under a good influence, are pleasing whenever they are pleased, and hand on the happiness to others, as a child, who, looking upon lovely things, looks lovely. Some leap to the strains with unapt foot, and make a halting figure in the universal dance. And some, like sour spectators at the play, receive the music into their hearts with an unmoved countenance, and walk like strangers through the general rejoicing. But let him feign never so carefully, there is not a man but has his pulses shaken when Pan trolls out a stave of ecstasy and sets the world a-singing.

Alas if that were all! But oftentimes the air is changed; and in the screech of the night wind, chasing navies, subverting the tall ships and the rooted cedar of the hills; in the random deadly levin or the fury of headlong floods, we recognize the "dread foundation" of life and the anger in Pan's heart. Earth wages open war against her children, and under her softest touch hides treacherous claws. The cool waters invite us in to drown; the domestic hearth burns up in the hour of sleep, and makes an end of all. Everything is good or bad, helpful or deadly, not in itself, but by its circumstances. For a few bright days in England the hurricane must break forth and the North Sea pay a toll of populous ships .... It is no wonder, with so traitorous a scheme of things, if the wise people who created for us the idea of Pan thought that of all fears the fear of him was the most terrible, since it embraces all. And still we preserve the phrase: a panic terror. To reckon dangers too curiously, to hearken too intently for the threat that runs through all the winning music of the world, to hold back the hand from the rose because of the thorn, and from life because of death: this it is to be afraid of Pan. Highly respectable citizens who flee life's pleasures and responsibilities and keep, with upright hat, upon the midway of custom, avoiding the right hand and the left, the ecstasies and the agonies, how surprised they would be if they could hear their attitude mythologically expressed, and knew themselves as tooth-chattering ones, who flee from Nature because they fear the hand of Nature's God! Shrilly sound Pan's pipes; and behold the banker instantly concealed in the bank parlour! For to distrust one's impulses is to be recreant to Pan.

There are moments when the mind refuses to be satisfied with evolution, and demands a ruddier presentation of the sum of man's experience. Sometimes the mood is brought about by laughter at the humourous side of life, as when, abstracting ourselves from earth, we imagine people plodding on foot, or seated in ships and speedy trains, with the planet all the while whirling in the opposite direction, so that, for all their hurry, they travel back-foremost through the universe of space. Sometimes it comes by the spirit of delight, and sometimes by the spirit of terror. At least, there will always be hours when we refuse to be put off by the feint of explanation, nicknamed science; and demand instead some palpitating image of our estate, that shall represent the troubled and uncertain element in which we dwell, and satisfy reason by the means of art. Science writes of the world as if with the cold finger of a starfish; it is all true; but what is it when compared to the reality of which it discourses? where hearts beat high in April, and death strikes, and hills totter in the earthquake, and there is a glamour over all the objects of sight, and a thrill in all noises for the ear, and Romance herself has made her dwelling among men? So we come back to the old myth, and hear the goat-footed piper making the music which is itself the charm and terror of things; and when a glen invites our visiting footsteps, fancy that Pan leads us thither with a gracious tremolo; or when our hearts quail at the thunder of the cataract, tell ourselves that he has stamped his hoof in the nigh thicket.

For Thought and Discussion

1. Are all the sights of nature beautiful and all her sounds delightful?
2. Why should the fire of Rome be referred to in a nature selection?
3. Of what poem are you reminded by the line—"charmed the hearts of upland ploughmen"?
4. Is the slime of the river really ugly?
5. Do butterflies refuse to dine upon filth?
6. Are gentle touches always significant of kindness?
7. Is nature always a benefactor?
8. Do you like orderly, conventional garden plots or gardens that run riot?
9. From what is the term *panic* derived? What does it mean?

10. Had the Greeks any cause for thinking of Pan as half man, half beast?   Give proof from mythology.
11. Note lines showing Stevenson's familiarity with the works of other authors.
12. Copy lines notable for poetic qualities.

A MUSICAL INSTRUMENT

ELIZABETH BARRETT BROWNING

WHAT was he doing, the great god Pan,
  Down in the reeds by the river?
Spreading ruin and scattering ban,
Splashing and padding with hoofs of a goat,
And breaking the golden lilies afloat 5
  With the dragon-fly on the river?

He tore out a reed, the great god Pan,
  From the deep cool bed of the river:
The limpid water turbidly ran,
And the broken lilies a-dying lay,   10
And the dragon-fly had fled away,
  Ere he brought it out of the river.

High on the shore sat the great god Pan,
  While turbidly flowed the river,
And hacked and hewed as a great god can
  With his hard bleak steel at the patient reed, 15
Till there was not a sign of the leaf indeed
  To prove it fresh from the river.

He cut it short, did the great god Pan,
  (How tall it stood in the river!) 20
Then drew the pith like the heart of a man,
Steadily from the outside ring,
And notched the poor dry empty thing
  In holes as he sate by the river.

'This is the way,' laughed the great god Pan, 25

  (Laughed while he sate by the river!)
'The only way, since gods began
To make sweet music, they could succeed.'
Then dropping his mouth to a hole in the reed,
  He blew in power by the river.   30

Sweet, sweet, sweet, O Pan,
  Piercing sweet by the river!
Blinding sweet, O great god Pan!
The sun on the hill forgot to die,

And the lilies revived, and the dragon-
　　fly　　　　　　　　　　　　　　　35
Came back to dream on the river.

Yet half a beast is the great god Pan,
　To laugh as he sits by the river,
Making a poet out of a man.

The true gods sigh for the cost and
　pain—　　　　　　　　　　　　　40
For the reed which grows never more
　again
As a reed with the reeds in the
　river.

For Thought and Discussion

1. Note thoughts in Mrs. Browning's poem which are similar to
   thoughts expressed in Stevenson's essay about Pan.
2. What new ideas are introduced in the poem?　Which is the
   most important?
3. Is destruction of one form of beauty sometimes prerequisite to
   the creation of other types of beauty?　Can such destruction
   be justified?　How?　Is wanton destruction ever excusable?
4. What lines indicate that there was an element of wantonness
   in the work of Pan?
5. What is connoted by the line "The *true* gods sigh for the cost
   and pain—"?
6. Quote lines indicative of the power of music.

Plus Work

Read the myths about Pan.

Write a paper showing how music is used both as an excitant
and as a sedative—in every day life, in times of war, and in the
treatment of nervous and mental disorders.

～

ODE TO THE WEST WIND
PERCY BYSSHE SHELLEY

[Akin to his own tempestuous
spirit was the force of the wind,
which, sweeping over Florence on an
autumn day, gave Shelley the inspiration for this magnificent ode.　Akin
to his other spirit, too—that gentler
spirit of his, so sensitive and responsive to the beauty and love of nature
—are the exquisite descriptions of
scenes and moods described in the
poem.　Some critic has affirmed that
in this poem, as in other of his nature
lyrics, Shelley has no definite message
for humanity, but others find in the
closing lines of the poem an inspiring
prophecy.]

O WILD West Wind, thou breath
　of Autumn's being,
Thou, from whose unseen presence
　the leaves dead
Are driven, like ghosts from an en-
　chanter fleeing,
Yellow, and black, and pale, and hec-
　tic red,
Pestilence-stricken　multitudes:　O,
　thou,　　　　　　　　　　　　5
Who chariotest to their dark wintry
　bed
The wingèd seeds, where they lie cold
　and low,
Each like a corpse within its grave,
　until

Thine azure sister of the spring shall blow
Her clarion o'er the dreaming earth, and fill 10
(Driving sweet buds like flocks to feed in air)
With living hues and odors plain and hill;
Wild Spirit, which art moving every-where,
Destroyer and preserver—hear, oh, hear!

Thou on whose stream, 'mid the steep sky's commotion, 15
Loose clouds like earth's decaying leaves are shed,
Shook from the tangled boughs of heaven and ocean,
Angels of rain and lightning; there are spread
On the blue surface of thine airy surge,
Like the bright hair uplifted from the head 20
Of some fierce Maenad,[1] even from the dim verge
Of the horizon to the zenith's height
The locks of the approaching storm. Thou dirge
Of the dying year, to which this clos-ing night
Will be the dome of a vast sepul-cher, 25
Vaulted with all thy congregated might
Of vapors, from whose solid atmos-phere
Black rain, and fire, and hail will burst—oh, hear!

Thou who didst waken from his sum-mer dreams
The blue Mediterranean, where he lay, 30
Lulled by the coil of his crystalline streams,
Beside a pumice isle in Baiae's bay,

[1] *Maenad,* a frenzied nymph.

And saw in sleep old palaces and towers
Quivering within the wave's intenser day,
All overgrown with azure moss and flowers, 35
So sweet, the sense faints picturing them! Thou
For whose path the Atlantic's level powers
Cleave themselves into chasms, while far below
The sea-blooms and the oozy woods which wear
The sapless foliage of the ocean, know 40
Thy voice, and suddenly grow gray with fear,
And tremble and despoil themselves—oh, hear!

If I were a dead leaf thou mightest bear;
If I were a swift cloud to fly with thee;
A wave to pant beneath thy power, and share 45
The impulse of thy strength, only less free
Than thou, O uncontrollable! If even
I were as in my boyhood, and could be
The comrade of thy wanderings over heaven,
As then, when to outstrip thy skyey speed 50
Scarce seemed a vision—I would ne'er have striven
As thus with thee in prayer in my sore need.
Oh! lift me as a wave, a leaf, a cloud!
I fall upon the thorns of life! I bleed!
A heavy weight of hours has chained and bowed 55
One too like thee: tameless, and swift, and proud.

Make me thy lyre, even as the forest is;

What if my leaves are falling like its
    own!
The tumult of thy mighty harmonies
Will take from both a deep, autumnal
    tone,   60
Sweet though in sadness.   Be thou,
    spirit fierce,
My spirit!   Be thou me, impetuous
    one!
Drive my dead thoughts over the uni-
    verse
Like withered leaves to quicken a new
    birth!

And, by the incantation of this
    verse,   65
Scatter, as from an unextinguished
    hearth
Ashes and sparks, my words among
    mankind!
Be through my lips to unawakened
    earth
The trumpet of a prophecy!   O Wind,
If winter comes, can spring be far
    behind?

For Thought and Discussion

1. Which of the titles applied to the West Wind do you think most fitting?
2. Does your knowledge of science and of nature bear out Shelley's suggestions as to the beneficent and the destructive qualities of the wind?
3. What terms here applied to the wind do you think might well be used to describe Shelley?
4. Of what does each of the divisions of the poem treat?
5. Account for Shelley's tone of sadness.
6. What are the resemblances between the conclusion of this poem and that of "To a Skylark"?
7. What is the meaning of the questioning but hopeful prophecy with which the poem is concluded?
8. Wherein do you think the beauty of this poem lies?   in the sentiment?   in the colorful language?   in the suggestiveness of the figures of speech?   in the comparisons?

∼✔

L'ALLEGRO

JOHN MILTON

[In Milton the cavalier impulses of his nature were at variance with his Puritanic tendencies. This is clearly shown in his companion poems "L'Allegro" and "Il Penseroso."[1]

In "L'Allegro" (the cheerful or light-hearted man), his cavalier traits predominate; he presents himself as a carefree person who banishes melan-choly and invokes the presence of mirth and her companions.

He then recounts the events of a typical day of pleasure as enjoyed by a country youth near enough to the village and the city to join in their evening pastimes. Told in simple language, uninvolved by Milton's classical style and mythological references, the account in brief runs thus:

[1]L'Allegro (lä lā′ grō).   Il Penseroso (ĕl pĕn′ rō′ sō).

To the song of the lark he awakes one morning, sees the cock strut forth in the barnyard and watches the sun rise in splendor. He listens to the hunter's hounds and horns, to the plowman's whistle, to the milkmaid's songs. He sees the mower whet his scythe and hears the shepherd count his flock. Each hour of the morning presents some new pleasure of an idealized country day. The landscape is lovely; the noonday dinner served at the shepherd's cottage between two aged oaks is savoury; the work of binding sheaves is picturesque. In the late afternoon, to the tune of fiddle music, he joins in the outdoor dances when the young and old of the upland village celebrate their holiday. Later with them he listens to tales of fairy folk told around a bowl of spicy ale. Then, while the villagers are being lulled to sleep by the wind, he takes himself to the city to enjoy its typical recreations— feasts, tournaments, comedies, and light music.]

HENCE, loathèd Melancholy,
  Of Cerberus[2] and blackest Midnight born
In Stygian[3] cave forlorn.
  'Mongst horrid shapes, and shrieks, and sights unholy,
Find out some uncouth cell,   5
  Where brooding Darkness spreads his jealous wings,
And the night-raven sings;
  There, under ebon shades and low-browed rocks,
As ragged as thy locks,
  In dark Cimmerian[4] desert ever dwell.   10
But come, thou goddess fair and free,

In heaven yclept[5] Euphrosyne,
And by men, heart-easing Mirth,
Whom lovely Venus, at a birth
With two sister Graces more   15
To ivy-crownèd Bacchus[6] bore;
Or whether (as some sager sing)
The frolic wind that breathes the spring,
Zephyr, with Aurora playing,
As he met her once a-Maying,   20
There, on beds of violets blue,
And fresh-blown roses washed in dew,
Filled her with thee, a daughter fair,
So buxom, blithe, and debonair.
Haste thee, Nymph, and bring with thee   25
Jest and youthful Jollity,
Quips and Cranks and wanton Wiles,
Nods and Becks and wreathèd Smiles,
Such as hang on Hebe's[7] cheek,
And love to live in dimple sleek;   30
Sport that wrinkled Care derides,
And Laughter holding both his sides.
Come, and trip it, as you go,
On the light fantastic toe;
And in thy right hand lead with thee[35]
The mountain nymph, sweet Liberty[8];
And if I give thee honor due,
Mirth, admit me of thy crew,
To live with her, and live with thee,
In unreprovèd pleasures free;   40
To hear the lark begin his flight,
And singing startle the dull night,
From his watchtower in the skies,
Till the dappled dawn doth rise;
Then to come in spite of sorrow,   45
And at my window bid good morrow,
Through the sweetbrier or the vine,
Or the twisted eglantine;
While the cock with lively din,
Scatters the rear of darkness thin;   50
And to the stack, or the barn door,
Stoutly struts his dames before;

[2]*Cerberus* (sûr' bēr ŭs), three-headed dog guarding the entrance to Hades.
[3]*Stygian*, referring to gloomy river Styx in Hades.
[4]*Cimmerian desert* (sĭ mē' rĭ ăn), land in which sun never shines.

[5]*yclept*, called.
[6]*Bacchus* (băk' ŭs), the god of wine.
[7]*Hebe* (hē' bē), the goddess of youth.
[8]*Liberty*, mountain nymph, so-called because mountaineers are usually freedom loving people.

Oft list'ning how the hounds and horn
Cheerly rouse the slumbering morn,
From the side of some hoar hill,   55
Through the high wood echoing shrill;
Sometime walking not unseen,
By hedgerow elms, on hillocks green,
Right against the eastern gate
Where the great sun begins his state,   60
Robed in flames and amber light,
The clouds in thousand liveries dight[9];
While the plowman, near at hand,
Whistles o'er the furrowed land,
And the milkmaid singeth blithe,   65
And the mower whets his scythe,
And every shepherd tells his tale[10]
Under the hawthorn in the dale.
Straight mine eye hath caught new pleasures
Whilst the landskip round it measures;   70
Russet lawns, and fallows gray,
Where the nibbling flocks do stray;

Mountains on whose barren breast
The laboring clouds do often rest;
Meadows trim with daisies pied;   75
Shallow brooks, and rivers wide;
Towers, and battlements it sees
Bosomed high in tufted trees,
Where perhaps some beauty lies,
The cynosure of neighboring eyes.   80
Hard by a cottage chimney smokes
From betwixt two agèd oaks,
Where Corydon[11] and Thyrsis[12] met,
Are at their savory dinner set
Of herbs and other country messes,   85
Which the neat-handed Phyllis[13] dresses;
And then in haste her bower she leaves,
With Thestylis to bind the sheaves;
Or if the earlier season lead,
To the tanned haycock in the mead.
Sometimes with secure delight,   91
The upland hamlets will invite,
When the merry bells ring round,

[9]*dight*, dressed.
[10]*shepherd tells his tale*, counts his sheep.

[11]*Corydon* (kŏr' ĭ dŭn), country fellow.
[12]*Thyrsis* (thûr' sĭs), another country man.
[13]*Phyllis* (fĭl' ĭs), *Thestylis* (thĕs' tĭ lĭs), country lasses.

And the jocund rebecks[14] sound
To many a youth, and many a maid [95]
Dancing in the checkered shade,
And young and old come forth to play
On a sunshine holiday,
Till the livelong daylight fail.
Then to the spicy nut-brown ale, [100]
With stories told of many a feat,
How Fairy Mab[15] the junkets eat.
She was pinched and pulled, she said,
And he, by Friar's[16] lantern led
Tells how the drudging goblin[17] sweat [105]
To earn his cream-bowl duly set,
When in one night, ere glimpse of morn,
His shadowy flail hath threshed the corn
That ten day-laborers could not end;
Then lies him down, the lubber fiend, [110]
And, stretched out all the chimney's length,
Basks at the fire his hairy strength;
And crop-full out of doors he flings,
Ere the first cock his matin rings.
Thus done the tales, to bed they creep, [115]
By whispering winds soon lulled asleep
Towered cities please us then,
And the busy hum of men,
Where throngs of knights and barons bold,
In weeds of peace, high triumphs hold, [120]
With store of ladies, whose bright eyes
Rain influence, and judge the prize
Of wit or arms, while both contend
To win her grace whom all commend.

There let Hymen[18] oft appear [125]
In saffron robe, with taper clear,
And pomp, and feast, and revelry,
With mask, and antique pageantry;
Such sights as youthful poets dream
On summer eves by haunted stream. [130]
Then to the well-trod stage anon,
If Jonson's[19] learnèd sock be on,
Or sweetest Shakespeare, fancy's child,
Warble his native wood-notes wild.
And ever, against eating cares, [135]
Lap me in soft Lydian airs,[20]
Married to immortal verse
Such as the meeting soul may pierce,
In notes with many a winding bout
Of linkèd sweetness long drawn out [140]
With wanton heed, and giddy cunning,
The melting voice through mazes running,
Untwisting all the chains that tie
The hidden soul of harmony;
That Orpheus[21] self may heave his head [145]
From golden slumber on a bed
Of heaped Elysian flowers, and hear
Such strains as would have won the ear
Of Pluto, to have quite set free
His half regained Eurydice. [150]
These delights, if thou canst give,
Mirth, with thee I mean to live.

---

[14]*rebeck*, a fiddle-like musical instrument found in country places.
[15]*Fairy Mab*, the mischievous queen of the fairies.
[16]*Friar's lantern*, Will-o'-the-wisp, a teasing, malicious sprite.
[17]*drudging goblin*, Robin Goodfellow, or Hobgoblin, or Puck, a house-elf, who helped the laborers and received a bowl of cream in return.

[18]*Hymen* (hī′ mĕn), the god of marriage, who presided at the wedding feast.
[19]*Jonson's learnèd sock*, Ben Jonson's comedies. The actor in comedy wore a low-heeled slipper, called a sock.
[20]*Lydian airs*, the softest of the Greek music.
[21]*Orpheus* (ôr′ fē ŭs), a Greek musician, who after the death of his wife, Eurydice (û rĭd′ i sē), visited the lower regions and gained Pluto's permission to take Eurydice back to earth with him, if he would not look back until he reached the open air. Eurydice followed his music. Orpheus forgot his promise and looked back. She vanished.

For Thought and Discussion

1. Have the notes on the poem been mastered?
2. Whom does the poet banish? Where is this character sent? Describe the place.
3. Whom does he call to be his companion? Give both names for this character.
4. Why does he imagine that Mirth is the child of Venus and Bacchus? of Zephyr (the west wind) and Aurora (the dawn)? Which parentage seems the more attractive to you?
5. What other companions does he ask Mirth to bring with her? What mood would you be in with these companions?
6. What sounds does the cheerful man hear? What does he see?
7. Who are Corydon and Thyrsis, Phyllis and Thestylis? Why are they mentioned?
8. What amusements do the country people enjoy? the city people?
9. Who was Orpheus? Why is he mentioned?
10. While one student reads this poem aloud to the class, let other members of the class select favorite lines and in turn read aloud the line or lines selected. The music and beauty of the lines become apparent through reading aloud.

Plus Work

A background study and test gives a class the necessary knowledge for understanding this poem. The teacher and the members of the class select twenty-five significant words, proper names, and phrases for study. The pupils study notes, the dictionary, and the stories of Greek and Roman mythology for two or three class periods. The teacher dictates the words, and the pupils write definitions and explanations. The papers are marked by the teacher or pupils and returned to the pupils, who are thus prepared to read the poem with a certain amount of understanding and appreciation.

～✌～

IL PENSEROSO
JOHN MILTON

[In contrast to "L'Allegro," "Il Penseroso" is a study of a man in a pensive, thoughtful mood. In this Milton as Il Penseroso (the melancholy or serious man) banishes Joy and invites Melancholy and her companions to join him. In the evening he walks alone in the moonlit garden and listens to the song of the nightingale and the sound of the far-off curfew bell. At midnight in a lonely tower he likes to view the starry heavens and read tragic dramas, and the works of such immortals as Homer, Plato,[1] and Chaucer

He enjoys a gray rainy morning, and when the sun begins to shine, he betakes himself to twilight groves and finds a smooth-flowing brook beside which he may sit and dream. Two of

[1]*Homer* and *Plato,* Greek philosophers.

[his chief delights are to walk in the
university grounds and to worship
where stained glass windows cast "a
dim religious light" and the sound of
organ music and pealing anthems lift
his heart to heaven. He pictures for
himself a peaceful old age devoted to
serious study.]

HENCE, vain deluding Joys,
    The brood of Folly without
      father bred,
How little you bested,[2]
  Or fill the fixèd[3] mind with all your
      toys;
Dwell in some idle brain,   5
    And fancies fond with gaudy
     shapes possess,
As thick and numberless
    As the gay motes that people the
      sunbeams,
Or likest hovering dreams,
    The fickle pensioners of Morpheus'[4]
      train.   10
But, hail! thou goddess, sage and holy,
Hail divinest Melancholy,
Whose saintly visage is too bright
To hit the sense of human sight,
And therefore to our weaker view 15
O'erlaid with black, staid Wisdom's
    hue;
Black, but such as in esteem
Prince Memnon's[5] sister might be-
    seem,
Or that starred Ethiope queen[6] that
    strove
To set her beauty's praise above   20

---

[2]*bested,* bestead, avail.
[3]*fixed,* steadfast.
[4]*Morpheus,* the god of sleep.
[5]*Prince Memnon's sister,* Prince
Memnon was an Ethiopian king, celebrated for his dark-skinned beauty.
The poet suggests that his sister was
also noted for her beauty.
[6]*starred Ethiope queen,* Cassiopeia,
who affirmed that her daughter was
more beautiful than the sea nymphs
and thus offended them. They attempted, without success, to cause the
destruction of Andromeda. Cassiopeia
was afterward changed to a constellation, hence *starred.*

The sea nymphs, and their powers
    offended.
Yet thou art higher far descended;
Thee bright-haired Vesta[7] long of
    yore
To solitary Saturn[8] bore;
His daughter she (in Saturn's reign 25
Such mixture was not held a stain)
Oft in glimmering bowers and glades
He met her, and in secret shades
Of woody Ida's[9] inmost grove,
Whilst yet there was no fear of Jove.[30]
Come, pensive nun, devout and pure,
Sober, steadfast, and demure,
All in a robe of darkest grain,
Flowing with majestic train,
And sable stole of cypress lawn   35
Over thy decent shoulders drawn.
Come, but keep thy wonted state,
With even step, and musing gait,
And looks commercing with the skies,
Thy rapt soul sitting in thine eyes; 40
There, held in holy passion still,
Forget thyself to marble, till
With a sad leaden downward cast,
Thou fix them on the earth as fast.
And join with thee calm Peace and
    Quiet,   45
Spare Fast, that oft with gods doth
    diet,
And hears the Muses in a ring
Aye round about Jove's altar sing.
And add to these retired Leisure,
That in trim gardens takes his plea-
    sure;   50
But first, and chiefest, with thee
    bring
Him that yon soars on golden wing,
Guiding the fiery-wheelèd throne,
The cherub Contemplations[10];
And the mute Silence hist along, 55

---

[7]*Vesta,* goddess of the hearth, representing purity.
[8]*Saturn,* represents solitude. Milton
thinks of Melancholy as the daughter
of Vesta and Saturn.
[9]*Ida,* a mountain in Crete.
[10]*cherub Contemplation,* medieval
theologians gave to cherubs the attributes of wisdom and divinity.

'Less Philomel[11] will deign a song,
In her sweetest, saddest plight,
Smoothing the rugged brow of night,
While Cynthia[12] checks her dragon yoke
Gently o'er th' accustomed oak.   60
Sweet bird, that shunn'st the noise of folly,
Most musical, most melancholy!
Thee, chauntress, oft the woods among
I woo, to hear thy evensong;
And missing thee, I walk unseen   65
On the dry smooth-shaven green,
To behold the wandering moon,
Riding near her highest noon,
Like one that had been led astray
Through the heavens' wide pathless way,   70
And oft, as if her head she bowed,
Stooping through a fleecy cloud.
Oft, on a plat of rising ground,
I hear the far-off curfew sound,
Over some wide-watered shore,   75
Swinging slow with sullen roar;
Or if the air will not permit,
Some still removèd place will fit,
Where glowing embers through the room
Teach light to counterfeit a gloom,   80
Far from all resort of mirth,
Save the cricket on the hearth,
Or the bellman's drowsy charm
To bless the doors from nightly harm.
Or let my lamp at midnight hour,   85
Be seen in some high lonely tower,
Where I may oft outwatch the Bear,[13]
With thrice great Hermes, or unsphere
The spirit of Plato, to unfold
What worlds, or what vast regions hold   90
The immortal mind that hath forsook
Her mansion in this fleshly nook;

And of those demons that are found
In fire, air, flood, or under ground,
Whose power hath a true consent   95
With planet, or with element.
Sometime let gorgeous Tragedy
In sceptered pall come sweeping by,
Presenting Thebes, or Pelops' line,
Or the tale of Troy divine,   100
Or what (though rare) of later age
Ennobled hath the buskined[14] stage.
But, O sad Virgin, that thy power
Might raise Musaeus[15] from his bower,
Or bid the soul of Orpheus sing   105
Such notes as, warbled to the string,
Drew iron tears down Pluto's[16] cheek,
And made Hell grant what Love did seek;
Or call up him[17] that left half told   110
The story of Cambuscan bold,
Of Camball, and of Algarsife,
And who had Canacè to wife,
That owned the virtuous ring and glass;
And of the wondrous horse of brass,
On which the Tartar king did ride;[115]
And if aught else great bards beside
In sage and solemn tunes have sung
Of tourneys and of trophies hung,
Of forests, and enchantments drear,
Where more is meant than meets the ear.   120
Thus, Night, oft see me in thy pale career,
Till civil-suited Morn appear,
Not tricked and frounced, as she was wont
With the Attic boy[18] to hunt,
But kerchieft in a comely cloud,   125
While rocking winds are piping loud,
Or ushered with a shower still,

---

[11]*Philomel,* the nightingale.
[12]*Cynthia,* goddess of the moon, whose chariot was drawn by dragons.
[13]*outwatch the Bear,* watch all night, since the constellation of the Bear never sets.

[14]*buskined,* buskins were high-heeled boots worn by actors of tragedy. "Il Penseroso" enjoyed reading tragedy.
[15]*Musaeus,* a mythical Greek poet, sometimes called the son of Orpheus.
[16]*Pluto,* the god of the underworld.
[17]*him that left half told,* Chaucer, who never finished the story of Cambuscan.
[18]*Attic boy,* Cephalus, loved by Aurora, the goddess of the dawn.

When the gust hath blown his fill,
Ending on the rustling leaves,
With minute drops from off the
   eaves.   130
And when the sun begins to fling
His flaring beams, me Goddess bring
To archèd walks of twilight groves,
And shadows brown, that Sylvan[19]
   loves,
Of pine, or monumental oak,   135
Where the rude ax with heavèd stroke
Was never heard the nymphs to
   daunt,
Or fright them from their hallowed
   haunt.
There in close covert by some brook,
Where no profaner eye may look, 140
Hide me from day's garish eye,
While the bee with honeyed thigh,
That at her flowery work doth sing,
And the waters murmuring,
With such consort as they keep,   145
Entice the dewy-feathered Sleep;
And let some strange mysterious
   dream
Wave at his wings, in airy stream
Of lively portraiture displayed,
Softly on my eyelids laid.   150
And as I wake, sweet music breathe

---

[19]*Sylvan,* god of the forest.

Above, about, or underneath,
Sent by some spirit to mortals good,
Or th' unseen Genius[20] of the wood.
But let my due feet never fail   155
To walk the studious cloister's pale,
And love the high embowèd roof,
With antique pillars massy proof,
And storied windows[21] richly dight,
Casting a dim religious light.   160
There let the pealing organ blow,
To the full voiced quire below,
In service high, and anthems clear,
As may with sweetness, through mine
   ear,
Dissolve me into ecstasies,   165
And bring all heaven before mine
   eyes.
And may at last my weary age
Find out the peaceful hermitage,
The hairy gown and mossy cell,
Where I may sit and rightly spell 170
Of every star that heaven doth shew,
And every herb that sips the dew,
Till old experience do attain
To something like prophetic strain.
These pleasures, Melancholy, give, 175
And I with thee will choose to live.

---

[20]*Genius,* presiding spirit.
[21]*storied windows,* stained glass windows depicting Biblical scenes.

For Thought and Discussion

1. Whom does the poet banish?
2. How does he cause this character to appear unattractive?
3. Whom does he call for his companion?
4. Identify these characters and explain why Milton mentioned.
   them:
     a. Morpheus
     b. Prince Memnon's sister
     c. starred Ethiope queen
     d. Vesta
     e. Saturn

5. Who are the companions of Melancholy?
6. To whom is Melancholy compared and why?
7. When the poet takes a walk, where does he go?
8. What sounds appeal to the melancholy man? What sights?
9. What are his favorite amusements?

10. What are his favorite literary selections?
11. What kind of music does he enjoy?
12. It is interesting to compare John Fletcher's poem "Sweetest Melancholy" with Milton's "Il Penseroso." Give the points of comparison and contrast between the two poems. What does Milton include that Fletcher does not?

Plus Work

The same type of background study and test given for "L'Allegro" may be used advantageously in the study of "Il Penseroso."

A Comparative Study of "L'Allegro" and "Il Penseroso"

1. Why are the poems, "L'Allegro" and "Il Penseroso," classified as pastorals? Under what other types of poetry may they be classified?
2. Do you note in the titles and in the poems themselves an indication of either or of both Puritanic and Cavalier tendencies in Milton? By referring to a biography of the poet and to the history of the period in which he lived, you may verify your conclusion.
3. What difficulty do you find in understanding the poems?
4. What reference books are needed for the study of these poems?
5. In what studies do you infer Milton was well versed?
6. Which of the activities or recreations mentioned by Milton do you also enjoy?
7. What hints do you find which suggest that if Milton were alive today, he would like picture shows and opera and certain other forms of recreation?
8. What clubs or leisure time activities, if any, do you suppose Milton would take part in if he were living at the present time?
9. Milton was the outstanding poet of the seventeenth century and was also prominent in the Puritan regime under Cromwell; for that reason you will have a better understanding of his literary and political importance after reading "The Puritan Age."
10. Part of the interest in reading Milton's poems lies in viewing his landscape miniatures. Describe a series of these from each poem.
11. Another part of the interest in reading these poems by Milton lies in noting the parallel structure of the two poems and seeing point by point the contrasts in the two. Point out parallel passages and enumerate the contrasts—a lark with a nightingale, sunshine with rain, and so on.
12. A third point of interest lies in comparing the recreations Milton describes with those of today. Make the comparisons.
13. Added pleasure will reward the pupil who studies the notes on these poems and reads the mythological stories to which they refer. Tell the story of Orpheus and Eurydice, and of Musaeus.

14. List five figures of speech in each poem.
15. Give examples of striking epithets.
16. Memorize passages which appeal to you. This will be easy if you listen to a Victor record of the two.

MILTON AS A BOY

JOHN MILTON 1608-1674

Milton's Birthplace. A home and a scrivener's shop combined called "The Spread Eagle" in Bread Street, Cheapside, near St. Paul's school in London, was the birthplace of Milton. Here his father carried on his broker's business and his legal work of drawing up wills, bonds, and mortgages, and in his leisure moments devoted himself to literature and music and to the encouragement of his son's literary ambitions.

College Years. Milton took his Master's degree at Christ College, Cambridge, in 1639. He did not particularly enjoy college life. His first tutor was not agreeable, and because of the infraction of a minor rule, Milton was at one time sent or withdrawn from school. Later, when with a brother he returned to the University, he was given a new tutor, and he finished his course with high honors. Milton was not at all effeminate, but in his youth his features were refined and delicate, and he was exemplary in his habits and very studious. For these reasons, probably, some of the rougher men of the college nicknamed him "The Lady"; nevertheless, they regarded him with respect and admiration.

Years of Retirement at Horton. After completing his college career, Milton retired to his father's country place and there spent six years in self-directed study, music and mathematics being his favorite studies. The fruits of his years at Horton are his so-called minor poems, the most perfect of their kind in English literature, a group including the pastorals "L'Allegro," "Il Penseroso," "Lycidas," an elegy in honor of his college friend, Edward King, and *Comus,* the one great masque after the time of Shakespeare.

Years of Travel. In April, 1638, Milton started on his long-dreamed-of visit to the historic and artistic centers of the continent. While in Italy the deep patriotism of the Italians aroused anew in him his old desire to write an epic that England would "not willingly let die," and probably he would have written such an epic at that time had it not been for the news that the English king had broken with Parliament. Because of that news he gave up his travels sooner than he had planned and renounced his literary ambitions, in order to return home and enter the fight for liberty.

Years of Service and Sacrifice. The year of Milton's return from the continent marks the beginning of what he termed his "left-handed writings," a number of pamphlets on divorce, education, free speech, the Episcopacy, the rights of the common people, and other problems relative to the execution of Charles I. In the struggle against the Royalists, these political pamphlets were so effective that Milton's pen has been compared to Cromwell's sword. Among the most notable of these works are *Areopagitica, a Speech for the Liberty of Unlicensed Printing,* and *Tenure of Kings and Magistrates.* After the writing of the latter, Milton was commissioned Secretary of Foreign Tongues, to the new commonwealth. His duties in that office were somewhat similar to those of the head of the present foreign office. In his day all the communications of the office were in Latin. Milton was admirably suited for this work, but his tasks were strenuously taxing, and his eyes, already weakened because of the strain of his early studies, began to fail rapidly. He was warned that further work would result in total loss of sight. With sacrificial courage, he continued writing his famous paper, "Defensio pro Populi Anglicano," which the government had asked him to write in reply to the Royalist's document "Defensio Regio pro Carlo I." Blindness fell upon Milton before his task was completed, and thus he made his second and his supreme sacrifice for his country. And as if blindness were not enough, poverty and persecution followed; his books were publicly burned, and, more racking than all else, the cause for which he had labored seemed irretrievably lost.

Milton's Theories of Education. After his return from abroad and before he was made Latin Secretary in 1649, Milton, in addi-

MILTON DICTATING "PARADISE LOST"

tion to his literary pursuits, tried out upon his nephews and a few other select pupils his theories of education as expounded in his memorable tract, "On Education." These pupils knew him as a schoolmaster severe in discipline but, nevertheless, one who delighted them with his conversation and with the "gaudy day," or holiday, which he gave them once a month. Readers will agree that Milton's contention that the purpose of education is citizenship, that the duty of a citizen is service, and that all services whether public or private, whether of peace or of war, should be performed "justly, skillfully, and magnanimously" sounds very much like pedagogic principles and democratic doctrines of today.

Milton's Home Life. Milton was thrice married. His relationships with his first wife, who was, if records are to be believed, rather a frivolous girl accustomed to the indulgence of a Royalist household, were not very pleasant. His second wife seemed to be a most admirable character, but she lived only a short time. Milton's children by his first wife were not very dutiful, and he was not very patient and reasonable in his treatment of them; hence the state of affairs in his home was most miserable until, surprisingly, his third wife, young Elizabeth Minshull, judiciously arranged for his daughters to leave home, ostensibly "to learn some curious and ingenious sorts of manufacture that are proper for women to learn, particularly embroideries in gold and silver." Elizabeth seemed to understand the disposition and needs of the blind poet, and she did much to comfort his last years.

About 1664 Milton moved to a very small house, at Artillery Walk, Bunhill Fields. There he resumed the joys of the leisure hours of his youth. He walked in his garden (one is happy to know that he could again have a garden), played on the organ, listened to his wife's singing, entertained his friends and completed in his old age "Paradise Lost," the matchless masterpiece he had planned in his college days, and also "Paradise Regained," and "Samson Agonistes."

Milton and His Readers. The casual reader can have no appreciation for Milton, the poet. The loftiness of his themes, the fixity of his purpose, the scholarliness of his diction and of his style, the breadth of his knowledge, and the profuseness of his gorgeous imagery are bars to superficial reading. The reader who would appreciate Milton must, in addition to a study of verse forms, metrical structure, and other poetic principles, make a special study of figures of speech.

It must be admitted that despite the beauty and variety of the verse structure, the melody of the organ-like cadences and the majesty of the theme, the average student will find little pleasure in reading Milton's epics, or even in reading his sonnets, unless he delights in discovering their philosophy of life; but a recent critic has affirmed that it would be difficult to overestimate the timeliness of his prose discussions concerning certain absurdities and evils which prevailed in his day, many of which have persisted well into the twentieth century.

❦

THE HEAVENS DECLARE THE GLORY OF GOD
PSALM 19

THE heavens declare the glory of
God;
And the firmament showeth his handiwork.
Day unto day uttereth speech,
And night unto night showeth knowledge,
There is no speech nor language,
Where their voice is not heard.
Their line is gone out through all the earth,
And their words to the end of the world.
In them hath he set a tabernacle for the sun,

Which is as a bridegroom coming out of his chamber,
And rejoiceth as a strong man to run a race.
His going forth is from the end of the heaven, and his circuit unto the ends of it;
And there is nothing hid from the heat thereof.
The law of the Lord is perfect, converting the soul;
The testimony of the Lord is sure, making wise the simple.
The statutes of the Lord are right, rejoicing the heart;

The commandment of the Lord is
pure, enlightening the eyes.
The fear of the Lord is clean, enduring forever;
The judgments of the Lord are true
and righteous altogether.
More to be desired are they than gold,
yea, than much fine gold;
Sweeter also than honey and the
honeycomb.
Moreover by them is thy servant
warned;
And in keeping of them there is great
reward.

Who can understand his errors?
Cleanse thou me from secret
faults.

Keep back thy servant also from pre-
sumptuous sins; let them not
have dominion over me;

Then shall I be upright, and I shall be
innocent from the great transgression.

Let the words of my mouth, and the
meditation of my heart, be acceptable in thy sight, O Lord,
my strength, and my redeemer.

LEISURE

WILLIAM H. DAVIES

WHAT is this life if, full of care,
We have no time to stand and
stare.

No time to stand beneath the boughs
And stare as long as sheep or cows.

No time to see, when woods we pass,[5]
Where squirrels hide their nuts in
grass.

No time to see, in broad daylight,

Streams full of stars, like stars at
night.

No time to turn at Beauty's glance,
And watch her feet, how they can
dance.   [10]

No time to wait till her mouth can
Enrich that smile her eyes began.

A poor life this if, full of care,
We have no time to stand and stare.

For Thought and Discussion

1. What is the difference between *having* no time and *taking* no
   time? Do people, as a rule, *have* no time or merely *take* no
   time for seeing the beauties of nature?
2. What does it take to make life rich and full?
3. The idea expressed in this selection is somewhat similar to that
   in "The World Is Too Much With Us." Which do you like
   better?
4. Which smile means more and never becomes mechanical, the
   one with the eyes or the one with the lips?
5. Do you object to the use of any certain word in this poem?
   Why? Can you suggest a more fitting one which will rhyme?

MY HEART LEAPS UP
WILLIAM WORDSWORTH

MY heart leaps up when I behold
    A rainbow in the sky.
So was it when my life began;
So is it now I am a man,
So be it when I shall grow old,   5
    Or let me die!
The child is father of the man;
And I could wish my days to be
Bound each to each by natural piety.

For Thought and Discussion

1. This brief lyric is said in theme to be the epitome of the longer "Ode on Intimations of Immortality." Point out respects in which this statement seems to be true.
2. Judging from this selection, what do you consider one of the chief sources of Wordsworth's pleasure in early and in later life?

THE RAINBOW
WILLIAM H. DAVIES

RAINBOWS are lovely things:
    The bird, that shakes a cold, wet
        wing,
Chatters with ecstasy,
    But has no breath to sing:
No wonder, when the air   5
Has a double-rainbow there!

Look, there's a rainbow now!
    See how that lovely rainbow
        throws
Her jewelled arm around
    This world, when the rain
        goes!   10
And how I wish the rain
Would come again, and again!

For Thought and Discussion

1. Do you think it a pretty fancy to suggest that a bird is moved to ecstasy by the beauty of the rainbow?
2. Which do you like better, the comparison of the rainbow to a "jewelled arm" embracing the world or the one used by Longfellow in "Hiawatha,"

> " 'Tis the heaven of flowers you see there;
> All the wild flowers of the forest;
> All the lilies of the prairie,
> When on earth they fade and perish,
> Blossom in that heaven above us."

3. Does *rain* connote rainbows and joy to you, or dark and gloomy days, or green fields, or plump sweet grains of wheat and corn? According to your answer label yourself as a romanticist, a realist, an optimist, a pessimist, or a philosopher.

∼✄

Additional Readings

Belloc, Hilaire: *Hills and The Sea*

Brooke, Rupert: *Letters From America*

French, Roy L.: *Recent Poetry*

Galsworthy, John: *The Inn of Tranquillity*

Gordon, Margery and King, Marie B.: *Verse of Our Day*

Hicky, Daniel Whitehead: *Bright Harbor*

Housman, A. E.: *Last Poems*

Hudson, W. H.: *Green Mansions*

Lucas, E. V.: *The Open Road*

Milne, A. A.: *Not That It Matters*

Rittenhouse, Jessie: *Little Book of Modern Verse*

    Second Book of Modern Verse

Voss, Elizabeth: *Shelter of Song*

Yeats, William Butler: *Wind Among the Reeds*

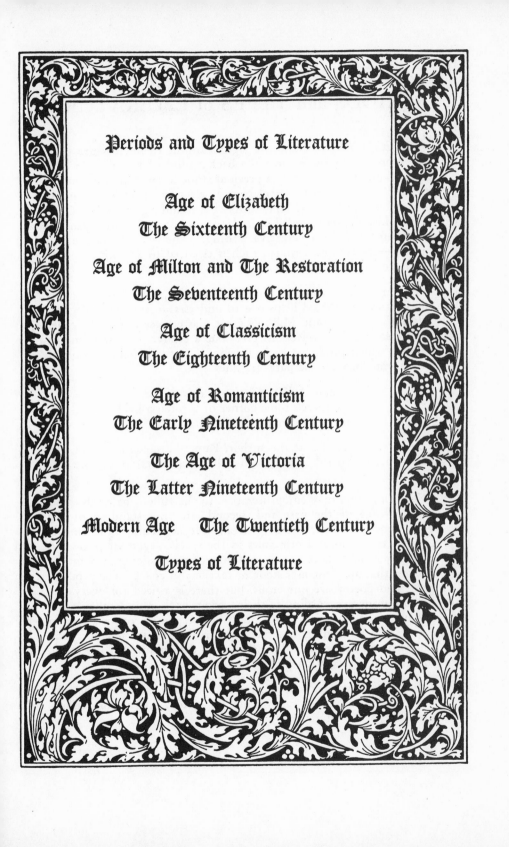

Periods and Types of Literature

Age of Elizabeth
The Sixteenth Century

Age of Milton and The Restoration
The Seventeenth Century

Age of Classicism
The Eighteenth Century

Age of Romanticism
The Early Nineteenth Century

The Age of Victoria
The Latter Nineteenth Century

Modern Age   The Twentieth Century

Types of Literature

PERIODS and TYPES of LITERATURE

SELECTIONS of literature significant in themselves are even more significant against the background of history to which they belong, for, as placing a precious stone in an exquisite mounting adds to its beauty, so, placing a selection of literature in its proper historical setting adds to its charm and significance. Conversely history, meaningful in itself, often becomes more meaningful when embodied in creative writing. The two—literature and history—are complementary; each is essential to the other and to a full understanding of life.

For instance, a study of the religious and political problems of the Restoration Period helps one to understand Bunyan's allegory, *Pilgrim's Progress*, and Milton's great masterpieces. On the other hand, reading these selections gives one a clearer understanding of the age which produced such writings. A further illustration of this is seen through the patriotic lines

> "If I should die, think only this of me
> That there's some corner of a foreign field
> That is forever England."

To one who knows that the author, Rupert Brooke, poet and war hero, does lie buried in a foreign field, these lines are doubly significant.

That a person may enjoy literature to the fullest, he needs, first, a knowledge of the past and, second, an understanding of the development of literature in general. He needs also some knowledge of the structural principles of the specific types of prose and poetry which authors use as mediums of expression much in the fashion that an artist uses stone or textile and color. The types of prose and poetry are numerous, but there is a need for every one because readers, according to their various backgrounds, their various moods, and their various needs are responsive on occasion to each. The discerning observer soon realizes that the more one knows of the historical and the structural development of literature, the greater appreciation he has for literature.

For the convenience of the reader the final section of the text gives a brief résumé of English literary history and a short discussion of types of literature.

PERIODS AND TYPES OF LITERATURE

A Brief Résumé of the Periods of English Literature

THE AGE OF ELIZABETH 1558-1625

The Sixteenth Century

Intense Interest in Life. The sixteenth century is one of the greatest in all literature, perhaps because it is rich in imagination and achievement. It is marked by zest and intense interest in life; by patriotism closely identified with praise of the queen; by appreciation of great personalities, portrayed in the plays of Shakespeare and Marlowe. The discovery and exploration of America in 1492 fired the imagination of the people and sent the adventurous on voyages to new lands. Along with the experimental voyage of Columbus and the discovery of a new world, a new attitude had come which cast aside many old superstitions and accepted the belief, "all is possible."

Heroes of the Age. Great dreams filled the minds of young men, and great enthusiasm spurred them on to accomplishment. The young man of this age was interested in court life, in war, in discovery and exploration and colonization, and in literature. This was an age for such heroes as Sir Walter Raleigh, the great courtier and explorer; Sir Philip Sidney, that famous exemplar of courtesy and courage; and Sir Francis Drake, the first navigator to sail around the world.

Sir Walter Raleigh. Sir Walter Raleigh, favorite of Queen Elizabeth, who according to tradition gained royal favor by throwing his cloak in her path, has always been one of the popular figures both in history and in literature. He was an important personage at court, sending out ships for exploration and colonization, yet he found time in his busy life to begin to write a *History of the World*.

Sir Philip Sidney. Another outstanding young man of the time, one who excited the admiration of the youth of that age, was Sir Philip Sidney. Very early in life Sidney made the choice of a career; he became a courtier and statesman, devoting himself to the fortunes of his country. The story of his heroic death, though familiar in history and in literature, merits re-telling. While he was in war in the Netherlands, he was seriously wounded. Suffering intensely, he asked for water. As he raised his flask to his lips, a young soldier lying near him pleaded for water, and Sidney passed the flask with the words, "Thy need is greater than mine." By Sidney's death, which soon followed, England lost one of her most high-spirited and gallant heroes. Elizabeth called him the jewel of her dominions.

The Drama. The popularity accorded to moving pictures of the twentieth century belonged in the Age of Elizabeth to the drama, which had its origin in the Middle Ages, when the church was the outstanding institution and dominated the lives of the people.

QUEEN ELIZABETH

Origin of the Drama. In the Middle Ages when books were scarce and few people could read, the church necessarily turned to dramatic presentation of outstanding Bible stories as a means of teaching. At first these stories were chanted by the priests and choir in dialogue form. Later, characters were introduced. At the festival of Corpus Christi elaborate pageants, or parades, were given. In the procession were images of the Virgin, of Adam and Eve carrying the Tree of Knowledge, of John the Baptist with a lamb, of Judas with his money bags, followed by the Devil taking him to Hades.

Episodes from the Bible were given by the priests before the altar. At Christmas the representation of the Holy Child worshipped by the Wise Men from the East made vivid the story of the birth of Christ. On Easter angels at the tomb in conversation with those who sought the body of Christ impressed the story of the Resurrection. These scenes attracted the knight and the ragged peasant alike in such crowds that the performances were moved from the altar to the nave, the space in front of the altar, and finally to the church porch outside. By this time laymen as well as priests took part. The language used became less dignified, and humorous touches crept into the plays. A typical case is found in the play of "Noah and the Ark." When Noah was ready to enter the ark, his wife refused to go, saying that Noah had been gone a hundred years without letting her know where he was and that he was always expecting calamity anyway. At last, after much entreaty on the part of Noah, she gave him a final box on his ears and entered the ark. This little scene of domestic comedy delighted the audience but displeased the church fathers, who soon withdrew from the performances because of the humorous incidents introduced.

Religious Play Cycles. Later on the trade guilds, the trade unions of that time, produced the religious plays, which were given once a year in an elaborate presentation lasting several days. Each guild assumed responsibility for either an episode, or a certain part of it, the boat-builders giving the play of "Noah and the Ark," and the bakers "The Last Supper." Large platforms built on wagons were used for the performances. Below these platforms were two rooms, one a dressing room, the other sometimes representative of Hades, with smoke pouring out, into which Satan might toss his victims. The wagons numbering from thirty to fifty were stationed in different sections of the city, each one moving on to the next station as soon as the play was finished so that all the people were able to see the play. The number of episodes given in different towns varied, but the cycle usually began with early biblical stories, as the "Fall of Lucifer from Heaven" or the "Creation of Adam" and extended down to the "Day of Judgment."

These plays were first given in England after the Norman Conquest in 1066; they were produced as late as the close of Elizabeth's reign, but at this latter date the wide appeal for the masses was gone. "The Passion Play," today given in various villages in Europe, is a survival of this drama of the Middle Ages.

The Morality Play. Players in the religious plays not only invented amusing episodes to relieve the serious tone, but they also introduced extra characters. Beelzebub often left the stage and went into the audience to take a collection. The frying pan he

THE GLOBE THEATER

used for the purpose was suggestive of an unpleasant hereafter for
the miser. Vice, equipped with horns and a tail, howled around
through the crowd, terrifying and delighting the audience. From
this beginning there developed a new type of drama, the morality

play, in which the characters were such abstractions as Death, Riches, Good-Fellowship, Envy, Greed, Beauty, Knowledge. In *Everyman*, one of the best known morality dramas, Death comes suddenly for Everyman, who pleads with his friends to go with him on this long journey from which there is no return. Good-Fellowship, Strength, Beauty, and others refuse to go; at last Good-Deeds accompanies him. The morality play, as can be readily seen, is an allegory in which there is a strong moral lesson; the characters represent virtues and vices.

Folk Plays. At the same time that the religious plays were flourishing, folk plays, springing from the customs of the people, were popular. May Day was celebrated in an elaborate fashion. A May Queen was chosen to preside over the dances around the Maypole. Another occasion of much merriment was Hallowe'en, the night on which all mischievous spirits roamed. The mummers, persons wearing grotesque masques and costumes, gave pantomimes. Many of these folk-play superstitions have been used by Shakespeare in his plays and by later writers as well, notably the great novelist, Thomas Hardy.

Interludes. Another popular dramatic form was the interlude. This was, as the name suggests, a short, witty dialogue to be given in the interludes, the pauses between acts of an elaborate production, or between the courses at a feast. This play created an appreciation for sprightly dialogue or conversation.

All of these different types of drama trained a play-going public; audiences were ready for Shakespeare, Marlowe, and other Elizabethan dramatists.

The First Plays. The first native, non-religious plays were probably written by schoolmasters to be given by choir boys for the proceeds to be realized from them. From 1550-1570 these plays, fashioned after the Latin and Greek models, were popular. *Ralph Roister Doister* and *Gammer Gurton's Needle* were the first English comedies and *Gorboduc*, the first English tragedy.

Theaters. Non-religious plays were first given in schools, innyards, or in vacant buildings. In 1576, the first playhouse, The Theatre, was built. Later, theaters were so profitable that there were ten or twelve in London, then (1600) a city of 200,000. Two of these, the Globe and the Blackfriars, have since become famous because Shakespeare held shares in them. These first theaters were octagon-shaped or rectangular, with a roof over the stage and balconies, but open to the sky in the center, or the pit. The performances, at first given in the afternoon, lasted several hours. The groundlings, those who occupied the pit, either stood or brought their own stools, along with lunches. The wealthy young sports about town bought seats upon the stage, where they enjoyed displaying the latest fashions in dress while they commented upon the play. In the balconies, extending around three sides of the theater, were the better class of patrons, men, because it was not quite respectable for women to attend the theater, although a few donned masks and went now and then. In the plays the women's parts were taken by boys until after the Restoration in 1661.

Christopher Marlowe 1564-1593. A number of dramatists preceding Shakespeare kept alive and increased the popular interest in plays. The outstanding figure was Christopher Marlowe, born in the same year as Shakespeare. He was killed at the height of his career. His plays reflect the spirit of the times in presenting swift action and great personalities in that eloquent style so dear to Elizabethans. His outstanding plays, *Tamburlaine, Doctor Faustus, The Jew of Malta,* and *Edward II,* are usually placed next to the tragedies of Shakespeare.

THE BIRTHPLACE OF WILLIAM SHAKESPEARE

William Shakespeare 1564-1616. Outstanding both in his own time and two centuries later is a fitting characterization of Shakespeare. To estimate his influence through the centuries would be a Herculean undertaking. When a negative opinion is expressed concerning the continued popularity of this great Elizabethan, one thinks of the new Shakespeare libraries and theaters. A few of the outstanding are the new theater at Stratford, the Folger Shakespeare Library in Washington, D. C., including a Shakespeare theater, and the Huntington Library in California.

The first Folio edition of Shakespeare's plays bore the imprint: "Mr. William Shakespeares Comedies, Histories, & Tragedies. Published according to the True Originall Copies. London: Printed by Isaac Iaggard, and Ed. Blount, 1623."

Prefacing this edition was a tribute by Ben Jonson to his "beloved Shakespeare." Thirty-six plays were included in the volume. Probably more than 500 copies were printed; the original price was £1 each. Approximately 180 copies survive, 114 in England and the remaining ones in the United States. King George V owned one; in the United States copies are to be found in various public and private collections. In 1905 First Folios were valued at £7,000. Later, volumes sold for £8,600 and £10,000. At the present, if offered for sale, an edition would command a fabulous price. Such is the value placed upon Shakespearean manuscripts by collectors of rare books.

THE ANN HATHAWAY COTTAGE

General Questions on the Age of Elizabeth

1. What were the outstanding characteristics of the Age of Elizabeth?
2. How many of these characteristics belong to the twentieth century? Name others of the twentieth century.
3. Who were the great heroes of the Age of Elizabeth?
4. Name one of the favorite types of entertainment of the Elizabethans?
5. What dramatic form has been the most popular in the twentieth century?
6. Where and when and why was dramatic representation first used?
7. With what subject matter did it deal?
8. What part did the trade guilds play in the development of the drama?

9. What is a morality play?
10. Name other types of the early drama.
11. Where and when was the first theater built?
12. What dramatist of his time ranks next to Shakespeare?

Oral or Written Reports

Attending an Elizabethan Play
The Story of *Everyman*
"Rare Ben Jonson"
Explorers of the Age
Francis Bacon as a Scientist
Edmund Spenser, the Greatest of the Non-dramatic Writers of the
    Elizabethan Period

References[1]

Bates, Katherine Lee: *The English Religious Drama*
Boas, R. P. and Hahn, B. M.: *Social Backgrounds of English Literature*
Boynton, P. H.: *London in English Literature*
Brawley, Benjamin: *Short History of English Drama*
Bushnell, N. S.: *Historical Background of English Literature*
Cruse, Amy: *Shaping of English Literature*
Curtis, M. I.: *England of Song and Story*
Davis, W. S.: *Life in Elizabethan Days*
Garnett, Richard and Gosse, Edmund: *English Literature*
Halleck, R. P.: *New English Literature*
Haney, J. L.: *English Literature*
Harrison, G. B.: *England in Shakespeare's Day*
Hartley, Dorothy and Elliot, M. M.: *Life and Work of the People of England*
Jusserand, F. F.: *Literary History of English People*
Lamb, Charles: *Tales of Shakespeare*
Long, W. J.: *English Literature*
MacCracken, H. N. and others: *Introduction to Shakespeare*
Macy, John: *Story of World's Literature*
Marshall, H. E.: *English Literature for Boys and Girls*
Martin, Dorothy: *First Book about Shakespeare*
Miller, E. L.: *English Literature*
Moody, W. V. and Lovett, R. M.: *History of English Literature*
Neilson, W. A. and Thorndike, A. H.: *Facts about Shakespeare*
    History of English Literature
Pancoast, H. S.: *Introduction to English Literature*
Quennell, Marjorie and Quennell, C. H. B.: *History of Everyday Things in England*

[1]Acknowledgment is made to the WILSON BULLETIN for permission to use *The Bibliography of Period Backgrounds*, Prepared for Senior High School English by Margaret R. Greer and the Minneapolis Senior High School Librarian.

Reynolds, George F. and Greever, Garland: *The Facts and Backgrounds of Literature*
Rolfe, W. J.: *Shakespeare, the Boy*
Shakespeare, William: *Merchant of Venice* (Avon Shakespeare), Introduction
Stevens, F. L.: *Through Merrie England*
Stuart, D. M.: *Boy Through the Ages*
Synge, M. B.: *Short History of Social Life in England*
Thorndike, A. H.: *Shakespeare's Theater*

Stories with a Historical Background

Bennett, Arnold: *Master Skylark*
Finger, Charles: *Courageous Companions*
Garnett, Richard: *Master Will of Stratford*
Jerome, Jerome K.: *Passing of the Third Floor Back*
Kingsley, Charles: *Westward Ho!*
Lucas, E. V.: *Slow Coach*
Major: *When Knighthood was in Flower*
Twain, Mark: *The Prince and the Pauper*

～✞

THE AGE OF MILTON AND THE RESTORATION
1625-1660, 1660-1688

THE SEVENTEENTH CENTURY

Civil War. Every country has a civil war; in fact, it is fortunate to have no more than one. The seventeenth century was a civil war period for England. The king and his adherents were opposed by Parliament. The king, Charles I, was finally executed. Then the great leader of the Parliamentary forces, Oliver Cromwell, a Puritan leader, established a new government and became the director with the title of Lord Protector of the Commonwealth.

Puritans and Cavaliers. The Puritan movement had a far-reaching influence, extending on down to the twentieth century. It was religious in origin, stressing purity of life and advocating strict religious principles and simpler forms of faith and worship as opposed to traditional forms. The opposition that the Puritans met caused many of them to leave England and settle a New England in America. Beginning as a religious reaction, their cause became identified with the political movement supporting Parliament and opposing the king on the grounds of heavy taxation and failure to respect the rights of Protestants. Opposed to them in their political and social attitude were the Royalists, or the Cavaliers. During the years the Puritans were in power, many of the Cavaliers left England to settle in the American colonies, and many others followed Prince Charles, the son of the executed Charles I, into exile in France. The Puritans were sturdy, pious, somewhat intolerant, condemning illiteracy and insisting upon education. The Cavaliers were gracious, courtly, cynical and cultured, gay devotees of pleasure, deriding the stern virtues of the Puritans. These two factions found expression in literature.

CAMBRIDGE

Milton and Puritan Trends. The great Puritan poet was John Milton, who renounced poetry for a time to defend the rights of the common people. His deep interest in religious subjects is evident in *Paradise Lost*; his leaning toward the grace and brightness of the Cavaliers is revealed now and then in his minor poems. John Bunyan wrote that great allegory, *Pilgrim's Progress*, Puritan in tone, though written after the fall of the Commonwealth. Minor prose writers of the period include Robert Burton, Sir

Thomas Browne, Thomas Fuller, Jeremy Taylor, Richard Baxter, and Izaak Walton. Carewe, Herrick, Suckling, and Lovelace, of the Cavalier school wrote gay, light, graceful lyrics that find appreciative readers today.

The Puritans closed the theaters for eighteen years, 1642-1660. Naturally there was not much drama written during this time. Some plays, however, excellent in technique, but unpleasant to read now because of the low moral tone, survive.

The over-severity of the Puritans caused the pendulum to swing back—too far as usual. After the death of Cromwell, the Commonwealth, lacking a strong leader, soon fell. In 1660 Prince Charles returned from exile and was crowned Charles II. With him came those pleasure-loving Royalists who had been with him in France. The social reaction that followed was pronounced; the severity of the Puritans was displaced by the looseness and gaiety of the Cavaliers.

Outstanding Writers of the Restoration. John Dryden, often called "the father of modern prose," was also a poet. He was the outstanding literary figure of the Restoration. Upon a man of affairs, Samuel Pepys, Secretary of the Navy, falls the distinction of furnishing the best background of this period. From 1660-1669 Pepys kept a diary, recording in shorthand in a charming and humorous manner the happenings of every-day life, the personal alongside the great events of the day.

Accession of William and Mary in 1688. As the seventeenth century was pre-eminently one of political upheavals, it is fitting to close this period with the last great political event. Charles II ruled by tact, refusing to enter into controversy, since, as he said, referring to his exile in France, he did not want to "set out on his travels again." His successor, James II, was obstinate and failed to please the English people, who deposed him and invited his eldest daughter, Mary, and her husband, William of Orange, to become rulers of England. At last the English people had emerged triumphant and had established the fact that the king rules only by the consent of the governed. The political liberty for which Milton had sacrificed much was, in a measure, secure, and an effective system of representative self-government was established. Constitutional government had become a realized ideal of the English people.

General Questions on the Age of Milton and the Restoration

1. What was the significance of the struggle of Parliament against the king?
2. Who were the Puritans and the Cavaliers? What attitude toward life did each have?
3. Who was the great poet of the Puritan Age?
4. What event checked the writing of drama in the Age of Milton?

5. What is meant by the "Restoration"?
6. Who was the great literary figure of the Restoration?
7. What Puritan writer is noted for writing one book, and that in the Restoration period?
8. Why is Samuel Pepys known today?
9. What English principle of government was established by the accession of William and Mary?

Oral or Written Reports

Milton's Appreciation of Nature
Milton's Appreciation for the Fine Arts
Milton's Attitude toward Public Questions—Education, Freedom of the Press
Milton as Latin Secretary under Cromwell
Significance of the Puritan Movement
John Bunyan and *Pilgrim's Progress*
The Great Fire in London
The London Plague
James Russell Lowell's "Essay on Dryden" from *Among My Books*

References

Gayley: *Classical Myths in English Literature*
Greene: *A Short History of England*
Macaulay: "Essay on Bunyan"
         "Essay on Milton"
Raleigh, Walter: *Milton*

Stories with a Historical Background

Dix, Beulah Marie: *Merrylips*
Howes, Charles B.: *Dark Frigate*

❧

THE AGE OF CLASSICISM 1688-1786

THE EIGHTEENTH CENTURY

New Influences. After the Restoration in 1660, changes in literary style were evident. During the Puritan rule, Royalists who went into exile in France had acquired an admiration for correctness and cleverness. They reverted to the Greek classics for models. This classic influence was soon felt and expressed in Restoration drama in adherence to the unities of time, place, and action. In poetry the heroic couplet, iambic pentameter lines rhyming in couplets, became the accepted form. John Dryden, poet laureate of the Restoration, and Alexander Pope of the eighteenth century both used the measure skilfully and effectively. In the eighteenth century, reason, rationalism, and common sense replaced

enthusiasm, freshness, and originality. Correctness, brilliance, epigrammatic heroic couplets, satire, not so bitter as in the Restoration
but clever and witty, represented the fashion of this new age, the
culmination occurring in the Age of Queen Anne.

Prose and Poetry: Leading Writers. The prose of the eighteenth century is significant because it is of interest to readers of
today and because out of it the present day novel has developed.
Daniel Defoe faked a journal of the plague year, which is modern
in its realism. He also wrote *Robinson Crusoe,* probably the first
and one of the best-liked adventure stories. Addison and Steele, in
The Spectator, made witty and wise comments on their time, creating the informal essay. This type of writing, which became exceedingly popular, was read at the breakfast table and over the teacups.
Jonathan Swift wrote *Gulliver's Travels,* which was famed in his
day as a masterpiece of bitter political satire but is known today
as an entertaining story for children.

The great poet of the age, Alexander Pope, was a model for
young writers long after the heroic couplet had gone out of style.
The number of familiar quotations to be found in his poetry testify
to its popularity.

Samuel Johnson, that kind old bear, was the literary dictator of
his time. He was the last conservative of the old order. The approaching wave of romanticism was not successfully stemmed by
Johnson, but perhaps he did his share in limiting the recognition
of that movement in his day. Associated with the name of Johnson
must necessarily be that of the poet, Oliver Goldsmith, who turned
to the past for literary forms, but was too liberal in nature and too
broad in his sympathies to be a close adherent to the old order. Another writer whose poetry indicated a new attitude was Thomas
Gray, who, like Goldsmith, found lowly life an attractive theme.
By this time a new age was coming, the Age of Romanticism, in
which there was a complete reaction against the literary forms and
subject matter of the eighteenth century. Robert Burns, the first
poet of the new order, wrote spontaneously of peasants and of
nature.

General Questions on the Eighteenth Century

1. What effect upon poetry, prose, and drama did the exile of the
   Royalists have?
2. What prose works written in the eighteenth century are read
   today?
3. Who was the outstanding poet of the eighteenth century?
   He was also the first writer to earn his living from writing.
4. What are the characteristics of Pope's literary style?
5. What does Pope say about honesty, learning?
6. Was Pope a radical or a conservative?
7. What type of satire did Addison write?
8. Who was Addison's co-worker on *The Spectator*?
9. Who were the outstanding writers of the eighteenth century?

Oral or Written Reports

The Johnson Circle
Johnson's Letter to the Earl of Chesterfield
Edmund Burke's Attitude toward the American Revolution
Purposes of *The Spectator*
London Coffee-Houses—From *The Spectator*
London in the Early Eighteenth Century
The "Marconi" or Beau of the Later Eighteenth Century

References

Addison and Steele: *The Spectator Papers*
Ashton, John: *Social Life in the Reign of Queen Anne*
Boswell: *Life of Johnson*
George, M. D.: *England in Johnson's Day*
Irving, Washington: *Life of Goldsmith*
Paul, H. G.: ed. *Sir Roger de Coverley Papers*
Reynolds, G. F.: *English Literature in Fact and Story*
Richardson, A. E.: *Georgian England*
Shelley, H. C.: *Inns and Taverns of Old London*
Ticknor, F. W.: *Social and Industrial History of England*
Trevelyan, G. M.: *England of Queen Anne*

Stories with a Historical Background

Dickens, Charles: *Barnaby Rudge*
Moore: *The Jessamy Bride*
Pyle: *Story of Jack Ballister's Fortune*

∾

THE AGE OF ROMANTICISM 1786–1832

EARLY NINETEENTH CENTURY

Political, Social, Economic, and Literary Signs of the Time.
The pendulum of political, social, and literary development took
a long swing from 1700 to 1800. Governmentally speaking it
swung from modified autocracy to modified democracy, and from
a literary standpoint it swung from classicism with its heroic
couplet and its coldly intellectual formalism to romanticism with
its lyrics and its warmly stimulating sympathy. It was well into
the nineteenth century, however, before England, turning away
from her affairs with France, diverted her attention to the needed
economic reforms at home. Then through the attention to such
problems as child labor, freedom of the press, extension of suffrage,
liberality in religion, popular education, and emancipation of slaves
in the colonies, England in reality bestowed upon the masses more
of the blessings of democracy. Likewise, although eighteenth cen-

tury writers like Gray, Goldsmith, Burns, and others with their themes of nature and their inspiring doctrine of the dignity of labor presaged the dawning of a new era, it was not until the nineteenth century that the second great creative movement of romanticism reached its zenith in the works of such men as Scott, Wordsworth, Coleridge, Shelley, Keats, and Byron.

New Movements in Literature: Magazines, Literary Criticism, Women Writers. The romantic period was marked by several notable developments. It was during the years between 1800 and 1830 that many of the present day English magazines had their origin. It was during this period, too, that literary criticism found its truest development, and that such critical and literary essayists as Hunt, Lamb, Coleridge, DeQuincey, and Hazlitt enriched English literature. More remarkable still, it was during this period that women for the first time achieved importance in the field of English letters. Of the notable women writers of this period, Mrs. Anne Radcliffe, though perhaps the most popular in her day, is now almost forgotten; but the works of Jane Austen, Marie Edgeworth, Hannah More, and Jane Porter are in current demand. To these women novelists and to Scott, the creator of the historical novel and the author of *Marmion, The Lady of the Lake,* and *Ivanhoe,* credit is largely due for the popularization of romantic literature.

Dominant Literary Characteristics. Nature and common humanity were dominant themes in the literature of the period. Other subjects treated were chivalry, medieval romance, the myths and dreams of a long past golden age, and the supernatural. While in general the literature was characterized by enthusiasm, or by a mingled tone of happiness and gentle melancholy, some of the writing, particularly certain works of Shelley and of Byron, was marked by a spirit of discontent and revolt. Despite the favor in which the novel, literary criticism, and the informal essay were held during the first half of the nineteenth century, the age was essentially one of poetry, and the prevailing types of poetry were the metrical romance and the lyric.

NOVELIST[1]

JANE AUSTEN 1775-1817

Life of Upper Gentry. Jane Austen belongs chronologically to the early nineteenth century, along with Sir Walter Scott, who expressed great admiration for her work. Her novels, however, have had greater popularity since her death than they had during her lifetime.

Curates, country squires, young ladies with matchmaking mothers, in short, the country life of the upper gentry furnished

---

[1]See index for Sir Walter Scott.

material for Jane Austen, the charming, pleasure-loving girl who had an acute sense of the ridiculous and a facile pen for portraying the daily lives of these people; their foibles, ambitions, parties—everything was food for the mill. Smiling over an awkward speech, observing an overbearing social climber, a fawning curate, a coxcomb of the army, watching all the love affairs out of the corner of her eye, she put this interesting array of characters in stories that move along rapidly.

Novels. *Pride and Prejudice* promises to hold its own in the future as in the past among readers who enjoy the novel of manners. This novel, written when the author was twenty-one, remained unpublished for sixteen years, because the publisher to whom it was submitted refused it. Finally after the publication and success of other novels, particularly *Sense and Sensibility* in 1811, *Pride and Prejudice* was brought out. However, *Persuasion* and *Northanger Abbey,* the first novels published under the name of Jane Austen, did not appear until in 1818, after her death.

Although she began writing very early in life, Jane Austen never took herself seriously as an author. She wrote for enjoyment; she was fond of her characters, probably because they mirrored her own enjoyment of life. She uses situations that are realistic but pleasant; she never leaves her leading character in the lurch. The reader can look forward to a satisfactory ending.

General Questions on the Age of Romanticism

1. What were the political, the social, and the literary signs of the Age of Romanticism?
2. What new type of publication appeared during this period?
3. Who were the leading essayists of the period?
4. Who were the leading women writers of the period? What was their chief type of writing?
5. In this age which was predominant, poetry or prose?
6. In what subjects were the Romanticists interested?
7. Why is Burns classed as a Romanticist?
8. What subject was of paramount interest to Wordsworth, and what was his point of view?
9. Upon what subjects did Coleridge write?
10. How (aside from his poetry) did Byron find expression for his ideas on freedom?
11. What interest of Scott's childhood found expression in his works?
12. What was Shelley's attitude toward the world as he found it?
13. In what way did Keats's literary point of view resemble Scott's?

Oral or Written Reports

The Romantic Movement in Literature
The Songs of Burns
Wordsworth's Sonnets

Dorothy Wordsworth's Influence upon Wordsworth
The Lake Poets
Charles Lamb's Essays
Byron, The Champion of Freedom
Scott's Life at Abbotsford
Leigh Hunt—Popular Writer of His Day
The Songs of Thomas Moore

Stories with a Historical Background

Dickens, Charles: *Tale of Two Cities*
Eliot, George: *Silas Marner*

~~

THE AGE OF VICTORIA 1832-1900

LATTER NINETEENTH CENTURY

Social Changes. In 1785 inventions and improvements in machinery caused changes in the social organization which have continued to the present day, and seemingly the end is not yet in sight. When machine work replaced hand labor, many men necessarily looked for other occupations. They flocked to cities. There was a period of unrest and discontent, known as the Industrial Revolution. Necessarily such conditions called for reforms, many of which were agitated and effected during Victoria's reign.

Popularity of Prose. In the early half of the nineteenth century, Charles Lamb, Leigh Hunt, and others wrote interesting essays. Scott made the historical novel popular, and Jane Austen charmed readers with the novel of manners; but all of these were overshadowed by the poets—Wordsworth, Coleridge, Byron, Shelley, and Keats. In the latter half of the century, known as the Age of Victoria, the greater number of writers turned to prose and made it the outstanding literary form. In the twentieth century prose has completely overshadowed all other types.

Historians and Essayists. Thomas Babington Macaulay, 1800-1859, distinguished for his public services and famous for his brilliant speeches in Parliament, was the author of *History of England,* "Lays of Ancient Rome," and literary and critical essays.

Thomas Carlyle, 1795-1881, also a historian, in addition to *The French Revolution* and *Frederick the Great,* wrote philosophical treatises and literary essays; among the latter the most noted is his *Essay on Burns,* a critical estimate of his fellow countryman, whom he greatly admired.

Matthew Arnold, 1822-1888, who spent the major part of his life as an inspector of schools, found time to write critical essays of merit and some poetry, notably, *Sohrab and Rustum.*

Scientists. The outstanding scientists of the age contributed also to the interesting prose of the time. Thomas Huxley was noted for educational and scientific articles, and Charles Darwin for his famous book on evolution, *Origin of the Species,* which called forth a series of arguments not yet ended.

Art Critic and Social Reformer.   John Ruskin, 1819-1900, is the author of a delightful children's story, *King of the Golden River,* in addition to criticisms on art and architecture. In the latter part of his life he turned to social reform and devoted a fortune to the cause, in the meantime writing many volumes on the subject.

Poets.   Notwithstanding the fact that the literary interest of the age was in prose, some great poetry was written.   The two major poets, Tennyson and Browning, had many worthy contemporaries—Elizabeth Barrett Browning, Matthew Arnold, Edward Fitzgerald, notable translator of "The Rubaiyat" (Rö bäi yät), Dante Gabriel Rossetti, Christina Rossetti, George Meredith, and others.

NOVELISTS[1]

WILLIAM MAKEPEACE THACKERAY 1811-1863

Vanity Fair.   A gracious gentleman versed in arts and letters who has had the broadening influences of travel and of the best circles of society sits before a club window commenting in a gentle vein of humor and satire upon whatever he sees. Such is the picture drawn of William Makepeace Thackeray. Delicious scraps of moralizing make his comments more interesting and palatable. As the people of the world, Vanity Fair, pass before his eyes, he singles out the character whose ambition for money and position dominates her life to the exclusion of all else.   Grasping, unprincipled Becky Sharp, always moving in a straight line toward her goal, using everybody as a stepping stone, is amusing as well as interesting.   Neither noble nor great but supremely selfish and dishonest, she is the leading character in *Vanity Fair,* a book which appeals to him who reads slowly, re-reading from time to time leisurely for enjoyment.

Early Life.   Born in Calcutta, India, Thackeray was sent at an early age to England for his education.   Neither the year spent in grammar school nor the two years in Cambridge were enjoyed by Thackeray. Law, the study of which he decided to pursue, proved so dull that he abandoned it in favor of a career in art. When he failed to obtain the position as illustrator of Dickens's *Pickwick Papers,* he turned to writing and wrote many years before the publication of *Vanity Fair* brought recognition.   His other popular novels are *Henry Esmond, Pendennis, The Newcomes,* and *The Virginians.*

Appreciation of Works.   Thackeray's audiences will, probably, always be smaller but not less appreciative than Dickens's.   His

---

[1]See index for Charles Dickens and Robert Louis Stevenson.

characters, however, are not to be forgotten any more than are those of Dickens. Colonel Newcome is as appealing and pathetic as any character in literature, and blundering, blind Clive Newcome has too many prototypes in real life not to find sympathetic admirers. The background of India in *The Newcomes* is undoubtedly more or less autobiographical. Interesting characters, bits of philosophy, and a gentle vein of humor endear Thackeray to his readers.

GEORGE ELIOT (MARY ANN EVANS) 1819-1880

Methods of Character Portrayal. George Eliot understood human nature and portrayed it truthfully. Being realistic, her characters are neither too good nor too bad to seem genuine, and, as a rule, they are developing rather than stationary. They live; they are not merely tagged and placed upon a pedestal for observation. This is Eliot's method: she enters into the heart life of her characters; she gives a psychological analysis of their motives; and then she draws a moral lesson therefrom. As a rule her novels reflect the English countryside of her childhood. The people described are such as she associated with daily; in fact, many of the incidents told were events from the lives of her own family or the lives of people living in her own or in neighboring communities. Her works show that tragedy is as often the lot of common men as it is of those of higher stations in life.

Home Duties and Literary Activities. That George Eliot seemed to consider duty the supreme law of life and that she did not begin writing until she was almost forty has a logical explanation in the fact that at seventeen, because of the death of her mother, she was called upon to take charge of the family household. She had previously had some years of training in good private schools. Thereafter her education was gained largely from reading. However, she had the stimulus of good minds, and after her father's death she made a tour of the continent and upon her return to England became the assistant editor of a magazine.

Best Works. Among George Eliot's best works are *Scenes from Clerical Life, Adam Bede, The Mill on the Floss, Silas Marner, Romola, Felix Holt, Middlemarch,* and *Daniel Deronda*. It is just praise to say that one may read all of these consecutively and within a short period without tiring of the writer's style and characterization.

General Questions on the Age of Victoria

1. What were some of the social changes caused by the Industrial Revolution?
2. How did the Industrial Revolution affect literature?
3. Name the outstanding poets and prose writers of the Age of Victoria and classify their writings as essay, novel, poetry.
4. What two famous scientists belong to the Victorian Age?

5. What type of novel did Jane Austen write, and what class of people did she describe?
6. For what class of people did Dickens show great sympathy? What are your favorites among his novels?
7. Name two of Thackeray's best known novels and characterize each.
8. In what respect was George Eliot similar to Robert Browning?
9. On what great themes did Tennyson write?
10. In what respects was Robert Browning a challenging writer?
11. For what was Elizabeth Barrett Browning most celebrated?
12. In what does Robert Louis Stevenson's charm lie?

Oral or Written Reports

The Industrial Revolution
Machines Which Replaced Laborers
The Growth of the Factory System
The Growth of Cities
Scientists in the Age of Victoria
Outstanding Events in American History
Leading American Writers of the Latter Nineteenth Century
Charles Dickens as a Reformer
A Contrast between the Schools of Dickens's Time and the Schools of Today (See *Nicholas Nickleby*—Charles Dickens)
Mr. Micawber, a Character Frequently Met in Everyday Life (See *David Copperfield*—Charles Dickens)
The Novel of Manners—Introduced by Jane Austen

References

Brownell, W. C.: *Victorian Prose Masters*
Carlyle, Thomas: *Essay on Burns*
Gardiner: *A School History of England*
Gordon: *Men Who Make Our Novels*
Grierson: *Lyrical Ballads from Blake to Hardy*
Harper: *Wordsworth*
Hinchman and Gummerie: *Lives of Great English Writers*
Knight: *Dorothy Wordsworth's Journal*
Overton, Jacqueline M.: *Life of Robert Louis Stevenson*
Pace, Roy Bennett: *English Literature with Readings*
Peabody, Josephine: *The Piper*
Strachey, G. L.: *Queen Victoria*
Tappan, E. M.: *In the Days of Queen Victoria*
Trevelyan, G. M.: *British History in the Nineteenth Century*

Stories with a Historical Background

Dickens, Charles: *David Copperfield*
    Oliver Twist
Gallomb: *Spies*

THE MODERN AGE 1900-

The Twentieth Century

Literary Tendencies. The thousands of books printed in this century make an adequate treatment of the period impossible, especially since they reflect all the varied phases of the complex life of the time. Certainly one attitude, the democratic ideal, which has as one of its first champions Robert Burns, is firmly intrenched in the thought of this age. Liberalism has opposed tradition, and the spirit of rebellion is expressed not only in new modes of thinking but in experiments in literary style, for example, prose rhythms, free verse, clever and witty dialogue. The scientific spirit fostered by great developments in science has influenced literary output in style of writing, in exactitude of expression, and in variety of subject matter. Newly discovered psychological facts have been responsible for the "stream of consciousness" type of writing which has had a far-reaching influence. Social criticism has been responsible for portrayal of life, not only at its best but often at its worst. Individualism in literature, as in society, has run rife, but the new freedom has made life and literature more interesting. The old interests have not disappeared, and chief among the revivals is the study of personality ably expressed in well written biographies.

Prose Predominates. Novels, dramas, essays, sketches, short stories, travel stories, scientific articles, different types of the special article, which threatens to eclipse everything else—these present an interesting, if not heretofore unequalled, literary panorama. At any rate there is sufficient variety to satisfy all types of readers, and it is of the high standard of style that makes reading, even factual reading, a pleasant pastime.

Essays. In this, as in other fields, so many have written excellently that selection is difficult, but no doubt the works of Thomas Hardy, Gilbert K. Chesterton, George Bernard Shaw, Arnold Bennett, John Galsworthy, H. G. Wells, Max Beerbohm, and Hilaire Belloc will continue to attract readers.

Stories and Novels. Many of the authors listed as essayists are even more distinguished in the fields of the short story and of the novel. One who should be included in this group is Joseph Conrad, whose novels are unique not only in their exploitation of that interesting region, the South Sea Islands, but also for the author's own peculiar style, the attempt "to reach the emotions through the appeal to the senses." It is remarkable that Joseph Conrad, who was of Polish descent and learned no English until after he was twenty-one, should have become one of the greatest masters of English prose. A happy accident resulted in the publication of his first novel, *Aylmer's Folly*. John Galsworthy took a trip on the ship on which Conrad was the master. When the two became friendly, Conrad showed Galsworthy the manuscript of his novel, and later by following Galsworthy's advice found a publisher. At once he gained public favor. Among the most popular of his stories and novels are *Nigger of the Narcissus*, *Youth*, *Victory*, and *Lord Jim*.

Drama and Writers. In the field of the drama James Barrie and George Bernard Shaw are the two dramatic writers who rise above the mass in popularity and in influence.

JAMES BARRIE

Barrie. James Barrie had the distinction of belonging to two centuries. The nineteenth may claim his charming whimsical sketches and novels of Scotch life, but the twentieth has had the happy opportunity of seeing his thoroughly delightful plays which portray interesting characters, abound in fanciful and humorous turns, sentiment, and pathos, and introduce such interesting children as Peter Pan. The play of this name, together with *A Kiss for Cinderella* and *Dear Brutus*, represents the more fanciful type. *The Admirable Crichton* and *What Every Woman Knows* are slightly more realistic and serious. For those who love plays, Barrie's make good reading.

Shaw. George Bernard Shaw is a striking personality, often in the limelight, whether it be on account of learning to tango at seventy, sawing wood, taking a ten-mile walk, receiving the Nobel prize for literature but refusing the monetary remuneration, or expounding his views upon Soviet Russia. He always has many and interesting ideas. His plays abound in them. A humorist and a satirist, yet primarily a serious critic of life, he writes in paradoxes

GEORGE BERNARD SHAW

to provoke thought. His way of joking is to tell the truth—which is the funniest joke in the world. He attacks traditional institutions and modes of thought which he considers hindrances to progress. War he condemns as unintelligent and destructive of the forces of civilization. He has written novels, sketches, tracts, but mainly plays. Among the latter are *Man and Superman, Androcles and the Lion, Back to Methuselah,* and *Arms and the Man,* in which he laughs at the military hero. Though he has limitations, his popularity has an assurance of permanence.

Irish Literature. Shaw, though Irish, does not belong to the group of Irish writers who have consciously used old superstitions, faerie lore, and legends from the peasants for the nucleus of their work. Romantic poetry, highly imaginative, is represented by Yeats's *Land of Heart's Desire.* Humorous and realistic prose and poetry are found in such plays as Synge's *Playboy of the Western World*: poetic prose in *The Crock of Gold* by James Stephens, who is said to have the gift of Irish magic. The strong simple poetry of "An Old Woman of the Roads," by Padraic Colum, is a contribution of originality and freshness.

Poetry. New forms and experiments have had less influence upon English than upon American poetry. Yet democratic ideas, realism, the revolt against traditions, and new conceptions of beauty have affected poetry as they have every other art. Certain groups, or schools of writers, are outstanding, among them the vigorous, strong type represented by Henley and Kipling and the World War poets, who write of the suffering, the heroism, and the disillusionment of war. The simplicity and beauty of the poetry of today have made it more interesting and easier to read; in this field, as in others, so much excellent work has been done that there is a wealth of treasure from which to choose. Not to read the works of Thomas Hardy, Robert Bridges, A. E. Housman, William H. Davies, William Butler Yeats, Walter de la Mare, Wilfrid Wilson Gibson, John Masefield, Alfred Noyes, Padraic Colum, James Stephens, John Drinkwater, and James Joyce is to miss the large share of happiness and the deeper understanding of life which they are able to give.

General Questions on the Twentieth Century

1. Name the outstanding literary tendencies of this century.
2. Read the "New York Times Book Review" or any other good book review supplement for a number of issues, and take note of the number of new books and the different types of writing as well as the range of subjects.
3. How has the spread of the democratic spirit affected literature?
4. How has the interest in science affected both subject matter and style of writing?
5. Contrast the poetry of the twentieth century with that of the nineteenth.
6. If you were to select those writers who you think will be read one hundred years hence, what names would you place on the list?
7. Can you think of any way in which radio and television will affect literature?
8. What qualities make Irish poetry essentially different and original?

Oral or Written Reports

Arnold Bennett and *His Diary*
Barrie's Dramas
A Contrast between Heroic and Realistic War Poetry
John Galsworthy—A Leading Novelist of Today

Leading Poets Writing on the World War
Motion Pictures as New Forms of the Drama
Realism Reflected in Poetry Written after the World War
The Scientific Writing of H. G. Wells
George Bernard Shaw's Dramas as Criticisms of Life

❦

A BRIEF INTRODUCTION TO TYPES OF LITERATURE
PROSE

Literature is divided into two great classes, prose and poetry. Prose is classified under four well-defined heads—the narrative, the drama, the essay, and the oration. There are other less clearly defined divisions including letters, diaries, biographies, books of travel, philosophical and scientific treatises, and other similar factual types of writing. Subdivisions under the narrative are the short story, the tale, the novel, the romance, and the allegory. A brief introduction is here given to the short story, the drama, the essay— these being the outstanding types of prose included in this anthology.

The Short Story. A short story is a "short" story. It deals with one incident or a series of incidents that together create a situation. There are many ways of making a short story effective: by using characters of marked personality, by evolving an intriguing plot, by creating the atmosphere of a strange locality, by portraying a person in a crisis and working out his fate, by building up suspense so cleverly that the reader eagerly peruses the story to discover the solution. All of these or a combination of these may be used. A short story differs from a novel in length and in dramatic effect. It is a "little piece of life," as some particular writer sees it. A painter walks out with his easel and selects one scene; he does not try to put the whole world on one small canvas. A short story writer selects his situation and characters and uses his artistic skill to make a finished production. There are so many types and variations of stories that definition is difficult, but the short story differs from the special article, the essay, and other forms of short prose in that it is a story; it deals with characters who are involved in a conflict. There is a struggle in which individuals are arrayed against individuals or against forces of nature, circumstances, or society.

To study the conclusion of a short story is an interesting way to test its merit. Often the answer to the question "Does the story end satisfactorily?" depends upon whether the characters are left happy or unhappy. The proverbial happy ending in moving pictures satisfies almost all people. The artistic ending, however, is the one which results naturally from the situation without making use of improbable incidents and coincidences which usually *do not* happen in everyday life at the opportune time. Another interesting way to study a short story is to apply the test of reality to the characters. Would they, under the conditions prevailing, act in the specified manner?

The Drama. In a story the writer describes and interprets the characters for the reader, but in a drama the reader interprets the characters for himself by observing their actions, their conversation, and their expression and personal appearance, as when one meets a stranger, he forms a certain impression based upon the stranger's speech, dress, facial expression, and general appearance.

Plays vary in type and length. The one-act play has become popular, dealing, as does the short story, with a single incident or a series of happenings which create a situation. There is a single theme and a single problem, the solution of which is the end of the play. There is a conflict of will, which holds the audience. A dominant tone of comedy or tragedy is necessary to insure harmony of time or mood. The one-act play belongs almost entirely to the little theater, and the three-act play, more elaborate and pretentious, belongs to the stage proper. The three-act play is rather carefully constructed. It leads up to a climax; afterwards all problems are solved and the characters disposed of, or the solution is left for the audience. The five-act play was beloved of the Elizabethans, who flocked to the playhouses and enjoyed remaining half a day. In the five-act play the plot, probably including sub-plots, is complicated and elaborate, involving many characters. This play demands skilful construction with a carefully planned climax in the third act, after which the hero's fortunes decline or rise to a satisfactory level. Usually in Shakespeare's comedies the characters are paired off in a grand finale. A five-act play, as does all good drama, has a dominant tone of tragedy or comedy, though a tragedy may have a slight humorous relief plot, which cannot counteract but does lighten the mood.

A drama may be written in either poetry or prose. In the sixteenth century the Elizabethans liked poetic drama, Shakespeare's blank verse, for instance. In the twentieth century few take time to think long enough to understand poetry, unless perchance it is set to music; consequently, practically all drama is prose. At the present the most popular dramatic form, however, is the moving picture with its many scenes rather than acts; it is as yet without fixed standards of plot and tone, and its form is ever changing. Interesting similarities can often be found in the magnificent pageant-like Elizabethan plays and the more elaborate moving picture productions.

The Essay. The really delightful, informal essay of the present time seems, though of course such is not the case, an effortless composition full of spontaneity, sparkling with clever or humorous touches of human nature, and often appealingly whimsical or meditative. Whatever the mood of the writer, the reader seems to respond to it without effort. To reach its present status, the essay passed through many stages of development. Passages from the old Greek and Roman orations expressed the opinions and revealed the personality of the orator in much the manner of the modern essay. In the Bible are many essays on friendship, industry, riches, worship, good living, and similar ideals. The so-called modern essay, however, had its beginning in the writing of the French author, Michel Montaigne, in the year 1571. His essays were translated into English in 1601; a short while before that date, in the year 1597, Bacon's essays appeared. Thus Bacon shares with Montaigne the honor of introducing the essay type of writing to the English-speaking people; his work, however, was unlike that of the French essayist. Bacon's essays were of the formal, didactic, informative type, while Montaigne's were informal, and written with the thought of entertaining rather than with the purpose of instructing or reforming the reader. Addison and Steele were the best of the early Montaigne type of English essayists.

In an essay the writer speaks in his own character, makes his own observations, and reflects his own emotions. Usually he does this briefly; hence an essay might in one sense of the term be called a little lyric in prose. Indeed, the most delightful essays have a rhythmical, lyric quality much akin to poetry. So far as subject matter is concerned, an essayist often wanders from one phase of a subject to another, or wanders from one to another topic much after the fashion of a person engaged in conversation. He considers fit material for an essay any vagary or fancy that comes to his mind. The charm of an essayist depends upon his personal style, his ability to reflect his thoughts and moods entertainingly.

POETRY

The second of the two great divisions of literature is classified under four heads—narrative, dramatic, lyric, and didactic. Subdivisions under narrative poetry are the ballad, the epic, the metrical tale, and the metrical romance. Lyric poetry falls into five divisions—the ode, the sonnet, the elegy, the song, and the simple lyric. Sub-divisions under dramatic poetry are: the comedy, the tragedy, the historical drama, the mask, and the dramatic monologue. A descriptive poem is called a pastoral if it treats of simple country or shepherd life; it is called an idyl if it presents a "little picture."

Since description enters into almost every form of poetic composition and since satiric poetry is so designated because of the tone adopted by the writer, divisions of poetry, like divisions of prose, are necessarily somewhat overlapping. A descriptive poem may also be a didactic poem; a pastoral may be an elegy; an idyl may be a metrical tale. A given selection may be classed, and rightly so, under two or even more types of poetry. A brief introduction is given to the narrative, the dramatic monologue, didactic poetry, and the lyric.

Narrative Poetry. A narrative poem, as the word denotes, narrates or tells a story in verse. "The Pied Piper of Hamelin" is the story of how a group of children were led away by a piper. "The Highwayman" is the special type of narrative called a ballad. In a ballad there is a hero or central figure who has a heroic experience. It has certain characteristics of a song; such as, repetition of lines in the manner of a refrain and strongly marked rhythm. This story-song type dates from the earliest times when the minstrels sang songs about the brave and daring deeds of war chieftains. Many of these old ballads have love plots, tell of elopements, and end in death and disappointment. Stirring ballads were written by Scott. A narrative poem may be lengthy as is Byron's *Childe Harold's Pilgrimage,* the story of Childe Harold's wanderings over Europe, and Scott's *Lady of the Lake* and *Marmion.* Among those who use the narrative form skilfully in modern times are Rudyard Kipling, John Masefield, and Alfred Noyes.

One of the oldest forms of narrative verse is the epic, a lengthy and elaborate story with a central figure, a hero, who represents the feelings and traditions of a people, a race, a nation. It is written in a dignified and stately style. *Beowulf,* Homer's *Iliad* and *Odyssey,* and Milton's *Paradise Lost* are among the well known epics in literature. The metrical romance is a long love story with an involved and rambling plot; it was very popular in the Middle Ages. The metrical tale is somewhat briefer than the metrical romance, and it is told much more simply and realistically.

Dramatic Monologue. Another special type of poetry is known as the dramatic monologue in which one character tells the story, revealing the entire situation, his own character, and that of others also. "Juggling Jerry" and "My Last Duchess" are excellent illustrations of this form. Browning used the dramatic monologue extensively and effectively.

Didactic Poetry. Poetry which explains ideas or teaches moral lessons is termed didactic. Sometimes there is a mingling of types, the didactic being combined with the descriptive. It may include landscape pictures, descriptions of country life, the writer's ideas on problems of the times, his ideals and aspirations, as in the case of Goldsmith's *The Deserted Village.*

Lyric Poetry. A lyric is a brief expression of an emotion put into words that sing; it is music in words. As a baby's cry is said to be a universal language, the lyric may be said to be a universal form of literary composition; it belongs to all lands and all ages. The lyric seems to go back to the beginning of creation when the "morning stars sang together." Indeed nature and the lyric are almost inseparable; not always, but often nature forms the subject matter or at least the background for the emotional theme, particularly of the simple lyric.

The lyric is expressive of every phase of man's emotional life from babyhood until death. It is not concerned with telling a story; it is concerned with registering a person's emotional response to something which has affected him deeply. The song is one of the most natural and spontaneous of the lyric types of poetry. The child sings when he is happy; the Indian chants when he is sad. The song lyric is used in connection with all the significant rites and ceremonies and occasions of primitive and civilized life. There are bridal choruses and funeral dirges; songs of friendship, love, praise, and patriotism; hymns of worship; dithyrambics of hate and lyrics of supplication and of grief. Always in a lyric there is one central and clearly defined theme; sometimes, as in an elegy, there are two emotional themes, but one emotion is made secondary to the other.

The Italian sonnet, a clearly-defined subdivision of the lyric contains fourteen lines, usually in iambic pentameter. The octave, consisting of the first eight lines of the sonnet, gives the rising wave of emotion, the question, the problem, the hope or the desire; the last six lines carry the thought to a conclusion. The rhyme scheme of the octave is usually *a b b a a b b a*; the rhyme scheme of the sestet varies. Instead of the octave-sestet arrangement, the English sonnet is made up of three quatrains with alternating rhyme and a concluding rhyme couplet often epigrammatic in force. The ode is the majestic type of lyric, exalted in mood and expressive of noble ideals. It is often used in commemoration of great public events. The structure of the ode is irregular, in harmony with the thought expressed. While the elegy is a lyric expressing grief and giving reflections on death in general, it, as a rule, suggests hope and faith. The song differs from other types of lyrics in that it is intended to be sung. A lyric is called a simple lyric when it cannot properly be classified under one of the above heads.

General Questions on Types of Literature

1. Into what two great divisions is literature divided?
2. Classify prose under four well-defined heads.
3. List other divisions of prose.
4. Explain the term narrative and list its subdivisions.
5. How does a short story differ from other divisions of the narrative?
6. How may one test the effectiveness of a short story?
7. Explain the differences between the one-act play, the three-act play, and the five-act play and tell to what each belongs.
8. In what respects is an essay similar to a lyric?
9. Mention one of the oldest forms of the essay and tell where it is found.
10. What French and what English writer shared the honor of

introducing the essay type of writing to the English-speaking people? At what time did each write?

11. How did the essays of Addison and Steele resemble and differ from those of Bacon and Montaigne?

12. Upon what does the charm of an essayist depend?

13. What are the chief types of poetry?

14. List the subdivisions of narrative poetry and explain the nature of each.

15. List the types of lyric poetry and explain each.

16. How does a comedy differ from a tragedy?

17. How does a pastoral differ from an idyl?

18. Name and give the authors of several narrative poems.

19. What is an epic? List several.

20. What Victorian writer used the dramatic monologue extensively?

21. What are the requirements of the Italian sonnet? of the English sonnet?

22. How does the sonnet differ from the ode?

23. How does the song differ from other types of the lyric?

MAP   847

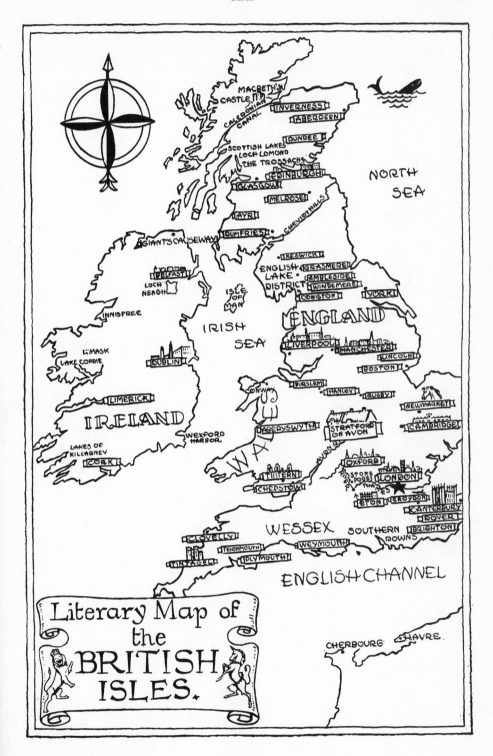

Literary Map of
the
BRITISH
ISLES.

CHRONOLOGICAL INDEX

THE AGE OF VICTORIA 1832-1900
LATTER NINETEENTH CENTURY

THE TWENTIETH CENTURY

INDEX OF TYPES

LYRIC

NARRATIVE POETRY

SHORT STORY

INDEX OF AUTHORS

A PRONOUNCING INDEX

[Use the table below for letter sounds for pronouncing new words.]

ā as in ate
a as in senate
â as in rare
ă as in cat
ä as in far
ȧ as in sofa

ē as in eve
ė as in event
ĕ as in end
ẽ as in writer

ī as in ice
ĭ as in if

ō as in cold
ô as in obey
ô as in cord
ŏ as in stop

ū as in unit
ů as in circulate

ŭ as in cut
ú as in focus
û as in burn

ōō as in moon
ŏŏ as in foot

Abazai (ăb ȧ zī')
Abou Ben Adhem (ä bōō bĕn' ä' dĕm)
Abu (ä' bōō)
Abydos (ȧ bī' dŏs)
Acheron (ăk' ẽr ŏn)
Acme (ăk' mē)
Adonis (ȧ dō' nĭs)
Adonais (ăd ō nā' ĭs)
Aershot (âr' shŏt)
Agonistes (ăg ō nĭs' tēs)
Aix (āks)
Alastor (ȧ lăs' tŏr)
Alcalde (ăl kăl' dĭ; äl käl' dä)
Aldersgate (ôl' dẽrs gāt)
Aleppo (ȧ lĕp' ō)
Algarsife (är' gä sēf)
Alloway (ăl' ō wä)
Altama (ăl' tȧ mä)
Amalek (ăm' ȧ lĕk)
Anacleto (än ä clä' tō)
Antony (ăn' tō nĭ)
Apollo (ȧ pŏl' ō)
Arcadia (är kā' dĭ ȧ)
Arcady (är' kā dĭ)
Arden (är' dĕn)
Armour (är' mẽr)
Areopagitica (ăr ē ŏp ȧ jĭt' ĭ kȧ)
Ashur (ä' shōōr)
Asolando (ä sō län' dō; ăs ō län' dō)
Assyrian (ȧ sĭr' ĭ ȧn)
Aurora (ô rō' rȧ)
Avon (ā' vŏn)
Aylmer (āl' mẽr; ĕl' mẽr)
Ayr (âr)
Azores (ȧ zōrz')

Baal (bā' ăl)
Bacchus (băk' ŭs)
Baiae (bī' ē)
Ballantyne (băl' lȧn tīn)
Banquo (băn' kwō)
Barrie (băr' ĭ)
Bathsheba Everdene (băth shē' bȧ ĕv' ẽr dĕn)
Beerbohm (bēr' bōm)
Belloc (bĕ lŏk') Hilaire (hĭll' ȧ rē)
Bellona (bĕ lō' nȧ)

Belshazzar (bĕl shăz' ȧr)
Beltarbet (bĕl tär' bĕt)
Berenice (bĕr ē nī' sē; bā rā nēs')
Bideford in Devon (bĭd' ē fẽrd; dĕv' ŭn)
Birnam (bẽr' năm)
Blenheim (blĕn' ĕm)
Boom (bōm)
Bombay (bŏm bā')
Bonnivard (bŏn' nĭ vȧrd)
Brunswick (brŭnz' wĭk)
Buchan (bŭk' ȧn)
Bukloh (bōō' klō)

Caithness (kāth' nĕs)
Calais (kȧ lā')
Caliban (kăl' ĭ băn)
Cambridge (kām' brĭj)
Cambuscan (kăm' bŭs kăn; kăm bŭs' kăn)
Campbell (kăm' bĕl; kăm' ĕl)
Canace (kä' nȧ sē)
Casa Guida (kä' sä gwē' dȧ)
Cawdor (kô' dôr)
Cenci (chĕn' chē)
Cerberus (sûr' bẽr ŭs)
Chapaco (chä pä' kō)
Chekhov (chĕ kôf')
Chillon (chĭl ŏn'; Fr. shē yôn')
Christabel (krĭs' tȧ bĕl)
Christendom (krĭs' 'n dŭm)
Cimmerian (sĭ mē' rĭ ăn)
Claret (klăr' ĕt)
Claus of Innsbruck (klaus ĭns' brōōk; ĭns' prōōk)
Colmekill (kŏm' kĭl)
Coleridge (kōl' rĭj)
Colum, Padraic (cŏl' um păd' rĭc)
Comus (kō' mŭs)
Coppée, François (frän-swä' kō pā')
Cortez (kôr tĕz')
Corydon (kŏr' ĭ dŭn)
Cossack (kŏs' ăk)
Coverley (kŭv' ẽr lĭ)
Crécy (Fr. krā' sē; krĕs' ĭ)
Creole (krē' ōl)
Crichton krī' ton)

Croisic (kroi′ sĭk)
Cruikshank (krŏŏk′ shănk)

Dante (dăn′ tē; dän′ tā)
Darien (dā rĭ ĕn′)
Deesa (dē′ să)
De la Mare (dĕ lȧ mâr′)
De la Casse (dĕ lȧ kȧs)
De Quincey (dē kwĭn′ sĭ)
Deronda (dĕ rŏn′ dä)
Derwent (dûr′ wĕnt)
Devonshire (dĕv′ ŭn shēr)
Diodati (dē ō dä′ tē)
Dirck (dûrk)
Donalbain (dŏn′ ăl bān)
Don Juan (dŏn jū′ ăn; Sp. dōn whän)
Duffeld (dû′ fĕlt)
Dumfries (dŭm frēs′)
Dunbar (dŭn bär′)
Dundee (dŭn dē′)
Dunsany (dŭn sā′ nĭ)
D'Urberville (dēr′ bēr vĭl)

Edinburgh (ĕd′ 'n bŭr ō)
Elaria (ē lä′ rē ȧ)
Elia (ē′ lĭ ȧ)
Elgin (ĕl′ jĭn)
Elizabethan (ē lĭz ȧ bē′ than; ē lĭz ȧ bĕth′ ăn)
Elysian (ē lĭzh′ ȧn; ē lĭzh′ ĭ ăn)
Endymion (ĕn dĭm′ ĭ ŏn)
Epicurus (ĕp ĭ kū′ rŭs)
Erebos (ĕr′ ē bŭs)
Ethiope (ē′ thĭ ōp)
Euphrosyne (ū frŏs′ ĭ nē)
Eurydice (ū rĭd′ ĭ sē)

Faustus (fôs′ tŭs)
Fennel (fĕn′ ĕl)
Fenwick (fĕn′ wĭk)
Ferrara (fĕr rä′ rä)
Fife (fīf)
Firwanna (fīr vä′ nä)
Fleance (flē′ ȧns)
Flores (flō′ rĕs)
Forres (fôr′ rĕs)
Forster (fôr′ stēr)
Fra Pandolf (frä pän′ dôlf)

Galileo (găl ĭ lē′ ō)
Galsworthy (gôlz wûr′ thĭ)
Gammer Gurton (găm′ ēr gēr′ tŏn)
Geoffrey (jĕf′ rĭ)
Ghent (gĕnt)
Giles (jīlz)
Girondist (jĭ rŏn′ dĭst)
Glamis (glăm′ ĭs; glämz)
Gloucester (glŏs′ tēr)
Golgotha (gŏl′ gō thȧ)
Gorboduc (gôr′ bō dŭk)
Gorgon (gôr′ gŏn)
Gootland (gōt′ lônd)
Graemes (grāms)
Grasmere (grȧs′ mēr)
Gunga Din (gōong′ gȧ dēn)

Hampden (hăm′ dĕn)
Hasselt (häs′ ĕlt)

Haydon (hā′ dŭn)
Hazlitt (hăz′ lĭt)
Hebe (hē′ bē)
Hecate (hĕk′ ȧ tē)
Hellespont (hĕl′ ĕs pŏnt)
Hermes (hēr′ mēz)
Hippocrene (hĭp′ ō krēn)
Hunt, Leigh (lē)
Hymen (hī′ mĕn)
Hyrcan (hûr′ kăn)

Il Penseroso (ēl pĕn′ sā rō sō)
Innisfree (ĭn′ ĭs frē)
Innsbruck (ĭns′ brŏŏk; ĭns′ prŏŏk)

Jagai (jȧ gī′)
Jamaica (jȧ mā′ kȧ)
Joris (jôr′ ĭs)
Juliet (jū′ lĭ ĕt)

Kala Nag (ä′ lä näg)
Kamal (kȧ′ mȧl)
Keats (kēts)
Kenilworth (kĕn′ ĭl wûrth)
Kubla Khan (kōō′ blä kän)

La Belle Dame (lä bĕl′ däm)
L'Allegro (lä lā′ grō)
Lagerlöf (lä′ gēr löf)
Lammermoor (lăm′ mēr mŏŏr)
Landor (lăn′ dēr)
Lannes (län; lăn)
Leander (lē ăn′ dēr)
Lear (lēr)
Leghorn (lĕg′ hôrn)
Leman (lē′ mȧn)
Lethe (lē′ thē)
Leviathan (lē vī′ ȧ thăn)
Lochinvar (lŏk′ ĭn vär)
Lokeren (lōk′ ēr ĕn)
Lowndes, Humphrey (loundz, hŭm′ frĭ)
Lucero (lōō kȧ′ rō)
Lycidas (lĭs ′ dȧs)
Lyeys (lē′ ĭs)

Macbeth (măk bĕth′)
Macduff (măk dŭf′)
Macaulay (mȧ kô′ lĭ)
Madeira (mȧ dē′ rȧ)
Maenad (mē′ năd)
Magdalene (môd′ lĭn)
Malcolm (măl′ kŭm)
Malvern (măl′ vērn)
Mannering, Guy (măn′ ēr ing, gī)
Marmion (mär′ mĭ ŏn)
Marathon (mär′ ȧ thŏn)
Maskell (măs′ kĕl)
Masefield (māz′ fēld)
Matadore (măt′ ȧ dōr)
Mecheln (mĕk′ ĕln)
Memnon (mĕm′ nŏn)
Menteith (mĕn tēth′; mĕn tīth′)
Merlin (mēr′ lĭn; mûr′ lĭn)
Micawber (mĭ kô′ bēr)
Midlothian (mĭd lō thĭ ȧn)
Milne (mĭln)
Miranda (mĭ răn′ dȧ)

Morpheus (môr' fŭs; môr' fē ŭs)
Morte d' Arthur (môrt där' thẽr)
Mossgiel (mŏs' gēl)
Moti Guj (mō' tĭ gōōj)
Musaeus (mū sē' ŭs)
Musgrave (mŭs' grāv)

Narcissus (när sĭs' ŭs)
Nazim (nä zĭm)
Neptune (nĕp' tūn)
Nice (nēs)
Norweyan (nôr wā' ăn)
Noyes (noiz)

Oisin (ō' shĕn)
Orestes (ō rĕs' tēz)
Orion (ō rī' ŏn)
Orpheus (ôr' fŭs; ôr' fē ŭs)
Othello (ō thĕl' ō)

Padua (păd' ū á)
Palacio, Vicente Riva (pä lä' sī ō vē
  sĕn' tĕ rē vá)
Pallas (păl' ás)
Pambamarco (păm bă mär' kō)
Paracelsus (păr á sĕl' sŭs)
Parnassus (pär năs' ŭs)
Peggoty (pĕg' ŏ tĭ)
Pelops (pē' lŏps)
Pepys (pēps; pĕps; pĕp' ĭs)
Peran Wisa (pĕr' än wē' sá)
Persepolis (pẽr sĕp' ō lĭs)
Philomel (fĭl' ō mĕl)
Phoebus (fē' bŭs)
Phyllis (fĭl' lĭs)
Pierian (pī ē' rĭ ăn)
Pippa (pĭp' á)
Pisa (pē' sä; pē' zä)
Plato (plā' tō)
Pleiades (plē' yădz; plē' ădz)
Pluto (ploō' tō)
Poitiers (Fr. pwá tyā'; poi tērz')
Poges (pōgz; pŏg' ĭs; pŏg' ĭs; stōk)
Porphyro (pôr' fĭ rō)
Portsmouth (pôrts' mŭth)
Proculus (prō' kŭl ŭs)
Prometheus (prō mē' thōōs; prō mē'
  thē ŭs)
Prospice (prŏs' pĭ sē; Lat. prō' spĭ kĕ)
Proteus (prō' tŭs; prō' tē ŭs)
Pruce (prōōs' á)
Pylades (pĭl' á dēz)
Pyrrhus (pĭr' ŭs)

Ralph Roister Doister (rois' tẽr dois'
  tẽr)
Ratisbon (răt' ĭs bŏn)
Ravensheuch (rā' vĕns hū)
Ressaldar (rĕs ăl där')
Roland (rō' lănd)
Romola (rŏm' ō lá)
Romeo (rō' mē ō)
Rosalind (rŏz' á lĭnd)
Rossetti (rō sĕt' ē)
Rubaiyat (rōō' bäi yät)
Ruce (rōōs' á)
Rufe (rōōf)

Saint Colme (sānt kōm)
Satalye (sä tä lē' á)
Saturn (săt' ŭrn)
Scone (skōōn; skōn)
Senlac (sĕn' lăk)
Sennacherib (sē năk' ẽr ĭb)
Sestos (sĕs' tŏs)
Seyton (sā ton)
Shaw, Bernard (shô, bẽr' närd)
Shelley, Percy Bysshe (shĕl' ĭ, pẽr' sĭ,
  bĭsh)
Sienkiewicz (shĕn kyä vĭch)
Silverado (sĭl' vẽr ä dō)
Siguard (zē' gōōrt)
Siward (sē' würd)
Sohrab and Rustum (sō' răb rŭs' tŭm;
  sō' hräb' rŭs' tŭm)
Sotelo (sō tä' lō)
Southampton (south ămp' ton; sŭth
  ămp' ton)
Southey (sŭ' thĭ)
Stratford (străt' fôrd)
Stygian (stĭj' ĭ ăn)
Synge (sĭng)

Talisman (tăl' ĭs măn)
Tamburlaine (tăm' bẽr lān)
Tanaquill (tăn' ä kwĭl)
Tarquin (tär' kwĭn)
Tartar (tär' tár)
Tasso (tăs' ō)
Tatterdemalion (tăt ẽr dē māl' yŭn)
Tempe (tĕm' pē)
Thames (tĕmz)
Thais (thā' ĭs)
Theocritus (thē ŏk' rĭ tŭs)
Thestylis (thĕs' tĭ lĭs)
Thucydides (thōō sĭd' ĭ dēz)
Thyrsis (thŭr' sĭs)
Timon (tī' mŏn)
Timotheus (tĭ mō' thōōs; tĭ mō' thē ŭs)
Tintagel (tĭn tăj' ĕl)
Tolstoy, Leo (tŏl stoi')
Tongres (tôn' gr)
Torcuato (tôr kwä' tŏ)
Trafalgar (trá făl' gär; trá făl gär')
Tramyssene (trä mĭs sä' ná)
Triton (trī' tŏn)
Troy (troi)
Turkye (tür kē' á)
Twickenham (twĭk' 'n am)

Vicar of Wakefield (vĭk' ẽr)
Voltaire (vŏl târ')

Weser (vā' zẽr)
Westminster (wĕst' mĭn stẽr)
Woolwich (wōōl' ĭch)
Worcester (wōōs' stẽr)
Wordsworth (wûrdz' wûrth)

Xanadu (zăn' á dōō)
Xenophon (zĕn' ō fŏn)

Yeats (yāts)
Ypres (ē' prĕs)

Zephyrus (zĕf' ĭ rŭs)
Zeus (zūs)

GENERAL INDEX

WRITING WOMEN'S WORLDS